Sociology

Sociology

Richard P. Appelbaum

University of California, Santa Barbara

William J. Chambliss

The George Washington University

HarperCollins*CollegePublishers*

Acquisitions Editor: Alan McClare
Developmental Editor: Melissa Mashburn
Project management, art direction/coordination, text and cover design: York Production Services
Cover Illustration: José Ortega
About the Cover Artist: José Ortega, creator of the cover art for *Sociology*, was born in Ecuador in 1965 and came to the United States at the age of five. He graduated from the School of Visual Arts in 1988. His first professional commission from The New York *Daily News* attracted several further inquiries and Ortega's striking technique soon became widely recognized and admired. Ortega has contributed illustrations, silkscreen prints and paintings to exhibitions in the United States, Venezuela and Japan. He has been the subject of a number of articles and received awards from several organizations including the Society of Illustrators, *Communication Arts* and *Graphis*. Most recently, he has completed a series of murals for the Metropolitan Transit Authority. José Ortega lives and works in New York City.
Art Studio: Dartmouth Publishing, Inc.
Photo Researcher: Karen Koblik
Electronic Production Manager: Chris Pearson
Electronic Page Makeup: American Book-Stratford Press
Printer and Binder: RR Donnelley & Sons
Cover Printer: Coral Graphics Services, Inc.

Library of Congress Cataloging-in-Publication Data

Appelbaum, Richard P.
    Sociology / Richard P. Appelbaum, William J. Chambliss.
        p.   cm.
    Includes bibliographical references and index.
    ISBN 0-06-500813-8
    1. Sociology.   I. Chambliss, William J.   II. Title.
HM51.A64 1995
301--dc20

95 96 97 9 8 7 6 5 4 3 2

To Karen and Pernille

Brief Contents

Contents

Maps

Instructors' Preface: *Why This Textbook?*

During the past quarter century, the world has experienced an accelerating rate of economic, political, institutional, and cultural globalization. Examples of this are not hard to find: the end of the Cold War, the democratization of South Africa, the increasing economic interdependence of nations, and the rapid growth of transnational businesses, to name but a few. *Sociology* is the first textbook to make **globalization** a core focal point while providing full and comprehensive coverage of the fundamentals of sociology as applied to the understanding of American society. It examines the effect of globalizing forces on our society and students' daily lives. *Sociology* explores the social implications of developments such as organizations and institutions that span national borders, globalized media and culture, and worldwide environmental problems. In addition to examples and discussions in each chapter, *"globalization" boxes* and *end-of-chapter globalization sections* explore the impact of globalizing forces on standard sociological topics. Chapter 10 (*Global Inequality*) focuses on recent changes in the world stratification system. Extensive *full color maps* featuring global, regional, and U.S. projections convey sociological information and orient students to global geography.

In an ever more interdependent world, an understanding of and appreciation for human diversity is increasingly important. *Sociology*'s emphasis on **diversity** will help students overcome ethnocentrism and appreciate the importance of multicultural understanding. Chapters on *Race and Ethnicity* (10), *Sex and Gender* (11), and *Aging* (12) focus directly on issues of diversity and inequality, while *"Silenced Voices" boxes* and numerous discussions and examples incorporate issues of race and ethnicity, gender and sexuality, class, age, and cultural diversity throughout the text.

Sociology's emphasis on **critical analysis** will help students realize that statements about facts and theories—whatever their source—must be scrutinized in light of one another, and that one of the tasks of sociology is to demystify both common-sensical and scientific understandings. *"Critical Thinking" boxes* in each chapter examine sociological and more popular writing, while *"Critical Assessment"* sections weigh the strengths and limitations of major theories.

THE ORGANIZATION OF THIS TEXTBOOK

Part I provides students with an **Introduction to Sociology**. Chapter 1, *The Sociological Perspective*, highlights the principal themes of the textbook and sets out the major issues and theoretical frameworks in sociology. Chapter 2, *The Process of Inquiry*, extends the explorations of the first chapter, arguing that there are numerous approaches to sociological understanding and offering detailed discussions and examples of the major ones.

Part II examines the relationship between **The Individual and Society**, focusing on the intersections between the micro, organizational, and macro levels. In Chapter 3 we explore the nature of *Culture*, learning that human cultures are multiple, diverse, and socially constructed. This provides the foundation for understanding the various forms of human *Societies* discussed in Chapter 4, which presents major sociological concepts and theories, as well as analyses of recent changes in industrial society. Chapter 5 examines the central importance of *Socialization and Social Interaction* in the development of both individual and society, looking at the principal agents of socialization across the life span. Chapter 6 applies this understanding to the level of *Groups and Organizations*. Both conformity and individualism are explored, as well as the importance of both bureaucratic and innovative forms of social organization. Chapter 7 extends this discussion to encompass *Deviance and Crime*, emphasizing the importance of social definitions as well as social structure in understanding an important contemporary social issue.

As the United States becomes more diverse, there is increasing demand for bilingual education. Currently, out of 2.4 million students who have difficulty with English, only about 350,000 have access to bilingual classrooms, although bilingual education is mandated by federal law.

Other studies have drawn similar conclusions. A study of student-teacher interaction in a largely African-American kindergarten found that such labels as "fast" or "slow," which the teacher had assigned by the eighth day of class, tended to stay with the student throughout the year (Rist, 1970). Another study found that female and Asian-American students frequently received classroom grades that were higher than their actual test scores, while Latinos, African Americans, and white males received lower grades (Farkas et al., 1990a, 1990b). The differences had to do with the teachers' perceptions of a student's "attitude." Those who appeared to be attentive and cooperative were judged to be hard workers and good students, and they were graded up; those who appeared to be indifferent or hostile were graded down.

Classroom labeling occurs in other cultures as well. Paul Willis, in a highly influential study, found that British boys from working-class families were systematically labeled as low academic achievers and taught to think of themselves as only capable of having working-class jobs (Willis, 1981, 1990). The boys understood quite well that this labeling process worked against them, and they resisted it by the use of humor and other challenges to authority. This rein-

forced their teachers' perception that the boys would never make it and would eventually drop out of school and assume their "rightful position" in the working class. The boys thus tacitly accepted their teachers' labeling, creating a self-fulfilling prophecy in which they wound up in working class-jobs.

EDUCATION AND INEQUALITY

Education is a two-edged sword. For some, it can help to reduce inequality by opening up new possibilities for social mobility. For others, it can reinforce existing inequality by providing unequal educational opportunities according to one's race, ethnicity, social class, or gender.

The Challenges of Cultural Diversity

The United States is one of the most culturally, ethnically, and racially diverse countries in the world (see Chapter 10). This poses unusual challenges for public education, leading to many debates over how best to provide equal opportunities for all groups. One highly contentious issue, for example, concerns **bilingual education,** *the offering of instruction in a non-English language as well as in English.* Nearly 13

A Beijing, China, street sweeper wears a surgical mask for protection against air pollution. China experiences extremely high levels of pollution, an experience typical of newly industrializing countries that are too poor to invest in antipolluting technologies. Global industrialization is a major source of global pollution today.

The Effects of Urbanization

Industrialization and urbanization go together, and when people in industrializing societies move to cities they create additional environmental problems beyond those associated with population growth and industrialization alone. Apart from creating their own miniclimates (urban areas are "heat islands," some 5 to 9 degrees Fahrenheit hotter than surrounding areas), cities are highly inefficient users of energy. The average U.S. city consumes 150 gallons of water per person each day, along with 3.3 pounds of food and 16 pounds of fossil fuel. In the process 120 gallons of sewage per person is produced, as well as 3.3 pounds of garbage, and 1.3 pounds of air pollution. New York City by itself produces enough garbage each year to cover Central Park's 1.3 square miles to a height of 13 feet (Spirn, 1984).

While rural areas tend to rely on local supplies of food, fuel, and water, cities typically bring these necessities from distant places. Residents in low-income urban areas in India and Africa, for example, often must obtain wood for cooking and heating from nearby forests, resulting in massive deforestation. One study of nine major Indian cities found that it took less than ten years to deplete forests within 60

miles by an average of 30 percent (Bowonder *et al.,* 1985). The growth of cities in an unplanned sprawl requires the use of energy just to move people and goods around. The use of private automobiles increases pollution: Streets and highways become clogged, and pollution reaches the levels for which cities such as Los Angeles, Mexico City, and Bangkok are infamous. Although air quality standards in the United States have actually reduced automobile pollution in recent years, urban Americans nonetheless manage to burn 416 gallons of gasoline per person in 1986, four times as much as their counterparts in European cities (which have far more efficient public transportation serving more compact urban areas, as well as more fuel-efficient cars), and ten times as much as Asian urbanites (who still rely heavily on their bicycles and feet for transportation).

Usually food must be shipped long distances to reach cities, requiring energy for transportation, refrigeration, processing and packaging, and storage. Water must be imported from far away as well. Los Angeles and much of southern California, for example, are semidesert areas that are entirely dependent on water from northern California, the eastern slope

CRITICAL THINKING BOXES

To further enhance students' critical thinking skills and stimulate discussion, the authors have integrated boxed inserts within each chapter which examine controversial issues and ask students to weigh the strengths and weaknesses of opinions expressed.

Box 13.1

Critical Thinking

Is There a Ruling Elite?

Some 30 years ago, political scientist Robert Dahl began studying political power in New Haven, Connecticut. By focusing on decision making in a number of specific cases, he formulated what became the classical pluralist theory of state power. Dahl argues that no single elite rules American society, but rather that power is shared by a large number of groups and interests that are constantly contending with and offsetting one another. Dahl summarizes his position as follows:

> Important government policies [are] arrived at through negotiation, bargaining, persuasion, and pressure at a considerable number of different sites in the political system—the White House, the bureaucracies, the labyrinth of committees in Congress, the federal and state courts, the state legislatures and executives, the local governments. No single organized political interest, party, class, region or ethnic group would control all of these sites (Dahl, 1967, p. 37).

Sociologist G. William Domhoff (1978, 1983, 1990) has been studying political power nearly as long as Dahl. Yet his conclusions are the exact opposite. According to Domhoff, power in American society is exerted by a ruling elite, consisting of the owners and managers of major corporations, political leaders, major advisors to the government, people occupying positions on the most important government commissions and agencies, and military leaders. In Domhoff's view the members of this elite are highly interconnected. They often attend the same schools and

colleges, marry into one anothers' families, belong to the same clubs, and sit on the same corporate boards of directors. They even camp out together at places like northern California's rustic Bohemian Grove, where, according to Domhoff, the most powerful figures congregate each year to renew old acquaintances and make business deals (Domhoff, 1974). Domhoff claims that this picture has not changed fundamentally since he began his research 30 years ago:

> As the 1990s began...the same old power elite was in the saddle as never before...On balance, given the power of American elites and the problems of organizing large numbers of people, the prospects for greater fairness and equality did not look very good as the 1990s began. There will be no natural evolution to a better future for everyone, only a natural evolution to the rich getting richer and the poor getting poorer, for that is how capitalism works without intervention by a countervailing political party and the state. But the power elite...is precisely in the business of making sure that such intervention does not happen (Domhoff, 1990, pp. 283–284).

How would you reconcile such conflicting viewpoints on the same issue? What differing assumptions between the pluralist and social conflict theories of state power might lead to such different conclusions? Can you think of a study you might conduct that would enable you to decide which viewpoint is more likely to be correct?

or less unified upper-class power elite exerting control over politics, the economy, and the military (Berle and Means, 1982, orig. 1932; Mills, 1956; Miliband, 1969; Domhoff, 1983; 1990; Mintz and Schwartz, 1985). This theory was introduced to contemporary sociology by C. Wright Mills in The Power Elite (1956). In his classic study, Mills argued that the United States is controlled by an elite group dominating the political, economic, and military

institutions. Although these officials are not seen as conspiring behind closed doors to run the country, Mills argues that they do share similar socioeconomic backgrounds, attend the same Ivy League schools, and incorporate the ethos of capitalism as they assume leading roles in managing the affairs of society. Often the same individuals can be found going through a "revolving door" consisting of top positions in law, business and government. Mills' theory

---

Robert K. Merton and Structural Strain Theory

Although Durkheim's theory sought to explain deviant behavior in broad terms, he did not specifically offer a functionalist explanation of different forms of deviance. That task fell to an American sociologist, Robert K. Merton, who in 1938 adapted

Durkheim's concept of anomie to explain deviance as resulting from a person's position in the social structure. According to Merton's theory, **structural strain** is *a form of anomie that occurs when a gap exists between the goals society sets for people and the means society provides for people to achieve those goals* (See Table 7.1).

CRITICAL ASSESSMENTS

Each chapter presents fair and frank assessments of the strengths and limitations of the major theories being discussed.

Critical Assessment. Merton's strain theory of deviance implies that groups with access to legitimate means for achieving culturally prescribed goals should have low rates of deviance. The fact is, however, that deviant behavior is commonplace among all groups in modern societies, including those with ready access to legitimate means for achieving their dreams (Coleman, 1994; Adler and Adler, 1994). For example, one of the most prevalent and costly forms of deviant behavior in modern societies consists of crimes committed by high-status persons in connection with their work (see the section entitled "Who Commits Crime?" at the end of this chapter).

Similarly, one would not expect to find high rates of deviant behavior on college campuses if anomie theory is correct. College students are much more likely to find compatibility between cultural goals and legitimate means for achieving them than most other groups. Yet forms of deviance such as under-age drinking, using false identification, consuming illegal drugs and theft are in fact quite common (Elliot and Huiznga, 1983; Schreiber, 1993; Johnston et al., 1992). It seems clear that structural strain is not enough to explain the existence of deviant behavior in many parts of American society.

The Sociological Perspective

CHAPTER OUTLINE

THINGS TO LOOK FOR

1. What are the key social forces shaping our world today, and what special insights does sociology bring to bear in explaining them?
2. What are the central concerns of sociology, and how does the sociological imagination help us to better address them?
3. What is the nature of scientific inquiry? How does sociological inquiry differ from that of the natural sciences, and how is it similar?
4. Who are the key founders of sociology, and how did their underlying perspectives differ on the nature of social relations?
5. To what extent has sociology excluded the voices of women and people of color since its founding in the nineteenth century?

INTRODUCTION: SOCIOLOGY— A GLOBAL FOCUS

Imagine you are standing before an enormous clock on which the hands tick away the years of the earth's history. The clock is set so that 24 hours represent the nearly 5 billion year history of our planet. On this cosmic scale, a single second equals nearly 60,000 years; a single minute, 3.5 million years. The first life on earth—the simple one-celled organisms that emerged in the oceans some 2.5 to 3.5 billion years ago—do not make their appearance until at least 7 hours on the clock have passed by. The dinosaurs appear at about the twenty-third hour; they walk the planet for less than 42 minutes, then disappear forever. On this 24-hour clock, the first humanlike creatures appear during the last 2 minutes, and *Homo sapiens* emerges in the last 4 seconds. What we call human history has barely appeared at all. Written languages, cities, and agriculture, which date back some 12,000 years, emerge only in the last quarter second—representing not even a tick!

On a planetary scale human beings are very recent arrivals indeed, and what we proudly refer to as human history barely registers. Yet although we arrived only an instant ago, we have certainly made our presence known. Our population has exploded a thousandfold during the last 17 seconds on the planetary clock, from 5 million people before written language heralded the dawn of human history to 5 billion people today. Within 40 years, yet another 5 billion people will be added to our already overcrowded planet. Human beings already have spread into every corner of the earth, crowding out other forms of plant and animal life. Thanks to modern science, technology, and industry, each of us is today capable of consuming a vastly greater amount of the planet's limited resources than were our prehistoric ancestors. The damage we have already done to our planet is well known.

Now shift your imagination to the last few years—a time too brief to register on the planetary clock, yet a significant portion of your own life. In terms of the brief span of human history, this has been a watershed period. The Cold War, which had made deadly opponents of the United States and the Soviet Union, came to an abrupt end. The Soviet Union, in an act without parallel in modern history, in 1991 voted itself out of existence, leaving in its wake numerous independent but highly troubled nations. Along with the Soviet Union went much of its military might, including its threat as a nuclear superpower. Global thermonuclear annihilation, which had menaced all life on the planet for some 40 years, at least for the moment appeared to recede as a danger. The military arms race also slowed, as both the United States and the former Soviet republics reduced their military spending. The nations of Eastern Europe, formerly under Soviet control, became independent states. Overnight, Soviet-style communism virtually ceased to exist. Yet these same changes contributed to economic collapse throughout the former Soviet republics and much of Eastern Europe. Ancient ethnic hatreds resurged in Germany, Yugoslavia, Armenia, Georgia, and other countries. A violent and brutal war erupted between Serbs, Croats, and Muslims in what had formerly been Yugoslavia. If the end of the Cold War brought renewed optimism for a peaceful global future, it also rekindled growing strife between different peoples and nations.

During the same brief period, representatives of 170 nations gathered in the Brazilian city of Rio de Janeiro, declaring their commitment to saving the planet's fragile environment. At the 1992 Rio Conference, the world's nations sought to balance their economic growth with environmental protection, seeking global cooperation in the fight against acid rain, deforestation, ozone depletion, global warming, species extinctions, and other human-made sources of environmental destruction. The conference acknowledged that however diverse the peoples of the planet might be, they share a common home and therefore a common interest in its preservation.

Two years after the Rio Conference, 11,000 scientists and other experts from all nations gathered in Yokohama, Japan at the tenth international conference aimed at coordinating global efforts to end the scourge of AIDS. Acquired Immunodeficiency Syndrome,

Vice President Al Gore addressed representatives of 170 nations in Rio de Janiero at the Rio Conference in 1992, a major international conference recognizing the global environmental interdependence of all people on earth. A major focus of the conference was the need to balance economic development with environmental protection.

which was identified as a deadly disease barely a decade earlier, by then had afflicted an estimated four million victims worldwide in an epidemic that threatened to infect as many as 110 million people by the year 2000. A global health epidemic, like global environmental destruction, requires a global response—and both Rio and Yokohama provided the beginnings of just such an effort.

Closer to home, the United States experienced a major change in its global role, one that has deeply affected all of our lives. A long economic expansion, which created favorable job and economic opportunities for Americans who entered adulthood during the third quarter of this century, came to an end. Today, in every city and in many small towns, increasing numbers of destitute people can be seen pushing shopping carts and sleeping on the streets. Two out of every five children living in a family headed by someone under 30 years of age live in poverty, while the gulf between rich and poor grows wider every year (Children's Defense Fund, 1992; Shapiro and Greenstein, 1991). And a diverse range of jobs, from factory work to engineering, have already been lost to Asia, Latin America, and other places where people work for a fraction of American wages. Many of you wonder about what kinds of jobs you will be able to get when you receive your college degree. To many observers, the centers of global economic power appear to be shifting west to Asia, and east to Europe.

It is clear that we live at a major turning point in human history—an incredibly exciting and challenging time to be alive. Students who are in college today will help determine the fate of our troubled planet and nations. Yet this is also a terribly unsettling time as well. From ethnic and racial conflicts to global environmen-

tal destruction to worldwide disease epidemics to an uncertain role for the United States in the emerging world, there is much that cries out for sociological analysis and understanding.

Sociologists use the term **globalization** to refer to *the processes by which the lives of all people around the planet become increasingly interconnected, along with our awareness of such interconnections* (Robertson, 1992). We believe this is a key feature of life as we move into the twenty-first century—an issue so important that it is becoming a central feature of our sociological understanding. That is why we emphasize it in every chapter of this book.

There is nothing new about globalization. Five hundred years ago, when Columbus sailed from Spain to the Caribbean, the world changed forever. Many thousands of years before that, when people crossed what is today called the Bering Sea from Siberia to Alaska, another enormous process of globalization occurred: human beings spread to virtually every location on earth. What is different today is the pace at which globalization is occurring, and the degree of global interdependence that is the result. It took early humans thousands of years to move from Asia to North America. It took Columbus three months to cross the Atlantic Ocean. Another half century passed before Cortez and Pizarro conquered the native Aztec and Inca empires of Mexico and Peru, and yet another half century went by before English colonies were founded at Jamestown and Plymouth. Today, however, events that occur in Europe or Asia or Africa affect us instantaneously. Thanks to modern computer technology, an American business decision can influence the lives of thousands of Japanese workers—and vice versa. When farmers or corporations in Brazil or Malaysia burn down the forests in search of farmland, the resulting climate changes affect everyone on earth. When a war breaks out in a seemingly remote corner of the planet, it is certain to be televised on the evening news the very same day.

Studying sociology will help you better understand issues such as these. At first thought, this might seem surprising. How can sociology provide insights into problems of the environment, or health, or the economy? The answer is simple: all of these problems are at root problems of human beings and the social relations they have created. The central task of sociology is to ask how the social world is organized and maintained, in order to better understand how people create—and change—their social world.

THE SOCIOLOGICAL IMAGINATION

The sociological study of social relations contributes to critical thinking about the social world. Instead of accepting things as they are, the sociologist asks why things occur in a particular way, and under what set of social relationships might they be otherwise. By **critical thinking,** sociologists mean *a willingness to ask any question, no matter how difficult; to be open to any answer that is supported by reason and evidence; and to openly confront one's biases and prejudices when they get in the way.* One of sociology's most important founders, Max Weber (see below), captured this spirit in two simple words, when he said that a key task of sociological inquiry was to openly acknowledge "inconvenient facts" (Gerth and Mills, 1946). In each chapter of this textbook we will highlight critical thinking, both in assessing different theories and in special critical thinking boxes.

A generation ago a well-known sociologist, C. Wright Mills (1959), called such a critical understanding the **sociological imagination.** According to Mills, this refers to *the ability to grasp the relationship between our lives as individuals and the larger social forces that help to shape them.* As we go about our daily routines, we often forget that they are in many ways affected by larger economic, political, and cultural forces that are all but invisible to us. When a young man engages in illegal activities that land him in prison, we are tempted to dismiss it as the result of personal failings or bad luck (Box 1.1). But when a country has one of the highest incarceration rates in the world—as the United States does today—sociologists turn to other explanations for this seemingly "personal" problem. Why should a large part of the young male minority population be in prison? What social forces have come together to produce a widespread pattern of illegal activities and disproportionate incarceration among members of a particular social class, racial or ethnic group, or gender? The sociological imagination enables sociologists to study how such factors as racism, lack of employment opportunities, segregation of impoverished minority groups into inner-city ghettos, governmental policies, and a multibillion dollar illegal drug economy combine to produce an escalating rate of imprisonment in the United States today (Chapter 7).

Mills argued that the sociological imagination enables us to understand the relationship between private troubles (such as getting arrested for selling drugs), and public issues (such as the emergence of a lucrative drug economy in impoverished inner-city neighborhoods where few legal economic opportunities exist). Mills believed that by understanding these relationships, we will be better able to take charge of our lives. After all,

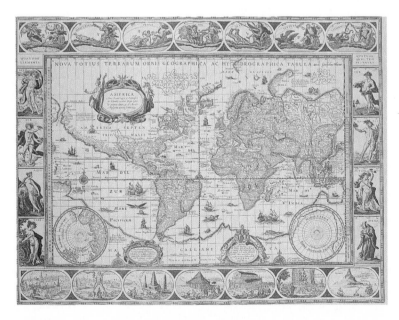

Maps, which will appear throughout this book, often tell important sociological stories. This French map, which was published in 1646, reminds us that the process of globalization began long ago. It also shows that Europeans had a distorted view of the geography of lands that were geographically distant. What might a Chinese map of the same period reveal?

Advanced communications technologies, such as AT&T's Global Communications Center, are partly responsible for the rapid acceleration of globalization during the past quarter century.

if we are to avoid becoming victims of large, seemingly distant events, we must study them in order to better understand how they affect us on a daily basis. Only then can we hope to make decisions and take actions to improve our lives.

Sociologists sometimes refer to Mills' distinction between private troubles and public issues as a difference between the micro and macro levels of social relations (Turner, 1986). The **micro level** refers to *social relations that involve direct social interaction with others,* including families, friends, coworkers, and fellow students. This level is termed micro because it is small-scale, almost as if we used a microscope to focus on a tiny range of social processes requiring our direct involvement. The **macro level** refers to the *larger, more invisible, and often more remote social processes that help to shape the micro world.* These include the political, economic, cultural, and other large-scale social forces we have just discussed. In this textbook, Part II deals primarily with micro-level relationships, providing the building blocks for the more macro-level topics that will be found in the remainder of the text. But it is important to remember that the distinction between mi-

cro and macro is partly artificial. As we have just seen, the macro-level global economy touches our micro-level daily lives in countless ways. At the same time, the actions we take in our micro worlds, whether it be as students in our universities or as citizens in our communities, will have an impact on the macro world as well. A key objective of this textbook is to enable us to understand how our daily lives are both shaped by larger historical processes, and how we are at the same time the makers of history.

PRINCIPAL THEMES IN SOCIOLOGICAL RESEARCH

Of the many themes that recur in sociological research, a number are of central importance in understanding our world today. In this textbook we pay special attention to three themes that we believe are transforming our lives at the end of the twentieth century. These include (1) an appreciation of the enormous diversity of peoples on our planet; (2) explaining the nature of inequality among people, groups, and nations; and (3) understanding the unprecedented social changes that are

Box 1.1

Critical Thinking

Why Did Robby "Turn Bad"?

John Edgar Wideman and his younger brother Robby were raised by two caring, working-class parents in Homewood, an African-American ghetto in Pittsburgh, Pennsylvania. Both boys were superb athletes and excellent students.

John finished high school in a blaze of glory, receiving a scholarship to the prestigious University of Pennsylvania. At Pennsylvania John played basketball, was one of the best students in his class, and upon graduation received a Rhodes Scholarship to study English literature at Oxford University in England. Upon returning, he earned a Ph.D. in English, going on to a highly successful career as a university professor and novelist.

Robby's life was very different. Although he shared his brother's intellectual quickness and athletic ability, he stopped applying himself to academics when he was in high school during the 1960s. He turned his talents and energies to another purpose, becoming a leader in the Black social movement against racial injustice in American society. As he was drawn into the angry protest and lifestyle experimentation of that period, he started using drugs and "getting into trouble." Although his brother and parents tried to change Robby's ways, no amount of preaching or punishment seemed to work. A string of petty crimes escalated into more serious ones. At age 25, Robby and two of his friends killed a man while committing a holdup. Today, 30 years later, Robby is serving a life sentence for murder and armed robbery.

In his book *Brothers and Keepers* (1984), John Edgar Wideman poignantly retells Robby's story, based on his brother's recollections as well as his own. After reading these two excerpts from Widerman's book, ask yourself how the sociological imagination might enable you to account for their divergent paths. What evidence might you gather to test your ideas? What biases do you hold that might get in the way of a dispassionate and impartial analysis?

John: A brother behind bars, my own flesh and blood, raised in the same houses by the same mother and father; a brother confined in prison has to be a mistake, a malfunctioning of the system. The fact that a few twists and turns of fate could land you here with the bad guys becomes a stark message about my own vulnerability. It could easily be me behind bars instead of you (pp. 47–48).

Robby: How you gon feel sorry when society's so corrupt, when everybody got their hand out or got their hand in somebody else's pocket and ain't no rules nobody listens to if they can get away with breaking them? How you gon apply the rules? It was dog eat dog out there, so how was I spozed to feel sorry if I was doing what everybody else was doing. I just got caught is all. I'm sorry about that, and damned sorry that guy Stavros got killed, but as far as what I did . . . ain't no way I gon torture myself over that one (p. 90).

occurring as the result of the rapidly accelerating globalization of virtually all aspects of life. Although these themes will be discussed in separate chapters throughout the book, a few words should be said about their importance at this time.

Diversity

Diversity refers to *the social relations and interaction of many different kinds of people.* It is obvious that there is enormous plant and animal diversity in the world, a diversity which not only makes the world an interest-

ing place in which to live but which many biologists now regard as important for human survival. At the Rio Conference, delegates debated a treaty to preserve the biological diversity of the millions of plant and animal species that are currently threatened with extinction. Among other reasons, such "biodiversity" is important because a diverse range of plants and animals means a greater variety of medicines, more foods for human use, and ecologically stable environments.

The same is true with human diversity. There is an enormous range of human beliefs, behaviors, and forms of social organization on the planet today. Such diversity brings with it a richness of experience, customs, and knowledge that, when openly shared, can prove crucial to the quality of our common human future. At the same time, as with plant and animal diversity, human social and cultural diversity is today challenged.

One challenge to human diversity is a relatively new one—globalization. This challenge carries with it both promises and problems. Globalization entails the emergence of a single, unified global economy, which today touches people in even the most remote reaches of the planet; global culture, in which television, film, and other forms of mass communication create similarities of style, beliefs, and behavior; and global political organizations such as the United Nations, which alter local political practices.

The other challenge is a very old and familiar one—widespread human intolerance of anything that is different. Human history abounds with examples of groups of people who have lashed out at others whose religion, language, or customs differed from their own. All too often the perception of such difference has led to conflict, war, and even the destruction of entire peoples. If you read a newspaper or watch any television news broadcast, you will see many examples of such fear and prejudice at work in the world today. These are found not only in such troubled places as Rwanda or the former Yugoslavia but in our own backyard as well, where the past two decades have witnessed a resurgence of white supremacist organizations that call for the elimination of Asian Americans, African Americans, Jews and homosexuals.

People everywhere tend to be **ethnocentric;** they have a *tendency to judge other cultures by their own standards, regarding their values and way of life as "normal" and "better."* One of the challenges of diversity is to recognize the limitations of such a narrow viewpoint: peoples and communities differ from one another, and from a sociological perspective no one can be said to be more "natural" or "human" than any other. Vast differences separate people from different countries, and even people within the same country. In poor countries, simple survival is of fundamental importance, and starvation and death are commonplace experiences. Within the United States the lives of poor people living in the mountains of Appalachia differ greatly from those of poor people living in downtown New York or Los Angeles, and the lives of both groups differ from the wealthy teenagers and young adults depicted on the popular television series *Beverly Hills 90210.*

In this book we will emphasize diversity, focusing on the differences as well as similarities between peoples and cultures, not only around the globe but among different groups within the United States. The acceptance of diversity is of particular importance in today's rapidly shrinking world, because it is increasingly impossible to remain isolated from beliefs and customs which challenge one's own.

Inequality

Sociologists use the term **inequality** to refer to *differences in wealth, prestige, power, and other valued resources.* Since sociology emerged as a field of study a century and a half ago, many of its leading figures have attempted to explain why there are rich and poor, and why the gap between them grows or shrinks. This is a question that has enormous importance to everyone, not just sociologists. In recent years, the gap between rich and poor has grown significantly in the United States (Barancik and Scott, 1992). A generation ago, most college students correctly assumed that their degrees would help assure them a good job and a steadily growing income. Today that is no longer the case; a college degree no longer provides an automatic key to a secure job and lifetime prosperity.

One common explanation for why some people are poor and others are wealthy is that inequality is the result of individual differences in talent and hard work. Although sociologists do not deny that such individual factors can play a role, they prefer to focus on more systematic social forces that characterize society as a whole. For example, discrimination can place entire groups of people at an economic disadvantage relative to other groups. A great deal of research has now demonstrated that women earn less money for the same work than men even when they are equally talented, educated, and hard-working (Chapter 11). The same is true for African Americans and Latinos relative to whites (Chapter 10). Alternatively, the economy as a whole can contribute to inequality. When business is booming and jobs are plentiful, many people find their income increasing: a rising tide carries all ships. Conversely, when the economy is stagnant, well-paying jobs are scarce, and people who have worked hard all their lives may suddenly find their living standards drop despite their efforts (Chapter 8).

This textbook will devote a great deal of attention to inequality, not only because it is an important topic in sociology but also because changes in the global economy will have a major impact on inequality in the United States during the coming decade. The interplay between globalization and inequality will impact not only unskilled or partly skilled workers but college graduates as well.

Globalization

The pace of social change that has occurred in the past five years is, in many ways, without precedent in world history. The maps of Europe and much of Asia have been transformed virtually overnight. Once-poor coun-

Among the more visible manifestations of growing poverty in the United States is the presence of homeless people sleeping on grates or living in card-board boxes. This homeless person lives across the street from the White House.

tries in Asia now pose economic challenges to the United States and Europe. Poverty and homelessness have increased in America, at the same time that glass and steel skyscrapers have transformed the formerly impoverished Asian cities of Hong Kong and Singapore into two of the most modern metropolitan areas in the world today. The pace of social change today is tied to the processes of globalization that we will focus on throughout this book. Let us briefly see what this means by discussing the relationship between globalization and the American economy, politics, culture, and the environment. We will return to each of these themes throughout this book.

Globalization and the American Economy

Americans benefit in many ways from what might be called a "global assembly line," since virtually everything we consume is made, at least in part, somewhere else in the world (Box 1.2). When you buy a pair of Air Jordan athletic shoes, you are helping to pay the wages of thousands of factory workers in Indonesia, the high fees of designers and advertising agencies in the United States, and, of course, Michael Jordan. When you buy a Gap shirt in Atlanta, the sale is recorded in a central computer that enables the company to estimate exactly how many shirts of that particular style need to be re-ordered from hundreds of factories around the world.

Our increasingly globalized world economy has had negative impacts on the lives of college students as well. As we have mentioned, many jobs that were once the mainstay of the American economy have been lost to workers in other countries. Lost jobs mean lost wages, lost wages mean smaller tax revenues for all levels of government, and smaller tax revenues mean less money to spend on such things as education, roads,

and health care. When government has less money to spend on state colleges and universities, it is necessary to raise fees and tuition. Although many of you have experienced this rising cost of getting a college education, you may not have suspected that it is an indirect result of economic globalization. But it, like many of our economic difficulties today, is partly a result of the emergence of a global economy.

Globalization and Politics

Decisions made by governments in other countries affect our daily lives whether or not we are aware of it. When Japan's Ministry of International Trade and Industry decides to support long-term research in artificial intelligence or aircraft design, it is likely that Japanese industry will play an increasingly dominant role in these areas, with a direct impact on the American economy. That, at least, is what happened in the automobile industry during the 1980s. As the governments of Europe take the final steps to become a single economic community with a single currency, the result is the largest unified economy in the world. That, in turn, will have an enormous impact on the United States. The recently ratified North American Free Trade Agreement (NAFTA) will change the lives of millions of North Americans, Canadians, and Mexicans. Some U.S. workers will find their jobs moving across the border to Mexico, where impoverished people are quite willing to make clothing or assemble electronics for $5 a day. Other U.S. workers will find new employment by creating products for Mexican consumers. There is great debate among sociologists and economists as to whether on balance Americans will be better or worse off as a result.

Sociology is concerned both with the political pro-

Globalization

You, the Global Consumer

Try a simple experiment. Walk through your dorm room, apartment, or house, and make a list of every product that you find. Include all electronic equipment, such as your stereo, television, computer, or calculator. Look for information on where your CDs were actually manufactured as disks. Go through your closet and drawers, checking the labels on your clothing. What about your bicycle? Your car? If you are a good detective, you will find that much of what you consume was actually made by the hands of people who live in countries far away from the United States.

By way of example, consider the clothing you wear. Currently, at least a quarter of all clothing purchased in the United States is manufactured in some other country, twice the percentage of only a decade ago. Globally, the total dollar value of world trade in apparel today is well over a hundred times greater than it was a mere 40 years ago, having nearly tripled in the past 15 years alone. The richest countries in the world are the principal consumers of clothing that is increasingly made in the poorest countries (Dickerson, 1991; Appelbaum, Smith, and Christerson, 1994). In fact, the ability of Americans to buy all sorts of products, from clothing to cars, has a lot to do with the emergence in the past 20 years of a truly global production process based on the use of cheap labor around the world. While this has lowered the cost of many of the things we consume, it has also contributed to the loss of jobs and lower wages in the United States as well as the employment of millions of people around the world in low-wage factories. It remains an open question for sociological investigation who benefits and who loses as a result of the explosive growth in global production.

cesses by which such decisions are made, and the impact of these decisions on our daily lives. In this textbook, we will try to understand how the role of government is changing in the face of globalization, and how these changes are affecting the ways we live and interact with one another.

Globalization and Popular Culture

Music, television, and movies do not respect national boundaries. Rock music, which began as a combination of African rhythms, African-American blues and jazz, gospel, and country and western music, today has fused with musical forms from around the globe. Today one can hear rock and roll in the Chinese metropolis of Shanghai, or the small Mayan community of Ixtahuacan in the Guatemalan highlands. And in either place, it is common to find people wearing Levi jeans or surfing T-shirts. Japanese television now features MTV, while reruns of *Dallas* help to shape European images of American life, as do Clint Eastwood films in Asia. U.S. films are popular worldwide, and help to foster images of American lifestyles abroad. The Academy Awards are reportedly watched by more than a billion people worldwide.

Cultural diversity within nations is one result of the sweeping changes occurring in the world today, which have contributed to an enormous flow of immigrants from poor nations to wealthy ones. Virtually every industrial nation in the world has substantial and growing numbers of people who arrive in search of work and a better life. The United States, which has always been a nation of immigrants, is currently experiencing an enormous wave of migration from Asia and Latin America that helps bring diverse cultures into daily contact.

When immigrants come to the United States, they bring their cultural beliefs and practices with them. Soccer, one of the most popular sports in the world, is becoming increasingly popular in the United States as well, partly because of the influx of immigrants from Latin American countries where soccer is the premier sport. One result: for the first time, the United States hosted the world soccer championships in 1994. Rock and roll was forever transformed by the "British Invasion" of groups like the Beatles and Rolling Stones in the 1960s, just as it was altered by the "Caribbean Invasion" of reggae music in the 1970s and 1980s. American art was influenced by such European artists as Picasso early in this century; Picasso, in turn, was influenced by African art. Today millions of immigrants from Mexico, Central America, and Asia have brought with them their customs, language, and cuisine. Mexican-style fast-food restaurants are today a fixture across America, Chinese restaurants are commonplace, and even the most cautious diners have probably experimented with Japanese *sushi* or hot dishes from Thailand.

While the spread of culture around the globe has contributed to the emergence of some common shared aspects, it has also triggered a backlash of fear and intolerance. Hate crimes directed against native ethnic minorities and immigrants are, unhappily, common almost everywhere on the planet. In the United States, languages such as Spanish, Chinese, or Korean have been challenged by the "English only" movement, just as such economic imports as Japanese cars have been challenged by the "buy American" slogan.

Globalization and the Environment

Finally, it is obvious that pollution of the land, seas, and atmosphere shows little respect for national boundaries. When the giant Soviet nuclear power plant at Chernobyl suffered a meltdown in 1986, the radiation clouds poisoned the air across Europe, leaving millions of people living on contaminated ground. Acid rain from U.S. factories is killing forests and fish in the northern reaches of Canada, as well as across the Arctic Ocean in Siberia. DDT, once a popular pesticide used to kill deadly malaria-carrying mosquitoes and other insects, is today found in Antarctic penguins. We have good reason to believe that chemical propellants in our hairsprays and underarm deodorants are contributing to the depletion of ozone high in the earth's atmosphere, resulting in increased chances that today's sun-worshippers will suffer skin cancer later in life.

The rapid atmospheric growth of carbon dioxide and other "greenhouse gases"—major causes of global warming—are partly a result of the efforts of the impoverished people in poor nations to obtain a higher living standard. When China announced a five-year plan for industrial development, some experts feared that the projected level of industrial growth would *double* the amount of carbon dioxide in the earth's atmosphere. Yet such industrial development will eventually result in more clothing, running shoes, electronics, telephones, automobile parts, and other commodities that people in the United States will eagerly consume, while raising the standard of living of millions of Chinese. Sociology is directly concerned with these interconnected social and environmental processes.

SOCIOLOGY AND SCIENCE

Sociologists are not content with common-sense answers to questions about human social relations. Rather, they gather information in a systematic way, and try to develop systematic explanations based on that information. In other words, sociologists address social questions with the tools of science, although the word "science" may be used in many different ways.

Science and Scientific Theory

Science emerged as a challenge to religion, which had long argued that truth is revealed by God, rather than being discovered through disciplined inquiry. **Science**

The government of East Germany erected the Berlin Wall in 1961, separating that country from the West. With the disintegration of the Soviet Union, the two Germanys were reunified and the wall was torn down. The destruction of the wall was a symbol of the end of the Cold War and the ushering in of an era of global hopes for peace.

Population growth and poverty are two of the forces that have led people in poor nations to burn their forests in an effort to claim land for farming. As the world's rainforests rapidly disappear, some environmentalists are predicting global warming and other worldwide repercussions. How do you weigh such long-term global effects against the immediate survival needs of people in a particular country?

is a way of learning about the world *that combines systematic theory and observation to provide explanations of how things work.* **Scientific theories** consist of *a set of logically consistent ideas about the relationships between things, which permit those ideas to be checked against observations through scientific research.* **Scientific research** refers to *the different methods used by scientists to achieve the goal of systematic observation and information-gathering.* If scientific research yields observations that are inconsistent with scientific theories, then one or the other must be wrong. The various approaches to research employed by sociologists are discussed in the next chapter.

Natural scientists (for example, physicists, chemists, biologists, geologists, and astronomers) *study the nonhuman or purely physical aspects of the natural world.* Their research almost always begins with an explicit, well-formulated theory (Kuhn, 1970; Popper, 1959; Suppe, 1974). Theories tell the natural scientist which facts to look for; indeed, the theory often tells the scientist what a relevant fact *is.* Theories help the scientist to see what is happening; facts help the scientist to construct and evaluate the theory. Theories and facts require one another, and each continually modifies the other in a never-ending process that is the hallmark of science.

Two scientists observing the same event often have different interpretations, depending on the theory they bring to their observations. For example, an astronomer looking at the sunset knows that the sun appears to be setting only because the earth is rotating about its axis—it is the motion of the earth, not the sun, that gives the appearance of the setting sun. Before astronomy came to accept this theory, however, astronomers

trained in the scientific method believed that the earth remained still while the sun slowly moved below the horizon. This was because their theory—which stemmed from both common sense and religious beliefs—stated that the earth, as God's prize creation, lay at the center of the universe. If a scientist of today were to sit side-by-side with a scientist of the fourteenth century and observe a sunset, the two would interpret their observations differently.

A good theory has the following six characteristics:

1. **It is useful:** it provides answers to important questions.
2. **It is logically consistent:** one part of the theory does not contradict another part.
3. **It is testable:** it leads to conclusions that are capable of being refuted by the available evidence, should the theory turn out to be wrong.
4. **It is valid:** it is consistent with all available evidence.
5. **It is as simple as possible:** simple theories are preferable to complicated ones, if both provide equally convincing explanations for the same thing.
6. **It is never the "final word":** it is based on the best research and thinking currently available, but may change as new information or better ideas become available.

Differences Between the Social Sciences and Natural Sciences

There are a number of important differences between the social and natural sciences (Table 1.1). One feature of the work of natural scientists is that their subject matter does not talk back to them: whether their concern is

Table 1.1   Principal Differences Between the Social Sciences and Natural Sciences

	Natural Science	Social Science
Object of study	"Natural" world	"Human" world
Object seen as	Passive	Active
Prediction is	Possible and desirable	Difficult
Guided by	Theory	Theory or observation
Generalizations	Universal	Conditional
Examples	Physics, chemistry, biology, geology, astronomy	Sociology, economics, anthropology, psychology, political science

with subatomic particles or the human gene, they are focusing on objects that lack a human consciousness. On the other hand, **social scientists** (for example, sociologists, economists, anthropologists, psychologists, and political scientists) *study human beings and the social worlds that they consciously create.* The subjects of social science study can and do talk back, and in this lies a fundamental difference between the social and natural sciences. As the social scientist gains an understanding of how some aspect of the social world operates, the actors in that world may then go out and change their behavior—sometimes on the basis of what the social scientist has discovered.

For example, over the past quarter century many social scientists have studied the ways in which women are treated unequally as wage earners (Chapter 11). Scholars—particularly female social scientists—have documented the fact that women employees are often paid less than men who do similar work (Bielby, 1993; Bielby and Bielby, 1988; Benkokraitis and Feagin, 1986; Marini, 1989; Morrison et al., 1987). This scientific understanding has contributed to changes in the ways in which female wage earners see themselves and has led to demands for equal pay for equal work. Women's changing awareness, due in part to social science research, has therefore resulted in demands for greater equality, which will change the findings of the research itself.

Because human beings are capable of thinking about their circumstances and exercising choice, human behavior is often said to be unpredictable. One of the characteristics of natural science is its ability to make extremely accurate predictions, particularly when explaining relatively large-scale phenomena. The laws of physics enable scientists to launch a satellite and know where it will be five years from now. In the social sciences, however, predictions are much more difficult to make. To the extent that people make choices, their individual behavior is hard to forecast. Yet while a sociologist may never be able to accurately predict whether

or not a particular person will become unemployed, it is possible to predict the percentage of people who will be unemployed under specific circumstances, particularly if the sociologist has a good theory about the causes of unemployment.

Another difference between the natural and social sciences is that while natural science research is almost always governed by an explicit theory, social science research may begin with observation and only later develop a theory (Chapter 2). This approach places a priority on detailed observation, although eventually theories emerge that will then be evaluated by means of further data collection.

One final difference between the social and natural sciences has to do with **generalization,** the ability to *draw a broad conclusion from a particular study and then to apply it to a larger range of phenomena.* Because no two human beings are exactly alike, it is often difficult do make such generalizations. If you study female employees in your school and find that on average they earn less than male employees, can you generalize from these findings to all universities in the United States? To all jobs in the United States? While a physicist may have little difficulty generalizing from the results of a single well-done laboratory experiment to the entire cosmos, sociologists seldom if ever enjoy this luxury. At best, sociologists are likely to draw **conditional generalizations**—generalizations that *apply only under a specified set of conditions.* For example, these may involve a particular type of university, certain kinds of jobs, or a single region of the country.

Sociology and the Social Sciences

Sociology is a particular discipline of the social sciences (Table 1.2). It is a social science because sociologists see themselves as engaged in the scientific study of human social relations. In this sense sociology differs from social work and other related fields that are more concerned with the application of sociological knowl-

Table 1.2   The Social Sciences and Their Subject Matters

Social Science	Object of Study
Anthropology	Culture
Psychology	The individual
Economics	Resource allocation
Political science	Government
Sociology	Social relations in general: groups, institutions, societies

edge, rather than with generating knowledge itself. Sociology includes numerous subfields; virtually every chapter of this textbook focuses on a different one.

Many other social science disciplines share sociology's goal of studying human social relations scientifically. What is unique about sociology is the assumption that *social relationships hold the key to understanding how all aspects of social life operate.* While the other social sciences tend to focus on particular areas of social life, sociology has broader concerns: it studies the social relationships that underlie disciplines such as anthropology, psychology, economics, or political science. For example, psychologists typically focus on individual behavior, attempting to explain someone's thinking, acting, or feelings in terms of their personal childhood or adult experiences. The sociologist would be more likely to focus on the larger web of social relations that shape individual personality, from family and peers to schools, colleges, workplace, popular culture, and other institutions of the larger society. The sociologist thus adheres to the principle of **embeddedness**—the notion that *economic, political, and other forms of human activity are fundamentally shaped by social relations* (Granovetter, 1985).

Differing Sociological Perspectives

Sociologists have a wide variety of perspectives on the social world. Indeed, as we shall see immediately below, on virtually any topic there are likely to be strong areas of disagreement as well as agreement. How can this be the case in a discipline that claims to be scientific?

Scientists, like all people, have differing ideas about how the world works. As we have seen, some of these ideas are logically interconnected in the form of *theories.* Theories are based in part on broad assumptions that can never really be tested. A **paradigm** is *a perspective or framework, containing assumptions about the world, that helps to shape scientific theories* (Kuhn, 1970; Suppe, 1974). To return to our earlier example,

for more than a thousand years astronomers adhered to a paradigm that envisioned the earth as the center of the universe, until that paradigm was successfully challenged by another, which viewed the sun as the center. Today, of course, neither paradigm is accepted as correct. A particular paradigm typically helps to frame a wide variety of theories, all of which share the paradigm's assumptions. Paradigms orient the theorist to what are believed to be important problems, and they suggest ways of studying them. They also raise questions, and thereby help in providing answers.

In sociology there are two predominant paradigms concerned with macro-level social processes, and one concerned with micro-level social relations (Table 1.3).

Macro-Level Paradigms: Functionalism Versus Social Conflict

The **functionalist paradigm** *seeks to explain social organization and change in terms of the roles or functions performed by individual members, groups, institutions, and social relations.* When explaining why schools exist, for example, a functionalist might ask "what purpose does schooling serve for the society as a whole?" Possible answers might include teaching people to think creatively and critically generating new ideas for science and industry, or preparing people for their place in the economy. The fact that not all people get to attend the best colleges and universities would be explained in terms of the different functions that people serve in society: just as society requires highly educated doctors and engineers, it also requires less-educated factory workers and retail clerks if it is to function properly.

One of functionalism's key nontestable assumptions is that society is similar to a living organism, in that both contain many parts that function to ensure the health of the whole. The human body requires a healthy heart, lungs, digestive tract, and so forth in order to function properly. Similarly, a healthy society requires a properly functioning economy, educational system, family, and government in order to function properly as a whole.

Table 1.3   The Three Principal Sociological Paradigms

	Functionalism	Social Conflict	Symbolic Interactionism
Level of Focus	Macro	Macro	Micro
Assumptions about Society	Society is like a highly interdependent living organism, with people and institutions contributing to the health of the whole; there is widespread consensus on what is good and just; all members of society can benefit if all work together ("win-win" situation).	Society is comprised of conflicting interests, with some groups prospering only at the expense of others ("win-lose" situation); conflict is universal; consensus is limited; inequality is widespread.	The "self" and society as a whole are comprised of interacting individuals; interaction is by means of symbols, whose meanings must be actively interpreted; humans are inherently social.
Key Concerns	What keeps society operating smoothly? What functions do different institutions and organizations serve for society as a whole?	What are the sources of conflict in society? Who wins, and who loses? How can inequalities be overcome? What is the role of power in social relations?	How do individuals experience one another? How do they interpret the meanings of particular social interactions? How do they actively construct both a sense of "self," and society as a whole?

Functionalism has been challenged by a competing paradigm that makes radically different assumptions about the social world. This perspective is termed the **social conflict paradigm** because *it seeks to explain social organization and change in terms of conflict that is built into social relations.* When explaining why schools exist, a conflict theorist would ask, "who benefits and who is hurt by the existing educational system?" One possible answer might be that middle class people benefit because they are able to take advantage of the best schools and colleges to advance their subsequent careers. Poor people, on the other hand, suffer since they are likely to wind up in more poorly funded or otherwise inadequate schools that foreclose the possibility of college, leaving them only eligible for poorly paid jobs later in life.

One of the social conflict paradigm's key assumptions is that there are always competing social groups with inherently conflicting interests, so that one group benefits at the expense of another. For example, according to the social conflict paradigm, far from working for the benefit of society as a whole, the educational system is seen as reproducing inequality and class differences (Bowles and Gintis, 1976). It is important to bear in mind that the social conflict paradigm does not assume that people are conflictive by nature; rather, it assumes that social relations are often structured so as to produce conflict.

These two paradigms make different assumptions about the social world, lead to different kinds of questions, and therefore result in different answers. Sociologists increasingly believe that the two paradigms are not mutually exclusive. A major tenet of this textbook is that all social relations involve both function *and* conflict. As we shall see in Chapter 16, the educational system both serves to prepare people for their social roles (functionalist paradigm), *and* serves to perpetuate inequality and class differences (social conflict paradigm). We do not think it useful to try to force most theories into one paradigm or the other, and then make a choice between them. Rather, throughout this textbook we will refer to both function and conflict as different and important aspects of all social relations.

Micro-Level Paradigms: Symbolic Interactionism

A number of paradigms exist that explain small-scale social relations. While some of these will be briefly discussed in Chapter 5 (for example, both behavioral and psychoanalytic psychology), within sociology a single micro-level paradigm predominates.

The **symbolic interactionist paradigm** argues that *both the human self and society as a whole are the result of social interactions based on language and other sym-*

bols. A **symbol** is *something understood as representing something else to a human mind;* symbols range from words and language to nonverbal gestures and signs (Chapter 3). As its name suggests, symbolic interactionism emphasizes the importance of both symbols and social interaction as the building blocks of human psychology on the one hand, and entire societies on the other.

Although the name "symbolic interactionism" originated with Herbert Blumer in 1937, the school was founded by the University of Chicago philosopher George Herbert Mead during the 1920s. We shall examine symbolic interactionist theories in some detail in Chapter 5 and will refer to them throughout the book.

The symbolic interactionist paradigm makes two important assumptions about social life. The first is that human beings cannot live their lives in isolation, and they acquire their sense of "who they are" only through interaction with other human beings. The second is that such interaction is sustained through the use of symbols, which means that the interpretation of symbolic meanings must be a primary concern of sociology. The beginning point of sociological inquiry thus lies not only with observing how people interact but more fundamentally with how people make their actions meaningful to themselves and to others.

A simple word like "man" or "woman," for example, may convey very different meanings to people in different societies, and even sometimes to different people in the same society. Through interactions with one another, people test out such meanings in an effort to arrive at the shared understandings that are necessary for communication to occur. Because of this, symbolic interactionism is sometimes said to be a type of **interpretive sociology,** an approach that is concerned with *the ways in which people interpret symbols in the course of arriving at shared understandings about their daily lives.*

Symbolic interactionism is by definition concerned with interacting individuals, and thus is difficult to apply at the macro level. While even the largest institutions can be seen as consisting of interacting individuals, macro sociology argues that such institutions should be studied in their own right. For this reason, throughout this textbook we shall rely on the functionalist and social conflict paradigms to understand how society operates at the macro level, while turning to symbolic interactionism when we seek to understand how such macro-level processes are in fact realized at the micro-level of immediate social relations.

THE EMERGENCE OF SOCIOLOGICAL THEORY

Sociology's roots can be traced to three historical events that gave birth to the modern world. First, the rise of science, beginning in the sixteenth century, led to the belief that science could be fruitfully applied to human affairs. During the eighteenth-century "Age of Enlightenment" numerous scholars, centered primarily in France, sought to develop a scientific understanding of social life, which they believed would enable human beings to realize their fullest human potential. Second, the growth of modern industry in large cities seemed to hold the promise of great wealth for all; yet millions of impoverished people were condemned to toil in factories and live in filthy slums. Early sociologists were concerned with the promises as well as the evils of industrialization. Finally, the concept of **social engineering** was born—the belief that *strong governmental leaders, advised by social scientists, could use social science to design a preferred social order.* This notion remains a central ingredient in modern sociological thought.

Sociology thus arose in Europe in response to the emergence of the modern era. It was concerned with the sweeping changes that were transforming life in Europe, not only in terms of its immediate past but also as a result of globalization. Through economic expansion and conquest, European nations were coming into increasing contact with very different peoples around the world. By studying the histories of their own societies, as well as looking comparatively at other societies around the world, the early sociologists sought to identify those features of modern, urban industrial society that they believed were unique in history.

The Nineteenth-Century Founding Fathers

Women and people of non-European heritage were systematically excluded from positions of influence in the European universities where sociology and the other social sciences originated in the nineteenth century. As a result, much of early sociology reflects the concerns of the men who founded it. It is also **Eurocentric,** in that its *knowledge is centered on European concerns and beliefs.* We shall explore the reasons for this after looking at four of sociology's principal founders. It should be noted that despite its Eurocentric origins and concerns, sociology from its outset sought to develop universal understandings that would apply to other times and places. In their efforts to achieve a scientific understanding of society, the founders in different ways left their stamps on sociology today.

Auguste Comte

Auguste Comte (1798–1857) was a French social theorist who is generally credited with founding sociology, largely because he coined the term and equated it with the scientific study of social relations. Comte believed that social science could be used to effectively manage social life. On the other hand, he feared mob rule and argued that social change should occur slowly. In his view, therefore, social engineering had to be accompanied by a strong respect for traditions and history (Lenzer, 1975).

Although Comte (1974; orig. 1830–1842) developed an elaborate three-stage theory of social change, his most enduring legacy was his insistence that sociology be a scientific "social physics." Comte argued that sociology must rely entirely on a single method, which he termed **positivism**—the *belief that knowledge should be guided by facts, rather than by imagination, pure logic, or any other nonfactual source.* Comte believed that facts could speak for themselves—that if we free ourselves from all biases, we will truly see things as they are. Such "positive" knowledge, Comte argued, is the keystone of science. In his view, sociology is the final science to enter the positivist phase. It is, in his words, the "queen" of the sciences, since it encompasses all the other forms of knowledge, studying all facets of social life. Because of their extensive wisdom, Comte believed that sociologists would someday help industrialists to govern society, providing the scientific understanding needed to harness industry for the common good.

Comte left an indelible stamp on modern sociology. First, his call for the scientific study of social organization continues to be the goal of most sociological research, although in the next chapter we will see that his hope for knowledge based solely on "the facts" is not possible. Second, his rather immodest vision of sociology as the "queen of all sciences" retains its appeal to sociologists, who are not shy about using their discipline to study any and all areas of social life. Finally, his strong belief that sociologists should sit as wise counsels to government and industry remains a somewhat frustrated hope of many sociologists today.

Emile Durkheim

If Comte founded and named the discipline of sociology, the French scholar Emile Durkheim (1858–1917) is generally credited with setting the discipline on its present course. Durkheim (1964a, orig. 1893; 1964b, orig. 1895; 1965, orig. 1912; 1966, orig 1897) established the subject matter of sociology, laid out rules for conducting research, and developed an important theory of social change.

Durkheim argued that unlike pyschology, sociology should focus not on individuals but rather on the social group. Sociology's subject matter consists of **social facts,** *qualities of groups that are external to individual members yet constrain their thinking and behavior.* Durkheim (1964b; orig. 1895) argued that social facts should be used to explain other social facts.

What exactly are social facts? To make a rough analogy with physics, individuals may be thought of as

Emile Durkheim (1858–1917) is generally regarded as the founder of modern sociology. His work has had an enormous impact on functionalist theory in sociology and anthropology, as well as quantitative approaches to studying the effects of social structure on human behavior.

atoms, each one different from the other. Groups are like molecules, comprised of many atoms, yet having their own unique properties. Just as atoms of hydrogen and oxygen combine into a molecule of water that is completely different from hydrogen and oxygen, so too do groups of individuals have **emergent properties**— properties that *differ from the characteristics of the individuals who comprise them.* Your behavior when you are alone may change when you are with a particular group of friends, and change again when you are in a more formal setting such as a classroom. You may feel constrained or "pressured" to act in certain ways under different circumstances, even if you do not openly acknowledge such pressures. The concept of social facts led Durkheim to appreciate the tremendous importance of **social structure,** *underlying regularities in how people behave and interrelate with one another.* People may change over time, but social structures usually remain relatively stable, at least over the short run.

In one of Durkheim's best-known research studies, he sought to explain suicide not in terms of the behavior of unhappy individuals but rather exclusively in terms of social facts that emphasized the importance of social structure. Instead of examining individual suicides, he focused on average *rates* of suicide as properties of different groups in France.

For example, drawing on official government statistics, Durkheim (1966; orig. 1897) found that higher percentages of people committed suicide in parts of France that were Protestant rather than Catholic. This was the case, he reasoned, because the social bonds and beliefs among French Catholics at the time were stronger than among Protestants, who as a consequence were more likely to feel unattached to others or to a strong belief in God. This lack of attachment made Protestants more disposed toward suicide than Catholics. Furthermore, Durkheim found that even Catholics were more likely to commit suicide if they lived in Protestant parts of France. He concluded that suicide was not due to the individual's religion itself but rather resulted from aspects of the larger social structure, such as the religious beliefs of the community. One of Durkheim's enduring legacies for sociology thus involves the statistical analysis of **structural effects,** *variations in human behavior that can be explained by the larger social structure rather than by individual differences.*

Durkheim's theory of social change, outlined in *The Division of Labor in Society* (1964a; orig. 1893), is concerned with the changing forms of **social solidarity,** the *bonds that unite the members of a social group.* In Durkheim's view, at the dawn of human history people lived in small, intimate groups in which they all spoke the same language, shared the same beliefs and values, and did pretty much the same kinds of work. There was very little division of labor and members typically shared what Durkheim termed a **collective conscience**—*common values, outlooks, interpretations of events, languages and dialects, and, in general, identical ways of thinking that characterize preindustrial societies.* People in such groups were united by what Durkheim termed **mechanical solidarity**, *strong social ties and shared beliefs that are based on similarity.* In modern industrial countries, by way of contrast, the only thing that connects people is a highly complex and interdependent set of social roles and organizations. People may speak different languages, have different values and beliefs, and engage in tens of thousands of different kinds of occupations. According to Durkheim, the common glue that unites people in modern society is their mutual interdependence: each citizen performs a particular duty that is essential for the continued operation of the entire society. Durkheim termed this **organic solidarity**—*social ties that are based on difference and functional interdependence, similar to the unity of a living organism comprised of many interdependent parts, in which each part has its own specialized role to play.*

Durkheim's analysis of society as a unitary organism makes him the founder of the functionalist paradigm in sociology. Durkheim argued that the function of the division of labor is to provide a basis for social solidarity, one that shifts over time from mechanical to organic. Unfortunately, the latter is often a poor substitute for the former, since it is often impersonal and remote. In extreme cases, the differences between people are so great that the result is **anomie**—*a state of confusion that occurs when people lose sight of the shared rules and values that give order and meaning to their lives.* In this unhealthy situation social order breaks down, people are no longer guided by widely shared rules, and pathological behavior such as suicide increases (1973; orig. 1922). Durkheim strongly advocated *moral education* to reinfuse people with a set of shared values, as well as social engineering to help a nation's leaders design institutions capable of ensuring harmony and social order.

Karl Marx

Karl Marx (1818–1883) was born in Germany but did much of his important writing in exile in France and England. Marx had a substantial impact on the emergence and subsequent development of sociology, even though he did not think of himself as a sociologist (Tucker, 1977; Appelbaum, 1988; Zeitlin, 1987). He was primarily concerned with explaining the shortcomings of capitalism, using his theories to rally intellectuals and workers in an effort to change a system he believed to be inherently unjust. Marx did not believe in being an "armchair intellectual," commenting on social life from a safe distance. Nor did he believe that the task of social scientists was to work with industrialists or capitalists to engineer a more humane form of capitalism. Rather, to paraphrase one of his more famous statements, he believed that his task was "not to simply interpret the world, but to change it" (Marx, 1845–1846).

Yet at the same time Marx did not believe people could change the world simply on the basis of their wishes or desires. Rather, effective change can occur only if people adequately understand how society operates, and how their actions can influence its course. The future is not determined by the present; nor is it freely created by individual actors. Rather, the scientific study of society enables us to understand the relationship between larger social structures, and people's actions. This is what we have previously called the "sociological imagination."

Marx saw himself as a revolutionary, providing the theoretical underpinnings for an international labor movement that would eventually transform all of the world's industrial nations. The revolutions that created the former Soviet Union (1917), the current People's Republic of China (1949), Cuba (1959), and numerous other countries were based in his ideas, although it is

Karl Marx (1818–1883) argued that capitalism inevitably produces growing inequality and conflict between social classes, leading to its eventual demise. His ideas had a significant impact on the social sciences and are the origin of conflict theory in sociology. They also led to communist revolutions in Russia, China, Cuba, and other poor nations throughout the world.

debatable how closely the resulting societies actually resembled Marx's views. As recently as the late 1980s, as many as one out of every three people on the planet lived in countries that claimed Marxism to be their guiding social and economic philosophy.

Because these ideas called for the radical transformation of capitalism, they have almost always been outside the mainstream of sociological thought, particularly in the United States (Appelbaum, 1988). Nonetheless, they have had an incalculable influence on the development of sociology, even on those who disagreed with them (Zeitlin, 1987). Marx, unlike the other theorists of his time, emphasized the negative consequences of capitalism for the lives of working people and sought to develop a theory of social change that would hasten its downfall. Whereas writers such as Comte and Durkheim believed capitalism to be the end point of history, Marx claimed it was not—that another type of social order would eventually emerge that would be more humane and capable of satisfying the needs of everyone. This new social order would build on the strengths of the old one but would reject its weakness. Specifically, it would

harness the power of science, technology, and industry for the benefit of all, rather than only for the wealthy and powerful. The system that would accomplish this Marx termed **communism**—the *abolishment of private ownership of factories and other means of producing wealth, which would then be cooperatively owned and run by the workers themselves* (Marx, 1848, 1867).

One of Marx's principal contributions to sociology was his notion of **social class,** a concept that refers to *unequal social position based on income, wealth, and—more generally—a person's location in the economic system.* In Marx's view, capitalism ultimately tends to divide people into two broad classes: those who own factories and other sources of wealth, and those whose labor actually makes the products. The former, termed **capitalists,** includes the *factory owners, merchants, and bankers.* The latter, termed **proletariat** (from the Latin term for "common person"), primarily includes *factory workers.* In Marx's analysis, capitalism makes enemies of these two broad groups, since the former prospers at the expense of the latter. Class conflict is the inevitable result; Marx (1848) believed that "the history of all hitherto existing society is the history of class struggles." Marx claimed that if workers were to succeed in raising their wages and their standard of living, the profits of the capitalists paying the wages would be reduced. In order to survive, Marx argued, capitalists would try to cut labor costs, both by replacing workers with machines and by finding cheaper workers elsewhere in the world. Both of these predictions have proven at least partially correct. Automation has displaced workers in many high-technology factories, while numerous jobs in American manufacturing have been lost to low-wage areas throughout the world.

Marx's ideas thus provide important insights into the process of globalization. The large part of his work was concerned with the analysis of capitalism, and many of his conclusions remain invaluable. At the same time, there have been many changes in capitalism that neither Marx (nor any social scientist) could foresee a century and a half ago. Many workers have prospered in capitalist countries, and even though poverty remains, Marx's anticipated worldwide anticapitalist revolutions have not taken the course he anticipated. Moreover, since the late 1980s many of the political systems based on Marx's ideas have moved rapidly toward adopting capitalist economies.

Yet Marx's important contributions to contemporary sociology are many. These include his emphasis on the importance of social class, his analysis of capitalism as a global economic system, and his recognition that conflict and change are the central features of social life. Because of his emphasis on the universality of social conflict, Marx is generally credited with being the founder of the social conflict paradigm in sociology.

Max Weber

Max Weber (1864–1920), a German sociologist who wrote at the turn of the century, may well have had the greatest influence on sociology (as well as political science) of any of the figures we have mentioned. Weber's influence, like Durkheim's, partly has to do with sociological method, and partly with the theoretical understanding he brought to bear on the emergence of the modern social world. His writings on sociological method are best-known for two claims: (1) that a direct knowledge of pure facts is not possible; and (2) that sociology should be concerned with how human understanding occurs in social interaction.

Concerning the nature of facts, Weber—unlike Comte, Durkheim, and Marx—believed that sociological ideas could never exactly capture the realities they sought to describe. This is because all ideas—sociological or otherwise—are at best a partial view of a complex and multifaceted reality (Burger, 1976). For example, when Weber (1958; orig. 1904–1905) sought to describe "Protestantism," he acknowledged that it was necessary to extract certain beliefs and practices from the enormous range of things that Protestants actually claim to believe. This led Weber (1949; orig.

Max Weber (1864–1920) is one of the most influential theorists in the social sciences. His studies of the relationship between values and economic institutions have proved an enduring legacy, as has his notion that modern societies are becoming increasingly bureaucratized. He also argued that sociological explanation was concerned not only with cause and effect, but with the understanding of meanings as well.

1903–1917) to conclude that sociologists could never present pure facts, but then should instead seek to formulate **ideal types**—*sets of sociological ideas that best capture the essential features of some aspect of social reality according to the theoretical concerns of the sociologist.* A sociologist who wants to describe the nature of "bureaucracy" should look at real-life examples of bureaucracies, extracting those features that are common to most. Such a description is then judged according to how well it captures the essential features of the actual bureaucracies it purports to describe, as well as how useful it is to sociologists for the subsequent development of a theory of bureaucracy.

Weber's second claim about sociological method was that sociologists should begin their analysis with individuals rather than social groups (Gerth and Mills, 1946). He thus rejected Durkheim's call for the study of social facts. Rather, Weber argued, an adequate explanation of the social world must begin with the individual, and take into account the *meaning* of the things people say and do. Groups can neither think nor act; only people are capable of this. And, because people live in a symbolic world of words and images, a given thought or action may not mean the same thing to two people. For example, a sign that says "maximum speed limit 55" means one thing to an ordinary motorist, another thing to an ambulance driver, and yet something different to a police officer.

Weber argued that in order to adequately explain what people do, we must employ **verstehen,** the common term for *interpretive understanding;* we must be able to figuratively "stand under" the people we study, to walk in their shoes and see the world through their eyes. A dirt mound teeming with thousands of termites would produce revulsion in most Americans, but among Venezuela's Yanomamo Indians roasted termites are viewed as a delicious source of nourishment, and so the same mound would be regarded as a potential feast. Sociologists must be extremely careful not to let their own cultural biases interfere with their efforts to see the world through the eyes of the people they study. Weber's writings on *verstehen* greatly influenced interpretive sociology, including the symbolic interactionist paradigm.

Weber wrote extensively on the importance of cultural values in shaping human society. Unlike Marx, who tended to emphasize the importance of economic factors in accounting for social change, Weber (1958; orig. 1904–1905) argued that religious beliefs were in large part responsible for the emergence of capitalism in northern Europe (Chapter 17). In his account, traditional Protestant values—particularly as embodied in the teachings of early theologians such as John Calvin (1509–1564)—motivated religious followers to work hard and to live austere lives for the greater glory of

God. Such people became the entrepreneurs and laborers alike in capitalistic enterprises: the former reinvested all their profits in their businesses (since God condemned ostentatious living), while the latter provided a diligent and tireless workforce.

Weber's theories of social and economic organization have also been highly influential (Weber, 1979; orig. 1921). Weber believed that there is a general trend in the modern world toward ever-greater reliance on the use of logic and reason. While most social organizations throughout history were based on habit, custom, and tradition, modern organizations seek to be as efficient, rational, and scientific as possible, showing little concern for tradition. One of Weber's most famous demonstrations of this argument is found in his study of **bureaucracies,** *organizations that are governed by an extensive number of written rules and regulations intended to promote organizational efficiency.* Weber feared that modern life would come to be bureaucratized in every respect. However efficient bureaucracies might be, Weber felt that they would result in highly unsatsifying lives, rendering us prisoners in what he termed an "iron cage." This process of bureaucratization was global in scope and would eventually extend to social organizations around the world. In this prediction Weber proved to be truly farsighted.

Although Weber shared some of Marx's pessimism about capitalism, he did not believe that some alternative utopian form of social organization would emerge. Nor did he believe that sociologists enjoyed privileged insights about the social world that would enable them to wisely counsel rulers and industrialists, as Comte (and to some extent Durkheim) had thought. Although Weber did become involved in advising the democratic German government immediately after World War I, he was extremely realistic about the shortcomings inherent in the use of social science to solve all social problems.

Founding Mothers and People of Color

The four towering figures of early sociology that we have just discussed were men born in one or two European countries. Why is our list so limited?

First, there were few women writing as sociologists in the nineteenth century, and virtually no people of color. Second, the few women who were writing were not taken seriously by the academic community. Both reasons reflect discrimination on the part of the male-dominated intellectual community, including many early sociologists. Between 1840 and 1960, for example, almost no women held senior academic positions in any sociology department at any European or American university, with the exception of exclusively

Abdel Rahman Ibn-Khaldun (1332–1406), a North African Arab who lived in Tunis and Spain more than six centuries ago, might well be considered the true founder of sociology. Schooled in mathematics, history, and the Koran, the Muslim holy book, he advanced such modern notions as social forces, social facts, and social laws. In his study of such institutions as the state and religion, Ibn-Khaldun emphasized the importance of strife and conflict as well as social solidarity, making him a predecessor of both the functionalist and social conflict paradigms. Yet because his work was largely unknown to sociologists until relatively recently, he had little influence on the emergence of the discipline.

"women's colleges" (Ritzer, 1992). Women were pushed to the fringes of the discipline, and gender issues were not a central sociological concern. The exclusion of women from academia, of course, was not unique to sociology; it was—and to some extent still is—found in all academic fields.

Although the French Revolution (1789) and the American Constitution (drafted in 1787) were supposed to have ushered in periods of democracy and equality in both countries, in fact women did not get the right to vote until 1920 in the United States and 1945 in France. French women were not even given the right to attend secondary schools until 1880, nearly one hundred years after the French Revolution. In 1848, when a woman, Jeanne Deroin, attempted to run for the French National Assembly, its all-male representatives ruled her efforts unconstitutional. Twenty years later, when Julie Daubie won a prize from the Lyon Academy for her essay "Poor Women in the Nineteenth Century," France's Public Education Minister denied her diploma on the grounds that he would be "forever holding up his ministry to ridicule" (Kandal, 1988). It is small wonder that sociology, which was born in such an environment, did not include many influential women theorists.

Under these discriminatory conditions, it is also not surprising that important European male sociologists typically mentioned only their male predecessors, thus perpetuating the notion that there were no important female influences. Thus, for example, Emile Durkheim traced the important roots of his sociology to other male figures such as Rousseau, Montesquieu, and Comte. Marx spent a great deal of his writings debating the ideas of prominent male economists such as Adam Smith, or male philosophers such as Hegel. The vast number of citations in Weber's work seldom include women scholars, although his wife, Marianne Weber, was an accomplished scholar and political activist, who wrote on gender roles and authority, gave public lectures in support of the women's movement, and was the first woman member of the local provincial government. Whether such selectivity merely reflects the lack of women scholars at the time or is the result of anti-female biases on the part of the "founding fathers" is a topic that is only now being explored by social historians (Kandal, 1988).

While neither women nor people of color were silent when sociology was born (Box 1.3), their voices have been effectively silenced by most of those who have recorded sociology's history. In this textbook we shall pay special attention to these voices, acknowledging the importance of their scholarship and drawing attention to their exclusion when they have been ignored.

Twentieth-Century American Sociology

Although sociology was born in Europe, it took firm root in American soil, where it was heavily influenced by rapid turn-of-the-century industrialization and urbanization. Strikes by organized labor, corruption in government, an explosion of European immigration, and the growth of city slums all helped to shape early sociological thought.

The first sociologists were disproportionately men from small midwestern towns, a large number coming from ministerial backgrounds. They were often imbued with a liberal enthusiasm for social reform, a mistrust of government, and an aversion to big city life. It is perhaps not surprising that the infant discipline cut its teeth on urban social problems such as crime, delinquency,

and poverty (Ritzer, 1992; Bramson, 1961; Hinkle and Hinkle, 1954). From the very beginning, American sociology typically championed the cause of those who were exploited and oppressed by society, and many early sociologists were activists pressing for change.

Yet at the same time, early American sociology was not immune to the prevailing racial prejudices of the period. For example, an early book review in the *American Journal of Sociology,* the discipline's new journal, concluded that "it is still only through full recognition that the average Negro is still a savage child of nature that the north and south can be brought to unite in work to uplift the race" (Ellwood, 1907). One of the most prominent social commentators of the time, W. E. B. DuBois (1868–1963), was largely ignored by the discipline, even though he was the first African American to receive a Ph.D. from Harvard and was the author of some 20 books and more than a hundred scholarly articles on race and race relations. DuBois' pathbreaking

W. E. B. DuBois (1868–1963) was a prominent and outspoken African-American sociologist whose writings on race relations and the lives of American blacks are now seen as fundamental. Yet at the time, his ideas were too radical to find wide acceptance in the sociological community.

Box 1.3

Silenced Voices

Scholars Outside the Mainstream

Although there were not as many female scholars as male scholars when sociology was founded, there were nonetheless a large number of highly accomplished women writers whose ideas were largely ignored, both in Europe and the United States. There were also some prominent African-American sociologists whose voices were also effectively excluded from the mainstream of sociological thought, at least until recent times.

Sociology as a discipline emerged during the first modern flourishing of feminism, which grew as a movement from the 1830s to the 1930s (Kandal, 1988). The British scholar Mary Wollstonecraft's (1982; orig. 1792) *A Vindication of the Rights of Women,* for example, argued that scientific progress could not occur without allowing women to become men's equals, a goal that could be achieved only through universal education. Around the same time, the English writer Catherine MacCaulay published her *Letters on Education,* advancing similar arguments. In France, a feminist newspaper was published from 1836 to 1838, and in 1843 Flora Tristan called upon male workers to grant equal rights to their female counterparts, "the last remaining slaves in France." The first feminist daily newspaper, *Women's Voice,* was published in England in 1848. The League for Women's Rights was founded in 1861, and the First International Congress for Women's Rights in 1878. Aline Valette published *Socialism and Sexism* in 1893, nearly three-quarters of a century before the term "sexism" found its way into spoken English.

Two examples will help show how important women scholars were largely excluded from early mainstream sociological discourse. One was a prominent British sociologist; the other an African-American writer and activist.

Harriet Martineau (1802–1876), acclaimed as the first woman sociologist (Rossi, 1973), is best known for her translation of Auguste Comte's six-volume work on politics. Martineau's meticulous editing helped make Comte's often obscure and excessive prose accessible to the English-speaking world, thereby ensuring his stature as a founder of sociology. Yet Martineau was a distinguished scholar in her own right, arguably a far better sociologist than the man she translated. She was the author of dozens of books, countless articles, and more than a thousand newspaper columns. Her works included important studies of democratic beliefs and practices in America, sociological research methods, British industry and agriculture, and political economy, leading some sociologists to regard her now all-but-forgotten work as in many ways comparable to the discipline's acknowledged founders (Terry, 1983; Deegan, 1991).

Ida B. Wells-Barnett (1862–1931), born into slavery in Mississippi, became an internationally recognized writer, lecturer, and crusader for the rights of women and African Americans. She was best known for her systematic sociological studies of lynching, a common southern practice in which mobs of white citizens hung blacks who had offended the white community. Wells-Barnett wrote several highly influential books and countless newspaper articles on the topic. She also crusaded for women's suffrage and was a founding member of the National Association for the Advancement of Colored People (NAACP) (Deegan, 1991; Lerner, 1972). Yet despite these important achievements, her work was all but forgotten until the 1970s, when a growing number of scholars began systematic efforts to "rediscover" the voices of once-influential women and minority writers that had long been ignored by mainstream social science disciplines.

1899 study, *The Philadelphia Negro* (1967), was not even reviewed in the *American Journal of Sociology.* His call for the scientific sociological study of race relations, as well as his insistence that educated black leaders should lead the fight for Black liberation in the United States and Africa, were viewed by many whites as too radical for the times (Stuckey, 1993; Omi and Winant, 1986).

Although the earliest college courses actually entitled "sociology" were offered in the 1880s, the first de-

Ida B. Wells-Barnett (1862–1931), born a slave, emerged as one of the most influential writers of her time on the vicious practice of lynching blacks that was common in the south. She also fought for women's voting rights, and was a founder of the National Association for the Advancement of Colored People.

partment devoted exclusively to the emerging discipline was founded in 1892 by Albion Small at the University of Chicago, which dominated the discipline for much of the first half of the twentieth century (Ritzer, 1992). Robert Ezra Park (1864–1944), Ernest Burgess (1886–1966), and their students founded the "Chicago School" of sociology, which conducted numerous studies of social life in the rapidly growing city. No topic or group was exempt—from hoboes and flophouses to movie houses, dance halls, and slums; from youth gangs, crowds, and mobs to residents of lakefront mansions. Florian Znaniecki and W. I. Thomas conducted a major study of the problems experienced by Polish peasant immigrants. E. Franklin Frazier, an African-American student of Park, conducted studies of race relations, calling for the assimilation of racial and ethnic minorities into the mainstream American

culture (Omi and Winant, 1986). Park himself was a strong advocate of racial inclusion, having once served as a personal secretary to the great African-American educator, Booker T. Washington. Park and Burgess's 1921 textbook, *An Introduction to the Science of Sociology,* shaped the discipline for years afterward (Ritzer, 1992; Bramson, 1961; Hinkle and Hinkle, 1954).

Despite its liberal leanings, the Chicago School was not entirely free from the prejudices of the period. On the one hand, at a time when women were excluded from most universities, the sociology department admitted female graduate students, employed female faculty members, and opposed sex-segregated classes. Yet at the same time, in its scholarly writings it advanced the prevailing sociological belief that a woman's proper place was in the home. Furthermore, Park and Burgess strongly believed that the task of sociology was to scientifically study society and not engage in social reform. Perhaps this is why the department's five female faculty members never achieved regular full-time faculty status, or why female sociologists at the University of Chicago were eventually separated into a newly founded school that prepared people for social work (Deegan, 1988).

One of sociology's preeminent figures, Jane Addams (1860–1935), never obtained a regular position in the university, which even denied her an honorary degree. Yet Addams wrote eleven books, hundreds of articles (including several in the *American Journal of Sociology*), and eventually won the Nobel Peace Prize. Addams is perhaps best known as the founder of Hull House, a settlement house for the poor that became a center for feminists, political activists, social reformers, and even University of Chicago sociology professors. But she also pioneered studies of social problems in Chicago, and her *Hull House Maps and Papers,* published by Hull House residents in 1893, helped to shape the interests of the Chicago School more than a decade later (Deegan, 1988; 1991).

After World War II, the dominance of Chicago sociology ended. The discipline began to turn away from the study of social problems, and toward more sophisticated statistical modeling of social processes. A renewed interest in the grand theories of the founding fathers was kindled by Harvard sociologist Talcott Parsons (1902–1979), who reintroduced such theorists as Durkheim and Weber (but not Marx) to American sociologists. Parsons's own theories sought to develop a functionalist explanation of social relations, in which all institutions were seen as contributing to the stability of the social system as a whole (Ritzer, 1992; Bramson, 1961; Hinkle and Hinkle, 1954).

At Columbia University, Robert K. Merton's (1910–) **theories of the middle range** sought to

Jane Addams (1860–1935) is perhaps best known as the founder of Hull House, a Chicago settlement house for the poor. She received the Nobel Peace Prize in 1931, and she was also a widely published sociologist, whose research on Chicago neighborhoods strongly influenced the men who are generally credited with founding American sociology.

bridge European-style grand theory and more narrowly focused research. His studies of public opinion, technology, deviance, reference groups, and voting behavior helped to advance the functionalist paradigm in sociology. Merton argued, for example, that human actions have two different kinds of functions for the larger social system. **Manifest functions** are *social consequences that are intended by the actor;* **latent functions** are *those that are neither intended nor expected* (Merton, 1968). Merton thus sought to demonstrate that not all functions work to strengthen the social organism, as Durkheim and other early functionalists implied. He identified these as **dysfunctions**—*maladaptive consequences of actions that weaken the social organism.* It is important to ask for whom an action is likely to be functional, and for whom is it likely to be dysfunctional (Ritzer, 1992).

Another Columbia University sociologist, C. Wright Mills (1916–1962), influenced the thinking of many sociologists who began teaching in the 1960s and 1970s, even though he was himself very much an outcast from the discipline during his lifetime. We have already noted the importance of Mills's concept of the sociological imagination. Mills, who described himself as a "plain Marxist," scathingly condemned the injustices he perceived in American society. One of his best-known studies was a highly critical analysis of "white collar" professionals, whom Mills believed constituted a new and powerful social class. Another study analyzed the workings of the "power elite," a small group of businessmen, military leaders, and politicians that Mills believed ran the country in their own interests.

Mills wrote partly in reaction to functionalism, seeking to redefine sociology as a discipline concerned with radical social change (Ritzer, 1992).

MAKING HISTORY

It is our hope, as authors, that this textbook will enable you to better understand how human beings are both the changer and the changed. The world in which we live today is changing as never before in the brief history of the human race. In some ways these are deeply troubling times, beset by economic dislocation, environmental damage, and other worries that seem to grab at us every time we turn on the television or pick up a newspaper. At the same time this is an extremely promising and hopeful time. The most powerful nations on earth seem more willing than ever before to lay aside their differences, and work toward common solutions to the economic and environmental problems they have created. The technological advances that threaten us also hold the promise of bringing us together in a global community—a "spaceship earth" on which we all share the same problems and the same promises.

The decisions we make today will prove decisive for the future of our planet. Yet we cannot simply invent a better future out of our fantasies. To act effectively in the world, we must first understand how the world op-

The 5.4 billion people of this planet truly live in a global community, in which the lives of different peoples can no longer be seen as separate from one another. Sociology can help provide a better understanding of the global interdependencies that shape our problems as well as promises for the future.

erates, from the immediate events of our daily lives to distant social forces that reverberate around the globe. This textbook is intended to provide you with the be-ginnings of such an understanding, with the hope that you will become more effective actors in a world that desperately needs your engagement.

CHAPTER SUMMARY

1. Sociology is centrally concerned with the social group, and the processes that characterize its oper-ation. Unlike the other social sciences, sociology is especially concerned with the ways in which po-litical, economic, and other organizations are **em-bedded** in social relationships.

2. The **sociological imagination** enables us to better understand the linkages between personal experi-ences and "private troubles" and seemingly remote "public issues." Sociology is thus concerned with the interplay of the **micro** and **macro** levels of so-cial relations.

3. Sociology also develops an appreciation of human **diversity,** which is both fostered and threatened by the process of globalization. Mass communication helps to make us aware of our differences, while creating pressures to blend those differences into a common culture.

4. Another function of sociology is to explain **in-equality** within and between countries in terms of larger social processes, such as economic global-ization and discrimination.

5. A final key task of sociology is to understand the implications of **globalization** on the economic, po-litical, cultural, and environmental processes that are transforming our lives. Although globalization is as old as human history, its pace has rapidly ac-celerated during the past twenty years.

6. Science relies on theories to explain how things are related in the world, to generate hypotheses which can then be checked against observations obtained through **scientific research.** Facts can never "speak for themselves;" all scientific knowledge is a combination of theoretical insight and observation.

7. Early sociologists believed that the tools of science could lead to a better life. They thus sought to un-derstand the impact of industrialization, urbaniza-tion, and globalization on the social world.

8. The founders of sociology differed deeply on the nature of the discipline and its role in social change. While Durkheim, Comte, and Weber viewed their research as helping to improve on the existing social order, Marx saw his research as helping to radically transform it.

9. Although sociology generally traces its origins to a small group of nineteenth century male intellec-tuals from Europe, there were important women writers at the time whose ideas often had an unacknowledged impact on sociological thinking; discrimination, however, seriously limited their role.

10. In the United States, sociology originated primar-ily at the University of Chicago, with a focus on the problems stemming from indusrialization and urbanization. Its founders tended to be liberal re-formists. Although there were some notable ex-ceptions, women and people of color remained largely excluded from the discipline until well into the twentieth century.

QUESTIONS FOR DISCUSSION

1. According to C. Wright Mills, the "sociological imagination" consists of being able to make con-nections between one's personal experiences and larger social forces. Use the sociological imagina-tion to account for some personal concern of im-portance to you at the present time.

2. To what extent can the approaches of natural sci-ence be used to study human affairs? In what ways does sociology differ from the natural sciences?

3. The earliest influences on the development of soci-ological thought were men from a small number of European countries. Why was this the case? Is it possible that other influential figures are simply not known today? Discuss why this might be so.

4. In what ways are processes of globalization affect-ing your life today? In what ways can you say that you might be better off in five years because of these processes? In what ways might you be worse off?

KEY TERMS

anomie: A state of confusion that occurs when people lose sight of the shared rules and values that give order and meaning to their lives.

bureaucracy: An organization that is governed by an extensive number of written rules and regulations intended to promote organizational efficiency.

capitalists: In Marx's theory, a propertied social class that includes factory owners, merchants, and bankers.

collective conscience: Common values, outlooks, interpretations of events, languages and dialects, and in general the identical ways of thinking that characterize early preindustrial societies.

communism: A political-economic system that abolishes the private owernship of factories and other means of producing wealth, which would then be cooperatively owned and run by the workers themselves.

conditional generalization: A generalization that applies only under a specified set of conditions.

critical thinking: A form of thinking characterized by a willingness to ask any question, no matter how difficult; to be open to any answer that is supported by reason and evidence; and to openly confront one's biases and prejudices when they get in the way.

diversity: The social relations and interaction of many different kinds of people.

dysfunctions: In Robert K. Merton's theory, the maladaptive consequences of actions that weaken the social organism.

embeddedness: The notion that economic, political, and other forms of human activity are fundamentally shaped by social relations.

emergent properties: Properties of groups that differ from the characteristics of the individuals who comprise them.

ethnocentrism: The tendency to judge other cultures by the standards of one's own culture, regarding one's own values and way of life as "normal" and "better."

Eurocentric: Knowledge that is centered on European concerns and beliefs.

functionalist paradigm: A macro-sociological perspective that seeks to explain social organization and change in terms of the roles or functions performed by individual members, groups, institutions, and social relations.

generalization: A broad conclusion that is drawn from a particular study and then applied to a larger range of phenomena.

globalization: The processes by which the lives of all people around the planet become increasingly interconnected in economic, political, cultural, and environmental terms, along with an awareness of such interconnections.

ideal type: According to Max Weber, a set of sociological ideas that best captures the essential features of some aspect of social reality according to the theoretical concerns of the sociologist.

inequality: Differences in wealth, prestige, power, and other valued resources.

interpretive sociology: An approach to sociology that is concerned with the ways in which people interpret symbols in the course of arriving at shared understandings about their daily lives.

latent functions: In Robert K. Merton's theory, social consequences that are neither intended nor expected by the actor.

macro level: Larger, more invisible, and often more remote social processes that help to shape the micro world.

manifest functions: In Robert K. Merton's theory, social consequences that are intended by the actor.

mechanical solidarity: In Emile Durkheim's theory, strong social ties and shared beliefs that are based on similarity.

micro level: Social relations that involve direct social interaction with others.

natural scientist: A scientist who studies the nonhuman or purely physical aspects of the natural world.

organic solidarity: In Emile Durkheim's theory, social ties that are based on difference and functional interdependence, similar to the unity of a living organism in which each organ has its own specialized role to play.

paradigm: A perspective or framework containing assumptions about the world that helps to shape scientific theories.

positivism: Auguste Comte's belief that knowledge should be guided by facts rather than by imagination, pure logic, or any other nonfactual source.

proletariat: In Marx's theory, an unpropertied class that primarily includes factory workers (from the Latin term for "common person").

science: A combination of systematic observation and theory that provides explanations of how things work.

scientific research: The different methods used by scientists to achieve the goal of systematic observation and information-gathering.

scientific theory: A set of logically consistent ideas about the relationships between things that permits those ideas to be checked against observations through scientific research.

social class: Unequal social position based on income, wealth, and—more generally—a person's location in the economic system.

social conflict paradigm: A macro-level perspective that seeks to explain social organization and change in terms of the conflict that is built into social relations.

social engineering: The use of social science, usually by government, to design a preferred social order.

social facts: Qualities of groups that are external to individual members yet constrain their thinking and behavior.

social scientist: A scientist who studies human beings and the social worlds that they consciously create.

social solidarity: The bonds that unite the members of a social group.

social structure: The underlying regularities in how people behave and interrelate with one another.

sociological imagination: C. Wright Mill's notion of the ability to grasp the relationship between one's life as an individual and the larger social forces that help to shape it.

structural effects: Variations in human behavior that can be explained by the larger social structure rather than by individual differences.

symbol: Something understood as representing something else to a human mind

symbolic interactionist paradigm: A micro-sociological perspective arguing that both the human self and society as a whole are the result of social interactions based on language and other symbols; originates in the writings of George Herbert Mead.

theories of the middle range: Robert K. Merton's name for theories that seek to bridge European-style grand theory and more narrowly focused research

verstehen: The German term for interpretive understanding; in Weber's work, a research method that involves empathy with the persons being studied.

RECOMMENDED FOR FURTHER READING

Appelbaum, Richard P. (1988). *Karl Marx.* Newbury Park, CA: Sage.

> An examination of the theories of Karl Marx that presents and evaluates his critical philosophy, economic analysis, and political theory.

Deegan, Mary Jo. (1988). *Jane Addams and the Men of the Chicago School, 1892–1918.* New Brunswick, NJ: Transaction Books.

> A study of the highly influential role played by the founder of Hull House in the formation of the Chicago School of Sociology and the reasons why this history remains largely unknown.

Gerth, Hans, and C. Wright Mills (eds.). (1946). *From Max Weber: Essays in Sociology.* New York: Oxford University Press.

> A collection of some of Weber's most important essays on politics, economics, and science, along with a useful introductory essay that summarizes his work and biography.

Kandal, Terry R. (1988). *The Woman Question in Classical Sociological Theory.* Miami: Florida International University Press.

> An important study of the emergence of nineteenth-century European sociology and its relationship to feminist social movements; provides a detailed examination of the role of women in the theories of the discipline's founders.

Mills, C. Wright. (1959). *The Sociological Imagination.* New York: Oxford University Press.

> A once-influential book that examines the strengths and weaknesses of different forms of sociological thinking, along with a call for a sociological understanding that links individual experience with larger historical currents.

Ritzer, George. (1992). *Sociological Theory* (3rd ed.). New York: McGraw-Hill.

> A detailed examination of the major schools and figures in sociology over the past two centuries, with special attention to the historical circumstances that helped to shape the discipline.

The Process of Inquiry

CHAPTER OUTLINE

THINGS TO LOOK FOR

1. What are the differences between scientific inquiry and other ways of obtaining knowledge about the world?
2. What are the limitations of social science research, in comparison with research in the natural sciences?
3. How would you devise a strategy for researching a topic of importance to you? What different methods might you employ, and what are the strengths and weaknesses of each?
4. What are the ethical implications of studying other human beings?

INTRODUCTION

William Julius Wilson, a prominent, highly respected African-American sociologist, stirred up a storm of controversy when he published *The Truly Disadvantaged: The Inner City, the Underclass, and Public Policy.* In his book, Wilson (1987) argued that during the past 20 years a new social class had emerged: the urban underclass. It is found in the inner-city core of most major metropolitan areas, living in substandard housing and public housing projects. According to Wilson, the underclass consists of people living in poverty, lacking education, job skills, and hope. It includes unskilled, unemployed men, as well as single welfare mothers and their children. In Wilson's view, most members of the underclass are trapped in a vicious cycle of poverty, drugs, gang-related violence, and crime, from which few can ever hope to escape. The loss of jobs in the American economy has prevented people in the underclass from obtaining work that pays a living wage.

Wilson's book remains highly controversial. Some sociologists argue that his book is unintentionally racist, since it depicts the underclass as mainly black. While Wilson countered that society is in fact to blame for creating such an underclass, his critics responded that the very idea of an underclass fuels false stereotypes of racial minorities who prefer to live off welfare and deal drugs than work at an honest job. Yet since Wilson himself is African American, his arguments could not easily be dismissed.

Most importantly, Wilson's book contained a great deal of research to back up his claims, from governmental statistics to studies conducted by Wilson and his coworkers. Wilson's theory of the underclass was not simply based on his opinion; it was supported by facts as well. That did not necessarily make the theory correct, but it did mean that it was more likely to be taken seriously. Politicians cited the results in support of their policies, academics bestowed awards on Wilson, and his critics conducted their own studies to counter his results. Wilson's theory and its reception show the importance of research for obtaining sociological understanding.

SOCIOLOGICAL UNDERSTANDING, FAITH, AND COMMON SENSE

A central difference between sociological and other forms of thought is that in sociology we put our biases, assumptions, and conclusions to the test. Sociological inquiry requires that sociologists be open to changing their minds in the face of information that contradicts their expectations.

Some ideas about society are based on beliefs that, however compelling, can never be proven wrong. This is true, for example, of religious beliefs, which are simply accepted as articles of faith—that is, we do not question their fundamental truth or authenticity. Such beliefs may be said to have originated in God's Word, as revealed in sacred texts or scriptures. They are powerful sources of human spirituality and comfort. But they are not scientific, because there is no way that they can be tested and proved false. If they are to be scientific, sociological ideas must be formulated in such a fashion that they can be falsified—that is, *it must be possible to know if they are incorrect.* This is termed the **principle of falsification** (Popper, 1959), and it is one of the most important doctrines of scientific inquiry.

Unlike natural scientists, sociologists can seldom design studies that clearly satisfy the principle of falsification. Society is not a laboratory where ideas can be tested under rigorously controlled conditions. For example, suppose a sociologist wanted to test Wilson's notion that job shortages are partly responsible for the growing urban underclass. The sociologist clearly could not choose a city and, keeping everything else the same, remove half the jobs to see if the number of people in its underclass increased. But sociological ideas can still be tested by indirect means. By comparing the size of the underclass in different cities, for example, it is possible to test Wilson's idea that there is an association between job availability and the size of the underclass. If the underclass is larger in cities with fewer available jobs, we may decide that this is an adequate test of Wilson's ideas.

Not all sociological research is oriented toward testing scientific ideas. Some research is **descriptive**—that is, *it seeks to paint a detailed picture of a particular*

Abandoned slum housing in Philadelphia indicates the formidable problems of poverty that plague American cities. Sociologist William J. Wilson has argued that the loss of jobs in the inner city contributes to the creation of an urban "underclass," trapped in a vicious cycle of poverty, drugs, and crime. Wilson's theories have proved highly controversial, stimulating a great deal of fruitful research.

phenomenon. Although such an approach does not rule out examining a particular theory, the emphasis is on richness of detail rather than theory-testing. An example is Martin Sanchez Jankowski's *Islands in the Street* (1991), a study of Irish-American, Jamaican, Dominican, Central American, Puerto Rican, Chicano, and African-American urban gangs. Jankowski's study was based on ten years of observation obtained by participating in gang-related activities in a number of U.S. cities. The book provides a powerful and unforgettable description of life in gangs, even though it was not conducted in such a way that a particular set of ideas could be scientifically falsified. On the other hand, Jankowski's descriptive research was intended to generate

ideas that could be tested by others (Jankowski, 1991, p. 17).

Sociological knowledge differs not only from beliefs that are held on religious faith but from common-sense understandings as well. Consider the following ideas, all of which are commonly believed to be true by many Americans, and all of which are false:

■ *Americans are among the best-educated people on earth.* In fact, American high school students typically rank among the lowest in math and science test scores among the industrial nations of Europe and Asia. Taiwanese, Korean, and Japanese high school students spend almost one-third more hours in class

Sociologists have long had a fascination with youth gangs. Although studying gangs can place difficult demands on the researcher, their increased prominence has led to a resurgence of sociological interest. These women are members of the Grand Bassett gang in Los Angeles.

than their American counterparts (*World Monitor,* 1992)

■ *Hard work and education will always pay off.* In fact, men typically earn more than women and whites earn more than blacks, even when they work in the same occupation and bring to it the same educational background. For example, women with college degrees today earn on average less than men with high school diplomas, while college-educated African-American men average only four-fifths of what college-educated white men earn (Faludi, 1991; Bergman, 1986; Blau and Ferber, 1987; U.S. Commission on Civil Rights, 1978; Granovetter and Tilly, 1988).

■ *People are homeless because they are unwilling to work hard.* In fact, homelessness is the result of a decline in jobs; a shortage of low-rent housing; the closure of state-run mental institutions; and cutbacks in governmental programs for the poor. Many homeless people have full-time jobs but still don't earn enough to pay the rent (Rossi, 1989; Wright, 1989; Dreier and Appelbaum, 1992; Burt, 1992).

A key task of sociology is to hold such common-sense beliefs up to scientific scrutiny. This is not to argue that common sense does not have an important place in everyday thinking, or that other beliefs, including religious beliefs, are not of value. Sociology does not claim to provide answers to questions about ultimate truth, nor does it provide practical guidelines for everyday life. It does, however, subject all claims of truth to critical examination, insofar as they can be stated in a way permitting them to be studied scientifically.

MEASURING SOCIOLOGICAL CONCEPTS

A **concept** is *an idea or mental construct that focuses upon specified properties common to a set of phenomena, to the exclusion of other properties* (Singleton et al., 1993). All thought involves concepts. If I observe a four-legged furry animal wagging its tail, I would probably attach the concept "dog" to it, ignoring any characteristics that might lead me to classify it as something else. If the animal turns out to be a wolf, I have used the wrong concept, as I might subsequently discover to my regret. Similarly, if I encounter a young man sleeping on a sidewalk surrounded by bags of clothing, I may conceptualize him as a "homeless person" with no other place to go. Alternatively, I might choose the concept "drifter," which focuses on voluntary movement from place to place in search of adventure, rather than homelessness. If the sidewalk is in front of a European train station I might think of the person as a student bumming around on a summer vacation. The concept I choose will in part shape what I "see," and how I subsequently interpret the event.

From Concepts to Operational Measures

The difference between common sense and sociological concepts is that the latter are more precisely defined and usually derive from an explicit social theory. In many cases, sociological concepts are defined in such a way that they can be measured as well.

One of the principal tasks of sociological research is to systematically develop concepts and evaluate how they conform to the world they purport to describe. For example, one of the most important sociological concepts is social class. How do we know that social class exists? The first step is to give a precise definition of the term, so that all sociological researchers will observe the same thing. In the previous chapter we defined social class in terms of a person's economic standing in relationship to the larger economy.

Once the sociologist has defined a concept, the next step is to figure out how to observe it in the world. On the one hand, the concept can be defined in terms of **qualities**—*discrete categories (usually indicated by words or labels) that enable us to make nonnumerical distinctions among the things we observe.* Thus we may talk of the "upper class" to refer to anyone who is extremely wealthy, as indicated by a fancy home, an expensive car, and a lavish lifestyle. Or we may talk of the "underclass" to refer to anyone who lives in a city, dropped out of high school, is unable to get a job, and whose parents lived under similar circumstances. Much important sociological research has been conducted with such qualitative concepts. Research that emphasizes their use is often termed **qualitative sociology,** because it *is based on descriptive rather than quantitative forms of analysis.* Although qualitative sociology may sometimes make use of statistical measures, its emphasis is primarily nonnumerical (Singleton et al., 1993).

At the other extreme, a concept can be defined in terms of **quantities**—*explicit numerical distinctions that enable us to make relatively precise measurements* (Singleton et al., 1993). This type of research, which is the most common type in sociology, is sometimes termed **quantitative sociology,** because *it calls for research based primarily on numerical measurement and analysis.* The first step in quantifying a concept is to make an **operational definition**—that is, to *define the concept in terms of operations or measurements that can be performed on it.* The researcher then collects data based on the operational measure. For example, "upper class" might be operationally defined in terms of a yearly after-tax income exceeding $1 million. The researcher could then precisely identify members of the upper class by adding up an individual's annual income, subtracting out taxes, and determining whether the remainder exceeded $1 million dollars. "Underclass" might be operationally defined in terms of residence in an inner-city area, legal income under half of the poverty level, lack of a permanent job, and a less than high school education.

Testing Hypotheses

In order for a sociological explanation to be scientific, it must be capable of generating predictions about the actual world. Predictions that are derived from scientific theories are termed **hypotheses;** these are often little more than *theory-driven ideas about the world that are capable of being disproved when tested against observations.* Strictly speaking, it is easier to test hypotheses through the use of quantitative rather than qualitative measures. Hypotheses enable scientists to check the accuracy of their theories. For example, a sociological theory about inequality may hold that gender discrimination accounts for at least part of the income differences between men and women. This theory might lead to the hypothesis that salaried women will earn less money then men who are doing comparable work. In order to test the hypothesis, a sociologist might compare the salaries of women and men with identical education, experience, and skills, all of whom are doing similar work in similar jobs. If a difference is found, the hypothesis is sustained, and at least for the moment this aspect of the theory is supported.

Validity and Reliability

Both qualitative and quantitative research are necessarily concerned with accuracy. In both cases, it is important to know whether or not we are actually observing what is "out there," and faithfully reporting the results. **Validity** is concerned with *whether or not our concepts and their measurement are congruent with the world they are claiming to represent.* Sociologists have distinguished different kinds of validity, of which two are especially important. **Face validity** refers to *the extent to which our operational definitions appear to measure the concepts they are intended to measure.* Does the operational definition of "underclass" given above accurately capture what we mean when we speak of an underclass? Were we correct in including lack of education as a part of the operational definition? Should we have included some measure of involvement in illegal activities? **Construct validity** refers to *whether*

or not we are in fact measuring the concept itself. Once we have operationally defined the underclass, have we actually succeeded in measuring it? One way to answer this question is to measure other things that our theory tells us go along with being a member of the underclass, such as membership in gangs or receiving welfare. If people we identify as members of the underclass also turn out to possess these other characteristics, we may conclude that our construct has been validated (Singleton et al., 1993). Finally, **bias** refers to a *result that lacks validity in a particular direction.* For example, if members of the underclass consistently exaggerate their income and education when responding to interviewers, then the resulting statistics will have an upward bias: the average reported income and education will be higher than the average actual income and education.

Researchers are also concerned with the **reliability** of their results—the *extent to which their findings are consistent between different studies of the same thing, or for the same study over time.* A study is said to be reliable if two different measures of the same thing produce the same result, or if the same measurement produces the same result at two points in time. For example, ten years ago the U.S. government attempted for the first time to estimate the total number of homeless people in the United States (see Box 2.1). The resulting estimates were highly unreliable, because different scholars studying the same homeless population came up with wildly different numbers. Because of the many problems with the government's study, its results were eventually dismissed as bearing little relationship to the actual number of homeless people (Appelbaum, 1986).

A study can produce valid results that are unreliable, or reliable results that are invalid! Think about two bathroom scales. One gives extremely erratic results— every time you get on it tells you a different weight, although the overall average just happens to be accurate. The average is thus said to be a valid estimate of your weight, even though individual estimates are unreliable. The second scale gives you exactly the same result every time you step on it; the only problem is, the scale adds ten pounds to your actual weight each time. This second scale is highly reliable, but extremely invalid, since there is a consistent bias to its results. For a bathroom scale—or a study—to be useful, its results should be both reliable and valid.

In qualitative research, it is often hard to determine whether or not the results are both valid and reliable. To overcome this difficulty, qualitative researchers may share their field notes with other experts, invite other scholars to reproduce their research, and even share their results with the people they are studying to see if they agree with the observations and interpretations. Quantitative researchers, on the other hand, have developed

Box 2.1

Critical Thinking

The HUD Homeless Study and Some Pitfalls of Doing Research

During the early 1980s, the problem of homelessness exploded on the American scene. Shelter providers and others who worked with the homeless claimed there were already more than two million homeless people in the United States. The U.S. government, under increasing pressure to provide funding for food, shelter, and emergency services, claimed there were far fewer. In order to settle the question once and for all, the U.S. Department of Housing and Urban Development (HUD) decided to conduct a scientific study of homelessness in cities and towns across the country (U.S. HUD, 1984). Government researchers analyzed all the existing studies, and then called homeless service providers and other experts in 60 cities and asked them to estimate the number of homeless people in their communities. As a result of this research, the government concluded that there were about 250,000 to 350,000 homeless people in the United States, only a fraction of the previous estimate.

The HUD figures were widely cited and used in other studies, although they were eventually discredited as well (Tucker, 1989, 1990; Burt, 1992; Appelbaum, 1985). The HUD homeless study provides a textbook example of poorly conducted research (Appelbaum, 1986; Appelbaum et al., 1991). First, HUD's **operational definition** of homelessness was based on people on streets and in shelters, and effectively excluded homeless people in abandoned buildings or cars, or temporarily sleeping on someone's sofa. Second, HUD based its figures on highly **unreliable** "guesstimates" from shelter providers, police officers, and other local experts who often admitted they were only guessing at the number of homeless in their communities. Finally, the figures HUD obtained contained an in-built **bias** toward underestimating the number of homeless people, since they were based almost entirely on homeless estimates for the downtown areas of big cities, excluding the numerous homeless people who lived in surrounding cities and suburbs. As a result of these problems, HUD's estimate of a national homeless figure lacked any **validity.**

Many homeless advocates questioned HUD's **objectivity** as well (U.S. House of Representatives, 1984). The Reagan Administration had publicly denied there was a major homeless problem, and HUD's budget for low-cost housing programs had already been slashed by billions of dollars. A low homeless figure was clearly in the government's interest, since it would be difficult to justify further cuts in government housing programs if the number of homeless people was large and growing. There was even evidence that governmental researchers had "doctored" their data to fit their conclusions, by ignoring estimates they regarded as too high (U.S. House of Representatives, 1985). Subsequent research has confirmed that there may be as many as a million homeless in the United States (Burt, 1992).

---

very precise methods for determining validity. These typically involve different ways of measuring the same thing, to see if cross-checks provide the same results.

Relationships Among Variables

As we have seen, quantitative research is based on **variables,** *operational measures that vary (increase or decrease in value) according to the value of the thing they are measuring.* A simple kind of variable, termed a **nominal variable,** tells you *whether or not something falls into a particular category*—for example, male or female. The variables used in qualitative research are likely to be nominal. **Ordinal variables** measure *rank order,* as in the example of class: a person might be classified as lower class, middle class, or upper class, based on income, wealth, and lifestyle. This provides the beginning of quantitative research. More precise quantitative measurement is obtained with **ratio variables,** which permit *absolute measurement along a scale with a meaningful zero point.* Income, for example, may vary from zero to billions of dollars; age from zero to a hundred or so. The advantage of ratio variables is that they permit mathematical computations to be performed. For example, we know that someone who is 20 years old is twice as old as someone who is 10, or that a corporation executive whose annual income is $3 million earns a hundred times as much as a high school teacher who receives $30,000. We cannot make such comparisons with ordinal variables, however; a person who is upper class, for example, cannot be said to be three times higher in terms of social class than a person who is lower class.

Sociologists often seek to estimate the relationship between two or more variables (see Figure 2.1). Let's assume they want to know whether education is associated with higher earnings. By asking people about their years of schooling and annual income, they could estimate the degree of **correlation** (literally, the co-relationship) between the two—that is, *the degree to which the two variables regularly vary together.* Such research would reveal that in general the greater the education the higher the income, although the correlation would be far from perfect, since there are many exceptions to this rule.

Often when sociologists study the relationship between two variables, they believe that there is a **causal relationship** between the two—that is, *one variable is said to be the cause of another.* In such a relationship,

it is the **independent variable** *that is believed to bring about a change in the other* variable; the **dependent variable** is the one *that is believed to have changed as a result of the other.* It is important to recognize that "causation" is a slippery concept that originates in our theories about the world, rather than in the observations themselves. We may notice, for example, that when the number of people out of work increases, so does the size of the underclass. But no matter how often we observe this, we can never state that joblessness is the cause of the underclass on the basis of observations alone: correlation is not causation. Rather, we must have a theory that links the two together. For example, we might argue that when the economy turns downward factories close, jobs are lost, unemployment rises, and the number of people who can never realistically expect to find work increases, thereby swelling the ranks of the underclass.

Sometimes an observed correlation between two variables is the result of a **spurious relationship**—a *statistical association between two or more variables that is actually the result of something else that is not being measured, rather than a causal link between the variables themselves* (Singleton et al., 1993, p. 525). For example, one study found a positive correlation between the number of storks in parts of northwestern Europe, and the number of babies that were born in the same areas (Wallis and Roberts, 1956; reported in Singleton et al., 1993). Although the explanation that storks actually do bring babies might have some appeal in children's fables, the association is clearly spurious. In fact, both the number of storks and the number of babies are the result of the same underlying cause, which in this example was not measured: the number of human beings living in an area. More people meant more buildings, chimneys, and other nesting places for storks, just it as it meant more people to have babies. By failing to take into account the number of people before computing a correlation between babies and storks, we are led to the wrong conclusion.

It is obvious that extreme care should be taken in developing our theories, specifying relationships between variables, deriving operational measures, and collecting suitable data. Quantitative research methods often give impressive statistical results, but that does not always make them right.

Figure 2.1   **Hours Studying and Grades: The Experience of Ten Students Taking Soc 1**

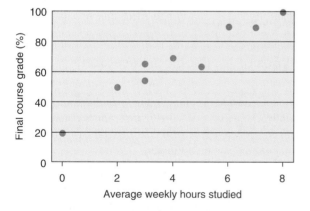

Scatterplots are graphs used by sociologists to represent correlations. This scatterplot shows that in general, the more hours studied the higher the grade. The student who did no studying earned a grade of 20 percent, while the student who averaged 8 hours a week received 100 percent. Still, the relationship is not perfect: Two students studied 3 hours a week, yet one got 55 percent and one got 65 percent, while the one who studied 5 hours did slightly worse than the one who averaged 4 hours. Hours per week studied is important, but it is not the only factor determining grades.

THE PROBLEM OF OBJECTIVITY

Scientists, like all human beings, have biases and prejudices, passions and dislikes, preconceived ideas and unrecognized assumptions. These predispositions are often thought of as interfering with a scientist's **objectivity**—*the ability, during research, to represent the* *object of study as truthfully as possible.* The task of scientific research is to be aware of personal biases and assumptions, to make them explicit, and to try not to let them get in the way of what one observes and reports.

Max Weber recognized this problem, and nearly a century ago set forth the position that most sociologists continue to hold today. Weber (1946, orig. 1919) argued that the values and beliefs of social scientists can and should enter into their selection of a topic for study. Once the research question has been framed, however, they should seek to be as **value neutral** as possible—that is, *their personal beliefs and opinions should not influence the course of their research.*

Objectivity can be a special problem for sociologists and other social scientists, because they are often studying groups, organizations, and societies of which they are members. As ordinary citizens, they will likely have strong opinions about such things as poverty, homelessness, racial inequality, or unequal pay for men and women. When they put on their hats as research sociologists, it is important that they become aware of these opinions, openly acknowledge them when they write up their work, and put them aside as best they can when they conduct their research. We mentioned the importance of having an open mind in the first chapter, as a central aspect of the sociological imagination.

How can we best achieve objectivity? First, recall that the goal of research is not to prove our ideas correct but to find out if they are wrong. To accomplish this, we must be willing to allow the data we collect to contradict ideas that we may hold with passionate conviction. The goal of research should be to extend human understanding, not to prove a particular point of view. When we read sociological studies, we must always ask ourselves if this fundamental condition is being met.

A second way of achieving some measure of objectivity is to invite others to draw their own conclusions about our data. This is achieved through **replication**—*constructing research strategies that can be duplicated by other scholars.* At a minimum, replication requires making data available to others, to see if they draw the same conclusions that we have drawn.

Perhaps the most important way that objectivity is achieved is through openly sharing the results of research, subjecting it to the critical scrutiny of experts. Sociologists seek to publish their research results in scholarly journals, where a panel of experts will determine whether or not it meets the journal's standards for publication. Once published, other scholars will read it with a highly critical eye, particularly if they disagree with its conclusions. Some scholars may seek to replicate the study in a different setting, perhaps drawing upon a different research strategy, in order to see if the conclusions remain the same.

CONDUCTING SOCIOLOGICAL INQUIRY

Sociological inquiry requires that the researcher first develop an overall strategy to guide the research, and then select from among a large number of methods to actually conduct it.

Developing a Research Strategy

A **research strategy** is a *clearly thought-out plan to guide sociological inquiry.* Its ultimate purpose is to fill in some gaps in our understanding about the social world. Its more immediate objective may be to evaluate the adequacy of a well-formulated theory, or to obtain some preliminary knowledge that will enable us to formulate a theory later on. It addresses the question, "how can we best learn about such-and-such a topic, in a way that will provide us with the greatest confidence that our results are accurate?"

A research strategy will suggest different approaches to answering this question. These approaches include different **research methods,** which are *specific techniques for systematically gathering data while conforming to rules that have been agreed upon by a community of scholars.* Some research methods are better suited to providing certain types of information than others. Some may appeal to us personally as well; others may be the last way in the world we want to spend our time. As we develop our research strategy, we will become clear about the pluses and minuses of different research methods as techniques that we might fruitfully use to answer a research question.

Types of Sociological Research

Sociologists employ a variety of methods to learn about the social world (Table 2.1). These methods are not mutually exclusive; a good research strategy may entail several of them. The principal methods used by sociologists include the following.

Survey Research

Surveys are probably among the most common, and certainly most well-known, sociological research techniques. A **survey** typically entails *administering a precisely worded questionnaire to a group of people in order to determine their characteristics, opinions, and behaviors.* The issue of generalizability is of central concern in conducting this form of research. First, the researcher has to define a **population universe** to which the study applies—*the group of people for whom generalizations are to be made.* If we wish to study peoples' voting preferences for a presidential candidate, do

Survey research is an important source of information on people's attitudes and characteristics. Although surveys may be done face-to-face, as in this public opinion poll conducted in a shopping mall, they are usually less expensive when conducted by telephone or mail. Each method has advantages and disadvantages.

we want to be able to generalize to all people over 18 years of age who are qualified to vote? Only registered voters who are likely to actually vote? Each of these groups is said to be a different population universe.

Once the population universe is identified, a **sample**—*a subset of cases that will represent the larger population*—must be selected, since it is seldom economically feasible, nor desirable, to interview everybody in a chosen population universe. The science of **statistics** is concerned with *generalizing from samples to the larger populations they represent.* Two principal types of sampling are used by sociologists: random or probability sampling, and nonprobability sampling. In a **random sample**, *everyone in the underlying population has an equal chance of being chosen for the sample.* The researcher might put the names of all registered voters into a hat, and then blindly draw 400 names to be surveyed. In **nonprobability sampling**, *subjects are chosen because of their specific characteristics.*

Among all registered voters, men between 18 and 25 who have never before voted might be targeted for special study. Although random samples are most desirable from the standpoint of generalizing to the larger population, often they are not practical. If only one out of every 20 voters in a population is an 18-to-25-year-old male, then a sample of 400 might result in only 20 interviews, a number too small to yield valid or reliable results. Doubling the sample size might work, but that would also double the costs of the study. In such a case, nonprobability sampling may be needed in order to generate a sizable number of cases at a reasonable cost. The researcher would over-sample 18-to-25-year-olds, in order to come up with a sufficient number of cases.

Once the sample is constructed and drawn, the questionnaire is administered. Questionnaires primarily have closed-ended questions, where the respondent checks a box indicating the preferred response. This, of course, forces the respondent to choose from among predetermined alternative responses. Closed-ended questions are easier for the researcher to code into a computer, and, if properly constructed, permit precise measurement. Questionnaires may contain open-ended questions as well. For example, respondents may be asked to state their opinion about a political candidate in a few words, or to describe their occupations. In this case, the researcher will have to code the responses into different categories once the questionnaires are collected.

Administering questionnaires can be difficult. Ideally, surveys are best conducted in person or by telephone, since these typically produce response rates of 80 to 90 percent. Mail surveys, on the other hand, are typically returned by fewer than half of the people who receive them, although with proper follow-through higher response rates can be achieved (Dillman, 1978; Heberlein and Baumgartner, 1978; Yammarino, Skinner, and Childers, 1991; Singleton et al., 1993). It is important to remember that unless the sample represents the underlying population, the survey is probably useless.

Surveys have several significant advantages. They provide the researcher with exact responses that have known margins of error, and so are easily coded into variables for analysis. They permit the researcher to draw conclusions about large numbers of people on the basis of a much smaller number of interviews. This is a major advantage in terms of time and money. Finally, and perhaps most importantly, they often permit the researcher to see patterns that would not be evident from other forms of research. For example, systematic differences in responses between men and women, old and young, or wealthy and poor can be simultaneously measured, and the joint impact of these and other variables can be estimated.

Table 2.1   Some Major Sociological Approaches to Inquiry: How to Choose?

Approach	When Appropriate
Surveys	Basic information about a large population is desired (including its underlying social patterns and relations), and sampling is a feasible strategy
Interviews	In-depth information is desired, and direct access to informants is possible
Detached observation	Information must be gathered but direct access is not possible or data-gathering must be as unobtrusive as possible
Participant-observation	First-hand knowledge of the direct experience of subjects is desired, including greater depth of knowledge about what is "really" happening
Participatory research	A primary goal is empowerment—training of people to acquire the necessary skills to do the research themselves
Experiments	Precise control is desired to isolate specific causes of social processes
Using available information	Direct acquisition of data is either not feasible or desirable, either because the event being studied occurred in the past, or because it would be too costly or difficult for researchers to gather data

On the other hand, surveys also have a number of significant weaknesses. Surveys can be somewhat superficial, since in order to be economically feasible they usually call for brief responses to closed-ended questions. Extreme care must be taken to ensure that these questions and their possible responses capture the respondent's point of view, not merely that of the researcher. Surveys are also more likely to reveal what people say rather than what they actually do. As a result, responses are sometimes self-serving, intended to make the interviewee look good in the eyes of the researcher. While a well-constructed survey can partly compensate for these shortcomings, a survey is not the ideal instrument to provide the rich, detailed information that gives a concrete sense of people's actual experiences.

Fieldwork

Fieldwork, sometimes called **ethnography** (from *ethno,* "people," and *graphos,* "depict"), is as old as human curiosity about the lives of others. When Marco Polo recorded his travels in China during the thirteenth century, he was conducting a form of fieldwork. Although fieldwork is often rooted in a particular community or society, it can also be used to shed light on global processes, as it is increasingly called upon to do today (Box 2.2). Ethnography has its strongest roots in anthropology, where it remains the principal method of gathering data: anthropologists typically immerse themselves in the daily life of another culture, study its language and its customs, and then report on what they have learned. But sociologists have also relied on ethnographic techniques to conduct some of the discipline's best-known studies.

Classic examples of ethnographic work include William F. Whyte's (1943) *Street Corner Society,* a study of Italian-American working class men; Herbert Gans' (1962) *Urban Villagers,* a study of Boston's Italian-American neighborhoods; Elliot Liebow's (1967) *Talley's Corner,* a study of urban African-American men; and Carol Stack's (1974) *All Our Kin,* a study of African-American families. More recently, Mitch Durnier's (1992) *Slim's Table* examines the lives of older African-American men who congregate at a well-known Chicago southside restaurant; Arlie Hochschild (1989) looks at working mothers in *The Second Shift,* as well the elderly in her earlier (1978) research; Mary Romero (1992) examines Chicana household workers in *Maid in the USA;* Martin Sanchez Jankowksi (1991) looks at gangs in *Islands in the Street,* while Anne Campbell (1991) focuses on *The Girls in the Gang;* Barrie Thorne's (1993) research highlights differences in boys' and girls' gender play; and Patricia Zavella (1987) looks at cannery workers in *Women's Work and Chicano Factories.*

As we have already noted, conducting fieldwork can be extremely demanding. The researcher often has to strike a delicate balance between personal involvement and scientific detachment. The strength of this method is that it can provide a deep, sympathetic, extremely rich and detailed understanding of the lives of others. Its weaknesses include the fact that it can be extremely time-consuming, requiring years "in the field" to collect and analyze information. Mountains of field notes will be written and hours of taped interviews may be recorded, all of which will have to be distilled down to a valid and reliable set of conclusions. There is also an ever-present danger of researchers becoming so identified with the people they are studying that objectivity is lost. Ethnography is a highly interpersonal type of

Box 2.2

Globalization

The Study of Global Social Processes

As the processes of globalization have intensified, sociologists and other social scientists have increasingly turned their attention to conducting research that is global in scope. Sometimes such research simply compares social processes that occur in different countries in order to better understand which features are common to all countries and which are unique to particular ones. Such comparative-historical studies are among the oldest form of sociological research; all of the founders of sociology discussed in Chapter 1 at some point in their research used this method.

Another type of research, however, focuses on global social processes. Economic globalization provides one powerful example that will concern us throughout this book. Researchers have examined the ways in which global industries are managed across national borders, and the impact of economic globalization on the world of work. Let us consider an example of each, looking at studies that have drawn upon a wide variety of different research methods. (For yet another example, see Box 14.1.)

Gary Gereffi's (1992; Gereffi and Korzeniewicz, 1990; 1994) research on such industries as apparel, electronics, pharmaceuticals, and footwear examine how a company might design its product in Los Angeles, hire a New York advertising agency to market it, use a Hong Kong company to oversee fabrication in Chinese factories, and eventually sell the product in American, European, or Mexican retail outlets. Gereffi uses a variety of different research methods to study these processes. He analyzes government statistics and corporate business documents, observes working conditions in factories, and conducts lengthy interviews with people throughout these industries. His research is complicated by the fact that his sources are found across the world: statistics differ from country to country, documents may be in a variety of languages, and linguistic and cultural differences often pose barriers to observation and interviews.

Maria Patricia Fernandez-Kelly (1982, 1983) has focused on workers themselves in global industries. Her research studies the largely female workforce in Mexico's border industries, many of whom are migrants from rural Mexico who seek work in U.S. factories on the Mexican side of the border, where wages are low and health and safety regulations poorly enforced. The opening of the U.S.-Mexico border to American factories has had an enormous impact on the Mexican workforce as well as on those American workers who have lost jobs to their much more poorly paid Mexican counterparts. The massive movement of people and jobs across national boundaries is an important aspect of the global economy, and Fernandez-Kelly's research—which includes extensive observations, interviews with workers, and documentary film-making—has provided a vivid description of working and living conditions on the global assembly line.

Globalization provides new opportunities and challenges for sociological inquiry, particularly for sociologists who are comfortable with living in other cultures, willing to acquire language skills, and concerned with avoiding ethnocentric biases in their research.

---

research requiring intense involvement with other people and finely developed "people-oriented" skills.

Let's look at a number of different techniques that have been developed in connection with field work.

Interviews. An **interview** *is a detailed, in-depth interrogation.* The researcher comes to the interview with a series of open-ended questions that allow the respondent to provide a full and detailed answer in his or her own words. In the **structured interview,** the researcher has a *detailed list of specific questions to ask;* in the **semistructured interview,** the researcher has a *list of topics to cover but trusts to the interview situation itself to determine the course of questioning and the details of the questions.* A good interviewer must be extremely sensitive to the respondent, subtly probing for detail and

Ethnographic research provides invaluable information about the lives of people. Ethnobotanist Mark Plotkin is attempting to understand how the Tirió Indians in the Amazon rain forest use their plants for healing. Plotkin believes such research is vital, as globalization threatens people like the Tirió—as well as their knowledge—with extinction.

steering the interview without putting words into the respondent's mouth. It is especially important to avoid asking **leading questions**—questions that *solicit a particular response.*

Interviews are an especially useful way of gathering in-depth information from well-selected informants. On the other hand, because interviews are detailed and time-consuming, they are not usually an appropriate strategy for gathering systematic information from a broad cross section of people. The trade-off between conducting interviews or doing a survey is often a choice between getting thorough information from a

small number of informants, or more superficial information from a larger and more representative sample.

Detached Observation. Sometimes the research strategy requires that researchers stay at arm's length from the people they are studying, simply observing what is going on but otherwise remaining detached or disengaged. A sociologist studying crowd behavior at a rally or student participation in a seminar would be an example. The researcher tries to be a "fly on the wall"—invisible, unobtrusive, yet constantly recording what is going on. Although this technique is useful for

Sociologist Mitch Durnier spent five years conducting research at a southside Chicago cafe, in an effort to understand the lives of a small group of men who hung out at "Slim's Table." Ethnographic research often requires deep immersion in the culture or subculture being studied.

particular situations, it is difficult to base all of one's research on such passive observation, since the information obtained may be partial and impressionistic.

Participant-Observation. Research often requires a mixture of active participation and detached observation; it can range from one to the other extreme. In his study *Islands in the Street,* Martin Sanchez Jankowski (1991) offers an example of an extremely high degree of participation. He became friends with many gang members, was accepted even though it was known that he was conducting research, and was present for illegal as well as lawful gang activities. In fact, the gangs often "tested him" by breaking some law and then waiting to see if Jankowski would report them. As a researcher, he was exposed to many of the dangers of gang life and often had to engage in fights with gang members to prove his courage. During his ten years of research, he was seriously injured twice. According to Jankowski (1991, p. 13), "I ate where they ate, I slept where they slept, I stayed with their families, I traveled where they went, and in certain situations where I could not remain neutral, I fought with them." His research provides important sociological understanding into the social organization of gangs, showing why young people join them, how they routinely operate, and how they relate to the larger community.

Participant-observation is a principal approach to conducting fieldwork. One of its main advantages lies in the fact that participation often enables the researcher to experience and observe situations that would simply remain unknown to the detached observer. On the other hand, when the degree of participation is extremely high, remaining detached and objective can be a major challenge. Participant-observation research frequently raises fundamental ethical questions as well. Although Jankowski (1991) states that he never participated in any illegal activities himself, he admits that he observed many during the course of his research. To report such illegal activities to the police would have violated his trust with the gangs and would have ultimately rendered his research impossible to conduct. Yet failure to report such activities may have had harmful consequences for the victims of some of the crimes he observed. These are difficult questions which participant-observers may have to face.

Participatory Research

Occasionally a research strategy is designed to involve the subjects of the research in the research process itself (Park, 1993; Whyte, 1991; Freire, 1972). This type of research is usually tied in with community action. It is conducted when a group or community wants to engage in some form of social change but lacks the expertise to

do so. The researcher is invited to become a fully engaged member of the social change process, helping the members of the group to conduct necessary research and training them in the techniques for doing so.

In one example, a group of poor people from a rural county in the Appalachian Mountains discovered that a toxic dump had been illegally located in their community and wanted to do something about it. The people from the community lacked the formal education and training needed to effectively document the abuses themselves, or to provide convincing testimony to regulatory agencies far away in the state capital. Working closely with researchers from the Highlander Folk School (1985), a leading advocate of participatory research, they were able to successfully train themselves, gather the necessary data, and force the dump to be removed.

Participatory research is an appropriate strategy when a primary goal is to empower people in a community or organization to acquire the necessary expertise to conduct their own research. Its principal shortcoming lies in its highly engaged approach to research, which may make detachment and objectivity difficult.

Experiments

Although experimental design is the classic scientific approach for the study of causal relationships, it is not commonly used in sociological research. This is because the social world seldom conforms to a scientific laboratory, and it is therefore extremely difficult to simulate real-world situations in a laboratory setting where the researcher attempts to isolate and measure the effect of a single cause. In a typical experiment, volunteer subjects will be randomly assigned to two groups. The first, called an *experimental group,* receives some special attention, based on the cause being studied; the second, the *control group,* does not. The subjects do not know to which group they have been assigned, and seldom know the true purpose of the experiment.

In one series of studies of the effect of violent images in the media, for example, one group of undergraduate male students was shown films that were sexually explicit and violent (the experimental group), while others were shown no films at all (the control group). The students were then inteviewed to determine how sympathetic they were to a woman who had been raped. The studies found that students in the experimental group were less sympathetic than those in the control group, leading the researchers to conclude that exposure to violence in the media increases men's tolerance of actual violence against women (Linz, Donnerstein, and Adams, 1989; Linz, Donnerstein, and Penrod, 1988; Linz, 1989).

The advantage of laboratory studies is that they permit precise control of the experimental conditions, enabling the researcher to isolate such specific causes as exposure to violent images in the media.

This advantage is also the principal weakness of laboratory studies, which are in many ways artificial. To the extent that the laboratory fails to duplicate a more natural setting, it is difficult to generalize the results of laboratory experiments to the larger society. As a result, sociologists sometimes use field experiments, in which a real-life situation is simulated as best as possible. In one classic example, Philip Zimbardo (1972) converted the basement of a Stanford University building into a makeshift prison, randomly assigning his students to be prisoners and guards in order to better understand how people take on social roles. The simulation was so realistic that it had to be called off in less than a week, because of the stress it was producing among the subjects of the experiment.

Field experiments, while sometimes providing a useful simulation of real-world conditions, nonetheless remain artificial, resulting in problems of generalizability. Additionally, they can be difficult to administer and costly to run.

Working with Available Information

A fifth major research strategy involves working with data collected by other people, almost always for purposes other than the research at hand. Often such data are the only information available. Examples include statistical data, documentary analysis, and comparative-historical research.

Statistical Data. This includes numerical information obtained from government agencies, businesses, and other organizations that collect data for internal or external use. The U.S. Census, for example, provides a rich source of information, compiled every ten years, on an enormous range of individual and household characteristics. Additional government surveys of business, manufacturing, agriculture, labor, farming, and housing are routinely conducted by the Census Bureau and other government agencies. The United Nations collects annual data on economic trade between countries. Many businesses publish annual reports that contain basic economic information on their financial performance.

The primary advantage of using such data is that it is already there—it is available, someone else has collected it, and it is usually relatively inexpensive to acquire. It may be extremely comprehensive, including a wealth of information that most researchers would not have the time or resources to go out and collect. A disadvantage is that since it was not originally collected with a researcher's specific purposes in mind, it may not provide the exact information that is required. Another disadvantage is that statistical data may be of questionable validity and reliability, although any problems with government sources are usually studied in detail and therefore well known.

Documentary Analysis. This technique involves the analysis of written materials—studies that have been done, records of meetings, newspapers, and other forms of test—produced by individuals, government agencies, private organizations, and other sources. For example, Francis Fox Piven and Richard Cloward's *Poor People's Movements* (1977) is an important study that draws heavily on documents that were available to them as founding activists in the National Welfare Rights Orga-

In the "Stanford Prison Study," psychologist Phillip Zimbardo randomly assigned student volunteers to be either prison guards or inmates in a makeshift prison. The students quickly became so immersed in their roles that Zimbardo had to cancel the experiment prematurely. His research shows the importance of social roles in structuring behavior.

nization (NWRO). Although their research is based on a number of different methods, one source of information about the history of the NWRO consisted of minutes of meetings, memos, and other internal documents. Such records provide a rich source of detailed information, if the researcher is able to obtain them. At the same time, it is important to exercise caution in the use of such materials, because they may not have been compiled with accuracy in mind. People who keep records are often mindful that others will see the documents, and so may take pains to ensure that nothing unflattering is recorded. Minutes of meetings may be incomplete, or may be deliberately slanted to reflect the viewpoint of the notetaker. It is therefore important that the researcher look at such materials with a highly critical eye, double-checking other sources for accuracy where possible.

Comparative-Historical Research. This technique typically entails studies of several different countries, as well as examination of changing historical patterns in a single country. The conclusions drawn are based on similarities and differences between countries, as well as on changes over time. Comparative-historical research in sociology often differs from the research conducted by historians: sociologists usually seek to identify patterns common to the different times and places, whereas historians, by way of contrast, usually focus on a particular historical period and location and are less willing to draw broad generalizations from their research. Max Weber (1946, 1979), whose numerous studies helped to shape contemporary sociology, was an early master of the sociological approach.

The use of comparative and historical data contains all the pitfalls associated with the use of documents in general, as well as some additional problems. Data may be incomplete, inaccurate, and sometimes deliberately biased. Gaps in the historical record may sometimes exist. It may be difficult or impossible to obtain access to crucial information. Finally, documents may be in different languages, including languages no longer widely used in the modern world. Even when the language is familiar, the words may have had different meanings at earlier times.

Other Approaches to Inquiry

A number of other research methods employed by sociologists should be briefly mentioned. *Content analysis* consists of a variety of techniques for analyzing writing and other forms of communication. These typically involve coding the communication to be studied into relevant categories, taking a sample of elements of the communication, and then counting the occurrence of each category.

Biographical research involves the use of life histories, diaries, journals, and stories to reconstruct individual biographies. These can provide useful windows on past historical periods, as seen through the eyes of the person being studied. Autobiographies can also provide important sociological insights, as *The Autobiography of Malcolm X* indicates (Haley, 1965).

Conversation analysis is an entire field of sociological inquiry, which includes detailed methods for analyzing conversations and other forms of interactive speech (such as calls to emergency 911 numbers, or court proceedings). It holds that participants in a conversation actively construct their actions so as to form coherent sequences. Various sequencing procedures have been identified, including turn taking, fitting actions together, and correcting difficulties in hearing and understanding (Zimmerman, 1988; Boden and Zimmerman, 1991).

Evaluation research is concerned with evaluating the effectiveness of a program or policy (Rossi and Wright, 1977; Singleton et al., 1993). It may draw on any of the previously mentioned research methods, although most evaluation studies tend to rely on surveys, examination of statistical records, and other forms of quantitative analysis. Although most sociological research derives its focus from problems deemed important by sociologists, evaluation research is dictated by the needs of the agency requesting the study. This is an example of **applied sociology,** *sociological research whose primary purpose is to solve a practical problem rather than to advance sociological theory or understanding.*

How Intrusive Should You Be?

Because sociologists study the social world, their very presence often makes a difference to the people they study. Research methods differ greatly in the degree to which they intrude on people's everyday lives (Rossi, 1988). In *Street Corner Society,* sociologist William F. Whyte (1943) hung around with his subjects, went bowling with them, openly participated in their discussions, and joined their organizations. As he acknowledges in his book, his participation could not help but affect their behavior, which necessarily would have been different had he not been there. Even survey research, which is more impersonal than participant-observation, can have an impact: the people being interviewed may be asked questions about things they have never seriously thought about before, and—in formulating their responses to the interviewer—may form their opinions as well.

The only forms of sociological research that are completely unobtrusive are those which involve no contact whatsoever between the researcher and the people being studied. Analysis of existing documents, government statistics, and historical materials are examples of such nonintrusive research methods. Of course, the census-taker who collected the original government statistics had to interview someone face-to-face, a mildly intrusive activity that may well have imposed on that person's privacy as well as affected his or her responses. Spying is another relatively unobtrusive way to gather information, at least if the researcher is completely unobserved by those being studied. This approach raises serious ethical concerns, however, and is not commonly practiced by sociologists.

Unobtrusive measures are those that *are based on data collected with minimal impact on the persons being studied.* A sociologist who wants to study smoking behavior in an office environment may ask people how many cigarettes they smoke at work. Because of the stigma currently associated with smoking, even such a mildly intrusive approach might produce misleading responses. On the other hand, the sociologist might simply collect the ashtrays from the end of the day and count the cigarette butts, yielding an unobtrusive measure of workplace smoking behavior that is likely to be highly accurate.

The most famous study about the intrusive impact of the researcher on the persons being studied occurred at Western Electric's Hawthorne plant in the 1930s. Elton Mayo and his colleagues (Roethlisberger and Dickson, 1939) wanted to find out how to make a group of women workers increase their hourly output. The women, who worked together making electrical wiring connections, were studied over a period of time in order to test the adequacy of several ideas regarding

worker productivity. One idea, for example, held that lighting conditions in the room would make a difference; another emphasized seating arrangements; yet another stressed method of pay. What the researchers found, much to their surprise, was that *everything* made a difference: it didn't matter so much what was done to change working conditions, but merely that *something* was done. Subsequent interviews with the women revealed that they were motivated to work faster simply because they were getting a lot of attention from the researchers. They ordinarily experienced their work as repetitive and boring; for the first time, however, they felt that someone was genuinely interested in their performance.

This striking finding, the so-called **Hawthorne effect,** holds that *the researcher's impact on his or her subjects may actually affect the research results.* It acknowledges that human beings make conscious choices based on their immediate environment, and—if the researcher becomes part of that environment—then it follows that choices will often be affected by the research itself. It is important that sociologists be aware of this possibility and try to take it into account.

Sociology has another, larger-scale type of "Hawthorne effect": the results of sociological research are published and circulated, and subsequently may become the basis of social policy as well as everyday thinking (Giddens, 1990, 1991). Such basic notions as social class, racism and sexism, and inequality originated in social science research. Social science studies of the impact of segregated education on racial minorities were cited by the U.S. Supreme Court when it outlawed educational segregation in 1954. One important feature of life today is that we are constantly study-

Researchers must always take into account the possibility that their research itself will bias their results. In the celebrated 1930s study of Western Electric's Hawthorne plant, Elton Mayo and his colleagues were thwarted in their efforts to find out what made women workers more productive, since the researchers' very presence led to increased productivity.

ing ourselves, trying to use our understandings to alter our lives and our institutions, albeit with mixed success.

THE PROCESS OF SOCIOLOGICAL INQUIRY

Sociological inquiry seldom follows a cookbook approach that sets out exactly how to proceed from start to finish. Sociologists often have to feel their way as they go along, responding to the challenges that arise during research, adapting new methods that are required by the circumstances. The process presented here identifies rough stages of inquiry that are usually—but not always—followed. Even if you do not observe this exact sequence, however, all of these issues must at some point be addressed in the research process.

Define Your Research Question

Be clear about what you are studying. Formulating a clear statement about what interests you—about what you hope to learn—may be the single most important thing you do to ensure a successful research project. A muddled, confused research question will likely lead to equally muddled and confused results. The research question may be some unanswered issue derived from a careful reading of the existing research on the topic, or it may be something of personal concern to you. Often it is a question deemed important within a field of sociology; a topic deemed uninteresting or unimportant by leading figures in the discipline is likely to be ignored by most researchers as well (Box 2.3). Occasionally the research question may be given by someone else—the head of a research team, a program that must be evaluated, a government agency that wants a particular problem solved. But in all cases, your first task should be to clarify exactly what it is you hope to find out.

Review the Existing Knowledge Base

Sociological research cannot occur in a vacuum; others have surely studied some aspect of most research questions. You must therefore begin with an extensive review of the existing literature on your topic. This may consist of published studies, unpublished papers, books, government documents, periodicals and newspapers, and numerous other sources. This stage requires a great deal of detective work, and some technical skills as well. It is important that you learn how to use computerized methods of library research, since "looking up" sources electronically is faster and usually more accurate than most other methods. When you

read a particular study, you may want to look through the footnotes of other studies that are cited, obtaining those that seem relevant. Unpublished scholarly papers, especially those that have been presented at professional meetings, are an excellent source of the most recent research. Hard, diligent work is the key to success at this stage.

Select Appropriate Method(s) of Inquiry

By now you are ready to think about how your research question can best be answered. Which of the many methods reviewed above are best suited to your problem? Which method (or methods) will provide you with the best results for your particular research project? Which one best suits your personal style of inquiry? If you choose a method with which you are uncomfortable or poorly trained, your research will likely suffer.

Consider the Ethical Implications

Be familiar with the standards that exist at your university or research institution, and make certain you follow them carefully. Most agencies have specific forms that must be filled out and reviewed by "human subjects" committees. It is important to satisfy the legal requirements of doing research. Additionally, be aware of your own feelings about what you do: ultimately, you should only conduct research that conforms to your own ethical standards as well as the legal and professional requirements.

Conduct Your Inquiry

Conducting an inquiry is the central part of any research project—the most time-consuming and the most exciting. It is during this phase that you will acquire the new information and knowledge that will provide the base for making your own original contribution to the sociological understanding of your topic. Be aware of your biases and preconceptions, and strive to be as objective as possible. This does not mean you should not feel passionately engaged about your work, but it is important that you not let your feelings get in the way of conducting good, solid research.

Draw Your Conclusions by Analyzing Your Data

Once you have collected your information, you will want to figure out what it all means. If your project is quantitative, this will entail coding your data into a

Box 2.3

Silenced Voices

Inclusion and Exclusion in Sociological Research

The first step in the process of sociological inquiry is to define your research question. Yet as the following passage by Margaret L. Anderson and Patricia Hill Collins (1992, pp. 1–2) suggests, sociology's founders often defined their research questions so as to exclude entire groups of people. Broad theories were often based on studies of a small segment of the world population—the experiences and concerns of European males (see also Chapter 1). This passage challenges the Eurocentric nature of much social science. Most sociologists would agree that women and people of color have until recently been effectively outside of the mainstream of sociological inquiry.

Over the centuries Western thought has been centered on the experiences of a privileged few whose particular views of the world and experience within it have shaped what is known. How else can we explain that democracy and egalitarianism were defined as central cultural beliefs in the nineteenth century while millions of African Americans were enslaved? Why have social science studies been generalized to the whole population while being based only on samples of men? The exclusion of women, African Americans, Latinos, Native Americans, gays and lesbians, and other groups from formal scholarship has resulted in distortions and incomplete information not only about the experiences of excluded groups but also about the experiences of more privileged groups. Thus, the development of women's studies has also changed the way we see men; the study of racial-ethnic groups has transformed our understanding of white experience as well.

This exclusionary thinking has been increasingly challenged by scholars and teachers who want to include the diversity of human experience in the construction and transmission of knowledge. Those who ask us to think more inclusively want to open up the way the world is viewed, making the experience of previously excluded groups more visible and central in the construction of knowledge. Inclusive thinking shifts our perspective from the white, male-centered forms of thinking that have characterized much of western thought. Thinking inclusively means putting the experiences of those who have been excluded at the center of thought so that we can better understand the intersections of race, class, and gender in the experiences of all groups, including those with privilege and power.

---

computer and using a statistical program to analyze it. If it is more qualitative, this stage involves carefully reviewing and organizing your field notes, documents, and other sources of information. Most likely, it will involve a variety of methods, most of which require some special training. You should always be aware of the degree to which your data support your findings; avoid drawing conclusions that are speculative or unwarranted by your research. It is important to know if your results support or contradict your initial theory or hypothesis, or are simply inconclusive; all such findings must be reported. Finally, your results will have implications for larger theoretical questions. You should refer back to the theories on which your research was based, and consider how those theories are supported or might be modified in light of your results.

Communicate Your Results to Others

However fascinating your research may be to you personally, if others don't know about it, it cannot add to the larger sociological understanding. The most common way to let others in on your findings is to publish the results. Among sociologists, most research is initially published in specialized journals. Know which journals are concerned with your topic, as well as their standards for publication. Other forms of publication include books, popular articles, newspapers, and even video documentaries. Another way to communicate your findings is to give a presentation at a professional meeting. There are many such meetings of different associations each year; at least one will offer a panel suited to your topic. In some cases, high-quality undergraduate papers may be selected for presentation at special panels. If your paper is accepted for presentation, you will get excellent (although sometimes painful) feedback on your results from others who are expert in the field.

ETHICAL CONCERNS

An issue of major concern to social scientists has to do with special difficulties surrounding the conduct of research on other human beings. During World War II, the Nazis conducted horrible experiments on Jewish and other prisoners in concentration camps. Men, women, and children were frozen alive, burned, starved, and tortured in various ways as Nazi scientists sought to test their pet theories on live human subjects.

In one of the most celebrated studies in all social science, Stanley Milgram (1973) sought to discover whether such horrible behavior was unique to Nazi Germany, or if in fact ordinary Americans were capable of inflicting pain and even death on innocent people. Milgram and his associates at Yale University tricked volunteers into thinking they were administering painful and sometimes lethal electric shocks to other people (in fact, no one actually got a shock). The purpose of Milgram's study was to scientifically determine whether or not people would go along with an order to injure and possibly kill another human being, simply because they were told to do so by someone in a position of authority. While Milgram's findings have been important in helping us to better understand why people conform to orders, the volunteers for his study suffered enormous psychological stress during the experiment. (See Chapter 6 for a more detailed discussion of Milgram's research.)

Was Milgram's research ethical? When do the results of research justify subjecting human beings to physical or psychological discomfort, pain, embarassment, invasion of privacy, or deception? Social scientists have rightfully taken an increasingly strong position on the need to protect research subjects from overly zealous researchers. The Milgram study would not be permissible under the rules that exist in most American universities today, where faculty "human subjects" committees seek to ensure that all research meets the appropriate ethical standards.

The American Sociological Association has a stringent code of ethics that governs research on human subjects (Bailey, 1987). Sociologists are required to be extremely sensitive to the impact of their research on the people or organizations they study. Sociologists must not misrepresent their abilities, nor use their role to obtain information for any other purpose then their research. The people they study are entitled to privacy, confidentiality throughout the research process, and full anonymity when results are reported. If there is any possibility that risk or harm might result, subjects must be fully informed and their written consent obtained. When American sociologists conduct their research in other countries, they must be sensitive to any problems that might arise from differences in wealth, power, or political systems. They must scrupulously avoid providing any government with secret information obtained from their research.

Perhaps the most serious violation of the rights of research subjects occurred during a long-term study conducted by the U.S. Health Service, which in 1932 began a study of "untreated syphilis in the male negro" (Peters, 1955; Jones, 1989). The Tuskegee Syphilis Study, so-called because it was done at the Tuskegee Institute in Macon County, Georgia, sought to advance scientific knowledge about syphilis, a sexually transmitted disease that when untreated results in blindness and eventually death. A group of some 600 low-income African-American males, about 400 of whom were infected with the disease, were selected to be monitored. As the study continued it was periodically reviewed and extended by U.S. Health Service officials, until it eventually spanned 40 years.

During that time penicillin was identified as a treatment for the deadly disease, and by the 1950s it was widely used as a simple, inexpensive, and highly effective cure. Yet the scientists conducting the study decided not to administer penicillin on the grounds that it would interfere with their research on untreated syphilis. As late as the 1960s, the U.S. government itself, through the Center for Disease Control, authorized the study to be continued. In 1972 news of the research leaked to the general public, and U.S. Department of Health, Education, and Welfare ordered an end to the project. By that time, at least 28—and perhaps more than 100—of the subjects had died of syphilis (Allen, 1978). Many critics have noted that this study tells us as much about the nature of social relations in America at the time of the research as it does about the nature of the disease that it studied. It seems highly likely that had the subjects of this study been middle-class whites instead of poor blacks, the study would have been terminated as soon as a cure for syphilis was found.

In addition to physically or mentally endangering subjects, social science research raises a number of ethical concerns. Research may threaten an *invasion of privacy* of those being studied, in that their personal or professional lives may become the subject of investigation. Whether you seek to study student dormitory life, homelessness, or dealings in the corporate board room, people are entitled to have their personal lives remain private if they so desire. To ensure that subjects are aware that their privacy may be compromised, researchers typically must obtain from those who are being studied their **informed consent.** That is, *the subjects must agree to being studied, after having been fully informed of the nature of the research, any physical or psychological dangers that might be involved, and the uses to which the results will be put.* The subjects of the study are often also guaranteed *anonymity*—the assurance that their names will not be used in any written reports or publications, and their personal and social characteristics will be sufficiently disguised so that they cannot be identified in any way. Finally, the researcher should be aware of the uses to which the research may be put. Will anyone likely suffer as a result of the research?

Such guarantees are often not so simple as they may initially seem. Social science research often involves some degree of **deception**—that is, *the people being studied may not be fully informed of the nature or purposes of a study.* This is almost always the case in small group studies, where some degree of trickery, however mild, is necessary for the research to work. In one study, for example, Philip Goldberg (1968) asked students to evaluate edited versions of a half-dozen scholarly articles in terms of merit, persuasiveness, profundity, writing style, competence, and other characteristics. Although the students were told this was a study of their personal opinion of the articles and their authors, in reality it was a study of the students' own gender bias. Half of the students were falsely told the articles were written by women, in order to see if they systematically under-valued articles with female authorship. (They did.) In this research, the students were initially deceived about both the purpose of the research and the actual authorship.

Was this deception warranted? On the one hand, had the students truthfully been told that the study was concerned with their gender biases, they would have watched their words to prove they were openminded. The study would have been honest, but its results meaningless. On the other hand, the research resulted in important findings, although it did involve some deception. Virtually all scholars would agree that this study does not violate ethical standards: no one was physically or psychologically hurt in any way, and participants were immediately told the truth after they had completed their participation.

C H A P T E R   S U M M A R Y

1. Sociological understanding differs from faith and common-sense knowledge in that sociologists put their biases, assumptions, and conclusions to the test.

2. Sociological concepts are often operationalized into measurable **variables,** which permits quantitative research to occur. Quantitative research is particularly useful for understanding systematic social patterns and their complex inter-relationships. It is especially concerned with questions of **validity** and **reliability.**

3. Quantitative analysis permits **correlations** between variables to be measured, and **causal relationships** to be estimated. Care must be taken not to infer causation from correlation.

4. Qualitative research is often better suited than quantitative research for obtaining a deep understanding of the meaning of the social world to the people being studied. On the other hand, it is sometimes difficult to determine whether the results of qualitative research are reliable and valid.

5. Sociologists seek **objectivity** and **value-neutrality** in conducting their research. At the very least, they should seek to make their biases and assumptions known.

6. Research strategies are approaches for gathering information about the social world. They involve a plan for conducting research and choosing appropriate methods. It is important to carefully choose a suitable strategy before actually embarking on research.

7. A large number of different research methods are available to sociologists. Each has its own advantages and disadvantages, and the researcher should be familiar with each. Among other things, methods differ in their degree of intrusiveness into the lives of the people being studied.

8. Sociological inquiry involves several steps: clearly defining your research problem; reviewing the existing knowledge base; selecting appropriate methods; weighing the ethical implications of the research;

conducting the actual inquiry; drawing conclusions; and communicating the results to others.

9. To be ethical, research must be highly sensitive to the implications of invading the privacy of persons being studied. Safeguards include obtaining informed consent, guaranteeing anonymity if the subjects desire it, and being conscious of the uses to which your research may be put. The decision to deceive your subjects should be carefully taken, and it is especially important that subjects be fully informed of the nature of the research when the study is completed.

QUESTIONS FOR DISCUSSION

1. Imagine that you have decided to study homelessness by temporarily becoming a homeless person. Describe a research strategy, and discuss what you might and might not be able to learn from this approach. What are the ethical implications of this sort of research? How much of your true identity would you reveal to the people you are studying, and how might this affect your results?

2. Discuss the role of theory in research. To what extent is research best conducted with a purely "open mind," free from all theoretical ideas and biases? To what extent is it impossible to conduct research without having a prior theory to guide your efforts?

3. In what ways can research be said to be biased toward a particular social group or culture? Do you think that the sociological studies with which you are familiar have a Eurocentric or other type of bias?

4. Take any problem of interest to you, and choose three alternative research strategies by which you might study it. What are the strengths and weaknesses of each? What might you learn from each that you might not learn from the others?

KEY TERMS

applied sociology: Sociological research whose primary purpose is to solve a practical problem rather than to advance sociological theory or understanding.

bias: A result that lacks validity in a particular direction.

causal relationship: A relationship in which one variable is said to be the cause of another.

concept: An idea or mental construct that focuses upon specified properties common to a set of phenomena, to the exclusion of other properties.

construct validity: The degree to which a particular concept is in fact measured.

correlation: The degree to which two or more variables regularly vary together.

deception: In sociological research, when the subjects being studied are not fully informed of the nature or purposes of a study.

dependent variable: A variable that is believed to have changed as the result of another.

descriptive research: Research that seeks to paint a detailed picture of a particular phenomenon.

ethnography: A method of research in which fieldwork is conducted to depict the characteristics of a group of people as fully as possible.

face validity: The extent to which operational definitions appear to measure the concepts they are intended to measure.

Hawthorne effect: An effect on the subject being researched that actually results from the research process itself; named after the studies in which it was first observed.

hypothesis: An idea about the world, derived from a theory, that is capable of being disproved when tested against observations.

independent variable: A variable that is believed to bring about change in another.

informed consent: An agreement by the subjects of a research project to being studied, after having been fully informed of the nature of the research, any physical or psychological dangers that might be involved, and the uses to which the results will be put.

interview: A detailed, in-depth interrogation.

leading question: A question that solicits a particular response.

nominal variable: A variable that indicates whether or not something falls into a particular category.

nonprobability sample: A sample in which subjects are chosen because of their specific characteristics.

objectivity: The ability, during research, to represent the object of study as truthfully as possible.

operational definition: Defining a concept in terms of operations or measurements that can be performed on it.

ordinal variables: A variable that measures rank order.

population universe: The larger group of people for whom the conclusions of a survey sample are said to apply.

principle of falsification: The principle that a scientific theory must lead to testable hypotheses that are capable of being proved false.

qualitative sociology: A research strategy that is based on descriptive rather than quantitative forms of analysis.

qualities: Discrete categories (usually indicated by words or labels) that enable researchers to make nonnumerical distinctions among the things they observe.

quantitative sociology: A research strategy based primarily on numerical measurement and analysis.

quantities: Explicit numerical distinctions that enable researchers to make relatively precise measurements.

random sample: A sample in which everyone in the underlying population has an equal chance of being chosen for the sample.

ratio variable: A variable that permits absolute measurement along a scale with a meaningful zero point.

reliability: The extent to which researchers' findings are consistent between different studies of the same thing, or for the same study over time.

replication: Research strategies that can be duplicated by other scholars.

research method: A specific technique for systematically gathering data while conforming to rules that have been agreed upon by a community of scholars.

research strategy: A clearly thought-out plan to guide sociological inquiry.

sample: A subset of cases selected to represent a larger population.

semistructured interview: An interview consisting of a list of topics to cover, but in which the interview situation itself determines the course of questioning and the details of the questions.

spurious relationship: A statistical association between two or more variables that is actually the result of something else that is not being measured, rather than a causal link between the variables themselves.

statistics: A subfield of sociology concerned with generalizing from samples to the larger populations they represent.

structured interview: An interview consisting of a detailed list of specific questions.

survey: A precisely worded questionnaire administered to a group of people in order to determine their characteristics, opinions, and behaviors.

unobtrusive measure: A measure that is based on data collected with minimal impact on the persons being studied.

validity: The degree to which our concepts and their measurement are congruent with the world they are claiming to represent.

value neutrality: The belief that personal beliefs and opinions should not influence the course of a person's research.

variable: An operational measure that varies (increases or decreases in value) according to the value of the thing it is measuring.

R E C O M M E N D E D   F O R   F U R T H E R   R E A D I N G

Appelbaum, Richard P. (1986). "Testimony on *A Report to the Secretary on the Homeless and Emergency Shelters.*" In Jon Erickson and Charles Wilhelm, *Housing the Homeless.* New Brunswick, NJ: Rutgers University Center for Urban Policy Research.

> This brief article, written by one of the authors of this textbook, discusses the misuse of quantitative research to draw conclusions that are not warranted by the data. It critically analyzes a key governmental study that erroneously concluded there were only 350,000 homeless people in the United States.

Durnier, Mitchell. (1992). *Slim's Table.* Chicago: University of Chicago Press.

> An ethnographic study based on years of fieldwork at Valois Restaurant in a Chicago South Side neighborhood. The restaurant is a favorite congregating place for older black men who are neither part of an upwardly mobile middle class nor a dispossessed underclass.

Jankowski, Martin Sanchez. (1991). *Islands in the Street: Gangs and American Urban Society.* Berkeley: University of California Press.

A fascinating example of ethnographic research, based on ten years of participant-observation study of gangs across the United States.

Singleton, Royce, Bruce C. Straits, Margaret M. Straits, and Ronald J. McAllister (1993) *Approaches to Social Research.* New York: Oxford University Press.
A highly readable textbook that discusses four major research methods—experimentation, survey research, field research, and the use of available data. It calls for a multimethod strategy that treats these as complementary rather than mutually exclusive, and details the strengths and weaknesses of each.

Stack, Carol B. (1974) *All Our Kin: Strategies for Survival in a Black Community.* New York: Harper & Row.
A classic study that shows the strength and resilience of the African-American family, even under conditions of economic hardship and racial discrimination.

CHAPTER

3

Culture

CHAPTER OUTLINE

T H I N G S   T O   L O O K   F O R

1. What role does culture play in accounting for social conformity as well as individual differences?
2. To what extent is there a biological basis for human culture?
3. What is the role played by language in helping the members of a particular culture to shape their perceptions of "reality?"
4. How has globalization affected the degree of diversity found within cultures today? Why is cultural diversity an important issue to understand sociologically?
5. In what ways can it be said that a universal global culture is emerging? How is this tied to the resurgence of locally based cultures?

INTRODUCTION: A RAPIDLY CHANGING WORLD

Napoleon Chagnon has been researching the Yanomamö tribes in Brazil and Venezuela for almost three decades. The Yanomamö people were one of the few native cultures that remained largely untouched by the larger world. As recently as ten years ago, Chagnon discovered villages with no contact whatsover with the world outside the rain forest. When he returned to the Yanomamö in 1991, Chagnon (1992, pp. 212-213) found that many changes had occurred. Gold mining, logging of the rain forest, and missionaries had contributed to what he termed "catastrophic changes" and a tragedy of enormous proportions" in the Yanomamö's lives:

> In a short time over a hundred airstrips were cleared deep in Yanomamöland to support the mining operations. Scores of mining camps popped up almost over-night, some elaborate enough to have brothels, a general store, and a bar. The miners used destructive hydraulic pumps that sucked the river-bottoms of their gold-bearing ore, passed it through troughs into which toxic mercury compounds were added to extract the gold from the mud, and let the poisoned residue flow freely back into the rivers. They occasionally raped Yanomamö women and shot their men and children. The diary of a Brazilian gold miner in 1990, recites one hideous incident af-

ter another that his group of partners participated in or witnessed as they moved from camp to camp over a large area of Yanomamöland. Most of the officials of then President José Sarney's government turned a blind eye to this tragedy and accommodated even the slightest demands of the mining interests. . . .

> The aftermath of the illegal invasion of Brazilian miners is now a colossal problem. As many as 1,100 Brazilian Yanomamö may have already died and hundreds are still suffering either from new sicknesses introduced by the miners or from traditional maladies that became epidemic following the influx of so many miners. For most Brazilian Yanomamö groups, major aspects of their traditional culture and social organization have been forever changed.

As this excerpt indicates, people who until recently were completely isolated from the influence of North American, European, and Asian industrial nations are now rapidly becoming incorporated into a global economy and culture. Will globalization eventually eliminate all separate cultures, creating one homogenous, uniform culture that extends around the planet? To understand the implications of globalization for different cultures, we must first understand the nature of culture and the central role it plays in people's daily lives.

THE NATURE OF CULTURE

Culture shapes the way we think, the words we use, and the world of human-made objects we occupy. It creates enormous pressures for conformity, as well as the possibilities for change. Culture constitutes the materials out of which we construct our identities and our perceptions of the world. It comprises the lens through which we view the world, as well as the materials by which we might alter that lens and thereby the world itself.

Culture and Society

The term "culture" is popularly used in a variety of different ways. It originates in the Latin term for "cultivation," the preparation of land to produce crops. We retain that use when we think of someone as "cultured" because they show certain qualities that have resulted from their education and overall preparation. But for sociologists and anthropologists, the term **culture** is defined as *all of the beliefs, behaviors, and products common to members of a particular group.* These include the values and customs that we hold in common with others; the language that we speak; the rules we follow; the tools and technologies we use to make things; the goods that we make and consume; the organizations we belong to; and the larger institutions of society (Geertz, 1968; Tylor, 1958, orig. 1871; Brown, 1991a). **Institutions** can be defined as *clusters of relatively stable rules that govern social activities in a society; such rules also provide a shared understanding of the cultural meaning of those activities* (Meyer *et al.,* 1987). In Part IV we will discuss specific examples of institutions such as the family, work, education, religion, and medicine.

Society has traditionally been defined as *the interacting people who share a common culture*—that is, any group of people who speak a common language, share common beliefs and customs, belong to the same institutions and organizations, use the same tools and technology, and consume the same goods. Although the term "society" is sometimes also used to refer to people with a common culture who share the same territory, we prefer not to emphasize this geographical dimension: in modern society it is increasingly possible to share a common culture with people who are geographically dispersed.

Culture and society must be understood in terms of one another: culture consists of all the products shared within a particular society, which in turn consists of the interacting people who share the same culture. It is easy to understand these definitions if we think about the world as it existed more than a hundred years ago, when the words "culture" and "society" first began to acquire their present meanings. When Edward B. Tylor, one of the founders of modern anthropology, first published *Primitive Culture* in 1871, most people in the world lived and worked in small, relatively isolated, close-knit groups. Each group was unique in that its members spoke the same language, shared highly similar beliefs, used highly traditional tools, and dressed in similar clothing. Early anthropologists such as Tylor had a strong Eurocentric bias to their work (see Chapter 1). They assumed the existence of a common human culture, with "primitive" cultures at the lower end and European-style "civilization" at the higher. Eventually, however, anthropologists came to recognize that there are many different cultures, each with its own distinctive characteristics, and none instrinsically "better" or "worse" than any other.

The notion of discrete "cultures" and "societies" now has much less validity than in the past. Today, thanks to modern communications and industry, we interact with people a half a globe away; our lives are touched daily by ideas and products produced across the planet. At the same time, we continue to speak of "culture" and "society" in the more traditional, local sense: I may say I am a member of a society called the United States or that I share a common U.S. culture. These localizing forces remain strong; in fact, in some instances, local identifications with particular cultures and societies may be increasing alongside our more global identifications. The breakdown of the former country of Yugoslavia into warring factions is a tragic example of this process.

It is important not to confuse the sociological term "culture" with its more popular usage, which has to do with such personal qualities as proficiency in the arts or good manners. To make this distinction clear, sociologists use the term **high culture** to refer to *the fine arts, classical music, live theater, and other activities that usually require special preparation to fully appreciate.* This form of culture is routinely patronized by a relatively small elite group of mostly wealthy and highly educated people. Sociologists contrast high culture with **popular culture,** the *forms of culture that are pursued by larger numbers of middle- and working-class people.* These include spectator sports, television "soaps" and "sitcoms," amateur softball leagues, movies, and rock music. There is a strong potential element of evaluation in this distinction, of course, since "high" may imply "better" to some people. Sociologists do not use the terms "high culture" and "popular culture" in this evaluative way.

Individuality and Conformity

Americans tend to think of themselves as highly nonconformist, "rugged individuals" who bow down to no group or government official. The American Revolution, the colonization of America by Europeans, the expansion to the Western states, the Trade Union Movement, the Women's Movement: these and other major forces of social change in America are often described as the consequence of the efforts of strong-willed, independent individuals.

Americans pride themselves on their independence of spirit—represented by the lone eagle, America's national symbol. Thomas Jefferson's dictum "that government is best which governs least" and Hollywood's version of the maverick law enforcer or the frontier family in their isolated cabin on the prairie reinforce the image that the person who stands alone is to be revered and emulated.

High school and college students often see themselves as especially nonconformist. The hippies of the 1960s, the punks of the 1980s, and death rockers of the 1990s all sported highly distinctive clothing styles and haircuts. Yet how independent were they? Are young people with dyed hair or distinctive jewelry really acting independently, or are they simply conforming to the standards of a group of people that dress and act in a similar fashion?

Both the New York City Metropolitan Opera and Lollapalooza are examples of culture. Operas are a form of high culture, requiring some degree of special preparation to appreciate, while rock concerts are instances of popular culture, more likely to be pursued by middle- and working-class people.

One of sociology's central insights is that our lives and personalities are in large part constructed out of our shared culture. When we say we strongly believe in a particular value, for example, we are voicing often the beliefs of our family members, our friends, our teachers, or others who are significant in our lives. When we choose a word or a phrase to describe some important experience we have just had, that word or phrase acquires its meaning in a language we have learned from others.

Although we may make our own original contributions to culture, sociologists argue that such contributions must themselves be understood as shaped by the cultures in which we live. From such fundamental notions as time and space to newly emerging beliefs about work and marriage, all of our ideas are constructed out of materials provided by our culture. The ideas and institutions that precede us weigh heavily on our thoughts and actions.

Culture, in other words, is an important source of conformity. Although rugged individualism is a strongly held value in the United States (Bellah et al., 1985), in fact, like all people everywhere, we actually conform to cultural expectations most of the time. Think for a moment of how you have spent the past week or two. If you were to keep a detailed diary of everything you do, you would probably find that you awake at about the same time each weekday, that your morning bathroom routines are pretty much the same on Tuesday or Wednesday as they were on Monday, that you eat the same breakfast, put on your favorite clothing (the clothing that gives a certain "look" that is "you"), and habitually arrive at class the same few minutes late (or early), sitting in about the same seat each time. When you listen to the radio or watch television,

you almost always tune in to the same kind of music, most likely some form of popular music.

If you were to examine carefully the words that you use when speaking with your friends or writing in your diary, you would find that they, too, have a highly predictable quality. For one thing, they are likely to be in the English language, although an enormous number of other languages are spoken in the United States as well; Spanish, for example, is the spoken language in approximately one out of every twenty U.S. households (U.S. Bureau of the Census, 1990). In addition, if you were to pay close attention to your patterns of speech, you would find that you probably have a certain style of speaking that is shared by your friends. Young urban African Americans share a style of English that is very different from the style spoken by California surfers, which in turn differs from that spoken in New England boarding schools. Each group conforms to its own language expectations, without even being aware of its conformity.

The Evolution of Culture

According to archaeological evidence, as well as similarities in blood chemistry and genetics between chimpanzees and humans, scientists now believe that the first humans emerged from ape-like creatures on the African continent less than 8 million years ago. Evidence of human-type behavior dates back only 2 million years, and includes the use of stone tools, subsistence based on hunting animals and gathering nuts and berries, and a highly cooperative way of life. Because these early humans planned their hunts, they also must have possessed a capacity for abstract thinking and transforming their environments. About 250,000 years ago the human brain approached its present size, making these early ancestors the first true *Homo sapiens* (literally, "wise men"), although they still bore a strong resemblance to apes. Fire was first used about 500,000 years ago, and truly modern looking humans appeared 40,000 years ago (Jolly, 1993).

Early in their evolution, human beings developed a number of biological traits that have proved to be enormously successful for their survival. Although to varying degrees humans share some of these traits with other species, together they contributed to the creation of human cultures that enabled early humans to compensate for their relative physical weaknesses. These traits include a large and complex brain, which gives rise to intelligence; opposable thumbs, which enable humans to use tools and weapons; highly developed vocal cords and larynx, which, in combination with intelligence, permits the development of language and other forms of symbolic communication; upright posture, which frees the hands for purposes besides locomotion; and sociability, which fosters a high degree of cooperation within human society. Furthermore, because of their large brain size, human fetuses must be born early in their development, before their heads grow too large to pass through the birth canal. As a result, human babies are far less well-equipped for survival on their own than other species, and must spend an extended period of time in the care of adults. This, in turn, fosters a lengthy period of socialization during which the child learns its society's culture (Chapter 5).

Although early humans were far slower and weaker than many other animals, they could use their intelligence and toolmaking ability cooperatively to hunt down prey and protect against predators. The development of culture freed humans from dependence on their surroundings, enabling them to shape the world in their interests. As a result, in a mere instant of geological time we have become the dominant species on the planet, threatening many others (including perhaps ourselves) with extinction.

Early human cultures were strongly adapted to their physical environment, since they lacked the technological ability to significantly modify their immediate surroundings (Harris, 1975, 1977, 1980, 1987; Bennett, 1976). Food, clothing, and shelter were largely restricted to what was close at hand. Desert cultures, where water and food were scarce, differed significantly from jungle cultures where such natural resources abounded. People who lived in the frozen arctic developed cultures that were different from those that evolved in more temperate climates. Partly because of geological and climatic differences where hu-

man cultures were found, and partly because of human intelligence and inventiveness, an enormous variety of human cultures has emerged around the planet. As we will see at the conclusion of this chapter, modern technology, along with the forces of globalization, may soon render such variety a thing of the past.

Is There a Biological Basis for Human Culture?

One of the oldest debates in the social sciences concerns the question of "human nature." To what extent does a common human genetic heritage create cultural forms that are common to all people everywhere? To what extent do genetic variations account for the cultural and behavioral differences that are found among human societies? The debate has not led to any firm conclusions about what constitutes human nature. There are those social scientists who see humans as shaped by biological or genetic traits that determine, to varying degrees, the potential for everything from food preferences to language to propensity for violence. Others regard human beings as a blank slate on which anything can be written.

In recent years, this debate has been between sociobiologists and social learning theorists. **Sociobiologists** infer from the study of insects and other social animals that *there are genetic bases for competition, cooperation, aggression, envy, and other specific behaviors that are widespread among many cultures.* They argue that just as there is natural selection for hair color or skin pigmentation, so too there is natural selection for behavior: in both cases, differential reproductive success explains which traits or behaviors are genetically transmitted (Wilson, 1975, 1978). For example, among many animal species males will aggressively compete for females, asserting their domination over as many females as possible. Sociobiologists conclude from this evidence that since human males often behave in a similar fashion, there is a biological basis for male aggression, dominating behavior, and sexual promiscuity (Symons, 1979).

On the other hand, **social learning theorists** argue that *because human beings are social in nature, specific behaviors are always learned within a particular cultural context* (Bandura, 1977; Baldwin and Baldwin, 1981). They hold that there is no genetic basis for specific behaviors, since genes govern only the production of enzymes and other biochemical traits. Although human biochemistry clearly affects us physically, mentally, and emotionally, it does not determine specific behaviors. These must be socially learned. For example, a genetic predisposition toward excitability may be channeled into an intense passion for conducting scientific research, or into an equally intense passion for athletic excellence. Or, if men are indeed found to be aggressive and sexually promiscuous in many cultures, the reasons are to be sought in common sociological factors, and not in male biology (Symons, 1979).

We will explore this "nature-nurture" debate in greater detail in Chapters 5 and 11. For the present, we simply note that sociologists tend to adhere to the social learning viewpoint: specific behaviors are seen as the result of social factors that condition and modify biological predispositions, rather than resulting from genetics. Human behaviors are not considered **instincts**—*biologically fixed patterns of action.* They can instead be classified as responses that are learned within a particular culture. Human beings do have **reflexes**—*automatic responses to particular stimuli.* Babies will automatically "root" for their mother's nipple, without being taught to do so; an adult will withdraw a hand automatically from a hot stove to avoid being burned. Yet such simple reflexes do not explain most human behavior, particularly once infancy has been left behind. For human beings, social and cultural influences are so powerful that it is not possible to reduce the multiplicity of human behavior to any simple biological traits.

Evidence for the social learning position is found in the study of **cultural universals,** *features common to all cultures.* Such research suggests that human beings do not have a common, unchanging human nature that somehow gives rise to identical cultures everywhere on the planet. Early anthropologists who studied preindustrial societies were fascinated by the enormous variety of cultures they found, although they were also struck by what they regarded as the presence of common elements (Benedict, 1934; Murdock, 1945). A recent review of hundreds of studies concluded that while all known human cultures do in fact contain a number of common features, these do not dictate specific beliefs or ways of behaving. All societies, for example, contain such cultural universals as language, shelter, emotions, norms governing childhood socialization, a division of labor, a system of governance, rules governing sexual conduct, dance and music, and a taboo against incest (Brown, 1991a).

Cultural universals refer to the presence of very general features of society, rather than particular ways of thinking, acting, or other specific cultural traits. All cultures may provide for childhood socialization, but what and how children are taught varies enormously from culture to culture. An American child learns the multiplication tables from a teacher in a classroom, while a Yanomamö child learns to hunt in the jungle with older members of the tribe. All cultures have standards of beauty and ornamentation, but what is regarded as beautiful in one culture may be seen as ugly in another. Males in a number of Southeast Asian jungle tribes insert small pieces of bone or wood into their penises for ornamentation and the enhancment of sexual pleasure, a practice that would strike horror into the minds of most Americans. (Brown et al., 1988). Yet these same tribal peoples might look upon the idea of starving a woman to achieve the lean contours of a *Vogue* model, or body-building to "bulk up" and produce perfectly cut musculature, as being equally bizarre. Eating pork is forbidden for orthodox Jews and Muslims, while it is a dietary staple in China. All cultures thus have standards of good and bad, beauty and ugliness, right and wrong that vary enormously.

It should also be emphasized that the universal presence of a particular cultural trait does not mean that trait is necessary for a culture to exist. For example, Brown (1991a) claims that in all the cultures that have ever been known to exist, men dominated political life. Although this is a matter of debate today, even if it were true Brown is quick to point out that it would not mean that men *must* be dominant today. Whatever might have existed in the past, human beings are capable of constructing a culture based on principals of gender equality, if they so choose.

MATERIAL CULTURE

Sociologists and anthropologists have distinguished two different although interrelated aspects of human culture: physical objects (material culture) and the ideas associated with those objects (nonmaterial culture). Because of their importance, we shall devote a separate section to each. It is nonetheless important always to bear in mind that they are in a sense opposite sides of the same coin: each forms and is formed by the other.

Material culture includes *all the physical objects made by the members of a particular society to help shape their lives.* It includes the tools and technologies they use to make the goods they consume, the factories where such goods are made, the stores where such goods are sold, and the goods themselves.

Material culture is important in that it shapes our physical options and opportunities: the sorts of clothing we can wear, the kind of food we consume, the types of houses and cities in which we live, the settings in which we learn. Generally speaking, material culture provides the physical space in which we place our bodies, along with the physical resources we draw upon to interact with others (Foucault, 1979). These, in turn, strongly influence our options for behavior.

Try to imagine a world in which the material culture

were radically different, and think of how that might affect who you are and how you think. For example, what we call "learning" is powerfully shaped by the material culture in which it occurs. You probably spend much of your time learning by sitting quietly in a classroom or lecture hall, and taking notes from an instructor who lectures to you for extended periods of time. This physical learning format is such a commonplace of our material culture that we do not think of it as unusual; in fact, beginning with elementary school, most of us experience "education" in only this fashion. This form of education, however, is a relatively recent cultural innovation. The word "education" itself comes from the Latin term *educare,* which referred to the proper rearing of children and animals, and did not refer to formal schooling until the last two or three centuries.

Until recent times, very few people in most human cultures acquired knowledge through a formal classroom and a professor or other specialist providing them with vast amounts of information to absorb. The learning experiences of those few remaining Yanomamö who remain isolated from outside contact, for example, are probably much more typical of the ways in which people have learned throughout human history. Traditional Yanomamö youth learn partly by sitting in a circle with family members, listening to elders describe their experiences and dreams, and partly by direct, nonverbal experience in the field while hunting, fishing, and making their tools and weapons (Chagnon, 1992). The notion that knowledge could be acquired in a formal classroom setting, completely divorced from actual experience, would be incomprehensible to such

Yanomamö. On the other hand, the idea that knowledge could be primarily obtained by active engagement with the world, rather than "book learning," is equally alien to our way of thinking.

One of the most important aspects of material culture is **technology,** *the practical application of knowledge, through tools and techniques, to multiply and conserve human energy* (Levy, 1972). For the Yanomamö, traditional knowledge, passed on orally, enables young male warriors to fashion a bow and arrow that greatly extends their individual force: with these tools, they can kill large animals that otherwise would be too strong or fast for a single person to easily hunt. In modern society, the highly complex technology utilized in a Stealth bomber or Trident nuclear submarine provides a vastly greater (and more devastating) multiplication of human energy. Modern technology is based on the practical application of scientific knowledge, rather than on the oral transmission of traditional beliefs. It is constantly being revolutionized in such formal institutions as universities, research institutes, shops and factories, rather than being passed on largely unchanged from generation to generation, as with the Yanomamö.

Today, the material aspects of culture are rapidly becoming globalized. It no longer makes sense to speak of an exclusively "U.S. technology," for example, or a U.S. city, or even a U.S. car. Increasingly, all of these aspects of material culture are becoming global in nature: the "world car," with parts manufactured across the planet in a global assembly line, embodies technology developed in Japan, the United States, and Europe, and clogs the roadways of polluted "world cities"

Material culture bears directly on what is learned and how the learning process takes place. A Navajo woman is shown teaching a young girl how to use ancient methods to weave traditional patterns, in a one-on-one mentorship that reinforces long-standing social relations. Students in an electronic classroom, by way of contrast, use multimedia technology to learn. This approach is grounded not in tradition but rather in new technology and innovative teaching methods that communicate musical knowledge from all over the world. The relationship between teacher and student is more distant and less personal as well.

*Although modern manufac-
turing increasingly depends
on automation to perform
what was once done by hand,
technological advances do
not proceed at the same rate
in all industries. This recycling plant still relies on
hand-sorters to pick out glass
by color and to drop it into
separate bins, a process that
is relatively inefficient and
raises the costs of recycling.*

across the globe (Chapter 20). Classrooms the world over increasingly resemble one another; department stores (and McDonald's restaurants) can be found on nearly every continent; and—in general—U.S. travelers today would feel more at home in Bangkok or Buenos Aires than they would in the Philadelphia of 200 years ago (Levy, 1972). Today the traveler to a "remote" Indian village in Guatemala may well encounter young people wearing a combination of traditional clothing and California surfwear.

NONMATERIAL CULTURE

Nonmaterial culture consists of *all the nonphysical products of human interaction; that is, the ideas shared by people in a particular society.* It includes language, values, beliefs, rules, institutions, and organizations. For example, we have noted that the typical classroom, with its numerous fixed seats facing a professor, is an example of material culture. Such a classroom is the physical form taken by a modern, nonmaterial cultural institution—a formal system of mass education (in contrast to the informal sharing of experience in small groups among the Yanomamö). The institution we call "education" consists of a set of beliefs and ideas concerning how learning should be conducted in a particular society. Such belief systems play a crucial role in defining our mental options and opportunities, what we believe to be possible, good, bad, and even real. If you were a Yanomamö who lacked the idea of "professor" or the concept of the institution of "formal education," you would have no way of making sense of the behavior of modern university students, whom you would probably perceive as sitting in a strange, uncomfort-

able, and immobile manner for long periods of time, making incomprehensible squiggles on an unknown fiber for mysterious reasons, while confronted by an elder speaking a steady, rapid-fire stream of words.

In studying nonmaterial culture, sociologists have developed a number of ideas that have enabled them to better understand how culture works to shape human thinking and behavior. Among the most important are the concepts of values, norms, and language.

Values

Values are *highly general ideas about what is good, right, or just in a particular culture.* Sociologists disagree about the degree of consensus that actually exists over such core values. Functionalists tend to regard a given culture as characterized by widely shared common values, while social conflict theorists emphasize the degree to which values differ from group to group within a culture (Chapter 1). Studies of values common to all Americans have thus been conducted largely by sociologists who fall within the functionalist paradigm.

Talcott Parsons (1964), for example, argued that Americans share the value of **instrumental activism,** the *belief that individuals are responsible for actively achieving their goals through hard work.* This is also termed the American "work ethic": keep your eye on the prize, work hard, and your efforts will be rewarded with success. This value is exemplified by the hard-driving business executive, the professional athlete, and even the professional criminal: all three strive to achieve wealth and success, even though their methods differ considerably, and may sometimes be illegal. Another functionalist, Robert K. Merton (1938), argued that the most important values in our society were success, prestige, wealth, and power, although not everybody had equal access to achieving these goals. Other central U.S. values identified by sociologists (Bellah et al., 1985) include strong beliefs in the following:

■ The value of hard work for its own sake
■ The importance of accomplishments and success, particularly in material terms
■ The virtues of practical problem-solving or "know-how"—the "do-it-yourself" attitude
■ The capacity of science and technology to solve all of our problems
■ Freedom, equality, justice, democracy, and charity toward others
■ Patriotism, combined with a self-righteousness that judges (and often mistrusts) those who are different
■ Individualism—the belief that we are each responsible for our own fate, and that if we fail, we have no one to blame but ourselves
■ A desire for community

How widespread are these values in U.S. culture—and how stable are these values over time? The answer, not surprisingly, depends on the value in question. The National Opinion Research Center (NORC) each year asks a random sample of the U.S. adult population a series of questions. One of these questions asks whether or not respondents agree with the statement, "it is much better for everyone involved if the man is the achiever outside the home and the woman takes care of the home and family" (NORC, 1990). In 1977 two out of every three respondents were in agreement, while by 1989 only two out of five agreed (Figure 3.1). It seems clear that fundamental values regarding gender roles have changed significantly over time. There are many other examples of such changes in values, including growing environmental awareness and declining support for racial segregation among whites (NORC, 1990).

This shows that values do not exist in a vacuum; they are produced, sustained, and contested in the media, schools and colleges, religious groups, economic organizations, governmental bodies, and social movement organizations. The growing support for environmental protection or equality for women and minorities, for example, is the direct result of activism and education on the part of social movements in these areas (Chapter 21).

Let's take the value of individualism as an example. According to Christopher Lasch (1979), U.S. culture has become so individualistic that it is "narcissistic." Lasch claims that people from the United States are increasingly self-absorbed, selfish, and disdainful of the plight of others. To what extent is this true? Every fall

Figure 3.1   Woman as Homemaker

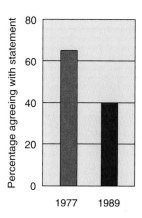

The percentage of Americans agreeing with the statement "It is much better for everyone involved if the man is the achiever outside the home and the woman takes care of the home and family" dropped sharply between 1977 and 1989, showing a change in cultural values.
Source: National Opinion Research Center (1990).

the American Council on Education (ACE) conducts a survey of entering first-year college students. In 1990 the ACE surveyed nearly 200,000 students at 382 two- and four-year institutions, representing the 1.6 million U.S. students beginning college that year. While more than half (62 percent) felt it was "essential" or "very important" to "help others in difficulty," only one in four felt the same way about "influencing the political structure" (21 percent) or "participating in community action" (26 percent). On the other hand, about two out of three felt it was "essential" or "very important" to "become an authority in my own field" (65 percent), while nearly three out of four felt the same way about being "very well off financially" (Figure 3.2). It is interesting to note that the percentage committed to being "very well off financially" is nearly *twice* the percentage found in the 1970 survey (74 percent versus 39 percent) (Astin, Korn, and Berz, 1990, pp. 5, 56).

These data would seem to suggest that there has been a sharp increase in individualism among students entering college since the early 1970s. One possible explanation is that in recent years many academics, business leaders, and government officials have persuasively argued for this belief (see, for example, Murray, 1984). Using the power of the presidency, Ronald Reagan was able to argue that public assistance programs designed to help the poor actually produced "welfare-dependent" individuals and families who preferred collecting welfare checks to hard work at regular jobs. Such well-publicized emphases on individual responsibility and "getting ahead" contributed to the shift in cultural values among entering college students.

Figure 3.2   Importance of Being "Very Well Off"

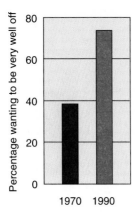

The percentage of entering college students feeling that it is "essential" or "very important" to be "very well off financially" nearly doubled between 1970 and 1990. Do you think this indicates a decline in idealistic thinking, or simply a more realistic concern with job prospects during uncertain economic times?
Source: Astin, Korn, and Berz (1990).

The Contradictions of Culture

Cultures often contain values that conflict with one another. Thus, for example, we have seen that the United States has a strong cultural value for individual accomplishment, yet at the same time values family and community. This can lead to a contradiction, as the former values can produce a sense of individualism and isolation, the very opposite of community (Bellah et al., 1985). The value for individualism can also come into conflict with the value toward showing charity to others who are "less fortunate." This contradiction sometimes leads Americans to blame others who are unsuccessful, holding them personally responsible for their plight; yet it also results in acts of compassion and service, such as volunteer work at a soup kitchen or homeless shelter.

Sometimes contradictions arise from **cultural lag,** a *tendency for different parts of nonmaterial culture to change at different rates in response to technological innovations or other sources of change in material culture* (Ogburn, 1964). Thus, for example, the previously mentioned cultural value of individualism partly reflects an earlier period in American history when many people lived on farms, and the ability to survive depended strongly on individual initiative and enterprise. Today, when most people live in cities and work in bureaucratic environments, such individualism may get in the way of more appropriate values calling for cooperation and conformity. Societies that have long emphasized the latter values—Japanese society being an outstanding example—often seem better able to moti-

vate their members to conform to the work requirements of modern society (Chapter 15).

Sometimes the contradictions between different cultural values simply reflect the fact that people do not always act according to their professed cultural beliefs. Although American culture emphasizes achievement, in many high schools today students who excel scholastically are derided as "nerds" or "geeks," and are treated harshly by their fellow students. **Ideal culture** refers to *the norms and values society professes to hold,* while **real culture** refers to *those that are followed in practice.* American culture claims to place a strong value on equality and justice, yet inequalities and injustices are common. The principal of equality requires that all people be treated equally; yet women are systematically paid less then men for comparable work (chapter 11), while African Americans and other racial and ethnic minorities frequently confront discrimination when they seek to buy or rent a house (Chapter 10). When sociologists study culture, they must take care to distinguish ideal from real culture. It is not sufficient to ask people what beliefs they hold dear; evidence for actual cultural practices must be sought out as well.

Norms

Norms are the *shared rules in a particular culture that tell its members how to behave in a given situation.* They are the specific "oughts" or "shoulds" that derive from more general values. Following a usage established by the sociologist William Graham Sumner in 1906, we can distinguish several different kinds of norms, roughly in order of increasing severity: folkways, mores (pronounced "*mor*-ays"), taboos, and laws (Table 3.1).

Folkways refer to *fairly weak norms (sometimes termed "conventions") that are passed down from the past, whose violation is generally not considered serious within a particular culture.* For example, although American folkways call for students to be reasonably dressed in most universities, it is not uncommon to find male students in cut-off T-shirts (or even going shirtless) on hot spring days. **Mores** are *strongly held norms whose violation would seriously offend the standards of acceptable conduct or righteousness of most people within a particular culture*—such as a university student who removed all clothing before attending class. Some behavior is said to be **taboo** in U.S. culture—that is, it is *forbidden, highly offensive, and even unthinkable;* incest is a common example. **Laws** are *norms that have been legislated by a governing body.* A local ordinance outlawing nudity in public places would be an example. Not all mores are enacted into law. For example, picking one's nose in public would be seen as

Table 3.1   Types of Cultural Standards and Rules

Type of Standard or Rule	Principal Characteristics	Example
Values	Highly general ideas about what is good, right, or just in a particular culture	The belief that all people should have equal opportunity
Norms	Culturally shared rules governing specific behaviors (the "oughts" or "shoulds")	The expectation that people should not engage in discriminatory behavior
Folkways	Fairly weak norms (sometimes termed "conventions"), passed down from the past, whose violation is generally not considered serious within a particular culture	The expectation that people will be equally pleasant to one another regardless of race
Mores	Strongly held norms whose violation would seriously offend the standards of acceptable conduct or righteousness of most people within a particular culture	The expectation that people will not insult one another by using offensive racial slurs
Taboos	Extremely strongly held norms whose violation is forbidden, highly offensive, and even unthinkable	A prohibition against injuring or killing another person because of his or her race
Laws	Norms that have been officially legislated by a governing body	Federal laws that make it a crime to deny someone a job or housing on the basis of race

an offensive violation of mores in American culture, although there is no law prohibiting it.

Norms can vary widely across cultures. Yanomamö from different villages, for example, greet one another with a symbolic act of gift-giving or other reciprocal exchange; the Yanomamö would interpret a casual American "how are you," without an accompanying response, as a normative violation, an insult that could well lead to violence. Norms vary within cultures as well. Among most Americans, for example, there is a norm that calls for direct eye contact for persons engaged in conversation; completely averting one's eyes is usually interpreted as a sign of weakness or rudeness. Yet in Navajo culture, there is a norm that calls for averting one's eyes as a sign of respect; direct eye contact, particularly between strangers, would be seen as violating a norm of politeness and consequently a serious insult. When a Navajo and a tourist encounter one another for the first time, the Navajo's cultural norms call for averting the eyes, while the tourist's cultural norms call for occasional direct eye contact. The result is likely to be a misunderstanding: the Navajo may see the tourist as rude and vulgar, while the tourist may see the Navajo as unforceful and weak. Each is likely to regard the other as behaving disrespectfully, a perception that stems from their cultural differences. Such cultural misunderstandings may grow into outright hostility and lead to unfair generalizations and stereotypes.

Norms, like the values they reflect, also change over time. In 1977, 42 percent of people interviewed reported smoking, including 49 percent of young people aged 18 to 23. Beginning with the U.S. Surgeon General's Report *Smoking and Health* in 1964, which reported definitive medical evidence linking smoking with cancer, heart and lung problems, and other serious health disorders, the U.S. government has waged a highly effective campaign to discourage people from smoking. As a result, by 1989 fewer than 30 percent of the population smoked, including only 32 percent of those aged 18 to 23 (National Opinion Research Center, 1990, pp. 819–820). Among some groups, a strong social norm toward smoking—once associated with independence, sex appeal, and glamour—has been replaced with an equally strong antismoking social norm that depicts smoking as unhealthful, unattractive, and selfish. As a result, smoking in the general U.S. population has declined by nearly one-third, while smoking for ages 18 to 23 has declined by more than one-half, in only a dozen years.

Since some degree of conformity to norms is necessary for any society to exist, one of the key tasks of the members of all cultures is to instill a willingness to conform. Broadly speaking, norms are obeyed for two reasons (Parsons, 1964). First, members of all cultures develop mechanisms for **internalization**—the social process by which norms and values *become thoroughly* *ingrained and are largely unquestioned as ways of thinking and acting "normally."* This is accomplished by a variety of techniques that reward behavior that is normative and punish behavior that is not (Chapter 5). Second, when socialization fails to produce the desired behavior, mechanisms of "social control" come into play to enforce conformity (Chapter 7). These range from such informal punishments as gossip and ostracism, to official forms of discipline such as imprisonment (Foucault, 1979). Emile Durkheim (1964; orig. 1893), one of the founders of sociology, argued a century ago that punishment serves not only to help guarantee conformity among those who would violate a culture's norms and values, but also to vividly remind others that the norms and values exist.

Symbols and Language

Human beings experience the world by means of organs that provide five different kinds of sensations: sight, sound, smell, touch, and taste. Although humans, like animals, may sometimes respond instinctively to sensations, unlike animals they are not compelled to do so. A male moth will attempt to mate with the ground-up remains of a female moth, so long as the odors of the female remain present to stimulate it. Needless to say, human beings do not ordinarily mate under such blind biological pressures. They are at least capable of interpreting the symbolic meanings of their sensory inputs before engaging in mating behavior. Prospective mates usually entertain such cultural notions as physical attractiveness, emotional or intellectual appeal, the appropriateness of the situation, and other norms governing human sexuality. They are likely to think the situation over themselves, as well as converse with others about it. The use of symbols, and particularly language, is one of the most important distinguishing characteristics of human beings.

Symbols

Human behavior is oriented toward symbols of "reality," rather than the reality itself. **Symbols** refer to *anything that represents something to the human mind.* Every culture provides a repertoire of symbols that its members learn to associate with different perceptions and experiences. Such symbols can represent a sensory input (for example, the image of a tree, the sound of a voice) or an abstract idea (the concept of culture, the mathematical symbol "+" or "−", the notion of romantic love). What is important to remember is that a symbol is a *representation*—literally, it "re-presents," or "makes present again," something that is not immediately present to our senses. As a representation, its

meaning is not automatically given, requiring instead an act of interpretation. It is through this act of interpretation that symbols free us from being prisoners of the physical world around us.

For example, you may have seen advertisements for a high-tech dog collar that administers a mild electric shock. This device is triggered by a small radio transmitter that can be set to a given distance; if the dog wanders, say, 100 feet from its home base, it feels a jolt of electric current on its neck. The dog is quickly conditioned to associate a shock with the rock or tree it encounters at 100 feet, and it will stop short to avoid the pain. Eventually, the transmitter can be turned off entirely; the dog has been conditioned to respond automatically and will no longer wander away from home.

Under the same circumstances, humans would seek

Higher primates, such as chimpanzees and gorillas, have exhibited a surprising ability to interpret symbols. During the past 20 years, Dr. Penny Patterson has taught a female gorilla, Koko, to recognize and communicate with some 500 to 700 symbols from the universal sign language for the deaf. Although Koko exhibits a remarkable range of human-like responses, it is important to remember that the symbolic repertoire of human beings is vastly greater than that of other animals.

to explain the meaning of the shock they were experiencing. Some might interpret it as God's punishment, others as the just or unjust exercise of governmental authority, still others as the laws of physics run amuck. Humans would not simply react blindly to the physical experience of being shocked, but rather would respond to the symbolic meaning that they interpret into the experience. Humans need not blindly react to physical reality; instead, they can respond to their symbolic interpretations of that reality.

Symbols may be written or unwritten, verbal or nonverbal. They may consist of words, gestures, images, or anything that conveys a meaning. Although higher primates also use symbols, as far as we know human beings have a far greater ability to use symbols than any other species.

Language

One of the most powerful forms of symbolization and a central feature of all human cultures is **language,** *a system of symbolic verbal and sometimes written representations learned within a particular culture.* It is an important constituent of what Berger and Luckmann (1963) termed "the social construction of reality." Language enables us to actively confer meaning on the world, and to derive meaning from it as well. Instead of blindly reacting to a stimulus, we interpret the meaning of an object or a situation, enabling us to choose alternative courses of action depending on our interpretations. The meanings of words are thus interpreted as they are used.

In the 1930s the anthropological linguist Edward Sapir and his student Benjamin Lee Whorf advanced the hypothesis that the words and language we use actually influence our perceptions. The accuracy of the Sapir-Whorf hypothesis—sometimes termed the **linguistic relativity hypothesis,** since it argues that *perceptions are relative to language*—has been sharply debated in anthropology (Malotki, 1983; Haugen, 1977; Witkowski and Brown, 1982). In its more

Map 3.1   **World Languages**

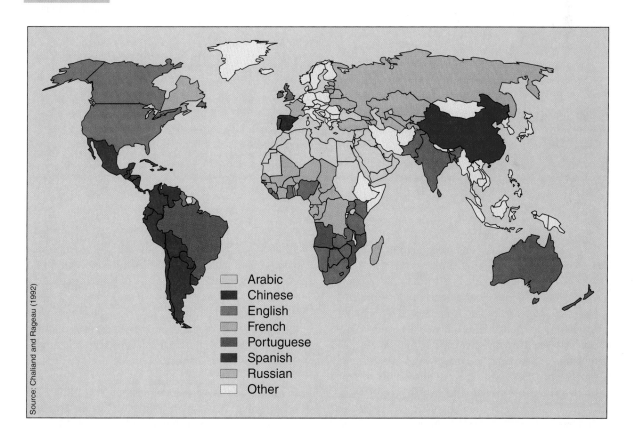

Source: Chaliand and Rageau (1992)

Arabic
Chinese
English
French
Portuguese
Spanish
Russian
Other

While thousands of languages are spoken around the world today, a relatively small number are predominant. These languages, an example of the globalization of culture, were spread largely through conquest, colonization, and the worldwide spread of science, technology, and industry.

Critical Thinking

Does "Newspeak" Influence How We Perceive Reality?

The writer George Orwell argued fifty years ago that governments carefully choose words to influence public opinion. In his famous novel *1984* he created a language, "Newspeak," which lacked any word or concept that might lead to criticism of the all-powerful state. Herbert Marcuse (1964) echoed this claim when he argued that modern governments develop a bureaucratic form of language that effectively silences criticism of public policies by muting the horrors of war.

Can well-chosen words be used by governments to influence how people perceive governmental policies? During the 1991 Persian Gulf War against Iraq, U.S. military strategists described the effects of missiles and bombs that accidentally struck civilian areas as "collateral damage" rather than as "civilian casualties." In one survey of 1,857 adults conducted by the Times-Mirror polling service (Rosenstiel, 1991), half of the respondents were asked if they were concerned about the amount of "collateral damage" resulting from allied bombing in Iraq, while the other half were asked if they were concerned about "the number of civilian casualties and other unintended damage." Barely

one in five of those interviewed (21 percent) reported being "very concerned" about "collateral damage," while nearly half (49 percent) reported the same level of concern for "civilian casualties." In what ways might such a careful choice of language have influenced public support for the war effort?

Consider the following examples from military terminology and how they might influence your opinion about the nature of warfare (Klare, 1991):

- *Peacekeeper* (the MX nuclear missile)
- *Friendly fire* (the accidental shooting or bombing of U.S. soldiers by their own comrades)
- *Daisy cutter* (a 15,000-pound fuel-air bomb that ignites a vapor cloud, creating an enormous fireball that incinerates everything within hundreds of yards)
- *Smart weapons* (computer-guided missiles and bombs)

What does this suggest about the relationship between the language we speak and the perceptions we hold about reality? How is your own thinking affected by the choice of words?

---

widely accepted form, the linguistic relativity hypothesis does not hold that language determines perception, only that one is most likely to attend to differences for which one has a word or a concept (see Box 3.1).

For example, an Indian from San Ildefonso Ixtahuacán in the highlands of Guatemala, whose language may possess well over a hundred words discriminating between diverse kinds of corn (Appelbaum, 1966), will perceive differences in corn that would likely escape the average U.S. grocery shopper, whose culture lacks such linguistic variety for this particular food product. On the other hand, the same Guatemalan Indian, on seeing a compact disc and a small silver frisbee for the first time, may well think they are the same thing, since both terms (and the underlying concepts) are absent from his or her language.

Language provides one of the most important sources of permanence for a culture. It outlives any particular member, affording a sense of history or cultural continuity, a feeling of "who we are." One of the central paradoxes of our time is that even as languages such as English and Japanese are becoming increasingly global in their usage, local attachments to language seem to be stronger than ever. For example, the French-speaking residents of Quebec, one of Canada's provinces, are so passionate about their linguistic heritage that they often refuse to speak English, which is the dominant language of Canada. In fact, there is a strong movement in Quebec seeking independence from the rest of Canada in part because of that province's linguistic and cultural distinctness.

In the United States there is a strong "English-only" movement to make English the official national language, outlawing the use of any other language in public education, on voting ballots, or in governmental publications. As of 1993, 19 states had passed legislation requiring all official federal and state publications to be in the English language. The English-only movement is partly a reaction to the rapid growth of Spanish and other languages spoken by recent immigrants to the United States, which some English-speaking cit-

Box 3.2

Silenced Voices

What Is "Real" English?

Through the globalizing influence of England and the United States, English has spread throughout the world. It is the official language of business and government in some Asian and African countries that were once colonies in the British empire, and it is widely spoken as a second language throughout the world. An estimated 334 million people regard English as their native tongue. As you can imagine, many different forms of the English language are spoken, ranging from vastly different sentence construction and vocabularies to mild variations in regional dialects and pronunciation. Young people in particular use their own special phrasing, grammar, and vocabularies, often to the dismay of their parents and teachers.

Sociologists who study language have long debated the social origins and linguistic aspects of "Black English vernacular," a variant of English spoken by Whites and Latinos as well as Blacks but rooted primarily among young urban African Americans. Although there is some debate over whether this form of English emerged out of slavery or much more recent efforts by African Americans to establish their own cultural identity, linguists agree that it is a fully functioning language system and deserves to be understood as such (Baugh, 1992; Smitherman, 1992; Speicher and McMahon, 1992; DeBose, 1992; Bailey and Bernstein 1990; Butters, 1989; LaBov, 1972, 1985). Yet the use of distinctive ways of speaking, such as Black English vernacular, may result in not being "heard" by the larger society; it is one way that subcultural voices can be silenced.

June Jordan, an African-American poet and teacher, captures this dilemma. Jordan (1990) was teaching a college class in which African-American female writers were being discussed. She noted that Alice Walker's *The Color Purple*, which was written in Black English vernacular, initially produced confusion among her African-American students. They initially objected to Walker's prose on the grounds that it sounded "funny" and didn't "look right," even though it is similar to the form of English they spoke among themselves. Through extended classroom discussions, Jordan and her students came to understand how "standard English" differed from Black English vernacular. They also came to realize that the larger culture stigmatized Black English vernacular, even though it was equally rich in expressiveness and complexity. Although there is extensive technical literature on the rules for Black English vernacular, Jordan's students decided to formulate some of their own, among them the following:

- Use the minimal number of words for every idea, to give the language greater poetic force.
- Strive for clarity.
- Avoid using tenses of the verb "to be," seeking more descriptive and precise verbs.
- Use "be" or "been" only to describe an ongoing state of affairs (for example, "she *be* at the office," meaning "she is always at the office").
- To say something really positive, use the negative (for example, "he bad" instead of "he's fabulous!").
- Be creative in inventing words (for example, "astropotomous" for an "astronomically huge hippopotamus").

Just like the linguists who had studied Black English vernacular, Jordan's students concluded that their own idiomatic way of speaking was as expressive and rich as more mainstream forms of English.

izens experience as threatening. In the Soviet Union, where Russian has been the official language for nearly seventy-five years, there are increasing demands to do business in the original languages of the newly independent Soviet Republics, now that the central government has lost its authority.

Passions often run high over languages and their associated cultures. It seems likely that controversies over language will increase in the coming years, as the creation of an increasingly globalized culture, combined with large-scale global migrations of poor people in search of economic opportunity, are experienced as threatening to local cultures and linguistic communities. Fierce loyalty to linguistic heritage can remain a strong feature of local cultures (see Box 3.2). Nonetheless, it is important to remember that no language today is "pure." The English language, for example, contains countless words that are of Latin, French, Germanic, and other linguistic origins.

Languages are constantly changing through use. The 1992 edition of the 200,000 word *American Heritage Dictionary,* for example, contains some 16,000 words added since the last edition was published ten years ago; they range from *junk bond, infotainment, couch potato,* and *Eurocentric* to *date rape, AIDS, chemical dependency,* and *serial killer* (Soukhanov, 1992). What do such words tell us about the rapid pace of social and technological change in recent years?

CULTURAL DIVERSITY

When speaking of the values and norms of a culture, it is important always to ask certain questions: Whose norms are being discussed? What is the relevant culture to which the norms refer? Does it make sense to think in terms of a common culture? Sociologists sometimes falsely assume the answer is "yes" and go on to speak of "middle class culture" as the common culture of all middle income U.S. citizens. Or they speak of "American culture," referring to all people living in the United States, or "Western culture," referring to all people living in North America and Europe. Such an assumption hides important changes that are occurring in the world today, changes that are giving rise to strong cultural identities among groups of people, some of which are much smaller than nations, and some of which are much larger. In the world of today care must be taken to appreciate the importance of **cultural diversity**—*the richness and variety of human cultural differences between and within countries.*

Subcultures

One way sociologists deal with cultural differences within a given nation is through the notion of **subcul-**

ture, *a smaller culture that exists within a larger, dominant culture yet differs from it in some important way.* For example, youth subcultures centering around such musical preferences as rap, heavy metal, or hip-hop may sport somewhat distinctive styles of dress, language, and behavior, while accepting other aspects of the dominant culture. Even professional thieves, who make their living engaging in such illegal activities as robbing banks, burglarizing grocery stores, or passing bad checks, share most of the values of U.S. society: they often marry and have children; they want to "make it" by accumulating wealth, power and prestige; they hope to avoid trouble as much as possible. They eat with knives and forks, drive on the right side of the road, and avoid violence whenever possible. Indeed, the subculture of thieves is comprised of people who subscribe to and believe in *almost* all of the values and norms of U.S. society.

An especially important basis of subculture in the U.S. today is found in racial or ethnic heritage (Chapter 10). These are the "hyphenated" groups of Americans whose subcultures can be partly traced to other countries. Examples include African-Americans, Mexican-Americans, Italian-Americans, Irish-Americans, and Asian-Americans. The degree to which these groups constitute subcultures varies from group to group and individual to individual. Although some members of any hyphenated group may have adopted all aspects of mainstream U.S. culture, others maintain some of the norms, values, and languages characteristic of their culture of origin. For example, many Italian-Americans in Boston's North End continue to speak Italian, celebrating street festivals and saints' days much as they (or their parents or grandparents) did in various regions of Italy. The same is true of virtually all ethnic groups, a fact that accounts for the richness of subcultural diversity in the United States.

In a sense, of course, all "Americans," with the exception of American Indians, are immigrants who could be said to be part of "hyphenated" subcultures. This has led to some confusion over the proper way to refer to those native cultures that long predated the European arrival. Many American Indians are today reasserting their distinctive cultural identities, in an effort to resist being absorbed into the American mainstream. In fact, some Indian political organizations resist the hyphenation "Native-American" on the grounds that their cultures were here long before Europeans renamed the continent "America" (after the Italian geographer, Amerigo Vespucci). In this textbook we will therefore follow the convention of the American Indian Movement, and generally use the term "Indian" rather than "Native American," even though we recognize that this is also an inaccurate label of European origin.

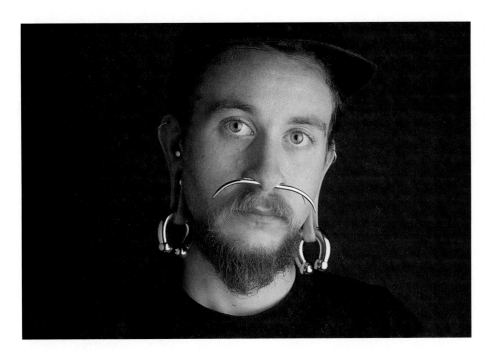

Subcultures abound in modern societies. Some groups stress the beauty of tattoos, others muscles, and yet others bright hair colorings. This man and probably his friends (but not necessarily his parents) place a high value on decorative objects that can be attached to the body. Men piercing their ears or other parts of their body is a relatively recent innovation in Western cultures, but it has been practiced for centuries elsewhere in the world.

Countercultures

A **counterculture** is a *culture that arises in opposition to the prevailing culture.* The hippies of the 1960s were highly countercultural, self-consciously claiming to "drop out" of a larger culture they regarded as overly money-hungry, technologically obsessed, and spiritually corrupt (Roszak, 1969). More current examples would include "dead heads" who continue to follow the music of the ageless hippies in the 1960s rock band the Grateful Dead, or skinhead advocates of white supremacy in the United States and Germany who provoke attacks on nonwhites and immigrants (Hamm, 1993).

The members of countercultures often tend to be youthful (Spates, 1976; Roszak, 1969), perhaps because young people have the motivation and time to experiment with alternative norms and values before accepting the responsibilities of adulthood. Although the 1960s saw thousands of young people flock to rural communes or urban countercultural enclaves such as San Francisco's Haight-Ashbury, the movement was short-lived, and most of the 1960s hippies have by now moved comfortably into middle-aged lives with middle-aged responsibilities. Yet there is evidence that many of the youthful rebels retain to this day some of the counter-cultural values they espoused a quarter century ago (Whalen and Flacks, 1989).

The distinction between a "counterculture" and a "subculture" is often difficult to sustain when applied to particular groups. Thus sociologists will speak of the 1960s counterculture but the subculture of delinquent gangs. The difference between the two is that the counterculture developed in self-conscious opposition to the prevailing culture, which it hoped to influence through its oppositional lifestyle. The delinquent gang, by way of contrast, is not trying to change the world into a world of delinquent gangs; they are rather defying the dominant culture with their behavior, dress, attitudes, and activities, while accepting such dominant cultural values as power and material success.

Sometimes subcultures will become countercultures. For example, during the 1970s gay and lesbian subcultures emerged in American cities such as New York and San Francisco. These subcultures soon became political, and today they are countercultural movements actively seeking to change the way the dominant culture thinks about and treats homosexuals. ACT-UP (AIDS Coalition to Unleash Power), GLAAD (Gay and Lesbian Alliance Against Defamation), and other homosexual organizations have had a major impact, from increased funding for AIDS research and prevention to the passage of laws prohibiting discrimination against homosexuals (International Gay and Lesbian Association, 1992; Plummer, 1981; Altman, 1982).

Assimilation or Multiculturalism?

U.S. schoolchildren are frequently taught that the United States is a vast melting pot, into which various ethnic groups are assimilated. **Assimilation** is *the process by which different cultures are absorbed into a single mainstream culture.* While it is certainly true that virtually all peoples living in the United States take on many common cultural characteristics, many groups strive to retain some subcultural identity as well. In fact, there is some indication that identification based on race or country of origin remains strong and may even be increasing, particularly among African Americans and immigrants from Asia, Mexico, and Latin America (Totti, 1987).

Given our country's enormous cultural diversity, a more appropriate metaphor than the assimilationist "melting pot" might be the culturally diverse "salad bowl," in which all of the various ingredients retain some of their original flavor and integrity, contributing to the richness of the salad as a whole. This viewpoint, termed **multiculturalism,** calls for *respecting cultural differences, rather than seeking to assimilate all subcultures into a larger, supposedly "better" culture.* Multiculturalism acknowledges that there are certain central cultural values shared by most people in a society, but it also acknowledges that there are important differences that deserve to be preserved (Anzaldua, 1990a, 1990b). Because of demands from African-American, Asian-American, Mexican-American and other ethnic groups, many colleges have begun to revise their general education programs to require exposure to the cultures of different ethnic groups and societies. The traditional views of the past are also being challenged by the growing recognition that "Western civilization," the mainstay of the core general education requirements of many colleges, is not the only culture in the world, however important its contributions may be.

Ethnic studies or "diversity" requirements reflect a growing awareness of the importance of different cultural traditions for American life. Apart from promoting a greater understanding of the contribution of different subcultures to American culture as a whole, such requirements serve another purpose: they help prepare American students to participate in a world where the United States is no longer the overwhelmingly predominant economic power. Understanding and appreciating cultural diversity will become increasingly important as globalization continues into the twenty-first century.

Ethnocentrism

In Chapter 1 we defined **ethnocentrism** as the *tendency to judge other cultures by the standards of one's own culture*—literally, making one's own people or group the center of things. We already have commented that cultural norms and values typically are internalized to the point where they seem to be a part of the natural order. For a member of a culture, "norms" are simply "normal." Because we are "inside" our culture, we are not aware of it being a "culture"; we simply assume that the ways we think and act are as natural as nature itself. It is in this sense that we say that thinking and acting appropriately become "second nature" to us. The ability of our language to help shape our perceptions reinforces this tendency to regard our culture as a part of the natural order of things.

Try to imagine what it would be like if you wore glasses with red lenses from the moment of your birth. You would be unaware that everything had an artificially reddish tint, having never experienced any other kind of world. Your red-tinted world would seem normal to you—just as your social world, viewed through the lens of your culture, seems normal to you.

In many cultures one's own culture is regarded as the standard by which all else should be judged. If you have ever traveled in a foreign culture you have probably experienced this ethnocentric tendency: after a particularly frustrating experience, you probably longed for home, where things were "normal" and life was "better." Such judgments are common, whether you are a U.S. citizen in Mexico, a Mexican citizen in Japan, or a Japanese citizen in the United States. Some societies even name themselves ethnocentrically. The Navajo, for example, call themselves *Dineh,* which means "the people," implying that others are not "the people" (Downs, 1972). The Yanomamö refer to people from outside the jungle as *nabo,* which in their language means "subhuman."

Although it often is difficult to avoid such judgments in daily life, when we are acting as sociologists we must resist this tendency. No culture occupies center stage for long, including the sociologist's own. Instead, sociologists argue for the stance of **cultural relativism**—*the attitude that the practices of another society should be understood sociologically in terms of that society's own norms and values, and not one's own.* Sociologists thus argue that there are no inherently "right" or "wrong" values, norms, folkways, mores, or laws. If, as sociologists, we regard our own culture as somehow better than others, our ability to understand other cultures will be impaired. This is not to say that as individuals we shouldn't have strongly held values and beliefs; only that we must suspend them as best we can when we are acting as sociologists.

As globalization has increased during the past quarter century, contact between peoples of different cultures has increased apace. When people move from one part of the globe to another, they take their cultures with them. This frequently can lead to conflict when the norms and values of the old culture clash with those of the new (see Box 3.3). Global businesses often require people of different cultures to work closely together, calling for a great deal of cultural sensitivity. Often, a culturally relativist stance is difficult to achieve if one understands neither the language nor the customs of the people one is dealing with. When the Sunbeam Corporation first began marketing a curling iron called "The Mist Stick" in Germany, it almost committed a costly

Box 3.3

Globalization

How Far Can We Push Cultural Relativism?

It is often extremely difficult to embrace cultural relativism fully. An example that has received recent attention involves young girls from certain African, Asian, and Middle Eastern ethnicities or tribal cultures who routinely undergo clitoridectomies or "female circumcision." This is a painful cultural ritual in which the clitoris and sometimes all or part of the vaginal labia are removed with a knife or sharpened stone, and the two sides of the vulva are partly sewn together as a means of controlling sexual activity.

In cultures where clitoridectomies have been practiced for countless generations, they are regarded as perfectly normal. For example, one study of more than two thousand men and women in two Nigerian communities found that nine out of ten women interviewed had been circumcised in their childhood, and that the large majority favored circumcision for their own daughters, primarily for cultural reasons. Yet at the same time, a significant minority believed the practice should be eradicated (Ebomoyi, 1987). Clitoridectomies are today regarded with abhorrence by most Europeans, Americans, and a growing number of women in the cultures where they are practiced (el Dareer, 1982; Johnson-Odim, 1991; Lightfoot-Klein, 1991).

In France, which has a large North African immigrant population, many African mothers follow their traditional customs and have clitoridectomies performed on their daughters. Some of those who are caught have been tried and convicted under French law for mutilating their daughters. These African mothers have argued that they were only engaging in the same cultural practice that their own mothers performed on them, that their grandmothers performed on their mothers. They felt that the French were being highly ethnocentric in judging their behavior by French customs. In this instance, globalization has led to a fundamental clash of cultural norms and values that have forced members of both cultures to confront some of their most deeply held beliefs. Feminists from Africa and the Middle East, while themselves strongly opposing clitoridectomies, have been critical of Europeans and Americans who sensationalize the practice as backward or primitive, without any understanding of the cultural and economic circumstances that sustain it (Accad, 1991; Johnson-Odim, 1991; Mohanty, 1991).

Suppose you are a sociologist studying a culture in which clitoridectomies are a normal practice. How will you conduct yourself and your research? Will you attempt to fully accept the practice, suspending your judgment while conducting research, or will you try to change people's beliefs about it?

---

linguistic blunder; in German, the word *mist* means manure. Americans like to tell jokes when they give public speeches, but jokes are especially difficult to translate from one culture to another. A U.S. Army general who ended a speech in Japan with the slang punch line, "show me, I'm from Missouri," created a real problem for his interpreter, who had absolutely no idea what he meant. In Japanese culture, the interpreter's inability to translate for the general would have been embarassing and shameful. Fortunately, the interpeter "saved face" by telling his audience in Japanese that "the general has made a joke and I'll be in trouble if you don't laugh." The audience burst out laughing, and the general assumed his joke was well-received (Wederspahn, 1993).

When people feel that their central beliefs and values are under assault, they often become ethnocentric in their response. Because of the rapid pace of change in the world today, there appears to be a rise in ethnocentrism in many countries. This is seen in the resurgence of a type of ethnocentrism termed **nationalism**—the *belief that the people of a particular nation have historical or God-given rights that supercede those of any other people.* Nationalism is not new. The relentless nineteenth-century western expansion of the United States was justified by a nationalist belief in the country's "manifest destiny" to conquer all the Indian tribes that lived between the Atlantic and Pacific Oceans. But today there appears to be an explosion of nationalist sentiment throughout the world. A horrifying current example is found in Serbian efforts to create a Greater Serbia out of what was once Yugoslavia, by "cleansing" entire villages of all other ethnic groups.

GLOBALIZATION: WILL A SINGLE GLOBAL CULTURE EMERGE?

We can now return to the question with which we began this chapter: do the powerful forces of globalization at work today mean that someday soon the enormous richness and variation in human cultures will be replaced by a single, homogeneous world culture (Featherstone, 1990)? There are both globalizing and localizing forces at work today in reshaping our understanding of the modern meaning of culture, producing similarities at the same time that they are reinforcing cultural differences.

Universal Culture

We noted earlier that most sociologists do not believe human beings have a common human nature that in turn leads to a common human culture. Nonetheless, such a common culture may emerge through social (rather than biological) processes. One of the key ways in which cultures come to resemble one another is through **cultural diffusion,** *the spread of one culture's characteristics to another.* Cultural diffusion has existed throughout human history, as cultures have influenced one another through conquest, trade, and even the casual contact of travelers. What is unique today is the accelerated rate at which diffusion occurs, and the fact that virtually no place on earth can long remain impervious to this process.

It increasingly is impossible for cultures to exist in isolation from one another, relying exclusively on their own cultural beliefs and practices for survival. There are few if any places on earth so remote as to escape radio, television, air travel, or the computer. A generation ago there were still Yanomamö tribes in Brazil and Venezuela whose way of life was completely untouched by the rest of the world. Today, many Yanomamö use machetes and other tools made in the United States or Japan; they wear T-shirts and shorts manufactured in garment factories in the Dominican Republic or Guatemala; they take medicine produced in Germany or Switzerland to combat diseases caught from the farmers and gold miners from Rio de Janeiro or Caracas who have pushed them off their land; and they tell their story to people around the world on network television. It seems likely that within another generation or two, all Yanomamö and other once-isolated tribes will be touched and transformed by global culture, despite persistent efforts to preserve their age-old ways of life.

Rock music, a form of popular culture the world over, provides a useful example of globalizing forces helping to create a universal culture today. "Rock and roll" originated in the United States in the 1950s, largely as a fusion of rural country-and-western white music and urban black blues. Country and western, in turn, had several international origins, including English, Irish, and Scottish folk music; blues came from the black gospel tradition, which itself combined U.S. southern Christian gospel songs with African rhythms and traditions. Since the 1950s, rock music has become globalized not only in its popularity but also in its sources, which today are as diverse as British rock, African sounds and rhythms, Caribbean reggae, and U.S. urban rap. Popular music is truly global. The "lambada," a recent Brazilian dance craze performed at the 1993 Academy Awards ceremony, is in fact a Bolivian song performed by musicians who are primarily from the African country of Senegal, whose music is produced by two Frenchmen. Rock music has become a multibillion-dollar industry worldwide, one that involves not only musicians but also musical instrument manufacturers, the electronics industry, advertising agencies, video makers, the recording industry, retailers, radio and television networks such as MTV, VH-1, and BET, and a host of other business people who—regardless of their nationality—share the common cultural value of making and selling music and video at a profit.

Other examples of forces producing an increasingly universal culture will be discussed throughout this book. These include the following:

- Television and radio, which daily bring U.S. culture (such as *Dallas* reruns) into homes throughout the world, while introducing people from the United States to the fortunes and misfortunes of people living half a globe away (Chapter 19).
- The film and video industries, which have turned Madonna (a U.S.-born Italian-American) and Arnold Schwarzenegger (an Austrian-born naturalized U.S. citizen) into globally recognized U.S. pop culture figures (Chapter 19).
- Electronic communications (telephone, FAX, electronic mail), which make instantaneous communication with any part of the planet not only possible but an integral part of daily life in the business world (Chapter 15).
- The emergence of a unified global economy, with businesses whose factories, management structures, and markets often span several continents and dozens of countries (Chapters 6, 9, and 15).

A Latin music festival in New York City's Central Park draws on cultural traditions from Africa, the Caribbean, and Latin America. Popular music provides many examples of cultural diffusion, illustrating the globalization of popular culture today.

■ "Global citizens" such as managers of large corporations, who may spend as much time in the air crisscrossing the globe as they do at home, identifying with a global, cosmopolitan culture rather that of their own nations (Chapter 15).

■ An international political, legal, and military framework, including United Nations agencies, regional trade and mutual defense associations, multinational banks and other global financial institutions, international labor and health organizations, and global tariff and trade agreements (Chapters 6, 13, and 15).

The Resurgence of Local Cultures

There is a seeming paradox about cultures in the modern world. At the same time that some aspects of culture are being globalized, local cultures remain strong and in many instances are being asserted with increasing vigor. Although people may move across the globe, they frequently continue to identify with their cultures of origin.

A striking current example can be drawn from the revolutionary changes in the former Soviet Union and Eastern Europe during the last ten years. Beginning in 1985, the Soviet Union began withdrawing its political and economic control over its Eastern European satellite countries, as well as over the republics that comprised the Soviet Union itself. As the central government loosened its grip, ethnic and cultural identities that had existed for years began to reassert themselves. People throughout the Soviet Union began insisting on their

cultural and ethnic differences, demanding their right to determine for themselves their institutions, folkways, mores, and norms. This happened not only in areas that the Soviet Union had acquired after World War II (such as the Baltic republics of Lithuania, Latvia, and Estonia), but in republics that had been a part of the Soviet Union for three-quarters of a century.

In 1991, when the Soviet Union finally disintegrated as a single nation, it became evident that even after so many years of tightly centralized state control over the economy, education, and virtually all sources of information, ancient cultural and ethnic ties remained strong. In many cases, in fact, such ethnic identifications had long been promoted by Soviet policies, which often favored one ethnic group over another in making appointments to top political and economic posts. At the first opportunity, people reasserted their heritages and demanded their right to separate themselves culturally, politically and economically from the central government. Today, many people of what is now called the Commonwealth of Independent States (CIS) still identify more strongly with their original nationalities than with their former country. People see themselves first and foremost as Russians, Kazakhs, Armenians, Georgians, Azerbaijanis, or any other of approximately one hundred nationalities and ethnic groups, many speaking their own language, rather than as citizens of a single country (Nahaylo and Swoboda, 1989, p. 360; Mandel, 1985).

A number of these groups are engaged in bloody wars with one another, as nationalist sentiments have

Despite (and sometimes because of) globalization, local cultures remain strong and in many cases resurgent. In the former Yugoslavia, local ethnic cultures—which had coexisted peacefully for many years—are today fighting one another for political and military supremacy. A woman weeps for one of the thousands of casualties of ethnic conflict in her war-torn country.

resurged. This is also true throughout Eastern Europe, where the collapse of former satellite countries of the Soviet Union has resulted in the surfacing of ancient ethnic identifications. Czechoslovakia has peacefully disintegrated into two ethnically based countries, while Yugoslavia has fractured into warring ethnic factions. The map of Eastern Europe is beginning to look much as it did a century ago: numerous tiny states based on ethnic differences, each ethnocentrically fearful of its neighbors.

While sociologists do not fully understand these processes, it is reasonable to hypothesize that they are in large part a result of globalization. As large corporations become increasingly important in a global economy, nations have become weaker (Chapters 13). This in turn has paved the way for the growth of old ethnic identifications and loyalties, as people search for bases on which to build a sense of community. When people cannot afford food or other essentials, they are especially likely to blame others for their problems. Economic decline in the former Soviet Union and Eastern Europe have contributed to the rise of nationalist sentiments and ethnic division. These processes will challenge sociological understanding for years to come.

C H A P T E R   S U M M A R Y

1. Human cultures have evolved over thousands of years, reflecting both the conditions where they emerged and the ability of human beings to use their minds to innovate novel and imaginative forms of social organization.

2. Most sociologists reject the notion that specific behaviors are biologically determined, arguing instead that biology and **social learning** interact in complex ways to produce an enormous variety of human cultures that cannot be reduced to biology alone.

3. Although there seem to be some **cultural universals** common to all societies, these consist of highly general characteristics rather than specific cultural traits or practices.

4. **Material culture** consists of all of the physical objects made by members of a society to shape their lives, such as tools and technologies, factories, consumer goods, offices, schools, places of worship, and cities and towns.

5. Tools and **technologies** are among the most important underlying aspects of material culture. While these once distinguished societies from one another, today they are becoming increasingly **globalized:** the same tools and technologies are now common to a growing number of societies around the world.

6. **Nonmaterial culture** consists of the ideas that lie behind material culture, including **language, values,** and **norms.** Although sociologists have iden-

tified a number of values common to all members of U.S. society, it is clear that not everyone holds all of these values, and that values change over time.

7. Culture shapes our thoughts and perceptions, and thus influences our behavior in powerful ways that we are often unaware of.

8. We live in a world of **symbols,** and one of our most important forms of symbolization is language. It helps to shape our very perceptions, while freeing us from responding **instinctively** to the world around us. Language is also an important source of

cultural continuity, and members of a culture are often passionate about their linguistic heritage.

9. **Ethnocentrism** runs counter to the sociological imagination; sociologists prefer **cultural relativism,** the attempt to understand a society relative to its own cultural norms and values.

10. Paradoxically, even as key aspects of culture are becoming globalized, local cultural identifications remain strong and even appear to be increasing in many places.

QUESTIONS FOR DISCUSSION

1. Discuss the difference between material and non-material culture. What are some examples of each? In what ways do each affect the ways in which we live our daily lives?

2. There is considerable debate over whether there are cultural universals common to all cultures. In what sense can such cultural universals be said to exist? What are some examples of cultural universals?

3. Is there a common American culture? Discuss, in terms of (a) common values, (b) subcultures, and (c) countercultures. Give concrete examples of each.

4. There are forces at work today that are simultaneously "globalizing" and "localizing" culture. Discuss, giving concrete examples that are familiar to you.

KEY TERMS

assimilation: The process by which different cultures are absorbed into a single mainstream culture.

counterculture: A culture that arises in opposition to the prevailing culture.

cultural diffusion: The spread of one culture's characteristics to another.

cultural diversity: The richness and variety of human cultural differences between and within countries.

cultural lag: A tendency for different parts of non-material culture to change at different rates in response to technological innovations or other sources of change in material culture.

cultural relativism: The attitude that the practices of another society should be understood sociologically in terms of that society's own norms and values, not one's own.

cultural universal: A feature common to all cultures.

culture: All of the beliefs, behaviors, and products common to members of a particular group.

ethnocentrism: The tendency to judge other cultures by the standards of one's own culture.

folkways: Fairly weak norms (sometimes termed "conventions") passed down from the past, whose violation is generally not considered serious within a particular culture.

high culture: The fine arts, classical music, live theater, and other activities that usually require special preparation to fully appreciate.

ideal culture: The norms and values a society professes to hold.

instincts: Biologically fixed patterns of action.

institution: A cluster of relatively stable rules that govern social activities in a society; such rules also provide a shared understanding of the cultural meaning of those activities.

instrumental activism: The belief that individuals are responsible for actively achieving their goals through hard work.

internalization: The social processes by which norms and values become so thoroughly ingrained that they serve as largely unquestioned natural ("normal") ways of thinking and acting.

language: A system of symbolic verbal and sometimes written representations learned within a particular culture.

laws: Norms that have been officially legislated by a governing body.

linguistic relativity hypothesis: A hypothesis, based on the theories of Sapir and Whorf, that perceptions are relative to language.

material culture: All the physical objects made by the members of a particular society to help shape their lives.

mores: Strongly held norms whose violation would seriously offend the standards of acceptable conduct or righteousness of most people within a particular culture.

multiculturalism: Respecting cultural differences, rather than seeking to assimilate all subcultures into a larger, supposedly "better" culture.

nationalism: The belief that the people of a particular nation have historical or God-given rights that supercede those of any other people.

nonmaterial culture: All the nonphysical products of human interaction; that is, the ideas shared by people in a particular society.

norms: The shared rules in a particular culture that tell its members how to behave in a given situation.

popular culture: Forms of culture that are pursued by large numbers of middle- and working-class people; in-clude spectator sports, television "soaps" and "sit-coms," amateur softball leagues, movies, and rock music.

real culture: The norms and values that a society follows in practice.

reflexes: An automatic response to a particular stimulus.

social learning theory: A theory that assumes that because human beings are social in nature, specific behaviors are always learned within a particular cultural context.

society: The interacting people who share a common culture.

sociobiology: A branch of science that studies the behavior of insects and other social animals to draw conclusions about human beings; it concludes that there are genetic bases for competition, cooperation, aggression, envy, and other common human behaviors.

subculture: A smaller culture that exists within a larger, dominant culture yet differs from it in some important way.

symbols: Anything that represents something to the human mind.

taboo: A strongly held norm whose violation is forbidden, highly offensive, and even unthinkable.

technology: The practical application of knowledge, through tools and techniques, to multiply and conserve human energy.

values: Highly general ideas about what is good, right, or just in a particular culture.

R E C O M M E N D E D   F O R   F U R T H E R   R E A D I N G

Anzaldua, Gloria. (1990). *Making Face, Making Soul: Haciendo Caras.* San Francisco: Aunt Lute Foundation.

    A collection of theoretical and creative essays by women of color that explores their experiences in American culture.

Baldwin, John, and Janice Baldwin. (1981). *Beyond Sociobiology.* New York: Elsevier.

    A well researched and thoughtful exploration and critique of sociobiology from the social learning perspective.

Brown, Donald E. (1991). *Human Universals.* New York: McGraw-Hill.

    An extensive survey of the anthropological literature examining the evidence for human universals and its implications for anthropology.

Chagnon, Napoleon. (1992). *Yanamamo: The Fierce People.* New York: Holt, Rinehart, & Winston.

    A recently updated examination of the shifting fortunes of one of the world's last isolated cultures, by an anthropologist who has spent some three decades researching them.

Featherstone, Mike.(ed.). (1990) *Global Culture: Nationalization, Globalization, and Modernity.* Newbury Park, CA: Sage.

A collection of essays by leading social scientists and humanists from many countries that explores a central theme of this textbook: to what extent is a global culture emerging, and with what effect on local cultures and the nation state?

Hamm, Mark. (1993) American Skinheads: The Criminology and Control of Hate Crimes. Westport, CT: Praeger

Harris, Marvin. (1986). *Good to Eat: Riddles of Food and Culture.* New York: Simon & Schuster

A survey of widely differing cultural practices throughout the world, by a leading exponent of the materialist approach to anthropology.

Societies

CHAPTER OUTLINE

THINGS TO LOOK FOR

1. What are the principal types of society that have existed since human beings first appeared on the planet? What is the likely fate of such societal diversity?
2. What are the principal "technological revolutions" described by sociologists, and how have they helped to shape the resulting societies?
3. In what ways are we experiencing a transition to a "postindustrial" society, and how is this likely to affect our lives?
4. To what extent is globalization transforming societies today? In what ways does globalization today differ from its earlier forms?

INTRODUCTION

We are today on the rising slope of a third technological revolution. It is a rising slope, for we have passed from the . . . stage of invention and innovation into the crucial period of diffusion. The rates of diffusion will vary, depending on the economic conditions and political stability of societies. Yet the phenomenon cannot be reversed, and its consequences may be even greater than the previous two technological revolutions that shaped the West and now, with the spread of industrialization, other parts of the world as well (Bell, 1989).

College graduates holding white-collar jobs are twice as likely to be fired from their jobs in the 1990s as they were in the 1980s, according to a recent study by a Princeton University sociologist (Farber, 1993). President Clinton predicts that 18-year-olds entering the labor force today can expect to change the nature of their work seven or eight times during their lifetimes. Many people who lose their jobs as a result of changes in the economy will never work again in the field for which they are trained. The changes that are occurring today are so profound that sociologists such as Daniel Bell (1989), an originator of the concept of postindustrial society, claim that a "third technological revolution" is taking place, as great as those that ushered in agriculturally based societies some 12,000 years in the distant past, or modern industrial society three centuries ago.

What do sociologists mean when they talk of different types of societies, with one type giving way to another? In this chapter we shall address this question. We will show that the changes that are occurring today take place on a global scale, one that leaves few societies on the planet untouched in the process.

WHAT IS A SOCIETY?

The concept "society," like the concept "culture," is one of the basic building blocks used by sociology to better understand the world in which we live. In the last chapter we defined **society** as *the interacting people who share a common culture.* This is an intentionally broad definition, since the concept of society must encompass virtually all of the organizations and institutions we will encounter throughout this book, from families to nations.

Yet because this definition is so broad, it leaves many questions unanswered. Is the United States one society or many? Is there a middle-class society that is different from working-class society? Is there a society of Italian Americans that is distinct from a society of African Americans? Is there a society of thieves that exists outside the society of law-abiding citizens? If we speak of "American society," are we referring only to people in the United States, or are we including people living in Canada? Do we want to include people from Mexico and Uruguay as part of "American society"?

There are no hard and fast rules that determine what constitutes a "society" and what does not. At one time the notion of *shared territory* was also a part of the definition of society, restricting the term to people who occupy a fixed geographical space. While such a definition made sense at a time when the vast majority of people had contact primarily with others who lived within a few miles, it no longer makes sense today. Modern communications technology enables us to interact by telephone, fax machine, and electronic mail with people thousands of miles away.

Many sociologists belong to the International Sociological Association, a society of people who share the common culture of sociology yet are dispersed around the world. Television fan clubs, labor unions, and religious organizations are but three of the thousands of societies that enable people who share a common culture to interact with one another, yet which are not bounded by geography. In fact, one of the key aspects of globalization is that it involves vastly increased social relations with people who are geographically distant, and therefore permits the creation of societies that are not territorially bounded.

SOCIAL STRUCTURE

To better understand how societies change, we must first understand the ways in which they are structured. A pile of bricks and lumber does not make a building; for this to happen they must be put together to form a physical structure. The structure of the building, in turn, shapes the activities that occur inside it.

The placement of rooms, doors, stairways, elevators, and other structural features of the building will help determine who interacts with whom, how quickly one can move from one place to another, and even the nature of power relations. The most important person in any large organization is likely to have an office at the top of the building, perhaps accessible by a private elevator. As one moves up the building, one simultaneously moves up the hierarchy of prestige and power.

The same is true of a collection of people. If 100 people live in an area and are not connected to one another, there is no social structure. In Chapter 1 we defined **social structure** as *the underlying regularities in how people behave and interrelate with one another.* One of the central insights of sociology is that social structures help to shape social life in important ways. In this book, when we speak of such things as economic structures or political structures, we are in fact talking about economic and political activities that are embedded in larger social structures (Granovetter, 1985).

For this reason, sociologists strive to find regularities as evidence of underlying social structures. Do almost all college students regularly attend classes, write exams and papers, get grades, and if they satisfy certain requirements receive an A.A., a B.A., or a B.S.? To the extent that this is the case, there is strong evidence that there is a common educational structure in the United States. The same could be said about relations between men and women, the world of work, and virtually every aspect of everything we do. Just as the physical structure of a building helps to determine movement within it, so does social structure help to determine social life.

Let's return for a moment to the example of a building. Sometimes its structure is unstable, perhaps because it was poorly designed, with too much stress placed on supports that cannot adequately bear the weight of the structure. Under such conditions, the building might shift, requiring that the underlying structural problems be repaired. Under extreme conditions no amount of repair will suffice, and the building will collapse entirely.

The same analogy can be applied to social structures, which may be unstable because of underlying tensions. We shall use the concept **structural contradiction** to refer to *those aspects of a social structure that are mutually incompatible with one another, and therefore result in structural instability* (Offe, 1984; Chambliss, 1988). For example, when business is bad, a company may be forced to cut costs if it hopes to survive. In recent years a number of major American businesses, from General Motors to IBM, have been forced to cut costs by laying off workers. Yet such actions, however necessary they might seem for such firms to survive, can also harm these firms as well. If enough companies lay off workers, the entire economy suffers; increasing numbers of people find themselves without money to spend on cars or computers. This further hurts sales, forcing additional layoffs, in what becomes a downward economic spiral. There is a structural contradiction between the need for companies to cut costs in search of profits (which led them to lay off workers in the first place), and their need to sell products (which

Buildings, an example of material culture, can tell us a great deal about the nature of society. Dr. Robert Shuller's opulent Crystal Cathedral in California reveals a society that produces a large surplus, of wealth and values conspicuous consumption. The modesty and physical closeness of buildings in a Basotho village in Africa shows a limited surplus and a high valuation on community.

requires that people be employed in order to be able to afford products).

Later in this chapter we will examine different kinds of societies, and the types of social structures that are likely to be found in each. We shall argue that each social structure contains its own contradictions, and that these have provided an important source of social change throughout history.

Institutions

Sociologists analyze social structure in terms of the institutions, groups, statuses, and roles that make it up. These terms are key conceptual building blocks in sociology. In Chapter 3 we defined **institutions** as *clusters of relatively stable rules that govern social activities in a society, which at the same time provide shared understandings of the cultural meaning of those activities.* The law is one such institution in most societies. It consists of a set of rules that the members of a society generally share and understand. The institution of law in modern society contains written rules governing behavior, as well as punishments for their violation. In societies without a written language, laws are passed down through parables, stories, and word of mouth. The family is another institution that exists in every society. Family relationships vary tremendously from one society to the next. In some societies the cousins, uncles, grandparents, and aunts may be as important as mothers and fathers; in others, only the biological parents will do. In the United States, some families have one parent, and some have two. Among two-parent families, each parent is usually a different sex, although same-sex parents are becoming increasingly common as well. Yet despite these variations, "the family" as an institution is a fundamental part of every society, even though the particular relationships that constitute a family vary from society to society and over time within a single society (Brown, 1991; Brody et al., 1988; Dornbusch et al., 1985; Thompson et al., 1992). Other institutions that exist in every society include politics, education, economics, medicine, and religion. We discuss each of these in Part IV.

Status

Institutions such as the family, education, and law are built around **statuses**—*established social positions in society that vary in terms of prestige.* In the institution of education, for example, the different statuses include teachers, students, principals, and college presidents. All individuals occupy many different statuses, organized around the family, work, education, religion, and the other institutions in which they participate. A stu-

dent may also be a floor advisor in a dorm, an employee at a bookstore, and a campus politician. A judge may also be a wife, a mother, and a daughter. Sometimes people use the term "status" to mean "high prestige." Among sociologists, however, the term does not have this evaluative aspect, although one might sociologically describe a status as "low" or "high" in terms of the prestige accorded it in a particular society (see Chapter 8).

The fact that everyone occupies many statuses is a source of potential conflict. Sociologists refer to this as **status inconsistency,** *a situation where a person occupies two or more statuses of different rank.* This can often occur as a result of the enormous geographical mobility that occurs in the world today. Many people have left their native countries in search of political freedom or greater economic opportunity. Once they arrive in their new homeland, however, they may find that they have a vastly different status from that which they enjoyed before they migrated.

One recent study, for example, found that Korean immigrants to southern California experienced such status inconsistency with regard to their occupation. Although many had worked in high-status professional occupations in Korea, once they arrived in Los Angeles their immigrant minority status severely limited their range of occupational choice. Many found themselves running liquor stores, grocery stores, and other small businesses in low-income, high-crime neighborhoods. They felt they were overworked in their new occupations, in constant physical danger, and looked down upon by their customers. Needless to say, this made adjustment to their new situation extremely difficult (Min, 1990).

People in modern societies typically experience many different **achieved statuses,** *statuses acquired by virtue of the social positions that people occupy.* Achieved statuses can change over time, as people move from one social position to another. The status of student gives way to that of worker; the status of doctor is replaced by that of retired person. Some statuses, however, are based almost entirely on personal characteristics over which we have little control. **Ascribed statuses** are *those that are given for life at the moment of birth.* In modern societies two of the most common bases for ascribing status are race and sex, two attributes that are unlikely to change regardless of other changes that might occur during a person's lifetime. Although statuses tend to be achieved rather than ascribed in modern society, the continued attribution of status on the basis of such unchanging personal characteristics as race and sex remains an important source of discrimination and inequality today (see Part III of this book).

Besides race and sex, there are many bases for ascription of social status in some societies. We will discuss **caste societies**—*societies in which social status is based almost entirely on ascription*—later in this chapter.

Roles

A **role** is *the expected behavior associated with a particular status.* The status of student, for example, carries with it certain role expectations: students are expected to attend class, read books, write papers, and socialize with other students. Some behaviors associated with a role may be highly specific and may even be written down as rules and regulations. At many universities, for example, the role of professor is spelled out in highly legal terms governing such things as the terms of employment, classroom responsibilities, and outside income. Yet there are many aspects of the role of professor that are highly vague and undefined. Although a professor may be expected to act and dress in a certain way, the numerous exceptions to this rule suggest that there is considerable leeway in this particular aspect of the professor's role. The role of student is especially undefined, as you will realize if you try to define a consistent set of role expectations that supposedly govern your behavior as student.

Just as statuses may contradict one another, so too may roles. **Role conflict** exists when *two or more roles contain contradictory behavioral expectations.* The role of parent may conflict with the role of full-time worker; it is difficult to find the time to be a "good" father or mother when one is working full-time to pay the bills or advance one's career. Students often experience role conflict when the expectations of their role as daughter, son, or companion conflict with the expectations of their role as student. Should I cram for the exam tonight, or help celebrate my best friend's birthday?

Sometimes the source of conflict is not between two roles but is rather within a single role. **Role strain** occurs when *contradictory expectations exist within a given role.* Professors are expected to be approachable, friendly, and supportive of students. They also are expected to judge the students and give them grades based on performance, which may make being friendly and supportive quite difficult.

Role conflict and role strain are examples of how larger social structures can create problems experienced at the personal level. Such problems originate in the ways in which social roles are defined within a particular society. Once people come to occupy social roles, they find themselves experiencing conflicts and strains that are structured into the roles themselves. Understanding the relationship between individual experience and social structure—between our own lives and the larger social forces that helps to shape them—is an example of what is called the "sociological imagination" in Chapter 1 (Mills, 1959).

Groups

Human beings, like animals and insects, from ants to gorillas, live in groups. A **social group** can be defined as *a collection of people who regularly interact with one another on the basis of shared expectations concerning behavior, and who share a sense of common identity.* Some social groups are extremely important in an individual's life. We will discuss groups in some detail in Chapter 6.

TYPES OF SOCIETIES

The institutions, statuses, roles, and groups that characterize a society once showed an almost infinite variation from society to society. Yet at least two major historical changes in the ways that societies provide for their sustenance have contributed to a growing similarity between societies today—the emergence of agriculture some twelve thousand years in the past, and the development of modern industrial production 250 years ago. Today, some sociologists are claiming that a third revolutionary change is under way—the exploding use of electronic information technology in all aspects of social life, including the production of wealth (Bell, 1973, 1989). As a result of these changes, many earlier forms of society are today converging on certain common features (Levy, 1972).

In order to understand the sweeping social processes that are today transforming societies around the globe, it is helpful to understand the different kinds of societies that have existed throughout history, how they emerged and how they changed. Although human beings have formed many different kinds of societies, anthropologists and sociologists have identified only a small number of basic types. The most widely accepted classifications are based on those activities that provide the principal means of economic support. At the risk of oversimplifying the many differences between societies that actually exist, we shall discuss six principal types (Table 4.1):

1. Hunting and gathering societies
2. Pastoral societies
3. Horticultural societies
4. Agricultural societies
5. Industrial societies, and
6. Postindustrial (sometimes called "informational") societies

Table 4.1   Types of Societies and Approximate Dates of Emergence

Type of Society	Time of Emergence (Number of Years Ago)
Hunting and gathering	500,000–250,000
Pastoral/horticultural	8,000–12,000
Agricultural	6,000–12,000
Industrial	250–300
Postindustrial	25

Hunting and Gathering Societies

From the emergence of *Homo sapiens* a quarter of a million years ago to the development of agriculture only 12,000 years ago, people survived largely on the basis of what they could catch from the wilds with their hands or with simple weapons. **Hunting and gathering societies** are *societies whose members derive their sustenance primarily from hunting wild animals, fishing, and gathering wild plants.* During this long period, the use of fire, technological developments such as slings, bows, and flint-tipped weapons, and social innovations such as group hunting enabled early humans to partly tame their environment.

But for the most part, human societies were utterly dependent on their immediate surroundings for survival. If the game left an area, so too did the society. If the weather changed so that nuts, berries, and wild veg-

etables became scarce, the society moved on to more promising surroundings. It was partly in pursuit of food that human societies spread from their African origins to the rest of the planet. Given the rudimentary technologies that existed, life could be difficult and short. Nonetheless, because many early hunting and gathering societies lived in hospitable areas where food was relatively plentiful, there was often ample time to make artifacts and engage in religious rituals (Sahlins, 1972). By the end of this period, there were only an estimated eight million human beings on the entire planet, far fewer than live today in Los Angeles, New York City, Tokyo, Mexico City, or any one of a dozen metropolitan areas in the world (Weeks, 1992).

A society's survival strategies have a major effect on the types of social structures that will emerge (Schrire, 1984). Hunting and gathering often required that a society be highly mobile, capable of moving daily

People in hunting and gathering societies *develop sophisticated and useful technologies, drawing on readily available resources. This painting shows Sioux Indians hunting buffalo in winter, using handcrafted snowshoes and lances and wearing warm clothing made of fur and hides.*

in pursuit of nourishment. Such a society was likely to be small in size, often barely larger than a handful of people related to one another by marriage and kinship. Its division of labor had to be rudimentary, since almost everybody who was physically capable had to be engaged in the gathering of food if the society was to survive. If conditions were relatively plentiful, as they are among the Yanomamö today in the jungles of Venezuela and Brazil, small villages might also emerge, along with somewhat more specialized roles.

As far as we know, hunting and gathering societies had some division of labor on the basis of gender, with the roles occupied by men and women generally accorded coequal importance (Leacock, 1978). The male role typically carried with it the expectation that the man would travel long distances, hunt animals, and return to his family with food if he was fortunate enough to encounter any. The female role called for gathering food, hunting small animals, protecting the children and the community from attack, making clothing, and providing stability while the men were away. This social structure most probably resulted from the fact that women who were carrying nursing babies in their arms could not easily hunt large animals. Other roles had to do with age; for example, elders, adults, and children were almost always distinguished from one another. In some cases roles based on leadership also emerged, with an individual or a group acquiring responsibility for making decisions that affected the entire society. But the leaders were expected to hunt or forage along with everybody else.

The norms and values of hunting and gathering societies typically demanded that the first loyalty of everyone was to the community as a whole, rather than to their mates or children. The roles in hunting and gathering societies thus typically had community-wide meaning. This was because under such fragile conditions of existence, group loyalty was often tantamount to group survival. Yet despite these similarities, human ingenuity was such that not all hunting and gathering societies developed the *same* institutions, statuses, roles, and norms. Indeed, anthropologists have identified an enormous range of different cultural forms among hunting and gathering societies—possibly greater diversity than is found among any of the other types we shall consider (Sahlins and Service, 1960).

The predominant form of social structure associated with hunting and gathering societies is **tribal.** The members of tribal cultures *share extremely strong customs and traditions, trace their lineage to a common (often mythological) ancestor, and submerge their individual identities to the larger group.* Such cultures have strongly defined values, norms, and roles, which means that it is clear to everyone how each individual contributes to the group's survival. The importance of the norms and the need for everyone to behave in accordance with their roles led the people of most hunting and gathering societies to create powerful rituals that all members embraced. Whereas a person in modern society may be excused for failing to attend religious services, among hunters and gatherers failure to pay homage to the god or goddess of the hunt was an unpardonable transgression.

The tribal social structure of American Indian societies contributed to their destruction at the hands of European settlers (Utley, 1963; see Box 4.1). The strong communal ties that bound each member to the tribe and united them against all others made it difficult for different tribes to share hunting and gathering sites. It also made it difficult for them to cooperate with one another against an outside enemy. Thus when the Europeans and then later U.S. citizens began their ceaseless march westward, they met resistance from individual tribes but rarely did the tribes combine into a military force sufficient to threaten the Europeans (Farb, 1968). The end result was the decimation of the native societies and the forced removal onto reservations of those who were not killed (Wright and Davison, 1993).

This process is an example of a structural contradiction: a strong sense of devotion and commitment to one's tribe that is incompatible with cooperation between tribes. The Europeans arrived with guns and other weapons that gave them superior military power, but they also had an organizational advantage because the American Indians seldom joined together to fight the common enemy. Tribal identity and a history of battles against one another was so firmly embedded in the tribal culture that it made it difficult for the different tribes to coalesce against a common enemy, thus giving the Europeans the ability to isolate and destroy the culture of the American Indian as it existed.

Today fewer than a million (and possibly as few as a quarter of a million) people continue to pursue hunting and gathering as their principal means of support, as globalization threatens the few remaining hunting and gathering societies with extinction (Wolf, 1983).

Pastoral Societies

A **pastoral society** is a society *whose members domesticate wild animals and rely on them for food and transportation.* Pastoral societies first appeared about 12,000 years ago. Raising animals provided a more predictable and manageable food supply than did hunting and gathering. Pastoral peoples were also able to pro-

Box 4.1

Silenced Voices

The First "Americans"

By the time the American colonists were waging their war of independence against Britain, the Sioux Indians had already occupied a vast territory far larger than the largest British colony. The Sioux claimed much of what was to eventually become Minnesota, Iowa, Nebraska, and North and South Dakota (Lazarus, 1991).

When the Europeans began arriving in large numbers during the nineteenth century, the life of the Sioux began to change irrevocably. In the following passage, Edward Lazarus (1991, pp. 8–11) describes how the culture of the so-called Teton group of Sioux was affected by contact with European culture in the Black Hills of what is today called South Dakota, even before the U.S. government had officially claimed their land.

As an old Teton Chief remembered: ". . . of all our domain, we loved, perhaps, the Black Hills the most. The [Teton group] named these hills the Sapa, or Black Hills, on account of their color. The slopes and peaks were so heavily wooded with dark pines that from a distance the mountains actually looked black. In the wooden recesses were numberless spring of pure water and numerous small lakes. There were wood and game in abundance and shelter from the storms of the plains.". . .

When the first white Americans came west, they found the Sioux in this homeland, spending the winters near these Hills, hunting on the undisturbed plain and feared by every enemy. To those Americans, like [Harvard University chronicler Francis] Parkman, who met the Sioux at the height of their power, they seemed untouched, beyond the long reach of the western world. . . .

But Parkman was wrong. Even by the early 1800s, when the Sioux still had not seen more than a few dozen white men, the influence of their distant and unknown world already was keenly felt. White man's guns in the hands of the Chippewa already had uprooted the Sioux from their previous habitat. White man's horses had revolutionized plains life and advanced Sioux dominion over their new home. And white man's diseases, somehow sparing the Sioux, had ravaged their foes along the Missouri—the Arikara, Omaha, and Mandan—abetting Sioux hegemony. Now, armed themselves, the Sioux used their guns to rout their rivals and increase the kill in the summer hunts.

Long before Parkman ventured west, the European world, in the form of the fur trade, had cast an outstretched arm into tribal life. Every fall the "mountain men," intrepid pioneers of the western wilderness, emissaries from the white world, semiliterate in European and native tongues, appeared at the great forks along the Missouri River (at the James River to the south and at the Yellowstone to the north), bearing guns and knives and cooking pots to barter for beaver skins and other hides. . . . In their wake, Sioux camps overflowed with modern conveniences: iron kettles, cooking utensils, steel knives and needles, sugar and coffee, luxuries that eased the rigors of nomadic life.

duce a **surplus**—that is, *they produced more sustenance than they required for immediate survival* (Dalton, 1967; Evans-Pritchard, 1940).

The production of a surplus, in turn, made it possible to store food for future use. Small settlements emerged, and forms of culture developed appropriate to people who were able to remain in one place for a time, rather than be constantly on the move. For example, many pastoral societies developed elaborate systems for controlling the size of their herds in order to steadily increase them. As the herds increased beyond the needs of the people in the society, they entered into trading relationships with other groups. These characteristics of pastoral societies had the potential for producing cooperation between different groups of people. Unlike hunting and gathering societies, which often competed with one another for access to wild animals or other forms of food, people in

Sheepherding, which has characterized pastoral societies since biblical times, is shown in what is today the country of Jordan. The domestication of animals was an important cultural advance that contributed to the production of a surplus, the development of trade, and the use of nonhuman energy sources to multiply human efforts in agriculture.

pastoral societies usually found it advantageous to be on friendly terms with other groups in order to trade their surplus for the surplus of others. Camels could be exchanged for goats and sheep, or goats and sheep could be exchanged for clothing, ornaments and a variety of food products.

Because of the demands placed on a geographical area by the increasing size of their animal herds, pastoral peoples could not be completely sedentary. Rather, they were forced to move from time-to-time in order to find feeding grounds for the herd. The fact that pastoral peoples produced a surplus not only encouraged cooperative relationships with their neighbors for purposes of trade, but it also made it possible for a fairly wide variety of specialized roles to emerge (Evans-Pritchard, 1940). At least some of the people in pastoral societies were free to explore activities other than those directly related to the problem of survival. Roles could emerge that were seen as enhancing the quality of life in ways not immediately connected with the food supply. Pastoral societies thus permitted the emergence of spiritual leaders, traders who bartered with people outside the society, ornament makers, craftspeople, and other specialized roles.

It is not surprising, then, that pastoral societies developed elaborate systems of religion that reflected their way of life. They often developed a belief in a god or goddess who looked after the peoples' needs, like a shepherd attending the flock. This might be accompanied by the belief that some individuals—a priesthood—possessed a special ability to carry the word of god. Three of the world's major religions—Christianity, Islam, and Judaism—all developed among pastoral peoples. All contain the idea that there is a god who watches over the people, and that there are special individuals ("pastors") who carry the god's message.

There are many pastoral societies still in existence today. These are concentrated mainly in North Africa, where vast desert lands are inhospitable to the development of agriculture or manufacturing. The pastoral societies of North Africa continue to depend on camels, goats, and sheep for their survival. Trading centers throughout the desert offer these people a chance to trade their surplus hides and meats for vegetables grown in places where water makes agriculture possible.

Horticultural Societies

Whereas pastoral societies are based on animal husbandry, **horticultural societies** rely on *the cultivation of plants by using a hoe or other simple tools.* Horticultural societies first appeared around the same time as pastoral societies. Often the lives of horticultural people were extremely harsh. The land could quickly become depleted of its nutrients, forcing the society to move. Droughts or excessive rains could disrupt the production of food as well. Some groups developed "slash and burn" techniques, in which forest cover or last year's crops would be cut and then burned to clear a field for this year's planting. While this technique was quick, efficient, and left behind ashes as natural fertilizers, it also contributed to erosion and in the long run made the land less productive.

Like pastoral societies, horticultural societies sometimes produced a surplus, particularly where the land was fertile. As we noted earlier, this meant that no longer did everybody have to be engaged in food production. The role of the shaman, a spiritual leader who cured the sick or implored the gods for good weather or abundant crops, could be supported by other members of society from the surplus food they produced. Roles could also be created for artisans, craftspeople, carvers and jewelers whose work embellished the life of those who worked in the fields. All of these roles emerged as people settled down into small communities near their gardens (Braudel, 1973, 1977, 1992).

Horticultural societies in a sense form a transition to the next type of society we shall consider, agricultural societies, since both depend on cultivating land to produce crops. What distinguishes them is the level of technology used for cultivation. The hand-held hoe and similar tools severely limited the productivity of horticultural gardens. Agricultural society, on the other hand, resulted from technological advances over these rudimentary methods of farming.

Agricultural Societies

Agricultural societies, like horticultural societies, are based on the domestication of plants. But whereas horticultural societies used simple implements like the hoe to tend what were essentially large gardens, **agricultural societies** relied on *plows, draft animals, or other technological advances for cultivating crops over an extended area.* The most important crops in an agricultural society were grains such as corn, wheat, rice, barley, and millet. Because of its enormous importance in contributing to social change, social scientists use the term **agricultural revolution** to refer to *the technological changes associated with the rise of agriculture and the domestication of farm animals.*

This is the first major technological revolution mentioned by Daniel Bell (1989) in the quote at the beginning of this chapter.

These changes took hold firmly in Europe, the Middle East, and along the Nile in North Africa some 5,500 to 8,500 years ago; in Southeast Asia, northern India, and China slightly earlier; and in sub-Saharan Africa, Central and South America somewhat later. While large draft animals such as cows or oxen were used in Asia, Africa, and Europe, in America the Maya, Aztec, Toltec, and Inca cultivated native crops such as corn by hand, along with squash, potatoes, and tobacco.

The new technologies permitted a greatly increased food supply, resulting in much larger populations than were found in earlier societies, and thereby contributed to numerous changes in the wider culture (Brooke, 1971). For one thing, women—who often had relatively high status in hunting and gathering and horticultural societies because they provided much of the food—now often found themselves subordinated to men (Fisher, 1979).

More food meant a greater surplus, which in turn supported bigger cities populated by merchants, craftspeople, religious leaders, and rulers who did not have to worry about producing their own food (Jacobs, 1970). The cities became centers of trade between agricultural societies, contributing to processes of economic and cultural globalization that date back thousands of years. In Europe, for example, farming methods, manufacturing techniques, and all sorts of popular foods and other products originated in Africa and Asia (Wolf, 1983).

Because they produced an economic surplus, agricultural societies often became stratified. A **stratified**

As the historian-sociologist Fernand Braudel pointed out, the potential for different types of societies is partly circumscribed by climate, geology and geography. In one example of an agricultural society, *a farmer tills part of the very limited land in Nepal flat enough to sustain agriculture.*

society is characterized by *systematic inequalities of wealth, power and prestige associated with a person's social status* (Gibbs, 1953; Pirenne, 1937; see Chapter 8). Stratification sometimes arose in response to structural contradictions. For example, because they produced a surplus, agricultural societies often prospered, grew, and expanded into neighboring areas. This threatened their neighbors, who resisted such expansion while coveting their wealth. The production of a surplus and economic prosperity thus contributed to warfare and conflict, which in turn favored the emergence of a stratum of warriors alongside the farmers. The farmers produced the surplus, part of which the warriors consumed in exchange for providing protection from the society's enemies. Another stratum that sometimes emerged consisted of the **nobility,** a *hereditary stratum possessing a highly elevated social status.* The nobility also lived off the labor of the farmers, organizing the warriors to protect against invasion and expand into new territories.

One form of stratification associated with agricultural society is **feudalism,** a social system in which *people are granted by those of higher status the right to occupy and use land, in exchange for performing designated services.* Feudalism emerged around the ninth century in parts of Europe, although feudal social relations were found in Japan and other parts of Asia as well. Under feudalism, a peasant farmer was allowed to farm a parcel of land to which the lord of the manor had title, in exchange for providing the lord with some of the crops that were harvested. The peasant's right to farm the land could be passed on to his children, but the peasant had no right to sell the land and move elsewhere. The lord above him, in turn, similarly held title to his own estates from those still higher in status. Some of the central ideas of feudalism have survived until the present time. The term "landlord," for example, derives from the feudal lord who had title to land. When a landlord rents you an apartment in exchange for money, it is the modern-day equivalent of a feudal lord "renting" out a parcel of land in exchange for some of the crops produced on it.

The feudal social structure essentially tied people to the land they tilled, in what became a complex system of land ownership and rights. The feudal social structure was in fact a caste system in which statuses were ascribed for life at birth. A peasant on an English manor in the twelfth century was not permitted to carry weapons, bake bread, press wine, cure people of illness, or keep records. The feudal caste system prescribed certain behaviors, including the kind of work one could do, where one could live and with whom one could associate and even marry. The roles for people in different castes were defined for all kinds of behavior (Bloch,

1961; Gibbs, 1953; Pirenne, 1937; see Chapter 8 for further discussion of caste society).

This particular social structure was well-suited to a society based on agriculture, where being tied to the land contributed to agricultural productivity. Feudalism provided a great measure of stability. It protected farmers not only against the incursions of distant tribes, but also from neighboring farmers who might covet their land or their crops if they were not all part of the same system of authority. Authority was based on long-standing traditions; peasants owed allegiance to their lords as a part of their birthright. A peasant's family might have farmed their lord's land for generations, as far back as people could remember. Norms and beliefs changed slowly, if at all; agricultural societies thus tended to be highly static.

Industrial Societies

Agricultural societies eventually gave way to a new form of society, one that first appeared in northern Europe about 250 to 300 years ago and today encompasses the globe. An **industrial society** is a society *whose principal means of support is based on the mechanized factory production of goods.* Like the agricultural revolution thousands of years earlier, the societal changes resulting from industrialization were so sweeping and important that sociologists use the term **industrial revolution** to refer to *the period during the eighteenth century when mechanized factory production first occurred.* This is the second great technological revolution described by Daniel Bell.

The industrial revolution grew out of a form of economic system that had begun to take root in Europe hundreds of years earlier, sometime between the fourteenth and sixteenth centuries (Cox, 1959, 1964; Wallerstein, 1974, 1980). This economic system, termed **capitalism,** is characterized by the *market allocation of goods and services, production for private profit, and private ownership of the means of producing wealth.* In order to better understand the nature of industrial society, it will be helpful to first look at the emergence of capitalism out of European feudalism.

The Transition from Feudalism to Capitalism

Although the European feudal social structure was well-suited to a society based on agriculture, it proved to be detrimental to one in which a capitalist economic system was rapidly emerging. In particular, its time-bound, traditional, unchanging ways—in which people were tied forever to the land they worked—became a

What we call "societies" today are often countries that have emerged as a result of conquest and colonization. Hundreds of years ago, countless societies existed in North America. Today, these have all been incorporated into three countries, whose boundaries bear no resemblance to the original societies. The same is true elsewhere in the world, for example in Africa (Map 4.2).

Map 4.1

North America: Indigenous Societies at the Time of Columbus, and Nations Today

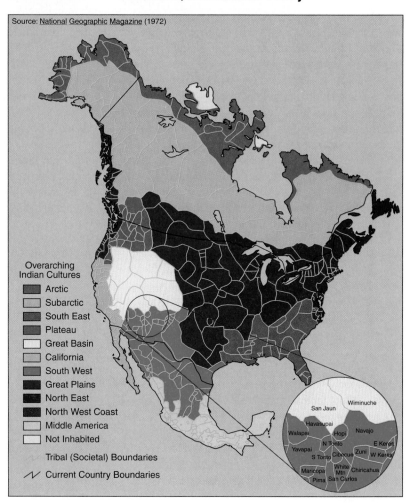

Source: National Geographic Magazine (1972)

Overarching Indian Cultures
- Arctic
- Subarctic
- South East
- Plateau
- Great Basin
- California
- South West
- Great Plains
- North East
- North West Coast
- Middle America
- Not Inhabited

⟋⟍ Tribal (Societal) Boundaries
⟋⟍ Current Country Boundaries

barrier to the free flow of people, goods, and ideas required by capitalism (Wallerstein, 1974, 1980).

The surplus generated in agriculture had created the opportunity for the production of new forms of wealth. Surplus agricultural products and handicrafts could now be traded for goods produced in distant lands. As a result, new social classes emerged: artisans who made clothing, tools, weapons, ornaments, and other goods; shopkeepers; and merchants who traded these goods at town marketplaces or in far-away lands.

The rise of new classes of merchants and artisans led to new contradictions in agricultural society. These new classes became increasingly wealthy and powerful. They demanded goods that could not be supplied by agriculture, such as spices, wool, and woven cloth. Home-based ("cottage") industries developed as men and women worked in their homes to produce clothing, furniture, tableware, and other specialized items that the traders purchased and in turn sold in distant markets.

During this same period, the most successful war-

riors became powerful kings, reigning over vast territories made up of numerous nobles with thousands of peasant farmers under their control. Commercial centers emerged where trading and commerce were common. The town-dwelling merchants, in the throes of creating a thriving commercial society, needed a strong central authority to facilitate trade and commerce. They needed roads and canals to transport goods, a "coin of the realm" or money that could substitute for the goods that were being bought and sold, and a means of regulating markets and trade fairs (Prestwick, 1985).

This in turn required institutions that could enforce agreements beyond the boundaries of a local community and across communities that had different norms governing agreements. As a result the law became standardized in more centralized governments, and such notions as "contract" and "private property" were invented to facilitate trade. The emerging legal and monetary system allowed exchange over a wide area without having to haul around bulky goods for barter

Map 4.2   Africa: Indigenous Societies Prior to European Colonization, and Nations Today

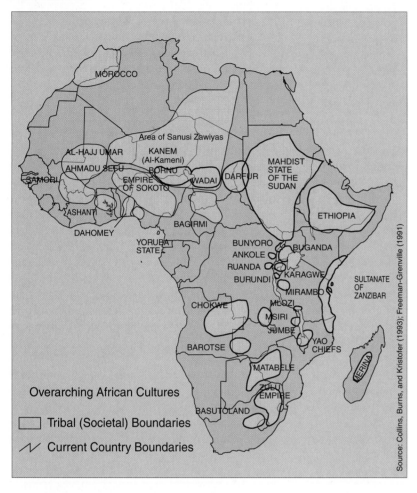

As elsewhere in the world, the countries found in Africa today often have little basis in the tribal societies which predated European colonization of the continent. In fact, the present map of Africa much more closely follows earlier colonial boundaries than those of the societies which are native to the continent.

Source: Collins, Burns, and Kristofer (1993); Freeman-Grenville (1991)

or trade. In some places people who refused to receive state-controlled money were even punished as criminals (Lenski, 1966; Kemp, 1978; Pirenne, 1937).

The merchants and traders found the feudal caste social structure an impediment to their commercial activities. Caste relations required that people marry within their caste and stay in one place. This conflicted fundamentally with the need of merchants for a mobile, flexible labor force. The cities needed workers, while the feudal lords needed peasant farmers. The conflicts between the landed aristocracy and the merchants of commerce grew ever more intense. The landlords and nobles fought to prevent their peasants from moving to the growing towns that promised a freer way of life. The townspeople protected themselves by building walls to defend against attacking nobles. In some places the merchants built armies that were more efficient than those of the landed aristocracy (Kent, 1986).

During the sixteenth and seventeenth centuries a major impetus toward the development of capitalism occurred with the voyages of European ships east to Asia and west to North and South America. Spain, Por-

tugal, the Netherlands, Britain, and France opened trade routes with the east, and conquered and then plundered parts of Asia and the Americas. The mining of precious metals such as gold and silver, and the increased trade in tea, spices, and silks from Asia, created an economic frenzy in Europe that in less than a century nearly doubled the price of goods and stimulated undreamed of commercial activity and wealth (Todorov, 1984; Robertson, 1986; Mintz, 1991; Blaut, 1989; Smith, 1991).

The Emergence of Industrial Society

All these changes laid the groundwork for the emergence of industrial society, which began in Britain in the mid-eighteenth century and quickly spread throughout Europe and then to much of the rest of the world (Wallerstein, 1980, 1989). Historians usually date the industrial revolution to the invention of machines that spun sheep's wool into fibers and wove the fibers into cloth, thereby providing a vast increase in goods to fuel the emerging capitalist system. Such machines, which came into use after 1760, permitted English weavers to produce wool fibers and textiles much more quickly than before, resulting in the rapid industrialization of the British textile and apparel industry.

The earliest machines were directly powered by natural forces such as moving water, but with the appearance of such fuel-powered devices as James Watt's steam engine in 1769, mechanization increased rapidly. Engines powered by steam and fossil fuels resulted in vast increases in **productivity,** *the amount of goods that a worker can produce in a given period of time.* Improvements in transportation soon followed, permitting manufacturers to more quickly get their goods from factory to market. One result was an enormous increase in average wealth; per-capita wealth in Britain, for example, quadrupled during the nineteenth century.

The industrial revolution soon spread throughout Europe and then to other parts of the world. Roads, canals, and, with the invention of the steam locomotive in the nineteenth century, railroads soon crisscrossed Europe and the United States. Belgium, with rich supplies of coal and iron, began to industrialize in the 1820s; France followed a decade later, along with Germany in mid-century. In the United States, the textile industry had already begun to industrialize by the end of the eighteenth century, when Samuel Slater, a textile worker who had immigrated from England, used machinery he had seen in England to open a cotton mill. Eli Whitney's cotton gin, invented in 1793, greatly increased the amount of cotton thread that could be used in textile factories. American industrialization exploded after the Civil War, and by 1900 the United States had surpassed Britain in the production of iron and cotton (Glen, 1984; Wrigley, 1988).

Japan began to industrialize during the early part of this century; the former Soviet Union during the 1930s; and China in the 1950s. Hong Kong, Singapore, Taiwan, and South Korea, the "newly industrializing counties" of East Asia, began a period of explosive industrial growth during the 1960s and 1970s, and today appear to be rapidly overtaking the older industrial powers (see Chapter 9).

Some Characteristics of Industrial Society

Industrial societies were characterized by improved health and increased life expectancy, mass public education, and the growth of democratic forms of governance. They were also usually more culturally diverse than earlier types of society, since their rapidly growing urban areas were typically populated by large numbers of immigrants from different cultures and subcultures in search of work. Specialized organizations emerged to deal with virtually all aspects of social life, including government, work, the economy, education, and religion. Although we will examine many of these in separate chapters, it will be helpful to bear in mind a number of the most important institutional changes that occurred.

Families As work became increasingly centered in factories, the home ceased to be the primary unit of production. On the one hand, this meant that the family decreased in economic importance; wage earnings, rather than the bounty of the hunt or the harvest, determined the family's economic well-being. The family also declined in importance as a source of education and training, since these functions were increasingly performed

The early years of industrial society *were characterized by the uncontrolled growth of factories where work hazards were a routine part of workers' daily lives. In the casting room of the lead factory shown here, workers were often injured by machinery and worked without adequate protection from the dangers of lead poisoning as well.*

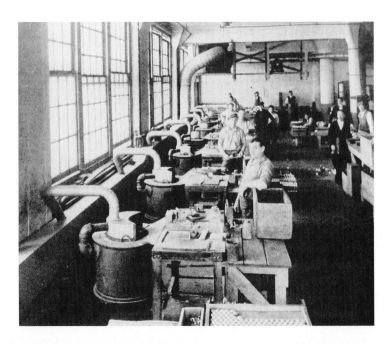

by specialized institutions such as schools or the workplace. On the other hand, families became increasingly important in terms of both consumption and emotional ties (Giddens, 1992).

Power Industrial society is characterized by a relatively high degree of centralization of power, whether it be in powerful governments, standing armies, or large business organizations. Although strong central governments are hardly new, what is unique to industrial society is the degree to which centralized power is today able to touch on the lives of virtually everyone in society. Once the industrial revolution had begun to spread, government became the arena of struggle between the new industrialists and the workers who toiled in their factories, thereby further enhancing its importance (Batchelder and Freudenberger, 1983; Gledhill, Bender, and Larsen, 1988; Harpham, 1985; Robertson, 1986; Hamilton and Hiszowicz, 1987; Mann, 1986).

Laws and Contracts Under feudalism, disputes were settled by the nobles. There were guidelines dictated by custom but no central authority to see that the guidelines were followed. Because commerce could not thrive in an environment where agreements made in one locale were not honored in another, the emerging capitalists fought for legislation enacting **contracts,** *binding agreements between parties that are enforced by a legal system backed by a centralized authority.* Contracts tended to reflect the relative power of the people who enacted them (Ibbetson, 1984; Teeven, 1983). Today, virtually every aspect of our daily lives, from marriage to sports, from religion to leisure, is governed by contracts.

Money In order for commerce to occur, it is important that a standardized and reliable system of money be recognized by everyone. The existence of such a monetary system, however, requires a government that has the legal right to issue money. The issuing of money and the creation of a monetary system was both a result and a cause of the growth of strong central governments and helped pave the way for the industrial revolution to occur (Spufford, 1988; Nightingale, 1990).

Technology As we have already seen, rapid technological change played a major role in the emergence of the industrial revolution. In addition to the previously noted changes, other inventions included ships that could navigate the globe, military weapons that gave first one country then another military superiority, and new forms of power that transformed the manufacturing process. Indeed, after the industrial revolution, "research and development" became branches of

industry. As we shall see in Chapter 15, much of this technological change resulted from businesses seeking cheaper ways of producing products, in the face of workers' struggles for higher salaries (Kemp, 1978; Inkster, 1991; Mathias and Davis, 1991; Braverman, 1976).

Bureaucracy Industrial society was accompanied by an enormous expansion in bureaucratic forms of organization. **Bureaucracies,** *formal organizations characterized by written rules, hierarchical authority, and a paid staff,* have long been found in government and religious organizations throughout the world (see Chapter 6 for a detailed discussion of bureaucracy). But the emergence of industrial society also saw the extension of bureaucratic forms of organization to a much wider range of activities. Indeed, virtually all of the institutions we will discuss in Part IV are today organized bureaucratically.

Social Norms The changes in political and economic forms accompanying the transition from an agricultural to an industrial society reached into every aspect of people's lives, affecting some of their most deeply held beliefs about the nature of social relationships. As we have seen, in hunting and gathering societies, the norms that defined specific role expectations were generally linked to the well-being of the entire community. Within at least one type of agricultural society—feudalism—behavioral norms were tied to one's membership in a particular caste. In industrial society, a large number of norms were concerned with ensuring that individuals accept and live up to the many contracts and agreements they entered into. Agreements were made between husbands and wives, employers and employees, government bureaucrats and factory owners, teachers and students.

The Emergence of Socialism

As we have seen, the industrial revolution was an outgrowth of an early form of capitalism based on commerce and the trading of goods produced by farmers and craftspeople. Once advanced technologies paved the way for factory production, industrial society and capitalism grew together. In fact, for a century and a half after the industrial revolution, all industrial societies had social structures based in capitalist economic relations (Baechler, Hall, and Mann, 1988; Jones, 1991).

This combination of industrial society and capitalist economics resulted in many changes, first in Europe, then North America, and eventually the entire world. It successfully harnessed the power of science and technology to transform the landscape. Drawing upon scientific advances in machinery and equipment, factories were able to produce far more goods than were previously possible. Enormous wealth was generated, and to some it seemed that before too long, human beings would never again have to suffer hunger and poverty. At the same time, industrial capitalism also resulted in the massive movement of farmers into cities, which soon became swollen with destitute people in search of work. Cities grew in size and squalor, with masses of people often crammed into tiny apartments where much of their pay went for rent. Workers labored long hours seven days a week, often under unsafe and unsanitary conditions. Workers were paid very little and could be fired for any reason; there were always thousands of others to take their place. Children as young as 10 or 12 could be found laboring alongside adults at all hours of the day or night (Chapter 15).

These characteristics of industrial societies based in capitalist economies led in the nineteenth century to the creation of an alternative vision of industrial society, one that would rely more on government than private enterprises to ensure the well-being of the citizenry. This vision, termed **socialism,** called for *the production and distribution of goods and services for the common good, by means of enterprises owned by the government* (Marx and Engels, 1977; orig. 1848). Under socialism, unlike capitalism, the state (rather than individuals) owns all economic enterprises, from the largest oil and steel companies to the smallest shops. Decisions about how many goods to produce or the price that should be charged for them are made by public officials, often located thousands of miles from the factory or the store.

Although socialism was never implemented in any European country during the nineteenth century, it was harnassed to the power of industrial society elsewhere in the twentieth. First in the Soviet Union in 1919, then in China in 1949, and subsequently in a number of other countries around the world, socialist economic relations were put in place by overthrowing capitalistic systems. We will discuss the fate of such societies below, as we examine recent changes that are today once again transforming industrial societies (see Chapter 15 for further discussion).

Postindustrial Societies

Both capitalism and socialism proved effective in creating industrial societies. In *industrial-capitalist* societies, gigantic corporations such as General Motors, IBM, AT&T, Toyota, Siemens, and Exxon generated more wealth than the vast majority of nations. While economic inequality and poverty continued to trouble industrial-capitalist societies, the overall level of wealth produced was unprecedented in human history. In *industrial-socialist* societies a parallel development took place: large state-owned organizations helped to rapidly transform countries like China and the former Soviet Union from impoverished agricultural societies into powerful industrial nations.

The Contradictions of Industrial Society

During the past two decades, both the capitalist and socialist forms of industrial society have confronted difficulties. We will examine a number of these difficulties in Chapters 6 and 15, but one particularly important problem should be mentioned at this point by way of example: the inefficiencies of the gigantic private or government organizations associated with industrial economies. Although such organizations can be effective in harnassing the powers of industrial production, they are also bureaucratic, inflexible, and incapable of responding rapidly to new ideas or changing circumstances.

Organizational inflexibility can be especially limiting at a time when business enterprises, whether run by the state or private individuals, must compete at a global level. In the United States, for example, Ford, General Motors, and Chrysler no longer are competing only with one another, but with Toyota, Honda, Hyundai, Volvo, Mercedes-Benz, and numerous other global automobile manufacturers. In the former Soviet Union, Aeroflot, the enormous state-run airline that once dwarfed all other airline companies in the world, found itself competing with United Airlines, American Airlines, Japan Airlines, British Overseas Airways, and many others that were struggling for a share of the world market. The gigantic enterprises that had worked reasonably well for many years were no longer working well to deliver the growing standard of living that people in all industrial societies have come to expect.

In industrial-capitalist societies, this contradiction between large size and responsiveness has threatened the survival of some of the largest and most powerful corporations in the world. In recent years such once seemingly invincible corporate giants as IBM, General Motors, and United Airlines have suffered enormous financial losses that have shaken them to their foundations.

In industrial-socialist societies the situation has been even worse. The enormous state bureaucracy that enabled the former Soviet Union to industrialize proved to be a barrier to further economic growth. As a result of years of economic stagnation and growing public discontent, the leaders of the Soviet Union overturned this system entirely in 1991, opting instead for a more capitalist one (Schoenfeld, 1991; Yakolev, 1989). Industrial-socialist societies throughout Eastern

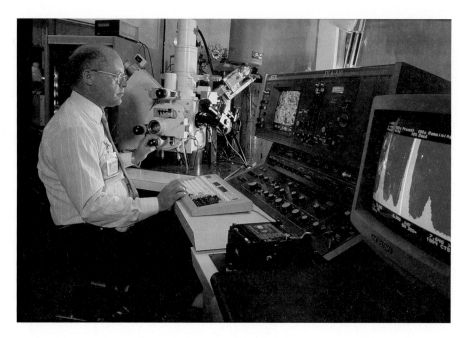

The scanning microanalyzer on which this man is working provides more information in a shorter time than was imaginable a generation ago. Such advances in electronics are contributing to the creation of a postindustrial society *based on information and knowledge as well as industrial production. The development of such technologies is one of the important forces contributing to globalization today.*

Europe have followed a similar route. The People's Republic of China, whose 1.1 billion people make it the world's largest socialist country, is rapidly transforming its economy in a capitalist direction as well, bringing to an end decades of tight state control over the economy.

Some Characteristics of Postindustrial Society

Highly centralized authority, whether it is located in a government office in Moscow or a corporate headquarters in New York, does not seem able to keep pace with a world where information can be transferred instantly anywhere on the planet by fax or electronic mail. As a result, according to some sociologists, we are witnessing the emergence of **postindustrial society,** a society *based on knowledge, information, and the provision of services rather than on the physical production of goods in factories* (Bell, 1973, 1989). This is not to say that factories are no longer important in postindustrial soci-

eties; it simply emphasizes the growing importance of human inventiveness and ingenuity in producing goods and providing services. This is the third great technological revolution identified by Daniel Bell.

Theorists of postindustrial society argue that the human mind is increasingly becoming the key to the creation of wealth and prosperity, aided by the information storage and computational abilities of the microchip. If industrial society is symbolized by smokestack factories whose workers perform simple repetitive physical tasks, postindustrial society will be symbolized by high-tech "smokeless" factories whose skilled engineers program computer-driven robots.

Sociologists have pointed to a number of features they believe will characterize postindustrial society, some of which we will discuss in detail in later chapters (see Table 4.2). The more optimistic forecasts include a much more central role for education and training, growing affluence and consumerism, and a decline in inequality as class differences come increasingly to reward knowledge and technical skills rather than the ownership of

Table 4.2   Some Principal Differences Between Industrial and Postindustrial Society

	Industrial Society	**Postindustrial Society**
Principal economic base	Manufacturing	Knowledge and information
Economic product	Goods	Services
Organization	Bureaucratic	Flexible
Geography	Centralized	Decentralized
Relationships	Moderately stable	Fleeting and unstable
Education to provide	Skilled workers	Thinkers and problem solvers

Box 4.2

Critical Thinking

Postindustrial Society

The following excerpts from two prominent sociologists present contrasting visions of the impact of postindustrial society on workers. Daniel Bell (1989), an originator of the concept of postindustrial society, presents a somewhat hopeful and optimistic vision. George Ritzer (1983, 1992), on the other hand, worries that computerized fast-food restaurants reveal the unskilled nature of future work, as more and more institutions of society become "McDonaldized." How would you judge the relative merits of these two arguments? Are they truly incompatible, or do they merely emphasize different features of postindustrial society?

[Postindustrial activities] are primarily processing, control, and information. It is a social way of life that is, increasingly, a "game between persons" [as opposed to nature or machines]. More important, there is a new principle of innovation, especially of knowledge and its relation to technology. . . . In a postindustrial society there is an expansion of new kinds of service. These are human services—education, health, social work, social services—analysis and planning, design, programming, and the like. . . . And the important fact is that the expansion of a postindustrial sector of a society requires the expansion of higher education and the education of

many more in the population in abstract conceptual, technical, and alphanumeric skills. . . .

An equally important change is in the role of women. . . .industrial work has largely been considered men's work (including the corporate sectors of management). Postindustrial employments are open, in skills and capacities, to women (Bell, 1989).

McDonald's does not yet have robots to serve us food, but it does have teenagers whose ability to act autonomously is almost completely eliminated by techniques, procedures, routines, and machines. There are numerous examples of this including rules which prescribe all the things a counterperson should do in dealing with a customer as well as a large variety of technologies which determine the actions of workers such as drink dispensers which shut themselves off when the cup is full; buzzers, lights, and bells which indicate when food (e.g., french fries) is done; and cash registers which have the prices of each item programmed in. . . . Because of such tools and machines, as well as the elaborate rules dictating worker behavior, people often feel they are dealing with human robots when they relate to the personnel of a fast-food restaurant. When human robots are found, mechanical robots cannot be far behind (Ritzer 1983, 1993).

property. According to this view, the most successful organizations will be smaller and more flexible. People will enter into a larger number of relationships of more fleeting duration, affecting family life, friendships, and communities. Businesses will become increasingly decentralized, as electronic communications makes it possible to perform virtually any activity from any location on earth—including one's home.

The most hopeful forecasts envision a growing concern for the well-being of all members of society, as experts in business and government work together to bring the fruits of modern technology to everybody. Under such a scenario, postindustrial society will be characterized by less and less conflict, as members come to recognize that by working together—aided by science and technology—they will be able to solve the principal

problems of society (Bell, 1973, 1978, 1988, 1989; Coenen-Huther, 1986; Touraine, 1971; Marien, 1977).

Some sociologists have argued that we are in the midst of a transition to a knowledge-based postindustrial society that will ultimately bringer greater prosperity to everyone. Others disagree, fearing that only those with highly specialized skills and talents will benefit, while others will be worse off. We will return to these issues in some detail in Chapter 15.

Critical Assessment There is considerable controversy over the extent to which postindustrial society currently exists and whether it likely to be the high-technology utopia envisioned by its more ardent proponents (Hill, 1974; Hourani, 1987; Miller, 1975; Neuberg, 1975; Schoonmaker, 1991; see Box 4.2). Critics

Roast duck may be one of the most popular dishes on the menu of Chinese restaurants. This Chinese boy is herding ducks by employing a technology reminiscent of ancient pastoral societies, *one that is unlikely to long endure the* industrialization *of food processing in China and elsewhere in Asia.*

point out that any transition to postindustrial society is likely to be a slow and uneven process. The United States, for example, will remain in many respects an industrial society, even though some aspects of postindustrial society may be found. For example, while such highly trained "knowledge workers" as clothing designers may travel the globe in person or electronically in search of new ideas and styles, the clothing itself is still made in "sweatshop" factories in U.S. cities—if it is made in this country at all.

Critics point out that while computers may be a driving force in postindustrial societies, in many ways they are currently contributing to increased inequality rather than reducing it. Many of the "high-tech" jobs that are now being created are in fact unskilled, and more and more occupations are being reduced to simple tasks that require less, rather than greater, mental ability. The checkout person in the department store who uses a bar code scanner to ring up sales, or the McDonald's clerk who presses the "Big Mac" button on the cash register, are both using computers in relatively low-skill jobs that pay low wages.

Some critics also claim that postindustrial society, rather than favoring the emergence of small and decentralized organizations, may instead result in greater coordination and control on the part of government agencies and large global corporations. The largest, most powerful organizations will have access to the highest-technology innovations, which they will use to enhance their control over the economic and political systems. Instead of promoting democracy, postindustrial society may lead to growing powerlessness on the part of those who lack the education and skills necessary to take advantage of the new technological developments.

Finally, the poorer, more agricultural nations of the world may have to become industrial societies themselves before they begin a transition to a postindustrial stage, if indeed they ever do. In fact, as we shall see in Chapter 9, in many ways the poorer nations of the world today provide low-wage factories for global enterprises based in the advanced industrial nations. If the United States is witnessing the appearance of "clean" high-tech factories, it is only because the older, high-polluting, low-tech factories have been displaced to the impoverished nations of the world (Frobel, Heinrichs, and Kreye, 1980, 1982; Ernst, 1980, 1987; Lipietz, 1986).

GLOBALIZATION: ARE SOCIETIES CONVERGING ON A SINGLE TYPE?

The world's societies have, in a sense, always been interconnected with one another (Wolf, 1983). Since human beings first appeared in Africa, they have spread their cultures and institutions throughout the world. The enormous variety of societies that have existed on the planet developed out of one another, through processes that often took tens of thousands of years (see Box 4.3). Trade between societies made its appearance about 30,000 years ago, and by the time of the industrial revolution was already global, with merchants helping to spread new ideas along with new products.

The European-based industrial revolution provided an enormous impetus to these processes, since the requirements of industrial societies for raw materials and cheap labor led to the extension of their economic con-

Box 4.3

Globalization

The "All-American" Student

Globalization brings the United States into contact with other societies; everything from the American economy to what we view on television is increasingly a part of a globally interdependent world. Yet while the pace of globalization may appear to be accelerating, there has never been such a thing as a closed society in the United States. America has always thrived on products and ideas from other cultures, as the following description of a "typical American student" proves (based on a concept by Linton, 1937).

The sun is barely up when our typical American student arises from her bed, an apparatus of ancient Middle Eastern design. She is alerted by the ring of a medieval European time-keeping device that she will be late for her exam if she doesn't hurry. She bathes in a large basin similar to one introduced four thousand years ago in the Middle East, scrubs her teeth with a brush devised by the Chinese, and avails herself of a toilet originating in classical Rome and perfected in Britain fifteen centuries later.

As she dresses, she reveals her preference for natural fibers such as cotton and wool, discovered in India and Greece many thousands of years ago and first woven into fabrics in southwestern Asia. Her clothing, of course, is much more contemporary, fashioned for American firms by Italian designers and made in Korean-owned factories located in Indonesia and Guatemala. Soon she is wide awake, well-fortified by several cups of a mildly narcotic drink invented by ancient Arabs using a popular African bean. Her bitter beverage is made more palatable by the addition of a white dairy substance first used in the Middle East, and a sweetener originating long ago in India and China.

She leaves her home on a self-propelled two wheeled device of Scottish origin and French design, listening to music on a tiny Japanese invention as she rides to school. Upon arrival, she first scans the pages of an innovation dating to medieval Germany, in hopes of catching up on yesterday's news. The medieval Germans, of course, had themselves relied on printing technologies invented five hundred years earlier in China.

She then engages in some last-minute cramming for her math exam, by problem-solving in a manner first devised in Iraq thousands of years before her birth. She is about to be tested on concepts that originated in ancient Greece, India, and North Africa, by making calculations on a medieval French device recently perfected in Japan. She records her answers on a thin, lightweight writing substance made out of plant fibers according to a process first used in ancient China, employing a Hungarian-invented writing implement with a small rounded point.

Later, in an effort to unwind after "acing" her math exam, she serves up another pair of aces, this time playing a court game originating in fourteenth-century Italy. She has the advantage of using a lightweight carbon fiber racket of recent British invention, buoyed by equally lightweight athletic shoes fashioned after a centuries-old design originating among Indians in Mexico.

Returning home, she enjoys her first free evening in many days, largely unaware of how so many different times and places have helped to make up the life of the typical American (a designation derived from Amerigo Vespucci, a sixteenth-century Italian mapmaker) student.

---

trol over many parts of the world. Yet this proved to be a two-way street as products, culture, and people flowed toward Europe and the United States as well as the reverse. Music, art, language, eating habits—all of these were transformed as industrial technology helped to make the world a smaller place.

Yet as recently as 50 years ago there were still many

societies around the globe that remained relatively insulated from one another. Hunting and gathering, horticultural, pastoral, and agricultural societies could be found alongside industrial societies. Although warfare and trade occasionally brought such societies into contact, most of the time they were able to pursue their traditional cultures for the most part unaffected by one another. The emergence of the computer age has changed all this.

If the industrial revolution shrank the world, the information revolution has shrunk it still further. The world's economy, political institutions, and cultures are increasingly interlinked. Societies that were once inaccessible to others are today easily reached, their low-cost labor tapped by global factories, their cultures impacted by satellite television. They, in turn, often send their people (and with them, their cultures) elsewhere, partly driven by economic hardship and the promise of better opportunities. Global migration today is contributing to a vast intermingling of societies, resulting in the richness of cultural diversity as well as growing ethnic strife and conflict (Chapter 20).

Globalization has also resulted in a vast increase in the possibility for societies to share their ideas with one another, as they grope for ways to solve their common problems. Fifty years ago the United States and the Soviet Union dominated the world; they offered two different approaches to economic development and politics and were not hesitant to use force to impose their beliefs on other societies. Today there are numerous models besides American-style capitalism and the former Soviet-style socialism—from the more "mixed" economies of Europe and Scandanavia to Japanese-style capitalism to the newly emerging industrial countries of East Asia (Chapters 9 and 15). Global conferences on the environment, global trade treaties, and global medical meetings on epidemics such as AIDS are other examples of such worldwide sharing of ideas.

It is possible that we are witnessing a convergence of societies previously unknown in human history. The enormous variety of hunting and gathering societies that existed thousands of years ago are today giving way to a global industrial society, in which individual societal differences are overlaid with features common to all. No matter in which society you might find yourself today, its economic and political institutions, sys-

Paradoxically, social institutions can embrace globalization yet prove resistant to change. This Japanese geisha is dressed in traditional attire, perhaps on her way to perform a tea ceremony in the same manner as it has been performed for many centuries. Yet she has no difficulty riding in a limousine and using a cellular phone to conduct her business.

tems of law, educational system, and even popular culture are increasingly likely to have a familiar feel. While such convergence of societal form is by no means universal, it may well become increasingly so as we move into the twenty-first century.

CHAPTER SUMMARY

1. All human societies can be understood in terms of **social structures** characterized by underlying regularities. Social structures can be further analyzed in terms of **institutions, statuses, roles,** and **groups.**

2. Social structures often contain **structural contradictions,** internal sources of instability that lead to social change.

3. Social structures vary depending on the type of society that people create. **Hunting and gathering,** **pastoral/horticultural, agricultural, industrial,** and **postindustrial societies** each have their own unique social structures.

4. Since the appearance of human beings about a quarter of a million years ago, societies were primarily of the **hunting and gathering** type, although **pastoral** and **horticultural** societies had also made their appearance. The **agricultural revolution,** the first major technological revolution, occurred nearly 12,000 years ago.

5. The second major technological revolution, the **industrial revolution,** began in eighteenth-century England and quickly spread throughout Europe and eventually the world.

6. **Industrial society** itself grew out of **capitalism,** an economic system that began to emerge out of European **feudalism** centuries before the industrial revolution.

7. The establishment of a **legal system** with guidelines for **contracts** and the protection of property was an important step in the development of industrial society. A strong **central government** set the framework for the protection of the new capitalist class.

8. During the twentieth century **industrial society** gave rise to another type of economic system, **socialism.** Emerging in Russia in 1917 and in China in 1949, socialism soon extended around the globe, although during the past five years many socialist economic systems have collapsed.

9. Many of the political and economic institutions of industrial society are large, bureaucratic, and unresponsive to the rapid changes that are occurring in the world today. This has contributed to the collapse of **socialism,** and changes in the institutions of **capitalist society.**

10. Today we are experiencing the emergence of **postindustrial society,** fostered by the third technological revolution—**information.** Much manual labor has been replaced by electronic machines and robots, the production of goods is giving way to the provision of services, and human knowledge is playing an increasingly important part in the creation of wealth.

11. Societies have been impacted by globalization throughout human history, although the pace has accelerated sharply during the past quarter century. The enormous variety of societies that once existed today appear to be converging on a common set of institutions that closely resemble one another.

QUESTIONS FOR DISCUSSION

1. How does the notion of structural contradiction help us to better understand change in societies?

2. Why did hunting and gathering societies eventually give way to agricultural societies? What were the characteristics of each, and why did they change?

3. What is industrial society, and what are the two principal economic systems associated with it? What are the strengths and weaknesses of each?

4. How does industrial society differ from postindustrial society? In what ways might the latter bring greater prosperity than the former? In what ways might it have the opposite effect?

5. What is the importance of globalization in the transformation of industrial into postindustrial society? What were some of the contradictions in the social structure of industrial society that contributed to this transformation?

KEY TERMS

achieved status: A status acquired by virtue of the social position a person occupies.

agricultural revolution: The technological changes associated with the rise of agriculture and domestication of farm animals.

agricultural society: A type of society whose members rely for their sustenance primarily on the cultivation of crops over an extended area, by means of plows, draft animals, or other technological advances.

ascribed status: A status that is given for life at the moment of birth.

bureaucracy: A formal organization characterized by written rules, hierarchical authority, and a paid staff.

capitalism: An economic system characterized by the market allocation of goods and services, production for private profit, and private ownership of the means of producing wealth.

caste society: A society in which social status is based almost entirely on ascription.

contract: A binding agreement between parties that is enforced by a legal system backed by a centralized authority.

feudalism: A social system in which people are granted by those of higher status the right to occupy and use land in exchange for performing designated services.

horticultural society: A type of society whose members rely for their sustenance primarily on the cultivation of plants by using a hoe or other simple tools.

hunting and gathering society: A type of society whose members derive their sustenance primarily from hunting wild animals, fishing, and gathering wild plants.

industrial revolution: The period during the eighteenth century when mechanized factory production first occurred

industrial society: A type of society whose principal means of support is based on the mechanized factory production of goods.

institution: A cluster of relatively stable rules that govern social activities in a society, which at the same time provide shared understandings of the cultural meaning of those activities.

nobility: A hereditary stratum in society, possessing a highly elevated social status.

pastoral society: A type of society whose members domesticate wild animals and rely on them as a principal source of food and transportation.

postindustrial society: A type of modern society based on knowledge, information, and the provision of services rather than on the physical production of goods in factories.

productivity: The amount of goods that a worker can produce in a given period of time.

role: The expected behavior associated with a particular status.

role conflict: A conflict that exists when two or more roles contain contradictory behavioral expectations.

role strain: The strain experienced when contradictory expectations exist within a given role.

social group: A collection of people who regularly interact with one another on the basis of shared expectations concerning behavior and who share a sense of common identity.

social structure: The underlying regularities in how people behave and interrelate with one another.

socialism: An economic system characterized by the production and distribution of goods and services for the common good, by means of enterprises owned by the government.

society: The interacting people who share a common culture.

status inconsistency: A situation where a person occupies two or more statuses of different rank.

statuses: Established social positions in society that vary in terms of prestige.

stratified society: A society characterized by systematic inequalities of wealth, power, and prestige associated with a person's social status.

structural contradiction: Those aspects of a social structure that are mutually incompatible with one another and therefore result in structural instability.

surplus: The production of greater sustenance than is required for immediate survival.

tribal structure: A type of social structure in which members share extremely strong customs and traditions, trace their lineage to a common (often mythological) ancestor, and submerge their individual identities to the larger group.

RECOMMENDED FOR FURTHER READING

Bell, Daniel. (1973). *The Coming Crisis of Postindustrial Society: A Venture in Social Forecasting.* New York: Basic Books.

A now-classic analysis of the emerging postindustrial society; anticipates some of the consequences and problems.

Mann, Michael. (1986). *The Sources of Social Power.* Cambridge University Press.

Identifies four basic networks of social interaction (economic, ideological, political, and coercive), challenging the concept of "society" and arguing that every historical period should be analyzed in terms of these networks of interaction.

Wallerstein, Immanuel M. (1989). *The Second Era of Great Expansion of the Capitalist World-Economy, 1730–1840s.* San Diego: Academic Press.

A detailed historical analysis of the later development of capitalism and industrial society, by the leader of the "world systems" approach to understanding capitalism as part of a global system of economic relations dating back to the sixteenth century.

Wolf, Eric R. (1983). *Europe and the People Without a History.* Berkeley: University of California Press.

An analysis of the history of Europe in relationship to the non-European world, including the considerable (and usually undocumented) impact of the latter on the former.

Wright, Ronald, and Peter Davison. (1993). *Stolen Continents: The Americas Through Indian Eyes Since 1492.* New York: Houghton Mifflin.

A survey and analysis of the systematic destruction by Europeans of American societies, from the Aztecs, Incas, and Mayan civilizations to the Iroquois and other North American Indians.

Socialization and Social Interaction

CHAPTER OUTLINE

THINGS TO LOOK FOR

1. How do people learn the statuses, roles, norms, and rules that prevail in their culture?
2. In what ways can socialization be regarded as a lifelong process?
3. What and who are the most important agents of socialization?
4. What can we learn about socialization through the study of social interaction, including ordinary conversations?
5. How does globalization affect socialization in the United States?

INTRODUCTION: THE IMPORTANCE OF SOCIALIZATION

Students should be taught to maintain order in their environment, make effective use of time and space, lead regulated lives, and, at the same time, understand the significance of manners and etiquette, and be able to act in any situation. (From a course of study for secondary schools in Japan; cited in Feiler, 1991).

The following description of the beginning of a day in a ninth grade class in Japan suggests a learning environment very different from its American counterpart:

The 45 students in the first homeroom class of the ninth grade were all seated at their desks when the opening notes of the Brahms symphony roared from the loudpeaker at precisely 8:30 A.M. Soon the violins faded, and a slow, synthesized pulse spread across the room, numbing the mind with its smooth, hypnotic gait. The room was cold and slightly dank. No sun shone through the plate glass windows overlooking the balcony. The clouds, like the students, were still.

In a moment, a soothing, resonant voice began to speak. "Good morning, boys and girls. Let's begin another *wonderful* day. Please close your eyes. . . ."

For ten minutes every morning the students at Sano Junior High sat in quiet meditation to prepare themselves for the day ahead. The principal, Sakamoto-*sensei*, had introduced this system, known as Method Training, several years earlier in order to quell the growing incidence of school "vi-

olence," mainly minor scuffles and hair violations. The program consisted of a sequence of 25 tapes for total mental and physical conditioning. Each day a different tape was played. . . .

After ten minutes the music dissolved, the voice disappeared, and Mrs. Negishi—standing erect before the class—took control of the homeroom meeting.

"Stand up," she commanded, and the students rose to their feet.

"Attention," she said, and they dropped their arms to their thighs.

"Bow."

It was 8:42 in the morning (Feiler, 1991).

People who are born and grow up in different cultures act and think very differently from one another. Bruce Feiler, an American who taught school in Japan, was struck by the ways in which Japanese schools socialized their students to become adult members of Japanese society. Deep respect for authority, long hours of focused learning, appropriate modes of dress, even proper ways to bow—all of these were central aspects of Japanese education that would be virtually unthinkable in most American schools today. Japanese educational practices, in turn, reflect widely shared norms and values that are found in Japanese families, workplaces, and indeed throughout Japanese culture.

Socialization: A Lifelong Process

For a society to endure across generations, its members must devise ways to pass their culture along to one another. Sociologists refer to the ways in which people acquire their society's core beliefs and practices as **socialization,** the *lifelong process through which people learn the values, norms and roles of their culture, and thereby develop their sense of self.* Socialization occurs throughout a person's lifetime, beginning with birth and ending with death. It is an active process in which individuals select among different cultural influences to construct their sense of who they are and how they should think and act as members of their culture.

As we shall see below, the principal agents of socialization often exert an enormous influence on the members of a society, particularly during the early years of life. Parents, teachers, television, and even friends constantly convey cultural norms and values. Although socialization involves a measure of conscious choice, much occurs "behind our backs"—it is carried in the language we speak, the roles we are given to play, and virtually every facet of our social interaction.

Maps 5.1, 5.2, 5.3

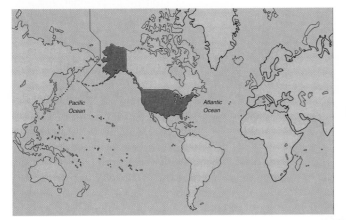

U.S. World View

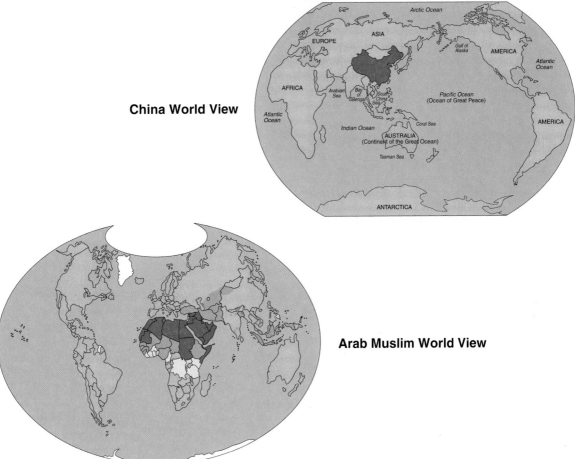

China World View

Arab Muslim World View

In many societies, including our own, people are socialized to regard their culture as the center of the world. The size and placement of a country on a world map can subtly convey information about the map-maker's beliefs regarding a country's relative importance. Map 5.1, the familiar Mercator projection, is both centered on North America and greatly exaggerates its size relative to Africa and Latin America. Map 5.2 is adapted from a Chinese atlas that shows China to be at the world's strategic center. Map 5.3 again recenters the world — this time on the nations and regions with large Arab or Muslim populations.

Nature or Nurture?

The question of how active a role we play in our own socialization is seen in the "nature-nurture" debate, which we first encountered in Chapter 3. To the extent that our personalities are determined biologically, socialization cannot involve a great deal of active participation and learning on our own part. Although the belief that "biology is destiny" held sway in the late nineteenth and early twentieth centuries, today most scholars no longer believe that there is a basic "human nature" that exists regardless of socialization. Very little of what we think of as typically human behavior comes naturally; rather, it must be explained in terms of socialization.

One way the importance of socialization might be assessed would be by studying human beings raised outside of all human contact. If there is a basic biological "human nature," it should be apparent even in such people. Studies of children deprived of significant contact with others find that they do not learn to talk, much less to interact effectively with other human beings. They develop very few "human" qualities (Rymer, 1993; Curtiss, 1977; Shattuck, 1980; Davis, 1949).

There have been numerous accounts of children reportedly raised by such animals as wolves, sheep, bears, panthers, and even pigs. Most stories of this sort are of extremely doubtful validity (Rymer, 1993). One of the more well-documented cases occurred nearly two hundred years ago, when a naked "wild boy" (later named "Victor") was discovered in Aveyron, a rural area of France (Shattuck, 1980). Victor could not speak, and although he stood erect, he ran using both his arms and legs like an animal. He was taken in by a young doctor, who kept a record of his socialization. Although Victor managed to learn a few words, he never spoke in complete sentences. He eventually learned to use the toilet, but he continued to exhibit "wild" behavior, including public masturbation. After his capture Victor proved incapable of all but the most rudimentary socialization.

Another way the impact of socialization can be studied is to examine unfortunate children kept in virtual isolation by their parents. "Genie" (a pseudonym) is one recent example that has been reported in some detail. Genie was almost completely isolated from contact with anyone for 12 years, from the time she was a year and a half old. She saw only her father, mother, and brother, and such brief encounters only occurred when they came to feed her baby food. Genie's father, who spent most of his time at home, did not allow his wife or Genie to leave the house or have anyone visit them. Genie was kept in a back room where she was ei-

ther strapped to a child's potty chair or placed in a sleeping bag that limited her body movements. Her contact even with her family was minimal, since she only saw them when they came to feed her. The family always spoke in whispers; isolated in a back room, Genie rarely heard any conversation. If she made noises her father punished her severely (Curtiss, 1977; Rymer, 1993).

When Genie was 13, her mother took her and fled the house. According to accounts by people who saw her shortly afterward, Genie was unable to control her bowels, eat solid food, cry, or even talk. Because of her tight confinement, she had not even learned to focus her eyes beyond twelve feet. She was constantly salivating and spitting, and had little use of her arms or legs (Rymer, 1993).

Gradually Genie learned some of the minimal social behavior expected of a 13-year-old. For example, she became toilet trained and learned to wear clothes. Although intelligence tests did not indicate reasoning disability, even after five years of concentrated effort on the part of a foster mother, social workers, and medical doctors, she never learned to speak beyond the level of a four-year-old, and did not engage others in conversation. Although she responded positively to people who treated her with sympathy and concern, Genie's social behavior remained severely underdeveloped. She never became a fully socialized adult member of society (Rymer, 1993).

Genie's case, like that of Victor the "wild boy," underscores the importance of socialization. Sociologists and other social scientists have developed a number of different theories to explain how socialization works. These theories differ in their assumptions about human behavior, and therefore emphasize different aspects of socialization. But they all share the belief that socialization is a crucial way that individuals become full members of their culture (see Box 5.1).

THEORIES OF SOCIALIZATION

Psychologists as well as sociologists have developed theories about socialization. While psychologists tend to focus on the impact of socialization on the individual, sociologists emphasize the interplay between individual experience and the larger society. Sociologists are especially concerned with explaining the impact of society on the individual, and particularly how socialization enables a culture to be sustained over time. Although some of the theories we shall consider were initially developed by psychologists, they all have important implications for sociology.

Box 5.1

Critical Thinking

Are Thieves Born or Made?

Can socialization explain why some people become criminals and others do not? Harry King was for many years a professional thief specializing in safecracking. In the following passage, Harry attributes his criminal career to his childhood socialization. What evidence does Harry provide that might shed light on the "nature-nurture" debate?

I was 10 or 12 years old and my mother and father broke up their family life and got a divorce. . . . [My mother] placed me in what was called a parental school. . . . It was while I was at this parental school that I learned that some of the kids had been committed there by the county for stealing bikes. They taught me how to steal and where to steal them and where to sell them. . . . I learned the names of legitimate dealers who would pay a dollar a piece for a bike. . . . I was no problem child at that time.

After about a year my mother took me home. . . . I was wandering around one day, I happened to go to the YMCA and there's racks of bicycles. All that day I never had it so good. I was riding them away as fast as I could. That was the start of it [my career in crime] as near as I can recall. I just went from there on up. I ran around with a group of kids. . . . We would break into grocery stores and steal cigarettes and things like that. I looked in the window of the post office one night. . . . There was a safe open and it was full of stamps. So I just climbed in the window and walked over to the safe and took out a whole bunch of stamps. The next day I walked out on the main street with a big bunch of stamps under my arm. I went from store to store selling them stamps at half price (King and Chambliss, 1984, pp. 4–5).

The Social Construction of the Self: Cooley and Mead

One of the most influential sociological theories of socialization originated with George Herbert Mead (1863–1931). As we noted in Chapter 1, Mead's approach emphasized the importance of symbolic interaction as the foundation of both the human self and the larger society. Although symbolic interactionism provides a framework for understanding social relationships in general, it has proved especially fruitful for understanding socialization (Mead, 1934, 1938; Blumer, 1969, 1970; Lindesmith and Strauss, 1956; Stryker and Schwartz, 1970).

Mead was strongly influenced by **behaviorism,** a *psychological approach that emphasizes the effect of rewards and punishments on observable human behavior* (Baldwin, 1986, 1988). Behaviorism arose during the late nineteenth century to challenge the then-popular belief that human behavior results primarily from inborn biological instincts and drives. Researchers such as Ivan Pavlov (1849–1936) and John Watson (1878–1958) had demonstrated that at least among animals, behavior can be changed by rewards and punishments. A rat that is rewarded with food pel-

lets will learn the fastest routes through a maze; one that is punished with electric shocks will learn to avoid painful routes. Furthermore, behaviorists showed that animals can learn to modify their environments in order to obtain rewards and avoid punishments: for example, a rat will learn to press a bar if it triggers the release of food (Watson, 1925; Skinner, 1938, 1953).

When they turned their study to human beings, behaviorists came to emphasize the importance of **social learning,** the *learning that occurs from observing and imitating others* (Baldwin and Baldwin, 1986; Rosenthal and Zimmerman, 1978; Bandura, 1977). Mead drew on these insights, emphasizing the importance of rewards and punishments in shaping human behavior (Baldwin, 1986). Unlike most behaviorists, however, Mead believed that humans actively interpret the significance of words and other symbols that serve as rewards and punishments in human interaction.

Mead drew on the ideas of Charles Horton Cooley (1864–1929), the sociologist who developed the theory of the **looking-glass self,** which is based on the belief that *our self-image results from how we interpret other peoples' views of ourselves* (Cooley, 1964; orig. 1902). According to Cooley, we are constantly forming ideas about how others perceive and judge us. These ideas serve as extremely important rewards and punishments as we formulate our own self-image, which in turn forms the basis for our social interaction with others. For example, a child gradually learns to self-apply words like "good" or "bad," "quick" or "slow," "nervous" or "easy-going," and to act accordingly.

Cooley recognized that not everyone is equally important in contributing to our self-image, arguing that **primary groups,** characterized by *intense positive and negative emotional ties, face-to-face interaction, intimacy, and a strong, enduring sense of commitment,* are an especially important source of the looking-glass self. Among the most important early primary groups are family and friends. But even **secondary groups,** which are *large, impersonal, and often involve fleeting relationships,* can be important as well, and the looking-glass self continues to develop throughout our lives (Barber, 1992; Berns, 1989). Both primary and secondary groups can serve as **reference groups,** in that both can *provide standards for judging one's attitudes or behaviors.*

Cooley's notion of the looking-glass self is reflected in Mead's concept of **role-taking,** *the ability to take the role of others in interaction.* Role-taking is an important part of the socialization process. Through role-taking, we come to see ourselves from another person's point of view and thereby are rewarded or punished according to the self-image we acquire through the eyes of others. Mead outlined four principal stages in socialization that reflect the ability to engage in more and more complex role-taking, resulting in an increasingly complete sense of self (Table 5.1).

According to Mead's theory, socialization consists partly of overcoming the extreme egocentrism of the newborn infant, and learning to see oneself through the eyes of other people and eventually society as a whole. In this sense, as we are socialized we increasingly acquire a "social" self.

During the **preparatory stage,** *children relate to the world as though they are the center of the universe.* They do not engage in true role-taking at this time and primarily respond to things in their immediate environment, such as their mother's breast, the color of an object, or the sound of a voice. Yet even at a very early age children are capable of some limited role-taking, as is seen in their playful interactions with others.

During the **play stage,** children *learn to take the attitude of the other people with whom they interact.* Mead refers to this as taking the role of **particular others,** *specific people who are important in their lives, whose views are important in their self-evaluations.* By playing at being their mother or father, for example, children come to see themselves as their parents see them. But, according to Mead, they do not yet acquire the complex sense of self that results from the ability to see oneself through the eyes of many different people. That takes place at the next stage.

During the **game stage,** children *learn to take on the role of multiple others.* In order to play a game, according to Mead, it is necessary to understand the role of everyone involved, simultaneously keeping a number of such roles in mind. When children go to bat in a game of softball, for example, they must see themselves through the eyes of the pitcher, the catcher, the person covering first base, and possibly other players as well.

This is a much more complex form of role-taking than that occurring in simple play, and it eventually enables the child to enter the **adult stage** by taking on the role of the **generalized other,** *the sense acquired by fully socialized adults that society has norms and values by which they evaluate themselves.* While initially the child's "generalized other" may consist only of the other children involved in a specific game, eventually he or she learns to take on the attitude of society as a whole. This is a crucial step, for it means conforming to a set of abstract principles that may or may not serve the child's immediate self-interest. By now the individual is capable of understanding extremely complex

Table 5.1   George Herbert Mead's Stages of Development

Developmental Stage	Role-taking	Self Seen Through the Eyes of
Preparatory	Highly limited	Primarily own eyes
Play	Particular others	Other individuals, one at a time
Game	Many others	Many other individuals
Adult	Generalized others	Society as a whole

In the play stage of development, according to George Herbert Mead, children learn to "take the role of the other." This process can involve role-playing with objects such as stuffed animals. Some children even invent imaginary playmates and learn social roles through imaginary interactions with them.

cultural symbols, such as love and hate, success and failure, friendship and morality.

To better explain the relationship between a person's sense of self and the larger society, Mead theorized that there are two aspects in the ongoing creation of the self—the "I" and the "me." These are best thought of as opposite sides of the same coin—two phases in the construction of the self. The **I** is the *impulse to act; it is creative, innovative, unthinking, and largely unpredictable.* The **me,** on the other hand, is *the image we believe others hold of us as we act, the looking-glass part of the self through which we see ourselves as others see us.* The "I" represents innovation; the "me" social convention and conformity. When the "I" initiates a spontaneous act, the "me" raises society's response: how would I be regarded by others if I acted in such a fashion? Human actions are constantly interrupted by such mental "discussions," which may happen so quickly that we are not even aware that they are occurring. They form a powerful source of social control and conformity.

Critical Assessment Symbolic interactionism provides a useful explanation of the ways in which people are socialized into society's norms and values. Like many sociological theories, Mead's approach emphasizes the importance of society in shaping individual psychology, rather than the reverse. Yet Mead's theory runs the risk of overemphasizing social conformity. Such concepts as role-taking, the generalized other, and the social "me" all highlight the ways in which people

are socialized to conform to the expectations of others. Mead assumes that all people have a strong basic need for the social approval of others. Yet such an assumption must be tested in particular cultures, since any "need" for social approval is itself acquired through socialization.

Biological Needs Versus Social Constraints: Freud

Sigmund Freud (1856–1939), a psychologist who lived in Vienna, Austria, had an enormous impact on the study of socialization as well as the discipline of psychology. His ideas have proved to be highly influential, even though many sociologists reject his overall theory. Freud (1905, 1929, 1933) founded the field of **psychoanalysis,** an *approach to the study of human psychology that emphasizes the complex reasoning processes of the human mind.* Unlike behaviorism, which was concerned with observable behavior, Freud focused on what could not be seen—the impact of the unconscious mind on human action. He also emphasized what he regarded as the overriding importance of early childhood socialization, arguing that the basic adult personality is established by age five or six. In addition, Freud sought to demonstrate that for a society to thrive, it must socialize its members to curb their needs and desires.

According to Freud, the human mind has three components: the id, the ego, and the superego. The **id** is the *repository of basic biological drives and needs,* which

Freud believed to be primarily bound up with sexual energy. ("Id" is German for "It," reflecting Freud's belief that this aspect of the human personality is not even truly human.) The **ego** is *the "self," the core of what is regarded as a person's unique personality.* The **superego** consists of *the values and norms of society, insofar as they are internalized by the individual.* It is similar to the notion of a conscience.

Newborn babies are all id, and therein lies a major problem for society. Left to their own devices, babies would constantly seek instant gratification in the form of food, physical contact, and nurturing care. They must therefore be socialized into learning that such gratification is not always possible; in fact, according to Freud the **reality principle** requires that *the members of any society renounce a substantial part of their desire for immediate pleasure in order to do the kind of work that is necessary for the society to operate smoothly.* Socialization is a principal responsibility of parents, who are constantly telling their children what is right and what is wrong, what they can do and what they cannot.

Such cultural "shoulds" and "should nots" form the basis for the child's superego, which is in constant war with the biologically based desires of the id. The task of the child's emerging ego is to serve as a sort of umpire between the two. To the extent that the ego succeeds in bending the desires of the id to the social demands of the superego, the child will grow up to be a well-socialized adult, more or less conforming to society's norms and values.

Unfortunately, this battle can prove highly damaging to the child's fragile ego. Desires that are repressed during the first few years of life do not necessarily disappear; rather, they are buried deeply in the unconscious mind, where they continue to cause trouble throughout a person's life. For example, according to Freud an infant who is severely punished during toilet training may become fixated at that stage of development, and for the rest of his or her life engage in compulsive hand-washing and other efforts to remain clean. Thus, even though a society successfully socializes its members to a high degree of cultural conformity, it may have done so at the cost of their psychological health. In Freud's view, the price of art, science, and all that he termed "civilization" can be a great deal of personal unhappiness (Freud, 1929).

Since a person's basic personality is established early in life, change does not come easily for adults. This is especially likely to be true if a person suffers from troubles that originate in experiences long repressed into the unconscious. For Freud, individuals must become fully conscious of the repressed reasons for their behavior, if they ever hope to change it. Much of his theory was therefore concerned with techniques intended to access deeply buried memories, since only by bringing them into conscious awareness can a person hope to confront them, challenge them, and eventually overcome their influence on behavior (Freud, 1933).

Critical Assessment Freud's discovery and exploration of the unconscious is generally viewed as an important contribution to understanding socialization. His belief that there are inherent biological drives that inevitably come into conflict with society's restrictions is more debatable, although some scholars have explored this possibility (see, for example, Marcuse, 1955; Robinson, 1969). Few people outside of orthodox psychoanalysis would accept the idea that socialization is completed by the age of five or six, although many would agree that the first few years are likely to be especially important because of an infant's enormous dependence on others (Seltzer, 1989).

Freud is also criticized for basing his theories almost entirely on his German middle- and upper-class patients and from them generalizing to all people in all societies. German society at the time of Freud was extremely repressive by today's standards, with severe methods of punishing children who were not well-behaved and conforming. Even if Freud's theories were true of some Germans at the time he was writing, it is doubtful that they can be generalized to other times, places, or cultures.

Finally, scholars have criticized Freud's theory for its biased accounts of women's experiences. For example, Freud's strong belief in repression led him to discount his female patients' stories about being sexually abused by their fathers or other male relatives during childhood. Although such recollections were commonplace, Freud came to regard them as repressed sexual fantasies rather than actual experiences.

Stages of Social Development: Piaget and Kohlberg

Some theories of socialization argue that all children necessarily go through certain developmental stages in order to become fully socialized adult members of society. The Swiss psychologist Jean Piaget (1896–1980) spent a lifetime conducting research on how young children develop the ability to think abstractly and make moral judgments (Piaget, 1926, 1928, 1930, 1932). His theory of **cognitive development,** based largely on studies of Swiss children at play, *argues that the ability to make logical decisions increases as a person grows older.* Like Mead and Freud, Piaget noted that infants are highly **egocentric,** *experiencing the world as if it were entirely centered on themselves.* Socialization entails an increasing ability to use language and symbols, to think abstractly and logically, and to see things from multiple perspectives. Piaget believed that while cognitive development involves a great deal of social learning, there is also a biological component; a given stage cannot be achieved until a child's mind has achieved the appropriate level of physiological development.

Piaget also developed a theory of **moral development,** which stated that *people at different ages learn to act according to abstract ideas about justice or fairness.* This theory parallels his theory of cognitive development, in that both are concerned with overcoming egocentrism and acquiring the ability to take other points of view. For very young children, rules are absolute; right is right, wrong is wrong. By playing games and engaging in other group activities, children eventually begin to realize that rules are made up by the group and therefore can be changed if the circumstances change. They learn to take the standpoint of others, and they come to realize that there is usually more than one side to the story. Eventually, children come to develop abstract notions of fairness; learning that rules should be judged relative to the circumstances. For example, they come to realize that whatever the rulebook says, it is fair to give a physically challenged child a head start in a foot race.

Lawrence Kohlberg (1969, 1983, 1984) extended Piaget's ideas about moral development, claiming to have identifed additional stages. Kohlberg presented hypothetical moral dilemmas to children and adults, asking them what they would do under specific circumstances and why they would do it. By evaluating their responses, Kohlberg was able to develop a complex scheme for moral development.

In Kohlberg's best-known study, subjects were told the story of "Heinz," a fictitious man who was unable to afford a drug that might save his wife from dying of cancer, since the druggist who developed the medication was unwilling to sell it except at a large profit. As the story unfolded, Heinz broke into the druggist's shop and stole the medication. Kohlberg asked his subjects what they would have done, emphasizing that there was no "right" or "wrong" answer.

According to Kohlberg, responses to this and other moral dilemmas suggest that there are three principal stages (and several substages) of moral development. During the **preconventional stage,** people *simply seek to avoid punishment or achieve some personal gain.* They go by the rules, simply trying to stay out of trouble. A person might support Heinz's theft on the grounds that his wife's death could create enormous problems; or oppose it on the grounds that Heinz might get caught and go to jail. Children are typically socialized into this rudimentary form of morality between ages 7 and 10.

During the **conventional stage,** the individual *seeks social approval.* The person is socialized into society's norms and values, and would feel guilty about violating them. Heinz's theft might be supported on the grounds that society would judge him callous if he let his wife die—or opposed because society would judge him a thief if he were caught. Children are socialized into this more developed form of morality at about age 10, and most people remain in this stage throughout their adult lives.

Finally, during the **postconventional stage,** the individual *invokes general, abstract notions of right and wrong.* Even though Heinz has broken the law, such law-breaking has to be weighed against the moral cost of sacrificing his wife's life. People at the highest levels of postconventional morality will go beyond social convention entirely, appealing to a higher set of abstract principles. For example, Heinz's theft might be supported on the grounds that adherence to the law is hardly worth a human life; or it might be opposed on the grounds that others more in need might be denied access to the scarce medicine. According to Kohlberg, very few adults ever reach this highest stage.

Critical Assessmant Although Piaget and Kohlberg have provided useful insights into how socialization contributes to different stages of cognitive and moral development, they have been criticized for drawing their conclusions from small-scale studies of largely middle class Europeans and Americans. It is extremely risky to generalize from such limited studies to other social groups and cultures. Still, the limited research that has been conducted outside of Europe and North America has found some support for Kohlberg's conclusions (Cortese, 1990; Gibbs, 1978; Simpson, 1974; Snarey, 1985).

Another criticism is that stage theories inevitably imply that later stages are somehow "higher" or "more advanced" than earlier stages. If the stages are based on the experiences of a particular group, then that group's "highest stage" becomes the yardstick by which all other groups are judged. This difficulty has led to some of the most telling criticisms of Piaget and Kohlberg, since most of the subjects they studied were male. This has led women scholars to argue that stages of development derived from male experience should not be applied to women.

Psychologist Carol Gilligan (1982; Gilligan et al., 1989), for example, argues that while men might be socialized to base their moral judgments on abstract principles of fairness and justice, women are socialized to base theirs on compassion and caring. This is partly because boys must learn to detach themselves from their mothers at an early age in order to form a male identity, while girls need not undergo such separation (Chodorow, 1978). As a consequence, Gilligan reasons, men learn to value detachment and impersonality, while women value attachment and intimacy. In the "Heinz" example, Gilligan's research showed that women were more concerned about how the decision would concretely impact the entire family, rather than with "higher" notions of abstract justice. Women therefore scored lower on Kohlberg's measure of moral development.

Gilligan's important criticisms of Kohlberg must not be taken to imply that there are natural differences in moral reasoning between men and women. Any differences that exist are due to socialization. Moreover, research based on Gilligan's ideas has found that men and women alike adhere to *both* care- and justice-based forms of moral reasoning, and that differences between the sexes are in fact small or nonexistent. In her effort to correct Kohlberg's onesided notions of moral reasoning, Gilligan may have contributed to stereotypes about differences between men and women (Tavris, 1993).

AGENTS OF SOCIALIZATION

Although socialization occurs throughout a person's lifetime, sociologists regard some sources of socialization to be especially important. These include family, schools, peer groups, workplaces, and the mass media (Figure 5.1).

The Family and Socialization

The family, a central institution in all societies, plays a key role in reproducing members' norms, values, and overall cultural understandings (Chapter 14). It is a primary group in which children are physically and emotionally dependent on adult members during the earliest years of their lives. As a result, the family is the first and usually foremost source of socialization in all societies.

In most societies children are raised in families consisting of blood-related parents and siblings. There are, however, important variations in the structure of family relations. In some cultures, for example, the mother's brother is the most important adult figure and

Figure 5.1   **Socialization: A lifelong process**

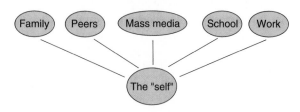

The family is the earliest and one of the most important sources of socialization, although once children reach age 2 or 3 their peers and the mass media (primarily television) have also become significant. Schooling soon becomes an important agent of socialization, in terms of not only formal curriculum but the "hidden curriculum" of society's norms and values. The workplace is the next important arena of socialization, although peers, family (both one's family of birth, and the family acquired through a long-term adult relationship) and mass media remain crucial throughout one's life.

is responsible for socializing his sister's children (Whiteford and Friedl, 1992). In other cultures "the family" consists of an extended group of people, including aunts, uncles, cousins and in-laws (Thompson, et al., 1992).

In the United States, family socialization differs somewhat depending on race and ethnicity (Starrels, 1992; Harrison et al., 1990). For example, African-American families typically share responsibility for child-rearing among a broader range of family members than do white families, reflecting a sense that children are the responsibility of extended families and even neighbors (Lubeck, 1985). This has also been found true of Afro-Caribbean immigrants (Ho, 1993), as well as the European-origin Amish of Pennsylvania.

Because of the diversity of U.S. culture, it is difficult to describe the "typical American family." As we shall see in Chapter 14, family patterns are changing rapidly, partly the result of a significant increase in divorce, separation, or remarriage (Brody et al., 1988; Cherlin et al., 1991; Crouter et al., 1984; DeLoache et al., 1987; Dornbusch et al., 1985; Emery, 1988; Furstenberg et al., 1983; Guidubaldi et al., 1987; Norton and Glick, 1986). The average number of children in a family has declined in the last 30 years. Mothers are much more likely to be employed at a full-time job out of the home than was the case in the past. More and more children are being raised by single parents as well. An increasing number of same-sex couples are raising children. Such changes directly affect the socialization process.

Child-rearing practices also tend to differ among

Conventional family roles are changing in the United States as women become more involved in the workforce and the struggle for equality of the sexes continues. In some families today, children are raised by "two moms," while in others a grandparent, single mother, or single father may do the parenting.

families of different social classes (see Chapter 8 for further discussion of social class). Parents whose jobs require them to be subservient to authority and follow orders without raising questions typically emphasize the importance of obedience and respect for authority within the family. On the other hand, parents whose work gives them considerable freedom to make their own decisions and be creative are likely to socialize their children into norms of creativity and spontaneity as well. Since most working-class jobs demand conformity while middle- and upper-middle-class jobs are more likely to emphasize independence, such workplace differences are strongly associated with social class (Kohn, 1965, 1976, 1977).

Yet it is important to bear in mind that these differences are more the result of the parents' experiences at work than social class itself. When middle- or upper-middle-class parents hold jobs that demand obedience, their socialization practices are likely to emphasize obedience; when working-class parents hold jobs that provide a measure of independence, their socialization practices will likewise emphasize independence. Given the fact that most of our waking hours are spent at work, it is not surprising that behavioral norms at work carry over into family life (Kohn, 1965, 1977).

The School and Socialization

Prior to the twentieth century most Americans lived and worked on family farms; school was far less important than family as an agent of socialization. Children in rural America started school relatively late in

life, spent fewer hours in the classroom, and were out of school for longer periods during the harvest and planting seasons. In the urbanized, industrialized world of today, however, the school and education have taken on a much more important role in socialization. Children often begin "schooling" when they enter day care or preschool at age two or three, and they stay in school for longer hours each day and for more days each year than was the case a hundred years ago (Coleman, 1992; West and Petrik, 1992).

The importance of education as socialization for entering the workforce has vastly increased as well. Few urban children learn skills from parents that will enable them to make a living. Such socialization extends well beyond such basic intellectual skills as reading, writing, and arithmetic. Today schools are also expected to teach manners, cleanliness, and respect for authority and to develop inquiring attitudes and basic social skills, although whether this is appropriate (indeed, whether it is possible) is a subject of considerable controversy today (Glaser, 1992). Indeed, some sociologists describe this as the **hidden curriculum,** *unspoken classroom socialization to norms, values, and roles* that a school provides along with the "official" curriculum (see Chapters 11 and 16).

Peers and Socialization

In American society adolescents spend far more time with their **peers,** *people of the same age, social standing, and class,* than they do with their family. This process of socialization begins with the first peer contacts

Over the past 100 years the school has become increasingly important in socialization. Children learn a hidden curriculum, consisting of prevailing cultural values, norms, and roles, as they acquire specific skills and knowledge. In this kindergarten classroom, students learn through bilingual education, reflecting the cultural diversity of the American population.

outside the family, when the child begins to play with other children during the first year of life. The intensity and importance of peer group interactions increases during adolescence and into adulthood (Sebald, 1992). So important are peer contacts that sociological theories often focus on this period of life to account for a wide variety of adult behavioral patterns such as career choices, ambition, and deviant behavior (Garden et al., 1986; Sebald, 1992; Sutherland, 1966; Cohen, 1958).

During adolescence, new language variations, new values, standards of dress, taste in popular culture (music, sports, and films), and new interpersonal allegiances develop. Children who learned at home to be polite often find other standards applied to their behavior by their adolescent peers. Rebellion against adult authority or, in the case of oppressed groups, against society at large, may become more important than the values learned at home.

From the point of view of socialization, not all peers are equal. Friendship groups constitute the most important peer associations that influence the socialization process. Because children cannot always choose their friends any more than their family, peer socialization depends in part on the friends they "happen to have." This, in turn, reflects circumstances over which children typically exercise little control, such as where they live or attend school. Of course, the attractiveness of some friends rather than others is also influenced by what children learn in their family, including their self-concept. In a study of college students, for example, it was found that people preferred to befriend others who

validated their self image through favorable responses (Chambliss, 1965).

People do not need to actually belong to a particular peer group for it to affect their socialization. Sociologists use the term **anticipatory socialization** to describe *adopting the behavior or standards of a group one hopes to emulate or join.* You may aspire to join a club, fraternity, or sorority, and so use its standards of dress or behavior as a guide to shape your own. Or you may train to become a better athlete in order to join your favorite team. A teenager may dress and act in ways that run counter to his family socialization, in order to be accepted by a particular group or "crowd." Anticipatory socialization is oriented toward future expectations, rather than to present experience.

Work and Socialization

For most Americans, the most immediate postadolescent experience with socialization occurs when they enter the workforce. We have previously noted that workplace norms calling for conformity or independence frequently extend into the home as well. Workforce expectations often differ substantially from those experienced in primary relationships such as the family and peer groups. While primary relations may develop around the workplace, the initial encounters are likely to be more impersonal.

People taking jobs for the first time realize that if they are to succeed, they often must balance opposing or contradictory role expectations. On the one hand, the employer will want them to work as hard as they can to produce as much as they can in as short a period of time as possible. In many work settings, people who work too long or too many hours can create similar work expectations that affect their coworkers. If this occurs, other employees will indicate rather clearly (and at times forcefully) that they expect eveybody to work at a comfortable pace. Such informal norms that develop in the workplace have long been known to be extremely powerful agents of socialization (Mayo, 1977; orig. 1933; Homans, 1950).

Employment also often involves socialization into the wider aspects of the social role itself, as well as learning the details of how to get the job done. Becoming a teacher, cook, factory worker, professor, lawyer, or thief involves learning the norms and values associated with each role, along with the specific skills the role requires. A professor is not only socialized into the proper way to lecture, grade papers, or give examinations but also into appropriate ways of dressing, interacting with other professors and administrators, and behaving in front of students.

The Mass Media and Socialization

In modern society, much of what we experience is filtered through the lens of **mass media,** *forms of communication that permit a one-way flow of information from a single source to a wide audience* (see Chapter 19 for further definition and an extended discussion). Newspapers, magazines, movies, radio, and television are all examples.

It is commonplace to read about the negative effects of the mass media on the socialization of children and teenagers. Children's television programs, for example, are blamed for everything from violence to the breakdown of cultural norms and values. Since the average American child spends from three to four hours a day in front of the television set, it seems reasonable to conclude that the content of television programming has a major effect on socialization. By the time the typical young American reaches 18, he or she will have seen 22,000 hours of television (Donnerstein et al., 1987, 1993; Huston et al., 1992; Staples and Jones, 1985.)

Television exposes children to definitions of reality and fantasy, to heroes and villains, role models and fools (Bierman, 1990). It informs children about how they can have fun and what they must buy to be happy. Children learn what it means to be a boy or girl, a man or woman. They learn about music and style, sex and violence (Donnerstein et al., 1993; Bierman, 1990; Huston et al., 1992; Tangney and Feshbach, 1988; Tracy, 1990; Waley et al., 1992).

During the past few years, the impact of media violence on children and young adults has received considerable attention. Five to six violent acts are depicted each hour on supposedly family-oriented prime-time television alone; all told, there are nearly two hundred such acts each week (Gerbner and Signorielli, 1990). By the time a child reaches junior high school, he or she has witnessed as many as 8,000 murders (Donnerstein et al., 1993). Three major media studies conducted during the past 20 years have all come to the same conclusion: media violence socializes many children, teenagers, and even adults into a greater acceptance of real-life violence. This is true of both males and females, whites and nonwhites (Donnerstein et al., 1993; Huston et al., 1992). Much media violence is directed against women, and a large body of research supports the conclusion that it helps socialize some men into condoning sexual violence, including rape (Donnerstein, Linz, and Penrod, 1987; Linz, Donnerstein, and Adams, 1989; Linz, Donnerstein, and Penrod, 1988; Linz, 1989).

GENDER SOCIALIZATION

An important aspect of socialization concerns the learning of culturally defined gender roles. We will discuss this in some detail in Chapter 11, but we can summarize that discussion in a few words: we are not born into our gender roles but rather learn them. Boys learn to be boys and girls learn to be girls, according to cultural norms and values. Such learning involves all the agents of socialization we have just reviewed: family, peers, schools, work, and media. By the time children have become teenagers, they have usually learned to do the sorts of things deemed appropriate for males or females in their culture.

Within the family, parents often hold stereotypical notions of how boys and girls should "be," and reinforce those behaviors in countless subtle and not-so-subtle ways (Marini, 1990; Katz, 1986; Jacklin et al., 1984; Ross and Taylor, 1989; Mosher et al., 1988; Siegal, 1987; Eccles et al., 1990). A girl may be treated as delicate or fragile, a boy as rough-and-tumble. Parents often serve as role models for "appropriate" gender roles, leading some sociologists to describe the home as a "gender factory" (Waite and Goldscheider, 1992).

Peer group gender socialization begins in young children's playgroups, where boys and girls characteristically engage in different activities reflecting cultural notions of gender-appropriate behavior (Cahill, 1989; Eisenhart and Holland, 1983). Although there is evidence that gender stereotyping is somewhat less pronounced among some racial or ethnic groups than

The role of television in socialization is not fully understood, although most sociologists agree it has a major impact. The average American child watches TV three to four hours daily, receiving images that convey information about gender roles, consumption, violence, and virtually every other aspect of social life.

others (for example, among African Americans; see Grant, 1983), such stereotyping is common throughout American culture.

Gender stereotypes are reproduced on television and other forms of the media, helping to socialize children from an early age. From children's cartoons to prime-time television, from advertisements to MTV, much television programming depicts males and females in stereotyped ways. Teenage girls, for example, are likely to be depicted as boy-crazy and obsessed with their looks; teenage boys as active and independent

(Cantor, 1987; Condry, 1989; Glazer, 1980; Silverstein et al., 1986; Steenland, 1988; Women's Institute for Freedom of the Press, 1986; see also Chapter 19).

Schooling is likely to reinforce differences in gender socialization in terms of not only peer group pressures, but also teachers' differing expectations for boys and girls (Best, 1983; Eisenhart and Holland, 1983; Sadker and Sadker, 1985). By the time children become teenagers, they are already likely to be "doing gender" in stereotypical ways. At this age, concerns over sexuality are likely to emerge, creating especially

Many families in the United States today consciously encourage nonstereotypical toys for their children in an effort to break down gender and other stereotypes. The little girl in this picture is playing with trucks, a toy traditionally reserved for boys. When girls play with trucks and boys with dolls, the assumption that girls will become homemakers and boys will become members of the paid workforce is subtly challenged.

strong pressures for conformity to stereotyped gender roles.

Gender socialization can be extremely difficult for adolescents who fail to conform to prevailing gender role expectations. Boys who lack athleticism, girls who grew up as "tomboys," or teenagers of either gender who focus on their schoolwork to the neglect of their social lives may experience exclusion by their classmates and peers. Some of the strongest norms regarding gender socialization in American society have to do with sexuality, which like all human behavior, is largely the result of socialization. Most children are socialized into norms of **heterosexuality,** *a sexual desire for persons of the opposite sex.* Those who grow up with orientations toward **homosexuality**—*sexual desire for persons of one's own sex*—can be cruelly stigmatized by their classmates and peers (see Box 5.2). We shall return to these issues in detail in Chapter 11.

TOTAL INSTITUTIONS AND RESOCIALIZATION

Although individuals typically play an active role in their own socialization, there is one setting where they experience little choice—**total institutions**—institutions *that isolate individuals from the rest of society in order to achieve administrative control over all aspects of their lives.* Examples include prisons, the military, mental hospitals, concentration camps, and sometimes even hospitals. The goal of total administrative control is achieved through rules that govern all aspects of daily life, subjecting inmates of such institutions to inflexible routines that are rigidly enforced by means of thoroughgoing staff supervision (Goffman, 1961).

A major purpose of total institutions is **resocialization,** the process of *altering an individual's personality through total control of his or her environment.* The first step in achieving resocialization is to break down

Box 5.2

Silenced Voices:

"Coming Out" As a Gay Man

Paul Monette is a 47-year-old homosexual writer and Person With AIDS (PWA). His autobiography *Becoming a Man: Half a Life Story,* which received the 1992 National Book Award for nonfiction, portrays his lifelong struggle to come to grips with the fact that he was "gay" (a term used to mean male homosexual). Monette grew up as a seemingly perfect example of the all-American upper-class male. He was born into a staunch New England Republican family, was a straight-A student at Phillips Andover Academy, won scholarships and honors at Yale University, and eventually became a successful poet and writer.

Yet throughout his life Monette experienced sexual desires for other men, which left him confused, unhappy, and ashamed. He somehow managed to keep all of this secret, and no one, not even his parents or his closest friends, knew that he was not a typical heterosexual male. Only when Monette met Roger Horwitz in 1975, his lover until Horwitz died of AIDS in 1987, was he able to accept himself as he was, to "come out of the closet" and put his shame behind him. Monette describes the conflicts of growing up gay in a heterosexual society in painful yet hopeful terms (Levine, 1992; Monette, 1993):

I was very witty and very charming and alone, alone, alone. . . . It doesn't matter how bright you are, or how well-educated you are, or how nice your people are. If you are in the closet and trying to pass [as a heterosexual] and telling that lie to yourself—and eventually you do tell it to yourself—your whole life becomes an act of ventriloquism. . . . Being gay is a central fact of my life; it is how I found love, and why I am an artist, finally. I might well have gone forward and written my gloomy poems and a novel or two of great irrelevancy. . . . but I've really come to glory in my difference.

I was given my heart back when I came out. . . . So I guess what I would say to my gay and lesbian brothers and sisters, especially to the gay and lesbian children of the next generation, and to all our friends and allies is: come out when you can. I know its not easy. But I would not give up what the last seventeen years of being out has meant to me. It has been a joyous experience, and that even includes the decade of AIDS.

the inmate's sense of self. Every aspect of life is monitored and controlled; all privacy is surrendered. Inmates are forced to give up all identification with the outside world on which their personalities are based. Shaved heads, standard prison uniforms, round-the-clock inspections, and constant humiliation and abuse contribute to this objective. In extreme situations, psychological and even physical torture may also be used.

Once the inmate has been "broken," the process of rebuilding the personality begins. Desirable behaviors are rewarded with small privileges; undesirable behaviors are severely punished. Since the goal is to change the inmate's attitudes as well as behavior, even a hint that he or she continues to harbor undesired ideas will result in disciplinary action.

How effective are total institutions at resocializing individuals? The answer partly depends on the methods employed, and partly on the individual. In one of the most extreme total institutions imaginable, Nazi concentration camps, some inmates came to identify with their guards and torturers, while others resisted resocialization until their deaths (Bettelheim, 1979). Inmates in U.S. prisons are often resocialized, although seldom to the norms of the wider society, as such "correctional" institutions would like to imply. Rather, they are often resocialized to the norms of other prisoners, with many emerging from prison more "hardened" in their criminal behavior than before.

Even when an institution is intially successful in its efforts at resocialization, when inmates return to their original social settings after release they often revert to earlier behavior. This provides further evidence that socialization is an ongoing process, one that continues throughout a person's lifetime as a consequence of specific social interactions.

LIFE-SPAN SOCIALIZATION

Although most theories of socialization focus on infancy and childhood, human beings do not stop growing and changing once they become adults. Yet it is only during the past quarter-century that social scientists began to take adult development seriously. As recently as 1968, for example, the *International Encyclopedia of Social Science* carried no entries under "adulthood" (Havighurst, 1973; Jordan, 1978).

Within the United States, there has been a growing interest in socialization throughout the life span, partly due to the fact that a rapidly growing proportion of the American population is elderly (see Chapter 12). For example, the number of Americans over 65 has doubled to nearly one in seven over the past 30 years (U.S. Bureau of the Census, 1991; Fosler et al., 1990. The "graying" of the American population has spawned a

small industry of popular books on the problems of adulthood, focusing on "midlife crisis" and other difficulties experienced by middle-aged (and, some sociologists would argue, mainly middle-class) Americans (Perun and Bielby, 1979; Giele, 1980).

There is much debate among social scientists concerning whether or not all people experience roughly the same stages of socialization as they grow older. Some theorists assume that physical changes associated with biological aging impact socialization in ways common to all cultures. Other theorists argue that biological age counts for relatively little in comparison with a person's specific experiences in life.

Perhaps the most influential stage theorist is Erik Erikson (1950, 1975, 1980, 1985), a German psychologist who compared childhood and adult development in a number of different cultures. Erikson's eight stages, along with the approximate ages at which they might typically occur in American culture, are as follows:

- Early infancy (birth–2 years)
- Later infancy (2–4)
- Early childhood (4–6)
- Middle and late childhood (6–early teens)
- Adolescence (early teens–early 20s)
- Young adulthood (early 20s–late 30s)
- Middle adulthood (late 30s–late 50s)
- Late adulthood (late 50s–death)

Although these stages cover the life span, they are heavily weighted toward the earlier years. As a result, a number of later theorists have focused on midlife or later years, adding stages of their own (Gould, 1975, 1978, 1980; Kegan, 1982; Levinson, 1978, 1980; Loevinger, 1980; Vaillant, 1977).

According to Erikson, each stage carries with it an overriding emotional conflict that must be addressed, before the individual can move on to the next stage. For example, Erickson claims that newborn infants must reconcile feelings of trust and mistrust in relationship to their mothers and others who provide nurturance. If infants encounter a warm, supportive environment, they become socialized into a trusting attitude that carries over throughout their lives. If they do not, they grow up mistrustful and suspicious. Or to take another example, adolescents are confronted with emotional conflicts stemming from their need to establish their own unique identities, while they are still subject to the powerful direct influence of parental socialization. If these conflicts are successfully resolved, adolescents will move into adulthood ready to choose a career and make independent life decisions. If not, they will grow up confused and uncertain about their role in life.

Although psychologists such as Erikson have tended to focus on age-related stages of life-span socialization, sociologists and social psychologists have emphasized the ways in which people are socialized in relationship to culturally influenced events in their lives (Hareven, 1982; Baltes and Nesselroade, 1984; Dannefer, 1984a, 1984b; Neugarten, 1970; Neugarten and Hagestad, 1976). Sociologists in particular have tended to downplay the impact of biological aging, while focusing on the way a particular culture constructs age-appropriate experiences (see Chapter 12).

In American culture, work, marriage, and parenting are among the most important experiences that shape socialization over the life course. Insofar as people differ in these experiences, their life-span socialization will differ as well. Socialization is therefore seen as an active process in which people shape their behavior according to their growing understanding of their life experiences (Kegan, 1982).

The following groupings are extremely rough guides to socialization in the United States today. Bear in mind that these are not biologically determined stages, but instead emphasize the social experiences typically associated with each grouping. Individuals are, of course, seldom "typical." A child may be socialized to compete as an adult chess grandmaster, while a 65-year-old may remarry, begin a second career, and decide to take up competitive sports.

Childhood corresponds to the *early, formative years that occur before the sexual changes associated with puberty.* This is typically a period of a high degree of dependency on parents and family, although such dependency varies enormously between societies and even subcultures within a single society. Some children may lead highly protected and insulated lives, while others grow up "streetwise," exposed to harsh adult conditions at an early age. In some places children may be expected to work on farms or in factories; even in the United States, child labor in "sweatshops" still occurs. As we have already noted, in the United States television, movies, and other forms of mass media today can expose very young children to situations once deemed appropriate only for adults.

Adolescence refers to the *teen years during which children mature sexually and begin to develop their own identities.* In American society this is likely to be a turbulent time, during which teenagers often come into conflict with their parents. Although sexual maturation and identity-formation occur in all societies, the notion of a "second childhood" termed "adolescence" is a relatively new invention of modern industrial society (Bakan, 1971). In most societies throughout human history, childhood led more or less directly into adult responsibilities such as work, early marriage, and child-rearing. During the early days of European and American industrialization children entered factories by ages 12 to 14; in many poorer countries today, fac-

tory work beginning at ages 15 or 16 is common (see Chapter 9). In the United States, working-class children experience a briefer adolescence than middle-class children, since many go directly to work after finishing high school.

Adulthood consists of *the years during which individuals develop their own careers, form families, and establish a life independent from their parents.* During the early years of adulthood, people often set goals for their lives, develop intimate personal relationships, form a family, and embark on a career. Some women may experience a conflict between their own professional ambitions and parental and peer expectations that they conform to more stereotypically feminine roles. Later adulthood often involves taking stock of one's life, including coming to grips with unfulfilled expectations. Adults who have children often have to redefine their roles once their children have grown. While this can be especially difficult for women, a growing number of women today are choosing to reen-

In Madagascar, an island off the east coast of Africa, dead ancestors are wrapped and rewrapped in traditional ceremonies. Learning to cope with death is a part of socialization in all societies, although some societies confront death more openly and directly than others. How would you expect the attitude toward death among the people of Madagascar to differ from your own? How are we socialized to view death in our society?

ter the workforce and develop careers later in life (U.S. Bureau of the Census, 1991).

Finally, **old age** includes *the years when one confronts the possibility of disengaging from important social roles, along with the realistic possibility of one's own death.* The age at which this occurs can vary significantly, with a growing number of elderly people leading active and economically productive lives well into their eighties or later. Theorists once argued that a primary task of old age is to disengage from roles and relationships that had long provided an important sense of one's own identity (Cumming and Henry, 1961). Today, however, there is a greater understanding that the elderly and society alike benefit when older people remain active and engaged as long as possible (Birren and Bengston, 1988; Butler et al., 1980; Neugarten, 1977; Rowe and Kahn, 1987).

Nonetheless, at some age virtually all people are forced to confront their own mortality. For those who are willing and able to do so, the final socialization consists of preparation for the inevitability of death (Kubler-Ross, 1969).

SOCIALIZATION AND SOCIAL INTERACTION

Socialization occurs primarily through social interaction, a seemingly simple phenomenon in which spoken words, gestures, body language, and other subtle cues come together in complex ways to create human communication. The task of the sociologist is to view such routine, everyday interaction as problemmatic—to try to identify the ways in which it occurs and the norms that make it possible.

Although all cultures socialize their members into unspoken norms concerning body positioning, eye contact, how close they can appropriately position themselves to friends or strangers, and so forth, socialization into norms governing the physical use of space varies enormously between cultures. In U.S. culture, for example, people avoid standing closer than a couple of feet from one another unless they share an intimate relationship (Hall, 1973). This unspoken norm applies with greater force to males than to females, since casual bodily contact is generally considered to be less acceptable among men than it is among women. Men are typically socialized to shun such displays of intimacy as walking arm-in-arm, while the same is not true of women. Yet although two men touching one another's buttocks might raise some eyebrows on Main Street America, "butt slapping" is a common display of manliness on the basketball court or football field. In the African country of Nigeria, on the other hand, it is typical for men walking together who are close friends or relatives to hold hands.

In American society, overt physical displays of affection among men are generally taboo. Yet the role of male athlete includes the expectation that men will engage in "butt slapping" or hugging during emotional moments. Perhaps because male athletes epitomize masculinity, they are partially excused from behaving in ways that might be culturally interpreted as too feminine for other men. Such notions of masculinity are changing in American society today.

In general, social interaction requires careful conformity to social convention. Thomas Scheff (1966) terms the fundamental rules that govern everyday social interaction **residual norms,** in that they *are simply there in the background—unspoken, unacknowledged, and yet central to competent behavior.* In fact, according to Scheff, the violation of such residual norms is generally interpreted as a sure sign that the person is "abnormal," perhaps even dangerously "crazy." A person in a crowded elevator who persists in loud, face-to-face conversations with strangers will be quickly avoided once the doors open, as will disheveled homeless people walking down the street muttering to themselves.

Erving Goffman and the Dramaturgical Approach

Erving Goffman (1961, 1963, 1967, 1972, 1973) drew on the ideas of George Herbert Mead and symbolic interactionism to study the social norms that govern interaction. Goffman employed what he termed the **dramaturgical approach,** the *study of social interaction as if it were governed by the norms of theatrical performance.* According to Goffman, much like actors on a stage, people are concerned with the **presentation of self**—the *creation of favorable impressions in the minds of others.* Such a concern with "impression management" occurs because, as Mead had argued, individuals are socialized to seek the esteem of others—to care what other people think. This, in turn, leads to social conformity, and as a consequence to social stability.

As people interact, they are constantly monitoring themselves and one another, looking for clues concerning how they are "coming across." This ongoing effort results in a continual realignment of individual actions, as people endlessly refit their roles together in a vast joint enterprise enabling society to run relatively smoothly. Such a constant alertness and preoccupation with image may seem exhausting, and Goffman identifies a number of conventions that ease the burden of performance. For example, he argues that people divide their interactions into different "regions," based on their perceived need to perform. **Frontstage** refers to the *places where they have to perform*—for example, answering a question in class, waiting on tables in a restaurant, asking for a date, going for a job interview, or even engaging in conversation with friends if the friendships are not secure. **Backstage** refers to the *places where they can avoid performance and "be themselves"*—for example, at home or with friends among whom they are truly comfortable.

People are also socialized to maintain interaction through norms that govern how much attention they should pay to one another. An example is the norm of **civil attention,** a *polite signal that they are conscious of another person's performance.* In American culture, this includes such behaviors as nodding one's head in apparent agreement, saying "uh huh" or "that's interesting," or responding with a question or comment when the conversation slows. Civil attention is one of the polite conventions of society that contributes to smoothly flowing social interaction, thereby reaffirming that the actors are competent in playing their social roles. There is some evidence that women are more strongly socialized to paying such civil attention than are men, in what has been characterized as "women's work in interaction" (Fishman, 1978).

Another common norm that Americans observe is **civil inattention,** a *polite signal that they are aware of another person's presence without indicating that they are also aware of his or her inappropriate or embarrassing behavior.* This enables others to "save face" and continue to play their roles. For example, at the conclusion of the U.S. Senate Hearing on Janet Reno's nomination for U.S. Attorney General, 85-year-old

Senator Strom Thurmond congratulated Ms. Reno on being appointed justice of the U.S. Supreme Court. Since Attorney General and Supreme court justice are two entirely different positions, there was a stunned moment of silence, until the chairperson continued the hearings without noting the senator's mistake. Indeed, no one mentioned this momentary lapse, and it received little press coverage.

Ethnomethodology and Conversation Analysis

It should be evident that routine, day-to-day conversations are among the most important building blocks of symbolic interaction and therefore the foundation of social institutions and ultimately of society itself. Something as fundamental to social structure as gender roles is learned through socialization into routine talk early in life, and continually reproduced through conversation.

Ethnomethodology

A branch of sociology concerned with understanding the fundamentals of social interaction is called **ethnomethodology**—literally, *the body of common-sense knowledge and procedures by which ordinary members of society make sense of their social circumstances and interactions.* ("Ethno" refers to "folk" or ordinary people; "methodology" to the methods they use to govern interaction—as distinct from the methods used by sociologists to study them.) Ethnomethodology emerged in the work of Harold Garfinkel (1963, 1985) in the early 1960s. It was influenced by symbolic interactionism on the one hand, and sociologists who were concerned with larger questions of social structure on the other (Heritage, 1989).

Garfinkel believed it was important to understand exactly what goes on in particular interactions, since even the most seemingly unambiguous interactions can involve multiple activities whose meanings depend on the context in which they occur. Garfinkel used the term **indexicality** to refer to the notion that *the meaning of any particular action or event depends on its context.* ("Indexicality" means "indicator of" some underlying context.) Clearly, social life would be impossible unless most people were socialized to assign meanings in similar ways. Garfinkel sought to understand how this is accomplished by studying the specific contexts of concrete social interactions.

Garfinkel reasoned that people develop an interpretation of what is happening by seeing a pattern emerge out of particular events. The pattern, in turn, enables them to interpret the meaning of the underlying events themselves. Garfinkel termed this the **documentary method of interpretation,** a theory stating that *peo-*

ple's interpretation of particular events and actions serves to "document" the presumed existence of an underlying pattern. This is dramatically illustrated by a common experience we have all had: we arrive at some point in a conversation, thinking that we have understood what was being said, only to discover through our partner's next remark that we have totally misunderstood all along. Suddenly, all the things said up to that point (the particulars of the conversation) take on a different meaning as we grasp them in a different context.

Garfinkel believed that all languages and cultures hold their members accountable for using procedures that enable people to make sense out of talk. Such procedures are not optional; people take it as their right to expect others to render what they say as intelligible, coherent, and understandable. Furthermore, he argued that such sense-making procedures are even more fundamental than cultural norms, since without such procedures talk and hence culture would not be possible. Because of the importance of sense-making procedures that govern conversations, another field emerged out of ethnomethodology that focused on talk itself: conversation analysis.

Conversation Analysis

The field of **conversation analysis** builds on the work of Garfinkel and other ethnomethodologists (Maynard and Clayman, 1991; Sacks, 1989, 1992; Sacks, Schegloff, and Jefferson, 1974; Schegloff, 1968, 1986, 1987, 1989, 1990, 1991). It is concerned with *how participants in social interaction produce and recognize coherent action on actual occasions.* Moreover, it assumes that people do this through specific conversational procedures that can be identified through careful research. And it accepts Garfinkel's finding that people hold one another morally accountable for the use of these procedures.

The term "conversation" must be broadly construed to include virtually any form of concrete human interaction, from routine "trivial" talk to emergency telephone calls to congressional hearings and court proceedings. Recent studies are particularly concerned with exploiting the potential of audio and video recordings of naturally occurring interaction (for example, see Heritage and Greatbatch, 1991; Hopper, 1991; Schegloff, 1989; Whalen and Zimmerman, 1987, 1990; Zimmerman, 1984, 1992).

Conversation analysis research has shown that social interaction is not simply a random succession of events. Participants in conversations actively construct their actions so as to fit one another in order to form a coherent sequence. One way in which conversations are sequentially organized by participants is through **turn-taking,** *specific procedures that enable utterances to be understood as responsive to earlier turns.*

Conversations are much more than the words that are spoken. How close a person sits beside another, hand gestures, the degree of eye contact—all convey meaning and are an integral part of the communication taking place. These Moroccan men understand cues that an American observer would have to learn in order to successfully communicate in their culture.

This is accomplished by using conversational procedures that indicate a person has understood the earlier turn and is ready to proceed to the next step. In general, utterances are usually regarded as responsive to the immediately preceding turn. For example, by responding "fine" to the question "how are you," you show that you have understood the previous question and are ready to move ahead in the conversation. A response such as "what do you mean" or "green" is not conventionally heard as indicating that you have understood the previous question and so is likely to lead to conversational breakdown. Conversational analysts have identified a number of techniques that are commonly used to repair such breakdowns.

While conversation analysis originally focused exclusively on the techniques people use to organize their conversations in coherent sequences, more recent research has emphasized the impact of the larger social structure on conversations as well (Wilson, 1991). Special attention has been given to the conversational use of power, whether it be the power of the dispatcher over

Box 5.3

Globalization

Changing Gender Roles in Japan

Gender relations in Japan are currently undergoing significant changes, partly as a result of Japan's emerging role as a global economic power. In traditional Japanese culture, men looked for a "good cook and a wise mother," but fewer and fewer Japanese women are willing to play these roles; many women do not want to give up their jobs and become housewives after marriage. (The Japanese word for wife, *kanai,* literally means "inside the house.") Japan's economy, propelled by its growing ability to sell products such as cars and electronics throughout the world, has contributed to a shortage of workers. This, in turn, has created new opportunities for Japanese women. Japanese women have become increasingly educated, and they have entered the workforce and acquired a degree of economic independence and assertiveness unknown in previous Japanese history. Women now surpass men in educational attainment, insist on having independent careers, marry later in life, seek more divorces, and have smaller families. Between 1975 and 1990, the proportion of unmarried women between 25 and 29 years old nearly doubled, from 21 percent to 40 percent, leading Kiyoko Yoshihiro, a Japanese feminist, to

claim that Japan is "at a turning point in the power balance between the sexes."

Japanese women are reportedly also much more selective in choosing a mate, demanding of their suitors the so-called "three highs:" high salary ($35,000 or more), high education (university degree, at a mimimum), and physical height (at least 5 feet 7 inches)! A leading women's magazine, *Nikkei Woman,* urged its female readers to accept nothing less than "goat man"—someone like the goat who is gentle but also strong and intelligent, has wide-ranging interests, and is willing to share household chores and child care with his mate. This is not to belie the fact that most Japanese women (like their American counterparts) still have less desirable jobs than men: they often serve the tea, work as secretaries, and earn half of what men earn. According to government statistics, Japanese women with jobs still somehow manage to spend an average of 4 hours and 21 minutes daily on housework, child care, and shopping—compared with 8 minutes for Japanese men. Nonetheless, it seems clear that in Japan, changes in a global role go hand-in-hand with changes in the traditional roles of men and women (Watanabe, 1992).

---

the caller in emergency phone calls (Whalen and Zimmerman, 1987; Whalen, Zimmerman, and Whalen, 1990; Zimmerman, 1984, 1992), in governmental hearings (Molotch and Boden, 1985), or the power exercised by men in male-female interactions (Fishman, 1978; Campbell et al., 1992; West, 1979; West and Zimmerman, 1977, 1983; Zimmerman and West, 1975, 1980).

GLOBALIZATION AND SOCIALIZATION

In modern society, the specialized knowledge originally developed by social scientists often feeds back into the more popular understandings of everyday life (Giddens, 1990). This is especially true in the area of socialization, where "pop psychology" self-help books

abound. A number of the most important theorists reviewed in this chapter, including Freud, Piaget, and Erikson, developed their ideas in Europe. These ideas, in turn, have been debated and refined around the world, subsequently contributing to virtually all of the theorists reviewed in this chapter.

While few American parents may have ever delved into Freud's writings, Freudian notions regarding breast-feeding, toilet training, and parental responsibility for the mental health of their children have long been a part of popular culture. Although Piaget has never become a household word, the Swiss psychologist nonetheless contributed enormously to theories about the appropriate age at which children should learn different cognitive skills and moral reasoning—theories that have found their way into scores of popular books on child psychology, not to mention *Sesame Street.*

We needn't turn to theories of socialization to see the impact of globalization; most fairy tales and folk heroes used to socialize American children into appropriate norms and values are foreign in origin as well. Santa Claus is derived from a Scandanavian fairy tale, while the Danish writer Hans Christian Andersen's "ugly duckling" and "little mermaid" have carried their moral messages to generations of American chidlren. Immigrants from Latin America or Asia bring with them their own stories and fairy tales with which to socialize their children, some of which will find their way into the wider culture. At the same time, global television today carries images from American culture to virtually every place on earth, where their impact on socialization and popular culture has yet to be assessed (Chapter 19).

One issue facing parents today is how to best socialize their children for the roles they will play in the globalized economy of the twenty-first century (Lotito, 1993). As we shall see in Chapter 15, a growing number of occupations require global travel, along with the ability to get along in a wide variety of different cultures. The challenge of socializing employees to working and living abroad has become a top priority of small businesses as well as large corporations (Oster, 1993). The socialization experienced as a result of living abroad can help to overcome ethnocentrism; college "study abroad" programs often provide an unparalleled opportunity for students to avail themselves of such socialization experiences.

We began this chapter with an example of how Japanese middle school children are socialized to distinctly Japanese cultural norms and values. Yet globalization today is having a significant impact on Japanese culture. In terms of gender socialization, for example, the traditional roles of Japanese women appear to be changing. Economic globalization has fueled the growth of the Japanese economy, drawing more and more women into the workforce. As increasing numbers of Japanese women work outside the home, they are socialized into far more independent and assertive roles than they previously experienced. Such socialization is reinforced by the increasing educational attainment of Japanese women, which now exceeds that of Japanese men (Box 5.3). In Japan, as elsewhere in the world, globalization holds the promise of changing gender roles, norms, and values.

C H A P T E R   S U M M A R Y

1. **Socialization** is a lifelong, active process through which human beings learn the customs, behaviors, roles, statuses, and ideas of their culture.

2. What we often refer to as "human nature" is in fact learned through socialization. Sociologists argue that human behavior is not determined biologically but is rather developed through **social interaction.**

3. Although socialization is a lifelong process, some theories emphasize the importance of the early years, while others argue that socialization remains important throughout the **life course.** The theories of Sigmund Freud and Jean Piaget are examples of the former; those of George Herbert Mead and Lawrence Kohlberg are examples of the latter.

4. According to Mead, children acquire a sense of social norms and values through **symbolic interaction** with others, including the other children with whom they play.

5. Building on the ideas of Jean Piaget, Lawrence Kohlberg argued that a person's sense of morality develops through different stages, from extreme **egocentricism** to the stage in which moral decisions are based on abstract principles.

6. Sociologists have described a number of key **agents of socialization.** One's immediate family provides the earliest and typically most important source of socialization, but peers, school, work, and the mass media all play a significant role.

7. There is some evidence that socialization differs by social class, with middle-class families placing a somewhat higher emphasis on independence and working-class families emphasizing conformity. These class differences, in turn, reflect corresponding workplace differences associated with social class.

8. All cultures have **tacit** or **unspoken norms** governing social interaction, including body placement and positioning and appropriate modes of public physical contact. Violation of these norms constitutes a form of **residual rule-breaking,** which provides a sign that the rule-breaker is somehow "abnormal" with respect to social norms.

9. According to Erving Goffman's **dramaturgical approach,** we are all actors concerned with the presentation of self in social interaction. In our efforts to maintain self-esteem, we are socialized to act in

culturally appropriate ways, thereby helping to ensure a degree of social conformity.

10. **Ethnomethodology** is the study of people's routine ways of interacting; it seeks to understand the basic nature of social organization at its most micro level.

11. **Conversation analysis,** which builds on ethnomethodology, is concerned with the ways in which participants in social interaction produce and recognize coherent action, studying the procedures by which they engage in **turn-taking,** fit their interactions together in close-ordered exchanges, and repair interactions when they break down.

12. Globalization changes the nature of socialization in two different ways. First, it contributes to the spread of diverse cultural understandings about how children should be raised and people should behave. Second, it results in the spread of scientific understandings about human development, which in turn affects popular understandings about how children should best be raised.

QUESTIONS FOR DISCUSSION

1. How can you account for the fact that the process of socialization creates a great deal of uniformity among people sharing the same culture, yet individual differences remain?

2. According to the different theories of socialization, how do people in a particular society acquire their sense of self, and how do they change?

3. Which is the most important agent of socialization in American culture? In what ways is this changing today?

4. Do all children in all cultures go through the same stages of social development? Discuss the arguments for and against such a position.

5. How is social structure "accomplished" in routine social interaction, such as ordinary conversations? Discuss this with reference to such things as power differences or gender roles.

6. In what ways might globalization contribute to a convergence in socialization practices throughout the world? In what ways might it contribute to greater diversity?

KEY TERMS

adolescence: The teen years, during which children mature sexually and begin to develop their own identities.

adulthood: The years during which individuals develop their own careers, form families, and establish a life independent from their parents.

adult stage: According to George Herbert Mead, the stage at which individuals learn to take on the role of the "generalized other."

anticipatory socialization: Adopting the behavior or standards of a group one hopes to emulate or join.

backstage: According to Erving Goffman, the places where people can avoid performance and "be themselves."

behaviorism: A psychological approach to socialization that emphasizes the effect of rewards and punishments on observable human behavior.

childhood: The early, formative years that occur before the sexual changes associated with puberty.

civil attention: According to Erving Goffman, a polite signal that one is conscious of another person's performance.

civil inattention: According to Erving Goffman, a polite signal that one is aware of another person's presence, without indicating that one is also aware of his or her inappropriate or embarrassing behavior.

cognitive development: A theory, developed by Jean Piaget, that the ability to make logical decisions increases as a person grows older.

conventional stage: According to Lawrence Kohlberg, the stage of moral development at which the individual seeks social approval in making moral decisions.

conversation analysis: A theory, based on the work of Harold Garfinkel and other ethnomethodologists, that studies how participants in social interaction produce and recognize coherent action on actual occasions.

documentary method of interpretation: The theory, developed by Garfinkel, that people's interpretation of particular events and actions serves to "document" the presumed existence of an underlying pattern.

dramaturgical approach: A theory of social interaction, developed by Erving Goffman, that regards interaction as if it were governed by the norms of theatrical performance.

ego: According to Freud, the part of the mind that is the "self," the core of what is regarded as a person's unique personality.

egocentricism: The theory that children experience the world as if it were entirely centered on themselves.

ethnomethodology: The body of common-sense knowledge and procedures by which ordinary members of society make sense of their social circumstances and interactions; also refers to the theory, developed by Harold Garfinkel, that studies such procedures

frontstage: According to Erving Goffman, the places where a person has to perform.

game stage: According to George Herbert Mead, the stage at which children learn to take on the role of multiple other people.

generalized other: According to the theories of George Herbert Mead, the sense we have that society has general norms and values by which we evaluate ourselves.

heterosexuality: A sexual desire for persons of the opposite sex.

hidden curriculum: An unspoken socialization to norms, values, and roles that a school provides along with the "official" curriculum.

homosexuality: A sexual desire for persons of the same sex.

I: In the interactionist theories of George Herbert Mead, the part of the self that refers to the impulse to act; it is creative, innovative, unthinking, and largely unpredictable.

id: According to Freud, the part of the mind that is the repository of basic biological drives and needs.

indexicality: The notion, developed by Harold Garfinkel, that the meaning of any particular action or event depends on its context.

looking-glass self: The theory, developed by Charles Horton Cooley, that our self-image results from how we interpret other peoples' views of ourselves.

mass media: Forms of communication that permit a one-way flow of information from a single source to a wide audience.

me: In the interactionist theories of George Herbert Mead, the part of the self that refers to the image we believe others hold of us as we act, that is, the looking-glass part of the self through which we see ourselves as others see us.

moral development: A theory, developed by Jean Piaget and Lawrence Kohlberg, that people at different ages learn to act according to abstract ideas about justice or fairness.

old age: The years when we confront the possibility of disengaging from important social roles, along with the realistic possibility of our own death.

particular others: According to the theories of George Herbert Mead, the specific people who are important in our lives, whose views are important in our self evalutations.

peers: People of the same age, social standing, and class.

play stage: According to George Herbert Mead, the developmental stage during which children learn to take the attitude of the other people with whom they interact.

postconventional stage: According to Lawrence Kohlberg, the stage of moral development at which the individual invokes general, abstract notions of right and wrong in making moral decisions.

preconventional stage: According to Lawrence Kohlberg, the stage of moral development at which the individual simply seeks to avoid punishment or achieve some personal gain in making moral decisions.

preparatory stage: According to George Herbert Mead, the developmental stage in which children relate to the world as though they are the center of the universe.

presentation of self: According to Erving Goffman, the constant effort to create favorable impressions in the minds of others during social interaction.

primary group: A group that is characterized by intense positive and negative emotional ties, face-to-face interaction, intimacy, and a strong, enduring sense of commitment. (The concept originated with Charles Horton Cooley.)

psychoanalysis: An approach to the study of human psychology that emphasizes the complex reasoning processes of the human mind; developed by Sigmund Freud.

reality principle: According to Freud, the assumption that the members of any society renounce a substantial part of their desire for immediate pleasure in order to do the kind of work that is necessary for the society to operate smoothly.

reference group: A group that provides standards for judging our attitudes or behaviors.

residual norms: According to Thomas Scheff, norms that are simply there in the background—unspoken, unacknowledged, and yet central to competent behavior.

resocialization: According to Erving Goffman, the process of altering an individual's personality through total control of his or her environment, usually within a *total institution.*

role-taking: The ability to take the role of others in interaction.

secondary group: A group that is large, impersonal, and often involves fleeting relationships.

social learning: The learning that occurs from observing and imitating others.

socialization: The lifelong process through which people learn the values, norms, and roles of their culture, and thereby develop their sense of self.

superego: According to Freud, the part of the mind that consists of the values and norms of society, insofar as they are internalized by the individual.

total institution: According to Erving Goffman, an institution that isolates individuals from the rest of society in order to achieve administrative control over all aspects of their lives.

turn-taking: According to the theory of conversational analysis, specific procedures that enable utterances to be understood as responsive to earlier turns.

RECOMMENDED FOR FURTHER READING

Gilligan, Carol. (1982). *In a Different Voice: Psychological Theory and Women's Development.* Cambridge: Harvard University Press.

Gilligan reviews different theories of social development, arguing that most have a built-in bias toward norms and values associated with male socialization in American culture.

Goffman, Erving. (1973). *The Presentation of Self in Everyday Life,* New York: Doubleday.

An influential work that employs the dramaturgical metaphor to analyze how people seek to manipulate and control their social world through their presentation of self to others.

Mead, George Herbert. (1934). *Mind, Self, and Society,* Chicago: University of Chicago Press.

Some of the most important lectures and writings of George Herbert Mead, one of the most influential theorists on socialization.

Rymer, Russ. (1993). *Genie: An Abused Child's Flight from Silence.* New York: HarperCollins.

A fascinating and well-researched case of a child raised in almost complete isolation. Particularly interesting because the author raises the ethical issues implicit in Genie's treatment by the social scientists engaged in rehabilitating and studying her.

Groups and Organizations

CHAPTER OUTLINE

THINGS TO LOOK FOR

1. What types of groups do sociologists study, and how do those groups affect the ways in which we interact with one another?
2. According to sociological theory, what are the different types of leadership, and how are they exercised in modern society?
3. What distinguishes bureaucracies from other types of organization? What are their advantages and disadvantages?
4. What new types of organization are emerging in the face of globalization today?

INTRODUCTION

The opening chords of "Nippon Denki Corporate Anthem" washed over a sea of earnest, eager young faces and 1,400 people in dark business suits rose to join in a vigorous rendition of what will henceforth be their own company song: "To build a culture of communication shall be our destiny! Nippon, Nippon, Nippon Den-ki!"

There followed uplifting pep talks from the chairman and president, the distribution of company lapel pins and names cards and finally the recital of the corporate pledge that made the assembled young people official employees of the computer and electronics giant known here as Nippon Denki K.K. (Nippon Electric Corporation) and around the world by its English initials, NEC.

At NEC and hundreds of other companies all over Japan, April 1 is the day for the *nyushashiki,* or entering-the-company ceremony. Roughly one million new graduates who finished high school or college last month started jobs that will last, in most cases, for the rest of their lives. . . . The employees will do what the company orders, and the company will watch out for the employees in good times and bad, virtually guaranteeing that these workers will never face a layoff and will not be fired for anything short of outright crime.

They will all wear their NEC lapel pins, use NEC health centers, vacation at NEC resorts, play on NEC sports teams and join the NEC company union. They will all have accounts at the Sumitomo Bank, because NEC is a member of the Sumitomo *keiretsu,* or corporate grouping.

In short, they will belong to NEC. (Reid, 1992).

In modern society much of our time is spent in groups and organizations. While sociologists have recognized the importance of this for over a century, during the past fifty years there has been a vast increase in their scientific study (Freeman, 1982; Aldrich and Marsden, 1988). As we approach the twenty-first century, the nature of groups and organizations appears to be changing, because of both globalization and the new information technologies. Important lessons can be learned about these changes by studying groups and organizations from other cultures.

Japanese business organizations such as Nippon Electric Corporation (NEC) have proved especially interesting to American scholars, since they are relatively successful in mobilizing their members to work hard and remain loyal. Yet as the above example indicates, by American standards Japanese organizations would seem rather strange. Many Japanese workers begin their lifelong affiliation with a single corporation by participating in a national "entering-the-company" ceremony which takes place every year on April 1. The new employees learn the corporate anthem, proper bowing techniques, deferential behavior toward superiors, company dress codes, business card exchange rituals, and even appropriate ways to serve tea. None of this would occur in an American corporation, where employees are provided with no such training, no lifetime job guarantees, and no expectations of company loyalty or proper etiquette.

The difference between Japanese and American business organizations is but one example of the ways in which organizations differ from one another. Sociology seeks to explain such differences, and the ways in which they impact our lives. Before we can examine organizations, however, it is necessary to look at the primary unit on which all organizations are built—the social group.

SOCIAL GROUPS

Sociology provides us with the insight that virtually everything of importance in our lives occurs through some type of social group. In Chapter 4 we defined a **social group** as *a collection of people who regularly interact with one another on the basis of shared expectations concerning behavior, and who share a sense of common identity.* People who belong to the same group identify with each other, expect each other to conform to certain ways of thinking and acting, and recognize the boundaries that separate them from others. Groups range in size from two people (such as roommates or a married couple) to large formal organizations (such as universities or corporations). They are distinguished by a sense of membership or belonging.

Groups are important sources of our values and

norms. As we saw in the preceding chapter, they can be powerful agents of socialization. Our ways of thinking and acting are shaped by our interaction with others, whether that occurs in an intimate two-person group or a large bureaucratic organization. We may sometimes feel that we are alone, but we are born into a family, hang out with groups of friends, receive our formal education in schools, play team sports, belong to churches or synagogues or mosques, work in offices or stores or factories, and in fact seldom find ourselves far away from one or another group or organization. Like all people everywhere, we are organizational junkies (Aldrich and Marsden, 1988).

Social groups can be distinguished from **social aggregates,** *simple collections of people who happen to be together in a particular location at a certain time but do not significantly interact or identify with one another.* People in crowds, or waiting for a bus, or sunbathing on a beach are said to be aggregates. Social groups also differ from **social categories,** *groupings that share some common characteristic but do not necessarily interact or identify with one another.* Examples include people of the same age, gender, race, or income group. Although social categories are often used in everyday life as well as by sociologists to explain how people think and act, they should not be confused with group membership.

The "sense of belonging" that characterizes social groups has led sociologists to further distinguish ingroups from outgroups. An **ingroup** is *a group toward which one feels particular loyalty and respect.* An **outgroup** is the opposite, *a group toward which one feels antagonism and contempt.* Unfortunately, one's sense

Figure 6.1   Learning to Bow from a Japanese Textbook for New Employees

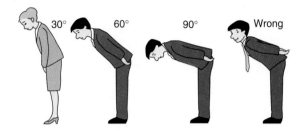

In Japan new company employees are taught the right way to bow: 30 degrees for a greeting at a reception, 60 degrees for a "normal" bow, and 90 degrees for making an apology. Women should cross hands in front when bowing. Employees should not raise their heads or smile.

of belonging to an ingroup often depends on finding an appropriate outgroup to scorn or hate (Sartre, 1965; orig. 1948). Racist skinhead groups, France's National Front, European and American Nazis and the Ku Klux Klan identify themselves as belonging to a "superior" white race by hating "inferior" Jews, Catholics, African Americans, or homosexuals. Similarly, the Serbian notion of "ethnic cleansing" in the former Yugoslavia is based on their ingroup belief that they are superior to other despised outgroups (such as Muslims) and therefore are entitled to use any means necessary to drive outgroup members from their lands. Less serious but

Workers and corporation executives develop different organizational practices depending on their society. Japanese workers at the Sumitomo Metal Works pray at the company shrine for their own and other workers' safety. Sociological research suggests that Japanese workers are more loyal to and proud of their companies than American workers, and Japanese companies are more loyal to their workers as well.

The Ku Klux Klan (KKK), a racist organization espousing white supremacy, marches in Houston, Texas, while people opposing their views protest. KKK members wear distinctive garb, one way of defining themselves as an ingroup *in opposition to the racial and religious minorities they regard as* outgroups.

closer to home, the members of a fraternity or sorority may bolster their own feelings of superiority by scorning their long-time rivals. To some extent, almost all people occasionally use ingroup/outgroup imagery to define their assumed strengths vis-a-vis some other group's presumed weaknesses.

Primary and Secondary Groups

Since groups differ greatly in how intensely they are experienced by their members, sociologists have made a fundamental distinction between primary and secondary groups. **Primary groups** are characterized by *intense positive and negative emotional ties, face-to-face interaction, intimacy, and a strong, enduring sense of commitment.* Charles Horton Cooley (1864–1929) termed such groups "primary" because he believed that they were the basic form of all human association (Cooley, 1902). Beginning with the first group to which most of us belong, a family, many of the groups that shape our personalities and our lives are primary groups. Families in particular are an important source of early socialization in all cultures (Chapter 5). Other examples of primary groups include friendship and other peer groups, sororities and fraternities, and social clubs.

By way of contrast, **secondary groups** are *large and impersonal, and often involve fleeting relationships.* We seldom feel we can "be ourselves" in a secondary group; rather, we are often playing particular roles. Secondary groups seldom involve intense emotional ties or powerful commitments to the group itself. While Cooley argued that people belong to primary groups

mainly because such groups are inherently fulfilling, people join secondary groups to achieve some specific goal: to earn a living, get a college degree, or compete in sports. Examples of secondary groups include business organizations, educational institutions, work groups, athletic clubs, and governmental bodies. Secondary groups can of course become primary groups for some of their members—for example, when students taking a course begin to socialize after class, forming bonds of friendship.

For most of the time that human beings have existed on earth, nearly all interactions were within primary groups. This began to change with the emergence of larger agrarian societies, and today the opposite may well be true: most of our waking hours are spent within secondary groups, although primary groups remain important.

Some sociologists, like Cooley, have worried that the declining importance of primary groups might lead to a loss of intimacy and closeness, as more and more of our interactions occur within the framework of larger, impersonal organizations. Others have recognized that primary groups can often be limiting, since they often enforce strict conformity to group standards (Durkheim, 1964a; Simmel, 1955). What appeared to Cooley as the growing impersonality and anonymity of modern life can also be seen as an increasing tolerance for individual differences. Primary groups such as families may be intimate, but they can also be suffocating. Impersonal secondary groups are more likely to be concerned with accomplishing the task at hand rather than with enforcing strict conformity to group standards of behavior.

Primary groups may be as small as two people, or much larger; what is important is the degree of intimacy and commitment that is shared. This reunion of a large extended family *from the Peruvian highlands constitutes a primary group, as does an American family comprised of a single parent and child.*

Reference Groups

Chapter 5 discusses the fact that we often judge ourselves in terms of how we think we appear to others, what Cooley termed the "looking-glass self." Groups as well as individuals may provide the standards by which we make evaluations. Robert K. Merton (1957), following Herbert Hyman (1942), elaborated on the concept of the **reference group,** *a group that provides a standard for judging one's attitudes or behaviors* (see also Hyman and Singer, 1968). The family is often an important reference group, as are peer groups or coworkers. All of these groups expect certain behaviors. An early major study of reference groups was conducted by Merton and Alice Kitt Rossi (1950), who found that morale among American soldiers was not so much the result of the harshness of their experiences as it was how they fared in comparison with other groups of soldiers. If soldiers felt they were "relatively deprived" in comparison with other soldiers, their morale would be low, even if their actual living circumstances were not that bad.

Reference groups may be primary or secondary

Sports are conducted in both primary and secondary groups. A "pick-up" game of basketball normally involves people in secondary group relations. A team of players who practice and play together for an extended period of time may develop intimate and lasting friendships, becoming a primary group of central importance in its members' lives.

groups, and they may even be fictional. One of the chief functions of advertising, for example, is to create a set of reference groups that will influence the buying habits of the consumer. When lean female models with flawless complexions are shown in ads for cosmetics, the message to women is simple: "if you want to look as if you were part of an ingroup of highly attractive, eternally youthful women, buy this product." In reality, of course, the models who are used in the ads seldom have the unblemished features that are depicted in the ads, which are constructed through artful lighting, photography, and computer enhancement techniques. Similarly, the happy-go-lucky, physically perfect young men and women seen sailing or playing volleyball or hang-gliding on beer commercials have little to do with the reality of most of our lives—or, indeed, with the actual lives of the actors in these commercials. The message, however, is otherwise: "drink this beer and you will be viewed by others as a member of the carefree ingroup depicted in this ad."

The Effects of Size

Another sociologically important way in which groups differ has to do with their size. A fascination with the effects of group size on social interaction goes back at least 2,500 years in Western thought, when the philosopher Aristotle claimed that the ideal size for a city was no more than 10,000 persons, since a larger size would make direct participation in governance nearly impossible (Mumford, 1961).

Sociological interest in small group size can be traced to the German sociologist Georg Simmel (1858–1918), who studied and theorized about the impact of small groups on people's behavior. Since Simmel's time, small group researchers have conducted a number of laboratory experiments to examine the effects of size on both the quality of interaction in the group, and the effectiveness of the group in accomplishing certain tasks (Bales, 1953, 1970; Homans, 1950; Hare et al., 1965; Mills, 1967).

The simplest group, termed by Simmel (1955) a **dyad,** obviously *consists of two persons.* Simmel reasoned that dyads were likely to be simultaneously intense and unstable, since they require the full attention and cooperation of both parties; if one person withdraws from the dyad, it ceases to exist. Dyads often involve both intimacy as well as conflict, and may require a great deal of cooperative behavior if they are to function smoothly. While they are often a source of our most important social bonds, they can be very fragile indeed. That is why Simmel believed that a variety of cultural and legal supports for marriage will be found in those societies where marriage is regarded as an important source of social stability.

Adding a third person substantially changes the nature of the group relationship. Simmel used the term **triad** to describe *groups comprised of three persons.* Triads can be more stable than dyads, since the presence of a third person releases some of the pressure on the other two members to always get along and put energy into the relationship. One person can temporarily withdraw attention from the relationship, without necessarily threatening it. Two of the members may have a disagreement, while the third plays the role of mediator. On the other hand, there is always the possibility that a coalition will form between two of the members, enabling them to "gang up" on the third, thereby destabilizing the group. Coalitions are most likely to form when no one member is clearly dominant, and all three members are competing over scarce resources. One rule of coalition-formation in triads is that a member will most likely choose the weakest of the two other members with whom a successful coalition might be formed. In revolutionary coalitions, the two weaker members unite to overthrow the stronger one. (Caplow, 1956, 1959, 1969).

Going from a dyad to a triad illustrates an important sociological principal, first identified by Simmel: as groups increase in size, their intensity decreases, while their stability increases. There are, of course, exceptions to this principle, but in many cases it is likely to apply. Increasing the size of a group tends to decrease its intensity of interaction, simply because there are a larger number of outlets for individuals who are not getting along (Figure 6.2). For example, in a dyad, only a single relationship is possible. In a triad, three different relationships can occur. Adding a fourth person leads to six possible combinations of relationships, not counting subgroups that may form. In a ten-person group, the number of possible two-person relationships explodes to 45!

Larger groups tend to be more stable than smaller ones because the withdrawal of some members does not threaten group survival. A marriage or love relationship falls apart if one person leaves, while a sorority or fraternity routinely survives the loss of its graduating seniors. Larger groups also tend to be more exclusive, since it is easier for their members to limit their social relationships to the group itself, avoiding relationships with nonmembers. This sense of being part of an ingroup or clique is sometimes found in fraternities, sororities, and other campus organizations. Cliquishness is especially likely to occur when the group consists of members who are similar to one another in terms of such social characteristics as age, gen-

Figure 6.2   The Number of Possible Two-Person Relationships (Dyads) Increases Exponentially with the Number of People

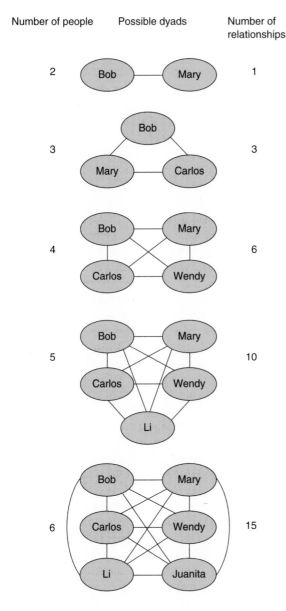

The larger the number of people, the greater the possible number of relationships. Note that this diagram illustrates only dyads; if triads and more complex coalitions were to be included, the numbers would be still greater (4 people yield 10 possibilities). Even a small, 10-person group can produce 45 possible dyads alone!

der, class, race, and ethnicity. On the other hand, a socially diverse membership is likely to foster a higher degree of interaction with people outside the group (Blau, 1977).

Beyond a certain size, perhaps a dozen people, groups will tend to develop a formal structure. Formal leadership roles may emerge, such as president or secretary, and official rules may be developed to govern what the group does. We shall discuss the nature of formal organizations later in this chapter.

Networks

Networks can be defined as *all the connections that link a person with other people, and through them to the persons with whom these people are connected.* Networks include people we know indirectly as well as directly—for example, our friends and our friends' friends. When we say that people are "well connected" or have "good connections," we are referring to their social networks.

Networks play an extremely important role in social interaction. As sociologist Mark Granovetter (1973) has demonstrated, there can be enormous strength in weak ties. Often, whom you know can be as important as what you know (Knoke, 1990; Wellman, Carrington, and Hall, 1988; Marsden and Lin, 1982). Some sociologists have argued that people at the top of government, industry, and the military belong to politically powerful networks. They often go to the same schools, sit on the same boards of directors of major corporations, belong to the same clubs and civic organizations, and in general develop extensive informal ties with one another (Knoke, 1990; Mills, 1956; Domhoff and Dye, 1984; Mizruchi, 1984). G. William Domhoff (1974) shows how social gatherings can provide an important network of connections for businessmen and politicians. When wealthy and powerful men get together for several days at northern California's "Bohemian Grove," they not only enjoy good eating, drinking, and entertainment, but they also make business deals and establish important political ties.

Organized crime groups in major cities of the United States are often depicted in the media and by the police as "Mafia families" consisting of tightly knit primary groups with strong ties of allegiance and highly developed mechanisms of social control. However, sociological research on organized crime has shown that organized crime groups more closely resemble networks than familes (Chambliss, 1988; Block, 1983, 1990). In Seattle during the late 1960s, for example, a network of gamblers, drug dealers, attorneys, bankers, real estate and insurance agents, police officers, prosecuting attorneys, and politicians controlled and managed a hundred million dollar a year business in crime (Chambliss, 1988). These people rarely interacted directly with one another, did not socialize together, did not use one another as a reference group nor did they particularly like one another. Nonetheless they constituted a network, coordinating their efforts to maximize their profits from crime and to minimize the risk of being caught.

Business interconnections are important in other cultures as well. In Japan, for example, the ownership of the leading corporations is "networked" into **keiretsu,** *enormous business and financial groupings that provide substantial coordination and control within the Japanese economy,* contributing to its strength in the global economy today. Firms like Toyota, Hitachi, and Matsushita include thousands of independent businesses that are networked together. These businesses buy goods and services from one another, sit on each other's boards of directors, and own shares of each others' stock. The top sixteen *keiretsu* account for fully a third of all the manufactured goods that are sold in Japan (Johnson, 1987; Orru, Hamilton, and Suzuki, 1989; Orru, Biggart, and Hamilton, 1991; Orru, 1991; Gerlach, 1992).

In Taiwan, by way of contrast, there are **guanxi,** *networks based primarily on social rather than purely economic foundations;* they include connections based on family, school ties, and region of origin. These are typical of Chinese business networks, and the resulting strong norms of trust have enabled Chinese business people to extend their influence throughout the world. A Chinese clothing manufacturer in Los Angeles might fax an order to his brother in Hong Kong, who works for a company that specializes in finding garment factories for Asian and American manufacturers. The brother, in turn, would contact a distant relative who lives across the border in China and owns a garment factory. Such extensive networks enable Chinese businesses to operate efficiently, inexpensively, and highly competitively. *Guanxi* is one reason that Chinese from Hong Kong and Taiwan have become powerful actors in the global economy (Wong, 1985; Hamilton and Kao, 1990; Kotkin, 1993).

While most people rely on their personal networks to gain advantage, not everyone has equal access to powerful networks. Some sociologists have argued that women's business and political networks are weaker then men's, thereby reducing their power (Brass, 1985). Another study found that young, professional, wealthy men had more extensive networks than other groups (Marsden, 1987). In Domhoff's (1974) study of the Bohemian Grove, he found that women were excluded from attending, except as entertainers. Former vice president Dan Quayle, who had never been in politics before 1976, went from congressman to senator to vice-president in the short space of 12 years. He was originally tapped to run for Congress because of his strong political connections in the state of Indiana, where for several generations his family had been among the state's most powerful newspaper publishers.

Leadership and Power

A **leader** is *a person who is able to influence the behavior of other members of a group.* All groups tend to have leaders, even if the leader is not formally recognized as such.

Studies of small group process have found that even in informal groups, a leader is likely to emerge. In early studies, Bales and Strodtbeck (1951) found that two different kinds of leadership seemed to naturally emerge in groups that had some task to accomplish. **Instrumental leaders** are *concerned with accomplishing the task at hand;* they are leaders who enable the group to "get the job done." ("Instrumental" refers to behavior that is calculated to achieve specific objectives.) **Expressive leaders** are more *concerned with the well-being of the group itself;* they seek to promote harmony and "good feelings" among group members. In their studies of juries, for example, Bales and Strodtbeck noted that while some members assumed a leading role in helping to arrive at a group decision, others were more concerned with keeping things running smoothly.

Groups typically do not set out to consciously select both kinds of leaders; in fact, the members may not even be aware that there is a difference between the two. While the same person initially is likely to provide both forms of leadership, when a group operates for an extended period of time the two functions tend to be split between two different people. This is not surprising, since instrumental leaders, who are usually officially in charge, are likely to displease other group members as they make unpopular decisions related to the task at hand. Under such circumstances, an expressive leader may emerge who is more focused on the emotional well-being of group members.

Another way to characterize leaders has to do with the degree to which they are concerned with routine group activities, as opposed to fostering major changes in the way the group operates. **Transactional leaders** are *concerned with accomplishing the group's tasks, getting group members to do their jobs, and making certain that the group achieves its goals.* This common type of leadership is termed "transactional" because it involves an exchange or transaction between the leader and the other members of the group. For example, a high school principal may give out salary bonuses and other forms of recognition to teachers, in hopes of motivating them to work harder. Transactional leadership is routine leadership.

Some leaders, however, are especially effective in motivating the members of their groups or organizations, inspiring them to achieve things that might not ordinarily be accomplished. Such **transformational leaders** go beyond the merely routine, *instilling the members of their groups with a sense of mission or higher purpose, and thereby changing the nature of the group itself* (Burns, 1978; Kanter, 1983). These are the leaders who are seen as "leaving their stamp" on their organizations—for example, Jaime Escalante, the inner-city high school teacher (depicted in the film *Stand and Deliver*) who transformed his classrooms into learning environments where once-failing students learned to score high on college entrance exams, or Bill Gates, who built the Microsoft corporation into the largest software manufacturer in the world.

For leaders to be effective, they must somehow get others to follow their lead. How is this accomplished? At one extreme, the leader can force people to obey whether or not they wish to do so; at the other extreme, people may willingly comply. The sociological notion of **power**—*the ability to mobilize resources and achieve a goal despite the resistance of others*—captures both extremes. Power can range from the raw exercise of physical force to **legitimate authority,** *power that is recognized as rightful by those over whom it is exercised* (Weber, 1947). Prison guards often rely on the use of force to ensure compliance with their orders, whereas professors depend on their legitimate authority to maintain a suitable learning environment in their classrooms.

Sociologists have typically found authority to be more interesting than the exercise of raw force, since the study of authority requires sociologists to explain why some people voluntarily yield freedom so others might lead. Sociologists and others who have studied leadership argue that leaders often exercise their power in two different ways. **Positional power** is *power that officially stems from the leadership position itself;* it is a form of legitimate authority that depends on the leader's role in the group. Leaders enjoy the power that is legally or formally associated with their position, whether it be the power to command the armed forces of the United States (a power given the U.S. President by the Constitution), or the power to test students (a power enjoyed by most teachers). Positional power includes the power to reward and punish group members (Hersey, Blanchard, and Natemeyer, 1987; Hersey and Blanchard, 1982; Raven and Kruglianski, 1975; French and Raven, 1959).

On the other hand, **personal power** does not derive directly from the leader's position in the organization, but *rather from the leader's personality;* it is a form of legitimate authority that depends on the ability to convince, rather than command. Personal power reflects a leader's expertise, access to information, personal connections, and, most importantly, the ability to inspire other members of the group. Jaime Escalante's ability to command the respect of his students derived in large part from personal qualities rather than from positional power tied to his role as a high school teacher.

In most situations, the effective exercise of personal power rather than positional power is more likely to result in highly motivated and satisfied group members. On the other hand, under some circumstances positional power seems to be preferred. For example, when group members are confused or ill-prepared to undertake a particular task, they seem to prefer the more command-oriented style associated with positional leadership. The members of high-risk, paramilitary organizations such as police department SWAT teams seem to prefer positional power as well (Hersey, Blanchard, and Natemeyer, 1987; Patterson, 1989; Podsakoff and Schriesheim, 1985).

Conformity

Sociologists have found that group pressure accounts for a great deal of conformity in all cultures. Because human beings are highly social animals, and because a great deal of socialization to norms and values occurs in primary groups such as the family, groups continue to exert a great deal of influence in shaping attitudes and behavior throughout life. How conformist are we, and under what circumstances are we most likely to conform? A great deal of research has explored the ways in which people conform to the expectations of others, particularly in group settings.

Obedience to Authority: Milgram's Research

In a classic experiment, Stanley Milgram (1963) set up what was portrayed to the subjects of the experiment as a scientific study of how people learn to memorize pairs of words. Male subjects who volunteered for the study were supposedly randomly divided into "teachers" and "learners." The "teacher" read pairs of words from a list that the "learner" was to memorize, so that when the "teacher" went back over the list and recited the first word of each pair, the "learner" would be able to correctly recite the second. Whenever the "learner" made a mistake, the "teacher" was to give him an electric shock by flipping a switch on a machine whose control board indicated shock levels ranging from "15

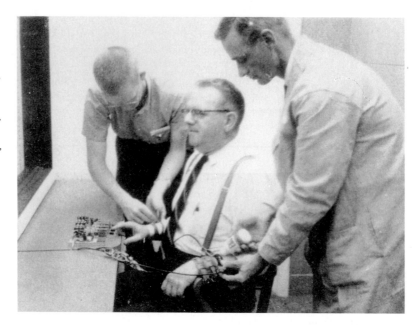

To determine the effects of authority on behavior, Stanley Milgram instructed student volunteers to "teach" a list of words to "learners" by administering increasingly painful electric shocks. Over half of the student "teachers" complied with authority to the point where the "learner" was presumably shocked into unconsciousness or possibly death. Even though the "learners" were not actually being shocked, such an experiment—however important the knowledge gained—would be considered unethical today.

volts—slight shock" to "450 volts—danger, severe shock." For each mistake, the voltage of the shock was increased, until it eventually reached the highest levels.

As the experiment progressed, the "learner"—who was typically concealed from the "teacher" by a screen—would scream out in pain for the "teacher" to stop giving him electric shocks. The scientist administering the experiment would order the "teacher" to continue, even when the "learner" could be heard shrieking about his "bad heart." The "teacher" was then confronted with a decision: should he obey the scientist and go along with the experiment, even if it meant injuring—and possibly killing—another human being? Much to Milgram's surprise, over half the subjects of the study kept on administering electric shocks until the maximum voltage was reached, and the "learner's" screams had subsided into an eerie silence as he presumably succumbed to a heart attack. Why did this occur? How could ordinary people so easily conform to orders that would turn them into possible accomplices to murder?

Milgram's experiment was not actually about learning at all. In fact, the "learner" was not even a volunteer for the experiment, but rather one of Milgram's employees. Nor was the "learner" actually receiving electric shocks; his screams were really on a prerecorded tape. The experiment was instead a clever deception of the "teacher," designed to reveal something about the nature of conformity. (Research such as this, which involves a high degree of deception and potential psychological damage to its subjects, raises serious ethical questions. As we noted in Chapter 2, it would no longer be allowed under the ethical guidelines of the American Sociological Association).

Milgram's research was intended to shed some light on what had happened in Nazi Germany ten years earlier. How could the German people go along with the mass extermination of millions of Jews, gypsies, and others who were judged to be inferior by the Nazis? The answer, according to Milgram's study, was that ordinary people would conform to orders given by someone in a position of power and authority—in this case, a white-coated scientist from Yale University—even when those orders had horrible consequences. In other versions of this experiment, Milgram found that conformity was especially likely to occur when the "teacher" was part of a group of people who were going along with the instructions to give electric shocks.

Total Institutions: The Zimbardo Prison Experiment

In the previous chapter we defined **total institutions** as *those which isolate individuals from the rest of society in order to achieve administrative control over all aspects of their lives.* As briefly mentioned in Chapter 2, Stanford University psychologist Philip Zimbardo (1972) constructed an ingenious "real life" experiment to examine the nature of conformity to arbitrary authority in a total institution. He converted the basement of a university building into a makeshift prison, randomly selecting half of his students to be "guards" and half to be "prisoners." There were no significant differences between the students chosen for each group, in terms of age, height, personality, intelligence, or other characteristics. All were males.

Zimbardo's plan was to observe the interaction between the two groups over a two-week period, seeing how each group adapted to their temporary roles. Prisoners were assigned to cells, from which they were allowed out only for brief periods of exercise and eating. Guards were responsible for overseeing the prisoners, maintaining order and discipline, and preventing prisoners from escaping. After only six days, however, he had to call the experiment off. The students had completely adapted to their roles: the guards had either become cruel and vicious, or passive in the face of those who were, while the prisoners had become meek and subservient. Some of the prisoners were depressed and crying much of the time, begging to be released—even though they were there as volunteers and could not be kept against their will. In one case, a student's parents came to plead for their son's freedom, which was denied. Yet any of the prisoners could have walked away any time they chose; there was no legal way they could have been confined against their will.

In fact, the power of the make-believe prison had become so great that most of the students appeared unable to recognize that they were voluntarily conforming to an increasingly terrifying situation. It was only after Zimbardo terminated the experiment that students began to come to their senses.

Zimbardo concluded that we are all powerfully socialized to conform to the standards of the groups that we belong to, even if the group is as transitory as the "Stanford Prison" group. He also concluded, with Milgram, that conformity to authority—even if it is arbitrary—is a powerful force in our culture. Another conclusion from Zimbardo's study is that total institutions can actually alter their members' perceptions. Not only did Zimbardo's "prisoners" and "guards" lose sight of the fact that they were actually volunteer students, but they came to perceive one another differently. According to interviews conducted after the experiment was over, students perceived the "guards" to be taller than the "prisoners"—even though as we mentioned above there was actually no difference between the two groups.

To the extent that we conform to the expectations of the group or the institution, we are in fact its prisoners—just as Zimbardo's "guards" and "prisoners" alike were the prisoners of a nonexistent Stanford prison. Such conformity helps to keep the group or the institution going; it is one reason why it often continues to exist even when it seems to have outlived its usefulness.

Groupthink and Group Pressures to Conform: Janis' Research

Although common sense tells us that "two minds are better than one," sociological research has found that pressures to "go along with the group" sometimes result in conformity rather than creative new solutions to problems. You have probably had the experience of being in a group that was struggling with a difficult decision and feeling uneasy at voicing your opposition to an emerging consensus. Irving L. Janis (1972, 1989; Janis and Mann, 1977) called this phenomenon **groupthink,** a *process by which members of a group ignore ways of thinking and courses of action that go against the consensus of the group.* Not only does groupthink stigmatize potential dissenters into conforming, it can also produce a shift in perceptions so that alternative possibilities are simply ruled out without being seriously considered. Although groupthink may facilitate reaching a quick consensus, the consensus may also be ill-chosen.

Janis engaged in historical research to see if groupthink characterized U.S. foreign policy decisions. Because high-level governmental decision-making is often recorded in minutes and on tapes as well as in the personal notes and diaries of the participants, he found rich sources of information to test his hypothesis. He examined several important decisions, including the infamous Bay of Pigs invasion of Cuba in 1961. In that decision, John F. Kennedy, the newly elected president, had inherited a plan from the previous administration to help Cuban exiles "liberate" Cub from the communist government of Fidel Castro. The plan called for U.S. logistical support and air cover for an invasion by an army of exiles at Cuba's Bay of Pigs. While a number of Kennedy's top advisors were certain the plan was fatally flawed, they refrained from bucking the emerging consensus, something they later admitted regretting at the time. The invasion was a disaster; the exile army was immediately defeated, and Kennedy suffered a great deal of public embarrassment.

There is an important lesson from Janis' research: even internationally prominent figures, sufficiently strongwilled to be top advisors to the president of the United States, will conform to group pressures if the pressures are sufficiently strong. It seems clear that if groupthink is to be avoided, group decision-making processes must ensure that all opinions are fully and openly entertained.

ORGANIZATIONS

An **organization** can be defined as *a group with an identifiable membership that engages in concerted collective action to achieve a common purpose* (Aldrich and Marsden, 1988). Since organizations enable us to pursue activities that we could otherwise not readily accomplish by ourselves, they are a central feature of all societies, and their study is a core concern of sociology today. Yet prior to 1947, neither of the two principal sociological journals made any reference to "organizations" in their indices (Freeman, 1982). This shift in sociological focus reflects a growing appreciation of the importance of organizations and the need to understand them sociologically. As organizations become increasingly global in scale, the study of organizations becomes an important key to understanding the processes of globalization itself.

Max Weber (1864–1920), one of the founders of the field of organizational studies (as well as sociology itself), demonstrated that in Europe and elsewhere there was a long-term historical trend toward increasingly rational forms of social organization (Weber, 1947). This is true in government, in the economy, and in organizations in general. According to Weber, until relatively recently in history the authority structure of organizations was mainly based on habit and custom: authority was legitimate if it was in accordance with long-standing traditional beliefs and practices. In modern society, however, authority is more likely to be based on reason: authority is legitimate if it is rationally designed to further the aims of the organization. Because of this long-term trend toward organizational rationality, organizations increasingly tend to be formal in modern society.

A **formal organization** is *an organization that is rationally designed to achieve its objectives, often by means of explicit rules, regulations, and procedures.* While all organizations are to some extent formal, they tend to be highly so in modern society. In fact, for an organization to acquire legal standing today it often must comply with a mountain of specific requirements imposed by a variety of government agencies. For a college or university to be legally accredited, for example, it must satisfy explicit written standards governing everything from grading policy to faculty performance to fire safety.

Types of Formal Organization

Although there are thousands of different kinds of formal organizations serving every imaginable purpose, a task of sociology is to simplify this by identifying the principal types. Amitai Eztioni (1975) has provided a useful classification based on the principal reasons people join formal organizations.

Utilitarian organizations are *those that people join primarily because of some material benefit or gain they expect to receive in return for membership.* You probably enrolled in college not only because you wanted to expand your knowledge but because you felt a degree would help you to get a better job or earn more money later in your life. In exchange, you probably paid tuition and fees, gave up some of your personal freedom and a great deal of your time, and agreed to submit to the rules and regulations that govern your particular institution. Many of the organizations we join are utilitarian, particularly those in which we earn our living.

Coercive organizations are *those in which people are forced to give unquestioned obedience to authority.* People are often forced to join coercive organizations, either for punishment (jails and prisons) or mandatory treatment (mental hospitals); some, however, may be joined voluntarily, although once one is a member one may not have the option of leaving voluntarily (the military). Coercive organizations require coercive mechanisms to ensure compliance with rules and regulations, and sometimes confinement. Guards, locked doors, barred windows, and constant monitoring are all features of such organizations. They are examples of "total institutions" that encompass all aspects of a person's life, often radically altering thinking and behavior.

Normative or **voluntary association** are *those a person joins on a voluntary basis to pursue a morally worthwhile goal without expectation of material reward.* Over 150 years ago the French social philosopher Alexis de Tocqueville (1835), on returning from travel in the United States, commented that Americans "are forever forming associations," and that this provided a fertile basis for democracy. Americans continue to be a nation of joiners. They affiliate with volunteer church groups such as the YMCA or Hillel, charitable organizations such as the Red Cross, political groups such as the League of Women Voters, and self-help groups such as Alcoholics Anonymous or Overeaters Anonymous. There are some 22,000 such organizations in the United States today (Gale Research Company, 1990), providing their members with a sense of connectedness while enabling them to accomplish personal goals.

One example of voluntary organizations that played a little-known but pivotal role in American history were antislavery organizations among African Americans at the time of the Civil War. Such organizations fought slavery before the war and provided charity for the poor throughout much of the ninteenth century. Numerous organizations of this type flourished in the North, and many existed in secrecy in the South prior to the abolition of slavery (see Box 6.1). In Philadelphia alone there were almost 60 African-American charitable associations in the 1830s, many of which were run by black women. After the Civil War, these organizations turned increasingly to teaching and charity, fighting for the rights of blacks, and to ending the abhorrent practice of lynching. They also fostered a strong sense of pride within the black community.

Bureaucracies

The authority structure of most large organizations today is often described as bureaucratic. Max Weber (1946) was the first sociologist to examine in detail the characteristics of **bureaucratic authority,** which he

Voluntary organizations play an important role in modern societies, reflecting the cultural value of helping others. Volunteers provide counseling for women in abusive relationships (as shown here), as well as food and shelter for the homeless, guidance for young people, education for prison inmates, fundraising for politicians, and a wide variety of social services.

defined as *authority based on written procedural rules, arranged into a clear hierarchy of authority, and staffed by full-time paid officials.* Although Weber showed that bureaucracies could be found in many different societies throughout history, he argued that they had become a dominant form of social organization only in modern society, where they touch all aspects of our daily lives: our schools, workplaces, governments, businesses, and even religions.

In order to better understand the nature of bureaucracy, Weber (1946) identified what he referred to as the "ideal type" of this form of organization—the characteristics that would be found if the perfect bureaucracy existed. While Weber recognized that no actual bureaucracy possesses all these characteristics, he argued that by clearly articulating them he was describing a standard against which actual bureaucracies could be judged. According to Weber, an ideal type bureaucracy has certain specific features.

Written Rules and Regulations The routine operation of the bureaucracy is governed by written rules and regulations, the purpose of which is to ensure that universal standards govern all aspects of bureaucratic behavior. The rules and regulations are typically contained in an organizational manual or handbook, which describes in great detail the requirements of each organizational position.

Specialized Offices Positions in bureaucracies are organized into "offices," creating a division of labor within the organization. Each office has its duties set forth in the organizational manual. Each specializes in one particular bureaucratic function to the exclusion of all others. Such specialization is one of the ways that

bureaucratic organization is said to be more efficient: bureaucratic officials are supposed to become experts at their particular tasks, efficient cogs in a vast organizational machine.

Hierarchy Bureaucracies are organized according to the principle of hierarchy: each office has authority over one or more lower-level offices, and each in turn is responsible to a higher-level office. The higher you are in the organizational chart, the more people you can give orders to, and the fewer people you have to take orders from. The organizational chart of a bureaucracy thus looks like a pyramid.

Impersonality in Record-Keeping Within the bureaucracy, communications are likely to be formal and impersonal. Such written forms substitute for a more personalized human contact, because bureaucracies must maintain written records of all important actions. Modern computer technology has vastly increased the ability of organizations to maintain and quickly access records. In some ways this may be seen as an advantage—for example, when you register for classes by touch-tone telephone, instead of standing in line for hours waiting to fill out forms. On the other hand, you may bemoan the resulting loss of human contact and the inflexibility of the process, however efficient it might be.

Technically Competent, Professional Administrative Staff Bureaucracies provide for ongoing fulfillment of the tasks required by each office. Staff are thus supposed to be replaceable: anyone who can fill the job description for a particular office is eligible for

Box 6.1

Silenced Voices

Voluntary Associations and African-American Women

Thousands of voluntary associations emerged among African Americans prior to the Civil War, where they played a key role in fighting for the abolition of slavery and equality for blacks. After the Civil War much of this organizational effort turned to promoting black pride, fighting racial injustice, and providing charity for the poor. During a period when thousands of black men were lynched by white mobs, much of the organizational work was devoted to abolishing this practice.

Born to a poverty-stricken black family in Macon, Georgia, Margaret Murray Washington (1865–1925) exemplifies this effort. Washington began teaching school at the age of 14, earned a degree from Fisk University in 1889, and became affiliated with the Tuskegee Institute, where she married the prominent black educator Booker T. Washington. She became president of the Afro-American Federation of Colored Women, and later president of the National Association of Colored Women. In the following passage (Washington, 1973; orig. 1929) Washington describes the work and goals of the National Association of Colored Women's Clubs, which had 300,000 members in the United States and other nations in 1929.

Margaret Murray Washington (1865–1925), born into poverty, became an important leader of the movement to create voluntary organizations among African Americans. She served as president of the Afro-American Federation of Colored Women and the National Association of Colored Women, and was a founder of the National Association of Colored Women's Clubs, which in 1929 had more than 300,000 members throughout the United States, Canada, Liberia, Haiti, and Cuba.

The School Question

How many people realize that even today in many parts of the country the school term for the colored child is not more than four months in a year? . . . No question today is of so vital an interest to the colored womans' club as this one which deals with the schools and the general educational advantages for their children and those of their sister club workers. . . .

Suffrage

Colored women, quite as much as colored men, realize that if there is ever to be equal justice and fair play in the courts everywhere for all races, then there must be an equal chance for all women as well as men to express their preference through their votes. . . . Our Department of Suffrage con-

ducts training classes in the Constitution of the country, and has given time to the study of all governmental affairs, so that women must be prepared to handle the vote intelligently and wisely when it comes to them.

"Anti-Lynching"

Our club women work incessantly to help mold sentiment against lynching, and although it is a slow process, there is a strong and growing feeling against this form of punishment for any cause whatsoever. . . . The Georgia State Federation of White Women's Clubs in their last convention came out strongly in favor of law and order as against mob violence and lynching. When the Women's State Federation of other Southern States takes a stand against this evil, the men in authority in these States will see it that lynching is put down and not until then will it be done. It is women's work now as always. . . .

Nothing has so changed the whole life and personnel of the colored woman and so surely brought her into her own as has the club life to which she has lent herself, inspired by the national association which has for its aim the development of its women, mentally, morally, and industrially, as well as along civic lines, and whose motto is, "Lifting as we climb. . . ."

---

the position. Work in the bureaucracy is a full-time job, ideally providing a career path for the bureaucrat, who must demonstrate the training and expertise necessary to fill the positions. In its pure form, therefore, the system is supposed to be a **meritocracy,** that is, a bureaucracy *in which positions are filled purely on the basis of a person's merit or qualifications.* This is typically demonstrated by performance on competitive exams, rather than by knowing the "right" people. In practice, of course—as with the other characteristics listed above—an actual bureaucracy is unlikely to fully meet this standard.

Bureaucracies: A Critical Evaluation

Is bureaucracy desirable or undesirable? Weber recognized that bureaucracies can be both. They can provide greater organizational efficiency in getting the job done, while at the same time creating an uncaring "iron cage" from which there is little escape in modern society (Weber, 1976; orig. 1904–1905). Yet his primary concern was with creating an ideal type model of bureaucracy that would serve as a useful guide for subsequent theory and research, rather than making judgments about the ultimate value of bureaucracies. Weber's ideal type has proved fruitful for evaluating the actual characteristics of real-life bureaucracies, in that they have been found to depart from his model in several significant ways (for example, see Hodges, 1981; Ferguson, 1984; Jacoby, 1963):

The Informal Structure of Bureaucracy

Although Weber presents a sometimes chilling picture of bureaucracies operating as vast, inhuman machines, we all recognize that in practice there is often a human face behind the counter. Somehow, most people manage to establish strong interpersonal ties in even the most rigid organizations. Peter Blau (Blau and Meyer, 1987, 1963; Blau and Scott, 1962), for example, stud-

ied the informal relations that exist in bureaucratic organizations, and showed that much of the work is actually done through personal connections rather than official channels. Staff members may get together for informal discussions over lunch to make a decision, rather than using the formal procedures required by the rule book. Students who wish to register late for a class may avoid getting a half dozen signatures, simply because they know the professor or a staffperson in the registrar's office.

In fact, much of the important work of bureaucratic organizations is done through such informal channels and connections. In our earlier discussion of networks, we showed how personal contacts play a key role in coordinating the affairs of business and government. Whether it is in the redwood forests of the Bohemian Grove, at country clubs, or just over a business lunch, layers of bureaucracy can often be sidestepped with a handshake.

The Dysfunctions of Bureaucracy

Sociologists have found that bureaucracies are not as efficient as Weber's ideal-type model might suggest. Bureaucracies can develop extremely inefficient, bloated staffs dedicated primarily to filling out paperwork and ensuring their own survival. Sociologists have identified a number of problems that plague bureaucracies, many of which will be familiar to you:

■ *Waste and incompetence:* In a large bureaucracy, it is often possible for administrators to "become lost" in the organization. As long as they are doing their job—filing forms, keeping records, responding to memos, keeping busy—nobody seems to question whether or not the organization as a whole is performing effectively or efficiently. Administrators become entrenched in their positions, and eventually lose touch with the larger goals of the organization. Secure in their positions, bureaucrats may

Figure 6.3   **An Organizational Chart of the Department of Defense**

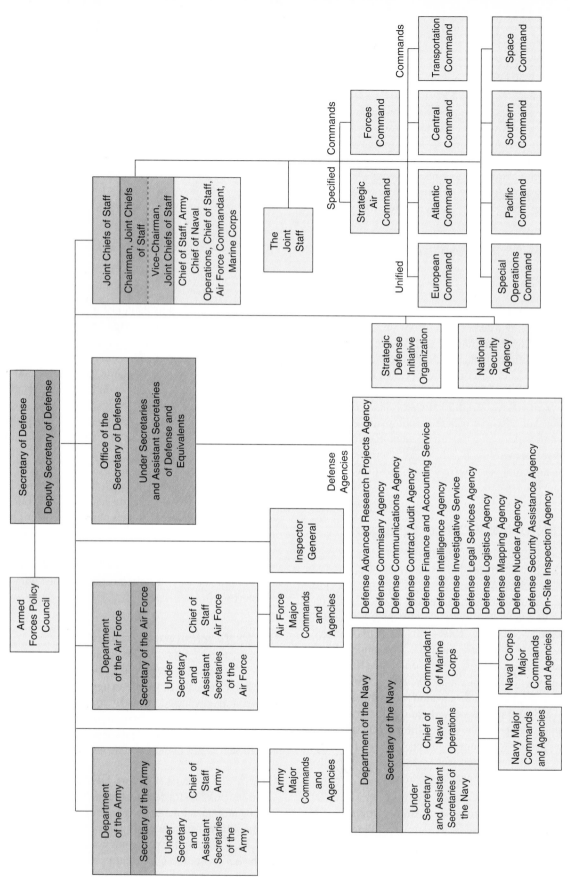

The U.S. Department of Defense is an example of a bureaucratic organization. A single person, the Secretary of Defense, is responsible for a vast number of offices and the employees who staff them, as well as all U.S. military forces. The secretary answers directly to the president, who is mandated by the Constitution as the "commander-in-chief" of the armed forces. Under the secretary are the three giant branches of the military: the departments of the Navy, Army, and Air Force. The secretary also supervises the Joint Chiefs of Staff, as well as his own office staff. Each one of these departments and divisions is an entire bureaucracy in itself. Those at the bottom of this hierarchy must go through countless levels of bureaucracy to get the attention of someone at the top—a virtual impossibility.

become inefficient, incompetent, and often indifferent to the clients they are supposed to serve.

■ *Trained incapacity:* We have all known bureaucrats who "went by the book," even when the situation clearly called for some fresh thinking. Thorstein Veblen (1899), a contemporary of Weber's, termed this **trained incapacity**—*a learned inability to exercise independent thought.* However intelligent they may otherwise be, such bureaucrats become "judgmental dopes" when it comes to making decisions that are not covered in the rule book. They become so obsessed with following the rules and regulations of their organizations that they frequently lose the ability to respond to new situations.

■ *Goal displacement:* Bureaucracies often lose sight of the original goals they were created to accomplish. Large corporations such as General Motors or IBM employ tens of thousands of "middle managers" whose job it is to handle the paperwork required in manufacturing automobiles or computers. Perhaps understandably, such people become more concerned with their own job security than with the original goals of the organization, which then becomes a sanctuary for well-paid bureaucrats who know and care little about making high quality cars or computers. This adds to costs, lowers efficiency, and can prove fatal to corporations that must compete in a global economy (Peters and Waterman, 1982; Reich, 1991).

Because of the shortcomings of bureaucratic forms of organization, some theorists have argued for alternative nonbureaucratic forms of organization. We will consider some of these alternatives later in this chapter (see also Box 6.2).

The Iron Law of Oligarchy

Max Weber argued that bureaucracies were an inevitable outgrowth of modern society, with its large-scale organizations, complex institutional structure, and concern for rationality and efficiency. Although it has been recognized that bureaucracies can be stifling, do they inevitably lead to a loss of freedom and democracy as well?

Robert Michels (1876–1936), a contemporary of Weber's, argued that bureaucracy and democracy are fundamentally incompatible. Michels observed that the socialist party in Germany, which was originally created to democratically represent the interests of workers, had become an enormous bureaucracy with tremendous power concentrated in its top leadership. He concluded that the transformation of the socialist

---

Box 6.2

Critical Thinking

Is There a "Feminine" Alternative to Bureaucracy?

Some scholars have argued that there is a "feminine" style of interaction that could constitute a humane alternative to bureaucratic organization (Ferguson, 1984). It is claimed that such a style can be traced to differences in male and female socialization in our culture, and emphasizes cooperation, caring, and personal connections with others, rather than the competition, abstract concern with rules, and hierarchy characteristic of most formal organizations (see Chapter 5). According to its proponents, such a "feminine" style may result in more humane and caring forms of organization in the future, particularly if greater numbers of women move into positions of power and influence in the business world, politics, and education (Bass, 1990; Gilligan, 1982; Gilligan et al., 1989; Loden and Rosener, 1991; Helgesen, 1990; Rosener, 1990).

This argument makes two principal assumptions. First, it assumes that men and women differ in their styles of interaction, along the lines just mentioned. Second, it assumes that such differences carry over into higher-level organizational roles—that the individual shapes the role he or she occupies, rather than the reverse. Based on what you have learned in this chapter and in Chapter 5, what evidence exists to support these assumptions? To refute them?

party into an undemocratic bureaucracy was an example of what he termed the **iron law of oligarchy,** *an inevitable tendency for large-scale bureaucratic organizations to become ruled by a handful of people in a highly undemocratic fashion.*

Michels, following Weber, argued that large-scale organizations require bureaucratic structures in order to function efficiently. Bureaucracies, as we have seen, are hierarchical in nature; the farther up you move, the greater is the concentration of power, since everybody is responsible to the person above. Furthermore, people typically get to the top because they are ambitious, hard-driving, effective in managing the people below, and often power-hungry as well. Once at the top, leaders have specialized access to information, resources, and important people, all of which reinforce their power. They often appoint subordinates who are loyal supporters, which further enhances their position. Such leaders may come to regard the bureaucracy as their personal organization, and run it virtually as a dictatorship.

Since democratic societies (indeed, all modern societies) require large-scale organizations to survive, democracies thus eventually sow the seeds of their own destruction: they breed bureaucracies that eventually grow into undemocratic oligarchies. Following his own logic, Michels was thus forced to the highly pessimistic conclusion that modern democracy is doomed to turn into oligarchy.

Critical Assessment How accurate was Michels analysis? It seems clear that there is more than a grain of truth in his concerns. One important study found a similar pattern in an American labor union (Lipset, Trow, and Coleman, 1977; orig. 1956). In recent years the U.S. government has been rocked with a series of scandals suggesting that our supposedly democratic governmental institutions are in fact remote and distant from the people they are supposed to serve. Beginning with Watergate, in which it was revealed that government intelligence agencies like the CIA were involved in spying on the Democratic Party in flagrant disregard of their own internal rules and procedures, there seem to have been an unending series of events proving Michels was correct in predicting that bureaucracies eventually come to function in very undemocratic ways.

In the mid-1980s, for example, the Iran-Contra affair uncovered the existence of a national security agency within the White House bureaucracy. This agency had arranged the sales of missiles to Iran in order to fund a U.S.-sponsored insurgency against the Nicaraguan government, even though both the missile sales and the funding operation were against explicit U.S. laws and policies at the time. More recently, in 1992 a majority of the members of the House of Representatives were found to have written bad checks on the House Bank at the taxpayers' expense. The House Bank was a large bureaucracy that had turned a blind eye to such practices for decades, permitting its leadership to act with impunity.

Yet despite such examples, it is important to recognize that in democracies, even powerful bureaucracies may eventually be held accountable. Watergate resulted in the humiliating resignation of U.S. President Richard M. Nixon, the imprisonment of many of his top advisors, and legislation that for a time restricted the operations of the intelligence agencies. The Iran-Contra affair received sustained public attention, which discredited the intelligence agencies that were implicated in the arms sales. The House Bank scandal resulted in the firing of the bureaucrat responsible for the questionable practices and a change in the rules of the bank, and it led to the "early retirement" of a number of representatives. It is probably more accurate to describe the relationship between democracy and bureaucratic oligarchy as one of tension, rather than as an "iron law" whereby democracy necessarily gives way to oligarchy.

Surveillance and Control in Organizations

Another way in which democracy and bureaucracy may prove incompatible has to do with the extensive record-keeping that is a central feature of bureaucratic organization. **Surveillance** refers to *the ability to monitor people, either through direct observation, or by keeping records.* The vastly increased ability of private and governmental organizations to monitor people is one of the central features of modern society (Giddens, 1990). One study of surveillance in the United States, Canada, Sweden, Germany, and France concluded that citizens increasingly are subject to surveillance by governments as well as private businesses (Flaherty, 1989).

Needless to say, computers have vastly increased the scope and efficiency of surveillance in modern organizations. Our motions are now routinely monitored by video cameras in stores, banks, and even gas stations. Every check cashed, credit card purchase, ATM advance or deposit, or telephone call is now routinely recorded on computers for future reference. The bad check you write today may come back to haunt you when you graduate and try to buy a car. In most colleges and universities, every student has a computerized file of grades, courses taken, transcripts, disciplinary actions, and virtually anything that is deemed worthy of being entered in the database. In many states, a routine traffic stop for a faulty taillight now triggers a national computer check from the patrol car's onboard computer, which will reveal any illegal activities (including unpaid traffic tickets) to the officer.

Surveillance *is an important feature of modern societies, whether it be through electronic record-keeping or direct visual observation. Technological advances have permitted a vast increase in the power of private organizations and government to monitor people's actions, as this photograph of security guards suggests.*

Sociologist Gary T. Marx (1985a, 1985b, 1988) has studied surveillance for many years. He has concluded that the new technologies pose a potentially serious threat to individual freedom. In Marx's view, the new high-tech forms of surveillance differ from older forms in a number of significant ways. First, they are able to overcome the impediments of distance, time, darkness, and even physical barriers. They are thus capable of monitoring previously inaccessible information and doing so over a much larger geographical space. Second, they make it easier to target entire groups of people for monitoring, rather than limiting one's surveillance to a single individual. Third, they require increasingly commonplace electronic equipment, rather than human spies; they are thus easier, safer, and often less expensive to utilize. Often, as we have noted, they require no special equipment at all—just the routine records that are now electronically kept by most organizations. Fourth, they are highly unobtrusive, making it much more difficult to avoid being monitored.

In modern bureaucratic organizations, physical surveillance is an important aspect of control. In the old-fashioned factory, workers typically sat at workbenches or on an assembly line, where their every motion could be monitored and measured by supervisers. While such monitoring was often crude, it did permit

management to determine the pace and organization of the assembly line (Braverman, 1976). In today's factories, the electronic recording of every operation permits a far higher degree of control over workers' activities. In fact, all phases in the production and sales of a good can be recorded for later retrieval, from the factory worker's quality and output to the sales history of the clerk where the good is sold. The optical scanner at the point of sales, for example, enables management to precisely monitor not only what is sold but how quickly and accurately the employee is conducting sales. This opens up the possibility of greater control over the pace of work and compensation (Sewell and Wilkinson, 1992; Rule and Brantley, 1992).

As computers come to pervade more and more aspects of our daily lives, the opportunities for surveillance will increase accordingly. This has led a number of scholars to conclude that the laws protecting citizens from abuse are inadequate to protect industrial nations like the United States from becoming what one writer has termed "maximum security societies" (Marx, 1988; see also Flaherty, 1989; Stephens, 1990).

Gender, Race, and Organizations

Organizations both reflect and reproduce society's social roles. Organizations that provide employment, for example, often define their jobs in terms of stereotypical male and female roles, the latter consisting mainly of low-wage jobs with little possibility for career advancement. Women are overwhelmingly found in such occupations, performing word processing, secretarial labor, and other forms of "women's work" (Taeuber and Valdisera, 1986; Matthews and Rodin, 1989). As a result of the sex segregation of work in organizations, women earn less than men even when their skills and educational profiles are the same. Racial differences in the workplace reinforce such gender differences, so that women of color often fare the worst in terms of employment and career opportunities (Hubler and Silverstein, 1992; U.S. Bureau of the Census, 1991).

There is, however, some evidence that occupational segregation is changing, albeit slowly. Women's career aspirations have grown in recent years, both because of changing cultural values and because the entry of large numbers of women into previously male-dominated jobs has forced some rethinking of women's roles. Federal legislation, beginning with the 1964 Civil Rights Act, has also been important, since most forms of workplace discrimination are now illegal (Jacobs, 1989; Reskin and Hartmann, 1986). Still, in most workplaces, occupational stereotyping by sex remains largely unchallenged (Milkman, 1987). Until this changes, organizations will continue to reflect the inequalities found in the larger society.

The Human Side of Organizations

In recent years, large-scale, impersonal bureaucratic organizations have come under attack from many quarters. We have already noted that sociologists have long been concerned with the informal "human" side of organizations (Blau and Meyer, 1987; Blau and Scott, 1962). In recent years, however, scholars have debated whether or not an entirely new organizational form might come to partly replace the bureaucracy altogether. In comparison with traditional bureacratic organizations, the new form would be less bureaucratic and hierarchical, would draw more deeply on the talents of its members, and would provide a more fulfilling environment in which to work. In this section we shall consider several examples of such an alternative approach to formal organizations.

Japanese Organizations

Many critics of large-scale organizations point to Japanese corporations, which they claim are smaller, less bureaucratic, and more cooperative than their U.S. counterparts. The interest in the "Japanese form of organization," sometimes termed "theory Z," naturally follows from the tremendous economic success of Japanese business (Ouchi, 1982). If Mazda can outcompete General Motors or if NEC can outcompete IBM, doesn't it follow that Mazda's or NEC's type of organization may be superior to that of its American counterparts?

Japanese businesses such as Mazda and NEC are run in a fashion that would strike Americans as a compromise between a collective and a bureaucracy. As we noted earlier, when workers join a large Japanese corporation, they are made to feel like they are joining a family, one they will remain with until they retire years later. Many workers and management do not have the "us" versus "them" attitude that characterizes U.S. labor relations. Workers at NEC or Mazda have lifetime job security; promotions and salary increases are based on age and length of service. Workers learn company slogans and songs, wear company uniforms, and participate in company rituals. They are regarded as part of the corporate family and are treated accordingly.

At Mazda, for example, ordinary assembly-line workers are routinely consulted by top management for their ideas and suggestions, on the theory that no one knows better about the car than the worker who is making it. Over the course of a year, tens of thousands of workers' suggestions are reviewed, and many are incorporated into design changes. The workforce is often organized into **quality circles,** *small groups of workers and managers who operate as a team to solve problems and improve product quality.* The performance of the team, not the individual, is the key to re-

ward. Many important decisions start in teams at the bottom, and work their way up to top management, rather than the reverse, as is the case in many American corporations. Pay differences between top management and ordinary workers are far smaller than in the United States. Workers receive general training in many aspects of factory production, rather than just specializing in one or two basic tasks. When a business experiences financial difficulties, as happend to Mazda in the mid-1970s, top management will take a pay cut before workers are fired.

When evaluating Japanese corporations, it is important to bear a number of things in mind. First, the original ideas for this mildly collectivist organizational form were not Japanese at all, but originated at Bell Laboratories in the 1920s. While they never found wide acceptance in the United States, they did in Japan. One reason for this is that Japanese culture emphasizes the importance of the group over the individual, and deeply respects the idea of sacrificing individuality for group performance. Furthermore, deep antagonisms between workers and managers, which makes cooperation difficult in U.S. businesses, are not found in most Japanese corporations. This is largely because Japanese businesses, in an effort to thwart workers' unions, agreed to unions' demands for lifetime employment and seniority-based promotions. The relatively small salary differentials between management and workers make it easier for workers to feel company loyalty in Japan.

Finally, as Japanese firms have themselves globalized, many of their organizational innovations are being threatened (Fukui, 1992). The system of lifetime employment and age-based seniority—which never applied to more than one-quarter of Japan's workers (Tsuda, 1981)—is now threatened as well (Miller, 1993). Such benefits are extremely costly, adding to the price of Japanese products, which in turn reduces their competitiveness in the global economy.

Quality circles may work well in Japan, but have not been quite as successful in factories in the United States. For example, some aspects of "Japanese-style management" have been introduced in General Motor's Spring Hill (Tennessee) factory, where the Saturn is made, as well as GM's joint venture with Toyota at its Fremont (California) plants. Particularly at the latter, workers have resisted some aspects of the new management system (Woodruff, 1992). Even though "quality" is an increasing concern of American corporations, most firms do not seek to improve quality by reorganizing the labor process into worker-manager teams (see Chapter 15).

In sum, while there are many advantages to the Japanese form of organization, it remains to be seen if this form can be exported as readily as Japanese cars or cameras. Not only may it be closely tied to Japanese culture, but it may also prove vulnerable to the very

Japanese manufacturers maintain that much of their phenomenal success since World War II can be attributed to worker participation in the manufacturing process. To enhance the quality of their products, factory management encourages worker input on quality control at this meeting of a quality *circle in a Japanese factory.*

processes of economic globalization that have otherwise worked so well for the Japanese economy.

Collectives

As part of the sweeping antiestablishment spirit of the 1960s, many youthful activists called for what they believed was a new form of antibureaucratic organization—the collective. As its name implies, a **collective** is a *small group of people that operate by agreement or consensus.* It is almost the exact opposite of Weber's notion of bureaucracy. Members of collectives shun hierarchy, avoid a division of labor based on expertise, and happily sacrifice efficiency in favor of more humanistic relations with one another or with the organization's clients. Collectives are concerned with democratic practices, and thus represent an organizational form intended to counter Michel's iron law of oligarchy.

In an important early examination of collectives, sociologist Joyce Rothschild-Whitt (1979) studied "alternative" newspapers, health clinics, and other organizations that self-consciously rejected bureaucracy in favor of more cooperative forms. In one health clinic, for example, all jobs were shared (to the extent legally possible) by all members: doctors would periodically answer telephones and clean the facility, while nurses and paramedical staff would conduct examinations and interview patients. While doctors were paid somewhat more than other staff members, the differences were not large and were the subject of negotiation by everyone who worked at the clinic. This health collective had two primary concerns: to provide personalized, inexpensive, high-quality medical service to a low-income community, and to treat all members of the collective as equal in value.

How successful were these early experiments? On the one hand, so long as the collectives remained small and committed to their cooperative values, they were able to function and provide services to their clients. On the other hand, vastly reduced pay differentials beteen professional and other employees, job-sharing, and collective decision making often made it difficult to compete with organizations that shared none of these values. In some of the collectives studied by Rothschild-Whitt, the original cooperative values tended to erode, and compromises were made with more conventional organizational forms.

Today, successful collectivist organizations include groups that are dedicated to helping their members solve personal problems. Among the most well-known "self-help" groups are those comprised of alcoholics, people with eating disorders (anorexics, bulimics, and compulsive overeaters), or people with mild psychological problems. These groups are initially formed by people with a particular problem or disability. They are small, informally run, and concerned with helping their members overcome their difficulties. They are nonbureaucratic, and shun specialists and experts. Instead, their meetings often consist of members recounting their difficulties, sharing experiences, and obtaining group support for their efforts. Many of the most successful groups are based on "12-step" programs designed to get their members to openly acknowledge their problem and take personal responsibility for its solution. As long as these groups remain small and informal, they continue to operate cooperatively. When they grow in size, they run the risk of developing bureaucratic structures and losing their more humane orientation.

Flexible Organizations

Some organizational theorists argue that large bureaucratic organizations cannot respond quickly or efficiently to the rapid changes occurring in the world today. In an environment that has been characterized as "permanent white water" (Vaill, 1989), where the only thing constant is change, any organization that suffers from too much bureaucratization is doomed. A number of writers have called for "flatter," "leaner," more flexible organizations, organized as networks rather than hierarchical bureaucracies, and with very few permanent employees (for example, Kanter, 1982; Toffler, 1984; Naisbitt, 1982, 1990; Peters, 1992).

The example of IBM is instructive in this regard. IBM had long been a "blue-chip" company whose computers dominated the business machine industry. IBM was large, bureaucratic, and highly successful. As a result, it was also inflexible in its ways of operating. The company was unwilling to risk investing in technologies that might undermine sales of its computers, and it was unable to alter an inflexible management style that had proved successful over many years. When global competition produced inexpensive desktop personal computers that were sufficiently powerful to challenge IBM's larger, more expensive mainframes, the company was slow to develop its own line of personal computers, partly out of fear of undermining sales of its larger machines. As a result, hundreds of "clone" companies filled the gap, developing their own powerful desktop computers that sold at a fraction of IBM's prices. The result? IBM has been forced to reorganize, lay off as many as half of its global workforce, and become less bureaucratic and more flexible in its response to changing market conditions. While this has improved IBM's sales, it has also cost workers thousands of jobs (Chapter 15).

We have already noted that there are many rungs in the bureaucatic ladder, and that this can impede the free flow of communication. Every member of the bureaucracy must go through proper channels, and by the time information reaches the top it may be too late to act. In a global economy, where lines of communication span the planet, such barriers can prove fatal to an organization. On the other hand, in more networked organizations members can access one another directly. There is a great deal of evidence that the presence of such networks partially accounts for the economic success of some ethnic groups, regions, and even entire nations (Kotkin, 1993; Piori and Sabel, 1984; Porter, 1990a, 1990b; Hamilton, 1990; Orru, Hamilton, and Suzuki, 1989; Orru, Biggart, and Hamilton, 1991; Orru, 1991).

Even today, it is possible to directly communicate with the top officer of one of the largest organizations in the world—the United States government. President Clinton (or at least his staff) can be sent electronic mail by anyone in the world with a computer and a modem. If you have access to electronic mail, try it: his E-mail address is CLINTON @ WHITEHOUSE.GOV.

GLOBALIZATION: ORGANIZATIONS THAT SPAN THE WORLD

Although there have long been organizations that are global in scope, such organizations have grown rapidly during the twentieth century and have virtually exploded during the past 50 years (Feld and Jordan, 1983; Jacobson, 1984). Organizations concerned with managing trade or international communications existed in the nineteenth century, but it wasn't until the creation of the short-lived League of Nations in 1919 that truly global formal organizations appeared, with elaborate bureaucracies and member nations around the world. The United Nations, created in 1945, is perhaps the most preeminent modern example of a truly global formal organization (see Box 6.3).

Scholars divide international organizations into two principal types, depending on whether their membership consists of nations or private organizations. Both types are characterized by regularly scheduled meetings of representatives from member groups or nations, formal procedures for making decisions, and a permanent headquarters where the principal business is conducted. Both types have grown apace with the world economy. Global businesses require stability to operate effectively, common manufacturing standards, currencies that can be easily exchanged for one another, and in general a secure and predictable global environment in which to operate. All of these have contributed to the growth of international organizations concerned with securing such conditions.

The first type of global organization is the **international governmental organization (IGO),** which consists of a group of *international organizations established by treaties between governments for purposes of conducting business between the nations comprising its membership.* Examples include the United Nations, the North American Treaty Organization (NATO), the European Community (EC), the Association of South East Asian Nations (ASEAN), and the North American Free Trade Agreement (NAFTA). IGOs often emerge for reasons of national security (both the League of Nations and the United Nations were created following highly destructive world wars), regulation of trade, social welfare or human rights, or, increasingly, environmental protection. Although there were only a handful of such organizations in the mid-ninteenth century, the number had grown to 50 by 1914, 80 by 1939, and well over 600 today (Jacobson, 1984).

Globalization

The United Nations—An Increasingly Important Global Organization

The United Nations is the preeminent example of an international governmental organization (IGO). It was founded in 1945 with 51 members, a number that has increased to 180 today—including 27 added since 1990 alone, mainly new nations created out of the former Soviet Union and its satellite countries in Eastern Europe. Its members reflect numerous different cultures and societies, speak a bewildering array of different languages, and present an enormous range of interests and concerns. Yet this global organization manages to function effectively in a number of vital areas and has assumed increasing importance in recent years

The United Nations is a formal bureaucratic organization that relies on a large number of specialized agencies to conduct its daily business, reflecting the range of problems and issues that exist in an increasingly interdependent world. Some agencies are concerned with fostering improved global communications in the areas of mail and telecommunications, aviation, weather, and ocean navigation. Others seek to enhance social welfare and promote peace. The latter include agencies concerned with global labor, food and agriculture, refugees, health, education, culture, banking

and finance, trade, and economic development.

Although the United Nations has engaged in a small number of peacekeeping and military operations, its major importance has been in other areas. For example, it has enacted a number of arms control treaties that restrict or prohibit the use of nuclear, biological, and chemical warfare. It has also adopted a "planetary management" perspective calling for action in areas deemed especially important to the future of the planet. These include the global population explosion and the growth of enormous, impoverished cities; the status of women and human rights; global poverty and hunger; the growth of deserts, and balancing economic development with protection of the planetary environment.

The United Nations, like all IGOs, is ultimately dependent on the goodwill of its member nations. In this it differs from formal organizations that exist within a single country, which (unlike the UN) often possess the means to enforce compliance with their decisions. When the decisions of IGOs such as the UN run counter to the interests of their most powerful member nations, they are usually powerless to act in an effective manner. Indeed, until the Cold War ended with the collapse of the Soviet

The United Nations, headquartered in New York City, is an example of a global international governmental organization (IGO). It has roughly 180 members who develop policies and programs concerning global communications, various aspects of global social welfare, international economics and trade, and world peace. The UN has also played a limited military role in war-ravaged areas around the world, working to put an end to the strife.

Union in the late 1980s, the UN was often unable to make decisions at all, particularly when the United States and the Soviet Union were in disagreement. During the 1980s, the United States even refused to pay its full share of membership fees, because it opposed UN policies.

As the nations of the world come to increasingly appreciate the global nature of the problems they confront, the United Nations may become more important as a global organization. While competing interests among powerful member nations make it unlikely that it will become the sort of "world government" some of its founders envisioned, the United Nations may continue to acquire increased authority for making and enforcing decisions in the years to come.

| Map 6.1 | Offices and Holdings of The News Corporation, a Global Organization |

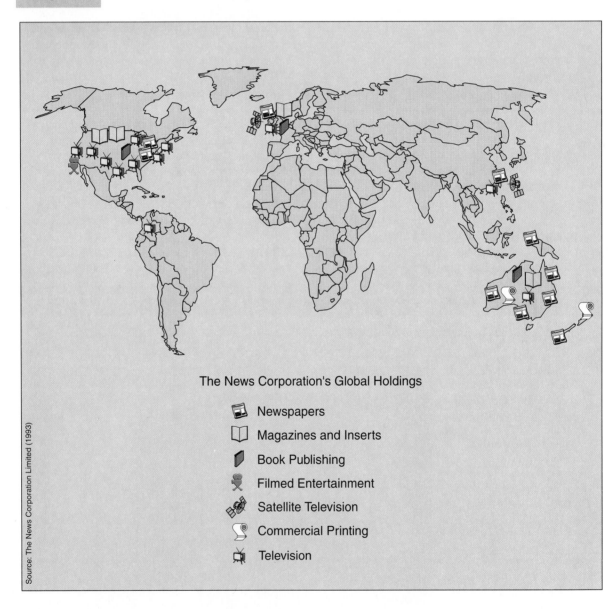

Source: The News Corporation Limited (1993)

The News Corporation's Global Holdings

- Newspapers
- Magazines and Inserts
- Book Publishing
- Filmed Entertainment
- Satellite Television
- Commercial Printing
- Television

News Corporation is an example of a global organization. It owns a wide range of businesses centered on mass media and publishing, including such diverse enterprises as Hong Kong's STAR satellite, newspapers, television systems, and publishing houses such as HarperCollins, publisher of this textbook.

IGOs can wield considerable power, provided that their member nations can agree to take action. Yet since nations ultimately control the use of military force, there are limits to the authority of even the most powerful IGOs, whose strength derives from the voluntary compliance of their member nations. The United Nations, for example, is entirely dependent on its members for finances and military power. Even though the UN has 180 member nations and a large number of important economic, cultural, and social programs, its political power is limited. Although it did mount a military effort to counter the Iraqi invasion of Kuwait in 1991, its military forces remained under their respective national commands. In the case of the former Yugoslavia, on the other hand, even though the United Nations condemned the atrocities that were occurring, it has been largely powerless to intervene.

The second type of global organization is the **international nongovernmental organization (INGO),** which consists of a group of *international organizations established by agreements between the individuals or private organizations comprising its membership.* Examples include the the World Federation of Trade Unions, the International Planned Parenthood Federation, the International Sociological Association, the International Council of Women, the African Football Confederation, and Greenpeace. Like IGOs, the number of INGOs has increased explosively in recent years—from a half dozen in the mid-ninteenth century

to 330 in 1914, 730 in 1939, more than 6,000 today, and a projected 11,000 by the end of the century (Jacobson, 1984; Feld and Jordan, 1983). Yet although they are far more numerous than NGOs, INGOs have far less power. Their activities are primarily concerned with promoting the interests of their members at the global level, largely through influencing the United Nations or individual governments. INGOs also engage in research, education, and the dissemination of information by means of international conferences, meetings, and journals.

There is a third type of international organization, but it does not fall neatly into either of these two categories. **Transnational organizations** are *bureaucratic organizations whose operations span national boundaries, but are centrally directed by citizens from a single country.* The principal examples are global businesses (sometimes termed *transnational corporations*) and religious bodies; these will be considered separately in Chapters 15 and 17.

International organizations arise, not surprisingly, when nations have a need to interact with one another. As national borders become less capable of containing key economic, cultural, and environmental activities, international organizations can be expected to grow in number and importance. Still, at the present time nations remain the primary actors on the global stage, with international organizations assuming a decidedly secondary role.

C H A P T E R   S U M M A R Y

1. There are two principal kinds of groups in society, **primary groups** and **secondary groups.** The latter are especially important in industrial and postindustrial society.

2. **Reference groups** provide a standard for judging our attitudes or behaviors. They are an important source of our self-image—what sociologist Charles Horton Cooley termed the "looking-glass self."

3. Group size is an important factor in group dynamics. Larger groups tend to be more stable than smaller groups, although their intensity may diminish as well. Groups of more than a dozen or so people usually develop a formal structure.

4. **Networks** constitute an important source of relationships, including connections that can be extremely important in business and politics. All members of society do not have equal access to the most influential economic and political networks.

5. **Leaders** are individuals who can influence the members of a group. Leaders may be concerned with group tasks, or the emotional well-being of the group. The most common form of leadership is **transactional**—routine leadership concerned with getting the job done. Less common is **transformational leadership,** which is concerned with changing the very nature of the group itself.

6. **Power,** the ability to mobilize resources and get things done, derives from two principal sources: the personal characteristics of the leader, and the importance of the position that the leader occupies.

7. **Formal organizations** are organizations that are rationally designed to achieve their objectives by means of rules, regulations, and procedures. They can be coercive, utilitarian, or normative, depending on the motivation for joining. One of the most common types of formal organizations in modern society is the **bureaucracy.** Bureaucracies are characterized by written rules and regulations, specialized offices, hierarchical struc-

ture, impersonality in record-keeping, a technically competent adminisrative staff, and professional management.

8. The **iron law of oligarchy** holds that large-scale organizations tend to overly concentrate power in the hands of a few people, who themselves may be hungry for more power. As a result, even supposedly democratic organizations, when they become large, tend to become undemocratic.

9. A number of organizational alternatives to bureaucracies exist. These include Japanese style organizations, which provide lifetime security and some degree of participation in decision making, **collectives,** which emphasize cooperation and humane working conditions, and networked organizations that increase flexibility by reducing hierarchy.

10 .Two important forms of global organization are **international governmental organizations (IGOs)** and **international nongovernmental organizations (INGOS).** Both play an increasingly important role in the world today, and IGOs—particularly the United Nations—may become key organizational actors as the pace of globalization increases.

QUESTIONS FOR DISCUSSION

1. To what extent do individuals in the United States tend to conform to authority? What is the evidence that most people are either conforming or nonconforming?

2. What are the principal characteristics of bureaucratic organizations? What are the advantages and disadvantages of this type of organization?

3. What alternatives exist to bureaucratic forms of organization? How do these differ from conventional organizations in terms of hierarchy and human relations within the organization?

4. What are the principal types of global organizations, and what role are they likely to play during the remainder of the twentieth century?

KEY TERMS

authority (*See* legitimate authority)

bureaucracy: A formal organization based on bureaucratic authority.

bureaucratic authority: Authority based on written procedural rules, arranged into a clear hierarchy of authority, and staffed by full-time paid officials.

coercive organization: An organization in which people are forced to give unquestioned obedience to authority.

collective: A small group of people that operate by agreement or consensus.

dyad: A group consisting of two persons.

expressive leader: A leader concerned with the well-being of the group itself.

formal organization: An organization that is rationally designed to achieve its objectives, often by means of explicit rules, regulations, and procedures.

groupthink: A process by which members of a group ignore ways of thinking and courses of action that go against the consensus of the group.

guanxi: Chinese business networks based primarily on social rather than purely economic foundations.

ingroup: A group toward which one feels particular loyalty and respect.

instrumental leader: A leader concerned with accomplishing the task at hand.

international governmental organizations (IGO): A group of international organizations established by treaties between governments for purposes of conducting business between the nations comprising its membership.

international nongovernmental organization (INGO): A group of international organizations established by agreements between the individuals or private organizations comprising its membership.

iron law of oligarchy: An inevitable tendency for large-scale bureaucratic organizations to become ruled by a handful of people in a highly undemocratic fashion.

keiretsu: Enormous business and financial groupings that provide substantial coordination and control within the Japanese economy.

leader: A person who is able to influence the behavior of other members of a group.

legitimate authority: A type of power that is recognized as rightful by those over whom it is exercised.

meritocracy: A bureaucracy in which positions are filled purely on the basis of a person's merits or qualifications.

network: All the connections that link a person with other people, and through them to the persons with whom these people are connected.

normative organization: An organization people join on a voluntary basis, to pursue a morally worthwhile goal without expectation of material reward; sometimes called a voluntary association.

oligarchy: Rule by the few.

organization: A group with an identifiable membership that engages in concerted collective action to achieve a common purpose.

outgroup: A group toward which one feels antagonism and contempt.

personal power: Power that derives from a leader's personality.

positional power: Power that officially stems from the leadership position itself.

power: The ability to mobilize resources and achieve a goal despite the resistance of others.

primary group: A group characterized by intense positive and negative emotional ties, face-to-face interaction, intimacy, and a strong, enduring sense of commitment.

quality circle: A small group of workers and managers operating as a team to solve problems and improve product quality.

reference group: A group that provides a standard for judging one's attitudes or behaviors.

secondary group: A group characterized by large size, impersonality, and fleeting relationships.

social aggregates: Simple collections of people who happen to be together in a particular location at a certain time but do not significantly interact or identify with one another.

social categories: Groupings that share some common characteristic but do not necessarily interact or identify with one another.

social group: A collection of people who regularly interact with one another on the basis of shared expectations concerning behavior, and who share a sense of common identity.

surveillance: The ability to monitor people, either through direct observation, or by keeping records.

total institution: An institution that encompasses all aspects of one's life; examples are prisons, the military, asylums, concentration camps, or hospitals.

trained incapacity: A learned inability to exercise independent thought; according to Thorstein Veblen, a characteristic of bureaucrats.

transactional leader: A person who is concerned with accomplishing the group's tasks, getting group members to do their jobs, and making certain that the group achieves its goals.

transformational leader: A person who is able to instill the members of a group with a sense of mission or higher purpose, thereby changing the nature of the group itself.

transnational organization: A bureaucratic organization whose operations span national boundaries but are centrally directed by citizens from a single country.

triad: A group consisting of three persons.

utilitarian organization: An organization that people join primarily because of some material benefit or gain they expect to receive in return for membership.

RECOMMENDED FOR FURTHER READING

Aldrich, Howard E., and Peter V. Marsden. (1988). "Environments and Organizations." In Neil J. Smelser, *Handbook of Sociology*. Newbury Park, CA: Sage.
   A review of the current state of thinking in the sociological study of organizations, and the ways in which they are shaped by their environments.

Bass, B. M. (1990). *Bass and Stogdill's Handbook of Leadership: Theory, Research, and Managerial Applications* (3rd ed.). New York: Free Press.
   A standard inventory of social science research on all aspects of management and leadership, reports the major theories and their findings.

Ferguson, Kathy E. (1984). *The Feminist Case Against Bureaucracy*. Phildelphia: Temple University Press.
   As the title suggests, this book reexamines the Weberian notion of bureaucracy from a feminist perspective, arguing that the hierarchical structure of authority reflects a patriarchal notion of social organization.

Kanter, Rosabeth Moss. (1983). *The Change Masters: Innovation for Productivity in the American Corporation*. New York: Simon & Schuster.
   A leading sociologist of business organizations examines the organizational leaders who are successful in changing their corporations to be competitive in a global economy.

Ouchi, William G. (1982). *Theory Z: How American Business Can Meet the Japanese Challenge*. New York: Avon Books.
   The now-classic statement of the Japanese style of management; urges American firms to adopt it before they lose out in global competition.

Deviance and Crime

CHAPTER OUTLINE

THINGS TO LOOK FOR

1. How do sociologists explain the existence of deviant behavior?
2. Under what circumstances have ordinary people engaged in unspeakably violent acts?
3. Has crime—or only the perception of crime—increased substantially in recent years?
4. Who commits crimes, and why?
5. What effect does globalization have on deviance?

INTRODUCTION: A BRUTAL BEATING

Around midnight on March 2, 1991, police in Los Angeles apprehended a black motorist, Rodney King, after a high-speed chase. As King got out of his car, the police knocked him to the ground and began beating him with their batons. A passerby happened to capture the incident on video, which was shown repeatedly on worldwide television. The brutality of the beating, which horrified viewers, is vividly captured in the following description by two sociologists:

> "[King was] twice impaled with wires from an electronic TASER gun . . . while being repeatedly beaten, blow after blow after blow—dozens of blows, 56 in all, about the head, neck, back, kidneys, ankles, legs, feet—by two police officers wielding their two-foot black metal truncheons like baseball bats. . . . A third officer . . . was stomping King" (Skolnick and Fyfe, 1993).

Four police officers were directly involved in the use of force; two other officers observed from a helicopter while shining a spotlight on the scene, another 14 stood by and watched while the beating took place, and seven others came by during the beating and left. No officer made a move to stop the beating.

The four police officers who did the actual beating, all of whom were white, were eventually brought to trial. The trial, however, was moved to a distant suburb populated disproportionately by retired police officers, on the grounds that the officers could not get a fair trial in racially divided Los Angeles. The virtually all-white jury found the officers "not guilty." The conclusion seemed inescapable that had the officers been tried by a multiracial jury in any American city they would have been found guilty (Skolnick and Fyfe, 1993). In fact, when they were brought to trial a second time for violating federal civil rights laws, they were indeed convicted, although on lesser charges.

Since the videotape was so graphic, showing the police repeatedly beating King while he was lying helpless on the ground, many people were astounded at the verdict. Nor was the Rodney King beating unique. Between 1987 and 1990 Los Angeles residents filed 4,400 misconduct complaints against the Los Angeles Police Department. The city of Los Angeles paid $9.1 million in 1989 and $11.3 million in 1990 to settle lawsuits filed against the police. Many residents in the predominantly black and Latino neighborhoods of Los Angeles regarded the King beating as just another example of police brutality, and the acquittal of the four officers as further proof that the standards of justice were different for whites and nonwhites. When the verdict was announced, nonwhite parts of the city erupted in rioting. People were beaten, stores looted, and buildings burned. More than a billion dollars in damage was done to the area, causing the loss of thousands of jobs.

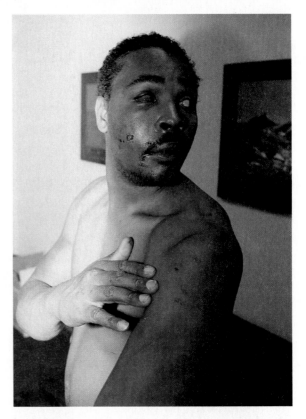

After being stopped for speeding following a high-speed chase, motorist Rodney King was severely beaten by four Los Angeles police officers while 14 others stood by and watched. Following the acquittal of the four officers by an all-white jury, rioting broke out, causing more than a billion dollars in damage. Both the police beating and the subsequent rioting are examples of behavior most Americans would define as deviant.

WHAT IS DEVIANCE?

Deviant behavior is behavior that *violates social norms and values shared by people in a particular culture.* It is "abnormal" behavior only in the sociological sense that it runs counter to prevailing social norms (*ab* means "away from," while *norm,* as we saw in Chapter 3, means a shared rule or standard). It is important to understand that sociologists do not use the term "deviant" to refer to something that is morally bad or wrong, only to describe behavior that is different in terms of the norms and values of a particular culture. Deviant behavior may range from violating relatively trivial norms, to actions that run counter to deeply held beliefs and values.

Was the police beating of Rodney King deviant? Clearly, many of the people who rioted thought it to be all-too-normal, at least in terms of routine police conduct in nonwhite communities. In fact, the police do have a great deal of authority to use whatever force they deem necessary, since their work is often extremely dangerous (Skolnick and Fyfe, 1993). Yet from the standpoint of most people who viewed the videotape, beating an unarmed motorist as he lay on the ground, even by the police, was plainly deviant in terms of the ordinary norms of conduct in American society.

Were the people who rioted deviant? Clearly, the police and most other Americans thought so; setting fires, looting, and beating innocent people are against the law and violate society's norms of acceptable conduct. Such actions are in fact instances of **crime,** a *particular form of deviance consisting of acts that violate norms that have been enacted into criminal law.* Yet many of the rioters apparently did not regard their actions as deviant, much less criminal; rather, their motives ranged from expressing outrage with the Rodney King verdict to simply seizing an opportunity to get their "share of the pie." This example illustrates the difficulty and challenge of the sociological study of deviance. The task of sociology is to explain deviance in terms of the norms and values of particular groups in society, as well as of society as a whole.

Deviance and Conformity

Up until now, we have emphasized the ways in which societies seek to ensure a high degree of conformity to their norms and values. Yet despite such pressures for conformity, deviance also flourishes in all soceities. Why is this the case?

Some degree of deviance results from prevailing societal attitudes toward conformity. Although people in all societies are expected to conform to group norms, in many societies they are also expected and encouraged to "be different" and "express their individuality."

In the cultures of Western Europe and the United States today, the life-cycle stage associated with adolescence, the teens, and even the early twenties is assumed to be one of experimentation and nonconformity. Young people traditionally sport a variety of nonconforming (from the point of view of adults) clothing and hairstyles.

Even in these "deviant" patterns, however, no matter how bizarre their appearances may seem to their elders, young people act in accordance with standards learned from their peers or from the media. The very fact that we are able to label a look as "grunge" or "hip-hop" suggests a standard of conformity that defines that particular style. Over time, what once was deviant becomes accepted. Long hair for men in the 1950s was considered so unusual that men who chose this style were stigmatized by their peers as deviant and often forced to cut their hair by school authorities. Earrings for men were unthinkable, since they were regarded as an exclusively feminine accessory. Long hair has since gone into and out of fashion several times, and today is no longer considered deviant, while single earrings are

Sociologists generally believe that what is labeled as deviant depends on cultural definitions and therefore is subject to change as definitions change. The "punk" look was a sign of rebellion and nonconformity when it first appeared, but many of its features have today become more widely accepted, and some are even copied among fashion designers.

worn by grade school boys and professional athletes alike.

The Pluralistic Character of Modern Societies

In order for an act to be regarded as deviant, it must violate social norms. Yet modern societies are **pluralistic;** they are *comprised of groups with diverse and often conflicting norms and values.* As a result, different groups may have different definitions of deviance (Rossi et al., 1974). For example, most people in American society would agree with the norm "thou shalt not kill." Yet in the United States (as in virtually all societies), circumstances exist under which killing another person is morally as well as legally approved. Examples might include soldiers in wartime, police officers in the line of duty, people defending themselves from assaults, and executioners carrying out court orders. Even here, however, people may disagree. Pacifists oppose killing under any circumstances, while some Americans oppose the death penalty. In fact, most industrial nations other than the United States lack the death penalty, and societal norms against violence are so strong in some that police officers are not permitted to carry weapons.

Furthermore, norms and values change over time; behaviors condemned as deviant at one time may be regarded as entirely normal at another. The highly sexualized content of much film and television is today taken for granted, yet images routinely depicted on MTV would have been regarded as scandalously deviant a single generation ago. Today, it is relatively common for "safe sex" to be publicly discussed in high school and even junior high school classrooms. Yet 30 years ago, a junior high school teacher who engaged in frank and explicit classroom discussions about any kind of sex would have been regarded as deviant and possibly fired.

The Banality of Evil

Under certain circumstances even the most seemingly extreme cases of deviant behavior, such as mass murder, can be regarded as perfectly normal, even commonplace. Consider the tragic but historically widespread example of **genocide,** *the institutionalized practice of systematically killing the members of a particular racial, religious, or ethnic group.* Policies of genocide were at times practiced against the American Indians by settlers who sought their land. They are practiced today by Serbs against other ethnic groups who stand in the way of their vision of a "greater Serbia" comprised of large portions of the former Yugoslavia, and by the Hutu majority against the Tutsi minority in the African country of Rwanda.

During World War II, the German government officially adopted a policy of genocide against Jews, gypsies, homosexuals, and people perceived as having mental deficiencies. Among the Jews alone, more than six million men, women, and children were killed by gassing, shooting, and various forms of torture. Rounding up so many human beings, transporting them by train to concentration camps in Germany and Poland,

Whether or not behavior is defined as deviant depends on the situation in which it occurs. These Somali teenagers are publicly displaying a pair of camouflage pants that they claim were taken from a soldier as a trophy of war. Although such behavior would ordinarily be considered deviant, during warfare there is invariably a suspension of otherwise strongly held norms.

executing them, and cremating their remains during a time of war required the coordinated effort of thousands of people. Responsibility for overseeing this effort fell to a middle-aged bureaucrat, Adolph Eichmann. Although Eichmann escaped from Germany in 1945, he was eventually captured by Israeli agents and brought to Israel to stand trial for his crimes.

What kind of a rare monster must Eichmann have been in order to be responsible for such horrific deviant acts? Hannah Arendt (1987) conducted an in-depth study of Eichmann at the time of his trial in hopes of answering this question. Her conclusion was shocking to many people: Eichmann's most remarkable characteristic was that he was entirely unremarkable. He was simply another faceless, colorless bureaucrat "doing his job," no different than thousands of other bureaucrats in modern society, except that his "job" was the complete extermination of all European Jews. Arendt concluded that what we call "evil" is actually **banal,** or

commonplace: under the right circumstances, the most ordinary people are capable of the most extraordinarily deviant acts (see Box 7.1).

BIOLOGICAL EXPLANATIONS OF DEVIANCE

Are some people born with a predisposition to be deviant? Most attempts to answer this question have focused on criminal behavior. On the one hand, some have argued that criminal behavior is determined by anatomical, biological, or other genetic differences inherited at birth. On the other hand, others have sought to explain deviance in terms of more social factors. Although the pendulum has swung in both directions, today most sociologists believe that criminal behavior is the result of socialization and other individual experiences. Before turning to sociological theories, however, let us briefly consider some influential efforts to

Box 7.1

Critical Thinking

How Can Ordinary Men Commit Extraordinary Crimes?

Christopher Browning (1992) studied the "ordinary" lower-middle and working-class men who comprised one of the German police units responsible for executing Jews in Poland. As you read the following account, ask yourself whether this provides evidence in support of Arendt's notion of the "banality of evil." What do you think you would have done under the circumstances?

On the morning of July 13, 1942, the police unit commander informed his men that they were to perform a "frightfully unpleasant task": It was their assignment to round up all the Jews in the town of Jozefow, Poland, separate out the men and send them to work camps, and then slaughter the remaining 1,500 Jewish women and children. Although the commander offered to excuse any of the older men who weren't up to such a task, only 12 out of 500 accepted the offer to be relieved from the mass murder of women and children. Browning

(1992, pp. 71–72) describes the commander's instructions:

> The men were explicitly ordered to shoot anyone trying to escape . . . those too sick or frail to walk to the marketplace, as well as infants and anyone offering resistance or attempting to hide, were to be shot on the spot. Thereafter, a few men of First Company were to escort the "work Jews" who had been selected at the marketplace, while the rest of First Company was to proceed to the forest to form the firing squads. The Jews were to be loaded onto the battalion trucks . . . and shuttled from the marketplace to the forest. . . .

Less than a fifth of the police balked at the actual killing, and as the unit moved on to other cities to conduct similar mass murders, its members "became increasingly efficient and calloused executioners" (p. 77).

account for deviance and crime in purely biological terms.

Early Studies: The Importance of Body Type

Cesare Lombroso, one of the most famous nineteenth-century proponents of the biological theory of crime, argued that criminals were a throwback to earlier, more ape-like human beings not yet completely eliminated from the species. Crime was therefore the result of inherited "stigmata" and "degeneration" (Lombroso, 1896). Following the search for biological causes of criminal behavior, Charles Goring later explained criminal behavior as a result of mental inferiority (Goring, 1972; orig. 1913) and Ernest Hooton (1939) theorized that there existed a "criminal stock" in the gene pool that cropped up from time to time. William Sheldon (1949) and Eleanor and Sheldon Glueck (1950, 1956) theorized that criminals could be distinguished from noncriminals on the basis of physique. They claimed to have discovered three basic physique types: muscular "mesomorphs," skinny "ectomorphs," and flabby "endomorphs." Criminals, they maintained, were concentrated among those with mesomorphic ("lean, muscular and thick skinned") body types.

Critical Assessment Much of the early research was based on comparing the physiques of prisoners with those of nonprisoners, which seriously biased the results. It is not surprising, for example, that male prisoners tend to be muscular ("mesomorphic"), since they often spend a great deal of time engaged in body building, physical conditioning, and athletics. Moreover, food is restricted in prison and alcohol is rarely available, further contributing to a lean, muscluar physique. Finally, many people who commit crimes (particularly "white-collar crimes") are not in prison, and so are excluded from prison-based research.

Contemporary Studies: Sociobiological Theories of Crime

Much research currently being conducted on the biological sources of criminal behavior is associated with **sociobiology,** which we defined in Chapter 3 as the effort to *infer from the study of insects and other social animals that there are genetic bases for competition, cooperation, aggression, envy, and other specific behaviors.* One promising avenue for research on humans has come from the comparison of twins. Identical twins have exactly the same genetic makeup, and so should exhibit exactly the same criminal behavior, if indeed biology determines criminality. Fra-

ternal twins, on the other hand, are like any siblings: They share some (but not all) genetic materials. Sociobiological theory would therefore predict that some (but not all) fraternal twins would exhibit the same criminal behavior.

In one early study, for example, Lange (1930) identified prisoners who were twins and then located and determined whether the remaining twin was also in trouble with the law. Of the 13 pairs of identical twins he found, 10 were both criminal. By way of contrast, only 2 of the 17 pairs of fraternal twins were both criminals. Until the 1960s, most twin studies were based on identifying an incarcerated twin, and then attempting to determine if the twin sibling was also criminal. More recent research has simply sought to identify pairs of twins in the general population, and then to determine the criminal records of each. These have tended to somewhat support the earlier conclusion that identical twins are more likely to have similar criminal records than fraternal twins (Christiansen, 1977) One of the best-known sociobiological studies of criminal behavior reviewed all the twin research conducted between 1929 and 1976 and concluded that a genetic component to crime had been demonstrated (Wilson and Herrnstein, 1985).

Critical Assessment There are three principal weaknesses to twin studies. First, most are based on extremely small samples, and so it is risky to draw general conclusions (Rose, et al., 1984). Second, identical twins often share socialization experiences that are far more likely to be similar than those of fraternal twins. Since identical twins are often difficult to distinguish from one another, they are likely to be treated the same, dressed alike, and sometimes even confused with one another by acquaintances, teachers, and friends. Their subsequent behavioral similarities undoubtedly reflect the extraordinarily high degree of similarity in their childhood and young adult experiences (Christiansen, 1977). Third, even among identical twins only about a third of all pairs exhibit criminal behavior for both siblings. If criminal behavior were genetically determined, *all* brothers (or sisters) of identical twins who are criminal should themselves be criminal as well.

FUNCTIONALIST EXPLANATIONS OF DEVIANCE

How do sociologists account for the enormous variability in what counts as deviant in a particular society? Not surprisingly, functionalism, conflict theory, and symbolic interactionism provide different although often complementary answers to this basic question, and we shall take up each in turn.

As we saw in Chapter 1, functionalists tend to regard societies as more or less unitary organisms in which each part contributes to the overall performance of the whole. From the functionalist perspective, society is characterized by a high degree of consensus over norms and values, and any explanation of deviant behavior must take such consensus into account.

Emile Durkheim: Deviance and Social Bonds

Functionalist theorists account for the existence of deviance as they would any other aspect of society, in terms of its function for society as a whole. It may seem puzzling at first to conclude that deviance exists because it serves some social function, but that is exactly the claim made by Emile Durkheim, the originator of functionalist theory more than a century ago. Durkheim (1951; orig. 1893) argued that deviance serves the function of defining the **moral boundaries** of society, *a sense of what is normal and acceptable behavior, achieved partly by identifying certain acts as deviant and punishing the people who commit them severely.* While Durkheim recognized that a certain degree of pluralism over norms and values exists in modern societies, he assumed that within any society there is a fundamental consensus concerning right and wrong "on which all healthy consciences agree." Acts violating that "conscience" are regarded as deviant; their punishment serves to reaffirm and reinforce society's shared consensus.

What happens when society's shared consensus breaks down? According to Durkheim, the outcome is **anomie,** *a state of normlessness resulting from a high level of confusion and conflict over norms, or an absence of norms altogether.* In his view, anomie is a potentially serious social problem in modern societies, and a major source of deviant behavior. In one of his most famous studies, Durkheim (1951; orig. 1893) sought to show how anomie was a principal cause of suicide in different parts of France. As discussed in Chapter 1, Durkheim claimed to show that when people lacked agreement on basic norms and values, they were more likely to take their own lives.

Durkheim therefore concluded that a certain amount of deviance is "normal," serving to remind people of society's normative boundaries. The absence of such boundaries, however, can also lead to deviance. Although subsequent research has led to qualification of his original findings on suicide (Douglas, 1967; Simpson and Conklin, 1989; Wasserman, 1989), Durkheim's overall notions about the functions of de-

viance have proved to be extremely durable for functionalist theory.

In one well-known study, for example, sociologist Kai Erikson (1966) drew on many of Durkheim's insights to explain the persecution of women as witches in Puritan New England. Erikson, like Durkheim, assumed that deviant individuals often provoke extreme anger in others, causing them to draw together in a common bond of righteous indignation. According to Erickson, when the moral authority of the Puritan communities began to weaken at the end of the seventeenth century, the public humiliation and execution of witches served the function of focusing community anger, bringing its members closer together. Erikson concluded that "crime waves" of witchcraft were actually created by the community in order to reestablish its fading moral boundaries.

Critical Assessment Functionalist theory has been criticized for overestimating the degree of consensus that actually exists in modern societies (Friedman, 1992). As pointed out above, modern societies are highly pluralistic, and even where consensus exists, not everybody follows the rules: People routinely exceed the speed limit, cheat on their taxes, and lie about their age.

Durkheim's notion that societies somehow create deviance to reaffirm their moral boundaries has also been faulted. Critics point out that "societies" don't create anything; only people do. According to this criticism, in order to really understand why something is defined as deviant in a particular society, one must look at how specific individuals or groups are able to make their definitions stick. Even if deviance does serve the function of reminding people of what is right and what is wrong, that does not explain why such a definition arose in the first place. For example, contrary to Erickson's assertion that the witchcraft "crime waves" in Puritan New England resulted from "the community's" need to reestablish its moral boundaries, more recent research suggests that the very notion of witchcraft was created by male religious leaders in an effort to thwart outspoken women who were challenging their authority (Chambliss and Seidman, 1982, pp. 197–201; Chambliss and Zatz, 1994).

Robert K. Merton and Structural Strain Theory

Although Durkheim's theory sought to explain deviant behavior in broad terms, he did not specifically offer a functionalist explanation of different forms of deviance. That task fell to an American sociologist, Robert K. Merton, who in 1938 adapted Durkheim's concept of anomie to explain deviance as resulting from a person's position in the social structure. According to Merton's theory, **structural strain** is *a form of anomie that occurs when a gap exists between the goals society sets for people and the means society provides for people to achieve those goals* (see Table 7.1).

According to Merton (1968; orig. 1938), in most societies there is a broad normative consensus on the goals people pursue as well as the legitimate means for achieving them. In American society, for example, there is wide agreement on the goal of success, as measured in terms of wealth, power, or prestige. Similarly, there is general agreement on how such a goal is best achieved: through education, hard work, and honest endeavor. For many people, society's goals as well as the means for achieving them are accepted as legitimate. People often work hard to achieve some measure of success; they avoid lying and cheating (at least most of the time) and in general abide by social norms. Merton referred to such behavior as *conformity.*

In Merton's view, deviance results from the strain between socially desirable goals and the socially acceptable means for achieving them. In general, he argued, the lower a person's social position, the more likely that person is to experience such a strain. This results in several different types of deviant behavior.

Merton calls the most common form of deviance *innovation,* because it involves an acceptance of society's goals but the adoption of innovative yet deviant means for achieving them. In Merton's view, lower-class people as a group are—like all Americans—under enormous pressures to achieve material success, yet because of their class position are often denied the means for achieving it. As a result, he predicts, members of this class are more likely than middle-class people to engage in innovative deviant behavior. Examples might include the street-corner dealer who hopes to become rich by selling drugs, the unskilled worker who engages in petty theft, or the shopkeeper who puts his or her children through college by failing to report income to the Internal Revenue Service. Even upper-

status people may innovate, however, as in the case of the high-level businessperson who embezzles company funds to support a costly standard of living.

A second form of deviance, *ritualism,* is the exact opposite of innovation: it occurs when a person rejects society's goals but nonetheless rigidly adheres to the socially approved means for achieving them. An example might be the low-level bureaucrat who has given up all realistic hope of achieving material success yet continues to work doggedly at his or her job. In Merton's view, people whose social position provides them with limited but tenuous rewards are likely to be ritualists, avoiding riskier forms of deviance such as innovation out of fear that they will lose everything if they are caught.

Retreatism describes yet another form of deviant response—a rejection of both the goals and the means for achieving them. Individuals who have retreated have "dropped out" of society. According to Merton, they include some poets, writers, and artists; alcoholics and drug addicts; some homeless people; and persons who have given up all hope.

Finally, *rebellion* characterizes those who reject society's goals and means but substitute alternative ones of their own making. Rebels have a vision of a radically different society, and they seek to implement it in their own lives and sometimes the lives of others. They are often part of a counterculture (Chapter 3), and may range from hippies to revolutionaries who are trying to completely transform the nature of society.

Critical Assessment Merton's strain theory of deviance implies that groups with access to legitimate means for achieving culturally prescribed goals should have low rates of deviance. The fact is, however, that deviant behavior is commonplace among all groups in modern societies, including those with ready access to legitimate means for achieving their dreams (Coleman, 1994; Adler and Adler, 1994). For example, one of the most prevalent and costly forms of deviant behavior in modern societies consists of crimes committed by high-

Table 7.1   Merton's Theory of Deviance: The Strain Between Culturally Defined Goals and the Means for Achieving Them

Individual Response	Cultural Goals	Legitimacy of Means
Conformity	Accept	Accept
Innovation	Accept	Reject
Ritualism	Reject	Accept
Retreatism	Reject	Reject
Rebellion	Reject/substitute	Reject/substitute

Source: Merton (1968; orig. 1938, pp. 230–246).

Members of the Branch Davidian religious group in Waco, Texas, committed mass suicide by setting fire to their compound after a prolonged armed standoff with federal officials. According to Merton's structural strain theory of deviance, the Branch Davidian form of deviance might have been labeled either retreatism *or* rebellion. *Federal officials decided on the latter definition, with controversial and disastrous results.*

status persons in connection with their work (see the section entitled "Who Commits Crimes?" at the end of this chapter).

Similarly, one would not expect to find high rates of deviant behavior on college campuses if anomie theory is correct. College students are much more likely to find compatibility between cultural goals and legitimate means for achieving them than most other groups. Yet forms of deviance such as under-age drinking, using false identification, consuming illegal drugs and theft are in fact quite common (Elliot and Huiznga, 1983; Schreiber, 1993; Johnston et al., 1992). It seems clear that structural strain is not enough to explain the existence of deviant behavior in many parts of American society.

Other Functionalist Theories of Deviance

Other efforts to account for deviance in functionalist terms have emphasized the importance of opportunities for deviance to occur and the failure of society to adequately ensure conformity. We shall briefly consider each of these two arguments, before turning to conflict theories of deviance.

Opportunities for Deviant Behavior

Richard Cloward and Lloyd Ohlin (1960) elaborated Merton's strain theory by pointing out that for deviance to occur, a person must first have access to appropriate opportunities for deviance. If a hard-driving executive is frustrated in her efforts to reach the top, for example, she may be tempted to *innovate* by cheating her company out of money. Unless she has access to others who will support her embezzlement, however, she is un-

likely to be able to do so effectively. Similarly, for a lower-class individual to take up safe-cracking as a means for overcoming his poverty, he must learn how to break open locked safes as well as "fence" the stolen goods. His success will depend to a great deal on his access to others, both to learn the required skills and dispose of the goods (King and Chambliss, 1984). The existence of extensive opportunities for drug trafficking in many urban neighborhoods helps to explain why this particular form of deviance is so widespread in U.S. cities today.

Cloward and Ohlin argue that in general, the existence of a particular opportunity structure will help to shape the type of deviance that occurs. Where opportunities for successful criminal activities exist, innovation is more likely to result. Conversely, where such opportunities are lacking, deviance may be more likely to take the form of *retreatism* or dropping out. In order to explain the existence of deviance, therefore, it is necessary to look not only at differences in social strain that are based on an individual's position in the social structure, but also at the social opportunities that exist for deviant activity.

Control Theories of Deviance

Gottfredson and Hirschi (1990) argue that since opportunities to deviate are everywhere, what needs to be explained is why most people live relatively conforming lives. Their explanation is that people conform unless the mechanisms that bind people to society are weak or nonexistent. Most deviant acts are spontaneous occurrences: A group of teenagers sees a drunken homeless man walking down the street and decides to rob him; a man knows of a house where people are on vacation and decides to burglarize it. The difference between those who succumb to the temptation and those who do not lies in the degree to which the individual has been successfully socialized to norms of conventional behavior.

There is some evidence in support of control theory. For example, delinquency is somewhat less common among youth who have strong family attachments, perform well in school, and in general have something to lose by becoming deviant in the eyes of others. Furthermore, delinquents tend to be deviant in all kinds of ways, not just in breaking certain rules: They are more likely to use drugs, be truant from school, talk back to teachers, and be seen by parents as "uncontrollable" (Gottfredson and Hirschi, 1990; Hirschi, 1969). This suggests that deviance may partly result from a general breakdown of social control for some members of society.

CONFLICT EXPLANATIONS OF DEVIANCE

Conflict theorists reject the notion that society is a unitary organism comprised of functionally interdependent parts. Rather, they argue, society consists of different groups or social classes with conflicting interests. For one group to benefit, another must pay. Furthermore, conflict theorists do not accept Durkheim's notion that societies are characterized by a consensus on which "all healthy consciences" agree. While some degree of consensus must exist for a society to operate at all, according to conflict theorists consensus is constantly being challenged.

Different groups will therefore have different standards of what is normal and what is deviant, based on their differing interests. More than a half century ago Thorsten Sellin (1938) pointed to the fact that the culturally diverse populations of modern societies such as the United States virtually ensured normative conflict, since norms and values held by some groups would surely be regarded as deviant by others. This is no less likely to be true today, given the large influx of immigrant subcultures into the United States during the past decade (Chapter 3).

How is it that certain acts come to be defined as deviant for the society as a whole? The answer, according to conflict theory, is that in any society there is a ruling group whose wealth and power enables it to define, legislate, and enforce those notions of deviance that reinforce its privileged position. Groups lacking the power to have their interests defined as normal are therefore seen as deviant and sometimes even criminal (Vold, 1958). Legislation outlawing marijuana usage during the 1930s, for example, was passed at a time when the principal users were poor Mexican immigrants, jazz musicians, and others of marginal status (Becker, 1963).

According to conflict theory, society's ruling groups are usually able to socialize others into accepting their notions of deviance, since they control the government, educational institutions, the media, and other important sources of information. But sometimes the ruling definitions of deviance are challenged by those who lack power. For example, conflict theorists would point to the civil rights movement as an example of how seemingly powerless people could successfully challenge laws they regarded as unjust, even when those laws were supported by the ruling groups in many states. As a result of conflicts created by the civil rights movement, acts of discrimination that were both normal and lawful 40 years ago are today deviant and illegal.

Structural Contradiction Theory

Structural contradiction theory is a *type of conflict theory that accepts Merton's notion that societies often contain strains that lead to deviance, but combines it with the notion that such strains result from aspects of a social structure which are mutually incompatible with one another* (Chambliss, 1988). According to this theory, for a capitalistic society to thrive firms must keep wages and salaries down, lest rising labor costs undermine profitability. Such downward pressures on wages have led to a loss of jobs and declining incomes in recent years (see Chapter 8). Yet at the same time society must promote extensive consumerism, since firms cannot profit unless they sell large quantities of products. This is an example of a structural contradiction.

Trapped between a norm of rampant consumerism and an economic system that makes such consumerism impossible for many, people experience enormous pressures to engage in deviant acts. Such acts may range from cheating on one's taxes to writing bad checks, from piling up unpaid bills to outright theft. It is not just lower-income people who are under pressure to engage in such "innovative" behavior, as Merton had argued, but everyone who wants to enjoy a higher standard of living than is currently possible.

Structural contradiction theory holds that societies with the greatest gap between what people earn and what they are encouraged to buy will have the highest levels of deviance. Since there are substantial differences between industrial societies in this regard, it is possible to test this theory. For example, societies such as Finland, Denmark, and Norway have a high level of wealth with a much smaller gap between rich and poor than the United States; hence they should have somewhat lower crime rates. There is some evidence that this is the case, with rates of assault, robbery, and murder anywhere from three to 35 times higher in the United States than in these countries, although there are numerous other factors which also explain these differences (Archer and Gartner, 1984).

Critical Assessment Although conflict theorists can point to numerous examples of how deviance is defined in ways that serve the interests of ruling groups, critics of the theory argue that it cannot account for norms and laws that define the behavior of the ruling groups themselves as deviant. For example, laws prohibit corporations from engaging in all kinds of potentially profitable activities. There are legal limits on the number of hours a person can be compelled to work each day, restrictions on the use of child labor, requirements for workplace safety and health safeguards, and guarantees of workers' right to strike. Yet clearly corporate owners and executives are powerful members of society's ruling groups, who strongly opposed such legislation when it was first introduced. Even though conflict theory claims that powerful groups are unlikely to permit their own activities to be defined as deviant, legislation that did so was nonetheless enacted.

Even the most powerful people in the world may be punished for engaging in acts that are defined as deviant. Billionaire bankers and stockbrokers go to jail for engaging in deals that are against the law, while politicians are forced out of office for such seemingly minor acts of corruption as failing to repay questionable loans from the House Bank. Richard Nixon was forced to resign when it was revealed that he was aware of illegal activities conducted by his reelection committee. Thus, even though conflict theory points to important differences in our ability to define deviant behavior, it is clear that factors other than power also lead to some acts being defined as deviant.

SYMBOLIC INTERACTIONIST EXPLANATIONS OF DEVIANCE

As we saw in Chapters 1 and 5, symbolic interactionism emphasizes the importance of the views of others in developing one's self-concept. According to this view, we see ourselves largely through the eyes of others, and the resulting sense we get of ourselves has a strong influence on how we behave. This idea has been fruitfully applied to deviant behavior.

Labeling Theory

An important application of symbolic interactionism is found in **labeling theory,** an approach which holds that *deviance (like all forms of human behavior) is the result of the labels attached to us by other people.* One of the founders of labeling theory, Edwin Lemert (1951), studied a group of people in the Northwest with an unusually high incidence of stuttering. By observing the interaction between people in this group, he concluded that stuttering was common partly because people were stigmatized and labeled "stutterers." According to Lemert, the labeling process has two steps: primary deviance and secondary deviance. **Primary deviance** occurs *when an activity (such as stuttering) is labeled as deviant by others.* **Secondary deviance** occurs *when a person labeled as deviant accepts the label as part of his or her identity, and as a result begins to act in conformity with the label.* Persons labeled as stutterers begin to see themselves through this lens, taking on the appropriate role—which includes a greater amount of stuttering than otherwise will have been the case.

In another well-known study, Howard Becker (1963) studied marijuana use among jazz musicians and came to the conclusion that important aspects of this form of deviance could also be explained by labeling theory. He found that people had to learn to label the physiological feelings associated with smoking

Stephen Hawking, the world's leading theoretical physicist, is afflicted with a degenerative neurological disease that has progressively lost him the use of motor control over his body. Hawking's accomplishments, which most people would regard as an insuperable challenge, are mirrored by other physically challenged people, who often consider such societal labels as "handicapped" or "disabled" to be greater barriers than their own physical limitations.

marijuana as pleasurable. Once certain reactions were labeled as appropriate, they would then come to be associated with marijuana use. Repeated use led smokers to label themselves as marijuana users, resulting in still more persistent smoking. As we noted earlier, Becker also pointed out that marijuana smoking was defined as deviant because others had the power to label it as such. He thus analyzed not only the process by which people come to acquire deviant labels, but the differential ability of people in society to assign such labels and make them hold.

A study of two deviant high school groups, conducted by one of the authors of this textbook (Chambliss, 1973), lends further support to the notion that power differences are important in labeling (see Box 7.2). Although both groups of boys were equally involved in deviant activity, only the lower-class group was labeled as delinquent. It is especially noteworthy that both groups accepted the labels that were attached to them, and behaved accordingly.

Support for labeling theory comes from studies of mental illness as well. While not all mental illness can be attributed to labeling, evidence suggests that once a label is attached the person will be more likely to exhibit the characteristics of "being mentally ill" associated with the label (Scheff, 1969, 1984; Szasz, 1970, 1987).

Cultural Transmission Theory

Another approach to the study of deviance, also derived from symbolic interactionism, argues that deviant behavior (again, like all behavior) is learned through interaction with others. This approach, which is complementary to labeling theory, draws attention to the ways in which deviant behavior is transmitted by subcultures whose behavior is seen as deviant by the dominant culture.

Albert Cohen (1958), for example, studied the subculture of teenage boys' gangs, in an effort to find out why members engaged in behavior defined as delinquent by the larger society. He concluded that the mainly working-class boys who joined such gangs were caught in a conflict between norms. On the one hand, their own subculture emphasized immediate gratification of one's needs and desires, urging them to enjoy life today without worrying too much about tomorrow. On the other hand, the more conventional middle-class values of the school emphasized hard work and deferring pleasure. This clash of values led the working class boys to delinquent acts, in an effort to reassert their own subcultural beliefs. Acts of vandalism against property, for example, were seen as delinquent by the larger society, yet experienced by the boys as a rejection of rules and regulations they simply did not share. Even violence and murder have been explained as reflecting the accepted behavioral standards of particular subcultures (Wolfgang and Feracutti, 1967; Erlanger, 1974).

One particularly important version of cultural transmission theory was first advanced nearly three-quarters of a century ago by Edwin Sutherland (1928), and later developed by one of his students, Donald Cressey (Sutherland, Cressey, and Luckenbill, 1992). The theory of **differential association** holds that *deviant behavior is largely the result of associating with other persons whose behavior is deviant.* According to this theory, the greater the degree of association, the greater the likelihood the behavior will be deviant. Sutherland sought to show that deviance was a function of such factors as the frequency and intensity of associations, how long they lasted, and how early they occurred in a person's life.

Critical Assessment Symbolic interactionism provides important insights into the ways in which deviant behavior is learned through interaction with other people. While functionalism and conflict theory emphasize the ways in which society as a whole can produce deviance, symbolic interactionism focuses on how particular individuals acquire deviant behaviors and identities. Unfortunately, the weakness of this approach is that it accounts for all forms of behavior, not just deviance. Neither labeling theory nor cultural transmission theory is exclusively concerned with how or why deviance arises in society. Instead, both explain how one learns all norms and values, regardless of whether they are defined as deviant or conventional by the larger society. In other words, both theories explain conformity as well as deviance.

One consequence of this shortcoming is that neither theory can truly explain why deviance is more prevalent among some groups than others, or why some groups have more power to label than others. Both functionalism and conflict theory, on the other hand, are better able to address these important issues. Taken together, the three approaches provide a more complete picture of deviance than any one by itself.

CRIME AND DEVIANCE

As we noted at the beginning of this chapter, crime is a particular type of deviant behavior consisting of acts that are against the criminal law. **Criminologists** are *social scientists who specialize in the scientific study of crime; they include sociologists, political scientists, and psychologists* (Sutherland, Cressey, and Luckenbill, 1992).

It is important to recognize that not all deviant acts are criminal, and that not all criminal acts are universally regarded as deviant. Dyeing your hair purple and

Box 7.2

Critical Thinking

The Roughnecks and the Saints

William Chambliss, an author of this book, studied two gangs of teenage boys for two years. With the permission and cooperation of the boys, Chambliss was able to follow them, talk to them, and watch them during and after school hours. One gang was labeled delinquent by teachers, the police, and others in the community. The other gang was seen as "good kids, headed in the right direction." As you read the following selection from his study (Chambliss, 1973), ask yourself which of the theories of deviance best explains the research results. How useful is labeling theory? Merton's stuctural strain theory?

Eight promising young men—children of good, stable, white upper-middle-class families, active in school affairs, good pre-college students—were some of the most delinquent boys at Hanibal High School. The Saints were constantly occupied with truancy, drinking, wild driving, petty theft, and vandalism. Yet not one was officially arrested for any misdeed during the two years I observed them. . . .

This record was particularly surprising in light of my observations during the same two years of another gang of Hanibal High School students, six lower-class white boys known as the Roughnecks. The Roughnecks were constantly in trouble with police and community even though their rate of delinquency was about equal with that of the Saints. What was the cause of this disparity?

Hanibal townspeople never perceived the Saints' high level of delinquency. The Saints were good boys who just went in for an occasional prank. After all, they were well dressed, well mannered and had nice cars. The Roughnecks were a different story. Although the two gangs of boys were the same age, and both groups engaged in an equal amount of wild-oat sowing, everyone agreed that the not-so-well-dressed, not-so-well mannered, not-so-rich boys were heading for trouble.

Why did the community, the school, and the police react to the Saints as though they were good, upstanding, nondelinquent youths with bright futures but to the Roughnecks as though they were tough, young criminals who were headed for trouble? Why did the Roughnecks and the Saints in fact have different careers after high school—careers which, by and large, lived up to the expectations of the community?

Differential treatment of the two gangs resulted in part because one gang was infinitely more visible than the other. This differential visibility was a direct function of the economic standing of the families. The Saints had access to automobiles and were able to remove themselves from the sight of the community. . . . Through necessity the Roughnecks congregated in a crowded area where everyone in the community passed frequently, including teachers and law enforcement officers. They could easily see the Roughnecks hanging around the drugstore.

To the notion of visibility must be added the difference in the responses of group members to outside intervention with their activities. If one of the Saints was confronted with an accusing policeman, even if he felt he was truly innocent of a wrongdoing, his demeanor was apologetic and penitent. A Roughneck's attitude was almost the polar opposite. When confronted with a threatening adult authority, even one who tried to be pleasant, the Roughneck's hostility and disdain were clearly observable. Sometimes he might attempt to put up a veneer of respect, but it was thin and was not accepted as sincere by the authority

Selective perception and labeling—finding, processing, and punishing some kinds of criminality and not others—means that visible, poor, nonmobile, outspoken, undiplomatic "tough" kids will be noticed, whether their actions are seriously delinquent or not. Other kids, who have established a reputation for being bright (even though underachieving), disciplined and involved in respectable activities, who are mobile and monied, will be invisible when they deviate from sanctioned activities. They'll sow their wild oats—perhaps even wider and thicker than their lower-class cohorts—but they won't be noticed.

When it's time to leave adolescence most will follow the expected path, settling into the ways of the middle class, remembering fondly the delinquent but unnoticed fling of their youth. The Roughnecks and others like them may turn around, too. It is more likely that their noticeable deviance will have been so reinforced that their lives will be effectively channeled into careers consistent with their adolescent background.

wearing nose rings are regarded as deviant by most Americans, yet they are not against the law. On the other hand, George Washington and Thomas Jefferson are seen as patriots for breaking unjust British laws, while Martin Luther King is similarly honored for leading thousands of people in acts of nonviolent disobedience against laws promoting racial segregation.

Crimes are usually punishable by fines, **incarceration** (*imprisonment*), or both. When most people think of crime they usually think of interpersonal violence (such as murder, assault, or rape) or property crimes (such as robbery, burglary, and theft). Sociologists point out, however, that this image of "crime" is much too narrow. In addition to interpersonal and property crimes, there are other categories of crime that sociologists seek to explain. For example, some illegal acts produce no victims, since the "victims" themselves are the perpetrators of the crime; gambling is one example.

Crime can also be categorized according to who commits it. Some crime is committed by individuals and gangs, some by groups of professional thieves, and some by organized groups of criminals. Some crimes are perpetrated by governments, while others are committed by "white-collar" business managers and executives. We shall turn to these issues after first considering some of the difficulties in measuring crime.

Measuring Crime

Is crime growing or declining? The two official sources of information on crime give different answers to this basic question. Data based on police department reports suggest that the United States is caught in the grips of an unprecedented crime wave, while interviews with randomly selected Americans reveal that crime is actually decreasing.

The first source of crime data, provided by local police departments throughout the country, is summarized in the Uniform Crime Reports of the Federal Bureau of Investigation (FBI, 1993). According to this source, overall levels of crime increased by nearly two-thirds over the past 20 years, while violent crimes more than doubled. This source does show a slight decline in 1992, however. According to the FBI, serious crimes reported to police dropped 3 percent between 1991 and 1992, while violent offenses dropped 1 percent.

On the other hand, when Americans are actually asked whether or not they themselves have been the target of specific criminal acts, they are less likely to say "yes" than they were 10 or 20 years ago. Every six months the National Institute of Justice asks a sample of some 83,000 Americans whether they have been victimized during the preceding six-month period. These "victim surveys" find that crime is actually decreasing

in virtually all categories, with overall levels of crime reaching a 20-year low (Figure 7.1). In fact, since the U.S. population is much larger today then it was 20 years ago, the *percentage* of the population that has been victimized has actually declined. For example, 20 years ago approximately one in three Americans reported experiencing some form of property crime or violent crime during the preceding six months. Today, that figure has dropped to one in four (Bureau of Justice Statistics, 1993; Ostrow, 1993).

How can total crimes reported to police have increased by two-thirds during the past two decades, while people actually report experiencing no overall increase?

There are several reasons for these discrepancies. First, about two-thirds of all crimes go unreported, so statistics on reported crimes are always suspect (Bureau of Justice Statistics, 1992a). Victim surveys provide a much more reliable source of information on crime than police department reports to the FBI. Second, most governmental statistics are gathered by agencies who have a strong stake in reporting increased crime (Chilton, 1993). Since police budgets are most likely to increase if crime is on the rise, it is often in their best interest to find as much crime as possible. During roughly the same 20-year period of declining crime, the number of police officers has doubled (Maguire, Pastore, and Flanagan, 1993). The "war on drugs" in particular has resulted in an increase in reported crimes and arrests, even though people who use or sell illegal drugs do not regard themselves as crime

Figure 7.1   **Surveys of Crime Victims Show Decreasing Crime**

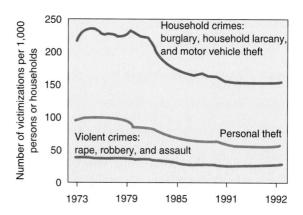

Since 1973, the Bureau of Justice Statistics has conducted nationwide surveys with a sample of some 83,000 people living in 42,000 households. Contrary to the widespread public perception that the country is caught in the grips of an escalating crime wave, these surveys show that the percentage of people victimized by crimes has actually declined during the past decade for most categories of crime. *Source:* Bureau of Justice Statistics (1992a).

"victims" and so would be unlikely to report these activities if asked by the victim surveys. Third, changing definitions of certain crimes has led to an increased reporting for some categories.

Finally, the public perception of rising crime is partly fueled by heightened government and media attention to violent crime, which creates the impression that almost everyone is in danger, even though the statistics indicate otherwise. In fact, apart from poor inner-city residents (whose likelihood of suffering a violent crime is two to three times as great as their suburban neighbors), most Americans are in less danger of violence than they were a generation ago (Bureau of Justice Statistics, 1992a). The increased availability and use of automatic "assault-type" weapons also makes the crimes that do occur especially deadly, often involving multiple victims and creating a random quality to violence that is especially terrifying.

Types of Crime

Interpersonal Violence

There are approximately 25,000 cases of murder reported to the police every year, or about one for every 10,000 people (Maguire, Pastore, and Flanagan, 1993, p. 358). This is by far the highest rate in the industrialized world—for example, nearly 20 times the rate reported in France (Archer and Gartner, 1984).

Unlike murder, crimes such as rape and assault often go unreported since they often involve family members, friends, and acquiantances, so exact figures are hard to come by. For example, estimates of the percentage of rapes reported to police range from a tenth to a half (Russell, 1984; Bureau of Justice Statistics, 1992a).

Contrary to what many people think, most interpersonal crimes, such as murder, rape, and assault, occur between acquaintances rather than strangers. Sociologists of crime point out that you are in much greater danger of being attacked, murdered, or raped by someone in your family or immediate friendship group than someone unknown to you (Fingerhut and Kleinman, 1990; Reidel and Zahn, 1985). Diana Russell (1984) found that only 16 percent of rapes reported in her survey were committed by a stranger, the same percentage as committed by dates and fewer than the number done by acquaintances (23 percent). In fact, she found that 84 percent of all rapes were committed by someone known to the victim (including dates, boyfriends, husbands or ex-husbands, relatives, friends, acquaintances, or authority figures). The data on murder show similar results. In the most reliable study to date, approximately 60 percent of the murders were either family or acquaintance murders and only 14 percent could be classified as stranger murders (Riedel and Zahn, 1985; Sanday, 1979; LaFree et al., 1992).

Assaults, legally defined as *unlawful attacks by one person upon another for the purpose of inflicting severe or aggravated bodily harm,* are more common than murder or rape. They include physical abuse of a spouse or child, as well as attacks that occur as a result of an argument, dispute, or interpersonal conflict. Even victim surveys cannot accurately estimate the number of assaults, since victims are reluctant to report that they have been assaulted if the perpetrator is a friend, spouse, or parent. One study estimates that violent abuse of a child by a parent occurs in about one-sixth of all families with children aged 3 to 17 (Strauss and Geles, 1986; Strauss et al., 1980).

It is estimated that as many as two million women are abused by their husbands each year (Strauss et al., 1980), while 30 percent of women who are murdered are victims of their husbands or boyfriends (FBI, 1993). As many as 30 percent will be the target of a violent sexual attack sometime in their lives, mainly by boyfriends, spouses, dates, or acquaintances (Johnson, 1980). As many as one in five women attending college will be the victim of a rape or attempted rape by the time they graduate (Meyer, 1984). A recent study of several thousand women in 32 colleges found that more than half had been sexually abused in some way. Fifteen percent had been raped, another 12 percent were the targets of attempted rape, and 26 percent had either been subjected to sexual coercion or unwanted sexual contact (Koss, Gidycz, and Wisniewski, 1987; see Chapter 11). Black and Latino women are more likely to be victims of violent crime than white women, primarily because of their greater poverty; low-income women are twice as likely to suffer violent crimes as high income women, and three times as likely to be raped (Bureau of Justice Statistics, 1992a).

Property Crimes

By far the most common crimes committed in industrial societies are property crimes, including **robbery** (*taking something by the use of violence or the threat of violence*), **burglary** (*unlawful entry of a premise with the intent to commit a crime*), and **larceny** (*the unlawful taking of property from someone other than one's employer*). Larceny—simple theft—is by far the most common form of crime, with nearly $4 billion lost each year to shoplifting alone.

Victimless Crimes

The term **victimless crimes** refers to *acts prohibited by law in which those who are affected are willing and voluntary participants.* Victimless crimes typically involve an exchange of illegal goods and services between consenting adults, or other illegal acts in which there is no victim. Vagrancy, purchasing drugs, and gambling are typical victimless crimes (Schur and

Bedau, 1974; Geis, 1972; Austin and Irwin, 1990). Although no individual is necessarily harmed by such "crimes," they are thought by some to be harmful to society as a whole (Schur and Bedau, 1974).

Who Commits Crimes?

From reading the newspapers and watching television, you might get the impression that only lower-income gang members from inner-city neighborhoods commit crimes. In fact, illegal activities are commited to some degree by nearly everybody in society. People who exceed the speed limit break the law, sometimes with lethal consequences. The same is true of those who drive after having a few drinks at a party. Many people routinely cheat on their taxes, lie about their age on application forms, or use illegal drugs. To better understand crime, it is useful to look at different groups that break the law.

Individuals and Gangs

Young men are more likely to commit violent crimes than any other category of people. For example, homicide rates among young males aged 15 to 24 are more than twice as high as the rate for the general population. One study found that in comparison with 21 other industrial nations, young men in the United States were on average ten times as likely to kill one another, and three times as likely to use firearms in the process (see Figure 7.2).

Three-quarters of all U.S. homicides among young males involved the use of guns, compared with one-quarter in other countries (see Figure 7.3). In 1987, for example, Japan had only 47 homicides involving young males; 8 of these involved firearms. In the United States, by way of comparison, there were 4,223 homicides among this group, 3,187 of which involved guns (Fingerhut and Kleinman, 1990).

Large urban areas have always spawned criminal gangs of various sorts. In fact, the study of urban gangs has been a topic of sociological study since the beginning of the century (e.g., see Thrasher, 1927). A **gang** can be defined as *a group of people, usually young, who hang around together and commit criminal acts either for economic gain or to protect their territory* (Thrasher, 1927; Short and Strotdbeck, 1965; Jankowski, 1991; Campbell, 1984; Moore, 1991; Moore and Pinderhughes, 1994). Recently, Martin-Sanchez Jankowski (1991) has provided a rich and extensive sociological analysis of a broad range of ethnically based urban gangs (see Chapter 2). Jankowski concludes that in poverty-stricken inner-city areas, gangs provide an important means by which individuals can band together in order to better compete for scarce resources.

Figure 7.2   **Homicide Rates for Young Men Aged 15–24 The United States and Other Industrial Nations, 1986–1987**

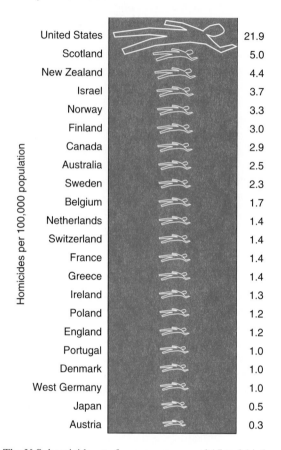

	Homicides per 100,000 population
United States	21.9
Scotland	5.0
New Zealand	4.4
Israel	3.7
Norway	3.3
Finland	3.0
Canada	2.9
Australia	2.5
Sweden	2.3
Belgium	1.7
Netherlands	1.4
Switzerland	1.4
France	1.4
Greece	1.4
Ireland	1.3
Poland	1.2
England	1.2
Portugal	1.0
Denmark	1.0
West Germany	1.0
Japan	0.5
Austria	0.3

The U.S. homicide rate for young men aged 15 to 24 is by far the highest among industrial nations. It is more than four times higher than Scotland, which has the second-highest rate, and nearly 44 times higher than Japan. *Source:* Fingerhut and Kleinman (1990, p. 3293).

Echoing Merton's "strain theory" of deviant behavior (see above), Jankowski argues that gangs develop norms that legitimize criminal activities as a necessary and even desirable way to achieve the American dream of material success—a dream that would otherwise prove impossible to achieve. Gang members denigrate people in their communities (including their own parents) for "selling out," and "toeing the line" when doing so gets them nowhere. The key to success—and therefore respect—lies in committing criminal acts that bring material gain.

In recent years gangs organized around the selling of illegal drugs have become prominent in many impoverished sections of U.S. cities. The gangs are organized along age lines with the older members supplying drugs to younger members who peddle them on the street. The gang leaders offer protection from other

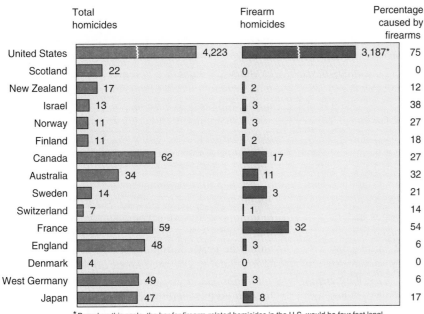

	Total homicides	Firearm homicides	Percentage caused by firearms
United States	4,223	3,187*	75
Scotland	22	0	0
New Zealand	17	2	12
Israel	13	3	38
Norway	11	3	27
Finland	11	2	18
Canada	62	17	27
Australia	34	11	32
Sweden	14	3	21
Switzerland	7	1	14
France	59	32	54
England	48	3	6
Denmark	4	0	0
West Germany	49	3	6
Japan	47	8	17

*Based on this scale, the bar for firearm-related homicides in the U.S. would be four feet long!

Figure 7.3

Firearm-Related Homicides Among Young Men Aged 15–24 The United States and Other Industrial Nations, 1986–1987

No country approaches the United States in terms of the absolute number of homicides among young men aged 15 to 24. In 1986 and 1987, for example, there were more than 4,200 homicides in the United States; there were 62 in Canada and 47 in Japan. Three-quarters of all homicides in the United States were caused by firearms, also by far the highest percentage of any industrial country. *Source:* Fingerhut and Kleinman (1990, p. 3292).

gang members, support in the event of an arrest, and training in how to avoid arrest and trouble (Williams, 1989, 1992; Campbell, 1984).

Professional Thieves

Some of the most efficient crimes are those committed by **professional thieves,** *people who earn their livelihood by committing crimes on a regular basis.* Like members of any profession, professional thieves acquire a great deal of specialized skill and experience, and often take pride in their work. There

are many different types of professional thieves including "confidence artists," safe-crackers ("boxmen"), bank robbers, check forgers ("laying paper"), and counterfeiters. Exact data on the number of professional thieves is not available (Sutherland, 1937; Jackson, 1972; King and Chambliss, 1984).

Organized Crime

Sociologists define **organized crime** as *crimes committed by criminal groups involving the provision of illegal goods and services* (Block, 1991). Gambling,

In most societies adolescent boys and girls form groups of friends. Adults and other adolescents may attach labels to these groups that have consequences for the members. Lower-class urban groups are often defined as gangs, a label carrying negative connotations. The typical gang in multicultural societies is ethnically or racially homogenous, as is the "Korat Boyz," a gang of Cambodian youth in Long Beach, California.

prostitution, illegal drugs, black marketeering, and money laundering (see below) are some of the most prominent activities of organized crime (Albini, 1971; Albanese, 1989; Walker, 1989). To meet the demand for such goods and services, criminal organizations have flourished in urban areas since the 1800s (Walker, 1989; Block, 1991; Block and Chambliss, 1981; Chambliss, 1988; Hess, 1973). Movies such as *The Godfather, Scarface,* and *Goodfellas* have popularized organized crime, helping to make it a part of American folklore.

Over the years criminal organizations have recruited members and leadership from the more impoverished groups in society, usually those who have most recently arrived in large cities with great hopes and limited means to achieve them. Thus organized crime in the United States has been dominated at various times by Irish, Jewish, Italian, and increasingly today African Americans (Albanese, 1989; Hess, 1973). Organized crime is a major industry in the United States, accounting for hundreds of billions of dollars in profits and considerable political influence. Today organized crime groups control a hundred billion dollar a year drug industry, illegal gambling throughout the United States and Europe, the smuggling of weapons, and international rings of prostitution (Block, 1991; Dorn et al., 1992; Inciardi, 1992).

State Organized Crime

State organized crime consists of *acts defined by law as criminal that are committed by state and government officials in the pursuit of their jobs as representatives of the government* (Chambliss 1989; Barak, 1992; S. Cohen, 1993). Needless to say, governments do not keep statistics on their own criminal behavior. Nonetheless we know that such crimes are not uncommon (Barak, 1991; Podesta, 1993; Chambliss, 1989;

Etzioni, 1984). An early example of state organized crime was state-supported piracy and smuggling. From the fifteenth to the eithteenth centuries the governments of various European countries gave licenses to pirates to attack the ships and colonies of nations competing with them for control of the gold and silver discovered in the Americas and being shipped to Europe (Best, 1980; Chambliss, 1989). This was done despite the fact that the laws of the nations issuing the licenses made piracy one of the most serious offenses in the criminal law (Best, 1980; Chambliss, 1989).

While piracy may seem to be a remote historical example, state organized crime continues today unabated in more modern forms. For example, there is evidence that in the 1960s and 1970s during the Vietnam War and in the 1980s during the Civil War in Nicaragua the U.S. Central Intelligence Agency (CIA) allowed Asian and Latin American international narcotics smugglers to ship opium, heroin, and cocaine into the United States on airplanes leased by the CIA. In return for this assistance the drug traffickers helped the U.S. government finance groups it supported in unofficial "secret" wars in Laos, Cambodia, and Nicaragua (McCoy, 1973, 1991; Owen, 1983).

In another prominent example, former National Security Advisor John Poindexter was found guilty in 1990 of lying to Congress about his role in the "Iran-Contra" scandal. The top-level agency he directed had secretly sold weapons to Iran, using the profits to illegally finance the "Contras," a group that was attempting to overthrow the government of Nicaragua. Congress had earlier explicitly outlawed the U.S. government from providing aid to the contras (Nemeth and Levin, 1990).

Governments, including the U.S. government, have also illegally financed elections, plotted the assassina-

The sinking of the Rainbow Warrior, *a ship owned by the environmental group Greenpeace, was an act of* state organized crime. *The* Rainbow Warrior *was headed for an area where the French were planning to test nuclear weapons in the ocean. French intelligence officers blew up the ship in an effort to stop the protest; one crew member died as a result.*

tions of foreign leaders, and in other ways criminally interfered with the operation of foreign governments. At Senate hearings held in 1976 it was admitted by U.S. government officials that they conspired to murder several heads of foreign governments, including Patrice Lumumba of Uganda, Kwame Nkrumah of Ghana, Fidel Castro of Cuba, and Salvador Allende of Chile (Pike, 1977; Earman, 1967). Evidence was also presented that the CIA enlisted the services of organized crime figures in the unsuccessful Castro assassination attempts. Such conspiracies, which were sometimes successful, constitute violations of American as well as international law, yet no member of the U.S. government has ever been charged with any of these crimes.

White-Collar Crime

White-collar crimes are *those committed by people of high social status in connection with their work* (Sutherland, 1949). There are two principal types of white-collar crime. Some are committed solely for the gain of the individual offender. Examples would include accountants who steal money from their employers by altering their books, or lawyers who overcharge their clients or otherwise cheat them out of money they are due. In a recent example, one prominent Virginia attorney was sentenced to five years in prison for cheating his clients out of $2.4 million (Hall, 1993).

A much more costly type of white-collar crime occurs when corporate executives commit criminal acts that benefit the company for which they work. In a recent example, the Prudential Corporation, one of the oldest and most powerful insurance and stock companies in America, was found guilty in 1993 of fraudulently selling stocks to hundreds of thousands of its customers. The company had to pay $41 million in fines and more than $330 million in claims to its customers (*Washington Post,* 1993). The Prudential was but one of thousands of such cases that occur every year (Clinard and Yeager, 1979; Sutherland, 1949; Geis and Meier, 1977).

Perhaps the most significant example of white-collar crime in recent years has been related to willful mismanagement in the savings and loan industry. During the 1980s, countless banks followed questionable lending procedures, resulting in hundreds of billions of dollars in bad loans. Many then sought to hide their practices from federal investigators. In one of the most notorious cases, Charles Keating, the owner of a large savings and loan association, was convicted of paying $1.4 million to five U.S. senators in 1987 in an effort to prevent his bank from being shut down. The result was that many people lost all the money they had deposited in the bank; this included a large number of elderly people who were cheated out of their life savings. "Bailing out" Keating's bank ultimately cost the U.S. taxpayers billions of dollars.

Clinard and Yeager (1979) studied the criminal, civil, and administrative violations of nearly 600 of the largest manufacturing, wholesale, retail, and service corporations in the United States. They also reviewed the records of 25 federal agencies and compiled data on legal actions either initiated or completed during 1975 and 1976. Firms were charged with violating a number of administrative, environmental, financial, labor, manufacturing, and trade laws. They found that three out of five manufacturing firms had been charged with at least one violation, while two out of five had been charged with multiple violations. A small number of firms (13 percent) accounted for more than half of

In a prominent recent example of white-collar crime, *Charles Keating was sentenced to prison for fraudulent acts connected with his savings and loan companies. Hundreds of savings and loan companies throughout the United States went bankrupt, accused of a variety of criminal acts that cost some depositors their life savings and U.S. taxpayer billions of dollars during the 1980s and early 1990s.*

all violations—an average of 24 per firm over the two-year period.

Some of the most serious corporate white-collar crimes involve deliberately withholding information about product dangers from the public, or violating worker health and safety regulations (Curran, 1993; Coleman, 1994). In one well-publicized example, several top executives of a corporation were sentenced to 25 years in prison for permitting the existence of hazardous working conditions that killed one employee by cyanide poisoning (Chambliss, 1988).

Crime Control

The United States imprisons a higher proportion of its citizens than any industrialized country in the world, and possibly any other country (Christie, 1992). There are nearly 900,000 inmates in state and federal prisons today, more than two and a half times as many as there were in 1980 (Figure 7.4). During the same period, the U.S. population grew only 12 percent. The number of inmates therefore increased 14 times faster than the population as a whole. It costs roughly $27,000 to keep a person in prison for a year—more than it costs to go to most colleges. A life sentence for a 25-year-old will eventually cost society more than a million dollars (Mandel and Magnusson, 1993).

Who Gets Arrested, and Why?

How can rates of imprisonment be rising, at a time when victim surveys actually show most categories of crime to be decreasing? The stereotype of crime control is the arrest and prosecution of violent criminals who have committed rape, murder, and robbery. Yet of the 14 million people arrested in 1992, only about 1 in 20 were arrested for violent crimes (Mandel and Magnusson, 1993). A study conducted in New Haven, Connecticut, reported that two out of three arrests were for minor offenses; for example, "crimes against morality" and "crimes against public order" accounted for twice as many charges as crimes against property or persons (Feeley, 1992). A study conducted for the National Council on Crime and Delinquency found that more than half of all federal and state prison inmates were guilty of crimes perceived by the public as minor offenses (Austin and Irwin, 1989).

Figure 7.4   The Explosion in State and Federal Prison Populations in the United States

The state and federal prison population in the United States has increased more than two and a half times during the past 12 years, to the point where the United States has the highest rate of imprisonment in the industrial world. Much of this imprisonment is due to drug-related offenses.

Source: Bureau of Justice Statistics (1992b).

Year	Prisoners
1980	329,821
1981	369,930
1982	413,806
1983	436,855
1984	462,002
1985	502,752
1986	545,378
1987	585,292
1988	631,990
1989	712,967
1990	773,124
1991	824,123
1992	883,593

 = 100,000 prisoners

A large part of the increase in arrest and imprisonment has to do with drug-related offenses. About 60 percent of federal prison inmates and 20 percent of state prison inmates are in jail for sale or possession of illegal drugs. Fewer than half of these inmates have been found guilty of a violent crime (Mandel and Magnusson, 1993). One recent study found that although drunk drivers kill more people annually than drugs (including overdose, disease, and the violence associated with the drug trade), the latter bring much harsher prison sentences; some states now mandate up to five years in prison for first-time possession (Mauer, 1993).

Nonwhites are arrested and imprisoned at much higher rates than whites. Currently, one-tenth of all Latino males in their twenties and one-fourth of all African-American males in that age group are in prison, on parole, or on probation. (The comparable figure for white males is 1 in 16.) It is estimated that as many as four out of five African-American males will be arrested at least once during their young adulthood, and many will have numerous arrests (see Box 7.3). Nearly half of all prison admissions today are black (Miller, 1992; Mauer, 1990; Bureau of Justice Statistics, 1993; Mandel and Magnusson, 1993).

There are a number of reasons why nonwhites are more likely to be arrested and imprisoned than whites. First, impoverished inner-city residents are disproportionately nonwhite (Chapter 8), and this is where the "war on drugs" has been focused. For many young, impoverished, poorly educated inner-city males, drug trafficking and other criminal activities are far more lucrative than any realistic alternative. One 1989 survey of young people in Boston estimated that criminal activities paid an average $10 to $19 an hour, compared with an average of $5.60 for legitimate work (Farrell,

1993). As a consequence, drug-related arrests fall disproportionately on nonwhites, particularly African-Americans and Latinos; alcohol-related arrests such as drunk driving, which are treated less severely by the criminal justice system, are concentrated among whites (Mauer, 1993).

Second, police work in general focuses on poor neighborhoods, where crowded living conditions force many activities onto the streets. Gambling or consuming drugs in a middle class suburban home is not likely to attract police attention; doing the same thing on the street, in an alley, or in some public place will likely bring a police response. Even violent arguments or domestic disputes are more likely to attract police attention in crowded neighborhoods than in dispersed suburban homes (Hindelang, 1978). When they are confronted by police, young Latino and African-American teenagers are much more likely to be treated harshly than are middle-class white teenagers, particularly if they "have an attitude" and fail to treat police with expected deference.

Finally, racism also partly accounts for greater arrest and imprisonment rates of nonwhites (see also Chapter 10). Even though many more whites are arrested for crimes than nonwhites, the latter are much more likely to serve time for their offenses. Black youths in particular have a much higher likelihood of being arrested and subsequently jailed than white youths, even when they commit the same crime. Numerous studies have found that although far more white than black juveniles are arrested for violent crimes such as murder, rape, aggravated assault, and robbery and assault, far more blacks actually wind up in custody or are tried as adults for their crimes (Harris, 1990, 1993; Mauer, 1994; Austin, Dimas, and Steinhart, 1992).

Even though federal statistics show that drug use is

A sculpture in front of the United Nation's building in New York City—showing a gun whose barrel has been tied into a knot—symbolizes that organization's commitment to ending war. Although most industrialized nations have not tied up their weapons to avoid war, they have outlawed or severely restricted the personal ownership of guns. The United States remains the principal exception, even though some experts argue that gun control would go a long way toward curbing violent crime.

Box 7.3

Silenced Voices

Young Black Men in Prison

Young black men comprise a disproportionate number of persons arrested and convicted for crimes. As many as one-fourth of those in their twenties are today under the control of the criminal justice system. In the following passage, Jewelle Taylor Gibbs (1994, pp. 141–143), professor of social welfare at the University of California and a leading authority on minority youth development, argues that black men are victims of social and economic injustice, not simply victimizers as they are commonly portrayed. What conclusions do you draw regarding the social causes of young black male imprisonment?

As the final decade of the twentieth century commences, young black males in America find themselves in an increasingly marginalized position, the unwitting heirs to over 370 years of slavery, segregation, and discrimination; the helpless victims of persistent poverty, social injustice, and economic inequality; and the convenient targets of political demagogues who use them as scapegoats for the social and economic problems of the larger society. The cumulative impact of these forces has resulted in a hostile and unpredictable environment for young black males in every institution of this society—the educational system, the social welfare system, the health-care system, the criminal justice system, and the economic system. . . .

In response to this exclusion from mainstream society's channels for achievement, personal development, and social mobility, young black males have found themselves increasingly socially isolated in inner-city ghetto neighborhoods, confined to low-skilled, dead-end jobs, subject to constant harassment by police and prosecutors, and manipulated by the mass media and unprincipled politicians. . . . They have responded to this victimization quite predictably, with feelings of rage and anger, fueled by even greater frustrations as they have seen the preferential treatment accorded to more recent immigrant groups who have been welcomed and encouraged to realize the American dream.

This society has chosen to address the symptoms and signs of black male anger rather than attack the underlying causes and conditions that have fueled that anger. The government has chosen to build prisons rather than low-income housing . . . and society has allowed the criminal justice system to warehouse young black males into jails and prisons rather than provide them with employment opportunities and incentives to education, thus completing the vicious cycle.

If this country does not adopt effective prevention strategies to rescue young black males from this escalating cycle of self-destruction and violence, it will lose another generation of black youth. . . . Are we willing to discard millions of young black men who have the potential to contribute to the economic, social, and cultural development of this nation?

---

higher among white youths than black youths, far more black youths are tried and convicted. White youths, particularly those of working- or middle-class background, are likely to be represented by private attorneys in court, and subsequently referred to their parents, drug treatment programs, or put on probation. Black youths are more likely to wind up in jail. Whatever its original intention, many experts conclude that the "war on drugs" has been a war on the poor (and blacks in particular) in its actual impact (Harris, 1990, 1993; Mauer, 1994; Austin, Dimas, and Steinhart, 1992).

The Impact of Punishment

There are a number of different forms of punishment, each with its own presumed impact on the offender. **Incapacitation** consists of *placing offenders in a location where their ability to violate norms is restricted.* For many years serious lawbreakers were exiled to remote places from which there was little possibility of returning. The colonial United States, as well as Australia, were favorite places for criminals to be sent from England. Today, most countries incapacitate deviants by imprisonment (Foucault, 1979).

Rehabilitation, which consists of *resocializing*

criminals to noncriminal norms and values, is a somewhat more controversial aspect of punishment, since there is conflicting evidence regarding whether the American penal system actually rehabilitates its prisoners. On the one hand, **recidivism,** *the rate at which ex-offenders are arrested for another criminal offense once they are released from jail,* is extremely high in the United States: Roughly two-thirds of offenders released from prison are returned to prison for committing another crime (Bureau of Justice Statistics, 1993). On the other hand, most of these are minor offenses, such as testing positive for drugs or failing to report regularly to their parole officer (Kahn and Chambers, 1991).

Furthermore, very few prisoners receive any significant job training, employment assistance, or treatment for substance abuse during or after their incarceration. Those who do have much lower recidivism rates; prisoners who get a high school or college diploma, for example, are half as likely to return to prison as other inmates (Kahn and Chambers, 1991; Rice et al., 1991; Keller and Sbarbaro, 1994).

Deterrence refers to *the impact of punishment on discouraging crime—not only on those who are punished but on others who learn by their example.* Clearly, given the high recidivism rates just noted, deterrence is not effective in most cases. This has led some to conclude that punishments are not sufficiently harsh (Wilson and Herrnstein, 1985; Mandel and Magnusson, 1993). Yet it is difficult to imagine a harsher punishment than the death penalty, and studies have concluded that even the death penalty does not effectively deter murder (Archer and Gartner, 1984; Bailey and Peterson, 1989; Bohm, 1991; Paternoster, 1991; Gibbs, 1981). In fact, one study claimed that the 36 states with the death penalty had slightly higher murder rates than other states (Bailey and Peterson, 1989), while another study found that murder rates actually declined in a half-dozen industrial nations that had abolished capital punishment (Archer and Gartner, 1984). What is clear is that the death penalty is highly selective in its application; of the 2,700 inmates on death row, all but 34 are men, and 40 percent are African Americans.

GLOBALIZATION, CRIME, AND DEVIANCE

As we shall show in Chapter 8, the creation of a global economy has resulted in the loss of jobs and growing poverty in the United States. This growing gap between what society deems desirable and what is actually possible for most people has had an especially harsh impact on inner-city areas, where joblessness and poverty afflict large portions of the population. As Merton noted more than 50 years ago, it is such groups that have the least to risk and the most to gain by turning to crime. Globalization has thus had an indirect impact on crime, at least for those groups that are bearing its most adverse economic effects.

| **Map 7.1** | **U.S. State-By-State Capital Punishment Figures During Past Decade, For Whites and Nonwhites** |

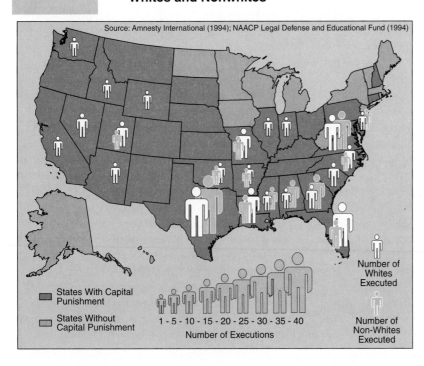

Source: Amnesty International (1994); NAACP Legal Defense and Educational Fund (1994)

States With Capital Punishment

States Without Capital Punishment

1 - 5 - 10 - 15 - 20 - 25 - 30 - 35 - 40
Number of Executions

Number of Whites Executed

Number of Non-Whites Executed

The use of capital punishment, as well as the number of people actually executed, varies widely by state. In all cases, however, a disproportionate number of those executed are non-white, leading some sociologists to conclude that the criminal justice system is racially biased in deciding who is guilty of a capital crime.

Some forms of crime have prospered directly from globalization. Consider the example of drug trafficking. Reduced transportation time and costs, advanced telecommunication technologies, and the weakening of national borders all favor an explosion of globalized businesses (Chapter 15), and these include the world drug trade. Cocaine and opium have been used in many parts of the world for centuries, but only in the last 50 to 100 years have these drugs become readily available to people in the United States and Europe. Much of the opium consumed in the United States (usually in the form of heroin) comes from the Middle East or Southeast Asia; most of the cocaine comes from Colombia and elsewhere in Latin America.

International business organizations engage in a number of criminal activities besides drug smuggling. To take one important example, the global banking system facilitates the secret transfer of profits from criminal enterprises, making detection all but impossible. **Money laundering,** *the practice of converting illegally acquired assets into legal businesses or foreign bank accounts,* is practiced by people who earn income from illegal activities such as drug trafficking or gambling. Money laundering is greatly facilitated by the existence of an international banking system that makes it as easy to deposit funds in banks in Switzerland as it is to use the ATM machine in the nearest shopping center. Even those who earn their income legally often manage to avoid taxes by setting up corporations in other countries (or in the state of Delaware, known world-wide for its business-friendly laws). Such practices often verge on illegality (McBarnet, 1991; 1993).

Globalization can also result in an increase in the *perception* that some behaviors are deviant. As we have noted above, deviance is behavior that violates the dominant cultural norms and values. When globalization brings cultures into contact with one another through immigration, members of the dominant culture are likely to perceive some of the behavior of the immigrant culture as deviant. This is especially likely to be the case if the immigrants are seen as threatening the jobs or livelihood of the country's nationals. Such labeling of different cultural traits as deviant can have deadly consequences (see Box 7.4).

Yet globalization can also point the way toward overcoming such ethnocentric definitions of deviance, by exposing people to different ways of thinking and acting that challenge their own. Growing intercultural contact, whether it be through business travel, tourism, immigration, or simply watching "foreign" films and television, has the potential of fostering greater cultural understandings and acceptance. This may even extend to the legal definitions of deviance. As the United States seeks to grapple with its drug problems, for example, it may look to the Netherlands and other European countries where a greater tolerance toward drug use has led to government programs that avoid criminalization in favor of regulation and treatment.

Box 7.4

Globalization

Immigration and Race Hatred

Globalization is contributing to the massive movement of people across national borders, as millions are lured by promises of better jobs and expanded economic opportunity. Yet immigration is sometimes perceived as a threat by citizens of the "host" country, especially those whose economic circumstances are marginal. When immigrants are seen as competing for scarce jobs, fear and hatred may go hand-in-hand.

In Europe and the United States, racist groups have attacked and killed immigrants, justifying their acts on the grounds that they are "foreigners," "dirty," or simply "different." "Skinhead" bands with names like *Skrewdriver, Brutal Attack, Condemned 84,* and *White Noise* implore their listeners to "stand together against the black tide" and other "foreign" influences. A Portland, Oregon skinhead group beat an Ethiopian immigrant to death with baseball bats in 1988. An estimated 70,000 yearly racial attacks in England have resulted in the murder of dozens of Pakistani and other East Indian immigrants (Hamm, 1993), while attacks on immigrants by German neo-Nazi youths occur regularly.

One of the important challenges facing nations today is how to manage the growing contact between cultures, so as to avoid negative labeling and race hatred.

CHAPTER SUMMARY

1. Notions of what constitutes **deviance** are relative to the norms and values of particular cultures. Even legal definitions of **crime,** a particular form of deviance, differ from place to place and over time, and depend on social and political processes.

2. The **pluralism** of American society makes it extremely difficult to establish universally accepted notions of deviance.

3. Even the most extreme forms of deviant behavior, including acts of **genocide,** can be done by ordinary people under particular circumstances; one task of sociology is thus to better understand the banality of evil.

4. Functionalist theorists explain deviance in terms of the functions it performs for society. Emile Durkheim argued that some degree of deviance services to reaffirm society's normative boundaries, while Robert K. Merton argued that deviance reflects **structural strain** between socially determined values, and the socially provided means for achieving those values.

5. Conflict theories explain deviance in terms of the conflict between different groups or classes in society. **Structural contradiction theory** argues that such conflicts are inherent in social structure; the sorts of structural strains identified by Merton are thus seen as built in to society itself.

6. Symbolic interactionist theorists argue that deviance, like all forms of human behavior, results from the ways in which we come to see ourselves through the eyes of others with whom we interact. Deviance is held to result largely from the labels others attach to us, which in turn reflects its cultural transmission through our **differential association** with others.

7. It is difficult to know with accuracy how much crime exists, since much crime goes unreported. One governmental source of information, based on crimes reported to police, shows rapidly growing crime. The other governmental source, based on surveys with crime victims, shows a decline in crime.

8. While the most heavily publicized crimes are violent crimes, the most common are property crimes and **victimless crimes.**

9. Although crime is depicted as being concentrated among poor racial minorities, in fact crimes are committed by people from all walks of life. **White-collar crime** and **state organized crime** are two examples of crimes committed by people in positions of wealth and power that have exacted enormous financial and personal costs on society.

10. Crime control in modern societies emphasizes the **incapacitation** of criminals through their **incarceration** in prisons. The United States currently has the highest proportion of its population in prison of any industrialized society.

11. A large number of nonwhites are arrested and incarcerated in the United States. This is partly due to a higher incidence of poverty among non-whites, and partly to **racism** in the criminal justice system, which results in a lesser likelihood of arrest and conviction for a particular crime if one is white.

12. Globalization has contributed to growing poverty in the United States, which has made crime an increasingly attractive source of income for some. Global migrations can lead to culture clashes, in which the dominant culture defines the behaviors of immigrant cultures as deviant. Moreover, such deviant or criminal acts as **money laundering,** drug trafficking, and tax evasion have flourished as a result of globalization.

QUESTIONS FOR DISCUSSION

1. What are the principal sociological explanations for the existence of crime and deviance among different groups in society?

2. Seemingly ordinary people have participated in the mass exterminations of entire peoples through-out history. Under what circumstances, if any, do you think this could happen in the United States today?

3. What are the principal types of crime, and who is most likely to commit them?

4. Why do victims' crime surveys report declining crimes, while police reports find an explosion in crime?

5. How do sociologists explain the differing arrest and conviction rates of different economic, racial, and ethnic groups in society?

6. What effects will globalization likely have on deviance and crime during the next decade or so?

K E Y   T E R M S

anomie: In Emile Durkheim's theory, a state of normlessness resulting from a high level of confusion and conflict over norms, or an absence of norms altogether (for Merton's reformulation, see *structural strain*).

assault: Legally defined as an unlawful attack by one person upon another for the purpose of inflicting severe or aggravated bodily harm.

banal: Commonplace or ordinary.

burglary: Legally defined as unlawful entry of a premise with the intent to commit a crime.

crime: A particular form of deviance consisting of acts that violate norms that have been enacted into criminal law.

criminologist: A social scientist who specializes in the scientific study of crime; includes sociologists, political scientists, and psychologists.

deterrence: The impact of punishment on discouraging crime—not only on those who are punished but on others who learn by their example.

deviant behavior: Behavior that violates social norms and values shared by people in a particular culture.

differential association: A theory that deviant behavior is largely the result of associating with other persons whose behavior is deviant; first developed by Edwin Sutherland.

gang: A group of people, usually young, who hang around together and commit criminal acts either for economic gain or to protect their territory.

genocide: The institutionalized practice of systematically killing the members of a particular racial, religious, or ethnic group.

incapacitation: Placing offenders in a location where their ability to violate norms is restricted, usually through imprisonment.

incarceration: Imprisonment.

labeling theory: An approach holding that deviance (like all forms of human behavior) is the result of the labels attached to a person by other people.

larceny: Legally defined as the unlawful taking of property from someone other than one's employer.

money laundering: The practice of converting illegally acquired assets into legal businesses or foreign bank accounts.

moral boundaries: A society's sense of what is normal and acceptable behavior, achieved partly by identifying certain acts as deviant and severely punishing the people who commit them. (The concept was developed by Emile Durkheim.)

organized crime: Crimes committed by criminal groups involving the provision of illegal goods and services.

pluralistic society: A society comprised of groups with diverse and often conflicting norms and values.

primary deviance: A process that occurs when an activity is labeled as deviant by others.

professional thief: A person who earns a livelihood by committing crimes on a regular basis.

recidivism: The rate at which ex-offenders are arrested for another criminal offense once they are released from jail.

rehabilitation: Resocializing criminals to noncriminal norms and values.

robbery: Legally defined as taking something by the use of violence or the threat of violence.

secondary deviance: A process that occurs when a person labeled as deviant accepts the label as part of his or her identity, and as a result begins to act in conformity with the label.

sociobiology: The effort to infer from the study of insects and other social animals that there are genetic bases for competition, cooperation, aggression, envy, and other specific behaviors.

state organized crime: Acts defined by law as criminal that are committed by state and government officials in the pursuit of their jobs as representatives of the government.

structural contradiction theory: A type of conflict theory that accepts Merton's notion that societies often contain strains that lead to deviance, but combines it with the notion that such strains result from aspects of a social structure which are mutually incompatible with one another.

structural strain: In Robert K. Merton's reformulation of Durkheim's theory, a form of anomie that oc-

curs when a gap exists between the goals society sets for people and the means society provides for people to achieve them.

victimless crimes: Acts prohibited by law in which those who are affected are willing and voluntary participants.

white-collar crime: Crime committed by people of high social status in connection with their work.

RECOMMENDED FOR FURTHER READING

Campbell, Anne (1984). *The Girls in the Gang: A Report from New York City.* London: Basil Blackwell.
    One of the few ethnographies of female gang members. A lucid description and interesting psychological account.

Chambliss, William J. (1988). *On the Take.* Bloomington, IN: Indiana University Press.
    A study of organized crime and its relation to politics based in Seattle, Washington, and extending to the international narcotics traffic.

Hawkins, Darnell. (1993). *Ethnicity, Race, and Crime.* Albany: State University of New York Press.
    A collection of articles by leading authorities on the relation of race and crime in the United States.

Skolnick, Jerome H., and James J. Fyfe. (1993). *Above the Law: Police and the Excessive Use of Force.* New York: Free Press.
    This book provides a useful analysis of police violence, and a careful examination of what constitutes "excessive force".

Williams, Terry. (1989). *The Cocaine Kids: The Inside Story of a Teenage Drug Ring.* Reading, MA: Addison-Wesley.
    This unique book studies a teenage drug ring from the inside. The profits, the lifestyle, and the incentives for becoming part of the ring are explored by a sociologist through interviews and participation in leisure activities.

Class and Stratification in the United States

CHAPTER OUTLINE

THINGS TO LOOK FOR

1. What are the principal components of social stratification in modern society, and how are they interrelated?
2. How do sociologists account for the existence of stratification?
3. What is the nature of the U.S. class structure, and how do people in different classes experience different lifestyles?
4. To what extent has inequality grown in the United States in recent years, and why has it grown?
5. In what ways has economic globalization affected the U.S. stratification system?

INTRODUCTION

The lifestyle of the wealthy is celebrated in American culture, from the pages of *People Magazine* to television shows such as *Beverly Hills 90210*. The poor and their lifestyle are seldom celebrated, although they are much more numerous than the wealthy.

Fortune magazine, which annually reports on the richest people in the world, estimated that in 1992 there were 233 individuals or families worth more than a billion dollars. The combined resources of the top 101 billionaires are valued nearly as much as the entire national income of Spain. The richest man in the world is the Sultan of Brunei, a tiny oil-rich country on the Asian island of Borneo. His $37 billion enabled him to commemorate the twenty-fifth anniversary of his rise to power by being drawn through the streets of Brunei on a golden chariot. Had this novel vehicle broken down, the Sultan would have had to make do with one of his 165 Rolls Royces. Four of the wealthiest ten are Americans. These include the Walton family, whose $23.5 billion stems from their discount Wal-Mart stores; the Mars family, best known for Mars Bars and M&M's; and the Newhouse and Kluge families, whose fortunes derive from mass media.

How much is a billion dollars? If conservatively invested, the interest alone would bring in more than $153,000 each day. A billion dollars would buy two years' worth of AIDS research at the U.S. Centers for Disease Control, or a year's supply of the drug AZT for 333,000 people with HIV-AIDS infection. It would operate all the public schools in the United States for a

day. It would put a year's worth of food on the table for a quarter of a million hungry families (*Fortune,* 1993).

At the other end of the scale, there are now as many as a million hungry and homeless people in America. A billion dollars would go a long way toward providing them with food and shelter, nearly doubling the amount that the federal government currently spends on homelessness each year. What is it like to be homeless in America today? The following description of a homeless family in San Antonio, Texas, is typical of the numerous accounts contained in Jonathan Kozol's *Rachel and Her Children* (1988, pp. 7–8):

In San Antonio I met a father with two boys who had been sleeping for four months next to a highway not far from the Hyatt Regency Hotel. He sold blood plasma twice a week to buy food for his kids. "They draw my blood, put it in a centrifuge, take the white cells, and inject the red cells back into my arm." If he showed up four weeks straight he got a bonus. In a good month he made $100. "The blood places," he told me, "poor people call them 'stab labs.' They're all over. He showed me a card he carried listing stab labs, with phone numbers and addresses, in a dozen cities. He had been an auto worker in Detroit. When he lost his job his wife became depressed and since was hospitalized. He had developed crippling asthma—"from the panic and the tension, I believe." He had thought mistakenly that San Antonio might offer health and labor and cheap housing that were not available in Michigan.

How can we explain the enormous differences in lifestyle that exist between people? Sociologists draw on a geological metaphor which assumes that groups of people, like the strata that comprise the earth's surface, can be layered from lowest to highest. Such layering is termed **social stratification,** which sociologists think of as the *systematic inequalities of wealth, power and prestige that result from social rank* (Weber, 1947). **Inequality,** in turn, can be defined as *the degree of disparity that exists in a society.* In the United States one form of inequality—economic—has increased sharply during the past quarter century.

What do sociologists mean when they define stratification in terms of "systematic" inequalities? The term "systematic" is used to highlight the belief that inequality is built into the social structure, rather than the result of chance occurrences such as winning a lottery. In fact, one of the central insights of sociology is that stratification is a feature of society, rather than resulting simply from a person's blind luck or personal effort. All societies in the modern world are seen as stratified on the basis of wealth, power, and prestige, as well as other factors such as gender, skin color (race), and national origin (ethnicity).

STRATIFICATION IN MODERN SOCIETIES: CLASS, STATUS, AND POWER

In Chapter 4 we saw that until the agricultural revolution, most people lived in societies with relatively simple stratification systems. In hunting and gathering societies, for example, there might have been hunters, food gatherers, healers, and perhaps a chief. These principal roles often coincided with gender (women were frequently food gatherers, men more likely to be hunters) and age (elders were more likely to be healers).

Agricultural societies, we noted, were more complex, with many additional roles for people to perform. Because such societies produced a surplus of food beyond that required for immediate survival, it was possible for some individuals or groups to acquire an unequal share of society's wealth, and as a result stratification became more pronounced (Dalton, 1967; Evans-Pritchard, 1940; Lenski, Lenski, and Nolan, 1991). The stratification systems in such societies increasingly came to resemble a pyramid, with a large number of people at the bottom and a successively smaller number of people as one moved toward the top.

With the industrial revolution, there has been a further increase in the complexity and interdependence of society. In modern industrial societies there are hundreds of thousands of different roles, giving rise to the differing forms of stratification we shall discuss below. The stratification systems in industrial societies somewhat resemble a teardrop, in which the numerically largest groups are usually found in the lower-middle ranges (the middle class).

Following Weber's (1947) approach, it is customary to regard stratification as having three separate although interrelated aspects. **Class** refers to *a person's location in a society's economic system, resulting in differences in the nature of work, income, and wealth.* Class position in society is a strong determinant of what is popularly called "lifestyle." **Status** refers to *a person's relationship to established social positions in society that vary in terms of prestige* (see Chapter 4). Status typically differs according to such things as occupation or family background. **Power** refers to *one's relationship to governmental and other political institutions;* it is manifested in the ability to mobilize

Although class, status, and power usually go together, some extremely powerful and high-status people renounce wealth altogether. Jesus was one such person, Mother Teresa another. This photo shows the earthly possessions of Mahatma Gandhi at the time of his death. Ghandhi, who led India to independence from British colonial rule through his teachings of nonviolence, could carry all of his belongings with him in his blanket, so simple was his lifestyle.

resources and achieve goals (Chapter 6). From a sociological perspective, class, status, and power are not regarded so much as attributes of individuals as they are aspects of the social structure itself.

Although class, status, and power for the most part go together and reinforce one another, it is important to remember that they do not necessarily overlap. Mother Teresa has neither upper-class wealth nor political power, yet she enjoys unparalleled international status for her selfless work on behalf of the poor in India and elsewhere. Colombian drug lord Pablo Escobar was reputedly once one of the richest and most powerful men in the world, yet enjoyed extremely low international status (although reportedly his status was high in his hometown of Medellin, because of numerous civic works he had performed). When Mahatma Gandhi died, his total worldly possessions could be carried in his blanket; although economically impoverished, he was the most powerful man in India at the time, and he was accorded the very highest status.

Social Class: Occupation, Income, and Wealth

Even though the term "class" is popularly used to refer to any social group with common economic, cultural, or political characteristics, sociologists restrict its meaning to highlight the economic dimension. Occupation, income, and wealth are important components of social class position. **Occupation** or *paid employment* is especially key, since it is an important source of income and wealth in modern societies. The *Dictionary of Occupational Titles* lists some 20,000 different kinds of jobs in the United States. Sociologists have used various classifications to reduce this massive number to a smaller number of categories. For example, jobs are classified as **blue collar** if they are *based primarily on manual labor* (for example, factory workers, truck drivers, miners), and **white collar** if they *mainly require mental skills* (for example, professionals such as doctors, lawyers, or managers). More recently, the term **pink collar** has been used to characterize jobs that *primarily employ women in nonmanual semiskilled work* (for example, secretaries, clerks, and typists).

Income refers to *the amount of money a person or household earns in a given period of time* (usually a year). Median U.S. household income was $28,910 in 1989 (U.S. Bureau of the Census, 1990). In that year the United States ranked eighth in per-person income among industrial countries, with higher incomes reported in Switzerland, Luxembourg, Finland, Norway, Sweden, Iceland, and Japan.

Wealth, which can be defined as *the value of everything a person owns,* is a far more important source of class position than income as one moves up the stratification system. An especially useful measure of wealth consists of **net financial assets,** the *value of everything one owns (excluding one's home and cars), minus the value of everything one owes.* Although people at the very top are certainly likely to have high incomes, most of their wealth comes not from income but from such financial assets as real estate, stocks, bonds, and other forms of investment. Most Americans do not enjoy such wealth; the top-earning fifth of the American population owns 90 percent of all net financial assets (Petruno, 1991).

According to a U.S. Census Bureau study, the net financial assets of the median U.S. household in 1984 was only $2,600. The Census Bureau found that about one-third of all U.S. households actually had zero or negative net financial assets (Francis, 1990). For some groups, the distribution of wealth is even more skewed downward. Among African Americans, for example, two out of three have zero or negative net financial assets.

Differences in wealth can often take the form of differences in privilege that can affect a person's life chances as much as money income. Members of Congress, high-level military officers in the Pentagon, or White House staff members do not have gargantuan salaries like the chief executive officers of corporations; what they do have, however, are privileges that translate into wealth. Members of Congress have their own bank, health spa, barbershop, and restaurant where they obtain services for a fraction of the cost that everyone else in the country must pay. White House staff members enjoy access to limousines and military aircraft, not to mention expense accounts that pay for many of their meals and hotel bills when they travel. Many businesspeople enjoy similar benefits, with expense accounts for travel and "frequent flyer" mileage accounts that enable them to fly their families to vacation spots free of cost. Ordinary working people typically do not enjoy such privileges.

Social Status

A considerable amount of research has gone into classifying occupations according to the degree of status or prestige they are granted in public opinion. Otis Dudley Duncan (Blau and Duncan, 1967) and Donald J. Treiman (1977) pioneered this research, polling people to find out what they thought of various occupations. Their studies show, not surprisingly, that white-collar jobs tend to be higher in prestige than blue-collar jobs (see Table 8.1). Doctors, attorneys, college professors, and scientists tend to be at the top of the prestige scale; maids and domestic workers, janitors and custodians, sanitation workers, and agricultural workers tend to be at the bottom. In general, occupations that involve working with ideas or people have higher prestige than occupations that involve working with one's hands or material objects (such as factory worker or plumber). Prestige rankings of specific occupations have been shown to be remarkably stable over time and across cultures, at least within industrial societies (Treiman, 1977).

In socialist societies, such as the Soviet Union prior to its breakup in 1991, Cuba, and the People's Republic of China, considerable public effort has gone into changing people's perceptions regarding different occupations. In these societies, farm work and blue-collar labor were officially claimed to be more important than most kinds of white-collar work, since according to Marxist theory people who work with their hands are the ones who actually provide society with the food, clothing, and shelter it requires to survive. Such efforts to change people's thinking met with only

Table 8.1   The Occupational Prestige Scale

Occupation	Prestige Score	Occupation	Prestige Score
Physician	86	Computer Operator	50
Lawyer	75	Postal Carrier	47
Professor	74	Secretary	46
Clergy	69	Welder	42
Psychologist	69	Farmer	40
Registered nurse	66	Security guard	37
Accountant	65	Child care worker	36
Athlete	65	Clothing salesperson	30
Airplane pilot	61	Truck driver	30
Computer programmer	61	Garbage collector	28
Sociologist	61	Taxi driver	28
Police officer	60	Waitperson	28
Actor	58	Farmworker	23
Firefighter	53	Janitor	22
Dental hygienist	52	Shoe shiner	9
Social worker	52		

White-collar workers
Blue-collar workers

Source: General Social Surveys (1991, pp. 827-835)

limited success, however, and have been challenged by the collapse of socialism in the former Soviet Union.

Power

An analysis of power clearly reveals a pyramid-like stratification system in the United States and most societies: at the very top are a handful of political and military figures, business people, and other leaders with substantial power; as one moves down, more and more people with less and less power are encountered. There has been considerable debate over the nature of power in the United States (see Chapter 13). One theory of power, termed **pluralism,** holds that *power is distributed among different groups that contend with one another on roughly equal footing* (Dahl, 1961). In this view, for example, the power of big business is matched by the "countervailing power" (Galbraith, 1956) of large labor unions, consumer groups, or environmental organizations. Individuals exert their power through organizations, and organizations provide a system of checks and balances on one another.

A second theory, termed **class dominance,** argues that *power is concentrated in the hands of a relatively small number of individuals who comprise an upper-class power elite* (Mills, 1956; Useem and Karabel, 1986; Domhoff, 1983, 1987, 1990). These individuals know one another personally, belong to the same organizations, and cycle in and out of top positions in

government, business, and the military. While ordinary people may think they can influence government through voting, testifying, or writing to their elected representatives, the class-dominant theorists believe that the real power occurs behind the scenes among the members of the power elite. Sociologist G. William Domhoff (1993), for example, estimates that fewer than 1 percent of Americans comprise a "ruling class" that owns 25 to 30 percent of the privately held wealth, runs the large corporations and foundations, and dominates the federal government.

A third theory, termed **structuralism,** holds that *individuals themselves are largely captives of their organizational roles,* whether they are at the bottom or the top of the organizational pyramid. Thus, although factory workers may seem powerless against the managers who hire and fire them, the managers themselves have little choice in the matter, since they too will lose their jobs if they do not turn a profit. For example, if profits are declining at General Motors because Japanese factories can produce more cars at lower costs, GM's top managers have little recourse but to replace their own workers with highly efficient robots that produce cars more quickly and cheaply. Once-powerful corporate executives may find themselves out of work if their corporations do not perform satisfactorily, as the founder of the Apple Computer Company—as well as his successor—both learned to their dismay.

CHANGES IN STRATIFICATION: CASTE, CLASS, OR CLASSLESS SOCIETY?

Stratification systems can be classified as relatively "open" or "closed," depending on the difficulty of moving from one stratum to another. It is useful to distinguish three principal types of stratification systems, based on their relative degree of openness. **Caste societies** are *those in which the strata are closed to movement, so that all individuals must remain throughout life in the stratum of their birth.* In caste societies, movement between strata is therefore extremely difficult or impossible. **Class societies,** on the other hand, are *those in which the strata are open to movement, so that changing one's stratum of birth is possible.* In class societies, membership in a particular stratum depends in part on individual effort. **Classless societies** are *those in which different economic strata do not exist at all.* All known societies fall into one of the first two categories, and most have some aspects of both. There are no known examples of classless societies, although twentieth century socialist revolutions throughout the world were largely inspired by a belief in their possibility.

Caste Societies

In caste societies, membership in a particular caste is based on **ascription;** that is, *it is acquired on the basis of personal characteristics—such as skin color, parental religion, or the caste of one's parents—that derive from birth and therefore are believed to be unchangeable.* A person is born into a caste and remains there for life. The "purity" of a caste is often maintained by rules of **endogamy,** the *prohibition against marrying or having sexual relations outside of one's social group.* Physical separation between the castes is ensured through prohibitions against **ritual pollution,** in which *contact between members of different castes is viewed as corrupting or contaminating the members of the higher caste.* Such pollution then requires the practice of culturally prescribed cleansing rituals in order for caste purity to be restored.

Caste systems are most widely associated with preindustrial societies. A caste system existed in Europe throughout much of the Middle Ages; remnants are present in Great Britain today. The British legislature, for example, is divided into two houses—a House of Commons based on popular elections, and a House of Lords based on "noble" parentage (although a certain number of memberships in the House of Lords can be purchased or conferred on "commoners"). Although rules of endogamy are no longer enforced, it still raises eyebrows in Britain when a highly visible member of the nobility marries a commoner—as, for example, when the second in line to the British throne, Prince Andrew, married Sara "Fergie" Ferguson in 1986, a vivacious but hardly aristocratic woman. (Eyebrows were raised again when their marriage broke up several years later.)

In the southern United States prior to the Civil War, African Americans were officially members of a lower caste; most were born as slaves and died as slaves, were prohibited from marrying across racial lines, and were legally treated as the property of their white "owners." While the Emancipation Proclamation officially put an end to slavery in 1863, aspects of the caste system remained in many southern states for another 100 years, while various forms of racial discrimination were practiced throughout the United States. Following a decade of struggle on the part of African Americans, the Civil Rights Act of 1964 legally abolished discrimination on the basis of race for the entire country. Although the treatment of African Americans as a separate caste is no longer legal in the United States, the discrimination and prejudice that remain throughout the country are residues of the former caste system (see Chapter 10).

Caste systems are still strong in parts of the world, the most well-known examples being found in India and in South Africa prior to 1992. The Indian caste system, which reflects Hindu religious beliefs, is more than two thousand years old. Prejudices associated with the caste system were legally abolished in 1949, the year before India achieved full independence from its British colonial status. Nonetheless, aspects of the caste system remain in full force today, particularly in rural areas. According to Hindu beliefs, there are four *varna* or castes, each roughly associated with broad occupational groupings. These range from the *Brahmins* (scholars, spiritual leaders) on top to the *Shudras* (common workers) on the bottom. Beneath the four castes are the "untouchables" (*Harijan*), who—as their name suggests—are to be avoided at all costs. These people are relegated to the worst jobs in the society: removing human waste, begging and foraging in garbage for their food.

In South Africa, the caste system termed *apartheid* (Dutch for "apart-hood") once rigidly separated black Africans, "coloreds" (people of mixed races), Asians, and whites. Whites, who comprise only 15 percent of the total population, historically controlled virtually all the of the country's economic wealth; they owned most of the usable land, they ran the principal businesses and industries, and had a monopoly on political power, since blacks lacked the right to vote. Blacks—who make up 73 percent of the population—were rigidly segregated into economically distressed townships and *bantustans* ("homelands"), from which they would emerge to work in virtual servitude for the white minority. Until recently, hundreds of laws governed ev-

Slavery, an example of a caste system, *was officially abolished in the United States in 1863. Many aspects of this caste system remained through the legal practice of racial* segregation, *until such nonviolent actions as sit-ins forced the federal government to end segregation as well. In this photograph, former civil rights activists celebrate the thirtieth anniversary of the sit-in at a Woolworth's Drug Store lunch counter in Greensboro, North Carolina.*

ery aspect of contact between the races. Laws determined where a person could live, as well as what social relations were permitted between the races. For example, until 1985 it was a crime for a white person to have sexual relations, marry, or live with anyone who was not white. The existence of apartheid, rampant discrimination, and oppression created intense conflict between the white minority and the black and mixed race majority. Decades of struggle against apartheid, often violent, finally proved successful in the 1990s. The most powerful black organization, the African National Congress, mobilized an economically devastating global boycott of South African businesses, forcing South Africa's white leaders to dismantle apartheid, which was abolished by popular vote among South African whites in 1992. In 1994, in the country's first-ever multiracial elections, the black majority won control of the government.

Class Societies

In class societies, class membership is at least in part the result of what one does rather than who one is according to birth (although birth remains an important determinant of class membership, as we shall see below when we discuss social mobility). Class systems

A global boycott of South African businesses contributed to the end of the caste system known as apartheid. *In 1994 Nelson Mandela was elected leader of the country's first postapartheid government; only four years earlier he had been released after 27 years of imprisonment. Mandela (wearing tie and jacket) is here seen talking to Jacob Zuma, a leading Zulu tribal member of Mandela's multiethnic party, the African National Congress.*

are thus in theory more open to social movement, even though caste-like barriers often remain in the form of discrimination based on race, ethnicity, religion, or gender. Still, it is possible for *some* people to rise or fall from one class to another. Social class membership is typically based on economic position, although there is a strong overlap with prestige and power as well. Unlike castes, which are sharply marked off from one another, class distinctions are blurred, so it is not clear when a person moves from one class to another.

Caste systems have largely given way to class-based ones in industrial capitalist societies (Berger, 1986). Modern industrial production requires that people move about freely, work at whatever jobs they are suited or able to do, and often change jobs frequently according to economic conditions. The rigid restrictions found in caste systems interfere with this necessary freedom. It seems reasonable to conclude that as modern industry spreads across the globe, most of the remaining caste societies will be replaced by class-based ones. Global capitalism in particular requires an enormous degree of mobility. Businesspeople must be free to jet around the planet, intermingling with others from different cultures. Large numbers of working people move into cities in search of jobs, where they are thrust into contact with persons from diverse backgrounds. Furthermore, as the world increasingly becomes a single economic unit, countries that continue to officially condone caste systems become more and more vulnerable to economic pressures to change their laws, as the example of South Africa illustrates.

There is some evidence that mature capitalist societies have increasingly open class systems, although they are far from classless. In 1955, the Nobel Prize–winning economist Simon Kuznets proposed a hypothesis that has since been called the **Kuznets curve:** *the observation that inequality increases during the early stages of capitalist development, then declines, and eventually stabilizes at a relatively low level.* Studies of European countries, the United States, and Canada suggest that inequality peaked in these places prior to World War II, declined through the 1950s, and remained roughly the same at least through the 1970s (Berger, 1986), although as we shall see below inequality has grown in the United States since that time.

Classless Societies

If caste systems have given way to class-based ones in most parts of the world today, is there any likelihood that classes themselves will someday disappear entirely? Karl Marx (1818–1883) argued that just such a society was possible. According to Marx, the earliest hunting and gathering societies were essentially classless, but only because they were so technologically backward that everybody was equally poor. Marx dubbed these societies "primitive communism," since he believed that they were organized cooperatively (Marx's sense of communism), yet at a primitive level of technological development. For classes to exist, Marx reasoned, a surplus of wealth must be produced—enough so that the poorer classes could support themselves by working, while having time left over for additional work needed to enrich the higher classes. When hunting and gathering societies settled down and took up more technologically advanced farming methods, they were able to produce such a surplus, and societies based on caste or class emerged.

Marx predicted that industrial capitalism would become so technologically advanced that it would eventually be possible for everyone to live reasonably well, without having one class of people labor long hours to support another. In Marx's view, communism would therefore eventually emerge out of capitalism—a classless society organized cooperatively for the common good, "from each according to his abilities, to each according to his needs."

Marx's vision of a classless society inspired successful communist revolutions in Russia (1917), China (1949), and Cuba (1959), as well as communist or communist-leaning governments in numerous smaller countries in Africa, Asia, Eastern Europe, and Latin America. Before the Soviet Union and Eastern Europe renounced communism between 1989 and 1991, as many as a fourth of the world's population lived in such supposedly classless communist societies. Economic inequality in most communist countries was indeed lower than in the United States and other capitalist industrial nations. In the former Soviet Union, for example, a doctor made roughly the same as a factory worker or manager (Lane, 1990). Yet despite greater economic equality, other types of class difference still remained strong. In the Soviet Union prior to 1991, membership in the Communist Party, when coupled with a governmental position, conferred enormous privileges: special summer vacation retreats, access to automobiles, better housing and health care, and the ability to obtain consumer goods that were otherwise unavailable to the larger population. Although no one became supremely wealthy by U.S. standards, such disparities angered ordinary Soviet citizens, who then supported new leaders who stripped Communist Party members of their wealth and privilege.

In sum, we may conclude that at least up until now, no classless industrial society has ever existed. Direct efforts to create classless communist societies have been somewhat successful in reducing inequality. Nonetheless, they have ultimately been judged failures by many of their members, who resented the class divisions that emerged, being poorer than their capitalist neighbors, and enjoying fewer political, religious, and personal freedoms than their capitalist neighbors.

WHY DOES STRATIFICATION EXIST?

There are two principal competing paradigms that seek to explain the fact that stratification is found in virtually all societies. Functionalist theories emphasize the ways in which stratification strengthens the society as a whole, arguing that all members ultimately benefit from some degree of inequality. Social conflict theorists argue that looking at society as a whole is misleading, since stratification results in conflict between those who win out at the expense of those who lose (refer back to Chapter 1 for further discussion of these two paradigms).

The Functionalist Explanation

The origins of functionalism are found in the writings of Emile Durkheim (1858–1917), who argued that social classes could be best understood as performing different functions for society as a whole. In this sense, social classes can be thought of as equivalent to the different organs in the human body (Durkheim, 1964; orig. 1893). Based on Durkheim's theory, a half-century ago Kingsley Davis and Wilbert Moore (1945) offered a functionalist theory of inequality that remains influential today. Davis and Moore theorized that inequality serves as an unconscious mechanism that helped to ensure that the most important positions were filled by the most qualified persons. Some degree of stratification is thus seen as necessary for society to exist. Davis and Moore asserted that all societies have some roles that are more important than others, and that these roles must be filled by the most qualified people to ensure the smooth working of society. Unconscious mechanisms, such as unequal rewards, therefore emerge to guarantee that the best and the brightest fill the most important roles.

The Davis-Moore theory has implications for public policy. It suggests that people become wealthy (or poor) largely because of their talents and efforts. Since according to this theory everyone more or less gets what they deserve, there can be little justification for government programs aimed at reducing inequality by redistributing income from rich to poor. In fact, such programs could be viewed as counterproductive, since they punish the most qualified people (by taxing their incomes) in order to reward the least qualified (through welfare and poverty programs).

Critical Assessment The Davis-Moore theory has been criticized on a number of grounds (Tumin, 1953, 1963, 1985; Wrong, 1959). Although most people would agree that some positions are more important to society than others, is it safe to assume that the actual difference in rewards between positions is always a measure of their relative worth? For example, if we take differences in income as a standard, professors in U.S. universities would be on average roughly four to five times as important to American society as their secretaries, corporate executives would be well over a hundred times more important than the workers in their factories, and convicted junk-bond financier Michael Milken's half-billion dollar 1988 income would have made him roughly 15,000 times as important as the person who won the "teacher of the year" award that year. Moreover, business executives would have to be rapidly increasing in importance to American society, since their average pay has escalated in recent years— even as the American economy has turned downward. And they would have to be far more important than their Japanese counterparts, who are paid far less even when their firms are thriving. Critics of the functionalist approach thus claim that rewards are not impartially allocated by some invisible societal mechanism that guarantees fairness but rather from decisions made by wealthy and powerful individuals who naturally tend to favor their own interests.

Other criticisms of the functionalist approach have also been made. People are often denied rewards on the basis of skin color, gender, and other ascribed characteristics that have nothing to do with their talents or motivations, but rather reflect prevailing prejudices (see Chapters 10 and 11). This results in an enormous waste of society's human skills and talents and is therefore dysfunctional for society as a whole. Furthermore, when people do acquire socially important, higher-status positions by virtue of their skills and efforts, they are then typically able to pass their wealth and status along to their children, even when their children are not particularly qualified themselves. Inequality in society then increases, leading to a growing mismatch between people's talents and the positions they occupy, producing anger and resentment among those who feel they are not being suitably rewarded. Again, these outcomes are dysfunctional for the entire society.

The Social Conflict Explanation

Unlike functionalist theory, which views classes as performing different functions that contribute to the effectiveness of society as a whole, social conflict theory holds that conflict is central to all forms of social organization, including societies (Dahrendorf, 1959, 1967; Chambliss, 1973; Coser, 1967; Rex, 1986). In this view, there is no such thing as a "society" that reflects the common interests of all people. Rather, what we falsely term "society" is seen as a collection of different classes, each with its own class interests, bound together in a fateful struggle for supremacy. Stratification, according to these theorists, thus reflects the winners and losers in that struggle.

Social conflict theory was originally formulated by Karl Marx, although there are aspects of conflict theory in the writings of Max Weber as well. As we saw in Chapter 1, Marx divides society into two broad classes, workers and capitalists. The workers do not own the factories and machinery that are required to produce wealth in capitalist societies; they possess nothing except their own labor power. The capitalists, on the other hand, own the necessary equipment, but require the labor power of the workers to run it. Thus the two classes require one another for survival, but their interests are seen as fundamentally opposed. Capitalists seek to keep labor costs as low as possible, in order to produce goods cheaply and thus remain competitive. Workers initially seek only to be paid a living wage, and later fight to obtain what they regard as their fair share of the pie. In Marx's famous statement, "the history of all hitherto existing societies is the history of class struggle" (Marx, 1977; orig. 1848).

Marx predicted that as a result of class struggle, capitalists would seek to replace workers with more efficient (and more compliant) machines; they would also move their factories to regions or countries where labor costs were lower. Workers would resist these trends, particularly if they acquired **class consciousness**—*an awareness of their own interests as a social class, along with an adequate understanding of the ways in which society operates to produce inequality.* Marx argued that such an understanding would grow out of the workers' experience in class struggle, provided that it was guided by an informed reading of his own theories. Eventually, in Marx's view, conflict would escalate, wealth and poverty would become increasingly polarized, and workers the world over would rise up in revolution. They would seize their factories and eventually create a conflict-free classless society, the first such society in modern history.

Max Weber (1947) rejected Marx's notion that the principal sources of conflict in society are exclusively economic in nature (Turner, 1986; Turner and Beeghley, 1981). Recall that Weber identified three dimensions of stratification: class, status, and power. Weber argued that conflict is likely to increase when these three dimensions are closely related to one another, and movement between strata is limited on all three. If a small group of people enjoys great wealth, high status, and enormous power, while all others are excluded from such privileges, people will be prone to conflict. Weber felt that such closed stratification systems were most likely to be found in traditional societies, where powerful figures would occasionally arise, sowing the seeds of conflict and promising sweeping change (see Chapter 13 for further discussion).

Critical Assessment There is ample evidence that conflict is found in many societies. As Marx anticipated, periodic conflicts between workers and capitalists are common, not to mention conflicts based on racial, ethnic, and other differences as well (Chapter 10). Weber was also correct in arguing that when people are simultaneously excluded from positions of wealth, status, and power, they are prone to conflict and to revolutionary leaders—as happened with Hitler's rise to power in Germany after Weber's death.

Nonetheless, many of the predictions of conflict theory have not been realized. This has been especially true of Marx's predictions concerning the overthrow of capitalism. First, as we have previously noted, his expectation of ever-increasing polarization between rich and poor in capitalist nations was not fulfilled, at least during the first three-quarters of this century. Second, Marx was clearly wrong in predicting that all social classes would be absorbed into the two great antagonistic classes of capitalists and workers. In fact, as capitalist societies have developed, a large middle class has emerged, consisting of better-paid workers, along with others who neither own factories nor labor in them: lawyers, doctors, teachers, engineeers, small business people, and so forth (see below, and Chapter 15). Finally, Marx's prediction that communist revolutions would topple the advanced capitalist nations has also proved false, although conflict between capitalists and workers occurs. While revolutions did lead to communism in largely agricultural societies such as Russia (in 1917), China (1949), and Cuba (1959), these societies are undergoing rapid changes in the face of global capitalism.

A PICTURE OF THE U.S. CLASS STRUCTURE

Following the theories of Max Weber, many sociologists identify social classes in terms of differences in wealth, status, and power, focusing in particular on differences in consumption and "lifestyle." We shall take this approach in order to provide a convenient snapshot of the current American class structure. Later on, we will offer two theories that give a somewhat different picture of both the number of classes and their relationship to one another. It is also important to bear in mind that class structures differ between societies. Unlike England, for example, the United States lacks a significant group of hereditary landowners, and so this class is missing from the following portrait. Furthermore, class structures change over time, as some classes grow while others shrink.

The Upper Class

This group consists of the very wealthiest Americans (fewer than 3 percent of the total population). Take as an example Thomas Frist, who became America's top income-earner in 1992 by receiving $127 million in salary and stock options from HCA-Hospital Corporation of America. Assuming that this hard-driving chief executive labors 10 hours a day, 6 days a week, 50 weeks a year, his annual $127 million package worked out to approximately $42,300 *per hour,* or about a third more than the typical U.S. household earned in that entire year.

The upper class includes the heads of major corporations, people who have made large amounts of money through investments or real estate, those fortunate enough to have inherited their wealth from their parents, some highly successful movie and television stars, a small number of the most successful professional athletes, and a handful of others. Most of them are "merely wealthy." They are likely to own a large suburban home as well as a townhouse or vacation home, drive expensive automobiles, fly first-class to vacations abroad, educate their children in private schools and colleges, and have their needs attended to by a staff of servants. Their wealth derives in large part from their substantial investments, from stocks and bonds to real estate. They are politically influential at the national level if they so choose, and at the state and local levels as well.

At the very top of this group are the super-rich, people who have accumulated vast fortunes enabling them to enjoy a lifestyle unimaginable to most Americans. Unlike most other people in American society, they are highly self-conscious of their unique social class posi-tion, which they believe entails both privilege and obligation. Their homes are often opulent, and sometimes filled with collections of fine art. They donate generously to the fine arts, hospitals, and charities. Their common class identity is fostered by such things as being listed in the coveted *Social Register,* or having attended the same exclusive private secondary schools (to which they subsequently send their own children). They sit on the same corporate boards of directors, belong to the same private clubs, and in general travel in the same circles. They contribute large sums of money to their favorite politicians, and are likely to be on a first-name basis with some members of Congress and perhaps even the president (Domhoff, 1987, 1990, 1993; Ostrander, 1984).

The emergence of a global economy has created extraordinary opportunities for the accumulation of such wealth, and as a result the number of super-rich Americans has exploded in recent years (see Figure 8.1). At the end of World War II, there were only 13,000 individuals valued at a million dollars or more in the United States, a number that grew to about 100,000 by the mid-1960s. Over the next decade, the number more than doubled, to 250,000 by 1976. The figure then increased sixfold by 1988, to 1.5 *million* millionaires. The number of *billionaires* grew from 2 to 51 during the same period (Phillips, 1991). Unlike "old money" families such as the Rockefellers or Vanderbilts, who accumulated their wealth in earlier generations and thus are viewed as a sort of American aristocracy, this "new wealth" often consists of upstart entrepreneurs like Microsoft Corporation's Bill Gates, the former "computer nerd" whose estimated $6.7 billion makes him at age 39 the twelfth richest man in the world (*Fortune,* 1993).

In societies divided into social classes, members of each class typically attend the same schools, have jobs similar to their parents, and marry within their own class. One way the upper class helps to reproduce itself is by institutionalizing mating practices that encourage class *endogamy. In this debutante ball in Atlanta, eligible unmarried upper-class women "come out" to meet eligible unmarried upper-class men.*

Figure 8.1 **Number of Millionaires in the United States from World War II to the Present**

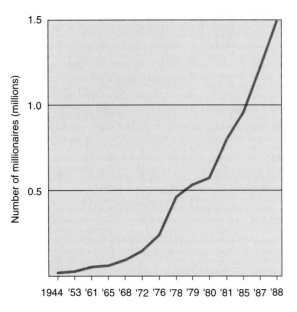

1944 '53 '61 '65 '68 '72 '76 '78 '79 '80 '81 '85 '87 '88

The global economy offers some people enormous opportunities to become wealthy. The number of millionaires in the United States has grown sharply in recent years, with the sharpest growth corresponding to the period of rapid economic globalization. Today there are more than 1.5 million millionaires, and more than 50 billionaires, an increase due in part to globalization.
Source: Phillips (1991).

The Middle Class

When Americans are asked to identify their social class, the large majority claim to be "middle class." This is partly because of the American cultural belief that the United States is relatively free from class distinctions; few people want to be identified as being too rich or too poor. Many-blue collar workers prefer to think of themselves as middle class rather than working class. This class is therefore in many ways a "catch-all" for a diverse group of occupations, lifestyles, and people who earn stable and sometimes substantial incomes at primarily "white-collar" jobs. The middle class grew throughout much of the first three-quarters of this century, although it appears to be shrinking today (see below), despite the fact that it currently includes about half of all American households. While it was once largely white, today it is increasingly diverse both racially and culturally, including Asian Americans, African Americans, and Latinos (Box 8.1). The increase in numbers of the last two groups has been especially pronounced during the past quarter century.

The middle class can be somewhat arbitrarily subdivided into two groups. The *upper middle class* consists of relatively high-income professionals and managers. It includes people who own or manage small businesses and retail shops, doctors and lawyers, engineers and professors, and even some large farm owners. Family incomes in this group range from about $50,000 to $150,000. Its members are likely to be college-educated, and many hold advanced degrees. Their children will almost always receive college educations as well. Their jobs are relatively secure (at least, relative to the lower middle class), and are likely to provide them with retirement programs and health benefits. They own comfortable homes, often in the suburbs or in trendy downtown neighborhoods; drive late-model cars; and have some savings and investments. They are likely to be active in local politics and civic organizations.

The *lower middle class* consists of some specially trained office workers, teachers, nurses, salespeople, and others who provide skilled services. Incomes in this group range between $25,000 and $50,000, and family incomes may run somewhat higher if more than one member of the household is working (which is increasingly likely to be the case). They may own a modest house, although many live in rental units. Their automobiles may be relatively late models, but they will not be the more expensive varieties. Almost all have a high school education, and some have college degrees. They want their children to have college educations, although this will most certainly have to be paid for with work-study and student loans. They are less likely to be politically active, beyond sometimes exercising their right to vote.

The Working Class

This group, which comprises about a third of all Americans, includes primarily "blue-collar" and "pink-collar" laborers. Its members are factory workers, mechanics, secretaries and office workers, sales clerks, restaurant workers, and others who earn a modest weekly paycheck at a job that involves little control over their working environment. Many blue-collar jobs in the United States are threatened by economic globalization, and so members of the working class today are likely to feel insecure about their own and their family's future.

The working class is racially and ethnically diverse. Its members typically earn under $25,000 annually, and more than one person in a household will surely have to work to make ends meet. Family income is just enough to pay the rent or the mortgage, put food on the table, and perhaps build a little surplus for a summer vacation. While older members of the working class may own a home that was bought a number of years ago, younger members are likely to rent. The home or

Box 8.1

Silenced Voices

Uncomfortably Middle Class

During the past 30 years many African Americans and Latinos from impoverished backgrounds have "made it" into the middle class. But such a journey is not always without pain. In the following passage Leanita McClain (1986) talks about running "a gauntlet between two worlds"—the poor inner-city world of her childhood, and the successful professional world of her downtown office. McClain, a journalist, was the first African American to sit on the editorial board of the *Chicago Tribune*. She took her own life at age 32, depressed by an outcry that resulted from an article she wrote on racial politics, as well as by the difficulty of being a role model for other African Americans.

I am a member of the black middle class who has had it with being patted on the head by white hands and slapped in the face by black hands for my success.

Here's a discovery that too many people find startling: when given equal opportunities at white-collar pencil pushing, blacks want the same things from life that everyone else wants. These include the proverbial dream house, two cars, an above-average school and a vacation for the kids at Disneyland. We may, in fact, want these things more than other Americans because

most of us have been denied them so long. . . .

I recall the girl I played dolls with who now rears five children on welfare, the boy from church who is in prison for murder, the pal found dead of a drug overdose in the alley where we once played tag.

My life abounds in incongruities. Fresh from a vacation in Paris, I may, a week later, be on the milk-run Trailways bus in Deep South back-country attending the funeral of an ancient uncle whose world only stretched 50 miles and who never learned to read. Sometimes when I wait at the bus stop with my attaché case, I meet my aunt getting off the bus with other cleaning ladies on their way to do my neighbors' floors.

But I am not ashamed. Black progress has surpassed our greatest expectations; we never even saw much hope for it, and the achievement has taken us by surprise.

In my heart, however, there is no safe distance from the wretched past of my ancestors or the purposeless present of some of my contemporaries; I fear such a fate can reclaim me. I am not comfortably middle class; I am uncomfortably middle class. . . .

I run a gauntlet between two worlds, and I am cursed and blessed by both.

---

apartment will be in a lower-income suburb or a city neighborhood. The household car, a lower-priced model, is unlikely to be of recent vintage. Children who graduate from high school are unlikely to go to college and will rather attempt to get a job immediately. Most members of the working class are not likely to be politically active even in their own community, although they may vote in some elections.

The Lower Class

This class, which comprises roughly one out of every four or five Americans, includes those who are only marginally working, or who do not work at all. Although some live in rural areas and eke out a living as family farmers or part-time workers, most are found

in cities. Those who are able will find employment in semiskilled or unskilled manufacturing or service jobs, ranging from making clothing in "sweatshops" to cleaning houses. Their jobs are "dead end," in that years of work are unlikely to lead to promotions and substantially higher income. Their work is probably part-time, and highly unstable. Even if they are fortunate enough to find a full-time job, there are no guarantees that it will be around next month or even next week. Many people in this class live in poverty. Very few own their own homes; most are renters, and some are homeless. If they own a car at all, it is likely to be second-hand. The lower class is disproportionately nonwhite. Its members are politically powerless; they do not participate in politics, nor do they vote.

An Urban Underclass?

Within the lower class, sociologists have recently identified a group they term the **underclass** (see Chapter 2). This group is seen as a *caste-like group that is "beneath" the class system in that it lacks access even to the lower parts of the working class.* It consists primarily of inner-city residents in the largest U.S. cities, many of whom are African American, who have been trapped for more than a generation in a cycle of poverty, from which there is little possibility of escape (Wilson, 1978, 1987; Wacquant, 1993). These are the poorest of the urban poor. Their numbers have grown rapidly over the past quarter century, and today include unskilled and unemployed (often never employed) men; young single mothers on welfare; teenagers from welfare-dependent families; and many of the homeless. They live in impoverished neighborhoods plagued by drugs, teenage gangs, drive-by shootings, and high levels of violence. They are the "truly disadvantaged," individuals who have little realistic hope of ever making it out of poverty.

The emergence of the underclass has been attributed to social forces that have come together during the past quarter century (Wilson, 1987; Wacquant, 1993; Sawhill, 1989). We have already mentioned that economic globalization has reduced the number of jobs available to unskilled workers. Since African Americans have historically been forced to provide much of the unskilled labor in the United States, they are particularly disadvantaged in today's labor market. Racial discrimination has made it especially difficult for them to compete for the dwindling supply of unskilled jobs. Second, government programs that once provided assistance for the poor were cut back sharply during the 1980s, leaving the poor with few resources that might be used to get ahead.

Finally, and much more controversially, sociologist William J. Wilson claims that the destruction of viable African-American inner-city communities is particularly responsible for the emergence of the underclass. After World War II, racial segregation brought middle and lower class African Americans together in thriving communities with churches, neighborhood newspapers, schools, social clubs, lodges, community organizations, and local businesses (Drake and Clayton, 1962). The economic growth of the 1960s and early 1970s, in combination with civil rights legislation that outlawed segregated housing, enabled the African-American middle class to move out of the inner city to the suburbs or other middle class neighborhoods. A "social buffer" of middle class values and role models thereby was lost, contributing to a self-destructive subculture among the impoverished families that remained behind, many living in now-decaying crime-ridden housing projects.

Critical Assessment Wilson's theory has come under much criticism. Edwards (1989), for example, argues that Wilson fails to adequately take into account worsening education and occupational opportunities that African Americans are facing today. Pettigrew (1989) similarly argues that Wilson downplays the importance of racism in U.S. society. One major objection is that his ideas perpetuate the notion of a "culture of poverty," whereby the poor are held responsible for their unfortunate fate (Willie, 1989; Wacquant, 1993). Sociologists often regard such ideas as "blaming the victims" for their plight (Ryan, 1976), rather than looking for the larger social forces that have produced poverty in the first place. Wilson has responded to his critics by saying that he does in fact address such sociological causes of poverty as job loss, economic stagnation, and

Social classes in the United States are usually residentially segregated. Chicago's southside Woodlawn neighborhood fought for years to preserve viable businesses, housing, and political institutions, yet nonetheless remains home to an underclass *of people trapped in poverty. The underclass lacks access to the education, jobs, and general opportunities available to people in other classes.*

racism. At the same time, he argues, sociologists have an obligation to acknowledge the consequences of underclass life itself, where generations of violence, crime, and isolation reinforce norms and values that run counter to those of the larger society—even if such research is unpopular (see Box 8.2).

THEORIES OF CLASS STRUCTURE

The picture of the American class structure we have just presented is largely descriptive, dividing people into classes on the basis of their lifestyles. We shall now examine two different theories of class structure that attempt to explain why certain classes exist. The first, Erik Ohlin Wright's theory of class location, emphasizes the roles that particular classes play in the larger economy. The second, Barbara and John Ehrenreich's theory of the professional managerial class, attempts to go beyond the notion of a "middle class" to explain the different white-collar roles that exist in society.

Wright's Theory of Class Location and Power

Erik Ohlin Wright's (1982, 1985) approach derives partly from Marx's analysis, which focuses on the degree of control that people have over their own labor, the labor of others, and in general the means of producing wealth in society. Wright divides the stratification system of industrial society into seven classes. Members of the first four classes are directly involved in large-scale, capitalist economic relations centered around factory production. Members of the last three classes are involved in other economic activities that are not centrally related to large-scale capitalist enterprises.

In Wright's formulation, among the four groups engaged in large-scale capitalist economic activities, the *bourgeoisie* are at the very top. These are the people who own the factories, corporations, and other principal means of producing wealth in society. They purchase the labor of others and have a great deal of authority and control over other people, while making the

---

Box 8.2

Critical Thinking

Will Dispersing the Underclass Help to Eliminate It?

William Julius Wilson's (1987) theory argues that a major reason the United States has an underclass is that the poorest of the poor are trapped in inner-city ghetto neighborhoods that lack employment opportunities as well as role models. One way to evaluate this theory would be to move members of the inner-city underclass into middle-class neighborhoods where such opportunities and role models exist, and see if their situation improves.

Just such an effort was made in Wilson's own city of Chicago. Under a program called the Gautreaux Project, nearly 4,000 low-income families were relocated from impoverished inner-city slums to Chicago neighborhoods and suburbs over a period of 15 years. According to research by the Northwestern University Center for Urban Affairs and Policy Research, "scattering" the poor into predomi-

nantly middle-class suburban neighborhoods has enabled the adults to find nearby work; 53 percent more found jobs than those who relocated to other inner-city neighborhoods. Virtually all of the children have graduated from high school, over half have gone on to college. Participants in the study report being highly satisfied with the program (Rosenbaum et al., 1991; Kaufman and Rosenbaum, 1991; Rosenbaum and Meaden, 1992; Rubinowitz, 1992).

Does this example support Wilson's theory? Do you think the special attention paid to the participants in this experiment might had have a bearing on its outcome (see, for example, the discussion of the "Hawthorne effect" in Chapter 2)? What other factors might account for its success?

key economic decisions. Under them are the *managers,* who occupy what Wright terms a **contradictory class location:** *their work partly gives them the power of the bourgeois class, yet at the same time, like members of the working class, they are in many ways denied such power.* On the one hand, managers have a great deal of power over others below them, and they are clearly involved in making important economic decisions. Moreover, they prosper as long as their business prospers, and many own stock in the business as well. On the other hand, managers do not own the means of production, nor do they have control over their own labor power. Rather, they work for the bourgeoisie, who can hire or fire them at will. Beneath the managers are the *supervisors,* who are also in a contradictory class location: Although they have power over the people they supervise, they do not make core economic decisions, nor do they truly control their own labor power. They are thus even weaker than the managers. At the bottom are the *workers,* who are subordinate in every way: They do not control their own labor, nor do they exercise any significant control over other people or key economic decision-making.

Among those who are engaged in other economic activities, the most independent are the *petty bourgeoisie,* who are self-employed small business people or professionals. These do not employ the labor of others, except perhaps for family members. They also enjoy considerable control over their own economic activities. Examples would include the owner of a small company that manufactures and sells clothing, or a person who owns a retail shop. The second group comprises *small employers* who own small shops or factories, employing limited amounts of the labor of others. They find themselves in a contradictory class location, since they lack real economic power: They are too small to control their own economic destinies, which often lie in the hands of the larger bourgeoisie, yet they themselves have power over their hired laborers. Examples of this group would be the owner of a small factory that makes minor automobile parts for General Motors, or the owner of a garment factory that employs a dozen workers who sew shirts for some large clothing manufacturer. Finally, there are the *semiautonomous employees,* who are technical and professional workers. These include doctors, lawyers, engineers, and others who are not self-employed but work for larger corporations, and therefore lack full control over their own economic activities. Their class position is therefore somewhat contradictory.

Wright's theory seeks to explain class conflict in terms of the degree to which a person occupies an unambiguous class position. Among those who are engaged in large-scale capitalistic economic activities, workers and bourgeoisie alone occupy positions that are not contradictory: Their interests are diametrically opposed to one another. Three other classes are caught in the middle, experiencing contradictory demands on their interests and loyalties. The remaining three classes lie outside the principal dynamics of the capitalist economy, and so their alliances depend on the specific circumstances of class struggle.

The Ehrenreichs' Theory of the Professional-Managerial Class

Like Wright, Barbara and John Ehrenreich (1979) define class membership in terms of the roles people play in the larger economy. They focus on a particular segment of the class structure: the middle class. They disagree with the Marxist notion that the middle class will eventually be absorbed into the two principal classes of capitalists and workers. They also disagree with the more conventional view that the middle class somehow lies "between" capitalists and workers, a growing segment of the population that differs from both. Rather, they argue, the very notion of a "middle class" is misleading.

The Ehrenreichs propose instead that the middle class be thought of as a **professional-managerial class,** consisting of *salaried workers who use their minds (rather than their hands), and whose function it is to help maintain a capitalist society.* This class is termed "professional" because its members require some specialized training, often of a scientific or technical nature. It is called "managerial" because its members are often involved in overseeing the labor of others. The membership of this class, accounting for 20 to 25 percent of all Americans, is highly diverse. It includes such occupations as engineers and scientists, administrators and managers, doctors and nurses, lawyers and bankers, welfare administrators and social workers, professors and teachers, entertainers and writers.

At one end of the professional managerial class are those whose interests and identity are closely bound up with the capitalist class, such as highly paid upper-level managers, lawyers, and engineers. The Ehrenreichs claim that 70 percent of all scientists and engineers work for business and industry; only about 15 percent are found in independent universities. At the other end are those whose daily activities are more working class in nature, such as nurses, social workers, or engineers doing routine inspection work. Such occupations are characterized by lower pay and less control over the conditions of employment.

The professional managerial class is caught in what Wright would term a contradictory class location. On the one hand, it is similar to the working class in that its members are salaried employees of business and government. They are not for the most part owners of capital (although the wealthier members of this class may own some stocks), but rather sell their services to others. Even though many members of this class see themselves as highly independent, in the last analysis they must take orders from others. This is true for the highly paid corporate lawyer as well as the nurse working in a hospital: both can be fired by their employers. Thus, according to the Ehrenreichs, members of the professional managerial class ultimately do not share a common interest with the capitalist class, even if they sometimes think otherwise.

Yet the professional managerial class does not share a common interest with the working class either. This is because a major function of this class is to manage and control members of the working class. Much work that is today performed by the professional managerial class was once done by the working class itself. A century ago workers performed highly skilled tasks, supervising their own labor. Today these functions are done by industrial engineers and managers (see Chapter 15). Workers have even given up production of their own culture to members of the professional managerial class, such as television scriptwriters who define the standards of working-class entertainment.

Thus, in contemporary capitalist society there is a three way polarization between the capitalist class, the working class, and the professional managerial class. The Ehrenreichs view the latter class as playing a strategic role in managing class conflict between the former two, while attempting to develop ever-greater power for itself. The emergence of postindustrial society will likely enhance the position of this class, whose power lies in its ability to work with ideas, information, and specialized knowledge.

INEQUALITY IN THE UNITED STATES

Between 1977 and 1989, average income in the United States grew by 10 percent, even after taking into account the declining purchasing power of the dollar due to inflation. Does this mean that all Americans experienced economic gains? A look behind the averages tells a very different story. As U.S. Labor Secretary Robert Reich has described it, the American stratification system now has two escalators in operation—a small one going up, and a larger one going down.

Furthermore, all groups in American society do not share equally in the wealth that is being produced. For example, the median income of Hispanic-origin households in 1992 was only 71 percent that of white households, while African-American households averaged only 58 percent (Table 8.2). Full-time women workers earned only 70 percent as much as men (U.S. Bureau of the Census, 1993a, 1993b). Such inequality is seen in a growing gap between rich and poor, declining income for families, increased poverty, and growing homelessness. We shall explore these trends below, examining racial, ethnic, and gender differences in greater detail in Chapters 10 and 11).

A Growing Gap Between Rich and Poor

In 1989 the wealthiest 1 percent of all Americans enjoyed net financial assets that averaged 237 times the amount of the remaining 99 percent. In fact, a Federal Reserve Board study found that the wealthiest 1 percent of American households had a total net worth of $5.7 *trillion* dollars, more than the bottom 90 percent combined. During a single 12-year period from 1977 to 1989, the wealthiest 1 percent of Americans saw their incomes nearly double, increasing by some $200 billion; most other Americans found their incomes stagnating or falling (Francis, 1990; Mandel, 1992; Phillips, 1991; Nasar, 1992).

Inequality in income and wealth in the United States is high today. In fact, the disparity between rich and poor is now the largest in nearly three-quarters of a century, and it is higher than in almost any other industrial nation (Shapiro and Greenstein, 1991; Phillips, 1991; Center on Budget and Policy Priorities, 1992. Figure 8.2 compares the concentration of income in the United States with other advanced industrial nations. The ratio of the average income of the wealthiest fifth of all households to the poorest fifth is presented. In the United States, this ratio is about 12 to 1—that is, the average income of the wealthiest 20

Table 8.2   Median Household Income and Poverty Rates for Whites, Blacks and Hispanics (1992)

	White	Black	Hispanic
Income	$32,368	$18,660	$22,848
Percentage of white income	—	57.6	70.6
Percentage in poverty	11.6	33.3	29.3

Source: U.S. Bureau of the Census (1993b).

Figure 8.2   Income Inequality in Industrial Nations: Ratio of Richest 20% to Poorest 20%

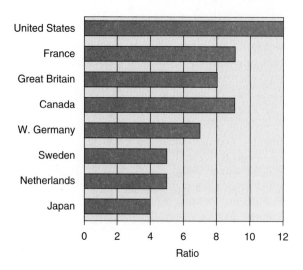

The richest fifth of all Americans are on average 12 times richer than the poorest fifth, the highest ratio in the industrialized world. In Japan, by way of comparison, the ratio is only 4 to 1.
Source: Phillips (1991).

percent of households is about 12 times that of the poorest 20 percent. Canada and France are tied for second, with ratios of 8.5 to 1, while Britain is third, with a ratio of 8 to 1. It is interesting to note that the two countries whose economies have proved to be among

This cartoon summarizes one aspect of Karl Marx's theory of stratification—namely, that polarization of rich and poor is a built-in feature of capitalist society. Although the gap between rich and poor in the United States declined throughout much of the twentieth century, during the past two decades it has grown. This is partly due to the effects of economic globalization.

the world's strongest in recent years—the former West Germany and Japan—have the lowest ratios of inequality, 4.5 to 1 and 4 to 1, respectively (Phillips, 1991).

One measure of growing inequality in American society can be obtained by comparing the average income of the heads of the largest corporations with that of other groups in society. In 1960, top corporate executives averaged approximately $190,000 in compensation, roughly 41 times as much as the workers in their factories (see Figure 8.3). By 1993, average CEO compensation reached $3.8 million, 157 times as much as the average factory worker salary of only $24,400. By far the largest portion of this exploding gap between rich and poor occurred after 1980, when executive

Figure 8.3   Salaries of U.S. Workers, Teachers, Engineers, and CEOs, 1960–1992

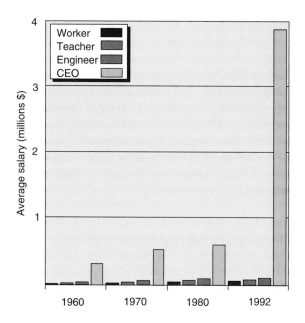

SALARIES

	worker	teacher	engineer	CEO
1960	$4,665	$4,995	$9,829	$190,383
1970	$6,933	$8,626	$14,695	$548,787
1980	$15,008	$15,970	$28,486	$624,996
1992	$24,411	$34,098	$58,240	$3,842,247

The gap in pay between top corporate executives and other Americans has exploded in recent years. In 1960 top executives earned about 19 times as much as engineers, 38 times as much as teachers, and 41 times as much as factory workers. Today, the ratios are 66 to one, 113 to one, and 157 to one. Most of this increase ocurred after 1980.
Source: Business Week (1993, pp. 56–57)

compensation increased sixfold, while worker salary increased by less than two-thirds (*Business Week,* 1993). The gap between executive pay and that of engineers and teachers grew comparably. By way of comparison, income (in U.S. dollars) for top executives at Britain's 30 largest companies averaged $1.1 million in 1991; for French and German executives it was $800,000; and for Japanese executives it was $525,000 (Crystal, 1991; see Chapter 6 for further discussion of Japanese business practices).

Declining Income Among Workers and Families

According to a study of men's employment prepared by Senator Paul S. Sarbanes (1992), Chairman of the Joint Economic Committee of Congress, between the end of World War II (1945) until the early 1970s, the average American male worker could expect his income to increase more-or-less continuously until the day he retired. Since the 1970s, however, this expectation has vanished for all men except the approximately 11 percent who complete four years of college. Although the median earnings of men nearly doubled during the 1945–1972 period, since that time it has actually declined. A young man aged 25 to 34 in 1959 could expect his income to increase by more than half over the next decade, and then continue to increase at a slower rate for the rest of his working life. Today, based on recent trends, the same young man could anticipate a modest gain of only about 10 percent over the next decade, followed by ten years of stagnation and then decline.

If one looks at young families instead of just male workers, the situation is still worse. Between 1973 and 1990, the inflation-adjusted income of young families with children (headed by someone under 30) declined by a third. Among young families headed by African Americans, the decline was even greater, nearly a half. The declines were greatest for high school dropouts, but astonishingly young families headed by a college graduate earned no more in 1990 than they had 17 years earlier (Children's Defense Fund, 1992).

Poverty in the United States

The U.S. government defines the "poverty level" as three times the cost of a nutritionally adequate diet. In 1991, for a family of four persons, that worked out to an annual cash income of approximately $13,924—an austere no-frills budget that assumes a nutritionally adequate diet can be purchased for only $3.18 per day, for each family member. Using this stringent standard, there are currently 36 million persons living below the "poverty line," or roughly one out of every seven Americans. About a third of all African Americans live in poverty, a quarter of all Latinos, one out of every seven Asian Americans, and one out of every eight whites (U.S. Bureau of the Census, 1992).

When President Lyndon B. Johnson's "War on Poverty" began in 1964, around 36 million Americans lived in poverty. Within a decade the number had dropped sharply, to around 23 million. But then, beginning in the early 1970s, poverty again began to climb. While there were many reasons for this, it was partly due to the increase in globalization that began

Because the U.S. population is so concentrated in urban areas, rural poverty often goes unnoticed. This West Virginia family lives in abject poverty and shares the caste-like status of the underclass urban poor.

MAP 8.1	Percentage of People in Poverty by County in the U.S., 1990

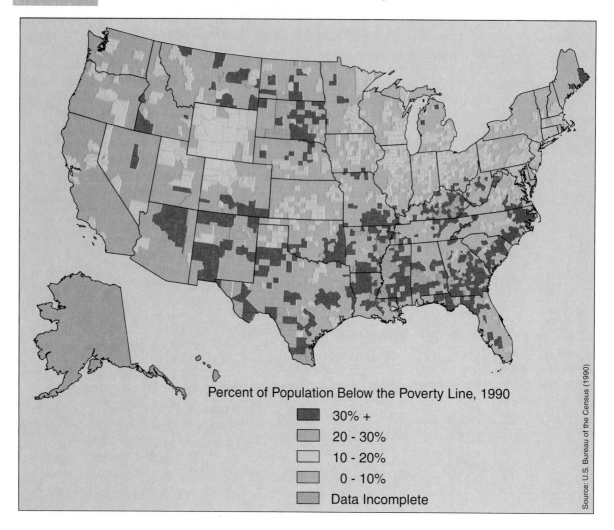

Percent of Population Below the Poverty Line, 1990

- 30% +
- 20 - 30%
- 10 - 20%
- 0 - 10%
- Data Incomplete

Source: U.S. Bureau of the Census (1990)

Poverty rates vary from region to region in the United States, and some regions have been more hard-hit by poverty than others. Poverty is most heavily concentrated in rural areas of the south and southwest, in the plains states, and in large metropolitan areas.

during that period, which resulted in growing loss of jobs to low-income countries. During the 1980s, the Reagan Administration sought to lower government spending, increasing the number of poor still further. Today there are 39.3 million people living in poverty, more people than at any time since the "War on Poverty" began (U.S Bureau of the Census, 1993c1994a; see Figure 8.4).

The U.S. poverty rate is the highest among the major industrial nations, more than five times that of Switzerland or Sweden. Many of these people are the **working poor**—*people whose earnings are insufficient to lift them above poverty.* About half of poor family members work at least part-time, and about one in six work full-time (U.S. Bureau of the Census, 1990).

Much of the growth in poverty is associated with the

feminization of poverty, an *increase in the proportion of the poor who are female.* Growing rates of divorce, separation, and single-parent family formation have placed women at a particular disadvantage, since it is extremely difficult for unskilled or semiskilled low-income women to simultaneously raise children by themselves, and find and hold a job that would raise them out of poverty. As a result, single-parent families headed by a woman are six times as likely to live in poverty as two-parent families, accounting for half of all poor families. The feminization of poverty is particularly acute among families headed by African-American women, but poverty rates are substantial among white and Latino female-headed families as well (U.S. Bureau of the Census, 1990).

Figure 8.4   **Percentage of Americans in Poverty, 1959–1992**

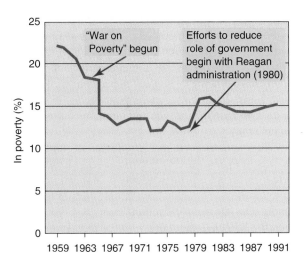

The percentage of Americans living in poverty dropped sharply during the late 1960s and 1970s, partly due to growth in the American economy, and partly to Medicare and government antipoverty programs. During the 1980s, it again increased, the result of globalization as well as changing gorvernmental priorities.
Source: US Bureau of the Census, (1993b).

These trends have also contributed to a rapid growth in the number of children living in poverty. The poverty rate for children in young families (headed by someone under 30) doubled between 1973 and 1990; two out of every five children in young families now live in poverty. Poverty rates among young African-American families have reached 68 percent; among young Latino families, 51 percent; and among female-headed families, 77 percent (Children's Defense Fund, 1992; Eggebeen and Lichter, 1991).

The reasons for growing poverty are many and much debated, but it is possible to identify a number of important causes. First, the impact of economic globalization on job loss and income decline has already been emphasized. Many of the jobs that are being created today pay too little to keep a family above the poverty level. In 1990, nearly one out of every five full-time workers failed to earn enough to lift a four-person family out of poverty (Associated Press, 1993). Second, the federal government cut spending on antipoverty programs throughout the 1980s, removing one small protection against poverty (Shapiro and Greenstein, 1991; Phillips, 1991). Third, women typically earn less for doing the same work as men (see Chapter 11). Finally, racism and discrimination continue to pose barriers to nonwhites in American society, particularly African Americans and Latinos (Chapter 10).

Homelessness

One of the most obvious indicators of the changes occurring in the American stratification system is the increase in **homelessness,** the type of *existence followed by a person who does not own a home, rent an apartment, or have a stable place to live.* The homeless are a common sight in nearly every U.S. city and town, and are increasingly found in rural areas as well. Only a generation ago the homeless were mainly elderly, alcoholic men who were found in the "skid rows" of the largest metropolitan areas. Today they are primarily young single men, often of working age, although the fastest-growing group of homeless consists of families with children. While the homeless are sometimes able to sleep in shelters provided by private charities, religious organizations, and local government, in most instances they have no choice but to sleep in abandoned buildings, cars and vans, subway stations, or out in the open (Blau, 1992; Burt, 1992; Hombs and Snyder, 1982; Wright, 1989).

No one really knows how many homeless people there are, since it is extremely difficult to count people who do not have a stable residence (Appelbaum, 1990). Estimates of the number of homeless vary widely (see Chapter 2, Box 2.1). The most widely accepted figures today range from three-quarters of a million to a million people at any given time, a number that continues to grow (Burt, 1992; Rossi, 1989; Wright, 1989).

Causes of Homelessness: Personal or Societal?

Although homelessness is found in other countries, the United States has an especially acute problem, with more homeless people than any other major industrial nation. Why is this the case? An adequate answer to this question illustrates the use of the sociological imagination (see Chapter 1), since it requires an understanding of the interplay between the personal characteristics of the homeless, and larger societal forces they confront.

Personal Causes of Homelessness Hundreds of studies have focused on the personal characteristics of the homeless population, and how various disabilities and shortcomings have contributed to their plight (Burt, 1992; Blau, 1992). One problem, according to these studies, is that about a third of the homeless suffer from mental illness, and a third are substance abusers; as many as half have both problems. This is sometimes attributed to **deinstitutionalization**—*the closure of many public mental hospitals, beginning in the 1960s, leaving mentally ill people with no insti-*

tutional alternative to a life on the streets or in homeless shelters. Such problems are compounded by the fact that many homeless people lack family, relatives, or other social networks to provide support.

Critical Assessment While there is some truth to the argument that many people are homeless because of their personal mental or physical disabilities, it leaves many questions unanswered. Why has the number of homeless people grown from a few thousand elderly men in the 1960s, to approximately a million men, women, and children today? Clearly, the number of substance abusers or mentally disabled individuals could not have increased by such an amount. Deinstitutionalization alone cannot account for the increase. The number of beds in state mental hospitals declined by 400,000, mostly before 1974; yet homelessness became an acute problem only in the 1980s (Burt, 1992). In fact, substance abuse and mental disability may be as much a *result* of living on the streets as a cause of it.

Societal Causes of Homelessness Among the societal causes of homelessness, sociologists point to a growing **affordability gap** between *what poorer people must pay for housing and what they can actually afford.* One side of the affordability gap, previously discussed, is a decline in income and a growth in poverty, partly due to the impact of economic globalization on the American workforce. The other side of the affordability gap is an increase in the cost of rental housing. Rents increased throughout the 1980s even as incomes were declining, to the point where the poorest families now pay over half their income on housing (Dreier and Appelbaum, 1992). Between 1970 and 1989, the number of low-income households increased by half, while the number of low-cost housing units declined by the same proportion. Together, these two trends have produced an estimated shortage of five million low-cost housing units for low-income people (Dolbeare, 1992). The affordability gap has been worsened by the loss of government programs aimed at providing low-cost housing for the poor, which were cut by four-fifths between 1981 and 1989. Thus, a crucial "safety net" was removed, just as poverty was increasing in the United States (Dreier and Appelbaum, 1992).

Personal and Societal Causes—A Sociological Explanation Personal characteristics interact with larger social forces to increase the risk of anyone becoming homeless. In general, the poorer a person is, the more he or she is likely to be vulnerable to any adverse economic condition. An unskilled worker struggling to pay the bills on a low-wage job has little margin for mistakes or misfortunes. The loss of the job, a drug or drinking problem, or a period of mental illness may lead to missed rent payments, eviction, and eventually homelessness. On the other hand, middle-class people with the exact same set of difficulties have a much lower risk of becoming homeless, since they will likely have other resources to fall back on: savings, investments, credit and loans, a larger array of job options, and probably friends and family who can afford to help out.

This is not to say that only poor people run the risk of becoming homeless: If you have ever volunteered at a homeless shelter, you may have been surprised to encounter formerly middle class families who "ran out of luck." But the people overwhelmingly at risk of becoming homeless are those who combine low-paying jobs, poverty, and high housing costs with a tangle of personal problems (Burt, 1992).

SOCIAL MOBILITY: WHO GETS AHEAD

Homelessness is an extreme consequence of one form of **social mobility,** or *movement through the stratification system, particularly as a result of changes in occupation, wealth, or income.* There are various kinds of social mobility. One set of distinctions has to do with the period of time over which mobility occurs. **Intergenerational mobility** refers to *movement that occurs across generations* (for example, being born into a working-class family, yet having a career as a college professor). This is distinct from **intragenerational mobility,** which is *movement that occurs within one's own lifetime* (for example, starting out as an assembly line worker and winding up the president of the corporation). A second set of distinctions has to do with the direction of social mobility. **Vertical mobility** refers to *movement that is up or down the stratification system.* It includes **upward mobility,** an *increase in occupational status* (for example, from worker to corporation president), and **downward mobility,** a *decrease in occupational status* (from worker to unemployed homeless person). **Horizontal** (or **lateral**) **mobility** refers to a *change in occupation that involves no change in status* (from autoworker to steelworker).

Structural Mobility

A final set of distinctions has to do with whether mobility results from personal efforts, or larger societal changes. **Structural mobility** refers to *movement through the stratification system that results from changes in the occupational structure of a society.* If the economy is growing, as was the case of the U.S.

economy for much of the twentieth century, there are likely to be more opportunities for upward mobility (Hauser and Featherman, 1976, 1977; Featherman, Jones, and Hauser, 1974). This is because an expanding economy typically produces higher-status, higher-paying jobs. During the early phases of U.S. industrialization there was an enormous shift from agricultural to industrial work, which created substantial opportunity for upward mobility. This was the period when many impoverished immigrants came to the United States from Europe in search of fortune, fueling the "rags to riches" stories that are a part of U.S. folklore. As the U.S. economy matured it produced an expanding job base, and with it a growing middle class.

We have seen how this pattern has begun to change in the face of economic globalization and the resulting loss of jobs to low-wage countries. As a result, the "middle class bulge" in the U.S. stratification system appears to be thinning out at the bottom, with some middle class jobs replaced by lower-wage, lower-status jobs (Figure 8.5). The opportunities for upward mobility have thus been sharply curtailed by changes in the overall structure of the economy (Hout, 1988). A growing number of individuals are experiencing downward mobility, from middle class corporate managers who lose their jobs through "downsizing," to former factory

workers who are forced to find lower-paying work in such places as fast-food restaurants. The 1990 Census found that the middle class had shrunk significantly during the past decade (Knutson, 1992).

Positional Mobility

Regardless of whether the overall economy is expanding, contracting, or unchanging, some individuals will experience more upward or downward social mobility than others. **Positional mobility** refers to *movement through the stratification system that results from individual effort, accomplishments, or luck, rather than changes in the occupational structure.* Studies show that throughout much of the twentieth century, upward mobility has been more common than downward mobility, and that most mobility has been within a person's class of origin. For example, Blau and Duncan (1967) found that only about two out of five men born into blue-collar households experienced upward mobility into white-collar jobs, while fewer than a third of men born into white-collar households experienced downward mobility into blue-collar jobs. Contrary to the "rags to riches" myth, most mobility is thus short-range—that is, most sons do not move up or down a great deal in relationship to their fathers, unless a great deal of economic expansion is occurring (Blau and Duncan, 1967; Featherman and Hauser, 1978).

These findings do not apply to all groups of people, however. Women have been virtually absent from mobility research (Hout, 1988), since most sociologists have assumed that a woman takes on her husband's status when she marries. Sociology in general has focused on women's domestic roles to the exclusion of their participation in more "public" activities such as work, intellectual life, or politics (Elshtain, 1981). The assumption that a woman simply takes on her husband's status may have been partly justified when the majority of women were full-time homemakers, but it is clearly unwarranted now that women increasingly contribute to family income (and in many cases are the sole source of such income). Recent research has shown that women experience greater barriers to upward mobility than men and are often unable to move out of such lower-paying positions as secretaries, typists, and waitresses (Jacobs, 1989; Morrison et al., 1987; see Chapter 11).

African Americans and Latinos also tend to experience lower rates of upward mobility than whites, even during periods of economic expansion when the opportunities for structural mobility are high (Featherman and Hauser, 1978; Pomer, 1986). A good part of the economic gains made by African Americans and Latinos during the 1960s and early 1970s were due to structural mobility resulting from the economic expansion

Figure 8.5   **The Shrinking Middle Class, 1964–1989**

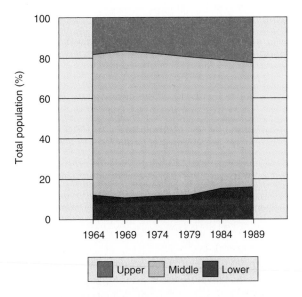

Since 1964, middle-income Americans have shrunk from 69 percent to 63 percent of the total, while high-income Americans have grown from 12 percent to 15 percent, and poor Americans have grown from 19 percent to 22 percent. *Source:* U.S. Bureau of the Census

of the period, as well as decreased discrimination resulting from civil rights legislation (Wilson, 1987). The economic stagnation of recent years has fallen most heavily on these same two groups, many of whom have experienced downward mobility, some into homelessness.

Social Mobility and "Cultural Capital"

Although individual mobility is explained by a number of factors, it is clear that family background has the strongest effect on a person's chances for success. Family background includes such factors as parental income, education, and occupation, all of which can work together to provide **cultural capital** for children in middle- and upper-class families. This includes the *verbal skills, knowledge base, and ways of thinking that help a person get ahead in society* (Bourdieu, 1984; DiMaggio, 1982, 1987). Cultural capital helps to explain why being born at the top of a stratification system is the best way of assuring that one remains there.

The old joke that "choosing one's parents is the best thing you can do to ensure material success in life" is partly true: cultural capital contributes to an accumulation of advantages, at least from the standpoint of social stratification.

Cultural capital results from a number of aspects of middle-class home life in U.S. culture. For example, there is often an emphasis on scholastic achievement, reinforced by exposure to books, magazines, and perhaps dinner-table discussions that enable children to develop the sorts of verbal skills that are rewarded as signs of intelligence in college classrooms. It is furthered by attendance at high-quality public or private high schools, which have the resources necessary to adequately prepare students for college. Strong parental expectations for higher education, combined with the financial resources to pay for it, are also important. And well-placed family "connections," which can help a person get started in business or a profession, also contribute to success.

It is not surprising, perhaps, that the University of

Box 8.3

Globalization

Low Wages in Other Countries Contribute to Low Wages in the United States

In addition to contributing to the flight of U.S. manufacturing jobs, low wages in developing countries have another adverse impact on stratification in the United States: They reduce the market for goods produced by American workers. According to labor specialist Richard Rothstein (1993), for example, higher wages in Mexico would lead to economic growth and lowered inequality in the United States. Why does Rothstein believe this should be the case?

Mexico's Constitution requires a minimum wage "sufficient to satisfy the normal material, social, and cultural needs of the head of a family and to provide for the mandatory education of his children." Yet recent Mexican governments have ignored this requirement. According to Rothstein, when the minimum wage in Mexico dropped by a half (to about 55 cents an hour) during the 1980s, many Mexicans who had previously bought U.S. products were now too poor to do so. As a result, the U.S. factories mak-

ing those products were forced to reduce production, laying off 300,000 American workers. Rothstein concludes that

> Wage growth in developing countries is thus essential not only for their own welfare but for the welfare of Americans as well. . . . Emphasizing the role of wage growth in Third World development strategies could help to stem the growth of poverty in the United States. It could begin to cure the 1980s epidemic in which the contagion of Third World poverty infected the living standards of the poorest American workers as well.

Do you agree with Rothstein's argument that the best way to preserve the American standard of living is to seek an increase in wages elsewhere in the world? What about the counter argument, that such wage increases would raise the cost of goods made elsewhere and sold in the United States?

California—which is required to admit the top 12 percent of California high school seniors exclusively on the basis of academic performance—overwhelmingly enrolls students from all-white, often wealthy California communities, leading one commentator to conclude that "the list of feeder high schools that send more than 100 students each to the University of California reads like a social register" (Brown, 1989). The one exception in recent years has been Asian-American students, whose high school grades and tests have made them highly competitive for UC admission. Again, however, such students typically come from homes that strongly emphasize academic achievement, giving them a great deal of cultural capital with which to compete.

Cultural capital partly explains why short-range mobility is far more common in the United States than long-range mobility. Christopher Jencks and his colleagues, for example, found that family background (as measured by parents' occupation, income, and education) was more important than one's own intelligence or education in explaining where one winds up as an adult. Together, family background, intelligence, and education, and other such factors account for only about half of all mobility; the remainder, according to this study, was due to a variety of individual factors including "luck" (Jencks et al., 1972, 1979).

Social Mobility and Individual Effort

We do not mean to imply that individual effort makes no difference in social mobility. Former U.S. presidents Dwight David Eisenhower and Richard Nixon, for example, both came from poor families that had experienced considerable economic hardship. Yet such examples are the exception, which is perhaps why they come so readily to mind. It may be useful to think of social mobility as similar to swimming across a fast-moving stream to get a reward at a given point on the opposite side. In this analogy, a person who starts the swim far upstream has a far easier chance of reaping the rewards of landing in the right place, since the current can be used to help get across. Such a privileged swimmer can be likened to an upper-class child, who can draw on cultural capital and other accumulated advantages to help ease mobility into an advantaged adulthood. On the other hand, a person who starts the swim far downstream needs to labor against the current, in order to achieve the same upstream landing on the other side. Such a disadvantaged swimmer is similar to the lower-class child, who must expend a far greater amount of effort in order to achieve mobility into a comparably advantaged adulthood.

GLOBALIZATION AND STRATIFICATION IN THE UNITED STATES: A SUMMARY

Throughout this chapter we have touched upon the various ways in which the emergence of a truly global economy affects stratification in the United States. We pointed out that the global spread of an industrial capitalist economy helps to undermine closed caste systems around the world, replacing them with more open class systems. The degree to which this process may result in greater equality will be explored in the next chapter.

Within the United States, this same process of economic globalization has meant that American workers are now competing with low-cost workers around the world for the same jobs (Box 8.3). This has had two primary impacts on stratification. First, it has led to the

In recent years, technological and organizational advances have made it increasingly easy and profitable for businesses to move their plants to low-wage countries. Many American factories have shut down as a result, as this photograph of an abandoned Detroit automobile plant shows. Plant closings and other adverse impacts of economic globalization have contributed to unemployment and declining wages for many U.S. workers.

loss of many of the jobs in manufacturing and business that once provided the economic foundation for the working class and segments of the middle class. Second, it has resulted in declining earnings in the United States, both because of competition for jobs from low-cost foreign labor, and because many of the remaining jobs pay far less than the jobs that have fled abroad.

As a result of these forces, three-quarters of a century of declining inequality in the United States appears to be reversing itself. There is evidence that economic polarization has occurred during the past quarter century, with a growing gap between rich and poor. The global economy has permitted the accumulation of vast fortunes at the same time it has contributed to declining wages, economic hardship, and poverty. Homelessness is one obvious manifestation of these processes, as is the emergence of an extremely impoverished urban stratum that some sociologists have characterized as an underclass. Although the working class is especially vulnerable to these changes, the middle class is not exempt, as a growing number of middle class households experience downward mobility. While it is too soon to predict the future of these changes, it seems likely that global economic integration will continue to increase for the foreseeable future. This could result in economic hardship for a growing number of Americans.

The world today is undergoing a transformation as profound as the industrial revolution. The impact of that transformation will reverberate well into the next century, touching our lives in every way. In the next chapter we will further examine the implications of this transformation for stratification and inequality in other countries in the world, especially the poorer countries that have recently begun to industrialize. In Chapter 15 we will return to the impact of globalization on work and the American economy.

CHAPTER SUMMARY

1. Societies are stratified on the basis of **class, status,** and **power.** Following Max Weber, these three sources of stratification are thought of as overlapping one another, with a great deal of wealth, prestige, and power concentrated in a relatively small number of people at the top.

2. Social class is based on **occupation, income,** and **wealth.** Wealth is unequally distributed in all societies, and in the United States a relative handful of people control the majority of wealth.

3. Sociologists have differing theories of power. Some hold **pluralistic** theories, which see power distributed among different groups; others adhere to **class dominance** theories, which see power as concentrated in a **power elite;** and still others hold to **structuralist** theories, which view power as constrained by institutional location.

4. **Class societies** are more open than **caste societies.** There is evidence that during industrialization in class-based societies, inequality first increases and then declines. There is also evidence that **inequality** is again beginning to increase with the advent of global postindustrial society.

5. Although caste-based societies are giving way to class-based ones, elements of caste based on race, ethnicity, and gender remain throughout the world and in the United States.

6. Although **classless societies** have long been a dream of social reformers and revolutionaries, they have yet to make their appearance in the modern world.

7. Functionalist theorists in sociology argue that inequality is necessary to motivate the most talented people to fill the most important roles, while social conflict theorists argue that inequality is the result of social classes and class conflict.

8. One way to view the U.S. class structure is to simply divide it into an upper class, middle class, working class, and lower class. Occupations, income, wealth, lifestyle, and power differ considerably for each. Sociologists debate whether or not an urban **underclass** can be found at the very bottom, caught up in a vicious cycle of poverty from which few escape.

9. Another way to view the U.S. class structure has to do with the different roles people play in the production of goods and services. The theories of Wright and Ehrenreich both avoid the notion of a "middle class," instead focusing on the extent to which a particular occupation involves such things as ownership of capital, control over the labor power of others, and the maintenance of a capitalist society.

10. Inequality is growing in the United States. During the last quarter century, partly as a result of eco-

nomic globalization, there has been a growing gap between rich and poor. Ordinary workers and families have seen their income drop, while incomes at the top have increased sharply. Poverty and **homelessness** have grown as well.

11. Much **upward mobility** in the United States has been short distance, within class, and has been due to the overall growth in the American economy during the first three-quarters of this century. Because of the changes that have occurred in the last 25 years, some middle-class people are experiencing downward mobility.

12. The emergence of a global economy has had a major impact on the U.S. stratification system and will continue to do so well into the next century.

QUESTIONS FOR DISCUSSION

1. Sociologists and economists have long argued that one result of industrialization is a decline in inequality. To what extent is this thesis supported by recent changes in the U.S. stratification system? Why do you think such changes have occurred?

2. "All you need to get ahead in our society is hard work and effort." What theory supports this statement? What theory refutes it? What is the evidence for and against each theory?

3. "Although American society is a class society, elements of caste remain." Discuss the evidence for and against this statement, and discuss the nature of class and caste in the U.S. stratification system.

4. Inequality in the U.S. is among the highest in the industrial world. Why do you think this might be so? What arguments might be used to justify such inequality? To criticize it?

5. How has globalization in the past 15 to 20 years affected social stratification in the United States?

KEY TERMS

affordability gap: The difference between what poorer people must pay for housing and what they can actually afford to pay; one source of homelessness.

ascription: The acquisition of one's position in the stratification system on the basis of personal characteristics that derive from birth and therefore are believed to be unchangeable; associated with caste societies.

blue collar: Work that requires manual labor.

caste society: A society in which the strata are closed to movement, so that all individuals must remain throughout life in the stratum of their birth.

class: A person's location in a society's economic system, resulting in differences in the nature of work, income, and wealth.

class consciousness: An awareness of one's own interests as a member of a particular social class, along with an adequate understanding of the ways in which society operates to produce inequality.

class dominance: The theory that power is concentrated in the hands of a relatively small number of individuals who comprise an upper-class power elite.

class society: A society in which the strata are open to movement, so that changing one's stratum of birth is possible.

classless society: A society in which different economic strata do not exist.

contradictory class location: A class position in which members have some of the power of the bourgeois class (for example, control over the work of others), yet like the working class are ultimately denied such power (since they are ultimately accountable to the bourgeois class).

cultural capital: The verbal skills, knowledge base, and ways of thinking that help a person get ahead in society.

deinstitutionalization: The closure of many public mental hospitals, beginning in the 1960s, which has contributed to the growing number of homeless mentally ill people on streets and in shelters.

downward mobility: Movement through the stratification system that results in a decrease in occupational status.

endogamy: A prohibition against marrying or having sexual relations with persons outside of one's social group or caste.

feminization of poverty: An increase in the proportion of the poor who are female.

homelessness: The type of existence followed by a person who does not own a home, rent an apartment, or have a stable place to live.

horizontal (or lateral) mobility: Movement through the stratification system that involves no change in status.

income: The amount of money a person or household earns in a given period of time.

inequality: The degree of disparity that exists in a society.

intergenerational mobility: Movement through the stratification system that occurs across generations.

intragenerational mobility: Movement through the stratification system that occurs within a person's lifetime.

Kuznets curve: The observation that inequality increases during the early stages of capitalist development, then declines, and eventually stabilizes at a relatively low level; advanced by the economist Simon Kuznets.

net financial assets: The value of everything one owns (with the exception of one's home and cars), minus the value of everything one owes.

occupation: Paid employment.

pink collar: Work that primarily employs women in nonmanual semiskilled work.

pluralism: The theory that power is distributed among different groups that contend with one another on roughly equal footing.

positional mobility: Movement through the stratification system that results from individual effort, accomplishments, or luck, rather than changes in the occupational structure.

power: A person's relationship to governmental and other political institutions, manifested in the ability to mobilize resources and achieve a goal despite the resistance of others.

professional-managerial class: A class that consists of salaried workers who use their minds (rather than their hands), and whose function it is to help maintain a capitalist society.

ritual pollution: The belief that contact between members of different castes will corrupt or contaminate the members of the higher caste.

social mobility: Movement through the stratification system, particularly as a result of changes in occupation, wealth, or income.

social stratification: The systematic inequalities of wealth, power, and prestige that result from social rank.

status: A person's relationship to established social positions in society that vary in terms of prestige.

structural mobility: Movement through the stratification system that results from changes in the occupational structure of a society.

structuralism: The theory that power is highly constrained and shaped by a person's organizational role.

underclass: A caste-like group that is "beneath" the class system in that it lacks access even to the lower parts of the working class; consists primarily of inner-city African Americans who have been trapped for more than a generation in an unending cycle of poverty from which there is little possibility of escape.

upward mobility: Movement through the stratification system that results in an increase in occupational status.

vertical mobility: Movement that is up or down the stratification system.

wealth: The value of everything a person owns.

white collar: Work that requires mental skills.

working poor: People whose earnings are insufficient to lift them above poverty.

R E C O M M E N D E D   F O R   F U R T H E R   R E A D I N G

Blau, Joel. (1992). *The Visible Poor: Homelessness in the United States.* New York: Oxford University Press.

A thoughtful examination of the nature and causes of homelessness, which analyzes societal forces as well as individual problems. Contains much useful historical and public policy materials as well.

Crystal, Graef S. (1991). *In Search of Excess: The Overcompensation of American Executives.* New York: Norton.

An examination of the recent escalation in pay for America's top corporate executives, which examines some of the causes and implications. Much useful statistical information, including compensation comparisons with other countries.

Weber, Max. (1947). *The Theory of Social and Economic Organization.* New York: Free Press.

A collection of essays debating the merits and weaknesses of the "underclass debate." The classic study of the nature of stratification, by one of the founders of modern sociology.

Willie, Charles (ed.). (1989). *The Class and Caste Controversy on Race and Poverty: Round Two of the Wilson-Willie Debate.* New York: General-Hall.

A collection of essays debating the merits and weaknesses of the "underclass debate."

Wilson, William Julius. (1987). *The Truly Disadvantaged: The Inner City, the Underclass, and Public Policy.* Chicago: University of Chicago Press.

In this seminal study that launched the "underclass debate," Wilson uses statistical and historical materials to argue that an underclass exists in American society. Contains much useful information on past and proposed public policy as well.

Global Stratification

CHAPTER OUTLINE

THINGS TO LOOK FOR

1. Why are the nations of the world economically stratified? Which nations fall into which strata, and how does this impact the quality of life in each?
2. Why do global starvation and famine persist in a world that has actually shown an increase in per-person food production?
3. What are the different theories that claim to explain global inequality? What are the strengths and weaknesses of each?
4. Why have the newly industrializing countries (NICs) of East Asia been able to rapidly industrialize, moving into the front ranks of world economic power?
5. What is the likely future of global inequality, and how will it impact the United States?

INTRODUCTION: GLOBAL STRATIFICATION—A MULTICLASS SYSTEM?

Two of my brothers died in the plantation. The first, he was the eldest, was called Felipe. . . . They'd sprayed the coffee with pesticide by plane while we were working, as they usually did, and my brother couldn't stand the fumes and died. . . . The second one . . . his name was Nicolas . . . died when I was eight. He was two then. When my little brother started crying, crying, crying, my mother didn't know what to do. . . . He lasted fifteen days.

The little boy died early in the morning. We didn't know what to do. Our two neighbors were anxious to help my mother but they didn't know what to do either—not how to bury him or anything. Then the overseer told my mother she could bury my brother in the plantation but she had to pay a tax to keep him buried there. My mother said, "I have no money at all." He told her, "Yes, and you already owe a lot of money for medicine and other things, so take his body and leave". . . . It was impossible to take his body back to the highlands. . . . So my mother decided that even if she had to work for a month without earning, she would pay the tax to the landowner, or the overseer, to bury my brother in the plantation. . . . One of the men brought a little box, a bit like a suitcase. We put my brother in it to

be buried. . . . That night the overseer told us: "Leave here tomorrow."

This tragic story was recounted in the autobiography of Rigoberta Menchu (1983), an Indian woman from the rural highlands of Guatemala who won the Nobel Peace Prize in 1992 for her efforts to focus the world's attention on the plight of her people. Her story recounts the terrible working conditions on one of Guatemala's rural coffee plantations, where thousands of Indians work in extreme poverty.

Yet when Indians flee political violence and grinding poverty in rural Guatemala, they often find conditions are no better in the cities. Many wind up working in factories, where they labor long hours at low wages, under extremely unhealthy conditions. Some work in apparel factories, making clothing for well-known American manufacturers whose labels are likely to be found on your jeans, jackets, and sportswear. These U.S. manufacturers do not themselves own the factories, however. Rather, the factories are likely to be owned by Guatemalans, or by immigrants to that country, many of whom come from Asia in pursuit of their own economic fortunes. Kurt Peterson (1992, p. 170) describes the experience of one young Guatemalan worker in such a factory:

Only 13 years old, "Maria" works at Sung Sil S.A., a 500-machine shop owned by Samsung, a Korean transnational corporation. Sung Sil is located in a recently constructed factory park ten miles outside Guatemala City. Maria lives with her two brothers, her parents, and her grandmother in a two-room shack on a dirt road near the modern factory. She does not attend school and cannot read. But Maria can sew—for 11 hours a day, 6 days a week she sews. When management requires, she works until 3:00 A.M., and then rises four hours later to begin again.

The compensation and conditions at Maria's factory are not commensurate with the restraints on her freedom. Maria rarely enjoys her paltry earnings, which total slightly more than U.S. $1 a day, because the income is used to pay family debts. "My paychecks are their paychecks," she said, pointing to her family. Finding the pressure to produce demoralizing and physically exhausting, Maria articulated her powerlessness: "The [supervisors] never let up on us, always pushing for more. Sometimes I just can't take it, and break down and cry. I am so young. Will I have to do this the rest of my life? Isn't there something we can do?"

Living on the brink of survival, Maria has few options: If she refuses to work extra hours or demands a raise, management will fire her, and her family will sink deeper into poverty; if she says nothing, she will endure physical and psychological abuse. Like most of her coworkers, Maria has opted for the latter, suffering in silence.

In today's global economy, prominent U.S. manufacturers may design clothing made by Guatemalan women and girls, in a factory run by a Korean immigrant to that country. American consumers benefit from this global economic arrangement, by enjoying well-made, inexpensive, yet fashionable clothing. The value of U.S. clothing imports from Guatemala grew from $6 million in 1983 to $350 million in 1991, a 58-fold increase in just eight years. The reason? Garment workers in the United States, who seldom earn as much as $60 a day, still cannot compete with impoverished Indians in Guatemala who are willing to work for only a dollar (Peterson, 1992).

During the past quarter century, the global stratification system has undergone an unprecedented change. More and more of the things we depend on for everyday life are produced on a "global assembly line" that spans the planet. This has altered working conditions in the United States and around the world. Global trade in clothing, for example, exploded from roughly $2 billion in 1963 to nearly $82 billion only 25 years later. As a result, even though your clothing may be designed by a prominent U.S. manufacturer, more than a quarter of all the clothing bought in the United States no longer bears a "made in USA" label. Half of all women's blouses, and two-thirds of all men's shirts, are made in factories in Mexico and Central America, South America, Asia, Africa, and the Middle East (Dickerson, 1991).

In this chapter we will examine global stratification as we approach the twenty-first century. We will avoid viewing the world as centered on the United States but will attempt instead to adopt a truly global perspective. Whereas in the previous chapter we focused on inequality within the United States, in this chapter we analyze global inequality. Just as sociologists have divided the people within a country into different socioeconomic classes, so too is it possible to divide the nations of the world into unequal economic strata. There are rich nations, poor nations, and nations in the middle. Furthermore, differences in wealth between nations, while substantial and in some cases increasing, are paralleled by growing differences within nations: Even the wealthiest nations today have growing numbers of poor people. As we shall see, both types of stratification—between nations, and within a single nation—reflect the same underlying social process: the rapid emergence of a single, unified global economy. We shall examine the impact of such stratification on people's daily lives.

WEALTH, POVERTY, AND GLOBAL STRATIFICATION

In Chapter 8 we defined **social stratification** in terms of *systematic inequalities in wealth, power, and prestige that result from social rank.* While in that chapter we were concerned with stratification in the United States, the same concept can more or less be applied to the world as a whole. Nations, like people, can be classified in terms of their role in a global stratification system, particularly with regard to differences between nations in wealth and power. What we found to be true for people within nations is true for nations as a whole: wealth and power generally go together. The wealthiest nations in the world are also the most powerful. (The third aspect of stratification, *prestige,* does not really apply at the global level, since there are no common

The "global assembly line" connects low-wage factory workers such as these women in Korea, with clothing designers in Paris, London, or New York. At least a quarter of all clothing purchased in the United States today is made for U.S. manufacturers by workers in other countries. As wages have risen in countries like Korea, their clothing factories have also shut down, reopening in much lower-wage countries such as China, Indonesia, or Guatemala.

global cultural norms or values by which one might judge differences in social status between nations.)

Global stratification has been characterized in various ways by sociologists and other social scientists. Prior to the 1990s, it was common to speak of "three worlds" occupying our planet. The **first world** consisted of *the industrial capitalist nations of the world*—the United States and Canada, the nations of Western Europe, Japan, Australia, and New Zealand. With the obvious exception of Japan, all of these nations were culturally European in origin. All had capitalist economic systems and democratic political systems. All were relatively wealthy. The **second world** consisted of the *socialist or communist nations* of the world—the former Soviet Union, the nations of Eastern Europe, China, Cuba, Vietnam, North Korea, and a handful of African nations such as Zambia and Angola. These nations were characterized by state-managed economies and political systems that were tightly controlled by the Communist Party of each country. While none of these nations was as wealthy as nations in the first world, most of them had achieved an adequate standard of living for a large part of their population, which typically included the provision of mass education, health care, and low-cost housing.

The **third world** included *the remainder of the world—a catch-all category comprised of countries that did not fit neatly into the other "two worlds."* These countries included Mexico, the nations of Central and South America, and non-Communist countries in Africa and Asia. Approximately two-thirds of the world's population fell into the third world. The economies of these countries tended to be preindustrial. Their citizens fed themselves—often barely—primarily by crops and animals tended on family farms, although many of these countries also had large plantations that produced fruit, coffee, sugar, cotton, and other basic products to be sold to the first and second worlds. The political systems of these countries ranged from democracies to military-run states in which human liberties were virtually nonexistent. One thing virtually all third world countries had in common was poverty: With the exception of a handful of wealthy and powerful citizens educated in the other two worlds, the vast majority of people in the third world had little cash income, minimal property, and many lived on the brink of starvation.

Even though the three-world distinction is still often used in sociology textbooks, by the 1990s it had outlived whatever usefulness it might have once had as a way of describing the nations of the world. For one thing, the second world of socialist and communist nations had come to an abrupt end with the dissolution of the Soviet Union and its Eastern Europen allies. While it remains too early to anticipate exactly what economic and political form these formerly second-world countries will eventually have, at the moment they are adopting capitalist economies and somewhat more open and democratic political systems. Even China, which officially remains a socialist society, is rapidly moving down what its leaders once derisively referred to as the "capitalist road."

Also, the catch-all category of third world masked many differences among these nations, some of which—particularly those in East Asia—appear to be "catching up" with the first world. Finally, the ranking of first, second, and third worlds obviously reflected a value judgment, in which "first" meant "best" and "third" meant "worst." Sociologists and other theorists from the third world have adamantly rejected this term, offering others they regard as more accurately describing the circumstances in their countries. We will examine some of their theories later in this chapter. Even though it will complicate our discussion somewhat, we shall avoid using distinctions that overly simplify the world economic system. The world is rapidly changing today; it is not surprising that the concepts we use to describe it are changing as well.

Rich and Poor Nations

One simple way to stratify countries along the dimension of class is in terms of the wealth of their average citizens (see Map 9.1). This measure is usually calculated by dividing the total wealth of the country by its total population, yielding the **per-person gross national product (GNP)**, or *the country's yearly output of wealth per person.* The World Bank (1990, 1991), an international lending organization that provides loans for development projects in poorer nations, classifies countries into high-income (an annual per-person GNP of $6,000 or more, in 1988 dollars), upper-middle-income ($2,200–$6,000), lower-middle-income ($545–$2,200), and lower-income (under $545). It is important to understand that comparing countries on the basis on GNP alone can be extremely misleading, since measures of GNP tend to emphasize goods and services that are produced for sale. As we mentioned earlier, many people in low-income countries are farmers or herders who produce for their own families; the value of their crops and animals is not included in the statistics.

As Map 9.1 shows, with the exception of oil-rich countries like Saudia Arabia and European-settled countries like Australia and New Zealand, the high-income nations of the world are located in the northern regions, while the middle- and lower-income nations are located to the south. In general, the low-income countries include China, India, and most of the countries of Africa and Asia. The middle-income countries include Latin America, South Africa, the oil-rich countries of north Africa, and the newly industrializing countries of East Asia. Finally, the high-income countries include

Map 9.1	Low, Middle, and High Income Countries

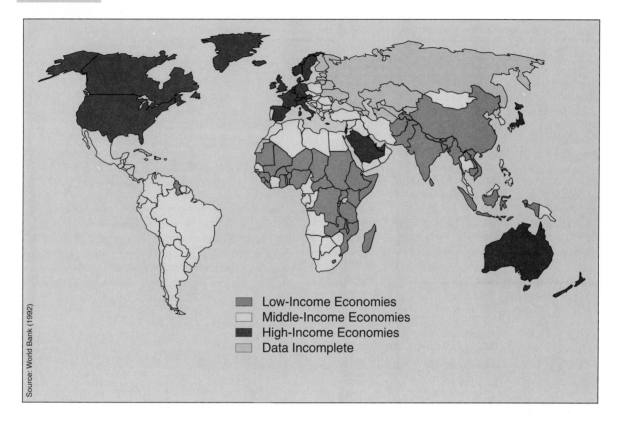

Source: World Bank (1992)

Low-Income Economies
Middle-Income Economies
High-Income Economies
Data Incomplete

Similar to members of individual countries, the countries of the world as a whole can be seen as stratified according to economic wealth. In general, those northern hemispheric countries that experienced industrialization the earliest are the wealthiest; some scholars have argued that this was partly achieved at the expense of poorer, weaker nations. Global stratification is changing today, with once poor countries of Asia becoming economic powerhouses.

Europe, the United States and Canada, Japan, Australia, and New Zealand. Figures 9.1 and 9.2 compare population and average incomes in high-, middle-, and low-income nations. They dramatically show that many people live in poor countries with extremely low average incomes, while very few people live in rich countries with substantially higher average incomes.

Table 9.1 compares these three groups of countries on a number of measures, including population, wealth and poverty, health, education and literacy, and energy consumption.

Population The low-income countries include 62 percent of the approximately five billion people reported in Table 9.1, while the high-income countries account for only 16 percent. Although death rates are similar between the three strata of nations, their birth rates are not: Low- and middle-income nations have more than twice the birth rate of high-income nations. As a result, the low-income nations are growing nearly three times faster than are high-income nations, so that by the year 2025 they are projected to have 65 percent

of the projected population of nearly 8 billion people. In that year, high-income countries will account for only 12 percent of the total. For every person in a high-income country today, there are approximately 3.7 people in low-income countries; by 2025, there will be 5.6.

Wealth and Poverty The gap between rich and poor nations is enormous. The average person in a typical high-income nation has 56 times the income of his or her counterpart in the typical low-income nation, where per-person annual income averages only $350. Furthermore, the gap between rich and poor countries appears to be growing, as Figure 9.3 indicates. Dividing the countries of the world into four income classes, we see that the richest nations have tripled their per-person income in the past 40 years; the middle income nations have doubled theirs; the poor nations have experienced a slight increase; but the poorest nations have been stagnant (Durning, 1989; for a sense of what poverty actually means, behind all the statistics, see Box 9.1.)

The average per-person income of the low-income nations lies at about the global per-person poverty line,

Figure 9.1   Population in Low-, Middle-, and High-Income Countries

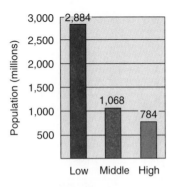

Like most countries, the world as a whole is highly strati-fied. More than three out of five people in the world live in low-income nations, while only one in six lives in high-income nations. The remainder—only about one in four people—lives in middle-income countries. (These data exclude the former Soviet Union and a small number of other countries.)
Source: World Bank (1992).

estimated by the World Bank at falling somewhere between $275–$370. By this meager standard, an estimated 1.2 billion people in the world live in poverty today, or nearly one out of every four, an increase over the past decade (World bank, 1990).

It is important to bear in mind that "poverty" in this context means conditions far worse than those experienced by most impoverished persons in the United States: It refers to an inability to meet the most basic biological needs for food, clothing, and shelter. Of those persons living in poverty, some 325 million live in sub-Saharan Africa (Africa south of the Saharan desert), where they number three out of every five persons; 675 million live in Asia, 150 million in Latin America, and 75 million in North Africa and the Middle East (Durning, 1989, p. 20). About one-third of the world's poor are undernourished. Most are rural, and almost all are illiterate. Many come from tribes or racial and ethnic groups that differ from those of the dominant members of their nations, and their poverty is at least in part the result of discrimination. Two-thirds of the world's poor are under the age of 15 (Durning, 1989), a fact that places enormous strains on education and training.

Women suffer particularly in terms of global poverty. Women experience lower education and literacy, work longer hours, and are paid lower wages than men. The poorest households tend to be female-headed throughout the world, in rich and poor countries alike (World Bank, 1990; Durning, 1989). The feminization of labor during the past quarter century throughout low-income countries has resulted in economic growth in

Figure 9.2   Average Income in Low-, Middle-, and High-Income Countries

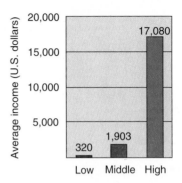

Income disparities between rich and poor nations are substantial. The average income of the people who live in high-income nations is 56 times that of those who live in low-income nations. Thus, although rich nations account for only a fraction of the world's population, their combined income vastly exceeds that of the world's majority. (These data exclude the former Soviet Union and a small number of other countries.)
Source: World Bank (1992).

some places, but it has also meant that growing numbers of women labor in the sorts of factories described earlier in this chapter (see Chapter 11 for further discussion of the impact of the global economy on women).

Health The average life expectancy at birth of people in high-income nations is 22 years longer than that in low-income nations. One major cause of this difference is infant mortality; the infant death rate is eight times higher in low-income than high-income countries. Food intake, as measured by total calories, is only 71 percent as high—one indication of the degree of malnourishment. Low-income countries generally have inadequate health facilities that seldom serve their poorest people, lack proper sanitation, suffer from pollution of drinking water, and in general suffer from a greater risk of communicable diseases.

Education and Literacy Not surprisingly, education and literacy are considerably higher in high-income than low-income countries, with middle-income countries occupying an intermediate position. While virtually everyone attends high school in high-income countries, only 38 percent do in low-income countries; the rate for women is even lower, at 31 percent. Nearly two out of five people are unable to read and write in low-income countries, an illiteracy rate that rises to about half for women.

Table 9.1   Global Stratification: Selected Indicators

	Income Level		
	Low	**Middle**	**High**
Number of Countries	43	58	24
Population			
Population (millions)	3,058	1,088	816
Deaths per 1,000 people	10	8	9
Infant deaths per 1,000 births	69	48	8
Births per 1,000 people	30	29	13
Yearly population growth, 1980–1990	2.0%	2.0%	0.6%
Population projected to 2025	5,154	1,878	915
Wealth and Poverty			
Per-person wealth	$350	$2,220	$19,590
Health			
Daily kilocalories per person (1989)	2,406	2,860	3,409
Life expectancy at birth (excluding China and India)	55	66	77
Education and Literacy			
Percentage of high school age group in school (1989)	38	55	95
Percentage of females in high school (1989)	31	57	96
Percentage of total adult illiteracy	40	22	4
Percentage of female adult illiteracy	52	27	5
Energy Consumption (pounds of oil equivalent)			
1965 per-person energy consumption	273	1,570	7,862
1990 per-person energy consumption	747	2,992	11,371

Source: World Bank (1992, Tables 1 and 5, pp. 26–29).

Notes: All figures are for 1990, unless otherwise indicated. Nonreporting countries include the former Soviet Union, the former German Democratic Republic (East Germany), Romania, Poland, Czechoslovakia, Bulgaria, North Korea, Namibia, Cuba, and the former Spanish Sahara. Countries with populations of less than a million are excluded from the table.

Most of the world's 5.4 billion people live in densely populated low-income countries. Crowds such as the one shown here on a street in India are commonplace throughout the less developed world, as people flock to cities in hope of finding greater economic opportunities. Overcrowded slum housing, abject poverty, and severe health problems are often the result.

Figure 9.3   Adjusted Income per Person for Four Economic Classes of Nations, 1950–1988

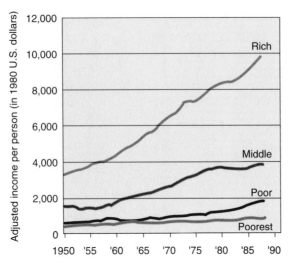

The income gap between rich and poor countries is large and growing. Per-person income in the world's poorest nations has remained stagnant during the past 40 years, while income in the richest nations has tripled. Nations in between have shown more moderate increases.
Source: Adapted from Durning (1988, p. 11).

Energy Consumption Finally, compared with people in low-income countries, people in high-income countries are energy hogs. In 1990 the per-person consumption of petroleum, natural gas, and other forms of energy was 15 times higher in high-income nations. If China and India are excluded (these two industrially developed low-income countries consume signifi-

cantly more energy than the others), the disparity is far greater, reaching 74 to one! These differences between low- and high-income countries have declined somewhat during the past quarter century, not because wealthier nations are conserving energy and consuming less, but because the poorest nations have nearly tripled their per-person energy consumption as they adopt modern transportation and industrial technologies. If the low-income nations of the world are successful in industrializing over the next quarter century, their consumption of energy may begin to approach that of the high-income nations today. The understandable desire of the low-income nations to "catch up" with the wealthy nations will add substantially to the already severe strain on the planet's fragile environment (see Chapter 20).

Global Starvation and Famine

Famines, one of the many so-called "natural disasters" that plague the world today, are nothing new (see Box 9.2). What seems to be new today is the *pervasiveness* of famine and starvation—the fact that so many people in the world today appear to be on the brink of starvation (World Commission on Environment and Development, 1987). According to estimates by the World Bank and the United Nations Children's Fund, more than 100 million Africans are believed to lack minimally adequate nourishment, while as many as a half million children died worldwide in 1988 as a direct result of their poverty (Durning, 1989). Famine is particularly widespread in Africa, where climate changes have resulted in lowered rainfalls and the rapid spread of deserts into once-fertile areas. While famine-

Low levels of economic development, combined with vulnerability to a harsh environment, makes famine a reality for people throughout the African continent. During the 1990s, a deadly combination of famine and warfare in Somalia took the lives of hundreds of thousands of people, despite a worldwide effort to provide food and medicine as well as peace-keeping military forces. This is a photograph of a French "feeding center" in Somalia.

Box 9.1

Globalization

Poor Families in Ghana and Bangladesh

A Poor Subsistence Household in Ghana

In Ghana's savannah [prairie] region a typical family of seven lives in three one-room huts made from mud bricks, with earthen floors. They have little furniture and no toilet, electricity, or running water. Water is obtained from a stream a 15 minute walk away. The family has few possessions, apart from three acres of unirrigated land and one cow, and virtually no savings.

The family raises sorghum, vegetables, and groundnuts on its land. The work is seasonal and physically demanding. At peak periods of tilling, sowing, and havesting, all family members are involved, including the husband's parents, who are 60 and 70 years old. The soil is very low in quality, but the family lacks access to fertilizer and other modern inputs. Moreover, the region is suscepti-

ble to drought; the rains fail two years out of every five. In addition to her farm work, the wife has to fetch water, collect firewood, and feed the family. The market town where the husband sells their meager cash crops and buys essentials is five miles away and is reached by dirt tracks and an unsealed road that is washed away every time the rains come.

None of the older family members has ever attended school, but the eight-year-old son is now in the first grade. The family hopes that he will be able to stay in school, although there is some pressure to keep him at home to help with the farm in the busy periods. He and his two younger sisters have never had any vaccinations and have never seen a doctor.

Map 9.2   Ghana

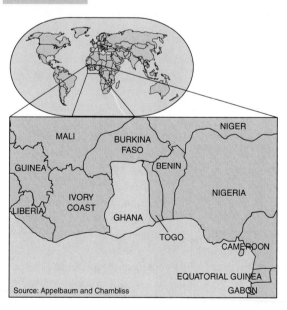

Source: Appelbaum and Chambliss

A Poor Landless Laborer's Household in Bangladesh

In a rural community in a drought-prone region of Bangladesh a landless laborer and his family attempt to get through another lean season.

Their house consists of a packed mud floor and a straw roof held up by bamboo poles from which dry palm leaves are tied to serve as walls. Inside there is straw to sleep on and burlap bags for warmth. The laborer and his wife, three children and niece do not own the land on which the shack is built. They are lucky, however, to have a kindly neighbor who has indefinately lent them the plot and a little extra on which they are able to grow tumeric and ginger and have planted a jackfruit tree.

The father is an agricultural day laborer and tends to be unemployed most of the year. During slow agricultural periods in the past he could sometimes find nonagricultural wage labor—for example, in construction in a nearby town—but he lost the strength to do much strenuous work after a bout of paratyphoid. He therefore engages in petty services around the village for very low pay.

The wife typically spends her day cooking, caring for the children, husking rice, and fetching water from the well. She is helped in these tasks by her 13-year-old niece, whose parents died in a cholera epidemic some years ago. The woman and her niece are always on the lookout for ways to earn a little extra. Such work as husking rice, weeding fields, and chopping wood is sometimes available from better-off neighbors. The nine-year-old son attends school a few mornings a week in a town an hour's walk away. The rest of the day he and his seven-year-old sister gather fuel and edible roots and weeds. The sister also looks after the baby when her mother or cousin cannot. . . . The household spends about 85 percent of its meager income on food—predominantly rice. Family members are used to having only two meals a day.

Source: World Bank (1990 pp. 24-25).

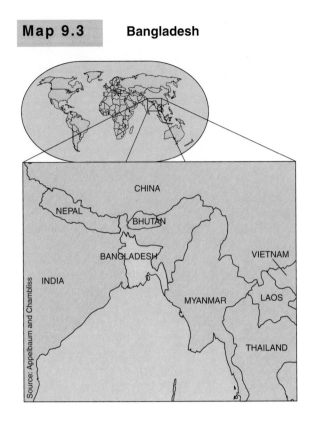

Map 9.3   **Bangladesh**

Source: Appelbaum and Chambliss

stricken Somalia is well-known to American television viewers, numerous other countries suffer the same tragic problem. It is estimated that as many as 1.2 billion people will be threatened by encroaching deserts in the year 2000 (World Commission on Environment and Development, 1987).

It is not known whether these changes are the result of short-term cycles in annual rainfall, or long-term trends resulting from population growth, over-farming and over-grazing of once-fertile lands, and the growth of cities (Dotto, 1988; World Commission on Environment and Development, 1987; Brown and Jacobson, 1987). But in general, we can say that most famine and starvation in the world today is the consequence of a combination of natural and social forces. The social causes of famine and starvation include:

- War, as in Yugoslavia and Somalia in 1992 and 1993.
- Explosive population growth, resulting in overgrazing and overfarming of land, which contributes to the spread of deserts.
- The conversion of family "subsistence" farms into large corporate-owned plantations where crops are produced for sale to other countries, which reduces the amount of land available for family farms.
- Long- and short-term changes in weather resulting from the growth of cities, atmospheric pollution, and other human activities.

- The development of hybrid strains of plants that reduce their hardiness and variety, making them more susceptible to crop disease and failure.

We will consider many of these problems in greater detail in Chapter 20. What is certain is that the countries affected by famine and starvation are for the most part too poor to pay for new technologies that would increase their food production, or to purchase sufficient food imports from elsewhere in the world.

Paradoxically, at the same time as world hunger grows, food production in the world as a whole continues to increase. Between 1953 and 1987, for example, world agricultural production grew from approximately 546 to 682 pounds per person (World Commission on Environment and Development, 1987). But this growth is not evenly distributed around the world. In much of Africa, for example, per-person food production has actually been declining in recent years. Surplus food produced in high-income nations such as the United States is seldom affordable to the countries that need it most. In fact, some experts (Lappe and Collins, 1979) have shown that even impoverished countries like Bangladesh produce more food than they consume, but much of it is produced on large farms for sale to the world market, reducing the amount of food available for local consumption (see Box 9.3).

Box 9.2

Critical Thinking

Are "Natural" Disasters Really Natural?

In recent years a number of "natural disasters" have been widely covered on American television. The juxtaposition of two of these tells a great deal about the role that global inequality plays in determining the impact of such disasters on human life. In the spring of 1991 a deadly typhoon struck the country of Bangladesh. A half year later Hurricane Andrew, the most destructive storm in Florida's history, devastated the southern part of the state.

In Bangladesh, the storm and subsequent flooding claimed an estimated 125,000 lives. In Florida, despite the enormity of the hurricane's devastation, only 55 people died, even though it caused an estimated $30 billion dollars in property damage, flattened entire communities, and left tens of thousands of people temporarily homeless. Why were two seemingly similar "natural" disasters so different in their impacts? To answer this question, sociologists look beyond the "natural" force of the two storms to analyze the underlying social conditions that help to shape their impact in the two countries.

Because Florida is part of a high-income industrial society, numerous existing institutions were able avert the brunt of "natural" disasters. Early warning systems alerted the population to the impending disaster, while civil defense organizations arranged an orderly evacuation before the fury of the storm reached low-lying communities. Since most people were able to afford housing built ac-

cording to structural and safety codes, much of the housing was spared by the storm. In fact, the housing that suffered the greatest damage tended to be occupied by the poorest people, who often lived in trailers or inadequately-built structures. After the storm hit, numerous institutions—from the American Red Cross to the armed forces—were ready to move in with disaster relief. An entire nation watched in judgment on television, a partial guarantee that politicians during an election season would act quickly and decisively to alleviate the suffering.

In Bangladesh, which is an impoverished and densely populated nation in which millions of people live and farm on the mud flats at the mouth of the Ganges River, few if any of these institutions are in place. People are too poor to afford well-constructed houses, and too dependent on wet-rice farming to live in upland areas away from the flood plains where the rice must be grown. Governmental institutions have few of the resources necessary to evacuate and feed the numerous people who lie in the path of a storm. After a devastating typhoon passes, the government is almost entirely dependent on foreign charity to feed and shelter the hundreds of thousands of survivors who are left stranded.

While a typhoon, hurricane, earthquake, fire, or other "natural" disaster can strike anywhere, the effect will have a lot to do with the social conditions that characterize the potential victims.

Hurricane Andrew, the most destructive storm in Florida's history, claimed 55 lives and $30 billion in property damage in the fall of 1991. A comparable storm in Bangledesh earlier that year killed 125,000 people. High-income industrial societies such as the United States are far better prepared for "natural" disasters than poor countries, since they can afford such things as early-warning systems, mass evacuations, and costly building codes.

To better understand the social forces responsible for famine and starvation, we must turn to the theories that sociologists and other social scientists have developed to explain the existence of global inequality.

THEORIES OF GLOBAL INEQUALITY

In this section we will examine three different kinds of theories attempting to account for global inequality. Each is based on a different set of assumptions concerning the nature of the global economy, and each as a result offers widely differing explanations of the sources of global inequality.

"Market-Oriented" Theories

One highly influential group of theories argues that unrestricted capitalism, if allowed to fully develop, is the best possible avenue to economic growth. These are sometimes termed **market-oriented theories,** because they assume that *the best possible economic consequences will result if individuals are free to make their own economic decisions, uninihibited by any form of governmental constraint.* No government bureaucracy should dictate which goods to produce, what prices to charge, or how much workers should be paid. Followers of market-oriented theories are convinced that the blockages to economic development that exist in the world's low-income countries are largely self-imposed, because in a variety of ways the hand of government has attempted to set prices or wages, or otherwise attempted to direct the economy (Viner, 1953; Rostow, 1961; Berger, 1986).

One of the most influential early theoretical proponents of such theories was W. W. Rostow, an economic advisor to former president John F. Kennedy whose ideas helped shape U.S. foreign policy toward Latin America during the 1960s. Rostow's theory is a type of market-oriented theory termed **modernization theory,** because it *lays out the conditions under which traditional societies can become fully modern.* According to Rostow (1961), the barriers to development in low-income countries result primarily from cultural values and social institutions that prevent their economies from operating effectively. For example, many people in low-income nations, in Rostow's view, lack a strong work ethic; they would sooner consume today than invest for the future. Large families are partly responsible, since a breadwinner with many mouths to feed can hardly be expected to save money for investment purposes. But the problems are even deeper, since the cultures of such countries according to modernization theory tend to support fatalism—a value-system that views hardship and suffering as unavoidable features of daily life, and thereby discourages people from working hard to overcome their fate. National poverty, in this view, is largely due to the cultural failings of the people themselves. Such failings are reinforced by government policies that set wages and control prices, and they are seen as generally interfering in the efficient operation of the economy.

According to this theory, how can low-income countries hope to break out of their poverty? Rostow viewed economic growth as going through several stages, which he likened to the journey of an airplane. The first stage, or traditional stage, is the one described above; it is characterized by low rates of savings, the lack of a work ethic, and a fatalistic value system. This

One survival strategy of people in less developed countries is the creation of food cooperatives. These women in Mali partly control their own food supply by working collectively. More often, however, farming is controlled by large landowners, with little benefit to rural people.

Box 9.3

Silenced Voices

Herbert José de Souza Fights Against Hunger and Inequality in Brazil

Brazil, a country of 161 million people, has become the world's third largest producer of food for sale to other countries, and the world's second largest market for executive jets. Yet as many as a third of Brazil's population survives on less than two dollars a day, and a quarter go to bed hungry every night. Widespread poverty has resulted in hunger and malnutrition, forcing many people into virtual slavery in sugar cane plantations, gold mines, ranches, and charcoal factories (Brooke, 1993).

Herbert José de Souza is a sociologist who heads the Brazilian Institute of Economic and Social Analysis. As the founder of the Citizenship Committee Against Misery and for Life, he has campaigned for greater economic equality, denouncing what he terms the country's "savage capitalism." De Souza recently launched an antihunger campaign entitled "a new millennium without misery," which has received the strong support of Brazil's president. Although many Brazilians have expressed doubt that such a goal can be achieved, de Souza remains optimistic, contending that "despair is the disease of the elites."

De Souza knows personally what it means to overcome despair, since he is dying of AIDS, contracted during a blood transfusion for hemophilia. He brother has already died of the disease. He minces no words in attributing the dire poverty that exists in his country to the greed and indifference of Brazil's elites, rather than to food shortages or technological backwardness (Brooke, 1993):

> Looking at the human and natural resources of Brazil, I have never found any scientific reason why we cannot feed our [people].. . . The problem is that the Brazilian elites don't see the poor. . . .
>
> What has happened that is concrete in the struggle against hunger? The concrete is this: a beginning of a change in consciences. Brazilian society is beginning to realize that misery is not acceptable.
>
> We either have to definitively accept that poverty and misery are part of our culture, and therefore consolidate our social apartheid . . .

or we have to review our history, our vision of the world. There is no reason, no argument, no theory that justifies the existence of this misery.

> This is cultural—there is still the plantation house and the slave house mentality. . . . The Brazilian elite is highly inhuman, highly insensitive. The elite is not able to elaborate a concept of humanity that includes the poor.

Assuming that de Souza's analysis is correct, how might Brazil's elites be brought to show more compassion for the poor? Do you agree that the problem is cultural, as de Souza suggests—or do you think that world economic conditions somehow also explain the enormous disparities between rich and poor in that country?

Map 9.4   **Brazil**

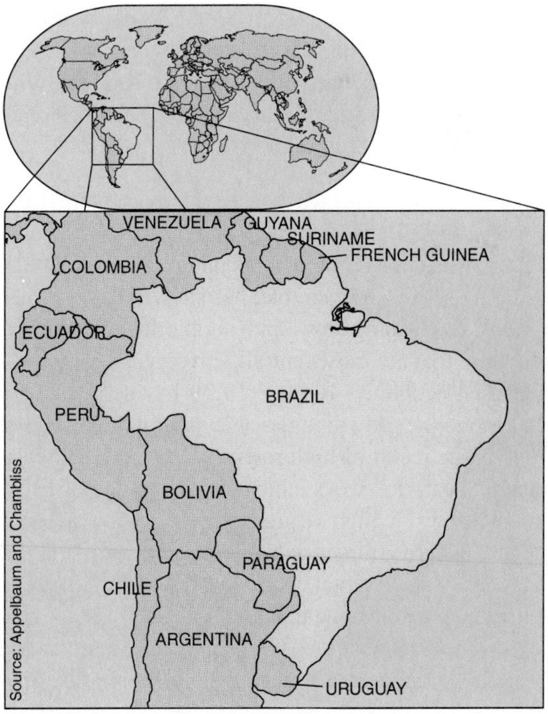

Source: Appelbaum and Chambliss

stage can give way to a second one, Rostow argued—the take-off to economic growth. This occurs when poor countries begin to shed their traditional values and institutions, and start to save and invest money for the future. Capitalist institutions are the key to this transformation—for example, the growth of privately owned businesses that are free from governmental interference. Modernization theorists estimated that if approximately 10 percent of national wealth were saved to be invested by businessmen in new technologies and industries, low-income countries would break out of their vicious cycle of poverty. The role of wealthy countries, like the United States, was to help this happen. For instance, American advisors would help low-income countries set up birth control programs in order to relieve the costly burden of large families. The U.S. government would provide low-cost loans and other forms of financial assistance, to help poor countries develop electrical power, build roads and airports, increase their agricultural production, acquire new technologies, and establish new industries.

Eventually, with the help of money and advice from high-income nations, the airplane of economic growth would taxi down the runway, pick up speed, and become airborne. The country would then enter the third phase—the drive to technological maturity. Extending the aeronautical metaphor, it would slowly climb to cruising altitude, improving its technology, reinvesting its recently-acquired wealth in new industries, and adopting the institutions and values of the high-income nations. Finally, the country would reach the phase of high mass consumption when people would be able to enjoy the fruits of their efforts by achieving a high standard of living. The airplane would cruise along relatively effortlessly, mainly on automatic pilot, having entered the ranks of high-income nations.

Critical Assessment There is some evidence to support Rostow's claim that the adoption of modern, capitalist institutions leads to economic development. Warren (1980), for example, has shown that the most rapidly developing low- and middle-income nations are those that are most centrally involved in the global capitalist economy. Berger (1986) has demonstrated that economic growth in the once-poor nations of East Asia is the result of high rates of savings and investment, a "can-do" work ethic, and—most importantly, in his view—a high degree of reliance on markets rather than government to cause economic growth. But there are fundamental weaknesses with market-oriented theories. For one thing, they tend to assume that low-income countries exist in isolation from the world economy, condemned to be economic backwaters be-

cause of their own failure to establish appropriately "modern" values and institutions. Yet this is hardly the case. Virtually all countries in the world today are part of a global economic system, and prosperity in one country is often bought at the cost of the exploitation of the natural resources or workforce of another country. Equally questionable is the notion that the most successful economies in the world are those in which the government plays absolutely no role. In fact, as the example of East Asia demonstrates, government often plays a key role in supporting, regulating, and directing economic growth (see below, "Sociological Lessons from the NICS").

Marxist Theories

While Marx focused on inequality *within* capitalist countries, he also argued that capitalism would eventually result in inequality *between* countries as well. In Marx's view, this is because businesses in industrial capitalist nations would eventually look outside their borders for new sources of profit. Three such strategies can serve as examples.

First, in order to profit from sales of coffee, cotton, sugar, or other agricultural products, a European or U.S. company might acquire land in a semitropical country such as Guatemala or El Salvador where these crops can be grown in abundance.

Second, petroleum, copper, iron, and other natural resources required for industrial economies are found throughout the world, and so it is to be expected that businesses in powerful high-income countries will set up oil wells, mines, and refineries wherever such valuable goods can be found. Sometimes these two economic strategies resulted in **colonialism,** a *political-economic system under which powerful nations establish rule over weaker peoples or nations for their own profit.* Although colonialism typically involved European nations administering territories in North and South America, Africa, and Asia, some Asian countries (such as Japan) have had colonies as well. Colonialism came to an end throughout most of the world shortly after the end of World War II.

A third economic strategy, one that is increasingly followed today, involves the relocation of factories from high-wage to low-wage countries. This economic strategy is pursued when the wages in advanced capitalist countries grow to the point where they seriously threaten profits.

During the 1960s, a number of theorists began to address these issues. They especially questioned such market-oriented explanations of global stratification as Rostow's modernization theory. Many of these critics were sociologists and economists from the low-income countries of Latin America and Africa. These theorists rejected the idea that their countries' economic backwardness was somehow due to cultural or institutional failings. Discouraged by the failure of their countries to "take off" into economic growth, they turned to Marx's ideas to explain their countries' poverty as resulting from the role they played in sustaining economic development in the high-income industrial nations of the world. They argued specifically that low-income nations are not *under*developed as much as they are *mis*developed, as a result of exploitation by the wealthier nations of the world (Prebisch, 1967, 1971; Frank, 1966, 1969a, 1969b, 1979; Amin, 1974; and Emmanuel, 1972).

These sociologists and economists were termed **dependency theorists** because they believed that *the poverty of low-income nations was the immediate consequence of their exploitation by wealthy ones.* Ac-

Dependency theorists *argue that low-income nations are "misdeveloped" as a result of the policies and interests of the developed nations. How might a dependency theorist interpret this picture of an elderly woman begging in front of an expensive store in Mexico city?*

cording to this theory, global capitalism had locked the poor countries of the world into an unyielding downward spiral of exploitation and poverty. Andre Gundar Frank (1966, 1969a, 1969b), the leading dependency theorist, referred to this as the "development of underdevelopment," which he argued forced a clear choice on the peoples of impoverished nations: either "underdevelopment or revolution." According to this theory, dependency results from the fact that important economic and political decisions are made by foreign businesses for their own advantage, without regard to what is in the best interests of the local people. Local businesses that might compete with foreign corporations are prevented from developing. With the exception of a handful of local politicians and businessmen who serve the interests of the foreign corporations, the population becomes impoverished. Peasants are forced to choose between starvation, and working at near-starvation wages in foreign-controlled plantations, mines, and factories. The national economy becomes increasingly misdeveloped, with a wealthy sector profiting from producing goods that are sold to other countries, while the remainder of the population sinks deeper into poverty.

Dependency theorists further argue that whenever local leaders emerge to question these arrangements, they are quickly suppressed. Unionization is usually outlawed and labor organizers are jailed and sometimes killed. Occasionally, when the people elect a government opposing these policies, that government is likely to be overthrown by the country's military, often backed by the armed forces of the industrial nations themselves.

Critical Assessment Although dependency theory seemed to account for the experiences of most low-income countries during the 1950s and the 1960s, it could not explain the differences in development that were occurring throughout the world (Berger, 1986). In Africa, for example, some impoverished nations (for example, Ethiopia) had never been European colonies, while more prosperous nations (for example, Kenya) had been colonies (in this case, of Britain). In Asia, Hong Kong and Singapore, two city-states rapidly "taking off" into economic development, had once been colonies; Hong Kong, in fact, will remain a British colony until it becomes a part of China in 1997. Dependency theory, by ruling out the possibility that poor countries might ever develop within the world capitalist system, could not explain the dramatic economic growth that began in East Asia in the 1950s. In fact, some critics of dependency theory have argued that closer ties with global capitalism are the key to successful development, rather than the principal barrier (Berger, 1986).

In response to these concerns, Fernando Cardoso, a Brazilian sociologist and currently that country's president, argued that **dependent development** was indeed possible (Cardoso and Faletto, 1979). That is, *under certain circumstances, poor nations could still hope to develop economically, albeit in ways shaped by their dependence on wealthier nations.* In particular, the governments of these countries could play a key role in steering a course between dependency and development (Evans, 1979).

World Systems Theories

Marxist theories tend to view global inequality as the result of high-income nations exploiting low-income ones. But as the global economy emerged with force in the 1970s, it became apparent that nations themselves might not be the appropriate unit of analysis for understanding global inequality. **World systems theory** argues that *the world capitalist economic system must be understood as a single unit, not in terms of individual countries.*

Immanual Wallerstein's (1974, 1979, 1990) version of world systems theory argues that capitalism has long existed as a global economic system, beginning with the extension of markets and trade in Europe in the sixteenth century. In Wallerstein's view, the world economic system can be divided into three levels: the core, the periphery, and the semiperiphery. The **core countries** consist of *the most advanced industrial nations, who realize the lion's share of profits in the world economic system.* The **peripheral countries** consist of *low-income, largely agricultural nations that are often manipulated by core countries for the economic advantage of the latter.* Natural resources, such as agricultural products, minerals, and other raw materials flow from periphery to core—as do the profits. Finally, the **semiperipheral countries** occupy an *intermediate position: these are semiindustrialized, middle-income countries that extract profits from more peripheral countries, while in turn yielding profits to core countries.* Relations between core, peripheral, and semiperipheral countries are not purely economic: They are political as well. Core countries essentially call the shots in the world economic system, exploiting the countries in the semiperiphery and periphery. When their economic power is challenged, they can always fall back on their superior political and military might. The semiperiphery, while to some degree controlled by the core, is also able to exploit the periphery. Moreover, the greater economic success of the semiperiphery holds the promise of similar development to the periphery.

Although Wallerstein's original theory focused on the early development of capitalism in Europe, a related theory examines the division of labor in the global economy today. This theory, termed the **New International Division of Labor (NIDL),** argues that *the division of labor characterizing industrial societies has now been extended to cover the entire planet, relegating low-income nations to the role of providing cheap labor for firms based in high-income countries* (Frobel, Heinrichs, and Kreye, 1980, 1982; Ernst, 1980, 1987; Lipietz, 1986). For example, most of the tasks involved in making an "American" automobile were at one time broken down into specific activities located within a few factories, almost all owned by a single company such as Ford or General Motors, all located within a single country, and most located geographically close to one another. Today, according to NIDL theory, a division of labor still exists—except that the different factories are now located all over the world. Computerized technology, which makes it possible to tightly coordinate industrial activities no matter where they are located on the planet's surface, has made this possible.

According to NIDL theorists, the drive to find ever-cheaper labor has led transnational corporations (see Chapter 15) to locate their factories wherever the cheapest labor can be found. Within this global division of labor, high-income industrial nations retain such profitable high-skill activities as design, engineering, and marketing, while less profitable activities requiring unskilled or semiskilled labor are farmed out to factories in low-income nations. This process thus tends to reinforce inequality between nations.

Most recently, a number of theorists—including one of the authors of this book—have attempted to rethink world systems theory from the standpoint of global economic activities, rather than from that of individual nations (Gereffi, 1992; Appelbaum and Gereffi, 1994; Appelbaum, Smith, and Christerson, 1993; Gereffi and Korzeniewicz, 1994; Porter, 1990a, 1990b). The global nature of economic activities is captured in the notion of the **commodity chain,** *a network of labor and production processes whose end result is a finished commodity* (Hopkins and Wallerstein, 1986; Gereffi, 1992; Gereffi and Korzeniewicz, 1993). This network consists of all the activities that are pivotal in the production process—the extraction of raw materials, the design or engineering of the commodity, its actual manufacturing, marketing and sales, and so forth. These activities can be seen as links in a tightly interlocked "chain" that extends from the raw materials to the final consumer.

Think about a typical sport shirt, for example. The key activities in its commodity chain might include oil drilling and refining in Saudi Arabia (since petroleum is the source of polyesters such as nylon, rayon, or spandex), cotton farming and processing in Guatemala, the spinning and dying of polyster filaments and cotton threads in a Caribbean factory, the weaving of these filaments and threads into fabric in American textile mills, designing the shirt in a Los Angeles designer's studio, cutting the fabric into suitable patterns and sewing them into a shirt in a Hong Kong garment factory, transporting them in Korean container ships to Los Angeles, creating an advertising campaign in New York City, and finally distributing the finished shirts through a network of retail outlets owned by a major American department store.

As you can see, this process is complex and geographically dispersed around the world. The commodity chain approach avoids viewing profits as simply being made in "core" countries. Rather, it examines the commodity chain itself to find out the different activities by which profits are made. Sometimes these activities are found in core nations; sometimes they are not. Thus, instead of regarding countries as falling into the core or periphery, the commodity chain approach suggests that different activities on the chain itself are core or peripheral. **Core activities** *are those where the profits are made,* while **peripheral activities** *are those from which profits are taken.*

The important question, then, is not "which countries are core or periphery," but "where does the commodity chain 'touch down' geographically, why, and with what consequences for the well-being of the people of that country?" In low-cost production (as in the garment industry), the principal profits are not realized in sewing or other aspects of factory production, but rather in marketing, retailing, and design. While such activities are typically found in the "core" countries, often lower-income countries that begin with low-profit manufacturing may themselves "move up" into more profitable parts of the commodity chain. Today, many countries in Asia are increasingly prospering by developing their own profitable "core" activities on the commodity chain, while thousands of "peripheral" sweatshops are found in U.S. cities like Los Angeles and New York.

Critical Assessment The various forms of world systems theory have made important contributions to our understanding of the origins and development of the global economy. In its original formulations, the theory often remained bound to the notion that the key actors in the world economic system were nations, rather than transnational corporations. The three-part division of nations into core, semiperiphery, and periphery reflected this assumption.

The NIDL theory, while taking a more global (and therefore less nation-based) standpoint, still erred by emphasizing the importance of cheap labor as the main determinant of factory location. Its critics have pointed out that many of the activities that have "gone global" have opened their factories in such high-income nations as Japan, Germany, and England, rather than in low-income ones. For example, South Korea's three largest manufacturers of consumer electronics—Daewoo, Samsung, and Goldstar—have opened television and VCR factories in France, Italy, Great Britain, and Germany. When low-income nations do become the sites of factories from high-income ones, it does not always follow that they are mercilessly exploited to benefit the latter: Workers in the high-income countries may themselves lose jobs and suffer falling wages, while the low-income countries may build new industries that eventually lead to rising wages for their workforce (Gereffi, 1989, 1992; Appelbaum and Gereffi, 1994; Schoenberger, 1988; Scott, 1988; Storper and Christopherson, 1987; Porter, 1990a, 1990b; Nakarmi and Reichlin, 1992).

The commodity chain approach also has a number of weaknesses. First, it tends to look at global manufacturing only from the standpoint of business, as if the global organization of production were determined entirely by the profit-and-loss considerations of powerful transnational corporations. But workers also play a key role in shaping the global economy. Sometimes they do so merely by moving to another country. For example, the movement of millions of poor immigrants from Mexico and Central America to Los Angeles has fueled the growth of low-wage manufacturing industries there. Sometimes workers organize and fight for higher wages and better working conditions, as they did in Korea during the 1980s, when they were successful in overturning that country's military government.

Second, the commodity chain approach sometimes underestimates the power of nations in a global economy. Governments still exert considerable control over working conditions, worker training and education, trade relations, and economic development.

Finally, commodity chain theory often fails to appreciate the extent to which production is tied to a particular place. Although it correctly recognizes that businesses are increasingly "footloose" in a global economy, that does not imply that all places are equal except for wage levels. It is obviously more expensive, difficult, and risky to try to get a finished shirt to Los Angeles from an Indonesian factory than from a factory located across town. There are also business advantages for an industry that remains in a particular location, in that networks of suppliers and related industries may be found nearby that "know the business" and make it viable and healthy (Porter, 1990a, 1990b; Scott, 1988; Piore and Sabel, 1984; Storper and Christopherson, 1987).

Summary and Evaluation of Theories of Global Inequality

Social theories do not originate in a social or historical vacuum. The theories we have just reviewed must be evaluated in light of the times and places in which they were conceived. *Modernization* and other *market-oriented theories* originated in the United States and other high-income industrial nations during the 1950s and 1960s, and reflect the belief that "any country can make it if it does it our way." These theories inspired U.S. government foreign aid programs, such as the Alliance for Progress, which attempted to spur economic "take-off" in low-income countries by providing them with money, expert advisors, and technology.

The failure of these programs was partly responsible for the emergence of *dependency theories* at roughly the same time. The latter originated in the low-income countries themselves, and grew out of the anger and desperation felt by sociologists and economists from these countries, many of whom believed that their countries' poverty was directly due to exploitation by U.S. and European businesses. Since dependency theorists believed that such exploitation made it impossible for their countries to ever achieve economic growth, they typically called for revolutionary changes that would get rid of foreign corporations altogether. Such theories, however, could not explain the occasional "success story" among low-income nations. During the 1960s and 1970s, it appeared that countries like Brazil, Argentina, and Mexico might achieve significant economic growth, even though they were clearly part of a world capitalist system. Moreover, Japan had already achieved outstanding success, and other countries in East Asia were beginning to follow suit. *Dependent development* theories acknowledged these facts, arguing that under certain conditions—notably, the presence of a strong national government committed to economic growth—dependent nations could still hope to develop economically.

By the late 1970s, it was becoming evident that the capitalist economic system was becoming increasingly global, dominated by transnational corporations that freely operated in many countries. These changing conditions led to a major rethinking of the causes of global inequality. Building on the insights of *world systems theory,* economists and sociologists argued that a *new international division of labor was emerging* that should shift our focus from individual countries to the global processes of production itself. *Commodity chain theory* represents the most recent effort to account for these processes in global terms. It is clear that any theory today must take into account the spectacular success of one group of countries that has escaped from grinding poverty during the past two decades. It is to these countries that we now turn for a better understanding of global inequality today.

THE NEWLY INDUSTRIALIZING COUNTRIES (NICS)

By the mid-1970s, it was clear that a number of low-income countries in East Asia were undergoing a process of "late industrialization" that would soon challenge the global economic dominance of the United States and Europe (Amsden, 1989). This process began with Japan in the 1950s but quickly extended to the **newly industrializing countries (NICs),** *the rapidly growing economies of the world,* which in Asia included Hong Kong in the 1960s, and Taiwan, South Korea and Singapore in the 1970s and 1980s. Other Asian countries are not far behind—notably Malaysia and Thailand.

Singapore is one of the most thoroughly modern cities in the world, immaculate in appearance and efficient in operation. Part of what has been called the "Asian Miracle," Singapore—along with Taiwan, South Korea, and Hong Kong—was transformed from a low-income nation to a relatively properous newly industrialized country (NIC) in only a few decades. Can such countries provide developmental models for poor countries in Asia, Africa, and Latin America?

China, the world's most populous nation, and Indonesia, the fifth most populous, also appear poised for rapid economic growth. These are all countries that were once in the economic periphery, as identified by world systems theorists. Today most are in the semiperiphery, and some have even made it into the core.

It is useful to look at the economic growth statistics of the East Asian region to understand the importance of what has happened in the last quarter century (Figure 9.4). Between 1965 and 1988, for example, the Japanese economy grew at a per-person rate of 4.1 percent, in comparison with only 1.7 percent in the United States. The average Japanese growth rate, per person, was nearly two and one-half times that of the United States. This meant that Japanese wealth, per person, more than doubled in 25 years; in the United States, it failed to increase by half. Astonishingly, the East Asian NICs grew even faster. For example, yearly per-person economic growth in Hong Kong averaged 6.2 percent, Singapore 6.5 percent, and South Korea a phenomenal 7.1 percent (World Bank, 1992, Table 1).

Causes of Economic Growth in the NICs

Social scientists have identified several factors that explain the success of the East Asian NICs which, taken together, provide an understanding of the complexity of global stratification today. They help to answer the question, "can the rapid economic growth of the East Asian NICs be repeated by other countries?" While some factors are historically unique, others suggest some lessons that might be learned by other countries seeking economic growth.

Are the East Asian NIC's Historically Unique?

There are a number of unusual historical circumstances that enabled the East Asian NICs to move up in the global stratification system, which are unlikely to recur in the near future.

First, none of the four countries were subject to the kinds of economic, social, and political exploitation by industrial powers that so often fell to countries in Latin America and Africa. Although Taiwan and Korea were once part of the Japanese empire, and Hong Kong and Singapore were British colonies (as already noted, Hong Kong will remain a colony until 1997), in many ways they benefited from their colonial relationships. Japan eliminated large landowners who opposed industrialization, and both Britain and Japan encouraged industrial development, constructed roads and transportation systems, and established relatively efficient governmental bureaucracies. Britain also actively developed both Hong Kong and Singapore as trading cen-

Figure 9.4   Average Yearly Economic Growth, 1965–1988: United States and Selected Asian Countries

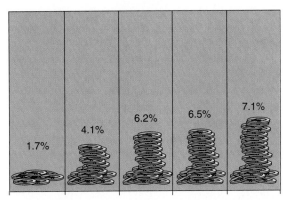

United States   Japan   Hong Kong   Singapore   South Korea

During the past 30 years, economic growth in the Asian NICs has greatly outstripped that of the United States, with economies such as those in Hong Kong, Singpore, and South Korea growing three to four times faster. Currently, China has one of the fastest-growing economies in the world.
Source: World Bank (1992, Table 1).

ters (Moulder, 1977; Morishima, 1982; Amsden, 1979, 1989; Gold, 1986; Cumings, 1987).

Second, the region benefited from a long period of world economic growth. Between the 1950s and the mid-1970s, the growing economies of Europe and the United States provided an enormous market for the clothing, footwear, and electronics that were increasingly being made in East Asia—a "window of opportunity" for economic development that did not exist before and has not existed since. Furthermore, periodic economic slowdowns in the United States and Europe forced businesses to cut their labor costs, fueling the relocation of factories to low-wage East Asian countries (Henderson and Appelbaum, 1992).

Third, this period coincided with the high point of the "Cold War," where the United States and its allies—largely in hopes of creating a bulwark against communist China—poured substantial economic and military resources into the region. Direct aid and loans were provided to invest in such new technologies as transistors, semiconductors, and other electronics, fueling the development of local industries. All of this contributed to economic growth, while military assistance favored strong (often military) governments that were willing to use repression to keep labor costs low (Frobel et al., 1980; Deyo, 1987; Henderson, 1989; Mirza, 1986; Okimoto et al., 1984; Amsden, 1989; Haggard and Cheng, 1987).

One especially virulent form of prejudice is **racism,** *the belief that a particular racial or ethnic group is naturally inferior, so that their unequal treatment is justified.* As we shall see throughout this chapter, racism runs deep in most cultures, including that of the United States, where white prejudice toward blacks has been especially pronounced. Research based on national survey data does suggest that whites report becoming less prejudiced toward blacks since the early 1970s (Ransford and Palisi, 1992).

One form that prejudice takes is **stereotyping,** *generalizing a set of characteristics to all members of a group.* Stereotyping occurs, for example, when a person observes someone of a particular ethnicity behaving in a certain way, and then concludes that the behavior is characteristic of all members of the ethnic group. The stereotype then serves to justify treating people differently, on the basis of the presumed characteristics. The historically established relationship between groups in society has a strong influence on the development of stereotypes.

For example, consider the historical origins of stereotypes regarding blacks in the United States. Enslaved Africans in the United States were allowed no education; teaching slaves to read and write was illegal. Slaves were treated as children, even though slave men performed grueling physical labor in the fields, while slave women worked hard in their "masters'" homes, raising the master's children, cooking, and cleaning. Slave women also were sometimes forced to bear children, since slave children represented valuable property (Collins, 1991). The resulting stereotypes reflected this forced division of labor: blacks were seen as "childlike," the men "naturally" strong, the women motherly and obedient "breeders." Such stereotypes still exist today. Black men are streotyped as "naturally athletic," which is then used to account for their success in sports (see Box 10.2); black women as sexually active, eager to bear children—the image of the irresponsible "welfare mother" (Collins, 1991; Sklar, 1992).

Today as during slavery, such negative stereotypes

Box 10.2

Critical Thinking

Why Do Blacks Seem to Dominate Certain Sports?

Although we have noted that African Americans make up about 12 percent of the U.S. population, they occupy a predominant position in most professional sports. Blacks also contribute 60 to 70 percent of the basketball players in Division 1A college basketball (National Collegiate Athletic Association [NCAA], 1993). Between 1970 and 1990 the number of blacks employed in athletics rose from 2,127 to 7,178 (Hacker, 1992). How can this be explained? One popular belief attributes black success in sports to anatomical or biological differences. According to this view, blacks have larger leg muscles, a greater supply of fast-twitch muscles, thinner hips, longer legs, or some other anatomical advantage which accounts for their performance (Burfoot, 1992). Such stereotypes, which closely resemble historical beliefs about male slaves having unusual strength, are not supported by empirical research. There are substantial physical differences between blacks from different parts of the world, and considerable overlap between blacks, whites, and other racial categories.

The sociological explanation for black predominance in certain sports is simple: In virtually all other fields, there are far fewer opportunities for blacks to achieve economic success than there are for whites. Elgin Baylor, one of the great basketball players of the 1960s, was once jokingly asked when the National Basketball Association would accept white players. His response was not humorous: "when corporations accept blacks." Sports is perceived as one place where a person's ability speaks for itself, regardless of race or ethnicity.

That this system is inherently exploitative is demonstrated by the fact that African-American college athletes are less likely to graduate from college than any other group of college students (NCAA, 1993). Since most college athletes cannot expect to have careers as professional athletes, the end result of playing sports for four years in college is only that: an opportunity to play sports for four years in college. Young men who drop out of school in hopes of "making it" in professional sports usually wind up failing and discouraged (Gaston, 1986).

serve to justify prejudice and discriminatory behavior against blacks. Yet it is important to remember that stereotypes can and do change. The growing economic and political power of blacks, for example, have resulted in an erosion of the old stereotypes and their replacement with new ones. In films and on television, black men and women are today often depicted as aggressive, sexual, and with "attitude" (Bogle, 1990). We shall examine media stereotypes about blacks and other minority groups in Chapter 19.

Stereotypes are not always negative. Asian Americans, for example, are frequently stereotyped as intelligent and educated, well-disciplined, hardworking, thrifty, and ambitious. These are traits that are generally valued in U.S. culture (Takaki, 1989). Even such positive stereotypes may sometimes prove damaging, however. The notion that Asian Americans constitute a "model minority" has been roundly criticized by scholars, who point out that this stereotype overlooks the fact that many Asian Americans have low-paying jobs or confront the same barriers to economic achievement as do other minority groups (Woo, 1985, 1992; Lai, 1992; see also Chapter 11, Box 11.2). One recent study, for example, found that while Asian Americans as a whole had the highest median family income of any minority group in the United States, a substantial minority (30 percent) were on welfare—a figure that reached 77 percent for Laotion and Cambodian immigrants in California (Ong et al., 1994). Furthermore, such positive stereotypes can then be used to justify blaming other minority groups for failing to enjoy the presumed success of the "model minority" (Collins, 1991; Fitzgerald, 1989; Suzuki, 1977; Woo, 1985, 1992).

Another form that prejudice takes is **scapegoating,** *blaming another person or group for one's problems.* The importance of scapegoating has been recognized at least since the fourteenth century, when the Arab social philosopher Ibn-Khaldun observed that the perception of an outside threat serves to increase solidarity within a society. During the 1930s, when Germany's economy was in a shambles and the country was still humiliated as a result of its defeat in World War I, Hitler rose to power partly by scapegoating others for all of his country's woes. By painting a picture of a "Jewish-communist conspiracy" that was somehow economically bankrupting the country while undermining its "racial purity," Hitler was able to mobilize the German people against Jews, gypsies, homosexuals and communists. Hitler's effectiveness in blaming others for Germany's problems contributed to his eventual rise to power, World War II, and the genocidal extermination of millions of people (Scheff, 1994).

As the example of Germany illustrates, scapegoating often appeals to individuals and groups who are relatively powerless, since it identifies and blames other, more powerful groups for their plight. In the United States today, the Ku Klux Klan and other white supremacist groups appeal especially to lower-class whites, whose eroding economic position can be conveniently blamed on Jews or blacks. Throughout the world today, immigrants are frequently scapegoated for taking jobs away from local citizens (see Box 10.3). This is currently true for Latino immigrants to the United States, who are often blamed for costing American citizens their jobs—even though most work for subminimum wages as factory workers, housecleaners, gardeners, farm laborers, and other jobs few citizens seem willing to take (Ong, 1989; Pastor, 1993).

DISCRIMINATION

While prejudice refers to attitudes, **discrimination,** *the unequal treatment of individuals on the basis of their membership in a group,* refers to actual behavior. As with prejudice, discrimination can be positive or negative: One may engage in actions that benefit the members of a particular group, or in actions that are harmful. At one time racial and ethnic discrimination in the United States was fairly open. As we have already noted, prior to the passage of federal civil rights legislation it was legal for a business, restaurant, or bus company simply to say "whites only" or "Jews need not apply." Today such overt forms of discrimination are no longer legal. Nonetheless, they often continue in more subtle forms (Feagin and Hodge, 1992).

For example, the Fair Employment Council of Greater Washington (D.C.) recently conducted an experiment in which similarly qualified blacks, whites, and Latinos applied for the same job. (Bendick, Jackson, and Reinoso, 1993). When an equally qualified black and white applied, whites received preferential treatment 29 percent of the time, compared with only 5 percent for blacks. When a white person was paired with a Latino, the white received preferential treatment 25 percent of the time. In a similar vein, a recent newspaper investigation in Los Angeles found that local businesses were secretly instructing employment agencies to illegally discriminate on the basis of age, gender, race, and ethnicity by using "code words" that secretly communicated their preferences for a person of a particular group. In one case, a business seeking to hire Latinos told the employment agency to "talk to Maria," while one that preferred whites said "talk to Mary." "Talk to Mary Ann" indicated a preference for blacks, "no Z" meant "no blacks," while "young environment" meant "no older workers" (*Time,* 1992).

Another example of discrimination occurs when

Box 10.3

Globalization

France Discourages Marriages with African Citizens

Blaming others for one's problems is called *scapegoating*. As economic globalization results in the massive relocations of jobs and workers, such scapegoating can be expected to increase. In France, the recently elected conservative government, riding a backlash of resentment against foreign immigrants, has pledged itself to "zero immigration." In a country where 11 percent of the population is out of work, the country's 4.1 million foreign workers are frequently blamed for taking jobs away from French citizens.

One way the French government hopes to realize "zero immigration" is by cracking down on marriages between French citizens and foreigners. There are presently some 31,000 such "mixed" marriages in France. The government argues that such marriages are frequently arranged so that the foreign spouse can obtain French citizenship.

June 19, 1993, was to be the wedding day for Fabienne Bricet, a 24-year-old student, and Ahmed Khelifa, her 25-year-old fiancé. The problem was that Bricet was French and Khelifa was an Algerian, a former university student who had remained in Paris after his temporary residence permit expired.

When the couple showed up at the local police station in response to a written request, Khelifa was arrested, handcuffed, interrogated, and then deported to Algeria. According to Bricet's attorney, throughout France public officials were informing the police of such marriages, especially when the foreign spouse was black or from Muslim North Africa.

Bricet followed Khelifa to Algeria, where she sought to persuade the French consulate to marry them. The Consulate declined on the grounds that Khelifa was not a French citizen. Their efforts to obtain a French visa so he could return to Paris were similarly thwarted. In desperation, the couple attempted to get married in Algeria, but that also failed because Bricet lacked an Algerian work permit. She eventually returned to France, without her fiancé.

"I am completely bewildered," she later told journalists. "The French state does not want me to get married. And against the state, I seem to be powerless. Why? I have gone around so many times. . . . A whole series of beliefs I had about my country and the rights of the individual here have just collapsed" (Cohen, 1994).

---

banks refuse to lend money to people or businesses who live in minority neighborhoods. This practice is termed **redlining,** *the banking practice of figuratively drawing a red line through an area to indicate that it is off-limits to lending activity.* Redlined neighborhoods are typically poor, and virtually always are comprised of racial or ethnic minorities. Once an area is redlined, even qualified residents are unlikely to secure loans. Although the practice violates federal law, it is nonetheless a common way that banks can avoid making loans to minority residents. Studies have found that banks loan less money to minority neighborhoods than to white neighborhoods, even when the residents have similar economic profiles (Dreier, 1993; Hacker, 1992; Wilson, 1993; Finn, 1989; Shlay, 1989; Canner and Smith, 1991).

Job discrimination and redlining are examples of **institutional discrimination,** *unequal treatment that has become a part of the routine operation of such major social institutions as businesses, schools, hospitals, and the government.* Although discrimination on the part of individuals can be hurtful, when discrimination results from the practices of large institutions it is likely to have more far-reaching effects on peoples' lives. It is because of institutional discrimination that minorities are systematically disadvantaged relative to whites—for example, as shown in studies finding that blacks experience twice the infant mortality rates of whites, have shorter life expectancies, or are much more likely to be rejected for social security disability insurance benefits when they have serious ailments (General Accounting Office, [GAO], 1992; Laveist, 1993).

RACIAL AND ETHNIC GROUPS IN THE UNITED STATES

The United States is made up of people from many different cultures. As Map 10.1 indicates, there is a high degree of ethnic diversity in different regions of the country.

Some people became part of what is today American society because they wanted to; others had little choice in the matter. Long before Europeans found their way to this continent, it was occupied by numerous indigenous societies, some organized into extensive nations. Many of these societies were conquered by the European settlers and their armies. The European settlers, in turn, were eventually incorporated into the the predominantly English-descendent colonies and their territories. It is estimated that during the colonial period almost half of the Europeans came as **indentured servants,** *people who by law were bound to service to someone for a specified period of time, usually seven years, in order to pay for their passage.* At about the same time, beginning in the seventeenth century, millions of slaves were brought from Africa; by the time of the first U.S. Census in 1790, about 750,000 of the nearly four million Americans, nearly one in five, was of African origin (U.S. Bureau of the Census, 1993, Table P-12). Thus a substantial proportion of the colonial population on the eve of the American revolution had arrived in servitude, either as indentured servants or as slaves; some estimates place the figure as high as two out of every three people (Daniels, 1990).

Once the colonies won their independence from England, the newly formed United States began to expand westward in search of its "Manifest Destiny," defeating and absorbing the remaining native populations who had thus far remained independent. It was only beginning in the mid-nineteenth century that large numbers of immigrants, predominantly European but including many Asians, began to arrive. Most were driven by poverty and attracted by the rapidly expanding American industrial economy (Figure 10.1). Today there are still other groups of immigrants, originating in Latin America and Asia, adding further to the country's racial and ethnic diversity. Of the nearly 60 million immigrants who arrived in the United States between 1820 and 1991, it is estimated that about 64 percent came from Europe, 17 percent from Latin America, 11 percent from Asia, 7 percent from Canada, and 1 percent from Africa (U.S. Immigration and Naturalization Service, 1992; see Figure 10.2).

Map 10.1   Racial and Ethnic Diversity in the U.S. by County

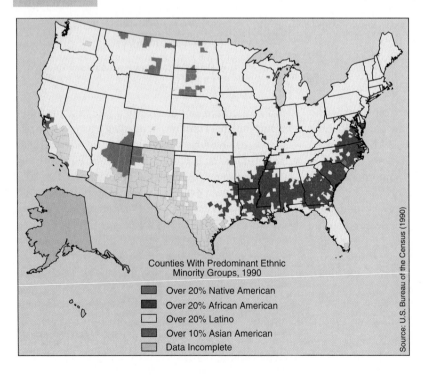

Counties With Predominant Ethnic Minority Groups, 1990

- Over 20% Native American
- Over 20% African American
- Over 20% Latino
- Over 10% Asian American
- Data Incomplete

Source: U.S. Bureau of the Census (1990)

Geographical concentrations of different racial and ethnic groups vary widely, reflecting the historical experiences of each group. African Americans tend to be concentrated in the east coast and south, as well as in large metropolitan areas throughout the country. Latinos are disproportionately found in the southwest and west, areas that are close to (and in some cases were once part of) Mexico. Native Americans are concentrated in the southwest, while Asian Americans are primarily found on the west coast.

Figure 10.1   **Number of Immigrants Arriving in the United States, 1820–1990**

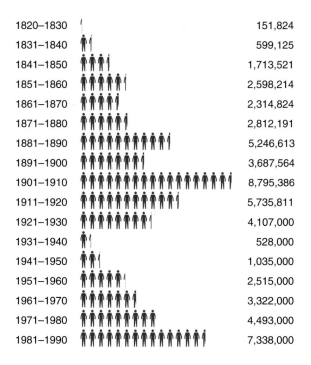

1820–1830	151,824
1831–1840	599,125
1841–1850	1,713,521
1851–1860	2,598,214
1861–1870	2,314,824
1871–1880	2,812,191
1881–1890	5,246,613
1891–1900	3,687,564
1901–1910	8,795,386
1911–1920	5,735,811
1921–1930	4,107,000
1931–1940	528,000
1941–1950	1,035,000
1951–1960	2,515,000
1961–1970	3,322,000
1971–1980	4,493,000
1981–1990	7,338,000

 = 500,000

The number of immigrants has ebbed and flowed not only on the basis of economic conditions in the United States relative to the rest of the world, but in response to U.S. politics as well. In 1882, for example, the Chinese Exclusion Act was passed to reduce the number of Chinese immigrants, since their labor—once prized on the transcontinental railroad and in California's gold and silver mines—was now seen as a threat to the white labor force. Similarly, the 1924 Quota Law favored Western European immigrants while barring Asians; the 1986 Immigration Reform and Control Act (IRCA) sought to limit illegal immigration from Latin America.
Source: U.S. Bureau of the Census (1993, Population Table 5).

The descendents of all of these different peoples today comprise American society: Native Americans, the original European settlers, indentured servants, slaves brought from Africa, immigrants from all over the world. As we look at these different racial and ethnic groups, it is important to remember that each has been shaped by a difference experience. People who became "Americans" as a result of conquest or slavery are likely to have a different relationship to American society than are those who came voluntarily in search of a better life.

Figure 10.2   **Immigrants to the United States by Place of Origin, 1820–1991**

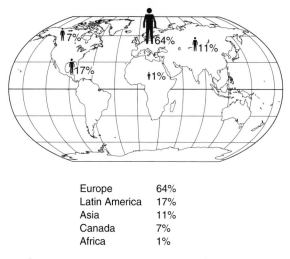

Europe	64%
Latin America	17%
Asia	11%
Canada	7%
Africa	1%

Total immigrants: 58.8 million

Nearly two-thirds of the nearly 59 million immigrants to the United States originated in Europe. Nineteen percent of these came from Germany, 15 percent from Italy, 14 percent from England, 13 percent from Ireland, and 9 percent from the former Soviet Union. Of the Latin American immigrants, nearly a half came from Mexico. Of those from Asia, 17 percent came from the Philippines, 15 percent from China, 8 percent from India, 7 percent from Japan, and 7 percent from Vietnam.
Source: World Almanac and Book of Facts (1992); U.S. Immigration and Naturalization Service (1992).

Table 10.1 summarizes current and projected changes in minority population, based on projections by the U.S. government derived from recent trends in immigration. While it is always speculative to make projections a half century into the future, the anticipated trends are striking. The four minority groups listed in the table presently account for one out of every four Americans. If the government statisticians are correct, "minorities" will account for nearly half the U.S. population by the year 2050. Latinos will double their share of the population to 21 percent, while Asian Americans will more than triple theirs to 10 percent. It will he helpful to bear this table in mind during the following discussion of specific groups.

American Indians

When the English, Spanish, French, and other Europeans arrived during the sixteenth century, they en-

Table 10.1   Minority Populations in 1990 and Projected for 2000 and 2050

	1990		2000		2050	
	Number (thousands)	**Percentage of Population**	**Number (thousands)**	**Percentage of Population**	**Number (thousands)**	**Percentage of Population**
African American	29,986	12.1	33,834	12.3	57,316	15.0
Latino	22,354	9.0	30,602	11.1	80,675	21.1
Asian American	7,273	2.9	11,582	4.2	38,765	10.1
American Indian	1,959	.8	2,096	0.7	4,078	1.0

Source: U.S. Bureau of the Census (1993).

countered numerous separate societies, ranging from tiny isolated hunting and gathering tribes to extensive pastoral and agricultural nations (see Chapter 4). There is no agreement on how many people lived in North America at the time. Estimates range from as high as ten million people to as low as two million, with five million the most likely figure. Encounter soon became conquest, and although the indigenous peoples resisted, they were eventually defeated and their lands occupied. It is believed that between 1500 and 1800—a span of only three centuries—the North American Indian population was reduced to 600,000 people, the result of European diseases for which they lacked immunity, forced labor and slavery in mines and on plantations, starvation and poverty, and systematic extermination by their conquerors. In the Caribbean island that is today called the Dominican Republic, for example, a population of one million Indians was re-

duced to approximately 500 in less than 50 years (Brown, 1991; Haggerty, 1991; Harjo, 1993; Schaefer, 1993; Thornton, 1987).

Although a number of European countries originally laid claim to different parts of North America, during the nineteenth century the rapidly expanding United States acquired these lands and their native societies. Sometimes this was accomplished by purchasing the lands from European governments who claimed to "own" them; well-known examples include the Louisiana Purchase from France in 1803, which doubled the country's size by acquiring what eventually became the plains and rocky mountain states; and the purchase of Alaska from Russia in 1867. Since the indigenous peoples understandably did not recognize these purchases, military force was frequently necessary to ensure their compliance, resulting in a number of wars between Indian tribes and

U.S. history books often speak of how Europeans "discovered" America, even though the continent had been populated for tens of thousands of years prior to the Europeans' arrival. In this cartoon such a Eurocentric *view is turned upside down, as the local inhabitants "discover" the Europeans upon their arrival.*

Drawing by Richter; © 1991
The New Yorker Magazine, Inc.

the U.S. government. The Indian survivors of these wars were forced onto **reservations,** *tracts of land set aside by the U.S. government for occupation and use by Indians.*

The Indian population has increased to nearly two million people during the past century, about 0.8 percent of the total U.S. population (U.S. Bureau of the Census, 1992). Although they are frequently grouped together under the name "American Indians" or "Native Americans" (refer to Box 10.1), they include members of some 500 different tribes and other groupings. Although most live in urban areas, about a third (38 percent) remain on reservations (Schaefer, 1993; U.S. Bureau of Indian Affairs, 1990).

American Indians are the poorest ethnic minority in the United States. They have significantly lower life expectancy, higher infant mortality, and unemployment rates on the reservations reaching 50 percent. More than half of all Indian children are born into poverty, three times the white rate (U.S. Bureau of the Census, 1993).

Despite the near-genocide of American Indians and the devastating poverty to which they have been subjected throughout their history, many have retained a strong sense of the value and importance of their own culture (Trafzer, 1993). In recent years, some have engaged in militant political action in an effort to force the U.S. government to honor treaties and improve their situation. The American Indian Movement (AIM), founded in 1968, has organized over 150 demonstrations protesting the treatment of American Indians. Violence between American Indians, local police and federal law enforcement officers began occurring on Indian reservations throughout the western states some

30 years ago (U.S. Senate Hearings of the Judiciary, 1976), and continues sporadically today.

Indian nations have sued the government, sometimes sucessfully, for compensation for lands taken from them and for the return of lands annexed by the United States. The fact that their ancestors were conquered remains an important aspect of the relationship between American Indians and the rest of society: Unlike other minority groups, American Indians have legal standing as independent peoples, including the right to their own land and the ability to negotiate directly with the U.S. government. In the words of one native American:

> Our struggle is to avoid being subjugated and to preserve our land, our water, our traditions, and our unique legal rights. Indian nations are inherently sovereign and have negotiated approximately 600 treaties with the U.S. government, In this, we are different from racial and ethnic minorities. . . . Although many provisions of the treaties have been broken unilaterally by the United States, the treaties are still the "Supreme Law of the Land," as they are characterized in the U.S. Constitution. Nothing is more doomed to failure than an effort to toss Indian people into the general melting pot or to deal with Indian people on a strictly racial basis. Our legal status requires that we be dealt with on a government-to-government basis (Harjo, 1993, p. 7).

African Americans

African Americans are the largest minority group in the United States, comprising just over 12 percent of the

In 1990 American Indians organized the "Bigfoot Memorial Ride" in South Dakota to commemorate the centennial of one of the last and bloodiest battles of the European conquest of America: the massacre of American Indians by U.S. soldiers at Wounded Knee.

population. The experience of African Americans in the United States can be divided into several critical periods. Slavery, which lasted more than 250 years, forcibly brought more than nine million Africans to North and South America. During the colonial period of the seventeenth and eighteenth centuries, more than four times as many Africans as Europeans arrived in the American colonies (Daniels, 1990). Most of the slaves were used to develop agriculture in the south, but the use of slaves was widespread throughout the colonies.

Slave revolts were often a threat to slave owners. In 1831 Nat Turner, an African slave in Southampton, Virginia, organized a rebellion that nearly succeeded in capturing Richmond, Virginia, the state capitol (Tragle, 1971). Turner's rebellion was not unique; it was one of at least 250 black uprisings against slavery (Rubenstein, 1970).

Slavery was officially abolished in 1863 by Abraham Lincoln's Emancipation Proclamation during the height of Civil War, and came to an end with the defeat of the southern states two years later. During the immediate post-civil war period, most former slaves remained in the South. Some continued to work on plantations for white owners, others became sharecoppers and a few gained ownership of small farms. During the period of Reconstruction, which continued throughout the remainder of the nineteenth century, African Americans moved to establish political and economic equality. Within months after the end of the Civil War, for example, James Rapier, a black Reconstructionist, gave a keynote address to the Tennessee Negro Suffrage Convention demanding "the vote . . . free speech, free press, free schools, and equal rights for all" (Schweninger, 1982, p. 79).

Some of these demands came to pass. African Americans gained the right to vote, and in some jurisdictions they were a majority of registered voters. In Louisiana, for example, more than 130,000 African Americans were registered to vote in 1896 alone. Black legislators were elected in every southern state. Between 1870 and 1901, 22 African Americans served in the U.S. Congress, while hundreds of others served in state legislatures, on city councils, and as elected and appointed officials throughout the South (Holt, 1977).

Any political power that African Americans enjoyed was, however, short-lived. "Jim Crow" laws were soon passed that mandated segregation in schools, restaurants, and public buildings, effectively turning blacks into second class citizens. These laws also effectively prevented blacks from exercising their newly won right to vote, by requiring the payment of poll taxes that few impoverished ex-slaves could afford. Some places also enacted literacy requirements that

virtually no one could achieve. When blacks sought to register to vote, the white citizens responsible for the literacy tests demanded a flawless recitation of such documents as the preamble to the Constitution and the Bill of Rights. Even though few whites could pass such a test, only the blacks were failed.

As a consequence of such restrictions, by 1901 the registration of black voters had dwindled to a mere handful (in Louisiana it went from 130,000 in 1896 to 1,342 eight years later). Not surprisingly, the representation of African Americans in local, state, and federal government declined sharply. In Mississippi, for example, the number of black representatives in the state legislature was 31 in 1870; 20 years later it was only one (Morrison, 1987).

As a result of Jim Crow laws, by the twentieth century blacks found themselves only slightly better off than they had been under slavery. To replace the slave labor lost with emancipation, white plantation owners and farmers created a system of "share-cropping" in which former slaves worked the land owned by their former masters and received a small share of the crop.

Although social and political discrimination also existed in the North, its higher degree of industrialization offered a promise of economic opportunity. As a result, the migration of African Americans from the South to industrialized northern cities took place in large numbers beginning in the 1920s, intensifying during and after World War II. Between 1940 and 1970 over five million southern black Americans left the rural South for what they hoped would be a better life in the North (Lemann, 1991). But by the end of this period the manufacturing base of the cities had begun to decline, closing off avenues to upward mobility that had previously been enjoyed by earlier immigrant groups (Sowell, 1983; Wilson, 1987; see Chapter 8).

By the 1950s—almost 100 years after slavery ended and James Rapier demanded political, social, and economic equality—most African Americans were still denied their fundamental rights in the United States. Jim Crow laws were strongest in the south, where blacks had to sit in the back of public buses, forgo eating in restaurants as long as whites were waiting to be served, use separate toilet facilities, and attend all-black schools. Although the U.S. Supreme Court ruled in 1954 that segregated schools violated the U.S. Constitution, when black students sought to attend the universities of Arkansas and Mississippi in 1957, they were barred from entering by local police and National Guard units. Five years after the Supreme Court decision, virtually all southern black elementary and high school students still attended segregated schools (Branch, 1988; Issel, 1985).

In 1955, however, segregation received its first major challenge when a middle-aged black woman was arrested in Montgomery, Alabama, for refusing to give up her seat on a bus to a white man. Rosa Parks, who worked for a black civil rights organization, had decided to break a law she knew to be unjust. Her single action, which triggered Martin Luther King's successful year-long boycott of public transportation in Montgomery, became a symbol that ignited a generation of blacks and whites in the Civil Rights Movement. Between 1950 and 1970, black activists captured center stage in the political arena. Some, such as Martin Luther King Jr. and Malcolm X were martyred for their beliefs; others, such as Jesse Jackson, remain prominent today.

The Civil Rights Movement used strikes, boycotts, voter registration drives, sit-ins, and freedom rides to achieve racial equality. In 1964, following what was at the time the largest march on Washington in the nation's history, the federal government passed the first in a series of civil rights laws that would eventually make it illegal to discriminate on the basis of race, sex, religion, physical disability or ethnic origin. Although the Civil Rights Movement was committed to nonviolent forms of protest, more militant actions also occurred during this period. Riots erupted in predominantly black areas of dozens of American cities, including New York, Chicago, Los Angeles, Detroit, Philadelphia, and Washington. In some instances neighborhoods were burned, stores were looted, and military units were required to restore the peace. Al-

though there were many reasons for the urban riots, in part they reflected the impatience of many African Americans with prejudice and discrimination still experienced a century after the Civil War (National Advisory Commission on Civil Disorders, 1968).

The actions of the 1960s, both nonviolent and militant, resulted in a number of legal gains for African Americans. These, in turn, have contributed to a growing economic split in the black population. On the one hand, blacks are disproportionately lower-income or impoverished (Bonacich, 1989; Wilson, 1991; Lieberson, 1988; Hacker, 1992). Figure 10.3 shows the income distribution of white and black families at two points in time, 1970 and 1990. Black income currently averages 58 percent of white income, and black families have an income distribution that is virtually the mirror opposite of whites: a large percentage at the bottom (37 percent earn near poverty-level wages under $15,000, compared with 14 percent for whites), and a small percentage at the top (15 percent earn over $50,000, compared with 33 percent for whites). Since 1970, the middle class "thinned out" for both categories, although much more so for blacks. Black families earning $15,000 to $35,000 dropped from 42 percent of all families to 34 percent, while white families in that category dropped from 38 percent to 33 percent. A much larger proportion of whites than blacks moved upward in the income distribution; a much larger proportion of blacks moved downward. (Hacker, 1992).

Nearly half of all blacks are employed in such unskilled or semiskilled services as household servants,

Until the 1950s, Jim Crow laws in the south prohibited African Americans from attending the same school, eating at the same restaurant, using the same water fountain or public toilet, or riding in the same part of the bus as white people. Rosa Parks sparked a boycott that eventually led to the end of Jim Crow, when she sat in the white section of a Montgomery, Alabama, bus and refused to give up her seat. She is shown here being fingerprinted after being arrested for her "crime."

Figure 10.3   Income Distribution for Black and White Families, 1970 and 1990

(1990 dollars)

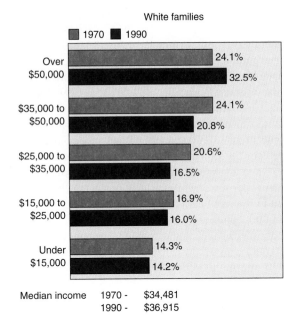

White families

■ 1970 ■ 1990

Over $50,000	24.1% / 32.5%
$35,000 to $50,000	24.1% / 20.8%
$25,000 to $35,000	20.6% / 16.5%
$15,000 to $25,000	16.9% / 16.0%
Under $15,000	14.3% / 14.2%

Median income   1970 - $34,481
                1990 - $36,915

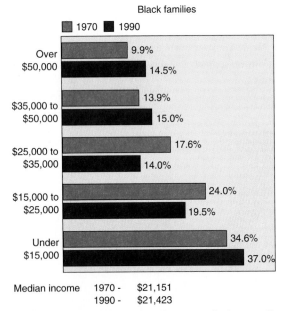

Black families

■ 1970 ■ 1990

Over $50,000	9.9% / 14.5%
$35,000 to $50,000	13.9% / 15.0%
$25,000 to $35,000	17.6% / 14.0%
$15,000 to $25,000	24.0% / 19.5%
Under $15,000	34.6% / 37.0%

Median income   1970 - $21,151
                1990 - $21,423

Black families have almost the mirror opposite income distribution of white families: fat on the bottom and lean on the top. While both "thinned out" at the middle class levels between 1970 and 1990, black families did so primarily by moving downward (although a significant number also moved up); whites by moving upward. These changes reflect the economic changes of the past two decades, which saw a loss in the lower-income jobs traditionally available to minorities in the United States.
Source: Hacker (1992).

dishwashers in restaurants, janitors, custodians, and sanitation workers; the comparable figure for whites is only 27 percent. Average unemployment rates for blacks typically run at three times the white rate, reaching as high as 50 percent among black teenagers who are seeking work. Nearly half of black males between 25 and 34 are currently unemployed or work at jobs that pay less than poverty-level wages. As a result of these factors, the number of blacks living in poverty has increased by a half during the past decade, to nearly 30 percent of all blacks; nearly half of all black children are born into poverty, nearly three times the white rate (U.S. Bureau of the Census, 1992; Pollard, 1992; Wilson, 1978, 1987; Wacquant, 1993; U.S. Bureau of the Census, 1993).

Yet on the other hand, more African Americans than ever before have achieved middle class professional or managerial occupational status. Fifteen percent of black families earned over $50,000 in 1990, compared with 10 percent in 1970 (Hacker, 1992). Income gains reflect gains in black education. Black high School graduation rates doubled between 1970 and 1990, as did the number of black Ph.D.'s during the 1980's (U.S. Bureau of Census, 1992). Nonetheless, these figures are still low in comparison with the total number of blacks in the American population.

Blacks have also achieved substantial gains at the political level. In 1963 there were only 103 African Americans holding public office throughout the United States. By 1992 the number of black public officials had increased to more than 5,000 (Morrison, 1987). In 1992, 16 new black members of Congress were elected, and for the first time in U.S. history a black woman, Carol Moseley Braun, was elected to the U.S. Senate. The total number of black members of Congress rose to 40, the largest number in U.S. history (See Chapter 13, map 13.1). There are more than 250 black mayors, including many of the major cities in the United States. While advances of African Americans at the top of the American class system are impressive, the majority of the African-American population lives well below white standards in the United States.

Latinos

As previously mentioned, the category "Latinos" includes people from the many different cultures that share the Spanish language as part of their ethnic heritage. The history of some predates that of the present-day United States, going back to a time when the southwestern states were a part of Mexico. Following its defeat in the 1846-1848 war, Mexico was forced to sell two-fifths of its territory to the United States. The war, which was prompted by Mexico's earlier refusal to voluntarily sell to the U.S. government what became

Texas and California, enabled the United States to acquire all of its southwestern states, including California. Along with this vast territory came the people who occupied it, including tens of thousands of Mexicans who forfeited their property and were subject to various forms of discrimination (Valenzuela Arce, 1992).

According to official estimates, there are 22 million Latinos living in the United States, comprising 9 percent of the total population (U.S. Bureau of the Census, 1992). These figures no doubt underestimate the total Latino population, given that there is a sizable but unknown number who have entered the country illegally and are therefore missed by the census. Latinos are increasing in numbers more rapidly than any other minority group, and within a decade will surpass African Americans as the largest one (U.S. Bureau of the Census, 1993). By that time California will be nearly one-third Latino, and Los Angeles more than half (California Department of Finance, 1993). Eventually, by 2050, Latinos are expected to number a fifth of the total population (see again Table 10.1).

Although some Latinos can trace their roots to the Mexicans who lived in the Southwest when it was still a part of Mexico, most are relatively recent immigrants from different Spanish-speaking countries (Table 10.2). Sixty-one percent of the Latino and Hispanic population traces its origins to Mexico, 13 percent to Central and South America, 12 percent to Puerto Rico, and 5 percent to Cuba.

As with other minority groups, Latinos often experience discrimination in American society. Forty percent of Latino children are born into poverty, two and a half times the white rate. About 30 percent of all Latinos live in poverty, while 47 percent hold unskilled and semiskilled service sector jobs. All of these figures are about twice the comparable rates for white Americans (U.S. Bureau of the Census, 1992).

Mexican Americans

The largest group of Latinos are of Mexican origin. The majority of the Mexican American population lives in California, New Mexico, Texas, and Arizona. Immigration of Mexican-Americans has long reflected the immediate labor needs of the U.S. economy (Barrera, 1979; Hansen, 1988; Moore and Pachon, 1985; Majka and Majka, 1982; Muller and Espenshade, 1986; Reichert and Massey, 1982). During the 1930s, state and local governments forcibly sent hundreds of thousands of Mexican immigrants back to Mexico, but when the United States experienced a labor shortage in World War II, immigration was once again encouraged. This policy continued after the war under the *bracero* program, which enabled some four million Mexicans to work as temporary farm laborers in the United States, often under conditions of extreme exploitation. (In Spanish, "bracero" refers to someone who uses his or her arms.) Following the repeal of the *bracero* program in 1964, Mexican immigration was once again discouraged, but by the 1980s it was apparent that a floodgate had opened, with millions of Mexicans fleeing poverty by crossing the border. Subsequent efforts to halt migration, such as the restrictive Immigration Reform and Control Act (IRCA) of 1986, have thus far proved futile.

As with other minority groups, the Mexican-American population has a growing middle class, but the growth of the very poor is increasing even more rapidly (U.S. Bureau of the Census, 1991). Yet Mexican-American communities exhibit a high degree of resilience, with extremely strong extended family networks and community and religious institutions. Household members often find work in lower-paying jobs in manufacturing, or services such as housecleaning, child care, and gardening (Moore and Vigil, 1993).

Puerto Ricans

In 1917 the United States made Puerto Rico a protectorate and Puerto Ricans became U.S. citizens. In the next 70 years, more than two million Puerto Ricans migrated to the United States, mostly to the East Coast. Over half of all Puerto Ricans living in the United States

Table 10.2   Origins of Latino Population in the United States

Country of Origin	Percentage of Latino Population
Mexico	61
Central and South America	13
Puerto Rico	12
Cuba	5
Other Latino	9

Source: Moore and Pinderhughes (1993, p. xvii).

For years Latino, Filipino, and other ethnic groups worked the vineyards and farms of the Southwest. Work conditions were generally harsh and the wages the lowest paid to any workers in the country. César Chavez (pictured here with walking stick) and some fellow-workers organized the United Farm Workers of America (UFW), forcing growers to collectively bargain with the union over wages and work conditions. Chavez died in 1993, but the UFW continues its work on behalf of farm workers.

reside in New York City. In terms of education, employment, and income Puerto Ricans share with blacks similar problems of prejudice and discrimination. Like other Latinos, they also face problems of adjusting to school and work in a foreign language. Thirty-eight percent live below the poverty line, the highest rate of any Latino group (U.S. Bureau of the Census, 1991). They have been adversely impacted by the loss of the manufacturing jobs that traditionally have provided employment for immigrant groups. One result is high unemployment and a growth in the informal economy (Ricketts and Sawhill, 1988; Sullivan, 1989).

Cuban Americans

When Fidel Castro came to power in Cuba in 1959, Cubans who opposed his regime sought to imigrate to the United States. These included some of Castro's political opponents, but primarily consisted of middle class Cubans whose standard of living declined, the result of Castro's programs to help the poor as well as the U.S. economic embargo. Unlike most other immigrants who had entered the United States illegally, the Cubans were for the most part welcomed by the U.S. government, since they were regarded as refugees from communism (Forment, 1989). About a half million entered the United States, most of them in Florida, only 90 miles away from Cuba.

The Cuban community in Miami is by far the most successful Latino immigrant group, having created numerous successful businesses and acquired a great deal of political power (Forment, 1989; Stepick and Grenier, 1993). The reasons for this success are not hard to discern. Unlike most immigrants, who tend to come from the poorer strata of their native countries, many Cuban immigrants were highly educated professionals

and businesspeople before they fled to the United States. They brought with them a considerable reserve of training, skill, and, in some cases, wealth.

Furthermore, the U.S. government provided financial assistance, such as small business loans. It also provided language classes, job-training programs, and recertification classes for physicians, architects, nurses, teachers, and lawyers who sought to reestablish their professions in the United States. About three-quarters of all Cubans arriving prior to 1974 received some form of government benefit, the highest rate of any minority community. The reasons for the U.S. government's largesse were largely political: the Cubans were fleeing Castro's communist regime, and thus were seen as bolstering the U.S. side in the Cold War against communism (Mohl, 1990; Stepick and Grenier, 1993; Wilson and Portes, 1980; Forment, 1989).

Asian Americans

There are presently 7.2 million Americans who trace their origins to Asian countries, about 3 percent of the total population (Table 10.3). The number of Asian Americans is growing rapidly, primarily due to immigration; U.S. government statisticians project their numbers at a tenth of the U.S. population by the mid-twenty-first century (see again Table 10.1). As with Latinos, the extraordinary ethnic diversity of this category cannot be captured by the term "Asian American."

Many Asian Americans can trace their origins to the mid-nineteenth century, when massive construction projects in the western states contributed to a severe labor shortage. The building of the transcontinental railroad, as well as gold and silver mining in California, demanded a large number of unskilled laborers; young

Table 10.3   Asian-American Population, by Country of Origin: 1990

	Population
Chinese Americans	1,640,000
Filipino Americans	1,407,000
Japanese Americans	840,000
Asian Indians	815,000
Korean Americans	799,000
Vietnamese	615,000
Laotian	149,000
Cambodian	147,000
All Other	854,000
TOTAL	7,274,000

Source: U.S. Statistical Abstracts (1993).

Chinese men provided a ready supply (Jackson, 1991; Gittins, 1981; Saxton, 1971). Some came voluntarily; others were kidnapped by ship captains and brought to the West Coast. (The nineteenth-century term "shang-haied," which refers to capturing young men and forcing them to serve as shiphands, can be traced to the Chinese city where this practice was common.)

The Asian-American population has experienced considerable prejudice and discrimination. During

During the mid- to late-nineteenth century hundreds of thousands of Chinese immigrants entered the United States as part of a national policy to find cheap unskilled labor to build railroads and work in the gold and silver mines of the west. Chinese immigrants passing through Angel Island in San Francisco left behind photos of families and other personal items that poignantly tell of their hardships and hopes.

World War II, for example, Japanese Americans were forcibly placed in internment camps and their property confiscated, on the false grounds that their allegiances were likely to be with Japan rather than the United States. Most historians agree that anti-Asian racism contributed to this action. (No such steps were taken against the Germans, who were allied with Japan during the War.)

Nonetheless, the Asian-American population has been relatively successful in gaining an economic foothold. According to one recent study (Ong et al., 1994), Asian Americans as a whole have the highest median family income of any minority group ($35,900), the lowest rates of divorce (3 percent) and teenage pregnancy (6 percent), and the lowest rate of unemployment (3.5 percent). Between 1972 and 1987, the number of Asian-American–owned businesses increased tenfold.

Yet the same study found that while some Asian Americans enjoyed relative economic success, many others lived in poverty (Ong et al., 1994). For example, for each family earning in excess of $75,000, there is another earning less than $10,000. As mentioned above, 30 percent of all Asian Americans are on welfare, with substantially higher rates among immigrants from Southeast Asia. Among Asian Americans over 25 years old, a third have a college degree, yet a quarter lack a high school diploma. There are also enormous differences within the Asian-American population. Nearly half of all Indian Americans, for example, are professionals, compared with less than a quarter among Korean Americans. Poverty and hardship are acute among those from Southeast Asia, particularly immigrants from Cambodia and Laos. The study attributes these problems partly to discrimination, and partly to the traumatic wartime experiences that spurred immigration from that region during the past two decades.

The economic success of many Asian Americans is

partly due to a high cultural valuation on education and entrepreneurial activity. It also reflects the fact that recent Asian immigrants tend to come from higher socioeconomic backgrounds, and therefore bring with them greater financial resources than more impoverished immigrants. Family networks and kinship obligations also play an important role. In many Asian-American communities, informal community-based lending organizations provide capital for small business, families and friends support one another as customers and workers, and profits are reinvested in the community (Kasarda, 1993; Sanders and Nee, 1987; Portes, 1981; Portes and Jensen, 1987; Nee and Sanders, 1987; Gilberston and Gurak, 1993; Forment, 1989; Light and Bonacich, 1988).

White Ethnic Americans

According to the 1990 Census, among white Americans 60 million people identify their ethnic background as German, 39 million as Irish, 33 million as English, 13 million as French, 12 million as Italian, and 9 million as Polish (U.S. Bureau of the Census, 1991, 1993). There are also smaller numbers of Slavs, Greeks and Russians. Jewish immigrants first arrived when the colonies were established. Among the English, French, and Spanish settlers were 23 Jews who had been expelled from Portuguese colonies in Brazil, arriving in the United States in 1619. In the next 160 years they were joined by Jews from England and the Caribbean, so that by 1790 there were over 2,000 Jewish citizens of the United States spread from New England to Georgia.

Because their European origins were similar to those of the dominant American culture, these European immigrants found acculturation to be easier (and often more desirable) than immigrants from Latin America or Asia. In addition, white ethnic groups could more easily assimilate than could American Indians, Latinos, Africans, and Asians, because for the most part they were not easily distinguishable physically from the dominant population. In some cases the European immigrants also had access to funds for investment. The groups that arrived at the beginning of industrialization found a ready demand for their labor, which enabled them to advance economically.

To facilitate assimilation many families changed their names, encouraged their children to speak English only, and whenever possible sent their children to school with other whites. Although they came with visions of finding fulfillment through the "American dream," many first had to overcome substantial barriers of prejudice and discrimination (Calavita, 1984). In mid-nineteenth century Boston, for example, the Irish were stereotyped as drunken, criminal and generally immoral; they comprised a large portion of the city's poor (Handlin, 1968). The term "Paddy Wagon" to describe the police van that picks up the drunk and disorderly is based on the belief that it was the Irish who were the van's most frequent occupants. ("Paddy" was a commonly used derogatory name for the Irish at the time.) In Massachusetts "alcoholism" was frequently recorded as a cause of death for Irish Catholics but not English-descent Protestants (Sklar, 1993).

New Immigrants

As previously indicated in Figure 10.1, there has been an enormous upsurge in immigration to the United States during the past decade or so. Yet the profile of these immigrants differs markedly from that of most previous groups. Only about 10 percent of recent immigrants have originated in Europe, which has accounted for nearly two-thirds of all immigrants since 1820, as was shown in Figure 10.2. On the other hand, 47 percent came from Latin America, including 1.7 million from Mexico alone (23 percent), while 37 percent

U.S. immigration policy reflects not only the need for different kinds of workers but prejudices against different racial and ethnic groups as well. The ship The Golden Venture *was carrying hundreds of illegal Asian immigrants to the United States when it sank. The survivors shown here are being transported to shore, where they face arrest and deportation.*

Immigrants face many barriers, not the least of which is language. Language classes are not available for many immigrant groups, and the wait for a class may be anywhere from four months to three years. This photograph shows an English as a second language (ESL) class being offered at Riverside Church in New York City.

came from Asia (U.S. Immigration and Naturalization Service, 1992).

These "new immigrants" are thus almost entirely Latino and Asian. Some are refugees from war-torn countries, including those who fled political repression and military violence in Guatemala, El Salvador, and, most recently, Haiti. The large influx of Vietnamese immigrants, following U.S. defeat in the Vietnam War in 1975, also falls into this category. But by far the largest number of these immigrants have arrived for economic reasons. In most cases these are people who lived in extreme poverty in their own countries, and hoped that the United States would afford them greater opportunity.

This is especially true of the immigrants from Mexico and other parts of Latin America. The global economy has brought with it an enormous differential in economic conditions between the wealthy industrial nations and the poorer regions of the world (Chapter 9). Wages for unskilled labor in Los Angeles, for example, are 10 to 15 times higher than those for comparable work in Mexico or Central America (Bonacich et al., 1994; Peterson, 1992). It is not surprising that millions of people are willing to cross the U.S.-Mexico border, many illegally, in search of work. In 1991, for example, one out of every seven immigrants to the United States wound up in Los Angeles, a city close to Mexico with a large low-wage economy and substantial Latino population (Appelbaum and Bonacich, 1993). Many of these immigrants retain close ties with their original communities, sending back part of their paychecks to help support children or parents who remained behind.

Not all of the new immigrants are impoverished, however. Some, particularly those from Asian countries

such as Hong Kong and Korea, often arrive with significant resources at their command. Many are highly educated, with backgrounds in the professions or business. These immigrants may wind up as entrepreneurs in the United States, starting small businesses that draw on the resources of the ethnic enclave economy. Since Asian countries such as Korea and Hong Kong themselves have relatively prosperous economies, immigrants from those countries are sometimes able to start businesses whose customers are in their native countries (Light and Bonacich, 1988; Hess, 1990).

The new immigrants contribute substantially to the ethnic diversity of the United States, bringing with them customs that differ from those of the European-originating majority. Whether or not they will be accepted into an increasingly multicultural society depends in part on whether or not the U.S. economy can absorb them without threatening the livelihood of its current workforce (Archdeacon, 1992). If not, it is possible that they will be scapegoated for many of the economic problems in the United States, and the doors on future immigration from Latin America and Asia tightly shut.

GLOBALIZATION, RACE AND ETHNICITY

Globalization has contributed to increased racial and ethnic contact, both directly as the result of migration of people in search of work (Chapter 15), and indirectly as a result of global television and other forms of mass media (Chapter 19). This increased contact can lead to growing racial and ethnic strife, or to a better understanding and appreciation of cultural differences.

Pluralistic societies may generate interethnic conflicts. At their ugliest, such conflicts spawn hate groups that attack immigrants and other minorities, vandalizing their homes and businesses. A recent neo-Nazi rally in what was formerly East Germany raises the specter of the Holocaust, *which killed more than 11 million members of minority groups in Europe, including 6 million Jews.*

A Rise in Racial and Ethnic Conflict?

Although racial and ethnic violence are hardly new to human history, such acts appear to be on the increase today. Within the United States, many acts of violence reflect the strain between immigrant groups and other members of American society. The Federal Bureau of Investigation estimated that in 1991 there were some 20,000 hate-crime incidents involving hostile acts against people for no reason except their race, religion, ethnicity, or sexual orientation (FBI, 1992). Some incidents involve extraordinary acts of interpersonal, racially motivated hatred, such as the 1993 New Year's day murder of a young black man in Florida, who was doused with gasoline and burned to death by white racists. Others, however, are the result of long-simmering tensions between different racial and ethnic groups, as the following examples illustrate:

• In South Central Los Angeles there are recurrent tensions between Korean immigrants who own small stores and factories, and the black and Latino residents who provide their customers and factory workers. These tensions nearly erupted in a riot in 1991, when Soon Ja Du, who with her husband owned a small neighborbood store in a black neighborhood, shot and killed 15 year-old Latasha Harlans after a scuffle over an alleged attempt to steal a bottle of orange juice (Miles, 1992).
• In Brooklyn, Henry Kwok Lin Lau, a Chinese immigrant from Hong Kong, was stabbed to death in 1990 by a man yelling racial slurs against Asians.
• During the same year, also in Brooklyn, a car driven by a Hassidic Jew went out of control in the racially mixed Crown Heights neighborhood after running a red light. One black child was killed, and another seriously injured. Long-standing tensions between Jews and blacks exploded; within hours, a group of neighborhood black youths sought revenge by killing a Jewish passerby. Four nights of rioting erupted; some demonstrators carried signs that said "Hitler didn't do the job" (Bullard, 1991; Allis, 1991; Anti-Defamation League, 1991).
• In a widely publicized incident in 1988, Mulugeta Seraw, an Ethiopian student living in Portland, Oregon, was brutally bludgeoned to death with baseball bats by a group of youths belonging to the East Side White Pride Skinhead Gang, an offshoot of a national racist organization, the White Aryan Resistance (WAR). One of the boys later convicted of the killing, previously nicknamed Ken Death, was renamed "Batman" because his bat had cracked on Seraw's head (Bullard, 1991).

Although there are many reasons for such acts of violence, they are in part the result of globalization. First, the creation of a global economy has meant an increasingly borderless world in which businesses can locate anywhere they choose. This has had a mixed impact on many industrial nations, including the United States, since many jobs have been lost to low-wage areas elsewhere in the world (Chapters 8 and 15). As we noted earlier in this chapter, when peoples' livelihoods are threatened, they often scapegoat others. Second, the massive immigration of recent years has contributed to a great deal of contact between different races and ethnic groups. Immigrants offer a convenient target for scapegoating, both because they are readily perceived as competing for scarce jobs and because their cultural differences can be seen as threatening.

Racial and ethnic conflicts are not unique to the United States. Today there are more than 50 wars and many other violent conflicts taking place throughout the world (see Map 10.2), although the U.S. news media gives prominence to only a few. In Europe right-wing political parties are thriving by blaming foreign ethnics for economic problems, and racist organizations engage in acts of terrorism and violence against foreign workers and ethnic minorities (Echikson, 1992; Rumer and Rumer, 1992).

Globalization has contributed to these conflicts. To take but one recent example, in January 1994 Indians in the Mexican province of Chiapas started a revolution against the local government. Armed Indians occupied several cities before they were finally driven into the mountains by Mexican Army forces. The Indians were protesting years of poverty, along with their long-standing treatment as second-class citizens because of their ethnic status. But the immediate cause of their insurrection was the Mexican government's signing of the North American Free Trade Agreement (NAFTA), which called for eliminating state subsidies for corn, tobacco, and other crops on which the Indians depended for their survival. NAFTA is a step toward economic globalization, but one that is seen as harmful by Mexico's Indian minority population.

The most prominent current examples of ethnic violence are currently found in both Europe and Africa. When Yugoslavia broke up in 1991, people who iden-tified with being Croatian or Muslim declared their regions to be independent. The once-dominant Serbian majority resisted these efforts, engaging in war against the Croatians and Muslims. The Croatians, in turn, fought not only for independence from Serbian contol, but against the Muslim minority as as well. The Serbians soon embarked on a policy of "ethnic cleansing" in territories occupied by Croatians and Muslims. This included murder, rape, the mass deportation of Croats and Muslims from their homes, and the confiscation of their property. One eyewitness report from the Muslim town of Kozarac, Bosnia, recounted how a local resident of Serbian ethnicity pointed out Muslim judges, parliamentary representatives, police officers, businessmen, restaurant owners, and even local sports heroes, who were arrested and promptly executed (Battista, 1992).

In the African country of Rwanda, ethnic violence between the Hutu and Tutsi tribes has led to the open practice of genocide. In 1994 the Hutu majority embarked on a systematic program to exterminate the Tutsi minority. Within a few months, hundreds of thousands of people were killed. Entire families were hunted down and massacred, and over a million refugees fled to neighboring countries.

Global Prospects for Racial and Ethnic Peace

If globalization is partly the cause of racial and ethnic strife throughout the world, it also holds the promise for solutions. Perhaps the most hopeful example is South Africa, where the dismantling of the system of racial *apartheid* and the open election of Nelson Man-

When the former Soviet Union decentralized authority, age-old ethnic strife led to internal conflicts in many countries, including Georgia, Ukraine, and the former Yugoslavia. In this picture, women in Bosnia-Herzegovina, part of what was once Yugoslavia, grieve the killing of their loved ones in what has become a violent ethnic war.

Map 10.2   Global Racial and Ethnic Strife, 1993

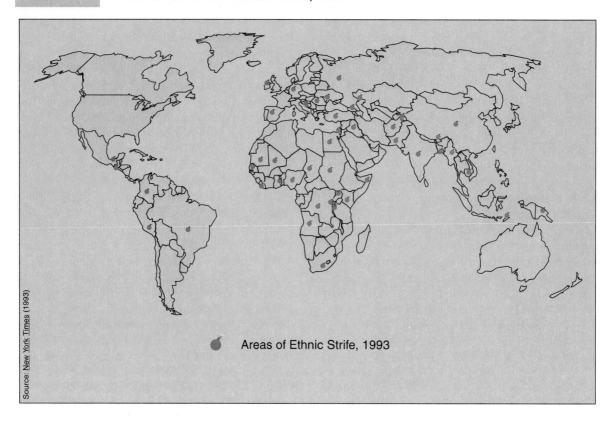

Source: New York Times (1993)

🔴 Areas of Ethnic Strife, 1993

As the Cold War has ended, violent racial and ethnic conflicts appear to have increased. From the former Yugoslavia to Rwanda, millions of people have been uprooted from their homelands and subjected to violent persecution.

dela as the first black president resulted from a global economic boycott of companies that did business in the country (see Chapter 8). In a global economy, many businesses have factories and sell products around the world. When consumers in the United States and other industrial nations refused to buy goods sold by businesses that had South African investments, the businesses began to withdraw their investments from the country. This, in turn, put enormous economic pressure on the minority white South African government. Public opposition to *apartheid*'s racist policies, which consigned three-quarters of the country's population to servitude while excluding them from any political or economic power, also forced the U.S. government to take a stand. As a result of these international pressures, South Africa's white population eventually voted to abolish *apartheid* altogether.

Global media has been important in shaping world opinion about South Africa, as well as other countries where racial and ethnic strife occur. During World

War II, the extent of the Holocaust was concealed until the concentration camps were liberated at the end of the war. Today, thanks to global television, it is extremely difficult for any country to conceal acts of ethnic or racial genocide from the rest of the world.

Televised images of starving Somalian children, victims of that country's ethnic strife, eventually prompted the United Nations to take action to reduce the conflict. A UN military peacekeeping force was dispatched to Somalia, in hopes of forcing the warring parties to agree to peace. In Yugoslavia, television helped to bring the terrifying meaning of "ethnic cleansing" into people's homes around the world. In early 1994, when Serbian forces shelled a public market in the city of Sarajevo during the course of a two-year seige, television viewers got an unforgettable close-up view of the carnage. The United Nations called for military action to end the seige, and the North Atlantic Treaty Organization (NATO) forced the Serbians to withdraw from the neighboring hills under threat of airstrikes from the United States and other NATO forces.

In Rwanda, where hundreds of thousands of civilians have been killed in ethnic strife between the Hutu majority and the Tutsi minority, chilling photographs of the slaughter led to calls for United Nations intervention. Yet thus far the international community has been powerless to enforce peaceful solutions in any of these examples, and individual countries are reluctant to commit large numbers of soldiers for active intervention.

One last example will serve to illustrate the complexity of achieving racial and ethnic harmony in the world today. The country of Israel was created by the United Nations in 1948. It was conceived as a homeland for Jews throughout the world, particularly the remnants of the millions who had died in the Holocaust just a few years earlier. The land itself was a biblical homeland to Christians and Muslims as well as Jews, and by the twentieth century it had become home to many different ethnic groups, primarily Arab and Palestinian, but also including Jews from Europe and the Soviet Union.

Many Arabs and Palestinians resisted the creation of a new country on what they regarded as their land. Ongoing racial and ethnic strife, including two major wars with its neighboring Arab States, have plagued the country of Israel since its inception. Until the Soviet Union collapsed in 1991, Israel was caught up in the "Cold War" as well, with the United States providing substantial military and economic support to Israel, while the Soviet Union did the same for the Arab nations surrounding Israel. Today, although conflict persists, it seems that for the first time world pressures may contribute to a resolution of these problems.

Solutions to the world's racial and ethnic problems are not easily found. For one thing, they can be costly. Military intervention, even when conducted on humanitarian grounds, must be paid for, and the taxpayers of the "peacekeeping" nations are the ones who must foot the bill. There is also the danger that a limited intervention will escalate into a major war. Economic pressures, such as boycotts, are less likely to lead to warfare, but they can also be difficult to achieve. The case of South Africa, however, suggests that they can ultimately succeed.

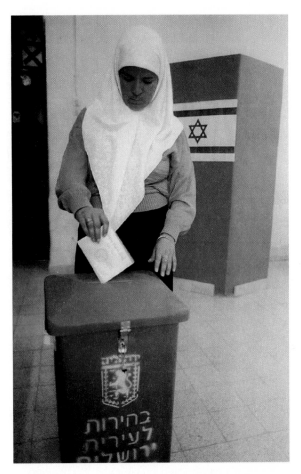

The Middle East has long been home to ethnic strife, particularly between Israel and its Palestinian and Arab neighbors. Yet significant strides toward peace have been made in the past few years, as this photograph of a Palestinian woman casting her vote in Jerusalem's 1993 mayoral election shows. The writing on the ballot box is in Hebrew.

As the world becomes an increasingly interdependent economic, political, and cultural system, racial and ethnic strife in one region can affect people everywhere. By the same token, the countries of the world become dependent upon one another in ways that may make it possible for global pressures to become ever more effective. It remains to be seen under what conditions ethnic conflict can be overcome by international, political, economic, or military pressures.

CHAPTER SUMMARY

1. Sociologists argue that **race** is not a biological category but rather a social construct. Its importance derives from the fact that people in a particular culture believe race makes a difference, and then act on the basis of that belief.

2. The same is true of **ethnicity,** a concept that emphasizes the cultural differences between people that are believed to be important.

3. **Minority groups,** typically based on race or ethnicity, often suffer **prejudice** and **discrimination** in society. Different models of minority-majority relations emphasize **assimilation** and **acculturation, segregation,** or **pluralism.**

4. Racial and ethnic segregation are widespread in American society, despite two decades of civil rights legislation outlawing its open practice.

5. Prejudice is often accomplished through **stereotyping,** and frequently manifests itself through **scapegoating.** During difficult economic times, scapegoating is likely to increase, often with highly adverse effects for minority groups.

6. Although discrimination is against the law in the United States, it is still widely practiced. **Institutional discrimination** in particular has resulted in unequal treatment of minorities in terms of jobs, housing, education, and other important societal institutions.

7. An understanding of race relations in the United States requires an understanding of the unique histories of different racial and ethnic groups. Groups that became part of American society by conquest or enslavement have a different relationship to society than those who voluntarily joined it through immigration.

8. The United States is a multiethnic, multiracial society. Approximately one-fourth of all Americans belong to the principal minority groups today, including African Americans, Latinos, Asian Americans, and American Indians. This figure is projected to rise to nearly half by the middle of the next century.

9. Although the vast majority of immigrants historically have come from Europe, in recent years the pattern has changed, with most coming from Latin America and Asia.

10. With a few exceptions, all minority groups are disadvantaged in the United States relative to the majority white population. This is true in terms of such things as average income, the proportion living in poverty, and the quality of education.

11. Globalization has brought with it an increase in acts of racial and ethnic violence. Changing economic conditions threaten many people, while global migration brings members of different groups together, increasing the possibilities for scapegoating.

12. Globalization also carries the possibility for solutions to racial and ethnic strife, since the global institutions that are being created may provide a framework for resolving some of the problems that cause it..

QUESTIONS FOR DISCUSSION

1. What do sociologists mean when they assert that "race" and "ethnicity" are social constructs, rather than constructs based purely on the biological or natural characteristics of different groups of people?

2. What changes in migration have occurred in recent years? How are they likely to affect racial and ethnic diversity in the United States?

3. What do sociologists mean by "institutional discrimination," and how does it affect the lives of minorities? What steps might be taken to overcome it?

4. What is the relationship between prejudice, stereotyping, scapegoating, and racial violence?

5. What are the principal problems of race and ethnicity that appear to be worsened by globalization? How might they be resolved within a global framework?

KEY TERMS

acculturation: Adopting the norms, values, and life-ways of the dominant culture.

assimilation: Absorption into the dominant mainstream culture.

cultural pluralism: The belief that minority groups should retain their distinct cultural identities but only within a framework that ensures their overall equality.

discrimination: The unequal treatment of individuals on the basis of their membership in a group.

ethnic economic enclaves: Neighborhoods comprised primarily of members of an immigrant ethnic group who provide one another with mutual economic support.

ethnicity: The attribution of characteristics to groups of people who share a common cultural (including religious) heritage.

indentured servants: People who by law were bound to service to someone for a specified period of time, usually seven years, in order to pay for their passage.

institutional discrimination: Unequal treatment that has become a part of the routine operation of such major social institutions as businesses, schools, hospitals, and the government.

minority group: A group of people, distinguished on the basis of perceived racial or cultural differences from the dominant group in society, who are disadvantaged as a result of their status.

prejudice: A preconceived belief about an individual or a group that is not subject to change on the basis of new evidence.

race: A category of people whose biologically based common physical characteristics are believed to make them socially distinct.

racism: The belief that a particular racial or ethnic group is naturally inferior, so that their unequal treatment is justified.

redlining: In banking practice, figuratively drawing a red line through an area to indicate that it is off-limits to lending activity.

reservation: A tract of land set aside by the U.S. government for occupation and use by Indians.

scapegoating: Blaming another person or group for one's problems.

segregation: The physical and social separation of different categories of people.

stereotyping: Generalizing a set of characteristics to all members of a group.

RECOMMENDED FOR FURTHER READING

Collins, Patricia Hill. (1991). *Black Feminist Thought: Knowledge, Consciousness, and the Politics of Empowerment.* New York: Routledge, Chapman & Hall.

> This study traces the stereotypes of black women, and black women's responses. It demonstrates the politics of empowerment as well as the obstacles to liberation.

Du Bois, W. E. B. (1968; orig. 1903) *The Souls of Black Folk.* New York: Fawcett World Library.

> In this classic and brilliantly written study, Du Bois, one of America's important early sociologists, recounts the experiences of blacks under slavery and Reconstruction, and their struggle for liberation. The solutions offered nearly a century ago are well worth considering today.

Hacker, Andrew. (1992). *Two Nations: Black and White, Separate, Hostile, Unequal.* New York: Ballantine Books.

> An excellent brief summary of race relations in the United States, providing a wealth of statistical data and a well-written text that places the data in a sociological context.

Moore, Joan, and Raquel Pinderhughes (eds.). (1993). *In the Barrios: Latinos and the Underclass.* New York: Russell Sage Foundation.

> Over the years Joan Moore and her students have provided among the best ethnographies on Mexican-American gangs and life in Mexican-American communities. This book summarizes earlier findings and compares impoverished Mexican Americans and African Americans.

Root, Maria O. O. (ed.). (1992). *Racially Mixed People in America.* Newbury Park, CA: Sage.

> A collection of 26 essays that explore the meanings of multiracialism from the perspective of people whose own racial heritages are mixed.

Takaki, Ronald. (1989). *Strangers from a Different Shore: A History of Asian Americans.* Boston: Little Brown.

> A historical study of Asian immigrants to the United States, from one of the leading scholars of Asian-American studies.

Sex and Gender

CHAPTER OUTLINE

THINGS TO LOOK FOR

1. What is the difference between sex and gender? What is the relative contribution of biology and socialization to gender identity?
2. How do traditional sociological and feminist theories differ in their accounts of gender in modern society?
3. What is the extent of gender inequality in the workplace, in the home, in the mass media, and in politics? How is this changing?
4. How has the sociological understanding of homosexuality changed in recent years, and how has the homosexual community contributed to such changes?
5. What is the impact of globalization on gender inequality?

INTRODUCTION

■ "A male . . . shall be valued at 50 silver *sheckels;* if it is a female, she shall be valued at 30 *sheckels*" (God's commandment to Moses, as recorded in the Bible, Leviticus 27:4).
■ According to the U.S. Census Bureau, the average full-time U.S. woman worker earns about 70 cents for every dollar earned by a full-time male worker, a figure that has not changed a great deal in recent years (U.S. Department of Commerce, 1991a, 1992b).

Although more than 3,300 years separate the ancient Israelites and modern U.S. societies, their monetary valuations of women relative to men show a startling similarity. In fact, in virtually all cultures around the world today, most women occupy positions that are economically subordinate to those of men. Sociologists do not believe that such differences are ordained by God; nor do they believe they are merely coincidental. Rather, they derive from cultural values that disadvantage women.

In this chapter we shall examine gender relations and differences, asking why they exist and how they are changing. After first examining the nature of human sexuality, we turn to different theories concerned with gender in society. This will enable us to examine

the ways in which men and women acquire their gender roles, an important basis for the various forms of gender inequality that we shall consider in some detail. We conclude with a look at recent changes in sexual orientation, along with an assessment of the changing nature of gender relations in the world today.

SEX, GENDER, AND SEXUALITY: SOME KEY DISTINCTIONS

Although some degree of controversy surrounds the relative importance of "nature" and "nurture" in accounting for behavioral differences (Chapter 5), sociologists give far greater weight to social influences in accounting for behavioral differences between men and women. To highlight the distinction between biological and social factors, sociologists use the term "sex" to refer to biological differences, and "gender" to refer to social ones.

Sex and Biology

Sex refers to *anatomical or other biological differences between males and females that originate in the human gene.* Many of these differences, such as difference in genitalia, are normally present at birth. Other differences, triggered by genetically controlled male or female hormonal secretion, develop later in life—for example, female menstruation, differences in muscle mass, facial hair, height, and vocal characteristics (Fausto-Sterling, 1985; Hudson, 1978; Marini, 1990). It is important to emphasize that apart from a few obvious anatomical differences that distinguish most males and females, what is striking is the overlap between the two sexes. Although men are on the average taller then women, for example, in a roomful of people many of the women will be taller than many of the men (see Figure 11.1).

Gender and Society

Because some biological differences exist between men and women, it may seem reasonable to assume that biological differences are responsible for behavioral differences. Yet sociologists do not make this assumption. Rather, sociologists generally argue that differences in behavior between males and females are largely learned through social interaction. The term **gender** is used to refer to *behavioral differences between males and females that are culturally based and socially learned.* Cultures differ widely in their norms and values regarding **gender roles,** *the normative expectations concerning appropriately "masculine" or "feminine" behavior in a particular culture.* We will

Figure 11.1   Although Boys' Average Scores on Math Tests are Higher than those of Girls, There Is a Great Deal of Overlap Between the Sexes

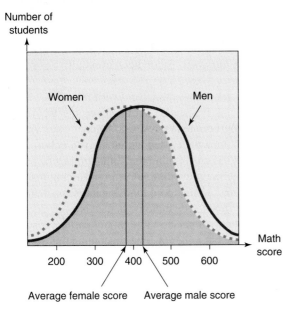

The shaded area indicates overlap between male and female scores. Although there are minor differences, what is striking is the degree of overlap.
Source: Adapted from Tavris (1992, p. 42).

therefore reserve the terms "male" and "female" for sex differences that are biological in origin, while using the terms "masculine" and "feminine" to refer to the corresponding culturally specific gender differences that are social in origin.

Some research has sought to determine whether biological sex determines gender. Most of this research has concluded that the answer is no. To cite one intriguing example: There is the well-studied case of a seven-month-old male identical twin whose penis was accidentally injured during circumcision, a routine procedure (in the United States) for removal of the foreskin on the penis. His parents decided to surgically alter his anatomy from male to female, and raise him as a girl. The parents held fairly traditional ideas of how boys and girls should be raised, encouraging their now-"daughter" to play with dolls and otherwise act in feminine ways. Their "daughter's" twin brother, in traditional fashion, was encouraged to play with toys and tools and to be masculine. As the "daughter" grew older, "she" developed stereotypically feminine traits; her brother, on the other hand, became a "typical" little boy. The "daughter's" parents reported her as a model "little girl"—neat, clean, organized, and "[lov-

ing] to have her hair set" (Money and Ehrhardt, 1972; Money, 1975).

If biology alone determined gender, the two children should have grown up with the same masculine behavior, regardless of how they were raised. Both of them were genetically male, as well as genetically identical to one another in all other respects. Yet their genders diverged, suggesting that their differing socialization experiences were more important than their genetic similarities.

Other research comes to the same conclusion: Social learning, rather than biology, largely accounts for **gender identity,** *the ways in which individuals in a particular culture come to think of themselves as male or female, and learn to act accordingly* (Imperato-McGinley et al., 1979; Money and Ehrhardt, 1972; Fausto-Sterling, 1985; Marini, 1990). This includes attitudes, behaviors, and social roles that are traditionally associated with being "masculine" or "feminine." A person's gender identity is learned early in childhood and subsequently reinforced throughout life. Some scholars have argued further that cultural attitudes surrounding gender, rather than innate biological mechanisms associated with one's sex, are responsible for the need to "choose" between only two sexes in the first place (Butler, 1990, 1993; Kessler and Mckenna, 1985; Martin, 1992). These scholars would point to the above-mentioned case of the parents who chose to raise their surgically altered son as a daughter, in which the possibility of raising their child in a third gender role was not even entertained.

Are differences in childhood socialization to gender roles long-lasting? The previous case of the twins provides conflicting answers to this question. Once "she" reached adolescence, the "daughter" began to experience problems, leading her to question her feminine identity. Although this has suggested to some scholars that biology was ultimately more important than socialization in determining her gender, other factors may account for her ambivalence about being a girl. Her schoolmates cruelly taunted her because of her increasingly masculine appearance, the result of normal hormonal changes resulting in the development of many secondary masculine physical sexual traits. Since "she" had been told that she was born a boy and was now being ridiculed because of her emerging masculine features, it seems reasonable that she came to question her adopted female gender (Williams and Smith, 1979; Diamond, 1982.). This study illustrates the difficulties of isolating biological factors from social ones in the study of humans.

One final source of evidence for the importance of socialization (as opposed to biology) in acquiring gender comes from studying the effects of hormones on behavior. Much of the research on this topic has been conducted on animals. For example, male monkeys whose testes have been removed become less aggressive, while female monkeys given male hormones (such as testosterone) become more aggressive. It is difficult to infer from monkeys to humans, however, since far more social learning occurs with humans. Most studies conclude that there is no consistent evidence that hormones cause gender differences in behavior, or that hostility and aggressiveness are significantly higher in males or associated with testosterone levels (Rutter and Giller, 1984; Maccoby and Jacklin, 1974; Ehrhardt and Meyer-Bahlburg, 1981; Meyer-Bahlburg, 1977; Tourney, 1980; Money, 1988; Hyde, 1984; Marini, 1990). Once again, most sociologists conclude from this research that gender is socially acquired.

Sexuality

Sexuality refers to *the ways in which people construct their erotic or sexual relationships, including norms governing sexual behavior.* Sexuality, like gender, is socially constructed; it reflects the norms and values of particular cultures and subcultures (Plummer, 1984).

An important aspect of sexuality concerns the degree to which sexual behavior is socially regarded as acceptable. Societies differ in their degree of sexual restrictiveness or permissiveness. Although the United States historically has been more sexually restrictive than many other industrial societies, there is evidence that people's actual sexual behavior reflects more permissive attitudes than traditional social norms would suggest. For example, the first major studies of sexuality in the United States, based on interviews with some 11,000 adults, were conducted during the late 1940s and early 1950s, a time of much greater sexual restrictiveness than today. Yet even these studies found that a majority of Americans (women as well as men) had experienced premarital intercourse, while two out of five men had extramarital sex (Kinsey, 1948, 1953).

Sexual permissiveness is much greater today. For example, a federal governmental survey of nearly 12,000 high school students found that by their senior year, three out of four boys and two out of three girls reported having had sexual intercourse, over half within the previous three months (Center for Disease Control, 1992). Even as early as ninth grade, about half of all boys and a third of all girls claimed to have had intercourse. By way of comparison, in Japan only about 1 out of 20 boys or girls report having had sex by age 15 (Toufexis, 1993).

A second important aspect of sexuality concerns **sexual orientation,** *a person's desire or attraction for a sexual partner of a particular sex.* Because in all cultures there are two biological sexes, the possibilities for sexual orientation would seem to be fairly straightforward. As with so many aspects of human behavior, however, this turns out not to be the case. As noted earlier, the fact that in most cultures there are only two principal choices based on biological sex may itself be culturally determined.

The normative sexual orientation in all cultures, including our own, is for **heterosexuality,** *a sexual attraction or desire for persons of the opposite sex* (*hetero* comes from the Greek word meaning "other" or "different"). Specific norms governing what constitutes appropriate heterosexual behavior (as with all behavior) must be learned within a given culture. It is important to bear in mind that although heterosexuality may be the prevailing norm in most cultures, it is not "normal" in the more fundamental sense that it is somehow dictated by biology. In fact, biology does not by itself cause a person to be of any particular sexual orientation, but rather operates in conjunction with social factors.

A second sexual orientation, **homosexuality,** entails a *sexual desire for persons of one's own sex* (*homo* comes from the Greek word meaning "same" or "similar"). Today, the term "gay" is often used interchangeably with homosexual to refer to a male whose sexual orientation is toward other men, while "lesbian" is used to refer to homosexual women. (The term derives from the name of the Greek island Lesbos, the birthplace of Sappho, the renowned ancient Greek poet.) Specific behaviors associated with homosexuality, as with heterosexuality, must be socially learned. Both heterosexuality and homosexuality appear to be the result of a complex interplay between biological and social factors (see below, "Homosexuality, Biology, and Social Learning").

Heterosexuality and homosexuality do not exhaust the possibilities of human sexuality. A third sexual orientation, **bisexuality,** involves a *sexual desire for persons of both sexes* (the prefix *bi* means "two"). **Transsexuality** involves *people of one sex whose sexual identity is with persons of the opposite sex,* which further increases the range of possibilities for human sexuality. Transsexuals are men and women who feel like they are trapped inside the body of the other sex. (As one transsexual male put it, "I am female, with those things [penis and testes] stuck on;" quoted in Green, 1974, p. 47). Transsexuals also may have "same," "opposite," or "bisexual" orientations. As these examples illustrate, although there might be only two biological sexes, human beings can and do learn a wide range of behaviors associated with sexuality. Sociologists who study human sexuality think in terms of multiple sexualities rather than simply two basic possibilities (Plummer, 1984, 1991).

SOCIOLOGICAL THEORIES ABOUT GENDER

Until relatively recently, the most influential sociological theorizing about gender assumed that prevailing gender differences were both normal and functional for society as a whole. Today, largely as a result of feminist scholarship, this assumption is no longer held by most sociologists.

Classical Sociological Theory: Gender Differences as Normal

A common theme running through nineteenth century sociological theory was the notion that men and women "naturally" possessed the traits found in European society. Sociological founders Auguste Comte and Emile Durkheim (Chapter 1), drawing on earlier philosophers such as Jean-Jacques Rousseau, believed that women were best suited to "private" family roles that involved nurturance, childbearing, and raising a family. Men, on the other hand, were seen as possessing inherent advantages when it came to roles outside the family in such "public" spheres as science, industry, and government. Women were in many ways regarded as "naturally" subordinate to men (Comte, 1975; Durkheim, 1964, orig. 1895; Elshtain, 1981; Kleinbaum, 1977).

The reasons for such presumed social differences were sought in biological differences between the sexes. In one popular (but erroneous) theory, women were reported to have smaller brain capacity than men, a belief that was based on comparing the skulls of deceased men and women. (By this standard, elephants should be more intelligent than humans, because their skulls are far larger.) Because of these alleged differences in brain size, men were assumed to be biologically more rational than women, who were in turn seen as inherently emotional.

Although sociologists no longer believe that biological differences determine gender-appropriate social roles, until relatively recently sociology persisted in arguing that role differences based on sex were functional for social stability. For example, Talcott Parsons (1955), one of the most influential American sociologists during the middle third of this century, offered a functionalist theory of gender differences. Parsons argued that in industrial society women make their societal contribution by raising children and maintaining the family unit; men by earning the family income through outside labor. Parsons did not attribute such role specialization to biology; rather, he argued, it was the result of differences in social learning. Women were socialized to acquire such "expressive" qualities as sympathy and emotionality, which later served them

well as homemakers. Men, on the other hand, were socialized into such "instrumental" qualities as rationality and competitiveness, required for the workplace.

Comtemporary Feminist Theory: Countering Patriarchy and Sexism

Feminism refers to *the belief that social equality should exist between the sexes.* (It is also used to characterize the social movements aimed at achieving that goal.) Feminism emerged in the United States in connection with the abolitionists and other antislavery groups during the 1830s, which gave birth to the struggle by women to achieve rights for themselves. The founding year of the "first wave" of the women's movement is generally traced to 1848, when Elizabeth Cady Stanton and Lucretia Mott held a convention in Seneca Falls, New York, to push for women's issues. The 1963 publication of Betty Friedan's *The Feminine Mystique* helped to initiate the "second wave" of the women's movement, along with women's experiences in the Civil Rights and anti-Vietnam War social movements (Bernard, 1981, 1982; Epstein, 1988; Friedan, 1963, 1981; Lipman-Blumen, 1984).

One of the contributions of feminist thinking to sociological theory has been a better understanding of the nature of **patriarchy,** *any set of social relationships in which men dominate women.* Although some researchers have sought to find evidence of nonpatriarchal societies (Gimbutas, 1982, 1989; Eisler, 1988), Brown's (1991) extensive survey of anthropological research concludes that all known societies have thus far been patriarchal to some degree. Patriarchy is often justified on the basis of **sexism,** *the belief that one sex is innately inferior, and therefore its domination is warranted.* In patriarchal societies, men typically regard themselves as superior to women, and as a result various forms of discrimination against women are common. Nor are all sexist attitudes and behaviors necessarily limited to men. If patriarchal norms and values go unchallenged, many women may accept them as normal too.

Although there are numerous differences among the women (and men) who identify themselves as feminists, all believe that patriarchy and sexism should be abolished. By the same token, not everyone who opposes gender inequality sees themselves as feminist or identifies with feminism. At the risk of greatly simplifying an on-going discussion with many points of divergence as well as agreement, several broad streams of feminist thinking can be identified.

Liberal feminism holds that *women's inequality is primarily the result of imperfect institutions, which can be corrected by reforms that do not fundamentally alter society itself.* In Britain, liberal feminism dates at least as far back as 1792, when Mary Wollstonecraft's *Vindication of the Rights of Women* argued for women's equality. A major milestone in the development of liberal feminism in this century was the publication of *The Feminine Mystique,* previously mentioned, which argued that traditional values surrounding femininity were in many ways oppressive to women, preventing them from realizing their full potential. Today, liberal feminists fight to elect women to the House and Senate, to enact the Equal Rights Amendment, and argue in favor of a woman's right to choose an abortion.

Socialist (or Marxist) feminism, on the other hand, regards *women's inequality as largely the result of capitalistic economic relations that must be transformed fundamentally before women can achieve equality.* This viewpoint originates in the writings of Marx and Engels, who argued that inequality, including that of women, was an inevitable feature of capitalism (Chapters 1 and 8). Engels (1942; orig. 1884), for example, sought to demonstrate that the family unit was historically based on the exploitation and ownership of women. Late nineteenth and early twentieth century socialists such as Charlotte Perkins Gilman, Alexandra Kolontai, and Rosa Luxembourg extended these ideas. Socialist feminism in the United States reemerged in the 1960s, when liberal feminists became frustrated with the pace of social reform and began to seek more fundamental sources of women's oppression. By focusing on women's economic roles, both in the secondary labor market and as unpaid labor in the home, socialist feminism has sought to demonstrate the ways

in which exploitation of women's labor, both paid and unpaid, is a major source of wealth in capitalist societies (Eisenstein, 1979; Hartman, 1979, 1984; Kuhn and Wolpe, 1978; Mitchell, 1975; MacKinnon, 1982, 1989; Reed, 1970; Rowbotham, 1973; D. Smith, 1979, 1987, 1990; Vogel, 1984; Zaretsky, 1976).

Socialist feminists have often looked to socialist nations for examples of nonoppresive gender relations, but overall the results have been disappointing. Although countries such as Cuba, China, and the former Soviet Union often passed laws guaranteeing women's rights, in reality women in these countries still tend to work largely in "women's jobs" with lower pay and status than men, and in general experience various forms of discrimination (Gray, 1989; Andors, 1983; Nazzari, 1983).

Radical feminism, mindful of the fact that true equality for women has yet to be achieved under any existing economic-political system, argues that *women's inequality is fundamental to all other systems of inequality, including economic.* It grew in part out of women's frustration with the civil rights and antiwar movements of the 1960s and 1970s, groups that were headed by male leaders who often treated women as second-class citizens. While the men were making speeches about equality, women were often relegated to doing such stereotypical "behind the scenes" women's work as mailing flyers, making posters for demonstrations, or cooking meals. Radical feminists concluded that to truly improve the situation of women, patriarchy must first be abolished (Barry, 1979; Dworkin, 1981, 1987, 1989; Firestone, 1971; Griffin,

Liberal feminists *seek changes within the existing social system, in their efforts to obtain equality for women. For example, institutionalized bias in medical research has meant that less money has been spent for research on "women's diseases" such as breast and ovarian cancer, than on many other forms of illness. Women's groups have lobbied and demonstrated to change such priorities.*

1978, 1979, 1981; Millet, 1970; Morgan, 1970). As one way of redressing male-female inequality, some radical feminists have called for the creation of alternative institutions, communities of women working around issues of health, media, day care, shelters for battered women, and rape crisis intervention.

While feminism today draws on all these strands, it seeks to go beyond the earlier discussions—which primarily involved white middle class women in Europe and North America—by incorporating the voices and concerns of women of color everywhere (see Box 11.1). Although there is no agreed-upon name for this current rethinking of feminist ideas, we will use the term **multicultural feminism** to describe feminism that focuses on *understanding and ending inequality for all women, regardless of race, class, nationality,* *age, sexual orientation, or other characteristics* (B. Smith, 1990). Racism, along with economic privilege and patriarchy, are seen as the root causes of women's oppression (Anzaldua, 1990a, 1990b; B. Smith, 1990; Baca Zinn et al., 1990; Davis, 1981; Andersen and Collins, 1992; Segura, 1989; Mohanty et al., 1991).

Multicultural feminists have analyzed gender inequality in a wide variety of settings. U.S. sociologist M. Jacqui Alexander (1991), for example, has examined the role of the state in trying to enforce conventional norms and values in the Caribbean nation of Trinidad and Tobago, focusing on legislation that served to criminalize gay and lesbian sex. She was especially interested in the racial aspects of the debates over the legislation, a legacy of the country's status as a former British colony whose black population once

Box 11.1

Silenced Voices

I Am Your Sister

Audre Lorde was an African-American lesbian and mother, the author of more than a dozen books of nonfiction as well as poetry. She was born in New York City in 1934, and, prior to her death in 1992, taught at Hunter College. She was active in fighting for the rights of women, lesbians, and people of color. In this passage, taken from a talk she gave to women at the predominantly black Medgar Evers College in Mississippi, Lorde (1988) passionately explains what being black, lesbian, and feminist means to her.

When I say that I am a black feminist, I mean I recognize that my power as well as my primary oppressions come as a result of my blackness as well as my womanness, and therefore my struggles on both these fronts are inseparable.

When I say I am a black lesbian, I mean I am a woman whose primary focus of loving, physical as well as emotional, is directed to women. It does not mean I hate men. Far from it. . . .

I have heard it said—usually behind my back—that black lesbians are not normal. But what is normal in this deranged society by which we are all trapped? I remember, and so do many of you, when being black was considered *not normal,* when they talked about us in whispers, tried to pain us, lynch us, bleach us, ignore us, pretend we did not exist. We called that racism.

I have heard it said that black lesbians are a threat to the black family. But when 50 percent of children born to black women are born out of wedlock, and 30 percent of all black families are headed by women without husbands, we need to broaden and redefine what we mean by *family.*

I have heard it said that black lesbians will mean the death of the race. Yet black lesbians bear children in exactly the same way that other women bear children, and a lesbian household is simply another kind of family. . . .

Try to remember to keep certain facts in mind. Black lesbians are not apolitical. We have been a part of every freedom struggle within this country. Black lesbians are not a threat to the black family. Many of us have families of our own. We are not white, and we are not a disease. We are women who love women. . . .

I am a black lesbian, and I *am* your sister."

Map 11.2   **Females in Congress, 1970 and 1994**

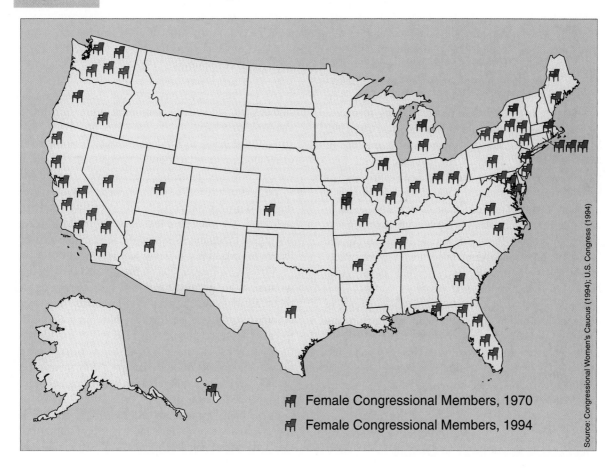

Source: Congressional Women's Caucus (1994); U.S. Congress (1994)

🪑 Female Congressional Members, 1970

🪑 Female Congressional Members, 1994

Women have been historically under-represented in politics in the United States, especially at the national level. Reflecting recent changes in the role of women in American society, however, growing numbers of women are seeking and gaining national elective office, even though they still remain a small minority of the total.

other study that tracked thousands of men and women born after World War II over a 15-year period, Goldscheider and Waite (1991) found that in two-parent families with teenage boys and girls, the girls were assigned five times as many household chores as their brothers. On the other hand, the researchers also found that in highly educated families, husbands did significantly more sharing of housework, hopefully providing new role models for their children.

Politics

Prior to January 1993 there were only two women in the U.S. Senate (out of 100), three female state governors (out of 50), and 29 female members in the U.S. House of Representatives (out of 435). The U.S. Supreme Court had its first and only female Justice (out of 9) appointed in 1981, and its second 12 years later. The United States had to wait until 1984 for a woman to be nominated as the vice-presidential candidate of

either major party, neither of which has ever nominated a woman for the presidency. In this regard the United States contrasts markedly with numerous other nations. Countries as diverse as Great Britain, Israel, Norway, Turkey, Canada, Pakistan, India, Nicaragua, and the Philippines have all had highly visible female heads of state in recent years, although some were elected partly because they were wives or daughters of powerful male politicians (Map 11.1). At the same time, it is important to remember that in much of the world women remain effectively excluded from power.

Typically, the more local the political office, the more likely it is to be occupied by a woman. Although men outnumber women in politics at all levels, women are often elected members of city and county governing boards, and female mayors are not uncommon. In most states, women are less likely to be found as representatives to state government than they are at the local level, but even elected state-level women are more common than female representatives to Congress. This is partly because local politics is often part-time work, particularly in smaller cities and towns. It is thus a good candidate for "women's work," offering low pay, part-time employment, flexible hours, and the absence of a clear career path. The farther from home the political office, the more likely it is to be regarded as "man's work," providing a living salary, full-time employment, long and demanding hours, and a lifetime career.

On the other hand, women are starting to play a much more significant role in U.S. politics. The 1992 national elections saw an unprecedented number of women seeking office at the national level. Five women were elected to the U.S. Senate, tripling its female membership to six. One of these women was the first African-American woman in history to sit in the chamber. Symbolically, the Senate chamber was forced to add its first-ever female restroom. In the House of Representatives, 106 women ran for office, of which 47 were elected, nearly doubling the previous number of female representatives.

It remains to be seen whether or not this increase in the number of female elected officials will lead to any significant policy changes. Although some policies (such as requiring employers to provide maternity leave) have long been sought by women's political organizations, this does not mean that all women elected to office share these goals.

VIOLENCE AGAINST WOMEN

Violence directed against women is found in many societies, including our own. Some scholars have argued that increased depiction of violence in movies, television, and elsewhere in U.S. popular culture contributes to a climate in which women often are victimized (see Chapter 19). The most common manifestation of violence against women is rape, although sexual harassment increasingly is seen as a form of psychological (if not physical) violence as well.

Rape

Rape can be sociologically defined as *the forcing of nonconsensual vaginal, oral, or anal intercourse.* Sociologist Paulene Bart, who has studied different forms of relationships between men and women, offers the following classification (Bart and O'Brien, 1985):

- *Consensual sex:* Intercourse that is desired equally by both partners.
- *Altruistic sex:* One partner (usually female) "goes along" because she feels sorry or guilty for her partner.

- *Compliant sex:* One partner (usually female) goes along because she feels that the consequences of refusal would be worse than assenting to sex.
- *Rape:* one partner (usually female) is forced, often by actual or threatened violence, to have sex against her will (Brownmiller, 1986).

As one researcher has observed, between consensual sex and rape lies "a continuum of pressure, threat, coercion, and force" (Kelly, 1987, p. 58). Bart's classification understates the degree to which rape is an act of violence, rather than purely a sexual act. Rape is often carefully preplanned, rather than done on the spur of the moment to satisfy some uncontrollable sexual desire. Many rapes involve beatings, knifings, and even murder. Even when rape leaves no physical wounds, it is a highly traumatic violation of a woman's person that leaves long-lasting psychological scars.

Virtually all rapes are committed by men against women, although men rape other men in prisons and other all-male institutional environments. The most common forms of rape involve either violence or the threat of violence, but neither need be present for rape to occur; what is common to all forms of rape is the lack of consent. At least in principal, "No" means "no" when it comes to sexual relations in most courts of law in the United States.

It is difficult to know with accuracy how many rapes actually occur, since most rapes go unreported. One study estimated that as many as one in four women will be raped in their lifetime (Johnson, 1980). Most rapes are committed by relatives, acquaintances, or partners (Russell, 1984). One three-year study of some 6,200 students in 32 colleges and universities found that more than half of the women had been victims of some form of sexual abuse, including rape (15 percent), attempted rape (12 percent), sexual coercion (12 percent), or unsolicited sexual contact (14 percent). Of those rape attempts that were completed, four out of five female students knew the man who had raped them; two out of three were raped by their dates (Koss et al., 1987).

Strong anti-rape laws are relatively recent in the United States—many states still do not include in the legal definition of rape a husband's unwanted sexual advances toward his wife (see Chapter 14 for further discussion of domestic violence). In fact, the first state to repeal its marital exemption to anti-rape laws, Oregon, did so only in 1977; today, only two states—North Carolina and Oklahoma—still have laws that permit a man to force his wife to have sex against her will. Marital rape is nonetheless common; according to one study, 12 percent of women reported having been raped by their husbands (Finkelhor and Yllo, 1985).

Why Does Rape Occur?

Some writers have claimed that men are socialized to regard women as sex objects; in this view, rape is seen as one outcome of such male socialization (Brownmiller, 1986; Dworkin, 1981, 1987; Griffin, 1979). From seemingly innocent high school locker-room jokes, to TV commercials and magazine ads that depict women as sexually inviting, mindless bodies, to television and movie images equating masculinity with the conquest of women, many men grow up learning to believe that women exist for their pleasure.

The prevalence of "acquaintance rapes" suggests that many men are particularly likely to feel entitled to sexual access if they already know the woman. When a man goes out on a date with sexual conquest on his mind, he may force his attentions on an unwilling partner, overcoming her resistance through the use of alcohol, unrelenting persistence, or both. While such an act may not be legally defined as rape, it would be experienced as such by many if not most women. For example, one study of 19-year-old male undergraduates enrolled in an introductory psychology course found that the man was more likely to regard rape as justified if the woman "led him on" by coming over to his apartment, asking him out, or letting him pay for the date (Muehlenhard et al., 1985).

Such considerations have led Susan Brownmiller (1986) to conclude that the constant threat of rape contributes to a **rape culture,** *one that is the result of male socialization that reinforces male domination by fostering a state of continual fear among women.* One aspect of rape culture is male socialization to a sense of sexual entitlement, which can encourage sexual conquest and promote insensitivity to the difference between consensual and nonconsensual sex (Scully, 1990).

Although some aspects of male socialization may seem to condone and even glamorize rape under certain circumstances, the majority of men do not rape. Men are also socialized into norms and values that define rape as deviant. The existence of such contradictory cultural values, however, may make rape more acceptable to men than would be the case if cultural values were unambiguous. This would explain why rapes are more common when men believe that those norms condemning rape somehow do not apply—for example, with a spouse or date, or in times of war.

Rape as a Political Tool

During the civil war in Bosnia, Serbian soldiers systematically raped Muslim women as part of explicit military policy. In traditional Muslim faith, a family's honor is believed to be tied in part to the chastity of its female members. Unmarried women are severely punished if they do not remain virgins, and all women are expected to dress modestly to the point of completely covering their bodies and much of their faces. Rape, therefore, not only has a devastating impact on the woman who is violated, but it is perceived as a disgrace to the entire family as well. The military use of rape by the Bosnian Serb army was thus calculated to demoralize the Muslim population, in order to more effectively drive them out of the country.

The Serbian soldiers' actions, tragically, were far from unusual. For example, documents obtained from Iraqi sources reveal that some Iraqi prisons have rape rooms, where civil servants are employed to rape female prisoners as a means of coercing information. In 1937, during the infamous "Rape of Nanking," the Japanese army committed an estimated 20,000 acts of rape during the first month it occupied that Chinese city. More recently, after Bangladesh seceded from Pakistan in 1971, Pakistani soldiers were estimated to have raped 200,000 to 400,000 women, almost all of them Muslim (Makiya, 1993).

One instance of mass rape during World War II has recently received attention throughout the world: the tragic case of the so-called *jung-shindae* or "comfort girls," mainly from Korea, who were forced to serve as sex slaves for the Japanese army. As many as 200,000 girls and young women were dragged from their homes and forced to accompany Japanese soldiers, living in huts that served as movable brothels for Japanese troop encampments. These women were forced to have sex at 10 to 30 minute intervals with the Japanese soldiers who lined up outside. Those who resisted were tortured; some were branded with hot irons if they sought to escape. An unknown number died of disease, malnutrition, and suicide; most of those who survived were so shamed by the experience that they refused to speak of it. Only during the last few years has the Japanese government acknowledged that this occurred at all, and apologized to the surviving Korean women and the Korean people for its actions a half century ago (Lee, 1992a, 1992b; *Los Angeles Times,* 1992).

One does not have to turn to war to find examples of the political use of rape. Until 1863, when slavery was outlawed throughout the United States, black women in the southern states legally belonged to their white masters, who were free to sexually possess them as they saw fit. Women who resisted were punished and sometimes tortured. Rape, or the threat of rape, was thus used to keep black women subject to their "owner's" will. Although countless tens of thousands of slave women were forced to have sexual relations against their will, American history has not recorded this as an example of the mass rape of black women by white men. Yet after the Civil War, when the slaves

During World War II, the Japanese army forced as many as 200,000 Korean girls and young women to serve as "sex slaves" for soldiers. These "comfort girls" were repeatedly raped, suffering unspeakable pain, shame, and humiliation. Only recently have the survivors been able to speak out, as in this 1992 demonstration in front of the Japanese embassy in Seoul. Japan has finally admitted responsibility for their actions a half century ago.

were freed, thousands of black men were lynched on the grounds that they had raped or threatened to rape white women. Although rape was virtually unknown among black males at the time, the false belief that black men were sexually insatiable and uncontrollable served as a justification for the lynchings. In this sense, the myth of the black male rapist was used as a political tool to keep the newly freed black men "in their place" through fear of being lynched (Davis, 1981).

Sexual Harassment

Following the guidelines of the Federal Equal Employment Opportunity Commission, **sexual harassment** can be defined as (1) *unwelcome sexual advances, requests for sexual favors, or physical conduct of a sexual nature when such conduct is used as a condition of employment, instruction, evaluation, benefits, or other opportunities;* or (2) *when such conduct interferes with an individual's performance, or contributes to an intimidating, hostile, or offensive environment.*

Sexual harassment typically occurs in a situation of unequal power. It can range from crude and explicit efforts to coerce a clearly unwanted sexual relationship, to subtle innuendos that carry the same meaning. Employers have been found guilty of sexual harassment for fostering unwanted sexual attention on employees; therapists for engaging in sexual relations with their clients; clergy for becoming sexually involved with their parishioners; and faculty for seeking sexual favors in exchange for higher grades.

Sexual harassment occurs at all levels of the workplace, from top executives to the office staff. It is particularly likely to be found in previously male-dominated occupations (Gruber and Bjorn, 1982; Westley, 1982). One study of nearly a thousand female

attorneys in the United States found that three out of five had been harassed; 13 of them had suffered rape, attempted rape, or assault from their supervisors (Couric, 1989). A UCLA study of top female executives at the nation's largest firms found that three out of five had been sexually harassed at work (Brooks, 1993). Among 23,000 female U.S. federal employees at all occupational levels, more than two out of five reported some form of harassment (Stanko, 1985). Studies of other countries confirm that workplace harassment is common throughout the industrialized world. The International Labor Organization (1993; Briscoe, 1993), in a study of working women in 23 industrialized countries, found that up to 30 percent reported "serious, frequent" harassment; more than 8 percent had been harassed out of their jobs.

Sexual harassment is found in schools as well as the workplace. In one study of some 1,600 students from 79 high schools across the country, four out of five students reported having been sexually harassed at least once during all the years they had been at school, mainly by other students. Harassment ranged from unwanted sexual comments to forced sexual activity. Interestingly, only a moderately higher percentage of girls reported being harassed than boys, although girls were harassed more frequently. Sixty-five percent of the girls, and 42 percent of the boys, reported being "touched, grabbed, or pinched in a sexual way." About a quarter of the girls who had been harassed reported that the experience was so distressing it forced them to stay home or cut class, thereby interfering with their studies. The peak period of harassment occurred between sixth and ninth grade, although incidents were reported early in elementary school (AAUW, 1993).

Acts of sexual harassment are increasingly punishable under federal and state laws. The 1991 Civil Rights

Act gave victims of racial, religious, and sexual discrimination (which includes harassment) in the workplace the right to sue their employers for compensation and punishment. Students were given the right to recover damages from school officials in 1992. Many states also have laws prohibiting sexual harassment. Beginning in 1993, for example, California allowed schools to suspend or expel students in grades 4 through 12 who were found guilty of sexually harassing a classmate (Shogren, 1993). At most universities, there are explicit policies regarding harassment, as well as penalties for their violation.

HOMOSEXUALITY

The term "homosexual" was first used by the medical community in 1869 to characterize what was then regarded as a personality disorder. Homosexuality was not removed from the list of mental illnesses until 1973, a long-overdue step that occurred only under prolonged lobbying and pressure on the part of homosexual rights organizations. The medical community was belatedly forced to acknowledge that no scientific research had ever found homosexuals as a group to be psychologically unhealthier than heterosexuals (Burr, 1993).

Homosexuality, Biology, and Social Learning

Most sociologists currently believe that one's sexuality—be it homosexuality or heterosexuality—results from a combination of biological factors and social learning. Since heterosexuality is the norm in American culture, a great deal of recent research has focused on why some people become homosexual. A few scholars have recently argued that biological influences are the most important, predisposing certain people to become homosexual. One source of evidence for this claim consists of studies reporting that many homosexuals "always" felt different, exhibiting a great deal of gender noncomformity even as young children (for example, gay men who played with dolls when young; see Bell et al., 1981; Green, 1987). Other research has focused on presumed physiological differences between homosexuals and heterosexuals, such as differences in brain characteristics (LeVay, 1991; Maugh and Zamichow, 1991) or hormone production (Burr, 1993). All of these studies are inconclusive, both because it is virtually impossible to separate out biological from early social influences, and because studies based on physiological differences are based on an extremely small number of cases.

Yet another avenue of research is based on twin studies. Such studies hold promise for better understanding any genetic basis for homosexuality, since as we noted earlier identical twins share identical genes. In one recent study, Bailey and Pillard (1991, 1993) examined 167 pairs of brothers and 143 pairs of sisters in which at least one sibling defined himself or herself as homosexual (see Table 11.3) Some of these pairs were identical twins (who share all genes), some were fraternal twins (who share some genes), and some were adoptive brothers or sisters (who share no genes). The researchers hypothesized that if sexual orientation is entirely determined by biology, then virtually all of the identical twins should be homosexual: If one member of the pair is genetically homosexual, than the other member should be genetically homosexual as well, if biology determines sexual orientation. Among the fraternal twins, they hypothesized that some (but not all) pairs would be homosexual, since some (but not all) genes are shared. The lowest rates of homosexuality were predicted for the adoptive brothers and sisters.

The results of this study seem to show that homosexuality results from a combination of biological and social factors. Among both men and women, roughly one out of every two identical twins was homosexual, compared with one out of every five fraternal twins, and one out of every ten adoptive brothers and sisters (Bailey and Pillard, 1991, 1993; Maugh, 1991, 1993; Burr, 1993). These results offer some support for the importance of biological factors, since the higher the percentage of shared genes, the greater the likelihood that both siblings would be homosexual. On the other hand, since approximately half of the identical twin brothers and sisters of homosexuals were not themselves homosexual, a great deal of social learning must also be involved; otherwise, one would expect *all* identical twin siblings of homosexuals to be homosexual as well.

Yet even studies of identical twins cannot fully isolate biological from social factors. As we noted in Chapter 7, it is possible that even in infancy identical twins are treated more like one another by parents and peers than are fraternal twins, who in turn are treated more like one another than are adoptive siblings. Infant twins, for example, are often together, sharing similar experiences; when the twins look alike they are even more likely to be dressed identically, and otherwise treated as interchangeable. Thus childhood experiences may well have contributed to the fact that identical twins were more likely than others to share the same sexual orientation.

Homosexuality in the United States

Although it is currently estimated that from 2 to 5 percent of all women in the United States, and 4 to 10 percent of all men, are homosexual (Maugh, 1993; Burr, 1993), these figures are highly contested. First, many homosexuals are reluctant to report on their sexual ori-

Table 11.3   Percentage of Brothers and Sisters Who Are Both Homosexual, When One Member of the Pair Is Homosexual

	Identical twins	Fraternal twins	Adoptive siblings
Brothers (167)	52	22	11
Sisters (143)	48	16	6

Source: Bailey and Pillard (1991, 1993).

entation out of fear of being stigmatized. Second, as noted before, the very notion that "homosexuality" is a discrete category (one either "is" or "isn't") is debatable.

Homosexuals are found in all walks of life, in all cities and towns, in large urban areas as well as rural ones. Homosexuality has long been stigmatized in the United States, and in some states it is still a legally punishable crime. Twenty-four states, for example, outlaw anal intercourse, which is sometimes practiced by homosexual men; nine of these states, in fact, restrict the prohibition exclusively to homosexual anal intercourse. On the other hand, a nearly equal number of states have repealed such laws over the past 30 years (Cohn, 1992).

Homophobia, a term coined in the early 1970s to refer to *a generalized fear and hatred of homosexuals,* is widespread in U.S. culture. One national public opinion survey found that only 41 percent of Americans regarded homosexuality as an acceptable "alternative lifestyle," while barely a third believed that homosexual couples should be allowed to legally marry or adopt children. At the same time, fully 78 percent supported equal rights for homosexuals in job opportunities, suggesting that prejudice against homosexuals is strongest when it comes to family life (Wilson, 1992).

Homosexuality is increasingly depicted on television, in the movies, and on the news. MTV videos show same-sex couples in sexually suggestive activities, while Madonna's book *Sex* contains sexually graphic photographs of her with women as well as men. Movies such as *The Crying Game* and *Philadelphia* feature the lives and struggles of gay men. *Roseanne,* one of the most popular situation comedies on television, has had a lesbian character and *Melrose Place* has a homosexual male couple. Some popular rock stars are open about their same-sex sexual relations (Kopkind, 1993).

Social Movements for Homosexual Rights

Same-sex subcultures have existed throughout history, as far back as ancient Greece and Rome, in Europe dur-

ing the middle ages, and in Renaissance England. Homosexual bars called "Mollyhouses" could be found in England from the nineteenth century onward. Homosexual political organizations date to the middle of the nineteenth century, and continued into the twentieth (Boswell, 1980; Bray, 1982; Plummer, 1984; Bullough, 1976; Adam, 1979, 1987).

Until recently most homosexuals hid their sexual orientation, for fear that "coming out of the closet" would at the very least cause them embarrassment, and more likely cost them their jobs, families, and friends as well. Yet during the past 20 years many homosexuals have acknowledged openly their homosexuality. New York City, San Francisco, and other large metropolitan areas have thriving gay and lesbian subcultures. "Coming out" can be important not only for the person who does so, but for others in the larger society. "Closet" homosexuals come to realize they are not alone, while heterosexuals are forced to recognize that people whom they have admired and respected are homosexual (see Chapter 5, Box 5.2).

The current wave of gay and lesbian rights social movements began partly as an outgrowth of the social movements of the 1960s, which emphasized pride in racial or cultural identity. It was signalled by the Stonewall Riots on June 28, 1969, named for the Greenwich Village gay bar where they occurred (Weeks, 1977; D'Emilio, 1983). In that incident, gays, angered over continual police harassment, actively fought New York City police for two days, a public action that for most people (gay or not) was unthinkable at the time. The Stonewall Riots became a symbol of gay pride, heralding the "coming out" of homosexual men and women who insisted not only on equal treatment under the law, but on the complete end to stigmatization of their lifestyle. As Plummer (1984, p. 242) describes it, "the 1970s witnessed the growth of gay publishing, gay industries, gay bath-houses, gay counseling services, gay switchboards, gay churches, gay trade unions, gay political parties, gay fashion, gay discos, gay everything."

As of 1992, there were an estimated 1,600 gay and lesbian political, social, activist, and student organizations in the United States (Cohn, 1992). The press provided widespread and generally favorable coverage of the April 1993 march on Washington for gay and lesbian rights, attended by crowds estimated at between 300,000 and a million people (Houston, 1993). The previous June, some 200,000 people attended the annual Los Angeles Gay and Lesbian Pride celebration, watching some 5,000 marchers representing more than 250 gay and lesbian groups. Participants included prominent homosexual politicans, "leather contingents," "dykes on bikes," and the West Hollywood Cheerleaders—a group of men cross-dressed as women, sporting beehive hairdos and pompons. Similar parades were held in Boston, Chicago, Dallas, San Francisco and New York City. Such events would have been unthinkable a quarter century ago.

There is also some evidence of a growing backlash against homosexuality. This is due to long-standing homophobia in U.S. culture. As homosexuals have become more open and visible about their sexual orientation, those who fear homosexuality have felt increasingly threatened. But homophobia has also been deliberately fed by right-wing religious organizations that publicly condemn homosexuality as an abomination against God (*New York Native,* 1992). Reported "hate crimes" against homosexuals have increased, with nearly 2,000 incidents of "gay-bashing," fire bombings, and even murder reported in 1992 (Kopkind, 1993; Minkowitz, 1992a, 1992b, 1992c). One study of New York City, Chicago, San Francisco, Minneapolis-Saint Paul, and Boston found an increase in such "hate crimes" of nearly a third between 1990 and 1991 (*New York Times,* 1992). Another study of 500 homosexual New York City teenagers in 1990 found that one in five had been beaten because of their homosexuality (Kirtzman, 1992).

There is also a growing effort to pass antihomosexual legislation across the country. A 1992 Oregon referendum called on voters to classify homosexuality as "abnormal, unnatural, wrong, and perverse," and prevent the state from passing any laws that would protect homosexuals from discrimination. During the course of the campaigning, offices of groups opposing the referendum were repeatedly vandalized. Although the referendum was eventually defeated, two out of five voters supported it. In Colorado a less strident measure, which prohibited the state or any localities from passing laws specifically protecting homosexuals, was approved by the voters, although the measure was subsequently ruled unconstitutional. Although defenders of the measure argued that it simply sought to prevent the state from affording special protections to particular interest groups, homosexuals regarded it as a direct attack on their civil rights. Similar measures are currently under consideration in other states.

At the same time there is also evidence that many Americans are becoming more accepting of homosexuality. *Fortune Magazine* devoted a cover story to a highly sympathetic analysis of being "Gay in Corporate America," concluding that "in the company closet is a big, talented, and scared group of men and women. They want out—and are making the workplace the next frontier for gay rights" (Stewart, 1991). Corporations from Xerox to Pacific Gas and Electric have homosexual employee organizations; AT&T's gay and lesbian association, "League," boasts 20 chapters and 650 members (Noble, 1993).

The April 1993 march on Washington for gay and lesbian rights attracted as many as a million people, reflecting the growing power of the movement for homosexual rights in the United States. Many other cities have had rallies, marches, and demonstrations as well.

GLOBALIZATION AND GENDER INEQUALITY

Globalization has had a major impact on gender relations and equality. We will examine briefly three of these: the feminization of labor in the global economy, women's rights, and gay rights.

Economic Inequality in the Global Workplace

The feminization of labor, both at home and abroad, is one consequence of the emergence of a global economy (Chapters 8 and 9). As U.S. workers are forced to compete with low-wage workers around the world, declining wages and a loss of well-paying manufacturing jobs have helped draw women into the workforce, since it is increasingly difficult for a working-class household to make ends meet with a single breadwinner. At the same time, many of the jobs that have been lost in the United States are now occupied by women around the world, at a fraction of their original wages. The explosive early economic growth of such "newly industrializing countries" as Taiwan, Hong Kong, and Korea during the past two decades has been due in large part to their large pools of inexpensive female labor. Female seamstresses and electronics assemblers in these countries, often paid less than a dollar an hour, have provided Americans with inexpensive clothing, TV sets, computers, and televisions (Henderson and Appelbaum, 1992; Deyo, 1992; Cheng and Hsiung, 1992; Salaff, 1992; Castells, 1992).

In the long run, globalization may result in a higher standard of living for all people. Indeed, this has happened to a large extent in the "newly industrializing countries" of East Asia (Chapter 9). But for the immediate future, the feminization of the global workforce has brought with it the increased exploitation of young, uneducated, largely rural women around the world. These women labor under conditions that are often unsafe and unhealthy, at low pay and with nonexistent job security (see Box 11.3). According to a study by the Washington-based Population Crisis Committee, "over 60 percent of all women and girls in the world live under conditions that threaten their health, deny them choice about childbearing, limit educational attainment, restrict economic participation, and fail to guarantee them equal rights and freedoms with men" (Irwin, 1988).

Women's Rights

Since World War II women throughout the world have made economic and political gains, particularly in the industrializing societies. The spread of birth control technology has made it possible for women to exercise greater control over childbearing, providing them with some degree of choice between raising large families and working outside the home. Yet women have not achieved anything approaching political, economic, legal, or social equality with men. The United Nations Charter calls for equal rights for women, and a UN commission on the Status of Women was established

The global feminization of labor *has meant that many high-wage factory and service jobs in the United States have gone to low-wage women workers in poorer countries throughout the world. While this process is often experienced painfully in the United States, for women elsewhere in the world it has sometimes meant new skills and opportunties. In this photograph, a female mechanic repairs a motor scooter outside the garage where she works in Taipei, Taiwan.*

in 1948. The United Nations even declared 1975–1985 as the decade of the woman. Yet women remain in the poorest-paying industrial and service sector jobs in all countries, and in the less industrialized nations they are concentrated in declining agricultural sectors. Although women have gained increasing access to secondary and even advanced education in much of the world, their ability to achieve specialized education in science, engineering, business, and government has been limited. Women have obtained full legal equality with men only in communist or formerly communist nations, and as we have seen, even in these countries there remains a wide gap between women's legal rights and actual rights (Fox-Genovese, 1993).

Globalization has enabled women to learn quickly from experiences of other women, in countries geographically distant from one another. The experiences

Box 11.3

Globalization

The New Free Trade Heel

The following excerpt from an article in *Harper's Magazine* tells the story of Sadisah, one of thousands of women working in six Indonesian factories that manufacture Nike athletic shoes. The article indicates how a world economy helps to produce a major "gender gap" in earnings across the globe (Ballinger, 1992).

Her only name is Sadisah, and it's safe to say that she's never heard of Michael Jordan. But she *has* heard of the shoe company he endorses, Nike. Sadisah, like Jordan, works on behalf of Nike. You won't see her, however, in the flashy TV images of freedom and individuality that smugly command us to JUST DO IT!—just spend upward of $130 for a pair of basketball shoes. Yet Sadisah is, in fact, one of the people who *is* doing it—making the actual shoes, and earning paychecks in a factory in Indonesia.

In the 1980s, Oregon-based Nike closed its last U.S. footwear factory, in Saco, Maine, while establishing most of its new factories in South Korea, where Sung Hwa Corporation is based. Nike's actions were part of the broader "globalization" trend that saw the United States lose 65,300 footwear jobs between 1982 and 1989 as shoe companies sought nonunionized Third World workers who didn't require the U.S. rubber-shoe industry average of $6.94 an hour. But in the late 1980s, South Korean workers gained the right to form independent unions and to strike. Higher wages ate into Nike's profits. The company shifted new factories to poorer countries such as Indonesia, where labor rights are generally ignored and wages are but one seventh of South Korea's.

Today, to make 80 million pairs of shoes annually, Nike contracts with several dozen factories globally, including six in Indonesia. Others are in China, Malaysia, Thailand, and Taiwan. By shifting factories to cheaper labor pools, Nike has posted year after year of growth; in 1991 the company grossed more than $3 billion in sales— $200 million of which Nike attributes to Jordan's endorsement—and reported a net profit of $287 million, its highest ever. . . .

Sadisah earns $1.03 *per day.* That amount, which works out to just under 14 cents per hour, is less than the Indonesian government's figure for "minimum physical need. . . ." Sadisah's wages allow her to rent a shanty without electricity or running water. The profit margin on each pair is enormous. The cost of labor, to manufacture a pair of Nikes that sells for $80 in the United States, is approximately 12 cents.

Sadisah puts in six days a week, ten and a half hours a per day, for a [monthly] paycheck equivalent to $37.46—about half the retail price of one pair of the sneakers she makes. But how many Western products can people in Indonesia buy when they can't earn enough to eat? The answer can't be found in Nike's TV ads showing Michael Jordan sailing above the earth for his reported multiyear endorsement fee of $20 million—an amount, incidentally, that at the pay rate shown here would take Sadisah 44,492 years to earn.

---

and ideas of North American and European women have led women in other industrialized or industrializing societies to make similar demands for greater equality. Thus, for example, Japanese women educated in the United States have brought their new-found perspectives home with them, seeking to alter traditional attitudes that severely limit the role of women outside the home (Sterngold, 1993). Similarly, when women from the formerly communist nations of Eastern Europe sought to ensure their rights and power in the newly independent republics, they were aided by American female political activists, who raised money for meetings and eventually helped create the Network of East-West Women to exchange ideas (Nadle, 1992). Women who champion economic and political equality go to the same meetings around the world, belong to the same unions and organizations, and generally are able to support one another.

Children have always been an important part of the agricultural labor force. In Pampore, India, these girls are picking saffron flowers to be sold to people who can afford them. Despite some gains in women's status and wages, women remain in the poorest paid jobs, which are often in declining agricultural sectors.

This flow of information and ideas has been a two-way street. As noted above, women of color from Asia, Africa, and Latin America have caused a major rethinking of feminist theories in Europe and North America, as they have sought to develop their own concept of feminism, based in their own cultures rather than the cultural standards of middle-class white feminists (Mohanty et al., 1991).

For example, at the 1980 UN conference on women in Copenhagen, a great deal of debate occurred over the practice of clitoridectomies, a painful ritual form of female genital circumcision in which the clitoris (and sometimes the vaginal labia) are removed. This practice, which affects as many as a hundred million African and Middle Eastern women, was roundly condemned by feminists from Europe and the United States as a backward practice that revealed how men controlled and exploited the bodies of women throughout the world. African and Middle Eastern feminists, while opposing clitoridectomies, called on their European and American counterparts to better understand the cultural meaning of the practice and to focus their condemnation on the numerous other ways in which African women are exploited—including as cheap labor for European and American businesses (El Dareer, 1982; Lightfoot-Klein, 1989; El Sadaawi, 1980, 1983; Gilliam, 1991; Mohanty, 1991; Johnson-Odim, 1991).

The global changes of recent years have brought mixed results for women. The collapse of communism in the former Soviet Union and Eastern Europe brought with it a decline in many of the rights that women enjoyed under the former regimes. Although women had been central activists in many of the revolutions that toppled the communist governments, once the dust had settled they typically found themselves relegated to the sidelines by male politicians. Whereas under communism women had been legally guaranteed 20 to 25 percent of the seats in governing bodies, with democratic elections in countries like Bulgaria and Czechoslovakia they typically found their numbers reduced to under 5 percent. Paid maternity leave and day care were no longer provided under many of the reform governments, and worsening economic conditions meant that women increasingly were pushed out of the workforce as well. The rise of nationalism in the former Yugoslavia has meant that women more and more are called upon to play traditional roles as wives and mothers (Nadle, 1993). One can predict with certainty that traditional male dominance will have to be strongly challenged for women to gain significantly greater economic, political, and social equality in the immediate future.

Homosexual Rights

Globalization also has contributed to a growing international movement for the rights of homosexuals (International Lesbian and Gay Association, 1992). Gay rights movements are reported in more than 80 countries, and 50 countries now have newspapers that serve their homosexual communities. Nevertheless, 68 countries still outlaw sex between males, and 26 outlaw sex between women.

There are enormous differences in the degree of legalized homosexual discrimination between countries. In Africa, for example, male homosexual acts have been legalized in only 2 countries; they are explicitly outlawed in 22. (Female homosexuality is seldom mentioned in the law at all.) In South Africa, the official policy of the former white government was that homosexuality is a psychiatric problem that threatens national security; the black African National Congress called for full equality. In Asia and the Middle East, the situation is similar; male homosexuality is banned in 15 countries, while it is legal in 4. The predominantly Muslim countries outlaw homosexuality, and in Iran, which adheres to strict interpretation of Islamic law, homosexuality is punishable by death. Israel, on the other hand, completely bans discrimination against homosexuals, including in its highly effective armed forces, where virtually everybody—including homosexuals and women—is required to serve.

Europe has some of the most liberal laws in the world, with male homosexuality legalized in 28 countries, and female homosexuality in 23. Denmark legally recognizes same-sex marriages. The collapse of communism in the former Soviet Union may portend an easing of restrictions against homosexuals; in 1992, for example, Russian President Boris Yeltsin asked his legislature to end the long-standing criminal ban on "male love" (Gonzales, 1992).

On June 26, 1994, the twenty-fifth anniversary of the Stonewall Riots, a hundred thousand people attended the International March on the United Nations to Affirm the Human Rights of Lesbian and Gay People. The march, organized by the International Lesbian and Gay Association, called upon the United Nations to extend the Universal declaration of Human Rights to gays and lesbians. The United Nations was urged to take a number of specific actions aimed at ending discrimination against homosexuals around the world, in a growing effort by homosexuals to establish their universal right to the same guarantees of equality as other groups. Through such actions, made visible by global media, homosexuals have extended their long march out of the closet from a handful of cities in the industrial world to the far reaches of the planet.

CHAPTER SUMMARY

1. **Sex** refers to biological differences between males and females, while **gender** refers to differences that are socially learned. Gender is not determined by a person's biological sex, and much of what *feels* like biology is actually cultural.

2. Although the normative **sexual orientation** in all cultures is **heterosexuality, homosexuality** is also common, and other possibilities exist as well for human **sexuality**.

3. The United States has a strong undercurrent of restrictive norms and values regarding sexuality, although somewhat greater permissiveness has occurred in recent years.

4. Although functionalist sociological theorists have long regarded prevailing **gender roles** as functional for society, during the past two decades proponents of **feminism** have challenged the traditional views.

5. **Gender roles** are learned through social interaction with others. Early family influences, peer pressure, mass media, and the **hidden curriculum** in schools are especially important sources of gender socialization.

6. Children begin to learn culturally appropriate masculine and feminine **gender identities** as soon as they are born, and these roles are reinforced and renegotiated throughout life.

7. **Sexism** helps to support **patriarchy,** any set of social relations in which women are treated as inferior to men, resulting in their subordinate economic position and political power.

8. Gender inequality is pervasive in the workplace. Although the **feminization of labor** has resulted in a substantial increase in the number of women in the paid workforce, women typically occupy lower-paying occupations than men, and are paid less than men when they hold similar jobs.

9. Women do more housework than men in all industrial societies, even when they have paid employment outside the home.

10. Violence against women, including **rape,** is partly the result of male socialization and popular culture. In some countries rape has been used as a political tool and wartime strategy.

11. In the United States it is estimated that some 2 to 5 percent of all women and 4 to 10 percent of all men are homosexual. Although homosexuals have become increasingly open about their sexual orientation in recent years, homophobia remains strong in American society.

12. Globalization has resulted in the feminization of labor in the global economy, as well as an increasingly unified global struggle for women's rights. The movement for homosexual rights has also become increasingly globalized in recent years.

QUESTIONS FOR DISCUSSION

1. Discuss the difference between sex and gender. To what extent is gender identity biologically based? To what extent is it socially constructed? How do people come to acquire their gender identities?

2. In what ways is gender inequality found in the workplace? Discuss the "triple oppression" that affects lower-income women of color, and show how it operates in the economic sphere.

3. To what extent has gender inequality decreased in American society in recent years? How do you account for this trend?

4. What is the difference between consensual and nonconsensual sex? Under what circumstances might a man regard sex as consensual, and a woman regard it as rape?

5. What are some similarities and differences between the contemporary movements for women's rights and homosexual rights?

6. Discuss the impact of globalization on gender inequality. To what extent has globalization increased inequality? To what extent has it reduced it? What do you think are the prospects for the next quarter century?

KEY TERMS

bisexuality: Sexual desire for persons of both sexes.

feminism: The belief that social equality should exist between the sexes.

feminization of labor: The growing proportion of women in the workforce, often in the lowest-paying jobs.

gender: Behavioral differences between males and females that are culturally based and socially learned.

gender factory: A term used by sociologists to characterize the function of the home in reproducing society's traditional gender roles.

gender identity: The ways in which individuals in a particular culture come to think of themselves as male or female, and learn to act accordingly.

gender role: Normative expectations concerning appropriately "masculine" or "feminine" behavior in a particular culture.

glass ceiling: A seemingly invisible barrier to movement into the very top positions in business and government, which makes it difficult for some women to reach the top of their professions.

heterosexuality: sexual attraction or desire for persons of the opposite sex.

hidden curriculum: The unspoken socialization to norms, values, and roles that occurs in the classroom (see Chapter 5).

homophobia: A generalized fear and hatred of homosexuals.

homosexuality: Sexual desire for persons of one's own sex.

liberal feminism: A stream of feminist thought holding that women's inequality is primarily the result of

imperfect institutions, which can be corrected by reforms that do not fundamentally alter society itself.

multicultural feminism: A stream of feminist thought focusing on understanding and ending inequality for all women, regardless of race, class, nationality, age, sexual orientation, or other characteristics.

patriarchy: Any set of social relationships in which men dominate women.

radical feminism: A stream of feminist thought holding that women's inequality is fundamental to all other systems of inequality, including economic.

rape: The forcing of nonconsensual vaginal, oral, or anal intercourse.

rape culture: A culture resulting from male socialization that reinforces male domination by fostering a state of continual fear among women.

second shift: A phrase used by sociologists to characterize the unpaid housework that women typically do after they come home from their paid employment.

sex: Anatomical or other biological differences between males and females that originate in the human gene.

sexism: The belief that one sex is innately inferior, and therefore its domination is warranted.

sexual harassment: According to the guidelines of the Federal Equal Employment Opportunity Commission any behavior that entails (1) unwelcome sexual advances, requests for sexual favors, or physical conduct of a sexual nature when such conduct is used as a condition of employment, instruction, evaluation, benefits, or other opportunities; or (2) when such conduct interferes with an individual's performance, or contributes to an intimidating, hostile, or offensive environment.

sexual orientation: A person's desire or attraction for a sexual partner of a particular sex.

sexuality: The ways in which people construct their erotic or sexual relationships, including norms governing sexual behavior.

socialist (or Marxist) feminism: A stream of feminist thought holding that women's inequality is largely the result of capitalistic economic relations that must be fundamentally transformed before women can achieve equality.

stratification: Systematic inequalities of wealth, power, and prestige that result from a person's social rank (see Chapter 8).

tokenism: A situation in which highly successful women are seen as representing all women, rather than as individuals.

transsexuality: A sexual orientation that involves identification with persons of the opposite sex.

triple oppression: The extreme discrimination and inequality that is sometimes experienced by lower-income women of color.

R E C O M M E N D E D   F O R   F U R T H E R   R E A D I N G

Faludi, Susan. (1991). *Backlash: The Undeclared War Against Women.* New York: Crown.

A probing and troubling examination of the many forms of discrimination, inequality, and violence practiced against women.

Fausto-Sterling, Anne. (1985). *Myths and Gender: Biological Theories About Women and Men.* New York: Basic Books.

An examination of the biological bases for gender differences.

Goldscheider, Frances, and Linda Waite. (1991). *New Families, No Families: The Transformation of the American Home.* Berkeley: University of California Press.

This study followed thousands of younger and older "baby boomers" over a 15 year period, examining changing patterns of divorce and remarriage, single-parent families, gender roles within the family, and a trend toward the sacrifice of family for career.

Mohanty, Chandra Talpade, Ann Russo and Lourdes Torres (eds.). (1991). *Third World Women and the Politics of Feminism.* Bloomington: Indiana University Press.

A collection of feminist essays by women writers from the non-Western world, some highly critical of what they perceive as the Eurocentric bias in much feminist thinking.

Aging

CHAPTER OUTLINE

THINGS TO LOOK FOR

1. In what ways can aging be said to be a social rather than a biological process?
2. In what ways is America "graying," and what impact is this likely to have on future generations?
3. What are the principal sociological theories about aging in modern society?
4. Why are many of the popular stereotypes about the elderly unlikely to be true?
5. What is the impact of globalization on the role of the elderly in countries around the world?

INTRODUCTION: TURNING 100 WAS THE WORST BIRTHDAY OF MY LIFE

Sarah and Elizabeth Delany—"Sadie" and "Bessie" —turned 103 and 101 in 1993, the year their autobiography, *Having Our Say,* was published. Their father was born into slavery, and the two women grew up in a south in which blacks were rigidly segregated from whites and lynchings were commonplace. During their twenties, they moved north, joining more than a hundred thousand other blacks who settled in New York City's Harlem. There, surrounded by a Renaissance of black culture, both earned degrees at Columbia University, Sadie as a teacher and Bessie as a dentist. Their lives, which span a century of often-turbulent American history, encompassed the civil rights and women's movements, times of enormous change in the roles of women and minorities.

Fiercely independent, the two women still care for themselves in their shared home in New York City. In the following excerpts from their book (Delany and Delany, 1993, pp. 205, 208), Bessie and Sadie reflect on what it means to them to grow old:

Now, honey, I get the blues sometimes. It's a shock to me to be this old. Sometimes when I realize I am 101 years old it hits me right between the eyes. I say, "Oh Lord, how did this happen?" Turning 100 was the worst birthday of my life. I wouldn't wish it on my worst enemy. Turning 101 was not so bad. Once you're past that century mark, it's just not as shocking.

There's just a few things I have had to give up. I gave up driving a while back. I guess I was in my late eighties. That was terrible. Another thing I gave up was cutting back my trees so we have a view of the New York City skyline to the south. Until I was 98 years old, I would climb up on the ladder and saw those tree branches off so we had a view. I could do it perfectly well; why pay somebody to do it? Then Sadie talked some sense into me, and I gave up doing it.

Some days I feel as old as Moses and other days I feel like a young girl. I tell you what: I only have a little bit of arthritis in my pinky finger, and my eyes aren't so bad, so I know I could still be practicing dentistry. Yes, I am sure I could still do it.

Elizabeth ("Bessie") and Sarah ("Sadie") Delany were 103 and 101 years old when their best-selling autobiography was published in 1993. The sisters, who share a home in New York City, are highly independent. Their lives have encompassed Jim Crow laws and lynchings in the south, the "Harlem Renaissance," successful careers (Bessie as a dentist, Sadie as a teacher), and the civil rights and women's movements. Like a growing number of elderly people, they continue to live full and rewarding lives.

But it's hard being old, because you can't always do everything you want, exactly as *you* want it done. When you get as old as we are, you have to struggle to hang onto your freedom, your independence.—*Bessie Delany, age 101*

You know, when you are this old, you don't know if you're going to wake up in the morning. But I don't worry about dying, and neither does Bessie. We are at peace. You do kind of wonder, when's it going to happen? That's why you learn to love each and every day, child.—*Sadie Delany, age 103*

Growing old can be a fulfilling and rewarding experience, as it is with the Delany sisters. Or it can be filled with physical distress and social isolation. For most elderly Americans, the experience of aging lies somewhere in between, although more and more people today are leading active and satisfying lives as they grow old. In this chapter we shall examine the nature of aging in American society, exploring what it means to grow old in a world that is rapidly changing.

Table 12.1 The Median Age of the U.S. Population: Steady Increases into the Next Century

Date	Median Age (years)
1850	18.9
1860	19.4
1870	20.2
1880	20.9
1890	22.0
1900	22.9
1910	24.1
1920	25.3
1930	26.4
1940	29.0
1950	30.2
1960	29.5
1970	28.0
1980	30.0
1990	32.8
1991	33.1
1995	34.3
2000	35.7
2025	38.5
2050	39.3

Source: U.S. Bureau of the Census

THE GRAYING OF AMERICAN SOCIETY

Modern agriculture, sanitation systems, epidemic control, and medicine all have contributed to a decline in mortality throughout world. In most societies today, fewer children die in infancy, and more adults survive to achieve the status of elderly. These processes are much more pronounced in industrial societies such as the United States, which also experience low birthrates and hence relatively few children as well (see Chapter 20). As a result, the United States and other industrial societies are said to be **graying,** an *increase in the proportion of the population becoming elderly.* The average American newborn male today can expect to live to age 72; for female newborns, the figure is 79. (By way of comparison, the average life expectancy for men and women in most African countries is around 50, dropping to 40 in the poorest nations.)

The percentage of the American population over 65 has grown rapidly, from 4 percent a century ago to nearly 13 percent today. It is forecast to reach about 21 percent by the year 2030, totaling some 60 million people. The percentage of very elderly people 85 and older will nearly double, to 2.5 percent of the population (U.S. Bureau of the Census, 1991; Fosler et al., 1990; Clark, 1993). There are, however, significant racial and ethnic differences in the "graying" of the American population.

In 1850 half of the American population was under 18.9 years old. The median age has nearly doubled since that time, and today it is estimated at 34.3 years. By the middle of the next century it is forecast to be nearly 40 (Table 12.1). During the past decade, the median age of the U.S. population as a whole has increased 2.8 years (Figure 12.1). Whites have shown the largest increase (3.6 years), while Asians have increased the least (1.6 years). Hispanics, blacks and American Indians are intermediate. These increases in the median age for each racial and ethnic group are seen also in the proportion that are elderly (Table 12.2). Whites have by far the largest proportion; more than 14 percent of all whites are over 65, and 1.4 percent are over 85—between two and three times the percentages of all other groups except blacks (U.S. Bureau of the Census, 1993).

The "graying" of the American population is thus occurring most rapidly among whites, who have long life spans and relatively few children. Hispanics are "graying" the least, partly because this category includes many young immigrant workers with large families. We will explore some of the implications of these trends below, when we discuss the politics of aging.

Figure 12.1 **The "Graying" of the American Population, by Race and Ethnicity: Median Age, 1981 and 1991**

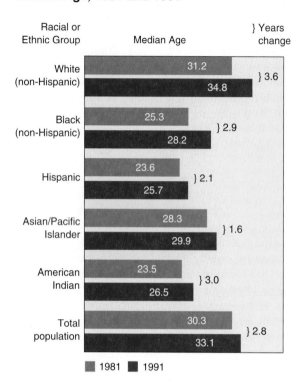

■ 1981　■ 1991

During the past decade, the median age (half are older, half are younger) has increased 2.8 years for the population as a whole, to 33.1 years. But this obscures important differences by race and ethnicity. Whites have "grayed" the most (3.6 years), and remain the oldest category by far (34.8 years). Asians have "grayed" the least (1.6 years) but are the second oldest group. American Indians and blacks have "grayed" similarly (roughly 3 years), although the Indian population remains younger on average than the black population. Hispanics, like Asians, have "grayed" relatively little and as a group are the youngest Americans (25.7 years). *Source:* U.S. Bureau of the Census (1993).

SOCIOLOGICAL PERSPECTIVES ON AGING

Aging can be sociologically defined as *the combination of biological, psychological, and social processes that affect people as they grow older* (Atchley, 1991; Riley, Foner, and Waring, 1988; Abeles and Riley, 1987). These three processes suggest the metaphor of three different although interrelated developmental "clocks:" (1) a biological one, which refers to the physical body; (2) a psychological one, which refers to the mind and mental capabilities; and (3) a social one, which refers to cultural norms, values, and role expectations having to do with age. There is an enormous range of variation in all three of these processes, as will be shown below. Our notions about the meaning of age are rapidly changing, both because recent research is dispelling many myths about aging, and because advances in nutrition and health have enabled many people to live longer, healthier lives than ever before.

It is important not to confuse the sociological meaning of age with the notion of **chronological age,** *the length of time a person has been alive.* Two individuals of identical chronological age may be very different from one another in biological, psychological, and social terms. Enormous differences exist between people of the same age, and the one generalization that can be made for certain about the elderly is that they are a highly heterogeneous group. As we shall see, social factors play a major role in shaping not only the psychological and social effects of aging, but the biological effects as well (Abeles and Riley, 1987). Chronological age is important primarily for official classification purposes. For example, the U.S. government defines people as "elderly" at age 65, at which time most people are expected to retire, becoming eligible for retirement benefits. This is a largely arbitrary number that has little to do with a person's competence,

Table 12.2 Percent of Population over 65 and over 85, for Different Racial and Ethnic Groups, 1991

Racial or Ethnic Group	Over Age 65(%)	Over Age 85(%)
White (non-Hispanic)	14.3	1.4
Black (non-Hispanic)	8.3	0.8
Asian/Pacific Islander	6.2	0.4
American Indian	6.0	0.5
Hispanic	5.2	0.4
Total population	12.5	1.2

Source: U.S. Bureau of the Census (1993).

effectiveness, or health. Although the use of such an arbitrary standard serves a bureaucratic function in modern society, it also can have the effect of marginalizing older people who are healthy, active, and capable of productive work (Atchley, 1991).

In examining the nature of aging in the United States as well as other societies, we will draw on the studies of **social gerontology,** a discipline concerned with the *study of the social aspects of aging.* The study of social gerontology is complicated by the fact that even as people grow older, society itself is changing. In particular, culturally defined values, norms, and roles regarding age themselves change over time, so that studying the process of aging is a bit like studying something that will not stand still (Riley, Foner, and Waring, 1988).

For example, Americans born in the 1910s grew up in a world where the average newborn baby could expect to live less than 55 years (Weeks, 1992), where a high school education was considered more than sufficient for most available jobs, and where "old age" often meant infirmity and disengagement from active work. Today, those very same people find themselves in their eighties, living in a world that differs dramatically from the one for which they were socialized. Among these differences are societal expectations concerning the elderly. The same is true for young people today. If you are a recently graduated high school student, you may think it reasonable to look to your grandparents for some idea about what your life will be like in the mid-twenty-first century, when you find yourself in your seventies. By that time, however, society will be very different than it is today. The role of the elderly will have changed, and you will have a hand in changing it.

Biological Aging

There are well-established biological effects of aging, although the exact chronological age at which they become apparent varies greatly from individual to individual, depending on genetics, lifestyle, and luck.

In general, for men and women alike, aging brings with it lowered physical viability and greater vulnerability to illness and disease (Atchley, 1991). Among the most obvious early manifestations of advanced age is a loss of skin elasticity, resulting in wrinkles. Muscle mass eventually decreases and overall muscle tone declines, resulting in less strength, slower response time, and longer recovery from exertion. Overall cardiovascular efficiency drops, and although this can be compensated somewhat by exercise, even among trained older athletes less oxygen can be inhaled and utilized during exercise than when they were younger. Hearing and eyesight also normally decline. For most people, however, such physical changes do not significantly prevent them from leading active, independent lives even well into their eighties. Eventually, of course, the biological clock runs out for everyone; 90 to 100 years seems to be the upper end of the genetically determined age distribution for most human beings (Atchley, 1991; Craig, 1980; Buskirk, 1985; Whitbourne, 1985).

Even though the overwhelming majority of older Americans today suffer no significant physical impairment and remain physically active, unfortunate stereotypes about the "weak and frail elderly" continue to exist and can become self-fulfilling prophecies (Heise, 1987). This is due more to the social than biological meaning of aging in American culture, with its preoccupation with youthfulness and corresponding fears about growing old and dying (Parsons, 1960). Women

Growing old chronologically does not mean a person cannot engage in physical activities. Whether it be a weekend hike, a daily walk, tennis, or competing in a triathlon, "senior citizens" today are challenging traditional American notions about what it means to be "old." These older surfers continue to enjoy the vigorous sport of their youth.

in particular suffer from these cultural expectations, since the preoccupation with being "forever young" applies with more force to women than to men (see Chapter 11). Yet the eternally youthful features of film and television stars are not only the result of lucky genes, healthy diet, obsessive exercise, and subtle hair coloring. They can often be traced to cosmetic medical procedures as well: repeated facelifts, which tighten sagging skin and remove wrinkles; expensive dental work; "tummy tucks," liposuction, and other surgical techniques for removing fat where it is not wanted; and breast implants and lip injections to alter appearance according to current standards of attractiveness.

Although the normal processes of aging cannot be avoided, they can be partly compensated and offset by good health, proper diet and nutrition, and a reasonable amount of exercise (John, 1988). Lifestyle can make a significant health difference for people of all ages. Today there are many people over 60 running in foot races, riding mountain bikes, and competing in tennis. In fact, only about one in five noninstitutionalized people over 65 are classified as having a severe disability requiring the assistance of others (Atchley, 1991). In terms of physical performance, the overlap between old and young is potentially great, particularly as older people in our society become more aware of the possibilities for long-term health and physical performance, while younger people shun exercise in favor of television viewing and junk food addiction.

Psychological Aging

The psychological effects of aging are much less well-established than the physical effects. Even though such things as memory, learning, intelligence, skills, and motivation to learn are widely assumed to decline with age, research into the psychology of aging suggests a much more complicated process (Birren and Cunningham, 1985; Schaie, 1984). Memory and learning, for example, need not decline with age for most people; less than a quarter of people 85 or older report frequent memory problems. On the other hand, the speed with which one recalls or analyzes information may slow somewhat, giving the false impression of mental impairment. Similarly, purely mental problem-solving abilities do not necessarily decline, unless they require physical dexterity to perform: An elderly person with slower physical reflexes obviously would appear impaired on a mental problem-solving test requiring that a button be instantly pushed to indicate the right answer. For the large majority of elderly people, such mental capabilities as motivation to learn, clarity of thought, and problem-solving capacity are less related to chronological age than social circumstances. For elderly people whose lives are stimulating and rich, such mental abilities do not appear to decline significantly until the late eighties (Atchley, 1991; Abeles and Riley, 1987; Schaie, 1979; Craik, 1977; Kohn and Schooler, 1982, 1983; Schooler, 1987; Baltes and Schaie, 1977; Craig, 1980; Arenberg and Robertson-Tchabo, 1980; Cutler and Grams, 1988).

Social Aging

Social age consists of the *norms, values, and roles that are culturally associated with a particular chronological age.* Ideas about social age differ between societies, and, at least in modern industrial societies,

As this photograph of a beauty shop in a California retirement home suggests, concern with appearance is found in all age groups. Since American culture places a premium on looking "forever young," as people grow older they may feel stigmatized by changes in their appearance associated with the normal effects of physical aging. Today's elusive search for the "fountain of youth" encompasses everything from creams and lotions to costly cosmetic surgery.

Cultural attitudes toward the elderly can differ substantially across societies. In traditional societies elders are often revered for their knowledge and perspective on life. The attentiveness of this young girl in Baños, Ecuador, as she combs her grandmother's hair, reflects a high degree of respect for the elderly in that society.

change over time as well. Social age is not a simple function of a person's chronological age; rather, it is constructed within a particular culture. One society may revere elderly people, regarding them as a source of historical memory and wisdom; another may dismiss them as nonproductive, dependent people who are out of step with the times.

To better take into account age-related aspects of social roles, sociologists and social psychologists have developed the notion of the **life course,** *a sequence of different roles a person is expected to assume during chronological aging.* For example, one sequence of roles associated with a "typical" American life includes infant, toddler, child, teenager, young adult, middle age, late maturity, and old age. This sequence is paralleled by other sequences having to do with educational, occupational, and family roles (Atchley, 1991). Although much scholarly effort has gone into identifying "typical" patterns of development over the life course, most people are far from "typical." Patterns of social aging vary widely. They differ by gender, race, and ethnicity, and they change over time (Atchley, 1991; Riley, Foner, and Waring, 1988). One study, for example, tracked a national sample of nearly 14,000 male and female high school graduates for eight years, reporting that the "typical" life course was followed by less than half of their sample (Rindfuss, Swicegood, and Rosenfeld, 1987).

Role expectations are extremely important sources of personal identity (Chapters 4 and 5). Social roles associated with aging are likely to take on particular importance, since there is no escaping them: although we can change many other roles, we cannot avoid growing older. Some of the roles associated with aging in

American society are positive, but others can be damaging, leading to lowered self-esteem and isolation. Like all people, the elderly are not simply the passive incumbents of their social roles, but active participants helping to shape and redefine them (Riley, Foner, and Waring, 1988). Later in this chapter, when we discuss aging and inequality, different social roles for the elderly in American society will be examined.

Retirement

The idea of a fixed age at which a person retires from paid employment is a relatively recent invention of industrial society (Falk et al., 1981; Townsend, 1981). In preindustrial societies, life ordinarily revolved around the household, and the elderly had little difficulty finding such useful things to do as helping with the cleaning and cooking, telling stories, or participating in religious rituals. In industrial society, where work and family are separate, retirement from the workforce has meant removal from those activities that have long provided a sense of being productive and useful. As noted above, the "official" age of retirement in the United States is 65, and fewer than a fifth of all people work past this age (U.S. Senate Special Committee on Aging, 1986).

Many people manage this transition well, even eagerly. Surveys of older adults report that the large majority feel favorably about their own retirement, women even more so than men. Those who are financially secure are especially likely to view retirement in positive terms (Atchley, 1991). Furthermore, research into aging claims that retirement has positive psychological and even physical effects on most retirees. Although it is often claimed that retiring from a lifelong

Nursing homes provide care for the infirm, but most retirement homes simply afford an opportunity for the elderly to share companionship while easing the burden of maintaining an independent home. Living in a retirement home can be costly, however, and thus is not an option available to everyone.

job can lead to depression and poor physical health, there is no evidence that this is the case. Retirement produces neither adverse physical nor mental consequences for the vast majority of retirees, and in fact may be associated with higher morale and greater happiness (Crowley, 1985; Palmore et al., 1985; Howard et al., 1986). Even social isolation does not typically increase with retirement, although it is higher for the fifth of all elderly men and half of all elderly women who are widowed (Parnes, 1985; Kunkel, 1989; U.S. Senate Special Committee on Aging, 1986).

SOCIOLOGICAL EXPLANATIONS OF AGING

Social gerontologists have offered a number of theories regarding the nature of aging in American society. Some of the earlier theories emphasized individual adaptation to changing social roles as a person grows older. More recent theories focus on the ways in which society shapes the social roles of the elderly, often in inequitable ways.

Functionalist Theories of Aging

The functionalist approach to aging emphasizes individual adjustment to changing social roles and the ways the roles of the elderly are useful to society. These theories, which were predominant in the 1950s and 1960s, assume that aging brings with it physical and psychological decline, and that changing social roles have to take such decline into account (Hendricks, 1992).

Talcott Parsons, one of the preeminent functionalist theorists of the 1950s, argued that American society needs to find roles for the elderly consistent with advanced age. He expressed concern that America, with its emphasis on youth and its avoidance of death, has failed to provide roles that adequately draw on the potential wisdom and maturity of a society's elders. Moreover,

given the "graying" of American society that was evident even in Parson's time, such failure could well lead to older people becoming discouraged and alienated from society. In order to achieve a "healthy maturity," Parsons argued, the elderly need to adjust psychologically to their changed circumstances, while society needs to redefine the social roles of the elderly. Old roles (such as work) have to be abandoned, while new forms of productive activity need to be identified (Parsons, 1960).

Parson's ideas anticipated those of **disengagement theory,** the notion that *elderly people should progressively pull back from social roles, freeing up those roles for others while preparing themselves for their eventual death* (Cumming and Henry, 1961; Estes, Binney, and Culbertson, 1992). According to this perspective, the increasing frailty, illness, and dependency of elderly people leads them to progressively disengage from society: They retire from their job, pull back from civic life, and eventually withdraw from other activities as well. Disengagement is assumed to be functional for the elderly because it enables them to assume less taxing roles consistent with their advancing age and declining health. It is assumed to be functional for the larger society because it opens up roles formerly taken by the elderly to younger people, who hopefully can fulfill them with fresh energy and new skills.

The idea that elderly people should completely disengage from the larger society took for granted the prevailing stereotypes about frail, dependent aged. Yet no sooner did the theory appear when these very assumptions began to be challenged, often by some of the theory's original proponents (Hendricks, 1992; Cumming, 1963, 1975; Henry, 1965; Maddox, 1965, 1970; Hochschild, 1975). The challenges to disengagement theory, in turn, gave rise to another theory, which draws the opposite conclusion. According to **activity theory,** *active people are more likely to lead fulfilling and productive lives, benefiting society as well as themselves.*

Activity theory regards aging as a normal part of human development and argues that elderly people can best serve themselves and society by remaining active. The theory found support in research showing that continued activity well into old age is associated with enhanced mental and physical health (Conner et al., 1985; Rowe and Kahn, 1987; Schaie, 1983; Birren and Bengston, 1988; Butler et al., 1980; Palmore, 1979; U.S. Bureau of the Census, 1994).

Critical Assessment Although few today would question the notion that elderly people should remain as active and engaged as possible, critics of functionalist theories of aging argue that such theories emphasize individual adaptation to existing conditions, rather than questioning whether society is producing conditions that are inequitable or unjust (Hendricks, 1992). What if society is not providing the sorts of roles that are most satisfying to the elderly, roles that draw on their particular strengths? A major challenge to functionalist theories of aging occurred during the 1970s and 1980s, when new theories looked at the ways in which American society allocated unequal social roles to its older members.

Social Conflict Theories of Aging

Unlike functionalist theories, social conflict theories emphasize the ways in which society produces inequities. According to conflict theory, problems of aging are related to other sources of inequality in society, including those based on class, gender, race, and ethnicity. All are seen as systematically produced through the routine operation of social institutions.

According to the conflict view, the elderly are struggling to get a share of society's scarce resources. Conflict theory points to the impact of globalization on a shrinking U.S. job base (see Chapter 8), with its potential to pit old against young in the competition for scarce jobs. Potential conflict is fueled by federal budget cutbacks, leading all social groups (including those based on age) to compete with one another for diminishing federal dollars. Conflict theorists further emphasize the impact of gender, race, and class on aging, pointing out that even among the elderly those who fare worst are women, low-income people, and minorities (Atchley, 1991; Estes et al., 1984; Estes, 1991; Estes, Swan, and Gerard, 1982; Estes, 1986; Hendricks and Hendricks, 1986; Hendricks, 1992; McKinlay, 1975).

Critical Assessment Conflict theories of aging have been criticized for overemphasizing the ways in which society structures opportunities for the elderly, often depicting them as hapless victims of larger social forces. In an effort to redress this imbalance, social gerontologists have come to look at the elderly as political actors who help to create the very social institutions that shape their lives. We shall turn to this topic below, when we discuss the politics of aging (Hendricks, 1992; Hendricks and Hendricks, 1986; Dannefer, 1989).

There was a time in the United States when older people were expected to become inactive. This role expectation has changed, and many older people now volunteer to participate in social services, such as this man holding an ill child in the hospital where he is volunteering his services.

GOVERNMENT SUPPORT FOR THE ELDERLY: MEDICARE AND SOCIAL SECURITY

Until the appearance of modern industrial society, the family was the principal source of financial and emotional support for the elderly. In the United States as in other industrial societies, however, a great deal of the financial burden has become the responsibility of government. The two principal governmental programs that provide financial support for the elderly are Medicare (instituted in 1965) and Social Security (instituted in 1935). The full benefits of Medicare and Social Security are available at age 65, although partial benefits are available to some people a few years earlier.

Social Security and Medicare are financed out of workers' payroll deductions, employer contributions, and taxes on those who are self-employed. Working Americans pay into these programs today, so they can draw on them when they are no longer able to earn a living. By providing a degree of economic support for the elderly, such programs also make it economically possible to retire; in the absence of the economic security such programs provide, elderly people would be under greater economic pressure to continue working as long as they were physically capable.

Medicare, which pays for acute medical costs for the elderly, reached some 35 million people in 1991, at a total cost of $114 billion. Social Security provides retirement pay for all elderly persons who have worked a minimal number of months during their lives and contributed a portion of their paycheck (typically matched by their employer) into a government fund. The program benefited some 40 million individuals in 1991, at a cost of about $264 billion. Most of these were retirees over 65, but some younger retirees and dependents of deceased workers received benefits as well (U.S. Social Security Administration, 1992).

Monthly benefits under Social Security depend in part on earnings prior to retirement. The maximum monthly payment is currently about $1,900, for those whose preretirement earnings exceeded $55,000. Those with earnings under $10,200 receive a monthly stipend of only $722, while the average stipend is about $1,450. Since retired women are less likely than men to have had continuous paid employment throughout their lives, their retirement income averages only slightly over half that of men (U.S. Social Security Administration, 1992; Belgrave, 1988).

Social Security and Medicare have been extremely important in lifting many elderly people out of poverty. In 1970, before Medicare was fully implemented and Social Security benefits had been increased to their present levels, one-quarter of all people over 65 lived in poverty—twice today's rate (U.S. Bureau of the Census, 1993). Yet even today, those who depend solely on this source of retirement income are likely to live modestly at best. For the typical retiree, Social Security accounts for only about 40 percent of income; most of the remainder comes from investments, private pension funds, and earnings. Low-income households, on the other hand, are likely to rely heavily on Social Security, which accounts for as much as three-quarters of all income for retirees living on less than $10,000 a year (Atchley, 1991).

AGING AND INEQUALITY IN THE UNITED STATES

Although Social Security and Medicare have helped to reduce economic inequality among the elderly, they are still not free from poverty and other forms of social inequality. Some recurrent problems include poverty, social isolation, ageism, physical abuse, and health.

Poverty

Twelve percent of all people over 65 live in poverty, or roughly one out of every eight (Figure 12.2). This is a slightly lower rate than for American society as a whole (14 percent). Although the incidence of poverty among the elderly is somewhat higher than it is for middle-aged working people, it nonetheless remains far below that of children under 16, 22 percent of whom are poor. As previously noted, the principal reason that poverty among the elderly is lower than poverty overall is because of the liberalization of Social Security benefits in 1972, and the enactment of Medicare in 1965.

Poverty rates for the elderly vary considerably by race, mirroring racial differences in poverty for other age groups. Among whites, only 10 percent of the elderly reported poverty-level incomes in 1991, compared with 34 percent for blacks and 21 percent for Latinos (U.S. Bureau of the Census, 1993).

Social Isolation

Although one of the common stereotypes about the elderly is that they are isolated from much human contact, this is not true for the majority of older people. About four out of five men aged 65 to 74 live with a spouse or mate; for those over 75, this remains true of three out of four. Elderly women do not fare so well, since women typically outlive men in American society. There are about 140 women for every 100 men over 60, a ratio that rises to about 160 at age 70. Partly due to the dearth of older men, only about half of all women aged 65 to 74 live with a mate; the proportion is less than a quarter for women over 75. The percentage living with a mate is somewhat lower for Latinos than it is for whites, and lower still for blacks (Atchley, 1991).

Figure 12.2   **Percent of Children and Elderly Living in Poverty, by Race and Ethnicity**

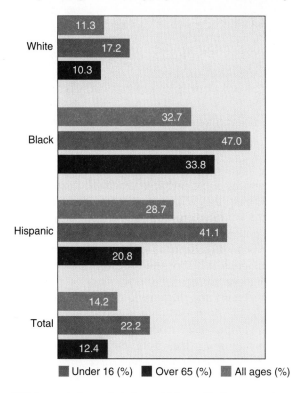

White
11.3
17.2
10.3

Black
32.7
47.0
33.8

Hispanic
28.7
41.1
20.8

Total
14.2
22.2
12.4

■ Under 16 (%) ■ Over 65 (%) ■ All ages (%)

Child poverty is nearly twice as high as elderly poverty in the United States. As with child poverty, elderly poverty is highest among blacks, among whom a third of all people over 65 are poor. Hispanics are intermediate, and whites are lowest. Elderly poverty dropped considerably during the 1970s, partly because of the enactment of Medicare in 1965, and partly because Social Security benefits were greatly increased in 1972. For poor children, the reverse has occurred: Federal antipoverty programs have been severely cut during the past decades.
Source: U.S. Bureau of the Census (1993, Table 739).

Four out of five older people have living children, and the vast majority of them can rely on their children for support if necessary (American Association of Retired Persons [AARP], 1989). In fact, norms of family obligation run high in American society; more than nine out of ten adult children report believing that maintaining parental contact is important, including the provision of financial support if it is needed (Finley, Roberts, and Banahan, 1988). Norms of family support run in both directions: Many studies have found that elderly parents continue to provide support for their adult children, particularly during times of difficulty such as divorce. Most elderly parents and adult children report feeling that the support they receive from the other is fair. Nor does geographical dispersal seem to deter familial support, since 85 percent of elderly people with children live close to at least one of them (Bengston,

Rosenthal, and Burton, 1990; Greenberg and Becker, 1988; Bankoff, 1983; Peterson and Peterson, 1988; Moss, Moss, and Moles, 1985).

Although most elderly people today do not suffer from social isolation, this may not be as true of future generations. Changing patterns of gender relations, including increased divorce and a decline in remarriage, may result in an increased proportion of elderly people living alone (Goldscheider, 1990). This, in turn, could well result in increased isolation and loneliness for a growing segment of those who become elderly in the next century (see Box 12.1).

Ageism

Ageism is *prejudice based on age,* and, like all prejudices, is fueled in part by stereotypes. Some common but false negative stereotypes depict the elderly as perpetually lonely, sad, infirm, forgetful, dependent, senile, old-fashioned, inflexible, embittered, and—in the title of a recent film about two elderly men— "crotchety." Such stereotypes inevitably impact the ways in which younger people view the elderly. For example, in one study college students were shown a photograph of the same man at ages 25, 52, and 73, and were asked to rate him in terms of a variety of personality characteristics. Ratings were significantly more negative for the man depicted at age 73, even though no information about him was provided (Levin, 1988). Although such prejudices can translate into acts of discrimination against the elderly, discrimination on the basis of age is today against federal law (U.S. Senate Special Committee on Aging, 1986).

Why should prejudice against the elderly exist? One reason may be found in America's concern with youthfulness, a value reflected in popular entertainment, advertising, and stereotypes about the elderly. A second has to do with attitudes toward death and dying. In the United States, as in other industrial societies, death is feared and postponed as long as possible. This negative attitude carries over into negative attitudes toward the elderly, who serve as a constant reminder of our mortality (Fry, 1980). Related to this is the popularity of the medical model of aging, according to which adverse physiological changes are assumed to be inevitable, capable of being corrected (within limits) only by costly medical procedures (Haber, 1983; Sankar, 1988; Matthews, 1993).

A final reason for prejudice against the elderly originates in the view that their knowledge and experience are of little value in today's rapidly changing technological society. Whereas prior to industrialization the elderly often were valued for their accumulated experience and wisdom, in industrial society constant change is seen as rendering much traditional learning obsolete

Box 12.1

Silenced Voices

The Isolated Elderly

Most research today strongly suggests that the elderly are neither isolated nor silenced. As is shown in this chapter, for the most part elderly people today are active and involved in networks of social relations, and they represent a potentially potent political force on issues that affect them.

Yet there are some social trends suggesting that future generations of elderly may find themselves more isolated than elderly people today. Partly because women's increased role in the paid workforce has given them a measure of economic independence from men, and partly because of changing norms and values regarding marriage resulting from the "gender revolution" (Chapters 11 and 14), divorce rates have risen and remarriage rates have declined. Whereas perhaps a quarter of today's elderly population has been divorced, the rate for elderly people is likely to double over the next 15 years (Goldscheider, 1990). Furthermore, remarriage rates also are declining, particularly among women (Sweet and Bumpass, 1987). Finally, there is some research suggesting that parents who get divorced have less contact with their adult children later in life. This is particularly true for fathers (Cooney and Uhlenberg, 1990).

In the following passage, sociologist Frances K. Goldscheider (1990) summarizes these conditions, raising the possibility that one unfortunate consequence of the "aging of the gender revolution" is that elderly people in the future may encounter far more isolation than is experienced by their counterparts today.

With the aging of the gender revolution the numbers of old unmarried men will grow dramatically; they will be much more difficult to ignore. The rapid growth in female labor force participation has provided a substantial number of women with substitutes for weak or problematic marriages. . . . [Those entering retirement years] will have experienced high rates of marital breakdown and decreasing probabilities of remarriage. Even among those who are remarried, high proportions will have problematic or *no* relationships with their biological children, which their stepchildren will not replace.

The family lives of those who are currently elderly may well be strong and supportive, for women and for men. But with the aging of the gender revolution, there will soon be new cohorts entering old age that will be very different, with a history of family ties that are broken, weak, and confused. How divorce is redefining intergenerational relationships of all kinds—not only between parents and children, but between grandparents and grandchildren and also among siblings—is an important area that requires systematic research. These research challenges are urgent ones, with equally urgent implications for social policies on aging. And we have barely begun to address them.

(Amoss and Harrell, 1981). The elderly are likely to be regarded as "old fashioned" and ignorant, the butt of jokes having to do with their presumed technical incompetence and general failure to develop the latest skills needed to use a computer or program a VCR.

Physical Abuse

It is difficult to estimate with any accuracy the number of older people who are physically abused, since most cases of abuse go unreported. Partly as a result of the increased public attention to abusive relationships of all sorts, however, there is an increased concern that elderly abuse is a widespread and significant problem. This concern in part reflects the stereotype of the elderly as frail and dependent, and therefore highly vulnerable to others.

Although cases of abuse certainly exist, most research suggests that it is not as widespread as is commonly perceived, and it is certainly well below the commonly cited figure of one out of every ten (Gelles and Cornell, 1990). One random survey among 2,000 noninstitutionalized elderly people in the Boston area found that only about 2 percent had experienced physical violence. Fewer than 1 percent reported being seriously neglected in terms of their daily needs, while

The elderly often suffer from stereotypes and discrimination in the same way that minorities and physically challenged people do. To counteract this image and fight for their political and economic rights, a group of elderly Americans joined together in 1971 to form the Gray Panthers.

about 1 percent claimed they were subject to chronic verbal aggression. Although these figures represent a small percentage of the elderly population, they do project out to a substantial 8,000 to 9,000 cases in the Boston area alone. While elderly men reported higher rates of abuse than did elderly women, 57 percent of the abused women (compared with 6 percent of the men) reported suffering injuries (Pillemer and Finkelhor, 1988).

Although it has been argued that abuse results from the anger and resentment adult children presumably feel when confronted with the need to care for their infirm parents (Steinmetz, 1983; King, 1984), most studies find that this is an incorrect stereotype. More than half of the abuse reported in the above-mentioned Boston study was perpetrated by a spouse; only a quarter occurred at the hands of an adult child (Pillemer and Finkelhor, 1988). Furthermore, when a child abuses an elderly parent, it is more likely that he or she is financially dependent on the parent, rather than the reverse. The child may feel resentment at such dependence, while the parent is unwilling to terminate the abusive relationship because of feeling obligated to the child (Pillemer, 1985).

Health Problems

Elderly people obviously suffer more from health problems than younger people, and health difficulties often increase with advancing old age. Older people experience a higher amount of long-term medical problems than do younger people, particularly such chronic problems as visual or hearing impairment, heart conditions, high blood pressure, and arthritis. Nonetheless, most elderly people rate their health as reasonably good and free from major disabilities. Fewer than 5 percent of people in their early eighties report conditions that severely limit their activities, and while this figure increases after age

85, even among this group only about a quarter need help with shopping and other routine tasks (Atchley, 1991; National Center for Health Statistics, 1989).

Unlike many other Americans, the elderly are fortunate to have access to health insurance and therefore medical services. Currently, the elderly account for about a third of all U.S. health care expenditures (Clark, 1993). While some 35 million Americans lacked health insurance in 1991 (about 14 percent of the population), among the elderly fewer than 1 percent lacked coverage. Ninety-six percent of the elderly are covered by the government's Medicare program, although nearly two out of three supplement Medicare with their own private insurance as well. Medicare currently covers about half of the health care expenses of elderly individuals (U.S. Bureau of the Census, 1992; Callahan, 1987). Yet despite such governmental support, the elderly still spend nearly one-fifth of their income on health care (Hess, 1990).

Medicare does not cover chronic or long-term illnesses that can prove financially catastrophic. Unfortunately, it is just such illnesses that are most likely to plague the elderly in the final years of their lives. As we shall see in Chapter 18, the cost of health care in the United States has exploded during the past decade, to the point where the bill for a few days' treatment in the hospital may run to thousands of dollars, and a year in a nursing home averages $30,000 (Eckholm, 1990). Needless to say, when the elderly contract a long-term, debilitating illness, their entire financial resources may be wiped out if insurance coverage is not adequate. The United States stands virtually alone among industrialized nations in failing to provide adequately for the complete health care of its most senior citizens, although the current debates over national health care reform may eventually result in full coverage (Hendricks and Rosenthal, 1993; Hendricks and Hatch, 1993).

When the elderly become physically unable to care for themselves, they may wind up in nursing homes. Although some facilities have a reputation for austerity and loneliness, the quality of most has improved in recent years, both because federal programs such as Medicare help to cover the cost of care and because of federal quality regulations. Only about 1 out of every 20 people over 65 are in nursing homes, a figure that rises to about 1 out of every 4 among people over 85 (Atchley, 1991; Lewin, 1990).

THE POLITICS OF AGING

In recent years programs such as Social Security and Medicare have come under fire on the grounds that they fail to promote **generational equity,** *the effort to strike a balance between the needs and interests of members of different generations.* For example, according to government figures there are today roughly five working-age people (19 to 64 years old) for every person over 65; by 2025, there will be only three (Clark, 1993). Such figures are often cited to argue that fewer and fewer people are being unfairly taxed to pay for a growing retired population (Box 12.2). Moreover, this "graying of America" is most pronounced among whites, and least pronounced among minority groups (U.S. Bureau of the Census, 1989; see again Box 12.2). Might this not lead to conflict between a predominantly white elderly retired population clamoring for benefits and a predominantly non-white working population that is forced to pay in order to keep the system financially solvent?

The Social Security system is currently expected to have reserves totaling nearly $7 trillion by 2015, more than sufficient to fund the people who will be retiring at that time (Quadagno, 1989; Atchley, 1991). Most workers today are better off than the people who are retiring, and they are able to afford paying into Social Security and Medicare. Furthermore, they will themselves benefit from these government programs when they retire. Without such programs, the elderly would likely become considerably more impoverished as a group, just like children and others in society who currently lack such support. It also seems probable that if Social Security and Medicare were significantly cut back or terminated, many older people would be forced back into the workforce to support themselves, where they would be competing with members of other generations for jobs. This would have the effect of worsening generational equity, rather than improving it (Bernstein and Bernstein, 1988; Quadagno, 1989).

The debate over generational equity indicates that growing old in American society has highly political implications. Governmental efforts to cut back on Social Security payments have been repeatedly rebuffed

Although most elderly people in the United States live independently, some are too infirm to care for themselves. Currently, 1 in 20 people over 65—and 1 in 4 over 85—live in nursing homes, where full-time care is provided. Nursing homes are costly, however, and the quality of care received by the elderly is largely dependent on their economic status.

in Congress, where representatives are fearful of losing their seats if they take on their elderly constituents. A 1988 law that extended Medicare to cover catastrophic illness was repealed the following year, when the elderly middle-class voters who would be eligible for coverage strongly objected to having to shoulder the entire cost of the program themselves. Public opinion polls repeatedly show that more than three-quarters of people in all age groups support more, not less, federal money for Medicare and Social Security (Quadagno, 1989). Furthermore, the elderly, now numbering more than 32 million people, constitute a potentially powerful political force. The American Association of Retired Persons (AARP), which is open to people 50 and over, claims to have 31 million members, comprising one quarter of all registered voters in the United States (Ornstein and Schmitt, 1990).

This is not to suggest that the elderly all hold the same political views; on the contrary, they are as politically heterogeneous as other groups in society. But voter turnout is much higher among the elderly than it is for other age groups (Atchley, 1991), and on issues

Box 12.2

Critical Thinking

Do the Elderly Get an Unfair Share?

The issue of generational equity was first raised by an organization called Americans for Generational Equity (AGE), created in 1984 by Dave Durenberger, a senator from Minnesota, to challenge the notion that elderly people were entitled to Social Security benefits (Quadagno, 1989). AGE's chief criticisms were targeted at the program's method of funding, which taxes people who are currently working in order to pay for the retirement of those who no longer work.

AGE argued that as the American population "grays," an ever-growing proportion of elderly people will become dependent on an ever-shrinking working population for their support. For example, according to government figures there are today roughly five working age people (19 to 64 years old) for every person over 65; by 2025, there will be only three (Clark, 1993). It would seem to follow that those who are working will bear an increasing burden for those who are not. AGE also argued that Social Security unfairly favors retirees over other needy groups in society. For example, AGE pointed out that retirees are sometimes wealthier than the working people whose taxes fund Social Security, and that there are more than three times as many impoverished children under 16 than impoverished people over 65 (13.1 million versus. 3.8 million). AGE predicted that job losses and economic decline resulting from globalization would ultimately lead to lower tax revenues, bankrupting Social Security and other programs financed out of this source (Ehrbar, 1980; Bladen, 1982; Peterson, 1982, 1987; Longman, 1982, 1985; Smith, 1987; Boyer, 1988; Quadagno, 1989).

Imagine that you are a U.S. senator being asked to reduce benefits for Social Security and Medicare on the basis of the generational equity argument. Based on what you have read in the text, does the available evidence support this argument, or challenge it? What additional evidence might you have to gather in order to vote intelligently?

---

they perceive as affecting their interests—such as retirement pensions and health care benefits—they can be expected to speak with a fairly uniform voice.

LIFELONG LEARNING

As American society continues to "gray," it will increasingly be forced to confront a growing elderly population that is unwilling to slip quietly into years of retirement and inactivity. It is by now well-appreciated that the elderly are capable of learning well into advanced old age and have much to offer long after having retired from paid employment. Mahatma Gandhi, Mother Teresa, Grandma Moses, Albert Schweitzer, and Henri Matisse all serve as important reminders of this fact. It is important for elderly people to maintain a readiness to learn, stimulated by participation in a wide variety of learning activities. As noted above, this can contribute to mental alertness, a positive psychological attitude, and even physical health (Plett, 1990; Plett and Lester, 1991; Dychtwald, 1990).

Educators have coined the terms **andragogy** to refer to *adult learning* (literally, "to lead adults"), and **geragogy** to refer to *older adult learning* (Knowles, 1980, 1984; John, 1988). In contrast to conventional notions of teaching, adult learning methods emphasize building on the extensive life experience of older people, rather than providing them with information in the standard undergraduate classroom format. Adults are not seen an "empty vessels" to be filled with others' knowledge by means of lectures and quizzes, but rather as highly knowledgeable in their own right. Adult learning tends to be informal, combining the learners' concrete experience with more theoretical sorts of knowledge. It draws on the interests and concerns of adult learners, who may be unwilling to spend time studying things that seem unrelated to their central concerns (Knowles, 1980, 1984; Nadler and Nadler, 1989; John, 1988; Plett, 1990).

American culture is beginning to recognize the importance of lifelong learning for the elderly, although little is as yet being done through government programs. There are a few state, federal, and local job-training programs, but these seem hardly adequate to serve the growing numbers of elderly people, during a period of deindustrialization when even young workers cannot find adequate jobs. Early retirement programs, sometimes termed "golden parachutes" or "golden handshakes," enable a small number of people (mainly middle class) to develop second careers after retiring from their principal work. Some American corporations have educational and retraining programs for their older workers, and many colleges and universities offer continuing education or adult education programs to the growing number of elderly people who are interested in taking classes. It seems likely that as the market for such services increases, so too will the oportunities available. Some scholars even have argued that by the early twenty-first century, "adult education" will become as important as "youth education" (Brookfield, 1986, 1987).

GLOBALIZATION: THE "GRAYING" OF THE WORLD POPULATION

Most societies in the world today are experiencing an aging of their populations as a result of both declining birth and death rates, although the poorer countries continue to have shorter life spans due to poverty, malnutrition, and disease (see Chapter 9). According to United Nations estimates (United Nations [U.N.], 1990; U.N. Population Fund, 1991), the world's average life expectancy had grown from 46 in 1950 to 50 in 1985 and will reach 71 by 2025. At that time, some 800 million people will be over 65, nearly a threefold increase in numbers from today. Among the very old (those over 80), where medical and service needs are the greatest, the number will increase by half in North America, while it will double in China and grow nearly one and a half times in West Africa (Sokolovsky, 1990). This will place major demands on resources in many countries that already are too poor to adequately support their populations.

Countries vary widely in what they are doing to cope with their growing numbers of older people. As we have seen already, the United States relies primarily on Social Security and Medicare to serve the financial and health needs of the elderly. Other industrial nations provide a much broader array of services. In Britain, while training programs aimed at increasing the job prospects of older workers are not a major part of government policy, a 1989 report did call for a pilot project to provide a small amount of money to unemployed people over 50 for education and training (Plett, 1990). In Japan, men and women remain active well into old age, both because Japanese culture encourages this, and because business policies often support postretirement work with the same company. A number of national

laws support employment and training of older workers, and private businesses also support retraining.

As mentioned above, in many preindustrial societies the elderly are highly valued. Because prior to modern times few people survived to old age (Chapter 20), the few who managed to do so did not place an undue economic burden on the society as a whole. Societies having large extended families, or practicing ancestor worship, were particularly likely to treasure their few surviving elders. In Thailand, for example, the elderly are traditionally revered; they are addressed with respect, have the seats of honor at public events, and are highly indulged by their families at home. Often they serve as informal advisors to community leaders (Seefeldt and Keawkungwal, 1985; Cowgill, 1968). In China and Japan, reverence for ancestors remains strong and ideally results in respect for one's elders (Glascock and Feinman, 1981; Falk et al., 1981).

Unlike industrial societies, preindustrial societies seldom define old age in purely chronological terms. A person is not immediately "old" on his or her sixty-fifth birthday but rather when routine adult duties can no longer be performed. In some societies old age is defined by deep-seated traditions as well—for example, completing five 12-year cycles on the traditional animal calendar in Thailand. In most societies, once older people become completely physically and economically dependent on others, they come to be regarded as an unwanted burden as well (Amoss and Harrell, 1981; Fry, 1980; Bass et al, 1990; Cowgill, 1968).

Globalization has begun to change the treatment of the elderly throughout the world (Cowgill and Holmes, 1972; Cowgill, 1986; Holmes, 1983; Fry, 1980; Hess and Markson, 1985). As more and more people live to old age, respect for them has tended to decline. This is partly because their growing numbers result in a greater economic burden on their families. Additionally, as previously agrarian societies become a part of the emerging global economy, traditional ways of thinking and behaving are likely to change. When extended families are uprooted from farms and move into cities in search of factory work, their ability to support nonworking members is likely to decline. In those societies that are highly family-oriented, the responsibility for supporting elderly parents and working for outside income often falls on young women. Research on Taiwan, for example, has found that young girls often work a full day in a nearby factory, returning home during lunch and after work to care full-time for infirm parents or grandparents (Cheng and Hsiung, 1992).

The combination of "graying" and globalization will shape the lives of elderly people throughout the world well into the next century. Traditional patterns of family care will be challenged, as family-based economies continue to give way to labor on the farms and in the of-

Map 12.1   The Graying of the World: Percent over 65 in 1990

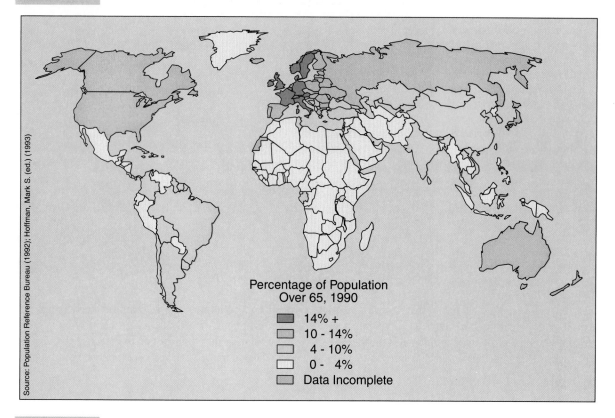

Source: Population Reference Bureau (1992); Hoffman, Mark S. (ed.) (1993)

Percentage of Population
Over 65, 1990

- 14% +
- 10 - 14%
- 4 - 10%
- 0 - 4%
- Data Incomplete

Map 12.2   The Graying of the World: Percent over 65 in 2010

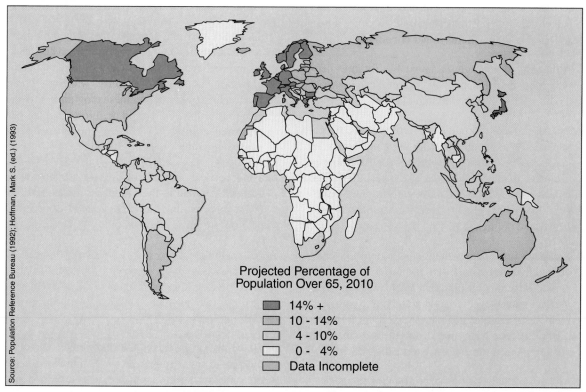

Source: Population Reference Bureau (1992); Hoffman, Mark S. (ed.) (1993)

Projected Percentage of
Population Over 65, 2010

- 14% +
- 10 - 14%
- 4 - 10%
- 0 - 4%
- Data Incomplete

The world population as a whole is aging, as birth rates and mortality decline. The industrial nations of Europe and North America, along with Japan and China, are experiencing the most significant "graying." The poorer nations of Asia, Africa, and Latin America, while also "graying," are forecasted to remain on average much younger than the more industrially-developed nations.

The social roles of the elderly depend on other social relations. As more parents are working, grandparents may become more important in child rearing. How might this elderly man caring for a baby in Taiwan reflect changes in the global economy that have produced rapid development in Taiwan?

fices and factories of global businesses. As with the industrial nations earlier this century, all societies increasingly will be challenged to find roles for their aging citizens. This challenge will include identifying new means of economic support, often financed by government programs. It will also entail identifying ways to incorporate rather than isolate the elderly, drawing on their considerable reserves of experience and talents.

C H A P T E R   S U M M A R Y

1. Biological, psychological, and social **aging** are not the same, and may vary considerably within and across cultures. It is important not to confuse a person's **social age** with his or her **chronological age.**

2. Although physical aging is inevitable, for most people proper nutrition, diet, and exercise can preserve a high level of health well into old age.

3. Because of low mortality and fertility rates, American society is rapidly **graying** or aging. Today 13 percent of Americans are over 65; this number is projected to reach 22 percent by the year 2030. The elderly are thus a large and rapidly-growing category that is extremely diverse economically, socially, and politically.

4. Although functionalist theories of aging originally argued that **disengagement** of the elderly from society is desirable, theorists soon came to emphasize the importance of continuing **activity** as a source of mental and even physical vitality. Conflict theorists, on the other hand, have focused on the ways in which society produces inequality among the elderly.

5. Most of the elderly in American society manage to lead independent lives that they report as largely satisfying and fulfilling. Still, there are some who suffer from poverty, social isolation, and costly medical problems, as well as from **ageist** prejudices.

6. Social Security and Medicare, by providing the elderly with retirement income and critical health care insurance, have helped to raise a significant number of elderly people out of poverty. Although there is some debate over whether these programs are overly generous to the elderly and therefore threaten **generational equity,** in fact their support levels are modest and their financing sound.

7. The elderly are capable of lifelong learning, and it seems likely that as their numbers increase, so will efforts at providing **andragogy** (adult-centered education) for those who want it.

8. Although the elderly are as politically and socially diverse as any group in society, on issues that affect their interests they are capable of exerting a great deal of political force. This will likely increase as their numbers grow.

9. Globalization threatens the traditional roles of the elderly in many societies, whose numbers are increasing as these societies experience their own "graying." The role of the elderly throughout the world is in a rapid state of transition.

QUESTIONS FOR DISCUSSION

1. What do you think is the proper role for the elderly in modern industrial society? What public and private policies might enable this role to be best achieved?

2. What effect is the "graying" of American society likely to have on economics and politics in the first quarter of the twenty-first century?

3. Does the current governmental system of providing retirement income and health care for the elderly promote generational equity? Why or why not?

4. What is the likely impact of globalization on the elderly throughout the world? How might this affect your own lives?

KEY TERMS

activity theory: A functionalist theory of aging, which holds that active people are more likely to lead fulfilling and productive lives, benefiting society as well as themselves.

ageism: Prejudice based on age.

aging: The combination of biological, psychological, and social processes that affect people as they grow older.

andragogy: Adult learning.

chronological age: The length of time a person has been alive.

disengagement theory: A functionalist theory of aging, which holds that elderly people should progressively pull back from social roles, freeing up those roles for others while preparing themselves for their eventual death.

generational equity: The effort to strike a balance between the needs and interests of members of different generations.

geragogy: Older adult learning.

graying: A term used to indicate that an increasing proportion of a society's population is becoming elderly.

life course: A sequence of different roles a person is expected to assume during chronological aging.

social age: The norms, values, and roles that are culturally associated with a particular chronological age.

social gerontology: A discipline studying the social aspects of aging.

RECOMMENDED FOR FURTHER READING

Atchley, Robert C. (1991). *Social Forces and Aging: An Introduction to Social Gerontology* (6th ed.). Belmont, CA: Wadsworth.

A standard textbook on aging from the perspective of social gerontology; covers a wide range of issues, such as individual aging, aging and social life, adapting to growing old, and society's role.

Brookfield, Stephen. (1987). *Developing Critical Thinkers: Challenging Adults to Explore Alternative Ways of Thinking and Acting.* San Francisco: Jossey-Bass.

An important book by a leading proponent of adult-centered learning, which argues for an andragogical approach to lifelong learning.

Dychtwald, K. (1990). *Age Wave: How the Most Important Trend of Our Time Will Change Your Future.* New York: Bantam Books.

A popularized book that reviews current demographic trends leading to the aging of society, and discusses their implications for everyone.

Hendricks, Jon, and Carolyn J. Rosenthal. (1993). *The Remainder of Their Days: Domestic Policy and Older Families in the United States and Canada.* New York: Garland.

A collection of essays that explore policy issues regarding the elderly, offering many useful comparisons between Canadian policies and those of the United States.

Sokolovsky, J. (ed.). (1990). *The Cultural Context of Aging: Worldwide Perspectives.* New York: Bergin and Garvey.

A collection of writings on the meaning of aging in different societies.

Politics and the State

CHAPTER OUTLINE

THINGS TO LOOK FOR

1. What are the defining characteristics of the modern nation-state?
2. Is government in America shaped by a plurality of contending groups and individuals, or by a relatively small power elite?
3. What is the role of the military-industrial complex in American society, and in the world generally? How might this role be changing?
4. Why do many Americans appear to be apathetic about politics?
5. How has globalization affected governance within and between nations?

INTRODUCTION: A TIME OF CHANGE

Although every era presents an enormous array of political challenges, the present period is witnessing changes in the world order that are in many ways without precedent.

During the span of a few short years, the former Soviet Union has been transformed from a major political and military power locked in mortal conflict with the United States, to a commonwealth of 11 independent nations struggling to create new political and economic forms. For nearly three-quarters of a century, the world was divided between two heavily armed camps, one championing socialism, the other capitalism (see Chapters 4 and 15). In this divided world, the United States and the Soviet Union were the two unquestioned superpowers, their vast military establishments possessing the nuclear capability to destroy all life on the planet. In fact, the world was brought to the brink of nuclear war in 1962, when President John F. Kennedy discovered that the Soviet Union had established nuclear missile sites in Cuba, a country 90 miles south of Florida that had recently allied itself with the Soviet Union. A direct confrontation was averted only when the Soviet Union backed down from a direct military challenge and agreed to remove its missiles (Allison, 1971; Blight, Allyn, and Welch, 1993).

Between the 1950s and the 1980s, there developed what came to be called the **Cold War,** a period of heightened *tensions between the United States and the Soviet Union.* Although the two superpowers never directly confronted one another on the battlefield (hence the term "cold"), the United States openly fought allies of the Soviet Union in Korea (1950–1953) and Vietnam (1964–1973), and was indirectly involved in numerous smaller wars, police actions, military coups, and insurrections in Guatemala, Chile, the Dominican Republic, Grenada, Nicaragua, Angola, Cambodia, and Mozambique. Even the numerous conflicts in the Middle East could in part be traced to the two superpowers' opposing interests in this oil-rich and militarily strategic region. In the view of U.S. policymakers, these conflicts were necessary to "contain communism" and "protect American interests."

All of this abruptly came to an end on Christmas day 1991, when Soviet President Mikhail Gorbachev's resignation signaled the final collapse of the Soviet Union. The Soviet Union's allies in Eastern Europe, heavily dependent on Soviet military and economic support, also soon ceased to exist as socialist nations. In the place of a single superpower were left numerous smaller countries and independent republics, all economically impoverished, and all seeking to establish capitalist economies. Some of these countries, although politically weakened, still possessed nuclear arsenals and large-standing armies. At the same time, another major socialist power, the People's Republic of China, was rapidly moving to adopt aspects of a capitalist economy. The conditions that had defined much of world politics throughout the twentieth century changed virtually overnight.

These global political changes are simultaneously hopeful and disturbing. Politics within the United States cannot be fully understood unless changes in the rest of the world are also taken into account. In this chapter we shall first examine the emergence and characteristics of modern nations, including theories of state power. We shall then turn to an examination of governance in the United States, including the key role played by the military. We shall conclude with a discussion of the impact of globalization on systems of governance throughout the world.

THE MODERN NATION-STATE AND THE RULE OF LAW

Max Weber (1864–1920), one of sociology's founders, defined the **state** as *a political apparatus possessing the legitimate monopoly over the use of force within its territory* (Weber, 1946a). By "legitimate" Weber simply meant that people regarded the state's exclusive right to use force as lawful (see Chapter 6). The modern **nation-state,** in turn, is *a particular form of state whose members are regarded as "citizens" possessing specified legal rights and obligations.* The idea of the nation-state is bound up with the modern idea that people can and should determine their own destiny, within the legal and political framework provided by a national government (Held, 1989). Although the term

One of the defining features of state power is a monopoly over the legitimate use of force. What constitutes legitimacy, however, can be a matter of dispute. In this 1987 photograph, South Korean workers and students fight the police, whom they regarded as defending an authoritarian and illegitimate government. Riots broke out in Seoul after a student was killed by riot police trying to break up a demonstration.

"nation-state" is properly used to refer to a society with these characteristics, in practice this term is today often used interchangeably with more common words such as "nation," "state," or "country."

The modern nation-state emerged in Europe between the twelfth and fifteenth centuries, when monarchs began claiming the ownership of all the territory within what were formerly independent feudal kingdoms (see Chapter 4). Many wars were fought during this period, as feudal Lords sought to resist the centralization of power and authority in the hands of a single king or queen (Keegan, 1993). The nation-state contributed to the rise of capitalism, which benefited from strong central governments and legal systems that regulated commerce and trade both within and across borders (Weber, 1979, orig. 1921; Wallerstein, 1974; Mann, 1986). Today, the nation-state as we have characterized it is with a few exceptions the only form of statehood found throughout the world (Giddens, 1985). All other forms of governance have all been absorbed into the approximately 180 nation-states that claim sovereignty over the world's 5.4 billion people.

There are several unique features of the modern nation-state that distinguish it from earlier forms of political organization. First, the government of the nation-state claims **sovereignty**—*final and total authority over its members, such that no greater authority can be found elsewhere* (Hinsley, 1986). While earlier governmental forms were often split by internal warring factions, the modern nation-state is more likely to be embroiled in conflicts with its neighbors (Held, 1989). Occasionally, a nation-state may cede some of its authority in a restricted area through international agreements, as when it signs a treaty agreeing to international laws regarding workplace conditions, human rights, or

respect for another nation's sovereignty. But such agreements are voluntary and can be enforced only if the international community is willing to do so and possesses superior force.

Second, underlying the organization of modern nation-states is a system of **law**, *the codified rules of behavior established by a government and backed by the threat of force* (Chambliss and Seidman, 1982). Since the nation-state's sovereignty depends in large part on the effective enforcement of its laws, it has a strong stake in seeing that its laws are enforced. Prior to the emergence of the modern nation-state, traditional beliefs ordinarily dictated how people should behave and how disputes would be settled. For example, if someone were robbed or injured in a dispute, the offended party and those accused of offending would attempt to settle their differences in keeping with local customs, with a local ruler acting as judge. What was important was that the parties to the dispute worked out a mutually acceptable solution in order to restore harmony. With the emergence of the nation-state, the offended party was no longer the individual but the nation itself. If its laws were violated, obtaining redress was essential; otherwise, its entire legal basis might be threatened. The government itself prosecuted violations of the law, rather than leaving this to the aggrieved parties. And the government itself determined the appropriate level of punishment (Chambliss and Zatz, 1994; Durkheim, 1964, orig. 1893; Jeffrey, 1956).

In the modern world the law touches everyone; the state extends into every aspect of life. People cannot be born, go to college, have children, get married, or even die without their behavior being circumscribed by law. Laws regulate all the institutions we discuss in this textbook—family, workplace, school, place of worship,

The U.S. Supreme Court is the court of last resort where citizens can appeal legal interpretations made in state and federal courts. The Court derives its legitimacy in part because it is viewed as being above politics. The fact that the justices are appointed by the president and must be approved by Congress, however, often invokes heated controversy over the Court's independence.

hospital, and government. From personal relations between parent and child to the impersonal operations of the economy, people no longer look to one another as the primary place where disputes are to be settled. Governments are expected to pass laws that will do everything from maintaining tranquillity in the home to regulating relations between nations.

Third, the members of nation-states are thought of as **citizens,** *individuals who are part of a political community in which they are granted certain rights and privileges, while at the same time having specified obligations and duties.* Citizens are regarded as participants in the political process itself. They are afforded legal protections from arbitrary rule and in turn are expected to perform duties such as military service, payment of taxes, and engaging in governance through voting or other activities. Whereas in earlier forms of governance people often were seen as subject to the arbitrary authority of their leaders, today citizens are regarded as sources of leadership themselves.

Citizenship rights can take several forms. **Civil rights,** which *protect citizens from injuries perpetrated by other individuals and by institutions,* include the right to equal treatment in the school or workplace regardless of race, gender, sexual orientation, or handicap status. **Social rights,** which call for *the governmental provision of various forms of economic and social security,* include such things as retirement pensions or guaranteed income after losing one's job. Finally, **political rights** *ensure that anyone who so chooses can participate in governance,* whether it be voting, running for office, or openly expressing political opinions. Although the extension of such citizenship rights is an ideal of the modern nation-state, in practice this ideal is not always met. In many places,

for example, women and members of racial and ethnic minorities lack the full rights of citizenship (see Chapters 10 and 11).

The rights and obligations of citizenship can often be mobilized into feelings of **nationalism,** a *powerful sense of identification with the nation-state that is expressed through a common set of strongly held beliefs* (Giddens, 1985). Modern nation-states often draw effectively on this sense of belonging, in order to mobilize popular support for everything from economic sacrifice to going to war. Nationalism appears to be especially appealing in the world today, as we shall note in the final section of this chapter.

POWER IN THE MODERN NATION-STATE

Although sociologists agree that nation-states exert a great deal of power over the lives of their citizens, they are not always in agreement on the ways in which power is exercised. Before we examine sociological theories of state power, however, it will be helpful to understand the relationship between power and authority in different societies. To do so, we shall briefly turn to the writings of Max Weber, whose ideas regarding political power have had an enormous influence on social scientists' understandings about the modern nation-state.

Types of State Power and Authority

In Chapter 6 we defined **power** as *the ability to mobilize resources and achieve a goal despite the resistance of others.* According to this definition, power can be

Social changes occurring in a society eventually affect every institution. The ban against openly gay men and women serving in the U.S. military has been increasingly challenged by gay service people, many of whom were thrown out of the military after their sexual orientation became known, sometimes after years of dedicated service. Here, uniformed men stage a "kiss-in" to protest what they consider to be an unjust and hypocritical policy.

assessed in terms of **domination,** *the likelihood that a command will be obeyed* (Weber, 1979; orig. 1921). Weber distinguished two pure forms (what he termed "ideal types"; see Chapter 1) of domination: (1) raw coercion, and (2) **legitimate authority,** *the use of power that is recognized as rightful by those over whom it is exercised.* Weber (1979) was much less interested in raw coercion then he was in authority people perceived to be legitimate, since it raised a sociologically interesting question: "Why do people voluntarily agree to give up power, allowing others to dominate them?" Weber's answer to this question, which was based on detailed studies of different societies throughout history, identified three "ideal types" of legitimate authority: (1) traditional, (2) rational-legal, and (3) charismatic. While Weber recognized that none of these existed in pure form, he did argue that particular societies tended to fall primarily into one of the three categories.

Throughout most of human history, according to Weber, state power has derived from **traditional authority,** *power based on a belief in the sanctity of long-standing traditions and the legitimate right of rulers to exercise authority under them* (Weber, 1979). Traditional rulers claim the right to rule on the basis of age-old norms and values that are frequently grounded in religious beliefs, and followers willingly agree with their claim. Much of the basis of authority therefore lies in habit; the rulers are legitimate simply because "it has always been that way." Traditional authority is inherently conservative and tends to be relatively stable over time. Traditional monarchies provide a good example. Authority is a birthright, which the king or queen commands because he or she was born into the royal fam-

ily. People are considered to be his or her "subjects" and are expected to be personally devoted to their ruler even if the ruler is incompetent. The same personal loyalty is expected toward the ruler's administrative staff and military forces.

Traditional authority, in Weber's view, impeded the rise of capitalistic economies, which are based on more rational forms of social organization. As capitalism began to develop during the later stages of feudalism, contractual relationships between monarch and subject began to limit the former's power (Chapter 4). Eventually, traditional authority gave way to **rational-legal authority,** *power based on a belief in the lawfulness of enacted rules and the legitimate right of leaders to exercise authority under such rules* (Weber, 1979). Rational-legal authority derives from a belief in the rule of law. One does not do something simply because it has always been done that way, as with traditional authority; rather, one does it because it conforms to established legal procedures. Laws can change, and with them the basis for legitimate authority.

A leader is regarded as legitimate so long as she or he acts according to law; personal loyalties are not supposed to be important. The president of the United States swears to uphold the U.S. Constitution and can be held accountable for doing so. Laws, in turn, are enacted and enforced through formal, bureaucratic procedures (Chapter 6), rather than reflecting custom and tradition or the whim of a ruler. Weber argued that rational-legal authority was most compatible with modern economies, and that as a consequence was rapidly replacing more traditional forms of authority. The march of history, in Weber's view, was a march toward rational-legal authority.

Weber did, however, identify a third form of authority that often threatened the other two. **Charismatic authority** is *power based on devotion inspired in followers by the presumed extraordinary personal qualities of a leader* (Weber, 1979). Charismatic authority derives from the "gift of grace," the belief that an individual has a "gift" of superhuman (and often divine) powers. Prominent historical examples would include Moses, Jesus Christ, Mohammed, and Buddha; more recent figures would include Hitler, Martin Luther King Jr., Mahatma Gandhi, and Mother Teresa.

Weber analyzed charismatic authority not in terms of whether or not a leader actually possesses such near-magical powers but rather in terms of the ways in which followers acquire and institutionalize their beliefs. As long as charismatic leaders are able to demonstrate their power, they are likely to be able to exercise authority. But when they waver, their authority is threatened. Moreover, when charismatic leaders die, much of their power dies with them, since their power is based on their personal qualities. While their immediate advisors may seek various ways to "routinize" their leader's charisma, this is unlikely to be successful in the long run. As a result, charismatic authority eventually gives way to one of the other two forms, traditional or rational-legal authority.

Weber felt that charismatic authority was particularly important in modern times: As people become frustrated with rational-legal authority, they are prone to the appeal of charismatic figures who promise answers to all problems. This could have highly destabilizing consequences for modern nation-states, particularly if people become disenchanted with impersonal bureaucracies and governments that are unable to deliver on their promises. A chilling proof of Weber's prophetic concern was provided soon after his death by the rise of Adolph Hitler, a leader with enormous charismatic appeal to Germans experiencing political humiliation and economic privation following Germany's defeat in the World War I (Scheff, 1994). Charismatic individuals continue to have appeal today, as globalizing processes contribute to economic dislocation, the loss of traditional beliefs and values, and the ability of modern nation-states to govern effectively.

Theories of State Power

Sociologists and political scientists have developed different theoretical approaches to account for the exercise of rational-legal authority in modern nation-states. We shall focus on two that differ markedly in their views of just how widely power is actually shared—functionalist and social conflict theories. These theories are based largely on governance in the United States today, although they can be applied also to other modern societies. In the following discussion, we shall use the terms "government" and "the state" interchangeably to refer to those governing institutions that possess legitimate authority in society.

Functionalist Theories of State Power
Functionalist theory argues that the modern nation-state reflects people's desire for a form of political organization that will make their social life more predictable and secure. In this view, the nation-state has thrived in part because relatively strong central governments serve to enhance economic development while assuring a degree of social stability. One way that governments achieve these goals is to work out differences that arise between individuals and groups whose interests conflict with one another. Functionalists thus view the state as contributing to the preservation of social order, by helping to manage conflicts and problems that are inherent when people live together (Alford and Friedland, 1985).

Functionalist theories of state power originally assumed a high degree of consensus on society's norms and values. For example, as Durkheim saw it, the state's ideal role was to educate people for their place in society, to regulate the economy to the extent necessary for its harmonious operation, and to provide for the necessary administration of public services (Durkheim, 1956, orig. 1922; 1964, orig. 1893; 1973). In Durkheim's view, the state primarily translated widely shared values and interests into fair-minded laws and effective policies. Yet it is clear that in modern societies there is not always universal agreement and consensus on all issues. While consensus is assumed to exist on such general values as freedom or equality, when it comes to more narrowly defined interests people are likely to diverge. Contemporary functionalist theory therefore argues that modern societies are **pluralistic,** in that they are *comprised of groups with different and often conflicting values and interests on specific issues, which contend with one another on roughly equal footing* (Dahl, 1961, 1982, 1989; Friedman, 1990). The role of the state in a pluralistic society is to then manage debate and conflict in such a way that the important interests and viewpoints are represented. The state is thus seen as a neutral umpire, impartially adjudicating between different groups.

The functionalist theory of state power has tended to focus on how power is exercised on specific issues, seeking to explain who can most effectively access and influence the governmental decision-making process. The foremost proponent of this view, political scientist Robert Dahl (1961, 1982, 1989), originally studied decision making in a single community—New Haven, Connecticut—where he concluded that politics was "dominated by many different sets of leaders, each having access to a different combination of political resources" (Dahl, 1961, p. 86). Dahl argued that in their efforts to exert political influence, individuals coalesce into **interest groups,** *groups comprised of people who share the same concerns on a particular issue, and therefore unite in an effort to influence governmental policy.* Interest groups may be short-lived, such as a local citizens' group that bands together to have a road repaved or a school built; or they may be long-lasting, such as a labor union or a manufacturers' association.

According to pluralistic theory, although interest groups may differ in their resources, influence, and capabilities, these factors are less important than the fact that there are many groups attempting to exert power. The notion that there exists a plurality of contending groups has given rise to the theory of **countervailing powers,** *a theory holding that the influence of one group is offset by that of another.* For example, if a major paper company wants to clear-cut a forest, an environmental organization will likely oppose it. In a similar fashion, big businesses and organized labor are seen as routinely facing off against one another, so that neither can exercise undue influence on the political process. When two powerful interests oppose one another, compromise is seen as the likely outcome, and the role of the government is to mediate solutions that benefit as many interests as possible.

Critical Assessment Critics of the functionalist theory of state power argue that it is based on a number of assumptions that are not substantiated by empirical research (Domhoff, 1978, 1983, 1990; Chambliss and Seidman, 1982). One of these assumptions is that modern societies are characterized by a high degree of consensus on important beliefs and values. Critics of functionalism argue that modern nation-states are comprised of extremely diverse populations, often including people from different racial and ethnic groups, immigrant backgrounds, social classes, and regions of the country. Such diversity may impede consensus on basic values. Furthermore, the complex nature of economic and political issues confronted by government officials cannot possibly be subject to widespread citizen debate, which is a precondition for the formation of consensus.

Critics of functionalist theory also dispute the assumption that government is somehow a neutral mediator between conflicting interests. They claim that legal systems are largely the result of power struggles between different social groups, and they consequently tend to favor the interests of the winners. In their view,

laws favor some groups over others, so that the legal deck is stacked from the beginning. For example, critics of functionalism point to the fact that when the U.S. Constitution was framed, landed property owners were favored over the landless, whites were favored over blacks and Indians, and men were favored over women. They note that American immigration laws at times specifically excluded Chinese, Japanese, and other nonwhites, often denying them citizenship and the right to vote (Friedman, 1985, 1990; Takaki, 1989). Land laws have been biased against Native Americans, blacks were rigidly segregated in many states prior to 1954, homosexual sex is still punishable by law in numerous states, and American women could not vote prior to the ratification of the Nineteenth Amendment to the U.S. Constitution in 1920. Women and minorities are still greatly underrepresented in government (see Map 13.1; see also Chapters 10 and 11).

Finally, critics of functionalist theory claim that regardless of how the legal deck is stacked, the game itself is often played unfairly in that some interest groups are far more powerful than others. In their view, government does not simply apply the rules in a neutral fashion, as functionalist theory claims. Rather, it bends the rules to favor the most powerful groups in society, including big business and other monied interests that finance increasingly costly political campaigns (Friedman, 1975, 1990; Feeley, 1992). As a consequence, critics of functionalist theory claim that even when laws are passed, they are somehow circumvented in ways that do not fundamentally alter the balance of power in society. For example, although school segregation has been outlawed since 1954 and most other forms of racial discrimination became illegal ten years later, racial segregation and discrimination continue to exist (Chapter 10). Women continue to earn only two-thirds as much as men, even though laws banning job discrimination on the basis of gender have been on the books for nearly 30 years (Chapter 11).

Social Conflict Theories of the State
The previous criticisms of functionalist theory reflect the social conflict theory perspective. Although social conflict theorists agree that the state serves certain functions for society, they ask the question, "for whom in society is the state functional?" In answering this question, conflict theorists reject the functionalist assumption that most people in society share a common interest on many important issues. Rather, they assume that society is comprised of different social groups, whose interests are fundamentally in conflict with one another. Unlike pluralistic theory, which views conflict as ultimately capable of being resolved through the give-and-take of political compromise, social conflict

Map 13.1   African-Americans in Congress: 1877 and 1994

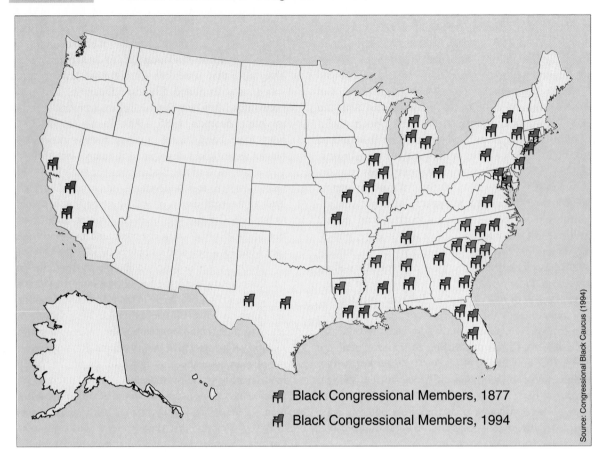

Source: Congressional Black Caucus (1994)

🪑 Black Congressional Members, 1877

🪑 Black Congressional Members, 1994

During the period of Reconstruction following the Civil War, numerous African Americans were for the first time elected to Congress from the Southern states. Representation of blacks in Congress dropped as low as zero during the "Jim Crow" period of rigid segregation, and only recently has begun to reflect their actual numbers.

theory sees the most important differences as irreconcilable. In this view, one group benefits at the expense of another; there is no overriding common interest. State power, according to conflict theory, inevitably benefits the most powerful groups in society.

Social conflict theory derives primarily from the ideas of Karl Marx, who claimed that the role of government in a capitalist society is to directly serve the interests of the capitalist class—to act, in his often-cited phrase, as "a committee for managing the common affairs of the whole bourgeoisie" (orig. 1848, in McClellan, 1977, p. 223). ("Bourgeoisie" was Marx's term for capitalist; see Chapters 1 and 8.) In Marx's original formulation, every type of society has a "ruling class" that controls the principal means of producing wealth. This class may rule directly, as it did under feudalism (see Chapter 4), or it may rule through a government that protects its interests, as it does in the modern era. In capitalist societies, Marx saw the government as directly serving the interests of a ruling class

that owns or manages the largest industries, corporations, and businesses of the country.

Although Marx occasionally wrote as if the "ruling class" exerted power with a single voice through a government that automatically did its bidding, in most of his writings he adopted the viewpoint that disagreements within the ruling class itself were played out at the level of politics (Appelbaum, 1988). Sometimes the capitalist class is divided on key issues; when this occurs, the different factions will be represented in government. Furthermore, the interests of other classes are occasionally represented in government, at least in societies where representatives are elected (Marx, 1851). The working class in particular, if well organized, can effectively press for such economic reforms as a shorter working day or the end of child labor (Marx, 1977; orig. 1867).

Marx's ideas led to a great deal of social conflict research, examining the relationship between government and the class structure of American society. This

gave rise to several different types of social conflict theory, each one emphasizing a somewhat different relationship between the government and class structure. **Class dominance theory** argues that *there is a more or less unified upper-class power elite exerting control over politics, the economy, and the military* (Berle and Means, 1982, orig. 1932; Mills, 1956; Miliband, 1969; Domhoff, 1983, 1990; Mintz and Schwartz 1985). This theory was introduced to contemporary sociology by C. Wright Mills in *The Power Elite* (1956). In his classic study, Mills argued that the United States is controlled by an elite group dominating the political, eco-

nomic, and military institutions. Although these officials are not seen as conspiring behind closed doors to run the country, Mills argues that they do share similar socioeconomic backgrounds, attend the same Ivy League schools, and incorporate the ethos of capitalism as they assume leading roles in managing the affairs of society. Often the same individuals can be found going through a "revolving door" consisting of top positions in law, business, and government. Mills' theory was highly compatible with Marx's approach to explaining class dominance, although Mills focused on the operation of the elites themselves rather than capi-

Box 13.1

Critical Thinking

Is There a Ruling Elite?

Some 30 years ago, political scientist Robert Dahl began studying political power in New Haven, Connecticut. By focusing on decision making in a number of specific cases, he formulated what became the classical pluralist theory of state power. Dahl argues that no single elite rules American society, but rather that power is shared by a large number of groups and interests that are constantly contending with and offsetting one another. Dahl summarizes his position as follows:

> Important government policies [are] arrived at through negotiation, bargaining, persuasion, and pressure at a considerable number of different sites in the political system—the White House, the bureaucracies, the labyrinth of committees in Congress, the federal and state courts, the state legislatures and executives, the local governments. No single organized political interest, party, class, region or ethnic group would control all of these sites (Dahl, 1967, p. 37).

Sociologist G. William Domhoff (1978, 1983, 1990) has been studying political power nearly as long as Dahl. Yet his conclusions are the exact opposite. According to Domhoff, power in American society is exerted by a ruling elite, consisting of the owners and managers of major corporations, political leaders, major advisors to the government, people occupying positions on the most important government commissions and agencies, and military leaders. In Domhoff's view the members of this elite are highly interconnected. They often attend

the same schools and colleges, marry into one anothers' families, belong to the same clubs, and sit on the same corporate boards of directors. They even camp out together at places like northern California's rustic Bohemian Grove, where, according to Domhoff, the most powerful figures congregate each year to renew old acquaintances and make business deals (Domhoff, 1974). Domhoff claims that this picture has not changed fundamentally since he began his research 30 years ago:

> As the 1990s began . . . the same old power elite was in the saddle as never before. . . . On balance, given the power of American elites and the problems of organizing large numbers of people, the prospects for greater fairness and equality did not look very good as the 1990s began. There will be no natural evolution to a better future for everyone, only a natural evolution to the rich getting richer and the poor getting poorer, for that is how capitalism works without intervention by a countervailing political party and the state. But the power elite . . . is precisely in the business of making sure that such intervention does not happen (Domhoff, 1990, pp. 283–284).

How would you reconcile such conflicting viewpoints on the same issue? What differing assumptions between the pluralist and social conflict theories of state power might lead to such different conclusions? Can you think of a study you might conduct that would enable you to decide which viewpoint is more likely to be correct?

talism as a political-economic system. A similar theory has been advanced by G. William Domhoff (1983, 1990), who in recent years has sought to document the existence of such a ruling elite (see Box 13.1).

Another version of social conflict theory emphasizes the importance of **structural contradictions,** which we defined in Chapter 4 as *aspects of a social structure that are mutually incompatible with one another, and therefore result in structural instability.* According to this view, the government in modern societies is inevitably caught up in a structural contradiction between the interests of the masses of people whose support is necessary for the government to be regarded as legitimate, and the powerful elites whose backing is also essential. This contradiction troubles both capitalist and socialist societies.

In capitalist societies, the role of the government is to ensure that businesses grow and prosper. Failure to do so will not only hurt the working- and middle-class people whose jobs may be threatened when business is doing poorly, but it will also anger the business elites who pour money into election campaign funds. It is difficult for government officials to be elected without support from the capitalist class. Yet at the same time, if government is perceived as favoring business over ordinary citizens, elected officials will not garner the votes necessary to remain in office. This can lead to a "crisis of legitimacy" for the state, which must act to benefit the capitalist class while obtaining the loyalty of other classes (Habermas, 1976, 1979; O'Connor, 1973; Offe, 1984; Held, 1989; Wolfe, 1977).

The contradiction between the need for popular legitimacy and elite support also is illustrated in the downfall of the Soviet Union. On the one hand, the basic beliefs of socialism, constantly buttressed by official government pronouncements, claimed that Soviet society was a "workers' paradise" in which all working people shared equally in the national wealth. On the other hand, people's everyday experience with economic hardship and corrupt public officials contradicted this claim. Two Russian sociologists describe the situation:

> The world around a Soviet person seemed to have a double-sided character. On the one side, there was the world of the most beautiful country with wise leaders and a happy population. On the other side, there was the world of mundane realities: [apartments] occupied by several families; bad, contaminated food; doctors incapable of curing anyone; the role of officials as capricious bribe-takers; and so on . . . The state acted as the main agent of exploitation and stood above the whole society as a gigantic and invulnerable divine force. State officials formed a kind of ruling elite . . . and hence enjoyed its privileges (Radaev and Shkaratan, 1992, pp. 301, 303).

A final version of social conflict theory, owing as much to the ideas of Max Weber as Karl Marx, emphasizes the **relative autonomy of the state,** *the belief that governments themselves exert a degree of power, independently of any class interests that may exist* (Weber, 1946b, 1979). Weber's work had sought to show the importance of bureaucratic organizations in modern society, with governments being among the largest and most powerful bureaucracies (see Chapter 6). This has led some sociologists to conclude that the government enjoys a degree of autonomy from the class structure of society. In this view, government interests may conflict with the interests of at least parts of the ruling class; a task of sociology is to better understand these conflicts (Tilly, 1975; Collins, 1974; Skocpol, 1979).

Critical Assessment Social conflict theory suffers from the opposite difficulty of functionalist theories—it tends to overemphasize the unified nature of the "ruling class" in capitalist society (Kolko, 1963). Large multinational corporations, small locally oriented businesses, banks, and owners of real estate do not necessarily share the same interests and frequently disagree on key issues. On central issues such as the legalization of drugs, abortion, women's rights, campaign reform, term limitations on elected officials, or national health service, American capitalists are deeply divided (Chambliss and Seidman, 1982; Chambliss and Zatz, 1994). Furthermore, there are many times when government decisions are in clear and direct opposition to the expressed interests and values of the most powerful capitalist groups. For example, the U.S. government passed laws legalizing trade unions and giving workers the right to bargain collectively against capitalists, even though both laws were opposed vehemently by the corporation executives and owners (McCormick, 1979; Klare, 1978; Chambliss and Zatz, 1994).

FORMS OF GOVERNANCE IN THE MODERN WORLD

The relationship between a society's government and its citizens can take a number of forms. In modern society, four forms of governance have proved to be especially important: (1) monarchies, (2) authoritarian regimes, (3) totalitarian regimes, and (4) democracies. Although we shall describe each of these, it is important to remember that in fact most systems of governance are unlikely to resemble any of these in pure form.

Monarchy

A **monarchy** is a *political system in which power resides in the personage of an individual or family and is*

passed from one generation to the next through lines of inheritance. As we mentioned earlier, monarchies derive their legitimacy from traditional authority. They were the primary form of governance in Europe between the twelfth and sixteenth centuries and were also important in most other parts of the world. Today, however, the formerly all-powerful royal families have been either dethroned or relegated to peripheral roles largely associated with ceremonial functions. The queens of England, Denmark, and the Netherlands and the kings of Sweden and Spain do not have any significant political power or formal authority to govern. Although a monarchy may still occasionally influence political events, as did the king of Spain in restoring democracy after 50 years of dictatorship, its influence is most often limited to the expression of opinions that are unlikely to be heeded by those who control the government.

There are, however, a few modern-day exceptions. King Hussein of Jordan and King Faisal of Saudi Arabia govern their countries and influence political, military, and economic decisions throughout the world. Saudi Arabia is a powerful member of the Organization of Petroleum Exporting Countries (OPEC), and as a result King Faisal is able to exert some influence over the price of oil, which in turn affects the economies of every country. Even these monarchs, however, govern with the consent of other powerful religious and financial groups.

Authoritarianism

In **authoritarian** political systems, *ordinary members of society are denied the right to participate in government.* Monarchies were typically authoritarian, in that citizens were regarded as subjects rather than as participants in governance. A more modern form of authoritarianism is the **dictatorship,** a *political system in which power rests in a single individual.* Because of the complexity of modern society, pure dictatorships are uncommon; even the most heavy-handed authoritarian leader requires some degree of support from military leaders, the intelligence apparatus, and major business leaders. As a consequence, authoritarianism often entails rule by an individual through a political party or organization that purports to serve the interests of all members of society. For example, the former authoritarian regimes of Eastern Europe and the Soviet Union claimed the right to rule on the basis of the "dictatorship of the proletariat" (working class), through the leadership of the Communist Party. Examples of authoritarian regimes include the former Soviet Union during its post-Stalin era, the Philippines under Ferdinand Marco in the 1980s, Cuba under Fidel Castro, and the People's Republic of China today.

Most authoritarian governments today tend to be of limited duration, since it is often exceedingly difficult to run a modern nation-state in this fashion. In previous years, authoritarian leaders have died (for example, Spain's General Franco in 1975), were overthrown by their enemies (as has been the case in many African and Latin American countries), or were ousted in popular revolutions (for example, when Cuba's Fidel Castro ousted Fulgenico Batista in 1959). More recently, however, once-powerful authoritarian regimes have allowed themselves to be voted out of existence, giving way to more democratic forms of governance. Such a transition has occurred in the former Soviet Union and most of its East European allies, as well as in Turkey and South Korea. This suggests the hypothesis that authoritarianism may prove to be fundamentally incompatible with the complexities of full participation in a global economic and political system. The case of China should prove instructive, since that country of 1.1 billion people is rapidly moving to integrate itself into the global economy while maintaining a highly authoritarian government at home.

Totalitarianism

When authoritarian dictatorships persist and become entrenched, the end result may be a totalitarian form of government. **Totalitarianism,** like authoritarianism, *denies popular political participation in government, but takes it one step further by seeking to regulate and control all aspects of the public and private lives of its citizens.* All opposition is outlawed, access to information is drastically controlled and limited, and citizens are required to demonstrate a high level of commitment and loyalty to the system. As the entire society becomes mobilized behind its rulers, daily life becomes highly regimented. External enemies, combined with claims of internal threats from "counter-revolutionaries," "terrorists," or "enemies of the people," are used as excuses to suspend individual rights and create extensive and intrusive security systems. Members are urged to inform on one another if the rules are broken or the leadership is criticized. Totalitarian governments sometimes derive their legitimacy from the perceived charismatic qualities of their leaders, who claim extraordinary abilities to serve the interests of their citizens.

Totalitarianism is a relatively new form of governance, because it requires a high degree of bureaucracy and advanced surveillance technology for a government to become so intrusive. Nazi Germany, the former Soviet Union during Stalin's dictatorship, General Pinochet in Chile, Franco in Spain, South Korea's military, and Saddam Hussein's regime in Iraq are all examples of totalitarian regimes.

Democracy

Democracy, *a political system in which citizens are able to directly or indirectly participate in their own governance,* literally means "the rule of the people." (The word comes from the Greek *demos,* "the people," and *kratos,* "rule.") Such a broad definition admits of many interpretations, and indeed a wide range of political systems in the world today call themselves democratic. This reflects the fact that throughout the world the *belief* in democracy has come to be widespread. Democratic political systems tend to be based in rational-legal authority, and they can take many forms.

The concept of democracy originated in the Greek city-state of Athens during the fifth century B.C., where it took the form of **direct democracy,** in which *all citizens fully participate in their own governance.* This was possible both because Athens was a small community by today's standards, and because the vast majority of its people (including women and slaves on whose labor its economy was based) were excluded from citizenship (Sagan, 1992).

Direct democracy is not possible today, given the enormous scale of most nations and the complexity of their affairs. Although some smaller New England communities in the United States still hold yearly town meetings where all adult residents can fully participate, most routine governance is still conducted through elected town councils. Most U.S. cities are far too populous to permit everyone to meet face to face, and nations are much larger still. As a result, democracy today typically takes the form of **representative democracy,** a *political system in which citizens elect representatives who are supposed to make decisions* that express the wishes of the majority who elect them to office. Popular participation is generally limited to voting for elected officials, who then enact laws that are administered by large bureaucracies staffed by permanent government employees. In this form, citizens retain the right to appoint and replace public officials through regular and institutionalized elections. The legitimacy of government officials derives from the popular support they gain in the electoral process.

Even though voting is the hallmark of representative democracy, the mere fact of voting does not necessarily ensure that a true democracy exists. Because most modern societies claim to be democracies, they may go through the motions of an election even though a meaningful choice of issues or candidates does not exist. In Iraq, for example, voters get to select only from among candidates belonging to the ruling Baathist Party; the candidates themselves are selected by the party leadership. The same was true in the former Soviet Union, where elections were limited to Communist Party candidates.

Forms of Governance and Economic Systems

It is important not to confuse a country's type of economy with its form of governance. Just because a capitalist society has a "free market" does not mean that its citizens are free to fully participate in governance. Similarly, just because the state exerts control over the economy in a socialist society does not mean that individuals enjoy no participation in governance whatsoever. Table 13.1 offers examples of various combinations of political regime and type of economic system.

Immediately following the end of the Civil War, African Americans gained a substantial share of state and federal elected offices. Jim Crow laws that discriminated against blacks reversed this process. Between 1900 and 1960 very few African Americans were elected to political office. In 1992 Carol Mosley-Braun became the first African-American woman to be elected to the U.S. Senate.

Table 13.1   Examples of Different Kinds of Modern Economic Systems and Political Regimes

Political Regime	Type of Economic System	
	Capitalist	Socialist
Democratic	United States, most industrial nations in the world today	??
Authoritarian	Singapore; South Korea (1961–1981); Philippines in later years; China today; Nigeria today	Cuba; former Soviet Union in later years; China today; Vietnam today
Totalitarian	Nazi Germany (1933–1945); Fascist Italy (1928–1945)	Soviet Union under Stalin (1927–1953); China during height of "Maoism" (1966–1971); Cambodia (1975–1979); North Korea today

Note: Although we have identified only two principal types of economic system (capitalist and socialist), we will suggest in Chapter 15 that there are many hybrid economies (called "industrial democracies") combining features of both—for example, free markets (a feature of capitalism) with some degree of central state economic regulation and planning (a feature of socialism). A number of northern European and Scandinavian countries fall into this "mixed" category.

There are no agreed-upon examples of socialist regimes with democratic forms of governance, although some scholars would argue that Nicaragua during the period 1979 to 1990 sought to achieve such a combination. Some leading scholars of Eastern Europe and the former Soviet Union believe, in fact, that the end result of the transformation of the Soviet Union will be the emergence of democratic socialist societies, not capitalist ones (Burawoy and Kortov, 1992; Burawoy and Lukacs, 1992).

THE AMERICAN POLITICAL SYSTEM

Politics in democratic societies is structured around competing political parties whose purpose is to gain control of the government by winning elections. Political parties serve this function by defining alternative policies and programs, building memberships, raising funds for candidates, helping to organize political campaigns, and linking citizens to officeholders. Yet political parties do not exist in a vacuum. Not only must candidates win elections and retain their offices, but their decisions, once in office, have enormous financial and social consequences. As a result, the American political system, as all political systems in democracies, is organized to influence both voters and legislators.

Political Parties and Voting

In the United States, unlike most other democracies, there are only two major political parties that play a significant role in electoral politics. During most of the twentieth century the Democratic Party has been seen as representing the interests of working- and middle-class Americans as well as racial and ethnic minorities. The Republican Party has also drawn much of its support from the middle class, as well as wealthy individuals and large corporations. There have been no important **third parties** (*any U.S. political party other than the Democrats or Republicans*) in national politics since Abraham Lincoln won as such a candidate in 1860.

In fact, since Lincoln's victory there have been only five presidential elections in which all minor parties combined got more that 10 percent of the vote. The most recent exception occurred in 1992, when H. Ross Perot, running at the head of his own party organization, won nearly 19 percent of the popular vote against incumbent George Bush and challenger Bill Clinton. This unusually high degree of support for a third-party candidate reflected voter dissatisfaction with the Democratic and Republican parties, which to many people no longer appeared to offer sufficiently different solutions at a time when economic problems had begun to threaten the middle class. According to one public opinion poll of 3,000 voters, only 33 percent consider themselves Democrats today, and 29 percent consider themselves Republicans. The largest group (39 percent) identify themselves as "independent" or "uncommitted" (Shogan, 1990).

This points to another fact of American politics: Differences between the two major parties often do not appear to be substantial, since in order to win elections both parties vie for the support of middle-of-the-road and uncommitted voters. In many other democracies there are a number of politically significant parties with sharply differentiated programs, including liberals, conservatives, socialists, communists, and environ-

When the U.S. colonies gained their independence from England, the doctrine that "all men are created equal" became one of the founding principles of the new nation. But slaves, women, children, and men who did not own property were excluded from voting and therefore were not "equal." Suffragettes in the early 1900s organized political demonstrations and attempted to force changes in the law through civil disobedience. After more than 150 years, the government was forced to acquiesce and women were given the vote in 1920.

mentally oriented "greens." Part of the reason for the difference between the United States and other democratic countries lies in the unique features of the American electoral system. Most other democratic societies have a **parliamentary system of government,** a *type of democracy in which the chief of state (usually called a prime minister) is the head of the party with the largest number of representatives in the legislature.* Party representation in the legislature is determined by voting in legislative districts. In some instances, only the party that wins the largest number of votes in a district sends its candidate to represent all district voters in the legislature. In other instances, all parties running candidates in a district send members to the legislature, in proportion to the number of votes they received. But in either case, it is the head of the party with the largest number of members in the legislature who becomes the country's leader. If no single party accounts for a majority of legislators, then parties are forced to form alliances with one another in order to build a majority coalition. Such a system favors the formation of numerous smaller parties, since even a tiny party that manages to win a few seats in the legislature has the possibility of entering into a coalition with the ruling party, and thereby playing a leading role in the government.

By way of contrast, the president of the United States is elected independently of his party's performance in legislative elections. Ronald Reagan, a Republican, was overwhelmingly elected president at the same time that the voters were sending Democratic majorities to both houses of Congress. Parties with narrow political interests and limited public support are thus effectively eliminated from the political process, since there is no avenue by which they can exert significant

political power. This silencing of minority voices is reinforced by the uniquely American system of electing presidents by actually voting for state electors, in which the candidate who gets the most votes in a state wins all of that state's electoral votes (see Box 13.2). There is thus a very strong incentive for all political groups to join one of the two major political parties, adopting centrist, middle-of-the-road positions with the widest public appeal, rather than forming smaller independent parties with well-defined positions. It is significant in this regard that H. Ross Perot, despite getting the support of nearly one out of every five voters, won no electoral votes for president and has had no discernible effect on congressional or presidential politics since losing the 1992 election.

Influencing the Vote: Money and Interest Groups, PACs, and Lobbyists

Influence is an important ingredient of democratic politics. It occurs at election time, when elected officials must spend a great deal of resources convincing the electorate to vote for them. It also occurs during the routine operations of government, when individuals and organizations seek to influence government officials to act on their behalf. Both of these sources of influence cost a great deal of money. Campaigning for office by means of television ads, radio, mailings, and media events can run into millions of dollars. Influencing an elected representative to pursue a favored project or vote in a particular way is also costly. Research on the role of interest groups, political action committees, and lobbyists suggests that, in keeping with the social conflict theories discussed above, a relatively small number of people and groups in America

Box 13.2

Silenced Voices

The American Voter

The U.S. system of voting for president discourages the formation of smaller parties that represent specific interests, since such parties are highly unlikely to have any significant effect on the outcome of presidential elections or congressional politics. One reason for this, explained in the text, is the American system of voting for the president and legislative representatives separately. A second is the electoral college system, provided for in the U.S. Constitution as a means to safeguard against a direct popular vote for president, which many of the founders feared would place the presidency in the hands of the masses of propertyless voters. At the time the Constitution was framed, the 13 states limited the vote to property-owning white males, estimated at less than 5 percent of the total U.S. population (Hellinger and Judd, 1991).

Under the electoral college system, voters in a state do not actually vote for president or vice president, but rather for a slate of "electors" from each candidate's political party. The "electors" of the winning candidate, in turn, get to cast all their votes for their party's candidate, in the electoral college vote approximately one month later. Each state has the same number of electors as its combined congressional delegation (House of Representatives and Senate). Thus, a populous state like California has 54 electors, accounting for a tenth of the total U.S. presidential electoral vote; small states like Delaware, Montana, or Vermont have only 3. The system is "winner-take-all," in which a presidential candidate who gets only one vote more than the leading opponent gets all of the state's electoral votes. In 1992 third-party candidate H. Ross Perot garnered 19.2 million votes across the country, one-fifth of the total votes cast; yet he received no electoral votes, because he failed to emerge the victor in any state. Bill Clinton, who won with only 44 percent of the popular vote, received a landslide victory in the electoral college, with nearly 70 percent of the votes, since he won the states with the largest number of electoral votes. In Utah, Perot actually out-polled Clinton in the popular vote, yet the state's five electoral votes all went to Bush, who received the largest number of popular votes in that state (45 percent).

One consequence of the lack of choice between many different party alternatives is a high degree of political apathy in the United States, reflected in extremely low voter turnout. One public opinion poll found that nearly a third of all those interviewed "completely agreed" with the statement "generally speaking, elected officials in Washington lose touch with the people pretty quickly" (Shogan, 1990). In the United States about half of the potential voters are silent in presidential elections; an even larger number are silent in off-year elections for congressional, state and local candidates. Many eligible voters do not register to vote, and, among those who register, many do not bother to vote.

As a consequence, the president of the United States is usually elected by less than a third of the potential voters. In 1988, for example, George Bush got the vote of only 27 percent of voting-age adults. Bill Clinton's share four years later was only 25 percent, since H. Ross Perot drew a sizable number of voters. Even Ronald Reagan, in his landslide victory over Walter Mondale in 1984, could only muster 29 percent of the potential vote. In all of these elections, the resounding voice among Americans old enough to vote proclaimed "none of the above." Those who are most likely to be silent at election time are lower-income people, blue-collar and service workers, and racial and ethnic minorities. In other countries voter turnout is much higher, reaching four-fifths of all potential voters in many European countries (Marger, 1987).

It is telling that in 1992, when Perot's presence on the ballot gave many American voters the sense of having an alternative, nearly 10 million more people voted than in the preceding two elections, raising the turnout to almost 50 percent. The surprising appearance of "Perotism" suggests that in future elections the silent American voter may be silent no longer. This is especially likely to be the case if the two major parties continue to fail to offer what voters regard as viable solutions.

exert disproportionate influence at the national level (Alexander, 1987).

Money and Interest Groups

Interest groups represent an enormous range of concerns in American politics. Conservation groups such as the Sierra Club seek to control corporate activities that are detrimental to the environment; the American Medical Association presses for doctors' interests on such issues as national health care; the National Rifle Association attempts to defeat gun control legislation; the National Organization of Women seeks equal rights for women. Interest groups range from a handful of individuals to corporations to enormous organizations with millions of members.

Political campaigns are extremely costly, and thus offer an important opportunity for interest groups and wealthy individuals to seek to exercise their influence on elected officials. Between January 1991 and November 1992, congressional candidates spent more than a half a billion dollars trying to get elected (Federal Election Commission, 1992). The presidential campaign costs each candidate more than $150 million. In states with large populations candidates may spend over $10 million running for the Senate, and half of that amount running for the House of Representatives.

In 1992, for example, Alfonse D'Amato of New York spent $11.3 million in his Senate race, while his unsuccessful opponent spent $6.3 million. Two years later, Michael Huffington of California spent $27 million of his own money, in his unsuccessful bid for a U.S. Senate seat. In the overwhelming majority of congressional races money talks; the candidate who spends the most on the election is usually the candidate who wins (Domhoff, 1990). Incumbents usually have an edge in this process, since they are able to raise large sums of money from individuals and interest groups they have favored during their tenure in office. As a consequence, incumbents are more likely to be re-elected, although the 1994 election proves this is not always the case.

In order to raise large sums of money, a candidate must either be extremely wealthy or rely on the contributions of others. Although candidates occasionally finance most of their own campaigns (H. Ross Perot and California's Michael Huffington are recent examples), the vast majority depend on raising funds from others. Contributors, in turn, naturally expect something in return for their donations, usually in the form of votes, favorable legislation, or projects that serve their interests. To take one example, during the 1988 elections 249 Republican Party contributors joined the prestigious "Team 100," by contributing more than $100,000 to the campaign. "Team 100" members included 66 individuals from investment and banking, 58 from real estate and construction, 17 from the oil industry, and 15 from food and agriculture (Cobb et al., 1990). During the 1988–1992 Bush presidency, 11 businessmen who had each contributed more than $100,000 to the Republican Party were nominated for ambassadorships (Sinai, 1992). During the first half of 1992, 19 businesses and individuals contributed more than $100,000 each to either the Democratic or Republican parties (see Table 13.2).

Political Action Committees (PACs)

Some of the most influential special interests in the United states today are organized into **political action committees (PACs),** *organizations formed by interest groups to raise and spend money in order to influence*

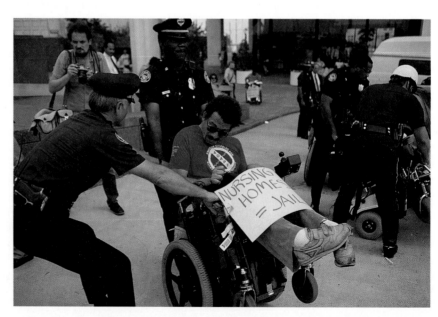

Social protest through demonstrations is an important part of the political landscape in all democratic societies. The protest may involve breaking the law in order to draw public attention to an issue of importance. In this photograph, demonstrators blocking the entrance to a nursing home are arguing that nursing homes are being used as "dumping grounds" for physically challenged persons who are not given a fair chance to be contributing members of society.

Table 13.2   Major Contributors to Political Parties

Contributor	Total	To Republicans	To Democrats
Archer Daniels Midland, Decatur, Ill.	$416,500	$370,000	$46,500
American Financial Corp., Cincinnati	345,000	345,000	0
Edgar M. Bronfman, New York City	200,000	200,000	0
RJR Nabisco, Wilkes-Barre, Pa.	186,000	105,000	81,000
U.S. Tobacco Co., Greenwich, Conn.	176,174	118,174	58,000
Atlantic Richfield, Co., Los Angeles	158,350	136,000	22,350
Decorating Den, Bethesda	150,000	150,000	0
FED-COM International Inc., Arlington	125,002	125,002	0
Occidental Petroleum Corp., Los Angeles	117,000	90,000	27,000
United Steelworkers of America, Pittsburgh	117,000	0	117,000
National Education Association, Washington	112,500	0	112,500
Phillip Morris Companies, New York City	101,330	78,330	23,000
The Sierra Nevada Group, Washington	100,000	100,000	0
Slim-Fast Foods Co., New York City	100,000	100,000	0
Stephens, Inc., Little Rock, Ark.	100,000	100,000	0
Sunrider International, Torrance, Calif.	100,000	100,000	0
Dwayne O. Andreas, Decatur, Ill.	100,000	100,000	0
Lawrence Kadish, Garden City, N.Y.	100,000	100,000	0
Blanchette Rockefeller, New York City	100,000	0	100,000

Note: Dwayne O. Andreas is chief executive officer of Archer Daniels Midland; Edgar M. Bronfman is CEO of Joseph Seagram and Sons, Inc.; Blanchette Rockefeller was the mother of Senator John D. "Jay" Rockefeller IV (D-W.Va).

Source: Goldstein (1991).

elected officials. In the 1992 presidential and congressional elections, PACs contributed over $170 million to congressional candidates (Federal Election Commission, 1992). Table 13.3 lists the leading corporate contributions to PACs during a ten-year period. These members of the Business Roundtable, a major interest group in American politics, have each contributed more than $1 million during the past decade in an effort to influence government policies and programs favorable to their interests.

PACs have played an important role in seeking to influence the outcome of the current national debate over health care reform (Table 13.4). PACs representing doctors, hospitals, insurance companies, and health-care workers have greatly increased their fund raising, contributions to political campaigns, and overall efforts to influence the outcome of the debate. The House and Senate leadership has averaged more than $250,000 each in campaign contributions from the health care industry during the past decade (Moyers, 1992), while a recent investigation of more than 200 medical industry PAC's found that they had given more than $60 million to congressional candidates during the last decade. The American Medical Association allocated $1.3 million to mount an advertising campaign opposing President Clinton's proposed health care re-

form. It currently maintains a Washington office, whose head is paid $422,000 annually to pressure Congress and the president to act in the interests of the medical profession (McCombs, 1993). Joseph Califano, former Secretary of Health, Education and Welfare, claims the following:

> Private interests and PAC contributors have acquired veto power in key committees over proposals that threaten them. . . . So long as private money clogs the corridors of power, any economic package President Clinton gets from Congress will include the same pay-offs to PACs that the House and Senate stuffed into the 647-page tax bill last year (Califano, 1992, p. A21).

Lobbyists

To influence lawmakers, interest groups often hire **lobbyists,** *paid professionals whose job it is to influence legislation.* Lobbyists scrutinize proposed legislation to see if there is any that affects their interests, and they propose legislation to further their interests. They often maintain an office in Washington or a state capital, and the most powerful lobbies are staffed by full-time employees. Lobbyists often work closely with those agencies and heads of congressional committees that

Table 13.3 Leading Corporate (Business Roundtable) Contributions of More Than $1 Million to Political Action Committees, 1983–1993

Company	Contribution
AT&T	$3,736,543
UPS	3,183,265
General Motors	1,985,712
Phillip Morris	1,952,917
Federal Express	1,915,478
GTE Corp.	1,859,281
BellSouth Corp.	1,769,192
General Electric	1,496,785
Union Pacific Corp.	1,469,750
Textron Inc.	1,200,106
Morgan Stanley	1,186,161
Ford Motor Co.	1,163,134
Nationsbank Corp.	1,133,795
Rockwell International	1,131,568
Citicorp	1,081,041
Martin Marietta	1,042,617
JP Morgan	1,024,575

Source: Common Cause (1994).

are responsible for regulating the activities of the interest groups they represent. Since lobbyists are often expert on matters that affect their interests, they may help in writing the laws that elected officials will introduce as legislation.

Lawyers and former governmental officials, including elected officials, and staff people who have worked for Congress or the executive branch, frequently are employed by lobbyists on the assumption that they can use their governmental contacts to their advantage. There is often a "revolving door" between lobbying organizations and government, which contributes to the substantial influence that many lobbyists enjoy (Birnbaum, 1992). To take one example, when Manuel Lujan Jr. was Secretary of the Interior he was responsible for regulating the use of federal lands for mining, grazing, and timbering. When Lujan left office, he accepted a job as a lobbyist for a company seeking to build a ski resort in New Mexico. The project required a boundary change for an area under the supervision of the National Park Service, and presumably Lujan's "insider's knowledge" was extremely valuable to the interest group seeking the boundary change.

One of the most important sources of influence in government is found within the government itself. As C. Wright Mills documented 40 years ago, the military

is heavily invested in governmental decisions. Not only does military spending comprise a large share of total government spending, but defense-related government contracts for everything from uniforms to advanced electronics can have an enormous impact on local economies. In fact, military-related spending is one of the principal businesses of government in many countries, including the United States. To understand the modern nation-state, therefore, it is necessary to understand the central role played by warfare and the military.

WAR AND THE MILITARY

Warfare was central to the formation of the modern nation-state (Tilly, 1975). The coalescence of thousands of societies throughout the world into fewer than 200 countries today has been achieved in large part through military conquest. Europe, for example, had hundreds of kingdoms and smaller states 500 years ago; today it has fewer than 50. The map of Europe was redrawn considerably during the two world wars, a process that continued with the breakup of the former Soviet Union (which added 11 countries to the map of Europe) and continues today with the civil war in what was formerly Yugoslavia.

Once democracy became firmly established as a feature of many nation-states, some political theorists believed that war would eventually be eliminated. This viewpoint was echoed after World War I, which was often referred to as the "war to end all wars." The history of modern nations unfortunately does not support such optimism. During the twentieth century alone, World War I was followed by World War II, wars in Korea, Vietnam, and the Persian Gulf, and a host of smaller conflicts around the world. In a century where nearly 100 million persons have lost their lives and world wars bear numbers for identification, warfare appears to be as firmly entrenched as ever (Keegan, 1993; Blainey, 1988). Nonetheless, there are some hopeful signs that warfare may eventually be regarded as an ineffective means of realizing national objectives.

The Military-Industrial Complex

General Dwight David Eisenhower was a leading American military hero of World War II. As head of the allied forces in Europe, he was responsible for the defeat of Germany and Italy, and therefore the end of the European conflict. After the war, Eisenhower became president of Columbia University and was later elected as the Republican Party candidate for U.S. President, an office he was to hold for two terms. As

Table 13.4   Top Political Action Committee (PAC) Contributors in the Area of Health Care 1989–1990 and 1991–1992

Organization	1989–1990 Total	1991–1992 Total	Percentage Change
American Medical Association	$2,375,537	$2,936,085	24
American Dental Association	817,428	1,420,958	74
American Academy of Ophthalmology	960,411	801,527	−17
American Chiropractic Association	173,350	641,746	270
American Hospital Association	502,689	505,888	1
American Podiatry Association	256,750	401,000	56
American Optometric Association	329,600	398,366	21
American Health Care Association	262,880	382,019	45
American College of Emergency Physicians	130,340	330,725	154
American Nurses Association	289,860	306,519	6
Association for the Advancement of Psychology	167,783	273,743	63
American Physical Therapy Association	149,750	198,941	33
Eli Lilly & Co.	175,740	195,530	11
Pfizer Inc.	137,300	188,100	37
Schering-Plough Corp.	126,434	186,050	47
Federation of American Health Systems	174,350	180,350	3
Glaxo Inc.	105,850	175,522	66
Corporation for the Advancement of Psychiatry	116,426	165,980	43
American Association of Oral & Maxillofacial Surgery	105,000	163,000	55
Abbott Laboratories	168,950	157,075	−7

Source: Goldstein (1991).

much as anyone else in the country, Eisenhower clearly understood the importance of the military and its role in American society. Eisenhower's words therefore had special meaning when, in his 1960 farewell presidential address to the nation, he warned of the dangers inherent in the overpowering coalition of what he termed the "military-industrial complex:"

This conjunction of an immense military establishment and a large arms industry is new in the American experience. [Its] total influence . . . economic, political, even spiritual . . . is felt in every statehouse, every office of the Federal government . . . We recognize the imperative need for this development. Yet me must not fail to comprehend its grave implications . . . for the very structure of our society. In the councils of government we must guard against the unwarranted influence, whether sought or unsought, by the military industrial complex. The potential for the disastrous rise of misplaced power exists and will persist (Eisenhower, 1960).

Eisenhower's warning was made more than 30 years ago, when the military-industrial complex had just emerged as a result of mobilization for World War II. Yet his words are no less important today. **Military-**

industrial complex is defined as the *interconnected institutions with a common interest in weapons and other defense spending.* It includes the military, the intelligence community, corporations with defense-related contracts, numerous government agencies, and university engineering and scientific research that has military applications. This network of governmental, military, and civilian officials is at the center of the American economy's high degree of dependence on military expenditures, and it helps account for the central role of military technology in scientific research and development in the United States.

The Department of Defense retains more than 24 million acres of land for its own use, an area greater than the combined states of Connecticut, Massachusetts, New Hampshire, Rhode Island, Vermont, and Delaware (Luttwak, 1984). One out of every five dollars in the federal budget goes to military spending, with the result that in many regions of the United States military spending is the foundation of local economies. For example, wages and salaries for personnel at Fort Ord, California, before it was closed, accounted for almost a third of the total for Monterey County. Maine's Bath Iron Works, which employs about 1 out of every 20 workers in that area, builds Navy destroyers (Congressional Budget Office [CBO], 1992).

Nuclear War and Mutual Assured Destruction (MAD)

After the European conflict in World War II had ended with Germany's surrender, the United States sought a quick end to the war in the Pacific. A decision was made to drop the newly developed atomic bombs on the Japanese cities of Hiroshima and Nagasaki. The devastation was unimaginable. In a flash the cities were entirely destroyed, their populations incinerated. Those who survived were exposed to radiation fallout, inflicting many with illness, disease, and early death.

The atomic bombs dropped on Hiroshima and Nagasaki were small in comparison with today's nuclear weapons. In addition to the instantaneous effects of blast, thermal, and nuclear radiation, thermonuclear weapons have a number of equally frightening delayed or secondary effects. Radioactive fallout is the most well-known danger associated with nuclear explosions, and it is the main reason the superpowers agreed to end atmospheric testing in the Limited Test Ban Treaty of 1963. A "nuclear winter" could prove equally destructive. Scientists have hypothesized that the dust and smoke thrown into the atmosphere by nuclear conflagrations could block the warming rays of the sun, cooling the planet and possibly leading to major species extinction (including our own). Given the total disruption that a general nuclear war would entail, it is exceedingly difficult to imagine how tightly-knit modern societies would survive (Gershwin, 1992).

Because nuclear weapons are so deadly, for a quarter century the United States and the former Soviet Union pursued identical military strategies dubbed **mutual assured destruction (MAD),** which called for *sufficient nuclear capability so that even after suffering a nuclear attack, it would be possible to completely destroy the attacker's society with a massive nuclear response.* Both sides believed that by maintaining the threat of a deadly "second strike" response to a "first strike" from the other, they could effectively deter a first strike from happening at all. MAD was thus supposed to make nuclear war impossible by the threat of mutual extinction (Kahn, 1978; Kissinger, 1985). Needless to say, such a strategy was highly risky and extremely costly. To maintain a credible "second strike" capability, each country had to build a nuclear arsenal that could destroy the world many times over, since many weapons would be lost in the initial attack. Armed and ready nuclear weapons had to be concealed in buried missile silos, on cruising submarines, and on high-altitude jet bombers continually in flight. Every technical advance by one side led to a corresponding technical development on the other side, with risks and costs mounting in an ever-increasing spiral.

At the time of its collapse, the Soviet Union possessed an estimated 27,000 nuclear weapons, about half of which were strategic weapons capable of reaching targets anywhere in the world, with the remainder consisting of smaller tactical weapons for battlefield use. The United States and its allies had comparable arsenals (Broder and Meisler, 1992). The world's nuclear weapons represented *3,000* times the explosive force of all bombs dropped during World War II, with a single nuclear submarine capable of demolishing all the major cities in Europe, Russia, or the United States (Sivard, 1993). It is estimated that since 1946 the United States has spent $2 trillion (in today's dollars) on all nuclear programs; the former Soviet Union has spent roughly the same amount, and the world total is perhaps $5 trillion (Sivard, 1993). The Strategic Defense Initiative ("Star Wars"), which envisioned putting up a "protective shield" in space to deter a surprise nuclear attack on the United States would have cost an estimated $100 billion had it been fully pursued (Center for Defense Information, 1991).

The world's major nuclear powers have long recognized the dangers of nuclear warfare, and international treaties to limit their use date back to 1959, when 40 nations (including the United States and the former Soviet Union) agreed to ban nuclear tests and dumping nuclear wastes in Antarctica. Since that time there have been nearly 20 agreements, with major breakthroughs in the past decade. The United States and the former Soviet Union agreed to limit their number of intercontinental nuclear missile sites in 1972, and, in 1988, to gradually eliminate all medium and shorter-range nuclear weapons. In 1991, as a result of the Strategic Arms Reductions Talks (START), the former Soviet Union and the U.S. agreed to reduce their nuclear arsenals by nearly one-third. The long-range strategic nuclear weapons forces of the two countries dropped by nearly a quarter between 1987 and 1992, from 23,600 to 17,900 warheads; if all goes as planned, they will further drop to 7,000 by the year 2003. As a result, the total destructive power of the world's nuclear weapons has been sharply reduced—it now represents only 1,620 times the total destructive power of World War II (Sivard, 1993; see Figure 13.1)!

For the moment, the collapse of the Soviet Union does not appear to have reversed this process, since both the United States and the Soviet Union's successor countries remain committed to reducing the threat of global nuclear destruction. Russia inherited the lion's share of the former Soviet Union's nuclear arsenal, although the Ukraine also has a sizable number, and Kazakhstan and Belarus smaller numbers. The United States currently has the largest number of nuclear weapons of any country in the world (Broder and Meisler, 1992).

Although the end of the Cold War hopefully por-

Scientists working for the U.S. military in World War II created the atomic bomb, by far the most destructive weapon ever invented. To hasten the end of World War II, the United States dropped atomic bombs on the Japanese cities of Hiroshima and Nagasaki, causing unprecedented devastation, as this photograph of the Nagasaki Medical College shows. Today, because of the end of the Cold War, some degree of nuclear disarmament has occurred, and the threat of global nuclear annihilation appears to be receding.

tends a decline in the nuclear arms race, there are some ominous signs as well. **Nuclear proliferation,** *the spread of nuclear weapons capability to additional nations,* remains a danger, even though a global treaty banning the sales of nuclear weapons technology was ratified by the world's major nuclear powers in 1968, nearly 30 years ago. A number of other countries have nuclear weapons, including Great Britain, France, China, Israel, and possibly South Africa. There is evidence that India and Pakistan also have nuclear weapons capability, which they were preparing to use against one another in a border dispute in 1990, a global disaster that was averted partly because of the active diplomatic intervention of the United States, several European countries, the former Soviet Union, and China (Broder and Meisler, 1992). North Korea, Iran, and Libya are believed to be seeking nuclear capability, and the 1991 Persian Gulf War was fought partly because U.S. strategists feared that Iraq was rapidly developing a credible nuclear weapons program.

Today, although the threat of MAD seems to have been reduced, it remains to be seen whether recent changes in the nation-state system portend an end to the nuclear arms race, or its escalation as newly independent nations strive to develop their own nuclear capabilities.

Conventional Warfare

The United States has been embroiled in ten "official" wars throughout its 200-year history, beginning with its founding in the Revolutionary War (Table 13.5). These wars have claimed more than a million American lives, and far greater numbers of lives in other countries, where most of the wars were fought. For example, it is esti-

mated that several million Vietnamese died in the Vietnam War, which claimed about 60,000 American lives. The one war the United States fought against itself—the Civil War—was, at least for Americans, by far the bloodiest war in American history. The half-million Americans killed in that war represented nearly 1 out of every 65 Americans alive at the time; a comparable war today would claim nearly four million American lives.

Under modern conditions, conventional war has become almost as destructive as nuclear conflict. Nearly 60 million people were killed in World Wars I and II alone (Sivard, 1983). A single nights' fire-bombing of Tokyo in March of 1945 resulted in the destruction of more than 15 square miles and the death of more than 80,000 people. It is estimated that in 1992, there were a total of 29 wars around the world that claimed a minimum of 1,000 lives each. In fact, the approximately 150 wars fought since World War II have claimed more than 23 million lives, twice the number of lives lost in wars during the entire nineteenth century, and seven times the number of lives lost in eighteenth century wars (Sivard, 1993). To take two recent examples, during the Persian Gulf War, the U.S. government estimates that upward of 150,000 Iraqis perished from the direct and indirect effects of the military campaign (Government Accounting Office [GAO], 1992). The Iran-Iraq War (1980–1988) lasted for eight years and claimed millions of lives.

Modern conventional warfare is highly technical. Automation, sensors, and information-processing capabilities increasingly enable anything to be targeted and destroyed, at night as well as during the day. Not only are conventional weapons exceedingly lethal, they are also extremely expensive. Globally, military ex-

Figure 13.1 **The Destructive Capacity of the World's Nuclear Arsenals**

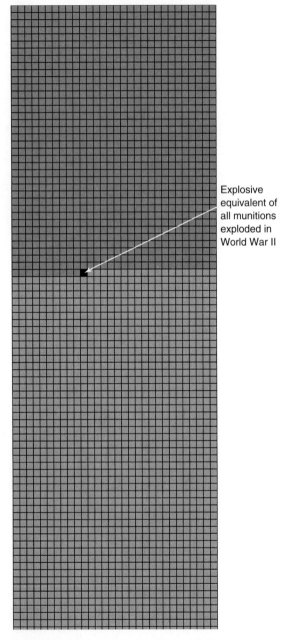

Explosive equivalent of all munitions exploded in World War II

The square at the center represents the explosive equivalent of all the destructive power of World War II, roughly six million tons of dynamite. By that standard, at their peak the destructive power of nuclear weapons represented approximately 3,000 World War II's (the entire box). Today, because of the nuclear disarmament treaties that have been negotiated between the United States and the former Soviet Union, the explosive power represented by the blue squares has been removed from the nuclear arsenals, leaving only the equivalent of 1,620 times the total destructive power of World War II. Once the projected nuclear disarmament is fully implemented, the destructive power of 900 World War II's will still remain.

Source: Adapted from Sivard (1993, p. 11).

penditures today approach $1 trillion annually (Sivard, 1993). The social and humanitarian costs associated with such high levels of military spending are considerable. Resources that might otherwise be devoted to improving health care, education, and alleviating world-wide hunger and starvation are siphoned off to meet military demands. It is estimated that if the lower-income nations were to divert half of their military spending to basic health services, as many as 10 million lives could be saved each year. The annual military spending of the world's industrial nations is roughly equal to the combined income of the world's poorest two billion people (Sivard, 1993).

The global sales of weapons is a major business, benefiting arms manufacturers and buttressing national economies. Prior to the end of the Cold War, the United States and the Soviet Union rivaled one another as the leading sellers of arms to the rest of the world. In 1989, for example, the Soviet Union accounted for approximately $18.6 billion in sales of weapons to other countries, and the United States accounted for $11.2 billion (U.S. Arms Control and Disarmament Agency, as reported in *World Almanac, and Book of Facts* 1992). With the end of the Cold War, the United States emerged as the undisputed leader in arms sales, accounting for 57 percent of such sales in 1990. China is also becoming an important arms merchant, having supplied billions of dollars in weapons and weapons-making capability to India, Pakistan, Iran, Iraq, Syria, and Saudi Arabia (Tong, 1992).

There are, however, some hopeful signs that the end of the Cold War may signal a slowing of the arms race (see Map 13.2). U.S. military spending fell from a 1988 high of $357.1 billion to $292.2 billion in 1994, a decline of nearly one-fifth—although it is still far higher than it was in 1981, when a major defense build-up began (Figure 13.2). As a percentage of national wealth, military spending is lower than at any time in the last two decades, standing at roughly 4.5 percent, down from a high of 6.5 percent in 1986 and 1987 (U.S. Department of Defense, 1993). Reflecting these trends, the United States will have reduced its armed forces from 2.1 million members in 1991 to 1.6 million by 1996 (Moskos, 1991).

World military expenditures also have declined slightly from their high point in 1989. This decline, however, has occurred almost entirely in the industrial nations. The poorer nations of the world, which can least afford it, have continued to increase their military spending (Sivard, 1993; see Figure 13.3). The global arms trade also has slowed, with total sales to nonindustrial countries dropping sharply to $24.7 billion between 1990 and 1991, the lowest level in seven years (U.S. Department of Defense and U.S. Arms Control

Table 13.5   American Casualties in Ten Wars, 1776–1993

War	Deaths	Casualties	Total
Revoluntionary War	25,324	8,445	33,769
War of 1812	2,260	4,505	6,765
Mexican-American War	13,283	4,152	17,435
Civil War	498,332	281,881	780,213
Spanish-American War	2,446	1,662	4,108
World War I	116,708	204,002	320,710
World War II	407,316	670,846	1,078,162
Korean War	54,246	103,284	157,530
Vietnam War	58,151	153,303	211,454
Persian Gulf War	148	Not available	—

Source: Adapted from *World Almanac and Book of Facts,* 1992.

Map 13.2   **Increase in Military Spending, By Nation: 1960 - 1990**

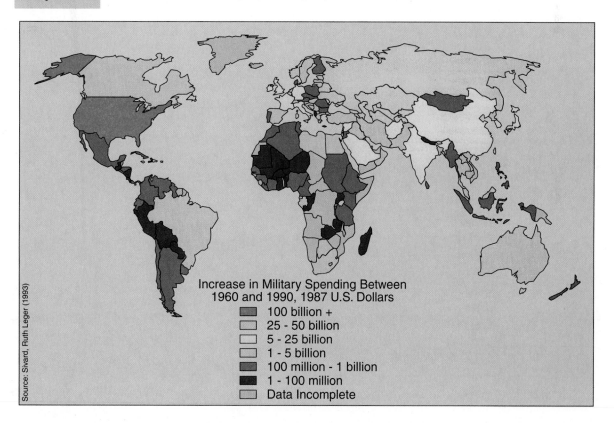

Increase in Military Spending Between
1960 and 1990, 1987 U.S. Dollars

- 100 billion +
- 25 - 50 billion
- 5 - 25 billion
- 1 - 5 billion
- 100 million - 1 billion
- 1 - 100 million
- Data Incomplete

Source: Sivard, Ruth Leger (1993)

World military spending grew sharply during the 20th century, peaking during the late 1980s. Not surprisingly, the largest increases have been in the industrial nations. Since then spending has declined somewhat, although not in the poorer countries of the world, which continue to buy weapons from wealthier ones.

Figure 13.2   **U.S. Defense Spending, Total and as a Percent of Gross Domestic Product, 1976–1994**

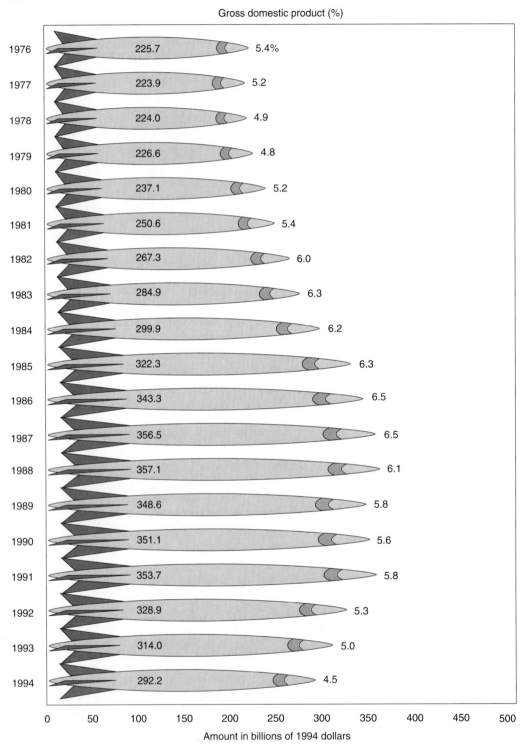

Gross domestic product (%)

Year	Amount	GDP %
1976	225.7	5.4%
1977	223.9	5.2
1978	224.0	4.9
1979	226.6	4.8
1980	237.1	5.2
1981	250.6	5.4
1982	267.3	6.0
1983	284.9	6.3
1984	299.9	6.2
1985	322.3	6.3
1986	343.3	6.5
1987	356.5	6.5
1988	357.1	6.1
1989	348.6	5.8
1990	351.1	5.6
1991	353.7	5.8
1992	328.9	5.3
1993	314.0	5.0
1994	292.2	4.5

0   50   100   150   200   250   300   350   400   450   500

Amount in billions of 1994 dollars

Military spending shot up rapidly during the Reagan presidency (1981–1988). In 1980 it stood at $237.1 billion, or roughly 5.2 percent of the total domestically produced national wealth (gross domestic product, or GDP). By 1988 military spending had reached $357.1 billion—a 50 percent increase in eight years of $120 billion (all figures are in constant 1994 dollars), representing more than 6 percent of GDP. Since that time, military spending has declined sharply, although it still remains higher than before the build-up. With the end of the Cold War and the collapse of the Soviet Union, military spending may be expected to drop even further, although this may hurt states and regions whose economies depend on military spending.
Source: U.S. Department of Defense (1933, Table 7.5).

Figure 13.3   World Military Expenditures, 1960–1991: Industrial and Lower-Income Nations

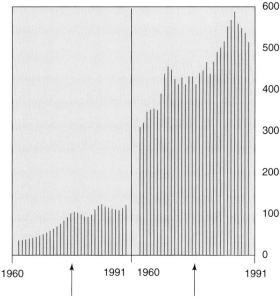

Military Expenditures
(in billions of 1987 dollars)

World military expenditures have increased sharply since 1960. In the industrial nations, they have nearly doubled since 1960, reaching a high of nearly $600 billion in 1989 (expressed in 1987 dollars). Since that time, they have declined slightly. In the lower-income nations of the world, they have continued to increase, although they have leveled off somewhat in the past few years.

Source: Adapted from Sivard (1993, p. 10).

and Disarmament Agency, as reported in World Almanac, 1992).

But as we noted above, the military-industrial complex plays a pivotal economic and political role in the United States as well as other countries, and as a consequence additional declines in military spending and the arms trade will not come easily. **Peacetime conversion,** the *transformation of defense-related industries to the production of nonmilitary goods and services,* is a formidable challenge confronting the United States today. The drop in defense spending and military personnel has contributed to overall economic decline in states that are highly dependent on defense-related industries or military bases. California, whose economy depends on both, has been especially hurt, revealing the difficulty of converting the military-industrial complex to peaceful purposes.

GLOBALIZATION: TOWARD A WORLD POLITICAL COMMUNITY?

We argued earlier in this chapter that nation-states were important in the development of capitalism. Strong central governments and codified legal systems served to manage business and labor, regulate trade, support investment in economic growth, and provide for the general social welfare. But as globalization has made it increasingly easy for workers and businesses to cross national borders, many of these functions are being assumed by international agreements and global business and political organizations.

Nelson Mandela is seen here sharing the Nobel Peace Prize with F. W. De Klerk, at that time president of South Africa, for their joint contribution to ending the system of apartheid. By supporting the internal African resistance struggle, globalization hastened the end of apartheid through an international economic boycott that proved damaging to the South African economy. Mandela was elected president of South Africa in 1994.

An increasingly unified world economy creates pressures for a unified body of rules and standards to help ensure that things run smoothly. Just as national systems of law developed when nation-based economies emerged, today an international system of law is important in a world economy based increasingly in global organizations (Chapter 6). When AT&T signs a contract with the Chinese government to produce high-technology electronics in Shanghai, it must be certain that the terms of the contract will be enforced. When General Motors and Toyota form a joint venture to together manufacture a car in a U.S. factory, they have to agree on thousands of engineering and technical specifications for the car, on techniques for jointly manag-

Box 13.3

Globalization

Is a Single World Government Likely to Emerge?

We have noted that one of the defining characteristics of the nation-state is sovereign control over its members. Nations are typically unwilling to give up significant sovereignty unless compelled to so so under the threat or actual use of force. While international treaties and other agreements necessarily involve some loss of national sovereignty, these are viewed as minor in comparison with the gains to be realized. Furthermore, nations will sometimes violate international agreements when it serves their interests and they believe they can do so without significant consequence.

The United Nations, an international organization comprised of about 180 member nations, is becoming increasingly important in the world political system. Zbigniew Brzezinski (1993a, 1993b), professor of political science at the School of Advanced International Studies at Johns Hopkins University and the national security advisor to former president Jimmy Carter, has even claimed that "the U.N.'s time has finally come. It is only within the framework of that global organization that the common problems of [humanity] can be collectively addressed" (Brzezinski, 1993b).

In recent years there have been some dramatic military examples of how the U.N. might play the increased role Brzezinski envisions. For example, when Iraq violated international law by invading Kuwait in 1990, the U.N. roundly condemned the action. When Iraq refused to comply with the U.N. decision and withdraw its troops, member nations, led by the United States, used overwhelmingly superior force to compel a withdrawal. The U.N. has also taken recent action to enforce peace in Somalia and Bosnia as well. Does this suggest that the U.N. may become a type of "world government,"

enacting international laws and using military power to enforce compliance?

A comparison of these recent U.N. interventions suggests that the U.N.'s ability to act effectively as a "world government" depends largely on which nations are violating the law, and which are seeking to uphold it. In the case of Iraq, international law was upheld but only because Iraq was powerless against the combined military might of powerful U.N. member nations willing to enforce the law. U.N. success in Somalia and Bosnia was much more limited, primarily because major countries were unwilling to use military force to achieve international objectives.

When a powerful U.N. member nation itself violates the law, it is highly unlikely that the law will be enforced at all. For example, in 1984 the United States mined Nicaragua's principal harbor in an effort to cut off military supplies and trade to that country. Although the United States had diplomatic ties with Nicaragua, it believed the country's government was overly sympathetic to communism, and so was supporting rebel forces attempting to topple the government. The U.S. action violated the U.N. charter, according to a decision by the U.N.'s World Court. Yet the United States simply refused to honor the Court's decision, and withdrew from its jurisdiction the following year. In this case no enforcement action was considered, given the superior power of the United States.

As the world becomes increasingly interdependent, international organizations such as the United Nations will likely be called upon to take more and more responsibility for making laws that apply to all nations. Their ability to enforce those laws appears unlikely to grow nearly as rapidly as their ability to enact them.

Table 13.6 Examples of Regional or Other International Organizations and Agreements Among Nations

Name	Number of member nations (1992)
International Criminal Police Organization (Interpol)	146
Organization of American States (OAS)	35
Organization of African Unity (OAU)	32
Organization for Economic Cooperation and Development (OECD)	24
League of Arab States (Arab League)	21
North Atlantic Treaty Organization (NATO)	16
Caribbean Community and Common Market (CARICOM)	14
Organization of Petroleum Exporting Countries (OPEC)	13
European Community (EC)	12
Economic Cooperation Organization	9
Group of Seven (G-7) (major industrial nations)	7
Association of Southeast Asian Nations (ASEAN)	6
North American Free Trade Agreement (NAFTA)	3

ing production, on common labor policies, and on ways to share profits.

As globalization leads to growing interdependence among nations, it seems reasonable to anticipate that the political institutions of different countries will increasingly come to resemble one another. Such a position is held by a group of theorists who study international organizations. According to the **institutionalist school** of organizational theory, *by becoming part of a global economic and legal system, countries and organizations are pressured into playing by a common set of international rules and regulations, as well as changing some of their internal rules and regulations to conform to international standards* (Meyer et al., 1987; Krasner, 1983; Meyer, 1980; Meyer and Hannan, 1979; Meyer and Thomas, 1980; Ramirez and Meyer, 1980; Thomas et al., 1987). Sociologists from the institutionalist school see most countries in the world eventually adopting similar institutional frameworks that permit them to freely interact with one another. Such convergence is seen not only in government organizations, but in education, law, and other areas as well. Institutional convergence may in the long run prove to be most compatible with democratic forms of governance, since rational-legal forms of authority and democracy go hand in hand.

To the extent that nations become organizationally similar and economically interdependent, it is possible that international organizations themselves will come to play an increasing role in world affairs. The emergence of regional trading blocks is an important step in the development of a global system of governance. Europe is moving to establish a European Community (EC), which will operate virtually as a single country. The EC will eventually have a single currency, a sin-

gle workforce, single minimal labor standards, and minimal restrictions on the movements of people or goods across the borders of its member nations. Although some member states have expressed concerns over excessive infringement on their national sovereignty, this movement toward a single, transnational system of governance could vastly increase Europe's economic power in a global economy.

The United States is following suit, with the North American Free Trade Agreement (NAFTA) now ratified by Canada, the United States, and Mexico. Unlike the EC, NAFTA will not create a single economy. It will, however, eliminate most restrictions on trade between the three nations. U.S. businesses wanting to open factories in Mexico, for example, can do so without having to pay special taxes on the goods that are made across the border. Similar efforts in Asia, the Middle East, and elsewhere are listed in Table 13.6.

The United Nations, which we discussed as an example of a global organization in Chapter 6, is likely to play an increasingly important role in the international system of nations. Now that it is no longer divided by Cold War politics, the U.N. may find itself in a better position to enforce an international system of law. For example, its member countries were virtually of one mind in supporting economic and military actions during the Persian Gulf War against Iraq in 1991, and they were willing to send peacekeeping forces to Somalia in hopes of ending ethnic warfare that was resulting in the mass starvation of hundreds of thousands of people. The U.N. presence in Bosnia, while somewhat more cautious, also reflects an openness to global intervention in the interests of promoting peace and protecting civilians from warfare.

Although individual nations are far from willing to

give up national sovereignty to any international organization, there does appear to be a greater willingness on the part of many nations to rely on one another for international standards as well as limited international law enforcement. Yet the failure of the U.N. to fully achieve peace in Somalia or Bosnia suggests that the world is a long way away from anything resembling a global government (Box 13.3).

Although global political coordination appears to be increasing, an opposite pattern is also in evidence: Some states are today fragmenting into smaller entities based on ethnicity. This trend reflects a resurgence of **ethnonationalism,** a *strongly held set of beliefs based on identification with an ethnic community that calls for nationhood based on ethnic ties.* We have already pointed to the breakup of the former Yugoslavia as an example of this trend. Countries like Yugoslavia, Georgia, Azerbaijan, and Armenia, once held together by strong central governments, have become warring factions of ethnic groups. Hundreds of thousands of people have died as different ethnic groups take up arms against one another, attempting to assert their own national sovereignty while seeking revenge for perceived historical wrongs.

As in any time of change, it is difficult to anticipate what the world will look like even a few years into the future. A decade ago few if any social scientists would have predicted such world-changing events as the collapse of the Soviet Union, the end of the Cold War, or the potential emergence of Communist China as a global capitalist powerhouse. No one can say for certain whether economic globalization will produce a corresponding political globalization, or whether it will prove so destabilizing that nations eventually disintegrate into ethnic rivalries.

C H A P T E R   S U M M A R Y

1. The modern **nation-state,** which characterizes almost all forms of governance today, is characterized by **sovereignty,** systems of **law,** and notions of **citizenship** in which members are seen as having both rights and obligations.

2. **Power** in the nation-state is typically realized through one of three kinds of **legitimate authority:** (1) **traditional authority,** based on custom and habit; (2) **rational-legal authority,** based on the belief in law; and (3) **charismatic authority,** based on the perceived inspirational qualities of the leader.

3. Functionalist theories of state power argue that the role of the state is to neutrally mediate between a **plurality** of contending interests, in which the influence of one group is usually offset by that of another group with an opposing view.

4. Social conflict theories of state power draw the opposite conclusion—that the state serves the interest of the most powerful groups in society, who are seen as having interests that conflict with most citizens. Some versions of social conflict theories argue for the **class dominance** of a ruling class or power elite, while other versions see **structural contradictions** in society itself as shaping the exercise of power.

5. Governance in the modern world has taken a number of forms, including **monarchy, authoritarianism** and **dictatorship, totalitarianism,** and **democracy.**

6. Democracy is one of the primary forms of governance in the world today, with most countries claiming to be democratic in theory if not in practice. Most democratic countries practice **representative democracy** rather than **direct democracy.**

7. Different forms of governance are compatible with different kinds of economic systems.

8. The American political system is presently characterized by widespread citizen indifference and apathy, reflected in low levels of voter turnout.

9. Elected officials are heavily dependent on financial support in order to get elected and remain in office. Partly because of this, **interest groups, PACs,** and **lobbyists** exert a great deal of political influence in American politics.

10. Warfare has been central to the formation of the modern nation-state, and remains important today. The United States and some other industrial nations possess a **military industrial complex** that is politically and economically dependent on military spending.

11. Militarization may be declining, largely as a result of the end of the Cold War. Military spending has dropped in the United States and Russia, and global

steps have been taken in the direction of limited nuclear disarmament.

12. The **institutionalist school** of organizational theory argues that globalization is reflected in a degree of convergence among the political institutions of the world's nations.

13. Regional agreements, as well as global political institutions such as the United Nations, suggest that increased world governance may also result from globalization.

14. At the same time that global political integration appears to be increasing, **ethnonationalism** is also growing, as some nations fragment into regional groupings based on strong ethnic ties and identifications.

QUESTIONS FOR DISCUSSION

1. What are the principal differences between the functionalist and social conflict theories of state power? How might each theory account for the existence of war and militarization today?

2. Does charismatic leadership potentially pose a serious challenge to democracy in the modern nation-state? Under what conditions might a charismatic leader acquire power?

3. Who rules America?

4. Are modern nation-states more likely to be authoritarian totalitarian, or democratic? What evidence exists in support of your answer?

5. Does globalization make warfare more or less likely as a means of settling international differences? Why?

KEY TERMS

authoritarianism: A political system in which ordinary members of society are denied the right to participate in government.

charismatic authority: Power based on devotion inspired in followers by the presumed extraordinary personal qualities of a leader.

citizens: Individuals who are part of a political community in which they are granted certain rights and privileges, while at the same time having specified obligations and duties.

civil rights: Legal rights that protect citizens from injuries perpetrated by other individuals and by institutions.

class dominance theory: A political theory, derived from the ideas of Karl Marx, which argues that there is a more or less unified upper-class power elite exerting control over politics, the economy, and the military.

Cold War: The period of heightened tensions between the United States and the Soviet Union, lasting from the 1950s through the 1980s. (The term "cold" was used because the two countries never openly confronted one another on the battlefield, although numerous wars were fought as a result of the conflict.)

countervailing powers: A theory holding that the influence of one group is offset by that of another.

democracy: A political system in which citizens are able to directly or indirectly participate in their own governance (literally, "the rule of the people").

dictatorship: A political system in which power rests in a single individual.

direct democracy: A political system in which all citizens fully participate in their own governance.

domination: The likelihood that a command will be obeyed.

ethnonationalism: A strongly held set of beliefs based on identification with an ethnic community that calls for nationhood based on ethnic ties.

institutionalist school: A theory of organizations stating that by becoming part of a global economic and legal system, countries and organizations are pressured into playing by a common set of international rules and regulations, as well as changing some of their internal rules and regulations to conform to international standards.

interest groups: Groups comprised of people who share the same concerns on a particular issue and therefore unite in an effort to influence governmental policy.

law: The codified rules of behavior established by a government and backed by the threat of force.

legitimate authority: The use of power that is recognized as rightful by those over whom it is exercised.

lobbyists: Paid professionals whose job it is to influence legislation.

military industrial complex: A phrase coined by former President Dwight D. Eisenhower to characterize the interconnected institutions with a common interest in weapons and other defense spending; it includes the military, the intelligence community, corporations with defense-related contracts, numerous government agencies, and university engineering and scientific research that has military applications.

monarchy: A political system in which power resides in the personage of an individual or family and is passed from one generation to the next through lines of inheritance.

mutual assured destruction (MAD): The defining nuclear strategy of both the United States, the former Soviet Union, and their allies throughout the Cold War, calling for sufficient nuclear capability so that even after suffering a nuclear attack, it would be possible to completely destroy the attacker's society with a massive nuclear response.

nationalism: A powerful sense of identification with the nation-state that is expressed through a common set of strongly held beliefs.

nation-state: A particular form of state whose members are regarded as "citizens" possessing specified legal rights and obligations.

nuclear proliferation: The spread of nuclear weapons capability to additional nations.

parliamentary system of government: A type of democracy in which the chief of state (usually called a prime minister) is the head of the party with the largest number of representatives in the legislature.

peacetime conversion: The transformation of defense-related industries to the production of nonmilitary goods and services.

pluralism: A political theory holding that society is comprised of groups with different and often conflicting values and interests on specific issues, which contend with one another on roughly equal footing.

political action committees (PACs): Organizations formed by interest groups to raise and spend money in order to influence elected officials.

political rights: Legal rights ensuring that anyone who so chooses can participate in governance.

power: The ability to mobilize resources and achieve a goal despite the resistance of others.

rational-legal authority: Power based on a belief in the lawfulness of enacted rules and the legitimate right of leaders to exercise authority under such rules.

relative autonomy of the state: A political theory, derived from the ideas of Max Weber as well as Karl Marx, which argues that governments themselves exert a degree of power, independently of any class interests that may exist.

representative democracy: A political system in which citizens elect representatives who are supposed to make decisions that express the wishes of the majority who elect them to office.

social rights: Legal rights that call for the governmental provision of various forms of economic and social security.

sovereignty: The final and total authority possessed by a nation-state over its members, such that no greater authority can be found elsewhere.

state: A political apparatus possessing the legitimate monopoly over the use of force within its territory.

structural contradictions: Aspects of a social structure that are mutually incompatible with one another and therefore result in structural instability.

third party: A phrase used to refer to any U.S. political party other than the Democratics or Republicans.

totalitarianism: A type of authoritarianism which, in addition to denying popular political participation in government, seeks to regulate and control all aspects of the public and private lives of its citizens.

traditional authority: Power based on a belief in the sanctity of long-standing traditions and the legitimate right of rulers to exercise authority under them.

R E C O M M E N D E D   F O R   F U R T H E R   R E A D I N G

Chambliss, William J., and Robert B. Seidman. (1982). *Law, Order, and Power* (rev. ed.). Reading: Addison-Wesley.

A textbook that examines the relationship between legal systems, the state, and political power from the conflict perspective.

Dahl, Robert A. (1961). *Who Governs?* New Haven: Yale University Press.

Domhoff, G. William. (1978). *Who Really Rules? New Haven and Community Power Reexamined.* New Brunswick, NJ: Transaction Books.

Reading this pair of books together will provide insight into some of the complexities of studying power. Dahl's book, the classical study of pluralism in an American community, concludes that no single group rules New Haven, Connecticut. Domhoff's reanalysis of Dahl's data draws exactly the opposite conclusion—that New Haven was indeed governed by a small group of people constituting a power elite.

Domhoff, G. William. (1990). *The Power Elite and the State: How Policy is Made in America.* New York: A. de Gouyker.

An argument for the existence of a power elite that governs America at the highest levels, based on years of research into the nature and operation of such a group.

Held, David. (1989). *Political Theory and the Modern State.* Stanford: Stanford University Press.

An analysis of different theories about the modern nation-state; examines questions of sovereignty, legitimacy, power, crisis, and the future of democracy.

Thomas, George M., John W. Meyer, Francisco O. Ramirez, and John Boli. *Institutional Structure: Constituting State, Society, and the Individual.* Newbury Park, CA: Sage.

A collection of essays from the "institutionalist school"; examines convergence among institutional structures in the nations of the world.

Families

CHAPTER OUTLINE

INTRODUCTION: WHAT IS A FAMILY?

In Waco, Texas, before their compound burned down in a confrontation with federal law enforcement officers, the followers of self-proclaimed religious messiah David Koresh lived together in what they referred to as a "family." Not far from their compound is a pet cemetery where a gravestone marks the resting place of "Buster, Not Just a Dog. He Was Family," and another that reads "Phemie Euphemie Fayette, Too Well Beloved to Be Forgotten, Our Little Girl" (McMurtry, 1993, p. 16). Charles Manson, who is serving a life sentence for a string of brutal ritual murders in the late 1960s, was leader of a group of young men and women which the media dubbed "the Manson family." One of the obligations of family membership was participation in the murders.

The Koresh and Manson families, as well as the existence of animals who are regarded as "family," suggest some of the difficulties encountered by sociologists as they attempt to study this topic. When people are asked what they mean by "the family," their responses suggest very little consensus (Trost, 1988). The social scientific definition reflects this ambiguity. Sociologists and anthropologists define a **family** as *a group of people who identify themselves as being related to one another, usually by blood, marriage, or adoption, and who share intimate relationships and dependency.* This definition emphasizes the fact that the meaning of "family" is socially constructed within a particular culture or subculture; it does not mean the same thing to everyone in all places or at all times. While "family" may be defined in terms of kinship based on birth or marriage, this need not be the case. There are numerous variations in family structures (Boutilier, 1993).

What constitutes a family is socially constructed. The members of a commune called the East Wind Community in Tecumsah, Missouri, define themselves as a family even though most of them are not related by blood. Because they are not legally defined as a family, however, they do not enjoy all the rights and protections of other American families.

BASIC CONCEPTS IN THE STUDY OF THE FAMILY

Just as with the concept of "family," the notion of "marriage" is culturally constructed and open to change. Sociologists define **marriage** as *a culturally approved relationship, usually between two individuals, that provides for a degree of economic cooperation, intimacy, and sexual activity.* Marriages may be legally certified by the government, as they are in industrial societies, or they may be authorized by religious organizations, kinship groups, or simply the norms of the prevailing culture (Parker, 1990). Although marriages usually involve partners of different sexes, this need not be the case, and same-sex marriages are becoming more common in the United States and other industrial societies. In some places, same-sex marriages are finding legal acceptance. Marriage typically provides the family framework within which children are born and/or raised.

In the United States, the most common family form is the **nuclear family,** *a social group consisting of one or two parents and their dependent children.* The meaning of "nuclear family" itself has changed over time, however. During the 1950s, four out of five children grew up with two biological parents who were married to each other. Today only half of all children can expect to spend their childhood in such a family, which today characterizes less than a quarter of all American households (U.S. Bureau of the Census, 1991; Whitehead, 1993). A significant number of families today have one or more of the following characteristics: They may involve only a single parent (usually the mother); include adopted children or children from previous marriages; be comprised of mates who are not legally married; or include same-sex couples. We shall examine these trends in some detail in the section entitled "Changing Family Values."

In many societies, and in some subcultures in the United States, people live in **extended families,** *social groups consisting of one or more parents, children, and other kin, often spanning several generations.* In addition to the basic nuclear family unit, an extended family might also include grandparents, aunts, uncles, cousins, or other close relatives. Most Northern European and American families are nuclear, while extended families are more common in Eastern and Southern Europe, Africa, Asia, and Latin America (Busch, 1990). In the United States, extended families are most likely to be found among lower-income households, families living in rural areas, and recent immigrants from countries where extended families are common. Economic necessity often contributes to the formation of extended families as a means of combining resources. During times when jobs are scarce, for example, young adults with their own children may move in with their parents simply to save money.

There are significant cultural variations in who takes responsibility for child rearing. Traditionally, the role of parent in Western European societies is assumed by the biological parents. However, this is only one of many variations in the world. Among the Baganda, a Bantu-speaking tribe of Central Africa, the responsibility for child rearing is the biological father's brother (Queen, Habenstein, and Adams, 1961). The Nayars of Southern India assign this role to the mother's eldest brother (Schneider and Gough, 1974). **Child-minding,** *an arrangement in which extended family members and friends cooperate in raising the children of a person who is living in another locale,* is common among Trinidadians and other Caribbean natives who have migrated to the United States in search of work (Ho, 1993; see Box 14.1). And nearly 5 percent of all American children under 18 now live with their grandparents, often without their own mothers present (Figure 14.1). This pattern is most common among blacks, where 12 percent live with their grandparents. Among whites, the figure is 4 percent; among Hispanics, 6 percent (U.S. Bureau of the Census, 1993).

Families vary also according to cultural norms governing the number of wives or husbands a person may have. The two basic cultural patterns are **monogamy,** in which *a person may have only one spouse at a time,* and **polygamy,** in which *a person may have more than one spouse at a time.* There are two types of polygamy—**polygyny,** in which *a man may have multiple wives,* and **polyandry,** in which *a woman may have multiple husbands.* Polygyny, which was accept-

Family patterns and definitions change over time. The gay couple in this photograph have just registered as domestic partners in New York City. Some states give registered gay and lesbian domestic partners many of the same legal rights given to heterosexual marriages.

The nuclear family *that is common to most industrialized nations consists of one or two parents and children. This Japanese nuclear family shows the impact of rapidly changing customs and traditions in that society, as revealed in the different styles of dress between parents and children.*

able in parts of Europe until the middle ages, is far more common than polyandry. In the United States, the best known example of polygyny was found among nineteenth century members of the Church of Latter Day Saints (Mormons). Since this practice violated dominant cultural norms as well as U.S. law, the Mormons left New York State for what later became Utah, in hopes of escaping persecution for their marital and other religious beliefs. When Utah was subsequently admitted as a state, the Mormon church agreed to give up the practice (Hardy, 1992).

Although monogamy is the law in the United States, anthropologist George Peter Murdoch's (1949) classic study of 862 societies found that only 16 percent required monogamy, while four out of five permitted polygyny. (Only four societies permitted polyandry.) Although monogamy is common in industrial societies, polygyny is apparently the rule in preindustrial societies (Barry and Schlegel, 1984). Ember (1974) theorized that in preindustrial societies warfare often decimated the male population, creating a "surplus" of women who necessarily had to share a smaller number of men if they hoped to have heterosexual relationships and bear children. Whatever the reasons for polygyny, however, today relatively few men actually practice it, even when it is permitted by social norms. Since the number of men and women is roughly equal in most societies, were some men to have more than one wife, others would necessarily have no wife at all.

Finally, in most societies marriages tend to be **endogamous,** *involving mates who come from the same kinship group, social category, or other social group.* While this is especially likely to be the case of preindustrial societies, it is frequently true of industrial societies as well. Even though in fiction we may celebrate

the wealthy aristocrat who marries the impoverished worker and lives happily ever after, most people choose mates who are from roughly the same social class, age, race, and ethnic group. Spouses typically have similar educational attainment, share the same beliefs and values, adhere to the same religious precepts, and often even live near one another or attend the same schools. Such constrained choices are not usually the result of deliberate decisions, except perhaps in the case of some members of the upper class who bow to family pressures to marry within their own exclusive social group (Domhoff, 1990). Rather, they reflect the importance of cultural norms and values in shaping people's perceptions of who constitutes an "appropriate" partner.

THEORETICAL PERSPECTIVES ON FAMILIES

When sociologists study the family, their views are often shaped by their overall perspectives on society as a whole. As with the study of other institutions, it is helpful to distinguish between the functionalist and conflict perspectives, so long as we bear in mind that these two approaches are not mutually exclusive but rather simply ask different questions and focus on different aspects of family life.

Functionalist Theory of the Family

Functionalist theory looks at families in terms of the functions they perform for the larger society. These are seen as including biological reproduction, which all societies require to perpetuate themselves; the nurturance and socialization of children; and the protection of those who are relatively helpless, including children,

Box 14.1

Globalization

Old Cultures and New International Families—Anne-Marie's Story

Anthropologist Christine Ho (1993) has examined what she terms "international families" that result from globalization. Focusing on mothers who emigrate from the Caribbean to the United States, Ho documents how they often rely on child-minding, an arrangement in which extended family members and even friends cooperate in raising their children while they pursue work elsewhere, often thousands of miles away. This practice adds a global dimension to cooperative child-rearing practices that are a long-standing feature of Caribbean culture. The story of Anne-Marie, a woman who migrated from the impoverished Caribbean island of Trinidad and Tobago in hopes of finding work in the United States, is illustrative.

Anne-Marie, the single mother of two infant sons, moved to New York City from Trinidad. She eventually got her "green card" and managed to find a job doing clerical work in a bank. But for her first five years in the United States, Anne-Marie's sons remained behind in Trinidad, in the care of her mother. Eventually, once she was financially stable, Anne-Marie's sons joined her, accompanied by her mother and her brother. The four then lived together in an extended family household.

Several years later Anne-Marie married a man who also came from Trinidad, and she and her new husband moved to Los Angeles in hopes that he would find work in the construction industry. Once again, she left her sons behind in the care of her mother, until she could get reestablished. After giving birth to a daughter she sent for her sons, and finally established a conventional nuclear family. This arrangement proved to be short-lived, however. In order to improve her career prospects, Anne-Marie decided to enroll in a year-long course in medical transcribing. Although her teenage sons were now old enough to be on their own after school, Anne-Marie wanted her daughter to get proper parental attention. The solution, once again, was child-minding: this time on the part of her husband's grandmother, mother, and younger sister, who lived in the Virgin Islands (also in the Caribbean). During the year of Anne-Marie's

schooling, her infant daughter lived with her husband's extended family.

Seven years later the situation once again changed. By now Anne-Marie's sons had grown and moved away from Los Angeles, and she needed someone to provide after-school care for her daughter, now eight, so she could work. Rather than rely on day care, Anne-Marie decided to send for her husband's sister in the Virgin Islands, the same young woman who had helped provide child-minding seven years earlier. The sister moved to Los Angeles, where she joined Anne-Marie's again-extended family, resuming the care of Anne-Marie's daughter while going to high school. In a sense, Anne-Marie and her husband were now providing child-minding for his younger sister, who was able to leave her own mother and grandmother in the Virgin Islands by joining her brother and sister-in-law in Los Angeles.

Nor were Anne-Marie, her husband, daughter, and husband's sister the only members of this extended family. Anne-Marie's husband had a daughter from a previous relationship who spent summers with them, and three other children. The couple also had a host of relatives living in Trinidad, the Virgin Islands, and in various places in the United States. This provided them with a large international family, an *extended family spanning several countries, yet characterized by intense interactions, strong emotional ties, and a binding sense of mutual obligation.*

Ho believes that such global family arrangements will enable Caribbean immigrants to avoid becoming fully "Americanized:" International families and child-minding are seen as providing a strong sense of continuity with their original Caribbean culture. She predicts that Caribbean immigrants will retain their native cultures by regularly receiving what she characterizes as "cultural booster shots," accomplished through the constant shuttling back and forth of family members between the United States and the Caribbean. At the same time, Ho notes, this process also contributes to the "Americanization" of the Caribbean region, which may eventually give rise to an ever-more global culture.

Figure 14.1   American Youths Under 18 Being Raised in Their Grandparents' Homes

Total
- ■ No parent present: 935,000
- ■ Living in grandparents' home: 3.2 million
- ■ U.S. youths: 69.3 million

Hispanic
- ■ No parent present: 86,000
- ■ Living in grandparents' home: 415,000
- ■ Total: 7.2 million

Note: Persons of Hispanic origin may be of any race.

Black
- ■ No parent present: 463,000
- ■ Living in grandparents' home: 1.2 million
- ■ Total: 10.0 million

White
- ■ No parent present: 452,000
- ■ Living in grandparents' home: 1.8 million
- ■ Total: 51.4 million

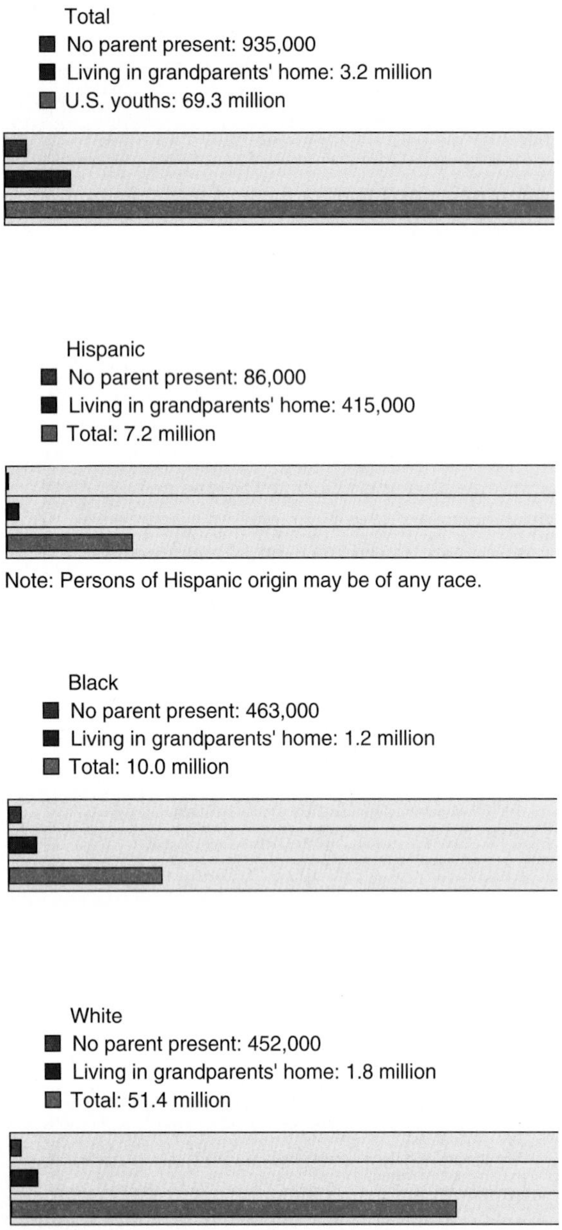

A substantial number of children today are living in their grandparents' homes, sometimes with a parent present, sometimes not. Nearly 5 percent of all Americans under 18, some 3.2 million youths, live with their grandparents. Of these, 29 percent have no parent present. The proportion living with grandparents differs considerably according to ethnic group; it is highest for African Americans (12 percent), lowest for whites (4 percent), and intermediate for Hispanics (6 percent).
Source: U.S. Bureau of the Census (1992).

the infirm, and the very elderly. Since human infants are helpless for a prolonged period after birth, it is especially important that all societies have strong cultural norms aimed at providing relatively stable family forms that help ensure protection of children. It is probably for this reason that very few cultures encourage childbearing outside of culturally sanctioned marriages. Socialization into society's cultural norms and values also occurs largely in the family, particularly during the first few years of life (Chapter 5).

Functionalists also see the family as providing a number of other important functions for society. For example, families help to regulate sexual behavior, although actual sexual norms vary considerably from society to society (Chapter 11). The family often serves to locate its members in the society's stratification system, since children normally acquire the social status of their parents and relatives. In caste societies, children retain their status positions throughout their lives, although in class-based societies mobility is possible (Chapter 8). Finally, the family serves to provide primary emotional support for its members, a topic we will return to in the section on "'Pure Relationships' and Romantic Love" (Blechman, 1990; Carter, 1993).

Critical Assessment In emphasizing the ways in which the family contributes to the maintenance and overall functioning of society, functionalist theory tends to view the family in terms of its contributions to social stability. Although few sociologists would question the assertion that families perform such important functions as socialization, placement into social statuses, or emotional support, some have pointed to the family's role in perpetuating divisions that exist within the larger society. Unequal power relations, gender inequality, and even violence may be features of family life that functionalist theory tends to ignore. The conflict theory of the family addresses such concerns.

Conflict Theory of the Family

Conflict theory focuses on the ways in which the family serves to reproduce societal inequality among its members, particularly between men and women. The family has been characterized as a **gender factory,** a setting in which *society's traditional gender roles are reproduced* (see Chapter 11). According to this view, the family serves to reproduce the relations of authority that exist in the wider society, centered around the authority of the father (Fenstermaker Berk, 1985; Waite and Goldscheider, 1992; Smart, 1984; Collins, 1985; Fine, 1992; Engels, 1968; orig. 1884). Conflict theory argues that in modern society women are expected to work without pay at home as wives and moth-

As functionalist theory indicates, the family can be an important source of early childhood socialization as well as emotional support for family members. The idealized picture of the two-parent, multichild American family applies to fewer and fewer families, however. Today, only a quarter of all American households fit this image.

ers, entering the paid workforce only when their labor is needed. This, according to conflict theory, is so that women can provide a cheap and ready source of labor to keep the economy running, while serving as a "safety valve" when the economy is slow: If women lose their paying job they can be expected to return home to their "primary" responsibilities as homemakers. Yet conflict theorists point out that even when they labor in the paid workforce, women are often expected to perform a **second shift** of *unpaid housework after they come home from their paid employment* (Hochschild, 1990; see Chapter 11).

Conflict theorists also point to a cultural contradiction in the role of the family: in capitalist societies, the family must promote consumption while socializing its members into an ethic that calls for hard work, deferred gratification, and a willingness to save for the future (Bell, 1978; Ehrenreich, 1989, 1992). In the United States, the family serves as the primary unit of consumption (Castells, 1983). Television advertisements project images of products into every American living room, carrying the never-ending message that happiness comes from instant gratification resulting from unending consumption. These television messages, which are constantly reinforced in movies and print media, are not lost on children, who are far more likely to prefer the pleasures of consumerism to the kinds of sacrifices that will eventually be required for them to become adult members of society. Barbara Ehrenerich (1989, 1992) has argued that this cultural contradiction between the ethics of work and the ethics of instant consumption results in a great deal of stress. Children constantly get a mixed message, "do your homework" versus "buy and play." Adults are caught in a similar bind: They must work to consume, and consume to compensate for the dissatisfactions of work.

Critical Assessment Conflict theory, in focusing on the oppressive aspects of family relationships, tends to overlook its important positive functions. Since the family serves as a microcosm of the larger society, it is a place where social change can begin. This is occurring, as spouses redefine their family roles, a topic we take up in the section on "Changing Family Values." Family members are not prisoners but participants in a crucial social institution that they themselves help to construct through their daily interactions. To better understand how the family serves as a flexible yet central institution, it will be useful to briefly examine its changing nature in modern society.

THE FAMILY IN MODERN SOCIETY

The family is, in a fundamental sense, a mirror of the larger society of which it is a part. As societies change, so too do families. Since the mid-eighteenth century, the impact of industrialization has had a profound impact on the nature of the family in modern society. The family, which once served as the primary place where children were socialized and all family members contributed to the production of society's wealth, no longer fulfills these roles to the same degree. Rather, the family has become a place where people expect emotional support, enjoying the fruits of their paid labor as consumers.

The Family's Changing Economic Role

Prior to the industrial revolution, the family played a key role as an economic unit. In societies based on agriculture, all family members were expected to work in order to contribute to family subsistence. Children were a valuable economic asset, since more children meant more hands for farming, handicraft, or work in the home.

Industrialization changed these family roles radically. Since industrialization resulted in a separation of home from workplace, most families now earned their subsistence outside the home. Not only did this lead to a devaluation of the economic importance of the family, but it resulted in a radical change in family roles as well: men became the principal "breadwinners" outside the home, while women—sometimes encouraged by law—remained at home as mothers and "homemakers" (Parker, 1990). The male role, which brought cash income into the home, came to be seen as the more important of the two, reinforcing patriarchal power relations. According to some sociologists, what we today understand as "home" and "motherhood" are actually inventions of modern society (Giddens, 1992; Dally, 1982; Badinter, 1981).

Children no longer provided hands to work the farm or make the family's clothing. Rather, they were to be educated in schools, which, like the workplace in industrial society, were specialized institutions outside the home. Eventually, the expectation of a primary school education was replaced by that of a secondary

The family, like all other institutions, is both an agent and a reflection of societal change. Although conflict theory has characterized families as gender factories *where stereotypical gender roles are reproduced, it is also a place where social change can begin, as this photograph suggests.*

school education, and then a college degree. Children came to be seen as an economic burden rather than an asset, and smaller families eventually became the norm (Headlee, 1991). As the socialization of children increasingly fell to institutions other than the family, children came to experience increased personal tensions in the face of conflicting demands from parents, peers, teachers, and friends (Tepperman and Wilson, 1993).

"Pure Relationships" and Romantic Love

Economic production, religious experience, education—all are now provided in specialized institutions such as the workplace, house of worship, and school. The family has become a haven of intimacy, providing the emotional support that is often difficult to find in the larger, more impersonal and bureaucratic institutions of society. These changes have brought with them a shift in the meaning of marriage.

In preindustrial societies, parents often selected their children's mates on the basis of the prospective spouse's social class, property, and traditional family ties. Marriages were usually based on economic considerations and family alliances, with more romantic encounters (at least for men) reserved for nonmarital affairs (Parker, 1990). Arranged marriages based on purely economic or social considerations have today given way to marriages based on notions of companionship, emotional fulfillment, and romantic love (Acampo, 1989; Giddens, 1992; Stone, 1982). In modern societies young people typically leave home to attend school or find work. They soon achieve a measure of economic independence from their parents, and with it, social freedom as well. One consequence is that few young people in modern society are likely to accept the notion that their parents should choose their spouse for any reason whatsoever.

Romantic love instead comes to be seen as the appropriate basis for selecting a marriage partner. This is reflected in the belief that marriage should entail a **pure relationship,** one that is *entered into purely for its own sake, and which is maintained only so long as it is mutually satisfying to both partners.* The pursuit of individual self-fulfillment, and the belief that such fulfillment can be found in a satisfactory relationship, is a relatively recent feature of human society. It is reinforced by the uniquely European-American belief in the overriding importance of the individual (Giddens, 1991, 1992).

As a result, marriage need not always be viewed as a lifetime commitment, enduring through bad times and good, "till death do us part." Rather, marriages come to be viewed as binding only so long as both partners are satisfied, although the presence of children may provide additional motivation for continuing an

Agriculturally based economies often foster large families as an economic necessity, as seen in this photograph of a turn-of-the-century Russian immigrant family in North Dakota. With industrialization, however, large families become an economic burden rather than an asset. Religion, custom, and knowledge are additional factors that help to determine family size.

otherwise unsatisfying relationship. In traditional societies, divorce is often an unthinkable public disgrace; in modern society, it is instead viewed as a private matter between the affected parties, a normal process resulting from individual growth and development. To the extent that the family has come to be seen as bearing the primary responsibility for the emotional well-being of spouses, it has become increasingly fragile as a social institution (Giddens, 1992).

CHANGING FAMILY VALUES

When Dan Quayle was vice president of the United States, he created a media storm when he called for the country to return to "traditional family values." Quayle criticized a popular television program, *Murphy Brown,* when the program's star character became pregnant and decided to have the baby despite being unmarried. The vice president objected to the program because, he said, it undermined "traditional family values."

Yet what are these "traditional family values?" On the night that Murphy Brown had her son, more than a third of all television-viewing Americans tuned in to share in the blessed event, most of this audience presumably sympathetic to what they were seeing (Whitehead, 1993). Any effort to characterize "traditional family values" quickly reveals an enormous diversity of opinion by social class, race, ethnicity, religion, and gender orientation (Pfeifer and Sussman, 1991).

During the 1950s, sociologists tended to focus on issues such as mate selection, divorce, and measures of marital satisfaction. Little attention was paid to those issues occupying center stage today—discrimination and gender inequality at home and in the workplace, family violence, and alternative notions of the family.

Changes in scholarship on the family reflect value changes in the wider society. Such societal changes have come about for many reasons: the civil rights, antiwar, and other protest movements of the 1960s, which caused many people to question gender relations as well as and other basic social institutions; the rapidly growing number of women in the workforce, providing some with a measure of economic and social independence from their spouses; and the rise of feminist thinking (Chapter 11).

As a result of these changes, the past two decades have seen a much wider openness to alternatives to traditional family life. Social scientists, along with the general public, have changed their thinking considerably on the significance of divorce, separation, single parenting, and other family forms (see, for example, Skolnick and Skolnick, 1992; Dizard and Gadlin, 1990; Stacey, 1990). During the 1940s, divorce was considered to be a disgrace; one sociology textbook characterized it as "the public acknowledgment of failure" (mentioned in Whitehead, 1993). But with divorce rates rising, such practices have found much wider acceptance. One study conducted during the 1970s, for example, reported that three-quarters of all Americans did not feel it was morally wrong for an unmarried woman to bear a child. Today, public opinion polls find that far fewer Americans value such things as being faithful to one's spouse, lifelong marriage, or parenthood than was true a generation ago (Whitehead, 1993). The greater diversity of family arrangements has even received official recognition: Beginning with the 1990 Census, the U.S. government has divided its long-standing "family households" category into two subcategories: "married couple family households" and "other family households" (Wetzel, 1990).

Work and Marriage

There is a high degree of commitment to marriage in the United States. Ninety-five percent of all people have been married by age 50, and a high percentage of divorced people remarry. Yet there is also an increasing tendency to postpone or avoid marriage altogether (U.S. Bureau of the Census, 1993; Glick, 1984). The median ages for men and women at the time of their first marriage began to rise in the early 1970s, when it was 23 for males and 21 for females. Today, both men and women are on average three years older than they were in the early 1970s at the time of first marriage (U.S. Bureau of Census, 1993). The **marriage rate,** *the ratio of the number of people who actually marry in a given year compared with the total number of people eligible to marry,* has been steadily declining since the 1960s, from 108 per 1,000 in 1966 to 78 per 1,000 in 1989 (Norton and Miller, 1992).

These changes reflect changes in the larger society, particularly the movement of women into the paid workforce. More women are in the workforce today than at any time since World War II, the result of economic pressures as well as changing attitudes toward female employment (Chapter 15). Three-quarters of all U.S. mothers now work outside the home, compared to less than a third only 20 years ago. The number of families where both spouses work has increased from about 23 million in 1975 to 31 million today (Figure 14.2), to the point where 46 percent of the workforce is today comprised of women (Figure 14.3). As more women have joined the workforce, family size has dropped steadily, from a "baby boom" high of 3.33 members in 1960 to only 2.62 today.

There is some evidence that these trends may be reversing. Female labor force participation appears to have peaked, and among younger women aged 20 to 24 has actually declined during the past several years (U.S. Department of Labor, 1994). Although the reasons for this are not fully understood, one possible explanation is that many of the jobs open to young women do not pay enough to offset the costs of childcare, transportation, and other expenses associated with working outside the home. As a result, women may have less incentive to seek paid work (Mahar, 1994). The labor force patterns of younger women are especially important for family formation and childbearing. It is too soon to tell whether or not these trends signal a partial return to more traditional families in which the husband alone is the wage earner.

Divorce and Single Parenting

Divorce and single parenting are increasingly common in American society, affecting all members of the family. We will examine these two interrelated changes in

Figure 14.2   Families in which Both Spouses Work, 1975–1991

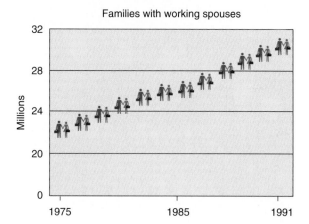

The number of families in which both spouses work has increased dramatically in recent years, from about 23 million in 1975 to nearly 32 million today. This reflects changing values toward work and family, as well as the economic necessity for two sources of income in families that have been adversely affected by recent economic changes resulting partly from globalization.
Source: Business Week (1993, p. 82).

Figure 14.3   The Number of Women in Workforce Is Now Almost Equal to the Number of Men

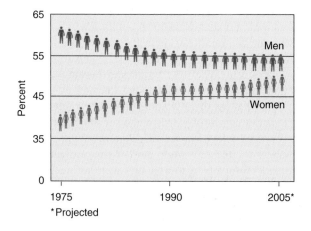

The number of men and women in the paid workforce has been converging for a number of years. In 1975 about 40 percent of the paid workforce was female; today, the figure is more than 45 percent. Within a decade, if present trends continue, almost as many women as men will be paid workers.
Source: Business Week (1993, p. 82).

Today more than half of all American women work outside the home, a figure that rises to three-quarters for women with children. This can create severe burdens for employed female caregivers, since the United States—unlike a number of European countries—does not provide for universal child care.

family life separately, before examining their impact on ex-spouses and children.

Divorce

Although the United States has one of the highest rates of marriage among industrial nations, its **divorce rate—** *the annual ratio of divorces to the total number of married households*—is among the highest as well. High rates of divorce are also common in Russia, Sweden, and Cuba, and throughout Eastern Europe. For every four new marriages that occur in the United States this year, there will be two divorces; in 1950, there was one (U.S. Census Bureau, 1993; see Figure 14.4). For the first time in American history, the rate of divorce is higher among families with children then it is among families where children are not involved. It is estimated that half of all marriages will end in divorce (Whitehead, 1993).

During the 1950s, in any given year fewer than 1 percent of all marriages in the United States ended in divorce. Whether or not married life was more or less satisfying 40 years ago is debatable, but it is clear that a much larger number of spouses chose to remain to-

gether at that time than do so today. This was partly due to the prevalence of stronger norms favoring marriage, and partly to a rapidly growing economy that enabled a single wage earner (almost always the husband) to earn enough to pay the household bills. The annual divorce rate began to climb in the mid-1960s, more than doubling to 2.3 percent of all marriages in 1979. Today, the figure has declined slightly, to about 2.1 percent (Whitehead, 1993). This is due partly to the "aging" of the U.S. population (see Chapter 12), since divorces typically occur in the earlier years of marriage. It also reflects a greater tendency of couples to postpone marriage, or to live together until they believe that marriage will work out.

There are many reasons for the high American divorce rate. The attitude toward an unsatisfying marriage has shifted from "stay together for the sake of the children" to "this marriage is simply not working out for either of us." Marriages are likely to be defined in terms of "pure relationships," and therefore are judged in terms of how well they meet the partners' emotional and sexual needs. The increasing economic independence, education, and autonomy of women has made it easier for women to end a marriage that is unsatisfactory, since they are no longer so financially dependent on their husbands as they once were. And finally, divorces have become easier to obtain. In 1970 California became the first state to permit **no fault divorce,** *allowing divorce purely on the grounds of incompatibility (termed "irreconcilable differences"),* rather than desertion, adultery, or "extreme cruelty" as had been the case since colonial days (Kitson, Babri, and Roach, 1985; Phillips, 1988; Miller, 1994).

Single Parenting

Although divorce and single parenting often go together, single parenting, unlike divorce, is not a new experience for American families. At the turn of the century, almost one out of every four children had lost a parent by age 15. But this was largely due to the death of a parent, the result of then-fatal illnesses or complications of childbirth (Whitehead, 1993). Today, single parenting is largely the result of divorce, separation, or the decision to bear children out of wedlock, and therefore carries a very different cultural meaning. Less than three-quarters of all American children under 18 live with both parents (Table 14.1). Twenty-four percent live with their mother, including 19 percent whose mothers have not remarried (U.S. Bureau of the Census, 1993). Each year, 1.2 million children move from two-parent to single-parent families. It is estimated that as many as half of all children born in the seventies will live in a single-parent household at one stage in their life before reaching the age of 18 (Bumpass, 1984).

Figure 14.4 **The Number of Divorces Each Year Now Half the Number of Marriages and Increasing**

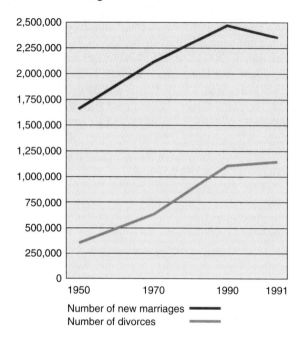

Number of new marriages ▬▬▬
Number of divorces ▬▬▬

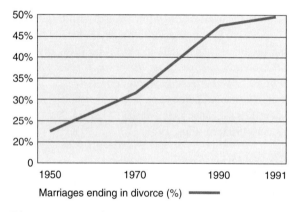

Marriages ending in divorce (%) ▬▬▬

Divorce appears to be becoming nearly as popular as marriage. In 1950 there were four new marriages for every divorce; by 1991, there were only two. This trend reflects changing values regarding divorce and marriage, the emphasis on marital satisfaction and compatibility, the increasing economic independence of women, and the greater legal ease of obtaining divorce.
Source: U.S. Bureau of Census (1993).

The Effect of Divorce and Single Parenting on Ex-Wives

The large majority of divorced women report on surveys that they are better off having ended their marriages (Whitehead, 1993). Divorced mothers report that they have greater confidence in their relationships with their children, are able to comfortably take on more responsibilities, and have a higher self-image (Kohen, Brown, and Feldberg, 1979). Although this may be true emotionally, the financial implications of divorce depend largely on the woman's social class and whether or not she has children. Half of all single mothers live in poverty. Many never remarry, and those who do spend an average of six years being single (McLanahan, 1988; Garfinkel and McLanahan, 1986; Whitehead, 1993).

Because women are often financially dependent on their husbands, divorce usually means a drop in income. Although the wealthier spouse (almost always the husband) may be required to pay spousal and child support, such payments are in fact hard to enforce. One study reported that three out of five divorced white mothers (and four out of five divorced black mothers) received no financial support from their ex-husbands at all, while other research reports that the income of divorced white mothers is only about half as much as their ex's income. Divorced black mothers average about two-thirds, but only because black men are on average much poorer themselves (McLanahan, 1988; Garfinkel and McLanahan, 1986; Whitehead, 1993).

Sociologist Lenore Weitzman (1981, 1985, 1990) has researched the impact of divorce on women's income for many years. Weitzman argues that women are systematically disadvantaged by divorce, as a result of declining spousal support awards and poor legal enforcement of the awards that are granted. Her startling statistic—that men experience a 42 percent improvement in their living standard after divorce, while women experience a 73 percent decline—has been widely cited to demonstrate that divorce benefits men at the expense of women (Weitzman, 1985).

Yet no sociological study has been able to duplicate Weitzman's dramatic finding, and she has been criticized for drawing conclusions that were not warranted by the research (Espenshade, 1979; Welch and Price-Bonham, 1983; Ellis and Lino, 1992; Faludi, 1992). One comprehensive survey of other studies concluded that women experience a drop of 10 to 30 percent, and men a small increase, after divorce (Sorenson, 1990). Although these differences are not as large as those originally reported by Weitzman, they do show that divorce continues to disadvantage women. U.S. policy has failed to adequately address this problem, although other industrial nations have attempted to do so. In Sweden, for example, the state pays child support to divorced parents, subsequently seeking reimbursement by billing the father. Child care is provided by the state as well, with parents paying according to their income (Rodger, 1991; Busch, 1990).

Table 14.1   Living Arrangements of Children Under 18, by Race and Hispanic Origin, 1992

	With Both Parents (%)	With Mother Only (%)	With Father Only (%)
All groups	73	24	3
Whites	79	18	3
Blacks	38	58	4
Hispanics	67	29	4

Source: U.S. Bureau of the Census, 1993, Table 79.

The Effect of Divorce and Single Parenting on Children

Twenty years ago, Carol Stack's (1974) highly influential book, *All Our Kin,* reflected the spirit of the time when it reported on the strengths of the single-parent family. Stack's research found that poor African-American mothers were remarkably successful in raising their children, thanks to kinship networks and their ability to marshal scarce resources. Twenty years later, however, the impact of divorce and single parenting on children is still being debated.

A number of studies have tracked children over time, attempting to determine whether divorce, separation, single parenting, and remarriage have any discernible impact on their emotional well-being. All the research agrees that divorce often has adverse and long-lasting financial consequences for the mother, which can contribute to family stress. More controversially,

some of the research also suggests that children of divorced families tend to have greater behavioral problems, do less well in school and are more likely to drop out, and generally have more difficulty adjusting to social relationships than children from families that remain intact. Yet the same studies frequently hasten to add that the majority of children of divorced parents do not have these problems, particularly once economic and class differences are taken into account (Zill, Furstenberg, and Peterson, 1987; Wallerstein and Blakeslee, 1990; Hetherington and Arasteh, 1988; Hetherington et al., 1992).

The problems that children of divorced parents do have often existed prior to the divorce as well: The divorce did not create the problems, nor did it alleviate them (Brody, Neubaum, and Forehand, 1988; Emery and Shaw, 1988). A study that followed some 15,000 British mothers over a number of years asked about

Map 14.1   Percent of Single-Parent Headed Households by U.S. County

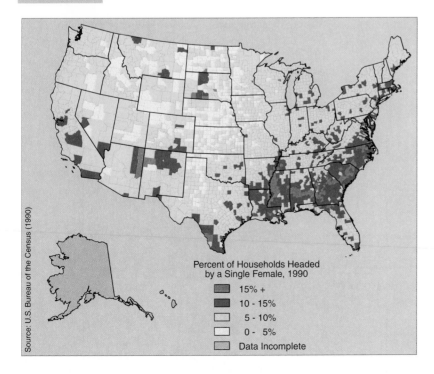

Source: U.S. Bureau of the Census (1990)

Percent of Households Headed by a Single Female, 1990

- 15% +
- 10 - 15%
- 5 - 10%
- 0 - 5%
- Data Incomplete

Single-parenting and poverty go hand-in-hand. The largest concentrations of single-parent households are found in the rural south, southwest, and west, as well as in large metropolitan areas across the country.

such children's problems as irritability, poor appetite, hyperactivity, sleepwalking, fighting, and vandalism. It found that the children who had such problems after divorce were the same children who had these problems when their parents were still married. A similar study of 1,700 families in the United States came to roughly the same conclusion (Cherlin, et al., 1991; Cherlin and Furstenberg, 1991).

In general, if the parent has a decent income, a satisfying job, and a good social support network, children being raised by one parent appear to do as well as if they were raised by both. Unfortunately, such favorable circumstances are often lacking. Parents who must raise their children alone are often poor, lack employment, and generally live highly stressful lives that contribute to behavior problems for their children. Although adequate child-care facilities have been shown to improve adjustment in young children, such facilities are rare in the United States (Hardey and Crow, 1991; Cadden, 1993).

Single Women With Children

The number of children born to single women has risen sharply in recent years, to nearly 1.2 million in 1990 (Figure 14.5). Five percent of all births were to unmarried women in 1950; today, the figure is close to 25 percent (Whitehead, 1993). Fifty-six percent of all children born to unmarried women are white, while 41 percent are black (U.S. Bureau of the Census, 1993). Between 1970 and 1990 the percentage of single women giving birth increased from 6 to 20 percent among white mothers, and from 38 to 65 percent among black mothers (U.S. Bureau of the Census, 1993).

A number of factors account for these increases. Mounting unemployment, particularly among the poor,

means that when pregnancy occurs fathers are often unable to support a family (Wilson, 1987). The woman may choose to have the child alone rather than marry someone whom she sees as incapable of contributing to the child's support. Religious beliefs and other values also play a role, in that some unmarried women who become pregnant do not want to have an abortion. A much smaller percentage of women have children without marrying simply because they prefer being single but still want children. Most births to unmarried women, however, occur to young women, suggesting that the birth was not planned: Nearly one-third occur to women under 20, and two-thirds to women under 25 (U.S. Bureau of the Census, 1993). Children born into such families face considerable financial hardship, since 77 percent of all children in female-headed families live in poverty (Children's Defense Fund, 1992; Eggebeen and Lichter, 1991).

Cohabitation

Cohabitation, *living together as a married couple without being married,* is today far more common than ever before during this century. The number of cohabiting American households has increased threefold in the past 30 years, a trend found throughout European societies as well (Blanc, 1984; Bumpass and Sweet, 1989; Parker, 1990). Cohabitation has increased for a number of reasons, including greater public toleration, more relaxed sexual norms, and the desire of couples to achieve emotional support while avoiding economic dependence or legal entanglements. For some couples, living together provides a kind of "trial marriage" that both parties believe will eventually culminate in a permanent alliance. This is especially common among couples who previously were married. Surveys of

Figure 14.5
Births Outside of Marriage, 1960–1990
A growing number of births are occurring outside of marriage, from slightly over 200,000 in 1960 to nearly 1.2 million today. These trends reflect changing economic circumstances as well as values toward marriage and child rearing. A quarter of all births today are to unmarried women, a significant cause of child poverty in the United States (three-quarters of all children in female-headed households live in poverty). *Source:* National Center for Health Statistics (1990).

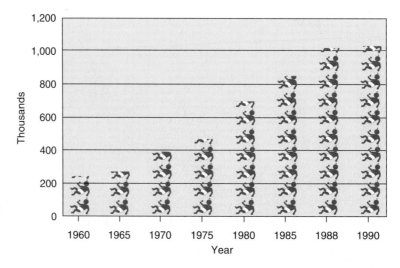

One of the goals of the gay and lesbian liberation movement is to change people's attitudes regarding homosexuality. This poster—showing a lesbian couple, one of whom is pregnant—seeks to make people aware that families can be different but still effective and valuable social units.

American college students indicate that a high proportion of those who cohabit expect to get married "sometime," although not necessarily to the person with whom they are living (Jackson, 1985).

Gay and Lesbian Couples

Homosexuality, while still stigmatized in the United States, is nonetheless finding increasing tolerance in American culture (Chapter 11). Homosexual marriages are legally sanctioned in a few communities, and homosexuality is now depicted on a number of popular television shows such as *Melrose Place* and *Roseanne.*

Homosexual norms toward the formation of stable families are partly the result of gender and age, much as in the heterosexual population. Younger homosexuals tend to be more sexually active than older homosexuals, and gay men more sexually active than lesbian women. The risk of contracting HIV-AIDS has had a significant impact in discouraging sexual activity within the homosexual community, particularly among younger gay men, who tended to be highly active before the risks of the disease were fully appreciated (Shilts, 1987).

Most homosexuals, like most heterosexuals, desire stable, emotionally supportive, long-lasting family relationships; for some, this includes children as well (Bell and Weinberg, 1978; Blumstein and Schwartz, 1983). Yet such fundamental goals can prove especially challenging for homosexual couples, who frequently encounter enormous social barriers in their pursuit of routine family relations. The courts are often unwilling to recognize same-sex marriages, and un-

likely to award custody of children to a homosexual parent in contested divorce proceedings. Adoption agencies are similarly reluctant to approve adoption when the prospective parents are homosexual. Even when homosexual couples do manage to have families, they must confront the difficulties that may arise from raising children who will have to fit into a predominately heterosexual (and frequently homophobic) society.

Stepfamilies

Although remarriage has always been common in the United States, during the past 30 years an increasing number of remarriages have involved the children of one or both spouses (Glick, 1984). One in four children growing up today will spend some part of their lives in "blended" stepfamilies as a result of the remarriage of one or both of their parents, acquiring stepparents and possibly stepbrothers and stepsisters as well (Whitehead, 1993).

The formation of stepfamilies is but one phase in a lengthy and sometimes difficult process which, from the child's standpoint, entails changes that are often unwanted and hard to comprehend. The process begins with the frequently painful experience of the parents' separation and divorce. The child must now live with one parent (usually the mother), visiting the other on weekends, although the growing popularity of joint-custody arrangements occasionally permits the child to move back and forth between two households. At some time, another adult may make an appearance, a new girlfriend or boyfriend of the parent. This may eventuate in remarriage, and the formation of an entirely new family, sometimes with new siblings. The new stepparent has no immediately apparent right to receive affection, yet usually expects to be accepted as "family" and granted parental authority. Often the biological father disappears from the picture altogether, with as many as half of all children of divorced parents reporting that they had not seen their father during the past year. Jealousy, confusion, and rejection of the new family members are not uncommon reactions under such circumstances. This is perhaps why as many as half of the children in one study report feeling "left out" in their stepfamilies (Wallerstein and Blakeslee, 1990; Cherlin and Furstenberg, 1991; Whitehead, 1993; Zill, Furstenberg, and Peterson, 1987).

Andrew Cherlin (1992), a sociologist who has written extensively on marriage and divorce, argues that remarriage is complicated by the fact that nearly all of the norms that govern it are ambiguous; there are no clear-cut cultural guidelines. Although some cultures have elaborate rules and clear standards for dealing with complex kinship systems resulting from remarriage (Radcliffe-Brown and Forde, 1950), American culture does not. The frustrations of deciding who is "in" and who is now "out" of the current family unit, as well as who should perform what roles and tasks, makes many American remarriages high-pressure relationships.

More often than not each stepfamily has to establish its own unique set of rules governing such things as the relation between children and stepparents, the type of authority that stepparents should have, whether there is a difference between the authority of the natural parent and the stepparent, and relationships with former spouses.

RACIAL AND ETHNIC DIVERSITY IN THE AMERICAN FAMILY

Although some generalizations apply to all families, there are many family differences associated with social class, race, and ethnicity. In this section we touch on a few of these differences. Once again, it is important to bear in mind that there are numerous exceptions to any patterns that might exist, and numerous families who do not fit neatly into any of these categories (see Box 14.2).

Social Class Differences in Families

Parents are often caught in a dilemma. They must instill some degree of conformity in their children, as they attempt to socialize them into the norms and values that will eventually prove appropriate for adult behavior.

Yet at the same time parents must seek to foster some degree of independence as well; after all, the child must eventually "leave the nest" and survive in the adult world. Given the tension between protection and instilling independence, it is to be expected that neither is fully achieved in most families. Although parents may understand that they need to help build their children's independence, too often they fail to trust their children's judgment, especially during adolescence. Parents may "hang on" to their children, prolonging their children's dependence long past the point where their children are ready to make decisions on their own. "Growing up" involves some degree of conflict no matter what formula is used.

There are, however, social class differences in parental attitudes toward children's independence. In American culture, middle- and upper-class families tend to value independence, self-direction, and individual initiative in their children. They attempt to control their children by reasoning with them, offering explanations and attempting to persuade. Working-class parents, on the other hand, are more likely to value respect for authority, obedience, and a higher degree of conformity, and to rely on punishment when these norms are violated. Sociologist Melvin Kohn, who spent many years studying class differences in child rearing, attributes them to differences in the parents' work experiences: middle- and upper-class jobs often require individual initiative and innovation, while working-class jobs tend to emphasize conformity (Kohn, 1977; see Chapter 5).

African-American Families

As Table 14.2 indicates, the percentage of blacks reporting that they have never been married is almost twice the white rate (37 percent versus 21 percent). Furthermore, the black rate has nearly doubled since 1970, when it was 21 percent. These figures are due to a number of influences. The general societal trend toward increasing cohabitation is especially pronounced among black families. Blacks also tend to defer marriage to a later age, have a lower likelihood of remarrying after divorce, and often avoid marriage altogether, even when children are present (Cherlin, 1992).

Nearly one-half (46 percent) of African-American households are headed by a woman with no husband present, compared with 14 percent for white households (U.S. Bureau of the Census, 1993, Table 66). As Table 14.3 shows, among black female-headed households, 42 percent of the women were never married, while another 19 percent were married but the husband was absent. As a result of these patterns, only 38 percent of all black children under the age of 18 are re-

Box 14.2

Silenced Voices

Deaf Culture and "Hearing" Families

There are as many as a 450,000 Americans who are completely unable to hear; about 250,000 were born deaf (Holt, 1994; Barringer, 1993). For them, family life poses unique challenges. As a consequence, many deaf people prefer to practice endogamy, marrying others who are deaf and therefore share a common experience.

There is a growing movement within the deaf community to redefine the meaning of deafness not as a form of disability, but rather as a positive culture (Lane, 1984b). A growing number of deaf people see themselves as similar to any ethnic group, sharing a common language (American Sign Language, or ASL), possessing a strong sense of cultural identity, and taking pride in their heritage. One survey reported that the overwhelming majority would not even elect to have a free surgical implant that would enable them to hear (Lane, 1992; Dolnick, 1993).

Roslyn Rosen is an example of a person who takes great pride in being deaf. Born of deaf parents and the mother of deaf children, Rosen is the president of the National Association of the Deaf:

> I'm happy with who I am, and I don't want to be "fixed." Would an Italian-American rather be a WASP [White Anglo-Saxon Protestant]? In our society everybody agrees that whites have an easier time than blacks. But do you think that a black person would undergo operations to be a white?" (quoted in Dolnick, 1993).

The desire for a deaf identity reflects the near impossibility of deaf people ever learning to communicate with "hearing" people (people who are not deaf) through lipreading and simulated speech. People who have never heard a sound find it virtually impossible to utter sounds that most "hearing" people can recognize as words. Lipreading is equally problematic and is fraught with error. Reading, which depends on an understanding of the meaning of spoken words, can prove to be a frustrating experience (Dolnick, 1993). Yet for those who "hear" and "speak" ASL, a rich form of com-

munication is possible, and with it comes a strong sense of shared identity (Lane, 1992).

Many deaf parents are wary when their deaf children get involved in relationships with "hearing" people, preferring that they remain within their own community. Among those who marry, 90 percent choose spouses who are also deaf (Dolnick, 1993). Although many deaf people have succeeded in the "hearing" world, the problems that confront them can be daunting (Spradley and Spradley, 1985; Lane, 1984a; Heppner, 1992; Sacks, 1990; Kisor, 1990). Most will never be able to speak in a way that is likely to be understood by "hearing" people, and most of the "hearing" people they encounter will not know ASL. It is not surprising that when it comes to intimate relations, most deaf people choose to marry others who share their own language and culture (Fischer and Lane, 1993; Padden and Humphries, 1988).

Although families ordinarily confer their own ethnic status on their children, this is not true for the nine out of ten deaf children who are born to "hearing" parents. Their parents are of one culture; they are of another (Dolnick, 1993). This can pose difficult choices for their families. On the one hand, "hearing" parents want the same sorts of things for their deaf children as do any parents: happiness, fulfillment, and successful lives as adults. Many would like their children to mainstream into the "hearing" world as best as possible. Yet they know that this will prove extremely difficult.

On the other hand, the deaf community argues that the deaf children of "hearing" parents can never fully belong to the "hearing" world, or, for that matter, even to their own "hearing" parents. Many leaders in the deaf community urge "hearing" parents to send their deaf children to residential schools for the deaf, where they will be fully accepted, learn deaf culture, and be with their own people (Lane, 1992; Dolnick, 1993). Fundamental questions about the meaning of "family" arise when the children and parents largely live in two different cultures.

Table 14.2   Marital Status by Race, Hispanic Origin, and Year: Percentage in each Category

Marital Status	Year			
	1970	1980	1990	1992
Total				
Never married	16	20	22	23
Married	72	66	62	61
Widowed	9	8	8	8
Divorced	3	6	8	9
White				
Never married	16	19	20	21
Married	73	67	64	64
Widowed	9	8	8	8
Divorced	3	6	8	9
Black				
Never married	21	31	35	37
Married	64	51	46	43
Widowed	11	10	9	9
Divorced	4	8	11	11
Hispanic				
Never married	19	24	27	28
Married	72	66	62	60
Widowed	6	4	4	4
Divorced	4	6	7	7

Source: U.S. Bureau of the Census (1993, Table 59).

ported as living with both parents (see again Table 14.1). Fully 58 percent live with the mother alone, in comparison with only 18 percent for whites (U.S. Bureau of the Census, 1993).

Why are there such pronounced differences between white and black family patterns? Sociologists have offered a number of explanations. One important factor is that a disproportionate number of blacks live in poverty, and their family patterns are similar to those of others who are poor. Another explanation focuses on the vastly different historical experiences of blacks rel-

ative to other racial and ethnic groups in the United States. Blacks were originally brought to America in chains, forcibly uprooted from their African families. Husbands, wives, and children were sold into slavery separately and were subsequently prevented from forming stable family relationships. After slavery ended, the migration of blacks from the rural south to large metropolitan areas across the country also left an imprint on black family formation, with black family patterns typical of rural populations elsewhere in the

Table 14.3   Percentage of Women Living in Households with No Spouse Present, by Race and Hispanic Origin, 1980 and 1992 (all persons 15 years and older)

	Whites		Blacks		Hispanic	
	1980	1992	1980	1992	1980	1992
Never married (single)	11	17	27	42	23	29
Married, spouse absent	17	17	29	19	32	26
Widowed	33	23	22	16	15	16
Divorced	40	43	22	23	30	30

Note: Persons of Hispanic origin may be of any race.

Source: U.S. Bureau of the Census (1993).

world (Lieberson, 1973; Sowell, 1981; Willie, 1989; McAdoo, 1993).

A related explanation is offered by William Julius Wilson, a leading African-American sociologist whose work is discussed at length in Chapter 8. Wilson argues that different family patterns between blacks and whites are caused in part by American society's creation of a permanent black urban underclass of unskilled, uneducated, and unemployable people entrenched in poverty (Wilson, 1987; 1990). In Wilson's view, poor inner-city black men who fall into this category are not viewed by black women as viable marriage partners. Because poor black women confront a shortage of viable mates, they choose to raise their children alone. Wilson's explanation is extremely controversial, since it seems to emphasize the limitations of impoverished black men rather than focusing on the societal conditions that produce racial discrimination and poverty (Willie, 1989; Edwards, 1989; Pettigrew, 1989; see Box 14.3).

Latino Families

As noted in Chapter 10, about one out of every ten Americans is Latino, a percentage that is expected to double by the middle of the next century (U.S. Bureau of the Census, 1993). Latinos currently account for nearly half of all recent immigrants from the Caribbean, Mexico, Central America, and other Spanish-speaking countries (U.S. Immigration and Naturalization Service, 1992).

Generally speaking, the more recent the immigration of a group, the stronger its ties to its former culture (Moore and Pinderhughes, 1993). Recently arrived immigrants frequently continue to reflect family patterns associated with their origin cultures. The family is of paramount importance in Latino culture, and a person's behavior is frequently judged in terms of how it reflects on their family. Other cultural characteristics of Hispanic families include a closeness between women family members of all ages, a high degree of respect for elders, friendship patterns that make men as well as women friends of the entire family rather than just the husband or wife, and a wide community of social support for family members (Sanchez-Aye'ndez, 1986).

These cultural characteristics are reflected in low rates of divorce (7 percent, compared with 9 percent for whites) and high rates of marriage (60 percent). Still, as with other groups, rates of marriage have declined during the past 20 years, while the percentage reporting being "never married" has increased (see again Table 14.3). Among Latina women who have no spouses, 29 percent report never having married, a figure that has grown during the past decade and is higher than that of whites (17 percent; see again Table 14.3). Two-thirds of all Latino children over 18 are reported as living with both parents, while 29 percent live with their mother alone (see again Table 14.1). The changes that are affecting all American families have affected Latino families, despite strong cultural values emphasizing the importance of families ties.

Asian-American Families

There are 7.2 million Americans who can trace their origins to more than a dozen Asian countries with highly diverse cultures. Chinese and Filipino Ameri-

Most societies have "rites of passage" associated with growing up. Facial and bodily scarring, religious confirmation services, high school graduation ceremonies, bar mitzvahs, and "coming out" parties are examples of practices found in different societies and ethnic groups. In this picture a Latina girl celebrates her Quinciniera *(fifteenth year) with her family in Austin, Texas.*

Box 14.3

Critical Thinking

The Politics of Studying the Black Family

The debate over the black family provides an example of how sociological research can become embroiled in political debates. In 1965 Daniel Patrick Moynihan, a former professor of sociology and currently a senator from New York state, published a highly controversial study of the African-American family that came to be known as *The Moynihan Report.* In that study Moynihan argued that lower-class black family life was often dysfunctional, reflected in high rates of dissolution, single parenting, and an overly dominant role of women. Moynihan attributed these difficulties to the legacy of slavery, which intentionally broke up black families. He also claimed that many rural blacks had failed to adequately adapt to urban environments. Moynihan concluded that lower-class black family life was in large part responsible for the failure of many lower-class blacks to make it into the American economic mainstream. Black poverty and urban violence, which exploded in the urban riots of the 1960s, were seen by Moynihan as partly the result of black family breakdown.

The Moynihan Report was strongly criticized as being racist and sexist, blaming the victims of racism and poverty (primarily black female heads of households) rather than economic conditions, racial prejudice, and discrimination. Moynihan's findings were largely disregarded, and sociologists avoided examining the connection between race, family characteristics and poverty for two decades. In 1987, however, sociologist William Julius Wilson revisited these same issues. As an eminent black sociologist, Wilson was less vulnerable to the charge of being racist than Moynihan had been. In Wilson's (1987, pp. 4–5) view:

> The controversy surrounding the Moynihan report had the effect of curtailing serious research on minority problems in the inner city for over a decade, as liberal scholars shied away from researching behavior construed as unflattering or stigmatizing to particular racial minorities. . . . Liberals have traditionally emphasized how the plight of disadvantaged groups can be related to the problems of the broader society, including problems of discrimination and social class subordination. . . . Despite pious claims about objectivity in social research, it is true that values influence not only our selection of problems for investigation but also our interpretation of the empirical data.

What does Wilson mean when he claims that researchers' values affect their research? How might this be taken into account when studying a controversial topic such as the black family?

---

cans constitute the largest group of Asian Americans, although significant numbers originated in Japan, Korea, Vietnam, Laos, and Cambodia as well.

Although Asian family patterns reflect the diversity among the Asian-American population, there are some common features as well. In general, Asian-American families tend to emphasize male authority and traditional gender roles, although these norms are changing. There is a strong sense of respect for one's cultural heritage, commitment to family loyalty, respect for elders, and a norm for mutual self-help. There is also a strongly felt obligation to succeed, seen in an emphasis on the importance of formal education. Asian Americans have higher rates of high school and college enrollment than

any other ethnic group (Gardner et al., 1985; Hurh and Kim, 1984; Kim and Hurh, 1988; Kitano and Daniels, 1988).

American Indian Families

American Indians are also highly diverse. There are nearly 500 different nations, although over half of all Native Americans come from just nine of these (Levitan and Johnston, 1975). American Indian families tend to be extended, often including uncles, aunts, grandparents, and others. Child rearing tends to be permissive, with children encouraged to be internally self-sufficient rather than externally motivated. There is an

An Algonquin mother in Quebec, Canada, smiles at her baby, who is strapped to a traditional cradleboard. This device was a useful way for American Indian women to carry their children the long distances they had to travel for food and water. The custom kept the child close to the mother's body for long periods of time. What difference do you think such close and on-going interpersonal contact might make on the child's personality?

emphasis on the group over the individual, stressing harmony in relationships, including sensitivity towards kin, tribe, and land.

Research on the Hopi and Pueblo Indians of the Southwest has reported that members of these groups do not see their children as belonging so much to a particular family as to the entire nation and its history— "the land, the sky, the tribe and its history, its customs and traditions" (Coles, 1977, p. 520). Yet the migration of American Indian families from reservations to urban areas has led to increased assimilation and acculturation, with urban Indian families often resembling those of the dominant culture.

DOMESTIC VIOLENCE

Domestic (family) violence, *the physical, sexual, or psychological abuse committed by one family member on another,* was a largely taboo topic within sociology until the past quarter century. Recent studies have found family violence to be all too common. Domestic violence can be perpetrated by adults toward children, by one spouse against another, among siblings, and occasionally by adult children against elderly parents.

Accurate information on family violence is difficult to obtain for a variety of reasons. Abused partners or children are reticent to call attention to the fact that they are abused. Police do not want to make arrests or be called upon to mediate family conflicts, while the courts are hesitant to get involved in what is often perceived as a "family matter" (Hayenjhelm, 1993; Sherman, 1993).

Reviewing existing studies in the late 1970s, Murray Straus proposed that aggression and violence within families was so widespread in the world that it could be regarded as a near-universal phenomenon.

Straus found that violence is most likely to be prevalent in societies where several conditions are met: Family relationships are characterized by high emotional intensity and attachment; there is a pattern of male dominance and sexual inequality; a high value is placed upon the privacy of family life; and violence is permitted or occurs in other institutional spheres (Straus and Gelles, 1990; Straus, Gelles, and Steinmetz, 1988; Straus, 1977).

The right of a husband to physically discipline his wife has deep roots in Anglo-American culture. British common law permitted a man to discipline his wife and children with a stick, provided it be no thicker than his thumb; the phrase "rule of thumb" originates in this practice. Through the end of the last century in the United States, men could legally beat their wives (Renzetti and Curran, 1992).

A number of studies have claimed that approximately one in six American women, one in five female children, and one in ten male children experience some form of violence each year, although these statistics are controversial and are widely debated (Straus and Gelles, 1985, 1988, 1990; Gelles and Straus, 1988). As we reported in Chapter 11, marital rape is not unusual, with as many as a tenth of all wives reporting that they have been raped by their husbands (Finkelhor and Yllo, 1985). Spousal battery is reportedly the largest single cause of injury to American women. As many as 4,000 women are killed each year by their mates, while estimates of other forms of abuse range from two to six million women—a figure that works out to about one every 5 to 15 seconds (U.S. House of Representatives, 1988; Browne, 1987; Saline, 1984).

Child abuse, involving *sexual and/or physical assaults on children by adult members of their family,* is also more common than is generally thought to be the

One of the contributions of conflict theory is to make us recognize the dysfunctional character of some families. Rape as well as child and spouse abuse are too common in modern society to be ignored, as this sign reminds us.

case. An estimated 6.9 million children in the United States are abused by their parents each year, 1.5 million seriously (Strauss and Gelles, 1990). Although boys and girls are equally likely to be physically abused, girls are more likely to be sexually abused as well. One study of nearly a thousand San Francisco women found that seven out of ten reported being sexually abused as girls (Russell, 1984, p. 172), while another study of college students reported that 19 percent of the women and 9 percent of the men had been sexually abused by an adult when they were children (Finkelhor, 1978). Research on child abuse draws varying conclusions regarding how likely it is that abusive parents will change their behavior with proper treatment and counseling; estimates range from as low as 16 percent to as high as 60 percent. Parents who are not likely to change are those who have a history of severe abuse themselves, are alcohol or drug abusers, or have serious psychological disabilities (Jones, 1987).

It is often believed that elderly abuse is also widespread, with estimates ranging as high as one in ten; the motivation, reportedly, is the resentment adult children feel at having to support their infirm parents (Gelles and Cornell, 1985; Steinmetz, 1981; King, 1984). Yet such stereotypes of elderly abuse are incorrect. The most careful studies report far lower rates of abuse, with most abuse occurring between elderly spouses. Only about a quarter of all elderly abuse occurs at the hands of adult children, and that primarily occurs when the child resents being financially dependent on the parent, rather than the reverse (Pillemer and Wolf, 1986; Pillemer and Finkelhor, 1988; Pillemer, 1985; see Chapter 12).

People have become far more aware of child and spouse abuse in recent years, largely due to efforts by the women's movement to bring such "family matters" to public attention. Shelters for battered women and

children have been created, enabling victims to be protected from violence while they are helped to reorganize their lives. The existence of shelters, while still limited in number, has enabled women to get counseling while terminating abusive relationships in relative safety (Hayjenhelm, 1991).

● GLOBALIZATION: IMPACTS ON THE FAMILY

World War II illustrates how sensitive the American family can be to events that occur thousands of miles away. During the war, when men were drafted into military service, women joined the labor force by the millions. The U.S. government strongly encouraged women to find employment in settings such as steel mills, weapons factories, and hospitals as part of their patriotic duty. A major governmental effort was mounted to convince "Rosie the Riveter" that welding seams on bombers was no less important than raising her children at home. Indeed, wartime propaganda sought to show that children would do fine when raised by relatives or babysitters, while mom served the war effort in the factory.

The American family changed dramatically as a result. Men went to the front, women went to work, and substitute parents had increasing responsibility for child-rearing. For the duration of the war, women became the principal family breadwinners. Yet these changes lasted only as long as the fighting. When the war ended and the men returned to reclaim their jobs, women returned to their traditional roles as homemakers. They were strongly encouraged to do so by official government films and leaflets, this time extolling the virtues of homemaking. Some of the more colorful governmental efforts painted dire pictures of unattended children playing with matches and accidentally starting fires, while their mothers selfishly pursued careers in the workplace. Family patterns once again changed, this time reverting to more traditional norms (Howe and Strauss, 1991; Weatherford, 1990).

Nor were the war's repercussions limited to four or five years of increased female employment. Since many young families had to postpone having children during the war, they compensated afterward by giving birth to the largest generation of children in U.S. history. The impact of the **baby boom,** *the unusually large number of children born in the decade after World War II,* has helped to shape family life ever since. The "baby boomers" fueled the growth of the U.S. economy, contributed to the suburbanization of America, and swelled the ranks of the workforce during the 1970s. Today, many of the readers of this textbook are themselves the children of these postwar "baby boomers."

While the echoing impacts of World War II show how global events can have an enormous impact on the family, economic globalization provides a more recent illustration whose impacts are felt throughout the American class structure. Among upper- and upper-middle class families, globalization has increased the demand for men and women with a high degree of skill and formal training as professionals, managers, ad-ministrators, and engineers. These positions often require lengthy periods of schooling, and eventually result in dual-career families in which the partners may decide to forgo having families in order to pursue their independent careers (Silberstein, 1992).

Among working- and middle-class families, many have found themselves confronting stagnant or declining incomes as a result of competition with a global workforce. The need for two incomes to make ends meet is one of the reasons for the dramatic increase in the number of women working outside the home. The movement of women into the paid workforce, in turn, has provided many with a degree of economic independence and an opportunity to rethink the meaning of marriage. As women join the paid workforce, some postpone marriage until they are older. Couples choose cohabiting as an alternative to marriage, and, when partners do decide to have children, their families are likely to be smaller.

Finally, among families at the lower end of the class structure, workers who lack globally competitive work skills have frequently lost their jobs to low-wage countries around the world. At the very bottom, this has fueled the growth of an urban underclass, with many families headed by unwed mothers, as discussed above (Wilson, 1987).

CHAPTER SUMMARY

1. There are enormous cultural variations in what comprises a **family** and the rules governing its formation. The meaning of "family" is socially constructed within a particular culture, and in the United States and other industrial societies that meaning is rapidly changing.

2. The institution of **marriage,** while found in all societies, need not be legally sanctioned; what is important is that it is culturally recognized.

3. The functionalist theory of the family looks at its functions for societal stability, emphasizing such things as biological reproduction, nurturance and socialization of children, protection of those who are relatively helpless, the regulation of sexual behavior, and the allocation of family members into society's system of stratification.

4. The conflict theory of the family looks at the ways in which the family reproduces societal inequality, emphasizing in particular the production of gender inequality. It also argues that the family is at the heart of a cultural contradiction—the need to so-cialize its members into conflicting norms regarding consumption and the importance of work.

5. In modern society, the roles of the family have shifted partly from socialization and production, to emotional fulfillment and consumption. This is because other, more specialized institutions have taken over some of the former roles.

6. The expectation that the family should serve as a source of **pure relationships** has contributed to its fragility, as have the economic changes associated with industrial and postindustrial society.

7. Unlike 50 years ago, today the majority of American mothers as well as fathers work outside the home. This reflects both changing family values, and the need for both spouses to earn an income.

8. The **divorce rate** in the United States is one of the highest in the world, with estimates that half of all marriages today will end in divorce. This reflects changing values regarding divorce and marriage,

the emphasis on marital satisfaction and compatibility, the increasing economic independence of women, and the greater legal ease of obtaining divorce.

9. Single parenting has also increased in recent years, with as many as half of all children today spending some of their childhood in a single-parent household. Ex-wives often suffer greater economic hardship than ex-husbands, while the impact of divorce and single-parenting on children is still being debated.

10. Other new family forms include a rise in unwed mothers, an increase in cohabitation, and a growing number of marriages involving same-sex couples.

11. There is enormous racial and ethnic diversity in American families, as well as differences associated with social class. One important and hotly debated issue has to do with the enormous problems faced by unwed mothers in the urban underclass.

12. **Domestic (family) violence** is a long-neglected topic that has only been seriously addressed during the last quarter century. Although precise estimates of the extent of violence are hard to obtain, it is believed to be widespread.

13. Globalization affects the family in times of war and in times of peace. Currently, economic globalization is a major source of America's changing work habits, which in turn impact family relations, although the effects differ by social class.

QUESTIONS FOR DISCUSSION

1. What are the principal differences between the functionalist and conflict theories of the family? Which do you believe better accounts for the changes that are occurring today, and why?

2. Describe the changing role of the family in modern society, and discuss how this might affect family stability.

3. There has been much discussion in recent years of changing "family values." What are some of these changes, and what are their impacts on family life? Discuss the ways in which scholars have viewed these changes in both positive and negative terms.

4. What are some of the principal differences in families among members of different social classes and racial or ethnic groups? To what extent might racial and ethnic differences overlap with class differences?

5. Discuss the impact of globalization on the recent changes that have occurred in the American family. Based on what you have read in this textbook, what future changes might occur if globalization continues to produce a world that is increasingly interdependent in terms of economics, politics, and culture.

KEY TERMS

baby boom: A phrase used to refer to the unusually large number of children born in the decade after World War II.

child abuse: A form of abuse involving sexual and/or physical assaults on children by adult members of their family.

child-minding: An arrangement in which extended family members and friends cooperate in raising the children of a person who is living in another locale.

cohabitation: Living together as a married couple without being married.

divorce rate: The annual ratio of divorces to the total number of married households.

domestic (family) violence: The physical, sexual, or psychological abuse committed by one family member on another.

endogamy: Marriage involving mates who come from the same kinship group, social category, or other social group.

extended family: A social group consisting of one or more parents, children, and other kin, often spanning several generations.

family: A group of people who identify themselves as being related to one another, usually by blood, marriage, or adoption, and who share intimate relationships and dependency.

gender factory: A term used by sociologists to characterize the function of the home in reproducing society's traditional gender roles (see Chapter 11).

international family: An extended family spanning several countries, yet characterized by intense interactions, strong emotional ties, and a binding sense of mutual obligation.

marriage: A culturally approved relationship, usually between two individuals, that provides for a degree of economic cooperation, intimacy, and sexual activity.

marriage rate: The ratio of the number of people who actually marry in a given year compared with the total number of people eligible to marry.

monogamy: A form of marriage in which a person may have only one spouse at a time.

no fault divorce: A relatively recent form of divorce, first adopted by the state of California in 1970, which permits couples to divorce purely on the grounds of incompatibility (termed "irreconcilable differences").

nuclear family: A social group consisting of one or two parents and their dependent children.

polyandry: a form of marriage in which a woman may have multiple husbands.

polygamy: A form of marriage in which a person may have more than one spouse at a time.

polygyny: A form of marriage in which a man may have multiple wives.

pure relationship: A relationship that is entered into purely for its own sake and is maintained only so long as it is mutually satisfying to both partners.

second shift: A phrase used by sociologists to characterize the unpaid housework that women typically do after they come home from their paid employment (see Chapter 11).

R E C O M M E N D E D   F O R   F U R T H E R   R E A D I N G

Cherlin, Andrew J. (1992). *Marriage, Divorce, Remarriage* (rev. ed.). Cambridge: Harvard University Press.

A scholarly examination of the effects of divorce and remarriage; draws on the author's extensive empirical research on the topic.

Dizard, Jan E., and Howard Gadlin. (1990). *The Minimal Family.* Amherst: University of Massachusetts Press.

A cleverly conceived debate between two sociologists as to whether the changes in family patterns sweeping the industrial world portend a growth in human freedom, or a decline in a fundamental social institution.

Hochschild, Arlie. (1990). *The Second Shift: Working Parents and the Revolution at Home.* New York: Avon Books.

A study of the "stalled revolution" in gender equality at work and at home, based on interviews with working fathers and mothers.

Parker, Stephen. (1990). *Informal Marriage: Cohabitation and the Law.* New York: St. Martin's Press.

An examination of the legal status of marriages that occur outside the law; includes a fascinating history of the institutionalization of marriage in modern society.

Skolnick, Arlene S., and Jerome H. Skolnick (eds.). (1992). *Family in Transition: Rethinking Marriage, Sexuality, Child Rearing, and Family Organization.* New York: HarperCollins.

A collection of writings on the changing nature of marriage and the family in society today.

Stacey, Judith. (1990). *Brave New Families: Stories of Domestic Upheaval in Late Twentieth Century America.* New York: Basic Books.

A well-written book telling the story of two women who live in Silicon Valley in nontraditional family arrangements; includes descriptions of "divorce extended families."

CHAPTER 15

Work and the Economy

CHAPTER OUTLINE

INTRODUCTION

To get a glimpse of China's economic boom, drive an hour north from the Hong Kong airport and turn left at the giant stainless steel archway. You've just entered Changan Inc., population 30,000. Cruise the palm-tree lined avenues and you'll pass a gleaming new cultural center, office towers, and a sprawling public recreation complex with an Olympic-size pool and a golf course. More than 100 two-story white townhouses with red tile roofs, sold for $100,000 to Hong Kong families, stand in neat rows with scores more under construction. . . . China is in a dash for prosperity. . . . [Its] emergence is already shaking the world (Barnathan et al., 1993).

The example of Changan is typical of the economic boom that has transformed southern China from a land of rice paddies to a global industrial powerhouse in the space of little more than a decade. An impoverished rural village only a few years ago, Changan today employs 100,000 workers from all over China. Its 700 city-owned factories produce Barbie dolls, precision tools, and a host of other products for foreign firms, and bring in some $40 million in rental revenues alone. The city is currently building an entirely new downtown, in anticipation of growth to over a million people by the end of the decade (Barnathan et al., 1993).

Until relatively recently, the People's Republic of China was a staunchly communist nation where privately owned businesses were illegal and foreign investors were decidedly unwelcome. In the past few years, however, China has begun to move down what its former leaders called the "capitalist road"—first haltingly, now with a vengeance. With nearly a quarter of the world's population, China is about to fully join the global economy, bringing close to a billion people to the world's labor market. Its present rate of economic growth—exceeding 12 percent per year—is by far the highest in the world. The southern province where Changan is located, which has some 60 million people, is growing even faster.

To a degree unprecedented in history, China's workers are competing with workers elsewhere in the world, including the United States, for the same jobs. From factory workers to engineers, Americans are finding themselves confronting a global pool of trained, motivated, and often extremely inexpensive labor. Businesses are "downsizing" not only their factories but their managerial and professional staffs as well.

Sociologists approach this topic by studying the social organization of work and economic life, tracing out the implications for other institutions. Schools and colleges must respond to changing work requirements, families are affected by new careers requiring flexibility and frequent job shifts, and governments face new roles as the political and economic borders between nations become weaker. In this chapter we will examine these issues, focusing on some of the challenges that today's college graduates will encounter as they enter the twenty-first century world of work.

THE ORGANIZATION OF WORK IN INDUSTRIAL SOCIETY

The industrial revolution of the seventeenth and eighteenth centuries gave birth to modern **industrial society,** a society in which *subsistence is based on the mechanized production of goods in factories* (Chapter 4). The modern factory system differed from earlier forms of economic organization in that it brought large numbers of laborers together under one roof for the purpose of producing goods for sale. In this it was unlike earlier **handicraft production,** *production in which workers typically labored independently on items of their own design, using their own tools, and at their own pace.*

While factory-like workhouses originally brought handicraft artisans together to share tools and common space, the workhouses soon evolved into the modern factory, involving a rigid division of labor, with each worker specializing in specific manufacturing tasks

China, with 1.1 billion people, is currently undergoing explosive economic growth. Its southern Guangdong Province, with some 60 million people, is perhaps the fastest-growing economic region in the world today. This photograph shows an empty field slated for development. Hundreds of square miles of former farmland and hills have been razed and converted to high-rise factories, office buildings, and apartments in the past decade.

rather than performing all the operations required to produce a final product. The use of machinery greatly increased the productive capacity of individual laborers, but it also tied the work process to the rhythms and requirements of the machinery itself. Moreover, machinery robbed the worker of control over the manufacturing process: Instead of using tools at their own pace, workers now labored at equipment that belonged to the owner of the factory, at a pace the owner determined.

Factory work thus called for *specialized, tightly coordinated work tasks, closely supervised by factory owners and their managers.* It contributed to the creation of a class society, including some people who owned the factories and equipment, and others whose labor set the machinery in motion (Chapter 8). The emergence of factories also led to the rapid growth of cities, since factories had to be close to markets, energy sources such as water or coal, transportation networks, and—most importantly—large numbers of workers (Glen, 1984; see Chapter 20).

The Alienation of Labor in Industrial Society

Nineteenth century industrial cities, such as Manchester, England (Engels, 1987; orig. 1844), were dirty and polluted. Smoke from factories intermingled with smoke from wood and coal used for cooking and heating. Raw sewage ran freely down the streets, and workers lived densely packed into slum housing. Disease and death were ever present features of urban life.

Conditions in the factories mirrored conditions in the surrounding neighborhoods. Factory work was often demanding, hazardous, and regimented. Workers labored at tedious tasks for 14 to 16 hours a day, 6 or 7 days a week. They were frequently exposed to toxic

chemicals and dangerous machinery, and they were constantly at risk of losing their jobs if economic conditions turned unfavorable or if they raised too many objections. Workers lacked any legal rights, leading to widespread exploitation of men, women, and children. Although workers in Europe and North America were eventually able to obtain legal protections against many abuses, the same conditions exist today in factories throughout the world (Chapter 9). And they are still found today in the United States, as Rebeca Martínez' story indicates (Box 15.1).

Karl Marx (1818–1883) provided an early theory of the experience of workers under such conditions. According to this theory, workers under industrial capitalism, suffered from a condition of **alienation** (or estrangement); they literally *experienced themselves as "strangers" during the many hours each day they labored in factories.* Marx believed that workers were alienated in a fourfold sense (orig. 1844, in McClellan, 1977; Ollman, 1971; Meszaros, 1970; Appelbaum, 1988). First, workers were *estranged from the products they made,* which belonged to the factory owner. Workers might labor all day in a factory producing clothing, yet be paid too little to afford the shirt or the pair of pants that they had made.

Second, workers were *estranged from the process of making things.* In earlier handicraft production, workers would consciously conceive of a product, design the technique for its manufacture, and then labor at all aspects of its making. In the factory, however, work was reduced to **detail labor,** *the execution of simple, highly repetitive, monotonous operations that required few if any skills.* The worker thus became one cog in a vast, impersonal machine, subject to the abuse and exploitation of the owner.

Third, workers were *estranged from their co-*

Silenced Voices

Rebeca Martínez, Garment Worker

Rebeca Martínez (not her actual name) came to the United States illegally from Guatemala at age 17. At the time of this interview, she had spent almost two years working on and off in the Los Angeles apparel industry, alongside some 120,000 other workers, many of them also illegal immigrants, most of them women. When Rebeca is able to find a job in one of Los Angeles' 5,000 garment "sweatshops," she earns $250 a week sewing for ten hours a day, six days a week. In Guatemala, she would be fortunate to earn $11 a week for the same amount of work. The following excerpts are taken from a 1992 interview in which Rebeca recounts her experiences as a seamstress in a small factory in Los Angeles' downtown garment district (Scott, 1993).

I didn't like working in this business. I dislike how workers are being mistreated, especially managers who don't give fair treatment to people. It didn't only happen with me, it is happening with a lot of people who are working in factories. Sometimes they accept the environment at work because they are desperate for money, or they are afraid of something. . . . I didn't like the way the manager shouted at everybody, and this made people nervous. When it was lunch time, or break time, and if there was a lot of work to do, the manager would let us have only ten minutes for break.

When I came here, I had never worked before, and so that was my first job. I used to cry a lot when I got home, because I disliked the situation that I just described. My oldest brother kept telling me that if I really wanted to work, I would become accustomed to the way it is . . .

I think the way they are treated is not right. People keep this hard feeling inside themselves, they feel everything inside, because maybe they are afraid of something like losing their job. Because of the workers' fears, they take advantage by telling you that if you don't like the job, then just beat it. I left for that reason. They can force people to leave the job because the managers are sure that a lot of people are looking for work.

I don't know what *explotación* ["exploitation"] is in English, but I guess it means taking advantage of people just because they need the money, and because they need the money they are treated like dogs. People are forced to work hard for very little money, and don't feel free to go from one place to another place for work. I think every regular individual deserves some respect, but in the factories, people don't receive any consideration. I dislike the way this happened.

Please remember, we breathe and feel the same as owners do.

---

workers. Rather than labor cooperatively and harmoniously toward a common goal, industrial capitalism pitted worker against factory owner, and worker against worker. The factory owner was forever seeking new ways to make a profit, usually at the expense of the worker. Workers who complained too much or were paid too much ran the risk of being fired, since they were constantly in danger of losing their jobs to more efficient machines or to the other workers with whom they were forced to compete.

Finally, workers were *estranged from their basic human nature.* When Marx wrote his theory of alienation, he believed that humans were biologically predisposed to experience pleasure when they used their minds creatively, and when they worked cooperatively

with one another. Human beings, in other words, were seen as both *conscious* and *social* animals. Industrial capitalism, in Marx's view, thus ran counter to human nature, since it reduced workers to mindless machines, and placed them in opposition to one another.

Critical Assessment Marx developed his theory of alienation when he was only 26 years old. It was based not on actual studies of workers' experiences in factories but rather on an analysis of what Marx believed to be human nature. Marx *assumed* that people were most completely fulfilled when they worked consciously and harmoniously together; his model of satisfying work seems to have been the artisan or craftsperson, making something at his or her own pace, for personal use. Since Marx knew this ran counter to conditions in factories, he concluded that the factory system violated human nature. A political conclusion followed from all this: Because they felt alienated from their own human natures, workers could be expected to resist the factory system and eventually rise up in revolution.

There are two shortcomings to this theory. First, it assumes that everybody shares a certain type of human nature. Sociologists tend to reject this idea, believing instead that so-called "human nature" involves the complex interplay of biological characteristics and social learning (Chapters 3 and 5). Thus sociologists argue that workers might eventually learn to enjoy even the most tedious factory work, particularly if such attitudes were reinforced in the home, the schools, and the work environment. In fact, Marx himself eventually abandoned his theory of human nature, arguing instead that growing polarization between rich and poor—rather than the more personalized experience of alienation—would eventually drive people to revolution (Althusser, 1971, 1986; Althusser and Balibar, 1990; Appelbaum, 1988). Second, because of the efforts by workers to better their circumstances, conditions in factories often improved as capitalism developed. As workers labored fewer hours and earned more money, their hostility to factory work often diminished.

Yet there is no question but that many workers today feel alienated from their work (Terkel, 1985). A recent study by the United Nations International Labor Organization (1993) described one form of alienation—job stress—as a "global phenomenon," estimating the annual cost of work-related stress at $200 billion due to lowered worker output, workers' compensation claims, absenteeism, health insurance costs, and direct medical expenses for stress-related illnesses. In a classic study of four industries, Robert Blauner (1964) found that worker alienation was high in the automobile and textile industries, where workers were virtually controlled by the machines they operated. On the other hand, alienation was lower in the printing industry, a traditional craft-like industry where workers continued to exert control over their labor process. And, most significantly, alienation was low in a highly automated chemical plant, where advanced machinery enabled workers to control their work to a high degree. In terms of Marx's theory of alienation, this suggested that worker control over the labor process might reduce at least one of the major sources of alienation.

Fordism and Taylorism

The modern industrial factory was organized with two principal objectives in mind. First, it was designed to maximize factory management's control over the worker. Second, it simultaneously sought to maximize **productivity,** the *amount of goods that a worker can produce in a given period of time.* These interrelated concerns were seen in Henry Ford's system of mass production, as well as Henry Winslow Taylor's principles of "scientific management."

Fordism: The Mass Production of Goods

The first modern factory was developed by Henry Ford (1863–1947), the American son of an Irish immigrant farmer. Ford made his first automobile in 1896, a gasoline-powered "horseless carriage" that eventually launched the company that still bears his name. By 1913, the Ford factory had introduced the system of **mass production,** which was based on an *assembly line that used a continuous conveyor belt to move the unfinished product past individual workers, each of whom performed a specific operation on it.* For example, as a car moved past, one worker would attach the door, another the windshield, another the wheels. The term **Fordism** has therefore been used to refer to the *large-scale, highly standardized mass production of identical commodities on a mechanical assembly line.*

Unlike the earlier handicraft system, which produced a smaller number of unique handmade items, the highly standardized system of mass production resulted in a large number of identical products at a considerable savings in cost. Furthermore, individual component parts of a final product could themselves be standardized; such things as doors or windows were identical on all cars and could thus be mass-produced in other factories. Henry Ford's famous "Model T" was one of the first automobiles to roll off an assembly line, and it revolutionized the system of manufacturing. Ford worried that poorly paid workers would not have sufficient financial resources to purchase the cars they were making. He accordingly paid them what was then a large salary ($5 a day), in order to help ensure a market for his products (Bryan, 1989; Collier and Horowitz, 1987).

Taylorism: Scientific Management of the Labor Process

The Fordist system of mass production reflected a theory that had been developed by Frederick Winslow Taylor (1856–1915), an industrial engineer who founded the field of **scientific management**—an effort to *apply the rules of engineering to scientifically reorganize the actions of the workers themselves.* In the 1880s Taylor began a series of time-and-motion studies at the Midvale Steel plant. He photographed workers' every movement, timing each distinct motion down to the nearest fraction of a second. It was Taylor's dream to be able to then redesign everything the worker did, in order to make it as efficient as possible, thereby maximizing worker productivity. Taylor's ideas, published in 1911 in his *Principles of Scientific Management,* enabled factory managers to greatly increase their control over the labor process. The worker was to do exactly as told by the factory's managers, no more and no less.

Although these changes were adopted to increase the overall efficiency (and hence profitability) of the factory, they had another effect that was arguably even more important. Work became **deskilled;** it was reduced to *detail labor consisting of extremely simple, highly repetitive, monotonous operations that required few if any skills or training.* Scientific management thus gave control over the production process to the factory's owners and managers, who became its "brains;" the workers were reduced to the status of bodies and hands, blindly executing their supervisors' ideas. A worker might spend an entire day welding a support bracket to a bumper, mounting an engine, or simply turning a bolt. Such deskilling robbed the workers of any discretion in their work, while making them highly vulnerable to layoffs, since they—like the components they were making—were standardized and therefore easily replaced (Braverman, 1976).

Primary and Secondary Labor Markets

Factory work in the United States contributed to a rising standard of living between the late 1940s and the early 1970s. This happened especially in such large-scale industries as steel and automobiles, where a small number of giant companies dominated world markets. Partly because workers in these companies belonged to powerful labor unions (see below), and partly because the companies themselves were highly profitable, many workers found themselves earning more and more money each year. They also enjoyed job security against being fired, health and retirement programs, and other benefits. Such workers became part of the American middle class.

Is the experience of automobile or steel workers typical of all workers in the United States? To answer this question, we first have to understand the concept of a **labor market**—*all those persons who are seeking to sell their labor to others for a wage or salary.* Some sociologists who study labor processes have concluded that rather than a single labor market, the United States has a **dual labor market**—one that is *divided into a lower strata of low-paying (and low-benefit) jobs that seldom provide opportunities for advancement, and an upper strata of well-paying jobs that provide career opportunity* (Bonacich, 1972; Roos, 1985; Bielby and Baron, 1986).

The **primary labor market** consists of *jobs that are reasonably secure, provide good pay and benefits, and hold the promise of career training and advancement.* Because of various forms of discrimination, including previous labor union exclusion of racial minorities, these jobs have historically tended to be disproportionately filled by native-born white males (Bonacich, 1972). A person who gains a foothold in the primary labor market could usually hope to advance in the U.S. economic system. At the bottom are unionized blue-collar workers in major industries, as well as such white-collar workers as bank tellers, office supervisors, computer programmers, and public school teachers. At the top, the primary labor market includes professionals, managers, and others whose work requires advanced training, special credentials, and specialized technical skills.

As we shall see below in the section on postindustrial society, the strength of the primary labor market has eroded considerably during the past quarter-century as the result of economic globalization. During the past two decades, many workers have seen their standard of living decline, and even managers and other professional workers have experienced layoffs as U.S. businesses struggle to cut costs in the face of global economic competition. It would seem that there are few, if any, jobs today that can claim to be as protected as primary sector jobs were once thought to be.

The **secondary labor market** includes *unstable jobs with little job security, low pay and few benefits, and little likelihood of career advancement.* Workers in this sector tend to be immigrants, female, and nonwhite. They are seldom unionized. This sector includes restaurant and fast food workers, clerks and typists, assembly-line workers in small factories and sweatshops, salesclerks, and the growing number of people employed by temporary work agencies. Although participation in this labor market may provide one with work, it is unlikely to result in mobility into the primary labor market, where the real opportunities for advancement are found (see Box 15.2). The secondary labor market has increased in recent years, also partly as a result of economic globalization.

There is also an **informal (or "underground") economy**—*goods and services sold by individuals and illegal businesses that do not pay taxes or register with federal, state, or local licensing authorities.* The informal economy includes everything from garage sales to unlicensed factories to drug dealing. Well-publicized examples include the widespread use of childcare "nannies," gardeners, and housekeepers who are paid "under the table," enabling upper-middle-class families to hire low-wage workers who are undocumented immigrants. Such employers avoid paying social security

Box 15.2

Critical Thinking

Are There Really "Dead-End Jobs"?

Thomas Sowell, a prominent African-American economist and a senior fellow at Stanford University's Hoover Institute, has stirred up controversy by arguing that the problems of poverty are in large part due to government welfare programs that subsidize the poor.

Sowell (1993) contends that while it may be important to retrain people for the high-technology jobs of the future, plenty of people are urgently needed in low-technology jobs in which they can make an immediate economic contribution. He cites "domestic" jobs, such as child care and care of the elderly, as examples of important occupations in which there is a significant shortage of qualified people.

Why is there a shortage? Sowell argues that part of the reason is that Americans have been led to believe that such work is menial and therefore unworthy. Additionally, he claims, government welfare and unemployment benefits help to promote welfare dependency by contributing to a mentality that prefers government "handouts" to useful (but poorly compensated) work. In support of his argument he points to Mexican-American immigrants who work hard, often for little pay, and almost never become beggars. He attributes their work ethic to the fact that most have not been in the country long enough to acquire the prevailing American "handout" mentality.

Sowell derides liberal intellectuals for dismissing such low-paying domestic service jobs as "dead-end." In his view they are often an important first step up the economic ladder. Moreover, he claims, when poor people work in the homes of those who are better off, they can broaden their interests, perhaps learning useful things from those who are more fortunate.

"There are no dead-end jobs," Sowell claims, only "dead-end people" who are the result of a liberal social philosophy and the welfare dependency it has created.

What is your response to Sowell's argument that government welfare programs can only produce dependency? What assumptions does Sowell make? How might you construct a study to subject Sowell's claims to empirical testing?

---

taxes or reporting the wages to the Internal Revenue Service. This practice received much attention recently when several of President Clinton's nominees for high government positions were forced to withdraw their names, when it surfaced that they had once employed such workers in violation of the law.

The informal economy provides an important source of work for low-income people, as well as cheap labor for businesses in the formal economy. For example, well-known brand name clothing companies may hire a licensed garment factory to make their clothing; the factory, in turn, may subcontract a portion of the sewing to unlicensed sweatshops in the informal economy. While such practices are illegal, they are also widespread (Efron, 1989a, 1989b, 1989c, 1989d, 1990)

(see the discussion on subcontracting below). Such practices are commonplace in poor countries around the world, where the informal economy is often a substantial part of the total economy (Vickers, 1991).

Labor Unions and Industrial Conflict

Labor unions are *workers' organizations concerned with improving various aspects of their members' working lives.* Unions reflect the belief that although workers as individuals have relatively little power in dealing with their employers, if they speak with a single voice they might be heard. In the United States, unions generally have been concerned with workers' pay and benefits, job security, working hours, and on-the-job health and safety conditions. In Europe, unions have also sometimes called for greater worker control over the work process, as well as a share in businesses' profits. One function of unions is to obtain legislation favorable to workers, by lobbying and making campaign contributions to public officials. Another function is **collective bargaining,** *negotiating with employers on behalf of the union's members;* any negotiated agreements are then legally binding on both employers and workers.

When unions and employers are unable to reach agreements on such fundamental issues as wages or working conditions, the union may call for a **strike** or *work stoppage.* Typically, union members will **picket** the employer, *marching in front of the doorway to the workplace so as to discourage other workers from entering until an agreement is reached.* The strike, if effective, will close down the factory and help force the employer to negotiate with the union. Strikes may last

Labor unions have played an important role in securing higher wages and benefits, shorter working days, and safer conditions for workers in America and throughout the world. Partly because globalization has created a global market for labor, however, many American workers have suffered job loss and declining wages in recent years, and union membership has suffered as a result.

a few days, months, or even years. If the union is sufficiently large, it may have enough money to help workers pay for their rent and food for the duration of the strike. When there are numerous unemployed workers who do not belong to the union, however, work stoppages are sometimes difficult to enforce, since there may be many workers willing to cross the picket line and disregard the strike.

The first American unions appeared in the late eighteenth century but did not really become significant until the advent of rapid industrialization a century later. The early unions were comprised of skilled craftsmen; women were excluded, not only from the unions but from the crafts themselves. Between the 1930s and the 1950s, unions were instrumental in the passage of federal legislation that guaranteed workers the right to strike, bargain collectively, receive a federally designated minimum wage, and enjoy certain health and safety protections in the workplace (Barbash, 1967; Boyer and Morais, 1955; Estey, 1981; Lipset, 1986).

Workers' rights were not easily won. The U.S. judicial system generally ruled that strikes were illegal throughout the nineteenth and well into the twentieth century, and strikes were often violently suppressed by private security forces, the local police, the state militia, and occasionally the federal government. Carnegie Steel's Homestead strike of 1892, for example, erupted in violence when the encampment of striking workers was fired upon by hundreds of armed private detectives, killing many people. The union movement remained weak until the Depression of the 1930s, when it began growing in strength, peaking in the late 1950s (Boyer and Morais, 1955; Wolff, 1965; Brierley, 1987; Goldfield, 1987).

In 1955 about one in every four American workers belonged to unions. That percentage has steadily declined to fewer than one in six, representing some 17 million workers today (Barbash, 1993; see Figure 15.1). This represents one of the lowest levels of unionization in any major capitalist industrial nation. The decline is most significant among workers in private industry. Among public sector employees, union membership is actually growing; nearly two out of every five union members in the United States today work for government agencies at the local, state, or federal level. The National Education Association (the teachers' union), for example, has 1.6 million members, while the American Federation of State, County, and Municipal Employees (AFSCME) has 1.2 million members. By way of comparison, the Teamsters' Union has 2 million members, and the United Auto Workers has 1.2 million (Encyclopedia of Associations, 1991).

The decline in private sector union membership partly reflects a growing frustration with the corruption

Figure 15.1 **U.S. Union Membership as a Percent of the Labor Force, 1955–1988**

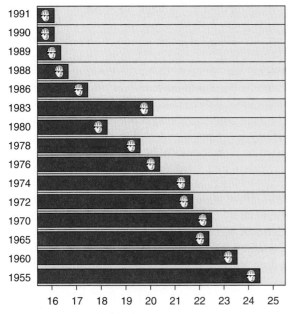

Union Membership as percentage of Labor Force

Union membership in the United States has declined throughout the post–World War II period, from about a quarter of the workforce in 1955 to a sixth today. Nearly two out of every five union members today are government employees. The traditional industrial labor union has declined as industrial jobs have been lost to low-wage countries around the world. By way of contrast, in Scandinavian countries most workers belong to unions, while in Western Europe unions maintain their strength by aligning themselves with political parties.
Source: Barbash (1993).

and inefficiency of some unions. But it is also due to the weakening position of American labor in the face of global competition. In a global economy, a steel plant in Pennsylvania or an automobile manufacturer in Michigan can close down its factory, fire its unionized workers, and reopen it in a low-income country where workers get a tenth of U.S. wages and unions are outlawed. It is difficult for unions to retain members when they can no longer guarantee job security or increasing wages. Significantly, the same Flint factory that saw the birth of one of the country's most powerful unions, the United Auto Workers, closed its doors in the late 1980s after General Motors had relocated its production facilities to Mexico.

In response to such changing conditions, some unions in recent years have been willing to work more closely with management, accepting wage cuts in exchange for greater participation in workplace decision making and a share in any resulting gains in produc-

tivity. Companies such as Xerox, AT&T, and Levi Strauss have all been willing to enter into such cooperative agreements with their unions, in an effort to increase their global competitiveness (Uchitelle, 1993). Some companies, such as United Airlines, are now even owned by their employees.

The Modern Corporation

If unions historically have symbolized labor, business is personified by the modern corporation. A **corporation** is a *formal organization that has a legal existence separate from its members.* Corporations are the principal economic actors in industrial society. Like people, they have rights and obligations: They engage in contracts and agreements, generate wealth, and pay taxes. Their income, debts, and legal responsibilities differ from those of their owners, who are legally protected from the corporations' liabilities. They range from giants like EXXON and AT&T to the mom-and-pop grocery store down the street. Although there are some 15 million such firms in the United States, most are small; fewer than 10 thousand firms employ more than 500 workers (U.S. Bureau of the Census, 1990b).

The largest corporations are usually publicly owned. This means that the corporation raises money by selling stock to anyone who wishes to buy it. The shareholders legally own the corporation; they elect its board of directors, hold regular meetings, and vote on important policies. In theory, this is intended to separate corporate ownership from management (Berle and Means, 1982; orig. 1932); the people who run the corporation are supposed to be accountable to the many owners of its stock. Some 43 million Americans own such stock, giving the illusion of popular control over corporate affairs (U.S. Bureau of the Census, 1991).

In fact, the reality of corporate ownership and control is quite different. Ownership of stock is almost always concentrated in a small number of hands that hold actual power. These may include the founders of the corporation, its top officers and managers, other corporations who have bought up a controlling interest, or simply wealthy investors. The large majority of stock today is held by institutional investors such as employee pension funds, mutual funds, insurance companies, savings banks, and the trust departments of commercial banks. Such large-scale institutional investors own more than $2 trillion worth of stock in publicly held American corporations; pension funds alone account for a third of the value of stock ownership. Most Americans who own stock therefore do so through their retirement plans and therefore have no direct contact with the corporation at all. Policies are seldom actually made at annual shareholders' meetings. They are rather made by the corporation's top officers and managers, and are then ratified by boards of directors that they largely appoint. The management is usually left alone as long as the corporation is doing well; only when sales or profits perform poorly is the board of directors likely to get involved (Zeitlin, 1989; Scott, 1980; Sethi, 1983).

A **monopoly** is said to exist *when a single firm accounts for all the sales in a particular market.* Prior to its government-mandated breakup a decade ago, AT&T had a virtual monopoly on telecommunications in the United States. Since they lack competition, monopolies are capable of exerting considerable power, including the power to set prices, a practice that is illegal in the United States. In some instances the federal government allows monopolies to exist, albeit tightly regulated, as was the case with AT&T prior to its breakup. An **oligopoly** exists when *several firms overwhelmingly dominate a market.* Oligopolies were common when American society was primarily based on domestic industries. In automobile manufacture, for example, the "big three"—General Motors, Ford, and Chrysler—completely dominated car sales in the United States for a quarter century. But economic globalization has almost ended oligopoly concentration, at least for the time being. Dozens of automobile manufacturers, from Japan and Korea to Germany, now challenge American dominance. In fact, the emergence of a global economy heralds a phase of increased economic competition for firms in every country, after a period in which national corporations often enjoyed unprecedented power in their own national markets.

Corporate power can become concentrated in another way—through **interlocking directorates** that *enable directors to sit on the governing boards of more than one corporation.* In this way, corporations with common interests will have overlapping board memberships, enabling a degree of coordination and control across corporations. A large manufacturer, the banks which lends it money, and the retailers who sell its products may all share people on one anothers' boards (Mintz and Schwartz, 1985; Useem, 1984). During the 1980s, yet another form of concentrated power emerged, the **conglomerate**—*an enormous corporation comprised of numerous subsidiaries, often consisting of unrelated business enterprises.* While corporations are typically identified with their principal products, conglomerates buy and sell corporations regardless of what goods or services they provide, so long as the transaction is profitable. A wave of mergers and acquisitions during the 1980s fueled the growth of conglomerates—and their subsequent collapse, when the economy turned downward at the end of the decade. Fueled by tolerant government regulations, easily acquired loans, and the enormous growth in corporate wealth made possible by economic globalization, corporations spent more than $1.3 trillion buying one another up—an amount equal to the national wealth of Germany. To take one example, the R. J. Reynolds tobacco company acquired food giant Nabisco for $25 billion, greatly enriching the top officers of both companies in the process (Sethi, 1993).

The most important corporate form today is the **transnational corporation (TNC),** *a corporation that operates in many different countries.* Fully a quarter of total world production is conducted by TNCs today, a figure that is expected to reach half by the turn of the

A quarter of the world's production comes from transnational corporations. The interests and profits of these companies are independent of any one nation, enabling them to move wherever the political and economic climate is most favorable. Chrysler workers outside a plant in Mexico are as important to the Chrysler corporation today as were Detroit workers 30 years ago.

Table 15.1   The 25 Largest Industrial Corporations in the World, 1990 (ranked by sales)

Rank	Company	Headquarters	Total Sales (in billions of dollars)	Employees
1	General Motors	U.S.	127.0	775,100
2	Ford Motor	U.S	96.9	366,641
3	Exxon	U.S.	86.7	104,000
4	Royal Dutch/Shell	U.K./Netherlands	85.5	135,000
5	IBM	U.S.	63.4	383,220
6	Toyota Motor	Japan	60.4	91,790
7	General Electric	U.S.	55.3	292,000
8	Mobil	Italy	51.0	67,900
9	Hitachi	Japan	50.9	274,508
10	British Petroleum	U.K.	49.4	119,850
11	IRI	Italy	49.1	416,200
12	Matsushita	Japan	43.1	193,088
13	Daimler-Benz	Germany	40.6	368,226
14	Phillip Morris	U.S.	39.1	157,000
15	Fiat	Italy	36.7	286,294
16	Chrysler	U.S.	36.2	121,947
17	Nissan Motor	Japan	36.1	117,330
18	Unilever	U.K./Netherlands	35.3	300,000
19	E. Dupont de Nemours	U.S.	35.2	145,787
20	Samsung	South Korea	35.2	176,947
21	Volkswagen	Germany	34.7	250,616
22	Siemens	Germany	32.7	365,000
23	Texaco	U.S.	32.4	37,067
24	Toshiba	Japan	29.5	125,000
25	Chevron	U.S.	29.4	54,826

Source: Sethi, 1993.

century (Modelski, 1979; Barnet and Muller, 1974). The largest TNCs are wealthier than most countries. General Motors, for example, had 1992 sales of $132 billion, greater than the gross national product of all but 24 countries (*Business Week,* 1993). The 25 largest TNCs together produce nearly $1.3 trillion in wealth, more than any country in the world except for the United States, Japan, and Germany. In 1990, 10 of the world's top 25 industrial corporations were headquartered in the United States; only a decade earlier, the number was 18 (see Table 15.1). Five of the top 25 were Japanese, as were the five largest banks in the world (Sethi, 1993). American dominance is increasingly being challenged by Japan, Korea, and other newly industrializing Asian countries (Chapter 9), as well as Germany and the recently formed European Community.

TNCs themselves are becoming increasingly global in terms of ownership and management. Although their principal headquarters may be in a single country, their shareholders are likely to be wealthy individuals and corporations from around the world, and their man-

agement may include people from the different countries in which they do business. Often, TNCs from one country will engage in joint business ventures with TNCs from another. As globalization intensifies, it is likely that TNCs will become increasingly international actors, with allegiances and accountability to no single country.

It is an open question whether the emergence of such powerful global corporate actors is beneficial or detrimental to people in the countries where they operate. Both are probably true. On the one hand, during the past quarter century, global corporations have enabled many countries in the world, especially in Asia, to greatly elevate their living standards. By operating globally, they create pressures for a common legal framework and political agreement between nations. On the other hand, they have often been involved in ruthless exploitation of workers in poor nations and have supported the violent overthrow of governments that were seen as unsympathetic to their interests. They have also contributed to massive environmental destruction (see Chapters 9 and 20 for further discussion).

POLITICS AND THE ECONOMY

Although industrialization occurred under capitalist forms of economic organization in England, France, Spain, and most of Europe, it took a socialist form in the former Soviet Union, China, and a number of other countries that industrialized much later (Baechler, Hall, and Mann, 1988). Although capitalism and socialism agree on the importance of economic growth and rising living standards, they differ profoundly in their ideas about how the economy should be organized so as to achieve this goal.

Capitalist Political-Economic Systems

Capitalism is a *political-economic system characterized by market allocation of goods and services, production for private profit, and private ownership of the means of producing wealth* (Chapter 4). Workers sell their labor to the owners of capital in exchange for a wage; capitalists are then free to make a profit on the goods their workers produce. Although capitalism emphasizes the importance of "free" markets and private economic decision making, in fact the economy is a social organization, in which social relations (including power relations) play a key role (Granovetter, 1985; Zukin and DiMaggio, 1990, Powell and DiMaggio, 1991). Concentration of ownership and interlocking directorates, discussed above, are two of the ways that economic elites help to shape the economy. Governments also play a key role in helping to shape economic life, even in countries such as the United States that pride themselves in keeping government's role to a minimum (Campbell et al., 1991; see Chapter 13).

Because capitalists are in competition with one another, they experience constant pressures to keep costs down. One important way this has been accomplished is through reducing the cost of labor. To achieve this objective, businesses have adopted technologies that increase workers' productivity, keep wages as low as possible, and relocate jobs to other parts of the country (or in other countries) where wages are lower. Capitalism thus frequently produces uneven development, inequality, and conflict between workers and their employers. On the other hand, it has also been successful in raising the living standards of large numbers of people in capitalist economies.

Capitalist systems are based on an individualist work ethic, which holds that if people work hard and diligently pursue their own individual goals, the society as a whole will prosper (Hamilton and Hirszowicz, 1987). There is accordingly a mistrust of the role of government in managing economic affairs. Nonetheless, there are wide variations in the degree to which individualistic beliefs and mistrust of government are held in different capitalist countries. In the United States, many Americans are passionate about being left alone to pursue their self-interest, and are deeply suspicious of government's ability to provide for the common welfare. On the other hand, other capitalist countries have more of a **collectivist orientation,** *the belief that members of society should assume responsibility for one another's welfare.* In Sweden, for example, this takes the form of trusting government to manage a wide range of economic and social affairs that would be unthinkable in the United States. Japan, on the other hand, does not expect government to take on such a major role but nonetheless expects businesses to assume almost family-like responsibility for the welfare of their employees.

Socialist Political-Economic Systems

Socialism is *a political-economic system in which the production and distribution of goods and services is pursued for the common good, by means of enterprises owned by the central government or its subunits* (Chapter 4). Socialist economic systems are based on a strongly collectivist work ethic. In practical terms, the central government is seen as representing the common good, and therefore the state owns all businesses, factories, farms, living units, and other means of producing wealth. The worker works for a state industrial enterprise, the farmer works for a state-run farm, the bureaucrat works in a state agency.

Socialist systems originated in the theories of nineteenth century philosophers and social scientists, and they were especially influenced by the ideas of Karl Marx. Marx believed that the interests of capitalists and workers were fundamentally opposed, leading to inevitable class struggle between the two. Marx predicted that workers would eventually prove victorious, capitalists and capitalism would be eliminated, and class struggle would come to an end. Since he also believed that governments existed primarily to protect the interests of capitalists, Marx concluded that once capitalism ended, so too would the need for government. During the short-term or socialist phase, however, the state would be required to manage the economy in the interests of the workers.

Needless to say, in all actual societies that have been modeled after Marx's theories, the short-term has come and gone. Far from withering away, socialist governments remained firmly in place, at least until recently, when they began to transform themselves—not into classless societies as Marx had expected but rather into different forms of capitalism. This has occurred in part because socialism itself proved to be too inflexible to manage a modern, postindustrial economy. As the 1991 collapse of the Soviet Union and its satellite countries in Eastern Europe made clear, the socialist requirement that tens of thousands of factories, farms, and other state-run enterprises run all of their decisions through the central government proved to be a deterrent to economic growth. Large state bureaucracies proved to be inflexible, inefficient, corrupt, and filled with people more interested in enriching themselves than doing their jobs. Furthermore, the fact that workers' pay was seldom tied to the amount of work they did proved to be a powerful disincentive to hard work.

At the same time, it is important to acknowledge that socialist systems have often been successful in reducing inequality, eliminating extreme poverty, and providing their populations with housing, health care, and basic social services. However successful they have been in these terms, they have nevertheless not proved to be effective in creating the flexible types of institutions necessary for postindustrial economies, nor have they provided the high levels of material consumption enjoyed by the middle classes in capitalist countries.

Industrial Democracy: A Middle Ground?

Is there a middle ground? Societies like Denmark, Sweden, Finland, Norway, and even Canada and England enjoy some degree of "socialist-like" welfare system, yet manage to follow successful "capitalist-like" strategies to run their economies. Such hybrid economic systems are sometimes termed **industrial democracies,** because they *seek some democratic controls over business, along with the public provision of basic social services.*

In Sweden, under the Meidner Plan, workers were able to gain some degree of control over the companies that employed them by buying shares of stock in their companies, a step recently taken by the employees of United Airlines in the United States, which, as we mentioned earlier, is now employee-owned. Sweden has long provided its citizens with extensive health-care programs, low-cost housing, generous unemployment benefits and workers' pensions, paid maternity leave, day care, and heavily subsidized education. Canada, England, and most European countries either have public health-care systems or ensure that all citizens have access to adequate and affordable private health care. In Denmark, for example, all residents receive free health care at public facilities; in Norway, the government pays full salary for 50 weeks in the case of long-term illness. Low-cost publicly owned or nonprofit housing is routinely provided to people who need it in England, Sweden, Germany, and parts of Canada—not to mention in such East Asian capitalist powerhouses as Hong Kong and Singapore (Dreier and Hulchanski,

1993; Green and Pinsky, 1989; Carnoy and Shearer, 1980; Appelbaum and Henderson, 1992; Stevenson, 1993).

Sluggish economic growth has recently forced many of these countries to rethink their public expenditures, which can be extremely costly and difficult to finance when the economy is weak (Melcher, 1992; Havemann, 1992). Yet they still enjoy a much higher degree of state involvement than exists in the United States.

POSTINDUSTRIAL SOCIETY

Industrial society has resulted in an ever-expanding standard of living for a large segment of the workforce in the United States. Yet at the same time, the organization of work in industrial society has resulted in the deskilling of labor, persistent inequality, a dual labor market, and the exploitation and alienation of segments of the workforce. As far back as 1973, sociologist Daniel Bell argued that we are entering a **postindustrial society,** *a society in which wealth is based primarily on knowledge, information, and the provision of services rather than on factory production* (Chapter 4). Postindustrial society, and the emergence of an increasingly unified global economy, go hand in hand.

Scholars typically depict the emerging postindustrial society in one of two ways: either as a prosperous high-tech utopia where electronic gadgetry frees people from alienating labor, or an increasingly stratified society in which a handful of technologically sophisticated professionals thrive while ordinary workers become superfluous. Will tiny, powerful, widely available supercomputers enable ordinary citizens to achieve greater control over their work and lives? Or will such technology enable business and government to exert ever increasing authority over the rest of us?

The Emergence of Postindustrial Society

Thirty years ago Marshall McLuhan (1964) wrote that we all live in a "global village." By this he meant that communications and transportation technology had radically shrunk the size of the planet, so that in effect we all resided in the same community. In 1900 it took several days to travel from New York City to Los Angeles by train, and weeks to cross the country by horse and carriage. Only 50 years later, commercial air travel had cut that time to 12 hours. Today, jet aircraft have cut that time by more than half, and the supersonic Concorde has reduced the New York–London travel time to only three hours. Instantaneous direct dial telephonic communication links most countries in the world today; it is now easier (and cheaper) to call Asia or

Europe from the United States than it was to phone coast-to-coast 40 years ago. Such changes in transportation and communication are giving rise to fundamental changes in our economy, our sense of nationhood, and our cultural identities.

The most significant changes were ushered in when scientists at the Intel Corporation invented the microprocessor in 1971. Although computers have long been used in science and industry, microprocessor technology reduced the computer from a roomful of wires and vacuum tubes to a single chip, eventually placing control over vast quantities of information in the hands of anyone with a laptop computer (Gilder, 1989). Within a few years the computational power of chips had increased enormously, giving birth to the desktop computer industry. Small businesses could now afford the computing power that only a few years earlier was reserved for industrial giants or governmental agencies (Zuboff, 1988).

The telephone, fax machine, and electronic mail are the most obvious current examples of this "information revolution." Business executives instantaneously cut deals a half a world away, and manufacturers make cars and clothing and computers on an assembly line that circles the planet (Chapter 9). Professors are able to conduct research and writing with colleagues in other countries, accessing entire libraries of information on CD-ROM disks or by means of electronic mail. In fact, much of this textbook was written utilizing just such technologies. These changes have radically reduced the **information float** (Naisbitt, 1990)—*the amount of time information takes to get from one place to another.*

Within a few years, existing technology will vastly extend even these storage and information capabilities. For example, the Janus Project, at Columbia University Law School, will create optical images of hundreds of thousands of books and publications by the end of the century, permitting researchers to electronically search for any word, phrase, or topic in a vast electronic library.

The Organization of Work in Postindustrial Society

The information revolution will significantly impact the nature of work and the organization of economic life in a number of ways. We shall briefly discuss six: the automation of manufacturing, flexible production, subcontracting, the growth of the service economy, the rise of the "symbolic analyst," and the "virtual workplace."

The Automation of Manufacturing

Automation refers to *the replacement of human labor by machines in the process of manufacturing.* Although the tendency to introduce labor-saving machinery has been present since the beginning of industrial capitalism, since the 1970s automation has increasingly entailed the use of computers to control all aspects of production. **Robots**—*computer-driven machines*—can now be programmed to do most phases of automobile manufacture, performing tedious and often dangerous work that once required the labor of hundreds of human workers. (The term "robot" comes from a Czechoslovakian novel about humanoid machines

Computers have changed the nature of work and economic life. They are today used to design everything from books to automobiles and have made it possible to reorganize many businesses on a global scale. In this photograph, textile designers employ computer technology to assist them in developing a fashionable fabric.

written in 1921 by Karel Capek; "robot," in Czech, means "worker.") Although U.S. factories are now beginning to employ robotic technologies, Japanese and German factories—which had to be built from scratch after being destroyed during World War II—have been highly automated for more than a decade. Japan currently leads the world in the production and use of robotic machinery.

In computer-integrated manufacturing (CIM), computers run assembly lines, program complex tasks to be performed by robots, and aid in designing new products. They are routinely used to design goods ranging from automobiles to airplanes, from clothing to athletic shoes. Modern apparel manufacturers, for example, can purchase a competitors' popular garment, scan it with an electronic device, and then redesign it on a computer screen and sell it under their own label (Dosi, 1984; Inkster, 1991; Martin and Rawthorn, 1986; Medland and Burnett, 1986; Hunt, 1990; Prasad, 1989).

We saw earlier that in industrial society, a division exists between those who work with their bodies and those who work with their minds. In nonautomated factories, workers are physically depleted in production processes that require lifting, moving, hauling, precise manual dexterity, and other forms of physical exertion. In highly automated factories, by way of contrast, much of the drudgery is performed by machines. Workers are increasingly removed from the physical process of production and instead are called upon to use their minds in what Shoshana Zuboff (1988) terms **intellective skill**—*the ability to think logically and abstractly, rather than relying on immediate physical experience.* Workers must make the decisions necessary to operate computer-driven processes, rather than use their bodies to run machines. Zuboff, who studied a number of high-tech industries, found that once workers had adapted to the new technologies, they preferred them to the older ones. Her findings echoed those of Blauner (1964), who, as we have seen, noted that worker alienation was lower in automated factories.

Although computerized factories are more productive, "cleaner," and potentially less alienating than the old machinery-based ones, they also employ far fewer workers. Indeed, one of the main objectives of automation is to produce more goods with fewer workers, thereby reducing the cost of production. Automation thus has two possible effects on the American workforce. First, it may reduce the demand for labor, thereby contributing to unemployment. A new Japanese technology, for example, permits a computer operator in Tokyo to direct a spray-painting robot in any factory in the world, thereby eliminating the need to employ workers as painters (Hamilton, 1992). Au-

tomation may thus mean that large numbers of unskilled and semiskilled workers will be displaced by machines and the handful of highly trained technicians that run them.

Second, since unskilled workers are no longer necessary when production is highly automated, countries with large pools of low-cost unskilled labor may have greater difficulty in attracting factories. One study found, for example, that while it cost three times as much to manually assemble electronic devices in the high-wage United States than in lower-wage Hong Kong, in highly automated factories the cost was the same in both countries—about a quarter of the original U.S. cost of doing the job by hand (reported in Rada, 1985). Although from the standpoint of the American worker this means that factories are less likely to move offshore in search of cheap labor, it does not necessarily mean that there will be many jobs in the highly automated factories that remain.

Flexible Production

One result of automation is greatly increased flexibility in the production process. Mass production technology made it difficult to tailor products to the needs of specific customers. To greatly change an automobile's design, for example, required the construction of a new factory or assembly line, a costly, risky, and time-consuming process. Automobiles changed but slowly, with perhaps a few embellishments every other year. Similarly, clothing styles changed once a year or so, and even the fashion-conscious were limited in the range of styles available. The 1950s were symbolized by the drab "man in a gray flannel suit" (Packard, 1959). Postindustrial society, on the other hand, is characterized by **post-Fordism,** *forms of industrial organization that emphasize flexibility rather than standardization* (Scott, 1988; Storper and Christopherson, 1987; Piore and Sabel, 1984). Unlike earlier generations of machinery, computer-driven tools and assembly processes can be quickly reprogrammed to alter the product that is being made. This permits rapid shifts to new products, constantly changing designs, and in general a much shorter time from manufacturer to buyer.

Clothing manufacturers like Benneton and The Gap produce six or more style changes a year. Their computers record and analyze millions of sales in thousands of outlets around the world, enabling them to more accurately anticipate the wants of specific customers: teenagers in Southern California may favor a different style than their counterparts in New York City or Tokyo. Orders can be placed quickly in clothing factories located in dozens of countries around the world, and the whole manufacturing process coordinated by computer. It is increasingly difficult for any company to survive today that cannot respond flexibly to shifting demands from its customers (Ewen, 1988; Swenson, 1990; Michman, 1991; Peters, 1992).

Subcontracting

The demand for flexibility is having a profound impact on the American workforce. Under the earlier mass production form of industrial organization, a single, gigantic firm such as General Motors typically employed a substantial workforce in all aspects of production, from raw materials processing to assembly to design and sales. Blue-collar workers belonged to unions and as a result had labor contracts that provided for some degree of job security, adequate pay, and health and other benefits. Under the postindustrial form of flexible organization, a rapidly growing number of businesses are reducing the number of their core employees to a minimum. This is accomplished through **subcontracting,** a *form of economic organization in which a firm hires other firms to provide specialized products or services* (Pfeffer and Baron, 1988; Peters, 1992). Businesses engage in subcontracting to reduce their labor costs, thereby enabling them to compete more profitably and realize greater profits.

An estimated 30 million Americans today—a third of U.S. workers—work at subcontracted jobs, including temporary workers, part-timers, independent subcontractors, and other forms of contingent workers. It is estimated that this number may reach half of all U.S. workers by the end of the century, approaching the percentage in Japan (Rosenblatt, 1993; Morrow, 1993; Orrú, Hamilton, and Suzuki, 1989; Gerlach, 1992). Manpower, Inc., the world's largest temporary employment agency, handles more workers each day than General Motors or IBM. Manpower and similar agencies now handle 1.5 million workers, three times as many as a decade ago (Castro, 1993).

Firms are able to become "lean and mean" by limiting their payrolls to a core group of highly skilled professional and technical employees, whose work is most profitable to the firm. This includes professional, technical, and managerial workers in such areas as product engineering and design, marketing, and retailing. The advice offered by one of today's top business consultants is to "contract out everything but your soul—what you do better than everybody else" (Kouzes, 1987). Yet even professionals are no longer ensured permanent full-time positions within firms. Lawyers, bank loan officers, engineers, and even senior executives can now be acquired on a temporary basis from firms that are the professional equivalent of Kelly Services or Manpower.

Factory work is especially likely to be subcontracted to other firms. For example, when you buy an athletic shoe or an item of clothing with your favorite U.S. brand label, the chances are that the company actually consists only of a handful of designers, accountants and tax experts, and marketing specialists. The actual making of the shoe or the sewing of the clothing is subcontracted to factories around the globe (Appelbaum and Gereffi, 1994; Bonacich and Waller, 1992; see Chapter 9). This enables businesses to substantially reduce their costs by paying only those subcontractors they require at the moment. A company that owns its own factories, on the other hand, must pay for its machinery and workers even if the economy is slow and the factory is idle.

Subcontracting can have highly negative consequences for the workforce, since subcontracted workers have none of the stability and protections that were once enjoyed by direct employees of the company. Wages are lower, and job security is nonexistent. There are no health benefits, pensions, paid vacations, training programs, or promotions. Subcontracted workers tend to be poor, nonunionized, disproportionately female, and subject to immediate layoff if they are not needed. When business is bad, there is nothing to prevent the company from reducing its subcontracted labor, since they lack the protections of regular workers. When the Bank of America merged with Security Pacific Bank in 1992, 3,600 jobs were eliminated; of its 65,000 remaining workers in California, nearly a third are part-timers who receive few benefits (Rosenblatt, 1993).

If subcontracted factories are located in low-wage countries, they often have health and safety conditions that would be illegal in the United States, a fact that is also true of many subcontracted "sweatshops" found in U.S. cities. Subcontracting has thus contributed to the creation of a dual labor market on a global scale. Factory jobs that once were part of a primary labor market in the United States have become part of a global secondary market due to subcontracting.

The Growth of the Service Economy

Economists have distinguished between three different parts of the economy. The **primary sector** is based on *the extraction of raw materials and natural resources;* it includes such industries as agriculture, livestock, mining, fishing, and forestry. Prior to the industrial revolution most people in society were engaged in such primary sector activities. Although the primary sector accounted for nearly half of all U.S. labor at the turn of the century, today it accounts for only 3 percent. The **secondary sector** entails the *production of finished* *goods from raw materials obtained in the primary sector;* factory manufacturing is a key example. Not surprisingly, such activities predominate in industrial society. In the United States, the number of people engaged in manufacturing activities actually declined by 1.4 million during the 1980s, to about 24 percent of all jobs by 1990 (U.S. Bureau of the Census, 1990a; Plunkert, 1990). The **tertiary sector** involves the *production of services.* **Services,** in turn, can be defined as *economically productive activities that do not directly result in a physical product.* This is the principal economic sector in postindustrial society, today accounting for 73 percent of the American workforce and roughly the same percentage of all new jobs. During the 1980s, the number of Americans working in services grew by an astonishing 29.4 million people, including 1.9 million in restaurants and fast-food places, along with nearly a million in grocery stores (U.S. Bureau of the Census, 1990a; Plunkert, 1990).

Although some services are high-paying, most are not. Between 1986 and 1989, for example, only about a third of all new jobs were in higher-paying service occupations such as professors, teachers, accountants, doctors, nurses, lawyers, bankers, entertainers, computer programmers, television announcers, wholesalers, and importers. On the other hand, 42 percent of all new jobs were in such low-paying service occupations as custodians, sales clerks, nurses' aides, restaurant workers, domestics, secretaries, and typists (U.S. Bureau of the Census, 1992). Service jobs generally pay much less than the manufacturing jobs they are replacing (U.S. Bureau of the Census, 1992).

Most successful business enterprises today are primarily engaged in the provision of services, even if we think of them as manufacturing a specific product. For example, only 10 percent of the sales price of the IBM personal computer goes to pay for the physical manufacture of the good itself, and much of this goes to factories that are located outside of the United States. The remaining 90 percent goes mainly for such services as research, design, engineering, sales, and repair (Reich, 1991).

The Rise of the Symbolic Analyst

The only jobs that are likely to be competitive in a global economy are those that cannot easily be done by anyone at another location. Such jobs require **symbolic analysts,** *people who work with symbols and ideas, rather than with things* (Bell, 1973; Drucker, 1993; Reich, 1991; Zuboff, 1988). Symbolic analysts invent things, design new products, engineer new technologies. They are creative people who "make things happen." They are organizers who bring people together, administrators who make firms run efficiently, and legal and financial experts who help firms to be profitable. They are professionals, managers, engineers, designers, and technical wizards whose skills and talents require specialized training and expertise. In a global economy where factory work can be subcontracted out to a global workforce, symbolic analysts still enjoy a measure of prosperity and job security, although as we noted above even these types of jobs are not immune from global competition.

Although there may be some jobs that require such a unique blend of skills and talents, it seems highly unlikely that in the near future the United States will retrain its civilian workforce of approximately 115 million people into symbolic analysts. In fact, there are

Postindustrial society is characterized by a growing number of jobs in the tertiary *or* service sector. *This photograph from Seoul, Korea, shows that these changes are global in nature. It also suggests the globalization of culture, since Dunkin Donuts is hardly a part of traditional Korean dietary customs.*

only 35 million people currently classified as professional, technical, or managerial—the closest Census approximation to this category (U.S. Bureau of the Census, 1990a). It seems certain that for the immediate future, most people in the U.S. workforce will increasingly find themselves competing with lower-cost labor in other countries.

It is important not to confuse symbolic analysts with workers who merely use high-technology equipment. Many office workers, for example, now rely on computers for writing, maintaining databases, and financial management. Yet such work does not necessarily enable the office workers to use their imagination or to exercise the degree of independence and autonomy associated with the role of symbolic analyst. Zuboff's (1988) research found that the computerization of office work can simply provide another form of managerial control over secretaries and clerical workers, unless the office managers are willing to share their authority and information.

The "Virtual Workplace" and "Telecommuting"

Modern telecommunications have greatly reduced the need for workers or service providers to be physically present in the same location as the company that employs them. An increasing amount of subcontracted work is today accomplished by means of the **virtual workplace,** *a work environment that is electronically rather than physically connected to its client.* Typically, the virtual workplace consists of a home office that is electronically connected to the outside world; the clients may be anywhere in the world. Lawyers, graphic designers, Hollywood sound engineers, accountants, soft-

ware writers, and even doctors today can **telecommute** out of their homes, *"traveling" to work electronically rather than physically by such means as telephone, fax, electronic data transfer, and electronic mail.*

It is estimated that as many as 6.6 million workers use computers and fax machines to electronically telecommute between their homes and their offices on a regular basis, about a sixth of the total number of people who work part- or full-time at home. Most telecommuters are white-collar professionals; men and women are about equally represented (Galen, 1993). Telecommuting is increasingly common not only in the United States but also elsewhere in the world. In Singapore and Hong Kong, for example, telephone ownership is high, and many workers telecommute from their homes or on portable telephones (Gordon and Peterson, 1992). From such electronic telecommuting to the relocation of manufacturing plants in remote areas, modern information technology has increasingly reduced the need for jobs to be centrally located. (Churbuck and Young, 1992). Companies from AT&T to ESPN have found it profitable to locate their principal facilities in remote suburban or even rural areas, where land is inexpensive, crime is nonexistent, and trained workers are willing to labor at lower wages.

The virtual workplace is changing the nature of work in the United States. It not only enables some professionals to work at home but also makes it possible for a low-cost workforce to be employed in areas that are geographically remote from the businesses that subcontract for their labor. High-transmission fiber-optic telephone lines have transformed the occupational structure of once remote American prairie towns. Workers in Lusk, Wyoming, a town of 1,500 in the

*Modern information technology has given rise to the vir-*tual workplace, *where physical location is less important than electronic access. This Arab businessman, garbed in traditional attire, conducts his business in a highly modern fashion.*

In Hong Kong, portable telephones are as common as fax machines, enabling business executives to do their work "on the run." It is not uncommon for persons who are doing business in neighboring China to remain in continual telephone contact with their offices across the border. By the end of this century global satellite cellular phone connection will greatly increase reliance on this technology.

state's least populated county, are now able to provide data-entry services for businesses located virtually anywhere. In Linton, North Dakota, women provide reservations services for the country's third-largest travel firm, operating out of a converted tractor dealership. Chippewa Indians in Belcourt, North Dakota, process data for the Internal Revenue Service and other clients (Churbuck and Young, 1992; Woutat, 1992). Gateway 2000, a fast-growing mail-order computer retailer whose sales exploded from under $300 in 1990 to nearly a billion in 1993, is headquartered in North Sioux City, South Dakota. Gateway has no retail outlets. Its 1,400 workers assemble and ship 250,000 personal computers annually, doing their business strictly by ads in computer magazines and an 800 telephone number (Walker, 1992).

Such an electronic dispersal of services does not necessarily create new jobs; often, it merely relocates jobs from high-wage to low-wage places. An economic bonanza for previously unemployed workers in rural prairie states may well result from the loss of jobs for workers in more costly metropolitan areas. The electronic uncoupling of work from specific locations

within the United States may prove to be a mixed blessing, particularly for highly paid workers.

Does Postindustrial Society Bring Prosperity?

It should be clear by now that not everyone prospers in postindustrial society. While some futurists envision a high-technology utopia (Naisbitt, 1982, 1990), in fact the transition to an information-based service economy may leave many people worse off than they were in industrial society. U.S. factory workers who traditionally enjoyed a fairly high standard of living have seen their jobs evaporate, relocated to low-wage areas around the world.

Hundreds of thousands of American autoworkers have lost their jobs since 1980, and more layoffs are announced each day (Table 15.2). IBM, which once had a policy of never laying off workers, has been forced to "downsize" its workforce from 400,000 to 275,000 (and it may eventually wind up with half that number). General Motors has cut some 200,000 blue-collar jobs during the past 15 years and may be forced to cut another 100,000 in the next few years (Nauss, 1993b). People who lose jobs with IBM or General Motors may find themselves providing low-wage services in restaurants, banks, supermarkets, or offices.

When USX (formerly called U.S. Steel) laid off some 2,000 workers from its Fairless, Pennsylvania, plant in 1991, workers lost jobs that paid $15 or more an hour and provided generous benefits, including health plans and retirement programs. Despite retraining efforts, the jobs that were finally available to most of the laid-off workers paid less than half that amount, and offered no benefits at all (Russakoff, 1993). Although some service jobs pay well and require the use of creativity and imagination, most do not. The transition to a postindustrial society currently threatens the comfortable standard of living most Americans have come to expect during the last half-century.

GLOBALIZATION: TOWARD A SINGLE WORLD ECONOMY?

The American economic order today is increasingly characterized by the emergence of a unified global economic system. In fact, some scholars have argued that it no longer makes sense to think of the United States or any other country as an isolated economic society at all: in many respects, the world can be regarded as a single economic unit (Lipietz, 1986; Dieter, 1987; Frobel, Heinrichs, and Kreye, 1980, 1982; Helleiner, 1990; Gereffi, 1992, 1994; Gereffi and Korzeniewicz, 1994).

Table 15.2   U.S. Companies that Announced the Elimination of at Least 10,000 Jobs Between January 1993 and March 1994

Company	Jobs to Be Eliminated	Details
General Motors	69,650	Plant closings and companywide cost-cutting program.
Sears, Roebuck	50,000	Mostly clerical and management; about two-thirds part-time.
IBM	38,500	Global cost-cutting, especially in headquarters and troubled mainframe computer business.
AT&T	33,525	Consumer communications jobs at all levels; middle managers; substantial cuts from NCR, its computer-making subsidiary.
Boeing	31,000	Production work force cut because of sluggish demand for planes.
GTE	27,975	Most cuts in telephone operations.
Nynex	22,000	Across the board.
Phillip Morris	14,000	Mostly in tobacco, food and beer units and corporate offices.
Procter & Gamble	13,000	Plant closings around the world.
Woolworth	13,000	Shutting 970 stores and shifting from core business to specialty chains.
Martin Marietta	12,060	Closing 12 plants and eliminating duplicated jobs after acquisition.
Eastman Kodak	12,000	All levels and all sectors.
Xerox	11,200	Service technicians to be hit hardest.
McDonnell Douglas	10,966	From commercial aircraft, space and military production units.
Raytheon	10,624	Various divisions.
Pacific Telesis	10,000	California economic slump blamed.

Source: New York Times (1994).

In November 1993, President Clinton met with members of the Asian-Pacific Economic Cooperation group in the state of Washington to discuss mutual cooperation among the Asian countries and the United States. Although there were conflicts at the meeting, the fact that it took place at all reflects the movement toward a single world economy that has been taking place at a rapid pace in the last decade.

Global Economic Interdependence

Throughout the first half of this century, most businesses in industrial societies were national businesses. Companies like General Motors and IBM were almost entirely owned by U.S. stockholders and run by U.S. managers who lived in U.S. communities. The products made by these companies were produced mainly in U.S. factories by U.S. workers, and sold largely to U.S. consumers. Although some international trade existed, it was small relative to the commerce that occurred within the United States. It made sense to think of an "American economy" even though Americans bought and sold some goods with other countries.

Most so-called "national" economies today are highly interdependent with one another. The value of U.S. products sold in other countries nearly doubled between 1986 and 1991, reaching $430 billion. Nearly one out of every eight dollars in national income now results from foreign sales of American products (Holstein, 1992). At the same time, nearly everything we buy involves labor from other countries (Box 15.3). Even businesses employing a handful of workers are capable of doing business abroad, thanks to

fax machines, toll-free 800 telephone numbers, electronic mail, and satellite computer hookups (Holstein, 1992).

It is important to recognize that it is not only consumers who have gone on a global shopping spree for cars, clothing, electronics, and other products. The commitment of U.S. business to "buy American" has declined even more rapidly than that of the average American household. Black and Decker, a prominent U.S. tool manufacturer, resupplied its factories with new state-of-the-art computer-driven lathes purchased from Japan. General Motors' subsidiary Hughes Aircraft, a leading defense contractor, is making a sonar system for U.S. navy helicopters—with key components imported from France. Nearly one-fifth of the airframe for Boeing's new 777 jetliner will be imported, as will nearly all the liquid-crystal displays used on U.S.-made laptop computers. When businesses are asked why they are importing so many goods, they typically mention better quality for lower labor costs (Grover and Barrett, 1992).

In a global economy, a growing national economy need no longer benefit all workers. The growth in the U.S. economy that began in 1993 did not result in an

Box 15.3

Globalization

The "All-American" Car

Labor Secretary Robert Reich, in his book *The Work of Nations,* described how nearly everything we consume is today manufactured by workers throughout the world. Reich offers the example of an "all-American" car, the Pontiac Le Mans, which turns out to have very little that is actually made in America:

When an American buys a Pontiac Le Mans from General Motors . . . he or she engages unwittingly in an international transaction. Of the $20,000 paid to GM, about $6,000 goes to South Korea for routine labor and assembly operations, $3,500 to Japan for advanced compo-

nents (engines, transaxles, and electronics), $1,500 to West Germany for styling and design engineering, $800 to Taiwan, Singapore, and Japan for small components, $500 to Britain for advertising and marketing services, and about $100 to Ireland and Barbados for data processing. The rest—less than $8,000—goes to strategists in Detroit, lawyers and bankers in New York, lobbyists in Washington, insurance and health-care workers all over the country, and General Motors shareholders—most of whom live in the United States, but an increasing number of whom are foreign nationals (Reich, 1991; p. 113).

increased number of manufacturing jobs or higher incomes for most workers. Rather, increased automation enabled businesses to produce more goods with fewer workers, while a growing number of goods were being produced in factories outside of the country. This same

Figure 15.2 **Economic Growth in the Industrial Nations Does Not Necessarily Mean More Jobs**

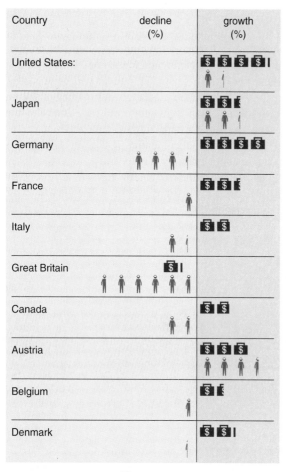

1992 Economic Growth: = .5% increase or decrease

1992 Jobs Growth: = .5% increase or decrease

Economic growth does not necessarily benefit all workers. Businesses in high-wage countries may prosper by using workers in low-wage countries, or by substituting advanced technology that replaces workers altogether. The 24 major industrial countries in the Organization for Economic Cooperation and Development (OECD) saw their economies grow by 1.5 percent in 1992, while the number of jobs declined slightly by 0.1 percent.
Source: Organization for Economic Cooperation and Development, cited in Havemann and Kempster (1993).

problem is being confronted by many countries throughout the industrial world: National economic growth does not necessarily mean more jobs. In Western Europe, unemployment has tripled in the past 20 years, to 10 percent or more of the workforce, and it is expected to rise still higher (Figure 15.2). Even Japan, whose unemployment remains below 3 percent, is experiencing a rise (Cooper and Madigan, 1992; Mandel et al., 1993; Kuttner, 1993; Havemann and Kempster, 1993; Uchitelle, 1994).

One consequence of increasing global economic interdependence is the emergence of regional trading blocks, in which national barriers to the free movement of goods and capital are greatly reduced or removed altogether (Chapter 13). The North American Free Trade Agreement (NAFTA), recently ratified between the United States, Canada, and Mexico, is an important example. NAFTA would create the world's largest trading block, comprised of 364 million people in a $6.2 trillion economy. Opponents of NAFTA argue that millions of U.S. jobs will shift to Mexico, since Mexican workers currently earn a tenth of U.S. wages (Baker et al., 1992). Supporters of NAFTA argue that free trade will bolster Mexico's economy, creating an enormous new market for U.S. products that will eventually lead to new jobs in both countries.

A Global Market for Labor

As a result of such economic globalization, a growing number of U.S. workers are competing with workers all over the world for the same jobs, a trend that will strongly affect the job prospects of many U.S. college students once they graduate. Currently, about one out of every four workers in the world are found in the industrial nations; by the year 2025, that ratio is projected to fall to one out of six (Bloom and Brender, 1993). Jobs will increasingly go wherever on the planet suitable workers can be found. Low labor costs, the absence of labor unions, and governments that enforce worker submissiveness through repressive measures are all factors influencing the globalization of labor (Chapter 9).

We have previously noted that the emergence of an increasingly global labor market has resulted in job loss and declining wages in many U.S. industries. U.S. firms already employ an estimated seven million workers in other countries (O'Reilly, 1992). It is likely that we are witnessing the emergence of a **global wage,** equivalent to the *lowest worldwide cost of obtaining comparable labor for a particular task, once the costs of operating at a distance are taken into account.* Al-

The signing of NAFTA—the North American Free Trade Agreement—was met with staunch support and concerted opposition. Businesses, the Clinton administration, and the Mexican government argued that it would build the economies of both countries, ultimately creating new markets and new jobs. U.S. trade unions (shown here protesting) insisted it would take jobs away from U.S. workers. Peasant farmers in Mexico staged a rebellion in Chiapas in anticipation of a loss of their livelihood when faced with the competition of U.S. agribusiness.

though the global wage varies according to how difficult and expensive it is to find and manage labor in geographically distant places, one thing is certain: For virtually any job, it is far lower than American workers are accustomed to receiving (Herzenberg and Perez-Lopez, 1990; Hecker, 1991). Hourly wages for high-quality labor in manufacturing are as low as 26 cents in China (Map 15.1). Much closer to home, Mexican workers are now among the most productive in the world. State-of-the-art factories turn out high quality televisions, VCRs, computers, and automobiles for American, European, and Japanese companies. Yet wages in Mexico are typically little more than a tenth of their American counterpart (Baker et al., 1993).

The global labor market is not limited to manufacturing; it appears that a global wage may be emerging for a wide range of professional and technical occupations as well. Electronic engineering, computer programming, data entry, accounting, and other highly specialized services can now be inexpensively purchased in such low-wage countries as India, South Korea, the People's Republic of China, and the Philippines. India, for example, graduates about 400,000 software engineers each year, more than any other country in the English-speaking world. Many of these engineers work in India for American companies, producing software that is electronically transmitted via satellite back to the United States (Gordon and Peterson, 1992). Given the lower cost of living in India, these engineers can be paid far less then their American counterpart. Moreover, one

of India's largest computer consulting corporations, Tata Consultancy Services, serves as a sort of global high-tech "temp" agency. Tata brings Indian programmers to the United States on temporary work permits, where they are subcontracted to U.S. software companies for a fraction of the $40,000 to $100,000 typically earned by American programmers (Eckhouse, 1992).

There are numerous examples of skilled clerical work that has "gone global." "Typing mills" in the Philippines word-process manuscripts for only 10 cents a double-spaced page; in China, it costs less than 4 cents. Workers in Jamaica make airline reservations, process toll-free 800 number calls, enter data, and process credit card applications for U.S.-based businesses. In the town of Fermoy, Ireland, workers process medical claims for a U.S. insurance company for one-third less than their U.S. counterparts (O'Reilly, 1992). All of these jobs at one time were relatively secure white-collar American jobs; today they are subcontracted on a global scale.

Today's Challenge: The Local and the Global

Yet at the same time that many jobs have left high-wage industrial countries for low-wage areas around the world, a reversal of this process has also occurred. Apparel manufacturing, for example, has shown a substantial increase in employment in the United States,

Map 15.1   **Hourly Manufacturing Wages, Selected Countries**

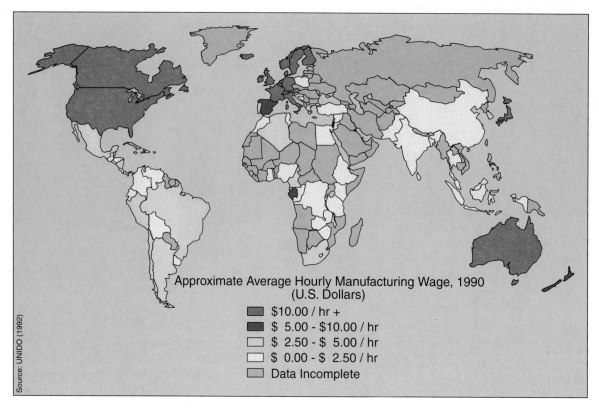

Approximate Average Hourly Manufacturing Wage, 1990
(U.S. Dollars)

▨ $10.00 / hr +
■ $ 5.00 - $10.00 / hr
□ $ 2.50 - $ 5.00 / hr
□ $ 0.00 - $ 2.50 / hr
▨ Data Incomplete

Source: UNIDO (1992)

Enormous wage differences exist between countries, a fact that explains both the migration of people from low- to high-wage countries, and the flight of manufacturing in the opposite direction. Some sociologists have argued that economic globalization will eventually result in rising wages in poor nations, along with declining wages in wealthy ones.

particularly in California (Appelbaum and Bonacich, 1993). There have also been some well-publicized cases of some major manufacturers bringing their factories back to the United States. General Motors, for example, recently decided to move production of some Chevrolet Cavaliers from its Mexican plant to Lansing, Michigan, resulting in as many as 1,000 new jobs for Michigan workers (Nauss, 1993a, 1993b).

There are a number of reasons why global industries might prefer to be located in industrial countries such as the United States, despite far lower wages elsewhere. For one thing, the emergence of a global wage has led to rising wages in lower-income countries, and lower wages in higher-income ones. In some industries, like apparel, this is largely due to a growing immigrant workforce that often works for less than the legal minimum wage (Appelbaum and Bonacich, 1993). In high-technology industries like automobile manufacturing, workers have accepted wage concessions and other agreements that have enabled the U.S. plants to become

more globally competitive (Uchitelle, 1993; Nauss, 1993a, 1993b).

But other considerations besides wages can be important. Even in the age of information, it is hard to put several heads together to come up with a new design or marketing plan if the heads are spread out around the globe. Printed circuits must be inspected to determine whether they meet acceptable standards, while fabrics should be felt to know if the garment will wear properly. Other things being equal, it is still better to have the company headquarters, research and development teams, and factories near each other. The United States remains the largest single national market for goods in the world; it is far preferable for most businesses to be close to their principal customers than elsewhere in the world.

One of the key issues facing businesses, workers, and government policy makers today is the challenge of retaining and creating jobs, in the face of an increasingly integrated global economy.

CHAPTER SUMMARY

1. Work in **industrial society** is typically organized in factories, and it entails specialization, tight supervision by management, and mass production.

2. Mass production, or "Fordism," resulted in the **deskilling** of labor, reducing workers to highly repetitive "detail labor." **Scientific management** sought to engineer the labor process so as to eliminate any independent thinking or control on the part of workers.

3. According to Marx, the capitalist factory system resulted in the widespread **alienation** of labor from their products and work, their fellow workers, and even their own human nature. Subsequent research has supported Marx's conclusions, although it has been suggested that alienation may be lower when workers control aspects of their work.

4. Industrial society exhibits a **dual labor market** consisting of a **primary labor market,** which offers opportunities for a decent wage and job advancement, and a **secondary labor market,** which is comprised of dead-end jobs.

5. **Labor unions** emerged to enable workers to speak with a unified voice, thereby increasing their power vis-a-vis management. Nonetheless, their strength has eroded significantly during the past 25 years, partly because of the decline in unionized jobs that has resulted from globalization.

6. **Capitalism** and **socialism** are the two principal types of political-economic systems that have emerged with industrial society. While all are committed to higher standards of living through economic growth, they differ on the desirability of private property and the appropriate role of the government. Socialism appears to be waning in importance, in the face of global capitalism and postindustrial society. Economic democracies may prove to be a viable middle ground.

7. The past quarter century has seen the emergence of a **postindustrial society** based on modern information technologies, flexible forms of economic organization, and increased **subcontracting** of labor. The provision of **services** replaces the production of goods, and people who work with ideas and information are better rewarded economically than people who do things with their hands.

8. Although postindustrial society holds the promise of prosperity for people who work with ideas and information, it has also meant new forms of exploitation of a global workforce, job loss in industrial societies, and the erosion of gains made by organized labor.

9. In the global economy, **transnational corporations** can draw on a global workforce, sell to global markets, and generally have few loyalties to any particular country. Many products in the world today are made by a global workforce, and the gap in earnings between **symbolic analysts** in the United States and factory workers in impoverished countries is enormous. Yet these same forces are giving rise to a **global wage,** which has already resulted in lower wages in the United States.

QUESTIONS FOR DISCUSSION

1. Discuss the changing nature of work in industrial and postindustrial society. What are the principal characteristics of work in each? What are the principal differences? Do you think work is likely to become more or less rewarding in the near future?

2. Explain the difference between capitalism, socialism, and communism, critically evaluating the strengths and weaknesses of each. What do you think might be a viable form of economic organization for the early twenty-first century?

3. Distinguish between "Fordist" and "post-Fordist" forms of work. Which do you believe is more likely to lead to worker alienation in Marx's sense of the term?

4. Account for the rise and decline of labor unions in the United States in terms of changes in the overall economy.

5. Describe the impact of the global economy on work in the United States. In what ways does the global economy help to bring prosperity to American workers? In what ways does it threaten their prosperity?

KEY TERMS

alienation: In Marx's formulation, the experience of estrangement resulting from capitalist forms of production. (Literally, to experience as a stranger the products of one's labor, the labor process, one's coworkers, and ultimately one's own human nature.)

automation: The replacement of human labor by machines in the process of manufacturing.

capitalism: A political-economic system characterized by the market allocation of goods and services, production for private profit, and private ownership of the means of producing wealth.

collective bargaining: Negotiating with employers on behalf of the union's members.

collectivist orientation: The belief that members of society should assume responsibility for one another's welfare.

conglomerate: An enormous corporation comprised of numerous subsidiaries, often consisting of unrelated business enterprises.

corporation: A formal organization that has a legal existence separate from its members.

deskilling: The reduction of work to detail labor consisting of extremely simple, highly repetitive, monotonous operations that require few if any skills or training.

detail labor: Extremely simple, highly repetitive, monotonous operations that require few if any skills.

dual labor market: A labor market that is divided into a lower strata of low-paying (and low-benefit) jobs that seldom provide opportunities for advancement, and an upper strata of well-paying jobs that provide career opportunities.

factory work: Specialized, tightly coordinated work tasks, closely supervised by factory owners and their managers.

Fordism: The large-scale, highly standardized mass production of identical commodities on a mechanical assembly line.

global wage: A wage equivalent to the lowest worldwide cost of obtaining comparable labor for a particular task, once the costs of operating at a distance are taken into account.

handicraft production: Production in which workers typically labor independently on items of their own design, using their own tools, and at their own pace.

industrial democracy: A political-economic system that seeks some democratic controls over business, along with the public provision of basic social services.

industrial society: A society in which subsistence is based on the mechanized production of goods in factories.

informal (or **"underground"**) **economy:** Goods and services sold by individuals and illegal businesses that do not pay taxes or register with federal, state, or local licensing authorities.

information float: The amount of time that it takes information to get from one place to another; now virtually zero for an increasing range of economic activities.

intellective skill: The ability to think logically and abstractly, rather than relying on immediate physical experience.

interlocking directorate: When directors sit on the governing boards of more than one corporation.

labor market: All those persons who are seeking to sell their labor to others for a wage or salary.

labor unions: Workers' organizations concerned with improving various aspects of their members' working lives.

mass production: Production based on an assembly line that uses a continuous conveyor belt to move the unfinished product past individual workers, each of whom performs a specific operation on it.

monopoly: The situation that exists when a single firm accounts for all the sales in a particular market.

oligopoly: The situation that exists when several firms overwhelmingly dominate a market.

NAFTA (North American Free Trade Agreement): An agreement between the United States, Mexico, and Canada, which will ease trade barriers between the three countries and lead to the creation of the world's largest trading bloc, with 364 million people in a unified $6.2 trillion economy.

picket: A labor action conducted by workers, involving marching in front of the doorway to the workplace so as to discourage other workers from entering (and working) until an agreement is reached.

post-Fordism: Forms of industrial organization that emphasize flexibility rather than standardization.

postindustrial society: A society in which wealth is based primarily on knowledge, information, and the provision of services rather than on factory production.

primary labor market: A labor market consisting of jobs that are reasonably secure, provide good pay and benefits, and hold the promise of career training and advancement.

primary sector: The sector of the economy that is based on the extraction of raw materials and natural resources.

productivity: The amount of goods that a worker can produce in a given period of time.

robots: Computer-driven machines.

scientific management: The application of engineering rules to scientifically reorganize the actions of the workers themselves (sometimes called *Taylorism* after its founder).

secondary labor market: A labor market that includes unstable jobs with little job security, low pay and few benefits, and little likelihood of career advancement.

secondary sector: The sector of the economy that is based on the production of finished goods from raw materials obtained in the primary sector.

services: Activities performed by an individual that do not directly result in a physical product.

socialism: A political-economic system in which the production and distribution of goods and services is pursued for the common good, by means of enterprises owned by the central government or its subunits.

strike: A work stoppage conducted by workers, usually to obtain higher wages or improved working conditions.

subcontracting: A form of economic organization in which one firm relies on other, more specialized firms to provide specialized products or services.

symbolic analyst: A person who works with symbols and ideas, rather than with things.

Taylorism: (*See* scientific management)

telecommuting: "Traveling" from home to work electronically rather than physically by such means as telephone, fax, electronic data transfer, and electronic mail.

tertiary sector: The sector of the economy that involves the production of services.

transnational corporation (TNC): A corporation that operates in many different countries.

virtual workplace: A work environment that is electronically rather than physically connected to its client.

RECOMMENDED FOR FURTHER READING

Appelbaum, Richard P. (1988). *Karl Marx.* Newbury Park, CA: Sage.

A brief and readable summary of the philosophical, economic, and political ideas of Karl Marx, whose views on the future of the labor process remain important for understanding the economic changes that are occurring in the world today.

Bell, Daniel. (1973). *The Coming of Postindustrial Society.* New York: Basic Books.

A classic study of the changing nature of industrial society, and its transformation into a postindustrial society based on the exchange of knowledge and information rather than the manufacturing of goods.

Braverman, Harry. (1976). *Labor and Monopoly Capital: The Deregulation of Work in the Twentieth Century.* New York: Monthly Review Press.

An extremely important examination of the nature of factory work, which argues that Taylor's "scientific management" was as much concerned with controlling workers as it was with increasing labor productivity.

Gereffi, Gary, and Miguel Korzeniewicz (eds.). (1994). *Commodity Chains and Global Capitalism.* Westport, CT: Greenwood Press.

A collection of articles that examine the changing global organization of work, including case studies of specific industries that have globalized their production processes in recent years.

Reich, Robert B. (1991). *The Work of Nations,* New York: Knopf.

A highly influential book about the future of work, written by the current U.S. Secretary of Labor. This book argues that a country's principal resource is its brainpower, and that only "symbolic analysts" will thrive in the global economy.

Zuboff, Shoshana. (1988). *In the Age of the Smart Machine: The Future of Work and Power.* New York: Basic Books.

An examination of the ways in which technology and information processing are changing tomorrow's workplace.

CHAPTER

16

Education

CHAPTER OUTLINE

THINGS TO LOOK FOR

1. In what ways do educational differences reinforce those of race and class? In what ways do they alter existing racial and class differences?
2. What is the "hidden curriculum" of education, and what role does it play in preparing young people for their roles in society?
3. What are the principal problems in American schooling today?
4. Just how violent are American schools?
5. How might schools better prepare students to effectively participate in an increasingly globalized world?

INTRODUCTION: EDUCATION AND THE GLOBAL MARKETPLACE

In recent years there has been a great deal of public concern about the quality of education in America. George Bush proclaimed himself the "education president," and Bill Clinton has made educational reform one of the top priorities of his administration. In the words of Nathan Glazer, a prominent sociologist of education, the United States is caught in the grips of:

A fever of concern about the quality of American education that has been unparalleled in the history of the Republic. We can date it from the 1983 report, *A Nation at Risk,* though of course the concern was evident for decades before. . . . The fever of concern is maintained by the steady evidence of American educational inadequacy as compared with the record of foreign nations, and by the relative decline of American economic power in an age when natural resources—in which we are still preeminent—are much less important than human resources" (Glazer, 1992, p. 57).

This concern arises in part because despite growing per-pupil spending on education, students' scores on standardized tests such as the SAT (Scholastic Aptitude Test) have not improved in a decade, after declining substantially from the 1970s (Figure 16.1). U.S. students currently place near the bottom on standardized test scores in mathematics and science compared to students in other industrialized nations (Figure 16.2).

The alarm is especially pronounced because Japan and newly industrializing East Asian countries such as Hong Kong, South Korea, Taiwan, and Singapore not

Figure 16.1   **Although Per-Pupil Public School Spending Has Doubled in the Past 20 Years, SAT Scores Have Declined**

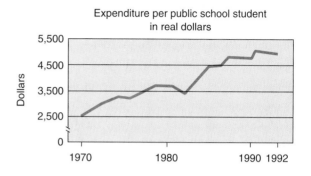

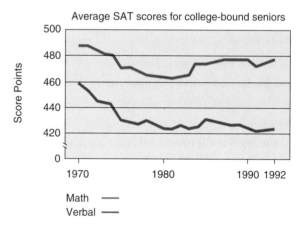

Verbal SAT scores declined sharply during the 1970s; math SATs showed less of a decline. During the 1980s, verbal SATs have fluctuated between 420 and 430, while math SATs improved somewhat, leveling off slightly below 480. These trends do not entirely reflect declining individual performance, however. They are also the result of the opening up of college education to lower-income minority students, greater numbers of whom began taking SATs in the 1970s. Because many of these students received less college preparation than middle-class students, average SAT scores declined.
Source: Levine (1992).

only outperform the United States in terms of average test scores but appear to be overtaking the United States in economic terms as well. American educators have long been mindful of the fact that many Asian cultures place an extremely high value on education, making extraordinary (by U.S. standards) demands on students to excel in school and perform well on examinations. It seems reasonable to conclude that the emergence of a growing number of Asian countries as economic powerhouses is due at least in part to their educational systems.

Figure 16.2   Average Test Scores by Country in Mathematics and Science

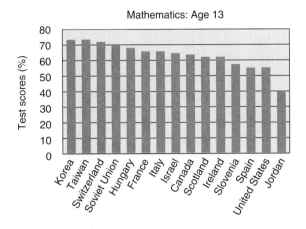

Mathematics: Age 13

Margin of error for test scores is +/−2.79 percentage points

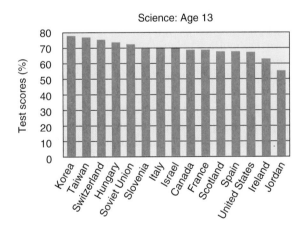

Science: Age 13

Margin of error for test scores is +/−2.78 percentage points

In a comparison with 15 other countries, 13-year-old U.S. students ranked fourteenth on standardized international mathematics tests and thirteenth on standardized science tests. The two top-ranking countries, South Korea and Taiwan, are among the newly industrializing countries of East Asia, but the United States is surpassed by countries from around the world. Educators worry that the United States will not be able to hold its own in the twenty-first century if its students are consistently outperformed by those from other countries.

Source: Educational Testing Service, as reported in *Washington Post* (1992).

As societies change, so too does the role of education. **Education** can be defined as *the transmission of society's norms, values, and knowledge base by means of direct instruction.* The term itself comes from a Latin word (*educare*) for proper rearing of the young (it was applied to animals as well as children), reflecting an upper-class concern for proper cultivation in manners as well as in the arts and humanities. **Formal education,** *education that occurs within academic institutions such as schools,* was restricted largely to the elite members of preindustrial society. For others, education typically occurred informally, within the family or immediate community. **Mass education,** the *extension of formal schooling to wide segments of the population,* became widespread throughout the world only with the advent of industrial society. Not only is mass education consistent with the democratic ideals that are professed in most industrial societies, but it is also the principal means by which people acquire the skills they need to participate effectively as workers and citizens (Chapter 13).

The existence of mass education raises a number of highly contested questions concerning the appropriate role of schools today. Should schools limit their mission to teaching academic subjects only, or should they enter into other areas of socialization, such as sex education or proper parenting techniques? Is it the responsibility of schools to play a central role in providing the skills required for global competitiveness, as the Glazer comment suggests? Is it the task of education to foster multicultural awareness and understanding, preparing students for participation in an increasingly borderless world? In this chapter we examine these issues, focusing on the changing role of education in modern society.

EDUCATION, INDUSTRIALIZATION, AND THE "CREDENTIAL SOCIETY"

The first educational institutions in the United States were created in the seventeenth century by the religious leaders of New England Puritan communities. Their original intent was to provide religious education; children were taught to read in order to study biblical scripture (Monroe, 1940). By 1647 the Massachusetts Bay Colony passed a law requiring every community of 50 or more people to establish a town school. The law was appropriately called "The Old Deluder Satan Act," intended to protect New England's youth from falling into the temptations of the devil.

Although schooling that focused almost exclusively on biblical study and religious training might have served the needs of seventeenth century Puritan com-

In the early years of industrialization a child's education was more likely to be in a factory or on a farm than in school. Demands by social activists and labor unions and the changing needs of industry led in time to the creation of mass, compulsory public education.

munities, as American society changed so too did its needs for education. By the time that industrial society began to appear two centuries later, schooling had begun to take on its modern form.

Industrialization vastly increased the need for **literacy,** *the ability to read and write at a basic level.* While such an ability might not have been necessary for shoveling coal or laying railroad ties, it was essential for other occupations that became increasingly important with industrial society. Operators of complex machinery, bookkeepers and accountants, inventors and designers, merchandisers, lawyers, and a whole range of occupations required not only basic literacy but a wide range of highly specialized skills as well. An educational hierarchy enabled the sons and daughters of the middle and upper classes to develop the knowledge and training appropriate for businesses and the professions, while the working and lower classes acquired technical skills required for factory work or farming (Vinorskis, 1992; Hellinger and Judd, 1991; Bowles, 1972; Bowles and Gintis, 1976).

When workers began forming labor unions in the nineteenth century, one of their demands was for free **public education** for their children, a *universal education system provided by the government and funded out of tax revenues rather than student fees* (Horan and Hargis, 1991; Hellinger and Judd, 1991). Political activists, philanthropic organizations, and newspapers joined with the unions in their demand. By the late nineteenth century public elementary schools were established in most of the industrial centers of the United States, and schooling soon spread throughout the coun-

try. In some states school attendance was compulsory for at least the first six years. The concept of public education was soon expanded to include high schools, and by the turn of the century the average American achieved eight years of schooling, while 10 percent had completed high school and 2 percent college or university (Vinorskis, 1992; Bettelheim, 1982; Walters et al., 1990; Walters and James, 1992).

With the creation of mass public education, the United States increasingly became a **credential society,** one in which *the qualifications needed for work and social status depended on the possession of a credential certifying the completion of formal education* (Collins, 1979). The possession of a credential serves as a filter, determining the kinds of jobs for which a person is eligible. People with a high school diploma have little chance to show whether or not they can perform a job requiring a college degree; nurses cannot do the work reserved for doctors, even when they have proven competence. Since a person's job is a major determinant of income and social class, educational credentials play a major role in shaping the opportunities for social mobility (Chapter 8).

THEORIES OF EDUCATION

What is the role of education in modern society? As with other institutions, sociologists differ in what they choose to emphasize. While functionalist theorists tend to look for the ways in which education serves society's needs, conflict theorists focus on the role of education in reinforcing social inequality. Interactionist theories help to illuminate both, by studying the actual processes that occur in the classroom.

Functionalist Theory of Education

Emile Durkheim (1956, 1973), the founder of functionalist theory in sociology, wrote extensively about the importance of education for modern societies. According to Durkheim, modern societies are highly complex, with numerous specialized yet highly interdependent institutions (Chapter 1). This creates a special problem for creating **social solidarity,** *bonds that unite the members of a social group.* The vast differences in modern society have led to a weakening of social ties. A partial function of education is to address this problem, by helping to socialize the members of society into the norms and values necessary to promote social solidarity. Durkheim termed this "moral education," and he believed it fell to the responsibility of institutions that were specialized for this purpose. Educational institutions therefore provide not only the knowledge and training necessary for members to fulfill their roles in modern society but also a sense of social solidarity as well.

Contemporary functionalist theories echo Durkheim's century-old concerns, emphasizing the function of formal education for socializing people into the norms and values as well as the skills that contribute to the overall functioning of society (Parsons and Mayhew, 1982). Following the insights of Robert Merton, however, contemporary functionalist theory distinguishes between the manifest and latent functions of education (see Chapter 1; Merton, 1968; Bourdieu and Coleman, 1991). The manifest or intended functions are the transmission of general knowledge and specific skills. The latent or unintended functions include the sorts of societal norms and values that Durkheim argued should be explicit concerns of moral education—what we have elsewhere termed the "hidden curriculum" (Best, 1983; see Chapters 5 and 11). For example, schools are one of the most important institutions where, beginning with kindergarten, children learn to organize their lives according to schedules, to sit at desks, to follow rules, and to show respect for authority. These values are especially important in producing a disciplined workforce (Gracey, 1993; Kohn, 1977; Vinorskis, 1992; Horan and Hargis, 1991; Bowles, 1972; Foucault, 1973).

Education is also seen as serving the latent function of allocating members of society into their appropriate adult roles, by enabling them to receive training commensurate with their talents, skills, and efforts (Chapter 8). From grades and report cards to standardized tests such as the SAT, GRE, or LSAT, schools function to channel students at every step (Oakes, 1985). According to functionalist theory, the final credential, whether it be a high school diploma, a specialized certificate, or an advanced degree, serves as a selection mechanism to help ensure that people get the jobs for which they are best suited and for which they are properly compensated (Figure 16.3). Functionalist theory argues that both society and the individual benefit as a result of this process (Clausen, 1991; Gottfredson, 1984; Davis and Moore, 1945).

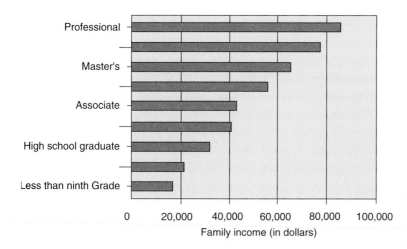

Figure 16.3   Median Family Income by Educational Attainment of Householder, 1991

There is a strong correlation between family income and education, with income growing steadily as education increases. In families where the head of household has less than a ninth-grade education, for example, the median income is $17,709—only about a fifth that of those with a professional graduate school degree ($89,919). It is clear that staying in school pays off for most people in a society where both formal education and a credential account for a great deal. *Source: Mortenson Report* (1993).

Family income (in dollars)

Critical Assessment Although education may serve the function of training and socializing students into society's norms and values, critics of the functionalist theory point out that it also has the paradoxical effect of undermining societal authority as well. Education can help students to develop an inquiring, critical spirit, by exposing them to ideas and ways of thinking that challenge their previously held ideas. That is one reason why pressures for social change often find fertile grounds on college campuses. Students who are urged to "question authority" in their classes often do so outside of class as well, and this can lead them to be highly critical of their own society. College students frequently become more liberal in their beliefs, and such changes often persist throughout their subsequent lives (Flacks, 1988; Flacks and Whalen, 1989; Newcomb, 1967; Alwin, Cohen, and Newcomb, 1991). From the civil rights and anti-Vietnam War protests of the 1960s, to the environmental movements of the 1990s, educational institutions have been forces for social change as well as supports for the status quo.

In fact, criticisms of existing institutions and demands for radical change often come from the most highly educated groups in society. This was true in the American and French revolutions of the eighteenth century, the communist revolutions of the twentieth century, the bloodless revolutions that led to the dismantling of communism along with the former Soviet Union in 1991, and the forces that are challenging the rule of the Communist Party in China today (Skocpol, 1979; Tilly, 1978; Foran, 1993; Moore, 1966; Wolf, 1969).

Conflict Theory of Education

Conflict theorists emphasize the ways in which educational institutions perpetuate social inequality. Schools are seen as socializing members of the working class to accept their class position by providing unequal access to the skills and training that are necessary in modern society. Children are taught at an early age to define their academic aspirations and abilities in keeping with the social class of their parents. The lower one's social class, the less likely one is to value higher education as a plausible avenue toward upward mobility, and the less likely one is to work to excel academically (Kozol, 1991; Clayton et al., 1990; Oakes, 1985; Mayberry, 1991; Bowles, 1972; Bowles and Gintis, 1976; Willis, 1981; Glaser, 1992).

Conflict theorists argue that educational opportunities differ by class, race, and ethnicity. Elite private secondary schools provide excellent education for those who are wealthy enough to afford them. Most middle-class children, however, are likely to attend fairly well-funded, high-quality public schools. Lower-class children, among whom are found a disproportionate number of racial and ethnic minorities, are often limited to poorly funded schools where educational resources are limited. The lower one's social class, according to conflict theorists, the poorer one's educational opportunities are likely to be, and the more limited one's opportunities as a result.

Conflict theorists also point to a school's role in socializing young people into culturally determined gender roles (Chapter 11). This includes not only the identity and behavior associated with being masculine or feminine in American society, but also the choice of academic subjects as well. Boys, for example, are more likely to receive support for excelling in math and science than girls (Box 16.1). Although such differences appear to be declining, they do help to account for the much larger proportion of boys who choose careers in math- and science-related professions (Best, 1983; Eccles and Jacobs, 1986; Felson and Trudeau, 1991; Garfinkel, 1989; Maugh, 1989; Feingold, 1988; Stumpf and Kliene, 1989; Sadker and Sadker, 1985, 1994).

Critical Assessment Critics of conflict theories of education point out that education, even in highly stratified societies, provides an important avenue of upward social mobility. If educational institutions served only to perpetuate the class system, it would be all but impossible for anyone from lower classes to make it into the middle or upper class, but this clearly is not the case. In fact, there is social mobility in American society, and education has been shown to account for a significant part of it (Jencks et al., 1973, 1979; see Chapter 8). Thus, although the educational system may in part reproduce the class structure, it also provides opportunities for change as well.

Symbolic Interactionist Theory

Symbolic interactionists study what actually occurs in the classroom, alerting us to the many subtle and not-so-subtle ways in which schools affect the self-image of students. By looking at the ways in which students are labeled, symbolic interactionists are able to shed light on how schools help to reinforce and therefore perpetuate differences among students.

In a classic study, Rosenthal and Jacobson (1968) conducted an intriguing experiment in which elementary school teachers were purposely misinformed about supposed intelligence test scores of selected students. Teachers were told, in confidence, that certain students had scored unusually high on standardized tests the previous year. In fact, these students were randomly se-

Theories that emphasize the role of education in reproducing existing societal norms and values may overlook its important role as a force for changing them. These Chicano students at UCLA are protesting university policy toward the study of Chicano history and experience in the United States. Their demands included the creation of a Chicano ethnic studies program and fellowships for Chicano students.

lected and were no different in intelligence than their peers. Rosenthal and Jacobson then observed the interactions between these students and their teachers, and monitored the students' academic performances. They found that the students falsely labeled as "exceptional" soon outperformed their peers, a difference that persisted for several years.

Rosenthal and Jacobson concluded that since these students had been labeled as "exceptional," their teachers behaved differently toward them. Teachers described them with such phrases as "more curious" or "more interesting," and communicated their heightened expectations by means of tone of voice, facial expressions, and praise. In what became a self-fulfilling prophecy, these so-called "exceptional" students came to see themselves through their teachers' eyes and began performing as if they were in fact more intelligent than their peers. This, in turn, confirmed the expectations of their teachers, who rewarded the "exceptional" students with still more positive attention. The younger students, whose self-image was more flexible than older students, exhibited the greatest improvement in performance.

Other studies have drawn similar conclusions. A study of student-teacher interaction in a largely African-American kindergarten found that such labels as "fast" or "slow," which the teacher had assigned by the eighth day of class, tended to stay with the student

This Calvin and Hobbes cartoon depicts one view of a child's day at school. Which aspects of education are conveyed by each of these images? Which sociological theory of education do they reflect?

CALVIN AND HOBBES
copyright 1993 Watterson.
Dist. by UNIVERSAL PRESS
SYNDICATE. All rights
reserved.

Box 16.1

Critical Thinking

Why Do Boys Do Better in High School Science and Math?

Even though girls often outperform boys in math during elementary school, by the time they reach high school the situation is reversed: Boys test better in math and science. One study of 338 suburban students in grades 5 through 12 found that girls score lower in math than in other subjects, even though their grades overall were higher than boys' grades. Furthermore, boys scored higher than girls on the math SATs, even though girls were as well prepared for the test as the boys (Felson and Trudeau, 1991). Why should this be the case?

One answer begins with early childhood socialization at home, and continues with formal education at school. Parents typically offer more encouragement to their sons than to their daughters when it comes to math and science. In one study of 4,000 students and 2,000 parents in southeastern Michigan, Jacquelynne S. Eccles, a University of Colorado psychologist, found that parents believed science to be less important for girls and tended to motivate only their sons to study science and math. This contributed to a loss of self-confidence on the part of the daughters, resulting in a considerable amount of "math anxiety" by junior high school. One

consequence is that twice as many boys as girls take high school physics, seven times as many male college graduates earn their degrees in physics, and 20 times as many men as women pursue careers as physicists (Eccles and Jacobs, 1986; Felson and Trudeau, 1991; Garfinkel, 1989).

Thus, by the time they are adolescents, many girls find themselves performing poorly on math and science tests. This poor performance contributes to a low self-image on these skills, leading many girls to avoid math and science courses. As a result, once they graduate from high school, relatively few girls go on to major in math or science in college, or to pursue subsequent careers in these fields. This in turn leads to a shortage of female math and science teachers, who might serve as role models for female students. A vicious cycle occurs, in which women are systematically discouraged from pursuing math and science at all levels. There is, however, some evidence that these differences are declining in recent years, perhaps as a result of changes in gender stereotypes (Maugh, 1989; Feingold, 1988; Stumpf and Kliene, 1989; see Chapter 11).

---

throughout the year (Rist, 1970). Another study found that female and Asian-American students frequently received classroom grades that were higher than their actual test scores, while Latinos, African Americans, and white males received lower grades (Farkas et al., 1990a, 1990b). The differences had to do with the teachers' perceptions of a student's "attitude." Those who appeared to be attentive and cooperative were judged to be hard workers and good students, and they were graded up; those who appeared to be indifferent or hostile were graded down.

Classroom labeling occurs in other cultures as well. Paul Willis, in a highly influential study, found that British boys from working-class families were systematically labeled as low academic achievers and taught to think of themselves as only capable of having working-class jobs (Willis, 1981, 1990). The boys understood quite well that this labeling process worked

against them, and they resisted it by the use of humor and other challenges to authority. This reinforced their teachers' perception that the boys would never make it and would eventually drop out of school and assume their "rightful position" in the working class. The boys thus tacitly accepted their teachers' labeling, creating a self-fulfilling prophecy in which they wound up in working class-jobs.

EDUCATION AND INEQUALITY

Education is a two-edged sword. For some, it can help to reduce inequality by opening up new possibilities for social mobility. For others, it can reinforce existing inequality by providing unequal educational opportunities according to one's race, ethnicity, social class, or gender.

The Challenges of Cultural Diversity

The United States is one of the most culturally, ethnically, and racially diverse countries in the world (see Chapter 10). This poses unusual challenges for public education, leading to many debates over how best to provide equal opportunities for all groups. One highly contentious issue, for example, concerns **bilingual education,** *the offering of instruction in a non-English language as well as in English.* Nearly 13 percent of all U.S. children aged 5 to 17 come from homes where the primary language is not English; 5 percent reportedly do not speak English "very well." This represents some 2.4 million students who potentially have difficulty with English-language instruction. Two-thirds of these students are Spanish-speaking, although the others speak some 200 different languages (Levitan and Gallo, 1993).

Bilingual education has been mandated by federal law since 1968, and currently reaches approximately 350,000 students (Levitan and Gallo, 1993). Yet the merits of bilingual education continue to be debated, and the federal government has reduced funding for bilingual programs while placing increasing restrictions on their use. Proponents of bilingual education argue that students who speak English poorly will fare poorly in school; instruction in their native language is seen as providing students with the same educational opportunities enjoyed by English-speaking students. Opponents of bilingual education counter that students in such programs will be hampered in developing the English-language skills that are necessary to excel in a predominantly English-speaking society. At present, studies on the effectiveness of bilingual education are inconclusive (Meyer and Fienberg, 1992; Levitan and Gallo, 1993; Moore, 1991).

Cultural differences can create other difficulties as well. Both formal and informal methods of assessing student performance may be biased against students whose cultural values differ from the dominant middle-class values of most teachers (Cohen, 1955; Willis, 1981; Horan and Hargis, 1991; National Commission on Testing and Public Policy, 1990; Rosser, 1989; Gifford, 1989). Subcultural norms concerning appropriate behavior may be misunderstood by other students and teachers, contributing to negative labeling. The Latino emphasis on honor and dignity may be perceived by white teachers as a quickness to take affront. The American Indian value of noncompetitiveness may make Indian students reluctant to directly answer questions in class, leading teachers to label them as inattentive, disinterested, or "slow." The assertive "in your face" attitude that characterizes many young people is especially pronounced in African-American culture; this can lead those who are more outspoken to be labeled as "problem" students. Across all subcultures, students may be torn between their roles as students and peers; those who go along with school authority may be criticized by their friends, suffering social ostracism as a result.

School Segregation

School segregation, *the education of racial minorities in schools that are geographically separated from those attended by whites and other ethnic groups,* is a long-standing pattern that persists today despite three decades of civil rights legislation intended to eliminate it (Jordan, 1992a). Before slavery was abolished in the United States, it was a crime to teach slaves to read and write; formal education was reserved solely for whites. Immediately following the abolition of slavery and the end of the Civil War, schools were integrated but "Jim Crow" laws soon initiated a century of discrimination

As the United States becomes more diverse, there is increasing demand for bilingual education. Currently, out of 2.4 million students who have difficulty with English, only about 350,000 have access to bilingual classrooms, although bilingual education is mandated by federal law.

against African Americans in the south. Such laws determined where blacks could live, where they could eat and shop, and where they would be educated (Chapter 10). In the north there were no laws segregating schools by race but segregated schooling occurred nonetheless as a consequence of residential segregation.

Black activists challenged the constitutionality of segregation numerous times, but the courts consistently found that the segregation of schools and public places did not violate the U.S. Constitution. For example, in its 1896 *Plessy vs. Ferguson* decision, the U.S. Supreme Court upheld the states' rights to segregate schooling and other public accommodations as long as the principle of "separate but equal" was followed. Thus segregation of schools by race remained the law in most southern states until 1954, when the Supreme Court reversed its earlier decisions. Relying on social science research showing that segregated schools were not in fact equal, the Court ruled in *Brown vs. Board of Education* that laws segregating public schools were unconstitutional.

The Supreme Court decision met with considerable resistance in the southern states, where segregation was the law. Governor George Wallace of Alabama personally blocked the entrance to the University of Alabama in an effort to stop black students from enrolling, while a black college student named James Meredith went to prison for trying to enroll and attend classes at the University of Mississippi. Black and white students who tried to integrate schools were beaten by police and citizens alike in their efforts to end school segregation in the south (Chong, 1991; McCartney, 1992; Branch, 1988).

Although racial integration of schools is today required by law, it has been effectively circumvented in many places. Thus, despite the end of legal segregation, **de facto segregation**—*school segregation based on residential patterns or student choice*—still exists. How is this possible? Students in the United States typically attend neighborhood-based schools, particularly at the elementary school level, but often for high school as well. In urban areas the movement of middle- and upper-class whites into suburban or outlying areas has left mostly poor minorities in the inner cities, where schools become entirely segregated as a result. Because residential racial segregation persists despite being against the law, most students attend schools with a high degree of racial segregation (Table 16.1). Because they are located in low-income neighborhoods, highly segregated schools also tend to be the most poorly funded as well.

Today two out of three black students and three out of four Latinos attend classes where most students are from minority groups. In Atlanta—a city with a population that is 67 percent black—the public schools are 92 percent black. In Washington, D.C., 91 percent of the public school enrollment is black. In 1970, 98,000 white children attended public schools in Detroit; in 1993 there were fewer than 14,000 (Usdansky, 1994).

To overcome racial segregation, the courts have required that local governments redraw the boundaries of school districts and that they bus students to schools outside their neighborhoods in order to achieve the goal of racial integration. Some white parents, in turn, have responded by pulling their children out of public school altogether, choosing to send them to private or parochial schools. The most recent Supreme Court decisions have limited the scope of previous laws aimed at promoting full integration and the tide to achieve full integration appears to be turning (Orfield and Montfort, 1993).

The chief exception to minority school segregation is found among Asian Americans, particularly those

Table 16.1   Percentage of Black and Latino Students Attending Schools That Are More Than Half Minority, for Selected States (1992)

	Blacks	**Latinos**
Illinois	88.8	85.0
New York	85.7	86.1
Michigan	84.6	NA
New Jersey	79.6	84.1
California	78.7	79.1
Maryland	76.1	NA
Wisconsin	75.3	NA
Texas	67.9	84.3
Pennsylvania	67.5	66.9
Connecticut	65.9	NA

Source: Orfield and Montfort (1993).

middle-class families who tend to be more assimilated into U.S. culture than other groups. As a consequence, middle-class Asian American students are almost entirely integrated into schools with whites. Still, the presence of Asian-American communities such as "Chinatown" or "Little Saigon" shows that there are exceptions to this rule, especially among recently arrived immigrants from China, Vietnam, Korea, and elsewhere in Asia (Orfield and Montfort, 1993; Loo, 1991; Chen, 1992).

Unlike other racial and ethnic groups in the United States, American Indians have not been legally mandated to integrate with the dominant society. This is because the various Indian tribes are recognized as separate nations whose rights are governed by treaties between them and the U.S. government. Treaties have sought to ensure free and comprehensive education on Indian reservations. Yet the teachers employed by the Bureau of Indian Affairs are ordinarily expected to teach in English, covering the standard subjects of American school curricula. This has created problems within the tribal communities, since such instruction is often seen by Indians as failing to respect their linguistic and cultural differences.

School Funding and Educational Opportunities

There are substantial differences in the amount of money spent on education in different states. In 1990 an average of $5,512 per pupil was spent on elementary and high school education in the United States (Figure 16.4), with some states (for example, Alaska, New York, and New Jersey) spending considerably more, while others (for example, New Mexico, Alabama, Idaho, and Louisiana) spending considerably less (Alsalam, et al., 1992; U.S. Bureau of the Census, 1993; Educational Resource Services, 1993).

Significant discrepancies in expenditures for education occur between different school districts in the same state as well. Schools are funded to a large extent out of property taxes. Since the value of homes and other property is generally higher in wealthier school districts, property tax collections are also higher, providing more money for education. The 47 largest urban school districts in the United States, for example, spend on average nearly $900 less per pupil than their wealthier suburban neighbors (see again Figure 16.4). The funding available to schools affects their classroom size, the availability of such things as computers, shops, textbooks, and equipment, and the overall atmosphere of the institution. Although per-pupil spending is not the only determinant of educational quality, it clearly plays an important role.

Urban schools generally spend less money on books and classroom instruction, and more on health and remedial education. Not surprisingly, students in urban school districts are more likely to drop out of school and to fall behind in learning at every grade level (Levitan and Gallo, 1993). Inner-city schools in Chicago have been described as "daytime warehouses for inferior students, taught by disillusioned and inadequate teachers" (Padilla, 1992). Jessica Siegel, a teacher at Seward Park High School, an inner-city school in New York City, describes Seward Park's condition on the first day of school:

> There is a huge hole in the roof, a crumbling ceiling in the faculty smoking lounge and a shortage of 200 window panes and glass panels, all on order for months. At a nearby annex that serves 900 freshmen and sophomores, a metal fence dented ten years ago has yet to be repaired (Freedman, 1991, as quoted in Glazer, 1992, p. 63).

Paying for education has become a highly controversial issue. On the one hand, educators recognize that many schools are in trouble and that a poorly educated population will be ill-equipped for work and citizenship in an increasingly complex, information-driven world (Chapter 15). On the other hand, taxpayers increasingly appear to be unwilling to foot the bill for significant educational reform. Partly this is due to the national eco-

Figure 16.4   **Spending Comparisons: Urban, Suburban, and Rural Schools, 1993**

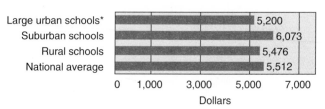

* The 47 largest school districts in the United States

A substantial gap exists in per-pupil spending according to school location. Schools in large urban areas spend the least (about $5,200), while suburban schools spend the most (about $6,100). This graph actually obscures some of the largest differences, since within large urban areas there are enormous differences by neighborhood, with schools in impoverished inner-city areas spending far less than those in wealthier areas. These differences in spending often result in differences in the quality of education available to children of different classes and racial and ethnic groups, thereby contributing to the perpetuation of inequality. *Source:* Educational Resource Services (1993).

Public schools in the United States are funded mainly from property taxes. Wealthier communities generate more property tax money, and therefore have more money to spend on schools. These photographs reflect two extremes in the state of Texas. One school is using a bucket as a basketball hoop on its playground, while the other has funding for a biology lab.

nomic slowdown of recent years (Chapter 8), which has been felt by those working- and middle-class Americans whose property taxes remain the largest single source of funding for education in most places. In some states, such as California and Massachusetts, a "taxpayers' revolt" against rising property taxes has resulted in substantially lowered property taxes for many households, which has meant less money for schools.

Financing schools on the basis of property taxes is itself controversial, since it often means that poorer school districts have poorly funded schools. This has led to numerous legal challenges to the current method of funding education. In Minnesota a citizens' group sought to have property tax funding of schools declared unconstitutional on the grounds that it did not provide equal education for everyone. The Minnesota Supreme Court ruled in 1994 that although the property tax system discriminated against poorer school districts, it nonetheless did not violate the state's constitution. More than 25 states are currently involved in lawsuits similar to Minnesota's. If the U.S. Supreme Court eventually determines that unequal school funding violates the U.S. Constitution, school financing could be radically altered.

Recently, the state of Michigan eliminated property taxes altogether as a means of paying for education (Walsh, 1993). The state's governor proposed substituting sales tax increases for property taxes and creating a more equitable distribution of funds to schools. A state-wide referendum was held in March 1994 in which the Michigan voters were asked to choose between reinstating property taxes to raise the $6 billion needed for public schools, increasing income taxes, or increasing sales taxes. The voters decided to increase sales taxes by 50 percent in order to pay for public education. This represents a major change in the funding of education, one which other states may follow as well.

Race, Class, and Educational Achievement

One of the most consistent findings in educational research is the close relationship between poverty and lack of education. Children born or raised in poverty are likely to have a much lower level of educational achievement than those born in economically better-off families, and this in turn increases the likelihood that they will remain relatively poor. For example, among children who have lived in poverty for at least a year, 71 percent have completed high school while only 8 percent have completed college. Among children who have never been poor, 94 percent have completed high school, and 33 percent have completed college (Levitan and Gallo, 1993).

Education and income go hand-in-hand. Between 1986 and 1990 people who did not finish high school averaged about 30 percent less income than people who completed high school, with larger differences among blacks than whites. People who completed four years of college averaged nearly 50 percent more income than those who did not (U.S. Department of Education, 1992). A recent analysis of 1991 U.S. Census Bureau data divided the 18 to 24 year-old population into four equally sized groups, based on family income (Table 16.2). Among the poorest fourth, whose family income was below $21,500, only 63 percent had graduated from high school. By way of contrast, the richest fourth—whose family income exceeded $61,600—had a 94 percent high school graduation rate. A similar pattern exists with regard to college enrollment and completion. Among the poorest fourth of young adults, 49 percent have been enrolled in college, while only 5 percent completed a B.A. by age 24. Among the richest fourth, 84 percent have been enrolled in college and 64 percent have completed their college degrees. In other words, children born into the wealthiest fourth of American families have nearly 17 times the likelihood of earning a college degree by age 24 as children born into the poorest fourth. The study also found that the rich-poor gap between rates of high school graduation, college attendance, and college graduation had increased over time (*Mortenson Report,* 1993b).

With the exception of Asian Americans, most minorities in the United States do not complete as high a level of schooling as whites (Figure 16.5). In 1992, 83 percent of the white population between the ages of 18 and 24 had completed high school, in comparison with 82 percent of Asian Americans, 75 percent of blacks, 66 percent of Native Americans and 57 percent of Latinos (Carter and Wilson, 1993). The low completion

Figure 16.5   Percentage of 18 to 24-Year-Olds Completing High School, for Selected Racial and Ethnic Categories

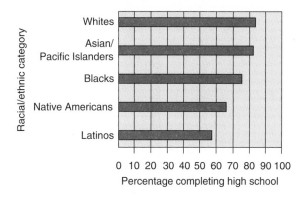

Sizable differences exist between high school completion by race and ethnic category, with whites and Asian Americans showing the highest completion rates, and Latinos the lowest (the low Latino rate partly reflects language difficulties confronted by recent immigrant children, as well as their need to work to contribute to family income). Since education is an important determinant of social class, these differences reinforce existing class distinctions between racial and ethnic groups.
Source: Carter and Wilson (1993); data come from different sources, and so results may not be strictly comparable.

rate for Latinos, however, is in part due to the fact that many are recent immigrants who speak little or no English, and often must drop out of school to work. High school completion rates have declined slightly in the past five years for African Americans, while they have increased among Latinos.

College enrollments exhibit a similar pattern (Figure 16.6). More than a third of all white 18 to 24 year-olds are presently enrolled in college, in comparison with a quarter of all African Americans and a fifth of all Latinos. All three groups have shown significant increases in enrollments during the past five years. Among young adults aged 25 to 29, 37 percent of Asian Americans, 27 percent of whites, 11 percent of blacks,

Table 16.2   Educational Attainment of Poorest Fourth of Children Aged 18–24, Compared with Wealthiest Fourth (1991)

Educational Attainment	Percentage of Poorest Fourth (income under $21,500)	Percentage of Richest Fourth (income over 61,600)
Completed high school	63%	94%
Enrolled in college	49%	84%
Completed college	5%	65%

Source: Mortenson Report (1993b).

Figure 16.6   **Percentage of 18 to 24 Year-Olds Enrolled in College, Selected Racial Categories**

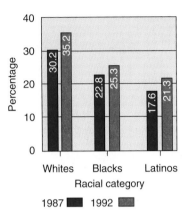

Whites   Blacks   Latinos
Racial category
1987 ■   1992 ▨

Racial and ethnic differences in college enrollments parallel those in high school completion, with whites having substantially higher enrollment rates than blacks or Latinos. Although all three categories showed improvement between 1987 and 1992, the largest gains were among whites, thereby widening the education gap.
Source: Carter and Wilson (1993).

and 9 percent of Latinos have graduated from college, holding bachelor's degrees or higher (*Mortenson Report,* 1993a).

Following the 1954 *Brown* v. *Board of Education* decision and a decade of civil rights activity, Congress enacted the Civil Rights Act of 1964 in an effort to increase educational opportunities for minorities. One part of the act allocated funds for research on the impact of racial segregation in schools. James Coleman, a University of Chicago sociologist, directed a team of sociologists who conducted an extensive study of the racial inequalities in education. To the surprise of many, the research—which gathered data from 570,000 students, 60,000 teachers, and 4,000 schools—concluded that although there were significant differences in the performance of white and black students, the differences could not be attributed to poorer school facilities, differences in spending, or teacher quality (Coleman et al., 1966). Coleman concluded that the major factors accounting for differences in school performance were the social class and family backgrounds of the students: Those from the lower classes performed less well than students from the middle and upper classes regardless of the quality of the schools. Black students exhibited lower levels of school achievement primarily because of family and class backgrounds, which left them "culturally deprived."

Critical Assessment   Although Coleman's research was supported by some later studies (Jencks et al.,

1973), other studies raised questions about the conclusion that students' family backgrounds, rather than the schools themselves, was responsible for low academic performance. Michael Rutter (1979), for example, conducted an intensive study of students in schools in poor neighborhoods over a four-year period. Rutter concluded that the quality of student-teacher interaction, the preparation of course materials, and the degree to which teachers were committed and caring were crucial in determining the outcome of education (Rutter, 1979). Rutter's study found that students from lower-class families were not receiving the same quality of education in the classroom as students from the middle and upper classes.

Rutter's findings were supported by other research (Rist, 1970, 1973, 1979). One case study of a black urban elementary school found that teachers segregated their classes into well-dressed and poorly dressed groups, with the well-dressed students seated closest to the teacher (Rist, 1970). The teachers knew which students came from welfare families and which did not; those who did not were given preferential treatment and were expected to perform better, which they invariably did (see Box 16.2). This finding was consistent with the Rosenthal and Jacobson research reported above. More recent studies by Hurn (1985) and further research by Coleman himself (Coleman et al. 1981) support the notion that school performance is substantially affected by the academic climate of the school, the quality of teaching, and the structure of school assignments, including homework.

Education can be an important avenue for social mobility throughout life, even among persons in prison. Many prisons offer the opportunity for prisoners to complete their high school or college degree while in jail. A study examining the effectiveness of such programs concluded that the higher the level of education achieved while in prison, the lower the likelihood that a prisoner would be rearrested or reimprisoned once released. Hollway and Moke (1986) compared the post-release arrest and imprisonment rates for prisoners released from the Ohio State Penitentiary. They found that those who had dropped out of high school were twice as likely to be arrested or sent back to prison during the first year on parole, compared to those who either completed high school or a two-year college course while in prison (Table 16.3).

CURRENT ISSUES IN U.S. EDUCATION

Education in the United States today often appears to be under a state of siege. Many of the challenges it faces stem from the unique characteristics of American society, while others reflect America's changing role in the world today. In this section we review some of the

Box 16.2

Silenced Voices

When Malcolm X Said He Wanted to Be a Lawyer

In his autobiography, Malcolm X, a prominent champion for the rights of African Americans who was assassinated in 1965, recounts how his high school English teacher encouraged him to be "realistic" and give up any hopes he might have had of becoming a lawyer. Such negative perceptions of the prospects of black students were common in Malcolm X's time, and in many schools continue to silence the voices of black students today.

Somehow, I happened to be alone in the classroom with Mr. Ostrowski, my English teacher. He was a tall, rather reddish white man and he had a thick mustache. I had gotten some of my best marks under him, and he had always made me feel that he liked me. . . . I know that he probably meant well in what he happened to advise me that day. I doubt that he meant any harm. It was just in his nature as an American white man. I was one of his top students, one of the school's top students—but all he could see for me was the kind of future "in your place" that almost all white people see for black people.

He told me, "Malcolm, you ought to be thinking about a career. Have you been given it thought?"

The truth is, I hadn't. I never have figured out why I told him, "Well, yes, sir, I've been thinking I'd like to be a lawyer." Lansing certainly had no Negro lawyers—or doctors either—in those days, to hold up an image I might have aspired to. All I really knew for certain was that a lawyer

didn't wash dishes, as I was doing.

Mr. Ostrowski looked surprised, I remember, and leaned back in his chair and clasped his hands behind his head. He kind of half-smiled and said, "Malcolm, one of life's first needs is for us to be realistic. Don't misunderstand me, now. We all like you, you know that. But you've got to be realistic about being a nigger. A lawyer—that's no realistic goal for a nigger. You need to think about something you can be. You're good with your hands—making things. Everybody admires your carpentry shop work. Why don't you plan on carpentry? People like you as a person—you'd get all kinds of work."

The more I thought afterwards about what he said, the more uneasy it made me. It just kept treading around in my mind.

What made it really begin to disturb me was Mr. Ostrowski's advice to others in my class—all of them white. Most of them had told him they were all planning to become farmers. But those who wanted to strike out on their own, to try something new, he had encouraged. Some, mostly girls, wanted to be teachers. A few wanted other professions, such as one boy who wanted to become a county agent; another, a veterinarian; and one girl wanted to be a nurse. They all reported that Mr. Ostrowski had encouraged what they had wanted. Yet nearly none of them had earned marks equal to mine.

Source: Malcolm X (1965, pp. 35–37).

principal issues that U.S. education must face as it moves into the twenty-first century.

Literacy

The U.S. Department of Education (1993a) recently completed the most comprehensive study of English literacy ever conducted in the United States. The study defined literacy broadly, testing 13,600 adults on the skills and knowledge required for reading, searching documents such as job applications or payroll forms for information, and using arithmetic for such things as

balancing a checkbook or calculating interest payments on a loan. The study categorized respondents into five categories of literacy:

■ Between 21 and 23 percent of all American adults (40 to 44 million people) fall into the lowest literacy category. These are people whose skills are limited to finding a single piece of information in a short sports article, locating the expiration date on their driver's license, or balancing their checkbook.

■ Another 25 to 28 percent of all adults (48 to 53 million people) fall into the second lowest proficiency

Table 16.3   Likelihood of Arrest or Return to Prison of High School and College Graduates and High School Dropouts

	Percentage Dropping Out of High School in Prison	Percentage Completing High School in Prison	Percentage Completing Two-Year College Course in Prison
Arrested during first year on parole	50	40	25
Returned to prison by end of first year on parole	29	16	12

Source: Holloway and Moke (1986).

level. These are people who can find two pieces of information in an article, locate an intersection on a street map, or determine the price difference between two movie tickets.

■ Only 18 to 21 percent all adults (34 to 40 million adults) performed in the two highest proficiency levels, requiring the ability to utilize complex information and specialized knowledge, or perform difficult arithmetic operations.

All told, some 90 million adults—nearly half of the adult population—had low literacy levels, even though most described themselves as capable of reading and writing reasonably well. Those performing at lower levels of literacy were on average more poorly educated, physically or mentally disabled, older, nonwhite, and immigrant. The study also found that literacy was strongly related to socioeconomic status. Those in the highest category reported incomes nearly three times as high as those in the lowest. The least literate group was far more likely to use food stamps, and less likely to have savings. In fact, nearly half of all those in the lowest literacy group lived in poverty, compared with only 4 to 8 percent of those in the two highest groups. When he issued the report, U.S. Secretary of Education Richard Riley concluded the following:

> This report is a wake-up call to the sheer magnitude of illiteracy in this country and underscores literacy's strong conection to economic status. It paints a picture of a society in which the vast majority of Americans do not know that they do not have the skills they need to earn a living in our increasingly technological society and international marketplace" (U.S. Department of Education, 1993b).

Yet even those who fall into the lowest literacy categories are likely to have attended some school. The overwhelming majority of people from all racial and ethnic groups between the ages of 18 and 24 years of age have completed high school (Carter and Wilson, 1993). As a result, the study's findings have been widely interpreted as a condemnation of education in America, even though the study itself did not draw such sweeping conclusions. Whatever the reasons, it seems clear that a large number of Americans are failing to develop the type of skills that will be required for work and citizenship in the twenty-first century.

Head Start Programs

One way to enhance literacy and improve education skills is to begin with the very young. In France, for example, 85 percent of three-year-olds (and all five-year-olds) are served by public preschools, while the national government offers special classes for schools in poor neighborhoods (Levine, 1992). In the United States, a much more limited approach to such programs exists.

Head Start, *a federally funded program in which enriched preschool environments are created for lower-income children in hopes of preparing them to do better in school,* was initiated partly as a result of the Coleman Report's call for programs intended to compensate for the "cultural deprivation" of lower-income students. These programs provide small classes for preschool children from impoverished inner-city neighborhoods, in which they are taught basic skills and knowledge that they have not learned at home. There are presently 12,000 Head Start centers serving some 721,000 children. Almost all are four to five years old, and most are minorities from female-headed homes. Head Start presently reaches about half of all poor four-year-olds; by way of contrast, two-thirds of children from families earning more than $30,000 attend preschools or other child-care facilities (Levitan and Gallo, 1993).

Teachers in Head Start programs are generally effective in enhancing the students' self-image and self-confidence, as well as in communicating the skills and learning needed to succeed in school. Head Start teachers often expect a great deal from their students, and communicate such expectations in a fashion that leads to positive labeling. Research tracking students from Head Start and similar preschool programs concludes that they consistently outperform other students, at least until around the sixth grade, when other influences begin to erode the effects of their earlier experience. Even at this point, however, former Head Start students who drop out of school do so at a later grade than other students, and are less likely to be arrested for delinquent behavior or become pregnant as teenagers (Levitan and Gallo, 1993; Milton S. Eisenhower Foundation, 1990; Zigler and Muenchow, 1993; Currie and Thomas, 1993; Cohen, 1993).

Busing, Private Schools, and School Choice

The concept of public education has been challenged in recent years, because of the many problems that beset public schools. **School busing,** *a court-ordered program to achieve racial integration by busing public school students to schools other than those they would normally attend,* has proved to be highly controversial, provoking criticism among academics and hostility among parents and policy makers. Furthermore, busing has not met with universal success, as minority students' performance has not always shown ap-

preciable improvement where it has been carried out (Rist, 1979; Orfield, 1978; 1991; St. John, 1975).

As a result of busing and other problems in public schools, **private schools**—*schools that are run by privately employed educators and paid for out of students' fees and tuition*—have become increasingly attractive to some parents. Private schools often provide some of the best education money can buy, but their principal shortcoming is that few people can afford the price (Table 16.4). Private schools, however high their quality, are not a viable solution to America's educational needs, since with few exceptions only wealthier students can afford to attend them. As a result, they tend to segregate students by class, race, and ethnicity. The educational opportunities and social contacts that come from private schools are available only to an elite few.

Colleges and universities can also be classified into public (state) and private, with the latter ordinarily far less expensive than the former (Table 16.5). Many of the most prestigious private universities cost more than $25,000 a year to attend. In recent years a number of public institutions have been forced to raise their tuition and fees, in response to dwindling revenues from financially strapped state governments. Fees for attending the University of California, for example, have more than tripled in recent years, reaching nearly $4,100 in the 1994–1995 academic year.

Some educational policy makers advocate making private schools more widely available to all segments of the population, through **school choice plans**—*programs in which the government provides families with educa-*

Table 16.4   Private Nonprofit School Tuitions: 1994–1995

Grade level	Tuition
Preschool	$6,353
Kindergarten	7,100
High school (average grades 1–12)	8,500

Source: NAIS Statistics Book, 1994. Washington, D.C.: National Association of Independent Schools.

Table 16.5   Mean Cost of Private and Public Undergraduate College and University Tuition, Room and Board: 1993–1994

Four-year college/university	Total	Tuition	Room	Board
Private undergraduate	$13,285	9,144	2,090	2,051
Public undergraduate				
In-state	4,983	2,483	1,868	1,632
Out-of-state	9,877	6,377	1,868	1,632

Source: National Center for Education Statistics (1994)

tional certificates or "vouchers" that can be redeemed for tuition payments at the private or parochial school of their choice. Much like food stamps, such vouchers would have a specified cash value that could be redeemed at participating schools; unlike food stamps, however, they would be available to all families with school-age children, and not just the poor (Conway, 1992).

Supporters of the voucher system argue that it would equalize educational opportunity while providing for greater freedom of choice than currently exists. Opponents claim that by drawing students away from public schools, the proposed voucher system would drain badly needed revenues from public schools, whose funding is tied to enrollments. Furthermore, critics claim, the amount of the vouchers will prove insufficient to enable lower-income families to send their children to costly private schools. The result would be to further segregate schools along the lines of class, race, and ethnicity, with predominantly white middle class families using their vouchers to help defray the cost of private school education, while all others are forced to send their children to financially strapped public schools.

Thirteen states have adopted school choice plans, but the response of parents has been less than enthusiastic. A study conducted by the Carnegie Foundation for the Advancement of Education found that fewer than 2 percent of the parents in these states utilize the plans. The study also found that school choice plans widen the gap between wealthy and poor districts. None of the states with school choice programs have shown any measurable improvement in student performance (Jordan, 1992b; Lawton, 1992; Lewis, 1992).

Magnet Schools

Magnet schools are schools that *seek to attract students by offering specialized, high-quality programs in math, science, arts, humanities or other subjects.* Often they offer specialized educational techniques as well. Magnet schools have been described as education's "quiet revolution." There are currently over 5,000 such schools, and about a fifth of the nation's high school students attend them (Toch, 1991; Feeley, 1992).

Originally designed to target high-achieving minority students, the schools have expanded and are now mainly located in middle- and upper-middle-income suburbs. Some, however, continue to serve inner-city residents, offering enriched programs and specialized instruction to their students. Some magnet schools today are bilingual, some take exceptional students regardless of race or class, and a few focus on international education (Toch, 1991). Teaching techniques tend to be innovative, homework is demanding, and

standards are unusually high. A few such schools are equipped with the latest in interactive multimedia technology, integrating video, sound, text, and images on computers equipped with CD-ROMS:

> At Thomas Jefferson High School for Science and Technology in Fairfax County, Virginia, five dishes download information from 130 different satellites, including research satellites that transmit only raw data. . . . Research is just a tap of the keyboard away: some 150 journals published full-text on CD-ROM—humanities as well as science publications—are accessible from any of the school's computer terminals (Feeley, 1992).

Magnet schools have been extremely successful as measured by the academic achievements of students attending them, although it must be remembered that they are likely to attract and enroll some of the highest-achieving students. The schools typically graduate a disproportionate number of National Merit Scholars, and in 1990 their students won half of the awards in the Westinghouse Science Talent Search competition, while accounting for over half of the 650 students who received the International Baccalaureate diploma in 1990 (American Council on Education, 1991; see Box 16.3).

Violence in Schools

Perhaps no single topic in the field of education has received as much public attention in recent years as school violence. Each day television and newspapers report incidents of armed students shooting and stabbing one another with seeming abandon, while school authorities and patrolling police officers find themselves powerless to stem the bloodshed. Consider the following stories, which typify routine news coverage on American education (U.S. House of Representatives, 1992; Lewis and Harriston, 1993; Lee, 1993):

■ On the morning of February 26, 1992, a student in Thomas Jefferson High School in Brooklyn, New York, shot and killed two of his classmates.

■ In September 1991, in the small town of Crosby, Texas, a 17-year-old varsity football captain was killed in the school cafeteria by a 15-year-old girl armed with a 38-caliber revolver.

■ At Valley Point Middle School in Georgia on a sunny afternoon in February an entire classroom including the teacher was held hostage by a 13-year-old boy carrying a loaded 22-caliber rifle.

■ The day after school opened in Washington, D.C. on September 9, 1993, two boys aged 14 and 15 fired

15 rounds of ammunition outside a junior high school.

■ Linda Floyd, a high school teacher in Rochester, New York, took a leave of absence after 24 years of teaching, on the grounds that she was emotionally and physically exhausted. A student she had expelled from her class was arrested for murdering another student, apparently because he wanted the student's jacket.

Some studies claim that as many as a quarter of all students have carried a weapon to school during the previous month, a figure that reportedly rises to half in impoverished metropolitan areas like Jersey City, New Jersey. It has been estimated that more than 100,000 students carry guns to school each day (*The Futurist*, 1990).

How accurate is such sensationalistic reporting of violence and weaponry in schools? A 1991 U.S. Department of Justice victimization survey reported that nearly one out of every four students in urban schools was afraid of being attacked at school; the figure for suburban schools was one out of five (Table 16.6).

Yet the most detailed surveys suggest that the actual incidence of violent acts is not as high as public perceptions suggest. A 1991 special U.S. Department of Justice victimization survey of students found that only about 9 percent of students aged 12 to 19 reported being the victim of a crime in or around their school over a six-month period (Bastian and Taylor, 1991; see again Table 16.6). The vast majority were property crimes, such as having something stolen from one's locker. Only about 2 percent reported being victims of violent crimes, such as being physically attacked. Most attacks, according to the survey, did not involve weapons and resulted only in cuts or bruises. These per-

centages did not differ greatly across racial and ethnic groups, although they were higher in urban schools (3 percent) than rural or suburban schools (Bastian and Taylor, 1991).

Although it is clear that violence is a problem in schools, it appears to be one that is greatly overplayed by politicians and the mass media.

GLOBALIZATION AND EDUCATION

Although the United States claims to provide public education for its entire population, only about three-quarters of all students graduate from high school. By way of comparison, almost everyone completes high school in Denmark, Finland, and Germany, while nine out of ten do so in Japan, France, and Switzerland (U.S. Department of Education, 1992). As shown in Figure 16.2, American students are consistently outperformed by Asian and European students on standardized tests. U.S. students spend less time in school than those from almost any other nation—180 days, in comparison with 210 for Germany and 243 for Japan (Map 16.1). Yet the percentage of national wealth spent on education is higher in the United States than in many other industrial countries, including Japan, Germany, Britain, and France. This is true not only for higher education, but for primary and secondary school education as well (Figure 16.7).

Globalization has created a highly stratified labor force, with an increase in low-wage, unskilled jobs at the same time that there is a growing demand for people in highly trained work (Chapters 9 and 15). A global labor market for a wide range of jobs means that those who lack the requisite training and skills are

Table 16.6   Students' Perceptions of School Violence and Crime

	Urban	Suburban	Rural
Percentage of students who said they were victims at school			
Of violent crime	8	7	7
Of property crime	2	2	1
Percentage of students who said they were afraid of attacks			
At school	24	20	22
To and from school	19	12	13
Percentage of students who said they had taken a weapon or other object to school for protection	3	2	1

Source: Bastian and Taylor (1991).

Figure 16.7   **Percentage of Gross Domestic Product Spent on Education, Selected Industrial Countries, 1989**

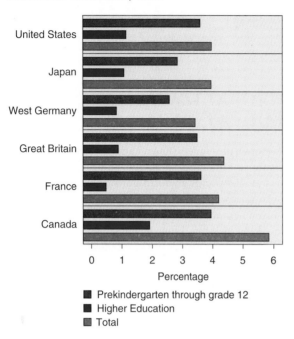

Prekindergarten through grade 12
Higher Education
Total

The United States spends a higher percentage of its gross national product (a measure of the total wealth produced each year) on education than many other industrial nations. Among the six comparison nations in this figure, only Canada outstrips the United States in spending on prekindergarten through twelfth grade and higher education. Yet the American educational system does not appear to be producing students whose performance, at least as measured by standardized tests, compares favorably with these other countries.
Source: Alsalam et al. (1992).

Becoming computer literate is now an essential aspect of acquiring an adequate education. These kindergarten students will be as familiar with working on computers as their parents were with pencil and paper. Unfortunately, all schools do not have equal access to this sort of technology; differences in education often parallel differences in societal stratification.

likely to be disadvantaged, finding themselves in lower-paid jobs as a result. A few short years ago, someone with basic skills in reading and writing could expect to find a reasonably well-paying blue-collar job in industry. This is no longer true; such jobs are readily found today in countries where people with comparable skills labor for a fraction of U.S. wages (Baldwin and Spille, 1991). A 1991 study by the Committee for Economic Development reported that only 12 percent of surveyed employers believed that high school graduates could write well, and only 22 percent believed they had a good mastery of mathematics (Levine, 1992). Even engineers and computer programmers are encountering growing global competition for their skills. Countries that cannot provide necessary training will lose economic ground to countries that do.

Computer literacy is one example of a globally valuable skill that is not yet provided in many U.S. classrooms. Although almost all U.S. schools have computers, a 1988 study by Congress's Office of Technology Assessment concluded that most teachers lack the necessary training to use them. When teachers do use computers, they do so primarily to teach students about the computers themselves, rather than as training tools for reading, math, and science. Most school computers lack CD-ROM players, innovative software, and the ability to connect electronically with remote databases (*Macworld,* 1992). Other countries are much more aggressively pursuing the use of advanced computerized multimedia technology in education. Both France and Japan, for example, have set national goals to promote computer literacy in the schools, have allocated funding for innovative pro-

Map 16.1   School Days Around the World

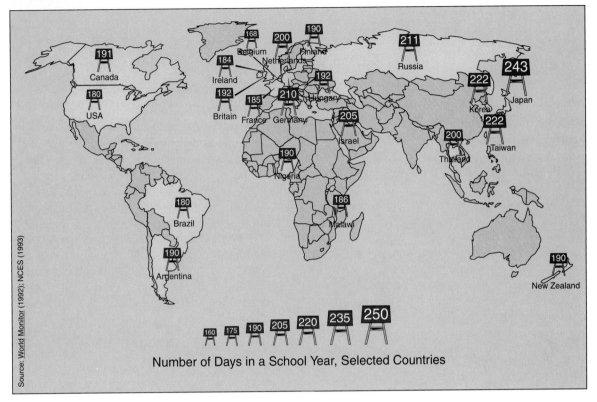

Number of Days in a School Year, Selected Countries

Secondary school students spend far more time in classrooms in some countries than others. In Japan, for example, students attend class on average 243 days each year; in the U.S., the figure is only 180. Some educators argue that such differences place the U.S. at a disadvantage relative to countries that provide more schooling.

grams, and have put high-level governmental officials in charge. Japan's Ministry of Education is in the process of equipping all schools, down to the primary school level, with computers (*Macworld,* 1992).

The abilities that will be required in the twenty-first century may well involve more than high-level skills in reading, writing, and mathematics. They will likely also require the ability to think analytically, to problem-solve, and in general to use one's intellect (Zuboff, 1988; Reich, 1991). It will be increasingly important for people to be aware of events taking place in other countries as well. High school and college curricula will likely reflect this need, and the most effective schools will provide training in comparative institutions, political geography, international relations, global economics, and languages. Educated people will be expected to know what the Masstricht Treaty was and what its impact on the world has been; what the European Community asks of its members, what the Gen-

eral Agreement on Tariffs and Trade stipulates, and what the implications are for Americans. There are already global educational programs that provide such training (Box 16.3).

It is clear that the United States must rethink its approach to education in light of globalization. Not long ago people in the United States were unaware and unconcerned about how their educational system compared with the education of people in other countries. If Japanese students went to school six days a week and had only one month's vacation, this was a matter of curiosity and an occasional expression of sympathy for the overworked Japanese child. Globalization has made comparisons of different country's educational systems a common practice, as educators and policy makers worry about their country's ability to remain globally competitive.

The United States is not alone in looking to other countries for ideas about how to improve education.

Box 16.3

Globalization

Education on a New Scale

Educational institutions are slowly responding to the opportunities and challenges posed by globalization. One example is the **International Baccalaureate Program,** *an international degree program intended to help students who are making a transition from high school in one country to higher education in another.* The program is recognized by colleges and universities throughout the world, with more than 300 schools in countries as culturally and geographically diverse as England, Germany, America, Brazil, Ethiopia, and Venezuela currently participating in programs that lead to the degree. These programs offer a combination of broad, liberal arts education as well as a high degree of specialization, affording students substantial curricular choice (Bruce, 1987).

The International Baccalaureate Program further cross-cultural understanding while providing the kinds of training and experience that will enable its graduates to become more effective "global citizens" in the years to come. Yet at the same time it is highly selective, enrolling a disproportionate number of students from the upper socioeconomic strata. As a result, the program reinforces social differences, further strengthening elite groups in the participating countries.

Some schools in the United States also offer opportunities in global education unheard of until recently. Long Beach Polytechnic High in California, for example, has created a Center for International Commerce that focuses on Pacific Rim economies and international relations (Tharp, 1991). It seems likely that there will be a growing number of such educational innovations in the years to come.

Students at California Polytechnic Institute in Pasadena are preparing for participation in the global village by playing a global "world game" as part of their studies. These students can anticipate working in a world in which knowledge about and familiarity with the economies and cultures of other countries may be as important as familiarity with their own.

Japan, for example, is seriously considering adopting the American practice of open competition among students, rather than continuing the Japanese tradition of disapproving of students who try to outshine their peers in the classroom (Tonegawa, 1992). In educational organizations, as in all organizations, countries can learn from one another, a practice that may lead to growing similarity in educational forms.

This is not to say that the responsibility for preparing citizens to participate successfully as global actors rests exclusively with educational institutions. Families, the government, and religious organizations will all play a role. But since a large part of the training of children and young adults today occurs in schools, it is clear that their contribution will be increasingly important in the years to come.

C H A P T E R   S U M M A R Y

1. The American educational system has come under attack in recent years for failing to adequately prepare students for their roles in an increasingly complex society. Students' performance on standardized tests, which lags below those of most other industrial countries, has been of special concern.

2. **Education** serves not only to transmit knowledge, information, and skills, but also to socialize children into the norms and values of society through what has been termed the **hidden curriculum.**

3. **Mass education** has spread with industrialization and the need for widespread **literacy.** As a consequence, all industrial societies today, including the United States, have a system of **public education** that continues through the high school level.

4. Functionalist theories of education emphasize the role of schools in serving the needs of society, while conflict theories emphasize their role in reproducing social inequality.

5. Interactionist theory, by focusing on the classroom itself, reveals the ways in which teachers' perceptions of students—and students' self-perceptions—help to create a self-fulfilling prophecy in which students often conform to their teachers' expectations.

6. Because the United States is a culturally diverse society, education confronts many unique challenges, such as the question of whether to provide **bilingual education** for non–English-speaking students.

7. American public schools have long been **segregated**—legally, prior to the 1954 Supreme Court ruling, and to a large extent **de facto** ever since. This is due partly to segregated residential patterns and

partly to the decision by many white parents to send their children to private schools.

8. There are significant differences in school funding by race, ethnicity, and class. This reinforces existing patterns of social inequality. In general, the higher one's social class, the more likely one is to complete high school or college. Conversely, low-income people are often trapped in a cycle of low educational attainment and poverty.

9. Lack of **literacy** is a major problem in the United States today, with a significant portion of the population performing poorly on literacy tests. **Head Start** programs are one way to overcome such deficits.

10. **School busing** has met with a hostile reception from many parents, and mixed results in terms of achieving its objectives.

11. Many parents have responded to the difficulties in **public schools** by sending their children to **private schools** instead; some are now seeking partial federal funding of private schools through **school choice plans,** a system of voucher programs.

12. **Magnet schools** are one type of educational innovation intended to improve public schools, but they are limited in scope and primarily reach middle-income students.

13. School violence, although a major concern in a wide range of schools, appears to be considerably less widespread than most people believe to be the case.

14. Globalization requires a major rethinking in the approach to education, since people must be prepared to work and live in an increasingly borderless world.

QUESTIONS FOR DISCUSSION

1. How does symbolic interaction theory complement functional and conflict theories of education?

2. What are the principal problems that trouble American schools, and how have educators sought to overcome them? How successful have these efforts been?

3. What is the relationship between race, class, ethnicity, and education?

4. In what ways are schools likely to be conservative institutions that reinforce the status quo? In what ways are they likely to be subversive institutions that undermine and seek to change it?

5. What role will education likely play in preparing people for the next century? How will globalization affect the type of schooling that students will ideally receive?

KEY TERMS

bilingual education: The offering of instruction in a non-English language as well as in English.

credential society: A society in which the qualifications needed for work and social status depend on the possession of a credential certifying the completion of formal education.

de facto segregation: School segregation based on residential patterns or student choice, which persists even though legal segregation is now outlawed in the United States.

education: The transmission of society's norms, values, and knowledge base by means of direct instruction.

formal education: Education that occurs within academic institutions such as schools.

Head Start: A federally funded program in which enriched preschool environments are created for lower-income children in hopes of preparing them to do better in school.

International Baccalaureate Program: An international degree program intended to help students who are making a transition from high school in one country to higher education in another.

literacy: The ability to read and write at a basic level.

magnet schools: A school that seeks to attract students by offering specialized, high-quality programs in math, science, arts, humanities or other subjects.

mass education: The extension of formal schooling to wide segments of the population.

private school: A school that is run by privately employed educators and paid for out of students' fees and tuition.

public education: A universal education system provided by the government and funded out of tax revenues rather than student fees.

school busing: A court-ordered program to achieve racial integration by busing public school students to schools other than those they would normally attend.

school choice plans: Programs in which the government provides families with educational certificates or "vouchers" that can be redeemed for tuition payments at the private or parochial school of their choice.

school segregation: The education of racial minorities in schools that are geographically separated from those attended by whites and other ethnic groups.

social solidarity: Bonds that unite the members of a social group.

RECOMMENDED FOR FURTHER READING

Alsalam, Nabeel, Laurence T. Ogle, Gayle Thompson Rogers, and Thomas M. Smith. (1992). *The Condition of Education: 1992*. Washington: U.S. Department of Education, National Center for Education Statistics.

A detailed study conducted for the U.S. Department of Education on virtually all aspects of the American educational system; provides hundreds of tables, graphs, and charts, along with an analysis of recent trends.

Best, Raphaela. (1983). *We've All Got Scars: What Boys and Girls Learn in Elementary School.* Bloomington: Indiana University Press.

A study of the "hidden curriculum" by which children are socialized to gender and other roles in elementary school.

Collins, Randall. (1979). *The Credential Society: An Historical Sociology of Education,* New York: Academic Press.

An examination of the importance of credentialling in modern society; focuses on the development and role of contemporary educational systems.

Freedman, Samuel. (1991). *Small Victories: The Real World of a Teacher, Her Students, Their High School.* New York: Harper & Row.

A vivid description of the difficulties, failures, and successes of teaching inner city students in a poorly funded school.

Glazer, Nathan. (1992). "The Real World of Urban Education," *The Public Interest,* 106 (Winter): 57–75.

Glazer sees the problem of schools in the breakdown of the family and community. He argues for "target" or "magnet" schools to educate the more talented and harder-working students.

Kozol, Johnathan. (1991). *Savage Inequalities: Children in American Schools.* New York: Crown Publishers.

Kozol, one of the most influential writers about American education, focuses on the fact that American schools are segregated and poorly funded, and provide inferior education. Kozol shows how this system serves to perpetuate inequality.

CHAPTER

17

Religion

CHAPTER OUTLINE

INTRODUCTION

As a society becomes increasingly modernized it inevitably becomes less religious. (Berger, 1982).

During the past century, only one social-science thesis has come close to universal acceptance by Western intellectuals—that the spread of modernization spells doom for religious and mystical belief. . . . In fact, the secularization thesis [that religion is dying in modern society] is at best a partial truth based on biased assumptions. In any event, by now it must be evident to all but the most devoted ideologues that the thunderous political activities taking place around the world are not dying spasms, but the lusty choruses of revival and uproar caused by the outbreak of new faiths (Stark, 1990).

Each of these two statements is by a prominent sociologist of religion. The first, which echoes a viewpoint that has prevailed since sociology emerged in the nineteenth century, holds that religion is incompatible with modern, technical, scientific society, and therefore is inevitably doomed. The second, which represents an emerging opinion among sociologists of religion, claims that religion is in fact alive and well in modern society, and even thrives in the face of challenges from science and other nonreligious ways of thinking.

Which viewpoint is correct? How can social scientists, looking at the same phenomenon, draw such vastly different conclusions? In this chapter we will attempt to answer this question, looking at the changing role of religion in modern society. We will examine the "death of religion" thesis, alongside the seeming explosion of religious beliefs of all sorts, including the highly traditional forms of religious thought that today are growing throughout the world.

THE SOCIOLOGICAL STUDY OF RELIGION

Religion is one of the oldest human institutions; cave drawings suggest that religious beliefs and practices existed more than 40,000 years ago. Sociologists define **religion** as *a cultural system of commonly shared beliefs and rituals that provides a sense of ultimate meaning and purpose, by creating an idea of reality that is sacred, all-encompassing, and supernatural* (Durkheim, 1965; Berger, 1967; Wuthnow, 1988). There are several key elements to this definition. First, religion is seen as a form of culture. You will recall from Chapter 3 that culture consists of the shared beliefs, values, norms, ideas, institutions, and organizations that create a common identity among a group of people. Religion shares all of these characteristics. Second, religion involves both beliefs and ritualized practices. Third, and perhaps most importantly, religion is seen as providing a sense of purpose—a feeling that life is ultimately meaningful. It does so by explaining in a coherent, compelling way that which transcends or overshadows everyday life, in ways that other aspects of culture (such as an educational system or a belief in democracy) typically cannot (Wuthnow, 1988; Geertz, 1973). For many people, such transcendence is achieved by belief in a supernatural force or power—God—that is regarded as the ultimate force behind the natural world. It is also often associated with a heightened sense of emotions that grows out of religious experience.

There are various ways that sociologists and anthropologists have classified different kinds of religions. It should be understood that these distinctions emerged among students of religion schooled in European and American religious traditions; their applicability to other religions is increasingly being questioned (Juergensmeyer, 1993; Smart, 1989; Wilson, 1982).

Animistic religions are those religions believing that *naturally occurring phenomena such as mountains and animals are possessed of indwelling spirits with supernatural powers*. Such religions are found throughout the world, particularly in parts of Africa, Asia, and among the indigenous peoples of Latin America. As traditionally practiced, for example, Japanese Shinto Buddhism is a form of animism. **Theistic religions** are *those that believe in one or more supernatural deities* (the term originates in the Greek word for "god"). Sometimes, although not always, such deities are seen as possessing human-like qualities. Theism is sometimes further divided into two categories, depending on the number of gods that are believed to exist: **polytheism,** which holds that *there are different gods representing various categories of natural forces* ("poly" means "many"), and **monotheism,** which holds that there is a *single all-knowing, all-powerful God* ("mono" means "one"). Ancient Greek and Roman religions, as well as some forms of Hinduism, are examples of polytheism; Judaism, Islam, and Christianity are examples of monotheism. Finally, there are **nontheistic religions,** which do not believe in the existence of gods at all, but rather *believe in the existence of divine spiritual forces.* Buddhism, as well as some forms of Hinduism are examples.

How Sociologists Think About Religion

It is important to recognize that when sociologists study religion, they do so as sociologists, and not as believers (or disbelievers) in any particular faith. This has several implications for the sociological study of religion.

Sociologists Are Not Concerned with Whether Religious Beliefs are True or False From a sociological perspective, religions are not regarded as decreed by God but rather as socially constructed by human beings. As a result, sociologists suspend their personal beliefs when they study religion. They are concerned with the human rather than the divine aspects of religion. Sociologists ask: How is the religion organized? What are its principal beliefs and values? How is it related to the larger society? What explains its success or failure in recruiting and retaining adherents? The question of whether a particular belief is "good" or "true," however important it might be to adherents of the religion under study, is not something that sociologists are able to address as sociologists. (As individuals they may have strong opinions on the matter, but care should be taken lest these opinions bias their research as sociologists.)

Sociologists Are Especially Concerned with the Social Organization of Religion Religions are among the most important institutions in society; they are a primary source of the most deep-seated norms and values. Yet at the same time religions are typically practiced through an enormous variety of social forms. Within Christianity and Judaism, for example, religious practice often occurs in formal organizations. Yet this is not necessarily true of such Asian religions as Hinduism and Buddhism. The sociology of religion is concerned with how different religious institutions and organizations actually function. The earliest European religions were often indistinguishable from the larger society, with religious beliefs and practices permeating many aspects of daily life. This is still true in many parts of the world today. In modern industrial society, however,

religions have become institutionalized, and so sociologists focus on the organizations through which religions must operate in order to survive (Hammond, 1992). As we shall see below, this has even lead some sociologists to view religions in the United States and Europe as similar to business organizations, competing with one another for members (Warner, 1993).

Sociologists Often View Religions as a Major Source of Social Solidarity To the extent that religions provide their adherents with a common set of norms and values, they are an important source of social solidarity. Religious beliefs, rituals, and bonds help to create a "moral community" in which all members know how to behave toward one another (Wuthnow, 1988). If a single religion overwhelmingly dominates a society, religion can be an important source of social stability. On the other hand, if a society's members adhere to numerous competing religions, then religious differences can lead to destabilizing social conflicts. Recent examples of religious conflict within a society include struggles between Sikhs and Hindus in India, Moslems and Christians in what was formerly Yugoslavia, and conflicts over abortion in the U.S.

Sociologists Explain the Appeal of Religious Movements in Terms of Social Forces Rather than Personal, Spiritual, or Psychological Factors For many people, religious beliefs are a deeply personal experience, involving a profound sense of connection with forces that transcend everyday reality. Although sociologists do not question the depth of such feelings and experiences, they are unlikely to limit themselves to a purely spiritual explanation for religious commitment. A person may claim that he or she became religious when God suddenly appeared in a vision, but sociologists are likely to look for more earthly explanations. Some researchers argue that people often "get religion" when their fundamental sense of social order is threatened by economic hardship, loneliness, loss or grief, physical suffering, and poor health (Berger, 1967; Glock, 1976; Schwartz, 1970; Stark and Bainbridge, 1980). Though there is certainly much truth in such accounts, sociologists would be more likely to focus on the disruption of social order rather than the psychological response of the individual.

Several types of social forces are likely to be of special interest to sociologists of religion; we will discuss these in greater detail throughout this chapter. First, sociologists sometimes focus on the ways in which religious fervor results from a crisis in prevailing beliefs. This occurred in the United States during the 1960s, when challenges included opposition to the Vietnam War, the civil rights movement, social movements among racial and ethnic minorities, and the youth-oriented counterculture. As a result, unusually large numbers of people were attracted to religious teachers ranging from Indian gurus to fundamentalist preachers, offering everything from meditation and yoga to astrology and "new age" religions (Wuthnow, 1988). Second, sociologists study the ways in which competition among religious organizations leads some to thrive and others to perish. This has led to the increased interest in the organizational dynamics of religious groups referred to above (Hammond, 1992; Finke and Stark, 1988, 1992; Roof and McKinney, 1987; Stark and Bainbridge, 1987). Finally, sociologists are concerned with the relationship between religion, ethnic identity, and politics. This is seen in the resurgence of ethnically based religion in pluralist societies such as the United States, as well as in the rise of religious nationalism throughout the world (Juergensmeyer, 1993; Lawrence, 1989; Sahliyeh, 1990; Merkyl and Smart, 1983).

TYPES OF RELIGIOUS ORGANIZATIONS

The sociological study of religion has identified several principal kinds of religious organizations, including church, sect, and cult. These concepts originated with such early theorists as Max Weber (1963; orig. 1921), Ernst Troeltsch (1931), and Richard Niehbur (1929). They are important to understand because they are key elements in the different theories of religious change that we shall consider in the following sections. Yet at the same time they are concepts that emerged out of the study of European and American religions, and, as noted above, there is much debate over their applicability to the non-Christian world.

Church

A **church** can be defined as a *religious organization that exists in a fairly harmonious relationship with the larger society* (Finke and Stark, 1992). In sociological language, churches are relatively *well integrated* with society; in everyday terms, they are "respectable" organizations that reflect a society's prevailing values and beliefs. Churches are likely to be formal organizations, more or less bureaucratically organized, that do not make waves. Their members tend to be middle- or upper-class "solid citizens" who read the prayer book and follow the rules (Niebuhr, 1929).

A church can take one of two forms, depending on whether or not it represents a state-sanctioned religion. An **ecclesia** is a *church that is formally allied with the state and is the "official" religion of the society.* As such, it is likely to enjoy special rights and privileges that other churches lack. In some instances, such as the Church of England in Great Britain, other religions are

The United States is one of the most religiously pluralist societies in the world, contributing to a resurgence of ethnically based traditions. This woman and her child are celebrating Kwanzaa, a week-long festival patterned after various African agricultural holidays, which begins on December 26. Kwanzaa, begun in 1966, is a celebration intended to foster familial and social values in the African-American community.

freely tolerated and practiced; in others, such as the official Shi'ite Muslim faith of Iran, other religions are strongly discouraged or repressed. On the other hand, a **denomination** is *a church that is not formally allied with the state.* The existence of denominations allows for freedom of religious choice, so that different denominations may openly compete with one another for membership. India and the United States offer examples of societies where freedom of religion has resulted in hundreds of religious denominations.

Sect

Unlike a church, which exists in relative harmony with the larger society, a **sect** is *a religious organization that exists in a high degree of tension with its environment* (Finke and Stark, 1992). Sects may be formal or informal organizations, but in sociological terms they are often at odds with the established churches. While churches tend to intellectualize religious practice, sects may emotionalize it, emphasizing heightened personal experience and religious conversion. They are less likely to be "respectable" middle class organizations, at least from the viewpoint of more mainstream churches, who often label them in negative terms. Sects often appeal to marginal individuals drawn from among lower-income households, racial and ethnic minorities, and the rural poor. Yet in Japan, India, and the United States today, some sects retain a strong middle-class appeal.

Sects often provide a new source of religious ideas and vitality outside the mainstream faiths of a society. When they are successful, they may grow in size, increasing their appeal to less marginal members of society. When this happens—when sects evolve into churches—they may become stodgy, losing their emotional appeal (Niebuhr, 1929). A new sect may then break off, seeking to return to its religious roots. This is what has occurred within both American Protestantism and Japanese Buddhism in recent years. Disturbed with the increasingly intellectualized and liberal direction taken by mainstream Protestant churches, numerous Protestant sects have broken off, seeking to return to what they view as the biblical roots of the Protestant faith (Finke and Stark, 1992). In a similar way, Buddhist sects in Japan are seeking a return to original Buddhist beliefs, in response to what they regard as the isolation and social irrelevance of mainstream Buddhist groups (Davis, 1991).

Cult

A **cult** can be most simply defined as *a religion that is unconventional with regard to the larger society* (Finke and Stark, 1992). Although cults can be formal or informal organizations, they are likely to be regarded as unique or unusual from the standpoint of the prevailing churches and sects. While sects often originate as offshoots of well-established churches, cults typically originate outside of a society's principal churches altogether. They are often led by a charismatic figure, who draws on a wide range of teachings to develop the cult's unique ideas. As a result, they are a source of fresh religious beliefs, while providing new opportunities for those who are religiously disaffected to "become churched" (Finke and Stark, 1992). Cults are likely to be in a high degree of tension with the larger society. A recent tragic example was the Branch Davidian cult, which committed mass suicide by setting fire to its Waco, Texas, compound after a lengthy armed standoff with federal officials.

As with sects, cults flourish when there is a breakdown in well-established and widespread societal belief systems. This is happening throughout the world today, in places as diverse as Japan, India, and the United States. When this occurs, cults may originate within the society itself, or they may be "imported" from outside. In the American context, examples of "indigenous" cults include "New Age" religions based on such things as spiritualism, astrology, religious practices adapted from Asia or Native Americans, and healing by means of crystals or pyramids. Examples of imported cults include the Reverend Sun Myung Moon's Unification Church ("moonies"), which originated in Korea, and Transcendental Meditation. It should be obvious that what is a cult in one country may well be an established religious practice in another. When Indian *gurus* (teachers) bring their beliefs into the United States, what might be considered an established religion in India is regarded as a cult in the United States. Christianity began as an indigenous cult in ancient Jerusalem, and in many Asian countries today, evangelical Protestantism is regarded as a cult imported from the United States.

THEORETICAL PERSPECTIVES ON RELIGION

Until relatively recently, much sociological research on religion was based on societies in which a single religion overwhelmingly predominated. As a consequence, it seemed reasonable to examine the relationship between a predominant religion and society as a whole. This was true in those European societies where the sociology of religion originated, as well as in the premodern societies that sociologists and anthropologists also studied. Within the past 50 years, however, this view has been challenged by some American sociologists. Based on their own experience in a society that is highly tolerant of religious diversity, these theorists have focused on religious pluralism rather than religious domination. Not surprisingly, their conclusions differ substantially from the earlier views.

Religion and Society: The Classical View

The classical view, as advanced in different ways by Durkheim, Marx, and Weber, regarded religion as inextricably bound up with the larger society. Religion was believed to reflect and reinforce society's values, or at least the values of those who were most powerful; provide an important source of solidarity and social stability; and serve as an important engine of social change. According to this view, religion's presumably irrational beliefs are threatened by the rise of **secular thinking**—*worldly thinking, particularly as seen in the*

the ruling class of Jewish religious leaders and their Roman conquerors. In more recent times, the role of black churches in spearheading the U.S. civil rights movement can be cited, from Martin Luther King and Jesse Jackson to countless lesser-known ministers and clergymen (Morris, 1984). Black churches have become centers of their communities, offering critiques of racism and actively working for social change in American society (Cone, 1969; Nelson and Nelson, 1975; Lincoln and Mamiya, 1990). Islam has also played an important role in leading African Americans—from Malcolm X to Black Muslims today—to militantly challenge racial inequality in the United States. Churches have played an extremely active role in providing sanctuary to illegal immigrants fleeing political persecution in their own countries (Wiltfang and McAdam, 1991).

Weber: Religious Values as Sources of Social Change

Max Weber, unlike either Marx or Durkheim, made the study of religion a major focus of his life's work. Weber planned to study all of the world's major religions, and, with the exception of Islam, managed to do so: Christianity, Ancient Judaism, Buddhism, Taoism, and Hinduism were all subjected to his meticulous historical scholarship. Weber was especially interested in the relationship between religious beliefs and economic life. In particular, he was concerned with explaining why capitalism emerged in such northern European countries as England, the Netherlands, France, and Germany, rather than in Spain, Italy, or China—countries that in different ways in the past had been far more advanced in terms of science, culture, and commerce.

The answer, Weber believed, was that capitalism first appeared in those parts of Europe where the Protestant Reformation had taken hold. This led him to conclude that something about Protestant beliefs must have been favorable for capitalist institutions, whereas the Catholic beliefs that prevailed elsewhere in Europe must have been barriers. In particular, Catholicism's belief in heavenly reward discouraged people from striving to improve their situation on earth; after all, if life is merely a veil of tears to be endured until a glorious afterlife occurs, why work to improve things in the here and now?

In his famous 1904–1905 study of *The Protestant Ethic and the Spirit of Capitalism* (1958), Weber analyzed the teachings of the founders of various Protestant sects, particularly those of John Calvin. He found that early Protestantism had two principal beliefs that together provided fertile ground for capitalism to flower. First, it held that God placed each person on earth to fulfill a particular "calling." Since whether or not one is to be saved is predestined by God, salvation cannot be changed by acts on earth. Evidence of salvation can be sought, however, in a life dedicated to hard work in whatever God called upon one to do. The peasant finds evidence of salvation by laboring long hours in the fields, the worker in the factory, the capitalist in the business office. Second, since Protestantism held that God abhors signs of wealth and ostentation, believers were expected to live extremely simple lives. In economic terms, this meant that Protestants not only had a strong work ethic but were inclined to save and reinvest their earnings rather than enjoy the fruits of their labor in the form of fancy houses, expensive clothing, or other forms of conspicuous consumption. A hardworking, frugal, sober population, reinvesting their earnings in new economic activities, is a surefire prescription for economic growth (Hunter, 1987).

Yet Weber also argued that capitalism's very success could undermine the Protestant ethic. Once capitalism takes hold, it traps people in an endless cycle of competition and work in order to survive, whatever their religious beliefs. Moreover, the modern combination of capitalism, scientific ways of thinking, and bureaucratic forms of organization all help to undermine religion in general. Weber was especially concerned with the growing disenchantment he believed would inevitably result from secularization. With the death of religion, he believed, life would lose its magical, meaningful qualities. Modern society, in Weber's famous image, would become an "iron cage," imprisoning people in endless, unsatisfying, and ultimately pointless work and a life bereft of spirituality.

Critical Assessment Weber's theory has powerfully influenced our understanding of the impact of culture on the economy. His idea that an ethic of hard work and frugality contributes to economic growth has been used to explain economic success around the world, from Basque settlers in Colombia to the "Japanese miracle" and new economic powerhouses of East Asia (Hagen, 1962, 1986; Morishima, 1982; Berger, 1986; Berger and Hsiao, 1988; Wong 1986; Redding 1990; see Chapter 9).

But Weber's analysis has been questioned on a number of grounds as well. First, Weber based his characterization of Protestantism on the teachings of its principal theologians, rather than by examining what Protestant workers, farmers, or capitalists actually believed or did. As we all know, there is often a major gap between the religious beliefs we espouse and our actions. Just because John Calvin preached a doctrine of austerity, sacrifice, and hard work does not mean that it was a part of the daily lives of the people who contributed to the rise of capitalism. Weber cites the writings of Ben Franklin, one of America's "founding fathers," as an example of the Protestant ethic, yet Franklin himself was far from puritanical in his everyday behavior. In fact, contrary to popular beliefs, most Americans during colonial times were not puritans; as Finke and Stark (1992, p. 23) note, "Boston's taverns were probably fuller on Saturday night than were its churches on Sunday morning" during the colonial period.

Second, the teachings of Calvin and other Protestant reformers occurred two centuries before modern industrial capitalism finally emerged. Protestantism itself changed considerably during that period, giving rise to denominations that no longer practiced the austere teachings of its founders. Finally, there is some evidence that capitalism developed among Jews and Catholics—and, for that matter, Hindus, Muslims, and Confucians—as well as Protestants, leading some scholars to question the exclusiveness of the Protestant ethic itself (Tawney, 1938; Robertson, 1933; Samuelson, 1961; Sombart, 1915; Fanfani, 1955; Cohen, 1980; Collins, 1980; Hunter, 1987; Lubeck, 1992; Abun-Nasr, 1965; Bordieu, 1962; Rodinson, 1978).

The Civic Functions of Religion in the United States

During the middle part of the twentieth century the most prominent American sociologists of religion followed Durkheim's lead, adopting a functionalist approach to account for the changing importance of religion in the United States. For example, Talcott Parsons (1960, 1967) argued that while the manifest or intended function of religion might be to provide individual salvation or a sense of purpose to life, its latent or unintended function is to maintain social stability. Religion was seen as accomplishing this by providing people with a set of overarching societal beliefs and values, along with the motivation to obey them.

The difficulty with Parsons' analysis was that it appeared to be incompatible with the secularization hypothesis. How could religion serve an important societal function if society is becoming increasingly secularized? One answer lies in rethinking the meaning of religion so as to encompass institutional secularization. After all, the weakening of religious institutions does not mean that people are necessarily becoming irreligious. On the contrary, religion can be redefined to include any activity that serves the function of providing people with a sense of solemnity, purpose, or higher meaning, whether that activity occurs in a place of worship or in the sanctity of one's private thoughts. Given this definition, it can be argued that religion is thriving in modern society (Luckmann, 1967; Mol, 1976; Wentworth, 1989).

Another, related answer extends the meaning of religion to include those nonchurch activities that serve the function of promoting a heightened sense of social solidarity. Robert Bellah, for example, argued that societies such as the United States possess a **civil religion**—*a set of religious beliefs through which societies interpret their own histories in light of some conception of ultimate reality* (Bellah, 1968, 1975). This usually consists of "god-language used in reference to the nation," including historical myths about the society's supposedly divine origins, beliefs about its sacred historical purpose, and sometimes even religious restrictions on societal membership (Wuthnow, 1988). Even if formal religion appears to be in danger of weakening, civil religions can remain strong, enshrined in (and reinforcing) belief in the nation itself.

One example is the American Pledge of Allegiance, which, in referring to "one nation, under God," seeks to infuse civic life with religious beliefs derived from a predominantly Judeo-Christian heritage. Although the Pledge of Allegiance has been used for over a century, the phrase "under God" was added by congressional legislation in 1954, during the height of Cold War fears about "Godless communism." Even though the Bill of Rights to the U.S. Constitution clearly called for a separation of church and state, in this instance a particular set of theistic religious beliefs was invoked as central to American citizenship.

The New "Religious Economy" Approach

One of the most recent approaches to the sociology of religion is tailored toward societies like the United States, which offer many different faiths to pick and choose from. Taking their cue from economic theory, **religious economists** argue that *religions can be fruitfully understood as organizations in competition with one another for adherents* (Hammond, 1992; Finke and Stark, 1988, 1992; Roof and McKinney, 1987; Stark and Bainbridge, 1987).

Like contemporary economists who study businesses, these sociologists argue that competition is preferable to monopoly when it comes to ensuring religious vitality. This is exactly opposite from the position of the classical theorists. While Durkheim, Marx, and Weber assumed that religion as a whole is weakened when challenged by different religious or secular viewpoints, the religious economists argue that competition increases the overall level of religious involvement in modern society. This is true for two reasons. First, competition makes each religious group try that much harder to win adherents. Second, the presence of numerous religions means that there is likely to be something for just about everyone. In a culturally

Fundamentalist Christian ac-tivists have campaigned heav-ily in recent elections. In Vista, California, fundamen-talists controlling the school board proposed that creation-ism—the belief that God liter-ally created the world in seven days—be taught as an alternative to the theory of evolution. In this photograph, fundamentalists attending a public meeting shout out the words "under God" as they recite the Pledge of Alle-giance. The proposal was eventually voted down when the school board was advised it was unconstitutional.

diverse society like the United States, a single religion will probably appeal only to a limited range of adher-ents, while the presence of Indian gurus, fundamental-ist preachers, and mainline churches is likely to en-courage a high level of religious participation.

This analysis is adapted from the business world, in which competition presumably encourages the emer-gence of highly specialized products that appeal to par-ticular market niches. In fact, the religious economists unabashedly borrow the language of business in de-scribing the conditions that lead to success or failure for a particular religious organization. According to Roger Finke and Rodney Stark (1992), a successful re-ligious group (in what they term "an unregulated econ-omy") must be internally well-organized for competi-tion, have eloquent preachers who are effective "sales reps" in spreading the word, offer beliefs and rituals that are packaged as an appealing product, and develop effective marketing techniques. Religion, in this view, is a business much like any other. Television evange-lists, whom we shall consider below, have been espe-cially good business people in selling their religious products. Thus religious economists such as Finke and Stark do not see competition as undermining religious beliefs and thereby contributing to secularization. Rather, they argue that modern religion is constantly renewing itself through active marketing and recruit-ment.

Critical Assessment A number of criticisms can be raised with regard to the religious economy approach. First, like the economic theory it emulates, it assumes that people rationally pick and choose between differ-ent religions, much as they might shop around for a new car or a pair of shoes. Although there is undoubtedly

some truth in this perspective, it seems unlikely that the choice of religion is as rational as this model implies. Religions also have a deeply spiritual component that may get overlooked if one assumes that religious buy-ers are always on spiritual shopping sprees. Wade Clark Roof's (1993) recent study of 1,400 "baby boomers"—Americans born after World War II, who are now in their middle ages—found that a third re-mained loyal to their childhood faiths, while another third continued to profess their childhood beliefs al-though they no longer belonged to a religious organi-zation. This leaves only a third who were actively look-ing around for new religions.

Second, some scholarship has questioned the evi-dence in support of the religious economists' major conclusion—that religious pluralism encourages, rather than reduces, the appeal of religion. While the religious economists' studies have found that religious involvement is higher when numerous religious groups abound (Finke and Stark, 1992; Stark and Bainbridge, 1980, 1985), other research has not supported this con-clusion (Land et al., 1991).

Third, religious membership per se is not the only measure of the degree of secularization in a society. Another indicator is the degree to which religious or-ganizations or beliefs exert power over government and other social institutions, or indeed over their own mem-bership. On this measure organized religion has be-come less powerful in the United States, as well as in most industrial societies (Hammond, 1992; Chaves, 1993, 1994).

Finally, the religious economy approach itself ar-guably applies only to the more liberal religious tradi-tions in the United States, which tend to favor a more rational approach to religious belief. It is questionable whether the more ethnically based or traditional American religions, not to mention most other religions throughout the world, can be understood through the lens of religious competition.

WORLD RELIGIONS

Although there are thousands of different religions throughout the world, six of them, encompassing an enormous diversity in beliefs and practices, are embraced by more than four-fifths of the people on earth. The sociology of religion has concerned itself with non-European religions since its origins in the writings of Durkheim and Weber. Nonetheless, there has frequently been a tendency to view all religions through concepts and theories that grew out of the European experience. For example, notions like "denomination" or "sect" presuppose the existence of formally organized religious institutions; they are of questionable utility for religions that emphasize on-going spiritual practice as a part of daily life, or the complete integration of religion with civic and political life. In recent years there has been an effort to create a more comparative sociology of religion, one that seeks to understand religious traditions from within their own frames of reference (Juergensmeyer, 1993; Smart, 1989; Wilson, 1982).

Christianity

Christianity, with its 1.7 billion adherents, encompasses enormously divergent denominations, sects, and cults. Common to all of these is the belief that Jesus of Nazareth was the Christ (Messiah, or "anointed one") foretold in the Hebrew Bible. Christians believe that Jesus' teachings while he lived, and his resurrection to heaven after he was crucified, hold the keys to an ethical life, freedom from sin, and ultimate salvation. While great doctrinal differences separate different Christian faiths from one another, almost all share the belief that at the beginning of time human beings fell from God's grace through their sinful acts, and that acceptance of Christ and his teachings provides the key to eternal salvation. Most Christians also believe in the biblical account of the Resurrection, according to which Jesus rose from the dead on the third day after crucifixion to ascend once again to heaven. All Christians adhere to a monotheistic belief in a single God, although in most Christian faiths God is also regarded as a trinity embracing a heavenly Father, his Son the Savior, and his sustaining Holy Spirit.

When Christianity originally emerged in Palestine some 2,000 years ago, it was a persecuted sect outside the mainstream of Jewish and Roman religious practices; yet within four centuries Christianity had become an *ecclesia* or official religion of the Roman Empire. In the eleventh century Christianity divided into the Eastern Orthodox Church (based in Turkey) and the Catholic Church (based in Rome). A second great split occurred within the Catholic branch, when the sixteenth century Protestant Reformation gave rise to numerous divergent Protestant denominations, sects, and cults. Protestants tend to emphasize a direct relationship between the individual and God, with each person responsible for his or her own salvation. Catholics, on the other hand, emphasize the importance of the Church hierarchy as the means to salvation, with the Pope in Rome as the final authority.

Christianity was spread through conquest and missionary work. The European colonization of much of Africa, Asia, and North and South America that began in the fifteenth century brought with it Christian teachings, churches, and large-scale conversion of native peoples, until today it has become the largest religion in the world, espoused by one out of every five people. Only in Asia are Christians a small minority (9 percent), largely because countries like Japan and China successfully resisted colonization and the Christianization that went along with it. In recent years, a substantial increase in the proselytizing efforts of Protestant evangelical groups has occurred, making significant inroads in traditionally Catholic countries (Bokenkotter, 1990; Hastings, 1991).

Islam

Islam is the second largest and fastest growing religion in the world today. There are an estimated billion or more Muslims (the name for those who practice *al-islam,* an Arabic term meaning submission without reservation to God's will), with the number increasing by 25 million each year. While Islam began and remains the official faith among Arab and other peoples of the Middle East, it has spread south into Africa, north into Europe and the former Soviet Union, and east to India, Pakistan, China, and Indonesia. Today far more non-Arabs than Arabs identify themselves as Muslims; there are some 140 million Muslims in Indonesia alone. Islam is also practiced by many Middle Eastern and Asian immigrants to the United States, as well as numerous African-Americans (Marsh, 1984).

Muslims believe in absolute, unquestioning, positive devotion to Allah (God). Although modern Islam dates to the seventh-century Arab prophet Muhammad (570–632), Muslims trace their religion to the ancient Hebrew prophet Abraham, who was also the founder of Judaism. The precepts of Islam were revealed to Muhammad and are contained in a sacred book dictated to his followers called the *Koran* (the common English

Map 17.1   Major Religions of the World

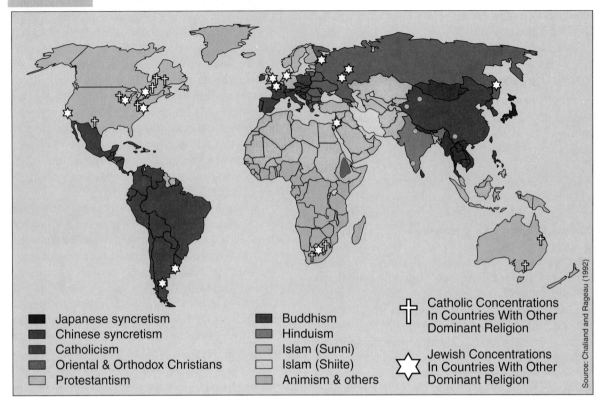

Japanese syncretism
Chinese syncretism
Catholicism
Oriental & Orthodox Christians
Protestantism

Buddhism
Hinduism
Islam (Sunni)
Islam (Shiite)
Animism & others

✝ Catholic Concentrations
In Countries With Other
Dominant Religion

✡ Jewish Concentrations
In Countries With Other
Dominant Religion

Source: Challand and Rageau (1992)

Missionaries and military force are two reasons that the majority of people in the world profess only a relative handful of religions today. Although Christianity (Catholicism and Protestantism) is the most widespread religion, it is rapidly being overtaken by Islam.

transliteration of *Qur'an,* which is closer to the Arabic pronunciation and which means *the Recitation).* Muhammad's ideas were not initially accepted in his birthplace of Mecca, so in 622 he and his followers moved to Medina (both are located in what is today Saudi Arabia). This migration, called the *hejira,* marks the beginning of Islam, which soon spread throughout Arabia. Today thousands of Muslims celebrate Muhammad's *hejira* each year by making a pilgrimage to a holy shrine called the *kaaba* in Mecca. Muhammad himself is not worshipped by Muslims. He is regarded not as a God or a Messiah but rather as a great teacher and prophet, the last in a line that includes Abraham, Noah, Moses, and Jesus.

Islam is a highly comprehensive religion. The sacred *sharia* (or *way)*—which governs all aspects of personal and social life—includes prescriptions for worship, daily life, ethics, and even government. *Sharia* originates in a number of different sources, including the writings of the Koran, customs derived from Muhammad's own life, past laws of the Islamic community, and current consensus on what is correct. Life is governed by the Five Pillars of Islam, which include: (1) acceptance of Allah as God and Muhammad as Al-

lah's messenger; (2) ritual worship, including facing toward Mecca and bowing in prayer at five prescribed times each day, no matter where one is or what one is otherwise doing; (3) *Ramadan,* a month of prayer and fasting during the daylight hours; (4) giving *alms* or donations to those who are poor or in need; and (5) making holy pilgrimage to Mecca at least once in one's lifetime (Weeks, 1988).

There is no separation of church and state in the Islamic code or in the countries where it predominates, and so Islam is typically an official religion in those countries, with the government regulating many aspects of private life. Although by American standards this may be judged extremely restrictive, traditional Muslims frequently view American life as spiritually undisciplined, corrupt and immoral (Arjomand, 1988; Kedouri, 1992; Abdul-Rauf, 1975; Esposito, 1984; MacEnoin and Al-Shahi, 1983; Martin and Islam, 1982).

Judaism

Judaism, with 14 million adherents worldwide, is by far the smallest of the world's major religions, yet it has exerted an influence greater than its limited numbers would suggest. First, as we have already mentioned, it is the source of the world's two largest religions, Islam and Christianity. Second, in European and American culture, Jews have played a role disproportionate to their numbers in such diverse fields as music, literature, science, education, and business. Third, the existence of Israel as a Jewish state since 1948 has given the Jewish faith international prominence. Israel has existed in a near-constant state of tension with many of its neighboring Arab countries since its founding, and in recent years has seldom been out of the news.

Judaism was one of the first religions to teach monotheism; an ancient and central prayer, often repeated, says "Hear Oh Israel, the Lord Our God, the Lord is One." Judaism, like many other religions, teaches that its adherents are God's chosen people, but it does not teach that observers have a duty to convert others to their faith.

Although Judaism in biblical times was a priestly religion centered around holy temples, today there is more emphasis on the family as an important location of worship. For example, many Jewish families light candles on Friday night in ritual observance. The primary religious writing for the Jews is the *Torah* (or *law*), which consists of a scroll on which the first five books of the Bible are inscribed (Genesis, Exodus, Leviticus, Numbers, and Deuteronomy). Although biblical tradition holds that Jewish law was given by God to Moses when he led the Jews out of slavery in Egypt about 3,500 years ago, the law has subsequently been elaborated by *rabbis* or teachers, and is codified in books called the *Mishnah* and the *Talmud.*

Jews have often suffered persecution at the hands of the surrounding society. From the twelfth century on, European and Russian Jews were often forced to live in special districts termed *ghettos,* where they lacked full rights as citizens, and were sometimes the target of harassment, attacks, and killings. Partly in reaction to these conditions, and partly because the Torah identifies the city of Jerusalem as the center of the Jewish homeland, some Jews embraced **Zionism,** *a movement calling for the return of Jews to Palestine and the creation of a Jewish state.* (*Zion* is a biblical name for the ancient city of Jerusalem). Zionists established settlements in Palestine early in the twentieth century, living peacefully with their Arab and Palestinian neighbors. Following World War II and the Nazi extermination of six million Jews during the Holocaust, the state of Israel was created as a homeland for the survivors.

Hinduism

Hinduism, which dates to about 2,000 years before Christ, is one of the oldest religions in the world and is the source of Buddhism and Sikhism. It is not based on the teachings of any single individual, and its adherents do not trace their national origins to a single God. Like other religions, Hinduism is an ethical religion that calls for an ideal way of life. There are today estimated to be nearly 700 million Hindus in the world, primarily in India, where Hindus comprise the large majority of the country's 866 million people.

As we saw in Chapter 8, the Indian social structure is characterized by a caste system in which people are believed to be born to a certain status that they must occupy for life. Although prejudices associated with the caste system were officially abolished in 1949, caste remains powerful to this day. The caste system has its

Islam, with a billion adherents worldwide, is the second largest and fastest-growing religion in the world today. Practitioners of Islam, called Muslims, are deeply religious. This photograph shows worshippers in the Istiolal Mosque, East Asia's largest, in Jakarta, Indonesia.

Judaism, with 14 million adherents worldwide, has had an influence beyond its numbers. Both Christianity and Islam trace their origins to early Judaism. Jewish religious observances emphasize the importance of family rituals, both at home and in the synagogue. In this photograph, children participate in a religious ceremony at Temple Beth Or in Everett, Washington.

origins in Hindu beliefs, which hold that an ideal life is partly achieved by performing the duties appropriate to one's caste. This is because Hindus, like Buddhists, believe in **samsara** or the *reincarnation (rebirth) of the soul according to one's karma or actions on earth.* One's rebirth into a higher or lower caste depends on the degree to which one is committed to *dharma* or the ideal way of life.

Hindu teachings hold that for upper-caste males there are four stages of life: (1) the *student stage,* a period of initial study and learning, which lasts from childhood until marriage; (2) the *householder* stage, during which one raises a family and participates in the larger society; (3) the *forest-dwelling stage* of spiritual seeking, which occurs after one's children have grown;

and (4) the *renunciation stage,* a period of achieving wisdom with age and giving up attachments to all wordly things in search of spiritual enlightenment. Eventually, if one is able to work out all past and present *karma* through leading a virtuous life according to Hindu precepts, one can be liberated from the cycle of rebirth and reincarnation altogether.

Perhaps because Hinduism does not have a central organization or leader, its philosophy and practice are extremely diverse. Religious teachings direct all aspects of life, ranging from enjoyment of sensual pleasures to stark renunciation of earthly pursuits. In modern times, Mahatma Gandhi can be taken as representative of one who led a virtuous life according to Hindu philosophy. Gandhi, the leader of India's

Hinduism, one of the oldest religions in the world, is the source of Buddhism and Sikhism, with some 700 million adherents, mostly in India. In Hindu tradition, any location may be sacred, and some homes have a shrine for worship, such as this shrine for Lord Krishna.

independence movement, devoted his life to the Hindu virtues of "honesty, courage, service, faith, self-control, purity, and nonviolence" (Potter, 1992).

Hindu religious services do not have to occur in a special place of worship. Although there are sacred sites on which temples and pilgrimage centers are located, any location may be a place of devotion. Hindus believe in the God-like unity of all things, yet they also venerate different gods representing aspects of the whole, such as the divine dimension of a spiritual teacher. Despite its teaching that life is *maya* or illusion, there is an earthly quality to Hindu religious beliefs (Schmidt, 1980; Basham, 1989; Kinsley, 1982; Potter, 1992).

Buddhism

Buddhism, founded in India by Siddhartha Gautama some five centuries before the birth of Christ, was originally an offshoot of Hinduism. According to legend, the young Siddhartha renounced an upper-caste life of material splendor in search for a more meaningful existence. A lifetime of wandering, occasional poverty, and different spiritual practices eventually taught him the way to achieve enlightenment, and he became the *Buddha—the awakened or enlightened one.*

Buddhism is more a prescription for righteous living than a doctrine of belief in a particular god. As a consequence, it is difficult to estimate with any accuracy the number of Buddhists in the world, since many people practice certain precepts of Buddhism without calling themselves Buddhists. It is estimated that there are some 300 million Buddhists in the world today, divided into several major groupings: the older *Theravada Buddhism* or "Way of the Elders," which is predominant in Burma, Thailand, and Sri Lanka; *Mahayana Buddhism* or the "Great Vehicle," practiced in China, Korea, and Japan; and *Vajrayana* or "Vehicle of the Thunderbolt," which is practiced in Tibet and Mongolia. In China, Buddhism is intertwined with Taoist folk religion and Confucian codes of ethical practice. In Japan, Buddhism interacts with traditional Japanese animism, *shinto* ("the way of the gods"), and with emperor worship. Offshoots of Japanese Buddhism include Nichiren and Zen.

Gautama Buddha's philosophy was contained in the Four Noble Truths: (1) All beings—gods, humans, and animals—are caught up in an endless round of suffering and rebirth, the result of their *karma* or actions. (2) Suffering results from desire or attachment. What we call "life" is fleeting and transitory; to the extent that we depend on wealth or friends or family or even religious beliefs for satisfaction, we are condemned to suffer unending frustration and loss. (3) Suffering can be overcome by breaking the endless cycle of karma and rebirth; when this occurs, *nirvana*—a blissful state of emptiness—is achieved. (4) The means to achieve nirvana is contained in what Buddha termed the Eightfold Path, which involves ethical behavior, a simple lifestyle, renunciation of material pleasures, meditation, and eventually enlightenment.

Buddhism, like all religions, has had to face growing modernization and secular thinking. A number of formerly Buddhist nations have become communist, and Buddhist practices have been repressed. Where Buddhism continues to be practiced, it has sometimes become politically aligned with nationalist movements, as in Sri Lanka. Its meditative lifestyle would

Buddhism, an offshoot of Hinduism, is more of an ethical system than a belief in a single god. Here children celebrate the Buddha's birthday by pouring holy water over his statue at the Zojoji Temple in Tokyo, Japan.

strike most people as highly incompatible with life in a modern industrial society, which instead emphasizes work, consumption, achievement, and all forms of *karma* that Buddhists regard as a barrier to enlightenment and happiness. Yet perhaps because of its anti-modern, meditative lifestyle, Buddhism continues to attract adherents (Kitagawa and Strong, 1992; Bechert and Gombrich, 1984; Robinson and Johnson, 1982).

Confucianism

Confucianism, whose name derives from the English pronunciation of its founder K'ung Fu-tzu (551–479 B.C.), is also more of a philosophical system for ethical living on earth than a religion concerned with a tran-scendental god (Fingarette, 1972). K'ung Fu-tzu never wrote down his teachings, but many of his sayings were compiled by his followers in a book called *The Analects.* They subsequently became the foundation of official ethics and politics for some two thousand years in China, and have had an enormous influence in countries bordering on south China (such as Korea and Vietnam) as well as Japan.

Confucianism emphasizes harmony in social relations, respect for authority and hierarchy, the importance of tradition, honoring one's elders, and learning through copying the behavior of wise and virtuous rulers. The group is seen as more important than the individual. Confucianism incorporates the Taoist notion that there is a **tao** or *"way of being"* prescribed by the natural harmony of the universe, and that the ideal life is led in accordance with this order (*tao* means "the way.") Rulers derive their wisdom and power from this *tao;* they have a mandate from heaven to maintain peace and harmony on earth. Followers emulate their rulers, and thus also may hope to live according to *tao.*

Confucianism teaches that opposites are not necessarily antagonistic, but rather together comprise a harmonious whole that is constantly in a creative state of tension or change. For example, it holds that there are two major principles in the universe, *yin* (the female principle) and *yang* (the male principle). These two principles are found in all things, and their dynamic interaction accounts for both harmony and change. The *I Ching* (Book of Changes) contains a series of philosophical teachings based on this view, along with a technique for analyzing present circumstances and determining a philosophically wise course of action.

Early in its history, Confucianism became an important philosophy for Chinese rulers and administrators, and although it subsequently went through periods of growth and decline, it eventually became an important part of Chinese thinking. During some periods, government positions were even filled by those who tested high in understanding of Confucius's writings. Confucianism also helped Chinese rulers to maintain their power, since it taught the masses of peasants to respectfully accept authority and live according to long-standing traditions. When China became communist in 1949, Confucianism was abolished as an official ethical system, although its influence has remained pervasive (Hansen, 1992; Lee, 1988; Fingarette, 1972).

Today, many scholars argue that such Confucian values as respect for authority and a highly disciplined work ethic are in fact partly responsible for the rapid economic growth in Singapore, Taiwan, China and other Asian countries today (MacFarquhar, 1980; Morishima, 1982; Berger, 1986; Berger and Hsiao, 1988; see also Chapter 9).

RELIGION AND GENDER

Although the major religions of the world are embraced by men and women alike, it is important to note that the principal deities, prophets, and leaders of many of these religions are largely male. Christianity and Judaism, for example, all contain teachings that view women as subordinate to men. God is depicted as male, beliefs typically emphasize male religious and political superiority, and women are often excluded from positions of theological power. The sociological explanation for this is straightforward: These religions were initially developed by men within patriarchal societies, and therefore reflect patriarchal norms and values (see Chapter 11).

According to the book of Genesis in the Jewish (as well as Christian) Bible, Eve, the first woman, violated God's word and tempted Adam to eat fruit from the tree of knowledge, thereby leading to their loss of innocence and expulsion from Eden. All human suffering can thus be traced to Eve's deception (Genesis 3). The Book of Proverbs instructs the good wife to oversee servants, care for her family, be kind, optimistic, busy, fertile, obedient, and sexually submissive to her husband. Given these conditions, it is perhaps not surprising that even today Orthodox Jews recite a daily prayer thanking God "that thou hast not created me a Gentile [non-Jew], a Slave, or a Woman."

For Christians, Saint Paul's teachings also asserted the authority of men over women. Saint Paul instructed wives "to submit yourselves to your husbands as to the Lord. For the husband is the head of the wife, even as Christ is the head of the church. . . . so also wives should submit to their husbands in everything" (Ephesians 5:23–24). He further counseled that "a woman

Although most of the world's principal religions traditionally espoused beliefs that view women as subordinate to men, this is being challenged in modern society. For example an increasing number of women are being ordained as Jewish rabbis and Protestant ministers. Jane Dixon, the third female bishop in the Episcopal Church, is here shown holding services in Saint Albans Cathedral.

should learn in quietness with and full submission. . . . suffer not a woman to usurp authority over men, but to be in silence" (1 Timothy: 11–12). This follows from Saint Paul's belief that a man "is the image of God and reflects God's glory; but the woman is the reflection of man's glory. For man did not come from woman; no, woman came from man" (I Corinthians 7:1–12, 11:7–9).

Many denominations and religious leaders today either reinterpret such teachings, or reject them altogether. There is some evidence that the role of women in Judaism and Christianity is changing, even if the process is a slow one (see Box 17.1).

RELIGION IN THE UNITED STATES

In comparison with other industrial nations, Americans are an unusually religious people. With few exceptions, "the United States has been the most God-believing and religion-adhering, fundamentalist, and religiously traditional country in Christendom [where] more new religions have been born . . . than any other country" (Lipset, 1991, p. 187). Even though secularization may have weakened the power of religious institutions in the United States, it has not thereby diminished the strength of religious beliefs.

According to public opinion polls, the overwhelming majority of Americans reportedly believe in God and claim they regularly pray (the majority daily). Seven out of ten Americans believe in an afterlife, and roughly two out of five report regular church atten-

dance (Roof and McKinney, 1987; Warner, 1993). Although there is a constitutional separation of church and state in the United States, American presidents all have attended church, and some—like Jimmy Carter (1976–1980), an acknowledged born-again Christian—have been deeply and publicly religious.

Roof's (1993) previously mentioned study of baby boomers, for example, found that even though two out of three dropped out of church or synagogue in their teens, for the most part they still remain *A Generation of Seekers* (the title of his book). Although less than a quarter have actively reaffiliated with a religious organization, three out of four claim to "definitely" believe in God, while one-third call themselves "born-again Christians." (For that matter, 70 percent also believe in "psychic powers.") Moreover, with many of the "boomers" raising families and approaching a mid-life reexamination, Roof believes they are turning back to religion for themselves and their children. Increasingly, however, religious experience is being sought outside of established religions, often in a highly personalized fashion.

Trends in Religious Affiliation

It is difficult to reliably estimate the number of people belonging to churches, since the U.S. government does not officially collect such data. Nonetheless, based on occasional government surveys, public opinion polls, and church records, sociologists of religion have concluded that church membership has grown steadily

Box 17.1

Silenced Voices

Women in Religion

In recent years there have been some efforts within Judaism and Protestantism to liberalize theological teachings in keeping with feminist thought. Women are also increasingly being ordained as clergy.

Within the Reform branch of Judaism, for example, out of a total of some 1,700 rabbis, approximately 200 are women. Women were officially allowed to become rabbis in 1972, and today nearly half of all newly ordained Reform rabbis each year are female. Almost all Protestant denominations now have female clergy, and the Episcopal Church ordained its first female bishop in 1989. Still, the number of women rabbis and ministers remains minuscule. The Catholic Church continues to officially regard the proper vocation of women as motherhood, and steadfastly opposes the ordination of women as priests, although some religious sister-

hoods have resisted this (Danzger, 1989; Davidman, 1991; Weaver, 1985; Higgins, 1985; Trible, 1979).

Recently, there has also been an upsurge of feminist spirituality, particularly within the United States. Some have turned to religious traditions that predate Judaism and Christianity, including the celebration of goddess-based religions. Others have sought reform within the mainstream religions, fighting for the rethinking of God as ungendered, calling for nonsexist language in scripture and services, and redesigning traditions and religious rituals along nonsexist lines. For example, Jesus has been found to have female disciples, while Jewish prayerbooks have been rewritten to reflect feminist principles (Christ and Plaskow, 1979; Starhawk, 1979; Weidman, 1984; Trible, 1979; Schussler Firoenza, 1983; Ehrenberg et al., 1983).

---

since the United States was founded. About one in six Americans were affiliated with a religious organization at the time of the Revolutionary War. That number had grown to about two in six at the time of the Civil War, three in six at the turn of the century, and four in six today (Finke and Stark, 1992).

One reason so many people belong to religious organizations is simply that there are an enormous number of such organizations one can belong to. The United States is the most religiously diverse country in the world, with more than 1,500 distinct religions (Melton, 1989); yet the vast majority of people belong to a relatively small number of religious faiths. About 58 percent of Americans identify themselves as Protestants, 25 percent as Catholics, 2 percent as Jews, and 1 percent as Muslims. Of the remainder, about half belong to a large variety of other religious groups, while half admit to having no religious preference at all (Roof and McKinney, 1987, p. 82).

A somewhat clearer picture of recent trends in American religion can be obtained if we break down the large Protestant category into major subgroups. Wade Clark Roof and William McKinney (1987) have analyzed some 17,000 interviews with a random sample of Americans obtained between 1972 and 1984.

They distinguished between several principal groupings of Protestant churches. *Liberal Protestants* include Episcopalians, Presbyterians, and the United Church of Christ (formerly Congregationalists). These were the churches that dominated early American history, and are part of the Protestant mainline, encompassing about 9 percent of all Americans. *Moderate Protestants* include those denominations that emerged in the nineteenth century and have a strong appeal to small-town and rural "middle America." The principal denominations are Methodists, Lutherans, Disciples of Christ, Northern Baptists, and the Reformed Churches, who together comprise about 24 percent of all Americans. *Conservative Protestants* include evangelical churches and sects that emphasize literal interpretation of the Bible, morality in daily life, and conversion through evangelizing. This category includes the Southern Baptist Convention, Churches of Christ, Church of the Nazarene, Assemblies of God, Seventh-Day Adventists, and numerous fundamentalists, Pentecostal, and holiness groups. Their members number about 16 percent of the American population. Finally, *Black Protestant* churches emerged among southern African Americans, where they provided an important source for the civil rights movement. Black leaders, including Martin Luther King and Jesse Jackson, emerged from this religious tradition. It primarily includes Black Methodist and Baptist churches, and comprises about 9 percent of the population.

As Figure 17.1 shows, the Catholic Church has shown by far the largest increase in membership, due in part to immigration of Catholics from Mexico, Central, and South America. Yet the growth in Catholic Church membership has also slowed in recent years, as some adherents have drifted away, either simply ceasing to identify as themselves Catholics or openly shifting to Protestantism.

Among Protestants, there has recently been an enormous growth in conservative Protestantism at the expense of the more liberal and moderate Protestant denominations. While all three groups showed a growth in membership from the 1920s through the 1960s, a major reversal has occurred since that time. Both liberal and moderate churches have experienced a decline in membership, while the number of conservative Protestants has exploded. The conservative denominations inspire deep loyalty and commitment, and they are highly effective in recruiting new members, particularly among young people. Today twice as many people belong to conservative Protestant groups as liberal

ones, and conservative Protestants may soon outnumber moderates as well (Roof and McKinney, 1987). Liberal Protestantism in particular has suffered. The aging members of liberal Protestant denominations have not been replaced by new young adherents, commitment is low, and some current members are switching to other faiths. Meanwhile, Black Protestant churches continue to thrive in the United States, as their members move into the middle class and achieve a degree of economic and political prominence (Roof and McKinney, 1987; Finke and Stark, 1992).

The number of Jews has declined in recent years, the result of low birth rates, intermarriage, and assimilation. Yet even assimilated Jews often identify themselves as Jewish, and in recent years there has been a resurgence of interest among some younger American Jews in rediscovering orthodox practices (Davidman, 1991; Danzger, 1989; Bamberger, 1992; Bernstein, 1951; Blech, 1991; Goldberg and Rayner, 1987; Eisen, 1983).

Among other denominations, it is possible that growing immigration from Asia could somewhat change the American religious profile; estimates of the number of Muslims in the United States run as high as three million, many originating in Asian countries (Haddad, 1979; Roof and McKinney, 1987; Finke and Stark, 1992).

Figure 17.1 Growth of Major Religious Groupings, 1926–1980

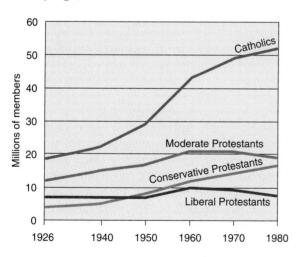

Although church affiliation has increased steadily throughout much of the twentieth century, among both liberal and moderate Protestant denominations the growth peaked around 1960 and has been declining ever since. Conservative Protestants have grown explosively, and today approach moderate Protestants in numbers. Catholics remain by far the largest religious group, their numbers fueled by immigrants from Catholic countries.
Source: Roof and McKinney (1987, Figure 7.1, p. 231).

Correlates of Religious Affiliation

There are substantial socioeconomic differences between the principal religious groupings in the United States. Among Protestants, as Table 17.1 indicates, *liberal Protestants* tend to be well-educated, somewhat upper income, and middle or upper class. They are over-represented in the northeastern states, and—to a lesser extent—in the west as well. Ethnically, they tend to be White Anglo-Saxon Protestants (WASPS), from English or German origins. *Moderate Protestants* are somewhat lower than liberal Protestants in terms of education, income, and social class; in fact, they are almost exactly typical of the national average on these measures. They tend to be disproportionately from the midwest, and, to some extent, from the west. They are from a variety of European ethnic backgrounds, including English, German, Scandinavian, Irish, and Dutch. *Black Protestants* are the least educated, poorest, and least middle class of any of the major religious groupings. Only 8 percent have graduated from college, only 15 percent report an income of more than $20,000, and fewer than one in three see themselves as middle class. *Conservative Protestants* have a similar profile, although they are marginally higher on all these measures. Like moderate Protestants, they include a di-

Table 17.1   Correlates of Religious Affiliation, mid-1970s

Grouping	College Graduate %	Income over $20,000 %	Middle Class/ Upper Class %	Region
Liberal Protestant	27	43	66	Northeast, West
Moderate Protestant	13	30	50	Midwest, West
Black Protestant	7	15	31	South
Conserative Protestant	8	22	37	South
Catholic	12	34	48	Northeast, West, Southwest
Jewish	38	50	80	Northeast
National average	14	30	47	—

Source: Roof and Mckinney (1987, Tables 4.2, 4.5).

verse profile of European ethnicities, although they include some African Americans as well.

Catholics strongly resemble moderate Protestants (which is to say the average American) in terms of their socioeconomic profile; they are largely concentrated in the Northeast, although they are over-represented in the west and southwest as well. Ethnically, the largest group is European in origin (primarily German, Italian, Slavic, and Irish, and to a lesser extent English and French), followed by Latinos from Mexico, Central, and South America.

Finally, *Jews* have the highest socioeconomic profile; nearly two in five have graduated from college, half reported an income over $20,000, and four out of five see themselves as middle class. Ethnically they are largely European in origin, particularly Slavic and German. They are overwhelmingly found in the northeastern states (Roof and McKinney, 1987).

What is most remarkable about these data is the striking relationship between the major religious groupings and socioeconomic status. Jews and liberal Protestants are the most heavily middle and upper class; moderate Protestants and Catholics are somewhat in the middle (although the growing number of poor Catholic Latino immigrants may be changing this); and conservative and Black Protestants are overwhelmingly lower class.

These groupings roughly correspond to social and political liberalism and conservatism as well. In terms of civil liberties (such as the right of atheists to speak in public or homosexuals to teach), racial justice (such as support for interracial marriage), women's rights (such as the right to have an abortion), Jews are by far the most tolerant. Liberal Protestants and Catholics are somewhat more tolerant than the average American, while moderate Protestants and Black Protestants are somewhat less tolerant. Conservative Protestants are the least tolerant of all religious groupings (Roof and McKinney, 1987).

Secularization or Religious Revival in America?

According to Phillip Hammond (1992), there have been three principal historical periods in the United States during which religion has undergone **disestablishment**—that is, *periods when the social and political influence of established religions has been successfully challenged.* The first such disestablishment occurred with the 1791 ratification of the first ten amendments to the U.S. Constitution (the Bill of Rights), which called for a firm separation of church and state. The second occurred between the 1890s and the 1920s, fed by an influx of some 17 million mainly European immigrants, many of whom were Catholic. For the first time, the notion of a predominantly Protestant America was challenged, and the mainstream Christian churches never regained their influence in politics or in defining national values. The third disestablishment occurred during the 1960s and the 1970s, when core religious beliefs and values were further eroded by the antiwar movement, the fight for racial equality, and experimentation with alternative lifestyles. Fundamental challenges came in such basic areas as sexuality, family authority, sexual and lifestyle preference, women's rights, and abortion (Roof and McKinney, 1978; Hammond, 1992; Wuthnow, 1976, 1978; Glock and Bellah, 1976; Hunter, 1987).

Yet despite this process of spiritual and political disestablishment, religious beliefs and affiliation appear to be as strong as ever. For one thing, beliefs have become increasingly privatized, as more and more people seek spiritual experiences outside of established religious organizations. As noted above, in his study of "baby boomers" Roof (1993) found that for many people religion had become a highly personal (rather than public) experience, leading him to conclude that almost all Americans are religiously oriented, although often outside of organized religion.

In their 1992 book on *The Churching of America*, Roger Finke and Rodney Stark argue that disestablishment is a normal process whereby mainstream groups become complacent, losing adherents to more competitively aggressive sects and cults that serve to replenish religious commitment. In fact, Finke and Stark question whether the third disestablishment occurred at all, noting that cult formation in the 1960s was only slightly higher than in the 1950s, while recent research suggests there are relatively minuscule numbers of people who belong to such groups as the Moonies (5,000 members), Hare Krishnas (3,000), Scientology (45,000), or other "new age" groups (20,000) (Melton, 1989; Kosmin, 1991). What has happened, most scholars agree, is that the most liberal, intellectualized, and inclusive religious denominations have lost members, while the most conservative, traditional, and exclusive ones have thrived.

The Resurgence of Evangelicalism

Evangelicalism refers to a *belief in spiritual rebirth (being "born again"), involving the admission of personal sin and salvation through Christ's acceptance;* *the literal interpretation of the Bible; an emphasis on highly emotional and personal spiritual piety; and a proselytizing commitment to spreading "the Word" to others* (Balmer, 1989). (*Evangel* comes from the Greek word for "bringing good news"; it originates in Martin Luther's rediscovery of the "good news" contained in the gospels of Matthew, Mark, Luke, and John.) Evangelicalism can be seen in part as a response to growing secularism, religious diversity, and in general the decline of once-core Protestant values in American life (Wuthnow, 1988). Between 1965 and 1985, membership in liberal Protestant denominations declined by nearly a fifth, yet membership in evangelical denominations grew by a third during this period (Hammond, 1986; Hunter, 1987). Enrollment in private evangelical schools nearly doubled between 1971–1978, to roughly 2.5 million students (Wuthnow, 1987). As of the mid-1980s, there were some 6,000 Christian bookstores, and some 1,200 members and affiliated stations of the evangelical National Association of Religious Broadcasters. In 1980, there were some 30,000 U.S. evangelical missionaries overseas (Hunter, 1987).

Evangelical organizations have been extremely effective in mobilizing resources to help achieve their re-

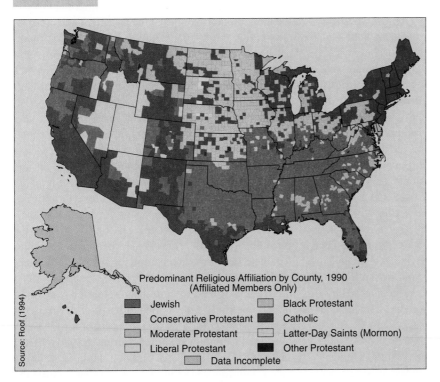

Map 17.2   **Religious Diversity in the U.S. by County, 1990**

Religious affiliation varies widely by region. Catholics are the most widespread, particularly in the northeast, west, and southwest (excepting the Mormon areas around Utah). Conservative Protestants are also widespread, especially in the east, southeast, and southcentral states. Jewish concentrations are found primarily in the larger metropolitan areas.

ligious and political objectives. In the business-like language used by the new religious economists, they have proved to be extremely competitive "spiritual entrepreneurs" in the "religious marketplace" (Hatch, 1989). Radio and television have provided one important new marketing technology for evangelicals to reach a much wider audience than was previously possible. Dubbed **televangelists** because *they conduct their evangelical ministries over television,* they depart from many earlier evangelicals in preaching a "gospel of prosperity"—the belief that God wants the faithful to be financially prosperous and satisfied, rather than to sacrifice and suffer (Hadden and Shupe, 1987). Luxurious temples, symbolized by Robert H. Schuller's "Crystal Cathedral" in Garden Grove, California, provide the televised settings for **electronic churches** whose *congregants are geographically dispersed and united primarily by means of electronic technology.* Theology and fund-raising are the staples of televangelism, which must support not only the television ministries themselves, but schools, universities, theme parks, and sometimes the lavish lifestyles of its preachers.

There is considerable debate over the number of people who watch such religious broadcasting. One of the most reliable studies, conducted in 1985 at the height of televangelism's popularity, estimated that the average quarter-hour audience for the top ten programs was about 8 million people. During a typical month, at least 34 million *different* American households tuned in at least once—about 40 percent of all households. Yet there is evidence that, at least for the moment, televangelism peaked in terms of viewership and profitability during the 1980s, and has declined somewhat since that time (Hadden and Swann, 1981; Hadden, 1990; Hadden and Shupe, 1987; Diekema, 1991).

Although some evangelicals combine a thoroughly modern lifestyle with traditional religious beliefs, others strongly reject many contemporary beliefs and practices. **Fundamentalists** are *evangelicals who are antimodern in many of their beliefs, calling for strict codes of morality and conduct, taboos against drinking, smoking, and other "worldly evils," biblical infallibility, and a strong belief in Christ's imminent return to earth* (Balmer, 1989). Their "old-time religion" clearly distinguishes good from evil, right from wrong, the sacred from the profane (Roof and McKinney, 1987).

Beginning with the reverend Jerry Falwell's "Moral Majority" in the 1970s, some groups of fundamentalists have become increasingly involved in what has been termed the "New Christian Right" in national politics, particularly in the conservative wing of the Republican Party (Kiecolt and Nelson, 1991; Simpson, 1985; Woodrum, 1988). Groups such as the Christian

Voice and the Religious Roundtable have advanced a political agenda that is compatible with fundamentalist beliefs. Antiabortion groups such as the Christian Action Council, Family America, and Prayers for Life were effective in getting the federal government to greatly restrict abortions between 1980 and 1992, despite public opinion polls showing that a majority of people favored a woman's right to choose. The National Federation for Decency and the Coalition for Better Television have fought for a more "Christian morality" in television programming (Hunter, 1987). Fundamentalist religious organizations helped to shape Republican Party policies and rhetoric during the Reagan and Bush administrations, contributing to its electoral success in three Presidential races during the 1980s, its defeat in 1992 (see Box 17.2) and its triumph in the 1994 midterm elections.

GLOBALIZATION AND RELIGION

Religion is one of the most truly global of all social institutions. As we have seen, nearly half of the world's population profess only two faiths, Christianity and Islam—religions that have bypassed national borders for more than a thousand years.

Religion has played a particularly important role in the global social changes of the past quarter century. In Vietnam in the 1960s, Buddhist priests burned themselves alive to protest the policies of the South Vietnamese government. Their willingness to sacrifice their lives for their beliefs, seen on television sets around the world, contributed to growing U.S. opposition to the war. During the 1970s and 1980s, a militant, activist form of Catholicism termed **liberation theology** combined *Catholic beliefs with a passion for social justice for the poor,* particularly in Central and South America and Africa (Berryman, 1987; Sigmund, 1990). Catholic priests and nuns organized farming cooperatives, built health clinics and schools, and challenged government policies that impoverished the peasantry. Many religious leaders paid with their lives for their activism, which government and military leaders often regarded as subversive.

In some of the East European satellite countries of the former Soviet Union, long-suppressed religious organizations provided an important basis for the overturning of Communist regimes during the early 1990s. In Poland, for example, the Catholic church was closely allied with the Solidarity Movement that toppled the Communist government in 1989. Yet as the socialist regimes have crumbled, religion has also all too often played a central role in reviving ancient ethnic and tribal hatreds. In the former Yugoslavia, to cite one ex-

Box 17.2

Critical Thinking

Winning Back the "Soul of America"

The following excerpt is taken from a May 1992 campaign speech by Patrick Buchanan, former speech writer for President Ronald Reagan and unsuccessful candidate for the 1992 Republican Party Presidential nomination. In this speech, Buchanan refers to what he characterizes as the "mob" involved in the 1992 Los Angeles riots, which engaged in looting and arson in lower-income parts of the city (see Chapter 7).

Buchanan's conservative call for a "culture war" against the "new barbarism" of those who threaten America's "Judeo-Christian truths and values" was seen by some commentators as reminiscent of Adolf Hitler's call for a "culture war" against Jews, Gypsies, homosexuals, and others whom Hitler believed threatened the German people's way of life. As you read Buchanan's commencement speech at Liberty University in Lynchburg, Virginia, ask yourself what assumptions are being made concerning the relationship between God, country, and national values. How can Buchanan's speech be seen as a reaction to secularization? What assumptions does it raise with regard to the separation of church and state, or religious pluralism in America?

But where did the mob come from?

Well, it came out of public schools from which God and the Ten Commandments and the Bible were long ago expelled. It came out of corner drug stores where pornography is everywhere on the magazine rack. It came out of movie theaters and away from TV sets where macho violence is romanticized. It came out of rock concerts where rap music celebrates raw lust and cop-killing. It came out of churches that long ago gave themselves up to social action, and it came out of families that never existed.

While we conservatives and traditionalists were fighting and winning the Cold War against Communism, we were losing the cultural war for the soul of America. And we can see our defeat in the smoking ruins of Los Angeles, in the laughter of the mob, in the moral absolution already being granted the lynchers and the looters. . . . Yet, relentlessly, for 30 years, the adversary culture, with its implacable hostility to Judeo-Christian teaching, has subverted [religion and morality].

The war for the soul of America will only be won with basic truths, and basic truths, Western civilization has discovered, are simple and straightforward. They are spelled out explicitly in the Old and New Testaments, and implicitly in our great literature and art. The challenge and duty facing this generation, who have the gift of an education rooted in Judeo-Christian truths and values, is to show your countrymen the way to recapture America's culture and our country—from the new barbarism. . . . so we must take back our cities, and take back our culture and take back our country.

God bless America.

Source: Los Angeles Times (1992)

ample, religious differences have helped to justify "ethnic cleansing," with Christian Serbs engaging in the mass murder and deportation of Muslims from communities and farmlands where they have lived for centuries.

Perhaps the most important trend in global religion today is the rise of **religious nationalism,** *the fusion of strongly held religious convictions with beliefs about a nation's social and political destiny.* In numerous countries around the world, religious nationalist movements have arisen that reject the notion that religion, government, and politics should be separate, calling in-

stead for a revival of traditional religious beliefs that are directly embodied in the nation and its leadership. These movements accept many aspects of modern life, including modern technology, politics, and economics. But they simultaneously emphasize strict interpretation of religious values, and completely reject the notion of secularization (Juergensmeyer, 1993).

The rise of religious nationalism is found throughout the world. In the Middle East, many Palestinian Muslims as well as orthodox Israeli Jews reject the notion of a secular democratic state, arguing—often violently—for a religious nation purged of nonbelievers.

Globalization, seen in the spread of religion, can also create an uneasy tension between modern society and more traditional religions. During the 1991 Persian Gulf War, Saudi Arabia sought to insulate its society from the presence of hundreds of thousands of American and European soldiers. Saudi Arabian soldiers are here seen kneeling in prayer outside their helicopters, prior to a combat mission.

Religious nationalism has triumphed in Iran (Box 17.3) and has made significant inroads in Egypt and Algeria. Hindus and Sikhs face off against one another in India, while religious revivals are found in Mongolia, central Asia, and in Eastern Europe. Some scholars believe this is being increasingly viewed as a "new Cold War," now that the old one between communism and capitalism has subsided—one that pits secular democratic nations

---

Box 17.3

Globalization

The Growth of Islamic Religious Nationalism

Islamic nationalism is one of the most visible examples of the religious nationalism that is today sweeping much of the world (Juergensmeyer, 1993). It seeks to combine strict Islamic religious observance with religious control over political institutions. Its appeal is partly a religious reaction to what many Muslims believe to be the corrupting influences of modern industrial society, including what is viewed as its excessive freedom of expression and political choice. Its appeal also reflects the experience many Muslim nations have had with centuries of control by outside nations, who are seen as having imposed alien and exploitive systems of governance in the name of capitalism or socialism. Islamic religious nationalism represents an effort by Muslims to find their own way in the modern world, drawing on their own religious values and political culture (Foran, 1993; Burke and Lapidus, 1988; Ghayasuddin, 1986; Dessouki, 1982; Juergensmeyer, 1993).

When a fundamentalist Islamic revolution under the Ayatollah Ruhollah Khomeini overthrew the corrupt, pro-American Shah of Iran in 1979, a wave of anti-American sentiment exploded in that country, which has since reverberated throughout the Muslim world. Although enormous public rallies condemning America as the "Great Satan" have quieted since Khomeini's death in 1989, Iran still calls for the global spread of traditional Islamic beliefs. With the collapse of the former Soviet Union, the appeal of Islamic nationalism has also spread to those former Soviet Republics containing large Muslim populations.

It remains to be seen whether religious nationalists will be able to live peaceably with their neighbors, or whether a "new Cold War" will emerge that pits the world's industrial democracies against religious nationalists both inside and outside their borders (Juergensmeyer, 1993).

against social movements for religious nationalism. This tension is fueled by global migrations and changing national boundaries, which often leave religious groups with strong nationalist ties to one country inside the borders of another.

Although religious nationalism is found among Christians, Jews, Muslims, Hindus, Sikhs, and numerous other religious groups, Islamic nationalism has received by far the most attention in the United States.

Islam will likely become the largest religion in the world sometime early in the next century. Within Islam, religious nationalists are often struggling against secular governments modeled after their European and American counterparts. What this might mean for global economics and politics is being hotly debated (Foran, 1993; Juergensmeyer, 1993; Burke and Lapidus, 1988; Esposito, 1987, 1990; Ghayasuddin, 1986; Dessouki, 1982; Keddie, 1983).

C H A P T E R   S U M M A R Y

1. **Religion** is both a cultural system consisting of shared beliefs, values, norms, and institutions, and an all-encompassing transcendental vision of reality that provides meaning and coherence to life.

2. The sociology of religion is not concerned with whether a particular religion is true or false, but with how it operates as an organization and its relationship to the larger society. Religions are viewed as arising from social relationships, and as providing a sense of social solidarity for adherents.

3. Sociologists have identified a number of different forms of religious organizations, depending on the degree of integration or harmony with the larger society. These include **churches, sects,** and **cults.**

4. The classical sociological view of religion sees religion as bound up with the larger society. In this view, religions are most likely to thrive if they are not in competition with other religions or **secular, (nonreligious) thinking.**

5. According to the classical view, religion in modern society is threatened by a long-term process of **secularization,** whereby the challenge of scientific thinking, as well as the side-by-side coexistence of numerous competing religions, inevitably lead to the demise of religion altogether.

6. The more recent **religious economy** approach draws the opposite conclusion: that competition among religious groups and the challenges of **secularization** force religions to work ever more diligently to win adherents, thereby strengthening the

various groups, and countering any trend towards secularization.

7. The two largest religions in the world today, Christianity and Islam, account for approximately half of the world population. Islam is the fastest-growing global religion in the world today.

8. Christianity, Islam, and Judaism are **monotheistic** religions with common origins in the Middle East. Hinduism, Buddhism, and Confucianism originated in Asia, and tend to consist more of ethical precepts and practices for living than worship of a single deity.

9. The United States is one of the most religious of all industrial nations. Although only about half of all Americans report regularly attending church, the large majority claim to believe in God and engage in regular prayer. Although church and state are legally separated in the U.S. Constitution, religious imagery and rituals pervade politics and civic life.

10. Mainline liberal and moderate religious groups in the United States have experienced declining memberships in recent years, while more conservative or **fundamentalist** groups have seen an increase.

11. Religion has always been one of the most global of all social institutions. One important development is the continuing growth of Islam as a world religion, which may have a significant impact on the emergence of global political and economic institutions.

QUESTIONS FOR DISCUSSION

1. Some sociologists have argued that secularization is inevitable—that religion is doomed in a modern, scientifically oriented industrial society. Others have claimed that the reverse is true—that religion addresses questions science cannot, and that competition between religious and other ideas results in stronger religious organizations. What is the evidence in support of each position? Which do you believe is correct, and why?

2. Is religion growing or declining in the United States today? Which religions are gaining adherents, and which are losing? How do sociologists explain these trends?

3. What are the principal trends in the globalization of religion today? What do you think these trends imply for the future of religion in the first years of the twenty-first century?

KEY TERMS

animism: The belief that naturally occurring phenomena such as animals or mountains are possessed of indwelling spirits or supernatural powers.

church: A religious organization that exists in a fairly harmonious, well-integrated relationship with the larger society.

civil religion: A set of religious beliefs through which societies interpret their own histories in light of some conception of ultimate reality.

cult: A religion that is unconventional with regard to the larger society.

denomination: A church that is not formally allied with the state.

disestablishment: Various periods in American history when the social and political influence of established religions has been successfully challenged.

ecclesia: A church that is formally allied with the state and is the "official" religion of the society.

electronic church: Churches in which the majority of congregants are geographically dispersed and are united primarily by means of electronic technology.

evangelicalism: A form of Protestantism characterized by a belief in spiritual rebirth (being "born again"), involving the admission of personal sin and salvation through Christ's acceptance; the literal interpretation of the Bible; an emphasis on highly emotional and personal spiritual piety; and a proselytizing commitment to spreading "the Word" to others.

fundamentalists: A group within evangelicalism that is highly antimodern in many of its beliefs, adhering to strict codes of morality and conduct, taboos against drinking, smoking, and other "worldly evils," biblical infallibility, and a strong belief in Christ's imminent return to earth.

liberation theology: A religious movement, centered primarily in Latin America, that combines Catholic beliefs, a passion for social justice for the poor, and actions aimed at achieving that passion.

monotheism: The belief in a single all-knowing, all-powerful god.

nontheistic religions: Religious based on a belief in the existence of divine spiritual forces rather than a god or gods.

polytheism: The belief that there are different gods representing various categories of natural forces.

profane: In Durkheim's view, the sphere of mundane, routine, everyday life.

religion: A cultural system of commonly shared beliefs and rituals that provide a sense of ultimate meaning and purpose, by creating an idea of reality that is sacred, all-encompassing, and supernatural.

religious economy: A theoretical framework, within the sociology of religion, which argues that religions can be fruitfully understood as organizations in competition with one another for adherents.

religious nationalism: The fusion of strongly held religious convictions with beliefs about a nation's social and political destiny.

sacred: In Durkheim's view, the sphere of life imbued with spiritual meaning.

Samsara: The belief, asssociated with Hinduism and Buddhism, that the soul is reincarnated (reborn) according to one's karma or actions on earth.

sect: A religious organization that exists in a high degree of tension with its environment.

secular thinking: Worldly thinking, particularly as seen in the rise of science, technology, and rational thought in general.

secularization: A rise in secular thinking and a simultaneous decline in the influence of religion, as seen in a weakening of the social and political power of religious organizations and typically accompanied by lessened religious beliefs and involvement.

tao The "way of being," according to the teachings of Taoism and Confucianism.

televangelism: Evangelical churches that conduct their ministries primarily over television.

theism: The belief in one or more supernatural deities or gods.

totem: Sacred objects believed to possess magical qualities connecting humans with the divine.

zionism: A movement calling for the return of Jews to Palestine and the creation of a Jewish state.

R E C O M M E N D E D   F O R   F U R T H E R   R E A D I N G

Finke, Roger, and Rodney Stark. (1992). *The Churching of America.* New Brunswick, N.J.: Rutgers University Press.

An examination of the growth of religious organizations in the United States, based on the religious economy perspective, which argues that religious affiliation is constantly replenished through the creation of new sects, cults, and other religious organizations.

Hammond, Phillip E. (1992). *Religion and Personal Autonomy: The Third Disestablishment in America.* Columbia: University of South Carolina Press.

A study of the impact of the social upheavals of the 1960s and 1970s on organized religion; focuses particularly on the survival of religion in an age that emphasizes personal freedom and choice.

Juergensmeyer, Mark. (1993). *The New Cold War? Religious Nationalism Confronts the Secular State.* Berkeley: University of California Press

This important recent study examines the rise of religious nationalism around the world, arguing that such movements are coming to be regarded as engaging in a new "Cold War" against the secular states that they challenge.

Roof, Wade Clark, and William McKinney. (1987). *American Mainline Religion: Its Changing Shape and Future.* New Brunswick, N.J.: Rutgers University Press.

A detailed empirical study of changes in American religious affiliation; looks at trends in the major religious denominations and sects.

Weber, Max. (1958; orig. 1904–1905). *The Protestant Ethic and the Spirit of Capitalism.* New York: Scribners.

One of the most important classical studies in the sociology of religion. Weber argues that capitalism arose in Europe because of the prevalence of Protestant values that emphasized glorifying God through thrift, hard work, austere living, and reinvestment (rather than consumption) of wealth.

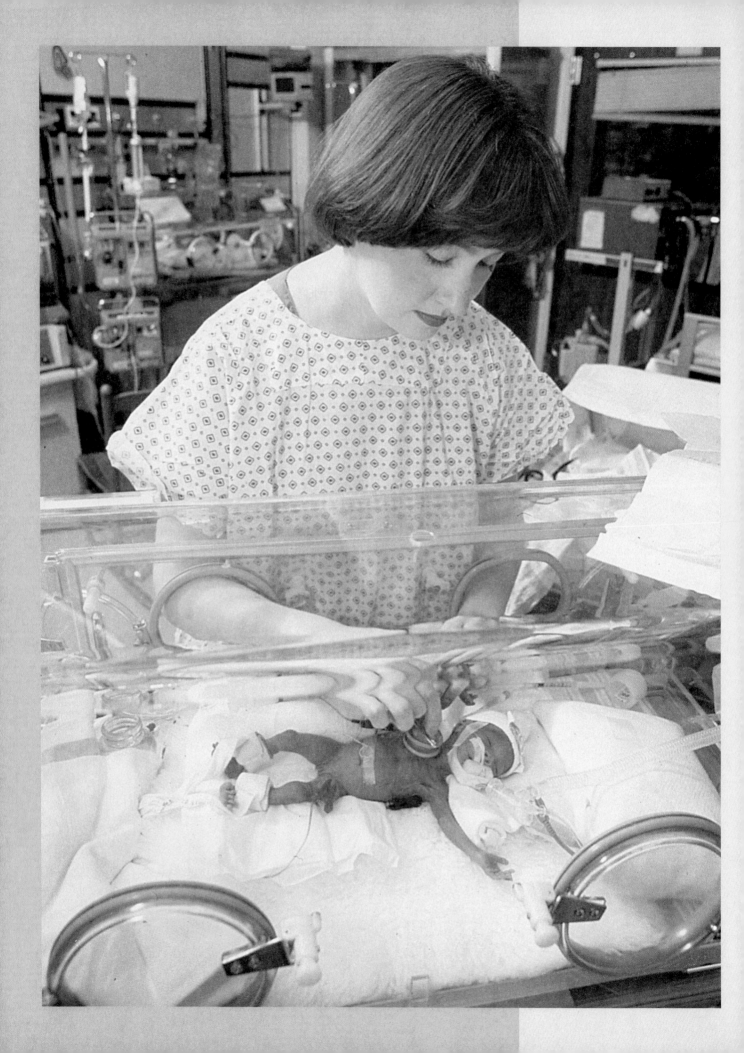

CHAPTER

18

Medicine and Health

CHAPTER OUTLINE

THINGS TO LOOK FOR

1. Why is the American health-care system one of the most costly in the world, yet unable to provide adequate and affordable health care to all Americans?
2. How has modern medicine evolved into its present form, and how else might it have been organized?
3. In what ways does the social organization of medicine reflect the social organization of society in general?
4. How can sociology help us to better understand something as seemingly technical as modern medicine?
5. Why is AIDS a global problem, and how can it be addressed with global solutions?

INTRODUCTION: SOCIOLOGY, HEALTH, AND MEDICINE

It is tempting to think of health and medicine in purely scientific or technical terms. If Acquired Immunodeficiency Syndrome (AIDS) has claimed more than 243,400 lives in the United States since it was first identified 15 years ago, or if 17 million people world-wide are infected with the HIV virus that causes AIDS (Cimons, 1992a; Maugh, 1994), surely it is up to biologists to discover a cure, while modern medicine is responsible for prolonging the lives of AIDS patients. Shouldn't we assume that AIDS is fundamentally a medical problem, the proper domain of medical researchers, doctors, nurses, and others trained in biology or the medical profession?

At one time people answered "yes" to such questions, and sociology and medicine went their separate ways. In the last half century, however, this situation has changed dramatically (Weiss and Lonquist, 1994; Coe, 1970). Today, it is widely accepted that sociology has a great deal to say not only about the causes of disease and illness but about their cure as well. Who suffers and who gets well, who is treated and who is not, how medicine and health care are organized as social institutions—all of these questions have made the sociology of medicine a timely field of study.

The Importance of Sociology for Medicine

At the beginning of the twentieth century, most doctors saw medicine and sociology as separate disciplines with little to offer one another (Coe, 1970; Weiss and Lonquist, 1994). A number of changes in the nature of disease and illness changed this, however. In the nineteenth century people died mainly from infectious diseases, while in the twentieth century they are living longer and are more likely to be chronically ill before dying. This has raised many nonmedical questions about the quality of life, the cost of keeping people alive, and who should be eligible for the most advanced medical technology. In addition, preventive medicine and public health services emerged as central features of medicine, requiring sociological understanding as much as medical knowledge.

As doctors began working together in clinics, and as hospitals grew in size and complexity, it became increasingly apparent that social scientists had important contributions to make to the practice of medicine. As medical practice became institutionalized in large, bureaucratic organizations, the growing body of sociological research into the dynamics of social interaction and organizational structure became increasingly important. Today most medical schools have sociologists on their staffs, and the sociology of medicine is one of the more active research areas in the discipline (Weiss and Lonquist, 1994; Mechanic, 1990).

Health and Medicine: A Basic Distinction

Although health and medicine are closely interrelated, sociologists have found it useful to distinguish between them. **Health** can be defined as *a state of mental, physical, and social well-being.* It involves not merely the absence of illness, but, more importantly, a positive sense of soundness as well. This definition, put forth by the World Health Organization, draws attention to the interplay of psychological, physiological, and sociological factors in a person's sense of well-being. While perfect health may prove to be an elusive goal for most people, this definition makes clear that such a standard cannot be achieved in purely physical terms. Health cannot be attained if the body is disease-free but the mind is troubled or the social environment is harmful.

Medicine can be defined as *an institutionalized system for the scientific diagnosis, treatment, and prevention of disease, illness, and other damage to the mind or the body.* It is concerned with the physiological and psychological conditions that prevent a person from achieving a healthful state. Medicine typically relies on the application of scientific knowledge, derived from physical sciences such as chemistry, biology, and physics, as well as psychology. As it has historically developed in the United States, medicine is usually viewed in terms of the failure of health: When people become ill, they seek medical advice to correct the problem. Yet, as the above definition suggests,

Health involves more than the absence of illness; it entails a complete state of well-being. During the past quarter century, Americans have become increasingly aware of the importance that environmental conditions can play in both illness and health. This once-pristine river is now contaminated by dioxin, a deadly industrial poison.

medicine and health can go hand in hand. The field of **preventive medicine**—*medicine that emphasizes a healthy lifstyle to prevent poor health before it actually occurs*—has been of growing interest in recent years.

CULTURAL DEFINITIONS OF HEALTH AND ILLNESS

What people view as sickness and health is greatly influenced by their cultural definitions. There are "sick roles" in every society, and to a large degree these are sociologically determined. According to Talcott Parsons's role theory of sickness in modern society, when someone is labeled as "sick" they are expected to behave in certain culturally appropriate ways and to receive culturally appropriate responses from others (Parsons, 1951, 1975; Meile, 1986; Myers and Grasmick, 1990). Parsons drew the following conclusions regarding the social construction of illness:

• Being healthy is a value in modern society; being ill is to be avoided.
• The role of "sick person" includes the right to be excused from social responsibilities and other normal social roles, as well as responsibility for the illness itself. Yet the role of "sick person" also includes a normative obligation to seek to get well, and to seek competent medical help in order to do so. Failure to do so can lead to a refusal of others to fulfill their own role obligations—that is, a refusal to treat the person as if he or she is truly sick.
• The norms of modern society include the idea that everyone has a right to medical care if they are sick.

Parsons's model helps us to understand sickness and health in modern society, for it underscores the fact that the "sick role" is to a large extent sociologically deter-

mined. Think, for example, of the difference in the culturally accepted response to someone who has cancer compared to the reaction to someone who is an alcoholic. The person with cancer expects to be treated with sympathy, patience, and understanding. He or she expects to be forgiven for days missed at work, for spending an inordinate amount of time in bed, or for asking others for special consideration and assistance. All of these and a host of other expectations and responses are contained in the role of "sick person." A person with a drinking problem, on the other hand, is not likely to be granted such a role.

The Social Construction of Illness

Some illnesses are culturally defined as legitimate, entitling those who contract them to adopt the role of "sick person." There is consensus that people who are ill with cancer, tuberculosis, leukemia, or heart disease are exempt from the role expectations of "normal" people. They are not expected to work, attend class, or engage in strenuous physical activity. Indeed, a chronically ill person who persists in leading a "normal" life is given considerable credit for an extraordinary exertion of effort.

Drug and Alcohol Use

Yet often there is considerable ambiguity in the social definition of an illness, and a corresponding definition in the role expectations that are associated with it. People who drink or use drugs may exhibit such obvious symptoms of illness as acute unsteadiness or incoherence, yet they are generally not clearly labeled as "sick." Rather, they are likely to be called such things as "alcoholics," "drug addicts," or "substance abusers," all of which imply that they are at least partly to blame

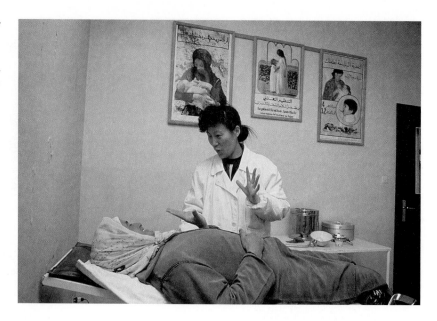

Preventive medicine can play an important role in maintaining individual health while lowering medical costs. During pregnancy, for example, women have often found it prudent to get periodic medical examinations, as shown by this Moroccan woman seeking advice from her doctor.

for their illness. Even though alcoholism and drug addiction are now often labeled as illnesses, those who have them are socially blamed in a way that cancer victims are not. Since they have presumably chosen to make themselves sick by engaging in behavior that results in social disapproval, they are not entitled to the more favorable social roles enjoyed by the person with cancer—even though the cancer may have been brought on by smoking (Langton, 1991; Schaler, 1991).

People addicted to cocaine or heroin are less likely to be considered sick and more likely to be blamed for their addiction than people addicted to alcohol, although there is no medical reason for this difference in social reaction. The legal response to drug use reflects this contradiction: People are placed in rehabilitation programs for drug addiction and in prison for drug possession. The first response reflects a social definition of drug addiction as an illness, entitling the person to a "sick role"; the second reflects a social definition of drug possession as a crime, assigning to the person a criminal role.

Chronic Fatigue Syndrome (CFS)

Social definitions of illness are often strongly contested, since such definitions are an important determinant of society's response to the illness. Someone who constantly complains of headaches, nausea or being tired but who is not diagnosed as having an illness will very likely be criticized and labeled "hypochondriac" rather than "sick." One example is **chronic fatigue syndrome (CFS),** *a persistent flu-like illness that can last for years or even decades.* CFS brings with it debilitating fatigue, difficulty in thinking, forgetfulness and irritability, sore throat and low-grade fever, and sometimes vision loss (Homes et al., 1988).

Yet is has proved extremely difficult for scientists

to pinpoint an organic source for the disease (Kruesi et al., 1989; Straus et al., 1985; Straus, 1987, 1988a, 1988b). This has prevented it from being labeled an illness, making it difficult for those who are afflicted to claim the full benefits associated with the "sick role." Because many CFS patients are middle-class women who are extremely depressed because of their illness, it was originally dismissed as the "Yuppie Flu," a minor psychological problem rather than a "serious" physical ailment (Goldstein, 1989; Kiken, 1992).

The name of an illness is an important part of the label attached to it. In the case of Chronic Fatigue Syndrome, public opinion polls and other research conducted by advocates for CFS patients found that the name "chronic fatigue" tended to trivialize the disease, leading the public to dismiss its importance (Iverson and Freese, 1990). As a result of research into the causes of the illness, as well as extensive lobbying efforts, the disease is now officially called Chronic Fatigue Immunodeficiency Syndrome (CFIDS), a label that does not equate the illness exclusively with being tired but rather links it with more generalized deficiencies in the body's immune system. This relabeling, which shares with AIDS the phrase "immunodeficiency syndrome," has coincided with greater government funding for CFS research.

Acquired Immunodeficiency Syndrome (AIDS)

The case of AIDS offers another constructive example in the sociological construction of illness (see Box 18.3). Some 402,000 Americans have suffered from AIDS, while perhaps a million are HIV positive, carrying the infection that will eventually lead to the disease (Cimons, 1992a; Maugh, 1994). Los Angeles

County is typical of major metropolitan areas in the United States: It is estimated that 1 out of every 2,000 people has AIDS, while 1 out of every 200 is infected with the virus that causes it (*Los Angeles Times,* 1992).

When the disease was first diagnosed in the United States in the early 1980s, it was widely believed to be the result of male homosexual practices and therefore confined to the gay population. Given the conservative political temper of the times, it was initially dismissed as a "gay disease," viewed by some as the deserved result of a morally reprehensible lifestyle. It took many years of activism on the part of the homosexual community before AIDS-related illnesses received governmental recognition and some degree of public acceptance.

One important social factor in the growing public acceptance of AIDS was the eventual medical realization that it was not a "gay disease" at all but could be transmitted in a variety of ways, including sexual contact between men and women, transfusion of HIV-positive blood, and the shared use of contaminated needles (Fee and Fox, 1988; Shilts, 1987). The spread of AIDS to the heterosexual population, which claimed the life of former tennis champion Arthur Ashe and infected basketball superstar Magic Johnson, all helped to enable its victims to legitimately claim the "sick role" rather than be thought of as deviants who were somehow being punished for violating society's norms and values.

As AIDS spread among heterosexuals, a growing number of women also contracted the disease. This created a major problem for the official definition of AIDS. In order to become eligible for such things as federally funded treatment, medications, and experimental vaccine trials, women who were infected had to show symptoms of illnesses that were officially recognized as AIDS-related. Since the federal guidelines had been based on men with AIDS, they did not include such uniquely female immunodeficiency illnesses as vaginal yeast infections or cervical cancer. As had previously occurred with AIDS in homosexual males, as well as with chronic fatigue syndrome, the official definition of the disease was altered only after political pressures were brought to bear on public health officials and government agencies (Filice and Pomeroy, 1991).

Mental Illness

Mental illness also illustrates the importance of the social construction of illness. In 1950 there were more than a half million mental patients living in approximately 300 state and county mental hospitals throughout the United States. These unfortunate people were generally regarded as hopelessly ill, consigned to spend their entire lives as virtual prisoners in large, impersonal, depressing facilities, heavily sedated and effectively cut off from the rest of the world. During the following decade, however, a major rethinking of the meaning of "mental illness" occurred. Some scholars argued that it was inhumane to warehouse people with mental illnesses in mental asylums, particularly those who could function adequately in the community with proper medical supervision and assistance. The development of new promising drugs for the treatment of many mental illnesses reinforced this position.

The result was a virtual rethinking of the meaning of mental illness, with a much less sharpened distinction between illness and normalcy (Scheff, 1969;

HIV-AIDS, which today afflicts as many as a million Americans and 17 million people worldwide, is a fast-growing, worldwide epidemic. At the present time there is no known cure for full-blown AIDS, which so weakens the body's immune system that death eventually results from a variety of diseases and infections. This person with AIDS (PWA) is shown in a San Francisco hospice, a home for people who are dying.

One activist organization seeking increased support for AIDS research and awareness is ACT-UP, whose tactics are often intended to shock people into action. This photo shows ACT-UP members leading a demonstration held during the 1992 Democratic presidential primary in New Hampshire.

Szasz, 1970). This movement to redefine the label culminated in 1963 legislation calling for the "deinstitutionalization" of many mental patients from state and county asylums, and their eventual relocation to small-scale community-based care facilities, such as "halfway houses" that would in theory enable them to lead seminormal lives (Mechanic and Rochefort, 1990; Mechanic, 1990). Within a decade, the number of patients living in state and county asylums had dropped dramatically, and today it is only about a fifth the number of 30 years ago (Mechanic and Rochefort, 1990).

The deinstitutionalization movement met with mixed results. Although some very successful community-based facilities were established, in many instances the necessary funding was not available. Furthermore, local residents often opposed the siting of community-based facilities in their neighborhoods, fearing that the residents might somehow prove to be dangerous.

Once again this illustrates the importance of the social construction of illness: Even though many psychologists and medical sociologists had changed their thinking about the nature of mental illness, most local residents and governmental officials had not. Today, some researchers attribute the upsurge in homelessness at least in part to deinstitutionalization, since many mentally ill people have no place to go except for streets and jails (Box 18.1). Although the impact of deinstitutionalization is often exaggerated, there is no question but that there are far more homeless mentally ill people than ever before, a fact that has led America's streets to be characterized as "open asylums" (Torrey, 1988; Bachrach, 1983; Brown, 1985; Jacob-

son et al., 1992; Dear and Wolch, 1987; Lamb, 1984; Johnson, 1990; Prior, 1993; Test, 1979).

The Doctor-Patient Relationship

One aspect of the social construction of illness is found in the doctor-patient relationship. In modern society, the doctor has assumed the role of authority in all matters related to health and medicine. This may seem fully understandable. Since doctors ideally possess the training and technical expertise to make the difference between life and death, it is not surprising that they are often treated by their patients with great respect.

Talcott Parsons (1951) viewed the unequal power between doctor and patient as functional for proper health care. Parsons argued that it is necessary for physicians to have authority over their patients because the doctors have the knowledge and necessary expertise, while the patients do not. The patient, for example, may intentionally or unintentionally misrepresent the illness, and the doctor must be in a position to control such a problem. On the other hand, the unequal relationship of authority between doctor and patient may enable the doctor to abuse his or her power. Moreover, some types of illness may respond better to this traditional authority system than others (Haug and Levin, 1981, 1983).

Most Americans ultimately defer to medical authority when it comes to matters of the body. Nor is this deference limited to acute illnesses. In the United States, childbirth—clearly one of the most basic of all human female biological functions—is almost always done under the watchful eye of a doctor in a hospital. (This is not true in many other industrial societies, in-

RECOMMENDED FOR FURTHER READING

Foucault, Michel. (1988). *Madness and Civilization: A History of Insanity in the Age of Reason.* New York: Vintage Books.

A difficult but highly influential study of the changing meaning of mental illness in modern society; focuses on the ways in which a scientific society grapples with the irrational.

Navarro, Vicente. (1992). *Why the United States Does Not Have a National Health Program.* New York: Baywood Publishing.

A collection of essays by well-known sociologists of medicine; explores the paradox that the United States is one of the few major industrialized nations in the world that does not provide health care for all of its citizens.

Shilts, Randy. (1987). *And the Band Played on: Politics, People, and the AIDS Epidemic.* New York: St. Martin's.

An important book about the early history of the AIDS epidemic in the gay community, showing how medical science, policy makers, and members of the community alike refused to acknowledge the seriousness of the illness until it had reached epidemic proportions.

Starr, Paul. (1982). *The Social Transformation of Medicine: The Rise of a Sovereign Profession and the Making of a Vast Industry.* New York: Basic Books.

An examination of the institutionalization of organized medicine and its emergence as an authoritative profession dominated by doctors and medical scientists.

Torrey, E. Fuller. (1988). *Nowhere to Go: The Tragic Odyssey of the Homeless Mentally Ill.* New York: Harper & Row.

A study of the explosion in the number of homeless mentally ill people who live on the streets and in homeless shelters, seen as victims of deinstitutionalization and the failure of society to provide alternative forms of treatment and shelter.

West, Candace. (1984). *Routine Complications: Troubles with Talk Between Doctors and Patients.* Bloomington: Indiana University Press.

A conversation analysis approach to understanding the verbal interactions between doctors and their patients; shows how the authoritative and often gendered relationship is reproduced and reinforced in language.

The Mass Media in Contemporary Society

CHAPTER OUTLINE

THINGS TO LOOK FOR

1. What is the impact of the mass media on their audiences?
2. To what extent is it possible for news to be "objective?"
3. In what ways does the news help to create reality for its audiences?
4. What relationship exists between the media and racial, ethnic, and gender stereotypes?
5. How do the mass media contribute to the globalization of politics and culture?

INTRODUCTION: HOOKED ON TELEVISION

During the 1991 Persian Gulf War, Americans were exposed to round-the-clock war news, which had all the riveting qualities of a made-for-TV movie: the massive military might of the United States; the media-cultivated personification of evil in Iraqi President Saddam Hussein; the latest high-tech weaponry. From a media standpoint, the war was unprecedented. Americans were exposed to live coverage of the war, from daily military briefing sessions to camera-equipped precision-guided missiles that carried the viewer, video-game style, into the target itself. While much of the official information was controlled by the government, numerous experts dissected, analyzed, and debated what was happening—all on prime time.

Did this intensive coverage leave Americans better informed about the causes and nature of the Persian Gulf War? The Center for Studies in Communication conducted a telephone survey with 250 randomly selected people in Denver, Colorado, during the height of the conflict (Jhally et al., 1991). This study found that while most of the people surveyed supported the war and could correctly identify such weaponry as the Iraqi "SCUD" and U.S. "Patriot" missiles, they had virtually no understanding about the actual events that led up to the war, or, for that matter, about Middle Eastern politics in general. The researchers concluded that the media, particularly television, had failed as "information providers." This was seen as a crucial shortcoming, since the less people knew the more they were likely to unquestioningly support the war.

News and information, as well as entertainment, are conveyed largely by means of **mass media,** *forms of communication that permit a one-way flow of information from a single source to a large audience.* Ninety-eight percent of all U.S. households have at least one television set, and many have more than one. Most Americans under 30 were raised on television, beginning with weekend cartoon marathons as young children, and culminating with hours of MTV or Video Soul as teenagers. American children under 11 average 28 hours a week watching television; teenagers average 23. Rates are even higher among blacks, Latinos, and the poor. Many adults spend hours watching television as well, whether it be soap operas or "sitcoms," sports or reenactments of shocking crimes, 24-hour news or 24-hour coverage of Congress (Donnerstein et al., 1993; Huston et al., 1992; Tangney and Feshbach, 1988; Tracy, 1990).

Why should a society that watches so much television be largely uninformed about the circumstances leading to the mobilization of a half million U.S. troops and the death of tens of thousands of people? In this chapter we shall seek to better understand the role played by the media in shaping people's perceptions about the world in which they live.

THE IMPORTANCE OF MASS MEDIA IN MODERN SOCIETY

We live today in what has been characterized as a **mass-mediated culture,** *a culture in which the mass media play a key role in both shaping and creating cultural perceptions* (Real, 1977). The mass media do not simply mirror society. They help to create the very world they purport to cover.

Communication is fundamental to human society. Long before people possessed even the most rudimentary forms of writing, they used words as symbols to represent ideas, feelings, and objects. But a culture based solely on the spoken word cannot easily extend its thoughts beyond its immediate world. Purely oral forms of communication require face-to-face contact, and the information that is passed from one person to another depends on fallible memory. The advent of writing, printing, and, in the fifteenth century, the movable-type printing press, greatly extended the ability of people to communicate with one another over ever-larger expanses of time and space.

As a result of these developments mass media eventually emerged and led to the creation of a **mass audience,** *a large collection of people who receive messages that are directed at them not as individuals but rather as a group.* Newspapers, magazines, photojournalism, radio, television, and film are all examples. The most important feature of the mass media is its one-directional flow, which gives the organization producing the media a great deal of potential influence over those who are viewing it. This is not only true for news and information but for entertainment as well.

Politics and warfare provide useful examples of this process. Television has played an important role in American politics since the 1960 presidential campaign, when 70 million viewers watched Senator John Kennedy debate Vice President Richard Nixon. Kennedy's narrow margin of victory was partly attributed to his more favorable television presence. Television viewers judged Kennedy to be more presidential, not necessarily because he had a clear edge in debating skills but rather because of his appearance: Kennedy's dark suit stood out regally against the lighter studio background, while Nixon's unfortunate "four o'clock shadow," which no amount of shaving or makeup ever seemed to erase, gave him a somewhat unkempt and haggard appearance. Today, almost all politicians "play to the camera," tailoring their pronouncements to what their advisors tell them will garner the most favorable attention on the six o'clock news.

Television's coverage of the Vietnam War, vividly seen on the growing number of color television sets in American homes during the late 1960s, helped to undermine public support for the war. Politicians and military planners have since been reluctant to engage U.S. troops in military actions, unless the engagement is limited, victory is ensured, and the media can be tightly controlled (as they were in the Persian Gulf War).

THE IMPACT OF MASS MEDIA

Radio and television penetrate into every home, bringing a bewildering variety of news and information from everywhere on earth to virtually every household in the United States. Sociologists have advanced a number of different theories to explain the impact of such media saturation on our daily lives. They vary between those viewing media as an all-powerful influence on just about everything people think and do, and those viewing media as simply reinforcing what people already choose to believe. We shall focus on the three principal theoretical frameworks that have emerged since World war II: (1) the limited-effects theory, (2) the class-dominant theory, and (3) the culturalist theory.

As its name suggests, the **limited-effects theory** of the 1940s and 1950s sought to demonstrate that *the media have minimal impact on people's attitudes and perceptions, since audiences are said to be highly selective in what they watch, perceive, and recall.* At the other extreme, the **class-dominant theory** of the 1960s and the 1970s questioned such claims, arguing that *society is dominated by a relatively small, powerful elite, whose viewpoint the media overwhelmingly tend to reflect.* Finally, **culturalist theory,** which originated in Great Britain in the 1970s but has impacted American sociology only in the last decade, embraces aspects of the other two media theories. It argues that *people play an active role in creating their own cultural meanings out of what they receive from the media.*

Limited-Effects Theory

Limited-effects theory argued that while the media may exert some influence under certain conditions, they are far from all-powerful. This theory arose as a response to a fear that in modern society, the media would become an all-powerful tool of business and government—a fear fueled in part by Hitler's highly effective use of the mass media to mobilize the German people.

In modern society, the mass media play an important role in shaping cultural perceptions. The entry of U.S. soldiers into Somalia was part of a well-publicized United Nations mission to restore peace to the famine-plagued, war-torn country. Their carefully staged arrival was met not by the anticipated armed opposition but by a phalanx of photographers and television cameras broadcasting images to the world.

Such fears reflected the belief that people were increasingly becoming part of a **mass society,** *one whose members are rootless, isolated, and lacking in strong social ties, and are thus defenseless against various forms of manipulation* (by the mass media in particular) (Kornhauser, 1968; Curran et al., 1982).

After World War II, a great deal of empirical research was devoted to testing these ideas (Merton, 1946; Berelson et al., 1954; Lazarsfeld et al., 1968; Katz and Lazarsfeld 1955; Trenaman and McQuail, 1961; Klapper, 1960; Feshbach and Singer, 1971; Gerbner and Gross, 1980). Drawing on the techniques and theories of group psychology, researchers conducted a variety of small-group studies to see if people who were exposed to specific media information were likely to change their views or actions as a result. These studies found that the ability of the media to influence opinions on such things as voting behavior was severely limited. In fact, according to this research, the media are most effective when they reinforce what people already know or believe to be true. For example, the studies found that when people are interested and generally well-informed about an issue, have strong prior personal opinions, or have direct personal sources of information that are generally in agreement with one another, they are unlikely to be swayed by what the media have to say. On the other hand, under circumstances where people are ill-informed and besieged with conflicting views, the media can help sway their opinion by providing them with "expert" information.

Critical Assessment While limited-effects theorists focused on whether or not the media can change people's minds, they ignored the powerful role of the media in helping to frame the nature of debate and discussion. This in turn influences the conclusions that viewers are likely to draw. While effects in the short-term may be limited, in the longer term the media can play an important role in shaping people's perceptions of reality. What can and cannot be talked about, whether candidates are limited to brief "soundbites" or are subjected to rigorous questioning and debate, the importance of a candidate's physical appearance—such features of media coverage can prove decisive in shaping public opinion.

For example, during the 1972 presidential debate between then-President Gerald Ford and challenger Jimmy Carter, Ford mistakenly stated that Poland was not dominated by the Soviet Union. This seemingly innocent error, while upsetting to Polish-American voters who wanted Poland liberated from Soviet control, went largely unnoticed by the general public: Polls taken a couple of hours after the debate showed Ford victorious by a 44 to 35 percent margin. Yet within 24 hours, once the news media had drawn attention to Ford's error in a way that reinforced the existing perception that he lacked intelligence, the public switched its view: now Carter was seen as the winner 61 to 19 percent (Schudson, 1992).

Furthermore, even though limited-effects theorists conceded that the media can play an important role when people are undecided on an issue, they tended to underestimate the important political role played by those who are undecided. Yet on many issues and candidates, many people do not make up their minds until it comes time to vote. The media's importance in swaying them one way or the other is indicated by the vast sums of money poured into television during the final days of a campaign (Fiske, 1987; Gitlin, 1980, 1983; Curran et al., 1982).

Class-Dominant Theory

Class-dominant theory views the media as a "kind of megaphone" that serves to amplify the ideas of society's ruling elites (Connell, 1980). According to this view, the media are increasingly controlled by a handful of large, powerful media conglomerates, resulting in a sharp decline in competition. Theorists point to the fact that during a brief seven-year period (1983–1990), the number of major media corporations declined by half (from 46 to 23). This leads class-dominant theorists to conclude that there has been a sharp increase in

"Since you have already been convicted by the media, I imagine we can wrap this up pretty quickly."

Although limited effects theorists claimed that the media have minimal affect in molding people's opinions, most scholars today would question that conclusion. This political cartoon makes the point that people accused of crimes are often "convicted" in the mass media (and consequently in public opinion), long before they can get a fair hearing in a court of law. Drawing by Richter; © 1991 The New Yorker Magazine Inc.

the dominance of global media monopolies, a handful of transnational corporations that own television satellites and stations, movie studios and theaters, newspapers, and publishing houses. This concentration of media ownership suggests the possibility that a handful of firms will effectively control what people around the world are able to read and view (Bagdikian, 1990; Gamson et al., 1992).

To use motion pictures as an example, in 1987 Paramount Pictures was owned by Gulf and Western, which had controlling interest in hundreds of movie theatres, the USA Network, and Madison Square Garden (including the New York Knicks). Coca-Cola owned Columbia Pictures (which it had merged with Tri-Star Pictures), while Turner Broadcasting System acquired MGM and United Artists (Jowett and Linton, 1990). Because of such interlocking ownership and control, whatever differences might separate individual media companies are viewed as minor in comparison with their agreements. As a consequence, the mass media are viewed as unlikely to go far toward questioning the status quo, challenging the opinions of their owners or their sponsors, or questioning fundamental economic or political values.

Class-dominant theorists argue that from their very beginnings, newspapers, radio, and television were dominated by commercial concerns that shaped their coverage and impaired their ability to be impartial. Even the doctrine of objectivity in the news is attributed in part to the media's recognition that unbiased, professional coverage would enhance their appeal to middle-class audiences (Schudson, 1978, 1990). Inasmuch as advertising is their major source of revenue, the mass media seek to appeal to as large an audience (with as much purchasing power) as possible. In general, the bigger the audience, the more sponsors are willing to pay for a spot (Gamson et al., 1992). For example, a 30-second ad on the 1994 Super Bowl, which was viewed by an estimated 80 million people, cost $850,000, or $28,000 a second—enough, in the view of class-dominant theorists, to provide advertisers with considerable clout.

Class-dominant theorists view this clout with concern, since it suggests that sponsors are likely to exert control over broadcasting. Programs that lack widespread appeal, that are controversial, or that otherwise might detract from a "buying mood" are likely to be shunned (Gamson et al., 1992; Herman and Chomsky, 1988). Similarly, the corporations that own the mass media are likely to avoid any programming that might prove personally embarrassing or raise general questions about corporate responsibility. For example, when NBC's *Today* show ran a segment on consumer boycotts in 1990, it focused on boycotts against

While class-dominant theorists portray the media as under the control of a handful of elite corporations, coverage does not necessarily reflect only the interests of the wealthy and powerful. This man helps to feed and house himself by selling Street News, *a newspaper published by homeless and formerly homeless people. The publication carries news, information, and analysis relevant to the plight and political struggles of the homeless.*

Philip Morris, Nike, Hormel, and other large corporations—but made no mention of General Electric, the company that owns NBC. The *Today* show's producers had little difficulty in declining to do a segment on what was at the time the largest consumer boycott in the country (Gamson et al., 1992).

Finally, class-dominant theorists argue that modern media technology itself encourages concentration of power. Cable television, used by some 50 million U.S. households, is typically monopolized by a single company in each community. Furthermore, a third of the nearly 8,700 local cable companies are owned by only two giant cable corporations. Thus, although cable has permitted an explosive growth in competing networks and channels, it has also contributed to the concentration of television access in many major TV markets.

Critical Assessment Class-dominant theory points toward important linkages between the mass media and the underlying economy. It raises questions about who owns and controls the media, their interconnections with one another, and how the media reflect the interests of their owners and advertisers. Yet at the same time, by viewing owners and advertisers as all-important and all-powerful, class-dominant theorists underplay the relative independence of those who are engaged in the day-to-day operations of media organizations. Even in locales where monopoly ownership of media exists, a good news organization may provide quality coverage. Studies of American and Canadian newspapers, for example, have found little statistical relationship between the quality of coverage and the degree of competitiveness in a particular media market (Entman, 1989; McCombs, 1988).

In fact, the media often serve as arenas in which those who are less powerful are able to successfully contend for public support (Gamson et al., 1992). Studies of media coverage of the environmental movement, U.S. intervention in Central America, the movement against nuclear power, and the anti-Vietnam war movement of the 1960s have all concluded that in each instance, challengers to governmental or corporate interests used the media effectively to mobilize public support for their positions (Gamson, 1988; Gamson and Modigliani, 1989; Gitlin, 1980; Hallin, 1987).

Class-dominant theorists also tend to assume that all people are "cultural dopes" (Hall, 1982), mindless consumers of information and images who never question what they read in the newspaper or see on television. In fact, the media often present contradictory information, and audiences are frequently engaged in interpreting the meaning of the information they receive. A number of studies have examined how viewers make sense out of the information they get from the media. It is to these studies that we turn in considering the third major theory of media power and influence.

Culturalist Theory

Culturalist theory adopts a position that is somewhere between the limited-effects and the class-dominant traditions. Although cultural theorists acknowledge that the media are owned and controlled by a relatively small number of conglomerates, they emphasize the role of audiences and media workers in actively shaping the audience-media relationship. It is therefore helpful to identify two streams of culturalist research. The first focuses on how audiences interact with the media, and seeks to demonstrate that audiences are not simply passive consumers but actively help construct what they perceive. The second looks specifically at the news, examining how news organizations develop a culture that helps determine what they report and how

they report it. We shall consider audience-media relations first and the role of news organizations in the next section.

Audience relations research is concerned with *the ways in which the media provide a set of meanings that viewers then interpret according to their own cultural understandings.* People rely on the media for their own opinions depending on (1) their familiarity with a topic, (2) their level of media consumption, and (3) the availability of alternative sources of information. Television viewers thus are regarded by culturalist theorists as active participants, not only in the mechanical sense of choosing from among a growing number of channels to view, but also in the sense that they will "read into" what they see and hear meanings that are consistent with their own experiences and cultural understandings. Viewers can withhold attention, check a competing broadcast, pop in a video, mute the sound, discuss what they are watching, create viewers' organizations (such as fan clubs), and in general actively participate in generating meaning through their viewing experience (Bielby and Harrington, 1992, 1994; Fiske, 1987; Grossberg, 1987; Hall, 1980; Kaplan, 1983; Swidler, 1986).

For example, in one study college students were asked to write down their reactions to two Madonna music videos, "Papa Don't Preach" and "Open Your Heart" (Brown and Schulze, 1990). When the results were analyzed, the researchers concluded that the students' interpretations differed widely according to such things as their race or how well they liked Madonna. While black students interpreted the words and imagery in "Papa Don't Preach" as being about the relationship between a girl and her father, white students were more likely to view it as being about teenage pregnancy. Neither group drew the same conclusion as professional critics, who had faulted the controversial video for romanticizing teenage pregnancy. While Madonna fans viewed "Open Your Heart" as the story about a professional female dancer and her son, students who disliked Madonna viewed it as being about sexual desire between an older woman and a young boy. Viewers' interpretations were so divergent that it was almost as if they were watching different videos. Other studies of "viewers' work" (Katz, 1990) have drawn the same conclusions—that viewers actively engage with what they perceive in the media, drawing their own conclusions in light of their past experiences and understandings (Graber, 1988; Hobson, 1980; Liebes and Katz, 1990; Livingston, 1990; Palmer, 1986).

Critical Assessment Much of culturalist research is unhistorical. It does not look at how specific media organizations develop, or how their unique histories shape what they do. The culturalist position has therefore been criticized for overemphasizing immediate audience relations to the neglect of larger questions of who owns the media and how they exert influence over what gets covered. The actual economics of media production thus tends to be ignored, in favor of studies that focus on how audiences make meaningful what they perceive. Many of the conclusions are based on small studies of viewer responses to a single program, making it difficult to draw conclusions about the media in general. Moreover, much of this research is focused on white middle-class audiences, ignoring other groups (Ewen, 1985; Tuchman, 1988; Williams, 1977).

In order to understand how the media are shaped, we must look at what actually occurs with the key actors and decision makers in the media world. We will examine the "news" as an example of how those in the media help to shape reality.

PRODUCING THE NEWS: HOW "NEWS" IS CREATED

Is it possible for the news media ever to be a completely neutral "mirror of reality?" The answer is clearly "no." Countless millions of events happen every hour around the earth, many of them life-and-death occurrences for the people involved. The news media have the difficult task of distilling this enormous amount of information down to a handful of stories that will appeal to their audiences, sell advertisements, and lend themselves to quick production for a 30-second news slot on the 22-minute "half hour" evening news.

To accomplish this task, the news media necessarily exercise considerable selectivity in choosing topics and preparing them for audience consumption. News is not simply reported; it is defined, selected, and actively constructed into stories as a routine part of the daily work of reporters, TV news writers, and others who have been socialized into the journalistic culture of news organizations. Sociologists who have extensively studied this process call it **agenda-setting**—*determining what "counts" as news and what does not.* They are concerned both with how agenda-setting occurs within the news organization, as well as its impact on different audiences. The term **framing** is used to refer to *the ways in which the images and content of news helps to shape audience perceptions* (Bachrach and Baratz, 1970; Bagdikian, 1990; Cohen and Young, 1973; Fishman, 1980; Gamson et al., 1992; Gans, 1979; Gitlin, 1980, 1983; Shaw and McCombs, 1977; Molotch, 1979; Molotch and Lester, 1974; Sigal, 1973; Tuchman, 1978; White, 1950).

Sociologists have identified a variety of ways in which news organizations operate in framing audience perceptions.

Favoring "Official" Sources of Information

Because reporters are few in number and cannot witness many events directly, they must have access to people and institutions that generate reportable information. Not only must such information be available, but it must be provided on a routine, on-going basis if reporters are to meet their deadlines. Much of what is called "news" is obtained on the reporter's "beat," which consists of regular contacts with a well-established network of sources who over time may shape the reporter's perspectives.

Within this network, the most important contacts are **official sources**—*government authorities, designated spokespersons, and others presumed to have specialized expertise on a topic.* Official sources almost always claim to speak on behalf of larger constituencies: the State Department spokesperson speaks for "the current administration," the civil rights leader for "African Americans," the Russian ambassador for "the Russian people." This gives their opinions greater weight and credibility. The need of people to rely on spokespersons tends to give greater weight to official opinions, topics, and viewpoints. Journalists value them because they are equipped to provide the steady stream of press releases, "leaks," and other information handouts journalists require to do their work. Furthermore, because journalists always wish to seem as if they are presenting "the facts," they often must find an official spokesperson if their reporting is to have credibility. As a result, the large majority of all people who "make the news" in print or on television represent official sources. Official sources are therefore well-positioned to control the flow and the content of news (Bagdikian, 1990; Fishman, 1980; Fiske, 1987; Gans, 1979; Gitlin, 1980; Hartley, 1982; Karp, 1989; Rock, 1973; Sigal, 1973; Terdiman, 1985; Tuchman, 1978).

One early study of several thousand first-page stories from the *New York Times* and the *Washington Post* found that official sources of information outnumbered all others two-to-one, while the most important single sources of information were U.S. government officials (Sigal, 1973). A study of media coverage of abortion found that in 1989 as well as 15 years earlier, the persons most likely to be quoted in the press were politicians, followed by religious officials. Low-income pregnant women, the group most affected by government-funded abortions, were almost never heard in the media (Grindstaff, 1992).

Another study monitored 865 programs on ABC's

The media rely heavily on official sources of information, which in turn helps frame public opinion. H. Ross Perot and Vice President Al Gore drew much attention when they debated the North America Free Trade Agreement (NAFTA) on Larry King Live. *Yet factory workers in Mexico and the United States, who will probably bear the immediate impacts of NAFTA, were largely ignored as sources of information by most mass media coverage.*

Nightline over a 40-month period in the mid- to late-1980s. During this period, the U.S. government was actively supporting an armed insurrection against the government of Nicaragua, and *Nightline* ran a number of stories on the subject. Only 2 out of 68 guests during the period opposed U.S. intervention, one of whom was the Nicaraguan foreign minister, who obviously had a stake in speaking out against U.S. policies aimed at overthrowing his government. Thus, while the programming gave the impression of providing open debate, in fact the principal criticism of U.S. policy came from a "foreigner," while high-ranking U.S. government officials represented the "American" view. In this fashion, official sources helped to frame the debate in a way favorable to administration policies (Gamson et al., 1992).

Deciding Which News Is Important

Given the bewildering variety of worldwide events that might be conceivably regarded as news, the media require some way to select a manageable number of items. One way this is accomplished is by **categorization of news,** *determining whether or not a given event "fits" into some preexisting category or "beat"* (Tuchman, 1978). The use of such categories as "politics," "the economy," "crime," "industry," "science," "sports," "opinion," "family life," or "foreign affairs" helps to define what is newsworthy, since events that do not fit neatly into categories are less likely to be regarded as news and can therefore be eliminated from consideration (Fiske, 1987). Such categories are well institutionalized throughout the media profession, contributing to a fair degree of industry standardization.

This is why there is a certain "sameness" to newspaper coverage or television broadcasts, not only within the United States but around the world as well.

Categorization not only limits the number of stories deemed worthy of coverage but also helps to determine how the coverage is framed. Thus, for example, a momentary jump in the unemployment rate might be categorized under "labor" and framed in terms of hardship for American workers, based on information provided by an official labor union source. Alternatively, if the same story is categorized under "the economy," it might focus on the globalization of business activities and the relocation of factories to low-wage areas around the world, featuring an interview with a government economist. The viewer's or reader's impression of the nature of the issue would depend on which category framed the coverage.

News categories also determine the distribution of stories throughout the pages of a paper, and the lineup of stories on television news programs. Newspapers and television news programs typically lead with the most important story and end with a lighter feature, reflecting a more general distinction that journalists make between "important," fast-breaking "hard" news and more human interest "soft" news (Tuchman, 1978). Economics, politics, and foreign affairs are all examples of front-page "hard" news. Child-raising, home-making, and volunteer community work fall into the softer "human interest" categories that appear in the middle sections of the newspaper or at the end of the TV news broadcast. This division is likely to consign women to the family pages, since if they are categorized as making news at all, it is likely to be of the "softer" variety (Hall, 1975; Tuchman, 1978; Hartley, 1982; Fiske, 1987). A recent study of 20 U.S. newspapers, for example, found that only 14 percent of the sources quoted in front-page news were women; another study of major newsmagazines found that only 13 percent of story references were to women (Women's Institute for Freedom of the Press, [WIFP], 1989a, 1990b).

Oversimplification of Complex Issues

News organizations, which face constant pressures of fixed deadlines and fickle public interest, often respond by streamlining the news down to headlines and slogans. This is true of all forms of mass media. Newspapers, which often run lengthy "feature" articles and give the impression of providing detailed reporting, are necessarily selective in their coverage and approach. It is most obvious, however, in radio and television, where news stories seldom last more than 30 to 45 seconds. A typical 22-minute television newscast may contain as many as 30 to 40 items, providing a highly fragmented, disconnected, and confusing sense of the world. Such fragmentation may leave the viewer with the impression that events are a series of self-contained episodes, rather than seeing them as resulting from social and political processes. One consequence, researchers claim, is that when viewers see a story about personal hardships such as homelessness or poverty, they are often likely to hold the individuals themselves responsible, rather than turning to larger social forces for an explanation (Gamson et al., 1992; Iyengar, 1991).

One way that simplification is achieved is through the use of slogans to represent a much more complex set of underlying problems and issues (Boorstin, 1964). For example, the use of the catch-phrase "war on drugs" immediately calls up an image of armed drug dealers shooting it out with better-armed police officers, in a sort of made-for-TV drama that emphasizes military approaches to dealing with the problem rather than the social and economic conditions that might have contributed to it (see Chapter 7).

A related form of simplification consists of reducing complex issues to "either-or" categories—one is either pro-abortion of anti-abortion, for gun control or against gun control, in favor of the administration's health-care plan or against it. While such simplification makes for potentially dramatic news coverage, it also reduces the audience's ability to understand the actual range of issues and positions. Officials and other newsmakers are well aware of the importance of "speaking in headlines," providing catchy soundbites if they hope to make even a brief spot on the evening news. Among presidential candidates, for example, the

average length of uninterrupted talk carried by the evening news declined from 42 seconds in 1968 to 9 seconds in 1988, to only 7.3 seconds during the 1992 presidential primaries (reported in Fishkin, 1992).

Simplification is also achieved by **personalizing the news,** *presenting it as resulting exclusively from the efforts of individuals rather than underlying social forces* (Fiske, 1987; Gamson et al., 1992; Gans, 1979; Gitlin, 1983). For example, when the women's movement first emerged in the late 1960s and early 1970s, it was primarily concerned with raising women's understanding of the ways in which they were oppressed. Since "consciousness-raising" about social forces was not easily personalized, it was generally ignored by the mass media. Most *New York Times* coverage appeared in the women's pages under the direction of a female editor (Tuchman, 1978). It was only after the women's movement became institutionalized in groups such as the National Organization of Women (NOW), which could then produce "newsworthy" leaders, was it considered worthy of front-page news coverage.

Stereotyping and Inequality in News and Entertainment

In both news and entertainment broadcasting, the mass media may reinforce gender, racial, and ethnic stereotypes. This is not to argue that viewers are imprisoned in the stereotypes they encounter on television or in the newspaper. As we saw earlier, people are not "cultural dopes" blindly accepting everything they see and hear. The antiwar movement of the 1960s initially had to overcome hostile media coverage, which did not prevent growing numbers of people (and eventually segments of the media themselves) from changing their thinking on government policies (Gitlin, 1980). The same has been true of social movements favoring the rights of women, minorities, and gays. Yet even though people are best understood as active viewers, listeners, and readers, it is important to also recognize the ways in which the media sometimes contribute to inequality in American society

Gender Stereotypes and Inequality

The stereotypes experienced by women in the larger society (Chapter 11) are reflected in the mass media. This is the case both in news and in entertainment.

Biases in the News Media

We have already mentioned that women are greatly underrepresented in the news. When women are the subject of front-page stories, such things as their gender, physical appearance, clothing, and marital status are likely to be mentioned, even when these attributes are clearly irrelevant to the story itself (Foreit et al., 1980). This tends to reduce their authority as credible spokespeople. Imagine the impact it would have on your thinking if you were to read in the newspaper, "President Clinton, boyishly handsome in a dark blue pinstripe with lightly accented matching socks and tie, recently announced that U.S. troops were being deployed to Haiti. . . ." A recent study examined newspaper coverage of U.S. Senate races and concluded that female candidates generally received less coverage than their male counterparts. Furthermore, when they were covered, reporting tended to be more negative and likely to focus more on their overall suitability for office rather than their position on issues (Kahn and Goldenberg, 1991).

The underrepresentation of women as sources and topics of news stories reflects their underrepresentation in the media profession itself. A recent study found that even after major gains during the 1980s, women hold only 16 percent of editorships and only 11 percent of the top positions in major media organizations (WIFP, 1990a). But the lack of female representation itself cannot explain gender bias in media coverage. Another study found that even when women edited the business section of a newspaper, coverage of women as topics or sources did not improve (Tuchman, 1978, 1979). This is partly because men predominate in events that are defined as news, and partly because of gender socialization that contributes to the perception, held by males and females alike, that "men's work" is more likely to be of historical significance.

At the same time, it is important to note that the all-male television news team appears to be a thing of the past, with female anchors—some prominent—now found on most news broadcasts. Still, female broadcasters tend to be young (only 3 percent are over 40, whereas more than half of all male anchors are) and attractive, qualities which are less important for men (Sanders and Rock, 1988; Craft, 1988; WIFP, 1989b).

Biases in the Entertainment Media

The depiction of gender in the entertainment media tends to reinforce stereotypical images of women as consumed with appearance and home life while men actively engage in the outside world. In the print media this is true in advertising as well as articles. On television, one study of 20,000 prime-time programs between 1955 and 1985 found that throughout the 30-year period, male characters outnumbered female characters two to one (WIPF, 1986). When females are portrayed, they tend to be younger, less mature, thinner, and more attractive than men, and they are more likely to be found in home or in family situations. One study found

that teenage girls are likely to be portrayed as primarily concerned with shopping, men, makeup, and their physical appearance. Programs like "Murphy Brown," "Roseanne," or "Golden Girls," which break with these traditional stereotypes, remain the exception (Cantor, 1987; Condry, 1987, 1989; Ferguson, 1983; Glazer, 1980; Phillips, 1978; Silverstein et al., 1986; Steenland, 1988).

MTV, Video Soul, and other music television programs seem to be challenging some of the gender stereotypes that prevail in popular music and the wider culture. On the one hand, analyses of music television videos have found that women are less likely to be featured than men and more likely to be portrayed as sex objects when they do appear. Yet at the same time

Gender biases in the entertainment media are slowly changing. Murphy Brown, the highly independent television journalist played by Candice Bergen, decided to have a baby during the 1992 TV series even though she wasn't married. This decision vaulted the program to national prominence when it was criticized by then Vice-President Dan Quayle for violating "traditional family values." In this photograph from the TV series, a visibly pregnant Murphy Brown celebrates her baby shower with real-life TV news broadcasters Mary Alice Williams, Paula Zahn, Faith Daniels, Joan Lunden, and Katie Couric, along with series regular Faith Ford.

women are as likely to be as aggressive as men, a characterization that runs against the prevailing stereotypes (Sherman and Dominick, 1986). There are prominent women musicians and vocalists whose "in your face" attitude both challenges gender stereotypes and reflects changing gender roles among youthful audiences. The impact of this medium on young people's attitudes about gender remains to be adequately studied.

Racial and Ethnic Stereotypes and Inequality

As is the case with women, media stereotyping of racial and ethnic minorities parallels their treatment in the wider society. Although some changes have occurred in recent years, minorities continue to receive unequal treatment in news and entertainment.

Biases in the News Media

News accounts of racial and ethnic minorities often focus on the poorest members of these groups and their accompanying social problems. Television news reporting abounds with reports on the black underclass, unemployment, violence, single parenting, and teenage pregnancy. On the one hand, this provides a corrective to the false view that all minorities have joined the American middle class. The above-mentioned study, for example, found that white students who watched news programs were more likely to perceive blacks as being worse off economically than those who did not (Armstrong, Neuendorf, and Brentar, 1992).

On the other hand, such problem-oriented coverage can also foster a "blame the victim" attitude (Gray, 1986a, 1986b, 1989). One study analyzed the content of the evening news on four Chicago television stations over a two-month period in 1989 and 1990. It concluded that coverage of crime and political news tended to portray blacks as more demanding and physically threatening than whites—an image that was all the more convincing because the presence of black journalists contributed to an impression that the coverage was racially unbiased (Entman, 1992). This was true 20 years ago as well; a 1970 study of Minneapolis newspapers found that two-thirds of minority group photographs depicted either political demonstrations or acts of violence, in comparison with fewer than one out of five photographs of well-established nonminority groups (Fedler, 1973).

The same biases are true of American media coverage of black issues when they occur outside the United States. One study examined coverage by the *Washington Post* and the *New York Times* of violence among black South Africans between 1986 and 1990. The study concluded that through the use of terms like "black-on-black violence" and other devices, the newspaper stories reinforced a stereotypical image of warring black tribes contrasted with a white government that represented law and order. While racial images of violence abounded, largely absent from the coverage was any examination of its underlying political and economic causes (Fair and Astroff, 1991).

The treatment of racial minorities in the media reflects larger social currents, and in recent years it has become increasingly unacceptable to stereotype or otherwise discriminate against racial or ethnic minorities. A major media landmark occurred with the 1977 miniseries "Roots," which depicted the struggles and triumphs of a black family over years of slavery, prejudice, and discrimination. "Roots" was viewed by 80 million people, revealing to millions of whites as well as blacks the impact of racism on the African-American experience. In addition to television programs like "Roots," the growth of minority-owned media has been found to help increase self-understanding among racial groups in the United States. A national survey of approximately 900 blacks, for example, found that those who read black newspapers and journals tended to have fewer negative stereotypes about other blacks than those who did not (Allen and Thornton, 1992).

The perception of racial and ethnic bias in media coverage is not restricted to nonwhites. A study of nearly 800 people representing 13 ethnic groups in Cleveland found that most felt the local television and newspapers did not adequately cover their ethnic communities. This negative perception was particularly strong among low-income people of the various ethnic groups (Jeffres and Hur, 1979).

Biases in the Entertainment Media

Racial stereotypes have long characterized films, television, and other forms of entertainment media, even if their impact is muted today. Blacks are still likely to be cast in roles associated with urban crime and drugs. Latinos are often depicted as strong but subject to violent outbursts, and Latino actors are often cast in roles associated with stereotypical problems such as immigration. Asians are frequently depicted as sneaky and cunning, while American Indians remain associated with tribal conflict and alcoholism (Bogle, 1990; Gerbner, et al., 1986; Omi, 1989; Russell, 1991). While a significant number of blacks have achieved media prominence, other minority groups have achieved less success, and women of color remain largely invisible. Even when minorities do achieve some degree of prominence, middle-class roles are likely to be depicted much more favorably than working-class or lower-class ones.

Blacks have resisted film stereotyping from the beginning of film. The 1915 film *Birth of a Nation,* which portrayed "civilized" white supremacists after the Civil War fighting "savage" blacks bent on rape and destruction, was met with demonstrations led by the National Association for the Advancement of Colored People (NAACP). The film was eventually banned in 5 states and 19 cities (Bogle, 1990). Since World War II, and particularly since the civil rights movements of the 1950s and 1960s, the most offensive stereotypes have largely disappeared from film and television, and today there are prominent nonwhite directors, actors, and writers, as even a cursory review of the local film or television listings will reveal. Much of popular music is dominated by nonwhite performers, and music such as rap or hip-hop remains a largely black expressive medium that is nonetheless enjoyed by white audiences (see Box 19.1).

The greater visibility of blacks in film and on television does not mean the end of racial discrimination, however. Many highly successful black media stars have often been cast into "tan" roles—essentially white middle-class characters who happen to have dark skin. "The Cosby Show," for example, which dominated prime-time television in the 1980s, depicted the upper-middle-class Huxtable family, in which the father was a doctor and the mother a lawyer. Although the program was widely acclaimed for breaking with stereotypical black roles, it did so by depicting a lofty socioeconomic status attained by very few people (Bogle, 1990; Gray, 1986b, 1989). Such programming gives viewers the impression that American society is completely open. One study, for example, found that among white university students, those who were the heaviest viewers of television entertainment programs were more likely to believe that blacks enjoyed high income, class standing, and education. This was especially true of those students who had experienced little actual interracial contact (Armstrong, Neuendorf, and Brentar, 1992).

Despite the phenomenal success of "The Cosby Show" and its offshoots, blacks, Latinos, and other nonwhite groups continue to be underrepresented on prime-time television; when they do appear they are more likely to be stigmatized in stereotypically unfavorable roles. One study of nearly 7,000 television characters found that about 90 percent were white, 8 percent were African American, 1 percent were Asian, and 0.6 percent were Latino, and only one was Native American (Williams and Condry 1988). Another study found that nearly half of all African-American prime-time characters on one network were criminals, entertainers, athletes, or servants (Staples and Jones, 1985). The few Latinos who appear on television were even more likely to be portrayed as criminals (Williams and

Condry, 1988). Racial minorities comprise less than 8 percent of all TV news directors (WIFP, 1989b).

VIOLENCE AND THE MEDIA

In an October 1993 episode of "Beavis and Butt-head," the "in-your-face" cartoon shown on MTV, the irreverent duo deliberately started a fire to be amusing. Shortly afterward, a five-year-old Ohio boy who had watched the show torched his family's mobile home. His two-year-old sister died in the blaze. MTV expressed its regret and vowed to reexamine the program, indirectly acknowledging responsibility for inspiring the tragedy.

As far back as 1961, the chairman of the Federal Communications Commission (FCC) decried television as a "vast wasteland [of] game shows, violence, sadism, murder, western badmen, western good men, private eyes, gangsters, more violence, and cartoons." Ten years later the U.S. surgeon general cited studies linking television violence with aggression in children; this resulted in the networks agreeing to a 7 to 9 P.M. "family viewing time" of supposedly nonviolent programming. Yet today there are five to six violent acts per hour on prime time, with four times as many during the Saturday morning children's shows, adding up to nearly 200 hours of violent programs each week (Gerbner and Signorielli, 1990). One study that tracked all Washington, D.C., channels from 6 A.M. until midnight counted more than 1,800 violent scenes during the 18-hour period (Lichter and Amundson, 1992).

The average child entering junior high school has viewed 8,000 murders and more than 100,000 other violent acts, a number that will double by the time of high school graduation. The average American 18-year-old has spent twice as many hours in front of the TV set as in school (Donnerstein et al., 1993; Huston et al., 1992; Staples and Jones, 1985). Moreover, with the rapid expansion of cable broadcasting and VCRs, a far greater range of programming is now available, from educational television to home movie channels. This provides a vastly increasing viewing opportunity for all sorts of programs, including violent ones.

Three major reports over the past two decades have examined the relationship between media violence and aggression. The first was done by the U.S. surgeon general in 1972, the second by the National Institute of Mental Health in 1982, and the third by the American Psychological Association in 1992. Each report drew on all scientific literature that was available at the time. All three concluded that violence in the mass media contributes to aggressive behavior and attitudes among people of both sexes, widely varying ages, and different racial and ethnic groups. Hundreds of studies have been conducted, some in artificial laboratory settings

Box 19.1

Silenced Voices

Is Rap Music the CNN of Its Youthful Audience?

Rap music or "hip-hop" has proved to be one of the most enduring and controversial forms of music to emerge in the past two decades. It began as black dance music in New York City's South Bronx during the 1970s, fusing reggae with the rapid-fire rhyming done by black disk jockeys to work up the crowds at house and block parties. What was originally an underground art form soon became big money, as major record labels and MTV tuned into rap's growing popularity. Today rap is a commercialized, high-tech digital medium, extremely profitable for its leading performers and their record labels (Powell, 1991; Shusterman, 1991).

Although there is white rap, Latino salsa rap, black women's rap, gay rap, country rap, and even Sesame Street rap, the predominant force in rap music remains tied to its early origins: black male experience in the often-violent inner city. It has been characterized as music self-consciously designed *by* urban blacks, *about* urban blacks, and *for* urban blacks (Wallace and Costello, 1990). Yet despite such an inward-looking focus, rap is no less popular in colleges or white middle-class suburban schools than it is in the inner city. Its driving rhythm,

hard-edge quality, antiauthority message, and sheer danceability all help to account for rap's appeal (Kuwahara, 1992).

Much rap music continues to glorify sexual conquest, urban violence, money, and self-absorption. In hard-core "gangsta rap" the lyrics sometimes glorify shooting and killing, insult women, and—as in the case of Ice-T's "Cop Killer" or Tupac Amaru Shakur's "APACALYPSE NOW"—call for "droppin' the cop." As a result, rap music has come under considerable criticism in recent years from groups as diverse as police departments, conservative parent associations, black churches, and liberal feminists. In New York City a group of black men and women, Masses United For Human Rights, has demonstrated against rap artists whose music is felt to degrade women. Black academics have been no less sharp in their criticism. Oberlin women's studies professor bell hooks argues that some rap music reinforces white stereotypes about blacks; racism, in her view, partly accounts for rap music's appeal outside the black community. Maulana Karenga, chair of the black studies department at California State University, Long Beach, claims that white-run record companies are only too happy to

Although rap music has often come under criticism for frequently having violent and sexist lyrics, rap artists counter that they merely depict the harsh realities of American urban life. Rapper Ice-T is shown here at a press conference in which he dismisses a 1992 boycott of his "Body Count" album, encouraged by police because it contained the controversial song "Cop Killer."

disseminate such a distorted view of black life, as long as it is profitable (Marriott, 1993)

Rap musicians defend their lyrics as reflecting the violence and sexism of the inner-city cultures from which they come. In their view, the larger society is responsible for creating the violent conditions that are a part of everyday life in their communities, and they are merely artists expressing widely felt frustration and rage. In the view of rap group Public Enemy's Chuck D, rap music is the "CNN of its audience," telling the truth about life in the black ghetto. It is the result of the pain and powerlessness that comes from being born poor and black in the United States today (Marriott, 1993; Wallace and Costello, 1990).

Is rap just another form of commercial exploitation, coupling the proven sales potential of sex and violence with white stereotypes about black culture? Or is it the voice of inner-city black youth who are oppressed by drugs, crime, and poverty, the authentic poetry of those who are unwilling to remain silent (Powell, 1991; Wallace and Costello, 1990)?

---

and some in "real-life" situations. Some studies monitored their subjects' youthful television viewing habits, and then followed up years later to see if they had any impact during adult life. Virtually all the studies found that increased television viewing of violent acts can lead to lasting changes in a person's overall aggressiveness (Donnerstein et al., 1993; Huston et al., 1992).

Some scholars have concluded that the media teaches young people that violence is socially acceptable, offers them violent role models to imitate, and desensitizes them to the actual experience of violence. Studies have also concluded that media depictions are especially likely to result in violent behavior if the viewer can easily identify with the aggressor, if the violent act is depicted as going unpunished, if it is realistic, or if it is sexually arousing (Donnerstein et al., 1993; Heusmann, 1986; Huston et al., 1992).

Media violence against women ranges from verbal abuse to rape, torture, murder, and mutilation. For example, one out of every eight Hollywood films shows a rape. Violent R-rated films are readily available to teenagers on cable and VCR, and have a measurable impact on their viewers (Donnerstein et al., 1993; Wilson et al., 1992, Yang and Linz, 1990). One series of studies exposed undergraduate male students to a variety of sexually explicit films and videos. Some viewers saw films that were both sexually explicit and violent (such as "slasher" films, or films depicting violent rapes), some saw films that were merely sexually explicit (nonviolent pornography), and some saw no films at all. The male viewers' feelings and responses were monitored throughout. After repeated viewings of such films, subjects were shown information about a sexual assault trial, in order to evaluate their degree of sympathy for the woman who had been raped. In general, the research found that exposure to sexually violent materials both desensitized viewers to rape, and reduced their sympathy for the rape victim. According to this research, sexually explicit material such as pornography does not by itself encourage men to think or act violently toward women, but when such materials are also violent they may well increase the viewers' willingness to tolerate and even commit violent acts toward women (Donnerstein, Linz, and Penrod, 1987; Linz, Donnerstein, and Adams, 1989; Linz, Donnerstein, and Penrod, 1988; Linz, 1989).

The public's fascination with violence is amply rewarded by the media, leading some scholars to argue that the media contribute to a "law and order" mentality that celebrates violence as well as the use of official repression to contain it. Challengers to official power are uniformly portrayed in an unfavorable light and inevitably get their deserved punishment, albeit only after holding the audience's rapt attention by committing crime after horrible crime. Such challengers may be depicted as deranged individuals or organized crime syndicates, local political dissidents or evil enemy powers, teenage gang members or sinister cyborgs; the message, however, is the same (Hall, 1980; Cohen and Young, 1973; Murdock, 1973; Chibnall, 1977; Whannel, 1979).

MASS MEDIA AND THE NEW INFORMATION TECHNOLOGIES

There is evidence that audiences are increasingly critical of the mass media, contributing to growing cynicism and apathy (Gamson et al., 1992). In a recent national survey of 1,700 adults, 40 percent reported having less confidence in the news than when they first started to follow current events. Three-quarters felt the media gave more coverage to stories that supported its own point of view, while 59 percent thought that the media had too much influence (Times Poll, 1993).

This influence may be challenged by newly emerging information technologies. Video, telephone, sound and computers seem to be merging into a new "multimedia technology" that can be transmitted in both directions via telephone line, cable, or satellite. Sounds and images are now readily converted into electronic information that can be stored and manipulated on an inexpensive laptop computer. Once today's copper phone lines are replaced by fiber optic cables or advanced satellite communication (something that has already begun in Asian countries such as Hong Kong, much of northern Europe, and in parts of the United States), it will be possible for "rivers of information" to flow between homes, businesses, schools, and offices. One can now buy hand-held computer/telephones capable of transmitting words, images, electronic mail, and faxes between any two points in the world via satellite; some analysts predict this technology will be as commonplace as portable telephones within a decade (Cole, 1992; Joseph Weber, 1992; Yang, 1992).

For at least 30 years, high-tech enthusiasts have generally been critical of the mass media, arguing that they

High-tech enthusiasts predict that the new information technologies will eventually lead to an information society where everyone carries pocket-sized computers connecting them with global "information highways." More pessimistic analysts envision a society that is stratified into those who have access to such technologies and those who do not. Apple's hand-held Newton, initially hailed as the first truly portable, popular gateway to the "information highway," failed to live up to its advance billing.

have far too much power and influence. In their view, the proliferation of hundreds or even thousands of television channels, cheap satellite dishes, home computers, and fast-transmission cabling will eventually enable people to bypass the mass media, thereby undermining their dominant position. Citizens are seen as electronically interacting with politicians, pursuing their education through direct access to information and data around the world, obtaining medical diagnoses, and even shopping without ever leaving their living room. Some even see such decentralized information technology as having the potential to topple governments and corporate bureaucracies alike, giving rise to new democratic forms of governance (Pool, 1966; Arterton, 1987; Gilder, 1992; Wriston, 1992; Naisbitt, 1990).

Sociologists tend to be skeptical about such predictions. While the new technologies may have the potential to foster a greater two-way flow of knowledge and information, they may also lead to increased central control (Box 19.2). At the very least, they are likely to result in some degree of stratification based on **technological literacy,** *mastery of the most recent technical innovations.* Such a system of stratification will doubtless reflect other systems of stratification in American society, as it will throughout the world. It seems reasonable to conclude that whatever the potential of the new information technologies, they are unlikely to replace the mass media in the foreseeable future (Arterton, 1987; Schudson, 1992; Fishkin, 1992).

GLOBALIZATION AND THE MEDIA: "IT ALL CAME FROM THERE"

From the Persian Gulf War to the fall of the Berlin Wall, from a million Chinese protesters at Beijing's Tienanmen Square to the genocidal war in Bosnia, people have become accustomed to watching history unfold live on camera. Borderless television emerged with full force during the 1980s. There are more than 300 satellite-delivered TV services in the world, more than half originating in the United States, ranging from Total Christian Television to MTV. Cable News Network (CNN) alone reaches 137 countries. It is estimated that there are more than a billion television sets in the world today, serving an audience of as many as half of the world's population (Map 19.1). The advent of direct broadcasting from satellites to dish antennas now makes it possible for people to receive programming even in the remotest areas. The cost of global transmission has dropped to well under $1,000 an hour,

Box 19.2

Critical Thinking

Do the New Technologies Strengthen the Hand of "Big Brother"?

In his novel *1984,* George Orwell (1959) described a terrifying world in which government, through its control over all forms of mass media, exerted virtually complete control over the lives and actions of all citizens. Television was used by "big brother" government not only as a means to circulate propaganda but also as an all-seeing "eye" to monitor a citizen's every movement. The year 1984 has come and gone without Orwell's dire predictions being realized, and today some high-technology enthusiasts argue that rather than undermining democracy, recent advances in information technology will actually enhance it (see text). Yet others have urged caution, fearing that history may yet prove Orwell correct—that information technology will permit all aspects of life to be monitored and recorded.

In the following excerpts, technology writer Herb Brody warns of the dangers inherent in new technologies that permit massive amounts of information on individual citizens to be stored and instantaneously accessed by government, law enforcement officials, and business. How do you reconcile Brody's account with the more hopeful viewpoints presented in the text?

Computers linked to telecommunications networks spread information and misinformation faster than it can be managed. As access in-

creases, so does the potential for loss of privacy. . . . Every time you pay taxes, buy insurance, use a credit card, or apply for a loan, you surrender a bit of personal information. Every time you call an 800 phone number the recipient gets a record of your phone number which can be traced to your address using the "reverse phone directories" that some telephone companies market. Both governments and businesses have amassed huge databases. Much of the information can be cross-referenced and aggregated using an individual's Social Security number, which has become (in direct opposition to the original intent) a national identification number. It's possible, knowing only a few pieces of information about individual people, to assemble dossiers on where they live, what they buy and who they associate with.

Ironically, digital technology offers, in principle, unprecedented privacy. It is possible to use a computer program to encode a message so that its meaning will be revealed only to someone possessing a digital key. [Yet] the Federal Bureau of Investigation has proposed legislation that would require all the switching computers in both the public telecommunications network and private organizations to be [accessible to law enforcement agents] (Brody, 1992).

bringing it well within the reach of even the smallest of networks (Lippman, 1992).

Television, films, and other forms of mass media all contribute to the globalization of culture around the world. This process favors those countries that currently dominate global programming. At the present time, this means a largely one-way flow from industrial nations, particularly the United States, to the rest of the world. Such an imbalance is of growing concern in many countries.

To take one prominent example, MTV, the world's largest global television network, reached 71 countries in Europe, Asia, and Latin America by the end of 1992.

Even Russians are among the 210 million households who can today watch Madonna or Pearl Jam in their living rooms. Viacom, the company that owns MTV, also owns VH-1, a baby-boomer music television network; Showtime, a cable movie channel; Nickelodeon, a children's channel; Nick at Nite, a channel which replays old television programs; and a number of local cable systems and radio and television stations. This single media conglomerate has a powerful influence on shaping youth culture in the United States and around the world (Landler, 1992). Yet Viacom's influence is challenged by companies such as Hong Kong's rapidly growing STAR TV, whose satellite broadcasts are capable of reaching as many as three billion people. Yet even these upstart companies are being acquired by transnational media giants (see Box 19.3).

Wheel of Fortune is possibly the most widely viewed television program in the world, reaching an estimated 100 million people in 25 countries (Tempest, 1992). Even if Pat Sajak and Vanna White are replaced by such local celebrities as Tarik Tarcan and Yesemin Kosal in Turkey, the format and the message are the same: the belief that glamour, luck, and good fortune can result in the good life. *Los Simpsons* is a top-rated show in Colombia and Argentina, while guerrilla insurgents in the Philippines were reportedly defeated by government soldiers when they were caught off guard watching MTV. Islamic censors in Egypt edit out kisses on reruns of *Dallas* and *Falconcrest,* while fashion broadcasting by CNN led Pakistani censors to run black bars across the screen to block out any exposed parts of women's bodies (Lippman, 1992).

Many nations in the world have reacted strongly to U.S. dominance in global media. The United Nation's 1980 MacBride Commission, for example, entitled its report "Many Voices, One World," and called for a correction to the imbalances in global communications flow. In 1984 the United States even withdrew from UNESCO, partly in response to that organization's efforts to restrain the activities of U.S. and European media in the poorer countries of Africa and Latin America.

The media have long been viewed as a potentially democratizing influence in countries whose governments seek to control the flow of information. The field of **development communication** argues that *the widespread dissemination of newspapers, radio, and eventually television are central to a society's movement from coercive forms of government to truly democratic forms* (Schiller, 1989; Sussman and Lent, 1991; Lerner, 1958; Lerner and Schramm, 1967; Schramm, 1964, 1977, 1979; Pool, 1966). Nepal's student uprising in 1991 was partly triggered when Nepalese students watched South African activist Nelson Mandela released after spending 27 years in jail. In China, government officials are concerned about the proliferation of backyard satellite dishes, which enable millions of Chinese to bypass government censorship and directly hook into foreign television transmissions (Kristof, 1993).

This spread of global journalism has been accompanied by the spread of VCRs, which makes it possible to widely disseminate "subversive" information

Map 19.1   Television Ownership Around the World

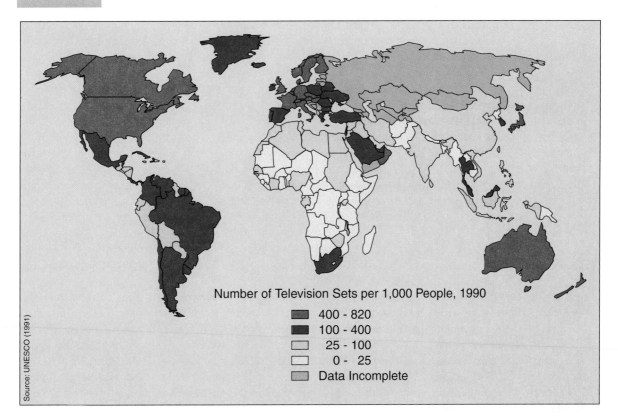

Number of Television Sets per 1,000 People, 1990

- 400 - 820
- 100 - 400
- 25 - 100
- 0 - 25
- Data Incomplete

Source: UNESCO (1991)

Television is one of the most powerful forms of media in the world today. Although TV ownership is greatest in Europe and North America, it is rapidly increasing throughout the rest of the world.

Box 19.3

Globalization

Will Hong Kong's STAR Televison Eventually Reach Three Billion People?

Bars in the vicinity of Lhasa's Potala Palace [in Tibet] have satellite dishes so they can offer STAR TV to customers. Young Tibetans tap toes to the latest video from Arrested Development, giving out low whistles of admiration. *Karen* insurgents in the Burmese jungle hang up their AK-47s to watch installments of *Santa Barbara* and *The Bold and the Beautiful* broadcast by STAR TV's general entertainment channel, STAR PLUS. . . . It's a world of soap operas without frontiers. And news, music videos, and movies, too. . . . The Global Village brought to you from geostationary orbit (Fitzpatrick, 1993).

At age 23, Hong Kong entrepreneur Richard Li is the founder of Satellite Television Asian Region (STAR TV). Bankrolled by his billionaire father's business empire, Li quickly built STAR TV into an Asian media powerhouse. Within three years, by 1993, STAR TV boasted a growing number of channels reaching an estimated 42 million homes, an increase from only 11 million in less than a year. Its range encompasses 53 countries with a combined population of 2.8 billion people in Asia and the Middle East, representing the world's largest untapped television and consumer market. With a borderless "footprint" extending a third of the way around the world, from Israel to Japan, STAR TV's potential audience speaks languages from Hebrew and Arabic to Urdu and Japanese, and includes more English speakers than are found in the United States and Canada combined.

The challenges of programming across such a vast multicultural area are daunting. How to satisfy Taiwanese teenagers hungry for Madonna without offending traditional Muslim beliefs in Pakistan? Broadcasters have decided not to air Madonna's "Erotica" video, and avoid advertising hard liquor. What language should a newscaster or "video jockey" speak to reach the widest possible audience? Plans are underway for educational channels that would broadcast in Mandarin Chinese, Urdu, Hindi, and Arabic. Yet despite the popularity of STAR TV, officials in target countries are not necessarily pleased with what India's Information Minister has characterized as a "cultural invasion." Still, popular programs originating in American culture currently dominate STAR TV's programming.

The success of STAR TV has not escaped the notice of the world's media conglomerates. In 1993 media magnate Rupert Murdoch's News Corporation bought a majority share in the company, although the Li family will remain in control of broadcasting. Murdoch's media empire includes Fox Broadcasting (with its 139 affiliated TV stations), Twentieth Century Fox films, and several major European and North American newspapers and publishing companies. It remains to be seen whether global broadcasting in the twenty-first century will be decentralized into numerous small competing media companies, or if a handful of giants will control the satellites and stations they transmit (Fitzpatrick, 1993; Goll, 1994; Rosenthal, 1993).

---

even when the government controls television broadcasting. Such videos were widely circulated in Eastern Europe before the communist governments were toppled, and reportedly played an important role in disseminating radical ideas. When asked what caused the downfall of communism in Eastern Europe in 1991, Lech Walesa, the leader of the Polish anticommunist Solidarity Movement, pointed to a TV set

and said, "it all came from there" (Lippman, 1992).

The media technologies of the future will make it easier and easier to bypass borders and frontiers in the world of the twentieth century. While their precise impact on economics, politics, and culture cannot be foretold, it is certain to be substantial. Walesa's attribution of Poland's sweeping changes to television may prove to be prophetic.

CHAPTER SUMMARY

1. **Mass media,** which emerged out of technological developments such as the printing press, permit a one-way flow of information from those who own or control the media to large audiences.

2. Television is the predominant mass media technology of the twentieth century. It has helped to shape our entertainment habits, consumption, and politics, and has contributed to the emergence of a **mass-mediated culture.**

3. According to the **limited-effects theory of media influence,** the mass media do not actually exert a great deal of influence over people, since they mainly give audiences what they already want to read, hear, or see.

4. **Class-dominant theorists** argue the opposite. They believe that the mass media are controlled by a handful of powerful ruling elites whose views they reflect.

5. **Culturalist theorists** argue that although the media may be controlled by elite groups, audiences nonetheless play an active role in determining both the content of media and how it is interpreted and understood.

6. The organizational culture of the mass media helps to **frame** the production of news, and thereby what viewers come to understand as news. Important framing devices include favoring **official sources,** deciding which news is worthy of coverage, and the oversimplification of complex issues.

7. The media tend to promote sexist thinking through the underrepresentation of women as well as depicting them in stereotypical roles.

8. The same is true of racial and ethnic minorities. Although blatant stereotyping is no longer common and representation has improved, there is still evidence that coverage is biased and reinforces stereotypes.

9. There is a great deal of evidence that violence in the media can result in violent and aggressive behavior among some viewers. Violent programming in particular seems to desensitize some viewers to rape and other acts of violence toward women.

10. Some high-tech enthusiasts believe recent developments in media technology will reduce the influence of mass media, permitting audiences a great deal more control over information as well as increased direct political access. Whether or not this will eventually prove to be the case remains controversial.

11. The globalization of mass media has spread images of American life and culture throughout the world, contributing to the creation of a global culture. While this is welcome in some places, in others it is resented and resisted.

12. Media technology also facilitates the spread of democratic political ideas and debate, and has contributed to the sweeping global political changes that are occurring today.

QUESTIONS FOR DISCUSSION

1. Can the news ever be truly "objective?" Discuss the various techniques employed by the media in "framing the news," and the effect this has on audience perceptions.

2. In what ways do the mass media promote inequality and stereotyping? In what ways has this changed in recent years?

3. In what ways do the mass media contribute to violence in society? What, if anything, do you think should be done about this?

4. What is likely to be the global impact of the media on politics and culture as we enter the twenty-first century?

KEY TERMS

agenda-setting: Determining what "counts" as news and what does not.

audience relations: A body of research, within the culturalist theory of media influence that is concerned with the ways in which the media provide a set of meanings that viewers then interpret according to their own cultural understandings.

categorization of news: A framing device that consists of determining whether or not a given event "fits" into some preexisting category or "beat."

class-dominant theory of media influence: A theory developed during the 1960s and 1970s arguing that society is dominated by a relatively small, powerful elite, whose viewpoint the media overwhelmingly tend to reflect.

culturalist theory of media influence: A theory developed during the 1980s and 1990s arguing that people play an active role in creating their own cultural meanings out of what they receive from the media.

development communication: A field of communication research arguing that the widespread dissemination of newspapers, radio, and eventually television are central to a society's movement from coercive forms of government to truly democratic forms.

framing: The ways in which the images and content of news help to shape audience perceptions.

limited-effects theory of media influence: A theory developed during the 1940s and the 1950s arguing that the media have minimal impact on people's attitudes and perceptions, since audiences are said to be highly selective in what they watch, perceive, and recall.

mass audience: A large collection of people who receive messages that are directed at them not as individuals but rather as a group.

mass media: Forms of communication that permit a one-way flow of information from a single source to a large audience; examples include newspapers, magazines, radio, and television.

mass-mediated culture: A culture in which the mass media play a key role in both shaping and creating cultural perceptions.

mass society: A society whose members are rootless, isolated, and lacking in strong social ties, and are thus defenseless against various forms of manipulation (by the mass media in particular).

official sources: Government authorities, designated spokespersons, and others presumed to have specialized expertise on a topic.

personalizing the news: A framing device that consists of representing the news as resulting exclusively from the efforts of individuals rather than underlying social forces.

technological literacy: Mastery of the most recent technical innovations.

RECOMMENDED FOR FURTHER READING

Bogle, Donald. (1990). *Toms, Coons, Mulattoes, Mammies, and Bucks: An Interpretive History of Blacks in American Films.* New York: Continuum.

Originally published in 1973 and recently updated, this book traces the racist treatment of blacks in the American mass media during the twentieth century. In successive chapters it runs through the first nine decades, combining sociological analysis with fascinating biographical accounts, and heavily laden with photographs of black film and television figures.

Gitlin, Todd. (1983). *Inside Prime Time.* New York: Pantheon.

A highly critical examination of prime-time programming; looks at how programming occurs, how decisions are made, and the limitations of commercial television.

Schiller, Herbert. (1989). *The Corporate Takeover of Public Expression.* New York: Oxford University Press.

An examination of mass media as big business, and how financial and commercial considerations shape what we are able to view.

Sussman, Gerald, and John A. Lent (eds.). (1991). *Transnational Communications: Wiring the Third World.* Newbury Park, Calif.: Sage.

A collection of essays on the globalization of media, focusing in particular on the impact of the United States and other industrial giants on the low-income countries of the world.

Tuchman, Gaye. (1978). *Making News: A Study in the Construction of Reality.* New York: Free Press.

A classic study of the social construction of news; critically examines the ways in which news is produced and shaped not only by commercial considerations but by the institutional requirements of news organizations as well.

Woolley, Benjamin. (1992). *Virtual Worlds: A Journey in Hype and Hyperreality.* Oxford, England: Blackwell.

A highly engaging and often amusing examination of the marriage between computers and media, and what it might hold for the future.

CHAPTER 20

Population, Urbanization, and the Environment

CHAPTER OUTLINE

THINGS TO LOOK FOR

1. What are the causes of global population growth, and what is likely to be its effect during the next century?
2. How have urbanization and the emergence of cities reflected the industrial organization of society?
3. What relationships exist between global population growth, industrialization, urbanization, and the environment?
4. What are nations doing today to deal with environmental problems?

INTRODUCTION: A GLOBAL PROBLEM

When our children are adults there will be no more Siberian tigers, African elephants, or cheetahs left in the wild. The major sources of diversity and evolution on this planet, the tropical rain forests, are falling at the rate of 100 acres a minute. At the rate we are going today, there will be no wilderness left on the planet within 30 years. The only remnants will be tiny islands which we set aside as parks and reserves—but when you have an island of wilderness, extinction within that island goes on. We are the *last* generation that will have any decision to make about wilderness because within our lifetimes it's all going to be gone. Around the world the skin of life is being torn apart by the deadliest predator ever known in the history of life on earth. (David Suzuki, biologist and anchor of Canadian Broadcasting Corporation series "Improving on Nature," in his keynote address at 1989 UCLA Conference on the Environment).

The predator Suzuki is refering to is of course humankind, and the most potent symbol of human destructiveness is the Brazilian rain forest. Rock stars have taken up the cause of "saving the rain forest," as have countless scientists, activists, and politicians. When Vice President Albert Gore, author of the best-selling *Earth in the Balance* (1993), visited the region in 1989, he was horrified by what he saw. He lamented that "the devastation is unbelievable. It's one of the great tragedies of all history" (Linden, 1989, p. 76).

The sheer vastness of the Amazon basin, which covers an area of some 2.7 million square miles, is hard to imagine. Nearly the size of the United States (excluding Alaska), the rain forest is a delicate web of interconnected life, containing an estimated one million plant and animal species. The National Academy of Sciences estimates that a typical four-square-mile patch contains 750 species of trees, 125 kinds of mammals, 400 types of birds, 100 varieties of reptiles, 60 kinds of amphibians, and more than 400 insect species. In 1988, 34 square miles of Brazilian rain forest went up in smoke each day, victim to hungry farmers, global beef producers, and logging companies. It was as if a country the size of Belgium—approximately 12,000 square miles—had been burned to the ground that year. Satellite photographs revealed tens of thousands of fires spread out over an area nearly equal in size to the United States east of the Mississippi River.

Brazil is typical of tropical countries where deforestation is occurring at an accelerating rate. From the jungles of Central America to Indonesia, Thailand, and Malaysia, the world's forests are being cut, logged, and burned at an alarming rate. Scientists fear that such destruction will result in catastrophic damage to the entire planet. For one thing, a major part of the planet's genetic biological diversity is threatened. Apart from the value of preserving plant and animal life for their own sake, this represents the loss of countless potential food sources for an increasingly hungry planet, as well as biochemicals that may disclose the genetic secrets for curing a wide range of human illnesses. As expressed by Thomas Lovejoy of the Smithsonian Institute, "the Amazon is a library for life sciences, the world's greatest pharmaceutical laboratory and a flywheel of climate. It's a matter of global destiny" (Linden, 1989, p. 77).

The Amazon illustrates not only the interconnectedness of plant and animal life, but of economics and politics as well. The government of Brazil, with money from world lending organizations, has sought to develop the region as a solution to the country's economic problems. Billions of dollars have been spent on the construction of roads and settlements in an effort to promote mining, ranching, family farming, and agribusiness—much as the American West was opened to pioneers a century ago. Population growth and a stagnant economy have resulted in massive urban joblessness and poverty in Brazil, as they have throughout much of the world.

Three quarters of Brazil's 121 million people now live in urban areas, including hundreds of thousands who reside in squalid squatter settlements found in every major city. Giant metropolitan areas continue to grow, swollen by people in search of work. Brazil's largest metropolitan area, Sao Paolo, has an estimated 18 million residents; its second city, Rio de Janeiro, has 12 million. The Brazilian government simply lacks the

The world's rain forests, important sources of biological diversity, are being logged at a rapid rate to make way for roads, cities, family farms, and large-scale agribusiness. The United Nations estimates that an area equivalent in size to the state of Washington is lost each year. Logging of the Amazon rain forest, depicted here, has been especially severe; Brazil lost some 12,000 square miles in 1988 alone.

money to deal effectively with the country's massive problems of unemployment and urban poverty. It is no wonder that many urban Brazilians join their impoverished counterparts from rural areas to seek their fortune through logging and farming in the jungle, or that the government has actively promoted rain-forest exploitation by constructing highways deep into its heart. As a result, the country is caught in a vicious cycle of economic poverty, public indebtedness, and ecological destruction (Linden, 1989; Smith, 1992; Hammond, 1990; Shabecoff, 1990).

Although the Brazilian example may seem dramatic, it is typical of the problems faced in a world where huge population increases have contributed to the growth of enormous cities filled with millions of impoverished people. As nations seek to develop their economies with the hope of providing jobs for their citizens, the planet's already fragile environment will be increasingly threatened. In this chapter we examine these complex interconnections, focusing in particular on the relationship between population growth, industrialization, urbanization, and the environment.

GLOBAL POPULATION GROWTH

It is well-known that the world population is rapidly growing and is at least partly responsible for ecological destruction, famine, and widespread starvation (see Chapter 9). Yet there is not universal agreement among social scientists that overpopulation is the root cause of the world's problems, or that population will continue to grow in the future as it has in the past.

Demography and Demographic Analysis

Demography, a subfield of sociology, is the *science of population size, distribution, and composition* (Keyfitz, 1993). Demographers have developed complex statistical techniques for predicting future population levels on the basis of current characteristics. Annual population growth or decline in a country is the result of four factors: (1) the number of people who are born in the country during the year; (2) the number who die; (3) the number who move into the country; and (4) the number who move out. In the language of demographers, population changes are based on **fertility** (*live births*), **mortality** (*deaths*), and **net migration** (*in-migration less out-migration*). Since there is no in-migration or out-migration to our planet for now at least, future population depends solely on fertility and mortality. Acting together over time, these demographic factors produce each country's **population pyramid,** typically depicted as *a graph that represents the composition of a country's population by age and sex.* Low-income preindustrial countries, which have high rates of fertility and moderate rates of mortality, tend to be much wider at the bottom than the top. High-income industrial nations, which have extremely low fertility and mortality, tend to be wider at the middle (Figure 20.1).

Demographers estimate future fertility on the basis of past fertility patterns of women of child-bearing age. Although it is possible to roughly estimate population growth on the basis of **crude birth rates**—estimated as *the number of births each year per 1,000 people*—a far more accurate measure consists of **age-specific fertility rates,** estimated as *the number of births typical of women of a specific age in a particular population.* Typically, demographers divide women into different five-year **cohorts**—*people born during the same*

Figure 20.1   **The United States, Mexico, and Sweden: Widely Differing Population Pyramids (Percent in Each Age-Sex Group)**

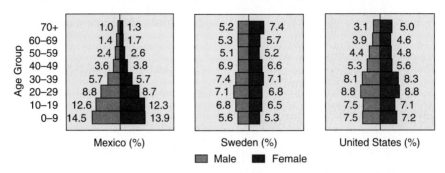

The three pyramids show the effects of different fertility rates. Mexico, with a birth rate nearly twice that of the United States (29 per 1,000) and a population growth rate of 2.2 percent annually, has an extremely young population, tapering off with increasing age. More than half of the Mexican population is under 19. The United States, with a growth rate of 0.8 percent, is largest in the middle age groups. Sweden, where the growth is only 0.4 percent, is "aging" the most rapidly of the three countries. The smallest age groups are among the young, and the largest among the middle-aged and elderly.
Source: PC Globe (1991).

time period—and who are therefore of approximately the same age today (for example, women 15 to 19, 20 to 24, 25 to 29, and so on). If the current average number of live births per thousand women is known for each of these age groups, it is relatively easy to project future fertility. Five years from now, for example, today's 15 to 19-year-old women will be 20 to 24, which means that the fertility rates of today's 20- to 24-year-old women can be applied to them. In this way, each successive cohort of women can be "aged" at five-year-intervals, yielding an estimate of total live births. Since fertility rates in most cultures typically peak during the late teens and twenties, the largest number of babies will be born to women in these age groups; thereafter, as the cohort "ages" into their thirties and forties, the total number of babies born to them will decline, dropping to zero as the cohort "ages" out of child-bearing age altogether.

The second source of population change is mortality. Although **crude death rates** (*the number of deaths each year per 1,000 people*) yield a rough measure, demographers prefer to rely on **age-specific mortality rates,** *estimates of the number of deaths typical of men and women of specific ages in the population.* As with age-specific fertility rates, these rates are then applied to successive cohorts of men and women as they age. Note that female mortality rates also affect the number of babies born, since as a cohort of females ages, some of its members will die, resulting in fewer women of child-bearing age.

One measure of the overall mortality of a society is its **life expectancy,** *the average number of years a per-*

son can expect to live once he or she has reached a given age. In almost all societies, the life expectancy at birth is longer for females than for males. In the United States, for example, the average life expectancy for baby girls is 79, while for baby boys it is 72. Life expectancy varies enormously among nations as well. Among the roughly 200 countries for which data are available, the United States ranks only thirty-ninth in terms of female life expectancy and forty-seventh for males. This is largely because of higher mortality rates among poorer Americans, particularly racial and ethnic minorities (see Chapter 10). For example, the mortality rate among impoverished inner-city African-American infants is higher than the rate for infants in countries like Poland, Hungary, and Cuba (Dreier, 1993). By way of comparison, Hong Kong ranks highest in terms of life expectancy at birth (84 for women and 77 for men), while the African country of Western Sahara ranks lowest (41 for women and 39 for men).

Because future population depends on assumptions about human behavior, it is extremely difficult to make predictions about population growth with much accuracy. If a country is effective in implementing family planning programs, for example, tomorrow's fertility may be very different from today's. Similarly, an unforeseen epidemic (such as AIDS) may greatly increase mortality, or, conversely, the development of new drugs (such as antibiotics) may greatly reduce mortality. For this reason, demographers often give a range of estimates for future population—a low estimate that assumes high mortality and low fertility; a high estimate that assumes low mortality and high fertility; and an intermediate estimate that represents a "best guess" somewhere in between.

There is one feature of population forecasting that is especially important when projecting future population: the number of young girls who constitute potential mothers at some time in the future. High-fertility societies typically have very large numbers of children, including female children who will grow up and enter child-bearing age. When they do so, they will provide a large base for having children, even if each one decides to have fewer children than was previously typical. For example, nearly half of India's 866 million people are under 20 years of age, including 204 million young women and girls, representing an enormous potential for future population growth, even if birth control leads to smaller cohorts in the future.

This is illustrated by the example of China, whose government decided to limit fertility in 1979 by rewarding one-child families with additional income and preferential treatment in terms of jobs, housing, health care, and education, while punishing those who refuse to keep their families small. This policy has succeeded in reducing fertility to 1.9 in 1992, its lowest level ever. Yet this does not mean the population of China has started to decline from its current level of 1.2 billion people. Because China has 171 million women under the age of 30 capable of bearing children—nearly a third of its female population—many demographers believe that even with low fertility rates the population will continue to grow for years to come, eventually peaking at 1.9 billion midway in the twenty-first century (see Box 20.1).

The Theory of the Demographic Transition

Demographers have noted that many societies seem to go through roughly the same stages of population growth: They begin with a stage of low growth resulting from high fertility and equally high mortality, pass through a transitional stage of high growth resulting from high fertility but low mortality, and end up in a final stage of low growth resulting from low fertility and low mortality. This model is termed the theory of the **demographic transition,** which assumes that *during industrialization declines in mortality precede but are eventually followed by declines in fertility, resulting in a period of population growth during the transition.*

In the past, agriculturally based preindustrial societies tended to have high fertility and mortality rates that more or less counterbalanced one another, resulting in a population that was either fairly stable or grew extremely slowly. Crude death rates as high as 50 per 1,000 people were caused by harsh conditions, unsta-

ble food supplies, and lack of disease control. Plagues, epidemics, and famines produced widespread illness and death, periodically reducing the population. Such societies had to develop strong beliefs and institutions in support of high fertility to prevent a decline in population. Children were therefore often valued for a variety of cultural and economic reasons, particularly where they made a contribution to hunting, farming, herding, weaving, and other tasks required of a household-based economy (Simon, 1981).

As these societies industrialized, their birth rates initially remained high, while their mortality rates plummeted as a result of improved food supply, sanitation and disease control, and eventually modern medicine. This resulted in rapidly growing populations. Eventually, however, mature industrialized societies also experienced a decline in fertility, as families came to realize that children are likely to be an economic burden for parents who live in cities, pay rent, buy groceries, and have to pay for child care and education. Although during the early stages of industrialization children often worked in factories and therefore contributed to family income, the hardships of child labor eventually led to the outlawing of such practices. Rather then being a source of income or other resources, children became an expense. People modified their reproductive practices accordingly, fertility dropped, and eventually population growth halted as low mortality was matched by equally low fertility. The demographic transition was completed.

Critical Assessment The theory of demographic transition nicely describes the historical experience of today's high-income industrialized societies, on which it is based. Unfortunately, it does not describe the experience of the remaining three-quarters of the world population nearly so well. These nations have seen their mortality rates decline *without* experiencing the sorts of economic growth that might lead their citizens to reevaluate the economic costs of having children. As a result, the first phase of the demographic transition (a decline in mortality) has not always been followed by the second (a decline in fertility), and population explosion has been the inevitable result. Mortality in these countries has dropped not because of economic growth, but because thanks to globalization they are able to obtain food, medicine (particularly antibiotics), agricultural technologies, knowledge of sanitation, and pesticides from the already industrialized nations. For example, DDT, which was developed as a pesticide in 1939, was widely used during World War II to wipe out mosquitoes that carried the deadly tropical disease malaria. In India alone a million people died of malaria each year before DDT reduced the number to below

Box 20.1

Globalization

What Is the Price of Zero Population Growth?

The Chinese government has long realized that the country's enormous population (currently 1.2 billion people) poses daunting challenges to economic development. With more than a fifth of the world's population requiring jobs, housing, food, health care, and government services, China could easily go the way of other populous low-income nations: a huge and growing gap between wealth and poverty.

In 1991, alarmed by the prospect of resurging population growth, the central government called for a new "responsibility system" to enforce existing programs intended to limit family size. It initiated a crackdown on people who violated family planning policies, and threatened to punish local officials if they were too lenient. In response, local family planning officials throughout rural China forced young women to submit to IUD insertion or sterilization. In 1991 alone, nearly 13 million women were sterilized. Families who had children in violation of government guidelines were assessed stiff fines. In some cases their homes were smashed, and possessions ranging from farm animals to television sets were confiscated by government officials. Violators were sometimes publicly beaten and shamed as well (Kristof, 1993; WuDunn, 1993b).

Although these programs have succeeded in reducing fertility to fewer than two children per family, their impact has been devastating for many people. In China, where children are culturally valued and male children in particular are highly prized, women have paid a stiff price for a lowered birth rate. Based on an analysis of birth registries and the normal ratio of female to male births, demographers estimate that 900,000 or more female infants simply "disappear" at birth. Some of these go unregistered, while others are aborted. Thanks to the technological globalization, even the smallest Chinese village can now avail itself of ultrasound equipment to determine the gender of unborn children, and female fetuses can be aborted. Occasionally, when the female baby comes to term, it may even be killed (Kristof, 1993; WuDunn, 1993b)

Although no one can contest the importance of global population control, the experience of China raises serious questions about the wisdom of even the best-intended policies. China's global economic ambitions, diagnostic equipment and birth control technologies imported from around the world, and ancient Chinese cultural beliefs all interact in a way that has proven costly to the Chinese people.

China's "one child" campaign has been highly effective in bringing the birthrate down—too effective, perhaps. In a culture where male children are the most highly prized, some families compelled to have only a single child have used ultrasound and other technologies to determine the sex of their fetuses, aborting those who are female. Nearly a million girls are unaccounted for annually, based on normal male-female sex ratios at birth.

5,000 (Dunlop, 1981). Part of India's population explosion can be directly attributed to the eradication of this single disease.

Yet at the same time, the low-income nations of the world have not industrialized, and there is considerable debate over whether or not they will be able to do so (see Chapter 9). Thus the conditions that might lead to changes in the economic value of large families have not occurred, and therefore fertility rates are not rapidly declining. Few if any children in most poor societies finish high school and fewer still go to college, so the cost of education is not a burden borne by most families. Laws protecting against the exploitation of child labor in factories are frequently lacking, or are poorly enforced. Large families thus continue to be culturally valued and economically useful, since children often contribute to family income by working on farms, in factories, or at numerous odd jobs to help make ends meet. High rates of fertility are often reinforced by religious beliefs that discourage birth control while strongly valuing childbearing.

The industrial nations have helped finance family-planning programs in low-income countries in order to educate people about birth control. In addition, they have provided condoms, pills, and other means of reducing fertility. While such programs have met with some success, they often run up against deep-seated religious and other cultural values. During the Reagan and Bush presidencies there were significant cuts in U.S. funding of such programs as well, since birth control efforts often violated the beliefs of some conservative supprters of those administrations. It is clear that global efforts at family planning are fraught with problems. It remains to be seen whether they will ultimately succeed in reducing fertility (and hence global population growth) in the absence of successful industrialization.

The Global Population Explosion

As Figure 20.2 shows, the world has experienced the detonation of a virtual "population bomb" during the last two centuries, an explosion that today threatens to engulf the entire planet (Ehrlich, 1968). The first doubling of the human population since the birth of Christ required 16 centuries to occur. The second doubling, by way of contrast, required only two centuries and by 1850 global population had reached one billion people. Although at that point the demographic transition had begun to slow population growth in Europe and the United States, explosive growth had begun in the rest of the world. Global population more than doubled during the next century, and again during the next 40 years. By 1950, global population had reached 2.3 billion; by 1993, it was 5.4 billion. The next doubling is projected to take about 40 years, yielding a population of 11 billion by 2030, 85 percent of whom will live in the low-income nations of the world. By the year 2100, given present trends in fertility and mortality, the number could reach 14.2 billion, nearly three times the present level. Even if moderate population control is achieved, according to one recent United Nations prediction, global population is likely to stabilize at 11.3 billion people, more than twice the current number (Weeks, 1992; United Nations Development Program, 1992; Smith, 1992; Feldman, 1989).

It is difficult to capture with words this extraordinary change in human population, which has occurred in the last instant on the global clock. An often-used

In this photograph a social worker in an Indian village explains the use of an intrauterine device (IUD). Such family-planning efforts have been employed in many low-income, high-fertility nations in an effort to curb population growth. Yet these efforts often encounter resistance in cultures where large families are prized for economic and other reasons. Some demographers assert that industrialization and economic growth are the best hopes for a demographic transition to a low-fertility, low-mortality society.

Figure 20.2   The Exponential Growth of Human Population

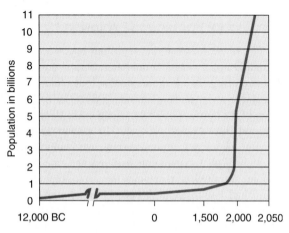

The world's population has grown explosively during the past several centuries. There were only about 8 million people when agriculture first developed 12,000 years ago, and 300 million by the time of the birth of Christ. As recently as five centuries ago, the number had only reached a half billion. The number doubled to a billion by 1850, and doubled again by 1950. Since that time it has doubled again, to 5.4 billion. The world population is projected to reach 11 billion by 2030.
Source: Weeks (1992); Oberai (1992).

metaphor points out that while it took as many as 20,000 generations to add the first two billion human beings to the planet, it only required a single generation to add the second two billion. It is estimated that by the year 2000, out of all the people who have ever been born in the history of the human race, one out of 13 will be alive at that time (Weeks, 1992). The conclusion is inescapable that the human species is in-

creasing in number with unprecedented speed and impact on planetary resources, and it will continue to do so for some time to come.

Malthus and Marx: How Many People Are Too Many?

This global population explosion may indeed seem alarming, but numbers alone do not tell the whole story. There is still a great deal of sparsely settled land in the world, and if the planet's 5.4 billion people were somehow crammed into the United States, the resulting crowding would be no greater than currently exists in the country of Taiwan. Is the world in fact overpopulated?

Malthus: Overpopulation and Its Natural Limits

The case that the world is overpopulated was first made more than two centuries ago, by the British social philosopher Thomas Malthus (1766–1834). Malthus (1926; orig. 1798) developed the theory of **exponential population growth**—the belief that, like compound interest, *a constant rate of population growth produces a population that grows by an increasing amount with each passing year.* Exponential increases thus exhibit a **doubling time**—*for a given rate of increase, the total number of people will keep doubling in a given time period.* For the United States, for example, the population will double in 87 years at the present rate of growth (0.8 percent each year); it will double again in the next 87 years, and so on again, until the growth rate changes. By way of comparison, with its current 1.9 percent annual growth rate, India will require only 37 years to double its population, roughly the same time as the world population as a whole. Saudi

A Tokyo subway illustrates some of the problems of the global population explosion. More people mean an ever-increasing strain on global resources, particularly when population growth is accompanied by industrialization.

Arabia, whose 4.2 percent annual growth rate is one of the highest in the world, will double in only 19 years.

Malthus claimed that while population grows exponentially, food supply does not—the earth's resources are finite, and so while population may continue to double, food is more likely to grow at a constant rate. The result, in Malthus' dire warning, is an ever-worsening pressure of people against food, which will eventually become self-limiting. Unless we take steps to control our population growth, Malthus predicted, nature will do it for us: Wars fought over scarce resources, epidemics, and famine will keep population in check.

Critical Assessment Was Malthus right? In fact, although war, epidemics, and famine have been sadly evident throughout human history, population has continued to grow exponentially, and the food supply right along with it. Malthus failed to recognize that modern technology can also be applied to agriculture, yielding exponential growth of food supplies—at least for a time. Yet even though Malthus' predictions of collapse have not yet been borne out, it seems clear that there is a limit to the carrying capacity of the planet. World population cannot continue to double forever. To take a crude example, were the United States' population to continue doubling at its present relatively slow rate of 87 years, in only ten doubling periods—roughly 900 years—the country's population would reach 256 *billion* people, nearly 50 times the current population of the entire planet! To sustain this number of people, every square mile of land would have to contain nearly 71,000 people. This clear impossibility reveals what demographers term the **doubling fallacy**—the *false assumption that a given rate of population increase can be sustained indefinitely.*

Marx: Overpopulation or Maldistribution of Wealth?

If Malthus pointed to unavoidable overpopulation and misery under conditions of growth, Karl Marx identified another important source of economic hardship: the unequal distribution of wealth. Marx was sharply critical of Malthus for having claimed that overpopulation was the central cause of human starvation and misery. In Marx's view (1967; orig. 1867), the central problem was not overpopulation relative to resources but the fact that resources were inequitably distributed: In all societies, as well as the world as a whole, a small number of people enjoy the lion's share of the wealth, while the majority get what is left over. We have already looked at the unequal distribution of wealth in the United States (Chapter 8) and in the world as a whole (Chapter 9). The gap in wealth between the richest and poorest fifth of all nations has doubled in the last 40 years. In 1960 the richest fifth of all nations were

on average 30 times as wealthy as the poorest fifth; in 1989, they were 60 times as wealthy (U.N. Development Program, 1992). The quarter of the world's population that lives in high-income industrialized nations currently consumes nearly three-quarters of the world's resources (Smith, 1992).

Marx argued that such maldistribution was the result of a capitalist economic system that divided people into unequal social classes (see Chapter 1). His argument was a powerful corrective to Malthus' pessimism, particularly if we bear in mind that Malthus and Marx were writing at a time when the world population was only around one billion people. Clearly Marx's criticism of Malthus has stood the test of time, since world population has doubled, redoubled, and nearly redoubled again since Malthus' predictions were made. Even today, some studies indicate that the present world population could be readily sustained if resources were more equitably distributed (Lappe and Collins, 1986), and that even growth to as many as eight billion people is sustainable with current technologies (Meadows, Meadows, and Randers, 1992). This is not to downplay the importance of bringing the global population explosion under control; it is only to highlight the complex interdependence of population and economic organization.

Critical Assessment Although Marx was right to point out that maldistribution of wealth is an important factor in determining poverty, he clearly underestimated the importance of population growth. At some point it seems clear that overpopulation will occur if population growth is not curbed, whatever technological solutions might be found to increase the food supply. As we shall see later in this chapter, and as the introductory quote illustrates, environmental stresses have grown substantially since Marx's time, and some scientists believe we are approaching a point of no return in terms of inflicting irreversible environmental damages. While some redistribution of wealth would go far to alleviate the problems of hunger and starvation in the world, ultimately the consequences of the population explosion must be faced. Since much of the world's population increase is currently being concentrated in urban areas, we will examine the impact of urbanization on modern life, before turning to the environmental effects of both.

URBANIZATION

Although words like "city," "urban," "rural," and "metropolitan" are commonly used in everyday language, for demographers and sociologists they have fairly well-defined meanings that are often shaped by the requirements of data collection. In the United

States, **rural** refers to *any human settlement of fewer than 2,500 people,* while **urban** is generally used to describe *a concentration of people engaged in nonagricultural activities.* A **city** is defined sociologically as *a permanent settlement of people who depend on others for the production of food,* but what counts as a legal "city" varies widely from country to country. In most parts of the United States, for example, a "city" in the legal sense is an urban settlement that has been legally incorporated or chartered. A large urban area is often referred to as a **metropolis,** which consists of *one or more central cities and their surrounding suburbs, forming a more or less integrated regional economy.* The U.S. Bureau of the Census offers two further distinctions: **Metropolitan Statistical Areas (MSA),** which consist of *counties with an urbanized area of at least 50,000 people,* and **Consolidated Metropolitan Statistical Areas (CMSA),** which are *groupings of the largest Metropolitan Statistical Areas.* As of the 1990 census, there were 284 MSAs and CMSAs in the United States, accounting for nearly four out of every five Americans—a proportion that continues to grow. Only 39 of these metropolitan areas contained 125 million people—half of the total U.S. population. The New York CMSA was the largest in the country, with 18 million people, followed by Los Angeles, Chicago, San Francisco, and Philadelphia.

As metropolitan areas grow, they often merge with one another to form what some urban theorists have termed a **megalopolis**—*a continuous stretch of metropolitan areas containing many cities and suburbs* (Mumford, 1961). In the United States, for example, the highly urbanized region that extends 600 miles from Boston to Washington, D.C., contains some 40 million people. Comparable areas extend from Chicago around the southern shore of Lake Michigan all the way to Detroit, and on the California coast from the Mexican border just south of San Diego for 200 miles to Ventura county north of Los Angeles.

Cities and the Rise of Industry

Preindustrial cities, which are *based on both agriculture and trade,* first appeared about 10,000 to 12,000 years ago. The development of settled agricultural areas enabled farmers to produce an **agricultural surplus,** *food beyond the amount required for immediate survival.* This surplus made it possible to sustain urban populations that were not primarily engaged in farming. The first known cities were small, with populations seldom exceeding a few thousand, since it required the surplus production of ten or more farmers to support one nonfarming city dweller. The need for access to transportation routes and rich soil for farming figured prominently in the siting of the earliest cities

along such major river systems as the Nile in Egypt, the Tigris and Euphrates in what is today Iraq, the Yangtze and Huang Ho in China, and the Indus in India (Hosken, 1993).

Early city residents included government officials, priests, handicraft workers, and others specialized in nonagricultural occupations, although many city dwellers engaged in farming as well. The early Greek city-states, which emerged some 2,500 years ago, were small and self-contained, and they generally lived within their resources, obtaining food and building materials from their neighboring areas (Mumford, 1961). Until modern times, very few cities in the world surpassed 100,000 people. Rome, at the time of Christ an enormous metropolis with 800,000 people, was comparable in population to a moderately sized U.S. city today.

The industrial revolution of the eighteenth century radically changed the nature of cities. While cities of the past had primarily served as centers of trade, **industrial cities** now emerged as *centers of manufacturing.* Although some of the earliest English factories were in smaller cities, by the nineteenth century industrialization went hand in hand with **urbanization,** *the concentration of people in urban areas.* At the beginning of the nineteenth century, there were barely 100 places in England with more than 5,000 inhabitants; by the end of the century, there were more than 600 such places, containing more than 20 million people. London alone grew from 1.1 million to 7.3 million people between 1800 and 1910 (Hosken, 1993; Brown and Jacobson, 1987). In the United States, the explosion of cities coincided with the onset of industrialization at the end of the nineteenth century. By the early twentieth century, most Americans could be classified as urban, and today, as we have noted, the large majority (78 percent) live in metropolitan areas.

Sociologists and the City

The early industrial cities were squalid and unhealthy places, with people living in shacks alongside factories. In the absence of sanitation and sewage systems, illness and epidemics were common, and many people died from typhoid, cholera, dysentery, and tuberculosis. Understandably, the earliest sociologists had a deep mistrust of urban life.

The German sociologist Ferdinand Toennies (1855–1936), one of the first to contrast traditional rural life with the then-emerging more cosmopolitan urban life, believed that the latter contained the seeds of "decay and death" (Toennies, 1963; orig. 1887). Toennies, termed traditional life **Gemeinschaft,** the German word for *community,* which was characterized by *intimate relationships, a strong sense of family, powerful folkways and mores, and pervasive religious beliefs.*

Urban life—termed **Gesellschaft,** the German word for *society*—is the opposite: *Relationships are impersonal, family life breaks down, traditional beliefs give way to cold calculation and impersonal reason, and religious conviction is replaced by shifting public opinion.* Toennies was deeply troubled by what he regarded as this unavoidable trend.

Georg Simmel, a German contemporary of Toennies, echoed this theme, although he emphasized the other side of the coin. In an important essay entitled "The Metropolis and Mental Life," Simmel (1964; orig. 1902) argued that the dense concentration of people in cities provides enormous amounts of mental stimulation for urban residents. People are constantly in contact with one another, and life is regulated by the "traffic light and the clock" rather than by the more organic rhythms of nature. In order to protect themselves against overstimulation, city dwellers of necessity adopt an attitude of indifference toward one another, stepping over the body of a drunkard or ignoring a cry for help. On the other hand, Simmel argued, the very impersonality of urban life creates an enormous opportunity for freedom, creativity, and lives that are free from the prying eyes and eternal gossip of neighbors in more rural settings.

During the 1920s and 1930s, researchers at the University of Chicago turned that city into a vast laboratory for urban studies. Many studies focused on such "social problems" as hoboes, the mentally ill, juvenile delinquents, criminals, prostitutes, and others who were seen as casualties of urban living (Box 20.2). In an important essay that synthesized many earlier ideas, Louis Wirth (1938) argued that urbanism constituted a specific "way of life" that resulted from the geographical concentration of large numbers of socially diverse people. One feature of urban living is that city residents frequently mistrust others who are different, segregating themselves on the basis of race, ethnicity, class, and even lifestyle into neighborhoods of like-minded people.

Some urban scholars, such as Robert Ezra Park, Ernest Burgess, and Roderick McKenzie (1925), believed that urban areas were similar to natural biological ones and could be analyzed according to ecological principles similar to those that governed natural habitats in the wild. Eager to be "scientific," the "Chicago School" argued that sociology should focus on **human ecology**—*the study of the spatial organization of people in their urban environment.* This consisted of analyzing the "natural" or "subsocial" processes that allegedly governed the physical organization of cities (Park, 1926; Burgess, 1925).

Box 20.2

Critical Thinking

How Pathological Are Cities?

Despite early sociology's frequent identification of city life with pathology, even in supposedly impersonal cities people manage to maintain intense social networks and close personal ties. Immigrant groups, for example, often recreate their home cultures, creating a strong sense of community (Gans, 1962a, 1962b; Fischer, 1982, 1984). Thus some sense of community can be reestablished even within the impersonality of the city in what Wirth termed a social mosaic. Wirth's (1928) study of a Jewish community in Chicago was but one in a long tradition of sociological research that rediscovered the existence of a small-town community within large cities. Other examples include studies of urban African-American men such as Elliot Liebow's (1967) *Talley's Corner* and Mitchell Durnier's (1992)

Slim's Table; studies of Italian-American communities such as William F. Whyte's (1943) *Street Corner Society* and Herbert Gans' (1962a) *The Urban Villagers;* and Gerald Suttles's (1968) *The Social Order of the Slum.*

Physical characteristics such as size or density do not by themselves account for urban problems; what is important is the way a particular society organizes itself in cities. Chinese cities such as Beijing or Shanghai manage to crowd millions of people into extremely dense neighborhoods, including the sorts of high-rise housing flats associated with crime and violence in the United States. Yet crime rates in Chinese cities, at least until recent times, have been low, and people have shared a strong sense of community.

In the view of the human ecologists, competition for scarce urban space naturally results in certain patterns of spatial organization that are common to all cities. The primary determinant of this spatial organization is the value of land, which is higher for more centrally located parcels. Downtown land is extremely expensive, and as a result banks, office buildings, high-priced stores, and factories all vie for space in downtown locations. (At the time this theory was first formulated in the 1920s, growing cities like Chicago had their factories downtown.)

Outside the downtown area, the city was seen as organized in concentric circles, with land values dropping as one moves away from the center (Figure 20.3). As the city grows, each zone "invades" the next outer one, spreading outward like ripples that form when a rock is thrown into a pond. For the early human ecologists, what was important about this model was its "naturalness;" human beings were seen as naturally competitive, imparting a shape to cities that was seen as inevitable and largely unalterable.

The human ecologists tested their theory on numerous cities in the United States and elsewhere, expecting to find this "natural" pattern reproduced under a variety of circumstances. What they found was that cities varied considerably in their spatial organization. The supposedly "natural" ecological laws dictating the concentric zone configuration could not account for such public open space as New York City's Central Park or the Boston Commons, whose central locations and correspondingly high land values should have yielded office buildings or factories rather than parks. The shape of cities is the result not of automatic ecological processes but of the interplay of economic, social, and political factors (Logan and Molotch, 1987).

Cities in the United States

Transportation and communication technologies have played an important role in helping to shape American cities. The automobile and urban rail and subway systems enabled cities to expand outward, by permitting increased separation between home and workplace. Similarly, modern construction technologies permitted cities to expand skyward, with 100-story office complexes such as New York City's World Trade Center housing as many as 50,000 employees on a few city blocks.

The Dynamics of Urban and Suburban Growth

However important the role of transportation and communication technologies might be, the principal forces shaping cities have been political and economic. Sociologists John Logan and Harvey Molotch have argued that cities are shaped by what they call the **urban growth machine,** consisting of *those persons and institutions that have a stake in growth in the value of urban land and comprise a power elite in most cities* (Molotch, 1976; Logan and Molotch, 1987; Warner, Molotch, and Lategola, 1992). These are said to include downtown businesses, real estate owners (particularly those who own commercial and rental property), land developers and builders, newspapers (whose advertising revenues are often tied to the size of the local population), and the lawyers, accountants, architects, real estate agents, construction workers, and others whose income is tied to serving those who own land. The

Figure 20.3   The Burgess "Concentric Zone" Model of the City

1. Central business district
2. Zone of transition
3. Zone of working class homes
4. Residential zone
5. Commuter zone

In the Burgess model, the more centrally located a parcel, the higher its value. Thus the central business district (CBD) is located downtown, containing office buildings, factories, and other high-cost land uses. The Central business district is surrounded by a "zone of transition," housing factory workers at extremely high densities in cheap tenement housing. As one moves outward, the land becomes more spacious, and the social class of its residents becomes progressively higher. All cities are supposed to more or less reproduce this configuration, which is seen as determined by underlying ecological processes.
Source: Burgess (1925).

The Chicago School of human ecology argued that urban growth reflected underlying economic processes. Yet the theory had difficulty accounting for such land uses as this downtown Chicago park, which, according to the theory, should have been filled with expensive office buildings. Urban theorists today argue that cities are shaped by conscious political processes as much as hidden economic ones.

growth machine is viewed as dominating local politics in most U.S. cities, with the result that cities often compete with one another for factories, office buildings, shopping malls, and other economic activities that will increase the value of the land owned by members of the growth machine.

The post–World War II development of U.S. cities and suburbs illustrates how the growth machine can operate at the national level. The rapid growth of suburbs during the 1950s and the 1960s is often attributed to the preference of Americans for suburban living, but in fact it is also due to a combination of economic forces and government policies designed to stimulate the postwar economy (Fischer, 1982; Mollenkopf, 1977; Logan and Molotch, 1987; Jackson, 1985). The relatively new federally insured mortgage system made it possible for banks to issue large, long-term loans to individuals who wanted to purchase a house, since the federal government assumed financial responsibility for repaying the loan if the buyer defaulted. Various federal programs helped to lower the interest rates on home loans, particularly for veterans. The 1949 Federal Housing Act, as amended during the 1950s, enabled cities to acquire large parcels of land with federal funds, which could then be used to build highways, office complexes, or shopping malls.

The 1956 Interstate and National Defense Highway Act established a highway trust fund, financed by a federal tax on gasoline at the pump. The act originated in the planning efforts of a powerful consortium of bankers, corporations and unions connected with the automobile, petroleum, and construction industries (Mollenkopf, 1977). The highway trust fund provided a self-renewing source of funding to construct high-

speed freeways connecting cities and suburbs across the country. The new freeways spurred the growth of the U.S. economy, both by improving transportation and by promoting the automobile and construction industries. The existence of freeways encouraged people to buy more cars and drive additional miles, which in turn provided still more gasoline tax revenues for additional highway construction in an upward spiral. Characterized by then-President Dwight Eisenhower as "the greatest public works program in history," the legislation eventually financed nearly 100,000 miles of highways—enough to build a "Great Wall" around the world 50 feet wide and 9 feet high.

The Highway Act, in combination with the new mortgage programs, spurred the growth of suburban living, and the high-consumption lifestyle that went along with it. All of this ushered in a quarter century of growth and relative prosperity for working- and middle-class Americans. Large numbers of people bought houses in the suburbs with federally insured and subsidized loans, commuted on federally financed highways to work in federally subsidized downtown office buildings, and even shopped in malls built in part with federal dollars. Those who remained behind in the cities often did so because they were too poor to afford either a home in the suburbs or a long-distance commute to work, if indeed they had a job.

Today, the emergence of postindustrial society has further encouraged development beyond the urban fringe (Stanback, 1991; Garreau, 1991; Hahn and Wellems, 1989; Moss, 1987; Castells, 1989). Modern information technology has made it easier to locate high-tech factories and office parks in once-remote suburban or even rural locations, taking advantage of relatively inexpensive land, wooded landscapes, and other amenities. Employees who benefit from such relocation tend to be highly-educated managerial, technical, and professional specialists. Those who lack specialized skills are likely to be left behind in declining inner cities. In 1959, only 27 percent of America's poor lived in central cities; by 1987, the figure had reached 43 percent (Kasarda, 1989, 1990; Persky, Sclar, and Wiewel, 1991).

As a result of these economic changes, cities have periodically experienced fiscal crises, even during the relative prosperity of the early 1970s. In today's much harsher economic climate, many major cities in the United States are close to bankruptcy. A 1992 survey of 620 municipalities conducted by the National League of Cities found that 54 percent had budget deficits, forcing many to lay off workers and defer spending (Pagano, 1992). As globalization further threatens the industrial job base of the United States, it seems likely that American cities will continue to suffer from a tangle of economic, fiscal, and social problems.

As cities have grown and declined, one of the most dramatic population shifts in U.S. history has been the rapid growth of **suburbs,** *a catch-all term for any urban development that occurs outside a city.* In 1950, cities contained 33 percent of the U.S. population, considerably more than their surrounding suburbs (23 percent). During the 1960s, the suburbs overtook the cities, and by 1990 suburban population reached 46 percent of the U.S. total, while city population had declined slightly to 31 percent (Frey and Speare, 1991).

The flight of middle- and upper-income households from the cities, although somewhat counterbalanced by movement in the other direction on the part of young professionals, has resulted in a growing income disparity between the cities and their surrounding suburbs. This has led some writers to speak of a new "suburban century" (Schneider, 1992), in which suburbanites will dominate the economy and politics (Edsall and Edsall, 1991; Stanback, 1991; Garreau, 1991). Yet it is important not to draw too sharp a distinction between cities and their suburbs. Many so-called suburbs are large cities themselves, with all of the problems of poverty, unemployment, homelessness, racism and segregation that plague their "downtown" neighbors (Dreier, 1993; Perksy, Sclar, and Wiewel, 1991).

Poverty, Segregation, and Discrimination in U.S. Cities

Although poverty has increased throughout the United States during the past two decades (Chapter 8), it has been particularly acute in the central cities of metropolitan areas, especially among racial and ethnic minorities. Inner-city neighborhoods have often become sites of crime, drugs, violence, and the racial tensions that have periodically exploded in riots, such as that which occurred in Los Angeles in 1992. Homeless men, women, and children are found in virtually every city in the country.

Reflecting the distribution of income, racial and ethnic segregation is common in American cities and suburbs. In many cities, nonwhites are now in the majority (Dreier, 1993). According to the 1990 Census, 30 percent of all African Americans live in neighborhoods that are almost entirely black, while most of the re-

Segregation, discrimination, poverty, and gang violence go together in many American cities. In this 1993 photograph, a group called "United For/In Peace" urges leaders of two rival Chicago gangs to work together to end violence and combat the effects of racism and poverty. The group is holding meetings with gang members across the country.

mainder (62 percent) live in neighborhoods that are 60 percent or more black. Segregation is similar among Latinos, although not quite so pronounced. Two-thirds of all whites live in nearly all-white neighborhoods. It is estimated that about 70 percent of the American population would have to move to achieve fully integrated neighborhoods (Massey and Denton, 1989; Gillmor and Doig, 1992; Dreier, 1993).

Why is racial and ethnic segregation so pronounced? Partly it is due to choice—the preference many people have for living with others whom they perceive as in some way similar to themselves. But it is also due to the effects of discrimination (Chapter 10). For example, many banks and other lending institutions routinely engage in **redlining,** a *policy by which they exclude entire low-income neighborhoods (particularly those occupied by racial or ethnic minorities) from loans for businesses, housing construction, or home improvements, thereby contributing to neighborhood deterioration.* Redlining reinforces segregation by isolating racial and ethnic minorities in physically declining neighborhoods. Although federal laws were passed in the mid-1970s outlawing redlining while requiring lenders to reveal the location of their loans, it is still widely practiced. A recent Federal Reserve Bank study of Boston found that even after taking into account economic differences between neighborhoods, white areas received 24 percent more loan money than black areas. A similar study conducted by the City of Boston, which focused on uninsured (and hence riskier) loans, estimated that white neighborhoods received three times the number of mortgages than black neighborhoods (Dreier, 1991, 1993; Finn, 1989).

Blockbusting is another illegal practice *in which lenders and real estate agents play upon racial fears to force down property values and drive current residents out of their neighborhoods, thereby profiting from increased sales, loans, and real estate commissions.* A recent study conducted in Boston, for example, documents how during the late 1960s and early 1970s, a consortium of leading lending institutions, in cooperation with city government, encouraged blacks to buy homes in Jewish neighborhoods. Real estate agents spread rumors in the community about violent crime, vandalism to Jewish places of worship, acts of anti-semitism, and declining property values, thereby inducing members of the Jewish community to sell their properties at any cost. One real estate broker later recounted how he was instructed to "just scare the hell out of them." Within a decade, the neighborhood went from all white to nearly all black. The banks profited from issuing new, higher-interest loans, while real estate agents benefited from the commissions they received on sales (Levine and Harmon, 1992).

Viable low-income neighborhoods have also been harmed by **urban renewal** *a federal government program that provides funds to localities for fixing up "blighted areas."* This usually has meant replacing low-cost housing (and the people who lived in it) with hotels, convention centers, high-rise office buildings, malls, and upscale residences. The low-income people who are displaced are seldom provided with comparable low-cost housing; as a result, many experience a growing rent burden, and some eventually become homeless (Gilderbloom and Appelbaum, 1988; Stone, 1993; Gans, 1962a). Government urban renewal programs have often been accompanied by **gentrification,** *a process by which upper-income professionals ("the gentry") buy low-cost downtown housing, fix it up, move in, and thereby convert the neighborhood from a low- to high-income area, displacing poor people as a result.* While this has resulted in an upgrading of "run-down" neighborhoods, like urban renewal it has also eliminated badly needed housing for the poor and in recent years has contributed to massive shortages of low-cost housing (Gilderbloom and Appelbaum, 1988; Goetze, 1979; Hartman, Keating, and LeGates, 1981; Palen and London, 1984; Stone, 1993).

World Urbanization Today

The problems of urbanization that trouble American cities were unknown throughout much of the world until relatively recently. In the low-income nations of the world, rapid urbanization did not begin until well into the twentieth century, when they began to become fully incorporated in the global economic system. Today they face problems of pollution, congestion, housing, poverty, and unemployment that eclipse those of American cities.

Some of the most highly urbanized countries in the world today are those that only a century ago were almost entirely rural. The metropolitan area that includes Mexico City, for example, had nearly 21 million people in 1991, and was the second-largest city in the world behind Tokyo, which contained 27 million (see Map 20.1). Mexico City is projected to reach 30 million by the end of this century. Sao Paolo, Brazil, is nearly as large as Mexico City, with some 19 million people today. In fact, of the 20 largest metropolitan areas in the world today (Map 20.1), 11 are found in low-income countries (Hosken, 1993; Gottdiener, 1994).

As recently as 1950, only 29 percent of the world's population lived in urban areas (Palen, 1986). A mere three and a half decades later that figure had grown to

Map 20.1   Population Projections for the World's 20 Largest Metropolitan Areas

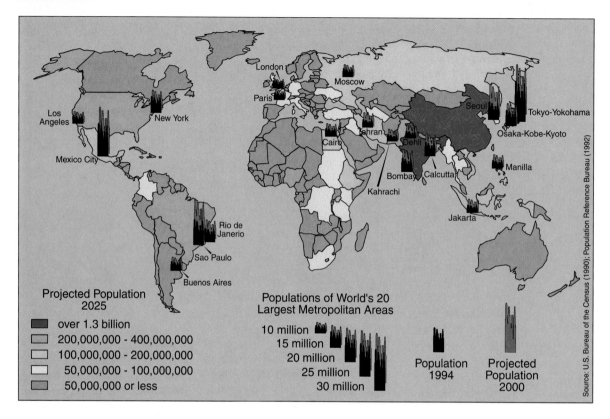

Projected Population 2025
- over 1.3 billion
- 200,000,000 - 400,000,000
- 100,000,000 - 200,000,000
- 50,000,000 - 100,000,000
- 50,000,000 or less

Populations of World's 20 Largest Metropolitan Areas
- 10 million
- 15 million
- 20 million
- 25 million
- 30 million

Population 1994   Projected Population 2000

Source: U.S. Bureau of the Census (1990); Population Reference Bureau (1992)

The world's largest metropolitan areas are expected to grow still larger throughout this century. Of these 20, only two (New York and Los Angeles) are in the United States. Many are in the poorest countries of the world, where they include large concentrations of impoverished people.

43 percent, and it is projected to reach 50 percent shortly after the turn of the century. During the next several decades, the number of people living in cities across the world is expected to double, with urban growth occurring three times faster in low-income than high-income nations. In many low-income countries, a large part of the total population lives in the capital city; nearly a quarter of Mexico's 90 million people, for example, live in Mexico City (Brown and Jacobson, 1987, p. 8).

This rapid urbanization has brought tremendous hardship to the people who swell these cities, since in many ways they resemble the squalid industrial cities of Europe and the United States in the last century—except that they are much larger. Millions of people live in shantytowns consisting of ramshackle huts made of oil drums, corrugated metal, or straw mats; the least fortunate sleep in the streets. Drinkable water, electricity, and sanitation are often unknown, and widespread pollution fills the air and contributes to ill-

ness and death. Although people come to the cities in search of work, many are unemployed or must eke out a marginal living as street vendors or in the "underground" or informal economy.

The Emergence of Global Cities

With the emergence of postindustrial society (see Chapters 4 and 15) **global cities** have appeared, *metropolitan areas that are highly interconnected with one another in terms of their roles as centers of global political and economic decision making, finance, and culture* (Friedmann and Wolff, 1982; Friedmann, 1986; Sassen, 1991; Soja, 1987; Smith and Timberlake, 1993). The information revolution of the past quarter century has in many ways eliminated space as a constraint on communication and coordination in far-flung business enterprises. Cities can no longer be understood in isolation from one another, as they increasingly become a part of a worldwide network of places

Tens of millions of people around the globe live in shacks erected on hillsides or on vacant land surrounding rapidly growing metropolitan areas. La Saline, a Haitian shantytown, is one example. Haiti suffers not only from population growth and extreme poverty but also from, until recently, a violent and repressive military government.

linked in a global economy. According to John Friedmann and Goetz Wolff, who first developed the idea of global cities, such places "constitute a worldwide system of control over production and market expansion" (Friedmann and Wolff, 1982, p. 310). The economic role of global cities is thus defined as much by their coordinating role in the global economy as it is by their economic role in their immediate geographic region. Examples of global cities include New York, London, Tokyo, Hong Kong, Los Angeles, Mexico City, and Singapore.

Saskia Sassen's *The Global City: New York, Tokyo, and London* represents the most complete and systematic attempt to theorize about world cities. Sassen (1991, pp. 3–4) identifies four principal functions of global cities:

1. They are "command posts" in the organization of the world economy.
2. They serve as key locations for businesses related to finance, accounting, marketing, design, and other highly specialized (and profitable) services that are replacing manufacturing as the leading economic sectors.
3. They are the most important sites of innovation and new product development.
4. They serve as the principal markets for global businesses.

In a far-flung global economy, overall coordination and control is found in global cities, where stateless corporations and international bankers maintain their headquarters. Yet at the same time, global cities often have growing numbers of poor people who work in low-wage services and low-skill factory production. Sweatshops coexist with the most profitable activities of international businesses in global cities; great poverty and equally great wealth are found side by side. In Los Angeles, for example, hundreds of thousands of immigrants from Mexico and Central America work in the shadows of the downtown skyscrapers that house the world's largest banks and corporations. These workers typically labor as janitors, domestics, or workers in small clothing factories that sew apparel for global garment manufacturers (Appelbaum and Arnold, forthcoming; King, 1990; Ross and Trachte, 1990; Sassen, 1991).

POPULATION GROWTH, URBANIZATION, AND THE ENVIRONMENT

The combination of rapid population growth, industrialization, and urbanization has taken its toll on the planetary environment. Additional people require increasing amounts of the planet's limited resources, and when the additional people are added to areas undergoing industrialization, they consume far more resources per person than did people in preindustrial times. The seven most industrialized countries in the world (which include the United States) account for almost half of human-caused carbon dioxide and other similar pollutants in the atmosphere (Smith, 1992). As they attempt to industrialize through their participation in the global economy, the poor nations of the world will likely join the wealthy ones in inflicting major damage to planetary ecology.

Growing World Industrial Production

To meet the growing needs of the world's people, global industrial output would have to increase some five times over present levels. Just three countries (China, India, and Brazil) today have 42 percent of the world's population; they alone will do significant harm to the world ecology if they industrialize without "clean" technology. Chinese factories today emit 15.5 million tons of sulfur dioxide into the atmosphere. That figure is projected to increase nearly a hundredfold by the year 2000, to 1.4 billion tons, if controls on pollution are not adopted (WuDunn, 1993a).

One source of this problem is the massive debt owed by the low-income nations of the world to the wealthy ones, which in 1989 amounted to more than two-fifths of their combined national wealth. To pay for this debt, poorer nations have frequently overexploited their natural resources, converting forests to farmland or pasture to produce cash crops, beef, and lumber for export. Within the next decade, a billion new jobs will be needed in these countries just to feed their growing populations. At the present rate, two out of every three countries that export tropical timber will soon be out of forests; yet they will still have enormous debts and a growing number of mouths to feed (Smith, 1992).

The Effects of Urbanization

Industrialization and urbanization go together, and when people in industrializing societies move to cities they create additional environmental problems beyond those associated with population growth and industrialization alone. Apart from creating their own miniclimates (urban areas are "heat islands," some 5 to 9 degrees Fahrenheit hotter than surrounding areas), cities are highly inefficient users of energy. The average U.S. city consumes 150 gallons of water per person each day, along with 3.3 pounds of food and 16 pounds of fossil fuel. In the process 120 gallons of sewage per person is produced, as well as 3.3 pounds of garbage, and 1.3 pounds of air pollution. New York City by itself produces enough garbage each year to cover Central Park's 1.3 square miles to a height of 13 feet (Spirn, 1984).

While rural areas tend to rely on local supplies of food, fuel, and water, cities typically bring these necessities from distant places. Residents in low-income urban areas in India and Africa, for example, often must obtain wood for cooking and heating from nearby forests, resulting in massive deforestation. One study of nine major Indian cities found that it took less than ten years to deplete forests within 60 miles by an average of 30 percent (Bowonder et al., 1985). The growth of cities in an unplanned sprawl requires the use of energy just to move people and goods around. The use of private automobiles increases pollution: Streets and highways become clogged, and pollution reaches the levels for which cities such as Los Angeles, Mexico City, and Bangkok are infamous. Although air quality standards in the United States have actually reduced automobile pollution in recent years, urban Americans nonetheless managed to burn 416 gallons of gasoline per person in 1986, four times as much as their counterparts in European cities (which have far more efficient public transportation serving more compact urban areas, as well as more fuel-efficient cars), and ten times as much as Asian urbanites (who still rely heavily on their bicycles and feet for transportation).

Usually food must be shipped long distances to reach cities, requiring energy for transportation, refrigeration, processing and packaging, and storage. Water must be imported from far away as well. Los Angeles and much of southern California, for example, are semidesert areas that are entirely dependent on water from northern California, the eastern slope of the Sierra Nevada Mountains, and the Colorado River, sources that are hundreds of miles away. The water from northern California must be pumped *over* the Tehachapi Mountains, requiring additional expenditures of energy. Mexico City must pump in water from an area 100 miles away and a mile lower in elevation. Once food, water, gasoline, and various forms of energy are consumed in urban areas, the resulting waste products must be collected, stored, treated, and disposed; this, too, requires the expenditure of large amounts of energy (Brown and Jacobson, 1987).

Global Environmental Problems

The environmental problems that exist today reflect the use of technologies developed around the world, as well as the rapid global economic changes that have occurred in the past quarter century. Problems occurring in one part of the planet often result from actions taken elsewhere and are likely to affect people everywhere. Consider, for example, the problem of deforestation with which we began this chapter. According to a 1990 study by the World Resources Institute and the United Nations, 40 to 50 million acres of tropical forest are lost each year, an area equivalent in size to the state of Washington. It reflects a loss of nearly 100 acres of forest *each minute,* 50 percent more than the United Nations had estimated a mere seven years earlier.

Brazil alone accounts for nearly half of the total global loss of forests; its burning forests added some five billion tons of carbon dioxide to the atmosphere in 1988, more than the world total a decade earlier (Marshall, 1989). Yet despite the increase in greenhouse gases resulting from deforestation in low-income nations, high-income industrial nations—which have far fewer people—contribute still more to global environmental damage, since they use (and waste) by far the largest share of global energy. The United States, for example, today *wastes* more energy than it consumed a mere 30 years ago; today more energy leaves smokestacks and tailpipes than was needed to power factories and automobiles in the 1960s. Between 1960 and 1989, total U.S. energy consumption increased 3.6 times faster than population: While population grew by one-fifth, energy consumption grew by four-fifths, and the amount of wasted energy doubled (*National Geographic,* 1991).

Many scientists argue that the release of carbon dioxide and other industrial and agricultural gases has contributed to a **greenhouse effect,** *the formation of a layer of gases in the upper atmosphere that traps heat at the planet's surface that otherwise would be reflected off into space.* Atmospheric carbon dioxide is known to have increased 25 percent in the last 100 years, due to increasing burning of fossil fuel, deforestation, and pollution; it will have doubled by 2030, at present rates of increase. By geologic standards this is an enormous change in a very short period of time. Some scientists fear that this might result in **global warming,** *a projected increase in average planetary temperatures by some 3 to 8 degrees Fahrenheit by the middle of the next century.* While there is a great deal of uncertainty in making such predictions, most researchers agree that a temperature increase at the high end of this range could have environmentally catastrophic effects (LaBrecque, 1989; Rosenberg and Crosson, 1988).

Although the industrial nations are today the major source of greenhouse gases, the far more populous low-income nations are likely to become the principal polluters as they seek to industrialize. China, for example, because of its enormous size and rapid move toward industrialization (see Chapter 9), is fast becoming the world's major contributor to greenhouse gases. Coal, a highly polluting source of energy, provides the country with three-quarters of its energy needs, creating so much pollution in some urban areas that residents must wear surgical masks for protection. Although China is committed to environmental protection, it is a poor country that lacks the resources to engage in widescale cleanups or conversion to cleaner technologies. In the southern and eastern part of the country, where urbanization and industrialization are proceeding at historically unprecedented rates, the environmental damage has been considerable. Yet the Chinese government has made it clear that economic development will not be subordinated to environmental concerns (WuDunn, 1993a).

Another critical environmental problem that results from industrialization and urbanization is the depletion of the ozone layer in the upper atmosphere. Ozone helps to shield against the sun's ultraviolet rays, which cause skin cancer and eye cataracts, as well as adversely affecting some plants, crops, and possibly the ocean plankton eaten by smaller fish. It is estimated that the ozone layer was depleted by some 5 percent between 1978 and 1991, and that a major ozone "hole" has appeared in the south polar region. Ozone depletion results from chemicals containing chlorine, such as the chlorofluorocarbons (CFCs) used in industrial solvents, dry cleaning, air conditioners, and refrigerators. Even though in 1991 the industrialized nations agreed to strict limits on CFC use, ozone depletion is expected to continue into the next century. This is because CFCs take many years to reach the upper atmosphere where they do their damage. As with other aspects of our environment, mistakes that are made today may take years before their full impact is realized (Stevens, 1991).

Global population and industrial, urban, and environmental systems form complex interconnections. Donella and Dennis Meadows's controversial 1972 study, *The Limits to Growth,* touched off a furor when their computer model of the planetary economy and

A Beijing, China, street sweeper wears a surgical mask for protection against air pollution. China experiences extremely high levels of pollution, an experience typical of newly industrializing countries that are too poor to invest in antipolluting technologies. Global industrialization is a major source of global pollution today.

ecology predicted global catastrophe within a century. Twenty years after their original study, the Meadows claim in their book *Beyond the Limits* (1992) that the human race must take dramatic steps to attempt to reverse damage that may already be irreversible. Their current global computer model draws on the interaction between 225 different measures of industrial output, natural resources, pollution, population, agriculture, and food supply. The model predicts that if nothing is done to significantly change current trends, the probable growth in population, pollution, food, and industrial output through the mid-twenty-first century will produce plummeting industrial output, famine, and rising mortality.

On the other hand, the Meadows also argue that a **sustainable development** scenario is possible, consisting of *programs that would create economic growth while preserving the environment.* This could be achieved through conserving nonrenewable resources such as forests and minerals, and by shifting to renewable sources of energy such as wind and solar power. If people, businesses, and nations were willing to pursue such policies, along with those that limit families to two children, population growth would halt while the world achieved a level of industrial output equivalent to Western Europe today.

GLOBALIZATION: PROGRESS TOWARD SUSTAINABLE DEVELOPMENT

The environmental problems that we confront are the direct result of the interaction between population explosion, urbanization, and industrialization. There is a growing recognition of the global nature of these problems, and an increasing willingness on the part of the world's nations to work together in the face of a looming catastrophe that knows no national boundaries. Just as globalization has contributed to the accelerated destruction of planetary ecology, so too it points the way to possible solutions. Of particular importance are global institutions such as the United Nations, which have provided a framework for disseminating information about family planning, as well as for negotiating treaties that would control ecologically unsound practices. In fact, the emergence of global institutions for dealing with planetary demographic, economic, political, and environmental concerns may well become one of the defining features of the next century, as the world comes to recognize that it is increasingly a single ecological, economic, and even political unit.

Signs of Global Progress

There has been some progress toward controlling population, energy waste, and ecological destruction in recent years. For example, although only one out of every ten fertile couples in the world used contraceptives in 1965, by the 1980s that figure had reached nearly half, thanks primarily to strong family-planning efforts by the United Nations and other global organizations. Currently, an estimated $3 billion in public and private monies is spent worldwide each year on family planning. The United Nations Population Fund estimates that spending an additional $2 billion would add another 1.2 billion couples to the roster of those using birth control by 2025, bringing the 2100 population down to 10.1 billion (Feldman, 1989).

Global population control efforts were hampered during the 1980s by the refusal of the U.S. government to fund United Nations programs that acknowledged abortion as a means of birth control, although U.S. policy changed in 1993. A number of low-income nations continue to oppose contraception, particularly in strongly religious Islamic and Catholic nations where birth control runs counter to religious beliefs. Yet most nations are committed to controlling population, and as we have already noted, China, the world's most populous country, has dramatically reduced its rate of population increase through strong government birth control policies, albeit at a substantial price to many individuals.

Yet the best hope for lowered population growth may be the changing role of women in the global economy. If industrialization continues to bring large numbers of women into the global workforce, it may also help to free them from traditionally subservient roles. Women who work often obtain a greater degree of economic independence as they develop a commitment to work and careers outside their homes. This, in turn, may lead them to limit their family size, as has happened in many industrial nations. In some European countries, where large numbers of women work and have full-time careers, population is actually declining, since the annual number of births has fallen below the number of deaths.

Other optimistic environmental signs include recent agreements between nations to limit CFC use, reflected in a decline in CFC production by nearly half between 1988 and 1991. The end of the Cold War has brought with it a decline in military spending, as well as reductions in nuclear warheads and delivery systems and the enormous dangers they posed. The production of natural gas, a relatively clean form of energy, has increased, as has reliance on solar and wind power. Genetic engineering promises to produce new, higher-yield forms of rice, sweet potatoes, and other foods in

The Norwegian ship Gaia *(named for the ancient Greek goddess of the earth) arrives in Rio de Janeiro for the 1992 United Nations Conference on the Environment and Development. A total of 170 nations met in an effort to work out a balance between economic growth and environmental protection. Such global efforts toward sustainable development offer hope that the peoples of the world will be able to work together to solve their common problems.*

low-income nations where the danger of starvation is ever-present. Many industrial nations have adopted recycling programs, and some have achieved considerable efficiency in energy use.

Japan's efficiency gains during the 1970s and 1980s were so great that today it uses half the materials and energy as the United States to produce equivalent output. Furthermore, in 1990 Japan adopted a 100-year plan for ecologically sound industrial development. U.S. corporations such as Monsanto, Dupont, and AT&T have pioneered "closed loop" manufacturing, which seeks to minimize waste and pollution discharges by using highly efficient technologies that recycle emissions and wastes into other phases of production. Even global cigarette smoking appears to be on the decline (Ellis, 1992; Briscoe, 1992; Smith, 1992).

The Rio Conference

In June 1992, 170 nations gathered at the United Nations Conference on the Environment and Development in Rio de Janeiro. The conference explicitly focused on the interconnection between environmental destruction, industrialization, and poverty. As the conference title suggests, low-income countries forced a discussion on the trade-off between the environment and development, pointing out the inequity that occurs when countries who have already achieved a relatively high standard of living suddenly call on those who have not to tighten their belts and do with less for the sake of environmental protection. Environmentalism, including birth control programs, is sometimes viewed with suspicion and mistrust in Africa and Latin America, as it is among people of color in the United States: It can easily be interpreted as an effort by predominantly white European and North American nations to

limit the options of nonwhite populations throughout the world (see Box 20.3).

At the Rio Conference, high-income countries sought international environmental standards, including a biological diversity treaty that would limit rain forest destruction, whaling, oceanic pollution, and species extinction. Global population control was also a high priority. Low-income countries, in exchange, sought a global climate treaty that would cut back carbon dioxide emissions, stabilizing at 1990 levels by the year 2000. They requested that programs for sustainable development be financed out of a $125 billion "green fund," controlled by the low-income nations, into which the wealthy nations would each contribute 1 percent of their wealth to be used in support of sustainable development projects. The low-income countries also demanded that part of their debt to the wealthy nations be forgiven, on the grounds that sustainable development is not possible as long as the poor nations are forced to log their forests and exploit their natural resources simply to pay the interest on their loans (Babbitt, 1992; Smith, 1992).

In short, the low-income countries seemed to be saying that if they are to accept global environmental standards that might restrict their economic development, the high-income countries must help pay the price. The industrial nations balked at some of these demands, fearful of placing too many restrictions on private businesses. The low-income nations, in return, refused to limit their ability to exploit their resources. While the Rio conference focused global attention on the interconnections between economic development, poverty, and environmental destruction, it also demonstrated that much more cooperation between wealthy and poor nations is required before these problems can be seriously addressed.

Box 20.3

Silenced Voices

Are Environmentalism and Family Planning Racist?

Edmund A. Peterson is an African-American member of the Environmental Policy Task Force, a group that seeks to balance environmental concerns with economic development programs aimed at low-income Americans. In these excerpts from an article entitled "It's Only Another Name for Genocide," Mr. Peterson (1993), a former U.S. Department of Energy official, expresses a view sometimes heard in the poor nations of Africa and Latin America, as well as among racial and ethnic minorities in the United States: that policies intended to protect the environment, including population control programs, primarily benefit whites at the expense of people of color.

"David Foreman, founder of the environmental group Earth First! has said: "I see no solution to our ruination of Earth except for a drastic reduction in human population."

Precisely where is this population cut going to come from? Certainly not the white population—the white birth rate was just 15.8 per 1,000 population in 1990, compared to 22.4 in the black community. By 2050, people of color are projected to be the majority in this

country. Does Mr. Foreman want to halt this trend?

. . . Tens of thousands of small companies, including bakeries, gas stations and dry cleaners, have been forced to close down due to excessive environmental regulations. The Joint Economic Committee [of Congress] calls this "green tape." On average, it costs $16,000 for a small firm to obtain a permit to operate under Clean Air rules. It doesn't take a genius to figure out that minorities are hurt disproportionately by these regulations, since most minority businesses are small. . . .

Environmental zealotry frequently slows economic development in African nations. It was pressure from environmentalists that caused the United Nations to force Zimbabwe to abandon its environmentally responsible elephant ranching program, which brought in much-needed foreign currency. Zimbabwe's wildlife department called the environmentalists "fat little yuppies from urban environments who don't know a thing about Africa."

In my view, this environmental colonialism must be stopped.

CHAPTER   SUMMARY

1. Population growth is the result of **fertility, mortality,** and **net migration.** The current explosion in population did not begin in earnest until the industrial revolution, with world population reaching 1 billion around 1850, 2.3 billion by 1950, and 5.4 billion in 1993.

2. Based on current trends, **demographers** predict that the global population will increase from its present level of 5.4 billion to as many as 14.2 billion people by the end of the next century, with potentially catastrophic consequences for the planet, unless people change their reproductive behavior.

3. The theory of **demographic transition,** which is based on the European experience, predicts that industrialization will lead to a drop in fertility and hence low rates of population increase. The low-in-

come nations of the world, however, have achieved low mortality rates without industrialization, and this has contributed to the global population explosion.

4. Two centuries ago Thomas Malthus predicted that overpopulation would lead to war, disease, and famine. Karl Marx, on the other hand, argued that inequitable distribution of wealth was responsible for starvation and suffering. Both arguments are partly correct, although Malthus' most pessimistic forecasts have yet to be realized.

5. Cities emerged when advanced agricultural techniques permitted societies to produce more food then they needed for immediate survival, resulting in an **agricultural surplus** that could be used to sustain people in cities. Today we are witnessing the

emergence of truly **global cities** that play a coordinating role in the global economy.

6. Although sociologists have often tended to view cities as a source of numerous pathologies resulting from their presumed harshness and impersonality, in fact research shows that many people form close friendship networks and tight communities even in the largest metropolitan areas.

7. American cities are typically shaped by local **urban growth machines** consisting of growth-oriented elites organized to enhance the value of land. The interplay of economics and politics (rather than any natural forces) explains the physical organization of cities.

8. The relatively recent combination of rapid population growth, industrialization, and **urbanization** has had a significantly adverse impact on the global environment. Major problems include widespread deforestation, species extinction, a **greenhouse effect** resulting from atmospheric emissions that portends possible **global warming,** and the partial depletion of the ozone layer.

9. Recent hopeful signs include increased public awareness of environment problems, global environmental treaties, and the call for **sustainable development** by the 170 nations at the Rio conference, which focused global attention on the interplay between environmental destruction, industrialization, and poverty.

QUESTIONS FOR DISCUSSION

1. In 1968, Paul Ehrlich claimed that a "population bomb" was ticking away that would eventually have catastrophic consequences for the planet. In what ways have his predictions been borne out? In what ways was Ehrlich, like Malthus two centuries earlier, overly pessimistic in his belief that population growth will necessarily outstrip the growth in food and other resources?

2. In many ways, cities reflect the economic conditions of the larger society. Show how this was true with the earliest agricultural cities, with industrial cities, and with the emerging global city.

3. What are the dimensions of global environmental problems today, and what insights does sociology bring to bear on understanding their causes and possible solutions?

KEY TERMS

age-specific fertility rate: The number of births typical of women of a specific age in a particular population.

age-specific mortality rate: The number of deaths typical of men and women of a specific age in a particular population.

agricultural surplus: The production of food beyond the amount required for immediate survival.

blockbusting: An illegal practice by which lenders and real estate agents play upon racial fears to force down property values and drive current residents out of their neighborhoods, thereby profiting from increased sales, loans, and real estate commissions.

city: A permanent settlement of people who depend on others for the production of food; in the United States, a legally incorporated or chartered urban settlement.

cohort: A group of people born in the same time period (for example, all people born between 1975 and 1980).

Consolidated Metropolitan Statistical Area (CMSA): According to the U.S. Bureau of the Census, groupings of the largest Metropolitan Statistical Areas.

crude birth rate: The number of births each year per 1,000 people.

crude death rate: The number of deaths each year per 1,000 people.

demographic transition: A theory arguing that industrialization is associated with movement from high fertility and mortality to low fertility and mortality, with the declines in mortality preceding declines in fertility such that a transitional period of rapid population growth results.

demography: A subfield of sociology concerned with the analysis of population size, distribution, and composition.

doubling fallacy: The false assumption that a given rate of population increase can be sustained indefinitely.

doubling time: Under exponential growth, the number of years it takes for the total population to double.

exponential population growth: The theory that a constant rate of population growth results in a population that grows by an increasing amount with each passing year.

fertility: Reproductive performance, as indicated by the number of live births actually born to a woman.

Gemeinschaft: The German word for *community,* which in Toennies's theory is characterized by rural- or town-based life, intimate relationships, a strong sense of family, powerful folkways and mores, and pervasive religious beliefs.

gentrification: A process by which upper-income professionals ("the gentry") buy low-cost downtown housing, fix it up, move in, and thereby convert neighborhoods from low- to high-income, displacing poor people as a result.

Gesellschaft: The German word for *society,* which in Toennies's theory is characterized by city life, impersonal relationships, the breakdown of family life, the replacement of traditional beliefs with cold calculation and reason, and the erosion of religious conviction in favor of shifting public opinion.

global cities: Metropolitan areas that are highly interconnected with one another in terms of their roles as centers of global political and economic decision making, finance, and culture.

global warming: A projected increase in average planetary temperatures by some 3 to 8 degrees Fahrenheit by the middle of the next century, resulting from the "greenhouse effect."

greenhouse effect: The formation of a layer of gases in the upper atmosphere that traps heat at the planet's surface that otherwise would be reflected off into space.

human ecology: A subfield of sociology, developed at the University of Chicago in the 1920s and 1930s, concerned with the study of the spatial organization of people in their urban environment.

industrial cities: Cities that are based on manufacturing.

life expectancy: The average number of years a person can expect to live once he or she has reached a given age.

megalopolis: A continuous stretch of metropolitan areas containing many cities and suburbs.

metropolis: One or more central cities and their surrounding suburbs, forming a more or less integrated regional economy.

Metropolitan Statistical Areas (MSA): According to the U.S. Bureau of the Census, all counties with an urbanized area of at least 50,000 people.

mortality: The deaths occurring in a population.

net migration: The difference between the number of people moving into a locale (in-migration) and the number of people moving out (out-migration).

population pyramid: A graph that represents the composition of a country's population by age and sex.

preindustrial cities: Cities that are based on both agriculture and trade.

redlining: A policy by which lending institutions exclude entire low-income neighborhoods (especially those occupied by racial or ethnic minorities) from loans for businesses, housing construction, or home improvements, thereby contributing to neighborhood deterioration.

rural: According to the U.S. Bureau of the Census, any human settlement of fewer than 2,500 people.

suburb: A catch-all term for any urban development that occurs outside a city.

sustainable development: Programs that create economic growth while preserving the environment through conserving nonrenewable resources such as forests and minerals, and by shifting to renewable sources of energy such as wind and solar power.

urban: A concentration of people engaged in non-agricultural activities.

urban growth machine: In Molotch and Logan's theory, persons and institutions that have a stake in growth in the value of urban land and comprise a power elite in most cities.

urbanization: The concentration of people in urban areas.

urban renewal: A federal government program that provides funds to localities for fixing up "blighted areas."

R E C O M M E N D E D   F O R   F U R T H E R   R E A D I N G

Brown, Lester R. (ed.). (1994). *State of the World, 1994: A Worldwatch Institute Report on Progress Toward a Sustainable Society.* New York: Norton.

A yearly anthology of writings on various aspects of the global environment, and what has been done (and can be done) to solve the problems that are identified. As its name implies, the Worldwatch Institute sees itself as an environmental watchdog; in addition to its annual "progress report," it publishes numerous "Worldwatch Papers" each year.

Ehrlich, Paul R., and Anne H. Ehrlich. (1990). *The Population Explosion.* New York: Simon & Schuster.

The now-classic textbook on the impacts of population growth, from the originators of the concept of the "population bomb."

Fischer, Claude. (1984). *The Urban Experience* (2nd ed.). New York: Harcourt Brace Jovanovich.

A textbook on cities and urban life by a principal urban sociologist.

Logan, John, and Harvey L. Molotch. (1987). *Urban Fortunes: The Political Economy of Place.* Berkeley: University of California Press.

A highly influential examination of the role of the urban growth machine in shaping politics, economics, and growth in U.S. cities.

Meadows, Donella H., Dennis L. Meadows, and Jorgen Randers. (1992). *Beyond the Limits: Confronting Global Collapse, Envisioning a Sustainable Future.* Post Mills, Vt.: Chelsea Green Publishing.

A controversial and upsetting examination of the interplay between population, industrialization, resources, agriculture, and the environment, which employs complex computer modeling to predict global catastrophe by the mid-twenty-first century unless strong actions are taken.

Sassen, Saskia. (1991). *The Global City: New York, London, Tokyo.* Princeton: Princeton University Press.

The principal presentation of the "global city" hypothesis, which looks at three of the world's leading metropolitan areas and their role in shaping the global economy.

Schnaiberg, Allan. (1980). *The Environment: From Surplus to Scarcity.* New York: Oxford University Press.

A sociological examination of the relationship between the environment and human society; analyzes the causes and consequences of dwindling environmental resources.

CHAPTER 21

Social Change, Collective Behavior, and Social Movements

CHAPTER OUTLINE

THINGS TO LOOK FOR

1. How do societies change, and what is the role of social movement organizations in the process?
2. What are the major differences between theories of societal change?
3. What is the relationship between collective behavior and social movements?
4. What is the role of social movements in shaping history today?

INTRODUCTION: APPROACHES TO UNDERSTANDING SOCIAL CHANGE

In a small office in downtown Moscow a commission appointed by Russian President Boris Yeltsin stays busy these days "reclaiming stolen names." The commission is charged with reviewing some 1,500 Communist place names, from "Street of the 26 Baku Commissars" to "Big Communal Farm Square." Its ultimate mandate: Restore the names that existed a century ago, before the Communist revolution. Leningrad, named after the Communist leader Lenin, is once again Saint Petersburg. Marx Avenue is now Hunters' Row, Gorky Park is "Not-Boring Gardens," and Godless Lane is godless no more. The changing of names to purge the country of reminders of Communist rule is a symbolic act reflecting much deeper social changes taking place in the former Soviet Union (Hiatt, 1992).

On December 25, 1991, the day that President Mikhail Gorbachev announced his resignation, the Soviet Union ceased to exist. Politically, it was transformed from a single highly centralized government ruling more than 350 million people, into a "Commonwealth of Independent States" formally committed to democracy and the transition to market-based economies. In the span of only a few short months, authoritarian rule by the Communist Party was replaced by a government pledged to holding democratic elections and instituting capitalist economic policies where privately owned industries would call the shots. Socially, people would no longer relate to one another as "comrades," but rather as citizens competing for a place in the market. The press would be free to criticize the government, while intellectuals would be free to write what they wanted.

How would sociologists characterize these events? To answer this question, it is first necessary to understand the ways in which sociologists have approached the study of social change. Some, following the "grand theory" macro-level tradition in sociology (Mills, 1959), have looked at large-scale patterns of change in entire societies. Others, adhering to a more micro-level approach, have looked at the collective behavior of individuals in crowds. Finally, some have examined the ways in which people consciously come together to create social movements oriented toward bringing about desired social changes. While the distinction between these three approaches is seldom tidy in reality, for the sake of simplicity we shall examine each one separately in turn.

THEORIES OF SOCIETAL CHANGE

Social change is all-encompassing, since it potentially includes everything from small group change to the processes of globalization that have been a central concern of this textbook. When sociologists speak of social change, however, they are generally referring to **societal change**—*changes that occur throughout the social structure of an entire society.* Societies, as we noted in Chapter 4, are defined sociologically as consisting of those people who share a common culture. Societal change can thus refer to changes in tiny, relatively isolated societies (for example, the Yanomamö); changes in large-scale modern societies (for example, the United States); or even changes common to a number of similar societies (for example, all industrial societies).

One way to classify a theory of societal change is in terms of its underlying assumptions regarding the nature of change. Based on the direction and abruptness of change, it can be helpful to think in terms of three different types of theory: functionalist theories, conflict theories, and cyclical theories. Since we have encountered most of these theories in other chapters, we shall briefly review only their highlights before turning to the study of social change in contemporary society.

Functionalist Theories of Societal Change

Most functionalist theories share the assumption that as societies develop they become ever more complex and interdependent. Within sociology, this assumption can be traced to Herbert Spencer (1860), who argued that societies change from "incoherent homogeneity to coherent heterogeneity." By this catchy phrase, Spencer intended to convey his belief that what distinguished premodern from modern societies was **differentiation,** *the development of increasing societal complexity through the creation of specialized social roles and institutions.* Premodern societies were seen as characterized by relatively few role and institutional

The 1991 collapse of the Soviet Union was hailed by the U.S. government and mass media as a triumph of capitalism and democracy over communism and authoritarianism. Yet by 1994 the Russian people, more impoverished than ever, were increasingly expressing their frustration with political bickering and free market ecomomic reforms. This pro-Communist rally in Moscow suggests that not all Russians support a U.S.-style market economy.

distinctions, requiring people to have a broad range of skills that enabled them to act relatively independently of one another. In modern societies, however, the reverse is said to be true: People master a narrow range of tasks within a large number of highly specialized institutional roles, thus leading to a great deal of interdependence (Chapter 4). Spencer's beliefs were reflected in Ferdinand Toennies's (1963; orig. 1887) argument that all societies evolve from *Gemeinschaft* to *Gesellschaft* (Chapter 20), as well as Emile Durkheim's notion that societies evolve from mechanical to organic solidarity (Chapter 1).

The earliest functionalist efforts within sociology were **evolutionary theories of societal change** in that they regarded all societies as *moving in a single direction on some important dimension of societal change.* This approach has generally taken two different forms. When anthropologists first began studying preindustrial societies, it was widely believed that all societies began as "simple" or "primitive" and eventually developed into more "complicated" and "civilized" forms. Such **unilinear evolutionary theories** *assumed all societies followed a single evolutionary path,* for example, from "savagery" through "barbarism" to "civilization" (Morgan, 1964; orig. 1877). During the twentieth century, as anthropologists collected more information on societies throughout the world, the notion of unilinear development became increasingly untenable: There were simply too many different ways that societies had actually evolved. **Multilinear evolutionary theory** (sometimes called **neo evolutionary theory**) thus argued that *multiple paths to societal change exist, depending on the particular circum-*

stances of the society (Service, 1975; Sahlins and Service, 1960). The particular interplay between technology, environment, population size, and social organization all play a role in determining the path.

Some evolutionary theorists view societies as eventually reaching an **equilibrium state** in which *no further change is likely to occur unless some external force sets changes in motion.* For example, Durkheim believed that primitive societies were basically unchanging, unless population growth resulted in such an increase in social relations that organic solidarity replaced mechanical solidarity. More recently, Talcott Parsons (1964) initially claimed that societies are basically equilibrium systems that constantly seek to maintain the status quo, unless something external interferes—for example, changes in technology or economic relations with other societies. He later came to argue, however, that societies do change, by becoming more complicated systems that are better adapted to their external environments (Parsons, 1966).

The most recent developments in functionalist theory have emphasized Spencer's original notion of differentiation, but with a twist: Instead of viewing differentiation as always contributing to greater functional *interdependence,* theorists such as Jeffrey Alexander and Paul Colomy have argued that differentiation can also lead to greater *independence* of some parts of society, contributing to social strain. "Dedifferentiation" can also occur: some institutions become less complex, the result of social groups that oppose the social changes that go along with modernization. Moreover, since different parts of society undergo these processes to varying degrees and at different times, considerable strain and conflict can arise (Alexander, 1985; Colomy, 1986, 1990; Alexander and Colomy, 1985, 1990).

Critical Assessment Although no one can deny that modern societies contain many more specialized roles and institutions than earlier societies, evolutionary theories also assumed that such social changes were progressive: "modern" societies (that is to say, European societies) were seen as "more evolved" than earlier, "primitive" forms. Such beliefs had an appeal in countries whose soldiers, missionaries, and merchants were conquering or colonizing much of the rest of the world, since they helped justify such actions as part of the "civilizing" mission of a more advanced people. These ideas were eventually rejected within the disciplines of anthropology and sociology (Lenski and Lenski, 1982; Nisbet, 1969), as is seen in the recent functionalist theories of Alexander and Colomy, who attempt to incorporate notions of conflict, strain, and uneven social change within their analyses.

Conflict Theories of Societal Change

Although evolutionary theories claim to explain societal change, in fact they depend on external forces to trigger change that occurs within a society (Appelbaum, 1970, 1979). Population growth, contact with other cultures, technological advances, and changing environmental conditions are all regarded as necessary causes of change. If none of these conditions occur, societies are seen as relatively stable—as tending toward equilibrium. **Conflict theories of societal change,** on the other hand, see *conflict as built into social relations.* Even if population is not growing or technology is unchanging, societal change is likely to occur. This is because all existing societies are seen as having in-built sources of conflict that eventually lead to sharp and sometimes violent breaks with the past. Karl Marx (1967, orig. 1867; 1977; orig. 1848), for example, held that conflict was inevitable in capitalist society, which he believed pitted the interests of workers against capitalists (see Chapters 1, 8, and 15).

Critical Assessment Marx's conflict theory adheres to its own evolutionary view of societal change, in which all societies advance to the same final destination: an economically classless society. We have earlier noted a number of weaknesses with this theory (Chapters 1, 8, and 15). Of particular importance was Marx's tendency to overemphasize economic conflict, while underestimating cultural conflict and other noneconomic factors, such as language, ethnicity, race, and nationalism, factors which increasingly are important in the world today.

In recent years there has been an effort to revive conflict theory. Some of the most influential efforts have followed Marx's lead in analyzing recent developments in the global economic system; these are discussed in some detail in Chapter 9. Others have sought to combine aspects of functionalism and conflict theory (Dahrendorf, 1959, 1967; Van den Berge, 1963; Collins, 1975, 1990). These theories tend to be highly eclectic, drawing on Marx, Weber, Durkheim, and other sociological theorists. They also focus more on interpersonal or organizational change, rather than on long-term processes of change in entire societies.

Rise and Fall Theories of Societal Change

Rise and fall theories of societal change *deny that there is any simple direction to societal change; rather, they argue that change is more likely to be one of growth and decline.* Such theories are common in the religious myths of many cultures, which view social life as similar to the lives of living creatures or the seasons of the year: a constant cycle of birth, maturation, old age, and death, with the end representing some form of return to the beginning. Sociology, emerging in an era that equated scientific and technological advance with progress, has tended to reject such cyclical metaphors in favor of more evolutionary ones that emphasize progress.

There have been a number of significant exceptions, however, among more historically oriented social theorists. Oswald Spengler (1918) sought to describe a war-torn Europe in *Decline of the West.* Pitirim Sorokin (1937, 1941), one of the best-known American historical sociologists during the mid-twentieth century, argued in his four-volume *Social and Cultural Dynamics* that societies alternate between three different kinds of mentalities: those that give primacy to the senses, those that emphasize religiosity, and those that celebrate logic and reason. More recently, historian Paul Kennedy has traced out the conditions that have been associated with national power and decline during the past five centuries, in *The Rise and Fall of the Great Powers* (1987). Kennedy argues that as nations grow in economic power they often seek to become world military powers as well, which in the long run proves to be their undoing. This, Kennedy claims, is because global military power eventually weakens the domestic economy, undermining the very prosperity that once fueled it. Kennedy forecasts that this might well be the fate of the United States.

The most important sociologist who could be considered a cyclical theorist, however, was Max Weber. Although Weber is generally credited with an evolutionary view of society as becoming increasingly politically and economically rational, he also emphasized the importance of cultural values in shaping human behavior (Gerth and Mills, 1946). In particular, as we discussed in Chapter 13, under certain circumstances rational-legal authority can break down altogether, leaving members of a society open to the highly emotional appeal of charismatic figures.

Critical Assessment Cyclical theories have not enjoyed great popularity among sociologists. Even Weber's theory is not truly cyclical; charismatic authority is a sort of wild card, providing for a somewhat unpredictable turn in the otherwise predictable march of societal change between traditional and rational-legal forms of authority. The more far-reaching versions of cyclical theory, such as Sorokin's theory of societal oscillation between three different world views, are framed in such broad terms as to be virtually impossible to prove right or wrong.

SOURCES OF SOCIAL CHANGE: COLLECTIVE BEHAVIOR

Social change ultimately results from human action. Sociologists who have studied the ways in which people effect changes have tended to look at the mass action of large numbers of people on the one hand, and at the more institutionalized behavior of organizations on the other. In this section we shall consider the former, examining theories of collective behavior. In the following section we shall look at the role played by social movements.

Collective behavior is *voluntary, goal-oriented action that occurs in relatively disorganized situations, in which society's predominant social norms and values cease to govern individual behavior* (Oberschall, 1973; Turner and Killian, 1987). Although collective behavior usually involves a disorganized aggregate of people, it can also occur in a highly regimented organization where order and discipline have broken down. The 1992 Los Angeles riots included numerous incidents of disorganized group action, including arson, looting, and beatings of passersby. The televised police beating of motorist Rodney King, whose acquittal triggered the riots, is an example of normative breakdown in a supposedly highly disciplined police organization.

This reveals another feature of collective behavior: It often consists of a group reaction to some initiating situation. Such a situation may appear to be sociologically unimportant—for example, street parties that erupt in a group rampage after the local team wins the pennant. But even seemingly trivial and spontaneous events may in fact be a group response to larger social conditions, heralding a larger movement for social change. The enormous crowds that supported Boris

Yeltsin when he defied Soviet authority in 1991 helped to trigger the final collapse of the Soviet Union, yet the crowds themselves were the result of long-standing social grievances and frustrations in Russian society.

Since its origins in the writings of the nineteenth-century French sociologist Gustave LeBon (1960, orig. 1896), the sociological study of collective behavior has been especially concerned with behavior of people in **crowds,** *temporary gatherings of closely interacting people with a common focus.* People in crowds are seen as prone to being swept up in group emotions, losing their individual ability to make rational decisions. The "group mind" of the crowd is viewed as an irrational and dangerous aspect of modern societies, insofar as they are comprised of rootless, isolated individuals who are prone to crowd behavior (Arendt, 1951; Fromm, 1941; Gaskell and Smith, 1981; Kornhauser, 1959).

Theories of Collective Behavior

Within contemporary sociology, the collective behavior perspective is rooted in the pre-World War II "Chicago School" of sociology, particularly George Herbert Mead's (1977) symbolic interactionism and Robert Ezra Park's (1972) writings on the crowd. These strands converged in the postwar writings of Herbert Blumer (1951), regarded by many as the founder of the study of collective behavior (McAdam et al., 1988).

It must be emphasized that theorists of collective behavior do not regard all crowds as potentially explosive. From the first major open-air rock-and-roll concert at Woodstock in 1968 to the giant Lollapalooza concerts of today, hundreds of thousands of people are able to enjoy a day of music and sun (or even rain) without rioting. What sociologists seek to explain are the conditions that can lead a group of people to engage in collective behavior. We shall focus on three principal sociological approaches: contagion theories, which emphasize nonsocial factors such as instincts; emergent-norm theories, which seek out some underlying social organization that leads the group to generate norms governing collective action; and value-added theory, which looks to a critical combination of personal, organizational, and social conditions.

Contagion Theories

This early approach, which originated with LeBon (1960; orig. 1896) and reached its fullest sociological statement with Herbert Blumer (1951), assumes that human beings can revert to herd-like animal behavior when they get together in large crowds. Blumer, drawing on symbolic interactionism, emphasized the importance of raw imitation: People in crowds may "mill

file members disappear; the militant thrust of the organization is then blunted (Piven and Cloward, 1977).

A related problem is that of **goal displacement,** which occurs when the SMOs *original goals become redirected toward enhancing the organization and its leadership* (Zald and Garner, 1966; McCarthy and Zald, 1973). The U.S. labor movement is an example; once labor unions became successful, many of them became large and prosperous bureaucracies that often seemed remote from the needs of their rank-and-file members.

In the last analysis, SMOs have to motivate people to support their cause, often with dollars as well as votes. Many groups engage in **grass roots organizing,** *attempts to mobilize support among ordinary members of the community.* This can range from going door-to-door to staging massive demonstrations. Most SMOs emerge from a group that has some grievance, and their active members consist largely of people who will directly benefit from any social change that occurs. The civil rights movement was typical in this regard; most of its leadership and rank-and-file members were African Americans who had suffered from discrimination and stood to benefit from its elimination.

Some SMOs are said to be dependent on **conscience constituents,** *people who provide resources for an SMO who are not themselves members of the aggrieved group whom the organization champions* (McCarthy and Zald, 1973). Such supporters are motivated by strong ethical convictions, rather than by direct self-interest in achieving the social movement's goals. The National Coalition for the Homeless, for example, consists primarily of public interest lawyers, shelter operators, and others who advocate on behalf of homeless people; yet only a relatively small number of homeless are themselves directly involved in the organization. Antiabortion organizations, which advocate on behalf of fetuses, are another obvious example.

Whether or not the SMO is comprised primarily of representatives of the aggrieved group, most are forced to go beyond their immediate constituencies for financial support. Homeless advocacy groups raise money from numerous sources, including media celebrities and direct mail to ordinary citizens (Blau, 1992). Similarly, much of the funding for the civil rights movements came from wealthy white liberal donors and private foundations (Jenkins and Eckert, 1986; McCarthy and Zald, 1973, 1977).

Macro-Level Studies

Apart from the efforts of particular SMOs, large-scale economic, political, or cultural conditions can contribute to success or failure. For example, the move-

ment for equality among African Americans benefited from the changing voter base of the Democratic Party, which reflected a growing black electorate to press for changes in the rural south and urban north. It also benefited from globalization, since as the United States sought an increasingly prominent global role it was increasingly sensitive to foreign criticism of its segregationist policies (McAdam et al., 1988).

Some political systems encourage social movements, while others repress them (Gale, 1986; Kitschelt, 1986). When a government is in crisis, it can respond by becoming more repressive, or it can create a space for social movements to flourish. The former occurred in China in 1989, when millions of students and workers, frustrated by deteriorating economic conditions and rigid government controls, took to the streets to demand greater economic and political freedom. The brutal crackdown at Beijing's Tienanmen Square, televised live to a global audience, momentarily ended the nascent social movement for democracy. On the other hand, as we have already noted economic stagnation and governmental paralysis in the Soviet Union enabled social movements to flourish in some of its East European satellite countries, which contributed to the decision by the Soviet leadership to transform the political and economic system. When a formerly repressive state collapses, revolutionary social change may result (McAdam et al., 1988; Skocpol, 1979).

Just as economic and political collapse can facilitate the rise of social movements, so too can prosperity. While impoverished people may lack the time or resources to engage in social movement activity, this is not equally true of the middle class. Prosperity helps to provide a basis for social movement activism. Resources are more abundant, mass media and other means of communication are more likely to be readily available, and activists are more likely to have independent means of supporting themselves. Prosperous societies are also more likely to have a larger class of well-educated people, a group that historically has provided the leadership of many social movements (McAdam et al., 1988; McCarthy and Zald, 1973; Zald and McCarthy, 1987). The activism of the 1960s, for example, occurred during a period of significant economic growth and prosperity, particularly among the middle-class college students who provided its core. Unlike students today, most were able to engage in social movement activities without compromising their economic futures.

Finally, even the spatial organization of society has been seen as having an impact on social movements. Dense, concentrated neighborhoods or workplaces facilitate social interaction, spurring the growth of social movements. A century and a half ago, Karl Marx recognized that cities and factories were powerful breeding grounds for revolutionary insurgency against capitalism, since they brought previously isolated workers together in single locations. Subsequent research has sustained his conclusion (Marx, 1977, orig. 1848; Tilly et al., 1975). The concentration of students in on campuses contributed to the rise of student activism in the 1960s (Lofland, 1985).

Micro-Mobilization Contexts for Building Social Movements

Certain arenas of action provide ideal conditions for incubating social movement organizations. These have been termed **micro-mobilization contexts,** *small group settings in which people are able to generate a shared set of beliefs to explain some social problem, along with the necessary social organization to do something about it* (McAdam et al., 1988). Such settings involve both formal and informal social networks, all of which make it easier to develop new understandings of why some troublesome micro-level problem (such as personally experiencing racism) is in fact the result of macro-level social forces (such as social institutions that promote racism). The Civil Rights Movement, for example, emerged at a time when the black community was developing strong local organizations, including schools, churches, and political groups. These highly interconnected institutions provided fertile grounds for the seeds of social activism (McAdam, 1982). Other examples include unions, student support groups, and even friendship networks.

Micro-mobilization contexts also create the basic organizational framework required to address the problem, including leadership, mass media, and other communications technologies, and specific roles for movement activists. Finally, micro-mobilization contexts also provide incentives for people to get involved. These can range from the emotional rewards that come from belonging to a group dedicated to a common cause, to paid salaries. Micro-mobilization contexts thus serve as the bridge that connects the personal concerns of individuals to collectivities hoping to create large-scale social change (McAdam, 1986; McAdam et al., 1988; Scott, 1990; Offe, 1985; Abrahams, 1992).

GLOBALIZATION AND SOCIAL CHANGE

Globalization has created an opportunity for the formation of global social movements, since many of the problems that exist in the world today are global in nature and require global solutions. This entire book has been concerned in large part with the impact of globalization on social change. Although we shall not review these impacts, it will be useful to briefly look at two related topics: the recent emergence of "new" social movements concerned with developing modes of thinking about the world and the probable direction of social change as we move into the twenty-first century.

The "New" Social Movements

Since the 1960s, a number of **"new" social movements** have emerged. While these movements may address economic and political issues, they are more *fundamentally concerned with the quality of private life, of-*

The "new" social movements are concerned not only with bread-and-butter political and economic issues but in changing the ways in which people think and act. In this photograph, a group of physically challenged people demonstrate to overcome being labeled as dependent and handicapped. They are calling for building code modifications that would enable them to enjoy the basic right of full physical access.

Box 21.1

Critical Thinking

How Effective Are "New" Social Movement Tactics?

The AIDS Coalition to Unleash Power (ACT-UP) is a "new" social movement organization, concerned in large part with the stigma surrounding AIDS. ACT-UP helps people with AIDS to fight against discrimination. The organization characterizes itself as "a nonpartisan group of diverse individuals united in anger and committed to direct action to end the AIDS crisis." It has achieved considerable media attention through its highly theatrical techniques in support of homosexual rights and the fight against AIDS. By using such tactics as "condom tosses," "die-ins," "body counts," and gay and lesbian "kiss-ins," ACT-UP has lived up to its name, often commanding media coverage through the sheer shock value of its actions. Like many of the "new" social movements, its membership is broadly middle class—primarily gay and lesbian, but with heterosexual members as well. Many of its members are HIV-positive or people with AIDS or AIDS-related illnesses.

Sociologist Josh Gamson (1991), who has studied ACT-UP for a number of years, argues that the organization's goals reflect two different types of objectives. The first, which is common to the "older" social movements, is to end discrimination against an oppressed group—in this case, all people (homosexual and heterosexual) infected with HIV-AIDS. To achieve this first objective, ACT-UP has engaged in demonstrations and educational efforts, pushing for such concrete objectives as greater access to AIDS-related treatment and drugs, increased "safer-sex" education, the end of

discrimination against people with AIDS in housing and jobs, and expanded funding for AIDS research. Its targets have ranged from government agencies to major pharmaceutical companies.

ACT-UP's second goal, however, is neither economic nor political, but cultural, and this is what makes it a "new" social movement. Its more outrageous demonstrations are intended to change people's perceptions about what it means to be gay, lesbian, and/or infected with HIV-AIDS. This goal is not directed against any particular organization or governmental policy, but rather it is concerned with changing popular cultural understandings. Tactics often involve taking a common symbol and turning it upside down, thereby hopefully shocking the public into rethinking the symbol's meaning. For example, ACT-UP activists believe that by throwing condoms in crowds, or having gay and lesbian "kiss-ins," they are able to force people to confront (and hopefully rethink) their negative stereotypes. Often these activities are conducted in such "all-American" settings as baseball games, shopping malls, cookouts, or front lawns, to dramatize the fact that people with AIDS are not "them" but "all of us."

ACT-UP assumes that real social change will come about not through "mere" economic or political gains but rather through sweeping changes in the nature of culture itself—of what people regard as normal. In what ways do you think that such a social change strategy, based on changing people's perceptions by confronting them with their stereotypes, is likely to prove successful?

ten advocating large-scale cultural changes in the ways that people think and act. Examples include movements that are concerned with gender and sexuality, individual freedom, personal identity, the environment, peace, and community control. They may be informal and even deliberately disorganized, preferring spontaneous and confrontational methods to more bu-

reaucratic approaches (Box 21.1). Part of their purpose in protesting, in fact, is not to force a distinction between "them" versus "us," but rather to dramatically draw attention to their own right to "be" (Omvedt, 1992; Touraine, 1985, 1988; Gamson, 1991; Offe, 1985; Eder, 1985; Cohen, 1985; Scott, 1990; Habermas, 1981; Klandermans, 1986; Tucker, 1991).

The new social movement organizations tend to be single-issue oriented. As a result, they are highly fragmented, and their organizations often resist establishing ties with one another. Such fragmentation helps to explain the vitality of many of the new SMOs, since it provides a diverse array of different organizations to attract fresh, new activists. Yet it also makes it difficult to generate a broad-based movement for social change. One movement that seems to have successfully bridged a range of concerns is India's Stri Mukti, an environmental organization that also champions women's rights (Box 21.2).

The new social movements are often comprised of professionals and other highly educated and technically skilled "knowledge workers." Whether or not such a base can provide a vehicle for social change remains to be seen. On the one hand, as we have argued elsewhere in this book (Chapter 15), "knowledge workers" constitute an increasingly important stratum in modern society. On the other hand, the large majority of people in all societies do not fall into this category, and it is difficult to imagine how significant social change could occur without a much broader base of popular support.

Box 21.2

Silenced Voices

"New" Social Movements in India Champion the Rights of the Environment—and Women

The Mukti Sangharsh is a "new" social movement organization in India that has emerged to challenge state-sponsored development projects. It is a mass-based movement whose members include peasants, members of tribal groups, and middle-class environmentalists. It raises its own funds, and, like other "new" social movements organizations, tends to be spontaneous rather than planned, informal rather than bureaucratized. It is not formally affiliated with any political party, and often expresses hostility toward organized politics.

Mukti Sangharsh directs its agitation toward the national government and transnational corporations, rather than local landlords or money lenders. It challenges large-scale public and private projects such as dams and other physical infrastructures that, although often favored by international development agencies, have displaced countless people and done major damage to India's environment. In the mid-1980s the movement made great strides when activists and peasants collaborated on research that showed how wells and rivers could be better utilized to preserve the fragile environment. A successful "people's science march" in 1985 demanded that professors conduct drought-related research on behalf of the drought-stricken communities.

During the same year the Stri Mukti Sangharsh Calval (Women's Liberation Struggle Movement) was formed by women from Mukti Sangharsh, who felt their central role in the antidevelopment struggle has been unacknowledged and largely ignored. The women fought against environmentally unsound development projects, attempting to place Indian women at the forefront of alternative technology and agricultural development. They also sought to educate women peasants around women's issues. Campaigns have centered on women who had been abandoned by their husbands and forced into exploitive work in order to survive, as well as more basic women's rights, including the right to own land or a home.

Stri Mukti's strongly ecological-feminist perspective is revealed in its slogan, "green earth, women's power, human liberation." Its focus on the intersection of global ecology, local environmentalism, and women's issues has sought to demonstrate that environmentalism is not confined to the physical use of land, but in important ways entails issues of survival and integrity for Indian women.

Source: Adapted from Omvedt (1992).

Social Change in the Twenty-first Century

It is impossible to predict social change with any degree of accuracy. A mere 20 years ago no one could have foreseen the collapse of Soviet communism, the end of the Cold War, or the impact of the computer on globalization. During the last half century, dozens of new nations have been formed, many of which could not have been anticipated only a few decades earlier (Map 21.1).

Human beings make their own history, and, as we argued in the first chapter of this textbook, they often do so in unpredictable ways. Yet as makers of history people are also constrained by existing institutions and social relationships. Social structures provide the resources for human action, even as the actions themselves are oriented toward changing those structures (Giddens, 1985).

The one thing that seems certain is that globalization will continue, its effects felt in all aspects of people's lives. The increasing societal complexity anticipated by Herbert Spencer in the mid-nineteenth century is today being realized at the global level. In purely economic terms, although the progress of globalization will proceed at different rates in different countries, the overall thrust will be toward increasing integration of the world into a single economic unit. While national boundaries may for a time remain partial barriers to the free flow of goods, they are less likely to impede the global exchange of information and services that the production of wealth increasingly requires. This means that the national economies of the world will become increasingly dependent upon one another for knowledge, physical labor, and markets for the goods and services that are produced.

Economic globalization, like most social processes, has both positive and negative impacts. On the one hand, it opens up the possibility for a vast increase in global productive capacity, technological advances, global cooperation, and an increase in the standard of living for people around the world. On the other hand, globalization can also lead to lowered wages and job losses in high-wage industrial countries, mirrored by gains in low-wage countries around the world. In some cases, people in low-wage countries may benefit; in others, they may be exploited. The reconstitution of national economies into a global economic system raises important questions about equity as well as about social processes.

The same is true of other forms of globalization. In

Global processes eventually are felt in specific localities. Nuclear power, for example, produces deadly, long-lasting wastes that must be deposited somewhere—often, where the local population is perceived as too politically powerless to object. The residents of Hillsboro, New Hampshire, demonstrate against solving this global problem in their locality.

this book we have seen how globalization is challenging the role of national power, leading to global political, legal, and economic frameworks that seem highly likely to become more important as countries become increasingly interdependent. We have also seen how forms of global culture are emerging, threatening the diversity of the local cultures in which they originated. And finally, we have examined a variety of social institutions, noting that in important respects they seem to be converging into a few common forms no matter where they are found.

We live at a moment in history that contains enormous possibilities as well as daunting problems. Without an understanding of these social forces, we will be unable to act intelligently to bring about the world we most desire. A sociological understanding of the forces shaping social change today may enable tomorrow's citizens to act more effectively to shape their world.

Map 21.1 **New Countries Since World War II, Grouped by Decade**

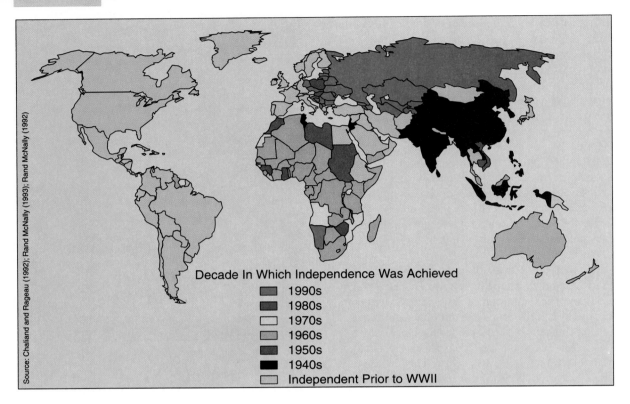

Source: Chaliand and Rageau (1992); Rand McNally (1993); Rand McNally (1992)

Decade In Which Independence Was Achieved
- 1990s
- 1980s
- 1970s
- 1960s
- 1950s
- 1940s
- Independent Prior to WWII

A host of new countries and borders have occurred since World War II, especially in Africa, Asia, and eastern Europe. This process continues today, as formerly socialist countries such as Yugoslavia or the Soviet Union fragment into separate nations. Yet at the same time, regional economic entities embracing many countries have also emerged, as seen in the European Community and the North American Free Trade Agreement.

C H A P T E R   S U M M A R Y

1. Sociologists differ on whether **societal change** is gradual or abrupt, and whether or not all societies are changing in roughly the same direction. **Evolutionary, revolutionary,** and **rise and fall theories of societal change** represent three approaches to these questions.

2. Early sociologists, fearful of mass society, viewed **collective behavior** as a form of group contagion in which the veneer of civilization gave way to more instinctive, animal-like forms of behavior.

3. A more sociological approach, emergent-norm theory, examines the ways in which crowds and other forms of collective behavior develop their own rules and shared understandings.

4. The most comprehensive theory of collective behavior, value-added theory, attempts to take into account the necessary conditions at the individual, organizational, and even societal levels.

5. **Social movements** have been important historical vehicles for bringing about social change. They are usually achieved through **social movement organizations (SMOs),** which can be studied using the tools and understandings of organizational sociology.

6. Social movements can be classified as **reformist, revolutionary, rebellious, reactionary, communitarian,** or "new" depending on their vision of social change.

7. **Resource mobilization theory** argues that the success or failure of SMOs cannot be explained by the degree of societal strain that might explain their origins, but rather with their organizational ability to marshal the needed financial and personal resources.

8. Many social movements depend heavily on **conscience constituents** for their support. **Micro-**

mobilization contexts are also important incubators of social movement success.

9. Globalization has created an opportunity for the formation of global social movements, since many of the problems that exist in the world today are global in nature and require global solutions.

10. **"New" social movements,** organized around issues of personal identity and values, are found throughout the world today.

Q U E S T I O N S   F O R   D I S C U S S I O N

1. What are the differing assumptions between evolutionary, revolutionary, and "rise and fall" theories of societal change? Which type of theory, in your view, best accounts for the social changes that are occurring today?

2. How do sociologists explain collective behavior? To what extent does it reflect more impulsive, unconscious processes, in which ordinary socialization to norms breaks down?

3. What are the principal factors that explain the success or failure of social movements?

4. How do the "new" social movements differ from the older, more traditional ones? Which do you think are likely to be most effective in achieving their goals, and why?

K E Y   T E R M S

collective behavior: Voluntary, goal-oriented action that occurs in relatively disorganized situations, in which society's predominant social norms and values cease to govern individual behavior.

communitarian social movement: A movement seeking to withdraw from the dominant society by creating its own ideal community.

conflict theories of societal change: Those theories that see conflict as built into social relations, such that societal change is likely to be abrupt and discontinuous.

conscience constituents: People who provide resources for a social movement organization who are not themselves members of the aggrieved group whom the organization champions.

craze: An intense attraction to an object, person, or activity.

crowd: A temporary gathering of closely interacting people with a common focus.

differentiation: The development of increasing societal complexity through the creation of specialized social roles and institutions.

equilibrium state: A condition of a society in which no further social change is likely to occur unless some external force sets changes in motion.

evolutionary theories of societal change: Those theories that regard all societies as moving in a single direction on some important dimension of societal change.

fad: A temporary, highly imitated outbreak of mildly unconventional behavior.

fashion: A somewhat long-lasting style of imitative behavior or appearance.

free rider problem: The fact that people can avoid the costs of social movement activism (such as time, energy, and other personal resources), and still benefit from its success without becoming active participants.

goal displacement: A problem that occurs when a social movement organization's original goals become redirected toward enhancing the organization and its leadership.

grass roots organizing: Attempts to mobilize support among ordinary members of the community.

micro-mobilization contexts: Small group settings in which people are able to generate a shared set of beliefs to explain some social problem, along with the necessary social organization to do something about it.

multilinear evolutionary theory (sometimes called **neoevolutionary theories**): Those theories argu-ing that multiple paths to societal change exist, depending on the particular circumstances of the society.

"new" social movements: Movements that have arisen since the 1960s that are fundamentally concerned with the quality of private life, often advocating large-scale cultural changes in the ways that people think and act.

panic: Massive flight from something that is feared.

reactionary social movement: A movement seeking to restore an earlier social system—often based on a mythical past—along with the traditional norms and values that once presumably accompanied it.

rebellion: A movement seeking to overthrow the existing social, political, and economic system, but lacking a detailed plan for a new social order.

reformist social movement: A movement seeking to bring about social change within the existing economic and political system.

resource mobilization theory: A theory about social movement organizations that focuses on their ability to generate money, membership, and political support in order to achieve their objectives.

revolutionary social movement: A movement seeking to fundamentally alter the existing social, political, and economic system in keeping with a vision of a new social order.

riot: A prolonged outbreak of violent behavior on the part of a sizable group of people, directed against people or property, and often illegal.

rise and fall theories of societal change: Those theories denying that there is any simple direction to societal change; rather, change is more likely to be one of growth and decline.

rumor: An unverified form of information that is transmitted informally, usually originating in an unknown source.

social movement organizations ("SMOs"): Formal organizations that seek to achieve social change through concrete actions.

social movement: A large number of people who have come together in a continuing and organized effort to bring about (or resist) social change.

societal change: Changes that occur throughout the social structure of an entire society.

unilinear evolutionary theories: Those theories that assume all societies follow a single evolutionary path.

RECOMMENDED   FOR   FURTHER   READING

Gitlin, Todd. (1980). *The Whole World Is Watching: Mass Media in the Making of the New Left.* Berkeley: University of California Press.

    A detailed examination of the role of the mass media in the emergence of 1960s student activism, by a former activist who is now a leading authority on the media.

Morris, Aldon. (1984). *The Origins of the Civil Rights Movement.* New York: Free Press.

    The now-classic study of the Civil Rights Movement in the United States, which shows that far from being a unique event, the movement grew out of a long struggle on the part of the African-American community for equality and social justice.

Piven, Frances Fox, and Richard A. Cloward. (1977). *Poor People's Movements: Why They Succeed, How They Fail.* New York: Pantheon.

    An important study of several social movements oriented toward the poor; advances the controversial thesis that success can be a movement's worst enemy: The power of social movements, the authors argue, lies in protesting from the outside, rather than becoming incorporated in government social service bureaucracies.

Whalen, Jack, and Richard Flacks. (1989). *Beyond the Barricades: The Sixties Generation Grows Up.* Philadelphia: Temple University Press.

By conducting follow-up studies with a comparison group of 1960s activists and more conservative fraternity and sorority members, the authors discredit the thesis that activists lose their commitment to social change once they enter adulthood.

Zald, Mayer, and John D. McCarthy (eds.). (1987). *Social Movements in an Organizational Society: Collected Essays.* New Brunswick, N.J.: Transaction Books

A wide-ranging collection of essays on social movements, by two theorists who have had an important impact on the development of social movement theory.

Glossary of Key Terms

acculturation: Adopting the norms, values and lifeways of the dominant culture.

achieved status: A status acquired by virtue of the social position a person occupies.

activity theory: A functionalist theory of aging, which holds that active people are more likely to lead fulfilling and productive lives, benefiting society as well as themselves.

adolescence: The teen years, during which children mature sexually and begin to develop their own identities.

adulthood: The years during which individuals develop their own careers, form families, and establish a life independent from their parents.

adult stage: According to George Herbert Mead, the stage at which individuals learn to take on the role of the "generalized other."

affordability gap: The difference between what poorer people must pay for housing and what they can actually afford to pay; one source of homelessness.

ageism: Prejudice based on age.

agenda-setting: Determining what "counts" as news and what does not.

age-specific fertility rates: The number of births typical of women of a specific age in a particular population.

age-specific mortality rates: The number of deaths typical of men and women of a specific age in a particular population.

aging: The combination of biological, psychological, and social processes that affect people as they grow older.

agricultural revolution: The technological changes associated with the rise of agriculture and domestication of farm animals.

agricultural society: A type of society whose members rely for their sustenance primarily on the cultivation of crops over an extended area, by means of plows, draft animals, or other technological advances.

agricultural surplus: The production of food beyond the amount required for immediate survival.

alienation: In Marx's formulation, the experience of estrangement resulting from capitalist forms of production. (Literally, to experience as a stranger the products of one's labor, the labor process, one's coworkers, and ultimately one's own human nature.)

andragogy: Adult learning.

animism: The belief that naturally occurring phenomena such as animals or mountains are possessed of indwelling spirits or supernatural powers.

anomie: In Emile Durkheim's theory, a state of confusion resulting from intense conflict over norms, or an absence of norms altogether. (For Merton's reformulation, see *structural strain.*)

anticipatory socialization: Adopting the behavior or standards of a group one hopes to emulate or join.

applied sociology: Sociological research whose primary purpose is to solve a practical problem rather than to advance sociological theory or understanding.

ascribed status: A status that is given for life at the moment of birth.

ascription: The acquisition of one's position in the stratification system on the basis of personal characteristics that derive from birth and therefore are believed to be unchangeable; associated with caste societies.

assault: Legally defined as an unlawful attack by one person upon another for the purpose of inflicting severe or aggravated bodily harm.

assimilation: The process by which different cultures are absorbed into a single mainstream culture.

audience relations: A body of research, within the culturalist theory of media influence that is concerned with the ways in which the media provide a set of meanings that viewers then interpret according to their own cultural understandings.

authoritarianism: A political system in which ordinary members of society are denied the right to participate in government.

authority (see *legitimate authority*).

automation: The replacement of human labor by machines in the process of manufacturing.

baby boom: A phrase used to refer to the unusually large number of children born in the decade after World War II.

backstage: According to Erving Goffman, the places where people can avoid performance and "be themselves."

banal: Commonplace or ordinary.

behaviorism: A psychological approach to socialization that emphasizes the effect of rewards and punishments on observable human behavior.

bias: Results that lack validity in a particular direction.

bilingual education: The offering of instruction in a non-English language as well as in English.

bisexuality: Sexual desire for persons of both sexes.

blockbusting: An illegal practice by which lenders and real estate agents play upon racial fears to force down property values and drive current residents out of their neighborhoods, thereby profiting from increased sales, loans, and real estate commissions.

blue collar: Work that requires manual labor.

bureaucracy: A formal organization characterized by written rules, hierarchical authority, and a paid staff.

bureaucratic authority: Authority based on written procedural rules, arranged into a clear hierarchy of authority, and staffed by full-time paid officials.

burglary: Legally defined as unlawful entry of a premise with the intent to commit a crime.

capitalism: An economic system characterized by the market allocation of goods and services, production for private profit, and private ownership of the means of producing wealth.

capitalists: In Marx's theory, a propertied social class that includes factory owners, merchants, and bankers.

caste society: A society in which the strata are closed to movement, so that all individuals must remain throughout life in the stratum of their birth.

categorization of news: A framing device that consists of determining whether or not a given event "fits" into some preexisting category or "beat."

causal relationship: A relationship in which one variable is said to be the cause of another.

charismatic authority: Power based on devotion inspired in followers by the presumed extraordinary personal qualities of a leader.

child abuse: A form of abuse involving sexual and/or physical assaults on children by adult members of their family.

child-minding: An arrangement in which extended family members and friends cooperate in raising the children of a person who is living in another locale.

childhood: The early, formative years that occur before the sexual changes associated with puberty.

chronic fatigue syndrome: A persistent flu-like illness that can last for years or even decades.

chronological age: The length of time a person has been alive.

church: A religious organization that exists in a fairly harmonious, well-integrated relationship with the larger society.

citizens: Individuals who are part of a political community in which they are granted certain rights and privileges, while at the same time having specified obligations and duties.

city: A permanent settlement of people who depend on others for the production of food; in the United States, a legally incorporated or chartered urban settlement.

civil attention: According to Erving Goffman, a polite signal that one is conscious of another person's performance.

civil inattention: According to Erving Goffman, a polite signal that one is aware of another person's presence, without indicating that one is also aware of his or her inappropriate or embarrassing behavior.

civil religion: A set of religious beliefs through which societies interpret their own histories in light of some conception of ultimate reality.

civil rights: Legal rights that protect citizens from injuries perpetrated by other individuals and by institutions.

class: A person's location in a society's economic system, resulting in differences in the nature of work, income, and wealth.

class consciousness: An awareness of one's own interests as a member of a particular social class, along with an adequate understanding of the ways in which society operates to produce inequality.

class dominance: A theory holding that power is concentrated in the hands of a relatively small number of individuals who comprise an upper-class power elite.

class dominance theory: A political theory, derived from the ideas of Karl Marx, which argues that there is a more or less unified upper-class power elite exerting control over politics, the economy, and the military.

class-dominant theory of media influence: A theory developed during the 1960s and 1970s arguing that society is dominated by a relatively small, powerful elite, whose viewpoint the media overwhelmingly tend to reflect.

class society: A society in which the strata are open to movement, so that changing one's stratum of birth is possible.

classless society: A society in which different economic strata do not exist.

coercive organization: An organization in which one is forced to give unquestioned obedience to authority.

cognitive development: A theory, developed by Jean Piaget, that the ability to make logical decisions increases as a person grows older.

cohabitation: Living together as a married couple without being married.

cohort: A group of people born in the same time period (for example, all people born between 1975 and 1980).

Cold War: The period of heightened tensions between the United States and the Soviet Union, lasting from the 1950s through the 1980s. (The term "cold" was used because the two countries never openly confronted one another on the battlefield, although numerous wars were fought as a result of the conflict.)

collective: A small group of people that operate by agreement or consensus.

collective bargaining: Negotiating with employers on behalf of the union's members.

collective behavior: Voluntary, goal-oriented action that occurs in relatively disorganized situations, in which society's predominant social norms and values cease to govern individual behavior.

collective conscience: Common values, outlooks, interpretations of events, languages and dialects, and in general the identical ways of thinking that characterize early preindustrial societies.

collectivist orientation: The belief that members of society should assume responsibility for one another's welfare.

colonialism: A political-economic system under which powerful nations establish rule over weaker peoples or nations for their own profit.

commodity chain: A network of labor and production processes whose end result is a finished commodity.

communism: A political-economic system that abolishes the private ownership of factories and other means of producing wealth, which would then be cooperatively owned and run by the workers themselves.

communitarian social movement: A movement seeking to withdraw from the dominant society by creating its own ideal community.

concept: An idea or mental construct that focuses upon specified properties common to a set of phenomena, to the exclusion of other properties.

conditional generalization: A generalization that applies only under a specified set of conditions.

conflict theories of societal change: Those theories that see conflict as built into social relations, such that societal change is likely to be abrupt and discontinuous.

conglomerate: An enormous corporation comprised of numerous subsidiaries, often consisting of unrelated business enterprises.

conscience constituents: People who provide resources for a a social movement organization who are not themselves members of the aggrieved group whom the organization champions.

Consolidated Metropolitan Statistical Area (CMSA): According to the U.S. Bureau of the Census, groupings of the largest Metropolitan Statistical Areas.

construct validity: The degree to which a particular concept is in fact measured.

contract: A binding agreement between parties that is enforced by a legal system backed by a centralized authority.

contradictory class location: A class position in which members have some of the power of the bourgeois class (for example, control over the work of others), yet like the working class are ultimately denied such power (since they are ultimately accountable to the bourgeois class).

conventional stage: According to Lawrence Kohlberg, the stage of moral development at which the individual seeks social approval in making moral decisions.

conversation analysis: A theory, based on the work of Harold Garfinkel and other ethnomethodologists, that studies how participants in social interaction produce and recognize coherent action on actual occasions.

core activities: According to commodity chain theory, the economic activities where the profits are made.

core countries: According to world systems theory, the most advanced industrial nations, who realize the lion's share of profits in the world economic system.

corporation: A formal organization that has a legal existence separate from its members.

correlation: The degree to which two or more variables regularly vary together.

counterculture: A culture that arises in opposition to the prevailing culture.

countervailing powers: A theory holding that the influence of one group is offset by that of another.

craze: Intense attraction to an object, person, or activity.

credential society: A society in which the qualifications needed for work and social status depend on the possession of a credential certifying the completion of formal education.

crime: A particular form of deviance consisting of acts that violate norms that have been enacted into criminal law.

criminologist: A social scientist who specializes in the scientific study of crime; includes sociologists, political scientists, and psychologists.

critical thinking: A form of thinking characterized by a willingness to ask any question, no matter how difficult; to be open to any answer that is supported by reason and evidence; and to openly confront one's biases and prejudices when they get in the way.

crowd: A temporary gathering of closely interacting people with a common focus.

crude birth rate: The number of births each year per thousand people.

crude death rate: The number of deaths each year per thousand people.

cult: A religion that is unconventional with regard to the larger society.

cultural capital: The verbal skills, knowledge base, and ways of thinking that help a person get ahead in society.

cultural diffusion: The spread of one culture's characteristics to another.

cultural diversity: The richness and variety of human cultural differences between and within countries.

cultural lag: A tendency for different parts of nonmaterial culture to change at different rates in response to technological innovations or other sources of change in material culture.

cultural pluralism: The belief that minority groups

should retain their distinct cultural identities, but only within a framework that ensures their overall equality.

cultural relativism: The attitude that the practices of another society should be understood sociologically in terms of that society's own norms and values, not one's own.

cultural universal: A feature common to all cultures.

culturalist theory of media influence: A theory developed during the 1980s and 1990s arguing that people play an active role in creating their own cultural meanings out of what they receive from the media.

culture: All of the beliefs, behaviors, and products common to members of a particular group.

de facto segregation: School segregation based on residential patterns or student choice, which persists even though legal segregation is now outlawed in the United States.

deception: In sociological research, when the subjects being studied are not fully informed of the nature or purposes of a study.

deinstitutionalization: The closure of many public mental hospitals, beginning in the 1960s, which has contributed to the growing number of homeless mentally ill people on streets and in shelters.

democracy: A political system in which citizens are able to directly or indirectly participate in their own governance (literally, "the rule of the people").

demographic transition: A theory arguing that industrialization is associated with movement from high fertility and mortality to low fertility and mortality, with the declines in mortality preceding declines in fertility such that a transitional period of rapid population growth results.

demography: A subfield of sociology concerned with the analysis of population size, distribution, and composition.

denomination: A church that is not formally allied with the state.

dependency theory: A Marxist theory of economic development arguing that the poverty of low-income nations is the immediate consequence of their exploitation by wealthy ones.

dependent development theory: A Marxist-influenced theory holding that although low-income countries are poor because of their exploitation by high-income countries, under certain circumstances they can hope to develop economically, albeit in ways shaped by their dependence on wealthier nations.

dependent variable: A variable that is believed to have changed as the result of another.

descriptive research: Research that seeks to paint a detailed picture of a particular phenomenon.

deskilling: The reduction of work to detail labor consisting of extremely simple, highly repetitive,

monotonous operations that require few if any skills or training.

detail labor: Extremely simple, highly repetitive, monotonous operations that require few if any skills.

deterrence: The impact of punishment on discouraging crime—not only on those who are punished but on others who learn by their example.

development communication: A field of communication research arguing that the widespread dissemination of newspapers, radio, and eventually television are central to a society's movement from coercive forms of government to truly democratic forms.

deviant behavior: Behavior that violates social norms and values shared by people in a particular culture.

dictatorship: A political system in which power rests in a single individual.

differential association: A theory that deviant behavior is largely the result of associating with other persons whose behavior is deviant; first developed by Edwin Sutherland.

differentiation: The development of increasing societal complexity through the creation of specialized social roles and institutions.

direct democracy: A political system in which all citizens fully participate in their own governance.

discipline: The coordinated regulation of people's behavior.

discrimination: The unequal treatment of individuals on the basis of their membership in a group.

disengagement theory: A functionalist theory of aging, which holds that elderly people should progressively pull back from social roles, freeing up those roles for others while preparing themselves for their eventual death.

disestablishment: Various periods in American history when the social and political influence of established religions has been successfully challenged.

diversity: The social relations and interaction of many different kinds of people.

divorce rate: The annual ratio of divorces to the total number of married households.

documentary method of interpretation: The theory, developed by Harold Garfinkel, that people's interpretation of particular events and actions serves to "document" the presumed existence of an underlying pattern.

domestic (or family) violence: The physical, sexual, or psychological abuse committed by one family member on another.

domination: The likelihood that a command will be obeyed.

doubling fallacy: The false assumption that a given rate of population increase can be sustained indefinitely.

doubling time: Under exponential growth, the number of years it takes for the total population to double.

downward mobility: Movement through the stratification system that results in a decrease in occupational status.

dramaturgical approach: A theory of social interaction, developed by Erving Goffman, that regards interaction as if it were governed by the norms of theatrical performance.

dual labor market: A labor market that is divided into a lower strata of low-paying (and low-benefit) jobs that seldom provide opportunities for advancement, and an upper strata of well-paying jobs that provide career opportunities.

dyad: A group consisting of two persons.

dysfunctions: In Robert K. Merton's theory, the maladaptive consequences of actions that weaken the social organism.

ecclesia: A church that is formally allied with the state and is the "official" religion of the society.

education: The transmission of society's norms, values, and knowledge base by means of direct instruction.

ego: According to Freud, the part of the mind that is the "self," the core of what is regarded as a person's unique personality.

egocentrism: The theory that children experience the world as if it were entirely centered on themselves.

electronic church: Churches in which the majority of congregants are geographically dispersed and are united primarily by means of electronic technology.

embeddedness: The notion that economic, political, and other forms of human activity are fundamentally shaped by social relations.

emergent properties: Properties of groups that differ from the characteristics of the individuals who comprise them.

endogamy: The practice of marrying with persons of one's own social group or caste.

equilibrium state: A condition of a society in which no further social change is likely to occur unless some external force sets changes in motion.

ethnic economic enclaves: Neighborhoods comprised primarily of members of an immigrant ethnic group who provide one another with mutual economic support.

ethnicity: The attribution of characteristics to groups of people who share a common cultural (including religious) heritage.

ethnocentrism: The tendency to judge other cultures by the standards of one's own culture, regarding one's own values and way of life as "normal" and "better."

ethnography: A method of research in which fieldwork is conducted to depict the characteristics of a group of people as fully as possible.

ethnomethodology: The body of common-sense knowledge and procedures by which ordinary members of society make sense of their social circumstances and interactions; also refers to the theory, developed by Harold Garfinkel, that studies such procedures.

ethnonationalism: A strongly held set of beliefs based on identification with an ethnic community that calls for nationhood based on ethnic ties.

Eurocentric: Knowledge that is centered on European concerns and beliefs.

euthanasia: Putting a severely ill person to death as an act of mercy; also known as "mercy killing."

evangelicalism: A form of Protestantism characterized by a belief in spiritual rebirth (being "born again"), involving the admission of personal sin and salvation through Christ's acceptance; the literal interpretation of the Bible; an emphasis on highly emotional and personal spiritual piety; and a proselytizing commitment to spreading "the Word" to others.

evolutionary theories of societal change: Those theories that regard all societies as moving in a single direction on some important dimension of societal change.

exponential population growth: The theory that a constant rate of population growth results in a population that grows by an increasing amount with each passing year.

expressive leader: A leader concerned with the well-being of the group itself.

extended family: A social group consisting of one or more parents, children, and other kin, often spanning several generations.

face validity: The extent to which operational definitions appear to measure the concepts they are intended to measure.

factory work: Specialized, tightly coordinated work tasks, closely supervised by factory owners and their managers.

fad: A temporary, highly imitated outbreak of mildly unconventional behavior.

family: A group of people who identify themselves as being related to one another, usually by blood, marriage, or adoption, and who share intimate relationships and dependency.

fashion: A somewhat long-lasting style of imitative behavior or appearance.

fee-for-service: A system of financing medical care in which the individual patient is responsible for paying the fees charged by the medical practitioner, clinic, or hospital.

feminism: The belief that social equality should exist between the sexes.

feminization of labor: The growing proportion of women in the workforce, often in the lowest-paying jobs.

feminization of poverty: An increase in the proportion of the poor who are female.

fertility: Reproductive performance, as indicated by the number of live births actually born to a woman.

feudalism: A social system in which people are granted by those of higher status the right to occupy and use land in exchange for performing designated services.

first world: The industrial capitalist nations of the world (the United States and Canada, the nations of Western Europe, Japan, Australia, and New Zealand).

folkways: Fairly weak norms (sometimes termed "conventions") passed down from the past, whose violation is generally not considered serious within a particular culture.

Fordism: The large-scale, highly standardized mass production of identical commodities on a mechanical assembly line.

formal education: Education that occurs within academic institutions such as schools.

formal organization: An organization that is rationally designed to achieve its objectives, often by means of explicit rules, regulations, and procedures.

framing: The ways in which the images and content of news help to shape audience perceptions.

free rider problem: The fact that people can avoid the costs of social movement activism (such as time, energy, and other personal resources), and still benefit from its success without becoming active participants.

frontstage: According to Erving Goffman, the places where a person has to perform.

functionalist paradigm: A macro-sociological perspective that seeks to explain social organization and change in terms of the roles or functions performed by individual members, groups, institutions, and social relations.

fundamentalists: A group within evangelicalism that is highly antimodern in many of its beliefs, adhering to strict codes of morality and conduct, taboos against drinking, smoking, and other "worldly evils," biblical infallibility, and a strong belief in Christ's imminent return to earth.

game stage: According to George Herbert Mead, the stage at which children learn to take on the role of multiple other people.

gang: A group of people, usually young, who hang around together and commit criminal acts either for economic gain or to protect their territory.

Gemeinschaft: The German word for *community,* which in Toennies's theory is characterized by rural- or town-based life, intimate relationships, a strong sense of family, powerful folkways and mores, and pervasive religious beliefs.

gender: Behavioral differences between males and females that are culturally based and socially learned.

gender factory: A term used by sociologists to characterize the function of the home in reproducing society's traditional gender roles.

gender identity: The ways in which individuals in a particular culture come to think of themselves as male or female, and learn to act accordingly.

gender role: Normative expectations concerning appropriately "masculine" or "feminine" behavior in a particular culture.

generalization: A broad conclusion that is drawn from a particular study, and then applied to a larger range of phenomena.

generalized other: According to the theories of George Herbert Mead, the sense we have that society has general norms and values by which we evaluate ourselves.

generational equity: The effort to strike a balance between the needs and interests of members of different generations.

genocide: The institutionalized practice of systematically killing the members of a particular racial, religious, or ethnic group.

gentrification: A process by which upper-income professionals ("the gentry") buy low-cost downtown housing, fix it up, move in, and thereby convert neighborhoods from low- to high-income, displacing poor people as a result.

geragogy: Older adult learning.

Gesellschaft: The German word for *society,* which in Toennies's theory is characterized by city life, impersonal relationships, the breakdown of family life, the replacement of traditional beliefs with cold calculation and reason, and the erosion of religious conviction in favor of shifting public opinion.

glass ceiling: A seemingly invisible barrier to movement into the very top positions in business and government, which makes it difficult for some women to reach the top of their professions.

global cities: Metropolitan areas that are highly interconnected with one another in terms of their roles as centers of global political and economic decision making, finance, and culture.

global wage: A wage equivalent to the lowest worldwide cost of obtaining comparable labor for a particular task, once the costs of operating at a distance are taken into account.

global warming: A projected increase in average planetary temperatures by some 3 to 8 degrees Fahrenheit by the middle of the next century, resulting from the "greenhouse effect."

globalization: The processes by which the lives of all people around the planet become increasingly interconnected in economic, political, cultural, and environmental terms, along with an awareness of such interconnections.

goal displacement: A problem that occurs when a social movement organization's original goals become redirected toward enhancing the organization and its leadership.

grass roots organizing: Attempts to mobilize support among ordinary members of the community.

graying: A term used to indicate that an increasing proportion of a society's population is becoming elderly.

greenhouse effect: The formation of a layer of gases in the upper atmosphere that traps heat at the planet's surface that otherwise would be reflected off into space.

gross national product (GNP): A country's yearly output of wealth.

groupthink: A process by which members of a group ignore ways of thinking and courses of action that go against the consensus of the group.

guanxi: Chinese business networks based primarily on social rather than purely economic foundations.

handicraft production: Production in which workers typically labor independently on items of their own design, using their own tools, and at their own pace.

Hawthorne effect: An effect on the person(s) being researched that actually results from the research process itself; named after the studies in which it was first observed.

Head Start: A federally funded program in which enriched preschool environments are created for lower-income children in hopes of preparing them to do better in school.

health: A state of mental, physical, and social well-being.

health care: All those activities intended to sustain, promote, and enhance health.

health maintenance organization (HMO): A group of doctors and health care specialists who work together and provide services for a set monthly or annual membership fee.

heroic measures: The practice of keeping patients with severe illnesses alive through the application of advanced medical technology.

heterosexuality: Sexual attraction or desire for persons of the opposite sex.

hidden curriculum: An unspoken socialization to norms, values, and roles that school provides along with the "official" curriculum.

high culture: The fine arts, classical music, live theater, and other activities that usually require special preparation to fully appreciate.

homelessness: The type of existence followed by a person who does not own a home, rent an apartment, or have a stable place to live.

homophobia: A generalized fear and hatred of homosexuals.

homosexuality: A sexual desire for persons of the same sex.

horizontal (or lateral) mobility: Movement through the stratification system that involves no change in status.

horticultural society: A type of society whose members rely for their sustenance primarily on the cultivation of plants by using a hoe or other simple tools.

human ecology: A subfield of sociology, developed at the University of Chicago in the 1920s and 1930s, concerned with the study of the spatial organization of people in their urban environment.

hunting and gathering society: A type of society whose members derive their sustenance primarily from hunting wild animals, fishing, and gathering wild plants.

hyperactivity: The inability to concentrate for more than a few seconds or moments without being distracted.

hypothesis: An idea about the world, derived from a theory, that is capable of being disproved when tested against observations.

I: In the interactionist theories of George Herbert Mead, the part of the self that refers to the impulse to act; it is creative, innovative, unthinking, and largely unpredictable.

id: According to Freud, the part of the mind that is the repository of basic biological drives and needs.

ideal culture: The norms and values a society professes to hold.

ideal type: According to Max Weber, a set of sociological ideas that best captures the essential features of some aspect of social reality according to the theoretical concerns of the sociologist.

incapacitation: Placing offenders in a location where their ability to violate norms is restricted, usually through imprisonment.

incarceration: Imprisonment.

income: The amount of money a person or household earns in a given period of time.

indentured servants: People who by law were bound to service to someone for a specified period of time, usually seven years, in order to pay for their passage.

independent variable: A variable that is believed to bring about change in another.

indexicality: The notion, developed by Harold Garfinkel, that the meaning of any particular action or event depends on its context.

industrial cities: Cities that are based on manufacturing.

industrial democracy: A political-economic system that seeks some democratic controls over business, along with the public provision of basic social services.

industrial revolution: The period during the eighteenth century when mechanized factory production first occurred.

industrial society: A society in which subsistence is based on the mechanized production of goods in factories.

inequality: The degree of disparity that exists in a society, measured in terms of wealth, prestige, power, and other valued resources.

informal (or "underground") economy: Goods and services sold by individuals and illegal businesses that do not pay taxes or register with federal, state, or local licensing authorities.

information float: The amount of time that it takes information to get from one place to another; now virtually zero for an increasing range of economic activities.

informed consent: An agreement by the subjects of a research project to being studied, after having been fully informed of the nature of the research, any physical or psychological dangers that might be involved, and the uses to which the results will be put.

ingroup: A group toward which one feels particular loyalty and respect.

instincts: Biologically fixed patterns of action.

institution: A cluster of relatively stable rules that govern social activities in a society; such rules also provide a shared understanding of the cultural meaning of those activities.

institutional discrimination: Unequal treatment that has become a part of the routine operation of such major social institutions as businesses, schools, hospitals, and the government.

institutionalist school: A theory of organizations holding that by becoming part of a global economic and legal system, countries and organizations are pressured into playing by a common set of international rules and regulations, as well as changing some of their internal rules and regulations to conform to international standards.

institutions: Clusters of relatively stable rules that govern social activities in a society, which at the same time provide shared understandings of the cultural meaning of those activities.

instrumental activism: The belief that individuals are responsible for actively achieving their goals through hard work.

instrumental leader: A leader concerned with accomplishing the task at hand.

intellective skill: The ability to think logically and abstractly, rather than relying on immediate physical experience.

interest groups: Groups comprised of people who share the same concerns on a particular issue and therefore unite in an effort to influence governmental policy.

intergenerational mobility: Movement through the stratification system that occurs across generations.

interlocking directorate: When directors sit on the governing boards of more than one corporation.

internalization: The social processes by which norms and values become so thoroughly ingrained that they serve as largely unquestioned natural ("normal") ways of thinking and acting.

International Baccalaureate Program: An international degree program intended to help students who are making a transition from high school in one country to higher education in another.

international family: An extended family spanning several countries, yet characterized by intense interactions, strong emotional ties, and a binding sense of mutual obligation.

international governmental organization (IGO): A group of international organizations established by treaties between governments for purposes of conducting business between the nations comprising its membership.

international nongovernmental organization (INGO): A group of international organizations established by agreements between the individuals or private organizations comprising its membership.

interpretive sociology: An approach to sociology that is concerned with the ways in which people interpret symbols in the course of arriving at shared understandings about their daily lives.

interview: A detailed, in-depth interrogation.

intragenerational mobility: Movement through the stratification system that occurs within a person's lifetime.

iron law of oligarchy: An inevitable tendency for large-scale bureaucratic organizations to become ruled by a handful of people in a highly undemocratic fashion.

keiretsu: Enormous business and financial groupings that provide substantial coordination and control within the Japanese economy.

Kuznets curve: The observation that inequality increases during the early stages of capitalist development, then declines, and eventually stabilizes at a relatively low level; advanced by the economist Simon Kuznets.

labeling theory: An approach holding that deviance (like all forms of human behavior) is the result of the labels attached to a person by other people.

labor market: All those persons who are seeking to sell their labor to others for a wage or salary.

labor unions: Workers' organizations concerned with improving various aspects of their members' working lives.

language: A system of symbolic verbal and sometimes written representations learned within a particular culture.

larceny: Legally defined as the unlawful taking of property from someone other than one's employer.

laws: The codified rules of behavior that have been officially legislated by a governing body and backed by the threat of force.

leader: A person who is able to influence the behavior of other members of a group.

leading question: A question that solicits a particular response.

legitimate authority: A type of power that is recognized as rightful by those over whom it is exercised.

liberal feminism: A stream of feminist thought holding that women's inequality is primarily the result of imperfect institutions, which can be corrected by reforms that do not fundamentally alter society itself.

liberation theology: A religious movement, centered primarily in Latin America, that combines Catholic beliefs, a passion for social justice for the poor, and actions aimed at achieving that passion.

life course: A sequence of different roles a person is expected to assume during chronological aging.

life expectancy: The average number of years a person can expect to live once he or she has reached a given age.

limited effects theory of media influence: A theory developed during the 1940s and the 1950s arguing that the media have minimal impact on people's attitudes and perceptions, since audiences are said to be highly selective in what they watch, perceive, and recall.

linguistic relativity hypothesis: A hypothesis, based on the theories of Sapir and Whorf, that perceptions are relative to language.

literacy: The ability to read and write at a basic level.

lobbyists: Paid professionals whose job it is to influence legislation.

looking-glass self: The theory, developed by Charles Horton Cooley, that our self-image results from how we interpret other peoples' views of ourselves.

macro level: Larger, more invisible, and often more remote social processes that help to shape the micro world.

magnet school: A school that seeks to attract students by offering specialized, high-quality programs in math, science, arts, humanities or other subjects.

managed competition: The Clinton administration's health-care proposal, consisting of a program in which everyone would belong to gigantic health maintenance organizations (HMOs) whose enormous bargaining power would in theory force insurance companies to lower their rates.

manifest functions: In Robert K. Merton's theory, social consequences that are intended by the actor.

market-oriented theories: Theories about economic development which assume that the best possible economic consequences will result if individuals are free to make their own economic decisions, uninhibited by any form of governmental constraint.

marriage: A culturally approved relationship, usually between two individuals, that provides for a degree of economic cooperation, intimacy, and sexual activity.

marriage rate: The ratio of the number of people who actually marry in a given year compared with the total number of people eligible to marry.

mass audience: A large collection of people who receive messages that are directed at them not as individuals but rather as a group.

mass education: The extension of formal schooling to wide segments of the population.

mass media: Forms of communication that permit a one-way flow of information from a single source to a large audience; examples include newspapers, magazines, radio, and television.

mass-mediated culture: A culture in which the mass media play a key role in both shaping and creating cultural perceptions.

mass production: Production based on an assembly line that uses a continuous conveyor belt to move the unfinished product past individual workers, each of whom performs a specific operation on it.

mass society: A society whose members are rootless, isolated, lacking in strong social ties, and are thus defenseless against various forms of manipulation (by the mass media in particular).

material culture: All the physical objects made by the members of a particular society to help shape their lives.

me: In the interactionist theories of George Herbert Mead, the part of the self that refers to the image we believe others hold of us as we act, that is, the looking-glass part of the self through which we see ourselves as others see us.

mechanical solidarity: In Emile Durkheim's theory, strong social ties and shared beliefs that are based on similarity.

Medicaid: A federal insurance program that provides health insurance for the disabled, the poor, and those on welfare.

medical care: An aspect of health care that is concerned with the diagnosis, advice, and treatment of illnesses by certified medical professionals such as doctors and nurses.

medicalization of deviance: The transformation of culturally defined deviant behavior into medical problems.

medicalization of health and illness: The process of giving all aspects of health and illness an exclusively medical meaning.

Medicare: A federal medical insurance program, begun in 1965, which provides medical insurance covering hospital costs for all people 65 years and older.

medicine: An institutionalized system for the scientific diagnosis, treatment, and prevention of disease, illness, and other damage to the mind or the body.

megalopolis: A continuous stretch of metropolitan areas containing many cities and suburbs.

meritocracy: A bureaucracy in which positions are filled purely on the basis of a person's merits or qualifications.

metropolis: One or more central cities and their surrounding suburbs, forming a more or less integrated regional economy.

Metropolitan Statistical Areas (MSA): According to the U.S. Bureau of the Census, all counties with an urbanized area of at least 50,000 people.

micro level: Social relations that involve direct social interaction with others.

micro-mobilization contexts: Small group settings in which people are able to generate a shared set of beliefs to explain some social problem, along with the necessary social organization to do something about it.

military-industrial complex: A phrase coined by former President Dwight D. Eisenhower to characterize the interconnected institutions with a common interest in weapons and other defense spending; it includes the military, the intelligence community, corporations with defense-related contracts, numerous government agencies, and university engineering and scientific research that has military applications.

minority group: A group of people, distinguished on the basis of perceived racial or cultural differences from the dominant group in society, who are disadvantaged as a result of their status.

modernization theory: A market-oriented theory of economic development arguing that low-income societies can become modern by "taking-off" into self-sustained economic growth only if they overcome fatalistic value systems, bring their population growth under control, eliminate government and other interference in private business, and achieve substantial rates of savings and investment (approximately 10 percent of GNP).

monarchy: A political system in which power resides in the personage of an individual or family and is passed from one generation to the next through lines of inheritance.

money laundering: The practice of converting illegally acquired assets into legal businesses or foreign bank accounts.

monogamy: A form of marriage in which a person may have only one spouse at a time.

monopoly: The situation that exists when a single firm accounts for all the sales in a particular market.

monotheism: The belief in a single all-knowing, all-powerful god.

moral boundaries: A society's sense of what is normal and acceptable behavior, achieved partly by identifying certain acts as deviant and severely punishing the people who commit them. (The concept was developed by Emile Durkheim.)

moral development: A theory, developed by Jean Piaget and Lawrence Kohlberg, that people at different ages learn to act according to abstract ideas about justice or fairness.

mores: Strongly held norms whose violation would seriously offend the standards of acceptable conduct or righteousness of most people within a particular culture.

mortality: The deaths occurring in a population.

multicultural feminism: A stream of feminist thought focusing on understanding and ending inequality for all women, regardless of race, class, nationality, age, sexual orientation, or other characteristics.

multiculturalism: Respecting cultural differences, rather than seeking to assimilate all subcultures into a larger, supposedly "better" culture.

multilinear evolutionary theory (sometimes called **neoevolutionary theories**): The theory arguing that multiple paths to societal change exist, depending on the particular circumstances of the society.

mutual assured destruction (MAD): The defining nuclear strategy of both the United States, the former Soviet Union, and their allies throughout the Cold War, calling for sufficient nuclear capability so that even after suffering a nuclear attack, it would be possible to completely destroy the attacker's society with a massive nuclear response.

NAFTA (North American Free Trade Agreement) An agreement between the United States, Mexico, and Canada, which will ease trade barriers between the three countries and lead to the creation of the world's largest trading bloc, with 364 million people in a unified $6.2 trillion economy.

national health service: A health care system that covers everyone in the country regardless of their ability to pay.

nationalism: The belief that the people of a particular nation have historical or God-given rights that supersede those of any other people.

nation-state: A particular form of state whose members are regarded as "citizens" possessing specified legal rights and obligations.

natural scientist: A scientist who studies the nonhuman or purely physical aspects of the natural world.

negative euthanasia: The withdrawing of vital life-support systems from a terminally ill person who will die as a direct result.

net financial assets: The value of everything one owns (with the exception of one's home and cars), minus the value of everything one owes.

net migration: The difference between the number of people moving into a locale (in-migration) and the number of people moving out (out-migration).

network: All the connections that link a person with other people, and through them to the persons with whom these people are connected.

New International Division of Labor (NIDL) theory: A theory of economic development arguing that the division of labor that characterizes industrial societies has now been extended to cover the entire planet, relegating low-income nations to the role of providing cheap labor for firms based in high-income countries.

"new" social movements: Movements that have arisen since the 1960s that are fundamentally concerned with the quality of private life, often advocating large-scale cultural changes in the ways that people think and act.

newly industrializing countries (NICs): The rapidly growing economies of the world, particularly the East Asian economies of Hong Kong, Singapore, Taiwan, and South Korea, but also including such growing Latin American economies as Mexico.

no fault divorce: A relatively recent form of divorce, first adopted by the state of California in 1970, which permits couples to divorce purely on the grounds of incompatibility (termed "irreconcilable differences").

nobility: A hereditary stratum in society, possessing a highly elevated social status.

nominal variable: A variable that indicates whether or not something falls into a particular category.

nonmaterial culture: All the nonphysical products of human interaction; that is, the ideas shared by people in a particular society.

nonprobability sample: A sample in which subjects are chosen because of their specific characteristics.

nontheistic religions: Religions based on a belief in the existence of divine spiritual forces rather than a god or gods.

normative organization: An organization people join on a voluntary basis, to pursue a morally worthwhile goal without expectation of material reward; sometimes called a *voluntary association.*

norms: The shared rules in a particular culture that tell its members how to behave in a given situation.

nuclear family: A social group consisting of one or two parents and their dependent children.

nuclear proliferation: The spread of nuclear weapons capability to additional nations.

objectivity: The ability, during research, to represent the object of study as truthfully as possible.

occupation: Paid employment.

official sources: Government authorities, designated spokespersons, and others presumed to have specialized expertise on a topic.

old age: The years when we confront the possibility of disengaging from important social roles, along with the realistic possibility of our own death.

oligarchy: Rule by the few.

oligopoly: The situation that exists when several firms overwhelmingly dominate a market.

operational definition: Defining the concept in terms of operations or measurements that can be performed on it.

ordinal variables: A variable that measures rank order.

organic solidarity: In Emile Durkheim's theory, social ties that are based on difference and functional interdependence, similar to the unity of a living organism in which each organ has its own specialized role to play.

organization: A group with an identifiable membership that engages in concerted collective action to achieve a common purpose.

organized crime: Crimes committed by criminal groups involving the provision of illegal goods and services.

outgroup: A group toward which one feels antagonism and contempt.

panic: Massive flight from something that is feared.

paradigm: A perspective or framework containing assumptions about the world that helps to shape scientific theories.

parliamentary system of government: A type of democracy in which the chief of state (usually called a prime minister) is the head of the part with the largest number of representatives in the legislature.

particular others: According to the theories of George Herbert Mead, the specific people who are important in our lives, whose views are important in our self-evaluations.

pastoral society: A type of society whose members domesticate wild animals and rely on them as a principal source of food and transportation.

patriarchy: Any set of social relationships in which men dominate over women.

peacetime conversion: The transformation of defense-related industries to the production of nonmilitary goods and services.

peers: People of the same age, social standing, and class.

peripheral activities: According to commodity chain theory, the economic activities from which profits are taken.

peripheral countries: According to world systems theory, the low-income, largely agricultural nations that are often manipulated by core countries for the economic advantage of the latter.

per-person gross national product (GNP): A country's yearly output of wealth, per person.

personal power: Power that derives from a leader's personality.

personalizing the news: A framing device that consists of representing the news as resulting exclusively from the efforts of individuals rather than underlying social forces.

picket: A labor action conducted by workers, involving marching in front of the doorway to the workplace so as to discourage other workers from entering (and working) until an agreement is reached.

pink collar: Work that primarily employs women in nonmanual semiskilled work.

play stage: According to George Herbert Mead, the developmental stage during which children learn to take the attitude of the other people with whom they interact.

pluralism: The theory that power is distributed among different groups that contend with one another on roughly equal footing.

pluralistic society: A society comprised of groups with diverse and often conflicting norms and values.

political action committees (PACs): Organizations formed by interest groups to raise and spend money in order to influence elected officials.

political rights: Legal rights ensuring that anyone who so chooses can participate in governance.

polyandry: A form of marriage in which a woman may have multiple husbands.

polygamy: A form of marriage in which a person may have more than one spouse at a time.

polygyny: A form of marriage in which a man may have multiple wives.

polytheism: The belief that there are different gods representing various categories of natural forces.

popular culture: Forms of culture that are pursued by large numbers of middle- and working-class people; includes spectator sports, television "soaps" and "sitcoms," amateur softball leagues, movies, and rock music.

population pyramid: A graph that represents the composition of a country's population by age and sex.

population universe: The larger group of people for whom the conclusions of a survey sample are said to apply.

positional mobility: Movement through the stratification system that results from individual effort, accomplishments, or luck, rather than changes in the occupational structure.

positional power: Power that officially stems from the leadership position itself.

positive euthanasia: The killing of a severely ill person who otherwise would live, as an act of mercy.

positivism: Auguste Comte's belief that knowledge should be guided by facts rather than by imagination, pure logic, or any other nonfactual source.

postconventional stage: According to Lawrence Kohlberg, the stage of moral development at which the individual invokes general, abstract notions of right and wrong in making moral decisions.

post-Fordism: Forms of industrial organization that emphasize flexibility rather than standardization.

postindustrial society: A type of modern society based on knowledge, information, and the provision of services rather than on the physical production of goods in factories.

power: A person's relationship to governmental and other political institutions, manifested in the ability to mobilize resources and achieve a goal despite the resistance of others.

preconventional stage: According to Lawrence Kohlberg, the stage of moral development at which the individual simply seeks to avoid punishment or achieve some personal gain in making moral decisions.

preindustrial cities: Cities that are based on both agriculture and trade.

prejudice: A preconceived belief about an individual or a group that is not subject to change on the basis of new evidence.

preparatory stage: According to George Herbert Mead, the developmental stage in which children relate to the world as though they are the center of the universe.

presentation of self: According to Erving Goffman, the constant effort to create favorable impressions in the minds of others during social interaction.

preventive medicine: Medicine that emphasizes a healthy lifestyle to prevent poor health before it actually occurs.

primary care: Medical services that focus on dealing with health problems as or before they arise rather than after they have become acute.

primary deviance: A process that occurs when an activity is labeled as deviant by others.

primary group: A group that is characterized by intense positive and negative emotional ties, face-to-face interaction, intimacy, and a strong, enduring sense of commitment; exemplified by family, peer, and friendship relations. (The concept originated with Charles Horton Cooley.)

primary labor market: A labor market consisting of jobs that are reasonably secure, provide good pay and benefits, and hold the promise of career training and advancement.

primary sector: The sector of the economy that is based on the extraction of raw materials and natural resources.

principle of falsification: The principle that a scientific theory must lead to testable hypotheses that are capable of being proven false.

private school: A school that is run by privately employed educators and paid for out of students' fees and tuition.

productivity: The amount of goods that a worker can produce in a given period of time.

profane: In Durkheim's view, the sphere of mundane, routine, everyday life.

professional-managerial class: A class that consists of salaried workers who use their minds (rather than their hands), and whose function it is to help maintain a capitalist society.

professional thief: A person who earns a livelihood by committing crimes on a regular basis.

proletariat: In Marx's theory, an unpropertied class that primarily includes factory workers (from the Latin term for "common person").

psychoanalysis: An approach to the study of human psychology that emphasizes the complex reasoning processes of the human mind; developed by Sigmund Freud.

public education: A universal education system provided by the government and funded out of tax revenues rather than student fees.

pure relationship: A relationship that is entered into purely for its own sake and which is maintained only so long as it is mutually satisfying to both partners.

qualitative sociology: A research strategy that is based on descriptive rather than on more quantitative forms of analysis.

qualities: Discrete categories (usually indicated by words or labels) that enable researchers to make non-numerical distinctions among the things they observe.

quality circle: A small group of workers and managers who operate as a team to solve problems and improve product quality.

quantitative sociology: A research strategy based primarily on numerical measurement and analysis.

quantities: Explicit numerical distinctions that enable researchers to make relatively precise measurements.

race: A category of people whose biologically based common physical characteristics are believed to make them socially distinct.

racism: The belief that a particular racial or ethnic group is naturally inferior, so that their unequal treatment is justified.

radical feminism: A stream of feminist thought holding that women's inequality is fundamental to all other systems of inequality, including economic.

random sample: A sample in which everyone in the underlying population has an equal chance of being chosen for the sample.

rape: The forcing of nonconsensual vaginal, oral, or anal intercourse.

rape culture: A culture resulting from male socialization that reinforces male domination by fostering a state of continual fear among women.

ratio variable: A variable that permits absolute measurement along a scale with a meaningful zero point.

rational-legal authority: Power based on a belief in the lawfulness of enacted rules and the legitimate right of leaders to exercise authority under such rules.

reactionary social movement: A movement seeking to restore an earlier social system—often based on a mythical past—along with the traditional norms and values that once presumably accompanied it.

real culture: The norms and values that a society follows in practice.

reality principle: According to Freud, the assumption that the members of any society renounce a substantial part of their desire for immediate pleasure in order to do the kind of work that is necessary for the society to operate smoothly.

rebellion: A movement seeking to overthrow the existing social, political, and economic system but lacking a detailed plan for a new social order.

recidivism: The rate at which ex-offenders are arrested for another criminal offense once they are released from jail.

redlining: A policy by which lending institutions exclude entire low-income neighborhoods (especially those occupied by racial or ethnic minorities) from loans for businesses, housing construction, or home improvements, thereby contributing to neighborhood deterioration.

reference group: A group that provides a standard for judging one's attitudes or behaviors.

reflexes: An automatic response to a particular stimulus.

reformist social movement: A movement seeking to bring about social change within the existing economic and political system.

rehabilitation: Resocializing criminals to noncriminal norms and values.

relative autonomy of the state: A political theory, derived from the ideas of Max Weber as well as Karl Marx, which argues that governments themselves exert a degree of power, independently of any class interests that may exist.

reliability: The extent to which researchers' findings are consistent between different studies of the same thing, or for the same study over time.

religion: A cultural system of commonly shared beliefs and rituals that provide a sense of ultimate meaning and purpose, by creating an idea of reality that is sacred, all-encompassing, and supernatural.

religious economy: A theoretical framework, within the sociology of religion, which argues that religions can be fruitfully understood as organizations in competition with one another for adherents.

religious nationalism: The fusion of strongly held religious convictions with beliefs about a nation's social and political destiny.

replication: Research strategies that can be duplicated by other scholars.

representative democracy: A political system in which citizens elect representatives who are supposed to make decisions that express the wishes of the majority who elect them to office.

research method: A specific technique for systematically gathering data while conforming to rules that have been agreed upon by a community of scholars.

research strategy: A clearly thought-out plan to guide sociological inquiry.

reservations: Tracts of land set aside by the U.S. government for occupation and use by Indians.

residual norms: According to Thomas Scheff, norms that they are simply there in the background—unspoken, unacknowledged, and yet central to competent behavior.

resocialization: According to Erving Goffman, the process of altering an individual's personality through total control of his or her environment, usually within a *total institution* (see definition).

resource mobilization theory: A theory about social movement organizations that focuses on their ability to generate money, membership, and political support in order to achieve their objectives.

revolutionary social movement: A movement seeking to fundamentally alter the existing social, political, and economic system in keeping with a vision of a new social order.

riot: A prolonged outbreak of violent behavior on the part of a sizable group of people, directed against people or property, and often illegal.

rise and fall theories of societal change: Those theories denying that there is any simple direction to societal change; rather, change is more likely to be one of growth and decline.

ritual pollution: The belief that contact between members of different castes will corrupt or contaminate the members of the higher caste.

robbery: Legally defined as taking something by the use of violence or the threat of violence.

robots: Computer-driven machines.

role: The expected behavior associated with a particular status.

role conflict: A conflict that exists when two or more roles contain contradictory behavioral expectations.

role strain: The strain experienced when contradictory expectations exist within a given role.

role-taking: The ability to take the role of others in interaction.

rumor: An unverified form of information that is transmitted informally, usually originating in an unknown source.

rural: According to the U.S. Bureau of the Census, any human settlement of fewer than 2,500 people.

sacred: In Durkheim's view, the sphere of life imbued with spiritual meaning.

sample: A subset of cases selected to represent a larger population.

samsara: The belief, associated with Hinduism and Buddhism, that the soul is reincarnated (reborn) according to one's karma or actions on earth.

scapegoating: Blaming another person or group for one's problems.

school busing: A court-ordered program to achieve racial integration by busing public school students to schools other than those they would normally attend.

school choice plans: Programs in which the government provides families with educational certificates or "vouchers" that can be redeemed for tuition payments at the private or parochial school of their choice.

school segregation: The education of racial minorities in schools that are geographically separated from those attended by whites and other ethnic groups.

science: A combination of systematic observation and theory that provides explanations of how things work.

scientific management: The application of engineering rules to scientifically reorganize the actions of the workers themselves (sometimes called *Taylorism* after its founder).

scientific research: The different methods used by scientists to achieve the goal of systematic observation and information-gathering.

scientific theory: A set of logically consistent ideas about the relationships between things that permits those ideas to be checked against observations through scientific research.

second shift: A phrase used by sociologists to characterize the unpaid housework that women typically do after they come home from their paid employment.

second world: The socialist or communist nations of the world (the former Soviet Union, the nations of Eastern Europe, China, Cuba, Vietnam, North Korea, and African nations such as Zambia and Angola).

secondary deviance: A process that occurs when a person labeled as deviant accepts the label as part of his or her identity, and as a result begins to act in conformity with the label.

secondary group: A group characterized by large size, impersonality, and fleeting relationships.

secondary labor market: A labor market that includes unstable jobs with little job security, low pay and few benefits, and little likelihood of career advancement.

secondary sector: The sector of the economy that is based on the production of finished goods from raw materials obtained in the primary sector.

sect: A religious organization that exists in a high degree of tension with its environment.

secular thinking: Worldly thinking, particularly as seen in the rise of science, technology, and rational thought in general.

secularization: A rise in secular thinking and a simultaneous decline in the influence of religion, as seen in a weakening of the social and political power of religious organizations and typically accompanied by lessened religious beliefs and involvement.

segregation: The physical and social separation of different categories of people.

semiperipheral countries: According to world systems theory, the countries that occupy an intermediate position in the global capitalist economy—semiindustrialized, middle-income countries that extract profits from more peripheral countries, while in turn yielding profits to core countries.

semistructured interview: An interview consisting of a list of topics to cover but in which the interview situation itself determines the course of questioning and the details of the questions.

services: Activities performed by an individual that do not directly result in a physical product.

sex: Anatomical or other biological differences between males and females that originate in the human gene.

sexism: The belief that one sex is innately inferior, and therefore its domination is warranted.

sexual harassment: According to the guidelines of the Federal Equal Employment Opportunity Commission, any behavior that entails (1) unwelcome sexual advances, requests for sexual favors, or physical conduct of a sexual nature when such conduct is used as a condition of employment, instruction, evaluation, benefits, or other opportunities; or (2) when such conduct interferes with an individual's performance, or contributes to an intimidating, hostile, or offensive environment.

sexual orientation: A person's desire or attraction for a sexual partner of a particular sex.

sexuality: The ways in which people construct their erotic or sexual relationships, including norms governing sexual behavior.

social age: The norms, values, and roles that are culturally associated with a particular chronological age.

social aggregates: Simple collections of people who happen to be together in a particular location at a certain time but do not significantly interact or identify with one another.

social categories: Groupings that share some common characteristic but do not necessarily interact or identify with one another.

social class: Unequal social position based on income, wealth, and—more generally—a person's location in the economic system.

social conflict paradigm: A macrolevel perspective that seeks to explain social organization and change in terms of the conflict that is built into social relations.

social engineering: The use of social science, usually by government, to design a preferred social order.

social facts: Qualities of groups that are external to individual members yet constrain their thinking and behavior.

social gerontology: A discipline concerned with the study of the social aspects of aging.

social group: A collection of people who regularly interact with one another on the basis of shared expectations concerning behavior and who share a sense of common identity.

social learning: The learning that occurs from observing and imitating others.

social learning theory: A theory that assumes that because human beings are social in nature, specific behaviors are always learned within a particular cultural context.

social mobility: Movement through the stratification system, particularly as a result of changes in occupation, wealth, or income.

social movement: A large number of people who have come together in a continuing and organized effort to bring about (or resist) social change.

social movement organizations ("SMOs"): Formal organizations that seek to achieve social change through concrete actions.

social rights: Legal rights that call for the governmental provision of various forms of economic and social security.

social scientists: A scientist who studies human beings and the social worlds that they consciously create.

social solidarity: The bonds that unite the members of a social group.

social stratification: The systematic inequalities of wealth, power, and prestige that result from social rank.

social structure: The underlying regularities in how people behave and interrelate with one another.

socialism: An economic system in which the production and distribution of goods and services is pursued for the common good, by means of enterprises owned by the central government or its subunits.

socialist (or Marxist) feminism: A stream of feminist thought holding that women's inequality is largely the result of capitalistic economic relations that must be fundamentally transformed before women can achieve equality.

socialization: The lifelong process through which people learn the values, norms, and roles of their culture, and thereby develop their sense of self.

societal change: Changes that occur throughout the social structure of an entire society.

society: The interacting people who share a common culture.

sociobiology: A branch of science that attempts to infer from the study of insects and other social animals that there are genetic bases for competition, cooperation, aggression, envy, and common human behaviors.

sociological imagination: C. Wright Mill's notion of the ability to grasp the relationship between one's life as an individual and the larger social forces that help to shape it.

sovereignty: The final and total authority possessed by a nation-state over its members, such that no greater authority can be found elsewhere.

spurious relationship: A statistical association between two or more variables that is actually the result of something else that is not being measured, rather than a causal link between the variables themselves.

state: A political apparatus possessing the legitimate monopoly over the use of force within its territory.

state organized crime: Acts defined by law as criminal that are committed by state and government officials in the pursuit of their jobs as representatives of the government.

statistics: A subfield of sociology concerned with generalizing from samples to the larger populations they represent.

status: A person's relationship to established social positions in society that vary in terms of prestige.

status inconsistency: A situation where a person occupies two or more statuses of different rank.

statuses: Established social positions in society that vary in terms of prestige.

stereotyping: Generalizing a set of characteristics to all members of a group.

stratification: Systematic inequalities of wealth, power, and prestige that result from a person's social rank.

stratified society: A society characterized by systematic inequalities of wealth, power, and prestige associated with a person's social status.

strike: A work stoppage conducted by workers, usually to obtain higher wages or improved working conditions.

structural contradiction: Those aspects of a social structure that are mutually incompatible with one another, and therefore result in structural instability.

structural contradiction theory: A type of conflict theory that accepts Merton's notion that societies often contain strains that lead to deviance, but combines it with the notion that such strains result from aspects of a social structure that are mutually incompatible with one another.

structural effects: Variations in human behavior that can be explained by the larger social structure rather than by individual differences.

structural mobility: Movement through the stratification system that results from changes in the occupational structure of a society.

structural strain: In Robert K. Merton's reformulation of Durkheim's theory, a form of anomie that occurs when a gap exists between the goals society sets for people and the means society provides for people to achieve them.

structuralism: The theory that power is highly constrained and shaped by a person's organizational role.

structured interview: An interview consisting of a detailed list of specific questions.

subcontracting: A form of economic organization in which one firm relies on other, more specialized firms to provide specialized products or services.

subculture: A smaller culture that exists within a larger, dominant culture yet differs from it in some important way.

suburb: A catch-all term for any urban development that occurs outside a city.

superego: According to Freud's, the part of the mind that consists of the values and norms of society, insofar as they are internalized by the individual.

surplus: The production of greater sustenance than is required for immediate survival.

surveillance: The ability to monitor people, either through direct observation, or by keeping records.

survey: A precisely worded questionnaire administered to a group of people in order to determine their characteristics, opinions, and behaviors.

sustainable development: Programs that create economic growth while preserving the environment through conserving nonrenewable resources such as forests and minerals, and by shifting to renewable sources of energy such as wind and solar power.

symbol: Something understood as representing something else to the human mind.

symbolic analyst: A person who works with symbols and ideas, rather than with things.

symbolic interactionist paradigm: A micro-sociological perspective arguing that both the human self and society as a whole are the result of social interactions based on language and other symbols; originates in the writings of George Herbert Mead.

taboo: A strongly held norm whose violation is forbidden, highly offensive, and even unthinkable.

tao: The "way of being," according to the teachings of Taoism and Confucianism.

Taylorism: (see *scientific management*)

technological literacy: Mastery of the most recent technical innovations.

technology: The practical application of knowledge, through tools and techniques, to multiply and conserve human energy.

telecommuting: "Traveling" from home to work electronically rather than physically by such means as telephone, fax, electronic data transfer, and electronic mail.

televangelism: Evangelical churches that conduct their ministries primarily over television.

tertiary sector: The sector of the economy that involves the production of services.

theism: The belief in one or more supernatural deities or gods.

theories of the middle range: Robert K. Merton's name for theories that seek to bridge European-style grand theory and more narrowly focused research.

third party: A phrase used to refer to any U.S. political party other than the Democrats or Republicans.

third world: All countries that do not fit neatly into the "first" and "second" worlds, comprising about two-thirds of the world's population (Mexico, the nations of Central and South America, and noncommunist countries in Africa and Asia).

tokenism: A situation in which highly successful women are seen as representing all women, rather than as individuals.

total institution: An institution that encompasses all aspects of one's life; examples include prisons, the military, asylums, concentration camps, and hospitals.

totalitarianism: A type of authoritarianism which, in addition to denying popular political participation in government, seeks to regulate and control all aspects of the public and private lives of its citizens.

totem: Sacred objects believed to possess magical qualities connecting humans with the divine.

traditional authority: Power based on a belief in the sanctity of long-standing traditions and the legitimate right of rulers to exercise authority under them.

trained incapacity: A learned inability to exercise independent thought; according to Thorstein Veblen, a characteristic of bureaucrats.

transactional leader: A person who is concerned with accomplishing the group's tasks, getting group members to do their jobs, and making certain that the group achieves its goals.

transformational leader: A person who is able to instill the members of a group with a sense of mission or higher purpose, thereby changing the nature of the group itself.

transnational corporation (TNC): A corporation that operates in many different countries.

transnational organization: A bureaucratic organization whose operations span national boundaries but are centrally directed by citizens from a single country.

transsexuality: A sexual orientation that involves identification with persons of the opposite sex.

triad: A group consisting of three persons.

tribal structure: A type of social structure in which members share extremely strong customs and traditions, trace their lineage to a common (often mythological) ancestor, and submerge their individual identities to the larger group.

triple oppression: The extreme discrimination and inequality that is sometimes experienced by lower-income women of color.

turn-taking: According to the theory of conversational analysis, specific procedures that enable utterances to be understood as responsive to earlier turns.

underclass: A caste-like class that is "beneath" the class system in that it lacks access even to the lower parts of the working class; consisting primarily of inner-city African Americans who have been trapped for more than a generation in an unending cycle of poverty from which there is little possibility of escape.

unilinear evolutionary theories: Those theories that assume all societies follow a single evolutionary path.

unobtrusive measure: A measure that is based on data collected with minimal impact on the persons being studied.

upward mobility: Movement through the stratification system that results in an increase in occupational status.

urban: A concentration of people engaged in nonagricultural activities.

urban growth machine: In Molotch and Logan's theory, persons and institutions that have a stake in growth in the value of urban land and comprise a power elite in most cities.

urban renewal: A federal government program that provides funds to localities for fixing up "blighted areas."

urbanization: The concentration of people in urban areas.

utilitarian organization: An organization that people join primarily because of some material benefit or gain they expect to receive in return for membership.

validity: The degree to which our concepts and their measurement are congruent with the world they are claiming to represent.

value neutrality: The belief that personal beliefs and opinions should not influence the course of a person's research.

values: Highly general ideas about what is good, right, or just in a particular culture.

variable: An operational measure that varies (increases or decreases in value) according to the value of the thing it is measuring.

verstehen: The German term for interpretive understanding; in Weber's work, a research method that involves empathy with the persons being studied.

vertical mobility: Movement that is up or down the stratification system.

victimless crimes: Acts prohibited by law in which those who are affected are willing and voluntary participants.

virtual workplace: A work environment that is electronically rather than physically connected to its client.

wealth: The value of everything a person owns.

white collar: Work that requires mental skills.

white-collar crime: Crime committed by people of high social status in connection with their work.

working poor: People whose earnings are insufficient to lift them above poverty.

world systems theory: The belief that the world capitalist economic system must be understood as a single unit, not in terms of individual countries.

zionism: A movement calling for the return of Jews to Palestine and the creation of a Jewish state.

Bibliography

Abdul-Rauf, Muhammad. (1975). *Islam: Creed and Worship.* Washington: Islamic Center.

Abeles, Ronald P., and Matilda White Riley. (1987). "Longevity, Social Structure, and Cognitive Aging." In Carmi Schooler and K. Warner Schaie (eds.), *Cognitive Functioning and Social Structure Over the Life Course,* pp. 161-175. Norwood, NJ: Ablex.

Abrams, Garry. (1989). "Ebbing Empire Televangelism: With His Medical Center Closed, Layoffs in His Ministry and Contributions Down from Their All-time High, Oral Roberts May Have Reason to Wonder: Have the Miracles Stopped?" *Los Angeles Times* (October 20): E-1.

Abrams, Naomi. (1992). "Towards Reconceptualizing Political Action," *Sociological Inquiry* 62 (summer): 327-347.

Abun-Nasr, J. (1965). *The Tijaniyya.* London: Oxford University Press.

Acampo, Elinor Ann. (1989). *Industrialization, Family Life and Class Relations.* Berkeley: University of California Press.

Accad, Evelyne. (1991). "Contradictions for Contemporary Women in the Middle East." In Chandra Talpade Mohanty, Ann Russo, and Lourdes Torres (eds.), *Third World Women and the Politics of Feminism.* Bloomington: Indiana University Press.

Adam, Barry D. (1987). *The Rise of a Lesbian and Gay Movement.* Boston: Twayne.

——— (ed.). (1979). "A Social History of Gay Politics." In Martin P. Levine (ed.), *Gay Men: The Sociology of Male Homosexuality,* San Francisco: Harper & Row.

Adams, Constance J. (1989). "Nurse-Midwifery Practice in the United States, 1982 and 1987," *American Journal of Public Health* 79 (August): 1038-1039.

Adler, Patricia A., and Peter Adler. (1994). *Constructions of Deviance: Social Power, Context, and Interaction.* Belmont, CA: Wadsworth.

Aguirre, B. E., E. L. Quarentelli, and Jorge L. Mendoza. (1988). "The Collective Behavior of Fads: The Characteristics, Effects, and Career of Streaking," *American Sociological Review* 53: 569-584.

Alba, Richard D. (1985). *Italian Americans: Into the Twilight of Ethnicity.* Englewood Cliffs, NJ: Prentice-Hall.

Albanese, Jay. (1989). *Organized Crime in America* (2nd ed.). Cincinnati: Anderson.

Albini, Joseph L. (1971). *The American Mafia: Genesis of a Legend.* New York: Appleton-Century-Crofts.

Aldrich, Howard E., and Peter V. Marsden. (1988). "Environments and Organizations." In Neil J. Smelser, *Handbook of Sociology.* Newbury Park, CA: Sage.

Alexander, Herbert. (1987). *Financing the Election.* Lexington, MA: Lexington.

Alexander, Jeffery C. (ed.). (1985). *Neofunctionalism.* Newbury Park, CA: Sage.

Alexander, Jeffery C., and Paul Colomy. (1985). "Neo-Functionalism," *Sociological Theory* 3: 11-23.

——— (eds.). (1990). *Differentiation Theory and Social Change: Comparative and Historical Perspectives.* New York: Columbia University Press.

Alexander, M. Jacqui. (1991). "Redrafting Morality: The Postcolonial State and the Sexual Offenses Bill of Trinidad and Tobago." In Chandra Talpade Mohanty, Ann Russo, and Lourdes Torres, *Third World Women and the Politics of Feminism.* Bloomington: Indiana University Press.

Al-Faruqi, Isma'il R., and Lois Lamya' al Faruqi. (1986). *The Cultural Atlas of Islam.* London: Collier Macmillan.

Alford, Robert, and Roger Friedland. (1985). *Powers of Theory.* Cambridge, England: Cambridge University Press.

Allen, Richard L., and Michael C. Thornton. (1992). "Social Structural Factors, Black Media, and Stereotypical Self-Characterizations Among African Americans," *National Journal of Sociology* 6 (summer): 41-75.

Allen, Brandt. (1978). "Racism and Research: The Case of the Tuskegee Syphilis Study," *Hastings Center Magazine.* Hastings-on-Hudson, NY: Institute of Society, Ethics, and the Sciences.

Allison, Graham T. (1971). *Essence of Decision: Explaining the Cuban Missile Crisis.* Boston: Little, Brown.

Allport, Gordon, and L. Postman. (1947). *The Psychology of Rumor.* New York: Holt.

Alsalam, Nabeel, Laurence T. Ogle, Gayle Thompson Rogers, and Thomas M. Smith. (1992). *The Condition of Education: 1992.* Washington: U.S. Department of Education, National Center for Education Statistics.

Althusser, Louis. (1971). *Lenin and Philosophy, and Other Essays.* London: New Left.

———. (1986). *For Marx.* London: Verso.

Althusser, Louis, and Etienne Balibar. (1990). *Reading "Capital."* London: New Left Books.

Altman, Dennis. (1982). *The Homosexualization of America.* Boston: Beacon.

Alwin, Duane F., Fonald F. Cohen, and Theodore M. Newcomb. (1991). *Political Attitudes Over the Life Span: The Bennington Women after Fifty Years.* Madison: University of Wisconsin Press.

American Association of Retired Persons (AARP). (1989). *A Profile of Older Americans.* Washington: AARP Fulfillment.

American Association of University Women (AAUW). (1991). *Shortchanging Girls, Shortchanging America.* Washington.

——. (1992). *The AAUW Report: How Schools Shortchange Girls.* Washington.

——. (1993). *Hostile Hallways: The AAUW Survey of Sexual Harrassment in American Schools.* Washington. Researched by Lewis Harris and Associates.

American Council on Education. (1991). "International Baccalaureate Programs." Washington.

Amin, Samir. (1974). *Accumulation on a World Scale.* New York: Monthly Review.

Ammott, T. L., and J. L. Matthaei. (1991). *Race, Gender, and Work: A Multi-cultural Economic History of Women in the United States.*

Amoss, P. T., and S. Harrell (eds.). (1981). *Other Ways of Growing Old.* Stanford: Stanford University Press.

Amsden, A. H. (1985). "The State and Taiwan's Economic Development." In P. Evans, D. Rueschemeyer and T. Skocpol (eds.), *Bringing the State Back In.* New York: Cambridge University Press.

——. (1989). *Asia's Next Giant: South Korea and Late Industrialization.* New York : Oxford University Press.

——. (1990). "Third World Industrialization; 'Global Fordism' or a New Model?" *New Left Review* 182: 5-31.

Anastasi, Ann. (1958). "Heredity, Environment, and the Question 'How?'" *Psychological Review* 65: 197-208.

Anderson, Elijah. (1993). "Abolish Welfare—And Then What," *Washington Post* (December 31): A-21.

Anderson, Margaret L. (1983). "Review Essay: Rape Theories, Myths, and Social Change," *Contemporary Crisis* 5: 237-242.

——. (1985). *Thinking About Women: Sociological Perspectives on Sex and Gender.* New York: Macmillan.

Anderson, Margaret L., and Patricia Hill Collins. (1992). "Reconstructing Knowledge: Toward Inclusive Thinking." In Margaret L. Anderson and Patricia Hill Collins, *Race, Class, and Gender: An Anthology.* Belmont, CA: Wadsworth.

——. (1992). *Race, Class, and Gender: An Anthology.* Belmont, CA: Wadsworth.

Anderson, Odin W. (1989). *The Health Services Continuum in Democratic States: An Inquiry Into Solvable Problems.* Ann Arbor, MI: Health Administration Press.

Anderson, Odin W., et al. (1985). *HMO Development: Patterns and Prospects, a Comparative Analysis of HMOs.* Chicago: Pluribus.

Andors, P. (1983). *The Unfinished Liberation of Chinese Women,* 1949-1980. Bloomington: Indiana University Press.

Anspach, Renee R. (1988). "Notes on the Sociology of Medical Discourse: The Language of Case Presentation," *Journal of Health and Social Behavior* 29 (December): 357-375.

Anti-Defamation League. (1991). "ADL Blasts Anti-Semitism in Crown Heights." Los Angeles: Anti-Defamation League of B'nai B'rith.

Anzaluda, Gloria. (1990a). "Haciendo Caras, Una Estrada." In Gloria Anzaluda (ed.), *Making Face, Making Soul: Haciendo Caras.* San Francisco: Aunt Lute Foundation.

—— (ed.). (1990b). *Making Face, Making Soul— Haciendo Caras: Creative and Cultural Perspectives by Women of Color.* SanFrancisco, CA: Aunt Lute Foundation.

Appelbaum, Richard P. (1966). "Seasonal Migration in San Ildefonso Ixtahuacan, Guatemala: Its Causes and Its Consequences," *Public and International Affairs* IV (spring): 117-142.

——. (1970). *Theories of Social Change.* Chicago: Rand McNally.

——. (1985). "Further Analysis of HUD Report on *Homelessness in America, Congressional Record* (December 4). Banking Committee Serial No. 99-56. Oral and written testimony before congressional hearings.

——. (1986). "Testimony on *A Report to the Secretary on the Homeless and Emergency Shelters.* In Jon Erickson and Charles Wilhelm, *Housing the Homeless.* New Brunswick, NJ: Rutgers University Center for Urban Policy Research.

——. (1988). *Karl Marx.* Newbury Park, CA: Sage.

——. (1990). "Counting the Homeless." In J. A. Momeni (ed.), *Homelessness in the United States,* Vol. 2, Issues and Data. New York: Praeger.

——. (1994). "Multiculturalism and Flexibility: Some New Directions in Global Capitalism." In Avery Gordon and Christopher Newfield (eds.), *Multiculturalism?* Minneapolis: University of Minnesota Press. Forthcoming.

Appelbaum, Richard P., and Christopher G. Arnold. (1993). "Space and the Global Economy: How Forces of Dispersal and Concentration Are Reshaping the Contemporary Los Angeles Garment Industry." To appear in Carville Earle, Leonard Hochberg, and David Miller, *Geographic Information Systems: A Handbook for the Social Sciences.* New York: Basil Blackwell. Forthcoming.

Appelbaum, Richard P., and Edna Bonacich. (1993). *A Tale of Two Cities: The Garment Industry in Los Angeles.* Los Angeles: Report to the Haynes Foundation.

Appelbaum, Richard P., and Harry Chotiner. (1979). "Science, Critique, and *Praxis* in Marxist Method," *Socialist Review* 9 (July-August): 71-108.

Appelbaum, Richard P., Michael Dolny, Peter Dreier, and John Gilderbloom. (1991). "Scapegoating Rent

Control: Masking the Cause of Homelessness," *Journal of the American Planning Association* 57 (spring): 153-164.

Appelbaum, Richard P., and Peter Dreier. (1990). Recent Developments in Rental Housing in the United States." In Willem van Vliet and Jan van Weesep (eds.), *Government and Housing: Developments in Seven Countries.* Newbury Park, CA: Sage.

Appelbaum, Richard P., and Gary Gereffi. (1994). "Points of Profit in the Garment Commodity Chain." In Edna Bonacich, Lucie Cheng, Norma Chinchilla, Norma Hamilton, and Paul Ong, *Global Production: The Apparel Industry in the Pacific Rim.* Philadelphia: Temple University Press. Forthcoming.

Appelbaum, Richard P., and Jeffrey Henderson (eds.). (1992). *States and Development in the Asian Pacific Rim.* Newbury Park, CA: Sage.

Appelbaum, Richard P., David Smith, and Brad Christerson. (1994). "Commodity Chains and Industrial Restructuring in the Pacific Rim: Garment Trade and Manufacturing." In Gary Gereffi and Miguel Korzeniewicz (eds.). *Commodity Chains and Global Capitalism.* Westport, CT: Greenwood.

Aptheker, Herbert. (1968). *Nat Turner's Slave Rebellion.* New York: Grove.

Archdeacon, Thomas J. (1992). "Reflections on Immigration to Europe in Light of U.S. Immigration History," *International Migration Review* 26 (summer): 525-548.

Archer, Dane, and Rosemary Gartner. (1984). *Violence and Crime in Cross-National Perspective.* New Haven: Yale University Press.

Archer, J., and B. Lloyd. (1985). *Sex and Gender.* New York: Cambridge University Press.

Arenberg, David, and Elizabeth A. Robertson-Tchabo. (1980). "Age Differences and Age Changes in Cognitive Performance: New 'Old' Perspectives." In R. L. Sprott (ed.), *Age, Learning, Ability, and Intelligence*, pp. 139-157. New York: Van Nostrand Reinhold.

Arendt, Hannah. (1951). *The Origins of Totalitarianism.* New York: Harcourt, Brace.

———. (1987). *Eichmann in Jerusalem: A Report on the Banality of Evil* (2nd ed.). New York: Penguin.

Arjomand, Said Amir. (1988). *The Turban for the Crown: The Islamic Revolution in Iran.* New York: Oxford University Press.

Armstrong, G. Blake, Kimberly A. Neuendorf, and James E. Brentar. (1992). "TV Entertainment, News, and Racial Perceptions of College Students," *Journal of Communication* 42 (summer): 153-176.

Arterton, F. Christopher. (1987). *Teledemocracy: Can Technology Protect Democracy?* Newbury Park, CA: Sage.

Asch, Solomon. (1955). "Opinions and Social Pressure," *Scientific American* 193: 31-35.

Asia Monitor Resource Center. (1988). *Min-Ju No-Jo: South Korea's New Trade Unions.* Hong Kong.

Associated Press. (1992). "In Philippines, Cultists Go on Tire-Deflating Spree," *Chicago Tribune* (December 29): 8.

———. (1992). "Women Worldwide Work Harder for Less, Study Says," (September 7): A-3.

———. (1993). "Study: Urban Poor Lack Adequate Food," *Santa Barbara News-Press* (June 12): A-4.

Astin, Alexander W., William S. Korn, and Ellyne R. Berz. (1990). *The American Freshman: National Norms for Fall 1990.* Los Angeles: Cooperative Institutional Research Program (American Council on Education, UCLA).

Atchley, Robert C. (1991). *Social Forces and Aging: An Introduction to Social Gerontology* (6th ed.). Belmont, CA: Wadsworth.

Atkin, C. (1982). "Changing Male and Female Roles." In M. Schwarz (ed.), *TV and Teens: Experts Look at the Issues.* Reading MA: Addison-Wesley.

Austin, James, Juanita Dimas, and David Steinhart. (1992). "The Over-Representation of Minority Youth in California Secure Facilities." San Francisco: National Council on Crime and Delinquency (September).

Austin, James, and John Irwin. (1989). *Who Goes to Prison.* San Francisco: National Council on Crime and Delinquency.

Babbit, Bruce. (1992). "The World After Rio," *World Monitor* (June): 28-33.

Baca Zinn, Maxine, Lynn Weber Cannon, Elizabeth Higgenbothem, and Bonnie Thornton Dill. (1990). "The Costs of Exclusionary Practices in Women's Studies." In Gloria Anzaluda (ed.), *Making Face, Making Soul: Haciendo Caras.* San Francisco: Aunt Lute Foundation.

Bachrach, Leona L. (ed.). (1983). *Deinstitutionalization.* San Francisco: Jossey-Bass.

Bachrach, Peter, and Morton S. Baratz. (1970). *Power and Poverty.* New York: Oxford University Press.

Badinter, Elizabeth. (1981). *Myth of Motherhood.* London: Souvenir.

Baechler, Jean, John A. Hall, and Michael Mann (eds.). (1988). *Europe and the Rise of Capitalism.* New York: Basil Blackwell.

Bagdikian, Ben H. (1990). *The Media Monopoly* (3rd ed.). Boston: Beacon.

Bailey, Guy, and Cynthia Bernstein. (1990). "The Idea of Black English," *The SECOL Review* 14 (spring): 1-24.

Bailey, J. Michael, and Richard C. Pillard. (1991). " A Genetic Study of Male Sexual Orientation," *Archives of General Psychiatry* 48 (December): 1089-1096.

Bailey, J. Michael, Richard C. Pillard, Michael C. Neale, and Yvonne Agyei. (1993). "Heritable Factors Influence Sexual Orientation in Women," *Archives of General Psychiatry* 50: 217-223.

Bailey, Kenneth D. (ed.). (1987). *Methods of Social Research.* New York: Free Press.

Bailey, William, and Ruth Peterson. (1989). "Murder and Capital Punishment: A Monthly Time Series Analysis of

Execution Policy," *American Sociological Review* 54: 722-743.

Bakan, D. (1971). "Adolescence in America: From Ideal to Social Fact," *Daedalus* 100: 979-995.

Baker, Stephen, Geri Smith, and Elisabeth Weiner. (1993). "The Mexican Worker," *Business Week* (April 19): 84-92.

Baker, Stephen, David Woodruff, and Elisabeth Weiner. (1992). "Detroit South: Mexico's Auto Boom: Who Wins, Who Loses," *Business Week* (March 16): 98-103.

Balassa, B. (1981). *Newly Industrializing Countries in the World Economy.* New York: Pergamon.

Baldwin, Janet, and Henry Spille. (1991). "GED Candidates in the Workforce: Employed and Employable," *Center for Adult Learning and Educational Credentials* (June 3): 1-6.

Baldwin, John. (1986). *George Herbert Mead: A Unifying Theory for Sociology.* Newbury Park, CA: Sage.

———. (1988). "Mead and Skinner: Agency and Determinism," *Behaviorism* 16: 109-127.

Baldwin, John, and Janice Baldwin. (1981). *Beyond Sociobiology.* New York: Elsevier.

———. (1986). *Basic Priciples in Everyday Life* (2nd ed.). Englewood Cliffs, NJ: Prentice-Hall.

Bales, Robert F. (1953). "The Egalitarian Problem in Small Groups." In Talcott Parsons (ed.). *Working Papers in the Theory of Action.* Glencoe, IL: Free Press.

———. (1970). *Personality and Interpersonal Behavior.* New York: Holt, Rinehart and Winston.

Bales, Robert F., and Fred L. Strodtbeck. (1951). "Phases in Group Problem-Solving," *Journal of Abnormal and Social Psychology* 46: 484-494.

Ballinger, Jeffrey. (1992). "The New Free Trade Heel: Nike's Profits Jump on the Back of Asian Workers," *Harper's Magazine* (August): 46-47.

Balmer, Randall. (1989). *Mine Eyes Have Seen the Glory: A Journey Into the Evangelical Subculture in America.* New York: Oxford University Press.

Baltes, Paul B., and J. R. Nesselroade. (1984). "Paradigm Lost and Paradigm Regained: Critique of Dannefer's Portrayal of Lifespan Developmental Psychology," *American Sociological Review* 49: 841-847.

Baltes, Paul B., and K. Warner Schaie. (1977). "The Myth of the Twilight Years." In S. Zarit (ed.), *Readings in Aging and Death: Contemporary Perspectives.* New York: Harper & Row.

Bamberger, Bernard J. (1992). "Judaism." In the *American Academic Encyclopedia* (on-line edition). Danbury, CT: Grolier Electronic Publishing.

Bandura, Albert, and R. H. Walters. (1977). *Social Learning Theory.* Englewood Cliffs, NJ: Prentice-Hall.

Bankoff, Elizabeth A. (1983). "Aged Parents and Their Widowed Daughters: A Support Relationship," *The Gerontologist* 38: 226-230.

Barak, Greg. (1992). *Crimes by the Capitalist State.* Albany: State University of New York Press.

Barancik, Scott, and Isaac Shapiro. (1992). *Where Have All the Dollars Gone? A State-by-State Analysis of Income Disparities Over the 1980s.* Washington: Center on Budget and Policy Priorities.

Barbash, Jack. (1967). *American Unions: Structure, Government, and Politics.* New York: Random House.

———. (1993). "Unions." In the *American Academic Encyclopedia* (on-line edition). Danbury, CT: Grolier Electronic Publishing.

Barber, Brian K. (1992). "Family, Personality, and Adolescent Problem Behaviors," *Journal of Marriage and the Family* 54 (February): 69-79.

Barber, Brian K., et al. (1992). "Parental Behaviors and Adolescent Self-Esteem in the U.S. and Germany," *Journal of Marriage and the Family* 54: (February): 128-141.

Barnathan, Joyce. (1993). "The AIDS Disaster Unfolding in Asia," *Business Week* (February 22): 52-54.

Barnathan, Joyce, Pete Engardio, and Lynne Curry. (1993). "China: The Making of an Economic Giant," *Business Week* (May 17): 55-68.

Barnet, Richard, and Ronald Muller. (1974). *Global Reach: Power and the Multinational Corporations.* New York: Simon & Schuster.

Barnett, Tony, and Piers Blaikie. (1992). *AIDS in Africa: Its Present and Future Impact.* New York: Guilford.

Barrera, Mrio. (1979). *Race and Class in the Southwest.* Notre Dame: University of Notre Dame Press.

Barringer, Felicity. (1993). "Pride in a Soundless World: Deaf Oppose a Hearing Aid," *New York Times* (May 16): 1.

Barroso, Carmen, and Cristina Bruschini. (1991). "Building Politics from Personal Lives: Discussions on Sexuality Among Poor Women in Brazil." In Chandra Talpade Mohanty, Ann Russo, and Lourdes Torres, *Third World Women and the Politics of Feminism.* Bloomington: Indiana University Press.

Barry, H., III, and A. Schlegel. (1984). "Measurements of Adolescent Sexual Behavior in the Standard Sample of Societies." *Ethnology* 23: 315-329.

Barry, Kathleen. (1979). *Female Sexual Slavery.* Englewood Cliffs, NJ: Prentice-Hall.

Bart, Pauline, B., and Patricia H. O'Brien. (1985). *Stopping Rape: Successful Survival Strategies.* New York: Pergamon.

Basham, A. L. (1989). *The Origins and Development of Classical Hinduism.* Boston: Beacon.

Bass, B. M. (1990). *Bass and Stogdill's Handbook of Leadership: Theory, Research, and Managerial Applications* (3rd ed.). New York: Free Press.

Bass, S.A., E.A. Kutza, and F. M. Torres-Gil (eds.). (1990). *Diversity in Aging.* Glenview, IL: Scott Foresman.

Bastian, Lisa D., and Bruce M. Taylor. (1991). *School Crime: A National Crime Victimization Survey Report.* Washington: Bureau of Justice Statistics (September).

Baszanger, Isabelle. (1985). "Professional Socialization and Social Control: From Medical Students to General Practitioners." *Social Science and Medicine* 20 (2): 133-143.

Batchelder, Ronald W., and Herman Freudenberger. (1993). "On the Rational Origins of the Modern Centralized State," *Explorations in Economic History* 20 (January): 1-13.

Bateson, Gregory. (1972). *Steps to an Ecology of Mind.* New York: Ballantine.

Battista, Mary. (1992). "A Town's Bloody 'Cleansing'," *Washington Post* (November 2): A-1, A-19.

Baugh, John. (1992). "Hypercorrection: Mistakes in Production of Vernacular African-American English as a Second Dialect," *Language and Communication* 12 (July-October): 317-326.

Bechert, Heinz, and Richard Gombrich (eds). (1984). *The World of Buddhism: Buddhist Monks and Nuns in Society and Culture.* London: Thames & Hudson.

Becker, Gary Stanley. (1976). *The Economic Approach to Human Behavior.* Chicago: University of Chicago Press.

———. (1991). *A Treatise on the Family.* Cambridge: Harvard University Press.

Becker, Howard. (1963). *The Outsiders.* Glencoe, IL: Free Press.

Belgrave, Linda Liska. (1988). "The Effects of Race Difference in Work History, Work Attitudes, Economic Resources, and Health in Women's Retirement," *Research on Aging* 10: 383-398.

Bell, A., and M. Weinberg. (1978). *Homosexualities: A Study of Diversity Among Men and Women.* New York: Simon & Schuster.

Bell, A., M. Weinberg, and S. Hammersmith. (1981). *Sexual Preference: Its Development in Men and Women.* Bloomington: Indiana University Press.

Bell, Daniel. (1973). *The Coming Crisis of Postindustrial Society: A Venture in Social Forecasting.* New York: Basic Books.

———. (1978). *The Cultural Contradictions of Capitalism.* New York: Harper Torchbooks.

———. (1988; orig. 1960). *The End of Ideology: On the Exhaustion of Political Ideas in the Fifties.* Cambridge: Harvard University Press.

———. (1989). "The Third Technological Revolution and Its Possible Socioeconomic Consequences," *Dissent* (spring): 164-176.

Bellah, Robert N. (1968). "Civil Religion in America." In William G. McLoughlin and Robert N. Bellah (eds.), *Religion in America.* Boston: Houghton-Mifflin.

———. (1975). *The Broken Covenant.* New York: Seabury.

Bellah, Robert N., Richard Madsen, William M. Sullivan, Ann Swidler, and Steven M. Tipton. (1985). *Habits of the Heart: Individualism and Commitment in American Life.* New York: Harper & Row.

Bendick, Marc, Charles Jackson, and Victor Reinoso. (1993). "Measuring Employment Discrimination Through Controlled Experiments." In *The Review of Black Political Economy.* Washington: Fair Employment Council of Greater Washington. Forthcoming.

Benedict, Ruth. (1934). *Patterns of Culture.* Boston: Houghton-Mifflin.

Bengston, Vern L., Carolyn Rosenthal, and Linda Burton. (1990). "Families and Aging: Diversity and Heterogeneity." In Robert H. Binstock and Linda K. George (eds.), *Handbook of Aging and the Social Sciences* (3rd ed.). New York: Academic.

Benkokraitis, Nijole, and Joe Feagin. (1986). *Modern Sexism: Blatant, Subtle, and Overt Discrimination.* Englewood Cliffs, NJ: Prentice-Hall.

Bennett, John W. (1976). *The Ecological Transition: Cultural Anthropology and Human Adaptation.* New York: Pergamon.

Berelson, Bernard, Paul F. Lazarsfeld, and William N. McPhee. (1954). *Voting; A Study of Opinion Formation in a Presidential Campaign.* Chicago: University of Chicago Press.

Berger, Peter. (1967). *The Sacred Canopy.* New York: Doubleday.

———. (1970). *A Rumor of Angels: Modern Society and the Rediscovery of the Supernatural.* Garden City, NY: Anchor.

———. (1982). "From the Crisis of Religion to the Crisis of Secularity." In M. Douglas and S. Tipton (eds.), *Religion and America.* Boston: Beacon.

———. (1986). *The Capitalist Revolution: Fifty Propositions About Prosperity, Equality, and Liberty.* New York: Basic Books.

Berger, Peter L., and Hsin-Haung Michael Hsiao. (1988). *In Search of an East Asian Development Model.* New Brunswick: Transaction.

Berger, Peter, and Thomas Luckmann. (1963). *The Social Construction of Reality.* New York: Doubleday.

Bergman, B. R. (1986). *The Economic Emergence of Women.* New York: Basic Books.

Berle, Adolf, and Gardiner C. Means. (1982; orig. 1932). *The Modern Corporation and Private Property.* Buffalo, NY: William S. Heim.

Bernard, Jessie. (1981). *The Female World.* New York: Free Press.

———. (1982). *The Future of Marriage* (2nd ed.). New Haven: Yale University Press.

Berns, Robert. (1989). *Child, Family, Community: Socialization and Support.* New York: Holt, Rinehart, & Winston.

Bernstein, Merton C., and Joan Brodshaug Bernstein. (1988). *Social Security: The System that Works.* New York: Basic Books.

Bernstein, Phillip. (1951). *What the Jews Believe.* New York: Farrar, Strauss & Young.

Berryman, Phillip. (1987). *Liberation Theology: Essential Facts About the Revolutionary Movement in Central America — and Beyond.* Philadelphia: Temple University Press.

Best, Joel. (1980). "Licensed to Steal." In R. Love, Jr., (ed.), *Changing Interpretations and New Sources in Naval History,* pp. 96-109. New York: Garland.

———. (1987). "Rhetoric in Claims-Making: Constructing the Missing Children Problem," *Social Problems* 34: 101-121.

———. (1990). *Threatened Children: Rhetoric and Concern about Child Victims.* Chicago: University of Chicago Press.

Best, Raphaela. (1983). *We've All Got Scars: What Boys and Girls Learn in Elementary School.* Bloomington: Indiana University Press.

Bestor, Arthur. (1950). *Backwood Utopias.* Philadelphia: University of Pennsylvania Press.

Bettleheim, Bruno. (1979). *Surviving and Other Essays.* New York: Knopf.

———. (1982). "Difficulties Between Parents and Children: Their Causes and How to Prevent Them." In Nick Stinner, et al., *Family Strengths 4: Positive Support Systems.* Lincoln: University of Nebraska Press.

Bielby, Denise D. (1992). "Commitment to Work and the Family," *Annual Review of Sociology* 18: 281-302.

———. (1993). "Explaining Gender Stratification and Inequality in the Workplace and the Household," *Rationality and Society* 5.

Bielby, Denise, and William T. Bielby. (1988). "She Works Hard for the Money: Sex Differences in Allocation of Effort to Work and the Family," *American Journal of Sociology* 93 (5): 1031-1059.

———. (1992a). *The 1992 Hollywood Writers' Report.* Hollywood, CA: Writers' Guild of America.

———. (1992b). "I Will Follow Him: Family Ties, Gender-Role Beliefs, and Reluctance to Relocate for a Better Job," *American Journal of Sociology* 97 (March): 1241-1267.

Bielby, Denise, D., and C. Lee Harrington. (1992). "Public Meanings, Private Screenings: The Formation of Social Bonds Through the Televisual Experience," *Social Problems* 3: 155-178.

———. (1994). "Reach Out and Touch Someone: Viewers, Agency, and Audience in the Televisual Community." In Jon Cruz, Justin Lewis, and Kathy Schwictenberg (eds). *Reconceptualizing Audiences.* Boulder, CO: Westview.

Bielby, William T. and Denise D. Bielby. (1989). *The 1989 Hollywood Writers' Report: Unequal Access, Unequal Pay.* Hollywood, CA: Writers' Guild of America.

Bielby, William T., and James Baron. (1986). "The Proliferation of Job Titles in Organizations," *Administrative Science Quarterly* 31 (December): 4.

Bierman, Jeffrey A. (1990). "The Effect of Television Sports Media on Black Male Youth," *Sociological Inquiry* 60 (fall): 413-427.

Bigler, Rose Johnson. (1994). "The Rights of Children," *The Criminologist* 19 (1): 1-10.

Birnbaum, Jeffrey H. (1992). *The Lobbyists: How Influence Peddlers Get Their Way in Washington.* New York: Times.

Birren, J. E. and V. L. Bengston (eds.). (1988). *Emerging Theories of Aging.* New York: Springer.

Birren, J. E., and W. Cunningham. (1985). "Research on the Psychology of Aging." In J. E. Birren and K. Warner Schaie (eds.), *The Handbook of Aging* (2nd ed.). New York: Van Nostrand.

Bladen, Ashby. (1982). "The Truth About Social Security," *Forbes* (December 6).

Blainey, Geoffrey. (1988). *The Causes of War* (3rd ed.). New York: Free Press.

Blanc, A. K. (1984). "Nonmarital Cohabitation and Fertility in the United States and Western Europe," *Population Research and Policy Review* 3: 181-193.

Blau, F. D., and M. A. Ferber. (1987). "Occupations and Earnings of Women Workers." In K. S. Koziara, M. H. Moskow, and L. D. Tanner (eds.), *Working Women: Past, Present, and Future.* Washington: The Bureau of National Affairs.

Blau, Joel. (1992). *The Visible Poor: Homelessness in the United States.* New York: Oxford University Press.

Blau, Peter M. (1977). *Inequality and Heterogeneity: A Primitive Theory of Social Structure.* New York: Free Press.

Blau, Peter, and Otis Dudley Duncan. (1967). *The American Occupational Structure.* New York: Wiley.

Blau, Peter, and Marshall Meyer. (1987). *Bureaucracy in Modern Society* (3rd ed.). New York: Random House.

Blau, Peter M., and W. Richard Scott. *(1962). Formal Organizations: A Comparative Approach.* San Francisco: Chandler.

Blauner, Robert. (1964). *Alienation and Freedom.* Chicago: University of Chicago Press.

Blaut, J. M. (1989). "Colonialism and the Rise of Capitalism," *Science and Society* (fall): 260-296.

Blech, Benjamin. (1991). *Understanding Judaism: The Basics of Creed and Deed.* Northdale, NJ: Aronson.

Blechman, Elaine. (1990). *Emotions and the Family: For Better or for Worse.* Hillsdale, NJ: L. Erlbaum.

Blight, James G., Bruce J. Allyn, and Daniel A. Welch. (1993). *Cuba on the Brink: Castro, the Missile Crisis, and the Soviet Collapse.* New York: Pantheon.

Bloch, Marc. (1961). *Feudal Society.* Chicago: University of Chicago Press.

Block, Alan A. (1983). *East Side—West Side: Organizing Crime in New York, 1930-1959.* New Brunswick, NJ: Transaction.

————. (1991a). *Perspectives on Organizing Crime.* The Netherlands: Kluwer.

————. (ed.). (1991b) *The Business of Crime: A Documentary Study of Organized Crime in the American Economy.* Boulder, CO: Westview.

Block, Alan A., and William J. Chambliss. (1981). *Organizing Crime.* New York: Elsevier.

Block, Alan A., and Frank A. Scarpitti. (1985). *Poisoning for Profit: The Mafia and Toxic Waste in America.* New York: William Morrow.

Bloom, David E., and Adi Bender. (1993). "Labor and the Emerging World Economy," *Population Bulletin* 48 (October): 1-39.

Blumer, Herbert. (1951). "Collective Behavior." In A. M. Lee (ed.), *Principles of Sociology.* New York: Barnes & Noble.

————. (1969). *Symbolic Interactionism: Perspective and Methods.* Englewood Cliffs, NJ: Prentice-Hall.

————. (1970). *Human Nature and Collective Behavior.* Englewood Cliffs, NJ: Prentice-Hall.

Blumstein, P., and P. Schwartz. (1983). *American Couples: Money, Work and Sex.* New York: William Morrow.

Boden, Deirdre, and Don H. Zimmerman (eds). (1991). *Talk and Social Structure: Studies in Ethnomethodology and Conversation Analysis.* Berkeley: University of California Press.

Bogle, Donald. (1990). *Toms, Coons, Mulattos, Mammies, and Bucks: An Interpretive History of Blacks in American Films.* New York: Continuum.

Bohm, Robert. (1991). *The Death Penalty in America: Current Research.* Academy of Criminal Justice Sciences Monograph Series. Anderson Publishing.

Bokenkotter, T. (1990). *A Concise History of the Catholic Church.* New York: Image.

Bonacich, Edna. (1972). "A Theory of Ethnic Antagonism: The Split Labor Market," *American Sociological Review* 38: 547-559.

————. (1989). "Inequality in America: The Failure of the American System for People of Color," *Sociological Spectrum* 9: 77-101.

Bonacich, Edna, Lucie Cheng, Norma Chinchilla, Norma Hamilton, and Paul Ong (eds.). (1994). *Global Production: The Apparel Industry in the Pacific Rim.* Philadelphia: Temple University Press. Forthcoming.

Bonacich, Edna, and Patricia Hanneman. (1991). "A Statistical Portrait of the Los Angeles Garment Industry." Unpublished manuscript. University of California/Riverside.

Bonacich, Edna, and David Waller. (1992). "The Restructuring of the Pacific Rim Garment Industry: A Perspective from the United States," University of California/Riverside: Department of Sociology.

Boorstein, Daniel J. (1964). *The Image: A Guide to Pseudo-Events in America.* New York: Harper & Row.

Boswell, John. (1980). *Christianity, Social Tolerance, and Homosexuality: Gay People in Western Europe.* Chicago: University of Chicago Press.

Boswell, Terry (ed.). (1989). *Revolution in the World System.* New York: Greenwood.

Bott, Elizabeth. (1954). "The Concept of Class As a Reference Group," *Human Relations* 7: 259-285.

Bourdieu, Pierre. (1962). *The Algerians.* Boston: Plenum.

————. (1984). *Distinction: A Social Critique of the Judgement of Taste.* Cambridge: Harvard University Press.

Bourdieu, Pierre, and James S. Coleman. (1991). *Social Theory for a Changing Society.* Boulder, CO: Westview.

Boutilier, Robert. (1993). "Diversity in Family Structures," *American Demographics* 15 (April): 4-6.

Bowles, Samuel. (1972). "Unequal Education and the Reproduction of the Social Division of Labor." In Martin Carnoy (ed.), *Schooling in a Capitalist Society.* New York: David McKay.

Bowles, Samuel, and Herbert Gintis. (1976). *Schooling in Capitalist America: Educational Reform and the Contradictions of Economic Life.* New York: Basic Books.

Bowonder, B., et al. (1985). *Deforestation and Firewood Use in Urban Centres.* Hyderabad, India: Center for Energy, Environment, and Technology, and National Remote Sensing Agency.

Boyer, Ernest L. (1988). "An Imperiled Generation," *The Generational Journal* 1 (April).

Boyer, Paul, and Stephen Nussenbaum. (1974). *Salem Possessed: The Social Origins of Witchcraft.* Cambridge: Harvard University Press.

Boyer, Richard Owen, and Herbert M. Morais. (1955). *Labor's Untold Story.* New York: Cameron Associates.

Brady, James P. (1982). "Arson, Fiscal Crisis and Community Action," *Crime and Delinquency* 28: 247-270.

Bramson, Leon. (1961). *The Political Context of Sociology.* Princeton: Princeton University Press.

Branch, Taylor. (1988). *Parting the Waters: America in the King Years, 1954-1963.* New York: Simon & Schuster.

Brandt, Allan M. (1983). "Racism and Research: The Case of the Tuskegee Syphilis Study." In Judith Waltzer Leavitt and Ronald L. Numbers (eds.), *Sickness and Health in America.* Madison: University of Wisconsin Press.

Brass, Daniel J. (1985). "Men's and Women's Networks: A Study of Interaction Patterns and Influence in an

Organization," *Academy of Management Journal* 28: 327-343.

Braudel, Fernand. (1973). *Capitalism and Material Life: 1400-1800.* New York: Harper & Row.

———. (1977). *Afterthoughts on Civilization and Capitalism.* Baltimore: Johns Hopkins University Press.

———. (1992). *Civilization and Capitalism, 15th–18th Century.* Berkeley: University of California Press.

Braverman, Harry. (1976). *Labor and Monopoly Capital: The Deregulation of Work in the Twentieth Century.* New York: Monthly Review Press.

Bray, Alan. (1982). *Homosexuality in Renaissance England.* New York: Gay Men's Press.

Brierley, William. (1987). *Trade Unions and the Economic Crisis of the 1980s.* Brookfield, VT: Gower.

Briscoe, David. (1992). "Some of World's 'Vital Signs' Improve, But Trouble Persists," *Santa Barbara News-Press* (December 18): A-3.

———. (1993). "Job Stress: U.N. Study Points to Growing Evidence of Problems Around the World Where Companies Are Doing Little to Help Employees Cope With the Strain of Modern Industrialization," *Los Angeles Times* (April 4): A-1.

Broder, John M. and Stanley Meisler. (1992). "Terrifying Quest for A-Arms," *Los Angeles Times* (November 19): A-1.

Brody, Gene H., Eileen Neubaum, and Rex Forehand. (1988). "Serial Marriage: A Heuristic Analysis of an Emerging Family Form," *Psychology Bulletin* 103 (March): 211-222.

Brody, Herb. (1992). "Of Bytes and Rights," *Technology Review* (November/December): 22-29.

Brooke, Christopher. (1971). *Structure of Medieval Society.* New York: McGraw-Hill.

Brooke, James. (1993). "A Hard Look at Brazil's Surfeits: Food, Hunger, and Inequality," *New York Times* (June 6): 20.

Brookfield, Stephen. (1986). *Understanding and Facilitating Adult Learning.* San Francisco: Jossey-Bass.

———. (1987). *Developing Critical Thinkers: Challenging Adults to Explore Alternative Ways of Thinking and Acting.* San Francisco: Jossey-Bass.

Brooks, Nancy Rivera. (1993)."Gender Pay Gap Found at Highest Corporate Levels," *Los Angeles Times* (June 30): A-1.

Brostoff, Steven. (1992). "Medical Malpractice Claims Fuel Health Care Cost Boom," *National Underwriter* 96 (January 13): 2.

Broude, Gwen, and Sarah Green. (1976). "Cross Cultural Codes on Twenty Sexual Attitudes and Practices," *Ethnology* 1: 409-428.

Brown, Dee. (1991). *Wonderous Times on the Frontier.* Little Rock, AK: August House.

Brown, Donald E. (1991a). *Human Universals.* New York: McGraw-Hill.

———. (1991b). Personal Communication, September 27.

Brown, Donald E., James W. Edwards, and Ruth B. Moore. (1988). *The Penis Inserts of Southeast Asia.* Berkeley, CA: Center for South and Southeast Studies.

Brown, Jane D., and Laurie Schulze. (1990). "The Effects of Race, Gender, and Fandom on Audience Interpretations of Madonna's Music Videos," *Journal of Communication* 40 (spring): 88-102.

Brown, Lester R. (ed.). (1994). *State of the World, 1994: A Worldwatch Institute Report on Progress Toward a Sustainable Society.* New York: Norton.

Brown, Lester R., and Jodi L. Jacobson. (1987). "The Future of Urbanization: Facing the Ecological and Economic Constraints," *Worldwatch Paper 77.* (May). Washington: Worldwatch Institute.

Brown, Phil. (1985). *The Transfer of Care: Psychiatric Deinstitutionalization and Its Aftermath.* Boston: Routledge and Kegan Paul.

Brown, Richard. (1980). *Rockefeller Medicine Man.* Berkeley: University of California Press.

Brown, Susan E. (1989). "The Zip-Code Route Into UC: GPA Counts, But Where You Live May Be Just As Critical," *Los Angeles Times* (May 3): Part 2, 7.

Browne, A. (1987). *When Battered Women Kill.* New York: Free Press.

Browning, Christopher R. (1992). *Ordinary Men: Reserve Police Battalion 101 and the Final Solution in Poland.* New York: HarperCollins.

Brownmiller, Susan. (1986). *Against Our Will: Men, Women and Rape* (rev. ed.). New York: Bantam.

Bruce, Michael G. (1987). "High School Graduation, International Style," *Phi Delta Kappan* 69 (September): 79-81.

Bruce, Steve. (1983). "Social Change and Collective Behavior: The Revival in Eighteenth-Century Rosshire," *British Journal of Sociology* 34: 554-572.

Bryan, Ford R. (1989). *The Fords of Dearborn.* Detroit: Harlo.

Bryant, Edwin. (1848). *What I Saw in California.* New York: Appleton.

Bryant, R. (1992). "The Boys in the 'Hood'—No KKK in South L.A.," *Los Angeles Sentinel* 47 (March 11): A-6.

Brzezinski, Zbigniew. (1993a). *Out of Control: Global Turmoil on the Eve of the Twenty-First Century.* New York: Scribner's.

———. (1993b). "Power and Morality," *World Monitor* (March): 22-28.

Buchanan, Pat. (1992). "Pat Buchanan Calls for Winning Back the 'Soul of America,'" *Los Angeles Times* (May 28): A-5.

Bullard, Sara. (1991). "Murder in Portland." In Sara Bullard (ed.), *The Ku Klux Klan: A History of Racism and Violence.* Montgomery, AL: Southern Law Center.

Bullough, Vern L. (1976). *Sexual Variance in Society and History.* New York: Wiley.

Bumpass, L. L. (1984). "Children and Marital Disruption: A Replication and Update," *Demography* 21: 71-82.

Bumpass, L. L., and J. A. Sweet. (1989). "National Estimates of Cohabitation," *Demography* 26: 615-625.

Burawoy, Michael, and Pavel Krotov. (1992). "The Soviet Transition From Socialism to Capitalism: Worker Control and Economic Bargaining in the Wood Industry," *American Sociological Review* 57 (February): 16-38.

Burawoy, Michael, and Janos Lukas. (1992). *The Radiant Past: Ideology and Reality in Hungary's Road to Capitalism.* Chicago: University of Chicago Press.

Bureau of Justice Statistics. (1992a). *Criminal Victimization 1991.* Washington: Department of Justice.

———. (1992b). *Prisoners in 1992.* Washington: U. S. Department of Justice.

———. (1993). *Highlights from Twenty Years of Surveying Crime Victims.* Washington: U. S. Department of Justice.

Burfoot, Amby. (1992). "White Men Can't Run," *Runner's World* (August): 89-95.

Burger, Thomas. (1976). *Max Weber's Theory of Concept Formation: History, Laws, and Ideal Types.* Durham, NC: Duke University Press.

Burgess, Ernest. (1925). "The Growth of the City." In Robert Ezra Park, Ernest Burgess, and Roderick McKenzie (eds.), *The City.* Chicago: University of Chicago Press.

Burke, Edmund, III, and Ira Lapidus (eds.). (1988). *Islam, Politics, and Social Movements.* Berkeley: University of California Press.

Burns, James MacGregor. (1978). *Leadership.* New York: Harper & Row.

Burr, Chandler. (1993). "Homosexuality and Biology," *The Atlantic Monthly* (March): 47-65.

Burrow, J. G. (1963). *AMA: The Voice of American Medicine.* Baltimore: Johns Hopkins University Press.

Burt, Martha R. (1992). *Over the Edge: The Growth of Homelessness in the 1980s.* New York: Russell Sage Foundation.

Busch, Ruth C. (1990). *Family Systems: Comparative Study of the Family.* New York: P.Lang.

Business Week. (1993a). "Figures on Number of Families in Which Both Spouses Work, 1975- 1991," and "Men and Women in the Workforce, 1975-2005." Based on Bureau of Labor Statistics Data. (June 28): 82.

———. (1993b). "The Widening Gap Between CEO Pay and What Others Make," (April 26): 56-57.

———. (1993c). *The 1993 Business Week 1,000* (special yearly issue).

Buskirk, Elsworth R. (1985). "Health Maintenance and Longevity: Exercise." In Caleb E. Finch and Edward L. Schneider (eds.), *Handbook of the Biology of Aging* (2nd ed.), pp. 894-931. New York: Van Nostrand Reinhold.

Butler, Judith P. (1990). *Gender Trouble: Feminism and the Subversion of Identity.* New York: Routledge.

———. (1993). *Bodies That Matter: On the Discursive Limits of "Sex."* New York: Routledge.

Butler, R. N., M. R. Oberlink, and M. Schecter (eds.). (1980). *The Promise of Productive Aging: From Biology to Social Policy.* New York: Springer.

Butters, Ronald R. (1989). *The Death of Black English.* Frankfurt, Germany: Peter Lang.

Cadden, Vivian. (1993). "How Kids Benefit From Child Care," *Working Mother* 16: 58-61.

Cahill, Spencer. (1989). "Fashioning Males and Females: Appearance Management and the Social Reproduction of Gender," *Symbolic Interaction* 12 (2): 281-298.

Calavita, Kitty. (1983). " The Demise of the 'Occupational Safety and Health Administration': A Case Study in Symbolic Action," *Social Programs* 30: 437-448.

———. (1984). *U.S. Immigration Law and the Control of Labor, 1820-1924.* London: Academic.

———. (1992). *Inside the State: The Bracero Program, Immigration and the I. N. S..* New York: Routledge.

Califano, Joseph A., Jr. (1992). "Break the Billion Dollar Congress," *Washington Post* (January 28): A-36.

California State Department of Finance. (1993). "Population Reports by Race/Ethnicity for California and Its Counties, 1990-2040." Sacramento: California Department of Finance Demographic Research Unit, Report 93 P-1 (April).

Callahan, Daniel. (1987). *Setting Limits: Medical Goals in an Aging Society.* New York: Simon & Schuster.

———. (1990). "Elder Abuse: Some Questions for Policymakers," *The Gerontologist* 28 (4): 453-458.

Campbell, Anne. (1984). *Girls in the Gang.* London: Basil Blackwell.

———. (1991). *The Girls in the Gang* (2nd ed.). Cambridge, MA: Basil Blackwell.

Campbell, John, J. Roger Hollingsworth, and Leon N. Lindberg. (1991). *The Governance of the American Economy.* Cambridge: Cambridge University Press.

Campbell, Keith, et al. (1992). "Conversational Activity and Interruptions Among Men and Women," *Journal of Social Psychology* 132: 419-421.

Canner, Glenn B., and Delores Smith. (1991). "Home Mortgage Disclosure Act: Expanded Data on Residential Lending." Washington: Federal Reserve Board (October).

Cantor, M. (1987). "Popular Culture and the Portrayal of Women: Content and Control." In B. B. Hess and M. M. Ferree (eds.), *Analyzing Gender,* pp. 190-214. Newbury Park, CA: Sage.

Caplow, Theodore. (1956). "A Theory of Coalition in the Triad," *American Sociological Review* 20 (August): 489-493.

———. (1959). "Further Development of a Theory of Coalitions in Triads." *American Journal of Sociology* 64 (March): 488-493.

———. (1969). *Two Against One: Coalitions in Triads.* Englewood Cliffs, NJ: Prentice-Hall.

Cardoso, Fernando H., and Enzo Faletto. (1979). *Dependency and Development in Latin America.* Berkeley: University of California Press.

Carlton, Jim. (1990). "Schuller's Big Soviet Coup May Prop Up U.S. Ministry," *Los Angeles Times* (July 1): A-1.

Carnegie Commission. (1979). *A Public Trust: The Report of the Carnegie Commission on the Future of Public Broadcasting.* New York: Bantam.

Carnoy, Martin, and Derek Shearer. (1980). *Economic Democracy.* New York: M. E. Sharpe.

Carr-Ruffino, N. (1982). *The Promotable Woman: Becoming a Successful Manager.* Belmont, CA: Wadsworth.

Carter, Deborah J., and Reginald Wilson. (1993). *Minorities in Higher Education.* Washington: American Council on Education.

Carter, Richard B. (1993). *Nurturing Evolution: The Family as a Social Womb.* Lanham, MD: Univeristy Press of America.

Castells, Manuel. (1983). *The City and the Grassroots.* Berkeley: University of California Press.

Castells, Manuel. (1989). *The Informational City: Information Technology, Economic Restructuring, and the Urban-Regional Process.* Cambridge, MA: Basil Blackwell.

Castells, Manuel. (1992). "Four Asian Tigers with a Dragon Head: A Comparative Analysis of the State, Economy, and Society in the Asian Pacific Rim." In Richard P. Appelbaum and Jeffrey Henderson (eds.), *States and Development in the Asian Pacific Rim.* Newbury Park, CA: Sage.

Castells, Manuel, L. Goh, and R. Y. Kwok. (1990). *The Shek Kip Mei Syndrome: Economic Development and Public Housing in Hong Kong and Singapore.* London: Pion.

Castro, Janice. (1993). "Disposable Workers," *Time Magazine* (March 29): 43-47.

Center for Defense Information. (1991). "Sounding Taps for Star Wars and the Stealth Bomber," *The Defense Monitor* XXV: 5.

Center on Budget and Policy Priorities. (1992). "Where Have All The Dollars Gone?" Washington: CBPP (August).

Chadwick, Bruce. (1983). "Book Sells; Movie Is Held," *Detroit Free Press* (September 12): 2-C.

Chafetz, Janet Saltzman, and Anthony Gary Dworwin. (1983). "Macro and Micro Process in the Emergence of Feminist Movements: Toward a Unified Theory," *Western Sociological Review* 14 (1): 27-45.

Chagnon, Napoleon. (1992). *Yanamamo: The Fierce People* (4th ed.) Fort Worth: Harcourt Brace Jovanovich.

Chambliss, William J. (1965). "The Selection of Friends," *Social Forces* 31 (March): 370-380.

———. (1973). "The Saints and the Roughnecks," *Society* (November): 24-31.

———. (1988). *Exploring Criminology.* New York: Macmillan.

———. (1988). *On the Take: From Petty Crooks to Presidents.* Bloomington: Indiana University Press.

———. (1989). "State Organized Crime," *Criminology* 27 (May): 183-208.

Chambliss, William J (ed.) (1973). *Sociological Readings in "The Conflict Perspective."* Reading, MA: Addison-Wesley.

Chambliss, William J., and Robert B. Seidman. (1982). *Law, Order, and Power* (rev. ed.). Reading, MA: Addison-Wesley.

Chambliss, William J., and Marjorie Zatz. (1994). *Making Law: Law, State and Structural Contradiction.* Bloomington: Indiana University Press.

Charliand, Gérard, and Jean-Pierre Rageau. (1992). *Strategic Atlas: A Comparative Geopolitics of the World's Powers* (3rd ed.). New York: HarperCollins.

Charon, Jean. (1970). *Cosmology: Theories of the Universe.* New York: McGraw-Hill.

Chaves, Mark. (1993). "Intraorganizational Power and Internal Secularization in Protestant Denominations," *American Journal of Sociology* 99(July): 1-48.

———. (1994). "Secularization is Declining Religious Authority," *Social Forces* 72 (March): 749-774.

Chen, E. K. Y. (1979). *Hyper-Growth in Asian Economies: A Comparative Study of Hong Kong, Japan, Korea, Singapore and Taiwan.* London: Macmillan.

Chen, Hsiang-Shul. (1992). *Chinatown No More: Taiwan Immigrants in Contemporary New York.* Ithaca, NY: Cornell University Press.

Cheng, Lucie, and Ping-Chun Hsiung. (1992). "Women, Export-Oriented Growth, and the State: The Case of Taiwan." In Richard P. Appelbaum and Jeffery Henderson (eds.), *States and Development in the Asian Pacific Rim.* Newbury Park, CA: Sage.

Cherlin, Andrew J. (1992). *Marriage, Divorce, Remarriage* (rev. ed.). Cambridge: Harvard University Press.

Cherlin, Andrew J., et al. (1991). "Longitudinal Studies of Effects of Divorce on Children in Great Britain and the United States," *Science* 252: 1386-1389.

Cherlin, Andrew J., and Frank F. Furstenberg, Jr. (1991). *Divided Families: What Happens to Children When Parents Part.* Cambridge: Harvard University Press.

Chibnall, Bernard. (1976). *The Organization of Media.* Hamden, CT: Linnet.

Chibnall, Steve. (1977). *Law-and-Order News: An Analysis of Crime Reporting in the British Press.* London: Tavistock.

Children's Defense Fund. (1992). *Vanishing Dreams: The Economic Plight of America's Young Families.* Washington: Children's Defense Fund.

Chilton, Roland J. (1993). "Crime Rates," *The Criminologist* (fall): 1-4.

Chodorow, Nancy. (1978). *The Reproduction of Mothering.* Berkeley: University of California Press.

Chon, Soohyun. (1992). "The Political Economy of Regional Development in Korea." In Richard P. Appelbaum and Jeffrey Henderson, *States and Development in the Asian Pacific Rim.* Newbury Park, CA: Sage.

Chong, Dennis. (1991). *Collective Action and the Civil Rights Movement.* Chicago: University of Chicago Press.

Christ, P., and J. Plaskow (eds.). (1979). *Womanspirit Rising.* San Francisco: Harper & Row.

Christiansen, Karl. (1977). "A Preliminary Study of Criminality Among Twins." In Sarnoff Mednick (ed.), *Biosocial Bases of Criminal Behavior.* New York: Gardner.

Christie, Andy. (1989). "Status Report: Home, Sweep Home," *Ms.* (April): 83.

Christie, Nils. (1992). *Crime Control As Industry.* London: Routledge.

Churbuck, David C., and Jeffery S. Young. (1992). "The Virtual Workplace," *Forbes* (November 23): 184-190.

Cimons, Marlene. (1992a). "New Study Boosts Forecasts of AIDS Infection," *Los Angeles Times* (June 4): A4-1.

———. (1992b). "AIDS Shows No Gender Bias, Researchers Report," *Los Angeles Times* (July 21): A-1.

Clark, Phillip G. (1993). "Public Policy in the United States and Canada: Individualism, Familial Obligation, and Collective Responsibility in the Care of the Elderly." In Jon Hendricks and Carolyn J. Rosenthal, *The Remainder of Their Days: Domestic Policy and Older Families in the United States and Canada,* pp. 13-48. New York: Garland.

Clausen, John S. (1991). "Adolescent Competence and the Shaping of the Life Course," *American Journal of Sociology* 96 (4): 805-842.

Clayton, Obie, et al. (1990). "Race Differences in College Attendance in the United States: Two Competing Theories," *Canadian Journal of Education* 15 (3): 245-263.

Clinard, Marshall B., and Peter C. Yeager. (1979). *Illegal Corporate Behavior.* Washington: Law Enforcement Assistance Administration.

Cloward, Richard A., and Lloyd E. Ohlin. (1960). *Delinquency and Opportunity: A Theory of Delinquent Gangs.* New York: Free Press.

Cobb, Jean, Jeff Denny, Vicki Kemper, and Viveca Novak. (1990). "All the President's Donors: The Mossbacher Connection," *Common Cause* (March/April): 19-28.

Cochran, Susan D., and Anne L. Peplau. (1985). "Value Orientations in Heterosexual Relationships," *Psychology of Women Quarterly* 9 (December): 477-488.

Cockerham, William. (1992). *Medical Sociology* (5th ed.). Englewood Cliffs, NJ: Prentice-Hall.

Coe, Rodney M. (1970). *Sociology of Medicine.* New York: McGraw-Hill.

Coenen-Huther, Jacques. (1986). "Postindustrial Society and Forms of Urban Sociability," *Revue Suisse de Sociologie* 12 (July): 91-102.

Cohen, Albert K. (1955). *Delinquent Boys.* New York: Free Press.

———. (1958). *Delinquent Boys: The Culture of the Gang.* New York: Free Press.

Cohen, Deborah. (1993). "Perry Preschool Graduates Show Dramatic New Social Gains at 27," *Education Week* (April 21): 3-9.

Cohen, Jean L. (1985). "Strategy or Identity: New Theoretical Paradigms and Contemporary Social Movements," *Social Research* 52: 663-716.

Cohen, Jere. (1980). "Rational Capitalism in Renaissance Italy," *American Journal of Sociology* 85: 1340-1355.

Cohen, Roger. (1994). "France Is a Match Breaker, Couple Says," *New York Times* (February 14): A-4.

Cohen, Stanley. (1993). "Human Rights and Crimes of the State: Culture of Denial," *The Australian and New Zealand Journal of Criminology* 26 (July): 97-115.

Cohen, Stanley, and Jock Young (ed.). (1973). *The Manufacture of News.* Beverley Hills, CA: Sage.

Cohn, Bob. (1992). "Discrimination: The Limits of the Law," *Newsweek* (September 14): 38-39.

Cohn, D'Vera, and Arbana Vobejda. (1993). "Women Surge in Professions, Not Trades," *Washington Post* (January 3): A-5.

Cohn, Lawrence D. (1991). "Sex Differences in the Course of Personality Development: A Meta-Analysis," *Psychological Bulletin* 109: 252-266.

Colby, Anne, and William Damon. (1987). "Listening to a Different Voice: A Review of Gilligan's *In a Different Voice.*" In M. R. Walsh (ed.), *The Psychology of Women: Ongoing Debates.* New Haven: Yale University Press.

Cole, Jesse. (1992). "It's in the Pocket," *Sky Magazine* (December): 82-89.

Coleman, James S., et al. (1966). *Equality of Educational Opportunity.* Washington: Government Printing Office.

Coleman, James S., Thomas Hoffer, and Sally Kilgore. (1981). *Public and Private Schools.* Chicago: National Opinion Research Center.

Coleman, James William. (1994). *The Criminal Elite: The Sociology of White-Collar Crime.* New York: St. Martin's.

Coleman, John C. (1992). *The School Years: Current Issues in the Socialization of of Young People.* New York: Routledge.

Coleman, Wanda. (1993). "Remembering Latasha: Blacks, Immigrants and America," *The Nation* (February): 187-205.

Coles, Robert. (1977). *Eskimos, Chicanos, Indians.* Boston: Little Brown.

Collier, Peter, and David Horowitz. (1987). *The Fords: An American Epic.* New York: Summit.

Collins, Patricia Hill. (1991). *Black Feminist Thought: Knowledge, Consciousness, and Politics of Empowerment.* New York: Routledge, Chapman & Hall.

Collins, Randall. (1974). *Conflict Sociology: Toward an Explanatory Science.* New York: Academic.

———. (1979). *The Credential Society: An Historical Sociology of Education.* New York: Academic.

———. (1980). "Weber's Last Theory of Capitalism: A Systemization," *American Journal of Sociology* 85: 925-942.

———. (1985). *Sociology of Marriage and the Family: Gender, Love, and Property.* Chicago: Nelson Hall.

———. (1990). "Conflict Theory and the Advance of Macro-Historical Sociology." In George Ritzer (ed.), *Frontiers of Social Theory: The New Synthesis,* pp. 68-87. New York: Columbia University Press.

Colliver, James, and Andrea Kopstein. (1991). "Trends in Cocaine Abuse Reflected in Emergency Room Episodes Reported to DAWN," *Public Health Reports* 106: 59-68.

Colomy, Paul. (1986). "Recent Developments in the Functionalist Approach to Change," *Sociological Focus* 19: 139-158.

———. (1990). "Strategic Groups and Political Differentiation in the Antebellum United States." In Jeffery C. Alexander and Paul Colomy (eds.), *Differentiation Theory and Social Change: Comparative and Historical Perspectives,* pp. 222-264. New York: Columbia University Press.

Colwill, N. K. (1987). "Men and Women in Organizations: Roles and Status, Stereotypes and Power." In K.S. Koziara, M. H. Moskow, and L.D. Tanner (eds.), *Working Women: Past, Present, Future.* Washington: The Bureau of National Affairs.

Common Cause. (1994). "Political Action Committee Contributions: 1983-1993." Washington: (February).

Comte, Auguste. (1974; orig. 1830-1842). *The Positive Philosophy.* New York: AMS.

———. (1975). *Auguste Comte and Positivism: The Essential Writings.* Gertrude Lenzer (ed.). New York: Harper Torchbooks.

Condry, J. C. (1989). *The Psychology of Television.* Hillsdale, NJ: L. Erlbaum.

Condry, J. C., and S. Condry. (1976). "Sex Differences: A Study of the Eye of the Beholder," *Child Development* 47: 812-819.

Cone, Cynthia A., and Berta E. Perez. (1986). "Peer Groups and the Organization of Classroom Space," *Human Organization* 45: 80-88.

Cone, James. (1969). *Black Theology and Black Power.* New York: Seabury.

Congressional Budget Office (CBO). (1992). *The Economic Effects of Reduced Defense Spending.* Washington: Government Printing Office.

Connell, Ian. (1980). "Television News and the Social Contract." In Stuart Hall, Dorothy Hobson, Andrew Lowe, and Paul Willis (eds.). *Culture, Media, Language.* London: Hutchison.

Conrad, P. (1975). "The Discovery of Hyperkinesis: Notes on the Medicalization of Deviant Behavior," *Social Problems* 23: 12-21.

Conrad, P., and J. W. Schneider. (1980). *Deviance and Medicalization: From Badness to Sickness.* St. Louis: Mosby.

Conway, George E. (1992). "School Choice: A Private School Perspective," *Phi Delta Kappan* (March): 561-563.

Cooley, Charles Horton. (1964; orig. 1902). *Human Nature and the Social Order.* New York: Schocken.

Cooney, T., and P. Uhlenberg. (1990). "The Role of Divorce in Men's Relations with Their Adult Children After Mid-Life," *Journal of Marriage and the Family* 52: 677-688.

Cooper, James C., and Kathleen Madigan. (1992). *Business Week* (December 21): 23.

Corcoran M., G. M. Duncan, and M. S. Hill. (1984). "The Economic Fortunes of Women and Children: Lessons from the Panel Study of Income Dynamics," *Signs* 10: 232-248.

Cortese, Anthony Joseph Paul. (1990). *Ethnic Ethics: The Restructuring of Moral Theory.* Albany: State University of New York Press.

Coser, Lewis. (1967). *Continuities in the Study of Social Conflict.* New York: Free Press.

Couric, E. (1989). "An NJL/West Survey, Women in the Law: Awaiting Their Turn," *National Law Journal* 11 (December): S1, S12.

Cowgill, Donald O. (1968). "The Social Life of the Aged in Thailand," *Gerontologist* 8: 159-163.

———. (1986). *Aging Around the World.* Belmont, CA: Wadsworth.

Cowgill, Donald O., and L. D. Holmes (eds.). (1972). *Aging and Modernization.* New York: Appleton-Century-Crofts.

Cowley, Geoffrey. (1989). "The Electronic Goddess: Computerizing Bali's Ancient Irrigation Rites," *Newsweek* (March 6): 50.

Cox, Harvey. (1965). *The Secular City.* New York: Macmillan.

Cox, Oliver C. (1959). *The Foundations of Capitalism.* New York: Philosophical Library.

———. (1964). *Capitalism as a System.* New York: Monthly Review.

Craft, Christine. (1986). *Christine Craft: An Anchorwoman's Story.* Santa Barbara, CA: Capra.

————. (1988). *Too Old, Too Ugly, and Not Deferential to Men.* Rocklin, CA: Prima.

Craig, G. T. (1980). *Human Development* (2nd ed.). Englewood Cliffs, NJ: Prentice-Hall.

Craik, F. I. M. (1977). "Age Differences in Human Memory." In J.E. Birren and K. Warner Schaie (eds.), *The Handbook of Aging* (2nd ed.). New York: Van Nostrand.

Crouter, Ann C., Jay Belsky, and Graham Spanier. (1984). "The Family Context of Child Development: Divorce and Maternal Employment." In Grover J. Whitehurst (ed.), *Annals of Child Development* vol. 1, pp. 201-237. Greenwich, CT: JAI.

Crowley, Joan E. (1985). "Longitudinal Effects of Retirement on Men's Psychological and Physical Well-Being." In Herbert S. Parnes (ed.), *Retirement Among American Men,* pp. 147-173. Lexington, MA: Heath.

Crystal, Graef S. (1991). *In Search of Excess: The Overcompensation of American Executives.* New York: Norton.

Cumings, B. (1987). "The Origins and Development of the Northeast Asian Political Economy: Industrial Sectors, Product Cycles and Political Consequences." In F. C. Deyo (ed.), *The Political Economy of the New Asian Industrialism.* Ithaca, NY: Cornell University Press.

Cumming, Elaine. (1963). "Further Thoughts on the Theory of Disengagement," *International Social Science Journal* 15: 377-393.

————. (1975). "Engagement with an Old Theory," *International Journal of Aging and Human Development* 6: 187-191.

Cumming, Elaine, and William E. Henry. (1961). *Growing Old: The Process of Disengagement.* New York: Basic Books.

Curran, Daniel J. (1993). *Dead Laws for Dead Men: The Politics of Federal Coal Mine Health and Safety Legislation.* Pittsburgh: University of Pittsburgh Press.

Curran, James, Michael Gurevitch, and Janet Woollacott. (1982). "The Study of the Media: Theoretical Approaches." In Michael Gurevitch, et al. (eds.), *Culture, Society and the Media.* London: Methuen.

Currie, Janet, and Duncan Thomas. (1993). "Does Head Start Make a Difference?" Working Paper No. 4406 (July). Cambridge, MA: National Bureau of Economic Research.

Curtiss, Susan R. (1977). *Genie: A Psycholinguistic Study of a Modern-day "Wild Child."* New York: Academic.

Cutler, Stephen J. and Armin E. Grams. (1988). "Correlates of Everyday Self-Reported Memory Problems," *Journal of Gerontology: Social Sciences* 43 (3): 82-90.

Dahl, Robert A. (1961). *Who Governs?* New Haven: Yale University Press.

————. (1967). *Pluralist Democracy in the United States: Conflict and Consent.* Princeton: Princeton University Press.

————. (1982). *Dilemmas of Pluralist Democracy: Autonomy Vs. Control.* New Haven: Yale University Press.

————. (1989). *Democracy and Its Critics.* New Haven: Yale University Press.

Dahrendorf, Ralf. (1959). *Class and Class Conflict in Industrial Society.* Stanford: Stanford University Press.

————. (1967). *New Perspectives on the Theory of Social and Political Conflict.* London: Longmans.

Dally, Ann. (1982). *Inventing Motherhood.* London: Burnett.

Dalton, George. (1967). *Tribal and Peasant Economics.* Garden City, NY: Natural History Press.

Dandeker, Christopher. (1990). *Surveillance, Power, and Modernity: Bureaucracy and Discipline from 1700 to the Present Day.* New York: St. Martin's.

Daniels, Roger. (1990). *A History of Immigration and Ethnicity in American Life.* New York: Harper Perennial.

Dannefer, D. (1984a). "Adult Development and Social Theory: A Paradigmatic Reappraisal," *American Sociological Review* 49 (February): 100-116.

————. (1984b). "The Role of the Social in Life-Span Developmental Psychology, Past and Future: Rejoinder to Baltes and Nesselroade," *American Sociological Review* 49 (6): 847-850.

————. (1989). "Human Action and Its Place in Theories of Aging," *Journal of Aging Studies* 3: 1-20.

Danzger, Murray Herbert. (1989). *Returning to Tradition: The Contemporary Revival of Orthodox Judaism.* New Haven: Yale University Press.

Davidman, Lynn. (1991). *Tradition in a Rootless World: Women Turn to Orthodox Judaism.* Berkeley: University of California Press.

Davidson, L., and L. Gordon. (1979). *The Sociology of Gender.* Chicago: Rand-McNally.

Davies, James C. (1963). *Human Nature in Politics: The Dynamics of Political Behavior.* New York: Wiley.

————. (1969). "The J-curve of Rising and Declining Satisfaction as a Cause of Some Great Revolutions and a Contained Rebellion." In Hugh David Graham and Ted Robert Gurr (eds.), *Violence in America: Historical and Comparative Perspectives.* Washington: Government Printing Office.

Davis, Angela. (1981). *Women, Race, and Class.* New York: Random House.

Davis, Karen, and Diane Rowland. (1990). "Uninsured and Underserved: Inequities in Health Care in the United States." In Nancy F. McKenzie (ed.), *The Crisis in Health Care: Ethical Issues,* pp. 21-50. New York: Penguin.

Davis, Kingsley. (1949). *Human Society.* New York: Macmillan.

Davis, Kingsley, and Wilbert E. Moore (1945). "Some Principles of Stratification," *American Sociological Review* 10: 242-249.

Davis, Winston. (1991). "Fundamentalism in Japan: Religious and Political." In Martin E. Marty and R. Scott Appleby (eds.), *Fundamentalism Observed.* Chicago: University of Chicago Press.

Dear, Michael J., and Jennifor R. Wolch. (1987). *Landscapes of Despair: From Deinstitutionalization to Homelessness.* Princeton: Princeton University Press.

DeBose, Charles E. (1992). "Codeswitching: Black English and Standard English in the African-American Linguistic Repertoire," *Journal of Multilingual and Multicultural Development* 13 (1-2): 157-167.

Deegan, Mary Jo. (1988). *Jane Addams and the Men of the Chicago School, 1912-1918.* New Brunswick, NJ: Transaction.

———— (ed.). (1991). *Women in Sociology: A Biographical Sourcebook.* New York: Greenwood.

DeFleur, Melvin, and Sandra Bell-Rokeach. (1982). *Theories of Mass Communication.* New York: Longman.

Delany, Sarah A., and Elizabeth Delany (with Amy Hill Hearth). (1993). *Having Our Say: The Delany Sisters' First 100 Years.* New York: Kodansha International.

DeLoache, Judy S., Deborah J. Cassidy, and Jan Carpenter. (1987). "The Three Bears Are All Boys: Mothers' Gender Labeling of Neutral Picture Book Characters," *Sex Roles* 17 (3-4): 163-178.

D'Emilio, John. (1983). *Sexual Politics, Sexual Communities: The Making of a Homosexual Minority in the United States 1940-1970.* Chicago: University of Chicago Press.

DeMuro, Paul R., and Jerome C. Roth. (1993). "Fraud and Abuse Compliance Programs: Their Time Has Come," *Healthcare Financial Management* 47 (March): 50-52.

Dessouki, Ali E. Hillal (ed.). (1982). *Modern Islamic Political Thought: The Response of the Shi'i and Sunni Muslims to the Twentieth Century.* London: Macmillan.

de Tocqueville, Alexis. (1835). *Democracy in America.*

Deyo, F. C. (1989). *Beneath the Miracle: Labor Subordination in the New Asian Industrialism.* Berkeley: University of California Press.

————. (1992). "The Political Economy of Social Policy Formation: East Asia's Newly Industrialized Countries." In Richard P. Appelbaum and Jeffrey Henderson (eds.), *States and Development in the Asian Pacific Rim.* Newbury Park, CA: Sage.

———— (ed.). (1987). *The Political Economy of the New Asian Industrialism.* Ithaca: Cornell University Press.

Diamond, M. (1982). "Sexual Identity of Monozygotic Twins Reared in Discordant Sex Roles and a BBC Follow-up," *Archives of Sexual Behavior* 11: 181-186.

Dickerson, Kitty G. (1991). *Textiles and Apparel in the International Economy.* New York: Macmillan.

Diekema, David A. (1991). "Televangelism and the Mediated Charismatic Relationship," *The Social Science Journal* 28 (2): 143-162.

Dillman, D. A. (1978). *Mail and Telephone Surveys: The Total Design Method.* New York: Wiley.

DiMaggio, Paul. (1982). "Cultural Entrepreneurship in Nineteenth-Century Boston: The Creation of an Organizational Base for High Culture in America," *Media, Culture, and Society* 4: 33-50.

————. (1987). "Classification in the Arts," *American Sociological Review* 52 (4): 440-455.

DiTomaso, N. (1989). "Sexuality in the Workplace: Discrimination and Harassment." In J. Hearn, D. L. Sheppard, P. Tancred-Sheriff, and G. Burrell (eds.), *The Sexuality of Organization.* Newbury Park, CA: Sage.

Dixon, Jo, and Alan J. Lizotte. (1987). "Gun Ownership and the Southern Subculture of Violence," *American Journal of Sociology* 93 (2): 383-405.

Dizard, Jan E., and Howard Gadlin. (1990). *The Minimal Family.* Amherst: University of Massachusetts Press.

Dobash, R. Emerson, and Russell P. Dolash. (1979). *Violence Against Women.* New York: Free Press.

Dolbeare, Cushing. (1992). "The Widening Gap: Housing Needs of Low-Income Families," Washington: Low Income Housing Information Service.

Dolnick, Edward. (1993). "Deafness as Culture," *The Atlantic Monthly* (September): 37-53.

Domhoff, G. William. (1974). *The Bohemian Grove and Other Retreats.* New York: Harper & Row.

————. (1978). *Who Really Rules? New Haven and Community Power Reexamined.* New Brunswick, NJ: Transaction.

————. (1983). *Who Rules America Now? A View From the Eighties.* Englewood Cliffs, NJ: Prentice-Hall.

————. (1987). *Power Elities and Organizations.* Newbury Park, CA: Sage.

————. (1990). *The Power Elite and the State: How Policy Is Made in America.* New York: A. de Gryter.

Domhoff, G. William, and Thomas R. Dye. (1984). *Power Elites and Organizations.* Beverley Hills, CA: Sage.

Donnelly, Patrick. (1980). "OSHA: The Sociology of Worker Health and Safety." Ph.D. diss. University of Delaware.

Donnerstein, Ed, Daniel G. Linz, and Steven Penrod. (1987). *The Question of Pornography: Research Findings and Policy Implications.* New York: Free Press.

Donnerstein, Ed, Ron Slaby, and Leonard Eron. (1993). "The Mass Media and Youth Aggression." In *Violence and Youth.* Washington: American Psychology Association.

Dorn, Nicholas, Karim Murji, and Nigel South. (1992). *Traffickers: Drug Markets and Law Enforcement.* New York: Routledge.

Dornbusch, et al. (1985). "Single Parents, Extended Households and the Control of Adolescents," *Child Development* 56: 326-341.

Dosi, Giovanni. (1984). *Technical Change and Industrial Transformation.* New York: St. Martin's.

Dotto, Lydia. (1988). *Thinking the Unthinkable: Civilization and Rapid Climate Change.* Waterloo, Ontario: Wilford Laurier University Press.

Douglas, Jack (1967). *The Social Meanings of Suicide.* Princeton: Princeton University Press.

Downs, James F. (1972). *The Navajo.* New York: Holt, Rinehart & Winston.

Doyle J. (1985). *Sex and Gender.* Dubuque, IA: Brown.

Drake, St. Clair, and Horance R. Clayton. (1962). *Black Metropolis: A Study of Negro Life in a Northern City* (2 vols.). New York: Harper & Row.

Dreier, Peter. (1991). "Redlining Cities: How Banks Color Community Development," *Challenge* (November-December): 15-23.

———. (1993). "America's Urban Crisis: Symptoms, Causes, Solutions," *North Carolina Law Review* 71: 5.

Dreier, Peter, and Richard P. Appelbaum. (1992). "The Housing Crisis Enters the 1990s," *New England Journal of Public Policy* (spring-summer): 155-167.

Dreier, Peter, and J. David Hulchanski. (1993). "Social Housing: American Prospect, Canadian Reality." In John E. Davis (ed.), *The Affordable City.* Philadelphia: Temple University Press.

Drucker, Peter. (1993). "The Rise of the Knowledge Society," *Wilson Quarterly* (spring): 52-71.

Du Bois, W. E. B. (1967; orig. 1899). *The Philadelphia Negro.* New York: Schocken.

———. (1968; orig. 1903). *The Souls of Black Folk.* New York: Fawcett World Library.

———. (1970; orig. 1940). *Dusk of Dawn: An Essay Toward an Autobiography of a Race Concept.* New York: Schocken.

Duffy, John. (1993). *From Humors to Medical Science: A History of American Medicine.* Urbana: University of Illinois Press.

Dunlop, Thomas R. (1981). *DDT, Scientists, Citizens, and Public Policy.* Princeton: Princeton University Press.

Durkheim, Emile. (1956; orig. 1922). *Education and Sociology,* Sherwood L. Fox (trans.). New York: Free Press.

———. (1964a; orig. 1893). *The Division of Labor in Society.* New York: Free Press.

———. (1964b; orig. 1895). *The Rules of Sociological Method.* New York: Free Press.

———. (1965; orig. 1912). *The Elementary Forms of Religious Life.* New York: Free Press.

———. (1966; orig. 1897). *Suicide.* New York: Free Press.

———. (1973; orig. 1922). *Moral Education: A Study in the Theory and Application of the Sociology of Education.* New York: Free Press.

Durnier, Mitchell. (1992). *Slim's Table.* Chicago: University of Chicago Press.

Durning, Alan B. (1989). "Poverty and the Environment: Reversing the Downward Spiral." Worldwatch Institute, Worldwatch Paper 92. Washington (November).

Dworkin, Andrea. (1981). *Pornography: Men Possessing Women.* New York: Pedigree.

———. (1987). *Intercourse.* New York: Free Press.

———. (1989). *Letters from the War Zone: Writings 1976-1987.* New York: Dutton.

Dychtwald, K. (1990). *Age Wave: How the Most Important Trend of Our Time Will Change Your Future.* New York: Bantam.

Earman, J. S. (1967). *Memorandum for the Record: Report on Plots to Assassinate Fidel Castro.* Washington: Central Intelligence Agency (CIA).

Ebomoyi, Ehigie. (1987). "The Prevalence of Female Circumcision in Two Nigerian Communities," *Sex Roles* 17 (3/4): 139-151.

Eccles, Jacquelynne S., and J. Jacobs. (1986). "Social Forces Shape Math Participation," *Signs* 11: 367-380.

Eccles, Jacquelynne S., Janis E. Jacobs, and Rena D. Harold. (1990). "Gender Role Stereotypes, Expectancy Effects, and Parents' Socialization of Gender Difference," *Journal of Social Issues* 46 (summer): 183-201.

Echikson, William. (1992). "Europe's New Face of Fear," *World Monitor* (November): 30-35.

Eckholm, Erik. (1990). "An Aging Nation Grapples with Caring for the Frail," *New York Times* (March 27): A-1.

Eckhouse, John. (1992). "Programmers Losing Out," *San Francisco Chronicle* (May 6): B-1.

Eder, Klaus. (1985). "The 'New Social Movements': Moral Crusades, Political Pressure Groups, or Social Movements?" *Social Research* 52: 869-890.

Edsall, Thomas, and Mary Edsall. (1991). *Chain Reaction: The Impact of Race, Rights, and Taxes on American Politics.* New York: Norton.

Edwards, Harry. (1989). "Camouflaging the Color Line," In Charles Willie (ed.), *The Class and Caste Controversy on Race and Poverty: Round Two of the Wilson-Willie Debate.* New York: General-Hall.

Efron, Sonni. (1989a). "Sweatshops Expanding into Orange County," *Los Angeles Times* (November 26): A-1.

———. (1989b). "Mother's Plight Turns Home into a Sweatshop," *Los Angeles Times* (November 27): A-1.

———. (1989c). "Sweatshop Patrol: It's Tricky Duty," *Los Angeles Times* (November 28): A-18.

———. (1989d). "'Hot Goods' Law Revisited as Anti-Sweatshop Tool," *Los Angeles Times* (November 28): A-3.

———. (1990). "Targets Get Bigger in Sweatshop War," *Los Angeles Times* (February 5): A-3.

Eggebeen, David J., and Daniel T. Lichter. (1991). "Race, Family Structure, and Changing Poverty Among Women," *American Sociological Review* 56 (December): 801-817.

Ehrenberg, S., J. E. Lesley, D. B. Mandzuch, and S. Newman. (1983). "Feminist Shabbat Service." In L. Richardson and V. Taylor (eds.), *Feminist Frontiers,* pp. 381-383. Reading, MA: Addison-Wesley.

Ehrenreich, Barbara. (1989). *Fear of Falling: The Inner Life of the Middle Class.* New York: Pantheon.

———. (1992). "The American Family Vs. the American Dream," *The Family Therapy Networker* (September/October): 55-60.

Ehrenreich, Barbara, and John Ehrenreich. (1979). "The Professional-Managerial Class." In Pat Walker (ed.), *Between Labor and Capital.* Boston: South End.

Ehrhardt, Anke A., and H. Meyer-Bahlburg. (1981). "Effects of Prenatal Sex Hormones on Gender-Related Behavior," *Science* 211: 1312-1318.

Ehrlich, Paul. (1968). *The Population Bomb.* New York: Ballantine.

Ehrlich, Paul R., and Anne H. Ehrlich. (1990). *The Population Explosion.* New York: Simon & Schuster.

Eisen, Arnold M. (1983). *The Chosen People in America: A Study of Jewish Religious Ideology.* Bloomington: Indiana University Press.

Eisenberg, David M. (1990). "Alternative Therapies and Medical Practices," *New England Journal of Medicine* (January 28): 65-69.

Eisenhart, Margaret A., and Dorothy C. Holland. (1983). "Learning Gender from Peers: The Role of Peer Groups in the Cultural Transmission of Gender," *Human Organization* 42 (winter): 321-332.

Eisenhower, Dwight David. (1960). "Farewell Speech," *New York Times* (November 15): A-1.

Eisenstein, Zillah. (1979). *Capitalist Patriarchy and the Case for Socialist Feminism.* New York: Monthly Review.

Eisler, Riane. (1988). *The Chalice and the Blade.* San Francisco: Harper.

El Dareer, Asma. (1982). *Woman, Why Do You Weep? Circumcision and Its Consequences.* Westport, CT: Zed.

Elliot, Delbert S., and David Huiznga. (1983). "Social Class and Deliquent Behavior in a National Youth Panel," *Criminology* 21 (2): 149-177.

Ellis, James E. (1992). "Can Biotech Put Bread on Third World Tables," *Business Week* (December 14): 100.

Ellis, W., and M. Lino. (1992). "Payments of Child Support and Alimony," *Family Economic Reiew* 5: 2.

Ellwood, Charles A. (1907). Review of George S. Merriam, *The Negro and the Nation: A History of American Slavery and Enfranchisement,* in *American Journal of Sociology* 12 (July 1906-May 1907): 274-275.

El Sadaawi, Nawal. (1980). *The Hidden Face of Eve: Women in the Arab World.* London: Zed.

———. (1983). "Out of Egypt: A Talk with Nawal el Sadaawi, T. Patterson, and A. Gilliam," *Freedomways,* Special Middle East Issue, Part 2, 23: 3.

Elshtain, Jean Bethke. (1981). *Public Man, Private Woman.* Princeton: Princeton University Press.

Ember, M. (1974). "Warfare, Sex Ratio, and Polygyny," *Ethnology* 13: 197-206.

Emery, R. E. (1988). *Marriage, Divorce and Children's Adjustment.* Beverley Hills, CA: Sage.

Emery, Robert E., and Daniel S. Shaw. (1988). "Chronic Family Adversity and School Age Children's Adjustment," *Journal of the American Academy of Child and Adolescent Psychiatry* 27: 200-206.

Emmanuel, Araghi. (1972a). *Unequal Exchange: A Study of the Imperialism of Trade.* New York: Monthly Review.

———. (1972b). *Unequal Exchange.* London: New Left Books.

Encyclopedia of Associations. (1991). Detroit: Gale Research Company.

Engels, Friedrich. (1942; orig. 1884). *The Origins of Family, Private Property, and the State.* New York: International.

———. (1968; orig. 1884). "The Origins of Family, Private Property, and the State." In *Marx and Engels: Selected Works.* New York: International.

———. (1987; orig. 1844). *The Condition of the Working Class in England.* New York: Penguin.

Entman, Robert M. (1989). *Democracy Without Citizens.* New York: Oxford University Press.

———. (1992). "Blacks in the News: Television, Modern Racism and Cultural Change," *Journalism Quarterly* 69 (summer): 341- 361.

Epstein, Cynthia Fuchs. (1988). *Deceptive Distinctions: Sex, Gender, and the Social Order.* New Haven: Yale University Press.

Erickson, Kai T. (1966). *Wayward Puritans: A Study in the Sociology of Deviance.* New York: Wiley.

Erikson, Erik H. (1950). *Childhood and Society.* New York: Norton.

———. (1975). *Life History and the Historical Moment.* New York: Norton.

———. (1980). *Identity and the Life Cycle.* New York: Norton.

———. (1985). *The Life Cycle Completed: A Review.* New York: Norton.

Erlanger, Howard. (1974). "The Empirical Status of the Subculture of Violence Thesis," *Social Problems* 22: 280-292.

Ernst, Dieter. (1980). *The New International Division of Labour, Technology and Underdevelopment: Consequences for the Third World.* New York: Campus Verlag.

———. (1987). *Innovation, Industrial Structure, and Global Competition: The Changing Economics of Internationalization.* New York: Campus Verlag.

Espenshade, T. (1979). "The Economic Consequences of Divorce," *Journal of Marriage and the Family* 41: 615-625.

Esposito, John L. (1984). *Islam and Politics.* Syracuse, NY: Syracuse University Press.

———. (1990). *Voices of Resurgent Islam.* New York: Oxford University Press.

——— (ed.). (1987). *The Iranian Revolution: Its Global Impact.* Miami: Florida International University Press.

Estes, Carol L. (1986). "The Politics of Aging in America," *Aging and Society* 6: 121-134.

———. (1991). "The Reagan Legacy: Privatization, the Welfare State, and Aging." In J. Myles and J. Quadagno (eds.), *States, Labor Markets, and the Future of Old Age Policy.* Philadelphia: Temple University Press.

Estes, Carol L., Elizabeth A. Binney, and Richard A. Culbertson. (1992). "The Gerontological Imagination: Social Influences on the Development of Gerontology, 1945-Present," *Aging and Human Development* 35 (1): 49-65.

Estes, Carol L., J. Swan, and L. Gerard. (1982). "Dominant and Competing Paradigms in Gerontology: Toward a Political Economy of Aging," *Aging and Society* 2: 151-164.

Estes, Carol L., L. Gerard, J. Zones, and J. Swan. (1984). *Political Economy, Health and Aging.* Boston: Little, Brown.

Estey, Martens. (1981). *The Unions: Structure, Development, and Management* (3rd ed.). New York: Harcourt, Brace, Jovanovich.

Etzioni, Amatai. (1984). *Capital Corruption: The Attack on American Democracy.* New York: Harcourt, Brace, Jovanovich.

———. (1975). *A Comparative Analysis of Complex Organizations: On Power, Involvement, and Their Correlates.* (rev. ed.). New York: Free Press.

Evans, John. (1986). "Gender Differences in Children's Games: A Look at the Team Selection Process," *Canadian Association for Health, Physical Education, and Recreation Journal* 52: 4-9.

Evans, Peter. (1979). *Dependent Development.* Princeton: Princeton University Press.

Evans-Pritchard, E. E. (1940). *The Neur: A Description of the Modes of Livelihood and Political Institutions of a Nilotic People.* New York: Oxford University Press.

Ewen, Stuart. (1985). "Capitalist Realism," Review of Michael Schudson, *Advertising: The Uneasy Persuasion.* In *Journal of Communication* 35: 192-196.

———. (1988). *All-Consuming Images: The Politics of Style in Contemporary Culture.* New York: Basic Books.

Fackenheim, Emil L. (1988). *What Is Judaism? An Interpretation for the Present Age.* New York: Summit.

Fagot, B. (1978). "The Influence of Sex of Child on Parental Reaction to Toddler Children." *Child Development* 49: 459-465.

Fair, Jo Ellen, and Roberta J. Astroff. (1991). "Constructing Race and Violence: U.S. News Coverage and the Signifying Practices of Apartheid," *Journal of Communication* 41(autumn): 58-74.

Fairfield, Richard. (1972). *Communes USA.* Baltimore: Penguin.

Falk, G., U. Falk, and V. Tomashevich. (1981). *Aging in America and Other Cultures.* Saratoga, CA: Century Twenty-One.

Faludi, Susan. (1991). *Backlash: The Undeclared War Against American Women.* New York: Crown.

Fanfani, Amintore. (1955). *Catholicism, Protestantism, and Capitalism.* New York: Sheed & Ward.

Farb, Peter. (1968). *Man's Rise to Civilization as Shown By the Indians of North America from Primevel Times to the Industrial State.* New York: Dutton.

Farber, Henry. (1993). "The Incidence and Costs of Job Loss: 1982-1990," Brookings paper on economic activity, *Microeconomics.* Washington: The Brookings Institution.

Farber, S. L. (1981). *Identical Twins Reared Apart.* New York: Basic Books.

Farkas, George, Robert P. Grobe, Daniel Sheehan, and Yuan Shuan. (1990b). "Cultural Resources and School Success: Gender, Ethnicity and Poverty Groups Within an Urban School District," *American Sociological Review* 55: 127-142.

Farkas, George, Daniel Sheehan, and Robert P. Grobe. (1990a). "Coursework Mastery and School Success: Gender, Ethnicity and Poverty Groups Within an Urban School District," *American Educational Research Journal* 27 (4): 807-827.

Farrell, Christopher. (1993). "An Anguished Cry of 'Enough' in America's Killing Fields," *Business Week* (December 13): 80.

Fausto-Sterling, Anne. (1985). *Myths and Gender: Biological Theories About Women and Men.* New York: Basic Books.

Feagin, Joe R. (1991). "The Continuing Significance of Race: Antiblack Discrimination in Public Places," *American Sociological Review.* 56: 101-116.

Feagin, Joe, and Clairece Booher Feagin, (1990). *Social Problems: A Critical Power-Conflict Perspective* (3rd ed.). Englewood Cliffs, NJ: Prentice-Hall.

Feagin, Joe R., and Michael Hodge. (1992). "Fighting Racism: On Being Black and Middle Class," Paper presented at the annual meeting of the American Sociological Association.

Featherman, David L, F. Lancaster Jones, and Robert M. Hauser. (1974). *Assumptions of Social Mobility Research in the United States: The Case of Occupational Status.* Madison: The University of Wisconsin Institute for Research on Poverty.

Featherman, David L., and Robert M. Hauser. (1978). *Opportunity and Change.* New York: Academic.

Featherstone, Mike (ed.). (1990). *Global Culture: Nationalism, Globalization and Modernity.* Newbury Park, CA: Sage.

Federal Bureau of Investigation (FBI). (1992). *Hate Crimes in the U.S.* Washington: Government Printing Office.

————. (1993). *Crime in the United States: Uniform Crime Reports, 1970-1993*. Washington: Government Printing Office.

Federal Election Commission (FEC). (1992a). *Congressional Campaign Expenditures*. Washington: Government Printing Office.

————. (1992b). Personal communication (April 8).

————. (1993). "Contributions of Health Care PACs," Washington: Government Printing Office.

Fedler, Fred. (1973). "The Media and Minority Groups: A Study of the Adequacy of Access," *Jounalism Quarterly* 50 (spring): 109-117.

Fee, Elizabeth, and Daniel M. Fox (eds.). (1988). *AIDS: The Budens of History*. Berkeley: University of California Press.

Feeley, Malcolm M. (1992a). "Learning at the Cutting Edge," *Washington Post* (November 1): 5.

————. (1992). *The Process Is the Punishment*. New York: Russell Sage Foundation.

Feiler, Bruce M. (1991). *Learning to Bow: Inside the Heart of Japan*. New York: Ticknor & Fields.

Feingold A. (1988). "Cognitive Gender Differences Are Disappearing," *American Psychologist* 43: 95-103.

Feld, Werner J., and Robert S. Jordan. (1983). *International Organizations: A Comparative Approach*. New York: Praeger.

Feldman, Linda. (1989). "UN: World Population Heads for 14 Billion," *Christian Science Monitor* (May 17): 7.

Fenstermaker Berk, Sarah. (1985). *The Gender Factory: The Apportionment of Work in American Households*. New York: Plenum.

Fenstermaker, S., C. West, and D. Zimmerman. (1991). "Gender Inequality: New Conceptual Terrain." In R. Blumberg (ed.), *Gender, Family and Economy: The Triple Overlap*, pp. 289-307. Newbury Park, CA: Sage.

Ferguson, Kathy E. (1984). *The Feminist Case Against Bureaucracy*. Philadelphia: Temple University Press.

Ferguson, M. (1983). *Forever Feminine: Woman's Magazines and the Cult of Femininity*. London: Heinmann.

Fernandez-Kelly, Maria Patricia. (1982). *Feminization, Mexican Border Industrialization, and Migration*, Working Paper no. 3. Berkeley: University of California Center for the Study, Education and Advancement of Women.

————. (1983). *For We Are Sold, I and My People: Women and Industry in Mexico's Frontier*. Albany: State University of New York Press.

Feshbach, Seymour, and Robert D. Singer. (1971). *Television and Aggression: An Experimental Field Study*. San Franciso: Jossey-Bass.

Feuer, Louis. (1969). *The Conflict of Generations: The Character and Significance of Student Movements*. New York: Basic Books.

Filice, Gregory A., and Claire Pomeroy. (1991). "Preventing Secondary Infections Among HIV-Positive Persons," *Public Health Reports* 106: (September/October): 503-517.

Fine, Ben. (1992). *Women's Employment and the Capitalist Family*. New York: Routledge.

Fingarette, Herbert. (1972). *Confucius: The Secular as Sacred*. New York: Harper & Row.

Fingerhut, Lois A., and Joel C. Kleinman. (1990). "International and Interstate Comparisons of Homicide Among Young Males," *Journal of the American Medical Association* 263 (June 17): 3292-3295.

Finke, Roger, and Rodney Stark. (1988). "Religious Economies and Sacred Canopies: Religious Mobilization in American Cities, 1906," *American Sociological Review* 53: 41-49.

————. (1992). *The Churching of America*. New Brunswick, NJ: Rutgers University Press.

Finkelhor, David. (1978). *Sexually Victimized Children*. New York: Free Press.

Finkelhor, D., and K. Yllo. (1985). *License to Rape: Sexual Abuse of Wives*. Newbury Park, CA: Sage.

Finley, Nancy J., M. Diane Roberts, and Benjamin F. Banahan, III. (1988). "Motivators and Inhibitors of Attitudes of Filial Obligation Toward Aging Parents," *The Gerontologist* 28: 73-83.

Finn, Charles. (1989). *Mortgage Lending in Boston's Neighborhoods, 1981-1987*. Boston: City of Boston Redevelopment Authority.

Firestone, Shulamith. (1971). *The Dialectic of Sex*. London: Paladin.

Fischer, Claude. (1982). *To Dwell Among Friends: Personal Networks in Town and City*. Chicago: University of Chicago Press.

————. (1984). *The Urban Experience* (2nd ed.). New York: Harcourt, Brace, Jovanovich.

Fischer, Renate, and Harlan Lane (eds.). (1993). *Looking Back: A Reader on the History of Deaf Communities and Their Sign Languages*. Hamburg: Signum.

Fisher, Elizabeth. (1979). *Woman's Creation: Sexual Evolution and the Shaping of Society*. New York: Anchor-Doubleday.

Fisher, Marc. (1992). "Germany's Gypsy Question," *Washington Post* (November 1): F-1.

Fishkin, James S. (1992). "Talk of the Tube: How to Get Teledemocracy Right," *The American Prospect* 11 (fall): 46-52.

Fishman, Mark. (1980). *Manufacturing the News*. Austin, TX: University of Austin Press.

Fishman, Pamela. (1978). "Women's Work in Interaction," *Social Problems* 25 (April): 397-406.

Fiske, John. (1987). *Television Culture*. New York: Routledge.

Fitzgerald, Nora (1989). "Distorted Images," *Scholastic Update* 121 (April 7): 12.

Fitzpatrick, Liam. (1993). "Does Asia Want My MTV? An Interview with Richard Li, " *Hemispheres* (July): 21-24.

Flacks, Richard. (1967). "The Liberated Generation: An Exploration of the Roots of Social Protest," *Journal of Social Issues* 23: 52-75.

———. (1971). *Youth and Social Change.* Chicago: Markham.

———. (1988). *Making History: The American Left and the American Mind.* New York: Columbia University Press.

Flacks, Richard, and Jack Whalen. (1989). *Beyond the Barricades: The Sixties Generation Grows Up.* Philadelphia: Temple University Press.

Flaherty, David H. (1989). *Protecting Privacy in Surveillance Societies: The Federal Republic of Germany, Sweden, France, Canada, and the United States.* Chapel Hill: University of North Carolina Press.

Fleson, Richard B., and Lisa Trudeau. (1991). "Gender Differences in Mathematics Performance," *Social Psychology Quarterly* 54 (June): 113-126.

Fong, Eric. (1992). "Racial Interaction Patterns of American and Canadian Neighborhoods." Paper presented at the annual meeting of the American Sociological Association.

Foran, John. (1993a). "Theories of Revolution Revisited: Toward a Fourth Generation?" *Sociological Theory* 11 (March): 1-20.

———. (1993b). *Fragile Resistance: Social Transformation in Iran from 1500 to the Revolution.* Boulder, CO: Westview.

Foreit, K. G., et al. (1980). "Sex Bias in the News Treatment of Male-Centered and Female-Centered News Stories," *Sex Roles* 6: 475-480.

Forment, Carlos A. (1989). "Political Practice and the Rise of an Ethnic Enclave: The Cuban American Case," *Theory and Society* 18 (January): 47-48.

Fortune. (1993). "The Billionaires: The World's 101 Richest People," (June 28): 36-66.

Fosler, R. S., W. Alonso, J. A. Meyer, and R. Kern. (1990). *Demographic Change and the American Future.* Pittsburgh: University of Pittsburgh Press.

Foucault, Michel. (1973). *The Order of Things.* New York: Vintage.

———. (1979). *Discipline and Punish: The Birth of the Prison,* Alan Sheridan (trans.). New York: Random House.

———. (1980). *The History of Sexuality.* New York: Vintage.

———. (1988). *Madness and Civilization: A History of Insanity in the Age of Reason.* New York: Vintage.

Fox, Karen F., and Philip Kotler. (1980). "The Marketing of Social Causes: The First Ten Years," *Journal of Marketing* 44: 22-23.

Fox-Genovese, Elizabeth. (1993). "Women's Status Today." In the *American Academic Encyclopedia* (on-line edition). Danbury, CT: Grolier Electronic Publishing.

Francis, David R. (1990). "U.S. Middle Class Falls Short on Savings and Investments," *Christian Science Monitor* (March 30): 1

Frank, Andre Gundar. (1966). "The Development of Underdevelopment," *Monthly Review* XVIII (September).

———. (1969a). *Latin America: Underdevelopment or Revolution: Essays in the Development of Underdevelopment and the Immediate Enemy.* New York: Monthly Review.

———. (1969b). *Capitalism and Underdevelopment in Latin America: Historical Studies of Chile and Brazil.* New York: Monthly Review.

———. (1979). *Dependent Accumulation and Underdevelopment.* London: Macmillan.

Freedman, Samuel. (1991). *Small Victories: The Real World of a Teacher, Her Students, Their High School.* New York: Harper & Row.

Freeman, A. D. (1978). "Legitimizing Racial Discrimination Through Anti-Discrimination Law: A Critical Review of Supreme Court Doctrine," *Minnesota Law Review* 62: 1049-1110.

Freeman, Jo. (1979). "The Origins of the Woman's Liberation Movement," *American Journal of Sociology* 78: 792-811.

Freeman, John H. (1982). "Organizational Life Cycles and Natural Selection Processes." In Barry Shaw and L. L. Cummings (eds.), *Research in Organizational Behavior,* pp. 1-32. Greenwich, CT: JAI.

Freidson, Eliot. (1970a). *Profession of Medicine: A Study of the Sociology of Applied Knowledge.* Chicago: University of Chicago Press.

———. (1970b). *Professional Dominance: The Social Structure of Medical Care.* New York: Aldine.

———. (1989). *Medical Work in America: Essays on Health Care.* New Haven: Yale University Press.

Freire, Paolo. (1972). *Pedagogy of the Oppressed.* New York: Herder & Herder.

French, J., and B. Raven. (1959). "The Bases of Social Power." In D. Cartwright (ed.), *Studies in Social Power.* Ann Arbor, MI: University of Michigan, Institute for Social Research.

Freud, Sigmund. (1905). "Three Essays on Sexuality." In *Standard Edition,* vol. 7. London: Hogarth.

———. (1929). "Civilization and Its Discontents." In *Standard Edition* (vol. 21). London: Hogarth.

———. (1933). *New Introductory Lectures on Psycho-Analysis.* New York: Norton.

Freund, E. S., and Meredity B. McGuire (1992). *Health, Illness, and the Social Body.* Englewood Cliffs, NJ: Prentice-Hall.

Frey, William H., and Alden Speare, Jr. (1991). "U.S. Metropolitan Area Church Growth, 1960-1990: Census Trends and Explanations," *Research Reports No. 91-212.*

Ann Arbor: University of Michigan Population Studies Center.

Friedan, Betty. (1963). *The Feminine Mystique.* New York: Norton.

———. (1981). *The Second Stage.* New York: Summit.

Friedman, Emily. (1991). "Health Care's Changing Face: The Demographics of the 21st Century," *Hospitals* 65 (April 5): 36-40.

Friedman, J. B. (ed.). (1987). *TV Technology: A Look Toward the 21st Century.*

Friedman, Lawrence. (1975). *The Legal System: A Social Science Perspective.* New York: Russell Sage Foundation.

———. (1985). *A History of American Law.* New York: Simon & Schuster.

———. (1990). *The Republic of Choice: Law, Authority and Culture.* Cambridge: Harvard University Press.

———. (1992). *American Law.* Stanford: Stanford University Press.

Friedman, William J., Amy B. Robinson, and Britt L. Friedman. (1987). "Sex Differences in Moral Judgment," *Psychology of Women Quarterly* 11: 37-46.

Friedmann, John. (1986). "The World City Hypothesis," *Development and Change* 17: 69-83.

Friedmann, John, and Goetz Wolff. (1982). "World City Formation: An Agenda for Research and Action," *International Journal of Urban and Regional Research* 6: 309-344.

Frobel, Folker, Jurgen Heinrichs, and Otto Kreye. (1980). *The New International Division of Labor: Structural Unemployment in Industrialized Countries and Industrialization in Developing Countries.* Cambridge, England: Cambridge University Press.

———. (1982). "The Current Development of the World Economy: Reproduction of Labor and Accumulation of Capital on a World Scale," *Review* 5 (4): 507-555.

Fromm, Erich. (1941). *Escape from Freedom.* New York: Farrar & Rinehart.

Fry, C. L. (1980). *Aging in Culture and Society.* New York: Bergin.

Fukui, Haruhiro. (1992). "The Japanese State and Economic Development: A Profile of a Nationalist-Paternalist State." In Richard P. Appelbaum and Jeffrey Henderson (eds.), *States and Development in the Asian Pacific Rim.* Newbury Park, CA: Sage.

Fukuyama, Francis. (1992a). *The End of History and the Last of Man.* New York: Free Press.

———. (1992b). "Capitalism and Democracy: The Missing Link," *Journal of Democracy* 3 (July): 100-111.

Fullilove, Mindy T. (1993). "Perceptions and Misperceptions of Race and Drug Use," *Journal of the American Medical Association* 269 (August 5): 1034.

Furstenberg, Frank F., Jr., C. W. Nord, J. L. Peterson, and N. Zill. (1983). "The Course of Children of Divorce:

Marital Disruption and Parental Contact," *American Sociological Review* 48 (October): 656-667.

Futurist. (1990). "American Families at the Crossroads." Washington: Center for Family Studies.

Gagnon, J. (1977). *Human Sexualities.* Glenview, IL: Scott, Foresman.

Galbraith, Kenneth. (1956). *American Capitalism: The Concept of Countervailing Power* (rev. ed). Boston: Houghton-Mifflin.

Gale Research Company. (1990). *1991 Encyclopedia of Associations.* Detroit.

Gale, Richard P. (1986). "Social Movements and the State: The Environmental Movement, Counter Movement, and Governmental Agencies," *Sociological Perspectives* 29: 202-240.

Galliher, John F., and Cheryl Tyree. (1985). "Edwin Sutherland's Research on the Origins of Sexual Psychopath Laws: An Early Case Study of the Medicalization of Deviance," *Social Problems* 33 (December): 100-113.

Gamson, Joshua. (1991). "Silence, Death, and the Invisible Enemy: AIDS Activism and Social Movement 'Newness'." In Michael Buroway, et al. (eds.), *Ethnography Unbound: Power and Resistance in the Modern Metropolis.* Berkeley and Los Angeles: University of California Press.

Gamson, William. (1975). *The Strategy of Social Protest.* Homewood, IL: Dorsey.

———. (1988). "Political Discourse and Collective Action." In B. Kandermans, et al (eds.), *From Structure to Action: Comparing Social Movements Research Across Cultures.* Greenwich, CT: JAI.

Gamson, William A., David Croteau, Williams Hoynes, and Theodore Sasson. (1992). "Media Images and the Social Construction of Reality," *Annual Review of Sociology* 18: 373-393.

Gamson, William A., and A. Mogdiliani. (1989). "Media Discourse and Public Opinion on Nuclear Power," *American Journal of Sociology* 95: 1-37.

Gans, Herbert. (1962a). *The Urban Villagers.* New York: Free Press.

———. (1962b). "Urbanism and Suburbanism as Ways of Life." In Arnold M. Rose (ed.), *Human Behavior and Social Processes.* Boston: Houghton-Mifflin.

———. (1979). *Deciding What's News.* New York: Pantheon.

Garber, Howard L. (1988). *The Milwaukee Project: Preventing Mental Retardation in Children at Risk.* Washington: American Association on Mental Retardation.

Garden, Peggy C., Stephan A. Cernkovitch and M. D. Pugh. (1986). "Friendships and Delinquency," *American Journal of Sociology* 91 (March): 1170-1202.

Gardner, Robert W., Bryant Robey, and Peter C. Smith. (1985). *Asian Americans: Growth, Change and Diversity.* Washington: Population Reference Bureau.

Garfinkel, Harold. (1963). "A Conception of, and Experiments with, 'Trust' as a Condition of Stable Concerted Actions." In O. J. Harvey (ed.), *Motivation and Social Interaction.* New York: Ronald Press.

———. (1985). *Studies in Ethnomethodology.* New York: Basil Blackwell.

Garfinkel, Irwin, and Sara S. McLanahan. (1986). *Single Mothers and Their Children: A New American Dilemma.* Washington: Urban Institute Press.

Garfinkel, Simson L. (1989). "Gender Gap on the Science Track: Because of Stereotyping, Girls Don't Receive the Encouragement Boys Get to Give Science a Serious Try," *Christian Science Monitor* (May 9): 12.

Garfinkle, A. M., C. Lefcourt, and D. B. Schulder. (1971). "Women's Servitude Under Law." In R. Lefcourt (ed.), *Law Against the People.* New York: Random House.

Garreau, Joel. (1991). *Edge City: Life on a New Frontier.* New York: Doubleday.

Gaskell, George, and Patten Smith. (1981). "The Crowd in History," *New Society* 57 (August 20): 303-304.

Gaston, John. (1986). "The Destruction of the Young Black Male: The Impact of Popular Culture and Organized Sports," *Journal of Black Studies* 16 (June): 369-384.

Geertz, Clifford. (1968). "The Impact of Culture on the Concept of Man." In Yehuda A. Cohen (ed.), *Man in Adaptation: The Cultural Present.* Chicago: Aldine.

———. (1973). *The Interpretation of Cultures.* New York: Basic Books.

Geis, Gilbert. (1972). *Not the Law's Business: An Examination of Homosexuality, Abortion, Prostitution, Narcotics, and Gambling in the United States.* Rockville, MD: National Institute of Mental Health.

Geis, Gilbert, and Robert F. Meier (eds.). (1977). *White Collar Crime: Offenses in Business, Politics and the Professions* (rev. ed.). New York: Free Press.

Gelles, Richard J., and Clair Pendrick Cornell. (1985). *Intimate Violence in the Family.* Newbury Park, CA: Sage.

———. (1990). *Intimate Violence in Families* (2nd ed.). Newbury Park, CA: Sage.

Gelles, Richard J., and Murray A. Straus. (1988). *Intimate Violence.* New York: Simon & Schuster.

General Accounting Office (GAO). (1991). *Long-Term Care: Projected Needs of the Aging Baby-Boom Generation.* Report No. HRD-91-86. Washington: Government Printing Office.

———. (1992a). *Social Security Racial Difference in Disability Decisions.* Document #T-HRD-92-41. Washington.

———. (1992b). "Casualties in Desert Storm." Washington: Government Printing Office.

General Social Surveys (GSS). (1991). **Cumulative Codebook.** Chicago: National Opinion Research Center.

Gerbner, George, and Larry Gross. (1980). "The Violent Face of Television and Its Lessons." In Edward Palmer and Aimee Dorr (eds.), *Children and the Faces of Television: Teaching, Violence, Selling.* New York: Academic Press.

Gerbner, George, Larry Gross, N. Signorielli, and M. Morgan. (1986). "Television's Mean World: Violence Profile No. 14-15." Unpublished report, Annenberg School of Communication, University of Pennsylvania.

Gerbner, George, and N. Signorielli. (1990). "Violence Profile, 1967 Through 1988-89: Enduring Patterns." Unpublished report, Annenberg School of Communication, University of Pennsylvania.

Gereffi, Gary. (1989). "Rethinking Development Theory: Insights from East Asia and Latin America." *Sociological Forum* 4 (4): 505-533.

———. (1992). "New Realities of Industrial Development in East Asia and Latin America: Global, Regional, and National Trends." In Richard P. Appelbaum and Jeffrey Henderson (eds.), *States and Development in the Asian Pacific Rim.* Newbury Park, CA: Sage.

———. (1994). "The Organization of Buyer-Driven Global Commodity Chains: How U.S. Retailers Shape Overseas Production Networks." In Gary Gereffi and Miguel Korzeniewicz (eds.), *Commodity Chains and Global Capitalism,* pp. 95-122. Westport, CT: Greenwood.

Gereffi, Gary, and Miguel Korzeniewicz. (1993). "Commodity Chains and Footwear Exports in the Semiperiphery." In William Martin (ed.), *Semiperipheral States in the World Economy.* Westport, CT: Greenwood.

——— (eds.). (1994). *Commodity Chains and Global Capitalism.* Westport, CT: Greenwood Press.

Gerhardt, Kevin F. G. (1989). *The Silent Brotherhood: Inside America's Racist Underground.* New York: Free Press.

Gerlach, Michael. (1992). *Alliance Capitalism: The Strategic Organization of Japanese Business.* Berkeley: University of California Press.

Gershwin, L. (1992). "Threats to U.S." Transcript of speech delivered before Center for Defense Initiatives Conference ("Defense Against Ballistic Missiles: The Emerging Consensus in S.D.I."), September 23, Washington.

Gerth, Hans, and C. Wright Mills (eds.). (1946). *From Max Weber: Essays in Sociology.* New York: Oxford University Press.

Ghayasuddin, M. (ed.). (1986). *The Impact of Nationalism on the Muslim World.* London: Open Press, Al-Hoda.

Gibbs, J.C. (1978). *Stage Theories of Cognitive and Moral Development: Criticisms and Applications.* Cambridge: Harvard Educational Review.

Gibbs, Jack L. (1981). *Norms, Deviance, and Social Control.* New York: Elsevier.

Gibbs, Jewelle Taylor. (1994). "Anger in Young Black Males: Victims or Victimizers?" In Richard G. Majors and Jacob U. Gorson (eds.), *The American Black Male: His Present Status and His Future,* pp. 127-143. Chicago: Nelson-Hall.

Gibbs, Marion. (1953). *Feudal Order: A Study of the Origins and Development of English Feudal Society.* New York: H. Schuman.

Gibbs, Nancy. (1992). "Do You Want to Die?" *Time Magazine* 135 (May): 58-60.

Giddens, Anthony. (1985a). *The Constitution of Society.* Berkeley: University of California Press.

———. (1985b). *The Nation-State and Violence.* Berkeley: University of California Press.

———. (1990). *The Consequences of Modernity.* Cambridge, England: Polity Press.

———. (1991). *Modernity and Self-Identity.* Cambridge, England: Polity Press.

———. (1992). *The Transformation of Intimacy: Sexuality, Love, and Eroticism in Modern Societies.* Stanford: Stanford University Press.

Giele, Janet Z. (1980). "Adulthood as Transcendence of Age and Sex." In Neil J. Smelser and Erik H. Anderson (eds.), *Themes of Work and Love in Adulthood,* pp. 151-173. Cambridge: Harvard University Press.

———. (1988). "Gender and Sex Roles." In Neil J. Smelser, *Handbook of Sociology.* Newbury Park, CA: Sage.

Gifford, Bernard R. (1989). *Test Policy and Test Performance: Education, Language, and Culture.* Boston: Kluwer Academic.

Gilbertson, Greta A., and Douglas T. Gurak. (1993). "Broadening the Enclave Debate: The Labor Market Experiences of Dominican and Colombian Men in New York City," *Sociological Forum* 8 (June): 205-220.

Gilder, George. (1989). *Microcosm: The Quantum Revolution in Economics and Technology.* New York: Simon & Schuster.

———. (1992). *Life After Television.* New York: Norton.

Gilderbloom, John, and Richard P. Appelbaum. (1988). *Rethinking Rental Housing.* Philadelphia: Temple University Press.

Gill, Richard T., and T. Grandon Gill. (1994). "A Parental Bill of Rights," *Family Affairs* (winter). New York: Institute for American Values.

Gilliam, Angela. (1991). "Women's Equality and National Liberation." In Chandra Talpade Mohanty, Ann Russo, and Lourdes Torres, *Third World Women and the Politics of Feminism.* Bloomington: Indiana University Press.

Gilligan, Carol. (1982). *In a Different Voice: Psychological Theory and Women's Development.* Cambridge: Harvard University Press.

Gilligan, Carol, Janie V. Ward, and Jill M. Taylor (eds.). (1989). *Mapping the Moral Domain: A Contribution of Women's Thinking to Psychological Theory and Education.* Cambridge: Harvard University Press.

Gillmor, Dan, and Stephen Doig. (1992). "Segregation Forever?" *American Demographics* (January): 48-51.

Gimbutas, Marija. (1982). *The Goddesses and Gods of Old Europe, 6500-3500 B.C.: Myths and Cultural Images.* Berkeley: University of California Press.

———. (1989). *The Language of the Goddess.* New York: HarperCollins.

Gitlin, Todd. (1980). *The Whole World Is Watching: Mass Media in the Making and Unmaking of the New Left.* Berkeley: University of California Press.

———. (1983). *Inside Prime Time.* New York: Pantheon.

Gittens, Jean. (1981). *The Diggers from China: The Story of Chinese on the Goldfields.* New York: Quartet.

Glascock, A. P., and S. L. Feinman. (1981). "Social Asset or Social Burden? Treatment of the Aged in Non-Industrial Societies." In C. L. Fry (ed.), *Dimensions: Aging, Culture, and Health.* South Hadley, MA: Bergin & Garvey.

Glaser, Nathan. (1992). "The Real World of Urban Education," *The Public Interest* (winter): 57-75.

Glazer, N. (1980). "Overworking the Working Women: The Double Day in a Mass Magazine." *Women's Studies International Quarterly* 3: 79-95.

Gledhill, John, Barbara Bender, and Mogens Trolla Larsen. (1988). *State and Society: The Emergence and Development of Social Hierarchy and Political Centralization.* London: Unwin Hyman.

Glen, Robert. (1984a). *Urban Workers in the Early Industrial Revolution.* London: Croom-Helm.

———. (1984b). *Urban Workers in the Industrial Revolution.* New York: St. Martin's Press.

Glick, P. (1984). "Frequency, Duration, and Probability of Marriage and Divorce," *Journal of Marriage and the Family* 3 (May): 330-314.

Glock, Charles Y. (1976). "On the Origin and Evolution of Religious Groups." In Charles Y. Glock and Robert N. Bellah (eds.), *The New Religious Consciousness.* Berkeley: University of California Press.

Glock, Charles Y., and Robert N. Bellah (eds.). (1976). *The New Religious Consciousness.* Berkeley: University of California Press.

Glueck, Sheldon, and Eleanor Glueck. (1950). *Unraveling Juvenile Delinquency.* New York: Commonwealth Fund.

———. (1956). *Physique and Delinquency.* New York: Harper & Row.

Goetz, Ralf. (1979). *Understanding Neighborhood Change.* New York: Ballinger.

Goffman, Erving. (1961). *Asylums: Essays on the Situation of Mental Patients and Other Inmates.* Garden City, NY: Anchor.

———. (1963). *Behavior in Public Places.* New York: Free Press.

———. (1967). *Interaction Ritual: Essays on Face to Face Behavior.* Garden City, NY: Anchor.

———. (1972). *Relations in Public: Microstudies of the Public Order.* New York: Harper & Row.

———. (1973). *The Presentation of Self in Everyday Life.* New York: Doubleday.

Gold, T. (1986). *State and Society in the Taiwan Miracle.* Armonk, NY: M. E. Sharpe.

Goldberg, D., and J. Rayner. (1987). *The Jewish People.*

Goldberg, George A. (1983). *The Health Insurance Experiment's Guidelines for Abstracting Health Services Rendered By Group Health Cooperative of Puget Sound.* Santa Monica: Rand Corporation. Prepared for the U.S. Department of Health and Human Services.

Goldberg, Philip. (1968). "Are Women Prejudiced Against Women?" *Trans-Action* 5 (5): 28-30.

Goldfield, Michael. (1987). *The Decline of Organized Labor in the United States.* Chicago: University of Chicago Press.

Golding, Peter, Graham Murdock, and Philip Schlesinger (eds.). (1986). *Communications and the Political Process.* New York: Holmes & Meier.

Goldscheider, Frances K. (1990). "The Aging of the Gender Revolution: What Do We Know and What Do We Need to Know?" *Research on Aging* 12 (December): 531-545.

Goldschneider, Frances K. and Linda Waite. (1992). *New Families. No Families? The Transformation of the American Home.* Berkeley: University of California Press.

Goldstein, J. (1989). "CFIDS Is Not Depression," *CFIDS Journal* (January-February): 17-20.

Goll, Sally D. (1994). "New Crops's Star Reports Growing Pan-Asia Audience," *Wall Street Journal* (January 14): B6B.

Gonzales, Paul. (1992). "Being Gay and Lesbian," *Los Angeles Times* (December 1): H-6.

Goodman, Susan. (1990). "Agony Without Ecstasy: Alcohol and Violence," *Current Health* 2 (September): 28-29.

Gordon, Gil E., and David L. Peterson. (1992). "Telecommuting: Appropriate for the Asian Setting of the 1990s?" Paper presented at CommunicAsia '92 Conference in Singapore (June 4).

Gore, Albert. (1993). *Earth in the Balance: Ecology and the Human Spirit.* New York: Penguin Plume.

Goring, Charles. (1972; orig. 1913). *The English Convict: A Statistical Study.* Fairlawn, NJ: Patterson Smith.

Gottdiener, Mark (1994). *The New Urban Sociology.* New York: McGraw-Hill.

Gottfredson, Linda S. (1984). "The Role of Intelligence and Education in the Division of Labor," *Report No. 355,* Washington: National Institute of Education.

Gottfredson, Michael R., and Travis Hirschi. (1990). *A General Theory of Crime.* Stanford: Stanford University Press.

Gould, Roger L. (1975). "Adult Life States: Growth Toward Self-Tolerance," *Psychology Today* 8: 74-78.

———. (1978). *Transformations: Growth and Change in Adult Life.* New York: Simon & Schuster.

———. (1980). "Transformations During Early and Middle Adult Years." In Neil J. Smelser and Erik H. Erikson (eds.), *Themes of Work and Love in Adulthood,* pp. 151-173. Cambridge: Harvard University Press.

Graber, D. (1988). *Processing the News* (2nd ed.). New York: Longmans.

Gracey, Harry L. (1993). "Kindergarten as Bootcamp." In James Henslin (ed.), *Down to Earth Sociology.* New York: Free Press.

Granovetter, Mark. (1973). "The Strength of Weak Ties," *American Journal of Sociology* 78 (May): 1360-1380.

———. (1985). "Economic Action and Social Structure: The Problem of Embeddedness." *American Journal of Sociology* 91 (November): 481-510.

Granovetter, Mark, and Charles Tilly. (1988). "Inequality and Labor Processes." In Neil J. Smelser (ed.), *Handbook of Sociology.* Newbury Park, CA: Sage.

Grant, Linda. (1983). "Gender Role and Status in School Children's Peer Interactions," *Western Sociological Review* 14(1): 58-76.

Gray, F. D. (1989). *Soviet Women: Walking the Tightrope.* New York: Doubleday.

Gray, Herman. (1986a). "Racial Inequality as News and Ideology." Paper presented at the annual meeting of the American Sociological Association.

———. (1986b). "Television and the New Black Man: Black Male Images in Prime-Time Situation Comedy," *Media, Culture, and Society* 8: 223-242.

———. (1989). "Television, Black Americans, and the American Dream," *Critical Studies in Mass Communication* 6 (December): 376-386.

Green, F. (1987). *The "Sissy Boy" Syndrome and the Development of Homosexuality.* New Haven: Yale University Press.

Green, Mark, and Mark Pinsky. (1989). *America's Transition: Blueprint for the 1990s.* New York: Democracy Project.

Green, R. (1974). *Sexual Identity Conflict in Children and Adults.* New York: Basic Books.

Greenberg, Jan S., and Marion Becker. (1988). "Aging Parents as Family Resources," *The Gerontologist* 28 (6): 786-791.

Greif, Esther. (1980). "Sex Differences in Parent-Child Conversations," *Woman's Studies International Quarterly* 3 (23): 253-258.

Grenier, Guillermo, Doug Kincaid, Abe Lavender, Anthony Maingot, Betty Morrow, Alejandro Portes, Walt Peacock, Lisandro Perez, and Alex Stepick. (1993). "Black Miami: Searching for a Voice," *Footnotes* (May): 1-9.

Griffin, Susan. (1978). *Woman and Nature: The Roaring Within Her.* New York: Harper & Row.

———. (1979). *Rape, the Power of Consciousness*. New York: Harper & Row.

———. (1981). *Pornography as Silence: Culture's Revenge Against Nature*. New York: Harper & Row.

Grindstaff, Laura. (1992). "Abortion and Media Discourse: Mapping the Narrative Construction of 'Rights,' 'Life,' and 'Choice' in the Popular Press. Unpublished paper, University of California, Santa Barbara.

Grossberg, L. (1987). "The Indifference of Television," *Screen* 28: 29-45.

Grover, Ronald, and Amy Barrett. (1992). "Guess Who Isn't Buying American," *Business Week* (November 2): 26-27.

Gruber, J. E., and L. Bjorn. (1982). "Blue-Collar Blues: The Sexual Harassment of Women Autoworkers," *Work and Occupations* 9: 271-298.

Grunwald, Joseph, and Kenneth Flamm. (1985). *The Global Factory: Foreign Assembly in International Trade*. Washington: Brookings Institution.

Guidubaldi, J., J. D. Perry, and B. K. Nastasi. (1987). "Growing Up in a Divorced Family: Initial and Long-Term Perspectives on Children's Adjustment." In S. Oskamp (ed.), *Family Process and Problems: Social Psychological Aspects*, pp. 202-237. Beverley Hills, CA: Sage.

Gunsch, Dawn. (1993). "Benefits Program Helps Retain Frontline Workers," *Personnel Journal* 72 (February): 88-89.

Gurney, J. N., and K. T. Tierney. (1982). "Relative Deprivation and Social Movements: A Critical Look at Twenty years of Theory and Research," *Sociological Quarterly* 23: 33-47.

Gurr, Ted. (1970). *Why Men Rebel*. Princeton: Princeton University Press.

Gusfield, Joseph R. (1986). *Symbolic Crusade: Status Politics and the American Temperance Movement*. Urbana: University of Illinois Press.

Haber, C. (1983). *Beyond 65: The Dialemma of Old Age in America's Past*. New York: Cambridge University Press.

Habermas, Jurgen. (1981). "New Social Movements," *Telos* 49: 33-37.

———. (1976). *Legitimation Crisis*. London: Heinemann.

———. (1979). "Legitimation Problems in the Modern State." In Jurgen Habermas, *Communication and the Evolution of Society*. London: Heinemann.

Hacker, Andrew. (1992). *Two Nations: Black and White, Separate, Hostile, Unequal*. New York: Ballantine.

Haddad, Yvonne Y. (1979). "The Muslim Experience in the United States," *The Link* 12 (September/October): 3.

Hadden, Jeffrey. (1990). "Precursors to the Globalization of American Televangelism," *Social Compass* 37 (March): 161-167.

Hadden, Jeffrey, and Anson Shupe. (1987). "Televangelism in America," *Social Compass* 34 (1): 61-75.

Hadden, Jeffrey, and Charles Swann. (1981). *Prime-Time Preachers: The Rising Tide of Televangelism*. Reading, MA: Addison-Wesley.

Hagen, Everett E. (1962). *On the Theory of Social Change: How Economic Growth Begins*. Homewood, IL: Dorsey.

———. (1986). *The Economics of Development*. Homewood, IL: Dorsey.

Haggard, S., and T. J. Cheng. (1987). "State and Foreign Capital in the East Asian NIC'S." In F. C. Deyo (ed.), *The Political Economy of the New Asian Industrialism*. Ithaca: Cornell University Press.

Haggerty, R. A. (ed.). (1991). *Dominican Republic and Haiti: Country Studies* (2nd ed.). Federal Research Division, Library of Congress.

Hahn, Roland, and C. Wellems. (1989). *High-Tech Firms in the Baltimore Washington Cooridor: Growth Factors, Spatial Patterns, and Regional Development*. Baltimore: Johns Hopkins University Institute for Policy Studies.

Haines, Herbert H. (1984). "Black Radicalization and the Funding of Civil Rights: 1957-1970," *Social Problems* 32: 31-43.

Haley, Alex. (1965). *The Autobiography of Malcolm X*. New York: Ballantine.

———. (1967). *The Autobiography of Malcolm X*. New York: Grove.

Hall, Charles W. (1993). "Lawyer Gets Five Years for Bilking Elderly," *Washington Post* (October 23): B-5.

Hall, Edward T. (1973). *The Silent Language*. New York: Doubleday.

Hall, Stuart. (1973a). "A World at One with Itself." In Stanley Cohen and Jock Young (eds.), *The Manufacture of News*. Beverley Hills, CA: Sage.

———. (1973b). "The Determiniation of News Photographs." In Stanley Cohen and Jock Young (eds). *The Manufacture of News*. Beverley Hills, CA: Sage.

———. (1975). "Introduction." In A. C. Smith, Elizabeth Immirzi, and Trevor Blackwell, *Paper Voices: The Popular Press and Social Change 1935-1965*. London: Chatto & Windus.

———. (1980; orig. 1974). "Encoding/Decoding." In Stuart Hall, D. Hobson, A. Lowe, and Paul Willis (eds.), *Culture, Media, and Language*. London: Hutchison.

———. (1982). "The Rediscovery of Ideology: The Return of the Repressed in Media Studies," In Michael Gurevitch, Tony Bennett, James Curran and Janet Woolacott (eds.), *Culture, Society, and the Media*. London: Methuen.

Hall, Stuart, Chas Critcher, Tony Jefferson, John Clarke, and Brian Roberts. (1978). *Policing the Crisis*. New York: Holmes & Meier.

Hallin, D. (1987). "Hegemony: The American News Media From Vietnam to El Salvador." In D. Paletz (ed.), *Communication Research*, pp. 3-25. Norwood, NJ: Ablex.

Hamilton, Gary G., and Kao Cheng-shu. (1990). "The Insitutional Foundations of Chinese Business: The Family Firm in Taiwan," *Comparative Social Research* 12: 95-112.

Hamilton, Joan O. (1992). "Virtual Reality: How a Computer-Generated World Could Change the Real World," *Business Week* (October 5): 96-105.

Hamilton, Malcolm, and Maria Hiszowicz. (1987). *Class and Inequality in Preindustrial, Capitalist, and Communist Societies,* Brighton, Sussex: Wheatsheaf.

Hamm, Mark S. (1993). *American Skinheads: The Criminology and Control of Hate Crimes.* Westport, CT: Praeger.

Hammerle, Nancy. (1992). *Private Choices and Public Policy.* Westport, CT: Praeger.

Hammond, Allen L. (ed.). (1990). *World Resources 1990-1991.* Washington: World Resources Institute.

Hammond, Phillip E. (1986). "The Extravasion of the Sacred and the Crisis in Liberal Protestantism." In Robert Michaelson and W. Clark Roof (eds.), *Liberal Protestantism: Realities and Prospects.* New York: Pilgrim.

———. (1992). *Religion and Personal Autonomy: The Third Disestablishment in America.* Columbia: University of South Carolina Press.

Hammond, Phillip E., and James Davison Hunter. (1984). "On Maintaining Plausibility: The Worldview of Evangelical College Students," *Journal for the Scientific Study of Religion* 23: 221-239.

Handlin, Oscar. (1968). *Boston's Immigrants: A Study in Acculturation.* New York: Athaneum.

Handy, Robert. (1984). *A Christian America* (2nd ed.). New York: Oxford University Press.

Hannerz, Ulf. (1969). *Soulside: Inquiries into Getto Culture and Community.* New York: Columbia University Press.

Hansen, Chad. (1992). "Confucianism." *In American Academic Encyclopedia* (on-line edition). Danbury, CT: Grolier Electronic Publishing.

Hansen, Lee O. (1988). "The Political and Socioeconomic Context of Legal and Illegal Mexican Migration to the United States (1942-1984)." *International Migration* 26 (March): 95-107.

Hardesty, S., and N. Jacobs. (1986). *Success and Betrayal: The Crisis of Women in Corporate America.* New York: Franklin Watts.

Hardey, Michael, and Graham Crow (eds.). (1991). *Lone Parenthood: Coping with the Constraints and Making Opportunities in Single-Parent Families.* Toronto: University of Toronto Press.

Hardy, B. Carmon. (1992). *Solemn Covenant: The Mormon Polygamous Passage.* Urbana: University of Illinois Press.

Hare, A. Paul, et al. (1965). *Small Groups: Studies in Social Interaction.* New York: Knopf.

Hareven, Tamara K. (1982). "The Life Course and Aging in Historical Perspective." In Tamara K. Hareven and K. J. Adams (eds.), *Aging and Life Course Transitions: An Interdisciplinary Perspective,* pp. 1-26. New York: Guilford.

Harjo, Suzan Shown. (1993). "The American Indian Experience." In Hariette Pipes McAdoo (ed.), *Family and Ethnicity: Strength in Diversity.* Newbury Park, CA: Sage.

Harlan, A., and C. Weiss. (1981). "Moving Up: Women in Managerial Careers," working paper no. 86. Wellesley: Wellesley College Center for Research on Women.

Harpham, Edward J. (1985). "Class, Commerce, and the State: Economic Discourse and Lockean Liberalism in the Seventeenth Century," *The Western Political Quarterly* 38 (December): 565-582.

Harragan, B. L. (1977). *Games Mother Never Taught You: Corporate Gamesmanship for Women.* New York: Warner.

Harris, Marvin. (1975). *Cows, Pigs, Wars, and Riches: The Riddles of Culture.* New York: Random House.

———. (1977). *Cannibals and Kings: The Origins of Culture.* New York: Random House.

———. (1980). *Cultural Materialism: The Stuggle for a Science of Culture.* New York: Vintage.

———. (1987). *Cultural Anthropology* (2nd ed.). New York: Harper & Row.

Harris, N. (1987). *The End of the Third World: Newly Industializing Countries and the Decline of an Ideology.* Harmondsworth, England: Penguin.

Harris, Ron. (1990). "Blacks Feel Brunt of Drug War," *Los Angeles Times* (April 22): A-1.

———. (1993). "Hand of Punishment Falls Heavily on Black Youths," *Los Angeles Times* (August 24): A-1.

Harrison, Algea O. et al. (1990). "Family Ecologies of Ethnic Minority Children," *Child Development* 61: (April): 347-362.

Hartley, John. (1982). *Understanding News.* London: Methuen.

Hartman, Chester, Dennis Keating, and Richard LeGates. (1981). *Displacement: How to Fight It.* Berkeley, CA: Legal Services Anti-Displacement Project.

Hartman, Heidi. (1979). "Capitalism, Patriarchy, and Job Segregation By Sex." In Z. Eisenstein (ed.), *Capitalist Patriarchy and the Case for Socialist Feminism,* pp. 206-247. New York: Monthly Review.

———. (1981). "The Family as the Locus of Gender, Class, and Political Struggle: The Example of Housework," *Signs* 6 (3): 366-394.

———. (1984). "The Unhappy Union of Marxism and Feminism: Toward a More Progressive Union." In A. M. Jaggar and P. S. Rothenberg (eds.), *Feminist Frameworks,* pp. 172-188. New York: McGraw-Hill.

Hastings, Adrian (ed.). (1991). *Modern Catholicism: Vatican II and After.* New York: Oxford University Press.

Hatch, Nathan O. (1989). *The Democratization of American Christianity.* New Haven: Yale University Press.

Haug, Marie, and Bebe Levin. (1981). "Practitioner or Patient—Who's in Charge?" *Journal of Health and Social Behavior* 22: 212-229.

———. (1983). *Consumerism in Medicine.* Beverley Hills, CA: Sage.

Haugen, Einar. (1977). "Linguistic Relativity: Myths and Methods." In William C. McCormack and Stephen A. Wurm, *Language and Thought: Anthropological Issues,* pp. 11-28. The Hague: Mouton.

Hauser, Robert M., and David L. Featherman. (1976). *Occupation and Social Mobility in the United States.* Madison: University of Wisconsin Institute for Research on Poverty.

———. (1977). *The Process of Stratification: Trends and Analysis.* New York: Academic.

Havemann, Joel. (1992). "A Safety Net Snags on Its Costs," *Los Angeles Times* (April 21): A-1.

Havemann, Joel, and Norman Kempster. (1993). "The Case of the Disappearing Worker: What's Gone Wrong?" *Los Angeles Times* (July 6): H-1.

Havighurst, R. J. (1973). "History of Development Psychology: Socialization and Personality Development Through the Life Span." In P. B. Baltes and K. W. Schaie (eds.), *Life-Span Developmental Psychology.* New York: Academic.

Hayjenhelm, Amy. (1993). *Protecting Battered Women: The Problem the Police Avoid.* Washington: George Washington Press.

Headlee, Sue. (1991). *The Politcal Economy of the Family Farm: The Agrarian Roots of American Capitalism.* New York: Praeger.

Hebb, Donald O. (1980). *Essay on Mind.* Hillsdale, NJ: L. Erlbaum Associates.

Heberlein, T. A., and R. Baumgartner. (1978). "Factors Affecting Response Rate to Mailed Questionnaires: A Quantitative Analysis of the Published Literature," *American Sociological Review* 43: 447-462.

Hecker, Steven. (1991). *Labor in a Global Economy: Perspectives from the United States and Canada.* Oregon Books.

Heilbroner, Robert. (1990). "Reflections: After Communism," *New York Times* (September 10): 91-100.

Heise, David R. (1987). "Sociolocultural Determination of Mental Aging." In Carmi Schooler and K. Warner Schaie (eds.), *Cognitive Functioning and Social Structure Over the Life Course,* pp. 247-261. Norwood, NJ: Ablex.

Held, David. (1989). *Political Theory and the Modern State.* Stanford: Stanford University Press.

Helgesen, Sally. (1990). *The Female Advantage: Woman's Ways of Leadership.* New York: Doubleday Currency.

Helleiner, Gerald K. (1990). *The New Global Economy and the Developing Countries: Essays in International Economics and Development.* Aldershot, England: Brookfield.

Hellinger, Daniel, and Dennis R. Judd. (1991). *The Democratic Facade.* Pacific Grove, CA: Brooks/Cole Publishing.

Helm, Leslie. (1992). "Debts Put Squeeze on Japanese," *Los Angeles Times* (November 21): A-1, A-16.

Henderson, Jeffrey. (1986). "The New International Division of Labor and Urban Development in the Contemporary World System." In D. Drakakis-Smith (ed.), *Urbanization in the Developing World,* pp. 63-81. London: Croom-Helm.

———. (1989). *The Globalization of High Technology Production: Society, Space and Semiconductors in the Restructuring of the Modern World.* London: Routledge.

Henderson, Jeffrey, and Richard P. Appelbaum. (1992). "Situating the State in the Asian Development Process." In Jeffrey Henderson and Richard P. Appelbaum (eds.), *States and Development in the Asian Pacific Rim.* Newbury Park, CA: Sage.

Hendricks, Jon. (1992). "Generation and the Generation of Theory in Social Gerontology," *Aging and Human Development* 35 (1): 31-47.

Hendricks, Jon, and Laurie Russell Hatch. (1993). "Federal Policy and Family Life of Older Americans." In Jon Hendricks and Carolyn J. Rosenthal, *The Remainder of Their Days: Domestic Policy and Older Families in the United States and Canada,* pp. 49-73. New York: Garland.

Hendricks, Jon, and C. Davis Hendricks. (1986). *Aging in Mass Society: Myths and Realities.* Boston: Little, Brown.

Hendricks, Jon, and Carolyn J. Rosenthal. (1993). *The Remainder of Their Days: Domestic Policy and Older Families in the United States and Canada.* New York: Garland.

Henry, William E. (1965). *Growing Older: The Process of Disengagement.* New York: Basic Books.

Heppner, Cheryl M. (1992). *Seeds of Disquiet: One Deaf Woman's Experience.* Washington: Gallaudet University Press.

Herberg, Will. (1960). *Protestant—Catholic—Jew.* Garden City, NY: Doubleday.

Heritage, John. (1989). *Garfinkel and Ethnomethodology.* Cambridge, England: Polity.

Heritage, John, and David Greatbatch. (1991). "On the Institutional Character of Institutional Talk: The Case of News Interviews." In Don H. Zimmerman and Dierdre Boden (eds.), *Talk and Social Structure.* Cambridge, England: Polity.

Herman, E. S., and Noam Chomsky. (1988). *Manufacturing Consent.* New York: Pantheon.

Herman, J. (1980). "Children's Cognitive Maps of Large-Scale Spaces: Effects of Exploration, Direction, and Repeated Experience," *Journal of Experimental Child Psychology* 29: 126-143.

Hersey, P., and K. Blanchard. (1982). *Management of Organizational Behavior: Utilizing Human Resources.* Englewood Cliffs, NJ: Prentice-Hall.

Hersey, P., K. Blanchard, and W. Natemeyer. (1987). *Situational Leadership, Perception, and the Use of Power.* Escondido, CA: Leadership Studies.

Hertzenberg, Stephen, and Jorge F. Perez-Lopez. (1990). "Labor Standards and Development in the Global Economy." Paper delivered at the Symposium on Labor Standards and Development, Washington, December 12-13, 1988. U.S. Department of Labor, Bureau of International Labor Affairs.

Hess, B. B., and E. W. Markson (eds.). (1985). *Growing Old in America: New Perspectives on Old Age.* New Brunswick, NJ: Transition Books.

Hess, Darrel. (1990). "Korean Immigrant Entrepreneurs in the Los Angeles Garment Industry." Los Angeles: University of California, Los Angeles, Department of Geography.

Hess, Henner. (1973). *Mafia and Mafiosi: The Structure of Power.* Lexington, MA: Lexington Books.

Hess, John L. (1990). "The Catastrophic Health Care Fiasco," *The Nation* 250 (May 21): 698-702.

Hetherington, E. Mavis, and Josephine D. Arasteh (eds.). (1988). *Impact of Divorce, Single Parenting, and Stepparenting on Children.* Hillsdale, NJ: L. Erlbaum.

Hetherington, E. Mavis, W. Glenn Clingempeel, in collaboration with Edward R. Anderson, et al. (1992). *Coping with Marital Transitions.* Chicago: University of Chicago Press, for the Society for Research in Child Development.

Heusmann, L. R. (1986). "Psychological Processes Promoting the Relation Between Exposure to Media Violence and Aggressive Behavior by the Viewer," *Journal of Social Issues* 42 (3): 125-140.

Heyzer, N. (1986). *Working Women in Southeast Asia.* Milton Keynes: Britain: Open University Press.

Hiatt, Fred. (1992). "In Moskow, It's Bye-Bye Bolshevik Lane," *Washington Post* (April 12): B-1.

Higgins, P.J. (1985). "Women in the Islamic Republic of Iran: Legal, Social, and Ideological Changes," *Signs* 10: 477-494.

Highlander Folk School. (1985). *You've Got to Move* (video). New Market, TN.

Hill, Richard Child. (1974). "The Coming of Post-industrial Society," *The Insurgent Sociologist* 4 (spring): 37-51.

Hindelang, Michael. (1978). "Race and Involvement in Crimes," *American Sociological Review* 43: 93-109.

Hinkle, Roscoe, and Gisela Hinkle. (1954). *The Development of American Sociology.* New York: Random House.

Hinsley, F.H. (1986). *Sovereignty* (2nd ed.). Cambridge, England: Cambridge University Press.

Hirschi, Travis. (1969). *Causes of Delinquency.* Berkeley: University of California Press.

Ho, Christine G. T. (1993). "The Internationalization of Kinship and the Feminization of Caribbean Migration: The Case of Afro-Trinidadian Immigrants in Los Angeles," *Human Organization* 52 (spring): 32-40.

Ho, S. Y. (1990). *Taiwan: After a Long Silence.* Hong Kong: Asia Monitor Resource Center.

Hobsbawn. E. J. (1959). *Primitive Rebels.* New York: Norton.

Hobson, D. (1980). "Housewives and the Mass Media." In Stuart Hall, D. Hobson, A. Lower, and Paul Willis, *Culture, Media, Language,* pp. 105-114. London: Hutchison.

Hochschild, Arlie Russell. (1975). "Disengagement Theory: A Critique and Proposal," *American Sociological Review* 40: 553-569.

———. (1978). *The Unexpected Community: Portrait of an Old Age Subculture* (rev.ed). Berkeley: University of California Press.

———. (1990). *The Second Shift: Working Parents and the Revolution at Home.* New York: Avon.

Hochschild, Arlie Russell, and Anne Machung. (1989). *The Second Shift: Working Parents and the Revolution at Home.* New York: Viking.

Hodges, Donald C. (1981). *The Bureaucratization of Socialism.* Amherst: University of Massachusetts Press.

Hogue, Carol J., and Martha A. Hargraves. (1993). "Class, Race, and Infant Mortality in the United States," *American Journal of Public Health* 83 (January): 9-12.

Hollander, Paul. (1978). *Soviet and American Society in Comparison.* New York: Oxford University Press.

Holloway, Jerry, and Paul Moke. (1986). "Post Secondary Correctional Education: An Evaluation of Parolee Performance." Unpublished report, Wilmington College, Wilmington, OH.

Holmes, L.D. (1983). *Other Cultures, Elder Years: An Introduction to Cultural Gerontology.* Minneapolis: Burgess.

Holstein, William J. (1992). "Little Companies, Big Exports," *Business Week* (April 13): 70-72.

Holt, J. (1994). *Demographic Aspects of Deafness: Questions and Answers* (3rd ed.). Washington: Gallaudet Research Institute, Center for Assessment and Demographic Studies.

Holt, Thomas (1977). *Black Over White: Negro Political Leadership in South Carolina During Reconstruction.* Urbana: University of Illinois Press.

Homans, George. (1950). *The Human Group.* New York: Harcourt, Brace.

Hombs, Mary Ellen, and Mitch Snyder. (1982). *Homelessness in America: A Forced March to Nowhere.* Washington: Community for Creative Non-Violence.

Homes, G. P., et al. (1988). "Chronic Fatigue Syndrome: A Working Case Definition," *Annals of Internal Medicine* 108 (March): 387-389.

Hooker, Roderick, and Donald K. Freeborn. (1991). "Use of Physician Assistants in a Managed Health Care System," *Public Health Reports* 106 (January/February): 90-94.

Hooton, Ernest Albert. (1939). *The American Criminal: An Anthropological Study.* Cambridge: Harvard University Press.

Hopkins, Terence K., and Immanual Wallerstein. (1986). "The Organization and Locational Structure of Production Subcontracting." In Allen Scott and Michael Storper (eds.), *Production, Work and Territory: The Geographical Anatomy of Industrial Capitalism.* Boston: Allen & Unwin.

Hopper, Robert. (1991). "Hold the Phone." In Don H. Zimmerman and Dierdre Boden (eds.), *Talk and Social Structure.* Cambridge, England: Polity.

Horan, Patrick M., and Peggy G. Hargis. (1991). "Children's Work and Schooling in the Late Nineteenth Century Family Economy," *American Sociological Review* 56 (5): 583-596.

Hosken, Franziska. (1993). "City." In the *American Academic Encyclopedia* (on-line edition). Danbury, CT: Grolier Electronic Publishing.

Hourani, Benjamin T. (1987). "Towards the Twenty-First Century: The Organization of Power in Postindustrial Society," *Science and Public Policy* 14 (August): 217-229.

Houston, Paul. (1993). "Huge March Seeks Gay Rights," *Los Angeles Times* (April 26): A-1.

Hout, Michael. (1988). "More Universalism, Less Structural Mobility: The American Occupational Structure in the 1980's," *American Journal of Sociology* 93 (May): 1358-1400.

Howard, John H., Peter A. Rechnitzer, David A. Cunningham, and Allan P. Donner. (1986). "Change in Type A Behavior a Year After Retirement," *The Gerontologist* 26: 643-649.

Howe, Neil, and William Strauss. (1991). *Generations : The History of America's Future, 1584-2069.* New York: William Morrow.

Hubler, Shawn, and Stuart Silverstein. (1992). "Women's Pay in State Lags 31 Percent Behind Men's," *Los Angeles Times* (December 29): A-1.

Hudson, J. (1978). "Physical Parameters Used for Female Exclusion from Law Enforcement and Athletics." In C.A. Oglesby (ed.), *Women and Sport: From Myth to Reality.* Philadelphia: Lea & Febiger.

Hunt, V. Daniel. (1990). *Understanding Robotics.* San Diego: Academic Press.

Hunter, James Davison. (1985). "Conservative Protestantism." In Phillip E. Hammond (ed.), *The Sacred in a Secular Age.* Berkeley: University of California Press.

———. (1987). *Evangelism: The Coming Generation.* Chicago: University of Chicago Press.

Hurh, Won Moo, and Kwang Chung Kim. (1984). *Korean Immigrants in America: A Structural Analysis of Ethnic Confinement and Adhesive Adaptation.* Rutherford NJ: Fairleigh Dickinson University Press.

Hurn, Christopher J. (1985). *The Limits and Possibilities of Schooling: An Introduction to the Sociology of Education.* Boston: Allyn & Bacon.

Huston, A. C. et al. (1992). *Big World, Small Screen: The Role of Television in American Society.* Lincoln: University of Nebraska Press.

Hyde, Janet Shibley. (1984). "How Large Are Gender Differences in Aggression? A Developmental Meta-analysis," *Developmental Psychology* 20: 722-736.

Hyde, Janet Shibley, E. Fennema, M. Ryan, L.A. Frost, and C. Hopp. (1990). "Gender Comparisons of Mathematics Attitudes and Affect: A Meta-analysis," *Psychology of Women Quarterly* 14: 299-324.

Hyman, Herbert H. (1942). "The Psychology of Status," *Archives of Psychology* 38: 15.

Hyman, Herbert H., and Eleanor Singer. (1968). *Readings in Reference Group Theory and Research.* New York: Free Press.

Hymowitz, C., and T. D. Schellhardt. (1986). "The Glass Ceiling: Why Women Can't Seem to Break the Invisible Barrier," *Wall Street Journal* (March 24): D 1,4,5.

Ibbetson, David. (1984). "Sixteenth Century Contract Law: Slade's Case in Context," *Oxford Journal of Legal Studies* 4 (winter): 295-317.

Imperato-McGinley, H., R. Peterson, T. Bautier, and E. Sturla. (1979). "Androgens and the Evolution of Male-Gender Identity Among Male Pseudohermaphrodite with 5-Alpha Sign-Reductase Deficiency," *New England Journal of Medicine* 300: 1233-1237.

Inciardi, James A. (1992). *The War on Drugs II.* Mountain View, CA: Mayfield.

Inkster, Ian. (1991). *Science and Technology in History: An Approach to Industrial Development.* New Brunswick, NJ: Rutgers University Press.

International Labor Organization. (1993). *Condition of Work Digest: Preventing Stress at Work.* New York.

International Lesbian and Gay Association. (1992). "Being Gay and Lesbian: The Legal and Social Situation of Lesbians and Gay Men—A Country by Country Survey," *Los Angeles Times* (December 1): H-6.

Irwin, Don. (1988). "Women's Status: Sweden Put First, Bangladesh Last," *Los Angeles Times* (June 27): A-1.

Issel, William. (1985). *Social Change in the United States: 1945-1983.* New York: Schocken.

Iverson, M. M., and K. H. Freese. (1990). "CFIDS and AIDS: Facing Facts," *CFIDS Chronicle* (spring-summer): 37-43.

Iyengar, S. (1991). *Is Anyone Responsible? How Television Frames Political Issues.* Chicago: University of Chicago Press.

Jacklin, C., H. Dipietro, and E. Maccoby. (1984)."Sex-typing Behavior and Sex-typing Pressure in Child-Parent Interaction," *Archives of Sexual Behavior* 13: 413-425.

Jackson, Bruce. (1972). *In the Life: Versions of the Criminal Experience.* New York: New American Library.

Jackson, Donald Dale. (1991). "Behave Like Your Actions Reflect on All Chinese," *Smithsonian* 21 (February): 115-125.

Jackson, Kenneth T. (1985). *Crabgrass Frontier: The Suburbanization of America.* New York: Oxford University Press.

Jackson, P. G. (1985). "On Living Together Unmarried." In J. M. Henslin, *Marriage and Family in a Changing Society* (2nd ed.). New York: Free Press.

Jackson, Philip W. (1968). *Life in the Classrooms.* New York: Holt.

Jacobs, Jane. (1970). *The Economy of Cities.* New York: Vintage.

Jacobs, Jerry. (1989). *Revolving Doors: Sex Segregation and Women's Careers.* Stanford: Stanford University Press.

Jacobson, Harold K. (1984). *Networks of Interdependence: International Organizations and the Global Political System* (2nd ed). New York: Knopf.

Jacobson, John W., Sara N. Burchard, and Paul J. Carling (eds.). (1992). *Community Living for People with Developmental and Psychiatric Disabilities.* Baltimore: Johns Hopkins University Press.

Jacoby, Henry. (1963). *The Bureaucratization of the World.* Berkeley: University of California Press.

Janis, Irving L. (1972). *Victims of Groupthink.* Boston: Houghton-Mifflin.

————. (1989). *Crucial Decisions: Leadership in Policy-Making and Crisis Management.* New York: Free Press.

Janis, Irving L., and Leon Mann. (1977). *Decision-Making: A Psychological Analysis of Conflict, Choice, and Commitment.* New York: Free Press.

Janken, Kenneth Robert. (1993). *Rayford W. Logan and the Dilemma of the African-American Intellectual.* Amherst: University of Massachusetts Press.

Jankowski, Martin Sanchez. (1991). *Islands in the Street: Gangs and American Urban Society.* Berkeley: University of California Press.

Jeffres, Leo W., and K. Kyoon Hur. (1979). "White Ethnics and Their Media Images," *Journal of Communication* 29 (winter): 116-122.

Jeffrey, C. Ray. (1956). "The Development of Crime in Early English Society," *Journal of Criminal Law, Criminology, and Police Science* 47: 647-666.

Jencks, Christopher, et al. (1972). *Inequality: A Reassessment of the Effects of Family and Schooling in America.* New York: Basic Books.

————. (1973). *Inequality: A Reassessment of the Effects of Family and Schooling in America.* New York: Harper & Row.

————. (1979). *Who Gets Ahead? The Determinants of Economic Success in America.* New York: Basic Books.

Jenkins, Craig J. (1983). "Resource Mobilization Theory and the Study of Social Movements," *Annual Review of Sociology:* 527-553.

Jenkins, Craig, J., and Craig M. Eckert. (1986). "Channeling Black Insurgency: Elite Patronage and Professional Social Movement Organizations in the Development of the Black Movement," *American Sociological Review* 51 (December): 812-829.

Jenkins, Craig J., and Charles Perrow. (1977). "Insurgency of the Powerless: Farm Workers' Movements (1946-1972)," *American Sociological Review* 42: 249-268.

Jhally, Sut, Justin Lewis, and Michael Morgan. (1991). "The Gulf War: A Study of the Media, Public Opinion, and Public Knowledge." Oakland, CA: Center for Studies in Communication (February).

John, M. T. (1988). *Geragogy: A Theory for Teaching the Elderly.* New York: Haworth.

Johnson, Alan Griswold. (1980). "On the Prevalence of Rape in the United States," *Signs* 6: 136-146.

Johnson, Ann Braden. (1990). *Out of Bedlam: Myths of Deinstitutionalization.* New York: Basic Books.

Johnson, Benton. (1963). "On Church and Sect," *American Sociological Review* 28: 539-549.

Johnson, Chalmers. (1982). *MITI and the Japanese Miracle.* Stanford: Stanford University Press.

————. (1987). "Political Institutions and Economic Performance: The Government-Business Relationship in Japan, South Korea, and Taiwan." In Frederic C. Deyo (ed.), *The Political Economy of the New Asian Industrialism.* Ithaca, NY: Cornell University Press.

Johnson, G. (1939). "Personality in a White-Indian-Negro Community," *American Sociological Review* (August): 516-523.

Johnson-Odim, Cheryl. (1989). "Common Themes, Different Contexts: Third World Women and Feminism," In Chandra Talpade Mohanty, Ann Russo, and Lourdes Torres (eds.), *Third World Women and the Politics of Feminism.* Bloomington: Indiana University Press.

Johnston, Lloyd, Patrick O'Malley, and Gerald G. Bachman. (1992). *National Trends in Drug Use and Related Factors Among American High School Students and Young Adults 1975-1992.* Washington: Government Printing Office.

Jolly, Clifford. (1993). "Prehistoric Humans." In the *American Academic Encyclopedia* (on-line edition). Danbury, CT: Grolier Electronic Publishing.

Jones, David P. H. (1987). "The Untreatable Family," *Child Abuse and Neglect* 11 (3): 409-420.

————. (1991). "Ritualism and Child Sexual Abuse," *Child Abuse and Neglect* 15 (3): 163-170.

Jones, Gareth Stedman. (1991). "The Changing Face of 19th Century Britain," *History Today* 41 (5): 36-40.

Jones, James. (1989). "The Tuskegee Syphilis Experiment." In Phil Brown (ed.), *Experiments in Medical Sociology,* pp. 538-549.

Belmont, CA: Wadsworth.

Jones, Tamara. (1994). "Disturbed, Homeless and on the Edge," *Washington Post* (January 4): D-1.

Jordan, June. (1990). "Nobody Mean More to Me Than You and the Future Life of Willie Jordan." In Pat C. Hoy, II, Esther H. Schor, and Robert DiYanni (eds.), *Women's Voices: Visions and Perspectives.* New York: McGraw-Hill.

Jordan, Mary. (1992a). "Big-City Schools Became More Segregated During the 1980s, Study Says," *Washington Post* (January 9): A-3.

———. (1992b). "Where Available School Choice Is Embraced by Few," *Washington Post* (October 26): A-4.

Jordan, W. J. (1978). "Searching for Adulthood in America." In Erik H. Erikson (ed.), *Adulthood,* pp. 189-200. New York: Norton.

Journal of the American Medical Association (JAMA). (1903). 40 (May 2): 1238.

Jowett, Garth, and James M. Linton. (1990). *Movies as Mass Communication* (2nd ed.). London: Sage.

Judkins, David, Joseph Waksberg, and James Massey. (1992). "Patterns of Residential Concentration by Race and Hispanic Origin." Unpublished manuscript.

Juergensmeyer, Mark. (1993). *The New Cold War? Religious Nationalism Confronts the Secular State.* Berkeley: University of California Press.

——— (ed.). (1991). *Teaching the Introductory Course in Religious Studies: A Sourcebook.* Atlanta: Scholars Press.

Kahn, Herman. (1978). *On Thermonuclear War.* Westport, CT: Greenwood.

Kahn, Kim Fridkin, and Edie N. Goldenberg. (1991). "Women Candidates in the News: An Examination of Gender Differences in U.S. Senate Campaign Coverage," *Public Opinion Quarterly* 55 (summer): 180-199.

Kahn, Timothy J., and Heather J. Chambers. (1991). "Assessing Reoffense Risk with Juvenile Sexual Offenders," *Child Welfare League of America* (May-June): 333-345.

Kammerer, Dianne Anderson. (1992). "United States Anti-trust Law and the Control of Nurse-Midwifery." Ph.D. diss., George Washington University.

Kandal, Terry R. (1988). *The Woman in Classical Sociological Theory.* Miami: Florida International University Press.

Kanter, Rosabeth Moss. (1972). *Commitment and Community: Communes and Utopias in Sociological Perspective.* Cambridge: Harvard University Press.

———. (1977). *Men and Women of the Corporation.* New York: Basic Books.

———. (1982). "The Impact of Hierarchical Structures on the Work Behavior of Women and Men." In Rachel Kahn-Hut, Arlene Kaplan Daniels, and Richard Colvard (eds.), *Women and Work: Problems and Perspectives.* New York: Oxford University Press.

———. (1983). *The Change Masters: Innovation for Productivity in the American Corporation.* New York: Simon & Schuster.

Kaplan, E. A. (1983). *Regarding Television.* Los Angeles: American Film Institute Monograph Series/University Publications of America.

Karp, Walter. (1989). "All the Congressmen's Men," *Harper's* (July): 55-63.

Kasarda, John. (1989). "Urban Industrial Transition and the Underclass," *Annals of the Academy of Political and Social Science* 501 (January): 26-47.

———. (1990). "City Jobs and Residents on a Collision Course: The Urban Underclass Dilemma," *Economic Development Quarterly* 4 (November).

———. (1993). "Urban Industrial Transition and the Underclass." In William Julius Wilson (ed.), *The Ghetto Underclass.* Newbury Park, CA: Sage.

Katz, Elihu. (1990). *Viewers' Work.* Wilbur Schram Memorial Lecture, University of Illinois.

Katz, Elihu, and Paul F. Lazarsfeld. (1955). *Personal Influence: The Part Played by People in the Flow of Mass Communications.* Glencoe, IL: Free Press.

Katz, Phyllis A. (1986). "Gender Inequality: Gender and Consequences." In Richard D. Ashmore and Frances K. Del Boca (eds.), *The Social Psychology of Female-Male Relations,* pp.30-37. Orlando, FL: Academic Press.

Kaufman, Julie E., and James Rosenbaum, (1991). "The Education and Employment of Low-Income Black Youth in White Suburbs." Center for Urban Affairs and Policy Research Working Paper #WP-91-20 (spring). Evanston, IL.

Kay, N. M. (1984). *The Emergent Firm: Knowledge, Ignorance, and Surprise in Economic Organization.* London: Macmillan.

Kearney, Hugh. (1971). *Science and Change, 1500-1700.* New York: McGraw-Hill.

Keddie, Nikki (ed.). (1983). *Religion and Politics in Iran: Shi'ism from Quietism to Revolution.* New Haven: Yale University Press.

Kedouri, Elie. (1992). *Politics in the Middle East.* New York: Oxford University Press.

Keegan, John. (1993). *A History of Warfare.* New York: Knopf.

Kegan, Robert (1982). *The Evolving Self: Problem and Process in Human Development.* Cambridge: Harvard University Press.

Keil, Julian E., et al. (1993). "Mortality Rates and Risk Factors for Coronary Disease in Black as Compared with White Men and Women," *New England Journal of Medicine* 329 (July 8): 73-78.

Keller, Robert, and Edward Sbarbaro. (1994). *Prisons in Crisis.* Albany: Harrow & Heston.

Kelley, Dean M. (1972). *Why Conservative Churches Are Growing.* New York: Harper & Row.

Kelly, Liz. (1987)."The Continuum of Sexual Violence." In Jalna Hanmer and Mary Maynard (eds.), *Women, Violence, and Social Control.* Atlantic Highlands, NJ: Humanities Press.

Kemp, Tom. (1978). *Historical Patterns of Industrialization.* London: Longman.

Kennedy, Paul. (1987). *The Rise and Fall of the Great Powers: Economic Change and Military Conflict from 1500 to 2000.* New York: Random House.

———. (1993). "The American Prospect," *New York Review of Books* XL (March 4): 42-53.

Kent, Joan R. (1986). *The English Village Constable, 1580-1642: A Social Administrative Study.* Oxford, England: Clarendon Press.

Kessler, Suzanne J., and Wendy McKenna. (1985). *Gender: An Ethnomethodological Approach.* Chicago: University of Chicago Press.

Keyfitz, Nathan. (1990). *World Population Growth and Aging: Demographic Trends in the Late Twentieth Century.* Chicago: University of Chicago Press.

———. (1993). "Demography." In the *American Academic Encyclopedia* (on-line edition). Danbury, CT: Grolier Electronic Publishing.

Kiecolt, K. Jill, and Hart M. Nelson. (1991). "Evangelicals and Party Realignment, 1976-1988," *Social Science Quarterly* 72 (September): 552-569.

Kiken, Joyce. (1992). "The Research Bureaucracy, AIDS, and CFS." Ph.D. diss., The Fielding Institute, Santa Barbara, CA.

Kim, Kwang Chung, and Won Moo Hurh. (1988). "The Burden of Double Roles: Korean Wives in the U.S.A.," *Ethnic and Racial Studies* 11: 151-167.

King, Anthony. (1990). *Global Cities: Post-Imperialism and the Internationalization of London.* London: Routledge.

King, Dennis. (1989). *Lyndon LaRouche and the New American Fascism.* New York: Doubleday.

King, Harry, and William J. Chambliss. (1984a). *Harry King: A Professional Thief's Journey.* New York: Wiley.

King, Harry, and William J. Chambliss. (1984b). *Harry King: A Professional Thief's Journey.* New York: Macmillan.

King, Nancy R. (1984). "Exploitation and Abuse of Older Family Members: An Overview of the Problem." In J. J. Cosa (ed.), *Abuse of the Elderly,* pp. 3-12. Lexington, MA: Lexington Books.

Kinsey, Alfred C., et al. (1948). *Sexual Behavior in the Human Male.* Philadelphia: W. B. Saunders.

———. (1953). *Sexual Behavior in the Human Female.* Philadelphia: W. B. Saunders.

Kinsley, David. (1982). *Hinduism, a Cultural Perspective.* Englewood Cliffs, NJ: Prentice-Hall.

Kirtzman, Andrew. (1992). "Lessons in Hate: Routine Course of Violence for Gay HS Students," *Daily News* (May).

Kisor, Henry. (1990). *What's That Pig Outdoors? A Memoir of Deafness.* New York: Hill & Wang.

Kissinger, Henry. (1985). *Observations: Selected Speeches and Essays: 1982-1984.* Boston: Little, Brown.

Kitagawa, Joseph M., and John S. Strong. (1992). "Buddhism." In the *American Academic Encyclopedia* (on-line edition). Danbury, CT: Grolier Electronic Publishing.

Kitano, Harry H. L., and Roger Daniels. (1988). *Asian Americans: Emerging Minorities.* Englewood Cliffs, NJ: Prentice-Hall.

Kitschelt, Hebert P. (1986). "Political Opportunity Structures and Political Protest," *British Journal of Political Science* 16: 57-85.

Kitson, G. C., K. Babri, and M. Roach. (1985). "Who Divorces and Why," *Journal of Family Issues* 6 (September): 255-293.

Klandermans, Bert. (1986). "New Social Movements and Resource Mobilization: The European and the American Approach," *Journal of Mass Emergencies and Disasters* 4: 13-37.

Klapper, Joseph T. (1949). *The Effects of Mass Media.* New York: Columbia University, Bureau of Applied Social Research.

———. (1960). *The Effects of Mass Communications.* Glencoe, IL: Free Press.

Klare, Karl. (1978). "Judicial Deradicalization of the Wagner Act and the Origins of Modern Legal Consciousness, 1937-1941," *Minnesota Law Review* 62: 265-339.

Klare, Michael T. (1991). "High-Death Weapons of the Gulf War," *The Nation* (June 3).

Kleinbaum, Abby R. (1977). "Women in the City of Light." In Renate Bridenthal and Claudia King (eds.), *Becoming Visible: Women in European History.* Boston: Houghton-Mifflin.

Knoke, David. (1990). *Political Networks: The Structural Perspective.* New York: Cambridge University Press.

Knowles, Malcolm S. (1980). *The Modern Practice of Adult Education: From Pedagogy to Andragogy.* New York: Cambridge, The Adult Education Company.

———. (1984). *Andragogy in Action.* San Francisco: Jossey-Bass.

Knutson, Lawrence L. (1992). "Census: Poverty Has Eroded Middle Class," *Santa Barbara News-Press* (May 31): A-7.

Kohen J., C. Brown, and R. Feldberg. (1979). "Divorced Mothers: The Costs and Benefits of Female Control," In G. Levinger, *Divorce and Separation: Contests, Causes and Consequences.* New York: Basic Books.

Kohlberg, Lawrence. (1969). "Stage and Sequence: The Cognitive-Developmental Approach to Socialization." In

A. Goslin (ed.), *Handbook of Socialization Theory and Research.* Chicago: Rand-McNally.

————. (1983). *The Philosophy of Moral Development.* New York: Harper & Row.

————. (1984). *The Psychology of Moral Development* (vol. 2). New York: Harper & Row.

Kohn, Melvin. (1965). "Social Class and Parent-Child Relationships: An Interpretation," *American Journal of Sociology* 68: 471-480.

————. (1976). "Occupational Structure and Alienation," *American Journal of Sociology* 82: 111-130.

————. (1977). *Class and Conformity* (2nd ed.). Homewood, IL: Dorsey.

Kohn, Melvin L., and Carmi Schooler. (1982). "Job Conditions and Personality: A Longitudinal Assessment of Their Reciprocal Effects," *American Journal of Sociology* 87: 1257-1286.

————. (1983). *Work and Personality: An Inquiry into the Impact of Social Stratification.* Norwood, NJ: Ablex.

Kolko, Gabriel. (1963). *The Triumph of Conservatism.* New York: Free Press.

Koo, Hagan, and Eun-Mee Kim. (1992). "The Developmental State and Capital Accumulation in South Korea," In Richard P. Appelbaum and Jeffrey Henderson (eds.), *States and Development in the Asian Pacific Rim.* Newbury Park, CA: Sage.

Kopkind, Andrew. (1993). "The Gay Moment," *The Nation* (May 3): 577-602.

Kornhauser, William. (1959). *The Politics of Mass Society.* Glencoe, IL: Free Press.

Kosmin, Barry A. (1991). *Research Report: The National Survey of Religious Identification.* New York: City University of New York Graduate Center.

Koss, M. P., C. A. Gidycz, and N. Wisniewski. (1987). "The Scope of Rape: Incidence and Prevalence of Sexual Aggression and Victimization in a National Sample of Higher Education Students," *Journal of Consulting and Clinical Psychology* 55: 162-170.

Kotkin, Joel. (1993). *Tribes: How Race, Religion, and Identity Determine Success in the New Global Economy.* New York: Random House.

Kouzes, James M. (1987). *The Challenge of Leadership: How to Get Extraordinary Things Done in Organizations.* San Francisco: Jossey-Bass.

Kozol, Jonathan. (1988). *Rachel and Her Children: Homeless Families in America.* New York: Ballantine.

————. (1991). *Savage Inequalities: Children in American Schools.* New York: Crown.

Krasner, Stephen D. (1983). *International Regimes.* Ithaca, NY: Cornell University Press.

Kristoff, Nicholas D. (1993a). "China's Crackdown on Births: A Stunning, and Harsh, Success," New York Times (April 25): 1.

Kristoff, Nicholas D. (1993b). "Satellites Bring Information Revolution to China," *New York Times* (April 11): 1.

Kroeber, A. L. (1923). *Anthropology.* New York: Harcourt, Brace.

Kruesi, M. J. P., J. Dale, and Steven E. Straus. (1989). "Psychiatric Diagnosis in Patients Who Have CFS," *Journal of Clinical Psychiatry* 50 (February): 53-56.

Kubler-Ross, Elizabeth. (1969). *On Death and Dying.* New York: Macmillan.

Kuhn, Annette, and Ann Marie Wolpe (eds.). (1978). *Feminism and Materialism.* London: Routledge & Kegan Paul.

Kuhn, Thomas. (1970). *The Structure of Scientific Theories.* Chicago: University of Chicago Press.

Kulkarni, V. G. (1993). "The Middle-Class Bulge," *Far Eastern Economic Review* (January 14): 44-46.

Kunkel, Suzanne R. (1989). "An Extra Eight Hours a Day," *Generations* 13 (2): 57-60.

Kuttner, Robert. (1993). "The Productivity Paradox: Rising Output, Stagnant Living Standards," *Business Week* (February 8): 12.

Kuwahara, Yasue. (1992). "Power to the People Y'All: Rap Music, Resistance, and Black College Students," *Humanity and Society* 16 (February): 54-73.

Kuznets, Simon. (1961). *Capital in the American Economy: Its Formation and Financing.* Princeton: Princeton University Press.

LaBov, William. (1972). *Language in the Inner City: Studies in the lack English Vernacular.* Philadelphia: University of Pennsylvania Press.

————. (1985). *The Increasing Divergence of Black and White Vernaculars: Introduction to the Research Reports.* Philadelphia: University of Pennsylvania Press.

LaBrecque, Mort. (1989). "Detecting Climate Change I: Taking the World's Shifting Temperature," *National Science Foundation Mosaic* 20 (winter): 209.

Ladd, Everett Carl. (1966). *Negro Political Leadership in the South.* Ithaca: Cornell University Press.

LaFarge, Oliver. (1940). *As Long as the Grass Shall Grow.* New York: Alliance.

LaFree, Gary, Kriss A. Drass, and Patrick O'Day. (1992). "Race and Crime in Postwar America: Determinants of African-American and White Races, 1957-1988," *Criminology* 30: 157-189.

Lai, Tracy. (1992). "Asian American Women: Not for Sale." In Margaret L. Anderson and Patricia Hill Collins, *Race, Class, and Gender: An Anthology,* pp. 163-171. Belmont, CA: Wadsworth.

Lake, Alice. (1975). "Are We Born into Our Sex Roles or Programmed into Them?" *Woman's Day* (January): 25-35.

Lamb, H. Richard (ed.). (1984). *The Homeless Mentally Ill: A Task Force Report of the American Psychiatric*

Association. Washington: The American Psychiatric Association.

Land, Kenneth C., Glenn Deane, and Judith R. Blau. (1991). "Religious Pluralism and Church Membership," *American Sociological Review* 56 (April): 237-249.

Landler, Mark. (1992). "The MTV Tycoon: Sumner Redstone is Turning Viacom into the Hottest Global TV Network," *Business Week* (September 21): 56-62.

Lane, David. (1990). *Soviet Society Under Perestroika.* Winchester, MA: Unwin Hyman.

Lane, Harlan L. (1984a). *When the Mind Hears: A History of the Deaf.* New York: Random House.

———. (1992). *The Mask of Benevolence: Disabling the Deaf Community.* New York: Knopf.

——— (ed.). (1984b). *The Deaf Experience: Classics in Language and Education,* Franklin Philip (trans.). Cambridge: Harvard University Press.

Langberg, Mark, and Reynolds Farley. (1985). "Residential Segregation of Asian Americans in 1980," *Sociology and Social Research* 70 (October): 71-75.

Lange, Johannes. (1930). *Crime as Destiny.* New York: Charles Boni.

Langton, Phyllis, (1991). *Drug Use and the Alcohol Dilemma.* York, PA: Allyn & Bacon.

Lanning, Kenneth V. (1991). "Ritual Abuse: A Law Enforcement View or Perspective," *Child Abuse and Neglect* 15 (3): 171-174.

Lappe, Francis Moore, and Joseph Collins. (1979a). *Food First.* New York: Ballantine.

———. (1979b). World Hunger: Twelve Myths. New York: Grove Weidenfeld.

Larwood, L., and U. E. Gattiker. (1989). "A Comparison of the Career Paths Used by Successful Women and Men." In B. A. Gutek and L. Larwood (eds.), *Women's Career Development.* Newbury Park, CA: Sage.

Lasch, Christopher. (1979). *The Culture of Narcissism.* New York: Norton.

Laveist, Thomas A. (1993). "Segregation, Poverty, and Empowerment: Health Consequences for African Americans," *The Milbank Quarterly* 71 (1): 41-64.

Lawrence, Bruce B. (1989). *Defenders of God: The Fundamentalist Revolt Against the Modern Age.* San Francisco: Harper & Row.

Lawton, Kim A. (1992). "Court Ruling Gives School Choice a Chance," *Time Magazine* (April 27): 41.

Lazarsfeld, Paul F., Bernard Berelson, and Hazel Gaudet. (1968). *the People's Choice* (3rd ed.). New York: Columbia University Press.

Lazarus, Edward. (1991). *Black Hills, White Justice.* New York: HarperCollins.

Leacock, Eleanor. (1978). "Women's Status in Egalitarian Societies: Implications for Social Evolution," *Current Anthropology* 19 (June): 247-275.

Leavitt, Judith W., and Ronald L. Numbers (eds.). (1985). *Sickness and Health In America.* Madison: University of Wisconsin Press.

LeBon, Gustave. (1960; orig. 1896). *The Crowd: A Study of the Popular Mind.* New York: Viking.

Lecknus, Dave. (1993). "Some States Leading the Way," *Business Insurance* 27 (March 26): 35-36.

Lee, Don Y. (1988). *An Outline of Confucianism* (rev. ed.). Bloomington: Indiana University Press.

Lee, Felicia R. (1993). "Disrespect Rules," *New York Times* (April 4): 16.

Lee, Gary, (1992). "On Both Sides of the Leaf: U.S. Condemns Tobacco, Subsidizes Sales," *Washington Post* (June 4): A27-5.

Lee, John. (1992a). "One Comfort Girl's Chilling Account of Abuse," *Los Angeles Times* (April 25): B-2.

———. (1992b). "Ex-'Comfort Girls' End Silence on War Horrors," *Los Angeles Times* (April 25): B-2.

Lemann, Nicholas. (1991). *The Promised Land: The Great Black Migration and How It Changed America.* New York: Vintage.

Lembcke, Jerry. (1988). *Capitalist Development and Class Capacities: Marxist Theory and Union Organization.* New York: Greenwood.

Lemert, Edwin. (1951). *Social Pathology.* New York: McGraw-Hill.

Lenski, Gerhard. (1966). *Power and Privilege: A Theory of Social Stratification.* New York: McGraw-Hill.

Lenski, Gerhard, and Jean Lenski. (1982). *Human Societies* (4th ed.). New York: McGraw-Hill.

Lenski, Gerhard, Jean Lenski, and Patrick Nolan. (1991). *Human Societies: An Introduction to Macrosociology* (6th ed.). New York: McGraw-Hill.

Lenzer, Gertrude (ed.). (1975). *Auguste Comte and Positivism: The Essential Writings.* New York: Harper Torchbooks.

Lerner, Daniel. (1958). *The Passing of Traditional Society.* New York: Free Press.

Lerner, Daniel, and W. Schramm. (1967). *Communication and Change in Developing Societies.* Honolulu: University of Hawaii Press.

Lerner, Gerda. (1972). *Black Women in White America: A Documentary History.* New York: Vintage.

——— (ed.). (1973). *Black Women in White America: A Documentary History.* New York: Vintage.

Levant, R. F., S. C. Slattery, and J. E. Loiselle. (1987). "Father's Involvement in Housework and Child Care with School-Aged Daughters," *Family Relations* 36: 152-157.

LeVay, Simon. (1991). "A Difference in Hypothalamic Structure Between Heterosexual and Homosexual Men," *Science* (August 30).

Lever, Janet. (1976). "Sex Differences in the Games Children Play," *Social Problems* 23: 478-487.

————. (1978). "Sex Differences in the Complexity of Children's Play and Games," *American Sociological Review* 43: 471-483.

Levin, William C. (1988). "Age Stereotyping: College Student Evaluations," *Research on Aging* 10 (1): 134-148.

Levine, Bettijane. (1992). "Finding His Voice," *Los Angeles Times* (June 22): E-1.

Levine, Hillel, and Lawrence Harmon. (1992). *The Death of an American Jewish Community: A Tragedy of Good Intentions*. New York: Free Press.

Levine, Jonathan B. (1992). "Saving Our Schools," *Business Week* (September 14): 70-85.

Levinson, Alan. (1992). "Your New Global Workforce," *Fortune* (December 14): 52-66.

Levinson, Daniel J. (1978). *The Seasons of a Man's Life*. New York: Ballantine.

————. (1980). "Toward a Conception of the Adult Life Course." In Neil J. Smelser and Erik H. Erikson (eds.), *Themes of Work and Love in Adulthood,* pp. 151-173. Cambridge: Harvard University Press.

Levinson, Marc. (1992). "IBM, Please Call AT&T," *Newsweek* (December 28): 44-45.

Levitan, Sar A., and Frank Gallo. (1993). *Education Reform: Federal Initiatives and National Mandates*. Washington: George Washington University Center for Social Policy Studies.

Levitan, Sar A., and William B. Johnston. (1975). *Indian Giving: Federal Programs for Native Americans*. Baltimore: Johns Hopkins University Press.

Leviton, Daniel. (1991). *Hazardous Death, Health, and Well-Being*. New York: Hemisphere.

Levy, Marion J. (1972). *Modernization: Latecomers and Survivors*. New York: Basic Books.

Lewin, John C. (1992). "Hawaii: A Blueprint for Health Care Reform," *Business & Health* 10 (Mid September): 56.

Lewin, Tamar. (1990). "Strategies to Let Elders Keep Some Control," *New York Times* (March 28): A-1.

Lewis, Anne C. (1992). "Publis Education and Privatization," *Phi Delta Kappan* (April): 534-538.

Lewis, Nancy, and Keith A. Harriston. (1993). "Teen Held in Volley of Gunfire Near C. C. School," *Washington Post* (September 11): A-1.

Lewontin, R. C. (1982). *Human Diversity*. San Francisco: W. H. Freeman.

Lewontin, R. C., S. Rose, and L. J. Kamin. (1984). *Not in Our Genes: Biology, Ideology, and Human Behavior.* New York: Pantheon.

Lichter, R. S., and D. Amundson. (1992). *A Day of Television Violence*. Washington: Center for Media and Public Affairs.

Lieberson, Stanley. (1973). "Generational Differences Among Blacks in the North," *Journal of Sociology* 79: 550-565.

————. (1980). *A Piece of Pie: Black and White Immigrants Since 1880*. Berkeley: University of California Press.

————. (1988). *From Many Strands: Ethnic and Racial Groups in Contemporary America*. New York: Russell Sage Foundation.

Liebes, T., and Elihu Katz. (1990). *The Export of Meaning: Cross-Cultural Readings of "Dallas."* New York: Oxford University Press.

Liebow, Elliot. (1967). *Talley's Corner: A Study of Negro Streetcorner Men*. Boston: Little, Brown.

Lifton, Peter D. (1985). "Individual Differences in Moral Development: The Relation of Sex, Gender, and Personality to Morality." In A. J. Stewart and M. B. Lykes (eds.), *Gender and Personality*. Durham, NC: Duke University Press.

Light, Ivan H., and Edna Bonacich. (1988). *Immigrant Entrepreneurs: Koreans in Los Angeles, 1965-1982*. Berkeley: University of California Press.

Lightfoot-Klein, Hanny. (1989). *Prisoners of Ritual: An Odyssey into Female Genital Circumcision in Africa*. New York: Haworth.

Lim, L. Y. C. (1983). "Singapore's Success: The Myth of the Free Market Economy," *Asian Survey* 23 (6): 752-764.

Lincoln, C. Eric, and Lawrence H. Mamiya. (1990). *The Black Church in the African-American Experience*. Durham, NC: Duke University Press.

Linden, Eugene. (1989). "Playing with Fire," *Time Magazine* (September 18): 76-85.

Lindesmith, Alfred R., and Anslem Strauss. (1956). *Social Psychology*. New York: Dryden.

Linton, Ralph. (1937). "One Hundred Percent American," *The American Mercury* 40 (April): 427-429.

Linz, Daniel G. (1989). "Exposure to Sexually Explicit Materials and Attitudes Toward Rape: A Comparison of Study Results," *The Journal of Sex Research* 26 (February): 50-84.

Linz, Daniel G., Ed Donnerstein, and Steven M. Adams. (1989). "Physiological Desensitization and Judgments About Female Victims of Violence," *Human Communication Research* 15 (summer): 509-522.

Linz, Daniel G., Ed Donnerstein, and Steven Penrod. (1988). "Effects of Long-Term Exposure to Violent and Sexually Degrading Depictions of Women," *Journal of Personality and Social Psychology* 55 (5): 758-768.

Lipietz, A. (1986). "New Tendencies in the International Division of Labor: Regimes of Capital Accumulation and Modes of Regulations." In R. Peet (ed.), *International Capitalism and Industrial Restructuring*. Boston: Allen & Unwin.

Lipman-Blumen, Jean. (1984). *Gender Roles and Power.* Englewood Cliffs, NJ: Prentice-Hall.

Lippman, John. (1992). "How TV Is Transforming World Culture and Politics," *Los Angeles Times* (October 20): H-3.

Lippman, John, and Willaim Tuohy. (1992). "Who Will Rule the News?" *Los Angeles Times* (October 20): H-3.

Lipset, Seymour Martin. (1968). "The Activists: A Profile," *The Public Interest* 13 (fall): 46.

———. (1991). "Comments on Luckmann." In Pierre Bourdieu and James S. Coleman, *Social Theory in a Changing Society.* Boulder, CO: Westview.

——— (ed.). (1986). *Unions in Transition: Entering the Second Century.* San Francisco: Institute for Contemporary Studies.

Lipset, Seymour Martin, Martin Trow, and James Coleman. (1977; orig. 1956). *Union Democracy: The Inside of the International Typographical Union.* New York: Free Press.

Litoff, Judy Barrett. (1985). American Midwives: 1860 to the Present. Westport, CT: Greenwood.

Livingston, S. (1990). *Making Sense of Television.* London: Pergamon.

Loden, M., and J. B. Rosener. (1991). *Workforce America! Managing Employee Diversity as a Vital Resource.* Homewood, IL: Business One Irwin.

Loevinger, Jane. (1980). *Ego Development: Conception and Theories.* San Francisco: Jossey-Bass.

Lofland, John. (1985). *Protest: Studies of Collective Behavior and Social Movements.* New Brunswick, NJ: Transaction.

Logan, John, and Harvey L. Molotch. (1987). *Urban Fortunes: The Political Economy of Place.* Berkeley: University of California Press.

Lombroso, Cesare. (1896). *Crime: Its Causes and Consequences.* New York: Scribners.

Longman, Phillip. (1982). "Taking America to the Cleaners," *Washington Monthly* (November).

———. (1985). "Justice Between Generations," *The Atlantic Monthly* (June).

Loo, Chalsa M. (1991). *Chinatown: Most Time, Hard Time.* New York: Praeger.

Lorber, Judith. (1984). *Women Physicians: Careers, Status, and Power.* New York: Tavistock.

Lorde, Audre. (1988). *A Burst of Light.* Ithaca, NY: Firebrand.

Los Angeles Times. (1992a). "AIDS in Los Angeles County," (August 10): B-2.

———. (1992). "Buchanan Calls for Winning Back 'Soul of America,'" (May 28): A-5.

———. (1992). "Lawsuits Expected After Japan Refuses to Compensate Sex Slaves," (Febrary 23): A-26.

Lotito, Michael. (1993). "A Call to Action for U.S. Business and Education," *Employment Relations Today* 19 (winter): 379-387.

Lubeck, Paul. (1992). "Malaysian Industrialization, Ethnic Divisions, and the NIC Model: The Limits to Replication." In Richard P. Appelbaum and Jeffrey Henderson (eds.), *States and Development in the Asian Pacific Rim.* Newbury Park, CA: Sage.

Lubeck, Sally. (1985). *Sandbox Society: Early Education in Black and White America.* London: Falmer.

Luckmann, Thomas. (1967). *The Invisible Religion.* New York: Macmillan.

Luedde-Neurath, R. (1988). "State Intervention and Export-Oriented Development in South Korea." In G. White (ed.), *Developmental States in East Asia,* pp. 68-112. London: Macmillan.

Luria, Ella, and Eleanor W. Herzog. (1991). "Sorting Gender Out in a Children's Museum," *Gender and Society* 5: 224-232.

Luttwak, E. (1984). *The Pentagon and the Art of War.* New York: Simon & Schuster.

McAdam, Doug. (1982). *Political Process and the Development of Black Insurgency, 1930-1970.* Chicago: University of Chicago Press.

———. (1986). "Recruitment to High-Risk Activism: The Case of Freedom Summer," *American Journal of Sociology* 92: 64-90.

———. (1988). *Freedom Summer: The Idealists Revisited.* New York: Oxford University Press.

McAdam, Doug, John D. McCarthy, and Mayer N. Zald. (1988). "Social Movements." In Neil J. Smelser (ed.), *Handbook of Sociology.* Newbury Park, CA: Sage.

McAdoo, Hariette Pipes (ed.). (1993). *Family Ethnicity: Strength in Diversity.* Newbury Park, CA: Sage.

McBarnet, Doreen. (1991). "Whiter Than White Collar Crime: Tax, Fraud Insurance and the Management of Stigma," *British Journal of Sociology* 42 (September): 323-344.

———. (1993). "Legitimate Rackets: Tax Evasion, Tax Avoidance and the Boundaries of Legality," Oxford, England: Center for Socio-Legal Research.

MacBride, S. (1980). *Many Voices, One World: Communication and Society, Today and Tomorrow.* Unpublished report of the MacBride Commission, New York.

McCartney, John T. (1992). *Black Power Ideologies: An Essay in African American Political Thought.* Philadelphia: Temple University Press.

McCarthy, John D., and Mayer N. Zald. (1973). *The Trend of Social Movements in America: Professionalization and Resource Mobilization.* Morristown, NJ: General Learning.

———. (1977). "Resource Mobilization and Social Movements: A Partial Theory," *American Journal of Sociology* 82: 1212-1240.

McClain, Leanita. (1986). *A Foot in Each World: Essays and Articles.* Evanston, IL: Northwestern University Press.

McClellan, David (ed.). (1977). *Karl Marx: Selected Writings.* New York: Oxford University Press.

Maccoby, E. E., and C. N. Jacklin. (1974). *The Psychology of Sex Differences.* Stanford: Stanford University Press.

McCombs, M.E. (1988). "Concentration, Monopoly, and Content." In R. G. Picard, et al. (eds.), *Press Concentration and Monopoly.* Norwood, NJ: Ablex.

McCombs, Phil. (1993). "AMA's Doctor on the Case," *Washington Post* (February 4): C-1.

McCormick, Albert E., Jr. (1979). "Dominant Class Interests and the Emergence of Anti-Trust Legislation," *Contemporary Crises* 3: 199-417.

McCoy, Alfred W. (1973). *The Politics of Heroin in Southeast Asia.* New York: Harper Colophon.

———. (1991). *The Politics of Heroin: CIA Complicity in the Global Drug Trade.* New York: Lawrence Hill.

MacEnoin, Deni, and Ahmed Al-Shahi (eds.) (1983). *Islam in the Modern World.* New York: St. Martin's.

MacFarquhar, Roderick. (1980). "The Post-Confucian Challenge," *The Economist* (February 9): 67-72.

McKinlay, J. B. (1975). "A Case for Refocusing Downstream: The Political Economy of Illness." In P. Konrad and R. Kern (eds.), *The Sociology of Health and Illness: Critical Perspectives.* New York: St. Martin's.

MacKinnon, Catherine A. (1982). "Feminism, Marxism, Method, and the State: An Agenda For Theory. In N. O. Keohane, et al. (eds.). *Feminist Theory: A Critique of Ideology,* pp. 1-30. Chicago: University of Chicago Press.

———. (1989). *Toward a Feminist Theory of the State.* Cambridge: Harvard University Press.

McLanahan, Sara. (1988). "The Consequences of Single Parenthood for Subsequent Generations," *Focus* 11 (fall): 3.

McLuhan, Marshall. (1964). *Understanding Media: The Extensions of Man.* New York: Mentor.

McMurtry, Larry. (1993). "Return to Waco," *The New Republic* (June 7): 16-19.

Macworld. (1992). "America's Shame," (September).

Maddox, G. L. (1965). "Fact and Artifact: Evidence Bearing on Disengagement from the Duke Geriatrics Project," *Human Development* 8: 117-130.

———. (1970). "Themes and Issues in Sociological Theories of Human Aging," *Human Development* 13: 17-27.

Maguire, Kathleen, Ann L. Pastore, and Timothy Flanagan. (1992). *Sourcebook of Criminal Justice Statistics.* Washington: Department of Justice.

Mahar, Maggie. (1994). "A Change of Place," *Barrons* (March 21): 33-38.

Majka, L. C., T. J. Majka. (1982). *Farm Workers, Agri-Business, and the State.* Philadelphia: Temple University Press.

Makiya, Kanan. (1993). "Rape in Service of the State," *The Nation* (May 10): 627-630.

Malotki, Ekkehart. (1983). *Hopi Time: A Linguistic Analysis of the Temporal Concepts in the Hopi Language.* Berlin: Mouton.

Malthus, Thomas. (1926; orig. 1798). *First Essay on Population.* London: Macmillan.

Mandel, Michael J. (1992). "Who'll Get the Lion's Share of Wealth in the 90's? The Lions," *Business Week* (June 8): 86-88.

Mandel, Michael J., and Paul Magnusson. (1993). "The Economics of Crime," *Business Week* (December 13): 72-80.

Mandel, Michael J., Wendy Zellner, and Robert Hof. (1993). "Jobs, Jobs, Jobs: The Economy is Growing, but Employment Lags Badly," *Business Week* (February 22): 68-74.

Mandel, William. (1985). *Soviet, But Not Russian: The "Other" Peoples of the Soviet Union.* Palo Alto, CA: Ramparts.

Mann, Michael. (1986). *The Sorces of Social Power, vol. 1, A History of Power from the Beginning Until 1760.* New York: Cambridge University Press.

Marcuse, Herbert (1955). *Eros and Civilization: A Philosphical Inquiry into Freud.* Boston: Beacon.

———. (1964). *One-Dimensional Man.* Boston: Beacon Press.

Marger, Martin N. (1987). *Elites and Masses: An Introduction to Political Sociology* (2nd ed.). Belmont CA: Wadsworth.

Margo, Robert A. (1991). *Race and Schooling the South 1890-1940: An Economic History.* Chicago: University of Chicago Press.

Marien, Michael. (1977). "The Two Visions of Postindustrial Society," *Futures* 9 (October): 415-431.

Marini, Margaret Mooney. (1989). "Sex Differences in Earnings in the United States." In W. R. Scott (ed.), *Annual Review of Sociology* 15: 343-380. Palo Alto, CA: Annual Reviews.

———. (1990). "Sex and Gender: What do We Know?" *Sociological Forum* 5 (1): 95-120.

Marriott, Alice. (1945). *The Ten Grandmothers.* Norman: University of Oklahoma Press.

Marriott, Michel. (1993). "Hard-Core Rap Lyrics Stir Black Backlash," *New York Times* (August 15): 1.

Marsden, Peter. (1987). "Core Discussion Networks of Americans," *American Sociological Review* 52 (February): 122-131.

Marsden, Peter V., and Nan Lin. (1982). *Social Structure and Network Analysis.* Beverley Hills, CA: Sage.

Marsh, Clifton E. (1984). *From Black Muslims to Muslims: The Transition from Separatism to Islam, 1930-1980.* Metuchen, NJ: Scarecrow.

Marshall, George. (1989). *Rainforests, the Greenhouse Myth, and the Reforestation Fantasy,"* Green Letter (winter): 24, 35-38.

Martin, Emily. (1992). "Body Narratives, Body Boundaries." In Lawrence Grossberg, Cary Nelson, and Paula A. Treichler (eds.), *Cultural Studies.* New York: Routledge.

Martin, R., and R. Rawthorn. (1986). *The Geography of Deindustrialization.* Hampshire, England: Macmillan.

Martin, Richard C. (1982). *Islam, A Cultural Perspective.* Englewood Cliffs, NJ: Prentice-Hall.

Marwell, Gerald, and Pamela Oliver. (1993). *The Critical Mass in Collective Action: A Micro-Social Theory.* New York: Cambridge University Press.

Marx, Gary T. (1985a). "The Surveillance Society: The Threat of 1984-Style Techniques," *The Futurist* 19 (June): 21-26.

———. (1985b). "I'll Be Watching You: Reflections on the New Surveillance," *Dissent* 32 (winter): 26-34.

———. (1988). *Undercover: Police Surveillance in America.* Berkeley: University of California Press.

Marx, Karl. (1967; orig. 1867). *Capital.* New York: International.

———. (1977a; orig. 1845-1846). "Theses on Feuerbach." In David McClellan, *Karl Marx: Selected Writings.* London: Oxford University Press.

———. (1977b; orig. 1848) "The Communist Manifesto." In David McClellan (ed.), *Karl Marx: Selected Writings.* London: Oxford University Press.

———. (1977c; orig. 1851). "The Eighteenth Brumaire of Louis Bonaparte." In David McClellan (ed.), *Karl Marx: Selected Writings.* New York: Oxford University Press.

———. (1977d; orig. 1867). *Capital: A Critique of Political Economy,* vols. 1-3. New York: Random House.

Marx, Karl, and Friedrich Engels. (1977; orig. 1848). "Manifesto of the Communist Party." In David McClellan (ed.), *Karl Marx: Selected Writings.* New York: Oxford University Press.

Massey, Douglas S., and Nancy A. Denton. (1989). "Hypersegregation in U.S. Metropolitan Areas," *Demography* 26 (August): 373-391.

———. (1992). "Residential Segregation of Asian-Origin Groups in U.S. Metropolitan Areas," *Sociology and Social Research* 76 (July): 170-177.

Mathias, Peter, and John A. Davis. (1991). *Innovation and Technology in Europe: From the Eighteenth Century to the Present Day.* Oxford, England: Basil Blackwell.

Matthews, K. A., and J. Rodin. (1989). "Women's Changing Work Roles: Impact on Health, Family, and Public Policy," *American Psychologist* 44: 1389-1393.

Matthews, Sarah H. (1993). "Undermining Stereotypes of the Old Through Social Policy Analysis: Tempering Macro- with Micro-Level Level Perspectives." In Jon Hendricks and Carolyn J. Rosenthal, *The Remainder of Their Days: Domestic Policy and Older Families in the United States and Canada,* pp. 105-118. New York: Garland.

Mauer, Marc. (1990). *Young Black Men and the Criminal Justice System: A Growing National Problem.* Washington: The Sentencing Project.

———. (1993). *Does the Punishment Fit the Crime? Drug Users and Drunk Drivers, Questions of Race and Class.* Washington: The Sentencing Project.

———. (1994). "A Generation Behind Bars: Black Males and the Criminal Justice System." In Richard G. Majors

and Jacob U. Gordan (eds.), *The American Black Male: His Present Status and His Future.* Chicago: Newlson-Hall.

Maugh, Thomas H., II. (1989). "Sex Differences in Reasoning Skills Is on the Decline, Research Finds," *Los Angeles Times* (January 16): I-3.

———. (1991). "Survey of Identical Twins Links Biological Factors with Being Gay," *Los Angleles Times* (December 15): A-43.

———. (1993). "Genetic Compound Found in Lesbianism, Study Says," *Los Angeles Times* (March 12): A-1.

Maugh, Thomas H., II, and Nora Zamichow. (1991). "Medicine: San Diego Researcher's Findings Offer First Evidence of a Biological Cause for Homosexuality," *Los Angeles Times* (August 30): A-1.

Mayberry, Maralee. (1991). "Conflict and Social Determinism: The Deprivation of Education." Paper presented at the annual meeting of the American Educational Research Association, Chicago.

Maynard, Douglas W., and Stephen Clayman. (1991). "The Diversity of Ethnomethodology," *Annual Review of Sociology* 17: 385-418.

Mayo, Elton. (1977; orig. 1933). *Human Problems of Industrial Civilization.* New York: Aino.

Mead, George Herbert. (1934). *Mind, Self, and Society.* Chicago: University of Chicago Press.

———. (1938). *The Philosophy of the Act.* Chicago: University of Chicago Press.

———. (1977). *On Social Psychology: Selected Papers,* Anselem Strauss (ed.). Chicago and London: University of Chicago Press.

Meadows, Donella H. (1989). "Clouds of Dispute Cover Global Warming," *Los Angeles Times* (October 15): M-1, M-3.

Meadows, Donella H., and Dennis L. Meadows. (1972). *The Limits to Growth.* New York: Universe.

Meadows, Donella H., Dennis L. Meadows, and Jorgen Randers. (1992). *Beyond the Limits: Confronting Global Collapse, Envisioning a Sustainable Future.* Post Mills, VT: Chelsea Green.

Mechanic, David. (1990). "The Role of Sociology in Health Care," *Health Affairs* 9: 85-87.

Mechanic, David, and David A. Rochefort. (1990). "Deinstitutionalization: An Appraisal of Reform," *Annual Review of Sociology* 16: 301-327.

Medland, A. J., and Piers Burnett (eds.). (1986). *CAD-CAM in Practice.* New York: Wiley.

Meile, Richard L. (1986). "Pathways to Patienthood: Sick Role and Labeling Perspectives," *Social Science & Medicine* 22: 35-40.

Melcher, Richard A. (1992). "Sweden Fights to Come in from the Cold," *Business Week* (November 2): 46-47.

Melton, J. Gordon. (1989). *The Enclycolpedia of American Religions* (3rd ed.). Detroit: Gale Research.

Menchu, Rigoberta. (1983). *I, Rigoberta Menchu: An Indian Woman in Guatemala.* London: Verso.

Merkyl, Peter H., and Ninian Smart (eds.). *Religion and Politics in the Modern World.* New York: New York University Press.

Merton, Robert K. (1946). *Mass Persuasion: The Social Psychology of a War Bond Drive.* New York: Harper & Brothers.

———. (1968; orig. 1938). "Social Structure and Anomie," *American Sociological Review* 3: 672-682.

———. (1968). *Social Theory and Social Structure* (2nd ed.). New York: Free Press.

Merton, Robert, and Alice Kitt Rossi. (1950). "Contributions to the Theory of Reference Group Behavior." In *Studies in the Scene and Method of "the American Soldier."* New York: Free Press.

Meszaros, Istvan. (1970). *Marx's Theory of Alienation.* London: Merlin.

Meyer, Jack, and Marion Lewin. (1987). *Charting the Future of Health Care: Policy, Politics, and Public Health.* Washington: American Enterprise Institute for Public Policy Research.

Meyer, John W. (1980) "The World Polity and the Authority of the Nation-State." In Albert J. Bergesen (ed.), *Studies of the Modern World System.* New York: Academic.

Meyer, John W., John Boli, and George M. Thomas. (1987). "Ontology and Rationalization in Western Cultural Account." In George M. Thomas, John W. Meyer, Francisco O. Ramirez, and John Boli, *Institutional Structure: Constituting State, Society, and the Individual.* Newbury Park, CA: Sage.

Meyer, John W., and Michael T. Hannan (eds.). (1979). *National Development and the World System: Educational, Economic, and Political Change, 1950-1970.* Chicago: University of Chicago Press.

Meyer, John W., and George Thomas. (1980). "Regime Change and State Power in an Intensifying World State System." In Albert J. Bergesen (ed.), *Studies of the Modern World System.* New York: Academic Press.

Meyer, Michael, and Stephen Fienberg (eds.) (1992). *Assessing Evaluation Studies: The Case of Bilingual Education Strategies.* Washington: National Academy Press.

Meyer, Thomas J. (1984). "Date Rape: A Serious Problem That Few Talk About," *Chronicle of Higher Education* (December 5): 5-7.

Meyer-Bahlberg, H. (1977). "Sex Hormones and Male Homosexuality in Comparative Perspective. In D. Marshall and R. Suggs (eds.), *Human Sexual Behavior: Variations in the Ethnographic Perspective.* Englewood Cliffs, NJ: Prentice-Hall.

Michman, Ronald D. (1991). *Lifestyle Market Segmentation.* New York: Praeger.

Miles, Jack. (1992). "The Struggle for the Bottom Rung: Blacks vs. Browns," *The Atlantic Monthly* (October): 41-68.

Milgram, Stanley. (1963). "Behavioral Studies in Obedience," *Journal of Abnormal Psychology* 67: 371-378.

———. (1973). *Obedience to Authority: An Experimental View.* New York: Harper & Row.

Miliband, Ralph. (1969). *The State in Capitalist Society.* New York: Basic Books.

Milkman, Ruth. (1987). *Gender at Work: The Dynamics of Job Segregation by Sex During World War II.* Chicago: University of Chicago Press.

Miller, Jerome. (1992). "Young Black Males in the Criminal Justice System." Alexandria, VA: National Center for Institutions and Alternatives.

Miller, Joanne. (1988) In Neil J. Smelser (ed.), *Handbook of Sociology.* Newbury Park, CA: Sage.

Miller, Karen Lowry. (1993). "Land of the Rising Jobless," *Business Week* (January 11): 47.

Miller, Ruth Rhymer. (1994). "Alimony and Divorce: An Historical-Comparative Study of Gender Conflict." Ph.D. diss., The Fielding Institute, Santa Barbara, CA.

Miller, S. M. (1975). "Notes on Neo-Capitalism," *Theory and Society* 2 (spring): 1-35.

Millet, Kate. (1970). *Sexual Politics.* Garden City, NY: Doubleday.

Mills, C. Wright. (1956). *The Power Elite.* New York: Oxford University Press.

———. (1959). *The Sociological Imagination.* New York: Oxford University Press.

Mills, Theodore. (1967). *The Sociology of Small Groups.* Englewood Cliffs, NJ: Prentice-Hall.

Milton S. Eisenhower Foundation. (1990). *Youth Investment and Community Reconstruction: A Tenth Anniversary Report.* San Francisco.

———. (1993). *Investing in Our Children and Youth and Reconstructing Our Cities.* Washington.

Min, Pyong Gap. (1990). "Problems of Korean Immigrant Entrepreneurs," *International Migration Review* 24 (fall): 436-455.

Minkowitz, Donna. (1992a). "It's Still Open Season on Gays," *The Nation* (March 23): 368-370.

———. (1992b). "Many Lawmakers Fail to See Parallels Between Gay Bashing and Rape," *Advocate.*

———. (1992c). "Weekend form Hell," *Village Voice* (September 23): 16.

Mintz, Beth A., and Michael Schwartz. (1985). *The Power Structure of American Business.* Chicago: University of Chicago Press.

Mintz, F., and Michael Schwartz. (1985). *The Power Structure of American Business.* Chicago: University of Chicago Press.

Mintz, Sidney W. (1991). "Pleasure, Profit and Satiation." In H. C. Viola and C. Margolis, *Seeds of Change*, pp. 70-89. Washington: Smithsonian Institution.

Mirza, H. (1986). *Multinationals and the Growth of the Singapore Economy.* New York: St. Martin's.

Mitchell, Juliet. (1975). *Psychology and Feminism.* New York: Vintage.

Mizruchi, S. (1984). "Why Do Corporations Stick Together?" In G. William Domhoff and Thomas R. Dye (eds.), *Power Elites and Organizations.* Beverley Hills, CA: Sage.

Modelski, George (ed.). (1979). *Transnational Corporations and the World Order.* San Francisco: Freeman.

Mohai, Paul, and Bunyan Bryant. (1992). "Race and Class as Factors in the Distribution of Environmental Hazards: Evidence from the 1990 Detroit Area Study." Paper presented at the annual meeting of the American Sociological Association.

Mohanty, Chandra Talpade. (1991). "Under Western Eyes: Feminist Scholarship and Colonial Discourse." In Chandra Talpade Mohanty, Ann Russo, and Lourdes Torres (eds.), *Third World Women and the Politics of Feminism.* Bloomington: Indiana University Press.

Mohanty, Chandra Talpade, Ann Russo, and Lourdes Torres (eds.). (1991). *Third World Women and the Politics of Feminism.* Bloomington: Indiana University Press.

Mohl, Raymond. (1990). "On the Edge: Blacks and Hispanics in Metropolitan Miami Since 1959," The Forida Historical Quarterly 69: 37-56.

Mol, Hans. (1976). *Identity and the Sacred: A Sketch for a New Social Scientific Theory of Religion.* Oxford, England: Basil Blackwell.

Mollenkopf, John H. (1977). "The Postwar Politics of Urban Development." In John Walton and Donald E. Carns (eds.), *Cities in Change* (2nd ed.), pp. 549-579. Boston: Allyn & Bacon.

Molotch, Harvey L. (1972). *Managed Integration: Dilemmas of Doing Good in the City.* Berkeley: University of California Press.

———. (1976). "The City as a Growth Machine," *American Journal of Sociology* 82 (September): 309-333.

———. (1979). "Media and Movements," In Mayer Zald and John McCarthy (eds.), *The Dynamics of Social Movements.* Cambridge MA: Winthrop.

Molotch, Harvey, and Dierdre Boden. (1985). "Talking Social Structure: Discourse, Dominance, and the Watergate Hearings," *American Sociological Review* 50: 273-288.

Molotch, Harvey, and Marilyn Lester. (1974). "News as Purposive Behavior: On the Strategic Use of Routine Events, Accidents, and Scandals," *American Sociological Review* 39 (February): 101-112.

Monette, Paul. (1993). "The Politics of Scilence," *New York Times* (March 7): op-ed page.

Money, J. (1975). "Ablatio Penis: Normal Male Infant Sex-Reassigned as a Girl." *Archives of Sexual Behavior* 4: 65-72.

———. (1988). *Gay, Straight, and In-Between: The Sexology of Erotic Orientation.* New York: Oxford University Press.

Money J., and A. E. Ehrhardt. (1972). *Man, Woman, Boy, and Girl.* Baltimore: Johns Hopkins University Press.

Monroe, Paul. (1940). *Founding of the American Public School System.* New York: Macmillan.

Moore, Barrington, Jr. (1966). *Social Origins of Dictatorship and Democracy: Lord and Peasant in the Making of the Modern World.* Boston: Beacon.

Moore, Joan. (1991). *Going Down to the Barrio: Homeboys and Homegirls in Change.* Philadelphia: Temple University Press.

Moore, Joan, Robert Garcia, Carlos Garcia, Luis Cerda, and Frank Valencia. (1978). *Homeboys: Gangs, Drugs and Prison in the Barrios of Los Angeles.* Philadelphia: Temple University Press.

Moore, Joan, and Harry Pachon. (1985). *Hispanics in the United States.* Englewood Cliffs, NJ: Prentice-Hall.

Moore, Joan, and Raquel Pinderhughes. (1994). *In the Barrios: Latinos and the Underclass Debate.* New York: Russell Sage Foundation.

Moore, Joan, and James Diego Vigil. (1993). "Barrios in Transition." In Joan Moore and Raquel Pinderhughes, *In the Barrios: Latinos and the Underclass,* New York: Russell Sage Foundation.

Moore, Leonard J. (1991). *Citizen Klansman.* Chapel Hill, NC: University of North Carolina Press.

Morgan, Lewis Henry. (1964; orig. 1877). *Ancient Society, or Researches in the Lines of Human Progress, from Savagery though Barbarism to Civilization.* Cambridge: Harvard University Press.

Morgan, Robin (ed.). (1970). *Sisterhood Is Powerful: An Anthology of Writings from the Woman's Liberation Movement.* New York: Vintage.

Morishima, Michio. (1982). *Why Has Japan Succeeded?* Cambridge, England: Cambridge University Press.

Morris, Aldon D. (1984). *The Origins of the Civil Rights Movement: Black Communities Organizing for Change.* New York: Free Press.

Morrison, A. M., R. P. White, E. Van Velsor, and The Center for Creative Leadership. (1987). *Breaking the Glass Ceiling: Can Women Reach the Top of America's Largest Corporations?* Reading, MA: Addison-Wesley.

Morrison, Minion K. C. (1987). *Black Political Mobilization: Leadership, Power, and Mass Behavior.* Albany: State Univeristy of New York Press.

Morrison, Samuel Eliot. (1971). *The European Discovery of North America.* New York: Oxford University Press.

Morrow, Lance. (1993). "The Temping of America," *Time Magazine* (March 29): 40-41.

Mortenson Report. (1993). "Postsecondary Education Opportunity," 11 (February): 10.

Mosher, C., R. Anderson, and S. Tomkins. (1988). "Scripting the Macho Man: Hypermasculine

Socialization and Enculturation," *Journal of Sex Research* 25 (February): 60-84.

Moskos, Charles. (1991). "How Do They Do It? The Army's Racial Success Story," *The New Republic* (August 5): 16-20.

Moss, Miriam S., Sidney Z. Moss, and Elizabeth L. Moles. (1985). "The Quality of Relationships Between Elderly Parents and Their Out-of-Town Children," *The Gerontologist* 25: 134-140.

Moss, Mitchell. (1987). "Telecommunications, World Cities, and Urban Policy," *Urban Studies* 24: 534-546.

Moulder, F. (1977). *Japan, China and the Modern World Economy.* New York: Cambridge University Press.

Moyers, Bill. (1992). "Who Owns Our Government?" Washington: Public Affairs Television, *Listening to America* transcript 101.

Moynihan, Daniel Patrick. (1965). *The Negro Family: The Case for National Action.* Washington: Government Printing Office.

Muehlenhard, Charlene L., Debra E. Friedman, and Celeste M. Thomas. (1985). "Is Date Rape Justifiable?" *Psychology of Women Quarterly* 9 (3): 297-310.

Muller, Thomas, and Thomas J. Espenshade. (1986). *The Fourth Wave,* Washington: Urban Institute.

Mumford, Lewis. (1961). *The City in History: Its Origins, Its Transformations, and Its Prospects.* New York: Harcourt.

Munnell, Alicia H., et al. (1992). *Mortgage Lending in Boston: Interpreting HMDA Data.* Boston: Federal Reserve Bank of Boston.

Murdoch, George Peter, (1949). *Social Structure.* New York: Free Press.

Murdock, George Peter. (1945). "The Common Denominator of Cultures." In Ralph Linton (ed.), *The Science of Man in the World Crisis,* pp.123-142. New York: Columbia University Press.

Murdock, Graham, and Guy Phelps. (1973). *Mass Media and the Secondary School.* London: Macmillan.

Murray, Charles. (1984). *Losing Ground: American Social Policy 1950-1980.* New York: Basic Books.

Mydans, Seth. (1993). "Political Proving Ground for the Religios Right," *New York Times* (February 20): L-5.

Myers, Sheila Taylor, and Harold G. Grasmick. (1990). "The Social Rights and Responsiblities of Pregnant Women: An Application of Parson's Sick Role Model," *The Journal of Applied Behavioral Science* 26: 157-172.

Myrdal, Gunnar. (1944). *An American Dilemma: The Negro Problem and American Democracy.* New York: Harper & Row.

Nadler, L., and Z. Nadler. (1989). *Developing Human Resources* (3rd ed.). San Francisco: Jossey-Bass.

Nahaylo, Gordon, and Victor Swoboda. (1989). *Soviet Disunion: A History of the Nationalities Problem in the USSR.* New York: Free Press.

Naisbitt, John. (1982a). *Megatrends.* New York: Warner.

———. (1982b). *Megatrends: Ten New Directions for Transforming Our Lives.* New York: Warner.

———. (1990). *Megatrends 2000: The New Directions for the 1990s.* New York: Morrow.

Nakarmi, Laxmin, and Igor Reichlin. (1992). "Daewoo, Samsung, and Goldstar: Made in Europe?" *Business Week* (August 24): 43.

Nasar, Sylvia. (1992). "Fed Gives New Evidence of 80s Gain by Richest," *New York Times* (April 21).

Nation's Business. (1993). "Health Insurance: Uninsured Population Grows," 81 (March): 58.

National Advisory Commission on Civil Disorders. (1968). *Report.* New York: Bantam.

National Center for Health Statistics. (1989). *Physical Functioning of the Aged, 1984.* Vital and Health Statistics, Series 10 No. 167.

———. (1990). *Vital Statistics of the United States.* Washington: Government Printing Office.

———. (1993). *Vital Statistics of the United States.* Washington: Government Printing Office.

National Coalition for the Homeless. (1991). *Fatally Flawed: The Census Bureau's Count of Homeless People.* Washington (May 9).

National Collegiate Athletic Association (NCAA). (1993). *Annual Report.* Overland Park, KS.

National Commission on Excellence in Education. (1984). *A Nation at Risk: The Full Account.* Cambridge, MA: U.S.A. Research.

National Commission on Testing and Public Policy. (1990). *From Gatekeeper to Gateway: Transforming Testing in America.* Chestnut Hill, MA.

National Opinion Research Center (NORC). *An American Profile—Opinions and Behavior, 1972-1989.* New York: Gale Research.

National Geographic. (1991). (February): 18-19.

Nauss, Donald W. (1993a). "UAW Contracts Off to Friendly Start," *Los Angeles Times* (June 23): D-2.

———. (1993b). "GM to Shift Up to 1,000 Jobs from Mexico Plant," *Los Angeles Times* (June 22): D-1.

Navarro, Vincente. (1986). *Crisis, Health, and Medicine: A Social Critique.* New York: Tavistock.

———. (1992). *Why the United States Does Not Have a National Health Program.* New York: Baywood.

Nazzari, M. (1983). "The 'Woman Question' in Cuba: An Analysis of Material Constraints on Its Solution," *Signs* 9: 246-263.

Nee, Victor, and Jimy Sanders. (1987). "Reply: On Testing the Enclave-Economy Hypothesis," *American Sociological Review* 52 (December): 771-773.

Nelson, Hart M., and Anne K. Nelson. (1975). *Black Church in the Sixties.* Lexington: University Press of Kentucky.

Nemeth, Mary, and Bob Levin. (1990). "Guilty as Charged," *Maclean's* (April 16).

Neuberg, Leland Gerson. (1975). "A Critique of Postindustrial Thought," *Social Praxis* 3 (1-2): 121-150.

Neugarten, Bernice. (1970). "Dynamics of Transition of Middle Age to Old Age," *Journal of Geriatric Psychology* 4: 71-87.

———. (1977). "Personality and Aging." In J. E. Birren and K. W. Schaie (eds.), *The Handbook of Aging* (2nd ed.). New York: Van Nostrand.

Neugarten, Bernice, and G. O. Hagestad. (1976). "Age and the Life Course." In R. H. Binstock and E. Shanas (eds.), Handbook of Aging and the Social Sciences, pp. 35-55. New York: Van Nostrand.

Neuman, Graeme. (1979). *Understanding Violence.* New York: Lippincott.

Newcomb, Theodore, et al. (1967). *Persistence and Change: Bennington College and Its Students After Twenty-Five Years.* New York: Wiley.

New York Native. (1992). "Minister's Anti-Gay Tract, Sent to Student Group, Seen as Death Threat," (May 18): 10.

New York Times (1992). "Anti-Gay Crimes Are Reported on Rise in Five Cities," (April 20).

———. (1993). "Comatose Woman, Focus of Court Battles, Dies," (March 8): A1-4.

———. (1994). "Cutting the Most," (March 2): D-5.

Niehbur, Richard H. (1929). *On the Sources of Denominationalism.* New York: Holt.

Nieva, V. F., and B. A. Gutek. (1981). *Women and Work: A Psychological Perspective.* New York: Praeger.

Nightengale, Pamela. (1990). "Monetary Contraction and Mercantile Credit in Later Medieval England," *The Economic History Review* 43 (November): 560-675.

Nisbet, Robert. (1969). *Social Change and History.* New York: Oxford University Press.

Noble, Barbara Presley. (1993). "A Quiet Liberation for Gay and Lesbian Employees," *New York Times* (June 13): 4.

Nordhoff, Charles. (1975; orig. 1875). *The Communistic Societies of the United States.* New York: Harper.

Norton, A. J., and P. C. Glick. (1986). "One Parent Families: A Social and Economic Profile." In *The Single Parent Family: Special Issue of Family Relations.* New York: National Council on Family Relations.

Norton, Arthur J., and Louisa F. Miller. (1992). "Marriage, Divorce, and Remarriage in the 1990s." In U.S. Bureau of the Census, *Current Population Reports,* Special Studies, Series P-23 No. 180. Washington: Government Printing Office.

Oakes, Jeannie. (1985). *Keeping Track: How Schools Structure Inequality.* New Haven: Yale University Press.

Oakley, Ann. (1975). *The Sociology of Housework.* New York: Pantheon.

Oberai, A. S. (1992). "Assessing the Demographic Impact of Development Projects: Conceptual, Methodological and Policy Issues." United Nations Population Fund, New York: Routledge.

Oberschall, Anthony. (1973). *Social Conflict and Social Movements.* Englewood Cliffs, NJ: Prentice-Hall.

O'Connor, James. (1973). *The Fiscal Crisis of the State.* New York: St. Martin's.

Offe, Claus. (1984). *Contradictions of the Welfare State.* Cambridge, MA: MIT Press.

———. (1985). "The New Social Movements: Challenging the Boundaries of Institutional Politics," *Social Research* 52 (winter): 817-868.

Ogburn, William F. (1964). *On Culture and Social Change.* Chicago: University of Chicago Press.

Okimoto, D. I., T. Sugano, and F. B. Weinstein (eds.). (1984). *Competitive Edge: The Semiconductor Industry in the U.S. and Japan.* Stanford: Stanford University Press.

Oliver Relin, David. (1990). "The Census in History." In *Scholastic Update,* (teacher's ed.) 122 (January): 11.

Ollman, Bertell. (1971). *Alienation: Marx's Concept of Man in Capitalist Society.* Cambridge, England: Cambridge University Press.

Olson, Mancur. (1965). *The Logic of Collective Action.* Cambridge: Harvard University Press.

Omi, Michael. (1989). "In Living Color: Race in American Culture." In Ian Angus and Sut Jhally (eds.), *Cultural Politics in Contemporary America.* New York: Routledge.

Omi, Michael, and Howard Winant. (1986). *Racial Formation in the United States.* New York: Routledge & Kegan Paul.

Omvedt, Gail. (1992). "'Green Earth, Woman's Power, Human Liberation': Woman in Peasant Movements in India," *Development of Dialogue* 1 (2): 116-130.

Ong, Paul M. (1989). *The Widening Divide: Income Inequality and Poverty in Los Angeles.* Los Angeles: University of California, Los Angeles Graduate School of Architecture and Urban Planning.

———. (1994). *The State of Asia Pacific America: Economic Diversity, Issues, and Policies.* Los Angeles: University of California Asian-American Studies Center and LEAP: Asian Pacific American Public Policy Institute.

O'Reilly, Brian. (1992). "Looking Ahead: Jobs Are Fast Moving Abroad," *Fortune* (December 14): 52-66.

Orfield, Gary. (1978). *Must We Bus? Segregated Schools and National Policy.* Washington: Brookings Institution.

———. (1991). *Conservative Policy and Black Opportunity.* Chicago: University of Chicago Press.

Orfield, Gary, and Franklin Montfort. (1993). "Status of School Desegregation." Washington: National School Boards Association.

Organization for Economic Cooperation and Development. (1993). "The Controversy over Health Benefits." Washington.

Ornstein, Norman J., and Mark Schmitt. (1990). "The New World of Interest Politics," *American Enterprise* 1 (January-February): 46-51.

Orru, Marco. (1991). "The Institutional Logic of Small Firm Economies in Italy and Taiwan," *Studies in Comparative Economic Development* 26 (1): 3-28.

Orru, Marco, Nicole Woolsey Biggart, and Gary G. Hamilton. (1991). "Organizational Isomorphism in East Asia." In Walter Powell and Paul DiMaggio (eds.), *The New Institutionalism in Organizational Analysis.* Chicago: University of Chicago Press.

Orru, Marco, Gary G. Hamilton, and Mariko Suzuki. (1989). "Patterns of Intra-Firm Control in Japanese Business," *Organization Studies* 10 (4): 549-574.

Orwell, George, (1949). *1984.* New York: New American Library.

Oster, Patrick. (1993). "The Fast Track Leads Overseas," *Business Week* (November 1): 64-68.

Ostrander, Susan B. (1984). *Women of the Upper Class.* Philadelphia: Temple University Press.

Ostrow, Ronald J. (1993). "Crime Drop: Does Data Tell Whole Story?" *Los Angeles Times* (December 6): A-1.

O'Sullivan See, Katherine, and William J. Wilson. (1988). "Race and Ethnicity." In Neil J. Smelser (ed.), *Handbook of Sociology.* Newbury Park, CA: Sage.

Ouchi, William G. (1982). *Theory Z: How American Business Can Meet the Japanese Challenge.* New York: Avon.

Owen, John. (1983). *Sleight of Hand: The 25 Million Nugan Hand Bank Scandel.* Sydney, Australia: Calplorteur.

Packard, Vance. (1959). *The Status Seekers.* New York: McKay.

Padden, Carol, and Tom Humphries. (1988). *Deaf in America: Voices from a Culture.* Cambridge: Harvard University Press.

Padilla, Felix M. (1992). *The Gang as an American Enterprise.* New Brunswick, NJ: Rutgers University Press.

Pagano, Michael. (1992). *City Fiscal Conditions in 1992.* Washington: National League of Cities (June).

Palen, John J. (1986). *The Urban World* (3rd ed.). New York: McGraw-Hill.

Palen, John J., and Bruce London (eds.). (1984). *Gentrification, Displacement, and Neighborhood Revitalization.* Albany: State University of New York Press.

Palmer, P. (1986). *The Lively Audience: A Study of Children Around the TV Set.* Sydney, Australia: Allen & Unwin.

Palmore, Erdman. (1979). "Predictors of Successful Aging," *Gerontologist* 19 (October): 427-431.

Palmore, Erdman B., Bruce M. Burchett, Gerda G. Fillenbaum, Linda K. George, and Laurence M. Wallman. (1985). *Retirement: Causes and Consequences.* New York: Springer.

Park, Peter (ed.). (1993). *Voices of Change: Participatory Research in the United States and Canada.* Westport, CT: Bergin & Garvey.

Park, Robert Ezra. (1926). "Succession, an Ecological Concept," *American Sociological Review* 1 (April): 171-179.

————. (1967; orig. 1940). *On Social Control and Collective Behavior,* Ralph Turner (ed.). Chicago: University of Chicago Press.

————. (1972). *The Crowd and the Public and Other Essays,* Henry Elsner, Jr. (ed.). Chicago: University of Chicago Press.

Park, Robert Ezra, Ernest Burgess, and Roderick McKenzie (eds.). (1925). *The City.* Chicago: University of Chicago Press.

Parker, Stephen. (1990). *Infomal Marriage: Cohabitiation and the Law.* New York: St. Martin's.

Parnes, Herbert S. (ed.). (1985). *Retirement Among American Men.* Lexington, MA: Heath.

Parsons, Talcott. (1951). *The Social System.* Glencoe, IL: Free Press.

————. (1955). "The American Family: Its Relations to Personality and Social Structure." In Talcott Parsons and Robert F. Bales (eds.), *Family, Socialization, and Interaction Process,* pp. 3-33. Glencoe, IL: Free Press.

————. (1960a). "Some Comments on the Pattern of Religious Organization in the United States." In *Structure and Process in Modern Societies.* Glencoe, IL: Free Press.

————. (1960b). "Towards a Healthy Maturity," *Journal of Health and Social Behavior* 1: 163-173.

————. (1964). *Social Structure and Personality.* London: Macmillan.

————. (1966). *Societies: Evolutionary and Comparative Perspectives.* Englewood Cliffs, NJ: Prentice-Hall.

————. (1967). "Christianity and Modern Insdustrial Society." In Edward A. Tiryakian (ed.), *Sociological Theory, Values, and Sociocultural Change: Essays in Honor of Pitirim A. Sorokin.* New York: Harper Torchbooks.

————. (1969). "On the Concept of Value Commitments." In *Politics and Social Structure.* New York: Free Press.

————. (1975). "The Sick Role and the Role of the Physican Reconsidered," *Health and Society* (summer): 257-278.

Parsons, Talcott, and Leon Mayhew. (1982). *On Institutions and Social Evolution: Selcted Writings.* Chicago: University of Chicago Press.

Pastor, Manuel. (1993). *Latinos and the Economic Uprising: The Economic Context.* Claremont, CA: The Tomas Rivera Center.

Paternoster, Raymond. (1991). *Capital Punishment in America.* New York: Lexington.

Patterson, Don. (1989). "Power in Law Enforcement: Subordinate Preference and Actual Use of Power Base in Special Weapons Teams (SWAT)," Ph. D. diss., Fielding Institute, Human and Organizational Development Program, Santa Barbara, CA.

PC Globe. (1991). "Age Distribution," Tempe, AZ.

Pearson, J. L., and L. R. Ferguson. (1989). "Gender Differences in Patterns of Spatial Ability, Environmental Cognition, and Math and English Achievement in Late Adolescence," *Adolescence* 24: 421-431.

Pence, Gregory E. (1990). "Do Not Go Slowly into That Good Night: Mercy Killing in Holland." In Nancy F. McKenzie (ed.), *The Crisis in Health Care.* New York: Penguin.

Penn, Nolan, Percy Russell, and Harold J. Simon. (1986). "Affirmative Action at Work: A Survey of Graduates of the University of California, San Diego, Medical School," *American Journal of Public Health* 76 (September): 1144-1146.

Pennar, Karen. (1991). "Women Are Still Paid the Wages of Discrimination," *Business Week* (October 28): 35.

———. (1993). "A Crisis of Medical Success," *Business Week* (March 15): 78-80.

Persky, Joseph, Elliott Sclar, and Wim Wiewal. (1991). "Does America Need Cities?" Washington: Economic Policy Institute and the U.S. Conference of Mayors.

Perun, P. J., and Denise D. Bielby. (1979). "Midlife: A Discussion of Competing Models," *Research on Aging* 1: 275-300.

Peters, Jeffe J., James H. Peers, Sidney Olansky, John C. Cutler, and Geraldine Gleeson. (1955). "Untreated Syphilis in the Male Negro," *Journal of Chronic Diseases* 1 (February): 127-148.

Peters, Tom J. (1992). *Liberation Management: Necessary Disorganization for the Nanosecond Ninties.* New York: Knopf.

Peters, Tom J., and R. H. Waterman, Jr. (1982). *In Search of Excellence: Lessons from America's Best-Run Companies.* New York: Harper & Row.

Peterson, Candida C., and James L. Peterson. (1988). "Older Men's and Women's Relationships with Adult Kin: How Equitable Are They?" *International Journal of Aging and Human Development* 27 (3): 221-231.

Peterson, Edmund A. (1993). "It's Only Another Name for Genocide," *Pittsburgh Post-Gazette* (May 5).

Peterson, Kurt. (1992). "The Manquiladora Revolution in Guatemala." Occasional Paper Series 2. New Haven: Yale Law School, Orville H. Schell Jr. Center for International Human Rights.

Peterson, Peter G. (1982). "The Salvation of Social Security," *The New York Review* 35 (December 6).

———. (1987). "The Morning After," *The Atlantic Monthly* (October).

Peterson, Ruth D., and Laura J. Krivko. (1993). "Racial Segregation and Black Urban Homicide," *Social Forces* 71(June): 1001-1026.

Petruno, Tom. (1991). "A Bigger Piece of the Pie," *Los Angeles Times* (May 22): D-1.

Pettigrew, Thomas F. (1989). "The Changing—Not Declining—Significance of Race." In Charles Willie (ed.), *The Class and Caste Controversy on Race and*

Poverty: Round Two of the Wilson-Willie Debate. New York: General-Hall.

Pfeffer, Jeffrey, and James N. Baron. (1988). "Taking the Workers Back Out: Recent Trends in the Structuring of Employment," *Research in Organizational Behavior* 10: 257-303.

Pfeifer, Susan K., and Marvin B. Sussman. (1991). *Families : Intergenerational and Generaltional Connections.* New York: Haworth.

Phillips, F. B. (1978). "Magazine Heroines: Is Ms. Just Another Member of the Family Circle?" In Gaye Tuchman, A. K. Daniels, and J. Benet (eds.), *Hearth and Home,* pp. 116-124. New York: Oxford University Press.

Phillips, Kevin. (1991). *The Politics of Rich and Poor.* New York: HarperCollins.

Phillips, R. (1988). *Putting Asunder: A History of Divorce in Western Society.* New York: Cambridge University Press.

Piaget, Jean. (1926). *The Language and Thought of the Child.* New York: Harcourt, Brace.

———. (1928). *Judment and Reasoning in the Child.* New York: Harcourt, Brace.

———. (1930). *The Child's Conception of Physical Causality.* New York: Harcourt, Brace.

———. (1932). *The Moral Judgment of the Child.* New York: Harcourt, Brace.

Pike Report. (1977). *CIA.* Nottingham, England: Spokesman.

Pillemer, Karl A. (1985). "The Dangers of Dependency: New Findings in Domestic Violence Against the Eldery," *Social Problems* 33 (December): 146-158.

Pillemer, Karl, and David Finkelhor. (1988). "The Prevalence of Elder Abuse: A Random Sample Survey," *The Gerontologist* 28(1): 51-57.

Pillemer, Karl A., and Rosalie S. Wolf. (1986). *Elder Abuse: Conflict in the Family.* Dover, MA: Auburn House.

Piore, Michael J., and Charles F. Sabel. (1984). *The Second Industrial Divide: Possibilities for Prosperity.* New York: Basic Books.

Pirenne, Henri. (1937). *Economic and Social History of Medieval Europe,* I. E. Clegg (trans.). New York: Harcourt, Brace, World.

Pittard, Eugene. (1926). *Race and History.* New York: Knopf.

Piven, Frances Fox, and Richard A. Cloward. (1971). *Regulating the Poor.* New York: Pantheon.

———. (1977). *Poor People's Movements: Why They Succeed, How They Fail.* New York: Random House.

Plett, P. C. (1990). *Training Report: Training of Older Workers in Industrialized Countries.* Geneva: International Labor Organization.

Plett, P. C., and B. T. Lester. (1991). *Training for Older People: A Handbook.* Geneva: International Labor Organization.

Plummer, Kenneth. (1981). *The Making of the Modern Homosexual.* Totowa, NJ: Barnes & Noble.

———. (1984). "Sexual Diversity: A Sociological Perspective." In Kevin Howells (ed.), *The Psychology of Sexual Diversity.* New York: Basil Blackwell.

———. (1991). "Understanding Childhood Sexualities," *Journal of Homosexuality.*

Plunkert, Lois M. (1990). "The 1980's: A Decade of Job Growth and Industry Shifts," *Monthly Labor Review* (September): 3-15.

Podesta, Don. (1993). "Two Generals Convicted in Killing of Letelier: Chileans to Be Jailed for Washington Murder," *Washington Post* (November 13): A-19.

Podsakoff, Phillip, and Chester Schriesheim. (1985). "Field Studies of French and Raven's Bases of Power: Critique, Reanalysis, and Suggestions for Future Research," *Psychological Bulletin* 97 (3): 387-411.

Pollard, Kevin M. (1992). "African Americans in the 1990s," Washington: Population Reference Bureau.

Pomer, Marshall I. (1986). "Labor Market Structure, Intergenerational Mobility, and Discrimination: Black Male Advancement Out of Low-Paying Occupations, 1962-1973," *American Sociological Review* 51 (October): 650-659.

Pool, Ithiel de Sola. (1966). "Communications and Development." In M. Weiner (ed.), *Modernization: The Dynamics of Growth.* Washington: Voice of America.

Popper, Karl. (1959). *The Logic of Scientific Discovery.* New York: Basic Books.

Porter, Michael E. (1990a). "The Competitive Advantage of Nations," *Harvard Business Review* (March/April): 73-93.

———. (1990b). *The Competitive Advantage of Nations.* New York: Free Press.

Portes, Alejandro. (1981). "Modes of Structural Incorporation and Present Theories of Immigration." In Mary M. Kritz, Charles B. Keely, and Sylvano M. Tomasi (eds.), *Global Trends in Migration.* Staten Island, NY: CMS.

Portes, Alejandro, and Leif Jensen. (1987). "Comment: What's an Ethnic Enclave? The Case for Conceptual Clarity," *American Sociological Review* 52 (December): 768-771.

Potter, Karl H. (1992). "Hinduism." In the *American Academic Encyclopedia* (on-line edition). Danbury, CT: Grolier Electronic Publishing.

Powell, Catherine Tabb. (1991). "Rap Music: An Education with a Beat from the Street," *The Journal of Negro Education* 60 (summer): 245-259.

Powell, Walter W., and Paul DiMaggio. (1991). *The New Institutionism in Organizational Analysis.* Chicago: University of Chicago Press.

Prasad, B. (ed.). (1989). *Robotics and Factories of the Future* 3 vols. New York: Springer-Verlag.

Prebisch, Raul. (1967). *Hacia una dinámica del desarollo Latinoamericano.* Montevideo, Uraguay: Ediciones de la Banda Oriental.

———. (1971). *Change and Development—Latin America's Great Task; Report Submitted to the Inter-American Bank.* New York: Praeger.

Pressley, Sue Anne. (1993). "The People Ask: What's in a Name for the Navajo?" *Washington Post* (December 17): B-5.

Prestwick, Michael. (1985). "The Art of Kingship: Edward I, 1272-1307," *History Today* 35: 34-40.

Priest, Dana. (1993). "The Road to Health Care Reform," *Washington Post* (January 26): 12-17.

Princeton Survey Research Associates (PRSA). (1993). "What Do You Think Is the Most Important Problem Facing the Country Today?" National Opinion Poll. University of Connecticut: Roper Center for Public Opinion Research (December 9).

Prior, Lindsay. (1993). *The Social Organization of Mental Illness.* Newbury Park, CA: Sage.

Proverce, Sally, and Audrey Naylor. (1983). *Working with Disadvantaged Parents and Their Children: Scientific and Practice Issues.* New Haven: Yale University Press.

Quadagno, Jill. (1989). "Generational Equity and the Politics of the Welfare State," *Politics and Society* 17 (September): 353-376.

Queen, S. A., R. Habenstein, and J. Adams. (1961). *The Family in Various Cultures.* New York: Lippencott.

Raab, Earl (ed.). (1991). *American Jews in the 21st Century: A Leadership Challenge.* Atlanta, GA: Scholars.

Rada, Juan. (1985). "Information Technology and the Third World." In Tom Forrester (ed.), *The Information Revolution.*

Radaev, Vadim, and Ovsey Shkaratan. (1992). "Etacratism: Power and Property—Evidence from the Soviet Experience," *International Society* 7 (3): 301-316.

Radcliffe-Brown, A. R., and D. Forde. (1950). *African Systems of Kinship and Marriage.* London: Oxford University Press.

Ramirez, Francisco O., and John W. Meyer. (1980). "Comparative Education: The Social Construction of the Modern World System," *Annual Review of Sociology* 6: 369-399.

Randal, Judith. (1993). "The Jackson Hole Gang," *The Progressive* 57: 25.

Ransford, H. Edward, and Bartolomeo J. Palisi. (1992). "Has There Been a Resurgence of Racist Attitudes in the General Population?" *Sociological Spectrum* 12 (July-September): 231-255.

Raven, B., and W. Kruglianski. (1975). "Conflict and Power." In P. Swingle (ed.), *Structure of Conflict,* pp. 177-219. New York: Academic.

Real, Michael. (1977). *Mass-Mediated Culture.* Englewood Cliffs, NJ: Prentice-Hall.

Redding, S. G. (1990). *The Spirit of Chinese Capitalism.* Berlin:de Gruyter.

Reed, Evelyn. (1970). *Woman's Liberation.* New York: Pathfinder.

Reeves, Joy B., and Nydia Boyette. (1983). "What Does Children's Art Work Tell Us About Gender?" *Qualitative Sociology* 6 (winter): 322-333.

Reich, Robert B. (1991). *The Work of Nations.* New York: Knopf.

Reichert, Joshua S., and Douglas S. Massey. (1982). "Guestworker Programs: Evidence from Europe and the United States and Some Implications for U.S. Policy," *Population Research and Policy Review* 1 (January): 1-17.

Reid, T. R. (1992). "The Company Wedding: Bowing into a Japanese Firm Is for Life," *Washington Post* (April 2): A-21.

Reidel, Marc, and Margaret A. Zahn. (1985). *The Nature and Patterns of American Homicide.* Washington: U.S. Department of Justice.

Renzetti, Claire M., and Daniel J. Curran. (1992). *Women, Men, and Society* (2nd ed.). Boston: Allyn & Bacon.

Reskin, Barbara F., and Heidi Hartmann (eds.). (1986). *Woman's Work, Men's Work: Sex Segregation on the Job.* Washington: National Academy Press.

Rex, John. (1986). *Theories of Race and Ethnic Relations.* New York: Cambridge University Press.

Rhinegold, Howard. (1991). *Virtual Reality.* New York: Simon & Schuster.

Rice, D. P. (1986). "The Medical Care System: Past Trends and Future Projections," *New York Medical Quarterly* 6: 39-70.

Rice, Marnie E., Vernon L,. Quinsaey, and Grant T. Harris. (1991). "Sexual Recidivism Among Child Molesters Released from a Maximun Security Psychiatric Institution," *Journal of Consulting and Clinical Psychology* 59 (3): 381-386.

Ricketts, Erol R., and Isabel V. Sawhill. (1988). "Defining and Measuring the Underclass," *Journal of Policy Analysis and Management* 7 (2): 316-325.

Riley, Matilda White, Anne Foner, and Joan Waring. (1988). "Sociology of Age." In Neil J. Smelser (ed.), *Handbook of Sociology.* Newbury Park, CA: Sage.

Rindfuss, Ronald R., C. Gray Swicegood, and Rachel Rosenfeld. (1987). "Disorder in the Life Course: How Common and Does it Matter?" *American Sociological Review* 52: 785-801.

Risman, Barbara J. (1982). "College Women and Sororities: The Social Construction and Reaffirmation of Gender Roles," *Urban Life* 11 (July): 231-252.

Rist, Ray C. (1970). "Student, Social Class, and Teacher Expectations: The Self-Fulfilling Prophecy in Ghetto Education," *Harvard Educational Review* 40: 411-451.

———. (1973). *The Urban School: A Factory for Failure.* Cambridge: Harvard University Press.

———. (1979). *Desegregated Schools: Appraisals of an American Experiment.* New York: Academic.

Ritzer, George. (1983)."The McDonaldization of Society," *Journal of American Culture* 6: 100-107.

———. (1992). *Sociological Theory* (3rd ed.). New York: McGraw-Hill.

Ritzer, George, and David Walczak. (1988). "Rationalization and the Deprofessionalization of Physicians," *Social Forces* 67 (September): 1-22.

Robbins, John. (1987). *Diet for a New America.* Walpole, NH: Stillpoint.

Robertson, H. M. (1933). *Aspects of the Rise of Economic Individualism: A Criticism of Max Weber and His School.* Cambridge, England: Cambridge University Press.

Robertson, R. T. (1986). *The Making of the Modern World.* London: Zed.

Robertson, Roland. (1992). *Globalization: Social Theory and Global Culture.* Newbury Park, CA: Sage.

Robinson, J. G., and J. S. McIlwee. (1989). "Women in Engineering: A Promise Unfilled?" *Social Problems* 36: 455-472.

Robinson, Mile. (1992). "Running for Congress Gets Costlier Each Time," *Santa Barbara News-Press* (May 10): A-5.

Robinson, Paul A. (1969). *The Freudian Left: Wilhelm Reich, Geza Roheim, Herbert Marcuse.* New York: Harper & Row.

Robinson, Richard, and Willard Johnson. (1982). *The Buddhist Religion* (3rd ed.). Belmont, CA: Wadsworth.

Rock, Paul. (1973). "News as Eternal Recurrence." In Stanley Cohen and Jock Young (eds.), *The Manufacture of News.* Beverley Hills, CA: Sage.

Rodger, John J. (1991). "Family Structures and the Moral Politics of Caring," *The Sociological Review* 39 (November): 799-822.

Rodinson, M. (1978). *Islam and Capitalism.* Austin: University of Texas Press.

Roethlisberger, Fritz J., and Willaim J. Dickerson. (1939). *Management and the Worker.* Cambridge: Harvard University Press.

Romero, Mary. (1992). *Maid in the U.S.A.,* New York: Routledge.

Roof, Wade Clark. (1978). *Community and Commitment: Religious Plausibility in a Liberal Protestant Church.* New York: Elsevier.

———. (1993). *A Generation of Seekers.* San Francisco: Harper.

Roof, Wade Clark, and William McKinney. (1987). *American Mainline Religion: Its Changing Shape and Future.* New Brunswick, NJ: Rutgers University Press.

Roos, Patricia A. (1985). *Gender and Work: A Comparative Analysis of Industrial Societies.* Albany: State University of New York Press.

Roper Center for Public Opinion Research. (1993a). "Do You Think Race Relations in the U.S. Are Generally

Good or Generally Bad?" CBS/*New York Times* National Poll (March 28-31). Storrs, CT: University of Connecticut.

———. (1993b). "When Someone Refers to Your Race, Do You Prefer to Be Called Black, African-American, or Do You Prefer Some Other Term?" NBC News/*Wall Street Journal* National Poll. Storrs, CT: University of Connecticut.

Rose, Steven, R. C. Lewontin, and Leon J. Kamin. (1984). *Not in the Genes.* New York: Pantheon.

Rosenbaum, James E., and Patricia Meaden. (1992). "Harrassment and Acceptance of Low-Income Black Youth in White Suburban Schools," Center for Urban Affairs and Policy Research Working Paper #WP-91-6 (spring). Evanston, IL.

Rosenberg, Norman J., and Pierre R. Crosson. (1988). "Special Workshop—RFF Workshop on Greenhouse Warming," *Resources* (fall): 14-16.

Rosenblatt, Robert A. (1993). "Benefits Studied for Part-Time Workers," *Los Angeles Times* (June 16): D-14.

Rosencrance, John. (1985). "Compulsive Gambling and the Medicalization of Deviance," *Social Problems* 32 (February): 275-284.

Rosener, J. B. (1990). "Ways Women Lead," *Harvard Business Review* (November-December): 119-125.

Rosenstiel, Thomas B. (1991). "Americans Praise Media But Still Back Censorship, Postwar Poll Says." *Los Angeles Times* (March 25): A-9.

Rosenthal, Donna. (1993). "Linking Up with a Rising Star on the Global Dial," *Los Angeles Times* (August 7): F-1.

Rosenthal Robert, and Lenore Jacobson. (1968). *Pygmalion in the Classroom: Teacher Expectation and Student's Intellectual Development.* New York: Holt, Rinehart & Winston.

Rosenthal, S. J., and B. J. Zimmerman (1978). *Social Learning and Cognition.* New York: Academic.

Ross, H. and H. Taylor. (1989). "Do Boys Prefer Daddy or His Physical Style of Play?" *Sex Roles* 20 (January): 23-33.

Ross, Robert, and Kent Trachte. (1990). *Global Capitalisism: The New Leviathan.* Albany: State University of New York Press.

Rosser, Phyllis. (1989). *The SAT Gender Gap: Identifying the Causes.* Washington: Center for Women Policy Studies.

Rossi, Alice.(1973). *The Feminist Papers.* New York: Bantam Books.

Rossi, Peter H. (1988). "On Sociological Data." In Neil J. Smelser (ed.), *Handbook of Sociology.* Newbury Park, CA: Sage.

———. (1989). *Down and Out in America: The Origins of Homelessness.* Chicago: University of Chicago Press.

Rossi, Peter, Emily Waite, Christine Bose, and Richard Berk. (1974). "The Seriousness of Crimes: Normative

Structure and Individual Differences," *American Sociological Review* 39: 224-237.

Rossi, Peter, and S. R. Wright. (1977). "Evaluation Research: An Assessment of Theory, Practice, and Politics," *Evaluation Quarterly* 1: 5-12.

Rostow, W. W. (1961). *The Stages of Economic Growth.* Cambridge, England: Cambridge University Press.

Roszak, Theodore. (1969). *The Making of a Counterculture: Reflections on the Technocratic Society and Its Youthful Opposition.* New York: Doubleday.

Rothenberg, Stuart, and Frank Newport. (1984). *The Evangelical Voter: Religion and Politics in America.* Washington: Institute for Government and Politics.

Rothschild-Whitt, Joyce. (1979). "The Collectivist Organization: An Alternative to Rational-Bureaucratic Models," *American Sociological Review* 44: 509-527.

Rothschild, Joyce, and Alan Whitt. (1987). *The Cooperative Work Place: Potentials and Dilemmas of Organizational Democracy and Participation.* New York: Cambridge Univesity Press.

Rothstein, Richard (1993a). "Low Wages in Developing Countries = Poverty in the U.S.," *Poverty and Race* 2 (March): 6-7.

———. (1993b). "Continental Drift: NAFTA and Its Aftershocks," *The American Prospect* 12 (winter): 68-84.

Rowbotham, Sheila. (1973). *Woman's Consciousness, Man's World.* Middlesex, England: Pelican.

Rowe, R. H., and R. L. Kahn. (1987). "Human Aging: Usual and Successful," *Science Magazine* (July 10): 143-149.

Rubenstein, Richard E. (1970). *Rebels in Eden.* Boston: Little, Brown.

Rubinowitz, Leonard S. (1992). "Metropolitan Public Housing Desegregation Remedies: Chicago's Privatization Program," *Northern Illinois University Law Review* 12 (3): 589-669.

Rule, James, and Peter Brantley. (1992). "Computerized Surveillance in the Workplace: Forms and Distributions," *Sociological Forum* 7 (September): 405-423.

Rumer, Boris, and Eugene Rumer. (1992). "Who'll Stop the Next Yugoslavia?" *World Monitor* (November): 37-44.

Russakoff, Dale. (1993). "Changing Work Fractures Lives of Steel Families," *Washington Post* (March 28): A-1.

Russell, Diana E. H. (1984). *Sexual Exploitation: Rape, Child Sexual Abuse, and Workplace Harassment.* Beverley Hills, CA: Sage.

Russell, Margaret L. (1991). "Race and Dominant Gaze: Narratives of Law and Inequality in Popular Film," *Legal Studies Forum* 15 (3): 243-254.

Rutter, Michael. (1979). *Fifteen Thousand Hours: Secondary Schools and Their Effects on Children.* Cambridge: Harvard University Press.

Rutter, Michael, and Henri Giller. (1984). *Juvenile Delinquecy: Trends and Perspectives*. New York: Guilford.

Ryan, William. (1976). *Blaming the Victim* (rev. ed.). New York: Vintage.

Rymer, Russ. (1993). Genie: An Abused Child's Flight from Silence. New York: HarperCollins.

Sacks, Harvey. (1989; orig. 1964-1965). "Harvey Sacks: Lectures 1964-1965," Gail Jefferson (ed.), *Human Studies* 12 (3-4): 211-393.

———. (1992). *Lectures on Conversation: Harvey Sacks*, vols. 1 and 2, Gail Jefferson (ed.), with an introduction by Emanuel A. Shegloff (Lectures 1964-1972). Cambridge, MA: Basil Blackwell.

Sacks, Harvey, Emanuel Shegloff, and Gail Jefferson. (1974). "A Simplest Systematics for the Origin of Turn-Taking for Conversation," *Language* 50: 696-735.

Sacks, Oliver W. (1990). *Seeing Voices: A Journey Into the World of the Deaf*. New York: HarperCollins.

Sadker, Myra, and David Sadker. (1985). "Sexism in the Schoolroom of the 80's," *Psychology Today* 19 (March): 54-57.

———. (1994). *Failing at Fairness: How America's Schools Cheat Girls*. New York: Scribners.

Sagan, Eli. (1992). *The Honey and the Hemlock: Democracy and Paranoia in Ancient Athens and Modern America*. New York: Basic Books.

Sahlins, Marshall D. (1972). *Stone Age Economics*. Chicago: Aldine.

Sahlins, Marshall D., and Elman R. Service. (1960). *Evolution and Culture*. Ann Arbor: University of Michigan Press.

Sahliyeh, Emile (ed.). (1990). *Religious Resurgence and Politics in the Contemporary World*. Albany: State University of New York Press.

Salaff, Janet W. (1992). "Women, the Family, and the State in Hong Kong, Taiwan, and Singapore." In Richard P. Appelbaum and Jeffery Henderson (eds.), *States and Development in the Asian Pacific Rim*. Newbury Park, CA: Sage.

Saline, C. (1984). "Bleeding in the Suburbs," *Philadelphia Magazine* (March): 81-85, 144-151.

Salisbury, Richard F., and Elisabeth Tooker. (1984). *Affluence and Cultural Survival*. Washington: Proceedings of the American Ethnological Society.

Samuelson, Kurt. (1961). *Religion and Economic Action*. New York: Basic Books.

Sanchez-Aye'ndez, Melba. (1986). "Puerto Rican Elderly Women: Shared Meanings and Informal Supportive Networks." In Johnnetta Cole (ed.), *All American Women: Lines That Divide, Ties That Bind*, pp. 172-186. New York: Free Press.

Sanday, Peggy Reeves. (1979). *The Socio-Cultural Context of Rape*. Washington: Department of Commerce, National Technical Information Service.

Sanders, Jimy M., and Victor Nee. (1987). "Limits of Ethnic Solidarity in Enclave Economy," *American Sociological Review* 52 (December): 745-767.

Sanders, M., and M. Rock. (1988). *Waiting for Prime Time: The Women of Television News*. New York: HarperCollins.

Sandoz, Mari. (1961). *These Were the Sioux*. New York: Hastings House.

Sankar, A. (1988). " The Living Dead: Cultural Construction of the Oldest-Old." In Philip Silverman (ed.), *The Elderly as Modern Pioneers*, pp. 345-356. Bloomington: Indiana University Press.

Sarbanes, Paul. (1992). "Men at Work: Signs of Trouble, "Washington: Joint Economic Committee of Congress: (September).

Sassen, Saskia. (1991). *The Global City: New York, London, Tokyo*. Princeton: Princeton University Press.

Satre, Jean Paul. (1965; orig. 1948). *Anti-Semite and Jew*. New York: Schocken.

Sawhill, Isabel V. (1989). "The Underclass: An Overview," *The Public Interest* 96: 3-15.

Saxton, Alexander Plaisted. (1971). *The Indispensible Enemy: Labor and the Anti-Chinese Movement in California*. Berkeley: University of California Press.

Schaefer, R. T. (1993). *Racial and Ethnic Groups* (5th ed.). New York: HarperCollins.

Schaie, K. Warner. (1979). "The Primary Mental Abilities in Adulthood: An Exploration in the Development of Psychometric Intellegence." In Paul B. Baltes and O.G. Brim (eds.), *Lifespan Development and Behavior*, vol. 2. New York: Academic.

———. (1983). *Longitudinal Studies of Adult Psychological Development*. New York: Guilford.

———. (1984). "Midlife Influences Upon Intellectual Functioning in Old Age," *International Journal of Behavioral Development* 7: 463-478.

Schaler, Jeffery A. (1991). "Drugs and Free Will," *Society* 28 (September/October): 42-49.

Scheff, Thomas. (1966). *Being Mentally Ill*. Chicago: Aldine.

———. (1984). *Being Mentally Ill: A Sociological Theory* (2nd ed.). New York: Aldine.

———. (1988). "Shame and Conformity: The Deference-Emotion System," *American Sociological Review* 53: 395-406.

———. (1994). *Bloody Revenge: Emotions, Nationalism and War*. San Francisco: Westview.

Scheff, Thomas J., and Suzanne M. Retzinger. (1991). *Emotions and Violence: Shame and Rage in Destructive Conflicts*. Lexington, MA: Lexington.

Schegloff, Emanuel A. (1968). "Sequencing in Conversational Openings," *American Anthropologist* 70: 1975-1995.

———. (1986). "The Routine as Achievement," *Human Studies* 9: 111-152.

———. (1987). "Analyzing Single Episodes of Interaction: An Exercise in Conversation Analysis," *Social Psychology Quarterly* 50 (June): 101-114.

———. (1989). "From Interview to Confrontation: Observations on the Bush/Rather Encounter," *Research on Language and Social Action* 22: 215-240

———. (1990). " On the Organization of Sequences As a Source of 'Coherence' in Talk-in-Interaction." In Bruce Dorval (ed.), *Conversational Organization and Its Development*, pp. 55-77. Vol. 38 in the series, *Advances in Discourse Processes*. Norwood, NJ: Ablex.

———. (1991). "Reflections on Talk and Social Structure." In Don H. Zimmerman and Dierdre Boden (eds.), *Talk and Social Structure*. Cambridge, England: Polity.

Schiffer, J. (1991) "State Policy and Economic Growth: A Note on the Hong Kong Model," *International Journal of Urban and Regional Research* 15.

Schiller, Herbert. (1989) *The Corporate Takeover of Public Expression*. New York: Oxford University Press.

Schmidt, Roger. (1980). *Exploring Religion*. Belmont, CA: Wadsworth.

Schnaiberg, Allan. (1980). *The Environment: From Surplus to Scarcity*. New York: Oxford University Press.

Schneider, D., and E. Gough (eds.). (1974). *Matrilineal Kinship,* Berkeley: University of California Press.

Schneider, William. (1992). "The Suburban Century Begins," *Atlantic* (July): 33-39.

Schoenberger, E. (1988). "Multinational Corporations and the New Industrial Division of Labor: A Critical Appraisal," *International Regional Science Review* 11: 105-121.

Schoenfeld, Gabriel. (1991). "The End: The Total Collapse of the USSR," *New Republic* (January): 23-25.

Schooler, Carmi. (1987). "Cognitive Effects of Complex Environments During the Life Span: A Review and Theory." In Carmi Schooler and K. Warner Schaie (eds.), *Cognitive Functioning and Social Structure Over the Life Course*, pp. 24-29. Norwood, NJ: Ablex.

Schoonmaker, Sara J. (1991). "Trading On-Line: Communications and Power in Global Capitalism." Paper presented at the annual meeting of the American Sociological Association.

Schramm, W. (1964). *Mass Media and National Development*. Stanford: UNESCO and Stanford University Press.

———. (1977). *Big Media, Little Media*. Beverley Hill, CA: Sage.

———. (1979). *Mass Media and National Development, 1979.* Paris: UNESCO, International Commission for the Study of Communication Problems.

Schreiber, Leslie S. (1993). "Alcohol and Campus Sexual Deviance: Students' Neutralization of Responsibility," Ph.D. diss. George Washington University.

Schrire, Carmel (ed.). (1984). *Past and Present in Hunter gather Societies*. New York: Academic.

Schudson, Michael. (1978). *Discovering the News: A Social History of American Newspapers*. New York: Basic Books.

———. (1990). *Origins of the Ideal of Objectivity in the Professions: Studies in the History of American Journalism and American Law, 1830-1940*. New York: Garland.

———. (1992). "The Limits of Teledemocracy," *The American Prospect* 11 (fall): 41-45.

Schur, Edwin, and Hugo Adam Bedau. (1974). *Victimless Crimes: Two Sides of a Controversy*. Englewood Cliffs, NJ: Prentice-Hall.

Schussler, Firoenza, Elisabeth. (1983). *In Memory of Her: A Feminist Theological Reconstruction of Christian Origins*. New York: Crossroad.

Schwartz, Gary. (1970). *Sect Ideologies and Social Status*. Chicago: University of Chicago Press.Schwartz, Felice N. (1989). "Management, Women, and the New Facts of Life," Harvard Business Review 89 (January-February): 65-76.

Schweninger, Loren. (1982). "James T. Rapier of Alabama and the Noble Cause of Reconstruction," In Howard N. Rabinowitz (ed.), *Southern Black Leaders of the Reconstruction Era*. Urbana: University of Illinois Press.

Scott, Alan. (1990). *Ideology and the New Social Movements*. London & Boston: Unwin Hyman.

Scott, Allen J. (1988)."Flexible Production Systems and Regional Development," *International Journal of Urban and Regional Research* 12: 171-186.

Scott, Greg. (1993). "Achieving Dignity and Embracing Hope: Daily Battles for Justice in the Los Angeles Garment Industry." Report to the John Randolph and Dora Haynes Foundation (August 11). Santa Barbara, CA: Center for Global Studies, Pacific Rim Projects.

Scott, John. (1980). *Corporations, Classes, and Capitalism*. New York: St. Martin's.

Scully, Diana. (1990). *Understanding Sexual Violence: A Study of Convicted Rapists*. Boston: Unwin Hyman.

Seavy, C., P. Katz, and R. Zalk. (1975). "Baby X: The Effect of Gender Labels on Adult Responses to Infants," *Sex Roles* 1: 103-109.

Sebald, Hans. (1992). *Adolescence: A Social Psychological Analysis*. Englewood Cliffs, NJ: Prentice-Hall.

Sedney, M. (1987). "Development of Androgyny: Parental Influences." *Psychology of Women Quarterly* 11: 311-326.

Seefeldt, C., and S. Keawkungwal. (1985). "Children's Attitudes Toward the Elderly in Thailand and the United States," *International Journal of Comparative Sociology* 26: 226-232.

Segura, Denise A. (1989). "Chicana and Mexican Immigrant Women at Work: The Impact of Class, Race, and Gender on Occupational Mobility," *Gender and Society* 3: 37-52.

Sellin, Thorsten. (1938). *Culture Conflict and Crime*. New York: Social Science Research Council.

Spates, James L. (1976). "Cuntercultural and Dominant Culture Values: A Cross-National Analysis of the Underground Press and Dominant Cultural Magazines," *American Sociological Review* 41 (October): 868-883.

Specter, Michael. (1991). "Illegal Child Labor Resurging in U.S.: Immigrant Schoolgirls Toil in Modern-Day Sweatshops," *Washington Post* (November 12): A7-10.

Speicher, Barbara L., and Seane M. McMahon. (1992). "Some African-American Perspectives on Black English Vernacular," *Language in Society* 21 (September): 383-407.

Spencer, Herbert. (1860). *The Social Organism.* London: Greenwood.

Spencer, Rich. (1993). "Average Staff Doctor Said to Earn $139,700," *Washington Post* (February 4): A-3.

Spengler, Oswald. (1918). *The Decline of the West.* New York: Knopf.

Spiegel, Lyn. (1991). *Critical Perspectives on Media and Society: The Domestic Economy of Television Viewing in Postwar America.* New York: Guilford.

Spirn, Anne Whiston. (1984). *The Granite Garden:Urban Nature and Human Design.* New York: Basic Books.

Spradley, Thomas S., and James P. Spradley. (1985). *Deaf Like Me.* Washington: Gallaudet College Press.

Spufford, Peter. (1988). *Money and Its Use in Medieval Europe.* Cambridge, England: Cambridge University Press.

St. John, Nancy Hoyt. (1975). *School Desegregation: Outcomes for Children.* New York: Wiley.

Stacey, Judith. (1990). *Brave New Families: Stories of Domestic Upheaval in Late Twentieth Century America.* New York: Basic Books.

Stack, Carol B. (1974). *All Our Kin: Strategies for Survival in A Black Community.* New York: Harper & Row.

Stanback, Thomas M., Jr. (1991). *The New Suburbanization: Challenge to the Central City.* Boulder, CO: Westview.

Stanfield, James Ronald. (1990). "Keynesianism, Monetarism, and the Crisis of the State: A Review Article," *Journal of Economic Issues* 24 (12): 1139-1146.

Stanko, E. A. (1985). *Intimate Intrusions.* London: Routledge.

Staples, R. and T. Jones. (1985). "Culture, Ideology, and Black Television Images," *The Black Scholar* 16: 10-20.

Starhawk. (1979). "Witchcraft and Women's Culture." In P. Christ and J. Plaskow (eds.), *Womanspirit Rising*, pp. 259-268. San Francisco: Harper & Row.

Stark, Rodney. (1990). "Modernization, Secularization, and Mormon Success." In Thomas Robbins and Dick Anthony (eds.), *In Gods We Trust: New Patterns of Religious Pluralism in America.* New Brunswick, NJ: Transaction.

Stark, Rodney, and William Sims Bainbridge. (1980). "Towards a Theory of Religious Commitment," *Journal for the Scientific Study of Religion* 19: 114-128.

———. (1985). *The Future of Religion: Secularization, Revival, and Cult Formation.* Berkeley: University of California Press.

———. (1987). *A Theory of Religion.* New York: Peter Lang.

Starr, Paul. (1982). *The Social Transformation of Medicine: The Rise of a Sovereign Profession and the Making of a Vast Industry.* New York: Basic Books.

Starrels, Marjorie. (1992). "Attitude Similarity Between Mothers and Children Regarding Material Employment," *Journal of Marriage and the Family* 54 (February): 91-103.

Steenland, S. (1988). *Growing Up in Prime Time: An Analysis of Girls on Television.* Washington: National Commission on Working Women.

Stein, Jeannine. (1986). " Why Girls as Young as Nine Fear Fat and Go on Diets to Lose Weight," *Los Angeles Times* (October 9): View-1.

Stein, L. I., and Mary Ann Test (eds.). (1978). *Alternatives to Mental Hospital Treatment.* New York: Plenum.

Steinbrook, Robert. (1988). "AIDS Summit Delegates Adopt a Unanimous Call for Action," *Los Angeles Times* (January 29): I-3.

Steinem, Gloria. (1990). "Sex, Lies, and Advertising," *Ms.* (July/August): 18-28.

Steinmetz, Suzanne K. (1981). "Elder Abuse," *Aging*: 6-10.

———. (1983). "Family Violence Towards Elders." In Susan Saunders, Ann Anderson, and Cynthia Hart (eds.), *Violent Individuals and Families: A Practitioner's Handbook.* Springfield, IL: Charles C. Thomas.

Stephens, Gene. (1990). "High-Tech Crime Fighting: The Threat to Civil Liberties," *The Futurist* 24 (July-August): 20-25.

Stepick, Alex III, and Guillermo Grenier. (1993). "Cubans in Miami." In Joan Moore and Raquel Pinderhughes (ed.), *In the Barrios: Latinos and the Underclass Debate.* New York: Russell Sage Foundation.

Stevens, William K. (1991). "Here's Ozone News: Use Sun Protection," *Santa Barbara News-Press* (April 13): A-15.

Stevenson, Richard W. (1993) "Swedes Facing Rigors of Welfare Cuts," *New York Times* (March 14): 18.

Stewart, Thomas A. (1991). "Gay in Corporate America," *Fortune* (December 16): 42-56.

Stone, Lawrence. (1982). *The Family, Sex, and Marriage in England*, 1500-1800. Harmondsworth: Pelican.

Stone, Michael. (1993). *Shelter Poverty: New Ideas on Housing Affordability.* Philadelphia: Temple University Press.

Storper, M., and S. Christopherson. (1987). "Flexible Specialization and Regional Industrial Agglomeration: The Case of the U.S. Motion Picture Industry," *Annals of the Association of American Geographers* 77: 104-117.

Straus, Murray A. (1977). "Societal Morphogenesis and Intrafamily Violence in a Cross-Cultural Perspective," *Annals of New York Academy of Science* 28: 719-730.

Straus, Murray A., and Richard J. Gelles. (1985). "Societal Change and Change in Family Violence from 1975-1985 as Revealed in Two National Surveys," *Journal of Marriage and Family* 48: 465-479.

———. (1988). "Violence in American Families: How Much Is There and Why Does It Occur?" In Elam W. Nunnaly, Catherine S. Chilman, and Fred M. Cox (eds.), *Troubled Relationships,* pp. 141-162. Newbury Park, CA: Sage.

——— (eds.). (1990). *Physical Violence in American Families: Risk Factors and Adaptations to Violence in 8,145 Families.* New Brunswick, NJ: Transaction.

Straus, Murray A., and Richard J. Gelles, and Suzanne K. Steinmetz. (1988). *Behind Closed Doors: Violence in the American Family.* Newbury Park, CA: Sage.

Straus, Steven E. (1987). "EB or Not EB — That Is the Question?" *Journal of the American Medical Association* 257 (May 1): 2335-2336.

———. (1988a). "Allergy and Chronic Fatigue Syndrome," *Journal of Allergy and Clinical Immunology* 81 (May): 791-795.

———. (1988b). "Acyclovir Treatment of CFS," *New England Journal of Medicine* 319 (December): 26.

———, et al. (1985). "Persisting Illness and Fatigue in Adults With Evidence of Epstein-Barr and Viris Infection," *Annals of Internal Medicine* 102: 7-16.

Stuckey, Sterling. (1993). "W. E. B. DuBois." In the *American Academic Encyclopedia* (on-line edition). Danbury, CT: Grolier Electronic Publishing.

Stumpf, H., and Kleine, E. (1989). "Sex-related Differences in Spatial Ability: More Evidence for Convergence," *Perceptual and Motor Skills* 69 (3): 915-921.

Sullivan, Deborah, and Rose Weitz. (1988). *Labor Pains.* New Haven: Yale University Press.

Sullivan, Mercer L. (1989). *Getting Paid: Youth Crime and Work in the Inner City.* Ithaca, NY: Cornell University Press.

Sumner, William Graham. (1906). *Folkways: A Study of the Sociological Importance of Usages, Manners, Customs, Mores, and Morals.* Boston: Ginn.

———. (1913). *The Challange of Fact and Other Essays.* New Haven: Yale University Press.

Suppe, Frederick. (1974). "The Search for Philosophic Understanding of Scientific Theories." In Frederick Suppe (ed.), *The Structure of Scientific Theories.* Urbana: University of Illinois Press.

Sussman, Gerald, and John A. Lent. (1991). *Transnational Communications: Wiring the Third World.* Newbury Park, CA: Sage.

Sutherland, Edwin H. (1928). *Criminology.* Philadelphia: Lippencott.

———. (1937). *The Professional Thief.* Chicago: University of Chicago Press.

Sutherland, Edwin H., Donald R. Cressey, and David Luckenbill. (1992). *Principles of Criminology.* Philadelphia: Lippencott.

Suttles, Gerald. (1968). *The Social Order of the Slum.* Chicago: University of Chicago Press.

Suzuki, Bob H. (1977). "Education and the Socialization of Asian Americans: A Revisionist Analysis of the 'Model Minority' Thesis," *Amerasia Journal* 4: 43.

Swain, Tony. (1993). *A Place for Strangers: Towards A History of Australian Aboriginal Being.* Cambridge, England: Cambridge University Press.

Sweeney, Rosemarie, and James G. Jones. (1993). "The Case for Family Practice and Primary Care Research at the NIH," *American Family Physician* 47 (January): 37-39.

Sweet, J., and L. Bumpass. (1987). *American Families and Households.* New York: Russell Sage Foundation.

Swenson, Chester A. (1990). *Selling to a Segmented Market: The Lifestyle Approach.* New York: Quorum.

Swidler, Ann. (1986). "Culture in Action: Symbols and Strategies," *American Sociological Review* 51 (April): 273-286.

Symons, Donald. (1979). *The Evolution of Human Sexuality.* New York: Oxford University Press.

Symposium of Sickle Cell Disease. (1971). "Sickle Cell Diease; Diagnosis, Management, Education, and Research." St. Louis: Mosby.

Szasz, Thomas. (1970). *The Manufacture of Madness.* New York: Harper & Row.

———. (1987). *Insanity: The Idea and Its Consequences.* New York: Wiley.

Taeuber, C. M., and V. Valdisera. (1986). *Women in the American Economy.* Current Population Reports, Series P-23 No. 146. Washington: Government Printing Office.

Takaki, Ronald. (1989). *Strangers from a Different Shore: A History of Asian Americans.* Boston: Little, Brown.

Tamar, Lewin. (1993). "Man is Allowed to Let Daughter Die," *New York Times* (January 27): A12-4.

Tancred-Sherriff, P. (1989). "Gender, Sexuality, and the Labor Process." In J. Hearn, D.L. Sheppard, P. Tancred-Sheriff, and G. Burrell (eds.), *The Sexuality of Organization.* Newbury Park, CA: Sage.

Tangney, J. P., and S. Feshbach. (1988). "Children's Television-Viewing Frequency: Individual Differences and Demographic Correlates," *Personality and Social Psychology Bulletin* 14: 145-158.

Tannen, Deborah. (1990). *You Just Don't Understand.* New York: Ballantine.

Tavris, Carol. (1993). *The Mismeasure of Women: Why Women Are Not the Better Sex, The Inferior Sex, or the Opposite Sex.* New York: Touchstone.

Tawney, R. H. (1938). *Religion and the Rise of Capitalism.* Harmondsworth: Penguin.

Teeven, Kevin M. (1983). "The Emergence of Modern Contract Law in the Tudor Period," *Ohio Northern University Law Review* 10 (summer): 441-461.

Tempest, Rone. (1992). "'Wheel' Making a Fortune," *Los Angeles Times* (October 20): H-4.

Tepperman, L., and S. Wilson. (1993). *Next of Kin.* Englewood Cliffs, NJ: Prentice-Hall.

Terdiman, Richard. (1985). *Discourse/Counter-Discourse.* Ithaca, NY: Cornell University Press.

Terkel, Studs. (1985). *Working: People Talk About What They Do All Day and How They Feel About What They Do.* (rev. ed.). Harmondsworth: Penguin.

Terris, Milton. (1990). "A Wasteful System that Doesn't Work," *The Progressive* 54 (October): 14-16.

Terry, James. (1983). "Bringing Women. . . In: A Modest Proposal," *Teaching Sociology* 10 (January): 251-261.

Tesler, Lawrence G. (1991). "Networked Computing in the 1990s," *Scientific American* (September): 86-93.

Test, Mary Ann. (1979). "Continuity of Health Care in Community Treatment," *New Directions for Mental Health Services* 2: 15-23.

Test, Mary Ann, and L. I. Stein. (1978). "Community Treatment of the Chronic Pateint: Research Overview," *Schizophrenia Bulletin* 4: 350-364.

Tharp, Mike. (1991). "Creating a Port in a Storm," *U.S. News and World Report* 110 (May 27): 66.

Thrasher, Frederic M. (1927). *The Gang: A Study of 1,313 Gangs in Chicago.* Chicago: University of Chicago Press.

Thoma, Stephen J. (1986). "Estimating Gender Differences in the Comprehension and Reference of Moral Issues," *Developmental Review* 6: 165-180.

Thoman, E., P. Lieberman, and J. Olson. (1972). "Neonate-Mother Interaction During Breast Feeding," *Developmental Psychology* 6: 110-118.

Thomas George M., John W. Meyer, Francisco O. Ramirez, and John Boli. (1987). *Institutional Structure: Constituting State, Society, and the Individual.* Newbury Park, CA: Sage.

Thomas, William I., and Dorothy S. Thomas. (1928). *The Child in America: Behavior Problems and Programs.* New York: Knopf.

Thompson, Elizabeth, et al. (1992). "Family Structure, Gender and Parental Socialization," *Journal of Marriage and the Family* 54 (May): 368-378.

Thompson, L., and A. J. Walker. (1989). "Women and Men in Marriage, Work, and Parenthood," *Journal of Marriage and the Family* 51: 845-872.

Thorne, Barrie. (1993). *Gender Play: Girls and Boys in School.* New Brunswick, NJ: Rutgers University Press.

Thornton, Russell. (1987). *American Indian Holocaust and Survival: A Population History Since 1492.* Norman: University of Oklahoma Press.

Tilly, Charles. (1975). *The Formation of National States in Europe.* Princeton: Princeton University Press.

———. (1978). *From Mobilization to Revelation.* Reading, MA: Addison-Wesley.

———. (1986). *The Contentious French.* Cambridge, MA: Belknap.

———. (1993). *European Revolutions, 1492-1992.* Cambridge, MA: Blackwell.

Tilly, Charles, Louis Tilly, and Richard Tilly. (1975). *The Rebellious Century, 1830-1930.* Cambridge: Harvard University Press.

Time Magazine. (1992). "How Employers Discriminate," (December 1): 26-27.

Times Poll. (1993). "Poll Delivers Bad News to the Media," *Los Angeles Times* (March 31): A-16.

Toch, Thomas. (1991). *In the Name of Excellence: The Struggle to Reform the Nation's Schooling: Why It's Failing and What Should Be Done.* New York: Oxford University Press.

Todorov, Tzvetan. (1984). *The Conquest of America.* New York: Harper.

Toennies, Ferdinand. (1963; orig. 1887). *Community and Society* (Gemeinschaft and Gesellschaft). New York: Harper & Row.

Toffler, Alvin. (1984). *The Third Wave.* New York: Bantam.

Tonegawa, Keiko. (1992). "A Japanese Educator Tells What She Would Use from U.S. Programs," *The Education Digest* 57 (March): 16-19.

Tong, Shen, (1992). "China the Arms Merchant," *World Monitor* (June): 47-50.

Torrey, E. Fuller. (1988). *Nowhere to Go: The Tragic Odyssey of the Homeless Mentally Ill.* New York: Harper & Row.

———. (1994). "Jailing the Mentally Ill." Washington: National Alliance for the Mentally Ill.

Totti, Xavier F. (1987). "The Making of a Latino Ethnic Identity." *Dissent* 34 (fall): 537-542.

Toufexis, Anastasia. (1993). "Sex Has Many Accents," *Time Magazine* (May 24): 66.

Touraine, Alain. (1971). *The Postindustrial Society.* New York: Random House.

———. (1985)."An Introduction to the Study of Social Movements," *Social Research* 52 (4): 749-787.

———. (1988). *Return of the Actor.* Minneapolis: University of Minnesota Press.

Tourney, G. (1980). "Hormones and Homosexuality." In J. Marmor (ed.), *Homosexual Behavior.* New York: Basic Books.

Townsend, P. (1981). "The Structural Dependency of the Elderly: A Creation of Social Policy in the Twentieth Century," *Aging and Society* 1 (1): 5-28.

Tracy, D. M. (1987). "Toys, Spatial Ability, and Science and Mathematics Achievement: Are They Related?" *Sex Roles* 17: 115-138.

Tracy, L. (1990). "The Television Image in Children's Lives." *New York Times* (May 13): M-1. M-5.

Trafzer, Clifford E. (1986). *American Indian Identity: Today's Changing Perspectives.* Sacramento, CA: Sierra Oaks.

————. (1993). *Earth Song, Sky Spirit: Stories of the Contemporary Native American Experience.* New York: Doubleday.

Trangle, Henry Irving. (1971). *The Southampton Slave Revolt of 1831: A Compilation of Source Material.* Amherst: University of Massachusetts Press.

Trenaman, Joseph, and Dennis McQual. (1961). *Television and the Political Image; A Study of the Impact of Television on the 1959 General Election.* London: Methuen.

Trible, P. (1979). "Depatriarchalizing in Biblical Interpretation." In E. Koltun (ed.), *The Jewish Woman,* pp. 217-240. New York: Schocken.

Trieman, Donald J. (1977). *Occupational Prestige in Comparative Perspective.* New York: Academic.

Trieman, Donald, and Heidi Hartmann (eds.). (1981). *Women, Work, and Wages: Equal Pay for Equal Jobs of Equal Value.* Washington: National Academy Press.

Troeltsch, Ernst. (1931). *The Social Teaching of the Christian Churches.* New York: Macmillan.

Trost, J. (1988). "Conceptualizing the Family," *International Sociology* 3 (3): 301-308.

Tsuda, Shincho. (1981). "The Basic Perspective for a Japanese Theory of Management," *Keizai Hyoron* (July).

Tuchman, Gaye. (1978). *Making News: A Study in the Construction of Reality.* New York: Free Press.

————. (1979). "Women's Depiction by the Mass Media," *Signs* 4 (spring): 528-542.

————. (1988). "Major Media Institutions." In Neil J. Smelser (ed.), *Handbook of Sociology.* Newbury Park, CA: Sage.

Tucker, Kenneth H. (1991). "How New Are the New Social Movements?" *Theory, Culture and Society* 8 (May): 75-98.

Tucker, Robert C. (1977). *The Marx-Engels Reader.* New York: Norton.

Tucker, William. (1989). "America's Homeless: Victims of Rent Control," *The Heritage Foundation Backgrounder* 685 (January 12). Washington: The Heritage Foundation.

————. (1990). *The Excluded Americans: Homelessness and Housing Policies.* Washington: Regnery Gateway in cooperation with the Cato Institute.

Tumin, Melvin M. (1953). "Some Principles of Stratification: A Critical Analysis," *American Sociological Review* 18 (August): 387-393.

————. (1963). "On Inequality," *American Sociological Review* 28: 19-26.

————. (1985). *Social Stratification: The Forms and Functions of Inequality* (2nd ed.). Englewood Cliffs, NJ: Prentice-Hall.

Tumulty, Karen. (1992). "Global Competition: Can the U.S. Still Play by Its Rules?" *Los Angeles Times* (June 8): A-1.

Turner, Bryan. (1987). *Medical Power and Social Knowledge.* Beverley Hills, CA: Sage.

Turner, Jonathan H. (1986). *The Structure of Sociological Theory.* Chicago: Dorsey.

Turner, Jonathan H., and Leonard Beeghley. (1981). *The Emergence of Social Theory.* Homewood, IL: Dorsey.

Turner, Ralph H., and Lewis M. Killian. (1987). *Collective Behavior* (3rd ed.). Englewood Cliffs, NJ: Prentice-Hall.

Tygart, Clarence E. (1987). "Social Structural Linkages Among Social Movement Participants: Toward a Synthesis of Micro and Macro Paradigms," *Sociological Viewpoints* 3 (1): 71-84.

Tylor, Edward B. (1871). *Primitive Culture.* New York: Harper.

Uchitelle, Louis. (1994). "Job Extinction Evolving into a Fact of Life in the U.S.," *New York Times* (March 22): A-1.

Uchitelle, Louis. (1993). "Union Leaders Fight for a Place in the President's Workplace of the Future," *New York Times* (August 8): 32.

United Nations. (1990). *World Population Prospects.* New York.

United Nations Development Programme. (1992). Human Development Report. New York: Oxford.

United Nations International Labor Organization. (1993). "Job Stress: The 20th-Century Disease," Washington: International Labor Organization.

United Nations Population Fund. (1991). *World Population Prospects.* Oxford, England: Nuffield.

U.S. Bureau of the Census. (1976). *Historical Statistics of the United States, Colonial Times to 1970, Part I.* Washington: Government Printing Office.

————. (1980). "Detailed Occupation and Years of School Completed by Age for the Civilian Labor Force, 1980," PC-80-51-8. Washington: Government Printing Office.

————. (1986). "Projections of the Hispanic Population on the United States: 1983-2080. Series P-25 No. 995. Washington: Government Printing Office.

————. (1989). "Projection of the Population of the United States by Age, Sex, and Race: 1988 to 2080," *Current Population Reports,* Series P-25. No. 1018. Washington: Government Printing Office.

————. (1990a). "Detailed Occupation and Other Characteristics from the Equal Employment Opportunity File for the U.S., 1990," CP-5-1-1. Washington: Government Printing Office.

————. (1990b). "Money Income and Poverty Status in the United States: 1989." Washington: Government Printing Office.

————. (1990c). "Occupation of the Civilian Labor Force by Sex, Race, and Hispanic Origin, 1990." Washington: Government Printing Office.

———. (1990d). "Poverty in the United States: 1990." *Current Population Report: Consumers and Income.* Washington: Government Printing Office.

———. (1990e). *Statistical Abstract of the United States, 1990b.* Washington: Government Printing Office.

———. (1990f). *1990 Census of Population and Housing: Summary Tape File 3.* Washington: Government Printing Office.

———. (1990g). "Enterprise Statistics," Series ES87-1, *Large Companies, 1987.* Washington: Government Printing Office.

———. (1991a). "The Asian and Pacific Islander Population in the United States: March 1991 and 1990," P-20 No. 459. Washington: Government Printing Office.

———. (1991b). "The Black Population in the united States: March 1991." *Current Population Reports,* P-20 No. 464. Washington: Government Printing Office.

———. (1991c). "The Hispanic Population in the U.S.: March 1991." Series P-20, No. 455. Washington: Government Printing Office.

———. (1991d). "Vital Statistics." U.S. Statistical Abstracts. Washington: Government Printing Office.

———. (1991e). *1990 Census of Population.* Washington: Government Printing Office.

———. (1991f). *Current Population Report: Consumers and Income.* Washington: Government Printing Office.

———. (1991g). *Statistical Abstract of the United States, 1991.* Washington: Government Printing Office.

———. (1992a). "Annual Report of Income and Poverty in the United States: 1991." Washington: Government Printing Office.

———. (1992b). "Health Insurance Coverage." Washington: Government Printing Office.

———. (1992c). "Job Creation During the Late 1980s: Dynamic Aspects of Employment Growth," *Current Population Reports,* Series P-70 No. 27. Washington: Government Printing Office.

———. (1992d). *Statistical Abstract of the United States, 1992.* Washington: Government Printing Office.

———. (1992e). *U.S. Census of Population.* Washington: Government Printing Office.

———. (1993a). "1992 Annual Income and Poverty Reports." Washington: Government Printing Office (October 4).

———. (1993b). "Earnings of Year-Round, Full-Time Workers." Washington: Government Printing Office (January 22).

———. (1993c). "U.S. Population Estimates, by Age, Sex, Race, and Hispanic Origin: 1980 to 1991." *Current Population Reports* Series P-25 No. 1095 (February). Washington: Government Printing Office.

———. (1993d). "Vital Statistics." *U.S. Statistical Abstracts.* Washington: Government Printing Office.

———. (1993e). *Statistical Abstract of the United States, 1993.* Washington: Government Printing Office.

———. (1994). "Americans with Disabilities, 1991-1992," Series P-70 No.33. Washington: Government Printing Office.

———. (1994a). "1993 Annual Income and Poverty Reports." Washington, D.C.: U.S. Government Printing Office (October 6).

U.S. Center for Disease Control (U.S.C.D.C.). (1992). *Morbidity and Morality Weekly Report* 40 (January 3): 885-888.

U.S. Commission on Civil Rights. (1978). *Social Indicators of Equality for Minorities and Women.* Washington: Government Printing Office.

U.S. Department of Commerce, Bureau of the Census. (1994a). "The Earnings Ladder," Statistical Brief prepared by Jack McNeil (June). Washington, D.C.: U.S. Government Printing Office.

U.S. Department of Defense. (1993). "National Defense Budget Estimates for FY 1994, National Income Accounts (Purchases)," Table 7-5. Washington (May).

U.S. Department of Education. (1992). *The Condition of Education 1992.* Washington: Office of Educational Research and Improvement.

———. (1993a). "Literacy Levels Deficient for 90 Million U.S. Adults." Press release (September 8).

———. (1993b). *Adult Literacy in America.* Washington: National Center for Education Studies.

U.S. Department of Housing and Urban Development. (1984). *Homelessness in America.* Washington: Government Printing Office.

U.S. Bureau of Indian Affairs. (1990). "Federal Indian Reservations and Trust Lands." Washington: Department of the Interior.

U.S. Bureau of Labor. (1990). *Employment and Earnings* 37 (January): 1.

U.S. Department of Labor. (1994). "Monthly Labor Statistics." Washington: Bureau of Labor Statistics.

U.S. Health Care Financing Commission. (1991). *Care Financing Review,* (fall).

U.S. House of Representatives. (1984). "Report on Homelessness I." Hearing before the subcommittee on Housing and Community Development and the subcommittee on Government Operations, *Congressional Record* (May 24), Banking Committee Serial No. 98-91.

U.S. House of Representatives. (1985). "HUD Report on Homelessness II," Hearing before the subcommittee on Housing and Community Development, Congressional Record (December 4), Banking Committee Serial No. 99-56.

U.S. House of Representatives, Committe on Education and Labor. (1992). "Field Hearing on Violence in Our Nation's Schools," (May 4).

U.S. House of Representatives, Select Committee on Children, Youth, and Families. (1988). Women, Violence and the Law. Washington: Government Printing Office.

U.S. Immigration and Naturalization Service. (1992a). "Immigrants to the U.S., 1820-1991." Washington: Government Printing Office.

———. (1992b). "U.S. Population: Immigration by Country of Last Residence, 1820-1991." Washington: Government Printing Office.

U.S. Senate Hearings of the Judiciary. (1976). Washington: Government Printing Office.

U.S. Senate Special Committee on Aging. (1986). *Developments on Aging: 1985,* vol.3. Washington: Government Printing Office.

U.S. Social Security Administration. (1992). "Old Age, Survivors, and Disability Insurance." Washington: Government Printing Office.

U.S. Surgeon General. (1964). *Smoking and Health: A Report of the Surgeon General's Advisory Committee to the Surgeon General.* Washington: Government Printing Office.

Usdansky, Margaret L. (1994). "Segregated Schools Are Once Again the Norm," *USA Today* (May 12): 84.

Useem, Michael. (1984). *The Inner Circle: Large Corporations and the Rise of Business Political Activity in the U.S. and U.K.* New York: Oxford University Press.

Useem, Michael, and Jerome Karabel. (1986). "Pathways to Top Corporate Management," *American Sociological Review* 51 (2): 184-200.

Utley, Robert. (1963). *The Last Days of the Sioux Nation.* New Haven: Yale University Press.

Vaill, Peter. (1989). *Managing as a Performing Art: New Ideas for a World of Chaotic Change.* San Francisco: Jossey-Bass.

Vaillant, G. E. (1977). *Adaptation to Life.* Boston: Little, Brown.

Valenzuela Arce, Jose Manuel. (1992). "Permanencia y Cambio en las Identidades Etnicas: La Poblacion de Origen Mexicano en Estado Unidos," *Estudios Sociologicos* 10 (January-April): 103-125.

Van den Berghe, Pierre. (1963). "Dialectic and Functionalism: Toward Reconciliation," *American Sociological Review* 28 (October): 695-705.

———. (1978). *Race and Racism: A Comparative Perspective* (2nd ed.). New York: Wiley.

Van Velsor, E., and M. W. Hughes. (1990). *Gender Differences in the Development of Managers: How Women Managers Learn from Experience.* Greensboro, NC: Center for Creative Leadership. Report No. 145 (December).

Veblen, Thorstein. (1899). *The Theory of the Leisure Class.* New York: Macmillan.

Vickers, Jeanne. (1991). *Women and the World Economic Crisis.* Zed.

Viner, J. (1953). *International Trade and Economic Development.* Oxford, England: Clarendon.

Vinorskis, Maris A. (1992). "Schooling and Poor Children in 19th Century America," *American Behavioral Scientist* 35 (3): 313-331.

Vogel, Lise. (1984). *Marxism and the Oppression of Women: Towards a Unity Theory.* New Brunswick, NJ: Rutgers University Press.

Vold, George B. (1958). *Theoretical Criminology.* New York: Oxford University Press.

Wacquant, Loic J. D. (1993). "Redrawing the Urban Color Line: The State of the Ghetto in the 1980s." In Craig Calhoun and George Ritzer (eds.), *Social Problems.* New York: McGraw-Hill.

Wade, R. (1990). *Governing the Market: Economic Theory and the Role of Government in East Asian Industrialization.* Princeton: Princeton University Press.

Waitzkin, Howard. (1974). *The Exploration of Illness in Capitalist Society.* Indianapolis: Bobbs Merrill.

———. (1984). "Doctor-Patient Communication: Clinical Implications of Social Scientific Research," *The Journal of the American Medical Association* 252 (November 2): 2441-1446.

———. (1991). *The Politics of Medical Encounters: How Patients and Doctors Deal with Social Problems.* New Haven: Yale University Press.

Waley, Julia, et al. (1992). "Television and Political Memory," *Media, Culture, and Society,* 14 (October): 541-560.

Walker, Blair S. (1992). "Small PC Firm Reaps Big Profits," *USA Today* (May 13): 1p.

Walker, Samuel. (1989). *Sense and Nonsense About Crime: A Policy Guide* (2nd ed.). Monterey, CA: Brooks/Cole.

Wallace, David Foster, and Mark Costello. (1990). "Signifying Rappers," *The Missouri Review* XIII (2): 7-26.

Wallace, John M., and Jerald G. Bachman. (1991). "Explaining Racial/Ethnic Differences in Adolescent Drug Use," *Social Problems* 38: 333-357.

Wallerstein, Immanuel M. (1974a). *Capitalist Agriculture and the Origins of the European World-Economy in the Sixteenth Century.* New York: Academic.

———. (1974b). *The Modern World-System.* New York: Academic.

———. (1979). *The Capitalist World Economy.* Cambridge, England: Cambridge University Press.

———. (1980). *Mercantilism and the Consolidation of the European World-Economy, 1600-1750.* New York: Academic.

———. (1989). *The Second Era of Great Expansion of the Capitalist World-Economy, 1730-1840s.* San Diego: Academic.

———. (1990). *The Modern World-System II.* New York: Academic.

Wallerstein, Judith S., and Sandra Blakeslee. (1990). *Second Chances: Men, Women, and Children a Decade after Divorce.* New York: Ticknor & Fields.

Wallis, W. A., and H. V. Roberts. (1956). *Statistics: A New Approach.* New York: Free Press.

Walsh, Edward. (1993). "Michigan Ends Property Tax Funding of Schools," *Washington Post* (August 20): A-1.

Walters, H., and Huck, J. (1989). "Networking Women," *Newsweek* (March 13): 48-54.

Walters, Pamela Barnhouse, et al. (1990). "Schooling or Working? Public Education, Racial Politics and the Organization of Production in 1910," *Sociology of Education.* 63(1): 1-26.

Walters, Pamela Barnhouse, and David R. James. (1992). "Schooling for Some: Child Labor and School Enrollment of Black and White Children in the Early 20th Century South," *American Sociological Review* 57 (5): 635-650.

Walum, Laurel Richardson. (1977). *Dynamics of Sex and Gender.* Chicago: Rand-McNally.

Warner, Kee, Harvey L. Molotch, and Amy Lategola. (1992). "Growth Control: Inner Workings and External Effects." Berkeley: University of California Press, California Policy Seminar.

Warner, Steve. (1993). "Work in Progress Toward a New Paradigm for the Sociological Study of Religion in the United States," *American Journal of Sociology* 98 (March): 1044-1093.

Warren, B. (1980). *Imperialism: Pioneer of Capitalism.* London: Verso.

Washington, Margaret Murray. (1973; orig. 1929). "Club Work Among Negro Women." In Gerda Lerner (ed.), *Black Women in White America: A Documentary History.* New York: Vintage.

Washington Post. (1992). (February 6): A-4.

————. (1993). "Prudential Fined $330 Million," (October 22): B-1.

Wasserman, Ira M. (1989). "The Effects of War and Alcohol Consumption Patterns on Suicide: United States, 1910-1933," *Social Forces* 68 (2): 513-530.

Watanabe, Teresa. (1992). "In Japan, a 'Goat Man' or No Man," *Los Angeles Times* (January 6).

Watson, John. (1925). *Behaviorism.* New York: Norton.

Waxman, Sharon. (1992). "The New Sound of Hate," *Washington Post* (July 12): G-1.

Weatherford, Doris. (1990). *American Women and World War II.* New York: Facts on File.

Weaver, M. J. (1985). *New Catholic Women.* San Francisco: Harper & Row.

Weber, Jonathan. (1992). "And Now, for a Word from Our Future....," *Los Angeles Times* (October 20): H-11.

Weber, Joseph. (1992). "Look Ma—No Cable: It's Video-by-Phone," *Business Week* (November 16): 86.

Weber, Max. (1946a; orig. 1919). *From Max Weber: Essays in Sociology.* Hans Gerth and C. Wright Mills (trans. and eds.). New York: Oxford University Press.

————. (1946b). "Politics as a Vocation." In H. Gerth and C. Wright Mills (trans. and eds.), *From Max Weber: Essays in Sociology.* New York: Oxford University Press.

————. (1947). *The Theory of Social and Economic Organization.* New York: Free Press.

————. (1949; orig. 1903-1917). *The Methodology of the Social Sciences,* Edward Shils and Henry Finch (eds.). New York: Free Press.

————. (1958; orig. 1904-1905). *The Protestant Ethic and the Spirit of Capitalism.* New York: Scribners.

————. (1963; orig. 1921). *The Sociology of Religion.* Boston: Beacon.

————. (1977). *The Protestant Ethic and the Spirit of Capitalism.* New York: Macmillan.

————. (1979; orig. 1921). *Economy and Society: An Outline of Interpretive Sociology* (2 vols.). Berkeley: University of California Press.

Wederspahn, Gary M. (1993). "Don't Get Lost in the Translation," *Hemispheres* (February): 27-28.

Weeks, Jeffrey. (1977). *Coming Out: Homosexual Politics in Britain, from the Nineteenth Century to the Present.* New York: Quartet.

Weeks, John R. (1988). "The Demography of Islamic Nations," *Population Bulletin* 43 (December): 4.

————. (1992). *Population.* Belmont, CA: Wadsworth.

Weidman, J. L. (ed.). (1984). *Christian Feminism.* San Francisco: Harper & Row.

Weiss, Gregory L., and Lynne Lonquist. (1994). *The Sociology of Health, Healing and Illness.* Englewood Cliffs, NJ: Prentice-Hall.

Weitzman, L. (1979). *Sex Role Socialization: A Focus on Women.* Palo Alto, CA: Mayfield.

Weitzman, Lenore (1981). "The Economics of Divorce: Social and Economic Consequences of Property, Alimony, and Child Support Awards," *UCLA Law Review* 28: 6.

————. (1985). *The Divorce Revolution: The Unexpected Social and Economic Consequences for Women and Children in America.* New York: Free Press.

————. (1990). "Alimony: Its Premature Demise and Recent Resurgence in the United States." In Lenore Weitzman and M. Maclean (eds.), *Economic Consequences of Divorce: The International Perspective.* Oxford, England: Clarendon.

Welch, C., and S. Price-Bonham. (1983). "A Decade of No-Fault Divorce Revisited: California, Georgia, and Washington," *Journal of Marriage and the Family* 45 (May): 2.

Wellman, Barry (1984). "Domestic Work, Paid Work and Net Work." In Research paper no. 149, Center for Urban and Community Studies, University of Toronto.

Wellman, Barry, Peter J. Carrington, and Alan Hall. (1988). "Networks as Personal Communities." In *Social Structures: A Network Approach.* New York: Cambridge University Press.

Wentworth, William M. (1989). "A Dialectical Conception of Religion and Religious Movements in Modern Society." In Jeffrey Hadden and Anson Shupe (eds.), *Religion and the Political Order* vol. 3, pp. 123-134. New York: Paragon House.

West, Candace. (1979). "Against Our Will: Male Interruptions of Females in Cross-Sex Conversations," *Annals of the New York Academy of Science* 327: 81-97.

———. (1984). *Routine Complications: Troubles with Talk Between Doctors and Patients.* Bloomington: Indiana University Press.

West, C., and S. Fenstermaker. (1991). "Power, Inequality, and the Accomplishment of Gender: An Ethnomethodological View." In P. England (ed.), *Theory on Gender/Feminism on Theory.* New York: Aldine.

West, Candace, and Don H. Zimmerman. (1977). "Woman's Place in Everyday Talk; Reflections on Parent-Child Interaction," *Social Problems* 24: 521-529.

———. (1987). "Doing Gender," *Gender and Society* 1: 125-151.

———. (1983). "Small Insults: A Study of Interruptions in Conversations Between Unacquainted Persons." In Barrie Thorne and N. Henley (eds.), *Language Gender, and Society.* Rowley, MA: Newbury House.

West, Elliot, and Paula E. Petrik. (1992). *Small Worlds: Children and Adolescents in America 1850-1950.* Lawrence: University of Kansas Press.

Westley, L. A. (1982). *A Territorial Issue: A Study of Women in the Construction Trades.* Washington: Wider Opportunities for Women.

Wetzel, J. R. (1990). "American Families: 75 years of Change," *Monthly Labor Review* 113 (March): 4-13.

Whalen, Jack, and Richard Flacks. (1989). *Beyond the Barricades: The Sixties Generation Grows Up.* Philadelphia: Temple University Press.

Whalen, Jack, and Don H. Zimmerman. (1987). "Sequential and Institutional Contexts in Calls for Help," *Social Psychology Quarterly* 50: 172-185.

———. (1990). "Describing Trouble: Epistemology in Citizen Calls to the Police," *Language in Society* 19: 465-492.

Whalen, Jack, and Don H. Zimmerman, and Marilyn R. Whalen. (1990). "When Words Fail: A Single Case Analysis," *Social Problems* 35: 335-362.

Whannel, G. (1979). "Football, Crowd Behaviour, and the Press," *Media, Culture and Society* 1: 4.

Whitbourne, Susan K. (1985). *The Aging Body: Phisiological Changes and Psychological Consequences.* New York: Springer-Verlag.

White, D. M. (1950). "The 'Gatekeeper': A Case Study in the Selection of News," *Journalism Quarterly* 27: 383-390.

Whiteford, Michael B., and John Friedl. (1992). *The Human Portrait: Introduction into Cultural Anthropology.* Englewood Cliffs, NJ: Prentice-Hall.

Whitehead, Barbara Dafoe. (1993). "Dan Quayle Was Right," *The Atlantic Monthly* (April): 47-84.

Whittle, Jeff, et al. (1993). "Treatment of Black and White Heart in a VA Hospital," *New England Journal of Medicine* (August 25): 621-627.

Whyte, William F. (1943). *Street Corner Society: The Social Structure of an Italian Slum.* Chicago: University of Chicago Press.

———. (1991). *Participatory Action Research.* Newbury Park, CA: Sage.

Wideman, John Edgar. (1984). *Brothers and Keepers.* New York: Penguin.

Will, J. A., P. A. Self, and N. Dalton. (1976)."Maternal Behavior and Perceived Sex of Infant," *American Journal of Orthopsychiatry* 49: 135-139.

Williams, M., and J. C. Condry. (1988). "Living Color: Minority Portrayals and Cross-Racial Interactions on Television." Unpublished manuscript.

Williams, P., and M. Smith. (1979). Interview in *The First Question.* London: British Broadcasting System Science and Features Department.

Williams, Raymond. (1977) *Marxism and Literature.* New York: Oxford University Press.

Williams, Terry. (1989). *The Cocaine Kids: The Inside Story of a Teenage Drug Ring.* Reading, MA: Addison-Wesley.

———. (1992). *Crackhouse.* New York: Penguin.

Willie, Charles V. (1989a). "The Inclining Significance of Race." In Charles V. Willie (ed.), *Caste and Class Controversy on Race and Poverty* (2nd ed.), pp. 10-21. New York: General-Hall.

——— (ed.). (1989b). *The Class and Caste Controversy on Race and Poverty: Round Two of the Wilson-Willie Debate.* New York: General-Hall.

Willis, Paul. (1981). *Learning to Labor: How Working Class Kids Get Working-Class Jobs.* New York: Columbia University Press.

———. (1990). *Common Culture.* Boulder: Westview.

Wilson, B., Dan Linz, and Ed Donnerstein. (1992). "The Impact of Social Issue Television Programming on Attitudes Towards Rape," *Human Communications Research* 19 (2): 179-208.

Wilson, Bryan. (1966). *Religion in Secular Society.* London: C. A. Watts.

———. (1982). *Religion in Sociological Perspective.* New York: Oxford University Press.

Wilson, Edward O. (1975). *Sociobiology: The New Synthesis.* Cambridge: Harvard University Press.

———. (1978). *On Human Nature.* Cambridge: Harvard University Press.

Wilson, James D. (1992). "Gays Under Fire," *Newsweek* (September 14): 35-41.

Wilson, James Q., and Richard J. Herrnstein. (1985). Crime and Human Nature. New York: Simon & Schuster.

Wilson, Kenneth L., and Alejandro Portes. (1980). "Immigrant Enclaves: An Analysis of Labor Market Experiences of Cubans in Miami," *American Journal of Sociology* 86: 295-319.

Wilson, Thomas P. (1991). "Social Structure and the Sequential Organization of Interaction." In Don H. Zimmerman and Dierdre Boden (eds.), *Talk and Social Structure*. Cambridge, England: Polity.

Wilson, William Julius. (1978). *The Declining Significance of Race: Blacks and Changing American Institutions.* Chicago: University of Chicago Press.

———. (1987). *The Truly Disadvantaged: The Inner City, the Underclass, and Public Policy.* Chicago: University of Chicago Press.

———. (1991). "Studying Inner-City Social Dislocations," *American Sociological Review* 56 (1): 1-14.

——— (ed.). (1993). *The Ghetto Underclass.* Newbury Park, CA: Sage.

Wiltfang, Gregory, and Doug McAdam. (1991). "The Costs and Risks of Social Activism: A Study of Sanctuary Movement Activism," *Social Forces* 69 (June): 987-1010.

Wirth, Louis. (1928). *The Ghetto.* Chicago: University of Chicago Press.

———. (1938). "Urbanism as a Way of Life," *American Journal of Sociology* 44 (July): 1-24.

Witkowski, Stanley R., and Cecil H. Brown (1982). "Whorf and Universals of Number Nomenclature," *Journal of Anthropological Research* 38: 411-420.

Wojcik, Joanne. (1993). "Retiree Benefits: Firm Allowed to Cancel Cover," *Business Insurance* 27 (March): 3-4.

Wolf, Eric R. (1969). *Peasant Wars of the Twentieth Century.* New York: Harper Colophon.

———. (1983). *Europe and the People Without a History.* Berkeley: University of California Press.

Wolfe, Alan. (1977). *The Limits of Legitimacy.* New York: Free Press.

Wolff, Leon. (1965). *Lockout: The Story of the Homestead Strike of 1892.* New York: Cambridge University Press.

Wolfgang, Marvin. (1958). *Patterns in Criminal Homicide.* Philadelphia: University of Pennsylvania Press.

Wolfgang, Marvin, and Franco Ferracuti. (1967). *The Subculture of Violence.* London: Tavistock.

Wollstonecraft, Mary. (1982; orig. 1792). *A Vindication of the Rights of Women.* New York: Penguin.

Women's Institute for Freedom of the Press (WIFP). (1986). "1955 to 1985: Women in Prime Time TV Still Traditional, but New Treatment of Women's Rights Themes," *Media Report to Women* (November-December): 7.

———. (1989a). "Surveys of News Magazines Show Little Coverage of Women," *Media Report to Women* (November-December): 1.

———. (1989b). "Women Gain as Broadcast News Directors in New RTNDA Study," *Media Report to Women* (September-October): 6-7.

———. (1990a). "NFPW Study: Women Grossly Underrepresented in Newspaper Content, Editorial Decisions," *Media Report to Women* (July-August) 2-3.

———. (1990b). "Little Improvement Noted in Women's Page One Status," *Media Report to Women* (May-June): 3-4.

Wong, Siu-lun. (1985). "The Chinese Family Firm: A Model," *British Journal of Sociology* 36: 58-72.

———. (1986). "Modernization and Chinese Culture in Hong Kong," *The China Quarterly* 106: 306-325.

Woo, Deborah. (1985). "The Socioeconomic Status of Asian American Women in the Labor Force: An Alternative View," *Sociological Perspectives* 28 (July): 307-338.

———. (1992). "The Gap Between Striving and Achieving: The Case of Asian American Women," In Margaret L. Anderson and Patricia Hill Collins, *Race, Class, and Gender: An Anthology.* Belmont, CA: Wadsworth.

Woodruff, David. (1992). "Saturn," *Business Week* (August 17): 85-91.

Woodrum, Eric. (1988). "Moral Conservatism and the 1984 Presidential Election," *Journal for the Scientific Study of Religion* 27: 192-210.

Woodward, C. Vann. (1955). *The Strange Career of Jim Crow.* Oxford, England: Oxford University Press.

Woolley, Benjamin. (1992). *Virtual Worlds: A Journey in Hype and Hypereality.* Oxford, England: Basil Blackwell.

Woolsley, Christine. (1992). "Medicare Fraud Prompts Insurers to Recheck Files," *Business Insurance* 26 (December 28): 37.

World Almanac and Book of Facts. (1992). New York: Pharos Books. Licensed from Newspaper Enterprise Association, in conjunction with Microsoft Bookshelf.

World Bank. (1990a). *World Development Report 1990.* Washington.

———. (1990b). *World Development Report 1990:Poverty.* London: Oxford University Press.

———. (1991). *World Development Report 1991: The Challenge of Development.* London: Oxford University Press.

———. (1992). *World Development Report 1992: Development and the Environment.* London: Oxford University Press.

World Commisssion on Environment and Development. (1987). *Food 2000: Global Policies for Sustainable Agriculture: A Report of the Advisory Panel on Food Security, Agriculture, Forestry, and the Environment and Development.* London: Zed.

World Monitor. (1992). "The Map," (September): 11.

Wosik, Ramsay, and Jo Bryant. (1990). "A Longitudinal Study of Two Early Intervention Strategies: Project Care," *Child Development* 61 (December): 1682-1696.

Woutat, Donald. (1992). "Data Age's Boon in the Boonies," *Los Angeles Times* (September 19): A-1.

Wright, Erik Ohlin. (1985). *Classes.* London: Verso.

———, et al. (1982). "The American Class Structure," *American Sociological Review* 47: 709-726.

Wright, James D. (1989). *Address Unknown: The Homeless in America.* New York: A. de Gruyter.

Wright, Lawrence. (1993). "Remember Satan—Part II," *The New Yorker* (May 24): 54-76.

Wright, Robert, (1993). "The Technology Time Bomb," *New Republic* 208 (March 29): 25.

Wright, Ronald, and Peter Davison. (1993). *Stolen Continents: The Americas Through Indian Eyes Since 1492.* New York: Houghton-Mifflin.

Wrigley, Edward Anthony. (1988). *Continuity, Chance and Change: The Character of the Industrial Revolution in England.* New York: Cambridge University Press.

Wriston, Walter B. (1992). *The Twilight of Sovereignty: How the Information Revolution Is Transforming Our World.* New York: Scribners.

Wrong, Dennis H. (1959). "The Functional Theory of Stratification: Some Neglected Considerations," *American Sociological Review* 24: 772-782.

WuDunn, Sheryl. (1993a). "Chinese Suffer from Rising Pollution as Byproduct of the Industrial Boom," *New York Times* (February 28): 20.

———. (1993b). "To Punish Births: Fines, Beatings, Ruined Homes," *New York Times* (April 25): 12.

Wuthnow, Robert. (1976). *The Consciouness Reformation.* Berkeley: University of California Press.

———. (1978). *Experimentation in American Religion.* Berkeley: University of California Press.

———. (1987). "Religious Movements and Counter-Movements in North America." In James Beckford (ed.), *New Religious Movements and Social Change.* Paris: UNESCO.

———. (1988). "Sociology of Religion." In Neil J. Smelser (ed.), *Handbook of Sociology.* Newbury Park, CA: Sage.

X, Malcolm. (1990; orig. 1965). *The Autobiography of Malcolm X,* with the assistance of Alex Haley. New York: Ballantine.

Yakolev, Alexander. (1989). "Perestroika or the Death of Socialism." In S. F. Cohen and K. Vanden Heuval (eds.), *Voices of Glasnost: Interviews with Gorbachev's Reformers,* pp. 33-75. New York: Norton.

Yammarino, F. J., S. J. Skinner, and T. K. Childers. (1991). "Understanding Mail Survey Response Behavior: A Meta-Analysis," Public Opinion Quarterly 55: 613-639.

Yang, Dori Jones. (1992). "Microsoft's Other Pioneer Jumps into Multimedia," *Business Week* (November 30): 106-107.

Yang, N., and Dan Linz. (1990). "Movie Ratings and the Content of Adult Videos: The Sex-Violence Ratio," *Journal of Communication* 40: 28-42.

Yoors, Jan. (1971). *The Gypsies.* New York: Simon & Schuster.

Zald, Mayer, and Roberta Ash Garner. (1966). "Social Movement Organizations: Growth, Decay, and Change," *Social Forces* 44: 327-341.

Zald, Mayer, and John D. McCarthy. (1980). "Social Movement Industries: Competition and Cooperation Among Movement Organizations." In Louis Kriesberg (ed.), *Research in Social Movements, Conflicts and Change,* vol. 3. Greenwich, CT: JAI.

——— (eds.). (1987). *Social Movements in an Organizational Society: Collected Essays.* New Brunswick, NJ: Transaction.

Zald, Mayer N., and Gary L. Walmsley. (1973). *The Political Economy of Public Organizations.* Lexington, MA: Lexington Books.

Zaretsky, Eli. (1976). *Capitalism, the Family, and Personal Life.* New York: Harper Colophon.

Zavella, Patricia. (1987). *Women's Work and Chicano Families: Cannery Workers of the Santa Clara Valley.* Ithaca, NY: Cornell University Press.

Zeitlin, Irving M. (1987). *Ideology and the Development of Sociological Theory.* Englewood Cliffs, NJ: Prentice-Hall.

Zeitlin, Maurice. (1989). *The Large Corporation and Contemporary Classes.* New Brunswick, NJ: Rutgers University Press.

Zigler, Edward, and Susan Muenhchow. (1993). *Head Start: The Inside Story of America's Most Successful Educational Experiment.* New York: Basic Books.

Zill, Nicholas, Frank Furstenberg, Jr., and James Peterson. (1987). *National Survey of Children: Wave I, 1976 and Wave II, 1981.* Ann Arbor, MI: Inter-University Consortium for Political and Social Research, No. 8670.

Zimbardo, Philip. (1972). "Pathology of Imprisonment," *Society* 9: 4-8.

Zimmerman, Don H. (1984). "Talk and Its Occasion: The Case of Calling the Police." In D. Schiffrin (ed.), *Meaning, Form, and Use in Context: Linguistic Applications,* pp. 210-228. Washington: Georgetown University Press.

———. (1988). "The Conversation: The Conversation Analytic Perspective," *Communication Yearbook* 11: 406-432.

———. (1992). "The Interactional Organization of Calls for Emergency Assistance." In P. Drew and John Heritage (eds.), *Talk at Work: Interaction in Institutional Settings.* New York: Cambridge University Press.

Zimmerman, Don H., and Candace West. (1975). "Sex Roles, Interruptions and Silences in Conversations." In Barrie Thorne and N. Henley (eds.), *Language Gender, and Society.* Rowley, MA: Newbury House.

———— (eds.). (1980). "Language and Social Interaction," *Sociological Inquiry* 50: 3-4.

Zuboff, Shoshona. (1988). *In the Age of the Smart Machine: The Future of Work and Power.* New York: Basic Books.

Zukin, Sharon, and Paul DiMaggio (eds.). (1990). *Structures of Capital: The Social Organization of the Economy.* Cambridge, England: Cambridge University Press.

Zwerling, Craig, and Hilary Silver. (1992). "Race and Job Dismissals in a Federal Bureaucracy," *American Sociological Review* 57: 651-660.

Credits

MAP REFERENCES

Map 3.1
World Languages
Chaliand, Gerard and Jean-Pierre Rageau (1992) "Imperial Languages of the World," *Strategic Atlas*, 3rd ed. New York: HarperCollins, p. 39

Map 4.1
North America: Indigenous Societies at the Time of Columbus, and Nations Today
National Geographic Magazine (1972) "North American Cultural Areas and Tribal Groups, 1960," *National Geographic Magazine* (December): Map Supplement

Map 4.2
Africa: Indigenous Societies Prior to European Colonization, and Nations Today
Collins, Robert O., James McDonald Burns, and Erik Kristofer Ching (ed.) (1993) Problems in African History, rev. ed. New York: Markus Wiener
Freeman-Grenville, G.S.P. (1991) *The New Atlas of African History*. New York: Simon & Schuster

Map 5.1
U.S. World View
Chaliand, Gerard and Jean-Pierre Rageau (1992) "Imperial Languages of the World," *Strategic Atlas*, 3rd ed. New York: HarperCollins, p. 24

Map 5.2
China World View
Chaliand, Gerard and Jean-Pierre Rageau (1992) "Imperial Languages of the World," *Strategic Atlas*, 3rd ed. New

York: HarperCollins, p. 27

Map 5.3
Arab Muslim World View
Chaliand, Gerard and Jean-Pierre Rageau (1992) "Imperial Languages of the World," *Strategic Atlas*, 3rd ed. New York: HarperCollins, p. 28

Map 6.1
Offices and Holdings of The News Corporation, a Global Organization
The News Corporation Limited (1993) *Annual Report*. New York: The News Corporation

Map 7.1
U.S. State-by-State Capital Punishment Figures During Past Decade, For Whites and Nonwhites
Amnesty International (1994) "Fact Sheet on Death Penalty, 1994." Washington, D.C.: Amnesty International, Death Penalty Information Center
NAACP Legal Defense and Educational Fund (1994) "Death Row U.S.A." New York: NAACP Legal Defense and Educational Fund (spring)

Map 8.1
Percentage of People in Poverty by County in the U.S., 1990
U.S. Bureau of the Census (1990) *U.S. Census of Population*. Washington, D.C.: U.S. Government Printing Office

Map 9.1
Low, Middle, and High Income Countries
World Bank (1992) *World Development Report 1992: Development and the Environment*, pp. 200-201. London: Oxford University Press

Map 9.2
Ghana
Authors' maps

Map 9.3
Bangladesh
Authors' maps

Map 9.4
Brazil
Authors' maps

Map 9.5
East Asian Newly Industrializing Countries
Authors' maps

Map 10.1
Racial and Ethnic Diversity in the U.S. by County
U.S. Bureau of the Census (1990) *U.S. Census of Population*. Washington, D.C.: U.S. Government Printing Office

Map 10.2
Global Racial and Ethnic Strife, 1989-1994
New York Times (1993) "As Ethnic Wars Multiply, U.S. Strives for a Policy," *New York Times* (February 7)

Map 11.1
Female Heads of State Since World War II
Cantor, Dorothy W. and Tony Bernay (1992) *Women in Power: The Secrets of Leadership*. Boston: Houghton Mifflin

Map 11.2
Females in Congress, 1970 and 1994
Congressional Women's Caucus (1994) "Woment Members of Congress, 1917-1993." Washington D.C.: U.S. Government Printing Office

U.S. Congress (1994) "Directory, 103rd Congress." Washington D.C.: U.S. Government Printing Office

Map 12.1
The Graying of the World: Percent over 65 in 1993
Population Reference Bureau (1992) "World Population Data Sheet, 1992." Washington D.C.: Population Reference Bureau

Map 12.2
The Graying of the World: Percent over 65 in 2010
Population Reference Bureau (1992) "World Population Data Sheet, 1992." Washington D.C.: Population Reference Bureau
Hoffman, Mark S. (ed.) (1993) *The World Almanac and Book of Facts.* New York: Pharos Books

Map 13.1
African-Americans in Congress: 1877 and 1994
Congressional Black Caucus (1994) *Congressional Black Caucus, 103rd Congress.* Washington, D.C.: CBC

Map 13.2
Changes in Military Spending, By Nation: 1960–1993
Sivard, Ruth Leger (1993) *World Military and Social Expenditures, 1993,* 15th edition. Washington D.C.: World Priorities

Map 14.1
Percent of Single-Parent Headed Households by U.S. County
U.S. Bureau of the Census (1990) *U.S. Census of Population.* Washington, D.C.: U.S. Government Printing Office

Map 15.1
Hourly Manufacturing Wages, Selected Countries (1991 Dollars)
UNIDO (1992) *Industry and Development: Global Report.* New York: United Nations Industrial Development Organization

Map 16.1
School Days Around the World
World Monitor (1992) "The Map," *World Monitor* (September 11): p. 11.
NCES (1993) *The Condition of Education, 1993,* "Time in the Classroom," p. 128. Washington DC: U.S. Dept of Education, National Center for Education Statistics. U.S. Government Printing Office NCES

Map 17.1
Major Religions of the World
Chaliand, Gerard and Jean-Paul Rague (1992) "The Great Religions," *Strategic Atlas,* 3rd ed. New York: HarperCollins, p. 38

Map 17.2
Religious Diversity in the U.S by County, 1990

Roof, Wade Clark (1994) Dataset provided for on-going research project on mainline religions. Codebook and Technical Documentation provided by Roper Center for Public Opinion Research, "Churches and Church Membership in the United States, 1990." Storrs, CT: University of Connecticut, RCPOR

Map 18.1
The Global AIDS Epidemic
WHO (1993) "WHO Semi-Annual Statistics, January 1993." Geneva, Switzerland: World Health Organization, Global Programme on AIDS (April 4)
WHO (1994) *The HIV/AIDS Pandemic: 1994 Overview.* Geneva, Switzerland: World Health Organization, Global Programme on AIDS

Map 19.1
Television Ownership Around the World
UNESCO (1991) *UNESCO Statistical Yearbook, 1991.* Paris, France: United Nations Educational, Scientific, and Cultural Organization

Map 20.1
Population Projections for the World's 20 Largest Metropolitan Areas
U.S. Bureau of the Census (1990) *U.S. Census of Population.* Washington, D.C.: U.S. Government Printing Office
Population Reference Bureau (1992) "World Population Data Sheet, 1992." Washington, D.C.: Population Reference Bureau

Map 21.1
New Countries since World War II, Grouped by Decade
Chaliand, Gerard and Jean-Píerre Rague (1992) "Chronology of Decolonizations in the Eastern Hemisphere," *Stategic Atlas,* 3rd ed. New York: HarperCollins, p. 56
Rand McNally (1992) *Historical Atlas of the World.* Chicago, Rand McNally
Rand McNally (1993) *World Atlas of Nations.* Chicago: Rand McNally

TEXT CREDITS

p. 46
Excerpt from "Reconstructing Knowledge: Towards Inclusive Thinking" in RACE, CLASS, AND GENDER: AN ANTHOLOGY edited by Margaret L. Anderson and Patricia Hill Collins. Reprinted by permission of Wadsworth Publishing Company.

p. 54
Excerpts from YANOMAMO, Fourth Edition by Napoleon A. Chagnon, copyright © 1992 by Holt, Rinehart and Winston, Inc., reprinted by permission of the publisher.

p. 86
Excerpt from BLACK HILLS, WHITE JUSTICE by Edward Lazarus. Copyright © 1991 by Edward Lazarus. Reprinted by permission of HarperCollins Publishers, Inc.

p. 104
From LEARNING TO BOW by Bruce S. Feiler. Copyright © 1991 by Bruce S. Feiler. Reprinted by permission of Ticknor & Fields/Houghton Mifflin Co. All rights reserved.

p. 123
From "In Japan, a 'Goat Man' or No Man" by Teresa Watanabe from THE LOS ANGELES TIMES, January 6, 1992. Copyright, 1992, Los Angeles Times. Reprinted by permission.

pp. 142–143
Excerpt from BLACK WOMEN IN WHITE AMERICA by Gerda Lerner, editor. Copyright © 1972 by Gerda Lerner. Reprinted by permission of Pantheon Books, a division of Random House, Inc.

p. 130
Excerpt from "The Company Wedding: Bowing Into a Japanese Firm is For Life" by T.R. Reid from THE WASHINGTON POST, April 2, 1992. Copyright © 1992 by The Washington Post. Reprinted with permission.

p. 169
"The Saints and the Roughnecks" by William Chambliss from SOCIETY, November 1973. Reprinted by permission of Transaction.

p. 178
Excerpt from "Anger in Young Black Males: Victims or Victimizers?" by Jewelle Taylor Gibbs in THE AMERICAN BLACK MALE: HIS PRESENT STATUS AND HIS FUTURE edited by Richard G. Majors and Jacob U. Gordon. Reprinted by permission of Nelson-Hall.

p. 216
Excerpt from "The Maquiladora Revolution in Guatemala" by Kurt Peterson (1992), Occasional Paper Series, 2:170. Reprinted by permission.

p. 223
"A Poor Subsistence Household in Ghana" from WORLD DEVELOPMENT REPORT 1990, pp. 24–25. Reprinted by permission of The World Bank.

p. 275
Excerpt from "I Am Your Sister: Black Women Organizing Across Sexualities" from A BURST OF LIGHT by Audre Lorde. Copyright © 1988 by Audre Lorde. Reprinted by permission of Firebrand Books, Ithaca, New York.

PHOTO CREDITS

Index